PIRATES!

PIRATES!

Brigands, Buccaneers, and Privateers in Fact, Fiction, and Legend

Jan Rogoziński

Facts On File, Inc.

AN INFOBASE HOLDINGS COMPANY

For Paul Francis Hauch

Pirates!
Brigands, Buccaneers, and Privateers in Fact, Fiction, and Legend

Facts On File, Inc.
460 Park Avenue South
New York NY 10016

Library of Congress Cataloging-in-Publication Data
Rogoziński, Jan.
    Pirates! : brigands, buccaneers, and privateers in fact, fiction,
and legend / Jan Rogoziński.
       p.   cm.
    Includes bibliographical references and index.
    ISBN 0-8160-2761-7
    1. Pirates.   I. Title.
G535.R64   1995
910.4′5—dc20   94-12717

Facts On File books are available at special discounts when purchased in bulk quantities for businesses, associations, institutions or sales promotions. Please call our Special Sales Department in New York at 212/683-2244 or 800/322-8755.

Text design by Robert Yaffe
Jacket design by Paul Agresti

VB VC 10 9 8 7 6 5 4 3 2 1

This book is printed on acid-free paper.

Printed in the United States of America

CONTENTS

HOW TO USE
THIS BOOK

Pirates marauded during many eras and in all parts of the world. Many spoke languages other than English, and some wrote in other alphabets. Almost all followed a calendar different from the current one. *Pirates!* seeks to provide the essential facts in a consistent, clear, and interesting manner. The spelling of names and places is consistent with the usage of other historical studies and reference works.

The main heading gives the name by which an individual, topic, organization, or work of fiction is best known. A short phrase in parentheses after the name briefly describes that person or topic. The original language of literary and musical works and motion pictures is noted only when it is not English. If no language is mentioned, then the work first appeared in English.

Following this descriptive phrase, additional information within the parentheses tells where and when an individual or an institution existed or a literary work was produced. This information includes the ocean(s) or sea(s) in which a pirate operated. If possible, birth and death dates are given. When these are not known (the most frequent case), the years listed tell when a person was "active"—when he or she took part in piracy or in the other activities described. Unless "B.C." specifically is indicated, all years are "A.D." All dates have been changed to conform to the modern (Gregorian) calendar, with the year beginning on January 1.

Descriptions of nationality are given solely to help identify an individual's origins. Modern nations did not exist or had different boundaries in earlier centuries. Individuals thought of themselves as citizens of cities or regions. Take the example of Italy, created in 1871. In earlier eras, residents identified with cities such as Venice, Genoa, and Pisa, which often were at war. When this is known, *Pirates!* identifies an individual's native city or province. There is an important difference between a Genoese pirate that plundered the Pisan enemy (such as

Enrico PESCATORE) and one that tortured his fellow Genoese (as Michele BALBO did).

Within the text, words printed in small capital letters refer to another entry that gives additional information or that explains a technical term or phrase. Obvious words (e.g., galley) are cross-referenced only when of further use to the reader. These cross-references do not necessarily match exactly in terms of singular vs. plural, possessives, etc. For example, though the entry title is Rafael Sabatini, a cross-reference to it within another entry might be SABATINI's.

At the end of entries, additional cross-references ("see also") are given in parentheses. These include references to the Selected Bibliography, many of which indicate source material. Books are listed by the author's last name and an abbreviated title. The Bibliography gives the complete title and place of publication for every work. Throughout, all quotations and titles of literary works preserve the original spelling and punctuation of the author cited.

Sea raiders frequently used several names, and sources often spell the same name in various ways. When the differences are significant, these secondary names and variant spellings are provided. Special problems exist in transliterating names from foreign languages with alphabets different from our own, such as Greek, Arabic, and Chinese. Over the years, English-speaking scholars have adopted various systems of transliteration, none of which is universally accepted. *Pirates!* uses the same spelling as standard biographies and reference works, such as the *Oxford Classical Dictionary*.

Governments sometimes change the names of places and geographical features following wars and political revolutions. As with personal names, *Pirates!* uses the traditional name—that accepted at the time an event occurred and also found in other historical studies. When a new name later was adopted, it is given in parentheses following the traditional name. The spelling of these modern place names follows that of current maps and gazetteers.

In the articles on BOOTY and on individual pirates, no attempt has been made to give a current currency value for foreign monies in earlier eras. Any estimate of this type is bound to be wildly inaccurate.

Part of the difficulty lies in identifying comparable commodities and products. Assume, for example, that one is attempting to translate the value of Sir Francis DRAKE's booty into current dollars. Some items (such as food and housing) were much less expensive in 16th-century England, while others (iron and some types of clothing) cost as much as or more than they do today. And many items that Drake needed—such as antibiotics, radios, depth-finders, and accurate CANNON—could not be obtained at any price. Any comparison between older and current currency values can be only an imprecise approximation. Perhaps it is safe to say, for example, that the British pound in Drake's day had the buying power of something like a thousand pounds in current currency.

PREFACE

While they existed, pirates profoundly affected the course of human history. After pirates ceased to scour the seas, a rich pirate mythology developed; and "The Pirate" is among the oldest and most familiar images in literature and in the movies. While pirate reality and pirate fiction both are intrinsically engrossing and historically significant, they are not the same. Depending on whether reality or mythology is at issue, several principles have been followed in selecting topics for inclusion in *Pirates*.

In real life, pirates were seamen who robbed others. Most biographical entries tell about men who were both mariners and brigands. Other entries describe nautical and pirate culture as well as the methods used to capture prey and dispose of booty. Some men are present because they made it possible for pirates to commit their crimes. Every pirate needed HAVENS and assistance from governments at pirate ports. *Pirates!* thus includes important sponsors of piracy, even though some never went to sea.

There can be a question whether a mariner's acts really were piracy. As late as the 1860s, some governments gave out PRIVATEERING commissions, which allowed captains to attack ships from enemy nations. Absent are men that seized only belligerent vessels during wartime and followed governmental rules in disposing of their booty. Those included in *Pirates!* sometimes purchased commissions, often fraudulently. But they went on to commit acts not permitted by privateering rules. In some cases, as their biography explains, they acted legally on other occasions.

It has proved impossible to cite every mariner sailing on a pirate ship. However, most captains and masters are included—even when there is no proof that they took major booty. Pirates often were secretive so that evidence about their loot has not survived. It is reasonable to assume that a man received command of a vessel only after he had demonstrated his nautical and piratical skills. Also present are ordinary seamen who are famous for their non-piratical activities.

There is insufficient space to mention every work of pirate fiction and mythology. Dozens of volumes would be needed to describe every pirate novel, story, play, poem, and painting. In selecting works for inclusion, the first test has been accessibilty. Readers will be able to obtain most fiction cited in *Pirates!*. Books no longer in print usually are available at most public libraries. *Pirates!* does omit both most works never translated into English and pre-1900 works in English found only in a few research libraries, closed to the public.

Availability is determined by success, and success partly depends on literary quality. At least for pirate fiction, the best-selling works usually are the best-written. EXQUEMELIN's *Buccaneers of America*, Defoe's GENERAL HISTORY OF THE PYRATES, and Stevenson's TREASURE ISLAND have remained in print. When fictional works are rare, they often are of lesser literary worth. Because of this link between popularity and quality, *Pirates!* tells how a book or movie was received, when this can be determined.

Some uncommon books are listed because they influenced later, better-known works. For example, *Pirates!* reports on translations of fiction originally written in ancient Latin and Greek. Ancient works tell fascinating stories, which deserve to be better known. Moreover, their authors invented pirate legends and symbolism that were borrowed by modern writers. In this way, ancient legends were incorporated into current pirate mythology. Tracing their history and origins elucidates and enriches the meaning of modern pirate myths.

Pirates! includes virtually all English-language movies with a piratical theme. Some have not been re-released and are unavailable on videotape. However, they are likely to become more accessible in the future, especially with the increasing number of television channels devoted to movies.

I am grateful for the unflagging efforts and courtesy of Kathleen Carr, Lorrie Chase, and Mary Donald at the Inter-Library Loan Division of the Broward County Library. This work would have been impossible without their aid in obtaining books and journal articles—many old, truly obscure, and in uncommon languages. Esperanza de Varona generously arranged for photographs of rare books in the Special Collections of the University of Miami's Richter Library. As always, my greatest debts and primary loyalty are acknowledged by the dedication.

INTRODUCTION

Pirate Myth Vs. Pirate Fact

In *Gormenghast*, Mervyn Peake's 1950 fantasy novel, seven-year-old Titus, 77th Lord of Groan, daydreams about a

> posse of pirates . . . as tall as towers, their great brows beetl-ing over their sunken eyes, like shelves of overhanging rocks. In their ears were hoops of red gold, and in their mouths scythe-edged cutlasses a-drip. Out of the red darkness they emerged, . . . the water at their waists circling and bubbling with the hot light reflected from their bodies. . . . And still they came on, until there was only room enough for the smouldering head of the central buccaneer, a great salt-water lord, every inch of whose face was scabbed and scarred like a boy's knee, whose teeth were carved into the shapes of skulls, whose throat was circled by the tattooing of a scaled snake.

Peake's pirate chief is a terrifying, almost suprahuman outlaw. Yet so rich is pirate mythology that even Peake's dramatic vision catches only one of its multifold facets.

Except for a few marauders during the 1820s, pirates vanished from the Atlantic by 1725. Although they survived until 1830, the BARBARY corsairs long had posed only a minor menace. Almost 300 years have passed since pirates seriously threatened travelers and mariners in Euro-pean and American waters.

Without real brigands to provide a point of reference, pirate FICTION and MOVIES have been free to invent and adapt legends almost at whim. "The Pirate" provided a blank canvas on which anyone could draw whatever likeness he or she chose. As they created imaginary brigands, some artists captured mankind's deepest fantasies, fears, and desires—thus creating enduring myths. By the 20th century, many superimposed layers covered the canvas, preserving alternative and often contradic-tory images of piracy.

In early tales, the pirate is a cruel psychopath. This image was cre-ated by A. O. EXQUEMELIN and Daniel DEFOE, the prime sources mined by later authors. Mixing fact and fiction, each wrote just as a major epoch in pirate history ended. Exquemelin took part in Sir Henry MORGAN's 1671 Panama raid. Defoe's GENERAL HISTORY OF THE PYRATES (1724–1728) described the last brigands in the Atlantic.

In most respects, their fictional pirates are ordinary folk, who dress and live much like anyone else. Neither author paid much attention to pirate pleasures. Each instead emphasized violence and cruelty, convinced (correctly) that these would titillate their readers more than drunken orgies.

François L'OLONNAIS, Exquemelin's brutal hero, "ripped open one of his prisoners with his cutlass, tore the living heart out of his body, gnawed at it, and then hurled it in the face of one of the others." Perhaps trying to surpass Exquemelin, Defoe depicts Edward LOW slashing off ears, lips, noses, and other body parts (but no hearts). However, Defoe's most memorable creation, Edward TEACH alias BLACKBEARD, only torments and murders but does not eat his victims. Blackbeard's grotesque beard and clothing were intended as a broad joke. But generations of enthralled readers have accepted them as typical pirate dress.

Not all Defoe's pirate chiefs are as vile as Blackbeard. Defoe also invented the myth of the pirate as a virtuous outlaw, a nautical Robin Hood exiled by his inferiors. At MADAGASCAR, Defoe's Captain MISSON founds Libertalia, where kindly pirates care for the sick and old, and men of many colors live together in tender harmony.

Captain Misson is little known compared to villains like Blackbeard. In real life, Blackbeard was a mediocre robber. His exploits were nothing, for example, compared to those of Bartholomew ROBERTS. Yet Defoe's more accurate portrait of Roberts is overlooked precisely because it does not mention bestial tortures. For three centuries, Blackbeard's vile cruelties have eclipsed both Misson's utopia and Roberts's astonishing onslaughts. Defoe's (and Exquemelin's) stories became undying myths only when they provided the sadistic villains readers crave.

Unlike Exquemelin's Morgan and Defoe's Blackbeard, CAPTAIN KIDD—piracy's third major figure—was created by the popular culture and not by a specific author. It is significant that ordinary people invented this fiend, who buries his Bible and murders his own crewmen. With Kidd also came the myth that pirates buried their TREASURE— something real raiders never did.

The fundamental myths were firmly established by 1800. Most fictional pirates are savage murderers, a few are noble outlaws. Except for Defoe's Blackbeard, however, they resemble other seamen. Nineteenth-century authors and artists added the details of dress and behavior Mervyn Peake so vividly describes.

Accepting the myth that pirates were wicked, Victorian authors assumed they must have done everything that is wrong. Genteel society preached that certain pleasures are inherently evil, including DRINKING, sexuality, and SWEARING. Since pirates were evil, and these acts were evil, authors felt free to concoct the myth of pirate debauchery. Curiously, however, a note of envy often creeps in. How nice it would be, *The* LAST BUCCANEER implies, if we also could devote our lives to RUM and WOMEN of color.

Fictional pirates further set themselves apart by other filthy habits, such as dirty clothes and bare bosoms. By the end of the 19th century, some writers even fancied they wore EARRINGS and TATTOOS. Needless

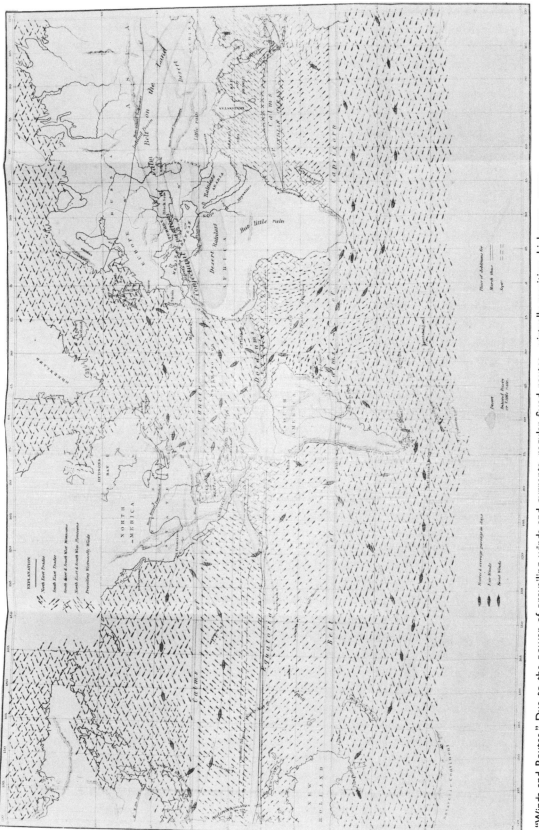

"Winds and Routes." Due to the power of prevailing winds and currents, regular fixed routes—virtually maritime highways—were favored both by merchantmen and by the pirates hunting them. Matthew Maury, *The Physical Geography of the Sea* (New York, 1855).

to say, they constantly blasphemed God and his Holy Bible. (Less stress was given to their use of tobacco, a habit not fiercely condemned until the late 20th century.)

Although they join together in orgies, fictional pirates never enjoy real friendships. They constantly betray their MATES and murder each other to steal buried treasure. All lust after GOLD, but most then hide it away. To conceal its location, they devise MAPS crammed with strange symbols.

The pirate's foul habits were exaggerated in popular children's books, anthologies, and melodramas. A note of buffoonery was present from the beginning. In Washington Irving's WOLFERT WEBBER (1824), the drunken ravings of a loutish ex-buccaneer frighten feeble tavern-goers. By the century's end, foolish captains were commonplace in vaudeville skits. These cartoon pirates were fondly satirized in The PIRATES OF PENZANCE and PETER PAN. Ironically, although HOOK lives in "Neverland" with other imaginary creatures, many grow up believing that his crew resemble real pirates.

In these main myths, pirates were either vile monsters or silly fools. However, authors occasionally revived Defoe's Libertalia, creating gentlemen bandits forced into crime. Patriotic novels such as WESTWARD HO! (1855) idolized English raiders who harassed the loathsome Spaniards. In Lord Byron's The CORSAIR (1814), the pirates similarly attack only heathen Turks. Byron's superb Captain Conrad is the finest example of the pirate chief as Romantic hero.

TREASURE ISLAND (1883) perfects the diverse myths about strange maps, buried treasure, and drunken seamen. (However, a boy's book could not mention sex or swearing.) Long John Silver's crew contains crude bullies, and Ben Gunn is a cackling madman. However, Silver himself shows elements of grandeur, like an incomplete version of Byron's corsair. Despite realistic appraisals of motivation, the novel has a fantastic air. Silver's PARROT is "maybe two hundred years old, and if anybody's seen more wickedness, it must be the devil himself."

By 1900, a complex pirate mythology incorporated many disparate strands. Pirates were ugly, sadistic brutes; between murders, they drank, sang songs, and toyed with compliant WENCHES. They captured finger-trickling treasures, but then hid them away and never returned. At the same time, a few captains were flawless gentlemen, whose victims deserved to be robbed. Yet a third tradition portrayed pirates as silly figures of fun—too drunk, stupid, or crazed to harm anyone.

Twentieth-century fiction and movies elaborated and exaggerated these myths. During the 1930s and 1940s, films (adapted from Rafael SABATINI's novels) gave the world pirate chiefs as arrogantly beautiful as Byron's corsair. In these epics, Errol FLYNN and Tyrone POWER enthrall gorgeous women while overcoming powerful forces of evil. In the 20th-century's greatest contribution to pirate mythology, their heroes excel in frenzied SWORD DUELS with fencing foils—a weapon only invented during the late 1600s.

Lacking equally charismatic stars, later SWASHBUCKLERS emphasized gory torture scenes that would have delighted Exquemelin and Defoe. From the 1940s, other movies parodied that stock vaudeville character, the Demented Captain, wildly rolling his eyes while bellowing fake-nautical curses.

Novels and movies increasingly mix several pirate myths. Somewhere in the mythical Caribbean, a bare-chested hero wades through rivers of Technicolor blood to rescue a voluptuous woman—but he fights merely a preposterous captain and his bumbling crew. Douglas Fairbanks's *The* BLACK PIRATE (1926), the earliest of these hybrids, successfully combined a noble and gymnastic hero, gruesome torture, and buffoonery. In some recent hybrids, the discordant ingredients fail to blend, and the FLOGGINGS and murders seem funny rather than terrifying.

Pirate Society and Culture

Fictional sea rovers are virtually a separate race, with a unique language, customs, weapons, and clothing. In real life, they resembled other sailors of their time period. Indeed, pirate crews often seemed to exaggerate and even flaunt the "lifestyle" they shared with other mariners.

Handling the rigging, steering, navigating, stowing cargo, and provisioning and maintaining the vessel—all required skills different from those of landsmen. There were no schools for seamen. Mariners went to sea as youths and spent their lives perfecting their craft.

During eras when men and women rarely traveled more than a few miles, sailors left their homes for months or even years. At sea, they formed a close-knit, interdependent community, whose members relied on each other for their lives. On larger vessels, men were divided into hierarchies of power and skill. However, tasks often were communal, and some could only be accomplished by many men. Even common seamen understood the purpose and rudiments of a specialist's tasks. An experienced sailor knew whether his ship was being operated correctly, even if he could not navigate it himself.

Mariners share certain traits, growing out of their unique way of life. They think of their ship's company as separate from and generally superior to landsmen. They tend to be independent and plain-spoken (and usually foul-mouthed). Although they have little respect for titles, they form close bonds with individuals they trust.

Pirates possessed these common nautical traits to an unusual degree. At sea, they were more isolated than other mariners, who could visit with passing vessels and dock at any port. This sense of alienation partially explains their willingness to assault and rob strangers. The prey was viewed as radically different from themselves, as outsiders, as "the other."

Among themselves, pirates were even more fiercely independent than other sailors. Naval squadrons always ran under military discipline, and European merchant ships became more authoritarian from the 16th century. Officers lived apart from common seamen, treated them as inferiors, and drove them with whips. By contrast, pirate life became radically democratic.

A pirate always was free to choose his own captain for each voyage. From the 1680s, as they undertook long, multi-year expeditions, pirate crews elected and fired captains while at sea. The ship's ARTICLES became a sacred covenant. Even though some had greater responsibilities, each crewman received an equal share of the booty. Physical punishments were rare and imposed only by majority vote.

Despite this extreme democracy—sometimes degenerating into anarchy—pirates felt a strong sense of community. Wounded men received an extra share of the loot. Crewmen and officers sailed as a team. Many formed strong attachments that sometimes matured into love. Pirates were as diverse as any other group of men. Their history does contain appalling brutality and foolish drunkenness. But it also records extraordinary seamanship and adventures, marked by moments of courage and unselfish brotherhood.

A

ABBAS, TUANKU *(Malayan pirate; South China Sea; active 1840s)* A brother of the rajah of Achin in northern Borneo, Abbas sponsored and led pirate raids. In 1843, he plundered an Indian vessel and imprisoned its owner and crew. The captives escaped and appealed to British authorities, who burned Abbas' village in February 1844.

ABBOTT AND COSTELLO MEET CAPTAIN KIDD *(motion picture; color; 1952)* Stranded on TORTUGA, the two comedians work as waiters and are asked to pass along a love letter. When they accidentally switch the letter for a treasure map, they are kidnapped by CAPTAIN KIDD (Charles Laughton), Captain [Henry] MORGAN (Leif Erickson), and Anne BONNY (Hillary Brooke), who head for Skull Island to find the buried booty. While this is one of the boys' less hilarious efforts, Laughton hams delightfully. Directed by Charles Lamont.

ABDULLA AL-HADJ *(British pirate; South China Sea; 1843)* In September, a British trading vessel stopped at Murdu in northern Borneo. While it was taking on cargo, Abdulla and the rajah's brother came on board. The visitors suddenly killed the captain and another officer, took over the ship, and stripped it bare.

Hoping to avoid punishment, the rajah of Murdu turned Abdulla over to the East India Company (but kept the loot). Abdulla was imprisoned for life at Bombay. During his trial, he stated that he was born in

Charles Laughton (center) in *Abbott and Costello Meet Captain Kidd* (1952).

England and taken to Arabia as a young boy. He had converted to Islam and somehow arrived at Murdu, where he became the rajah's chief advisor.

ABDULLA IBN MURRA *(Arab corsair; Mediterranean; active 707–708)* Sent to raid Sardinia by Musa Ibn Nusayr (the governor of North Africa, who conquered Spain in 711). He returned with 3,000 captives and treasures of gold and silver.

ABDUL-RAHMAN BARGACH AL-HADJ
(Moroccan corsair; Mediterranean, Atlantic; 1829)
One of the last corsairs operating from SALÉ. After his band captured several Austrian sailors, six warships bombarded and burned most of the Moroccan navy, thereby convincing the sultan to enforce laws against piracy.

ABDUL-RAHMAN BRITAL AL-HADJ *(Moroccan corsair; Mediterranean; 1829)* One of the last SALÉ corsairs. When he and ABDUL-RAHMAN BARGACH AL-HADJ captured some Austrian sailors, the Austrian navy's fierce reprisals ended Moroccan piracy.

ABDUL-RAHMAN CASTAGLI (KEUSTEKLY) REIS *(Barbary corsair; Mediterranean; active 1541–1554)* Castagli (from an Arabic word for "golden chain") captured Jean de LA VALETTE about 1541, made him a GALLEY SLAVE, and treated him with great harshness. Ransomed by his fellow KNIGHTS OF MALTA, Valette gained his revenge in 1554. His GALLEY defeated Abdul-Rahman's FUSTE, and the Muslim corsairs were condemned as oarsmen at Malta.

ABDUL-RAHMAN REIS *(Moroccan corsair; Mediterranean; active 1694–1698)* Captain of a warship (18 cannon and 130 crew), he sailed from SALÉ with his brother, BEN AÏSSA.

ABU HAFS *(Muslim corsair; Mediterranean; active 816–827)* Led adventurers who seized CRETE from the BYZANTINE EMPIRE in 827. After an unsuccessful uprising in Cordova, Spain, a large group of rebels fled with their families to Alexandria in Egypt. Profiting from local unrest, they chose Abu Hafs as their leader, took Alexandria in 816, and held it until the caliph's army ousted them in 827.

The defeated Spaniards were allowed to leave for Crete, which they already had raided at least once. Led by Abu Hafs, the band easily occupied the island. His descendants ruled as pirate emirs until the Byzantine reconquest in 962.

ACCOUNT, GOING ON THE *(nautical slang; all oceans; 16th–19th century)* An English saying, meaning that no wages were paid until BOOTY was taken. Both PIRATES and PRIVATEERS served "on account" when they agreed to ship's ARTICLES specifying NO PURCHASE, NO PAY. The phrase is popular with writers of pirate fiction, who exaggerate its significance. From the 15th century or earlier, other craftsmen and professionals (such as lawyers) also worked "on account."

ACCOUNT OF JOHN GOW *(biography; 1725)* Daniel DEFOE published this life of John SMITH, nicknamed Gow, on the day of his hanging. Defoe later shortened Gow's biography for the third edition of his GENERAL HISTORY. The revised version makes one major

(and romantic) change. Gow was captured at the Orkney Islands, where—the *General History* says—he was visiting the woman he loved.

ACHILLES TATIUS *(Greek novelist; second century)* Author of LEUCIPE AND CLEITOPHON. An orator and possibly a lawyer in Alexandria, Egypt. His name may refer to the god Tat.

ADMIRAL (1) *(nautical terminology; 1300 to present)* A naval commander of the highest rank, in charge of a squadron or fleet. The title is derived from the Arabic word *amir* ("commander"). In Muslim Spain and SICILY, the head of the nation's naval forces was called the *amir-al-ma* ("commander of the water") or the *amir-al-man* ("commander of the sea"). When Christian kings took over these countries, they kept the same office and the Arabic title. Genoese and French rulers copied the practice, and the English king also appointed an "Admyrall of the Se."

In England, LORD HIGH ADMIRALS were appointed from time to time until 1964. From about 1500, however, the same word also was used more loosely, when referring to anyone commanding the captains of several ships. In addition to naval squadrons, captains of fishing boats and merchant ships also might choose one man as "admiral."

English pirates sometimes elected an admiral when they agreed to act in CONSORT. The pirates operating from Irish ports made Richard BISHOP their admiral, and he commanded nine ships and 1,000 men in 1609. In 1668 and 1670, the governor of Jamaica commissioned Sir Henry MORGAN as admiral and allowed him to recruit captains for raids against the Spaniards.

(See also Guglielmo GRASSO, Enrico PESCATORE.)

ADMIRAL (2) *(novel; 1982)* Dudley POPE continues the adventures begun in BUCCANEER, as Ned Yorke and Sir Thomas WHETSTONE scour the Caribbean accompanied by their beautiful mistresses. Driven from Barbados for his royalist views, Yorke and other captains operate from PORT ROYAL, Jamaica, in 1660. When King Charles II regains power, Yorke could return to farming, but he decides that piracy is more exciting.

Yorke and Whetstone learn that the Spanish government, unable to pay for a TREASURE FLEET, has stored vast riches at PORTOBELO. Moreover, Spanish officials have removed soldiers from Portobelo and sent them to invade Jamaica. Yorke seizes this chance to grab Spanish gold.

The two captains go to TORTUGA. There the BUCCANEERS elect Yorke their admiral, with Whetstone his second-in-command. Since there are few ships to plunder, Yorke persuades the pirates to loot cities instead, with Portobelo as their first target. Leading 28 vessels and a thousand men, Yorke returns to Jamaica, where his pirates save the governor from a military rebellion.

With his soldiers away invading Jamaica, the Spanish governor quickly surrenders PROVIDENCE ISLAND. Going on to Portobelo, Yorke takes the town's four strong forts by trickery. The buccaneers anchor away from Portobelo and enter overland. A renegade Spaniard leads men dressed in Spanish armor seized at Providence Island. The pirates gain entry to the main stronghold, and they convince the other forts to surrender.

Less bloodthirsty than in later novels, Yorke does not massacre Spanish soldiers or civilians. His pirates return to Jamaica with millions in booty. Although London has outlawed piracy, the governor happily takes a share of their loot. Port Royal becomes the buccaneers' main haven.

Yorke's conquests are adapted from historical incidents. Providence Island was taken by Edward MANSFIELD in 1665. The surprise attack on Portobelo is based on Bartholomew SHARP's 1680 raid and not on Sir Henry MORGAN's more famous assault in 1668. However, no real-life buccaneer seized the king's treasure at Portobelo or any other fortress. The Spaniards did not send troops from Panama to invade Jamaica. They did not ferry the treasure from Portobelo to Cartagena in small ships.

(See also BUCCANEER; CORSAIR; GALLEON.)

ADMIRALTY COURT (British prize court; 14th century to 1875)

The LORD HIGH ADMIRAL settled maritime disputes until a formal Admiralty Court was created in about 1400. Its judge became an independent official, appointed by the king, during the 16th century. In 1875, the Admiralty and several other English courts were merged into one unified High Court of Justice.

The Admiralty Court had authority over everything happening at sea and as far inland as the first bridge crossing a river. In civil law, the court enforced shipping and insurance contracts as well as wage agreements between owners and sailors. During the 16th and 17th centuries, the court dealt with PASSES and judged contracts involving foreigners and between Englishmen overseas. In criminal law, the court punished all offenses at sea or relating to shipping. The Admiralty was the proper place to sue when a ship or cargo was damaged by another ship or by the negligence of sailors.

The Admiralty Court also was responsible for all aspects of PRIVATEERING and piracy. The court granted letters of MARQUE and REPRISAL. It guided the VICE-ADMIRALS, who appraised booty and collected the court's own fees as well as the shares due the admiral and king.

From 1589, the Admiralty Court regulated prizes and decided whether ships were legally captured. Foreign merchants and diplomats sued to recover their property, and English privateers turned to the court to settle arguments over booty. As England's only prize court into the 19th century, the Admiralty did the same work as the Maltese TRIBUNALE DEGLI ARMAMENTI.

The Admiralty Court enforced its decision by issuing orders to lower royal officials. The court could command them to recover stolen goods and arrest alleged pirates, but it did not try piracy cases. Under a 1536 law, the

Admiralty issued a commission to a special court in London, which convened a trial jury.

Despite its enormous powers, the court failed to control privateers during the 16th century. Powerful men like Sir Walter RALEIGH financed raids on friendly shipping as well as on the enemy. In these cases, the court could not enforce decisions that favored foreign owners. The situation improved during the 18th century, when the court judged thousands of cases involving prizes taken by naval ships.

The court also failed to control piracy, and English pirates with influential friends (such as John CALLICE) bought their freedom. When the BUCCANEERS became a problem after 1650, colonial officials refused to send pirates to London for trial. Many were acquitted by colonial jurors, who did not consider piracy a serious crime. To ensure that they would be punished, the government brought William KIDD and Joseph BRADISH to London in a warship.

The first effective laws against piracy were not passed until about 1700. The government set up a new system of vice-admiralty courts in nearly all the colonies, and it allowed panels of officials and naval officers to try pirates. Woodes ROGERS used this law to hang pirates at NEW PROVIDENCE ISLAND in 1719.

ADORNO, GIORGIO (Knight of Malta; Mediterranean; died 1558)

An Italian from Naples, elected CAPTAIN-GENERAL OF THE GALLEYS (in 1547, 1549, 1557, and 1558) as well as admiral (1547–1548). In 1547, his squadron captured a treasure ship that TURGUT REIS had dispatched to Constantinople, and it took other rich prizes in 1549.

ADRIATIC COAST (pirate haven; Adriatic Sea; 600 B.C.–A.D. 9, 800–1700)

The entire eastern coast of the Adriatic provides excellent HAVENS for sea bandits. Natural obstacles prevent invasion from inland regions. The Balkan peninsula is almost entirely mountainous, and the coastal ranges are harsh and lifeless. Large ships cannot navigate the few major rivers, while the ruggedly broken coastline and hundreds of islands provide many safe harbors for small boats.

Although difficult, passage from the interior is not impossible, and many different ethnic groups have settled in the region. Since the soil is poor and often sterile, these coastal peoples have always lived from the sea. Whenever the region's rulers have been either weak or bribable, many groups have turned pirate. Several devised special craft unique to the Dalmatian coast, including the LEMBOS, LIBURNIAN, and BRAZZERE.

In antiquity, ILLYRIAN tribes occupied the entire coast. From the 600s B.C., those to the south (in what is now Albania) pillaged their neighbors. The Adriatic Sea is narrow—only 45 miles wide at the Straits of Otranto between Italy and Albania. Pirates easily raided to the west or to the south until Roman armies crushed them between 229 and 168 B.C. Other pirate groups to the north (in ISTRIA and DALMATIA) were pacified by A.D. 9. All Illyria was subject to the Roman and later to the BYZANTINE EMPIRE, whose navies suppressed piracy.

Byzantine rule collapsed during the seventh century, and Slavic tribes occupied the coast. As Venice became a major trading power during the 800s, the NARENTANS along the northern coast again took to piracy. The Oriental trade that made Venice wealthy regularly traveled along the inhospitable Dalmatian shores. For nine centuries, Venice policed the region more or less successfully. Adopting a merciless policy, the Venetians killed any pirates they could capture and destroyed communities that harbored them.

Piracy thus thrived only when Venice was weak. After the Narentans were crushed in 998, the seas remained relatively peaceful until the 16th century. From the 1520s, the OTTOMAN EMPIRE occupied most of the region, Venice retained several coastal fortresses, and the Austrian Habsburgs ruled in northern Dalmatia. Taking advantage of disputes between these three empires, the USKOKS and other large bands ravaged the coast. Venice finally declared war to end Austrian support of the Uskoks, who were expelled in 1618.

(See also DEMETRIUS OF PHAROS; GENTHIUS; MICHAEL OF ZACHLUMIA; SCERDILAIDAS; TEUTA; SELECTED BIBLIOGRAPHY: West, *Black Lamb.*)

AELIANUS, CLAUDIUS *(Roman author; about 170–235)* In his *De Natura Animalium (On the Nature of Animals)*, the anecdotes teach moral lessons. In one story, from the fourth century B.C., he makes the point that even a pig knows his master's voice.

Pirates raid the TYRRHENIAN coast and carry off some pigs. When the pirates put to sea, swineherds shout to the pigs, who run to one side of the boat and overturn it. The pigs swim ashore, but the pirates drown. Chloe, the heroine of *Daphnis and Chloe*, uses a similar trick to rescue her lover.

AETOLIA *(Greek corsair haven; 300–186 B.C.)* Aetolia occupied a mountainous and wooded country in the center of Greece between Macedonia and the Gulf of Corinth. A warrior race, the Aetolians were among the last Greeks to develop commerce. In ancient times, every state waged war to enrich its citizens as well as to settle political disputes. But the Aetolians were unusual in making war and piracy their main business.

Often joining with corsairs from CRETE, the Aetolians ravaged the eastern Mediterranean during the third century. (After 150 CILICIA became the main pirate haven.) Most governments tolerated the Aetolians' raids and hired them to fight in their wars.

After Alexander the Great died in 323, ambitious generals fought to divide up his huge empire. Three relatively stable states emerged by 281—Macedonia, Ptolemaic Egypt, and the Seleucid or Syrian Empire. But none of these major powers attempted to make the seas

safe. Only RHODES never compromised with the corsairs, but one island could not defend the entire eastern Mediterranean.

The AETOLIAN LEAGUE was a nation of warriors and brigands, whose main profession was fighting as mercenaries for all the competing empires. When no one hired them, Aetolian bands plundered foreign states on their own account. The Aetolian League never created a navy. Instead, it tolerated piracy by individual captains, so long as they did not attack allied states. Indeed, the League encouraged piracy since it forced other nations to make treaties that favored Aetolia.

The Aetolians became noted as mercenary soldiers on land and then turned to the sea. The various city-states and empires always hired large numbers of mercenaries. From about 300 B.C. they also retained bands headed by an ARCHPIRATE to supplement their regular naval forces. All the empires used pirates during their frequent wars.

Even though Macedonia and Aetolia were traditional enemies on land, Macedonian kings often hired the services of Aetolians and other pirates. When Demetrius I besieged Rhodes from 305 to 304, a thousand private ships followed his navy, and the king put TIMOCLES and other corsairs on his payroll. In 276, an Aetolian band headed by AMEINIAS OF PHOCIS and MELATAS captured Cassandreia for Antigonus II, Demetrius' successor. In 204, Philip V secretly hired DICAEARCHUS to loot the Aegean islands. HYBRISTAS' Cephallian pirates in 190 may have been working for Antiochus of Syria.

Between wars, Aetolian corsairs raided for booty and slaves. Aetolian slave raids ravaged the Greek islands and mainland from about 250. SOCLEIDAS plundered the island of Amorgos, and another Aetolian band carried off 280 persons from Naxos. BUCRIS and others pillaged the coasts around Athens, and Aetolian slavers raided as far east as Cyprus. To buy immunity from pirate raids, dozens of islands and cities signed treaties with the Aetolian League.

The League encouraged these raids against foreigners and then pretended to know nothing about them. In 221, for example, two Aetolian chieftains raided the neighboring state of Messenia. Without seeking the League's approval, they sent out a pirate fleet, seized a Macedonian warship, sold its crew into slavery, and then pillaged coastal towns. In 220, the League's spring assembly, pretending it never had heard of these raids, declared that it was at peace with all other states. But it did not try to stop the same chiefs—this time joined by the Illyrian SCERDILAIDAS—from raiding Arcadia.

By this policy of public peace and private war, Aetolia gained booty without risk—much as England later profited from raids by Sir Francis DRAKE and Sir John HAWKINS.

AETOLIAN LEAGUE *(Greek military and pirate confederation; Mediterranean; 300–186 B.C.)*

During the fourth century B.C., the various tribes of AETOLIA formed a federal League made up of small towns and rural districts. This federal government dealt only with war and foreign policy, and the various districts remained autonomous in local matters. The League was the political voice of the Aetolian warriors, and all men of military age could vote at the Assembly's two yearly meetings. Day to day decisions were made by a general, elected annually, and his council. There was no admiral, for at sea Aetolia depended on private citizens licensed as PRIVATEERS.

From about 290, the Aetolian League expanded on land by taking in adjacent territories as full or affiliated members. It forced more distant regions to sign treaties accepting its dominance. By 240, the League controlled all of central Greece (except for the Athenian territories) and the western parts of the Peloponnesian Peninsula.

The Aetolian League used piracy to expand at sea during these same years. The League did not recognize any form of "international law," and it encouraged piracy against the citizens of a foreign state. The Aetolians became wealthy from pirate booty. Moreover, from about 250, the League encouraged piracy by individual captains as part of a "protection racket." Unable to defend their citizens against corsair attacks, dozens of Aegean and Ionian islands and several coastal cities signed treaties recognizing the League's supremacy.

Through these methods, the Aetolian League became the second strongest state in Greece after Macedonia. As the Romans extended their power, the Aetolians at first were their active allies. However, in 192, they made the mistake of turning on Rome, partly because they feared that Roman control of Greece would end their profitable plunder raids. With Roman victory, the Aetolians became subject-allies of Rome and could not make war without Roman approval. Their League lost its power, and pirates no longer found a safe haven in Aetolian ports.

AGAINST ALL FLAGS *(motion picture; color; 1952)* About 1700, British officer Brian Hawke (Errol FLYNN) is FLOGGED for deserting during battle. That night, Hawke escapes with two companions and rows to the MADAGASCAR shore. The beating was a ruse to fool the pirates. Hawke plans to spy out their impregnable stronghold at Diégo-Suarez.

The pirate captains drag Hawke before their court. Roc Brasiliano (Anthony QUINN) suspects Hawke's trick and wants him put to death. A fierce female pirate, Spitfire Stevens (Maureen O'HARA), saves Hawke's life, and he becomes the navigator on Roc's ship.

The pirates overcome an Indian ship and capture women from the imperial harem. Hawke learns that one of them is Princess Patma (Alice Kelley), the emperor's daughter. He protects her, angering Spitfire Stevens, who has fallen in love with him. When the princess is sold at

Errol Flynn and Maureen O'Hara in *Against All Flags* (1952).

auction, Flynn tries to buy her. Spitfire bids higher and takes the girl to her home.

Hawke signals the British fleet to attack, after his two assistants spike the pirate fort's cannon. Brasiliano catches Hawke and his men before they can flee the island with Princess Patma. At Roc's orders, they are tied to stakes at the water's edge, to be eaten alive by large crabs. Spitfire pretends to stab Hawke but really cuts his bonds.

The British ships attack. Stevens sails on Brasiliano's flagship, where Princess Patma is held captive. Hawke and his men sneak aboard. In a wild SWORD DUEL, Hawke kills Brasiliano and saves Stevens and the princess. Hawke is honored by the British admiral, who gives him custody of Stevens. They embrace as the ship sails away from the pirate island.

The film, directed by George Sherman, is fast-paced and contains some parody of other pirate films. At one point, Hawke (played by an unidentified stuntman) jabs his sword through a sail. While holding the hilt, he slides down the sail as his blade slits it—repeating Douglas Fairbanks' feat in THE BLACK PIRATE. The pirates and their city are immaculately clean, and the captains and Spitfire wear elaborately tailored costumes.

In contrast to his habit in CAPTAIN BLOOD (2) and THE SEA HAWK (3), the older Flynn never removes his shirt. But he is still handsome and athletic, and he performs many stunts himself. Quinn acts sneeringly villainous as Brasiliano. Until she melts into Flynn's arms,

O'Hara lives up to her name as Spitfire Stevens, a role based on the legend of Anne BONNY (2). In real life, Henry EVERY, not Roche BRASILIANO, who never visited Madagascar, plundered the emperor's ship.

AHMED ALCOUAR REIS *(Turkish corsair; Mediterranean; active 1768–1769)* Commanded a 22-gun sailing ship in the SALÉ fleet.

AHMED CUPRAT REIS *(Barbary corsair; Mediterranean; 1604)* The KNIGHTS OF SAINT STEPHEN captured Ahmed's large GALIOT near Corsica, as he raided from ALGIERS.

AHMED MUSTAGANY REIS *(Barbary corsair; Mediterranean; 1770)* Commanded a GALIOT in the SALÉ fleet.

AHMED PASHA *(Beylerbey of Algiers; Mediterranean; ruled 1586–1589)* Of Turkish origin, he favored the corsairs and, in 1587, personally commanded slave raids on Sicily, Naples, and Corsica.

AHMED REIS (1) *(Barbary corsair; Mediterranean; 1624)* From Smyrna in Turkey, Ahmed Reis commanded an Algerian GALLEY captured near Sardinia by the KNIGHTS OF SAINT STEPHEN.

AHMED REIS (2) *(Barbary corsair; Mediterranean; 1634)* Captain of a 40-gun Tripolitan GALLEY defeated near the Greek island of Aegina (Aiyina) by the KNIGHTS OF SAINT STEPHEN.

AHMED TURQUI REIS *(Turkish corsair; Mediterranean; 1773)* Commanded a five-gun GALIOT in the SALÉ fleet.

AHOY! *(nautical word; 18th century to the present)* A seaman's call (now rare) to attract attention, meaning "Hello there!" or "Hey there!"

AÏSA REIS *(Barbary corsair; Mediterranean; 1550)* Said to be TURGUT REIS' nephew, he courageously defended the port of Mahdia, east of TUNIS, against an overwhelming Spanish force.

ALCOHOLIC BEVERAGES See BUMBOO, DRINKING, GROG, PUNCH, RUM, RUMFUSTIAN.

ALDAY, JAMES *(English pirate; Atlantic; active 1540s)* A Dartmouth captain who frequently appeared before the ADMIRALTY COURT, often informing against his fellow pirates (including William COOKE). Early in 1546, Alday fell in with James LOGAN and Thomas MOUGHAM off the Spanish coast. Acting in CONSORT, the three captains entered Munguia harbor. There they looted three Portuguese ships, captured a well-laden Spanish merchantman, and carried their prize to Baltimore, Ireland. Alday's men ran the Spanish ship on a rock but managed to save some of their booty.

Alday was associated with the explorer Sebastian Cabot in the early 1550s. He unsuccessfully sought em-ployment with Sir Martin FROBISHER's 1576 expedition, and he perhaps already knew Frobisher during the latter's early days as a pirate.

ALESSANDRI, BROTHER VINCENZO *(Knight of Malta; Mediterranean; died 1657)* Commanding a private warship, he was captured and enslaved at Constantinople.

ALEXANDER THE GREAT *(Macedonian king, 356–323 B.C.)* From the 350s, the number of pirate bands in the Aegean Sea steadily grew, and Alexander the Great's expedition to Asia made matters worse. Fully occupied with the conquest of the vast Persian Empire (spring 334 to October 331), Alexander initially disbanded the Macedonian fleet. Pirate bands were free to plunder at will, and several also were used by Alexander's enemies.

Large corsair armadas—some including as many as 50 ships—joined forces with the Persians, who reoccupied the islands of Chios, Lesbos, and Tenedos from 334 to 332. Other corsairs worked with the Spartans in 331, when they rebelled against Alexander. At least some of the pirates sailed from cities in CRETE allied with Sparta and Persia.

In the spring of 331, Alexander ordered his admiral to conquer Crete and "to clear the sea of the pirate fleets." Because of this command, some of Alexander's biographers claim that he ended piracy throughout the Mediterranean. In fact, however, this relatively limited order refers only to the pirates aiding his Spartan and Cretan enemies.

Ancient writers sometimes described Alexander himself as merely a brigand on a larger scale. One legend (mentioned by the Roman author Cicero and repeated by Saint Augustine) makes the point that an unjust state is no better than a pirates' enclave. In the story, Alexander interrogates a captured pirate. "When he was asked what criminal impulse had driven himself to rampage across the sea in his one pirate boat, [the pirate] said, 'The same one that drove you to rampage across the world.' "

ALEXANDER OF PHERAE *(Greek tyrant; reigned 369–358 B.C.)* Alexander ruled Thessaly (in northeastern Greece) after the assassination of his uncle Jason. Alexander lacked his uncle's diplomatic skills. When important cities refused to recognize his rule, he tried to crush them by force. Desperate for money to pay his mercenary army, Alexander turned to piracy on a grand scale.

From 362, his ships raided the Aegean islands, seizing several and taking many captives. Their invasion of Peparethus the following year embroiled Alexander in hostilities with Athens, which considered the island part of its domain. Alexander's corsairs unexpectedly attacked the Athenian fleet sent to Peparethus, capturing six enemy warships. Carrying their raids to Athens' home waters, the pirates looted the port of Piraeus, seizing the coins from the tables of money changers. Pirate assaults ended only with Alexander's death in 358. His wife goaded her brothers to kill the tyrant while he was drunk; she locked them in the bedroom until the deed was done.

ALEYN, WILLIAM *(English pirate; Atlantic; active 1432–1448)* Aleyn was with William KYD's squadron in 1432, when it captured four British ships bound for Rouen, France. In 1448, he audaciously carried off vessels near Thanet in the Thames River.

ALGIERS *(Barbary pirate haven; 1525–1830)* A city-state on Africa's western coast, the most important center of Muslim piracy. Conquered by ARUJ and KHEIREDDIN BARBAROSSA, it furnished the base from which TURGUT REIS took TRIPOLI (1551) and ULUJ ALI conquered TUNIS (1574).

Algiers remained an autonomous part of the OTTOMAN EMPIRE until the French conquest in 1830. After Uluj Ali's death, the BEYLERBEYS sent by the Ottoman sultan had little influence, and the JANISSARY soldiers and the corsair's guild (TAIFE REISI) divided power. From 1626, the city was ruled by the Janissaries' divan (council) or (1659–1671) by their agha (general). In 1671, the corsairs' guild imposed rule by an elected DEY. But the Janissary's divan regained control in 1689, and it thereafter elected the dey from its own members.

Algiers' prosperity rose and fell with the success of its corsairs. During the 1560s, Turgut and other admirals campaigned in large fleets from Gibraltar to the Adriatic and Crete. Raids by individual captains or small squadrons became the norm from the 1570s.

Algerian corsairs generally headed for Majorca and then cruised along the coasts of Sardinia, Corsica, Italy, and Sicily. MURAT REIS raided the Canary Islands in 1586. Atlantic cruises became more frequent after 1600, as Simon SIMONSON, John WARD and other Christian RENEGADES helped to introduce sailing ships. Large squadrons plundered Madeira in 1617, ICELAND in 1617 and 1627, and England in 1631.

Atlantic raids fell off from about 1640, and the Algerians used both oared and sailing ships in the Mediterranean. During the 1640s, the fleet included 60 sailing ships, six GALLEYS, and many smaller vessels. The corsair fleet became smaller from the 1690s, as peace treaties protected French, British, and Dutch shipping. By the 1730s, Algiers had only eight small sailing ships, with six to 18 guns, and nine GALIOTS.

Most warships now belonged to the dey and his officials and not to individual corsairs, and the government usurped the authority of the corsair's guild. As rich prizes became rare, Algiers attracted fewer Muslim captains and Christian renegades. The impoverished city's population fell to fewer than 30,000 in 1800, down from 130,000 in 1620. Piracy dramatically revived during the era of the Napoleonic Wars (1791–1815), as HAMIDOU REIS rebuilt the fleet to 30 warships.

With peace in 1815, the European states asserted their power. Following the Second BARBARY WAR, the United States obtained a treaty protecting its ships. After a joint British-Dutch expedition bombarded Algiers in 1816, its rulers agreed not to enslave Christian captives. Nevertheless, piracy continued on a limited scale, and some smaller nations still paid tribute. The corsairs vanished only with the French occupation in July 1830.

British Wars and Treaties (1518–1830)

Algiers helped Britain during its war (1588–1604) with Spain, but conflicts arose as British piracy increased after 1604. While some British captains joined the corsairs (usually at TUNIS), others attacked Algerian ships, thus making their countrymen fair prey. Although they were less active in the Atlantic than SALÉ corsairs, Algerian corsairs enslaved hundreds of British seamen. In November 1620, Sir Robert Mansel brought six warships to Algiers but failed to burn the Algerian fleet.

A treaty in 1622 ended this undeclared war, but British captains continued to attack Algerian ships. Algiers had the advantage during the war that followed (1629–1646), and her corsairs even raided England and Ireland. By 1640, the city held at least 3,000 British slaves. Another treaty in 1646 also failed to end raids by either British or Algerian corsairs, although Sir Robert Blake brought a British fleet to Algiers in 1654.

Treaties in 1662 and 1671 established a system of PASSES. But new wars broke out because British ships carried passengers and goods for Algiers' enemies. A new treaty in 1682 fared better. France was increasingly hostile, and Algiers did not wish to fight both great powers at the same time. Britain and Algiers remained at peace until 1816, and corsairs did not attack British shipping.

French Wars and Treaties (1518–1830)

France and Algiers cooperated against Spain, their common enemy, during the 16th century. Kheireddin Barbarossa brought the Ottoman fleet to southern France in 1543–44, and Algiers had a French consul (ambassador) from 1579. Southern French merchants provisioned Algerian vessels, and they set up a fortified trading post—the so-called Bastion of France—near the border with Tunis.

The corsairs began to take French ships when France made peace with Spain in 1598. Simon SIMONSON poisoned relations by fleeing Algiers in 1609 with enormous booty and two brass cannon. The French held the Algerians in contempt and soon broke a treaty signed in 1628. French captains attacked Algerian ships, and the French navy refused to release Algerian GALLEY SLAVES. In 1637, French warships captured a vessel belonging to ALI BITCHNIN. Receiving permission to attack the Bastion of France, he killed or captured 317 French nationals in reprisal.

Both France and Algiers failed to enforce new peace treaties negotiated in 1642 and 1666. Most of the

KNIGHTS OF MALTA were French, and Maltese and French galleys depended on Algerian rowers, many illegally enslaved. Algiers declared war in October 1681, and French fleets savagely bombarded the city in 1682 and 1683. The DEY was willing to surrender, but the corsair MEZZOMORTO seized power and mounted a spirited resistance.

A French fleet again shelled Algiers in 1687 but was recalled as war in Europe became likely. A new treaty in 1689 regulated PASSES and the ransom of slaves by the French and Algerians. Calling for a "hundred years" of friendship, this delivered peace until 1798, when Napoleon invaded Egypt. Another treaty restored peace in 1802, and the French occupied Algiers in 1830 for domestic political reasons having nothing to do with piracy.

Spanish Wars and Treaties (1518–1830)

Until 1791, Algerian corsairs perpetually warred with Spain and the Spanish king's Italian possessions. Except from about 1600 to 1690, Algiers was at peace with France, Britain, and the Netherlands. Its corsairs occupied themselves with slave raids on Spain and Italy and attacks on Spanish and Italian coastal shipping. More pragmatic nations were willing to make treaties with Algiers to protect their commerce. For Spain and the Knights of Malta, the war against Algiers remained a religious crusade. Spanish public opinion never recognized the Muslim conquest of North Africa.

In 1708, taking advantage of European wars, Algerian troops occupied Oran, Spain's last important possession in North Africa. A mighty Spanish armada—more than 500 sailing ships and 30,000 soldiers—retook the city in 1732 and turned it into a base for savage raids on the Algerian and Tunisian coasts. In 1775, the Spanish sent an equally large fleet against Algiers itself. Landing on the same beach where Charles V's expedition had perished in 1541, it too ended in disaster.

The Spanish bombarded Algiers in 1783 and again in 1784 without ending corsair attacks. In 1785, Spain agreed to give up Oran and pay an annual tribute, but Spanish patriots forced the government to keep the city. Following a second treaty in 1791, Algiers regained control of Oran, and the two nations enjoyed peace for the first time in four centuries.

(See also BARBARY STATES; RENEGADES; SELECTED BIBLIOGRAPHY: Fisher, *Barbary*; Wolff, *Barbary*.)

ALI AL-HADJ REIS *(Moroccan corsair; Mediterranean; 1624)* Sailing from SALÉ, Ali took a Dutch ship off northern Spain. He tied together the captain and a sailor, beat them with a club, and threatened to throw them overboard—all to force them to say that the cargo belonged to French owners and thus was legal booty.

ALI AL-HAKIM REIS *(Moroccan corsair; Mediterranean; active 1672–1715)* Vice-admiral of the SALÉ fleet, he carried arms and ammunition to Agadir and then joined BEN AÏSSA in a raid on the Azores.

ALI BITCHNIN (PITCHNIN) REIS *(Barbary corsair; Mediterranean; active 1630–1643)* An Italian, perhaps Venetian, named Piccinio, he brought a pirate ship from the Adriatic to ALGIERS. Converting to Islam, he gained rich prizes, married the daughter of MURAT "THE GREAT" REIS, and became CAPTAIN OF THE SEA. He owned a large flotilla of warships, two palaces, a suburban villa, several thousand slaves, jewels, gold, and other valuable merchandise. He gave the city of Algiers a sumptuous bathhouse and a great mosque, and he indulged his Christian slaves.

Ali Bitchnin, who probably planned to take control of Algiers, maintained hundreds of soldiers and negotiated with tribal leaders. Several setbacks weakened his prestige. In 1638, he lost eight galleys and 2,000 slaves battling the Venetian fleet near Vlorë, Albania. In 1641, while personally commanding seven warships, he was outmaneuvered by one Dutch sailing ship and lost hundreds of men.

In 1643, Ali demanded that the OTTOMAN sultan pay in advance for Algerian assistance during wartime. But the JANISSARY army failed to support his revolt. He fled the city, was persuaded to return, and died soon after, probably poisoned by an enemy.

ALI CAMPOS REIS *(Moroccan corsair; Mediterranean; 1654)* A Spaniard who commanded a four-gun BARK at SALÉ.

ALI ISTAMBULI REIS *(Barbary corsair; Mediterranean; 1680s)* A Turk and captain of the *Europa*, a captured warship at TRIPOLI. In 1680, he visited Italy as ambassador to Francesco I dei MEDICI.

ALI LUEL AHMED REIS *(Barbary corsair; Mediterranean; 1766)* The Venetian consul at TRIPOLI granted Ali a PASS protecting against warships in the Adriatic and Aegean. His SHEBEC carried 10 cannon and four rock-throwers.

ALI MARCHIK REIS *(Barbary corsair; Mediterranean; 1657)* Commanded an ALGIERS sailing ship captured by a Dutch vessel near Tetouan, Morocco.

ALI MINIKSHALI (MENEXLY) REIS *(Barbary corsair; Mediterranean; active 1676–1679)* A Greek Muslim and CAPTAIN OF THE SEA at TRIPOLI from about 1676. He deserted in Crete with all his money in August 1679, after taking part in a failed rebellion the previous month.

ALI PEREZ (PIRIS) REIS *(Moroccan corsair; Mediterranean; active 1770s)* A descendant of Morisco (Spanish Muslim) refugees, he sailed from SALÉ and was sent to France as ambassador in 1781.

ALI REIS *(Barbary corsair; Mediterranean; 1552)* A Turk who raided from ALGIERS. Ali plundered both Muslims and Christians and brutally abused his GALLEY SLAVES. A Venetian squadron forced him to abandon his ship—a brand new GALIOT with several cannon—on the Albanian coast.

ALI SABOUNGI REIS *(Moroccan corsair; Mediterranean; 1773)* A Turk who commanded a five-gun GALIOT at SALÉ.

ALLARIA *(pirate haven; Mediterranean; third century B.C.)* Pirates from Allaria, in western CRETE, kidnapped men from Thera. The Allariotes gave them land to work, and they also forced them to join in pirate raids. Three years later, the Therans complained that the Allariotes had not shared the booty captured on a recent cruise. Their masters offered to free them in exchange for some Allariote prisoners detained at Thera.

(See also BOOTY, DIVISION OF.)

ALLISON, ROBERT *(English buccaneer; Caribbean, Pacific; active 1679–1680)* Commanding a small ship with 24 men, he left Jamaica in December 1679 with six other captains including Bartholomew SHARP. The pirates looted PORTOBELO in February and then set off across the isthmus to attack the city of Panama. Since they planned a swift raid, Allison remained in the Caribbean and guarded their ships.

ALRATCHE REIS *(Moroccan corsair, Mediterranean; 1627)* Captain of a SALÉ ship owned by Jan JANSSEN.

ALVEL, NICHOLAS *(English pirate; Ionian Sea; 1603)* Alvel and Christopher OLOARD plundered two Venetian ships and took them to Modone in Greece. Oloard was hanged, but Alvel apparently escaped punishment on this occasion.

ALVILDA *(mythical pirate; Atlantic; before 800?)* The medieval monk Saxo Grammaticus (active 1185–1208) tells Alvilda's story in his *History of the Danes*. He may have borrowed from legends about the Amazons, a mythical band of land-based female warriors.

Alvilda was a Gothic princess, living in what is now Sweden. Her father arranged her marriage to Alf, son of the king of Denmark. Alvilda instead recruited other young women to row her ship and became a pirate. After various raids, Alvilda's vessel ran into another pirate ship that had just lost its captain. The two groups joined forces, forming a band with about equal numbers of men and women. With Alvilda in command, they terrorized shipping along the Danish coast.

Prince Alf of Denmark took out a ship, and attacked the pirates. After a long battle, the prince's warriors boarded Alvilda's ship and killed most of the crew. The pirate captain, still dressed in armor and helmet, was brought before Alf for judgment. When the helmet was taken off, Alf took a long look at his foe and then proposed marriage. This time, Alvilda accepted his proposal and retired from piracy.

AMEINIAS OF PHOCIS *(pirate chief; Mediterranean; active 276–272 B.C.)* Ameinias came from Phocis, a small state in central Greece next to the AETOLIAN LEAGUE (which absorbed it in 254). In 276, he captured the port of Cassandreia (Néa Moudhaniá) for Antigonus II of Macedonia (ruled 283 to 239). Antigonus' troops, mainly barbarian mercenaries, could not take the strong fortifications guarding Cassandreia. The king turned to the Aegean pirates, allies of his father, Demetrius I.

Cassandreia withstood a 10-month siege until Antigonus gave Ameinias, "king of the pirates," a free hand. Ameinias at once opened sham negotiations, lulled the garrison into a sense of security, and then seized the city during a surprise night attack. Ten AETOLIAN pirates commanded by MELATAS led the column storming the walls. After this stunning victory, Ameinias gave up freelance piracy and became a general in Antigonus's mercenary forces. In 272, he defended Sparta against an enemy seige.

(See also TIMOCLES.)

AMERA TRABLESI (TRIPOLISSY) REIS *(Barbary corsair; Mediterranean; active 1760s–1770s)* After raiding from TRIPOLI, he commanded a GALIOT at SALÉ in 1772.

AMURAT BEY *(Barbary corsair; Mediterranean; about 1750)* A Frenchman originally named Sicart, he commanded TRIPOLI's best ship—an exceptionally fast 22-gun FRIGATE purchased from an English pirate.

AMYOT'S CAY *(novel; 1964)* Christopher Nicole (1930–) tells the story of Catherine Phillips, who founds a family of Bahamas planters. Born in 1695 to a whore on NEW PROVIDENCE ISLAND, Cath learns to love gold while robbing her mother's clients. George Bendel, a bookish Englishman, helps her hide when Spanish troops kill her mother in 1703. The pirates return, and Cath takes up the family trade, servicing Benjamin HORNIGOLD, Charles VANE, and BLACKBEARD among others. Blackbeard marries Cath but is killed in the Carolinas.

When Woodes ROGERS becomes governor, Cath and Bendel sail for the mainland with John AUGER, who returns to piracy. Governor Rogers hangs Bendel alongside the pirates but spares the pregnant Cath. He marries her to George Amyot, owner of a small island surrounded by treacherous reefs.

Cath never lives down her reputation as "Blackbeard's wife." When her husband dies of a stroke in 1733, Cath's nephew (and lover) and her white overseers charge her with murder. Helped by her African slaves, Cath blows 15 of her accusers to pieces with a cannon.

Buying new slaves to replace the rebels, Cath salvages rich treasures from Spanish galleons wrecked nearby. Although her slaves kill crewmen from at least one wreck, the governor protects her and takes a share of the loot. She dies when Spanish forces devastate the island in 1783, still the master of everyone—white and black—surrounding her.

Just after she murders her accusers in 1733, Cath tells the survivors that they are no better than she, only less resolute. "The cloud of righteousness hang above the criminal with the biggest cannon," she says, "for we are all criminals." Nicole seems to agree with his indomitable matriarch. With rare exceptions, his characters are motivated by greed and lust. The pirates are no worse than anyone else.

Nicole takes his stories of the New Providence brigands from Daniel DEFOE, and he neatly ties up the loose ends in Defoe's GENERAL HISTORY. Defoe claims, for example, that Blackbeard abused and beat his women. Nicole blames this brutality on sexual inadequacy caused by premature ejaculation.

(See also THE DEVIL'S OWN.)

ANAIA (pirate haven; Aegean Sea; 13th and 14th centuries)

A city (also known as Alto Luogo) near Kouch-Adassi, south of ancient Ephesus on the coast of Asia Minor. Under BYZANTINE rule, Anaia was a HAVEN for Italian and Greek privateers, including BULGARINO D'ANAIA and Giovanni de lo CAVO. From 1304 to 1329, the emirs of AYDIN made it the main base for their pirate fleets—mainly crewed by Christians or converts to Islam.

ANDRON (Greek corsair; Aegean Sea; about 294 B.C.)

Demetrius I of Macedonia (ruled 336–283) hired Andron during the wars to carve up the empire of ALEXANDER THE GREAT. Demetrius frequently employed corsairs, and many served him loyally. Andron, however, betrayed Demetrius when the other side offered him more money.

About 294, Demetrius held Ephesus on the coast of Asia Minor and, with pirate help, devastated neighboring territories. An enemy general bribed Andron, the most important pirate serving Demetrius in the region. One day Andron appeared in Ephesus, bringing with him a large number of "prisoners" for sale as slaves. The pretended prisoners in fact were enemy soldiers, who captured the city. Its new master paid off Andron and sent him on his way.

(See also TIMOCLES.)

ANGO, JEAN (French ship-owner and banker; Atlantic; 1480?–1551)

Operating from Dieppe in Normandy, Ango was among the greatest sponsors of mercantile and piratical expeditions, sending out larger fleets than English shipowners, such as Sir John WATTS. Like Sir John HAWKINS or Sir Walter RALEIGH but on a grander scale, he maintained a private navy that the ruler borrowed in wartime.

French governments were concerned with the Mediterranean and wars with the Habsburg rulers of Spain. (During these wars, French kings became allies of the OTTOMAN EMPIRE and the BARBARY PIRATES.) With little official support, Ango and other merchants financed private expeditions to West Africa and Central and South America.

Ango's father created a prosperous import-export business and was among the first to send ships to the Newfoundland fishing banks. Jean Ango perhaps sailed as a youth to Africa and the Indies. After his father's death, his enterprises prospered until he controlled, by himself or in syndicates with others, as many as 70 vessels.

Ango sponsored numerous expeditions to Brazil and Africa. In 1524, he equipped *La Dauphine* in which Giovanni da Verrazano explored North America's east coast and discovered the site of the future New York City. Jean and Raoul Parmentier in 1529 reached the East Indies in two of Ango's ships.

The Portuguese and Spanish tried to keep foreigners away from their colonies and trading posts. Ango's merchant vessels went armed and often battled Iberian ships. But he also sponsored voyages whose only purpose was piracy, and his warships plundered vessels returning from the Indies through the Azores and the Canary Islands. France and Spain frequently were at war. However, Ango's warships also raided during times of truce, and they attacked ships from Portugal and other neutral countries.

In 1523, Jean FLEURY, one of Ango's captains, captured two ships returning from Mexico with booty Cortés had looted from Montezuma's palace. These prizes opened Ango's eyes to the extraordinary treasures being transported from the Americas to Spain. He increased the size of his pirate fleets in the Azores and sent raiders in the West Indies themselves. French pirates, some undoubtedly financed by Ango, visited the Indies as early as 1528, and there were many assaults during the 1530s and 1540s. Spanish officials seldom captured enemy captains and reported only limited information.

With his vast earnings from commerce and piracy, Ango purchased financial, judicial, and military offices in Dieppe. By controlling the local government, he prevented any investigation of his activities or income. King Francis I generally favored Ango, used his ships during wars with Spain and England, and ennobled him in 1535. Ango's luxurious private life became legendary. He erected a large city palace and country mansion, both sumptuously decorated by prominent Italian artists and craftsmen.

Ango even conducted a private war against Portugal. In July 1530, after Portuguese coast guards had seized one of his ships, King Francis gave Ango a letter of MARQUE, allowing him to recoup his losses by looting Portuguese vessels. Ango virtually blockaded Lisbon with 30 ships carrying more than 800 soldiers. Astonished to find himself at war, the Portuguese king sent an ambassador to King Francis, who told him to see Ango, "since it's his business, not mine."

The Portuguese succeeded in bribing the ADMIRAL of France, and Ango surrendered his letter of marque in

1531 in return for generous compensation. The Admiral also issued an order prohibiting French ships from visiting Brazil or Africa. But Ango and other French shipowners ignored the ban and gave the Admiral a share of their profits.

Ango's rivals destroyed him after Francis I died in 1547. Much of his fortune was pledged to the king during a naval war with England (1544–1545). The loans were never paid back, and Ango was imprisoned for a time in 1549 for misconduct in office.

ANGRIA DYNASTY (Indian pirate kings; about 1704–1756)

A Muslim family of black Africans. Taking advantage of power struggles between local rulers and European trading companies, Angrian squadrons devastated shipping along India's western coast. Their castles—carved out of solid stone on isolated islands and cliffs—repelled three British fleets in the 1720s. The powerful Angrias took more booty than the Caribbean BUCCANEERS. Among European pirates, only the BARBARY and CILICIAN raiders are comparable.

The Angrias raided with large fleets of GRABS and GALLIVATS crewed by local seamen. These nimble craft easily outmaneuvered and sometimes captured larger European vessels, which were added to the Angrian fleet. Like other pirate commanders, the Angrias welcomed skilled recruits of any race. Europeans commanded captured warships and led their gun crews.

Angrian fleets pillaged hundreds of Indian coastal vessels and forced merchants to pay protection money. They also seized larger European vessels with rich cargoes, including 12 major British vessels taken during the 1750s. When British troops overran the family's capital in 1756, they destroyed 65 pirate ships and captured treasure worth £130,000.

(See also ANGRIA, CONAJEE; ANGRIA, SUMBHAJEE; ANGRIA, TOOLAJEE.

ANGRIA, CONAJEE (Indian pirate; Indian Ocean; died 1729)

Conajee (or Kanhoji) seized power as the declining Mogul Empire broke apart into many separate states. Among the most important was the Maratha Confederacy with its capital at Poona near the western coast. Despite frequent internal quarrels, the Maratha Rajahs long opposed the British East India Company and other foreign invaders.

Conajee Angria's father was shipwrecked on the coast and served in the Maratha Rajah's fleet. Conajee also joined the ruler's navy and became its commander in 1698. Angria soon made himself independent of the Maratha rajah and occupied 240 miles of coast between Bombay and Vengurla. In 1704, the East India Company ordered Angria to stop molesting British vessels. Because British captains had broken their word, Angria replied, he intended to seize their ships anywhere he could find them.

Angria carried out his threat for 25 years. In 1710, his troops captured and fortified Karanja and Kolaba

islands near Bombay, the Company's main port. His squadrons—including warships with up to 40 guns—looted Indian and European vessels and forced them to pay protection money. Captured British merchants were enslaved until they were ransomed. When one man was freed after ten years, the wounds from his chains were infected with gangrene. He made it back to England, but died when his leg was amputated.

Angrian squadrons attacked and overcame even the Company's largest ships, loaded with rich cargoes. In 1712, his raiders seized two British ships near Karwar, one the armed yacht of the Company's governor at Bombay. When the Company paid 30,000 rupees (£3,750) in ransom, Angria freed his British captives and ceased attacking British-owned vessels. But his squadrons continued to harass Indian merchants trading with Bombay.

During these years, European pirates based at MADAGASCAR also scoured the Indian Ocean. A new governor, Charles Boone, arrived at Bombay in January 1716 with orders to suppress piracy throughout the region. Boone fortified Bombay and created a formidable fleet aided by naval warships. Over the next five years, he sent three large expeditions against Angria's strongholds—all soundly defeated.

Early in 1716, Angria broke the truce by capturing two British ships and several Indian vessels under Company protection. In May, Boone sent an expedition to Gheriah (Vijayadurg) to retake the captured ships but found the place impregnable. An even larger fleet was thrown back from Karanja Island in November. When Angria's forces blockaded Bombay's harbor, the Company paid 70,000 rupees (£8,750) for another peace treaty, which Angria broke a few months later.

In September and October 1717, Angria's forces at Gheriah and Deoghur (Devgarh) beat off British attacks with specially built gunships. As they returned to Bombay, the Company's vessels ran into John TAYLOR, commanding the Cassandra and Victory. Taylor's pirates chased the British ships for two days and drove them into Goa harbor.

In 1721, the government sent Commodore Thomas Matthews from Britain with four men-of-war. In December, Angria's forces at Kolaba drove off a British-Portuguese attack by Matthews' warships and 6,000 soldiers and calvary.

Humiliated by the failure of the Kolaba expedition, the British gave up their efforts to destroy Angria's land strongholds. Governor Booth sailed for England in January 1722. Commodore Matthews left in December 1723 and later was convicted of trading with the Indian pirates.

Boone's successors tried to protect British ships along the coast with mixed success. Attacks on merchant vessels continued, and Angria's squadrons sometimes defeated British warships. After Angria died in 1729, his son Sumbhajee ANGRIA continued to devastate Indian and British shipping.

(See also SELECTED BIBLIOGRAPHY: Biddulph, *Pirates*; Downing, *Indian Wars*.)

ANGRIA, SUMBHAJEE *(Indian pirate; Indian Ocean; died 1743)*

After Conajee ANGRIA died, his sons disputed control of his territories in northwestern India. By 1735, Sumbhajee (Sambhaji) Angria ruled most of his father's forts from Srivardhan. His brother Mannajee retained a small territory around Kolaba, just south of Bombay.

Sumbhajee's warships routinely looted Indian merchants and also overcame larger European ships. His fleets were based at impregnable land fortresses. In 1738, his troops at Gheriah (Vijayadurg) repulsed a Dutch squadron that included seven men-of-war.

In January 1736, Angria's squadrons captured the East Indiaman *Derby*, heading for Bombay with a year's supply of gold to buy Indian goods. Nine of Angria's ships attacked from the rear so that the larger British vessel could not bring its guns to bear. After a short but fierce battle, the *Derby* and 115 crewmen surrendered. Her naval supplies equipped Angria's fleet, and the East India Company's commerce was devastated.

Early in 1740, Angria overran Mannajee's territories with 2,000 men and 40 or 50 ships. Since Angria's victory would threaten the very existence of Bombay, the East India Company sent a fleet that drove off his troops. But his pirates continued to cruise until his death in 1746.

(See also ANGRIA, TOOLAJEE.)

ANGRIA, TOOLAJEE *(Indian pirate; Indian Ocean; ruled 1743–1756)*

An illegitimate son of Conajee ANGRIA, Toolajee (Toolaji) succeeded his half-brother Sumbhajee ANGRIA and soon proved even more daring and aggressive. A few weeks after he gained power, his ships drove off two British East Indiamen and seized five vessels from their convoy. In October 1749, he personally commanded during a 24-hour battle and captured the *Restoration*, the finest British warship on the coast.

By 1750, Angria's warships controlled western India as far south as Cochin. During Britain's war with France, four warships patrolled the coast and convoyed Indian trading vessels. Angria's nimble vessels kept out of range of the big guns and snatched up victims within sight of the men-of-war. Only warships were safe from attack. During a stiff fight in 1754, his ships captured a Dutch vessel loaded with ammunition and blew up two large East Indiamen.

Angria was defeated when the British allied with the Maratha Confederacy, against which his father had rebelled. The British had gained prestige by defeating the French forces in India, and the Maratha ruler agreed to join an assault by land and sea. In April, four British warships assaulted Angria's fortress at Srivardhan. The fort surrendered on the third day after an ammunition depot exploded.

In February 1756, the British sent the largest fleet ever against Angria's capital at Gheriah (Vijayadurg). The navy supplied six men-of-war, and the Company sent 18 smaller ships. For two days and nights, more than 150 heavy guns bombarded the city and fort at close range. Sixty-five pirate vessels were destroyed, including 12 large warships with two to three masts. Angria was imprisoned at Bombay, and British troops seized an immense booty, including £130,000 in gold, silver, and jewels. (See also SELECTED BIBLIOGRAPHY: Biddulph, *Pirates*.)

ANNE BONNY *(novel, 1977)*

Anne BONNY (2), the 18th-century pirate, tells her own story in Chloe Gartner's novel. Gartner closely follows Anne's fictional biography in Daniel DEFOE's GENERAL HISTORY, adding several incidents to close gaps in Defoe's tale.

Anne's father emigrates from Ireland to Charleston, South Carolina. Growing up on the family plantation, she rides and hunts like a man. She loses her virginity at an early age but prefers men at least as tough as she is.

Anne's father betroths her to a mild-mannered medical student, whose father's plantation adjoins his own. Anne, aged 15, takes up with Benjamin HORNIGOLD, who sells loot to her father. Shocked by their affair, her ailing mother dies, and Anne murders the housekeeper. Her father insists that Anne go to Scotland to marry the medical student. To escape this fate, Anne marries James Bonny, a weak-willed pimp she does not love.

When Anne's father disowns her, she burns the plantation and flees with Bonny to NEW PROVIDENCE ISLAND in the Bahamas. She wants Hornigold, but he already has a woman on the island. Anne has a fling with Stede BONNET. She rejects only Edward TEACH (BLACKBEARD), because he never bathes.

Woodes ROGERS arrives to suppress the Bahamian pirates, led by Henry JENNINGS. Charles VANE and Jack RACKHAM, Vane's quartermaster, hold out for a time, but Rackham finally asks for a pardon. Anne convinces Rackham to return to piracy, with Anne disguised as Rackham's homosexual lover. She becomes pregnant and has the baby in Cuba.

When Rackham becomes an alcoholic, Anne seduces a sweet-natured crewman, who turns out to be Mary READ. Rackham sinks deeper into drunken lethargy, and the pirates are captured at Jamaica. Condemned to hang, Anne and Mary are reprieved when they reveal that they are women and pregnant. Mary dies in jail, but a Jamaican plantation owner buys Anne's freedom. She agrees to marry him but instead sneaks off and sails as a seaman.

Gartner's story accurately portrays Bahamian pirate life, and she smoothly weaves together fictional and historical characters. However, Defoe's assertion—that Rackham's crew believed Anne was a man—becomes even less plausible in the novel. Gartner frequently reminds the reader that Anne is a voluptuous beauty with large breasts. Caribbean pirates usually wore little or nothing above the waist. Surely Rackham's crew would have noticed that "Andy Bonny" never stripped, even on the hottest days.

ANNE OF THE INDIES *(motion picture; color; 1951)*
Jean Peters plays Anne, a female pirate. During the movie, her main crime is that she gives her love and confidence too quickly to a French naval officer, Captain Pierre François La Rochelle (Louis Jourdan). British officials seize La Rochelle's ship and wife. To gain their freedom, La Rochelle agrees to capture Anne and manages to get aboard her pirate vessel. Taking advantage of her feelings for him, he tricks her with a fake treasure map that leads her into a British ambush.

Anne escapes the trap and takes her revenge by kidnapping La Rochelle's wife, Molly (Debra Paget), from his ship. La Rochelle chases Anne and is captured. Anne cannot bring herself to sell Molly in the slave market. She schemes to maroon La Rochelle and Molly on a lonely cay. Once again, she softens, helps them escape, and goes to her death in a running sea battle with BLACKBEARD (Thomas Gomez).

Anne is fast-paced and action-crammed, as Peters takes on the mannerisms of male SWASHBUCKLERS. She leaps about swinging a sword and snarling "AVAST, there!" and "BLOW ME DOWN!" She fights a swift SWORD DUEL with Blackbeard, her mentor until they quarrel over La Rochelle.

ANSELL, JOHN *(English buccaneer; Caribbean; 1689)*
One of the captains who raided Maracaibo and Gibraltar, Venezuela, with Sir Henry MORGAN.

ANSTIS, THOMAS *(English pirate; Atlantic, Caribbean; active 1718–1723)*
Anstis left the Bahamas in 1718 with Howell DAVIS and sailed with Bartholomew ROBERTS after Davis was killed. During a West Indies cruise, Roberts captured an 18-gun BRIGANTINE,

Anne Bonny (Jean Peters) scans the horizon in *Anne of the Indies* (1951).

renamed it the *Good Fortune*, and made Anstis captain. Irritated by Roberts' growing arrogance, Anstis sneaked off with the *Good Fortune* in April 1721, as they approached Africa.

Anstis went back to the Caribbean and plundered three or four small merchant vessels. Daniel DEFOE wrote in the GENERAL HISTORY that his crew was especially brutal to the passengers of an English ship taken off Martinique. The pirates beat and wounded one man who tried to save a woman from rape. They then seized the woman, "twenty one of them forced the poor Creature successively, afterwards broke her Back and flung her into the Sea."

Some time after, Anstis seized a large ship and gave John FENN command. Although they had two strong vessels, the pirates quarreled and decided to break up the gang. In a joint petition to the king, they claimed that Bartholomew Roberts had forced them to join his crew. While waiting for a response, they camped on an uninhabited island off Cuba. For nine months, Defoe reported, "They pass'd their time in Dancing and other Diversions" including mock trials.

When no answer had been received by August 1722, Anstis and Fenn returned to piracy. Fenn wrecked his ship on Grand Cayman Island, and two British warships showed up as Anstis was rescuing his crew. Anstis was saved when the wind dropped. The pirates rowed the *Good Fortune* to safety, while the heavier warships were becalmed.

Anstis cruised throughout the Caribbean, took several prizes, and gave one to Fenn. In April 1723, a warship surprised the two crews while their ships were careened at Tobago. Fenn's vessel was captured, but Anstis outsailed his pursuers. Soon after, several recent recruits on the *Good Fortune* mutinied, murdered Anstis and the other officers, and gave themselves up at Curaçao.

ANTONIUS, MARCUS (1) *(Roman noble and general; died 87 B.C.)*
From 102 to 100, Antonius commanded the first Roman attack on the CILICIAN pirates. He was the father of Marcus ANTONIUS (2), who was given a similar command in 74, as well as the grandfather of the famous "Mark Anthony" (*circa* 83–32) who became Cleopatra's lover.

Antonius' forces cruised along the Cilician coast and attacked several pirate bases. They fought no major battles and did not permanently weaken the corsairs. Nevertheless, Anthony entered Rome in a triumphal procession late in 100 and was elected consul in 99.

ANTONIUS, MARCUS (2) *(Roman noble and general; died 71 B.C.)*
Son of Marcus ANTONIUS (1) and an easy-going man dominated by his wife. In 74, he was granted a special maritime command to fight piracy throughout the Mediterranean, receiving vast powers similar to those given to Gnaeus POMPEIUS in 67.

Unlike Pompey, however, General Anthony was utterly incompetent. Instead of attacking the main pirate havens in CILICIA, he operated along the coasts of Sicily and Spain (where he ruthlessly plundered the provincials). He then turned against the Cretans, who he accused of aiding both the Cilician pirates and MITHRIDATES OF PONTUS. The invasion of Crete ended in disaster for the Romans, and General Anthony was forced to conclude a humiliating peace shortly before his death.

APOLLONIUS OF TYRE (Latin novel; third century)

An anonymous work and possibly a translation of an earlier Greek ROMANCE. *Apollonius'* complicated plot includes many unrelated subplots and characters, and its pirate episodes are weaker than in other ancient romances. The pirates' characters are not developed, and they serve only to carry the heroine from one city to another. Despite its flaws, *Apollonius* remained popular during the Middle Ages, was translated into several languages, and provided the story for *Pericles, Prince of Tyre*, a play attributed to William Shakespeare.

The king of Antioch falls madly in love with and rapes his daughter. To keep her for himself, the king sets a riddle that her suitors must solve or lose their heads. One rich young man, Apollonius of Tyre, does solve the riddle. The king pretends that Apollonius is wrong but allows him to go to Tyre for 30 days.

Trying to return to Antioch, Apollonius is delayed by many adventures. In one of these, he is shipwrecked and cast ashore in North Africa, where he marries the king's daughter. One day, he learns that a thunderbolt has killed the evil king of Antioch and his daughter. Now lawful ruler of Antioch, Apollonius sails off to claim his kingdom.

During the voyage, his wife seems to die while giving birth to a daughter, named Tarsia. The wife's coffin is thrown in the sea and floats to Ephesus, where a skilled physician revives her. Leaving his daughter in Tarsus, Apollonius wanders in Egypt for 14 years. Tarsia grows up to be a great beauty. Her foster mother, whose own daughter is ugly, orders a slave to kill her. While Tarsia is saying her final prayers, pirates suddenly appear and carry her off to sea.

The pirates take Tarsia to Mytilene and sell her at auction to a brothel. Tarsia preserves her virginity by telling her sad story to her customers. Struck by her tale, they give her enough money to satisfy the brothel's owner. Apollonius finally shows up in Mytilene and rescues Tarsia. Later he recovers his wife at Ephesus, and the reunited couple live together happily, ruling over both Antioch and Tyre.

APOLLOPHANES (Corsair captain; Mediterranean; active 43–36 B.C.)

A former slave and pirate under Sextus POMPEIUS, whose ships raided Italy from Sicily. Pompey considered Apollophanes less skilful than MENAS and MENECRATES. He put Apollophanes and DEMOCHARES in command of his fleets in 38 only after Menecrates was killed and Menas went over to the enemy, Octavian Caesar. Apollophanes and Demochares defeated Octavian's squadrons in the Straits of Messina. The next day, a storm destroyed most of Octavian's remaining warships.

Apollophanes and Demochares shared command of Sextus' fleets until Octavian's forces drove the pirates from Sicily in 36. In 38, Apollophanes skirmished with the traitorous Menas. In the summer of 36, he commanded 45 warships during an inconclusive sea battle with Octavian's navy off the Sicilian coast. Octavian succeeded in landing part of his army in Sicily, and Apollophanes almost captured the future emperor as he returned to Italy on a single ship. Soon afterwards, Octavian's forces finally defeated Sextus' fleets at the battle of Naulochus (near modern Milazzo). Although his flagship was unharmed, Apollophanes surrendered to Octavian rather than joining Sextus Pompey in flight.

ARAGONA, FERDINANDO D' (Italian corsair; Mediterranean; 1600–1601)

From Naples, Ferdinando was captain of BERTONE, a sailing ship. He and Giacomo VINCIGUERRA took two richly laden Venetian prizes.

ARANDA, EMANUEL D' (Barbary captive; Mediterranean; 17th century)

A Spaniard enslaved at ALGIERS during the 1640s, he belonged for a time to ALI BITCHNIN. Unfortunately, there is no English translation of his lively description of life in Algiers, published as *Relation de la Captivité et liberté de sieur Emanuel d'Aranda* (Paris, 1665; Leyden, 1671).

ARCHEMBEAU (ARCHEMBO), CAPTAIN (French buccaneer; Caribbean; 1681)

When he returned from the Pacific coast in May 1681, the buccaneer-author William DAMPIER found at least nine pirate captains cruising off Panama. Dampier and many other Englishmen briefly sailed with Captain Archembeau before transferring to Captain WRIGHT's ship. In A NEW VOYAGE AROUND THE WORLD, Dampier claims he left Archembeau because his French seamen were "the saddest Creatures that I ever was among; for tho' we had bad Weather that requir'd may Hands aloft, yet the biggest part of them never stirr'd out of their Hammocks, but to eat or ease themselves."

ARCHER, JOHN ROSE (British pirate; Atlantic; died 1724)

Sailed under Edward TEACH (BLACKBEARD) in 1718. In 1723, Archer was on a merchantman captured by John PHILLIPS. He enlisted with Phillips' gang, became QUARTERMASTER, and was captured in April 1724. He and William White were hanged on June 12. John Jameson wrote, in *Privateers and Piracy in the Colonial Period*, that the Boston theologian "Cotton Mather ministered to them in their last days, adding, one would think a new horror to death."

ARCHPIRATE (nautical title, ancient Greek)

A pirate chief who commanded numerous warships and

sold his services to a king or city. An archpirate was a sea-going mercenary soldier rather than a small-scale robber, and the title was honorable. From Greek, it passed into Latin, and a Norse king signed himself *Archipirata* in the 10th century.

ARMADA DE LA GUARDA DE LA CARRERA DE LAS INDIAS *(Spanish naval squadron; Atlantic, Caribbean; 16th–18th centuries)*

The naval force (literally the "Fleet to Guard the Indies Sea Route") that protected the American TREASURE SHIPS. Responding to pirate attacks (from Jean FLEURY and others), the Spanish government in about 1521 established this squadron to patrol between Spain and the Azores. The cost was paid by a tax, known as the *avería*, which was placed on all ships, merchandise, and treasure arriving from the Americas. It later rose as high as 12 percent.

From the 1540s, the Indies Armada accompanied the convoys of merchant vessels sailing each year between Spain and the Caribbean. The warships usually transported the king's silver and gold and some private treasure. Although this was illegal, they often carried other cargo as well.

The number of ships in the Indies Armada varied with pirate threats and the availability of seaworthy vessels. Eight 600-ton GALLEONS (1) (each with 40 to 50 cannon) and three smaller ships normally guarded the Tierra Firme (Central American) convoy. Some 1,100 seamen and 900 soldiers manned the squadron. The smaller convoy to Mexico was protected by 500 men in two 600-ton galleons and two dispatch boats. However, 20 warships accompanied the fleets in 1595, when Sir Francis DRAKE and Sir John HAWKINS invaded the Caribbean.

In addition to employing its own warships, the government frequently hired private vessels, modifying them as needed. In either case, a specific and antiquated type of galleon was preferred into the 17th century. Relatively wide with shallow drafts, these vessels carried tall, lavishly decorated "castles" at either end.

The treasure galleons could carry large cargoes, and their size and many cannon protected them from pirate attack. But they were very slow, difficult to maneuver, and unable to sail against or near the wind. The galleons and merchant ships were safe as long as they stayed together. The pirates' low, close-sailing ships snapped up merchant vessels that fell behind the convoy.

ARNOLD, RICHARD *(English buccaneer; Pacific; active 1684–1686)*

Arnold invaded Central and South America with Peter HARRIS (2) who marauded in CONSORT with Edward DAVIS. Arnold served with either Harris or Davis until April 1686, when he and 38 companions returned to the West Indies.

ARQUEBUS *(firearm; 16th century)*

A smoothbore, matchlock gun that evolved into the MUSKET. It had a relatively short barrel, and the stock often was bent or curved. So called (from German *Hakenbühse*, hookgun) because, on early models, a hook near the muzzle gripped a wall to absorb the recoil.

ARSINE REIS *(Turkish corsair; Mediterranean; 1498)*

Arsine attacked shipping between Syria and Cyprus, forcing Christian merchants to travel in convoy.

ARTICLES, SHIP'S *(pirate rules; Europe and the Americas; all eras)*

From the earliest times, seamen have created bylaws to control behavior on board. Many pirate ships also operated under written regulations. The articles adopted by British and French pirates during the early 1700s are especially well known. Since pirates sail for plunder, their rules paid most attention to the division of booty.

When raiders operated from pirate HAVENS, the government enforced their articles. In ancient CRETE, treaties divided booty among vessels from different cities. From the 16th century, several nations created special laws and courts for pirates. In the BARBARY STATES, the pirate's union (TAIFE REISI) helped administer the rules. In MALTA, the TRIBUNALE DEGLI ARMAMENTI settled disputes over pirate contracts.

The English government allowed PRIVATEERS to plunder under certain circumstances. Owners, captains, and crews signed contracts enforced by the ADMIRALTY COURT. During the 17th century, colonial governors sometimes issued privateering licenses to Caribbean BUCCANEERS. The pirates continued to operate under articles even when they lacked commissions, and the practice continued into the 1720s.

Unlike privateering contracts, pirate articles could not be enforced in court. However, some rules were needed to run the ship and to fight battles. The articles also met psychological needs. By signing articles, the outlaws promised to work together as a community (or "company," in their words) for shared goals.

The entire crew assembled before every departure. Holding a Bible, each man swore a solemn oath and then signed or (if illiterate) made his mark on the articles. The meeting became a rowdy party with many bowls of PUNCH. New articles also might be signed when a group broke away and formed a crew on a different vessel.

Although each ship had its own articles, the basic provisions were similar and dealt with financial matters. In describing buccaneer articles, EXQUEMELIN mentions only booty and compensation to the wounded. The oldest surviving articles, from 1683, also concentrate on loot. Later articles kept these financial agreements and added other items as needed. Daniel DEFOE's GENERAL HISTORY prints the articles of Bartholomew ROBERTS (1719), George LOWTHER (1721), and John PHILLIPS (1723). Edward LOW's articles (1722) also are known. These forbid such crimes as fighting, desertion, cowardice, cheating while gambling, carelessness with fire, and bringing women or boys on board.

During the 19th century, Cheng I SAO imposed articles on her crews, perhaps copying the European custom.

(See also BIBLIOGRAPHY: Lydon, *Pirates*; Pringle, *Jolly Roger*.)

ARUJ BARBAROSSA (Barbary corsair; Mediterranean; 1474?–1518)

The creator—with his younger brother KHEIREDDIN—of the BARBARY STATES, Aruj can be compared to Spanish conquistadors such as Cortés and Pizarro. The brothers' nickname Barbarossa ("Red Beard") referred to their carrot-colored hair and also may be a corruption of Baba Uruj ("Father Uruj").

Aruj was the oldest of four brothers born (according to legend) to a retired Muslim solder and a Greek priest's daughter on the island of Lesbos. The natives of Lesbos—a haven for Italian, Catalonian, and Greek corsairs—remained pirates after the Ottoman conquest in 1462. On one voyage, the KNIGHTS OF RHODES captured Aruj and made him a GALLEY SLAVE. After his ransom or escape, an Egyptian emir outfitted the brothers as corsairs.

By about 1504 or 1505, Aruj and Kheireddin had moved to the western Mediterranean. The sultan of Tunis allowed them to use his ports, and they operated from the island of DJERBA. Off Elba, Aruj's small GALIOTS captured two much larger papal galleys. Later they took a Sicilian warship with 370 Spanish soldiers near Lipari. Drawn by his fame, other Levantine corsairs joined Aruj's band until he commanded perhaps a dozen vessels.

Aruj Barbarossa overpowers a papal galley about 1505. Aruj and his raiders had been captured and taken aboard the enemy ship. While the Italians looted his galliot, Aruj suddenly knifed his guard, and his men slaughtered the Christians with their own weapons. Illustration by Léopold Flameng in Charles Farine, *Deux Pirates* (1869).

During these same years, Spanish forces had occupied forts controlling the major ports. In 1512, the exiled ruler of Bougie invited the corsairs to drive out the Spanish. A cannon ball broke off Aruj's arm, and his men retreated in disorder. A second assault on Bougie in 1514 almost succeeded, until Spanish reinforcements arrived.

After this second failure, Aruj settled at the small port of Djidjelli, east of Algiers. The Tunisian sultan had turned against the Barbarossa brothers, but they received some aid from the Ottoman sultan. More important, they had won the esteem of the native peoples, who asked for their help against Spanish troops.

In 1516, Aruj's army of corsairs and tribesmen occupied Chercell and Algiers. Although the Spanish retained their fort (Peñón) in the harbor until 1529, Aruj controlled Algiers and murdered the existing sheikh. A savage storm destroyed a Spanish expedition attempting to retake Algiers in 1518.

Despite Aruj's brutal seizure of power in Algiers, factions in other towns sought his aid. Leaving Kheireddin in charge of Algiers, he marched south and west, taking Miliana, Médéa, and Ténès. The inhabitants of Tlemcen, the former capital, turned against their sultan, a Spanish puppet. Aruj quickly captured the city, and he seemed on the verge of creating a new kingdom. However, a Spanish expeditionary force, marching from Oran with some local warriors, trapped him in Tlemcen. After a six-month siege, Aruj and his few remaining corsairs fled by night but were caught and massacred by the Spaniards.

A SOFT FAREWELL (pirate slang; 17th and 18th centuries)

When two crews were in CONSORT, one sometimes slipped away at night to avoid splitting their BOOTY (one example being the crews of Thomas ANSTIS and Walter KENNEDY). The deserters were said to bid the other ship "a soft farewell."

ASSANTI, LIGORIO (Italian pirate; Mediterranean; 1341)

Responding to many complaints from the king of Cyprus, the KNIGHTS OF RHODES took away Assanti's feudal estate on the island of Nisyros, which he had turned into a "den of robbers."

ASSÉ REIS (Barbary corsair; Mediterranean; active 1805)

Captain of a FELUCCA cruising from TUNIS. During a sudden storm, he escaped to Tropea in southwestern Italy, where the local officials questioned him. During the previous two months, he had seized two fishing boats, two small coastal traders, and 21 prisoners.

ASSIA, BROTHER FREDERICO LANGRAVIO D' (Knight of Malta; Mediterranean; 1640)

CAPTAIN GENERAL OF GALLEYS, he raided the BARBARY COAST, capturing several oared vessels and (with only two GALLEYS) the 46-gun sailing vessel of KARA COGIA.

ATA IBN RAFI *(Muslim corsair; Mediterranean; died 703)* Sailing from Egypt, Ata Ibn Rafi raided Sardinia, took much booty, but perished with most of his sailors in a shipwreck off Africa during the return voyage.

ATHENODORUS *(Cilician corsair, Aegean Sea, first century* B.C.*)* Captured and sacked the island of DELOS during a daring raid in 69. To prosecute Rome's third war with MITHRIDATES, the Roman general LUCULLUS brought together a large fleet. But the Romans, led by C. Valerius Triarius, arrived too late to save Delos, which Athenodorus already had looted.

Inscriptions on five monuments in the ruins of ancient Delos mention Athenodorus' raid. The city's fawning citizens erected these monuments to ingratiate themselves with the Roman general. Without embarrassment, they lavishly praise Triarius for fortifying the city after Athenodorus had plundered it.

Athenodorus was the second CILICIAN pirate to sack the wealthy port of Delos. MENOPHANES had looted the city in 87, during Rome's first war with Mithridates. These attacks seriously damaged the Delian temples to Apollo and Diana. Another ancient inscription records a Roman law in 58, ordering their restoration and exempting the Delians from taxation.

ATKINSON, CLINTON *(English pirate; Atlantic; died 1583)* Born in southern England, Atkinson became a London retailer. At Studland (near Poole), a kinsman kept a tavern which Atkinson described as "the hell of the worlde."

In 1580, Atkinson was purser on the *Phoenix*, a merchantman commanded by Thomas HANKYN. He and Hankyn turned pirate, with Atkinson as captain. Consorting with Philip BOYTE, they seized an Italian merchantman off southwestern Spain. While fencing her valuable cargo at Topsham and Weymouth, Boyte and Atkinson were arrested. Confined at Exeter, Atkinson spent money lavishly, ingratiated himself with the mayor and jailer, and finally escaped.

In 1581, Atkinson appeared before the ADMIRALTY COURT in London to sue an owner of the *Phoenix*. Although a reward had been posted for his arrest, the court let him return to Studland without even posting bail. That same year, one of his creditors had him imprisoned for debt. He was freed in March 1582 after borrowing bail money, which he never repaid.

With two other captains, Atkinson seized a Scottish ship off Dungeness in July 1582. King James VI of Scotland wrote to Queen Elizabeth, reporting that the prisoners were taken ashore and tortured until they revealed their hidden money. The pirates knotted cords around their captives' heads and lit matches between their fingers, so that some lost their sight and hearing,

others their thumbs and fingers. Two captains commissioned to take pirates captured Atkinson in 1583, and he was hanged in London.

(See also BIBLIOGRAPHY: Ewen, "Organized Piracy.")

AUGER, BROTHER M. A. *(Knight of Malta; Mediterranean; 1679)* A "brother sergeant" (a non-noble member of the order) who was expelled for not registering his spoils with the TRIBUNALE DEGLI ARMAMENTI and for not paying his debts.

AUGER, JOHN *(British pirate; Caribbean; died 1718)* Governor Woodes ROGERS arrived at the Bahamas in July 1718. Although most pirates accepted a royal pardon, some later returned to their trade. In October, Rogers sent out three small ships to buy food at Cuba. All three captains—Auger, Henry White, and William Greenway—were among the pardoned pirates.

Two days out of NEW PROVIDENCE ISLAND, the ships anchored at uninhabited Green Cay. Led by Phineas BUNCE, another former pirate, the crews mutinied. Auger joined the mutineers, and they forced Greenway to go with them. Captain White and seven others were stripped naked and MAROONED on Green Cay. Auger and the other pirates hung around, took the castaways back aboard several times, and beat and abused them. They were rescued seven weeks later.

The pirates finally left Green Cay and lost their ships to Spanish coast guards at Long Island. Auger and about 15 others escaped to the island. They were recaptured in December by Benjamin HORNIGOLD and taken back to New Providence Island, where Auger and seven others were hanged.

(See also BIBLIOGRAPHY: Defoe, *General History*; Pringle, *Pirates*.)

AVAST! *(nautical expression; 17th century to the present)* A seaman's command to stop or cease a specific action. For example, "Avast heaving!" means stop pulling. The word lost its meaning in movie comedies, such as THE PRINCESS AND THE PIRATE and BLACKBEARD THE PIRATE, in which it is a nonsense word (usually used to express anger).

"AVAST BELAY" *(fictional pirate song; 1904)* The pirates in PETER PAN continually march around chanting "the same dreadful song."

> Avast belay, yo ho, heave to,
> A-pirating we go,
> And if we're parted by a shot
> We're sure to meet below.

The pirates are images from a child's fantasy, and their song is intended to be nonsense. Thus they keep on marching even though the first line means "Stop! Stop!"

(See also SWEARING.)

AVERY, JOHN See EVERY, HENRY.

AXABA REIS *(Barbary corsair; Mediterranean; active 1532–1533)* Commanding eight GALLEYS and GALIOTS, which sailed from ALGIERS for KHEIREDDIN BARBAROSSA, Axaba Reis was defeated by a larger Spanish squadron.

AXE, SAMUEL *(English pirate; Caribbean; active 1629–1645)* After serving with English forces in the Netherlands, Axe went to PROVIDENCE ISLAND in 1629 and built the main fort. Having quarreled with Daniel ELFRITH, he moved to Honduras in 1633 (with Sussex CAMOCK and Abraham BLAUVELT) but returned in 1636 to repel a Spanish attack. When a second Spanish expedition reoccupied Providence in 1641, Axe escaped to Saint Kitts. He was second-in-command from 1642 to 1645, during William JACKSON's Caribbean plunder voyage.

AYDIN, EMIRATE OF *(Muslim corsair's haven; Aegean Sea; 1304–1350)* A principality on Asia Minor's western coast. MEHMED BEY occupied ANAIA in 1304, and his son UMAR BEY completed the conquest of Smyrna in 1329. From these bases, their corsairs attacked shipping and raided the Greek mainland and islands. Although the emirs were Turkish, most corsairs were Christians or converts from a region long famous for its seamen's skills.

The corsairs met little coordinated resistance, since the BYZANTINE EMPIRE no longer had a navy, and squabbling Greek and Italian principalities divided the region. After years of discussion, Venice, Cyprus, the papacy, and the KNIGHTS OF RHODES assembled a joint expedition that captured Smyrna in 1344.

Umar Bey died trying to retake Smyrna in 1348. His brother Hizir made peace with the invaders, and the pirate threat became less serious. The Knights of Rhodes continued to defend Smyrna until its conquest by the Mongols in 1402.

AYDIN REIS *(Barbary corsair; Mediterranean; active 1525–1530)* A Turk nicknamed Cachidiablo ("Drub-devil") by the Spanish, Aydin Reis sailed from ALGIERS for KHEIREDDIN BARBAROSSA. In 1529, he and SALIH REIS (1), commanding 14 GALIOTS, raided the BALEARIC ISLANDS and southwestern Spain. Near Oliva, south of Valencia, they picked up 200 families of Moriscos (Spanish Muslims) fleeing slavery.

Returning to Algiers, the corsairs were surprised near Formentera Island by eight Spanish GALLEYS. Because he wanted to recapture the escaped Moriscos alive, the Spanish admiral did not fire, allowing the corsairs to board the much larger Spanish warships. After a brisk hand-to-hand combat, they captured seven of the eight galleys, freed their Muslim rowers, and took the prizes to Algiers.

Aydin was at TUNIS when Spanish forces invaded in 1535. According to one story, he unsuccessfully urged Kheireddin to kill 6,000 Christian slaves to prevent their joining the invaders. After Tunis fell, Aydin's band operated from Tajora, a few miles from the KNIGHTS OF MALTA at TRIPOLI. The Knights captured and enslaved him, but he escaped and helped TURGUT REIS attack Malta in 1551.

(See also SINAN REIS.)

AYLETT, CAPTAIN *(English buccaneer, Caribbean; died 1669)* Among the captains killed when Sir Henry MORGAN's flagship, the *Oxford*, caught fire and exploded during a drunken orgy.

(B)

BAGNIO (BAGNO, BAÑO) *(slave prisons; North Africa; 1550–1830)*

The presence of many Christian captives threatened security in the BARBARY states. By about 1550, government-owned slaves were kept in compounds called *bagnios* (Italian for "bath house"). Corsair captains built additional prisons for GALLEY SLAVES and also rented out space to other owners. ALGIERS had eight bagnios during the 17th century. The state prison held up to 3,000 captives; ALI BITCHNIN's contained 800. By 1750, as corsair raids plummeted, only three remained. TUNIS had nine bagnios in 1686, five in 1736. From the 1670s, the sultan of MOROCCO concentrated unmarried captives in a large prison in Meknes.

Only male slaves lived in the bagnios. Each prison contained open courtyards used as kitchens and living areas. These were surrounded by one or two stories of small cells rented out as sleeping quarters to as many as 20 men.

Most bagnios were locked only at night. Galley slaves and workers in the mines (and some captives held for ransom) were kept within, except when at work. Other captives and North African visitors could come and go during the day. Taverns—run by Christians with the government taking a cut—did a roaring business with slaves, Christian RENEGADES, and unobservant Muslims. Larger bagnios also contained workshops, hospitals, and Christian chapels staffed by captured clergymen or the REDEMPTIONIST fathers.

It is impossible to generalize about conditions in the bagnios. All accounts tell of disorder, noise, dirt, and crowds. Some descriptions from captives sound as if the guards were as brutal as those at modern concentration camps. A Spanish author, imprisoned during the 1640s, found the bagnios so entertaining that he often returned after he began living with his master. The *Philadelphia*'s crew was harshly treated during the First BARBARY WAR, possibly because the American navy was bombarding their captors.

BAHAMA ISLANDS

See NEW PROVIDENCE ISLAND.

BALANINI *(Malayan pirates; South China Sea; 19th century)*

Muslims who had their main HAVEN at Balanini Island in the Sula Archipelago. By the early 1840s, the Balanini had 150 vessels carrying at least 6,000 warriors. Most were MALAYS, but the pirates accepted recruits of many nationalities, including Europeans.

The Balanini worked closely with the ILANUNS, who often joined their expeditions. Second only to the Ilanuns in daring and ferocity, they preferred suicide to capture. Cruising between May and October, the Balanini often circled Borneo and frequently preyed on Brunei. They also visited the islands between Borneo and the Malay Peninsula and sometimes sold their loot at Singapore.

Balanini pirates plundered a British whaler off Timor Island in 1843. Near Brunei in May 1847, a British warship destroyed a Balanini squadron during a day-long battle. Thereafter, the Balanini raided in the Philippines. In the spring of 1848, a punitive force from Manila destroyed their fort at Balanini Island. The surviving pirates and their families were resettled in the northern Philippines.

BALBO, MICHELE *(Italian pirate; Aegean Sea; active 1270s)* From Genoa, Balbo seized a Genoese ship near Tenedos Island, torturing its passengers to make them reveal their treasures.

(See also MICHAEL VIII PALAEOLOGUS.)

BALDRIDGE, ADAM *(pirate fence; Indian Ocean; 1691–1697)* Baldridge arrived at SAINT MARY'S ISLAND, near MADAGASCAR, in January 1691 and helped the native peoples raid their enemies. For six years, he traded in slaves and sold supplies to visiting pirates for gold and booty. Baldridge's business was highly lucrative. He could buy slaves more cheaply than in West Africa. At the same time, the pirates paid dearly for alcohol, weapons, tobacco, and other necessities. They also bought passage home (under assumed names) on returning slave ships.

One of Baldridge's business associates was Frederick Philipse (1626–1702), politically influential and the richest merchant in New York. Philipse sent Samuel BURGESS to trade with Baldridge in 1696 and 1697. (Philipse's great-granddaughter married George Washington.)

Baldridge's business ended when he became too greedy. According to William KIDD, he tricked many natives on board a ship and sold them to the French at Réunion Island. In July 1697, the local tribes rebelled, destroyed Baldridge's warehouse, and killed at least 30 pirates. Baldridge escaped and went back to New York.

Amazingly, nothing Baldridge had done at Saint Mary's was illegal. However, his pirate customers had broken British laws. A new governor, Lord Bellomont, made Baldridge prepare a legal deposition in May 1699 detailing his transactions. Baldridge mentions dozens of famous pirates and often describes their voyages.

(See also SELECTED BIBLIOGRAPHY: Jameson, *Privateering*; Ritchie, *Kidd*.)

BALEARIC ISLANDS *(pirate haven; Mediterranean; all eras)* The group name for Majorca, Minorca, Ibiza, Formentera and several smaller islands, lying in the Mediterranean Sea midway between Spain and ALGIERS.

(See also AYDIN REIS; FRANCE, SOUTHERN).

BALESTRIER, CAPTAIN *(Majorcan corsair; Mediterranean; active 1709–1742)* Operated off Egypt and Palestine under license from the KNIGHTS OF MALTA and other piratical rulers.

BALLADS See "CAPTAIN KID'S FAREWELL TO THE SEAS"; "COPY OF VERSES, COMPOSED BY CAPTAIN HENRY EVERY, A"; "THE DOWNFALL OF PIRACY"; "SEAMAN'S SONG OF CAPTAIN WARD, THE"; "SONG OF DANSEKAR THE DUTCHMAN, THE"; SONGS, PIRATE; "VILLANY REWARDED."

BAMFIELD, JOHN *(English buccaneer; Caribbean; 1665)* Commanding the *Mayflower*, a small ship with only one gun, Bamfield invaded Saint Eustatius and Saba with Edward MORGAN.

BANDANNA/HEAD SCARF *(fictional pirate garb; 17th century)* Beginning with Howard PYLE during the 1880s, illustrations in pirate FICTION occasionally show BUCCANEERS wearing brightly colored headbands, and Douglas FAIRBANKS wears a bandanna in the film THE BLACK PIRATE (1926). Contemporary documents and historians, such as EXQUEMELIN, do not mention any such headgear. Seamen obviously could not wear loose hats, which would blow away. In cold climates (but probably not in the Caribbean), some mariners wore tightly fitting cloth or leather caps, sometimes with ear flaps.

(See also CLOTHING; EARRINGS.)

BANGKONG *(pirate ship; South China Sea; 19th century)* Oared warships built by the DYAKS of Borneo, bangkongs were similar to the Malay PRAHU but faster and lighter. Over 100 feet long and 10 feet wide, with an overhanging stem and stern, they were propelled by 60 to 80 paddlers. They were sturdy enough for long journeys at sea, even though they drew only a few inches of water and could turn at full speed in their own length.

(See also SELECTED BIBLIOGRAPHY: Rutter, *The Pirate Wind*.)

BARBARA *(pirate ship; Atlantic and Caribbean; 1540)* As far as is known, the first English ship used to commit piracy in the Americas, under John PHILLIPS.

BARBARY COAST *(pirate haven; Mediterranean; 1520–1830)* From the 14th century, the European name for the coastal regions of North Africa ruled from ALGIERS, TUNIS, and TRIPOLI. Until the late 18th century, MOROCCO often was included, although it had a different political system and did not live by piracy. *Barbary* initially was derived from Berber, the name of the original inhabitants. The word also referred to the region's "barbarous" pirates.

BARBARY PIRATE *(motion picture; black and white; 1949)* An inexpensively made supporting feature, directed by Lew Landers, which combines SWORD DUELS with stock shots and other production gimmicks. A traitor in Washington tells the pirates when valuable cargo is being shipped. To ferret out the informer, an army officer, Major Tom Blake (Donald Woods), goes under cover to TRIPOLI.

There Blake is captured and befriends Yusof, the ruling BEY. After fighting off MURAT REIS (played by John Dehner) and other villains and resisting scheming women in scanty costumes, Blake identifies the spy and rescues Anne Ridgeway (Trudy Marshall), an American captive. (See also BARBARY WAR, FIRST.)

BARBARY STATES (pirate havens; Mediterranean; 1520–1830)

ALGIERS, TUNIS, and TRIPOLI were city-states on the edge of a thinly populated desert. They were ruled by a "foreign legion" of Turkish troops nominally subject to the OTTOMAN sultan. The native peoples had no say in the government and rarely became corsairs.

Barbary rulers treated piracy as a business, regulated through the corsair's guild (TAIFE REISI). Sea captains, including many Christian RENEGADES, joined "the course" to make money. At the same time, the Barbary States justified their piracy as a form of religious warfare. Until the late 18th century, the corsairs usually did not molest Muslim shipping. Moreover, Barbary rulers forbade (or at least held down) attacks on ships from countries with which they had a formal peace treaty.

Until the 1580s, the Barbary States were the Ottoman Empire's western base in its global war with the Spanish Habsburgs—who also controlled much of Italy until 1713 and ruled the Holy Roman Empire until 1556. For the corsairs, attacks on Spanish and Italian shipping were a religious duty as well as a profitable business, and they usually did not attack Spain's enemies.

The Spanish began the war by occupying the port of Melilla in 1497, continuing the 800-year "Reconquest" that had driven the Moors from Spain in 1492. By 1511, Spanish forces had occupied many North African ports, including Oran, Algiers, and Tripoli. Over the next 60 years, famous corsair captains—ARUJ and KHEIREDDIN BARBAROSSA, TURGUT REIS, ULUJ ALI—retook all except Oran. Their squadrons of oared warships cruised the Mediterranean and laid waste the Spanish and Italian coasts. The Spanish government sent vast naval expeditions to reconquer North Africa. Tunis was reoccupied from 1535 to 1572. However, a great storm ended an invasion of Algiers in 1541, and the Ottoman fleet destroyed the Spanish invaders before DJERBA in 1560.

From the 1580s, Algiers, Tunis, and Tripoli conducted their own foreign policies. Thus a truce in 1581 between Spain and the Ottoman Empire did not include North Africa. The Barbary States remained at war with Spain and Portugal (united with Spain from 1580 to 1640) until the late 18th century. From about 1600, they also began to attack ships from France, Britain, and the Netherlands, as these nations made peace with Spain. The golden age of Barbary piracy continued until about 1650. Christian renegades—including John WARD, Simon SIMONSON, and Jan JANSSEN (at SALÉ)—taught the corsairs how to build and navigate sailing ships that could enter the Atlantic.

From the 1660s, Britain and France armed fleets of warships. The Barbary States could not compete in this naval race, and French naval bombardments devastated Algiers and Tripoli. Tunis made peace with Britain and France during the 1660s. Algiers submitted in the 1680s, and France imposed a treaty on Tripoli in 1692. The Dutch also gained peace by agreeing to pay the Barbary rulers an annual tribute.

Since these treaties protected the three largest merchant fleets, the number of corsairs and their influence on Barbary rulers steadily declined. The smaller European nations copied the Dutch in paying tribute, which compensated for the loss of booty. Piracy revived during the European wars between 1792 and 1815. When the wars ended, the Europeans again turned their power against North Africa. A French army occupied Algiers in 1830, and the French threat allowed the Ottoman Empire to take direct control of Tunis and Tripoli.

Europeans often referred to the Barbary States as "regencies," since they initially were ruled by a viceroy representing the OTTOMAN sultan. In fact, they had been conquered not by Ottoman armies but by daring adventurers. Aruj and Kheireddin Barbarossa seized Algiers between 1518 and 1525. TURGUT REIS conquered Tripoli (1551), and Uluj Ali occupied Tunis (1574).

These corsair chiefs set up the Barbary regencies as bases for maritime warfare—piracy, to their enemies—during a bitter struggle between the Ottoman Empire and the Habsburg rulers of Spain, Italy, and Austria. Piracy was highly profitable until about 1680, since Barbary governments received a share of BOOTY, European tribute, and subsidies from the Ottoman sultan. But the regency governments also received revenues from internal taxes.

The Barbary States had a dual nature, as both corsair havens and inland empires. Power thus was shared between two groups—the corsair's guild and the military garrison of JANISSARIES. Both groups were made up of outsiders and rarely accepted local Muslims as members.

From the beginning, the Barbary States were relatively autonomous. The sultan's authority rested in a BEYLERBEY sent from Istanbul. Although the sultan continued to confirm the man they nominated, the Janissary garrisons effectively controlled government and taxation from the 1590s. After considerable political anarchy, each nation came under a type of monarchy by about 1700. In Algiers, the Janissaries elected a DEY, who ruled until he died or was assassinated. In Tunis and Tripoli, hereditary civilian rulers usually managed to control the Janissaries. The Husanid (or Husaynid) family provided Tunis with hereditary BEYS, while the Qaramanli family ruled Tripoli as pashas.

Although they conducted an independent foreign policy, these Barbary rulers always affirmed their loyalty to the Ottoman sultan. The sultans confirmed the CAPTAIN OF THE SEA, and they awarded bonuses or higher offices to men distinguishing themselves in land or sea campaigns.

During wartime, the Barbary corsairs fought with the Ottoman navy, although ALI BITCHNIN tried to make the sultan pay in advance in 1643. All three regencies contributed substantial squadrons to the Ottoman naval wars with Venice during the 17th and 18th centuries. Algerian ships joined the Ottoman fleet that tried to drive Napoleon from Egypt in 1798, and Tunisian squadrons fought in Greece in 1821 and 1826. Like the KNIGHTS OF MALTA, the corsairs always remembered that piracy was a religious service as well as a business.

(See also SELECTED BIBLIOGRAPHY: Fisher, *Barbary*.)

BARBARY WAR, FIRST *(Tripoli versus the United States; Mediterranean; 1801–1805)*

In his 1796 treaty with the United States, Yusuf Qaramanli, BEY of TRIPOLI, settled for less than the rulers of ALGIERS and TUNIS and received no annual tribute. He was jealous of the 36-gun FRIGATE the United States had given Algiers and demanded a warship of his own. Failing to obtain satisfaction, he declared war on May 14, 1801, and dispatched Peter LISLE to look for American prizes.

The United States sent squadrons to the Mediterranean under Commodores Richard Dale (1801), Richard Morris (1802), Edward Preble (1803–1804), and Samuel Barron (September 1804–1805). Although American warships captured several vessels, they could not keep ships out of Tripoli's harbor. The American forces lacked both the small boats needed for a tight blockade and guns powerful enough to damage the city's fortifications.

By October 31, 1803, only two American ships remained at Tripoli. The 36-gun frigate *Philadelphia* was slightly east of the city, when lookouts sighted a SHEBEC running for the harbor. After chasing the enemy craft for more than two hours, the *Philadelphia* went hard aground on an uncharted sand reef. Unable to resist enemy gunboats, the 300 crewmen surrendered and were imprisoned at hard labor. Three days later, the Tripolitans refloated the *Philadelphia* and brought her into the harbor for repairs. On February 16, 1804, Stephen Decatur raided the harbor on the *Intrepid*, a captured Tripolitan ketch. Taking the enemy by surprise, Decatur's men seized and burnt the *Philadelphia*.

Augmented by gunboats acquired in Naples, the American ships bombarded Tripoli five times between August 3 and September 2, 1804. On the night of September 3/4, the Americans sent the *Intrepid* into the harbor loaded with gunpowder. This floating bomb exploded prematurely, killing the ship's 16 crewmen.

Unable to take Tripoli by frontal assault, the U.S. sponsored a political revolution. Yusuf Qaramanli had deposed his older brother Hamet. When Hamet promised to end the war, President Thomas Jefferson agreed to help him regain his throne. Thomas Eaton, formerly U.S. consul in Tunis, met Hamet in Egypt. Together they took a mixed force—about 400 men including seven U. S. Marines—on a harrowing six-week march (March 6 through April 24) across the Libyan desert to Derna.

Assisted by cannon fire from American ships in the harbor, Eaton's band charged the enemy and occupied Derna on April 27, 1805. (The Marine Corps hymn honors this expedition "to the shores of Tripoli.") News of Derna's loss frightened Yusuf Pasha, who received reports exaggerating Hamet's support. A compromise peace treaty ended the war on June 6. The United States paid $60,000 to ransom the *Philadelphia*'s crew and withdrew its support for Hamet Qaramanli, who returned to exile.

(See also BARBARY WARS.)

BARBARY WAR, SECOND *(Algiers versus the United States; Mediterranean; 1812–1815)*

The three BARBARY STATES revived piracy during the European wars from 1792 to 1815. HAMIDOU REIS and other Algerian corsairs were especially successful, and ALGIERS built up the largest pirate fleet in a century. But prizes became fewer by 1807. Britain and France had powerful navies, and the French tried to protect Italian vessels.

The U.S. signed a peace treaty with Algiers in 1795 and paid tribute until 1812. But the American navy had left the region after the First BARBARY WAR (1801–1805) with TRIPOLI. The DEY of Algiers permitted corsair attacks on American ships from 1807 and declared war in 1812.

As soon as war with Britain ended in 1815, President James Madison sent 10 warships under Commodore Stephen Decatur to end Algerian raids. On June 17, Decatur's ships took Hamidou Reis, Algiers' admiral, by surprise, and the Americans captured a second Algerian warship three days later. The American squadron reached Algiers on the 28th, and the Dey's government quickly submitted. A new treaty ended U.S. tribute payments and freed all American prisoners without ransom.

BARBARY WARS *(North African corsairs versus the United States; Mediterranean; 1801–1815)*

ALGIERS, TUNIS, and TRIPOLI depended on corsair booty to pay their troops. To protect their merchant fleets, European nations signed treaties with the Barbary governments and paid them an annual tribute. During the European wars between 1792 and 1815, the Barbary rulers maintained peace with Britain and France. The British tried to protect their Spanish and Portuguese allies, and Napoleon defended Italian interests after conquering Italy in 1801 and 1802. The Barbary corsairs could prey only on ships from the United States and the smaller European nations, such as Sweden, Denmark, and Holland.

The U.S. signed peace treaties with Algiers in 1795, Tripoli in 1796, and Tunis in 1797. The American government paid tributes in cash and naval stores, and it also gave the Dey of Algiers a 36-gun FRIGATE (the *Crescent*, renamed *El Merikana*). Despite these agreements, the rulers of Algiers and Tripoli humiliated American ambassadors and allowed the corsairs to seize American ships. The U.S. Navy, busy fighting an undeclared war with France, could not retaliate.

In June 1801—with the French war concluded—President Thomas Jefferson sent four warships to the Mediterranean. On arriving at Gibraltar, they found that Yusuf Qaramanli, pasha of Tripoli, had already declared war.

A series of American squadrons loosely blockaded Tripoli and subjected it to heavy bombardment during the summer of 1804. These naval efforts did not force Tripoli to submit. The United States finally gained peace (April 1805) by backing a land invasion by the pasha's brother.

During this war, the emperor of Morocco briefly supported Tripoli. Peter LISLE, the Tripolitan admiral, had abandoned the frigate MESHUDA at Gibraltar in 1801. The emperor purchased the ship, which the Americans captured on May 12, 1803, as it headed for Tripoli with guns and naval stores. Soon afterwards, the governor of Tangier licensed IBRAHIM LUBAREZ REIS to seize American ships. The United States sent four warships to Tangier, persuading the emperor to release all American prisoners and reratify the 1786 peace treaty. In August 1805, a similar show of force restored peace with the bey of Tunis, angered by the American capture of a Tunisian SHEBEC and her two Neapolitan prizes.

The 1805 treaty with Tripoli had left Yusuf Qaramanli in power. Moreover, the U.S. soon withdrew its forces as conflicts with Great Britain led to the War of 1812. The Algiers government was not impressed with American might. HAMIDOU REIS captured an American ship in 1805, while the U. S. fleet was still off Tripoli. Algiers ordered corsairs to attack American shipping in 1807 and declared war in 1812.

The Algerians quickly submitted when Stephen Decatur led a strong American squadron to the Mediterranean in the summer of 1815. Once the American squadron had left, however, the dey repudiated the peace treaty because the United States did not return an Algerian ship as promised. War nearly broke out again. Then came the British and Dutch bombardment of Algiers in August 1816. The dey accepted the American demands on December 23, and the United States did not again pay annual tribute. Although an American squadron stayed in the region for several years, there was no further need to use force.

(See also BARBARY WAR, FIRST; BARBARY WAR, SECOND; HAMIDOU REIS.)

BARBOLANI DEI CONTI DE MONTAUTO, FRANCESCO   *(Knight of Saint Stephen; Mediterranean; active 1590–1596)*   Sailing on his own account, Barbolani captured several Muslim merchant ships near Elba in 1590. In 1596, he commanded the order's squadrons, as they took many prizes along the BARBARY COAST.

BARBOLANI DEI CONTI DE MONTAUTO, GIULIO   *(Knight of Saint Stephen; Mediterranean; died 1619)*   From 1618, admiral of the order's galleys, which captured six Muslim vessels during their 1619 cruise.

BARDI, BROTHER GUALTEROTTI   *(Knight of Malta; Mediterranean; 1616)*   Bardi captured a small ship carrying rice from Egypt to Lebanon. Although its crew of Greek Christians did not resist, they were stripped naked and cast adrift in a small boat. The survivors sued Bardi in MALTA.

BARI   *(pirate haven; Adriatic Sea; 841–871)*   In 841, African and Sicilian soldiers seized Bari, a fortified city on the Italian coast. The freebooters plundered the countryside and passing merchant vessels. Although independent under their own "sultan," they collaborated fully with Muslim sea raiders from North Africa, SICILY, and CRETE.

In 867, a BYZANTINE squadron relieved Dubrovnik, besieged by Cretan corsairs. In 869 a larger Byzantine and Dalmatian fleet appeared off Bari, already blockaded on land by Louis II, king of Italy. Louis's troops finally occupied the city in 871.

BARK   *(type of ship; Mediterranean, Atlantic; 16th century to present)*   Until the 18th century, this name often was given to any small vessel. The word (spelled barque in Britain) later referred to a small ship with three masts, the first two being square-rigged and the after mast fore-and-aft rigged.

The fast-sailing bark was the favorite ship of Caribbean pirates, who sailed them to Africa and even MADAGASCAR around 1700. They sometimes held as many as 90 men, very closely packed together. After 1850, much larger barks, carrying up to five masts, were built, particularly for the trade around Cape Horn to South America's Pacific coast.

(See also SELECTED BIBLIOGRAPHY: Defoe, *General History*.)

BARKER, ANDREW   *(English pirate; Caribbean; died 1577)*   A Bristol merchant, Baker sailed for Panama in June 1576, with William COXE and Philip ROCHE commanding his two small ships. Baker claimed to be acting in REPRISAL, and his cruise was promoted by the earl of Leicester, a strong supporter of Sir Francis DRAKE. However, Barker had no royal commission, and he never tried to meet up with John OXENHAM, also raiding Panama at this time.

Barker's squadron reached Trinidad and worked westward along the coast, taking several valuable prizes. He was near Nombre de Dios before June 1577, but failed to make contact with the *Cimarrónes* (escaped African slaves). Barker subsequently seized a Spanish warship and made it his flagship. The captured crewmen either were set ashore (the English version) or thrown overboard to drown (according to Spanish reports). In about May 1577, Barker hanged a Spanish settler after unsuccessfully assaulting Veragua, in western Panama. However, Spanish officials of higher rank usually were released for ransom.

William Coxe continuously quarreled with Barker. In August, Coxe led a mutiny and Philip Roche, the other master, went along. The mutineers marooned Barker and a dozen others on Guanaja Island off Honduras. Spanish soldiers surprised Barker's party, killed them, and carried their heads and an unidentified person's hand to Trujillo as trophies.

BARKER, EDMUND *(English captain; Caribbean, Atlantic; died 1595)* A resident of London, Barker commanded the 60-ton *Mary* and captured a small prize in the West Indies in 1590. During James LANCASTER's unfortunate expedition (1591–1594) to the Indian Ocean, Barker was second-in-command of the *Edward Bonaventure*, and he later wrote a history of the voyage. He was killed during Lancaster's raid on Pernambuco, Brazil.

(See also: RANDOLPH COTTON; SELECTED BIBLIOGRAPHY: Foster, *Voyages*.)

BARKER, LEX *(American actor; 1919–1973)* Virile and athletic, he was cast as Tarzan five times between 1949 and 1953. After 1958, he frequently appeared in Italian and German adventure and western movies, including THE PIRATE AND THE SLAVE GIRL (1959) and SON OF THE RED CORSAIR (1963).

BARNES, CAPTAIN *(English buccaneer; Caribbean; 1677)* Raided Santa Marta, Venezuela, with Captain LAGARDE.

BARRE, CHEVALIER DE LA *(Maltese corsair; Mediterranean; 1663)* The French government protested his seizure of three Jews sailing—without PASSES—on a French ship in the Near East.

BART, CAPTAIN See SPEIRDYKE, BERNARD.

BATCHELOR'S DELIGHT *(English pirate ship; Pacific, Indian Ocean; 1684–1694)* A 26-gun Danish slave ship, which John COOK captured off West Africa in 1684. Cook and Edward DAVIS took the *Delight* on a four-year plunder cruise along South America's Pacific coast. Davis returned to Philadelphia in May 1688 and sold the *Delight* to some merchants.

The new owners sent the *Delight* to the East Indies. Its crew turned pirate—initially under a Captain Raynor—and visited MADAGASCAR in May 1689. The *Delight* took two rich Portuguese prizes during the next few months and looted an English ship near Bombay in January 1691. The pirates returned to New York with about £1,100 each and gave the *Delight* (and a £3,000 bribe) back to her owners.

BAUGHE, WILLIAM *(English pirate; Atlantic; active 1609–1612)* A ruthless pirate based at Leamcon, Ireland, from 1608 to 1611 and led by Richard BISHOP and Peter EASTON. Learning that more than £3,000 in cash was hidden aboard a captured Flemish ship, he instantly grabbed one of the petrified crew and "sawed his throte with a dagger untill the blood ran downe."

In June 1612, Baughe and his men surrendered at Kinsale, Ireland, under a general pardon that allowed them to keep their booty. Ignoring the terms of the pardon, an overzealous naval captain confiscated his ship and goods. Baughe successfully sued the captain in court and was awarded £2,586.

BEAUREGUARD, GUGLIELMO See GUADAGNI DI BEAUREGUARD, GUGLIELMO.

BEAVIN (BETHEWEN), THOMAS *(English pirate; Atlantic; active 1580–1583)* Originally a shoemaker, Beavin sailed from Studland Bay and Welsh ports, taking numerous prizes. Captured by royal ships in 1583, he was tried and hanged in London.

BEHEADING *(pirate punishment, all eras)* In China, beheading was the standard PUNISHMENT for many crimes, including piracy. Although HANGING became customary in Europe, captured pirates occasionally were beheaded. In some cases, aristocrats—such as Sir Hugh COURTNEY, Filippo MAZZA, Pietro EMO, Sir Walter RALEIGH—were beheaded out of respect for their social rank, since beheading is less painful and degrading than hanging.

BEKIR REIS *(Barbary corsair; Mediterranean; died 1652)* Son of a Greek RENEGADE who had been admiral of the OTTOMAN navy, he owned two galleys raiding from ALGIERS. In January 1647, he commanded a 22-gun sailing ship, captured off Sicily by six galleys of the KNIGHTS OF MALTA. Condemned to the oars, he was ransomed and returned to Algiers. A French official, captured by Bekir in 1651, described him as brutally mistreating his own GALLEY SLAVES. He died, while still young, when a violent storm sank both his galleys and killed most of their crews.

BELAY *(nautical word; 16th century to the present)* To coil a running rope around a cleat so as to fasten or secure it. In sailor's slang, to make fast or to stop. "Belay that yarn!" meant "Stop your lies; we've had enough of them."

BELLAMY, CHARLES *(British pirate; Atlantic; active 1717–1720)* Because both men marauded in the Atlantic about 1717, he often is confused with Samuel BELLAMY. Charles Bellamy raided with three ships off New England and New Brunswick during the summer of 1717. He set up a fortified camp at the Bay of Fundy, probably at Saint Andrew's, and plundered fishing and trading ships off Newfoundland's southern coast. A French warship, attacked by mistake in the Gulf of Saint Lawrence, badly mauled the pirate vessel and killed 36 men. Bellamy raided fishing vessels for some years from a new camp at Placentia Bay.

(See also SELECTED BIBLIOGRAPHY: Horwood, *Pirates*.)

BELLAMY, SAMUEL *(British pirate; Caribbean, Atlantic; died 1717)* In 1716, Bellamy sailed under Benjamin HORNIGOLD, who cruised in consort with Olivier LA BOUCHE. Hornigold left, perhaps in August, because he refused to loot British vessels. The crew elected Bellamy captain, and he and La Bouche captured several vessels near the Virgin Islands. Bellamy took over one large prize and gave command of his sloop to Paul WILLIAMS, his QUARTERMASTER. After losing contact with La Bouche during a storm, Bellamy and Williams cruised between Haiti and Cuba.

Early in March, the pirates captured the *Whydah,* a slave ship returning to London with gold, ivory, sugar, and indigo. Bellamy transferred to the *Whydah,* and sailed for Virginia with Williams. At least four more ships were pillaged, and one was added to the squadron under a man named Montgomery. After a severe storm drove the pirates toward the north, they made for Rhode Island, taking two more prizes on the way.

Sometime during the night of May 17, 1717 and the following morning, the *Whydah* and one of the prizes were wrecked during heavy fog. Her seven crewmen survived when the prize ran ashore at Orleans, Massachusetts. Meanwhile, the *Whydah* smashed into a sandbar three miles south of Wellfleet. Two of the 146 men aboard reached safety and were captured. A few others may have escaped, but Bellamy was killed. The nine seamen who reached the shore were tried in Boston, and seven were hanged.

Strenuous efforts were made to salvage the *Whydah's* cargo, reportedly worth £20,000. But the weather continued foul, and the wreckage was scattered along four miles of coast. Nothing of value was recovered and the search for Bellamy's booty continued. During the mid-1980s, divers working for Barry Clifford, a Cape Cod treasure hunter, finally brought up part of Bellamy's booty. Clifford claimed that his find was worth many millions of dollars.

In his GENERAL HISTORY, Daniel DEFOE invents speeches in which Bellamy condemns the British aristocracy as no better than pirates. As he tells one captive,

> They villify us, the Scoundrels do, when there is only this Difference, they rob the Poor under the Cover of Law, forsooth, and we plunder the Rich under the Protection of our own Courage; had you not better make One of us, than sneak after the A———s of those Villains for Employment?

These speeches, often quoted in books about pirates, were concocted by Defoe. However, judging by the testimony at the Boston trial, Bellamy shared Defoe's opinion of British gentlemen.

(See also SELECTED BIBLIOGRAPHY: Dow, *Pirates;* Jameson, *Privateering.*)

BEN AÏSSA, SIDI ABDULLA (*Moroccan corsair; Mediterranean; active 1672–1698*) Sometimes called Benache and the last of the SALÉ corsairs to command his own (rather than a state-owned) sailing ship. His devastating raids on merchant shipping from 1687 to 1698 led French officials to describe him as

their most deadly naval foe. He usually operated in the Atlantic, sailing from ALGIERS as well as from Moroccan ports. (The two nations' corsairs ignored their rulers' often hostile relations.) A bold navigator, he raided during the stormy winter season, when European captains did not expect to encounter pirates.

In both 1687 and 1691, Ben Aïssa took six merchantmen between March and May. In September 1691, he and FENNICH REIS captured six more vessels off the Canary Islands. Impressed by these continuing triumphs, Moroccan sultan Mawlay Isma'il (ruled 1673–1727) appointed Ben Aïssa ADMIRAL of the Salé corsair fleet and left him free to enjoy his great wealth.

From 1694, Ben Aïssa gave one captured ship to his brother, ABDUL-RAHMAN REIS, and assigned another to his son MOHAMMED REIS (5). Working together, the family commanded three of the five corsair ships still operating from Salé. On his final cruise in 1698, Ben Aïssa plundered five merchantmen in only 38 days.

In September 1698, Mawlay Isma'il sent him to France to request a royal princess in marriage. When he returned in 1699, supposedly with valuable gifts, the sultan's greedy son, Mawlay Affet, imprisoned and cruelly tortured Ben Aïssa. He paid a large fine to regain his freedom and the sultan's favor but never sailed again.

BERTAGNO, LUPO DE (*Spanish corsair; Aegean Sea; active 1452–1460*) A Catalan commanding a FUSTE, he took valuable booty from Venetian cities and shipping. In 1460, as OTTOMAN troops were occupying southern Greece, the inhabitants of MENEMVASIA accepted Bertagno's rule, but they soon expelled him and looked for other protectors.

BERTONE (*sailing ship; Mediterranean; 16th and 17th centuries*) A ship broad and rounded in appearance, with three masts and square sails, of medium tonnage and carrying about 60 crewmen. Very stable because of its solid hull and deep keel, the bertone (plural *bertoni*) provided an excellent gun platform, and it was favored by pirates as well as traders.

(See also ARAGONA, FERDINANDO D'; GERMAIN, JACQUES).

BEST, RICHARD (*English captain; Caribbean; 1594*) Commanded Sir John WATTS' 130-ton *Jewel.* After a rendezvous with two more of Watts' ships under John MYDDLETON and Richard Lane, Best took a CARAVEL near Havana in July. He went on to the Bay of Mexico, where he picked up an abandoned hulk carrying dyes, drugs, silk, and gems. Captain Best's report to the owner and government undoubtedly understates his prize's value. Booty of this kind—easily concealed and sold—invited embezzlement by the crew.

BEY (*Barbary officials; Mediterranean; about 1525–1830*) A military officer commanding land forces, subordinate to the BEYLERBEY or later the DEY of ALGIERS, TUNIS, and TRIPOLI.

BEYLERBEY *(Barbary rulers; Mediterranean; about 1525–1830)* Under the OTTOMAN EMPIRE, a title (meaning "bey of the beys") given to a governor-general commanding military governors (BEYS). The post of beylerbey existed in ALGIERS, TUNIS, and TRIPOLI until 1830, even though other officials usurped their powers. Each of the three BARBARY STATES had a separate governor-general, and the Ottoman sultan never appointed one man as beylerbey over all three. (Beylerbeys also used the honorary title of pasha after their personal names, e.g., HASAN VENEZIANO PASHA.)

Beylerbey meant something like "the big boss" when referring to military and naval officials. For example, contemporary records sometimes speak of the Ottoman Admiral (Kapudan Pasha) as beylerbey. ULUJ ALI ceased to be Beylerbey of Algiers in December 1571 when he became Kapudan Pasha. But, as such, he sometimes was informally referred to as beylerbey or beylerbey-of-the-sea.

(See also CAPTAIN OF THE SEA; KHEIREDDIN BARBAROSSA.)

BIANCO, JAMES *(Italian pirate; Mediterranean; 1303)* Consorting with Percival de la TURCHA, Bianco attacked a Venetian ship off Cyprus.

BICIAKI, CAPTAIN *(Greek pirate; Aegean Sea, Mediterranean; active 1820s)* Originally from Crete, Captain Biciaki fled to Naxos about 1825. Two years later, he forced the Naxiotes to outfit a vessel for a raid on the Turks. When the expedition failed, he turned to piracy and plundered ships belonging to Greeks and other Europeans.

BISHOP, RICHARD *(English pirate; Mediterranean, Atlantic; 1561?–1617)* A Yarmouth man, he commanded a PRIVATEER in 1591 and took Dutch letters of MARQUE in 1604, when England made peace with Spain. In 1605, he joined forces with John WARD in MOROCCO and sailed with Ward to TUNIS. He captured few prizes and took 60 men to the western Atlantic in 1608.

The Atlantic pirates elected Bishop—a man of "good temper and moderation"—admiral of their confederation. (Peter EASTON was vice-admiral.) In 1609, he was at Leamcon, Ireland, commanding nine ships and a thousand men. The following year, he requested a pardon. It was granted in 1611, and he settled near Schull, Ireland. He kept in contact with his old friends, and a pirate captain was arrested in his house in 1617.

(See also SELECTED BIBLIOGRAPHY: Senior, *Nation.*)

BLACKBEARD *(legendary fictional British pirate; 1724 to the present)* Daniel DEFOE's GENERAL HISTORY combined fact and fiction in narrating the life of Edward TEACH, alias "Blackbeard." To straightforward reporting of Teach's adventures, Defoe added lurid stories portraying him as a horrifying monster. Defoe invented these anecdotes, which are not found in official records or newspaper stories written at the time.

The highlight of Defoe's fiction is his description of Teach's bizarre beard and clothing (not mentioned by anyone who met Teach).

> This Beard was black, which he suffered to grow of an extravagant Length; as to Breadth, it came up to his Eyes; he was accustomed to twist it with Ribbons, in small Tails, . . . and turn them about his Ears. In Time of Action, he wore a Sling over his Shoulders, with three Brace of pistols, hanging in Holsters like Bandaliers; and stuck lighted Matches under his Hat, which appearing on each Side of his Face, his Eyes naturally looking fierce and wild, made him altogether . . . [worse than] a Fury, from Hell. . . .

Defoe's Blackbeard played appropriately devilish pranks on his crew. One of these tricks severely wounded Israel HANDS, his first mate. In another, Blackbeard made his ship into an imitation hell by closing up the hatches and burning brimstone until the sailors almost suffocated.

Defoe's Blackbeard had large appetites for both alcohol and women. He had at least 14 wives, and his escapades continued after he married an aristocratic North Carolina girl in 1718. Defoe wrote that Blackbeard often invited five or six of his brutal companions to his home, where he would force his wife "to prostitute her self to them all, one after another, before his Face."

Defoe's mythical Blackbeard is a fascinating fiend. But it is unfair to confuse this fictional character with Edward Teach. The real Teach did commit piracy and then cheated his crew out of their share of the booty. But there is no evidence that he ever murdered, maimed, or tortured either his captives or his crew or that he raped his wife or other women. In fact, a ballad written at the time ("THE DOWNFALL OF PIRACY") describes him as afraid of women and perhaps impotent.

Later authors picked up Defoe's tales and even embellished them, creating the legendary Blackbeard. In Robert Louis STEVENSON's MASTER OF BALLANTRAE (1889), James Durie joins Blackbeard's band. Stevenson repeats the GENERAL HISTORY's stories of DRINKING and DEBAUCHERY. However, he comments that Defoe's fiend carried his excesses to a ludicrous extreme, "like a wicked child or half-witted person." Since the drunken brute cannot catch prizes, Durie deposes him and takes over his ship.

Howard PYLE also believed that a drunk could not succeed as a pirate captain. In THE STORY OF JACK BALLISTER'S FORTUNES (1895), Pyle ignores Defoe's fictions and creates a brave and resourceful rogue. PETER PAN (1904) briefly mentions Blackbeard. In ANNE BONNY (1977), the heroine turns him down because he never bathes.

Defoe's bearded monster was too bizarre for the 1930s SWASHBUCKLERS. Movie heroes like CAPTAIN BLOOD gained prestige by overcoming worthier foes. Blackbeard came into his own in movie comedies spoofing the 1930s

Blackbeard buries his treasure. An entirely fictitious scene by Howard Pyle in *Harper's Monthly Magazine*, September 1887.

swashbucklers. Thomas Gomez is flamboyantly evil in ANNE OF THE INDIES (1951) as is Louis Bacigalupi in DOUBLE CROSSBONES (1952). However, critics award the prize for unrestrained garishness to Robert NEWTON in BLACKBEARD THE PIRATE (1952). Too preposterous to be truly frightening, Blackbeard is the perfect villain for children's movies, such as THE BOY AND THE PIRATES (1960) and BLACKBEARD'S GHOST (1967).

(See also MASTER OF BALLANTRAE, THE (2).)

BLACKBEARD'S GHOST (motion picture; color; 1968)

Disney fantasy-comedy, directed by Robert Stevens, opens with a flashback to Blackbeard's piracy. In the present, Silky Seymour (Jody Baker) and other criminals want to turn a small resort island into a casino. A track coach, Steve (Dean Jones), finds a witch's book and evokes Blackbeard's ghost (Peter Ustinov), who needs to do a good deed to gain eternal rest. Only Steve can see the ghost, a situation providing some of the sight gags. Through their help, Emily (Elsa Lanchester) and other little old ladies pay off the mortgage and save their island home.

BLACKBEARD THE PIRATE (motion picture; color; 1952)

Everything expected in a SWASHBUCKLER is here: land and sea battles, SWORD DUELS, FLOGGING, and TORTURE, buried treasure, mutiny, betrayal—and

even a few romantic kisses. These action episodes alternate with tongue-in-cheek jokes and sight gags.

Sir Henry MORGAN (Torin Thatcher) is sent to rid the seas of pirates like Blackbeard (Robert NEWTON). Jamaica's governor offers to pay anyone who can prove that Morgan still is working with the brigands. To collect the reward, pirate-surgeon Robert Maynard (Keith Andes) lets himself be shanghaied aboard a pirate ship. Joining him is Edwina, Edward MANSFIELD's daughter (Linda Darnell), who plans to marry Charles BELLAMY, the ship's captain. Once aboard, they discover that Blackbeard has taken over and hanged Bellamy.

Maynard quickly locates evidence that Morgan sponsored Bellamy's raids. Soon after, Blackbeard gets Edwina's maid Alvina (Irene Ryan) drunk. The shrieking biddy reveals that Edwina stole Morgan's treasure and hid it in her luggage. Blackbeard plans to keep the gold for himself, since he earned it by fighting with Morgan at Panama. (In real life, both Bellamy and Edward TEACH, known as Blackbeard, were born after Morgan died.)

After Maynard and Edwina become allies, Maynard damages the ship and is flogged almost to death. The pirates stop for repairs at an island filled with buxom native girls. Blackbeard and his first mate, Worley (William Bendix), bury Morgan's treasure, joined by Maynard (miraculously recovered from the flogging).

Robert Newton in *Blackbeard the Pirate* (1952).

Morgan's forces attack the island, kill or capture the pirates, and rescue Edwina. Blackbeard escapes by murdering a beachcomber who looks just like himself. Morgan finds the dead double and cuts off his head. Maynard singlehandedly sails a LONGBOAT back to Jamaica.

At PORT ROYAL, Morgan has taken over as governor. He holds Edwina prisoner and wants to hang Maynard. Edwina and Maynard run off to a ship in the harbor. Once again, Blackbeard controls the vessel, having freed his crew from prison. Morgan pursues Blackbeard in a captured Spanish galleon. Their ships battle with cannon, and Blackbeard is beaten off.

First Mate Worley digs up Morgan's treasure and brings it back to their vessel. Blackbeard kills Worley and locks up the mutineers. Trying to steal the treasure, Blackbeard accidentally drops it in the ocean. The outraged pirates bury him on the beach as the tide comes in, while Maynard and Edwina sail off in a longboat.

It is difficult to tell whether some scenes are intended seriously or as spoofs, and the sequence of events ignores history and physical possibilities. Reviewers agreed that Robert Newton's Blackbeard dominated the movie.

BLACK PIRATE, THE *(motion picture; color; 1926)* Directed by Albert Parker, this silent film stars Douglas FAIRBANKS as a handsome and amazingly acrobatic SWASHBUCKLER. Somewhere in the Caribbean, BUCCANEERS have just captured a vessel. Their captain, a bald-headed brute with a knife in his teeth, orders the brigands to blow up the captured ship and crew. Fairbanks and his father, the only ones to survive this massacre,

escape to a desert island. The father dies on reaching shore, and Fairbanks vows vengeance.

Arriving at the very same island to bury their captured loot, the pirates meet Fairbanks. The bald captain wants to kill this lone survivor because DEAD MEN TELL NO TALES. But Fairbanks (now known as the Black Pirate) persuades the captain to fight a SWORD DUEL, kills him, and joins the brigands.

The Black Pirate captures a merchant ship single-handedly after climbing up the stern of the vessel. In a series of sudden onslaughts, he quickly disposes of the men in his way. The most famous scene in the movie occurs during this attack. The Black Pirate climbs the mast to the dizzy heights of the top cross arms. He pierces the wide sail with his sword, grabs its hilt, and descends to the deck—his momentum retarded by the sword ripping the canvas as he comes down.

Some of the pirates turn on the Black Pirate and make him WALK THE PLANK. Fortunately, a sympathizer cuts his bonds with a knife, and he swims to shore to ride for his followers. The Black Pirate returns with perhaps 50 men—uniformly young and with large pectoral muscles. As they row toward the enemy ship, their boat sinks.

In the second most famous scene of the film, the Black Pirate has his men swim under water in formations something like those of airplane squadrons. Armed with CUTLASSES and knives, scores of these swimmers make their way to the pirate ship and capture its crew. The Black Pirate (who turns out to be a duke) has his vengeance. He also rescues a willowy princess, one of only two women in the cast.

Fairbanks and his director consulted a variety of technical advisors. The film often is true in the details of ship design, rigging, and weapons.

Although highly popular with movie fans, *The Black Pirate* was not a critical success. Many praised Fairbanks' acrobatics and the performances by several character actors. *The Black Pirate* was only the fourth full-length film made in Technicolor. The New York Times Film Critics Circle named *The Black Pirate* one of the 10 best films of 1926.

BLACK PIRATES *(African-American marauders; Caribbean, Atlantic, Pacific; about 1640–1730)* As sugar cane became their main crop, the French and English colonies imported many African slaves into the Caribbean. Slaves and freedmen—both black and of mixed race—also were numerous in Peru and Mexico, and smaller groups lived in Spain's Caribbean colonies. Some slaves and free blacks became sailors on coastal trading, fishing, and naval vessels. Others were servants on merchantmen, warships, and treasure galleons.

Caribbean pirates treated black sailors with color-blind pragmatism. When pirates captured a merchant vessel, they usually recruited able-bodied seamen of any color. Blacks belonged to pirate bands in the Caribbean and the Pacific during the 17th century. Others joined the

Douglas Fairbanks holds off attacking brigands in *The Black Pirate* (1926).

marauders sailing from the Bahamas and MADAGASCAR in the early 1700s.

Pirates of all races lived together without antagonism, but some prejudice probably existed. Only pirates of mixed blood were elected as officers. Moreover, pirates (both black and white) treated slave ships coming from Africa like any other booty. Newly arrived slaves, without usable maritime skills, were sold for cash.

Since they did not become officers, the names of many black crewmen are lost to history. However, evidence shows that black pirates took part in the largest and bloodiest raids. Diego GRILLO commanded a ship during Sir Henry MORGAN's sack of Panama in 1671. Peter CLOISE was an intimate friend of Edward DAVIS and accompanied him on all his raids between 1679 and 1688. After Davis captured a Spanish frigate off Peru in 1686, thirty-nine slaves enlisted on the BATCHELOR'S DELIGHT and helped sack towns in Guatemala and Peru. When Jean HAMLIN reached Saint Thomas in 1682, 16 white and 22 black pirates made up the crew of *Trompeuse*.

Many pirate ships raiding in the Atlantic and Indian oceans during the early 18th century had one or two

black seamen. Abraham SAMUEL was QUARTERMASTER for John HOAR. The *Good Fortune* of Rhode Island also had an officer of mixed origins, called Old South. When Bartholomew ROBERTS sailed to Africa in April 1721, his two ships carried 88 black crewmen but no black officers.

BLACK SEA   *(pirate abode; all periods)*   A large inland sea enclosed by Russia and Ukraine on the north and east, by Turkey on the south, by Bulgaria and Rumania on the west. Ships can reach the Mediterranean by a passage through the Bosporus, the Sea of Marmara, and the Dardanelles.

In antiquity, several Greek cities prospered along both the southern and northern coasts. The cities bordering the Straits of Kerch, which connect the Black to the Sea of Azov, were united into the kingdom of Bosporus from 438 B.C. to about A.D. 250. The eastern shore, where the Caucasus Mountains begin, was generally unsettled.

In 310 B.C., the Bosporan ruler Eumelus declared that he had totally eliminated the pirates sailing from the Caucasus region. If his claim was true, the brigands soon returned. Writing in about 20 B.C., STRABO noted that the Caucasian tribes infested the sea and lived by their robberies. Sailing in a slender, narrow boat (CAMARA), they darted into shore to capture prisoners and hold them for ransom. They found safe havens and go-betweens in the Bosporus kingdom, much as the cities of CRETE and CILICIA served the corsairs along their shores. To the west, other tribes occupied islands at the mouth of the Danube and caught ships as they left the river.

Piracy fell off during the first century A.D., after the Roman emperors stationed fleets at Sebastapol, Trabzon, and the mouth of the Danube. But it revived from the middle of the third century. Pressed by invasions on several fronts, the emperors had let the Roman fleet decay. Large bands of Germanic and native marauders controlled the Black Sea and made their way into the Aegean, plundering both shores as far south as Cilicia. The Cilicians returned to their buccaneering ways, and TREBELLIANUS even declared himself emperor.

The pirate attacks reached their climax in 268 and 269. Large bands—said to have 500 small ships—made their way into the Aegean, were repulsed before Athens, and chased away by the remaining Roman warships. The next year, raiders again entered the Aegean, this time without any Roman opposition, and halted near Mount Athos to repair their ships. Most disembarked and besieged Thessalonica and Cassandria, where the emperor Claudius (reigned 268–270) annihilated them. The survivors sailed south and attacked Rhodes, Crete, and Cyprus. One of the plagues ravishing the Mediterranean at this time struck them, and only a remnant returned home.

BLACK SWAN, THE (1) (novel, 1932)

Like Rafael SABATINI's other pirate heroes, Charles de Bernis is a chivalrous gentlemen forced into crime. In manners and methods, he closely resembles Sabatini's CAPTAIN BLOOD rather than Oliver, the more muscular captain of THE SEA HAWK (1). Like Blood, he is "a tricky, slippery devil, who had a way of defeating brute force by artifice."

The novel focuses on the love between Bernis and Priscilla Harradine, daughter of a recently deceased governor. A true Sabatini heroine, Priscilla is beautiful, strongminded, and pure. During the late 1680s, she is returning to England with Major Sands, a pompous fool who lusts after her inheritance.

Bernis joins them on the *Centaur* and relates his story. A French Protestant, he fled religious persecution and joined Edward MANSFIELD's colony on PROVIDENCE ISLAND. When Spanish troops massacred the English settlers, Bernis escaped and fought under Sir Henry MORGAN at PORTOBELO and PANAMA. He stayed with Morgan when he became governor of Jamaica and turned pirate hunter. Just recently, he resigned from Morgan's anti-pirate squadron to return to France. (In real life, Morgan retired some years earlier and never led ships against the BUCCANEERS.)

Soon after, Thomas Leach captures the *Centaur*. The last remaining pirate captain, Leach had rejected Morgan's offer of pardon. Now he marauds in the 40-gun *Black Swan*, stripping and sinking ships of every nation.

Leach kills the crew but spares Bernis, Priscilla, and Sands. Bernis persuades Leach that he knows the route of the Spanish TREASURE FLEETS. He promises to share the secret and takes command of the *Centaur*. He also convinces Leach to careen the *Black Swan* on an uninhabited island, where the two ships remain for several weeks.

The emotional atmosphere on the island is tense and stormy. Leach is a brutal, stupid scoundrel, a "treacherous, headstrong, violent beast." His 300 men are "monstrous wicked, lawless children" with "gross appetites" for "coarse delights." However, Sabatini does give more distinctive personalities to Leach's four officers.

Despite Major Sands' jealousy, Priscilla gradually comes to love Bernis. Leach accidentally sees Priscilla swimming naked and tries to rape her. Bernis kills Leach in a sword fight just before Morgan shows up with three warships. Priscilla discovers that the careening operation was a plot to trap Leach. She convinces Bernis to marry her, and they sail away, leaving the pirates stranded on the island.

BLACK SWAN, THE (2) (motion picture; color; 1942)

Along with THE BLACK PIRATE, CAPTAIN BLOOD, and THE SEA HAWK (3), one of the classic pirate spectaculars. Director Howard King keeps control over this exciting, full-blooded adventure movie. The actors' wild exuberance sometimes turns into unintentional parody. Unlike some later movie pirates, however, they do not deliberately caricature situations and dialogue.

Loosely following Rafael SABATINI's novel, the film presents a romanticized Sir Henry MORGAN (Laird Cregar). Pardoned and named governor of Jamaica, Morgan is ordered to suppress the other buccaneers. James Waring (Tyrone POWER) is one of Morgan's aides and a

Sir Henry Morgan (played by Laird Cregar), James Waring (Tyrone Power, on Cregar's right), and Tommy Blue (Thomas Mitchell) in a scene from *The Black Swan* (1942).

former pirate. He aggressively pursues but is spurned by Margaret Denby (Maureen O'HARA), the previous governor's daughter.

Meanwhile, two captains, Billy Leech (George Sanders) and the one-eyed Wogan (Anthony QUINN) refuse to submit. Morgan sends Waring and Tommy Blue (Thomas Mitchell) to capture them, and Waring kidnaps Miss Denby to keep him company during the voyage.

Leech and Wogan overpower Waring, who tries to convince them that he still is a pirate and married to Denby. (Leech investigates their cabin to make sure they share a bed.) Convinced that he is working for Governor Morgan, Wogan persuades Leech to tie up Waring. Blue and Waring's crew are locked in the hold.

Leech and Wogan attack Morgan's headquarters at Maracaibo (a Spanish colony in real life). During a ferocious battle between ships and shore batteries, all looks lost for Morgan's forces. Just then, Waring frees himself and his crew. He fights a wild SWORD DUEL with Leech, who wanders about pierced by Waring's weapon. After retaking his own vessel, Waring attacks and sink's Wogan's ship. Until the final victory, Waring is considered a traitor. As the movie ends, he is honored by Morgan and wins Margaret Denby's love.

The Black Swan was a box-office success, and Leon Shamroy won an Oscar for cinematography. As Theodore Strauss commented in the *New York Times*, the movie "is in the golden tradition of boyish adventures. . . . But a lot of grown-ups are going to like it too." His enormous body bedecked in wigs and finery, Cregar bellows and struts as Morgan. Despite a drooping mustache, Power's muscled torso makes him a vision of manly beauty, and O'Hara is ravishing in low-cut gowns. Sanders, sporting a thick red beard, and Quinn are conniving and sneering villains. The performances are enhanced by the lush color cinematography.

BLANC, CAPTAIN *(French buccaneer; Caribbean; 1697)* Took part in the Sack of CARTAGENA.

BLAUVELT (BLEWFIELD), ABRAHAM *(Dutch pirate; Caribbean; active 1631–1663)* A daring and resourceful sailor, after whom at least two places in the West Indies are named. In the early 1630s, Blauvelt explored the coasts of Honduras and Nicaragua for the pirates on PROVIDENCE ISLAND. He returned to England in 1637 and recommended a settlement near the town and river of Bluefields, Nicaragua.

After a Spanish expedition reoccupied Providence Island in 1641, Blauvelt briefly was a naval officer for the Swedish West India company. In 1644, he commanded his own ship, which raided Spanish shipping from Dutch New Amsterdam (New York) and a harbor in southwest Jamaica still called Blewfields Bay.

New Amsterdam no longer welcomed Blauvelt after the Dutch made peace with Spain in 1648. He disposed of his prizes at Newport, Rhode Island, in 1649, where his crew bickered over the booty. The governor declared one prize illegal, but he lacked the power to enforce his decision. Roger Williams, founder of the colony, was convinced that Blauvelt's crimes had permanently ruined Rhode Island's reputation. In 1650, he owned and commanded the French ship *La Garse*.

In 1663, Blauvelt lived among the Indians at Cape Gracias à Dios, on the Honduras-Nicaragua border, cutting LOGWOOD from a three-gun BARK. He joined Sir Christopher MYNGS' 1663 raid on Campeche Bay in Mexico.

(See also SELECTED BIBLIOGRAPHY: Dow, *Pirates*; Haring, *Buccaneers*; Newton, *Puritans*.)

BLONDEL, ROBERT *(French corsair; Caribbean; active 1553–1568)* Blondel commanded a vessel when François LE CLERC raided Puerto Rico and Hispaniola in 1553. In contrast to Le Clerc, however, he fought against rather than collaborating with English troops that occupied the French port of Le Havre in 1563.

As Sir John HAWKINS' third West Indian expedition (1557–1568) was passing West Africa, Hawkins was joined by French corsairs led by a "Captain Bland"— almost certainly an English version of Blondel. During the battle with Hawkins' fleet at SAN JUAN DE ULÚA, Mexico, the Spaniards captured Blondel's ship, and he was killed or taken prisoner.

BLOODING AND SWEATING *(type of torture; Atlantic, Caribbean; 17th and 18th centuries)* In 1718, George SHELVOCKE threatened to make a captured captain run the gauntlet naked, while the pirates struck him with sail needles. "Thus bleeding, they put him into a sugar cask swarming with cockroaches, cover him with a blanket, and there leave him to glut the vermin with his blood." In one documented case, Francis SPRIGGS omitted the final touch with the cockroaches.

(See also SELECTED BIBLIOGRAPHY: Kemp and Lloyd, *Brethren*.)

BLOUT, CAPTAIN *(French buccaneer; Caribbean; 1697)* Captain Blout took part in the SIEGE OF CARTAGENA.

BLOW ME DOWN! *(nautical slang; uncertain origin)* An expression used by movie pirates (and Popeye the Sailor), which communicates surprise or shock and refers to a sudden strong wind that overpowers a person or ship. A "blow" is a short but intense gale or storm.

BLUNDERBUSS *(firearm; 17th through 19th centuries)* A short MUSKET or large PISTOL, often of brass, with either an expanding bore or a flared muzzle, which could be loaded with balls, lead slugs, or buckshot. Like the modern shotgun, it scattered these projectiles in a wide pattern for hunting or close-up defense, such as repelling those boarding a ship.

BODULGATE, THOMAS *(English pirate, Atlantic; died 1471)* A friend of John TREVELYAN and

Richard PENPONS, Bodulgate had large estates and great political influence in Cornwall. Like Penpons, he often served on commissions investigating piracy by others while marauding on his own account. He personally commanded a ship that brought an Irish prize into Fowey in 1454. In 1460, two pirate vessels seized a Spanish freighter carrying British goods. They distributed her cargo at Fowey, with both Bodulgate and John Trevelyan taking major shares.

Bodulgate supported the House of Lancaster during the War of the Roses, and he was arrested when Edward IV became king in May 1461. In September, a royal commission—including Richard Penpons, his erstwhile friend—ruled that the politically incorrect Bodulgate had directed the sack of the Spanish freighter. He was ordered to pay £300 to the owners of her cargo.

BOGGS, ELI (American pirate; South China Sea; active 1850s)

Boggs enlisted with Chinese pirates by 1852, and his cruelty became legendary. One tale tells how he single-handedly boarded a JUNK, killed 15 men, and drove the rest overboard. Another story says his pirates captured wealthy Chinese merchants who were slow to pay ransom. To speed up negotiations, Boggs cut the body of one captive into four pieces and sent them ashore in a bucket.

A British vessel captured Boggs in September 1856, thanks to information from William HAYS, another American adventurer. Hays guided the warship to the Gulf of Liao-tung in northern China. After several days, Boggs' junk was sighted close to shore. Boarding parties in two boats were almost swamped when the junk exploded, seconds after Boggs dived overboard. Bully Hays dived after and caught him. Boggs attacked with a short sword, but Hays grabbed his wrist and knocked him out. He received a $1,000 reward and also helped himself to silver coins taken from the pirates.

Boggs was tried at Hong Kong in July 1857. He was acquitted of murder but sentenced to life imprisonment for piracy. According to A. G. Course's *Pirates of the Eastern Seas*, a reporter at Boggs' trial described him as "a handsome boy with carefully brushed hair, girlish face, charming smile, and delicate hands."

BOISBAUDRANT, BROTHER GABRIELLE CHAMBRES DE (Knight of Malta; Mediterranean; active 1634–1644)

A Frenchman famed for his daring in combat, Boisbaudrant commanded a GALLEY from 1634 to 1638, and became CAPTAIN GENERAL OF GALLEYS in 1642. In September 1644, his six galleys made an extraordinarily rich catch. About 70 miles from RHODES, they ran into an Istanbul-to-Alexandria convoy that included the "Galleon of the Sultan"—a heavily armed ship of more than 1,100 tons. Her passengers included Basseba, Sultan Ibrahim's favorite wife. A 19-year-old Circassian of legendary beauty, Basseba was taking her young son on a pilgrimage to Mecca.

Three galleys attacked the much taller GALLEON, which rained down missiles. Boisbaudrant had chased another vessel but returned and joined in the fight. The Maltese managed to board the galleon's bridge and finally took it after seven hours of hand-to-hand fighting. Boisbaudrant was among the first to fall, cut down by a MUSKET ball. He remained on board the bridge, covered with his own blood, to encourage his troops.

The captured galleon sank in heavy weather off the coast of southern Italy. However, the knights rescued much of her priceless cargo, the sultana's splendid jewels, and prisoners worth large ransoms. Basseba died soon after she arrived at Malta, and her son was brought up as a Christian.

This attack on the sultan's convoy had harsh consequences. Venice had enjoyed peace with the OTTOMAN EMPIRE since 1573, and the Venetians were themselves victims of Maltese piracy. Nevertheless, because the knights used Venetian ports on their way back to Malta, Sultan Ibrahim attacked Venetian-owned Crete in 1645. The Ottoman army soon overran the island, although the fortified capital of Candia (Iráklion) surrendered only in 1669.

BOLLATO (Barbary corsair; Mediterranean; about 1550)

The Italian nickname for a captain raiding from DJERBA with TURGUT's squadrons. Commanding a BRIGANTINE, he captured a BARK with 20 Christian pilgrims in the Gulf of Gaeta, between Rome and Naples.

BONFIGLIO, NICOLO (French pirate; Mediterranean; active 1495–1496)

Operating with a squadron of large sailing ships—one armed with 55 guns—Bonfiglio looted Venetian shipping along the BARBARY COAST.

BONITON, PETER (English pirate; Atlantic; 1609)

Boniton was from Cornwall and based in Ireland. Sailing to reconnoitre the Strait of Gibraltar, his ship was captured in a fierce fight off Faro by a French GALLEON sent to hunt pirates, and he was executed at Marseilles.

BONNET, STEDE (British pirate; Atlantic, Caribbean; hanged 1718)

According to Daniel DEFOE's GENERAL HISTORY, Bonnet was a middle-aged plantation owner on Barbados, educated and respected, who suddenly turned pirate to escape his nagging wife. (No mention of this has turned up in the Barbados records.) Most pirates stole their ships, but Bonnet bought the 10-gun SLOOP *Revenge* and recruited 70 crewmen.

Sailing in the spring of 1717, Bonnet plundered several ships off Virginia, New York, and South Carolina. He careened in North Carolina and then sailed for the Bay of Honduras. On the way, about March 1718, he met Edward TEACH (BLACKBEARD) commanding a much larger ship. Teach seized the *Revenge*, made his own man captain, and took Bonnet along as an involuntary guest.

Teach broke up his company in June, cheating Bonnet out of any share in the booty. Bonnet regained the

Revenge and appointed David HERRIOT sailing master. The governor of North Carolina granted him a royal pardon and permission to go to Saint Thomas to enroll as a PRIVATEER. (Britain recently had declared war on Spain.)

After unsuccessfully chasing Teach to Ocracoke, North Carolina, Bonnet returned to piracy and pillaged several ships off Virginia and in Delaware Bay. Since he had just been pardoned under his own name, he called himself Captain Thomas and renamed his sloop the *Royal James.*

In August, Bonnet sailed up the Cape Fear River in North Carolina, where he stayed for two months repairing the *Royal James.* News of his arrival reached Charleston, South Carolina, when the pirates seized a small ship. William Rhett, a prominent citizen, received a commission to arrest them and equipped two sloops. Rhett attacked on October 8, after wasting time looking for Charles VANE. The *Royal James* and the attackers ran aground and exchanged cannon fire for five hours before Bonnet surrendered. About 18 of Rhett's men and nine pirates were killed.

Bonnet and his men were tried at Charleston. There Bonnet was imprisoned in a private home, along with David Herriot and Ignatius PELL, who testified against the others. Bonnet and Herriot bribed the guards and escaped. Rhett pursued them to an island off the coast, killed Herriot, and rearrested Bonnet. He was convicted and hanged in November, together with 29 crewmen. Ignatius Pell and four others were acquitted.

(See also SELECTED BIBLIOGRAPHY: Hughson, *Carolina;* Pringle, *Jolly Roger.*)

BONNY (BONNEY), ANNE (1) *(British pirate; Caribbean; 1720)*

Bonny is one of the very few women pirates in European history. With Mary READ, she was captured in 1720, as Jack RACKHAM raided along Jamaica's northern coast. Early in November, a government ship seized Rackham's SLOOP, which carried the two women and nine men. Rackham and the other men were hanged. Because everyone knew they were women, Bonny and Read were tried separately. Their victims testified that they wore female clothing except during battles. Both joined in assaults carrying guns. The witnesses added that "they were both very profligate, cursing and swearing much, and very ready and willing to do anything."

After they were convicted, the judge asked if there was any reason why they should not be hanged as sentenced. "My Lord, we Plead our Bellies," Bonny and Read replied—the customary plea of pregnant women. Since hanging would kill the unborn child (who had committed no crime), women were reprieved until they gave birth. Bonny and Read were jailed, and nothing is known about their later fate.

The presence of two women on Rackham's sloop was highly unusual. Some ARTICLES specifically banned women and young boys, since the men fought to obtain their sexual favors. In this case, the pirates tolerated the women because they made themselves available to everyone in Rackham's small crew.

BONNY (BONNEY), ANNE (2) *(fictional pirate; Caribbean; 1720)*

Daniel DEFOE made Bonny famous through a melodramatic story inserted in his GENERAL HISTORY. In Defoe's fictional biography, Anne successfully disguised herself as a man while fighting beside her lover, Jack RACKHAM. Defoe's tale, which blends pornography and romance, often has been repeated as true. However, given the close quarters on Rackham's ship, Bonny could never have pretended to be a man for long. Even if Bonny and Rackham disguised their love as homosexual, the sanitary arrangements alone would have given Bonny away.

Defoe's story tells how Bonny was born in Ireland, the illegitimate child of a lawyer and his servant. Her father was forced to emigrate to South Carolina, along with Anne and her mother. The only heiress to a large fortune, Anne gave up everything to run away with James Bonny.

The two lovers went to the Bahamas, where Bonny was pardoned by Woodes ROGERS in 1718. Anne, who liked both money and men, soon began to sleep around. She eventually met Jack Rackham, who won her favor by lavishly spending his booty. When Governor Rogers threatened to whip Anne and Rackham, they stole a sloop and turned pirate together.

Putting on seaman's clothes, Anne fought beside the other pirates, who were convinced she was a man. She took shore leave in Cuba to have a baby, but rejoined the ship soon after. By this time, Mary Read, also wearing male attire, had joined the pirates. Mary learned Anne's secret when Anne seduced her, thinking her a pretty fellow. Everyone else was fooled until Anne and Mary revealed their secret in court. When the Jamaicans caught the pirate ship, only the women resisted, and Anne viciously condemned Rackham as a coward.

(See also ANNE BONNY (1); SELECTED BIBLIOGRAPHY: Defoe, *General History;* Pringle, *Jolly Roger.*)

BONTEMPS, JEAN *(French pirate; Atlantic; Caribbean; died 1570)*

During several Caribbean voyages, Bontemps (a nickname meaning "good weather") combined piracy and smuggling. Like Sir John HAWKINS, he collected slaves along the African coast for illegal sale to Spanish colonists.

A native of Normandy, Bontemps collaborated with the English troops occupying Le Havre in 1563 and looted merchant ships sailing from other French ports. In 1567, he sailed for the West Indies with at least four large ships and various smaller ones. (Pirates frequently added their prizes to their squadrons to impress victims.) Arriving in America, he ran into the Hawkins expedition under John LOVELL, and the two captains temporarily worked together.

Late in April, the pirates came into Borburata (Puerto Cabellos), Venezuela. They seized prominent citizens and threatened to kidnap them unless they were allowed to sell slaves and other wares. This threat failed, and only 26 Africans were sold by both fleets. (Bontemps also kept 1,500 pesos seized from the hostages.)

The English and French split up, and Bontemps reached RIO DE LA HACHA before Lovell. Despite a show of strength, the Spanish again refused to take his slaves. Bontemps sailed west, seized a richly laden ship traveling with a TREASURE FLEET, and used force to sell slaves at Santa Marta, Colombia.

As he returned to Europe, Bontemps raided ports in Hispaniola, including La Yaguana (Léogane) in the south and Puerto Plata, Monte Cristi, and Puerto Real on the northern coast. His squadron took at least 12 prizes and burned down Puerto Real. Returning to the Caribbean in 1570, Bontemps was killed at Curaçao while trying to force Spanish colonists to purchase his goods.

BOONETER, JAN GIJSBERTSZOON (Dutch admiral; Caribbean; active 1630–1631) In May 1630, Booneter took eight ships to the Caribbean for the DUTCH WEST INDIA COMPANY. He divided his fleet into several units, which attacked Spanish shipping and raided coastal towns. In the fall, he placed his ships under the command of Pieter ITA. When Ita returned to Europe, Booneter continued to plunder the Spanish Caribbean and blockaded Havana in June and July 1630. His squadron took substantial booty but probably not enough to pay its costs.

BOOTH, GEORGE (British pirate; Red Sea, Indian Ocean; active 1696–1700) Gunner on the Pelican and her successor, the Dolphin, which cruised in the Indian Ocean from about 1696. A British naval squadron trapped the Dolphin at SAINT MARY'S ISLAND in September 1699. The pirates burned their ship and escaped to nearby MADAGASCAR.

Before long, a French ship arrived to barter liquor and goods for slaves. Led by Booth, the pirates seized the vessel and later met and joined forces with John BOWEN. At Majunga in April 1704, the two pirate crews took over the Speaker, a 450-ton slave ship carrying 50 guns. Booth became captain of the Speaker and sailed to Zanzibar at the end of 1700. When they went ashore for provisions, Arab troops attacked the pirates. Booth was killed, and Bowen became captain.

(See also NORTH, NATHANIEL.)

BOOTY, DIVISION OF (throughout history)
Ancient Mediterranean
Ancient pirates divided their haul more or less equally, imitating military practices. Greek and Roman soldiers received equal portions, although a larger share might go to generals and men who had fought with special valor.

Greek customs were summarized by Xenophon, a mercenary soldier and historian (died about 355 B.C.).

> Whenever an army remained in camp and rested, individuals were permitted to go out after plunder, and in that case kept what they got. But whenever the entire army set out, if any individual went off by himself and got anything, it was decreed to be public property.

Prisoners became part of the common property and were guarded until they could be sold or given out. After the common goods were locked up, soldiers could keep any small items they found on the battlefield. Roman law similarly made captives state property, and soldiers expected their commander to distribute the take equally.

All the evidence shows that pirate practices were the same as those of regular soldiers. In Homer's poem, ODYSSEUS' men divide the spoils of piracy equally. The AETOLIANS and cities on CRETE encouraged piracy and drew up formal agreements dealing with anticipated spoils. In Cretan treaties, booty was divided according to the number of men each party committed. The city rulers first took a tenth off the top, supposedly for the god Apollo. In the EPHESIAN TALE, all share equally, but the captain chooses first. In the ETHIOPIAN ADVENTURES, the man first aboard the enemy vessel gets first choice.

Medieval
Among Christian pirates in the 14th-century Aegean (SANUDO reports), the captain received one-fifth of the loot, and the pilot also got a share off the top. When he owned the ship, the captain also took 150 percent of his expenses fitting it out for the voyage. His cut was higher (twice his expenses) if he attacked a fellow pirate—perhaps because of the extra risk.

When the Venetian government owned the ships, it kept one-third of the booty and gave the rest to the crews. In addition, it paid fighting men three ducats a head for every Muslim prisoner captured and enslaved.

Barbary States
In contrast to the Maltese, their main rivals in Mediterranean piracy, BARBARY corsairs followed relatively straightforward procedures. Christian observers commented on the lack of quarrels and the speed of justice.

Despite some variations over the centuries, the basic rules were simple. Crew members and soldiers kept whatever they pillaged from captured sailors or passengers, and the captain was entitled to everything in the cabins. The ship's equipment, the cargo, and the captives went into the common fund.

Unpaid debts and the government's cut came off the top. The Koran directed that the community receive one-fifth of booty. HASAN VENEZIANO PASHA enraged the corsairs by demanding the full fifth during the 1570s. Most rulers were satisfied with one-seventh to one-tenth of captives and cargo. Originally the ruler also received

Richest Prizes in the Indian Ocean and Red Sea, 1690–1722

Captain	Probable Value	Prize
John TAYLOR in the *Cassandra*, Olivier LA BOUCHE in the *Victory* (1721)	£500,000 in diamonds and treasure, £375,000 in other cargo. Divided into shares worth at least £3,600 each	*Nostra Senhora de Cabo*, a Portuguese vessel taken at Réunion Island
Henry EVERY in the *Fancy* and five other captains (1695)	£325,000 (estimate, probably low, by East India Company). The *Fancy* took most of the loot, about £1,000 cash per man plus jewels	*Fateh Mohammed* and *Gang-i-sawai* (*Gunsway*) taken in the Red Sea
Edmund CONDENT in the *Flying Dragon* (1720)	£150,000 (East Indian Company estimate) in money, drugs, spices, and silk. About £2,000 per share	A large (Arab?) ship taken near Bombay
Dirk CHIVERS and Robert CULLIFORD commanding the *Soldado* and the *Mocha* (1698)	£130,000 in cash. More than £700 per share	*Great Mohammed*, Indian ship taken in the Red Sea
John BOWEN in the *Speaker* (1700 or 1701)	£100,000	Indian vessel taken near the mouth of the Red Sea
Edward ENGLAND with the *Fancy* and the *Victory* (1720)	£75,000 according to some reports	*Cassandra*, an East India Company vessel taken at Johanna Island in the Comoros
Thomas HOWARD in consort with John Bowen in the *Speedy Return* (1703)	More than £70,000	Two Indian vessels taken in the Red Sea
John HALSEY with the *Charles* (1701)	£50,000 in cash	Two British ships taken at Mocha in the Red Sea
William KIDD in the *Adventure Galley* (1698)	£45,000 (estimate by Indian merchants), £22,500 (East India Company estimate)	*Quedah Merchant*, an Indian vessel taken off Cochin, India

Note New York witnesses said William MAY returned with rich booty from several prizes—£200,000 is mentioned in 1696, £300,000 in 1699. These reports, which exaggerated his take, cannot be confirmed from the Indian records.

the captured ship, but this rule was relaxed by the late 17th century. Additional fixed payments—usually two to three percent—went to maintain the harbor and to pay port officials and clergy.

The ship's owners and its crew each received one-half of the booty remaining after these taxes. Many ships were owned by syndicates, whose members divided their share in proportion to their investment. The crew's share was divided into several hundred shares, and individuals collected a certain number of these shares, depending on their rank.

Larger ships usually carried JANISSARY soldiers as well as sailors and oarsmen. Over time, the sailors gained a larger and the soldiers a smaller number of shares. (However, the Janissaries also drew their regular army pay while at sea.) Slaves—including Christians—received the same share as free sailors and oarsmen, but their owners took all or part of it.

At ALGIERS in 1634, the captain received 10 to 15 shares, in addition to whatever he might get as an owner. Senior officers and the Janissaries' general (Agha) took three parts each. Sailors, Janissaries, and gunners received two shares; the rowers each gained one share. By the late 1700s, Algerian captains took 40 shares, sailors three, and Janissaries only one-and-a-half.

Cargo and slaves were normally sold by auction. Certain Jewish merchants specialized in prize goods. After changing marks and altering bales, they either sold them to Christian merchants in North Africa or forwarded them to Jewish correspondents at European "free ports" such as LIVORNO.

Malta

Under the KNIGHTS HOSPITALERS, plunder was divided in extraordinarily complicated ways, and lawsuits were frequent. The island supported two pirate fleets—the order's navy and private ships under knights or secular captains. Booty taken by the naval fleet was not divided. The order kept all prizes, and it hired sailors and soldiers for wages. Knights sailing on their own ships turned over three-fourths to the order.

As a general rule, secular captains reported to the TRIBUNALE DEGLI ARMAMENTI, which sold their take and registered and distributed the proceeds. Accounting was difficult. Few Maltese corsairs captured rich cargoes, and the ship and crew often were the most valuable booty. Some ships went back to Malta under a prize captain, who earned additional shares for this dangerous job. But cargoes and captives captured in the Levant often were disposed of in local ports, with the purser recording the proceeds. In addition, corsairs often hunted in a pack (CONSERVA), which shared all prizes.

After the Tribunal's staff determined the amount coming to a specific ship, the grand master and the captain each took a fixed share off the top. The grand master received 10 percent, including one-tenth of all slaves. (Small shares also went to other officials and the nuns of Saint Ursula.) The captain collected 11 percent, but he shared this with his officers, especially the pilot.

The owners and crew divided the rest according to their contract. Under a common agreement, the *terzo buscaino*, the shareholders received two-thirds, and the crew shared equally in the other third. The owners thus took about half of all receipts, the crew about a quarter. Since the owners paid all ordinary expenses out of their share, they often ended up with little or nothing. Under another type of contract, *alla fratesca,* the crew kept anything found on individuals or on the decks. All other booty was split evenly between the investors and crew, after settling expenses.

Only proceeds from the ship, cargo, and captives were subject to the general share-out. Officers had complicated rights to the property and money of the passengers and crew. In addition, various crew members kept goods pertaining to their trade. Thus the cook seized the pots and pans, and the surgeon got the medical chest. All were supposed to pay 10 percent to the grand master.

These rules were difficult to enforce during the general confusion of boarding. Crew members grabbed whatever they could snatch and often treated prisoners brutally. For example, passengers and crews—even if obviously Christians—usually were stripped in the search for jewelry.

England

Raiders sailing from England divided plunder according to written contracts and verbal agreements. With few exceptions, pirates and PRIVATEERS followed the same rules. Many official expeditions commissioned by Queen Elizabeth I also were conducted under the traditional rules of plunder raids.

Prior to the 1580s, some owners took half the loot, and the captain and crew split the other half. In other cases, the captain and owner each received one-quarter, the crew one-half. Raids were much larger and semilegal during the Spanish War (1595–1603). Owners and suppliers took more, and the crew received a smaller share. After King James I outlawed piracy in 1603, multiship expeditions again became unusual. Captains owned and outfitted their own vessels, and split the whole take with their crews.

Under English law, raiders with commissions (letters of REPRISAL) had to declare prizes and booty with ADMIRALTY officials in each port. After appraising the goods, local officials immediately took out the government's cut as well as the normal import taxes. In return for registering their goods, owners and captains could bring disputes before Admiralty judges.

The government's share tended to increase over time. Some sources say the king originally claimed everything captured by private warships. By the 1580s, the LORD HIGH ADMIRAL took only a tenth—about the same as in MALTA or in the BARBARY STATES. When there was no admiral (as was usual after 1628), his share went to the king. From 1660 to 1673, the king's brother was admiral and got the tenth; the king imposed an extra fifteenth for himself. After 1673, the tenth went back to the king, and colonial governors took the fifteenth.

The king's share briefly rose to 20 percent in 1689. At that rate, few raiders bothered to obtain a commission. To encourage attacks on enemy shipping, the government abolished all taxes in 1708. By then, however, some VICE-ADMIRAL's courts took more than a fourth in fees.

After the government took its cut, owners and mariners shared what was left. Into the 19th century, crews received the least on ships operating under government privateering commissions and on naval vessels. The owners and suppliers took the largest share, and officers got much more than crewmen. The split was fairer on illegal raiders, which partly explains why so many mariners turned pirate.

Small vessels often belonged to one man, while two or more persons jointly owned larger ships. Wealthy adventurers (for example, the earl of CUMBERLAND) often used their own funds to outfit vessels. More prudent owners issued shares (called "bills of adventure") to their suppliers. During the 16th century, booty usually was split into thirds. The owners and suppliers each collected a third, from which they paid their expenses. The officers and crew received the remaining third.

The crew divided their allotted third into shares and distributed them according to rank. There was no one system of sharing, and disputes were common. Following Andrew BARKER's 1576 venture, the captain took eight shares, and the master got seven. Other officers collected between four and six shares, seamen collected two or

Richest Prizes by English Pirates, 1485–1620

Captain	Probable Value	Prize
Nine ships acting in CONSORT (1592)	£141,200 (seized by crown) to £500,000 (contemporary informed estimate)	MADRE DE DIOS, a 1,600-ton CARRACK returning from India and taken in the Azores
Sir Francis DRAKE with the GOLDEN HIND (1579)	£126,000 (registered gold and silver only) to £450,000 (contemporary informed estimate)	CACAFUEGO, 120-ton merchant vessel carrying treasure from Peru to PANAMA, taken off northern Ecuador
Sir Francis Drake commanding nine vessels (1587)	£114,000 (governmental accounting)	*San Felipe,* East Indian carrack taken in the Azores
Thomas CAVENDISH with the *Desire* and two smaller ships (1587)	£42,700 (registered gold and silver only) to £125,000 (reliable estimate)	*Santa Ana,* 700-ton MANILA GALLEON taken off Lower California
John WARD (1607) with the *Gift* and a PINNACE	£100,000 or more (official estimate)	*Reniera y Soderina,* 600-ton Venetian merchant vessel taken near Cyprus
Sir James LANCASTER with seven English and five French pirate ships (1595)	More than £50,000 (estimate)	The cargo from a wrecked East Indian carrack and other goods stored at Pernambuco, Brazil
William PARKER commanding two ships and a pinnace (1601)	More than £50,000 (estimate)	Looted PORTOBELO and took several prizes in the West Indies
Sir Richard GRENVILLE with the *Tiger* (1585)	More than £50,000 (estimate)	*Santa Marita,* part of the annual TREASURE FLEET and taken off Bermuda, plus other prizes
William LANE commanding four ships and a pinnace (1591)	More than £40,000 (estimated)	*Trinity* from the annual treasure fleet, plus other prizes taken in the West Indies

three shares, soldiers from one to four, and the ship's boys received a half share. However, some captains probably took more shares on other voyages.

The rule of thirds applied only to the cargo in the hold and valuable property. The victorious crew had a customary right called PILLAGE. This allowed them to seize all goods found above deck or among their captives' personal belongings, unless they were worth more than two pounds, a large sum at the time.

In theory, this legal pillage was brought to the mainmast and divided equally among the captors. Everyone above the rank of seaman also received the possessions of his opposite number among the vanquished. The captain took the enemy captain's sea chest, the master gunner received the enemy gunner's possessions, and so on. However, the rules of pillage varied in practice, and some versions gave the officers additional rights.

Elizabethan England

Although some operated under government license, English raiders frequently quarreled over booty during the Spanish War (1585–1603). In contrast, the BUCCANEERS and MADAGASCAR raiders (sailing from 1650 to 1720) usually split their take with few arguments.

While later pirates usually obeyed their ship's ARTICLES, Elizabethan raiders ignored customary rules of booty and pillage. When a prize was captured, perhaps after heavy fighting, any sense of fair play was swept aside. Gold, silver, or jewels quickly vanished into the sailors' pockets. Many officers also grabbed all they could lay their hands on.

In 1592, victorious raiders looted the MADRE DE DIOS, an East Indian carrack, so wildly they almost set the prize ablaze. Perhaps two-thirds of the booty never was accounted for. And looting and embezzlement also were normal conduct on official plunder ventures commanded by naval officers. In 1596, both seamen and soldiers were so busy looting Cadiz, that they allowed the Spaniards to burn the ships in the harbor.

Crewmen embezzled loose valuables and sometimes broke into the cargo in the hold partly because owners often cheated them. Many owners smuggled goods onto shore or bribed customs officials to undervalue them. Once the goods were disbursed and sold, it was easy for owners to lie about their proceeds.

In this web of competing thievery, amateur adventurers like the earl of Cumberland, Thomas CAVENDISH, and John CHIDLEY were robbed at every turn. Suppliers

Elizabethan booty. Aboard the *Golden Hind,* Sir Francis Drake (Rod Taylor, far left) shows Queen Elizabeth (Irene Worth) the treasures looted from the Spaniards during his three-year voyage around the world. From the movie *Seven Seas to Calais* (1963).

overpriced provisions, and captains and crews stole prize goods. In contrast, professional owner-captains (for example, Christopher NEWPORT) could make enormous profits. Since they were on hand throughout the voyage, they could keep their crews relatively honest and also avoid taxes and the Admiral's tenth by smuggling or bribery.

Buccaneers; After 1650

Booty was divided in unusually democratic ways by the Caribbean BUCCANEERS and pirates raiding in the Atlantic or from MADAGASCAR. By the 18th century, everyone on board received a virtually equal share of all loot.

In earlier eras, the crew kept only a fraction of the take. The government demanded 10 percent (or even more) off the top. Half to two-thirds was taken by those owning and supplying the ship. The crew divided what was left, but officers received four to six times as much as seamen.

Pirate rules were very different. Eighteenth-century ARTICLES set nothing aside for either the government or the ship's owners. The marauders apparently assumed they could steal both ships and supplies. In practice, however, pirates such as Edward COATES and Edward TEACH usually did bribe officials. Some pirate crews also

paid off shipowners, although nothing like the third common in earlier eras.

Everything of value on a captured ship was placed in a common fund guarded by the QUARTERMASTER. When two or more ships cruised in CONSORT, the vessels divided all booty taken, even if they were separated during battle. (Thus Thomas HOWARD and John BOWEN in 1703.) Each ship supposedly received a cut in proportion to the size of its crew, but consortships led to many arguments. Pirates on ships with smaller crews naturally wanted loot to be divided equally among the vessels. In 1698, two other crews refused to share with the *Pelican* because she had not taken part in the capture.

A vessel's common fund normally was divided at the end of the voyage. Before the booty was split, additional amounts were given to those who had lost an arm, a leg, or an eye. Oddly, the heirs of dead pirates got nothing special, although they were entitled to the deceased's share.

After these hardship payments, everything left was divided into shares of equal value. Each man received one or more shares, with the division becoming more democratic over time. During the 1660s, EXQUEMELIN wrote, the captain still took something for the use of his ship and also received five or six shares. The carpenter

"And So the Treasure was Divided." Illustration by Howard Pyle in *Harper's Monthly Magazine,* December 1905.

and surgeon received salaries as well as shares. By the 1720s, the officers received only a little more than the rest of the crew. At most, the captain got two shares, with lesser officers receiving only an extra half or quarter share.

Only gold or silver could be divided with rigid equality. When possible, other cargo was sold to fences (such as Adam BALDRIDGE) before the division. Otherwise, rough guesses had to be made. After John TAYLOR took a Portuguese prize in 1721, Daniel DEFOE relates, each man received 42 small diamonds

> or in less Proportion according to their Magnitude. An ignorant, or a merry Fellow, who had only one in this Division . . . muttered very much at the Lot, and went and broke it in a Morter. . . .

To prevent arguments, crews sometimes auctioned off captured goods. Before returning to the Caribbean in 1688, Raveneau de LUSSAN wrote, the French buccaneers shared out their gold and silver. Other items were auctioned off, and the receipts divided among the men.

BORG, EUGENIO (Maltese corsair; Mediterranean; 1704) Borg applied to the KNIGHTS OF MALTA for a corsair's license after commanding pirate vessels in the Near East.

(See also TRIBUNALE DEGLI ARMAMENTI.)

BOROUGH, ROBERT (English pirate; Atlantic; 1543) Borough, who came from Devonshire, commanded two ships licensed to take French prizes. He captured a Dutch merchantman and sold its cargo in Southampton. The ADMIRALTY COURT ordered him to make restitution.

BORRAS, CHEVALIER DE (Maltese corsair; Mediterranean; 1732) The Egyptian government levied heavy fines on French merchants after Borras attacked Muslim shipping near Alexandria and Palestine. Borras was French, Maltese investors financed his raids, and he flew the Spanish flag.

BOTADILLA, PEDRO DE (Spanish pirate; Mediterranean; 1518–1519) Botadilla attacked Italian shipping until a Genoese vessel captured his two ships off southern Italy in 1519.

BOTTOMRY BOND (pirate financing; Malta; 17th and 18th centuries) A mortgage on the prospective booty held by merchants loaning money or goods to outfit corsair vessels. Since the loans were repaid only if the pirates took prizes, the interest rate was as much as 40 percent a year.

(See also SELECTED BIBLIOGRAPHY: Earle, *Corsairs.*)

BOUCAN (pirate cooking; Caribbean; 17th century) A French word for a grill used to smoke meat for later consumption. Both the word and the *boucan* method may be native to the Americas. Spanish colonists called the same smoking process *barbacoa,* and this word has passed into English as "barbecue."

The boucan technique was especially important to the men illegally camping on Spanish Hispaniola (modern Haiti) from about 1620 to 1670. These squatters hunted the abundant wild cattle and pigs, and they used the boucan to preserve the meat for later use and for sale to passing ships. The hunters, who lived off the boucan, were known as *boucaniers* ("barbacuers"). English authors later used the same word to refer to pirates operating from Haiti and other Caribbean havens.

Richest Booty Taken in the Caribbean and along South America's Pacific Coast, 1628–1686

Captain(s)	Probable Value	Prize or Port
Piet HEYN commanding 31 vessels and some 2,300 men (1628)	11 to 14 million Dutch guilders	Spanish treasure fleet from Mexico taken off Cuba
Sir Christopher MYNGS commanding several warships (1658)	£200,000 to £375,000 (contemporary estimates)	Cuma, Puerto Caballo, and Coro, Venezuela
Laurens de GRAFF, Michel de GRAMMONT, Nicholas van HORN, and five other captains with about 1,000 men (1683)	800,000 pesos (£200,000) in treasure and jewels (contemporary estimate, possibly high)	SAN JUAN DE ULÚA and Veracruz, Mexico
Hendrick LUCIFER (1628)	1.2 million guilders	Spanish treasure ship from Honduras taken off Cuba
François L'OLONNAIS commanding eight ships and 660 men (1667)	260,000 pesos (£65,000) according to EXQUEMELIN	Several prizes; Maracaibo and Gibraltar, Venezuela
Sir Henry MORGAN with about 10 small ships and 500 men (1668)	250,000 pesos (£62,500) Exquemelin says	Puerto Principe, Cuba; PORTOBELO, PANAMA
Edward DAVIS, Captain LE PICARD, and George HOUT (1687)	200,000 pesos (£50,000) reported by Raveneau de LUSSAN and Spanish documents	Guayaquil, Ecuador
Christopher Myngs commanding 12 ships and about 1,500 men (1663)	150,000 pesos (£37,500) according to official reports	San Francisco de Campeche, Mexico
Henry Morgan with about eight small ships and fewer than 500 men (1669)	120,000 pesos (£30,000) according to Exquemelin and contemporary reports	Maracaibo and Gibraltar, Venezuela
Henry Morgan leading about 1,500 to 2,000 men (1671)	120,000 pesos (£30,000) reported by Morgan	Panama City, Panama
Edward MORGAN with six small vessels and about 300 men (1665)	£25,000 according to British and Dutch reports	Oranjestad, Saint Eustatius
Edward Davis and William KNIGHT (1686)	100,000 pesos (£25,000) reported by Spaniards	Saña, Peru
Pierre FRANÇOIS (date unknown)	100,000 pesos (£25,000) according to Exquemelin	Pearl fishing stations near RIO DE LA HACHA, Venezuela
John COXON and six other captains (1680)	£18,000 reported by British and Spanish documents	Portobelo

Note Pieter SCHOUTEN (in 1624) and Peter ITA (in 1628) both captured Spanish treasure ships, but the value of their booty is not reported.

A boucan had four vertical forked wooden posts supporting a rectangular wooden frame about two feet above the ground. Several green sticks were placed across the frame to form a grillwork of wood. Meat, poultry, or fish was placed on the grill and cooked for a relatively long time over a slow, smoky fire. As in the English word *barbecue*, boucan can mean the grill itself, the cooking technique, the resulting food, and the place where a grill was set up.

BOURNANO, CAPTAIN *(French buccaneer; Caribbean; active 1678–1680)* One of the first pirates to attempt the land route across PANAMA, Bournano led a force against Chepo in 1678. In February 1680, he sacked PORTOBELO with Bartholomew SHARP. He refused to go on to the Pacific with Sharp's party because he felt the jungle trail was too dangerous.

BOWEN, JOHN *(Welsh pirate; Indian Ocean, Red Sea, Persian Gulf; died 1704)* Born in Bermuda, Bowen moved to South Carolina and became captain of a ship trading in the West Indies. After some years, he was captured by French pirates. The French brigands crossed the Atlantic, pillaged along the African coast, and wrecked their ship on MADAGASCAR's southwestern coast.

About 18 months later, Bowen and the other survivors were picked up by a Captain Read. The pirates took over a larger Arab ship (but little booty) in the Persian Gulf. At this time (or perhaps earlier), Bowen enlisted with the pirates and was elected sailing master.

Returning to western Madagascar, Bowen's gang sailed in consort with George BOOTH. In April 1700, the two crews captured and took over the *Speaker*, a strong 50-gun slave ship. More than 200 pirates of many nationalities sailed to Zanzibar with George Booth as captain. Bowen took command at the end of 1700, when Booth was killed fighting Arab troops.

Near the mouth of the Red Sea, Bowen captured an Indian vessel with £100,000 in booty and (in November 1701) a British ship that was sold on the Indian coast. Returning to Madagascar, Bowen wrecked his ship on Mauritius Island but saved most of the men and treasure. In return for large bribes, the Dutch governor warmly welcomed the pirates and allowed them to buy a ship.

In April 1702, Bowen went back to Madagascar and set up camp on the eastern coast. Some time after, the pirates seized and took over the *Speedy Return*, which had stopped to buy slaves. After cruising alone with little success, Bowen joined Thomas HOWARD, and the two captains seized a rich British merchantman in March 1703.

After separating for a time, Bowen and Howard again joined forces. In August 1703, two Indian vessels and more than £70,000 were captured in the Red Sea. The pirates divided their plunder at Rajapura, India. Some stayed with Howard on the Indian coast. Bowen and 40 crewmen retired on Mauritius, where he died of disease about six months later.

(See also SELECTED BIBLIOGRAPHY: Defoe, *General History*; Grey, *Pirates.*)

BOY AND THE PIRATES, THE (motion picture; color; 1960)

Bert Gordon directed this children's movie. Helped by a pint-sized genie, young Jimmy Warren (Charles Herbert) goes back in time to visit BLACKBEARD (Murvyn Vye). After various skirmishes at sea, SWORD DUELS, and double-dealing, Jimmy rescues Katrina Van Keif (Susan Gordon) and escapes to safety.

BOYTE, PHILIP (English pirate; Atlantic; 1580)

From Portland, Boyte was captain of the 60-ton *Golden Hynde*. With Clinton ATKINSON, he seized a richly laden Italian merchantman off Spain and took her cargo to Weymouth, where he was captured. He was hanged in London.

BRADISH, JOSEPH (British mutineer; South China Sea; 1672–1701)

A native of Cambridge, Massachusetts, he sailed from London in March 1698 as boatswain's mate on the *Adventure*. The captain, Thomas Gulleck, starved and mistreated the crew. When Gulleck went ashore on an island near Singapore, Bradish led a mutiny and ran off with the ship. Several officers were sent ashore in a LONGBOAT.

Although they did not attack other vessels, the mutineers were outlawed as pirates. They sold some cargo at Mauritius and disposed of the rest at Block Island (near Rhode Island) in April 1699. The *Adventure* was burned, and about 25 men each received £1,600. Bradish took two and one-half shares as captain.

Bradish and 10 others were captured and imprisoned at Boston. The jailer, Bradish's cousin, let him escape, but he was recaptured by Indians. Taken to England on the same ship as William KIDD, Bradish was convicted of piracy and executed in 1701.

(See also SELECTED BIBLIOGRAPHY: Dow, *Pirates*; Ritchie, *Kidd.*)

BRADLEY, JOSEPH (English buccaneer; Caribbean; died 1671)

Bradley was among the captains attacking Costa Rica and PROVIDENCE ISLAND in 1665 with Edward MANSFIELD. In 1670, he seized a prize from a Spanish PRIVATEER in the harbor at Havana. While serving as one of Sir Henry MORGAN's commanders during the 1671 PANAMA raid, he was killed leading the attack on Chagres.

BRAN (BRAND), CAPTAIN (English buccaneer; Caribbean; 1668–1669)

Commanding an 80-man ship, Bran sacked PORTOBELO in 1668 with Sir Henry MORGAN and raided Campeche, Mexico, in 1669 with Roche BRASILIANO.

BRASILIANO, ROCHE (Dutch buccaneer; Caribbean; active 1650s and 1660s)

According to EXQUEMELIN, Roche (Roque, Rock) went to Brazil during the Dutch occupation. When the Portuguese expelled the invaders in 1654, he moved to Jamaica and shipped as a seaman. Joining a party of malcontents, he quarreled with the captain and stole a small boat. They soon captured a Mexican ship carrying gold and silver and brought it to Jamaica.

On one cruise, Roche was captured and imprisoned in Campeche, Mexico. To convince the governor not to hang him, Roche wrote a letter, which supposedly came from his friends outside. It warned that the buccaneers would kill every Spaniard they captured, if Roche were harmed. Taken to Spain, Roche soon escaped and returned to Jamaica.

During another Campeche raid in 1669, Roche's ship ran aground, and the 30 crewmen abandoned ship with nothing but a few MUSKETS. As they headed toward a pirate meeting place at Sad Gulf (modern Punta Holbox), they ran into Spanish cavalry. Exquemelin wrote that the pirates' muskets slaughtered the horsemen before they could get within pistol range. (However, Spanish records indicate the pirates ran from the calvary and escaped in canoes.)

The buccaneers killed the wounded Spaniards and took their horses and food. On the way to the Gulf, they

Roche Brasiliano. From Exquemelin, *Buccaneers of America,* first English edition (1684).

captured a small ship cutting LOGWOOD. With this vessel, they captured a Mexican ship loaded with merchandise and many pieces of eight. Captain Roche and his men took these two prizes to PORT ROYAL and enjoyed their spoils in a drunken orgy.

Exquemelin (and Spanish evidence) describe Roche as unusually brutal. When Roche was drunk, Exquemelin reports,

> he would roam the town like a madman. The first person he came across, he would chop off his arm or leg, without anyone daring to intervene, for he was like a maniac. He perpetrated the greatest atrocities possible against the Spaniards. Some of them he tied or spitted on wooded stakes and roasted them alive between two fires, like killing a pig. . . .

(See also SELECTED BIBLIOGRAPHY: Rogoziński, *Caribbean;* Weddle, *Spanish.*)

BRAZZERE *(pirate ship; Adriatic Sea; about 1540–1620)* The USKOKS' main vessel, named after the island of Brazza (Braca), it normally carried six to eight and no more than 16 oars. By crowding the boat with three or four men per oar and frequently changing places, the pirates could outrun naval galleys. The brazzere was ideally suited to the coast and small islands of DALMATIA. Small and maneuverable, it was easily hidden, pulled ashore, or sunk in shallow water to prevent discovery. The Dalmatian and ILLYRIAN pirates of antiquity had used similar small boats, such as the LEMBOS and LIBURNIAN.

BRETHREN OF THE COAST *(fictional name for Caribbean pirates; 19th and 20th centuries)* Modern writers give this name to the 18th-century Caribbean BUCCANEERS. However, there is no evidence that the buccaneers ever called themselves by this picturesque phrase.

The phrase *frères de la côte* does occur in 18th-century French authors. However, it refers to all the inhabitants of Saint Domingue (modern Haiti)—and not just the pirates. (Most colonists lived along the coast of that mountainous island.) In fact, some authors treat the pirates and the "brothers of the coast" as two distinct groups. After the Sack of CARTAGENA, for example, CHARLEVOIX wrote that the professional pirates cheated the "people of the coast"—the non-pirate colonists who had joined them for that raid.

BREWSTER, ADAM *(English buccaneer; Caribbean; active 1668–1669)* Captain of a ship during Sir Henry MORGAN's raids on PORTOBELO (1668) and Maracaibo, Venezuela (1669).

BRIG *(sailing ship; Atlantic, Pacific; about 1700 to present)* Ship that carried two masts, rigged in various combinations. The name originally was an abbreviation for BRIGANTINE, but the shorter form later was reserved for the modified versions, rerigged for greater sail power. Also, a slang term for a ship's prison.

BRIGANTINE *(type of ship; Mediterranean, Atlantic, Caribbean, Pacific; about 1400 to present)* Originally a small vessel, carrying both sails and six to 16 oars on each side. It received its name (the French version of the Italian *brigantino* meaning "brigand's ship") because it was a favorite vessel of Mediterranean pirates. In later usage, the term referred to a two-masted sailing ship, typically square-rigged on the foremast and having fore-and-aft sails on the main mast.

BRIGGEHO, WILLIAM DE *(English pirate; Atlantic; died 1228)* From Yorkshire, Briggeho was the first Englishman known to have been hanged for piracy.

BROCCHIERO DE ANAYA, DON DIEGO *(Knight of Malta; Aegean Sea; active 1583–1587)* A Spaniard captured by Venetian ships in February 1583 while anchored at Cerigo (Kithira) with two Turkish prizes. With other KNIGHTS OF MALTA and about 200 soldiers, he had taken booty worth 80,000 to 100,000 gold ducats. (His GALLEY had belonged to English raiders driven ashore at Malta by storms in 1582. The Roman Inquisition burned these Protestant pirates—among the first to invade the Mediterranean.)

The Spanish ambassador arranged Brocchiero's release from a Venetian prison. In 1587, he commanded a GALLEON (50 guns and 500 soldiers) that seized at least three Venetian merchant ships, inspiring the Venetian

Senate to condemn the knights as "corsairs parading crosses."

(See also SELECTED BIBLIOGRAPHY: Tenenti, *Piracy*.)

BROOKE, SIR JAMES *(British adventurer; South China Sea; 1803–1868)*
Born in India, Brooke was committed to the welfare of the native peoples. Having received a large inheritance, he sailed on a voyage of exploration in 1838. In August 1839, his yacht arrived at Kuching in Sarawak, a region in northern Borneo nominally subject to the sultan of Brunei.

MALAY nobles and the indigenous tribes (known as DYAKS) were rebelling against the Brunei government when Brooke reached Kuching. Unable to suppress the rebels, the Malay governor transferred his authority to Brooke, who became rajah in 1841. The sultan of Brunei granted him the region in 1842, and Great Britain recognized Sarawak as a sovereign nation in 1863. Brooke's family ruled until 1946, when Sarawak became part of British (now independent) Malaysia.

Rajah Brooke soon complained about the "formidable piratical hordes" over-running Borneo. These committed, he wrote, "the most fearful and dreadful outrages, there being no navy to keep them in check." Although the Brunei Malays fenced pirate booty, few were active raiders. The most enterprising Malay pirates were the ILA-NUNS and BALANINI, and several Dyak tribes also raided in large fleets. The two largest bands, known as the SARIBAS and the SEKRANG, operated from forts only 60 miles east of Kuching.

Brooke led anti-pirate expeditions, aided by British naval vessels. Brooke's Dyak allies joined in, hoping to crush their enemies and to gain "heads and plunder" (to quote one British captain). These auxiliary forces sometimes massacred everyone in villages supposedly inhabited by pirates.

In 1843, Brooke recruited the warship *Dido* commanded by Henry Keppel. The *Dido*'s boats and various Dyak vessels sailed up the Saribas River, burned pirate strongholds, and destroyed many guns and war boats. Keppel and the *Dido* returned the next year to help subdue the Sekrang raiders. Brooke razed the Sekrang villages, killed many, and forced their leader, Sherip SAHAP, to flee. In 1845, Brooke was assisted by eight warships. The British ships visited Brunei and bombarded a pro-pirate official. They moved on to Marudu Bay in northern Borneo and crushed Sherip OSMAN's band.

Despite these bloody victories, Saribas marauders renewed their assaults. Under a new leader, known as the *Laksamana* ("Admiral"), they killed over 300 persons in 1848. Brooke launched his most famous expedition in July. His squadron included the paddle-steamer *Nemesis*, three other British ships, and 70 PRAHUS manned by 2,500 Dyak warriors.

Brooke's force blockaded the Saribas River. Some 2,500 raiders in 110 warboats were trapped near the sandspit of Batang Maru. Under a bright moon, the pirates fought tenaciously for five hours, and more than a thousand died. Led by LINGGIR, one group made a supreme effort to board the *Nemesis*, which drove right through the struggling mass of prahus. The vessel's paddlewheels caught up boatsmen and crushed them to a pulp. After the battle, Rajah Brooke and his Dyak allies went up the Saribas, burning and plundering native villages.

The Batang Maru campaign largely ended Saribas piracy, but British critics accused Brooke of massacring innocent savages. By an 1825 law, moreover, naval vessels fighting pirates received generous prize money. Twenty pounds was paid for each pirate killed, £5 for every enemy present during the battle. The British naval forces requested the fantastic sum of £21,000, and one captain claimed almost £3,000 for his night's work. A commission of inquiry disagreed over the justice of Brooke's raids, but the law awarding prize money for killing "pirates" was revised.

(See also SELECTED BIBLIOGRAPHY: Keppel, *Expedition*; Runciman, *White*; Rutter, *Pirate*.)

BROUWER, HENDRICK *(Dutch general; Pacific; 1581–1643)*
Although the DUTCH WEST INDIA COMPANY ravaged Brazil and the Caribbean, Brouwer led the company's only expedition to South America's Pacific coast. Since all previous Dutch raids had ended in disaster, the Company preferred to assault the more accessible Atlantic coast.

By 1642, however, the Company had strengthened its hold on much of Brazil, first invaded in 1630. With a secure base in South America, the time seemed right for another Pacific adventure. The Company targeted Valdivia, a Spanish fort in southern Chile, abandoned in 1599 during an uprising by Araucanian Indians. By allying with the native peoples, the Dutch hoped to revive Valdivia's gold mines and to create a base for further raids.

Brouwer, a Company director and former governor-general of the East Indies, sailed in November 1642 with five ships and 600 men. After a brief stop in Brazil, the fleet sailed around the Cape Horn. By the end of April, less one lost ship, they were at Chiloé Island and began trying to make friends with the Indians. Several small forts were taken, but the Spaniards already had burned the main town at Castro. Brouwer died in August and was replaced by Elias HERCKMANS. His body was taken to Valdivia and ceremoniously buried, only to be dug up and burned in 1645 by Spanish troops.

(See also Simon de CORDES; Olivier van NOORT; Hugo SCHAMPENDAM; Joris van SPILBERGEN.)

BROWN, EDWARD *(British seaman; South China Sea; 1857)*
While employed on a Chinese merchant JUNK in February 1857, Brown was captured by a pirate commander named Ch'ing Ya-ling. He served as gunner on one of Ch'ing's craft and helped capture a

merchant vessel off Vietnam. After three months, he quarreled with the pirate crew, fled to a Cambodian village, and ultimately made his way back to Singapore. *Cochin-China, and my Experience of It*, the story of his captivity, was published in 1861 (London: Westerton) and reprinted in 1971 (Taipei: Cheng Wen).

BROWNE, JAMES *(Scottish pirate; Caribbean, 1677)* Operating under a French commission from the governor of Saint Domingue, Browne seized a Dutch slave ship off Venezuela. His English, French, and Dutch pirates killed the captain and several crewmen and landed the slaves in a remote bay in Jamaica. The Jamaican governor sent a frigate that seized Browne and eight of his men. Browne was hanged, but his crew were pardoned when they promised to give up piracy.

BUCCANEER *(novel; 1981)* Dudley POPE introduces Ned Yorke, a young aristocrat living on Barbados. During the English Civil War, Thomas Cromwell's Roundhead forces defeat King Charles I's Royalists. In 1655, Cromwell's fleet invades the Caribbean, carrying orders to arrest Yorke and other Royalists. Yorke's plantation will be seized by his neighbor, the sadistic, rum-swilling husband of Aurelia, the French refugee Yorke loves.

Fortunately, Yorke owns a small ship; and his foreman, Saxby, had deserted from the royal navy. Yorke, Aurelia, and Saxby flee attacking Roundheads. Most of Yorke's servants go along, including his formidable housekeeper, Mrs. Judd.

Yorke can not start another plantation because Cromwell's forces control the English islands. He unsuccessfully tries to smuggle goods into the SPANISH MAIN, but the Dutch monopolize illegal trading. As he travels west, he runs into a ship carrying Sir Thomas WHETSTONE and his mistress, Lady Diana. The two captains decide to prey on Spanish vessels and ports.

Under assumed names, Yorke and Whetstone make for Jamaica, just conquered by Cromwell's invasion fleet. Afraid of a Spanish counterattack, Cromwell's officers commission them as PRIVATEERS. Yorke and Whetstone steal a grain ship at RIO DE LA HACHA. With other captains, including Edmund MORGAN, they take rich booty at Santiago, Cuba, and fortify PORT ROYAL as a pirate HAVEN. (The real Thomas Whetstone did not reach Jamaica until 1661, and Sir Christopher MYNGS and not Whetstone plundered Santiago in 1662).

BUCCANEER, THE (1) *(motion picture; black and white; 1938)* Director Cecil B. De Mille's lavish spectacular adds fictional episodes to Lyle Saxon's biogra-

Frederic March (standing at balcony) as Jean Laffite in *The Buccaneer* (1938).

A French artist shows a Hispaniola buccaneer holding a flintlock musket. In fact, matchlock weapons were more common before the 1670s. Old clay pipes are still found on many Caribbean islands. The three smaller inset pictures show buccaneers smoking meat on a boucan, fighting a duel, and shooting at wild boar. From the first French edition (1684) of Exquemelin's *Buccaneers of America*.

phy of Jean LAFFITE (1). Frederic March is spirited and sometimes passionate as the wild-living pirate chief.

Laffite and Governor Claiborne's daughter Annette (Margot Grahame) are in love. Because of their relationship (invented for the movie), Laffite orders his men not to attack American vessels. One of Laffite's followers, a Captain Brown (Robert Barrat), cannot resist the bullion he noticed being loaded on the *Corinthian*. In the movie's one scene of piracy, Brown burns the vessel with its crew and passengers, including Governor Claiborne's other daughter. Laffite arrives on the scene, hangs Brown from the mast, and rescues a little Dutch girl (Franciska Gaal).

Laffite turns down a British offer of pardon and naval rank and reveals the British plans to General Andrew Jackson (Hugh Southern). The pirates come out of their hideaway bayous, and their uncanny skill with artillery wins the battle. At the victory ball, Laffite is about to achieve respectability and settle down with Annette. Suddenly she learns and tells the crowd that the pirates had scuttled the *Corinthian*. Laffite takes responsibility and sails away in disgrace, with the adoring Dutch girl at his side.

BUCCANEER, THE (2) *(motion picture; color; 1958)* A remake of Cecil B. De Mille's 1938 movie about Jean LAFFITE (played by Yul Brynner). (1). Anthony QUINN, then his son-in-law, took over as director when De Mille fell sick. De Mille's influence is evident in the opulent sets and costumes.

This version retains most of the 1938 plot, with some variations. The young cabin boy Miggs (Jeremy Hartleben) and not a Dutch girl now is the *Corinthian*'s only survivor. Captain Brown's daughter Bonnie (Claire Bloom) replaces the Dutch girl as Laffite's secondary interest, while Governor Claiborne's daughter Annette (Inger Stevens) remains his first love.

BUCCANEERS *(Caribbean pirates; about 1620–1720)* An English name for pirates cruising from Caribbean HAVENS, including PORT ROYAL, TORTUGA ISLAND, and Saint Domingue (modern Haiti). They primarily raided Spanish shipping and cities in the Caribbean and along the Mexican coast. From 1680 to 1688, many crossed the PANAMA isthmus and marauded along South America's Pacific coast.

Buccaneer captains were mainly English, French, and Dutch. Their crews contained adventurers of all sorts, including Spanish renegades, African slaves, and American Indians. With this diverse group, Sir Henry MORGAN captured Panama in 1671. French and English buccaneers continued to cruise in consort until the "Nine Years' War" (1688–1697), when they were coopted by their respective governments as auxiliary naval forces.

Most buccaneers did not attack shipping of their own nation. When possible, they operated with PRIVATEERING commissions, hoping that these would save them from hanging as pirates. During the 1660s and 1670s, Sir Thomas MODYFORD and other Jamaican governors gave out commissions to operate against the Spanish. The French governors of Tortuga and PETIT GOÂVE continued to issue licenses into the 1680s. However, the buccaneers were true pirates who operated for their own account with or without such commissions.

The French word *boucanier* ("barbecuer") originally referred to hunters who illegally camped in western Hispaniola (modern Haiti). (Some say the name is derived from the BOUCAN on which these hunters smoked meat.) English writers began to use the same word to describe pirates operating from Haiti and other Caribbean bases. The name became common after 1684, when EXQUEMELIN's history was translated into English as *The Bucaniers of America*.

It is easy to understand why the English used the same word for the hunters and pirates. Although some pirates never were hunters, many hunters practiced piracy at one time or another. Nevertheless, French authors call the Caribbean pirates *filibustiers* (FREEBOOTERS), the Dutch refer to them as *Zee-roovers* (sea rovers), and the Spanish prefer *corsarios* (corsairs).

BUCCANEERS AND MAROONERS OF AMERICA, THE *(history/fiction; 1891)* This compilation, by the artist and author Howard PYLE, contains EXQUEMELIN's *Buccaneers of America*. It adds the biographies of Edward TEACH, William KIDD, Bartholomew ROBERTS, and Henry EVERY from Daniel DEFOE's GENERAL HISTORY. Pyle modernized the authors' spelling and lightly edited their texts. Later editions are more accurate, but Pyle's version remains valuable because of his illustrations.

BUCCANEER'S GIRL *(motion picture; color; 1950)* Deborah McCoy (Yvonne de Carlo) is a wandering entertainer who stows away on a ship scuttled by Fredric Baptiste (Philip Friend). She falls for the handsome pirate, although at first he merely tolerates her.

After they arrive in New Orleans, Deborah attends a school for entertainers run by Madame Brizer (Elsa Lanchester). There she learns that Fredric actually attacks only ships owned by the conniving Narbonne (Rob-

Yvonne De Carlo in *Buccaneer's Girl* (1950).

ert Douglas), who had ruined his father. The seafaring Robin Hood turns over all his loot to a fund for mariners. On shore, he successfully masquerades as the fund's philanthropic administrator.

In addition to the usual sea battles and SWORD DUELS, *Buccaneer's Girl* includes a knock-down fight between Deborah and Arlene Villon (Andrea King), Fredric's snobbish fiancee. As Deborah, de Carlo performs several dances and sings three songs. At one point, she remarks that "I guess I'm not cut out for this occupation of pirate." Nevertheless, she finally sails into the sunset with both Fredric and the loot. Directed by Frederick De Cordova.

BUCCANEER SURGEON *(novel; 1954)* Using the pseudonym C. V. Terry, Frank Slaughter (1908–) mixes fictional and historical characters in his tale of Sir Francis DRAKE's 1585 Caribbean plunder raid. While critics generally ignored Slaughter's 60-plus historical romances, their total sales exceeded 70 million. Most feature a crusading physician (as was Slaughter himself), who is loved by two women—one wicked and depraved and the other wholesome and virginal. After many trials, the hero forsakes the voluptuous temptress and marries the good woman.

Bernal Fitzhugh is ship's surgeon during Drake's 1577 raid on Panama (which Slaughter, oddly, places after Drake's capture of the CACAFUEGO). Still working for Drake, Bernal goes to Madrid as a spy in 1585. There he encounters both Hernando Díaz and María Andreda, a Spanish noblewoman he instantly loves. Bernal is caught by the Inquisition (betrayed by María, he believes) and sentenced to hard labor in Santo Domingo.

The prisoners escape but are recaptured. While visiting Santo Domingo, Maria identifies Bernal, and he is about to be hanged. The prisoners escape again, seize a ship, and take a Spanish prize. Louis Leclerc, their captain, loses a leg in the battle and hates Bernal for taking command of his vessel.

To assist Drake's attack on Cartagena, Bernal recruits Africans who have escaped Spanish slavery. His new allies include Juana, a sultry woman of color, with whom he shares feverish sexual ardors. Bernal captures María in Cartagena, but he loves her too much to punish her supposed treachery. Enraged by jealousy, Juana connives with Leclerc to murder Bernal. He survives, Juana dies, and Drake hangs Leclerc.

Bernal takes Drake's wounded to a hidden anchorage. Hernando Díaz shows up with a galleon, massacres the wounded men, and captures Bernal. After telling Bernal that María is innocent, he ties Bernal to a rock which is under water at high tide. María eludes Diaz, swims to Bernal's rock, and cuts him free just before he drowns. Drake's fleet chases away the Spaniards, and Maria and Bernal consummate their love.

Slaughter portrays Drake as a charismatic tyrant, whose quick temper helps keep his ambitious captains in line. His description of Drake's 1585 expedition is accurate overall, although Spanish forces probably did not murder wounded English prisoners. Drake no longer used the GOLDEN HIND in 1585, and 16th-century CANNON were not as accurate as Slaughter supposes.

BUCRIS *(Greek pirate; Aegean Sea; active 239– 238 B.C.)* An AETOLIAN who raided near Athens, carrying many persons to CRETE for sale as slaves. His attack occurred during a war between the AETOLIAN LEAGUE and Macedonia, which dominated Athens at this time. But it clearly was an act of piracy, not related to any military operations.

BULGARINO D'ANAIA *(Italian pirate; Aegean Sea; 1275)* Sailing from ANAIA under license from Emperor MICHAEL VIII PALAEOLOGUS, Bulgarino captured a Venetian merchant ship near Andros, according to the VENETIAN CLAIMS.

BULL, DIXEY *(English pirate; Atlantic; 1632)* The first to plunder New England, Bull immigrated in 1631 and traded for beaver pelts along the Maine coast. In June 1632, French brigands stole his small ship and supplies. With some other wanderers, he unsuccessfully chased the Frenchmen. He then turned against his own people, plundered two or three small vessels, and took goods worth over £500 from a trading station at Pemaquid, Massachusetts. Some say he joined the French, others that he returned to England.

(See also SELECTED BIBLIOGRAPHY: Dow, *Pirates*.)

BUMBOO *(beverage; Caribbean; 17th and 18th centuries)* Consisting of RUM, water, and sugar flavored with nutmeg, bumboo was probably the most common alcoholic beverage among West Indians, including BUCCANEERS and pirates.

BUNCE, PHINEAS *(British pirate; Caribbean; 1718)* Bunce took a pardon when Governor Woodes ROGERS landed at NEW PROVIDENCE ISLAND in July 1718. In October, Rogers sent three SLOOPS for provisions. Bunce helped lead a mutiny, and he cruelly abused and MAROONED officers and men refusing to join his gang. While commanding one of the sloops, Bunce was captured by Spanish coast guards. He was wounded in the battle and died before he could be hanged.

(See also AUGER, JOHN; MCCARTHY, DENNIS; SELECTED BIBLIOGRAPHY: Defoe, *General History*.)

BURAK REIS *(Turkish corsair; Mediterranean; active 1485–1503)* After pillaging Christian shipping in the eastern Mediterranean, he joined the OTTOMAN navy and commanded a large sailing ship during a naval war with Venice from 1499 to 1503.

BURGESS, SAMUEL *(British pirate; Caribbean, Indian Ocean, Red Sea; died 1716?)* A former BUCCANEER, Burgess helped steal William KIDD's *Blessed William* in February 1690. William MAY became captain, and cruised from New York before taking the *Jacob* to

MADAGASCAR in December. Edward COATES later replaced May as captain, and Burgess returned to New York in April 1693 with £800.

Burgess bought a house and went to work for Frederick Philipse, New York's wealthiest merchant. During the next few years, he made several profitable voyages to Madagascar, where he sold the pirates supplies and guns for gold and slaves. Commanding the *Margaret*, Burgess ran into a British squadron at SAINT MARY'S ISLAND about September 1699. About 20 pirates accepted a pardon and bought passage home.

The *Margaret* reached Cape Town, South Africa, in late December. A Captain Lowth of the East India Company seized the ship and took it to Bombay. (Lowth was coldly received by the governor, who had told the Indians there were no English pirates on Madagascar.) In addition to £11,000 in pirate loot, Lowth seized another £6,000 and 80 slaves belonging to the *Margaret*.

The ship's owners sued the company, and Burgess was brought to London about 1701. Thanks to Robert CULLIFORD's testimony, Burgess was convicted of piracy while aboard the *Jacob*. He eventually was pardoned and sailed to the Pacific in 1693 as an officer on a PRIVATEERING vessel.

Burgess went back to Madagascar to trade liquor for slaves as first mate of the *Neptune*. A sudden storm destroyed the pirates' ships, and Burgess helped John HALSEY seize the *Neptune*. He became QUARTERMASTER but was ousted when Halsey died soon after. Burgess stayed at Madagascar, dealing in slaves with David WILLIAMS and other captains. A black chief poisoned him, the story goes, during an argument over prices.

(See also SAMUEL, ABRAHAM; SELECTED BIBLIOGRAPHY: Defoe, *General History*; Grey, *Pirates*.)

BURGH, SIR JOHN *(English soldier; Atlantic, Caribbean; 1562–1594)*

The third son of Lord William Burgh and the brother of Lord Thomas Burgh, lord-deputy in Ireland, Sir John Burgh spent his early years soldiering in France and the Low Countries. On his return to England, he became associated with Sir Walter RALEIGH.

In 1592, Burgh received command of the 300-ton *Roebuck*, part of a fleet that Raleigh planned to lead to the West Indies. Had the raiders reached PANAMA, Burgh would have commanded the land forces. Just before they sailed, however, the fleet instead was diverted to the Azores. Joined by squadrons under Christopher NEWPORT and John NORTON (2), Burgh's ships captured the MADRE DE DIOS, a Portuguese treasure ship. Rather than allowing the BOOTY to be divided into shares, the officers and mariners grabbed everything they could from the great prize. But Burgh's thefts seem to have been minor.

Burgh and Christopher Newport again worked together in 1593 during a raid on Venezuela, Trinidad, and Guyana sponsored by Raleigh and a syndicate of London merchants. Burgh commanded the *Roebuck* and the expedition, while Newport was captain of the London-based

Golden Dragon. At Margarita Island, Burgh suffered a heavy defeat when he attacked the capital rather than—like most raiders—the defenseless pearl fisheries. He probably went on to Trinidad and Guyana with little success.

In March 1594, Burgh was killed during a duel with John Gilbert, eldest son of Sir Humphrey GILBERT and a nephew and protege of Raleigh. The cause of their quarrel is not known.

(See also SELECTED BIBLIOGRAPHY: Andrews, *English Privateering*.)

BURY, MARK *(English pirate; Atlantic; 1589)*

Captain of the 70-ton *Bark Way*, Bury captured a Portuguese sugar ship and a French merchantman, which the ADMIRALTY court restored to its owner. Commanding the *Bark Burton* for Sir Walter RALEIGH, he seized a Mexican vessel in the Azores, carrying goods valued at £10,000.

BUTES *(corsair captain; Aegean Sea; ancient Greek legend)*

A son of the god Boreas (the North Wind), he led a band of men from Thrace, a region in northern Greece and Bulgaria. Butes' pirates sailed south and seized the uninhabited island of Naxos. They plundered passing ships and raided the Greek islands and mainland for slaves, particularly women.

During an assault on Thessaly in northern Greece, Butes' gang came upon women celebrating ecstatic orgies to honor the god Dionysus. Butes seized Coronis, one of the worshippers, and raped her. Answering Coronis' prayers for vengeance, Dionysus drove Butes insane so that he threw himself into a well and died.

Taking some of the women with them, the remaining pirates returned to Naxos. When they divided up their captives, two renowned chiefs killed each other over Pancratis, a woman of surpassing beauty. Despite this and other quarrels, the Thracians lived on Naxos for more than 200 years before abandoning it during a drought.

DIODORUS OF SICILY (first century B.C.) tells Butes' story and describes him as a mythical figure who lived long ago. Nevertheless, this myth may be based on folk memories of a real Captain Butes. Slave raids were common in ancient Greece. It is plausible that a corsair died while raping a priestess of Dionysus, the god of fruits (including wine) and sexual fertility. During their worship, the god possessed women. They went into a savage frenzy, spoke to plants and animals, and gained enormous physical strength.

BUTLER, JOHN *(Irish pirate; Caribbean; executed 1580)*

Second-in-command of John OXENHAM's 1576–1578 raid on PANAMA. Butler had spent 15 years in the Americas and promised that Oxenham would take rich booty. The Spaniards considered Butler, whom they called Cahlona, even more ruthless than Oxenham.

BUTLER, NATHANIEL *(English pirate; Atlantic, Caribbean; active 1619–1639)*

From Bedford, Butler went to sea as a youth and voyaged to North America and Guyana. He became a protege of Richard

Rich, earl of Warwick and Protestant leader, who made him governor of Bermuda from 1619 to 1622. Between 1625 and 1628, Butler commanded vessels during naval assaults in Spain and northern France. He was appointed a captain in the royal navy in 1637.

Butler became governor of Warwick's pirate colony on PROVIDENCE ISLAND in 1638. In about April 1639, he assembled a mixed fleet of Dutch and English vessels. After looting several smaller towns, the raiders descended on Trujillo, the chief port of Honduras. Trujillo had repelled Sir Anthony SHERLEY in 1597, but Butler's raiders took it by surprise and collected a ransom of £16,000. Butler apparently kept more than his fair share of the booty. Returning to Providence in September 1639, he sailed for England in great haste and secrecy.

Butler published the *Dialogicall Discourse Concerninge Marine Affairs* in 1634. An edition by W. G. Perrin appeared in 1929.

(See also SELECTED BIBLIOGRAPHY: Newton, *Puritans*.)

BYZANTINE EMPIRE *(pirate foe and sponsor; 395–1453)* A multi-ethnic empire with its capital at Constantinople (today Istanbul). Byzantium emerged from the Roman Empire and inherited its pretensions to universal rule. The empire's core included modern-day Greece, Turkey, and the eastern coast of the Adriatic Sea (ancient ILLYRIA). Muslim armies took Syria, Egypt, and North Africa during the 600s. The Normans conquered SICILY and southern Italy during the 11th century. From 1071, Asia Minor and Armenia were gradually absorbed by the Seljuk and later by the Ottoman Turks.

Until the 1050s, the Byzantine emperors maintained local fleets to fight pirates in the Mediterranean and the Black Sea. Naval power held together the far-flung empire. Its economy and tax revenues depended on trade between Asia and Europe, and Constantinople lived on imported food.

The entries for individual corsairs track the empire's success in suppressing piracy. When its navies were strong, pirates were few. When they decayed during the ninth century, Muslim corsairs occupied Cyprus, CRETE, and Sicily, and established forward bases in southern Italy. A revived fleet eliminated the pirates' Italian bases (875–917) and recaptured Crete (963).

Byzantine sea power again weakened from the 11th century. Merchants from Venice, Genoa, and Pisa gained control of the empire's commerce, and Italian mercenaries also manned the imperial fleet at Constantinople. This policy proved disastrous after 1182, when a mob massacred thousands of Italians living in the capital. The Byzantine navy collapsed. Genoa and Pisa allowed their citizens to exact reprisals anywhere in the empire, and many captains turned into full-time corsairs.

For the next seven centuries, piracy remained endemic throughout the Aegean and eastern Mediterranean. Any revival of Byzantine power became impossible after the Fourth Crusade sacked Constantinople in 1204 and divided the empire into small principalities. Although Emperor MICHAEL VIII PALAEOLOGUS recaptured Constantinople in 1261, western Europeans continued to rule the islands and large parts of Greece. During most of the 14th century, the coast of Asia Minor was split among various Turkish emirs.

These successors to the Byzantine Empire did not create organized navies. Most of the Greek, Latin, and Muslim lords encouraged piracy, and some personally led raids. The last Byzantine emperors relied on the Genoese or hired corsairs to defend their interests. (The imperial fleet was disbanded in 1284 and never rebuilt.)

The OTTOMAN EMPIRE reimposed unity as it subdued Asia Minor during the 14th century, occupied Constantinople in 1453, and conquered the various lordships in Greece. But corsairs—especially the KNIGHTS HOSPITALERS of RHODES and MALTA—continued to ravage the Aegean until the 1850s.

(See also BARI; GAFFORIO, CAPTAIN; GARIGLIANO, MONTE; GRASSO, GUGLIELMO; STIRIONE, GIOVANNI; TARANTO; VENETIAN CLAIMS.)

C

CACAFUEGO (Spanish treasure ship; captured March 1, 1579)

With the *Cacafuego*, Sir Francis DRAKE took one of the greatest booties of all time—certainly the largest haul ever by one ship with only 85 crewmen. Including smaller prizes, the Spanish ambassador later assessed Drake's total plunder at 1.5 million ducats (£450,000). Taking into account unregistered treasure and jewels, the Spanish estimate probably was close to the truth. The value in modern money would be at least a thousand times greater.

The *Cacafuego*, a 120-ton merchant vessel, was bound from Peru to Panama, where her treasure and passengers would cross the Isthmus and continue on to Spain. Although pirates had been raiding the West Indies for decades, Drake was the first to pass from the Atlantic to the Pacific coast of South America. Since the Spaniards did not expect to encounter marauders, most ships went unarmed. The *Cacafuego* originally was known as *Nuestra Señora de la Concepción* (*Our Lady of the Conception*). She received her vulgar nickname (meaning "Shitfire") because she was one of the few Spanish ships with even a few cannon.

Drake had been feverishly pursuing the *Cacafuego* for several days. On March 1, she was sighted near Esmeraldas, Ecuador. It was only midday, and Drake did not wish to attack before dark. He was afraid that reducing sail would arouse suspicions and trailed wine pots filled with water to slow his speed. Some nine hours later, Drake caught up to the *Cacafuego*. Expecting to meet only Spanish ships, her captain turned toward the stranger. Drake waited until the *Cacafuego* came alongside, then sent his boarders swarming to the attack. The *Cacafuego*'s crew quickly surrendered.

Drake led the captured ship out to sea beyond sight of the coast. Elated by this marvelous piece of good luck, Drake treated these captives generously. He dined with the officers and gentlemen (on their own provisions). All prisoners were released with presents appropriate to their rank.

Three days were needed to search the *Cacafuego* and to transfer her rich cargo. The ships separated on March 6. According to an anonymous history of the voyage, the English raiders enjoyed a wry comment by a Spanish youth. "Our ship," the Spaniard joked, "shall no more be called the *Cacafuego*, but the *Cacaplata* ["shit-silver"]. It is your ship that shall be called the *Cacafuego*."

Only Drake knew the amount of his booty, and he obeyed Queen Elizabeth's order never to reveal the secret. Spanish merchants in Seville claimed that the *Cacafuego* carried 400,000 pesos in illegal cargo in addition to registered treasure worth 360,000. If this estimate was accurate, Drake took some £266,000 in gold and silver. And he also seized jewels and other valuables concealed in the passengers' luggage.

When Drake landed at Plymouth in 1580, Queen Elizabeth grabbed his booty, and no accounting was ever made. Before the treasure was taken to London, Drake took out £10,000 pounds for himself, and £8,000 or so was distributed among the crew. Under the usual English BOOTY rules, the crewmen would have received a third of the entire plunder. But they had agreed to sail for set wages and thus had to accept whatever Drake gave them.

The remaining loot was stored in the Tower of London, and the queen and her courtiers furtively removed most of the treasure and all the jewels. The Tower still held 12 tons of silver and 100 pounds of gold in December 1585—only a small part of the original amount. Drake said his backers received £47 for each pound invested in his voyage, a profit of 4,700 percent.

(See also SELECTED BIBLIOGRAPHY: Wagner, *Drake's Voyage.*)

CADOUDJE REIS *(Barbary corsair; Mediterranean; January 1824)* Two British warships captured Cadoudje's 18-gun vessel as he returned to TRIPOLI with 17 Christian slaves.

CAESAR, JULIUS *(Roman statesman; 100–44 B.C.)* Later master of the Roman world, the young Caesar fought against and was captured by pirates based in CILICIA. In 78, Caesar briefly took part in SERVILIUS' Cilician campaign and then returned to Rome. Since his political ambitions temporarily proved fruitless, Caesar went to RHODES to study rhetoric. On the way (probably in 76), pirates seized his ship off Pharmacusa Island.

The arrogant Roman noble, aged 24, overwhelmed his captors. The Cilicians demanded the enormous sum of 20 TALENTS for his ransom. Caesar offered them 50, laughing at them for not knowing his importance. While his servants were borrowing the ransom money, the future ruler treated the pirates with nonchalant contempt. As the Greek historian Plutarch tells the story, Caesar

> made so little of them, that when he had a mind to sleep, he would send to them, and order them to make no noise. For 38 days, with all the freedom in the world, he amused himself with joining in their exercises and games, as if they had not been his keepers, but his guards. He wrote verses and speeches, and made them his auditors, and those who did not admire them, he called to their faces illiterate and barbarous, and would often, in raillery, threaten to hang them.

These boyish pranks amused the pirates, but Caesar had the last laugh. His ransom paid, Caesar was set ashore at nearby Miletus. He immediately hired ships and captured the pirates, still camped at Pharmacusa. The Roman governor, who wanted their booty, delayed the pirates' trial. Taking the law into his own hands, Caesar crucified the corsairs, the fate he had promised them during his captivity.

(See also SELECTED BIBLIOGRAPHY: Plutarch, *Life of Caesar.*)

CALEFATI, MARC ANTONIO *(Knight of Saint Stephen; active 1594–1599)* Calefati commanded five ships that invaded the Greek island of Chios in 1599 for plunder and slaves. Attacking at night, the Florentine forces quickly occupied the castle commanding the port. OTTOMAN troops counterattacked at dawn and ejected the invaders with heavy losses. After this failure, Jacopo INGHIRAMI replaced Calefati as admiral.

Genoa had ruled Chios until 1566, and the island still had many Italian inhabitants. Following Calefati's badly planned attack, Ottoman governors severely punished the Italians, killing some and seizing the property of many. The survivors fled Chios forever.

CALLICE (CHALLIS), JOHN *(English pirate; English Channel, Atlantic Ocean; active about 1574–1587)* Born in southeastern Wales, Callice moved to London as a youth, became a retailer and sailor, and joined the navy in about 1571. In early 1574, while commanding a royal ship, he seized an Italian merchantman and sold her cargo in Cardiff and Bristol.

For the next four years, Callice plundered mercilessly, and other captains sailed under his leadership. Arrested in May 1577, Callice was imprisoned in London and charged with six major cases of piracy and many minor ones. He was sentenced to hang for the six important crimes, which occurred near Cornwall, off France and Denmark, and as far south as the Azores.

Callice normally disposed of his booty in Wales, where he was intimate with local landowners and royal officials, including the VICE-ADMIRAL. He apparently had friends of even higher status, for Queen Elizabeth pardoned him in November 1577 at the request of Scotland's king. The ADMIRALTY COURT awarded the owners of his French prize £4,000 in 1579, but no payment ever was made. (An unknown source did pay £505 to Callice's Danish victims.) Callice was paroled in July 1578 but soon fled and became a pilot for Sir Henry KNOLLYS in Sir Humphrey GILBERT's expedition. Gilbert planned to plunder the Spanish Caribbean, but Knollys and Callice instead attacked ships in English waters.

From 1580, Callice raided in the north (he captured two ships near Hamburg, Germany) but continued to visit Wales. In August 1582, he was appointed captain by William FENNER (1), who had a commission to arrest pirates at sea. In March 1583, Callice instead looted two Scottish merchantmen and took their cargo to Portsmouth. He kept one Scottish prize—renamed the *Golden Chalice*—but abandoned her soon after to avoid arrest. The ship passed to Sir Humphrey Gilbert and formed part of his 1583 Newfoundland expedition.

In 1584, William Fenner was licensed to take Spanish and Portuguese prizes, and Callice served as his lieutenant. In December, Callice took command of a captured French warship and was separated from Fenner in foul weather. Although he was arrested in Ireland, he soon was released or escaped and captured several French vessels.

By 1585, Callice apparently felt that Wales and Ireland no longer were safe havens. (The 1579 judgement for £4,000 was still outstanding.) He henceforth operated from the BARBARY STATES, and was killed in the Mediterranean in 1586 or 1587.

CAMARA *(pirate vessel; Black Sea; first century B.C. and earlier)* Slender, narrow boats favored by the pirates of the Caucasus. They could hold 25 to 30 men, but were so light they could easily be lifted from the water and hidden in the scrub along the coast.

CAMBIANO, BROTHER ASCANIO *(Knight of Malta; Mediterranean; active 1602–1604)* CAPTAIN GENERAL OF GALLEYS (1602–1604) and admiral (1602–1603). During a severe famine on MALTA in 1603, the knights attacked OTTOMAN fortresses at Lepanto (Návpaktos) and Pátrai in Greece, which had large stores of grain. Cambiano's squadron included four GALLEYS and three GALLEONS and carried a thousand troops. The soldiers looted both fortresses and took 400 prisoners, and Cambiano's galleys captured three large sailing ships. In 1604, Cambiano's four Maltese galleys joined 11 from Naples in a raid on the Greek island of Cos. The knights received one-third of the booty and prisoners.

CAMETTO *(Barbary corsair; Mediterranean; about 1550)* Italian nickname for a captain sailing from DJERBA under TURGUT REIS. He commanded a FUSTE during a raid on Italy's west coast.

CAMOCK, SUSSEX *(English pirate; Caribbean; active 1628–1635)* Camock commanded ships for the earl of Warwick, a prominent Puritan politician. (His brother had married the earl's aunt.) In consort with Daniel ELFRITH, he took part in a profitless West Indian raid in 1628. Camock and some 30 men were marooned on San Andreas Island and rescued by a Dutch ship.

Camock returned to the pirate colony at PROVIDENCE ISLAND in 1633 and set up a trading post at Cape Gracias à Dio, on the Nicaragua-Honduras border. Camock found the work unrewarding, returned to England in June 1635, and became captain of a royal fort at Harwich. He left Samuel AXE and Abraham BLAUVELT in charge of the Honduran venture.

CANDIDE *(French novel; 1759)* In Chapters Eleven and Twelve of this comic satire by Voltaire (1694–1778), an old woman relates her sad life story. Born a pampered Roman princess, she and her mother are captured by SALÉ corsairs while traveling to Sicily. Led by their black captain, the pirates strip their captives, search their bodies for hidden gems, and repeatedly rape them.

When the pirates land in Morocco, a rival faction tries to steal their loot. Everyone except the princess dies in the battle. Found by a dishonest Italian eunuch, she is sold and resold in ALGIERS, TUNIS, TRIPOLI, and the Near East. There starving Turkish soldiers eat one of her buttocks before she finally makes her way to Holland.

The "Old Woman's Tale" presents an exaggerated horror story. Salé raiders usually operated in the Atlantic and not in Sicilian waters. There is no evidence that they raped female captives, which would have lowered their value as booty. Moreover most were Moriscos (Spanish Muslims) or European RENEGADES and not African blacks.

CANETE, JUAN *(Spanish corsair; Mediterranean; active 1540s)* Sailing from Majorca, he frequently plundered the North African coast, on one raid seizing persons sleeping under the walls of ALGIERS. Captured in 1550, trying to burn the Algerian corsairs' ships at night, he was executed in 1559. Juan GASCON revived his plan in 1567.

CANNIBALISM *(reputed pirate practice; 17th and 18th centuries)* Several stories accuse pirate captains of committing cannibalism—the eating of human flesh. There is no way of knowing whether these tales are true.

During the earlier 1600s, their Venetian enemies said the USKOKS ate the living hearts of their captives. EXQUEMELIN attributed the same atrocity to François L'OLONNAIS in the 1660s. On one raid, L'Olonnais was torturing his prisoners to obtain information. When they refused to talk, Exquemelin wrote, L'Olonnais ripped the living heart out of one captive and chewed it in order to terrify the others.

According to a Boston newspaper, Edward LOW fed human flesh to his captives in 1723. After capturing two whaling ships, Low made one captain eat his own ears. He forced a prisoner to eat the heart of the second captain.

CANNON *(ship's guns; about 1350–1850)* Muzzle-loading, smooth-bore guns fired by a slow match and propelling a solid round ball made from cast iron or (before 1600) stone. Small cannon were part of naval armament by the 1350s and were used to damage enemy rigging and sailors. By the 1480s, larger guns, cast from bronze or iron (from the 17th century), fired heavy missiles that could pierce an enemy vessel's hull.

The largest cannon weighed as much as 8,000 pounds, were 12 feet long, had openings eight inches across, and fired balls weighing up to 68 pounds. Worked by three to six men, each gun could fire about eight shots an hour. On sailing ships, cannon were fired from the main deck or through gun ports on one or two lower decks. They were mounted on small wheels, run out for firing, and brought back for reloading. Smaller swivel guns were used against boarders.

Gunnery (the art of firing) did not significantly change until the 1850s. Long-range artillery fire played a very small part in naval warfare. Cannonballs did little damage

A large cannon and a long-legged woman—a publicity photograph for the movie *The Princess and the Pirate* (1944).

them, although less rigidly. As they passed the enemy fleet, warships delivered broadsides one at a time, with each holding its fire as long as possible. To deliver these controlled broadsides, European navies built strong, heavy warships that also were slow and cumbersome.

Pirates preferred smaller, faster ships. Because they sought to board and not sink their prey, they had no need for large guns. They mainly attacked poorly armed merchantmen, and used cannon solely to frighten victims. Meetings with warships were rare, and the pirates simply outsailed rather than fighting them. From 1600 to 1730, although pirates were taken while at anchor, no warship ever overcame a Caribbean or Atlantic pirate ship at sea.

(See also SHIPS, PIRATE.)

CAPDEVILLE (CADOUILH, NEPEVILLE), JEAN *(French corsair; Atlantic, Caribbean; 1569)*

A lieutenant of Jacques SORES, Capdeville was as brutal as his leader. In 1569, he sailed from Normandy, with more than a hundred men. Off the Spanish coast, he seized a ship laden with sugar and added it to his own. The two pirate ships made for Venezuela, looted five or six frigates, and sacked Tolú, south of CARTAGENA. Capdeville continued on to Panama, decided Nombre de Dios was too heavily guarded to attack, and was prevented by a heavy undertow from sailing up the Chagres River. He returned to Tolú, this time burning it to the ground.

Spanish officials reported that Capdeville took rich booty while returning to Venezuela. Off Santa Marta, he captured a vessel from a fleet commanded by the governor of Cuba.

> Aboard which [were 265 persons, including] a Spanish lady and other women and her two children and more than 58 religious [nuns] and many other passengers and seamen. They say . . . that he threw them overboard and carried off the vessel with more than 100,000 ducats in goods to Brest in Brittany.

Two years later, Capdeville cruised in the Canary Islands with five vessels, including the CASTLE OF COMFORT, a powerful English warship. There he captured the GALLEON of the viceroy of Brazil, who died in the battle. Capdeville massacred 15 Jesuit missionaries and many other passengers and crewmen.

(See also SELECTED BIBLIOGRAPHY: Rogoziński, *Caribbean*; Wright, *Documents*.)

CAPTAIN *(ship's commander; all oceans; all eras)*

Captains traditionally have exercised almost unlimited authority over a ship at sea. During the late 18th century, British and Anglo-American pirates transferred some tasks from the captain to the QUARTERMASTER. Pirate captains generally retained unlimited power during battles, but they were subject to the quartermaster in many routine matters.

at long range, and cannon fire was highly inaccurate. No two guns—or cannonballs—were exactly alike, and gunpowder also varied. The loose-fitting balls did not emerge on a true center line, and the recoil changed the setting at each firing. There were no sights, and guns could not be traversed from left to right. Although most guns could reach several thousand yards, the maximum effective range was 200 to 500 feet. Significantly, the expression "a long shot" was adopted by gamblers.

Oared and sailing warships were modified to use heavier cannon. Galleys and galiots attacked on a widely extended line, much like a cavalry charge. Several smaller guns were mounted at the rear; one very large and several medium cannon faced forward. The fore guns were fired right before the galley rammed the enemy for boarding.

Initially, sailing ships also attacked in a wide front until the larger ships could grapple and board. From the 1560s, fleets advanced in a line, each immediately astern of the one in front. The English followed "line ahead" tactics from 1653, and the Dutch and French also adopted

CAPTAIN BLOOD (1) *(motion picture; black and white; 1924)* This silent film follows the plot of Rafael SABATINI's novel. Like the later 1935 movie, it omits the hero's assaults on Maracaibo and Cartagena. J. Warren Kerrigan plays Blood. Jean Paige is his true love, Arabella Bishop; and Wilfrid North is her wicked uncle, Colonel Bishop. The *New York Times* and other reviews considered Kerrigan to be uninspired, the other actors mediocre at best. Some of the shots of miniature ships are unconvincing. However, Director David Smith received general praise for the hand-to-hand fight and sea battles, especially the final scene in which Blood blows up two French ships.

CAPTAIN BLOOD (2) *(motion picture; black and white; 1935)* The first pirate movie with sound, *Captain Blood* made stars of Errol FLYNN (Peter Blood) and Olivia de Havilland (Arabella Bishop). The plot is relatively faithful to Rafael SABATINI's 1922 novel. Instead of Barbados, Blood is enslaved at PORT ROYAL, Jamaica (which was too strong to be attacked by a single pirate ship). Blood saves Arabella Bishop rather than a French woman from the evil Captain LE VASSEUR (Basil RATHBONE). This misses Sabatini's point that Blood idolized all women. Most significantly, Sabatini's Captain Blood attacked only Spanish ships. The movie Blood is a true pirate who also plunders English vessels.

When other actors were unavailable, Warner Brothers brought in the young Flynn and de Havilland for their first major film. With two novice leads, the studio decided to make do with model ships and clips from silent films. Perhaps for this reason, the movie leaves out the many episodes of piracy in the novel. These are replaced by

Errol Flynn ready to assault his prey in *Captain Blood* (1935).

a series of quick cuts showing Blood's crew boarding enemy ships.

With fewer sea battles, the movie focuses on its version of the love-hate relationship between Blood and Arabella. Director Michael Curtiz does supply numerous FLOGGING scenes and one major SWORD DUEL, when Blood and Le Vasseur fence down the beach and into the water itself. *Captain Blood* was nominated for an Academy Award as Best Picture. It features the first original background music by Erich Wolfgang Korngold, whose rich and resonant scores set the musical standard for movie spectaculars.

CAPTAIN BLOOD, HIS ODYSSEY *(novel; 1922)* The success of Rafael SABATINI's historical romance led to two sequels, and the series was adapted for several movies. A superb seaman, Blood out-thinks as well as outfights his foes. A true gentleman, he is loyal to friends, courteous to prisoners, and infinitely respectful toward women. Tall, dark, and handsome, he has striking blue eyes, "of singular penetration and of a steady hautiness." His voice "could woo seductively and caressingly, or . . . compel obedience." His men worship him and instantly obey his orders.

Captain Blood covers the years from 1685 to 1689. The plot centers around Blood's love for Arabella Bishop, niece of the villain who owns him at Barbados. Arabella is an independent colonial girl, slim, healthy, and brave. She initially rejects Blood as a "thief and pirate" but learns to love him deeply.

During the first episodes, Blood is loosely based on Henry Pitman. An English surgeon, Pitman was enslaved at Barbados after doctoring the wounded during a rebellion. Blood's adventures are similar to Pitman's until he escapes from Barbados. After Blood goes to TORTUGA, Sabatini freely adapts episodes from EXQUEMELIN, CHARLEVOIX, and other chroniclers. Since he started with Pitman's story, Sabatini transfers these events to the 1680s, when the BUCCANEERS had lost much of their power.

Blood escapes from Barbados in a captured Spanish warship. At Tortuga, he joins in consort with Jean LE VASSEUR (who never commanded a ship), but soon kills Le Vasseur to prevent a rape. Assembling 500 buccaneers, Blood plunders Maracaibo and Gibraltar in Venezuela. In describing Blood's raid, Sabatini copies Exquemelin's account of Sir Henry MORGAN's assault.

After some invented adventures, Sabatini has Blood join the French attack on CARTAGENA—which is moved from 1697 to 1689. Blood leaves before the buccaneers sack the city. After rescuing British officials, he seizes treasure taken from Cartagena by Baron de Pointis (Baron de Rivarol in the novel). Blood becomes governor of Jamaica and is united with Arabella in loving bliss.

Blood really is not a pirate, Sabatini insists, because he attacks only Spaniards, who are brutish, cruel, and greedy. Spain insists that she owns the Americas, and her huge fleets ravage British cities and vessels. Blood's victims thus are villains, his buccaneers Britain's sole defense against annihilation. In fact, Spain had no fleets in the Americas and never attacked a British town.

(See also CAPTAIN BLOOD RETURNS; FORTUNES OF CAPTAIN BLOOD.)

CAPTAIN BLOOD RETURNS (novel; 1931)
In this sequel to CAPTAIN BLOOD, HIS ODYSSEY, Rafael SABATINI recounts nine short adventures following Blood's escape from Barbados. The usual components are present. Blood fights the "cruel, treacherous, greedy, bigoted" Spaniards and rescues women in distress. While his own men are loyal, he must cope with coarse uneducated BUCCANEERS and stupid officials exiled to the colonies.

These stories emphasize Blood's mental agility. Despite Caribbean local color, the hero does not play a pirate's role. Although he fights several sea battles, Blood gains the gold by outsmarting his opponents. By the end, Blood resembles one of the more eccentric fictional detectives. Transported by accident to TORTUGA, he really belongs in an English country house or in a comedy of manners.

In three stories, Blood outwits Captain Easterling "a filthy pirate, a ruthless, bloodthirsty robber." In another, Blood disguises himself as a Spanish aristocrat to rescue his men from a Puerto Rican jail. Using the same ploy, he saves a French women, abducted (willingly, it turns out) by Spanish raiders. Despite bumbling British officials, he foils a Spanish invasion of Antigua.

Blood is, Sabatini stresses, a man of honor with firm moral convictions. He almost loses the gold at SANTA MARIA because he trusts a Spanish commander's word. Yet he also reflects light into an opponent's eyes to help a friend win a duel.

(See also FORTUNES OF CAPTAIN BLOOD, THE (2).)

CAPTAIN BRAND OF THE CENTIPEDE
(novel; 1864) A "Gothic" thriller by Henry Wise (1819–1869), complete with a citadel, dungeons, and tombs at midnight. Several imaginary details later became standard in pirate fiction—including PEG LEGS, EARRINGS, and victims forced to WALK THE PLANK. Because he assumes that his readers would find them strange, Wise carefully explains the earrings and plank-walking.

In 1805, during the Napoleonic wars, Captain Brand is helped by Don Ignacio and other corrupt Spanish officials. Brand lives in elegant luxury on a craggy island south of Cuba. He tyrannizes over his less-educated crewmen and his servant, a giant black woman who cannot speak. A drunken renegade priest serves his private chapel and the tomb of Dona Lucia, an innocent girl Brand had deceived. Only his surgeon, tricked into joining the brigands, resists Brand's evil orders.

Charles GIBBS, Brand's henchman, seizes a vessel carrying a French mother and infant. (In real life, Gibbs marauded some years later.) When her black servant resists, Gibbs throws the child into the sea. The servant crushes Gibbs' leg, and he later wears a wooden substitute. The pirates flee a British cruiser, stopping to pick up the floating infant.

Afraid of an attack, Brand blows up his hideaway, burying his treasure beneath the rubble. Before leaving, he ties up the surgeon and the child. But they live through the explosion, build a boat, and sail away.

Seventeen years later, the infant has grown into a handsome naval officer, serving with the surgeon. Captain Brand takes passage on their ship, escapes their trap, and visits his former stronghold. However, Don Ignacio already had taken Brand's buried gold before perishing in an accident. Brand's pursuers tie him to Dona Lucia's tomb, where birds tear at his living body.

Captain Brand lacks much of the pirate symbolism found 20 years later in TREASURE ISLAND. Brand does not drink to excess. His crewmen dress like other mariners, keep their ships and dwellings clean, and attend the renegade priest's Masses.

However, Brand's pirates do wear earrings. Many are African or Asian and retain their foreign customs. Writing in 1864, Wise assumes that white men do *not* sport earrings. Brand's pirates wear them only because they are standard garb in their native countries.

Captain Brand also contains an early reference to walking the plank. Before attacking the merchantman, Gibbs says, he captured a "Yankee schooner loaded with shingles and lumber; and as the skipper was sarsy, I just made him and his crew walk one of his own planks."

CAPTAIN GENERAL OF GALLEYS (Admiral of Malta; Mediterranean; 1553–1797) Charles V of Spain (and Italy), who granted MALTA to the KNIGHTS HOSPITALERS, frequently warred with France. Hoping to weaken French influence, he specified that their ADMIRAL must be an Italian. The Italian knights usually elected the head of their national organization, often an old man not suited to combat.

During the 1550s, the order's finances were severely strained. To gain funds, it strengthened its navy and turned to aggressive piracy. From 1553, the fleet commander received this title of "captain general," and the admiral's duties became ceremonial and administrative.

Until the 1670s, as Maltese piracy flourished, the captain general was elected from among the most skilled captains. He generally served for two years and could be of any nationality. (Ascanio CAMBIANO, an Italian, was both admiral and captain general.) The office was parallel to that of CAPTAIN OF THE SEA among the BARBARY pirates.

(See also CARAFA, FRANCESCO; CRÉMEAULX, FRANÇOIS; GATTINARO, SIGNORIO; ROMEGAS; SAINT AUBIN, PIERRE DE; STROZZI, LEONE; LA VALETTE, JEAN DE.)

CAPTAIN KIDD (1) (legendary English pirate; 1701 to the present) In popular legends, William KIDD still roams the seven seas, murdering, plundering, and burying gold. Thanks to the TREASURE ISLAND MOV-

Captain Kidd. Illustration by Howard Pyle, in *Harper's Monthly Magazine,* December 1902.

ies, Long John Silver probably is now better known. Ironically, Robert Louis Stevenson's novel borrowed many Kidd myths.

Kidd's reputation was blackened during political struggles in England. Folklore seized on Kidd's story and credited him with the crimes of other pirates. Meanwhile, Daniel DEFOE'S GENERAL HISTORY gave the dishonest trial records wide publicity. Relying on Defoe, even serious histories described Kidd's acts of shameless cruelty.

The real Captain Kidd was at best a second-rate pirate. Arriving at New York in 1690, he married a wealthy widow, and possibly raided as a PRIVATEER. He was a respected citizen, owned a pew at Trinity Church, and mingled with influential politicians.

Kidd went to England in 1695 to get a letter of MARQUE. He fell in with high-ranking officials, who arranged a license allowing him to capture and keep pirate booty. Kidd cruised from April 1697 to April 1698. He captured the *Quedah Merchant* near India, took her back to the Caribbean, and went on to New York in a small sloop. He was arrested in Boston in July 1699, arrived in London in April 1700, and was tried and hanged in May 1701.

The five great lords that arranged Kidd's pirate-hunting license belonged to the Whig faction. While he languished in prison, the Tories used Kidd to smear the Whigs. Tales were spread that the Whigs knew Kidd was a notorious pirate, who had committed foul deeds before his fateful voyage. Taverns buzzed, and the rumors were retailed in cheap pamphlets. Arrogant, boastful, and obscene, Kidd mocked God and the nation's flag.

Kidd's voyage embarrassed the Whigs, who did nothing to clear his name. Both factions preferred to hang Kidd and avoid a thorough sifting of the facts. He received a grossly unfair trial, during which the prosecuting attorneys detailed his alleged crimes in strong language.

> And there [off the Malabar coast]. . . he committed many great Piracies and Robberies, taking the Ships and Goods of the *Indians* and others at sea, *Moors* and *Christians,* and torturing cruelly their Persons. . .; burning their Houses and killing after a barbarous manner the Natives on the Shore; equally cruel, dreaded and hated both on the Land and at Sea.

The published versions of the trial record convinced the English public that Kidd was a ferocious and incorrigible pirate. Kidd harmed his cause by his behavior at the hanging. Condemned men were supposed to repent. Kidd arrived drunk and delivered a bitter and blasphemous tirade, copied down and printed in pamphlets.

Kidd's crimes were exaggerated in a ballad, "CAPTAIN KID'S FAREWEL," published on the day of his hanging. The song, long popular in America, became even harsher over time. Kidd became a monstrous Satanic rebel, who cursed God and his own family.

The second volume of Daniel Defoe's *General History,* published in 1728, provided Kidd's first biography. The *General History* combines fact and fiction, invents events, and describes pirates who never existed. Defoe's life of Kidd is relatively restrained and leaves out the most lurid stories. Perhaps for this reason, it secured Kidd's reputation as an evil man.

Defoe borrowed freely from the trial record. Kidd was honest, Defoe wrote, until he reached MADAGASCAR. He persuaded his men to turn pirate because he could not catch legitimate prey. Afraid to return to his employers empty-handed, "he resolved to do his Business one Way, since he could not do it another." After taking the *Quedah Merchant,* Kidd convinced himself he could buy a pardon.

Defoe's work remained popular and was frequently reprinted. Popular anthologies compiled the goriest bits and added lurid details from popular legends. Charles Ellms' best-selling PIRATES OWN BOOK plagiarized Defoe's biography and inserted falsehoods about Kidd's evil youth and buried treasure. Works of history also accepted the dishonest trial record enshrined by Defoe. In his famous *History of England* (published 1849–1861), Thomas Macaulay describes Kidd's acts of shameless cruelty. Nineteenth-century historians of New England and Madagascar likewise perpetuated the legend of Kidd's monstrous behavior.

The tide began to turn in the 1920s. Like Gosse, other historians noticed that Kidd was hardly the worst pirate ever. New biographies denounced Kidd's unfair trial, and some even argued that he was innocent of any crimes. By then it was too late, and Hollywood still portrays Kidd as a cruel and greedy pirate. Kidd is a cold-blooded murderer in CAPTAIN KIDD (2) (1945), and he plunders everyone in sight in CAPTAIN KIDD AND THE SLAVE GIRL and AGAINST ALL FLAGS (both 1952). His malevolence is mocked in DOUBLE CROSSBONES (1950) and ABBOTT AND COSTELLO MEET CAPTAIN KIDD (1952). (See also SELECTED BIBLIOGRAPHY: Bonner, *Pirate*; Defoe, *General History*; Gosse, *History*; Hinrichs, *Fateful*; Ritchie, *Kidd*.)

CAPTAIN KIDD (2) *(motion picture; black and white; 1945)* Kidd is the evil genius of myth and fiction in this film directed by Rowland V. Lee. As Kidd, Charles Laughton creates a chilling portrait of greed and ambition.

Marauding along the SPANISH MAIN and near MADAGASCAR, Kidd takes many rich prizes. Among them is Admiral Blaine's *Twelve Apostles*. Kidd and four henchmen sink both the *Apostles* and their own vessel, murdering all aboard. They bury their booty at a secluded bay, where Kidd kills one of the four, and return to England. Kidd wants wealth so he can enter the nobility, and he hires Carry Shadwell (Reginald Owen) as his valet to teach him etiquette.

King William III (Henry Daniell) gives Kidd the *Adventure Galley* and sends him to escort the *Quedah Merchant*. Kidd is joined by his comrades from the treasure cave, Cyprian Boyle (Sheldon Leonard), Jose Lorenzo (Gilbert Roland), and Orange Povey (John Carradine). He recruits a crew from condemned pirates, including Adam Mercy (Randolph Scott), Henry EVERY's chief gunner. Before they sail, Povey tells Kidd he has left behind a letter exposing Kidd's crimes.

Kidd plans to get the *Merchant*'s treasure and then pick up his own buried loot. He keeps a list of all those knowing about his plunder and crosses off each man's name as he dies. Povey is safe, but the others are killed one by one.

Kidd catches Mercy riffling through his cabin. Pretending to be a government spy, Mercy agrees to keep silent for a share of the booty. When Kidd meets the *Merchant*, he takes on board the treasure, the British ambassador, and his daughter, Lady Anne Falconer (Barbara Britton). Lorenzo plants a bomb that blows up the *Merchant*, and he kills the ambassador in a fake accident.

Lady Anne and Mercy instantly trust one another, and he tells her that he really is Adam Blaine, son of the *Twelve Apostles*' captain. When Lorenzo invades Anne's cabin, Mercy/Blaine kills him in a SWORD DUEL—one

more name checked off on Kidd's list. During the duel, Blaine loses a medallion with his family crest, and Kidd learns his true identity.

Kidd, Povey, and Blaine dig up Kidd's treasure. Blaine fights with Povey and falls into the ocean. He survives, swims to the *Galley*, and rescues Anne. Although Kidd's cannon sink their boat, the two escape and (miraculously) get home before Kidd. When Kidd swaggers into the king's council, Blaine and Anne confront him. He is hanged after an impassioned speech expressing the rage and pride of the cornered criminal.

Compared to traditional SWASHBUCKLERS, *Kidd* is relatively slow-paced and cheaply made. Yet Laughton's Kidd is an unusually believable pirate captain. Pirate movies often present the villain as a demented buffoon, constantly rolling his eyes and bellowing curses. Laughton's Kidd is terrifying precisely because he is sane while coldly plotting the murder of those around him.

CAPTAIN KIDD AND THE SLAVE GIRL *(motion picture; color, 1954)* Only the name connects this low-budget SWASHBUCKLER to the real William KIDD. A scheming earl saves Kidd (Anthony Dexter) from the hangman so he can steal his treasure. Accompanied by a beautiful slave girl (Eva Gabor), Kidd roams the seven seas, fighting off enemies and plundering victims. Directed by Lew Landers.

(See also CAPTAIN KIDD (1).)

CAPTAIN KIDD'S TREASURE *(imaginary riches; 1701 to the present)* While cruising near India in 1697 and 1698, William KIDD took only one significant prize. Although there were some coins and jewels aboard, the *Quedah Merchant* mainly carried luxury cloth. The owners claimed losses of £45,000. The East India Company, which had to reimburse them, estimated the *Quedah*'s value at only £22,500. When the booty was divided at MADAGASCAR, Kidd took 40 shares, somewhat less than 40 percent of the total take. However, he had to sell some cloth very cheaply in the Caribbean, and he left other cargo behind at Hispaniola as he deserted the *Quedah Merchant*.

When he arrived in New York, Kidd gave some money to his wife and friends, and he left about 50 pounds of gold with the owners of Gardiner's Island. Governor Bellomont diligently searched and recovered money and cargo worth about £14,000. This was about as much as Kidd could have possessed, leaving him with no treasure to bury.

Even before he returned to the Caribbean, rumors flew that Kidd had taken enormous riches—£70,000, £100,000, or even more. Perhaps the public remembered Henry EVERY's much richer haul in 1695, but Kidd encouraged rumors by his maneuvers in New York. He made matters worse by telling Bellomont that the abandoned *Quedah Merchant* still held goods worth £50,000 or £60,000. Most Americans believed that Bellomont did not recover all of Kidd's plunder. They were convinced

Captain Kidd buries his treasure on Gardiner's Island, New York, in this imaginary scene by Howard Pyle for *Harper's Monthly Magazine,* November 1894.

he must have left a horde behind somewhere between India and Boston.

The mystery surrounding Kidd's return sent treasure hunters off on a wild chase. By 1750, they had dug up almost every point of land and island along the New York coast. During the 19th century, nine companies dug for Kidd's loot, some in the Hudson River Valley, which Kidd never visited. Every coin found anywhere fostered belief in Kidd's treasure, and several well-planned hoaxes helped the story grow. The search still goes on. Two men were arrested for trespassing in 1983 while looking for Kidd's treasure in the South China Sea, another spot he never saw.

Washington IRVING drew on folk legends about Kidd's treasure in his 1824 stories "WOLFERT WEBBER" and "THE DEVIL AND TOM WALKER." Adding elements from European mythology, Irving turned Kidd into a Mephistopheles, who sold his soul to the devil. Secret markings marked the location of his gold, which was guarded by ghosts. James Fenimore COOPER similarly embroidered the Kidd legends in THE WATER WITCH (1830) and THE SEA LIONS (1849). Kidd's loot also figured in lesser, now forgotten novels and plays, including CAPTAIN KYD, an 1830 musical melodrama. Treasure remains crucial to the

plots of stories in Howard PYLE's STOLEN TREASURE (1907) and the 1945 movie CAPTAIN KIDD (2).

Robert Louis Stevenson borrowed from Irving and Cooper for TREASURE ISLAND (1883), which incorporates the legends about Kidd's gold at second hand. Through *Treasure Island,* the myth of hidden pirate caches was separated from specific references to Kidd. Later pirate stories and movies often include a buried treasure sequence. BLACKBEARD and Sir Henry MORGAN have been depicted burying booty—something never mentioned in first-hand accounts of their lives. In reality, pirates spent their loot as soon as they could.

(See also LABAT, JEAN-BAPTISTE; TREASURE, BURIED; SELECTED BIBLIOGRAPHY: Bonner, *Pirate;* Pringle, *Jolly Roger;* Ritchie, *Kidd.*)

"CAPTAIN KID'S FAREWEL TO THE SEAS"

(ballad; 1701)   An anonymous song supposedly reciting William KIDD's confession at the gallows, his pious regrets, and his moral warnings to others. In its original English form, the song was published on the day of Kidd's execution. The writer exaggerated Kidd's crimes, crediting him with five named prizes in addition to "many Moorish ships."

The ballad remained very popular throughout America for two centuries. It was frequently republished and sung at concerts and at religious revival meetings. Over the years, its 25 four-line stanzas took on a much darker tone, and the references to Kidd became less specific. The poem turned into the horrible lament of all souls damned by lust for gold.

Kidd (called Robert not William) is a fiend of deliberate and diabolical cruelty. He curses his kindly parents, outwardly disdains religion, and plunders ships of all nations.

The refrain "as I sail'd" frequently reoccurs, as in this stanza about Kidd's murder of William Moore.

> I murder'd William Moore as I sail'd, as I sail'd,
> I murder'd William Moore as I sail'd;
> I murder'd William Moore, and I left him in his gore,
> Not many leagues from shore, as I sail'd.

CAPTAIN KYD, THE WIZARD OF THE SEA

(four-act play; 1830)   J. S. Jones's melodrama, which includes seven songs, one a pirate chorus. *Captain Kyd* was produced in Boston and periodically revived there and in New York until 1856.

Robert of Lester actually is the bastard son of a pirate, Hurtel of the Red Hand, and Elpsy the Witch. Mark Meredith, the real lord of Lester, lives as a poor peasant. During an archery contest, Robert reveals his cowardice and jealousy and is trounced by Mark. He is spurned by Kate Bellomont and the other ladies present. When Witch Elpsy tells Lester about his true origins, he joins the pirates and turns into Captain Kyd, King of the Sea. Mark Meredith becomes Captain Fitzroy commanding the naval warship *Ger Falcon.*

Act Two is set in New York, where the taverns are filled with drunken Dutchmen. Their leader, Captain Horsebean Hemlock, describes Kyd's villainies. Meanwhile Kate Bellomont also has moved to New York, and Kyd (Lester) vainly tries to win her hand in marriage. Seeking a love charm, Kyd visits the witch's den of Elpsy, the Hag of Hell's Gate. After a fierce storm, the act ends with two lighted transparencies, showing a sinking pirate ship and a pirate swinging from a gibbet.

Kyd scuds through a storm "like the Flying Dutchman." He battles and takes the *Ger Falcon,* losing his own vessel. Captain Fitzroy escapes by swimming ashore. Horsebean Hemlock sings "CAPTAIN KYD'S FAREWEL." Kidd goes to the witch's den near Hell's Gate to bury treasure. Fitzroy and the other principal characters pursue and capture him. Remembering their days in England, Kate temporarily saves Kyd's life.

CAPTAIN MARGARET: A ROMANCE

(novel; 1908) John Masefield (1878–1967), named Britain's Poet Laureate in 1930, wrote *Captain Margaret,* a love story and a sea adventure set during the reign of James II (1685–1689). While not considered one of Masefield's best works, it is a reputable first novel.

Although it focuses on the relationships between its main characters, *Captain Margaret* contains a stirring battle scene and superb descriptions of ships and ports. Masefield published a history of pirate assaults on Panama and an edition of William DAMPIER's *New Voyage.* His descriptions of BUCCANEERS are knowledgeable and convincing.

Captain Cammock, a reformed pirate who commands the hero's ship, is especially memorable. Cammock cut LOGWOOD in Honduras, sacked PANAMA with Sir Henry MORGAN, and crossed to the Pacific with Bartholomew SHARP. Neither a fiend nor a hero, Cammock fell into piracy to make money. An uneducated yet shrewd seaman, he understood the strengths and weaknesses of the captains he followed.

Captain Charles Margaret is an English gentleman and poet, a man of intelligence and idealism. He deeply loves Olivia, but she foolishly marries Tom Stukeley, a coarse bully. Tall, powerful, and handsome, Stukeley lacks only brains and moral scruples. ("It is," Masefield wrote, "horrible to see any large thing without intelligence.") He steals money, rapes women, and kills a man in a duel. He married Olivia to get her money but finds that her trustees keep it under close guard.

Captain Margaret owns a SLOOP (named the *Broken Heart* in Olivia's honor) and hires Captain Cammock for a voyage to Virginia and the SPANISH MAIN. He dreams of an English colony in Panama, where former buccaneers will grow tobacco and trade with the Indians. By chance, Olivia and Tom Stukeley are visiting Margaret's port of departure in England, and he pays them a farewell visit. Stukeley is wanted for debt, forgery, and darker deeds. Pursued by royal officials shooting muskets, he and Olivia

row out to the *Broken Heart.* Margaret is so stirred by Olivia's narrow escape that he breaks the law by taking the Stukeleys with him.

In Virginia, Margaret persuades the governor (whom he has bribed for business reasons) not to arrest the company. Margaret and Cammock recruit 30 men who had sailed with Edward DAVIS. The little band sails to Springer's Cay, where Cammock had marauded with Bartholomew Sharp. There they are joined by buccaneers under Thomas PAIN and other captains.

Captain Margaret visits Tolú (now in Colombia) seeking permission to trade. Stukeley, who is fluent in Spanish, goes along as spokesman. He deserts to the Spaniards, who attack the English and wound Margaret. For Olivia's sake, Margaret goes back to Tolú to rescue Stukeley, accompanied by several buccaneer vessels. After taking Tolú in a gallant assault, Margaret discovers that Stukeley, now married to a Spanish woman, has just died of yellow fever. When Margaret returns from burying Stukeley, his drunken followers are plundering the city. Spanish troops counterattack, and Margaret barely escapes with his life. His crewmen desert to the buccaneers, who burn his fortress on Springer's Cay.

Margaret is heartsick over his participation in the bloody sack of Tolú. But Olivia finally recognizes Stukeley's beastliness and loves Margaret. She comforts the beaten man.

> There is no dishonor, Charles. You failed. The only glory is failure. All artists fail. But one sees what they saw. You see that in their failure.

CAPTAIN OF THE SEA (Barbary admiral; Mediterranean; about 1570 to 1830)

The official (usually referred to as "admiral" by Europeans) in ALGIERS, TUNIS, and TRIPOLI who commanded ship captains during wartime and who dealt with Christian governments. The captain was elected by the corsairs' guild (TAIFE REISI) and formally invested by the OTTOMAN sultan. He was (from about 1600) independent of the Admiral-in-Chief (Kapudan Pasha) in Istanbul, but followed his orders during wartime. "The greatest personage in the city" as piracy flourished during the 17th century, he had the unique honor of a lifetime appointment and a fixed salary.

(See also MURAT "THE GREAT" REIS; SELECTED BIBLIOGRAPHY: Fisher, *Barbary.*)

CAPTAIN PIRATE (motion picture; color; 1952)

Filmed in Britain (where it is titled *Captain Blood, Fugitive*) and based on Rafael SABATINI's novel CAPTAIN BLOOD RETURNS. Peter Blood (Louis Hayward), peacefully retired in the West Indies, is arrested and falsely accused of piracy. His pirate gang and his fiancee, Dona Isabela (Patricia Medina), manage to free Blood. He steals a ship from Hilary Evans (John Sutton) and searches for a villain who uses Blood's name during bloody raids on coastal towns.

After various adventures in disguise, Blood learns that Evans is the culprit and plans to raid PORTOBELO. He convinces the Spaniards he is a military attache and sinks his ship in the harbor. Evans' pirates arrive and founder on the sunken hulk, where Blood's cannon fire destroys them. Evans tries to escape, but Blood kills him in a SWORD DUEL. He frees Dona Isabela, imprisoned for her part in his escape. They marry and return to a peaceful life. Directed by Ralph Murray.

(See also FORTUNES OF CAPTAIN BLOOD.)

"CAPTAIN SHARKEY" (short story; 1897)
Sir Arthur Conan Doyle (1859–1930), creator of Sherlock Holmes, describes a pirate even more fiendish than BLACKBEARD. Doyle borrowed incidents from stories about Edward LOW and George LOWTHER in Daniel DEFOE's GENERAL HISTORY.

By the early 1700s, the BUCCANEERS have been replaced by solitary murderers, at war with the human race. Captain Sharkey is the worst among these heartless villains. His diabolical cunning outwits all opponents, while his savage cruelty revolts even other pirates. "From the Bahamas to the Main, his coal black barque, with the ambiguous name [*Happy Delivery*], had been freighted with death and many things which are worse than death."

An English captain stops at Saint Kitts. The ailing governor boards his ship, heavily dressed and wearing a wig and large green glasses. When the ship reaches England, the man reveals that he is Captain Sharkey and had cut the real governor's throat.

Some time after, Sharkey is hunting on Île-à-Vache while his ship is careened at Hispaniola. Stephen Craddock, a reformed Jamaican pirate, hopes to fool Sharkey by disguising another ship as the *Happy Delivery*. Sharkey turns the tables, sinks Craddock's ship, and takes him captive. Sharkey uses Craddock to sneak into Kingston harbor, but Craddock jumps off and dies to foil the plot.

In the third tale, Sharkey murders everyone on a prize, including Copley Banks' wife and sons. Banks, a wealthy Jamaica merchant, turns pirate: "It is Stede BONNET over again." After terrorizing traders for a year, Banks becomes Sharkey's consort and joins him in inhuman tortures. Coming to trust his partner, Sharkey joins a party on Banks' ship. Helped by a steward whose tongue Sharkey had cut out, Banks ties up Sharkey, surrounds him with gunpowder, and sets a fuse. "Then Copley Banks, his heart singing within him, touched his companion upon the shoulder, and they plunged together into the lonely jungle of the Caicos."

CAPTAIN SINGLETON (novel; 1720) In this
fictional autobiography, Daniel DEFOE combines foreign adventures and pirate stories. Both the hero and his friend, Quaker William, are fictitious. Defoe borrowed information about the East Indies from William DAMPIER's *Voyages*. His plot mixes incidents from the lives of various unnamed marauders. Henry EVERY is specifically mentioned—incorrectly, since Every never visited MADAGAS-

CAR. Captain Bob, as he calls himself, tells his own story. Bob is a fabulously successful villain, whose wicked character was formed during childhood. Seeking adventure with lawless abandon, he gradually learns to appreciate the usefulness of wealth.

Bob was kidnapped as a baby and sold to an old gypsy woman. When she is hanged, Bob is passed around and receives little education. Adopted by a ship's captain, he is taken on several Newfoundland voyages. Their ship is captured by BARBARY pirates, recaptured by Portuguese warships, and taken to Lisbon. The captain dies, and an aged Portuguese pilot makes Bob his servant.

They enlist on a ship to Brazil and Goa, and Bob learns how to be "an arrant thief and a bad sailor." Thanks to his charm, he becomes the steward's assistant and steals food and gold. When the voyage ends, Bob (now 17 or 18 years old) quarrels with the Portuguese pilot, who will not hand over his pay.

Before Bob can kill the pilot, he joins an unsuccessful mutiny, is marooned on Madagascar, and fails to persuade the other mutineers to turn pirate. With Bob as co-captain, the mutineers reach Africa and cross overland to the Atlantic coast, several thousand miles away. By cruelly exploiting the African natives, the men eventually reach their goal. Along the way, they gather up gold dust lying near rivers, and Bob returns to England a rich man.

Bob squanders his money and enlists on a ship headed for Spain. Led by a rogue named Wilmot, the crewmen mutiny and turn pirate in the West Indies. For about three years, they plunder ships of every nation—although Captain Wilmot was "particularly cruel when he took any English Vessel." Bob becomes an officer and rises to command a captured ship.

On one foray, Wilmot captures William Walters, a Quaker surgeon. At William's suggestion, Bob pretends to take him by force in case they are arrested. In time, William becomes the pirates' real leader, moderating their savagery by his cunning. William constantly reminds the crewmen that they became criminals to make money, and he discourages their fondness for battling other ships. Near Brazil, the men seize a derelict slave ship and want to kill the rebellious Africans. William rescues the slaves and sells them for a high profit.

The pirates go to the Red Sea and take many prizes. However, they foolishly let an English merchant live, and he alarms the coast. Escaping to Madagascar, they briefly join Henry Every. Without sharing his booty, Captain Wilmot leaves with Every.

Cruising on his own, Captain Bob raids as far east as China, looting European and native vessels. When they return to India, William convinces him that they are rich enough to retire. Rather than splitting with the crew, the two men sneak off with their plunder.

Suffering from guilt, Bob suggests that they give up their stolen goods. Quaker William points out that the original owners will not benefit, whereas he and Bob can do God's work with their money. Disguised as Armenian merchants, they return to England. Bob marries William's sister and carefully watches out for lawmen.

"CAPTIVE'S TALE, THE" (Spanish story, 1605)

A self-contained episode ("El Cautivo") in CER-VANTES' *Don Quixote de la Mancha*, told by an escaped slave from ALGIERS. Although the captive's story differs in some details from his own experiences, Cervantes based it on his years of captivity in Algiers.

Years earlier, the escaped slave (whose name is never given) joins the Spanish army, becomes an officer, and fights at LEPANTO in 1571. During the heat of battle, he jumps aboard the galley of ULUJ ALI, viceroy of Algiers. When Uluj Ali flees the Muslim defeat, the brave soldier is captured and condemned as a GALLEY SLAVE.

The sultan appoints Uluj Ali admiral of the OTTOMAN fleet. The enslaved oarsman witnesses several naval battles (like Cervantes himself) and the Ottoman conquest of TUNIS in 1574. According to the story, when Uluj Ali died in 1574, HASAN VENEZIANO PASHA inherited his slaves and took them to Algiers. (In fact, while Hasan did become viceroy of Algiers in 1574, Uluj Ali lived until 1587.)

At Algiers, a stroke of miraculous good luck enables the captive to escape with a beautiful Muslim girl. Hasan Veneziano normally abuses his slaves with fiendish cruelty. But he spares the captive and holds him for ransom in the state prison (BAGNIO). Across the street lies the palace of a wealthy former official (a friend of MEMMI "ARNAUT" REIS.)

One day, when the other slaves are at work, the official's daughter signals to the captive from a window. A secret Christian, the girl offers to use her father's wealth to free the (still handsome) captive, and he readily agrees to marry her and take her to a Christian country. Helped by a Christian renegade working at the prison, the captive and other prisoners buy a boat and flee with the girl—after marooning her father on a desert island. On the way to Spain, French pirates sink their ship. But the pirate captain proves merciful and lets his prisoners sail to Spain in his ship's small boat. When he meets Don Quixote, the captive is going home with his wife-to-be.

CARACCIOLI, FATHER

See MISSON, CAPTAIN.

CARAFA, BROTHER FRANCESCO (Knight of Malta; Mediterranean; active 1625–1627)

Commanding raids as CAPTAIN-GENERAL OF GALLEYS, Carafa captured six merchantmen and hundreds of slaves along the BARBARY COAST and in the eastern Mediterranean.

CARAFA, BROTHER FRANCESCO MARIA (Knight of Malta; Mediterranean; active 1669–1672)

As CAPTAIN GENERAL OF GALLEYS, Carafa in 1671 raided near Egypt with six galleys. Off Crete, his squadron met Algerian corsairs in three heavily-armed sailing ships. Although several captains refused to close with the enemy, the Maltese did capture one vessel, commanded by MEHMED BEY, son of the DEY of ALGIERS.

CARAMUSAL (type of ship; eastern Mediterranean; 16th through 19th centuries)

A common Turkish merchant ship, something like a GALLEON, with four sails and a high poop. Caramusals were relatively fast, and the largest could carry up to 900 tons of cargo.

CARAVEL (type of ship; Mediterranean, Atlantic, Pacific; 14th–17th centuries)

A relatively small trading vessel, with a simple curved bow and a plain transom stem. Mediterranean caravels had lateen (triangular) sails on two masts. During Spanish and Portuguese voyages of exploration, they developed into three-masted ships with a square rig on the two forward masts and a lateen-rigged mizzen. Three-masted caravels were about 80 feet long, and a few reached 100 feet.

CAREW, SIR PETER (English pirate; Atlantic; active 1560s)

A Devonshire landowner who carried out numerous raids on merchant shipping. In 1564, Carew chased pirates off Devon and Cornwall under a royal commission that allowed him to keep any booty he recaptured. Not finding any likely ships, he sailed to the Irish Sea, where he encountered and was decisively defeated by Sir Thomas STUKELEY.

Fifteenth-century caravel. From Jurien de la Gravière, *Les corsaires barbaresques* (1887).

CAREY, SIR GEORGE, SECOND BARON HUNSDON *(English promotor of piracy; Atlantic, Caribbean; 1547–1603)*

The eldest son of Henry Lord Hunsdon, the brother-in-law of Lord Admiral Charles Howard, and a kinsman of Queen Elizabeth I, Carey used his influence to gain personal wealth. As captain-general of the Isle of Wight (from 1582) and VICE-ADMIRAL of Hampshire, his power in the region was virtually unlimited. Crude and aggressive in manner, he enjoyed associating with pirate captains.

Queen Elizabeth ignored complaints from the local gentry about Carey's dictatorial ways. On one occasion, according to a contemporary writer, "an attorney coming to settle in the island was, by his command, with a pound of candles hanging at his breech lighted, with bells about his legs, hunted owte of the islands." When his victims sought justice from the ADMIRALTY COURT in London, Carey usually won the case through influence or by bribery.

Taking full advantage of his royal offices, Carey fenced pirate booty and other illegal spoils. In one case, a ship owned by Sir Walter RALEIGH captured a French prize. Raleigh's captain turned his prize over to John CALLICE, who returned the vessel to its owners but kept the cargo. Raleigh took some for his own use, but most was smuggled ashore by Carey's servants and his staff in the customs service. The French owners lost their suit in the Admiralty court because Callice and Carey bribed the chief judge, Sir Julius Caesar.

In September 1585, two small ships owned by Carey captured what is sometimes described as a Spanish prize. In fact, the ship was a Newfoundland fisherman owned by Frenchmen. Although they sued before the Admiralty court, the French owners never recovered their vessel.

From 1587 to 1591, Carey financed at least three fleets sent to plunder the West Indies. These ventures were headed by William IRISH, a gentlemen from the Isle of Wight who wore Carey's colors ("livery"). Although feudalism was somewhat old-fashioned by the 16th century, it benefited Carey in this case. Unlike many other pirate captains, Irish was consistently loyal to his employer.

Irish's 1591 venture was a financial disaster, and Carey's ships apparently kept to European waters in later years. He gave up plunder raids entirely after he succeeded his father as Baron Hunsdon in 1596. As treasurer for the Irish wars, he embezzled enormous sums by falsifying his accounts and by paying the troops in the debased Irish currency.

(See also MONSON, WILLIAM; SELECTED BIBLIOGRAPHY: *Dictionary of National Biography*.)

CARIA *(pirate haven; Mediterranean, Aegean; 16th through 13th centuries B.C.)*

The Greek name for a mountainous region in Anatolia (present-day Turkey), south of the Maeander River and just east of CILICIA. Its inhabitants—also known as Leleges in ancient Greek—lived in hilltop villages grouped around religious sanctuaries. During the 300s, the Carians, who were ruled from Miletus and Halicarnassus, lost their ethnic identity and adopted the Greek language and culture. During these later centuries, Carians often became mercenary soldiers and sometimes served as pirates under Cilician captains.

Many centuries before, however, the Carians (called LUKKA) had conducted daring raids against Cyprus and Egypt. According to THUCYDIDES, the Carians also moved west, practicing piracy from islands in the Aegean Sea. Thucydides knew only that the Carians had ruled the islands many centuries earlier. Other legends say they moved there after BUTES and his Thracian buccaneers left, perhaps during the 16th or 15th century.

Somewhat later, around 1350, King MINOS of CRETE, conquered the Aegean islands and drove out the Carian pirate chiefs. Minos took over the Carian fleets for his own purposes. HERODOTUS tells us that King Minos, instead of taxing the Carians, required them to man his warships. This hardy maritime folk proved far better warriors than the effete Cretan townsmen.

The Carians conquered many lands for Minos. And, Herodotus added, they made three discoveries that every other warrior soon copied. The Carians put hand-grips on their shields. They also bound plumes on their helmets and decorated their shields to distinguish themselves from the enemy during battle.

Despite the skills of the Carian seamen, the Cretan sea empire finally fell. In about 1150 B.C., invading barbarians occupied the Carian colonies on the Aegean islands. As sea commerce fell off, Carian pirates on the mainland ceased their raids. When civilization and trade revived centuries later, their maritime supremacy had passed to other peoples.

CARIBBEAN (1) *(motion picture; color; 1952)*

An 18th-century pirate takes his revenge in this film directed by Edward Ludwig. Captain F. Barclay (Sir Cedric Hardwicke) hates Andrew MacAllister (Francis L. Sullivan), who sold him into slavery and kidnapped his wife and daughter 20 years earlier. Barclay has become a dreaded pirate, while MacAllister now is a wealthy Caribbean plantation owner and slave-dealer. Barclay's wife is long dead. His child has been raised believing she is MacAllister's daughter, Christine (Arlene Dahl).

MacAllister hides on his well-fortified island with Christine, grown into a haughty island princess. To get his revenge, Barclay uses Dick Lindsay (John Payne), who looks like MacAllister's nephew. Lindsay manages to get on the island. He gains the confidence of the oppressed slaves and plans an uprising coinciding with MacAllister's annual slave sale. Meanwhile, he also falls in love with Christine, MacAllister's supposed daughter. In a vast general battle, the slaves rebel while Barclay

The final battle scene in *Caribbean* (1952).

attacks and takes over the island. This rousing melee somewhat compensates for the often illogical plot. Hardwicke and Sullivan play their characters with a florid lack of restraint.

CARIBBEAN (2)   *(novel; 1989)*   Pirates play a major role in *Caribbean,* a novel by James Michener (born 1907). In the book he tells the story of the fictional Spanish Ledesma family of CARTAGENA and the English Tatums of Barbados.

Don Diego, the first Ledesma to govern Cartagena, battles invaders led by Sir Francis DRAKE and Sir John HAWKINS. Michener describes the English attacks from Ledesma's viewpoint. Some incidents are invented, partly to connect the English raiders to Ledesma's Cartagena.

Later chapters detail the buccaneering exploits of Will and Ned Tatum. Two brothers, Will and Isaac Tatum, inherit a small farm on Barbados. Greedy and pompous, Isaac is dominated by his loathsome wife Clarissa. Through her lies, Will is tortured and exiled for blasphemy.

Will drifts to England, becomes a seaman, and is captured attacking a Spanish TREASURE FLEET (commanded by a Ledesma). He escapes from Cadiz and returns to Barbados hating all Spaniards. With his nephew Ned, aged 15, Will steals a vessel from Isaac and heads for TORTUGA. By 1667 there were few Spanish ships to plunder. Aided by Mompox, a "mixed-race buc-

caneer" who loves Ned, the Tatums cut LOGWOOD in Honduras and hunt cattle for the BOUCAN. Hearing about Sir Henry MORGAN's exploits, the three men join his assaults on PORTOBELO, Maracaibo, and PANAMA.

Accepting EXQUEMELIN's version of events, Michener portrays Morgan as both a brilliant tactician and a greedy murderer. Will and Ned fiendishly torture Spanish captives. After the Panama raid, Morgan flees to Jamaica with all the booty, leaving his followers penniless.

The Tatums and Mompox go back to Panama and help capture two small ships. Their adventures marauding along the Pacific coast are described in Ned Tatum's fictional diary. Michener borrows from Basil RINGROSE's account of Bartholomew SHARP's ventures during the 1680s. At JUAN FERNÁNDEZ, the pirates accidentally maroon the Indian WILLIAM (called David by Michener).

Along the way, the pirates capture a Spanish GALLEON carrying silver to Panama. Their captives include the daughter of the current Ledesma governor of Cartagena. Ned falls in love with the girl, but Uncle Will intervenes to prevent their marriage and also warns him away from Mompox.

The pirates make it to Barbados. Ned marries a local girl and opens a tavern, while Will enlists with Dutch pirates. Henry Morgan, now Jamaica's governor, arrests Will and sends him to Cartagena. Because Will had protected his daughter, Governor Ledesma pardons him, and he settles down with a Spanish widow.

English raiders condemned their Spanish victims as monsters, who used treachery and torture to monopolize the Americas. Authors of pirate fiction also portray all Englishmen as brave heroes, all Spaniards as villains deserving to die. Charles Kingsley's WESTWARD HO! forcefully preached this message, as do more recent authors, such as Rafael SABATINI and Dudley POPE. Michener, in contrast, finds heroes and villains on both sides of the English-Spanish battle.

CARLO EMMANUELE I *(Italian ruler; Mediterranean; 1562–1630)* Duke of Savoy from 1580, Carlo Emmanuele I unsuccessfully tried to enlarge his dominions by maneuvering between France and Spain. An enemy of the dukes of Tuscany, he sought to build up Villefranche and Nice as rivals to their port at LIVORNO, which prospered from fencing pirate booty.

Copying a policy of Fernando I dei MEDICI of Tuscany, Carlo Emmanuele opened Villefranche and Nice as "free ports" about 1611. Pirate booty was freely purchased and even stored in bonded warehouses. Peter EASTON received sanctuary at Villefranche in 1613 and lived as a wealthy courtier, but most of his men gradually drifted to other pirate havens.

CARRACK *(sailing ship; 16th through early 17th centuries)* The largest ship of its time, often reaching 1,200 tons, used by the Spanish and Portuguese for long commercial voyages to India, China, and the Americas. Like the three-masted CARAVEL, carracks were square-rigged on the fore and main masts and lateen-rigged on the mizzen. But they were larger, wider, and more robust than the caravel and carried very high fore- and aftcastles. The carrack was replaced by the GALLEON, which gained maneuverability by eliminating the high forecastle.

Obviously, all sea raiders hoped to capture an East Indian carrack carrying gold, jewels, and rare Oriental goods. But an individual pirate ship was powerless against these towering giants, whose guns could fend off even entire fleets of attackers. In 1587, Sir Francis DRAKE took the heavily laden *San Filippe* by surprise, approaching her without any distinguishing flags. He identified himself when he was so close that the carrack fired harmlessly over the tops of his little ships. The MADRE DE DIOS was captured by four English vessels in 1592 only after a hard fight. Two years later, the *Cinco Chagas* beat off the earl of CUMBERLAND's powerful force.

CARSTEN, JAN *(Barbary corsair; Mediterranean; 1608)* A Fleming (Belgian) and one of John WARD's captains at TUNIS. Commanding three warships, he was killed battling Venetian galleys off Modone in March 1608.

CARTAGENA *(treasure port; Caribbean; founded 1533)* A city between Panama and Venezuela, now part of Colombia. Cartagena soon became a major port, and it was one of only three cities visited by the annual TREASURE FLEETS between Spain and the Americas. In addition to valuable tropical products, the galleons collected gold and emeralds from provinces south of the city as well as pearls from the stations near Margarita Island and RIO DE LA HACHA. Many merchants from Guatemala likewise shipped their products to Cartagena to avoid buccaneers in the Gulf of Honduras.

This wealthy port attracted raiders from an early date. French corsairs sacked Cartagena in 1543 and perhaps also in 1549. Sir John HAWKINS bombarded the town in 1568, and Sir Francis DRAKE burned many buildings in 1586. Following Drake's attack, Spanish authorities designed strong defenses, with construction continuing during the 17th century.

Taking full advantage of the city's location, the Spaniards created a nearly impregnable fortress. Cartagena is located on a narrow spit of land between the sea and an arm of a wide, deepwater bay. An attack could not be mounted from the ocean side. The sea's bottom rises very gradually, so that ships could not approach within cannon range. A heavy surf breaks over the shallows and hidden reefs, making the shore dangerous even for small boats.

A hilly island, named Tierra Bomba, blocked the entrance to the bay. Ships originally could enter through two narrow channels on either side of Tierra Bomba—Boca Grande on the north and Boca Chica on the south. Boca Grande was filled in and served as a causeway linking Tierra Bomba with the walled city. The only passage into the harbor was the narrow Boca Chica channel, treacherous for vessels without local pilots.

A coral wall surrounded the city. Three massive bastions dominated the Boca Chica passage, and a convent east of the city (La Popa) also was fortified. The causeway and bridges linking the town to the mainland passed over the island of Imanie (Getsemaní), which also was enclosed with stout walls.

Because of its strong defenses, Cartagena was the only major Spanish port never attacked by the BUCCANEERS. It was taken in 1697 by a large expedition combining French naval forces and pirates. A British naval fleet was driven off after six weeks in 1741. Colombian rebels captured the city in 1815 and 1821 only after sieges lasting many months.

(See also CARTAGENA, SACK OF; SELECTED BIBLIOGRAPHY: Rogoziński, *Caribbean*; Wood, *Spanish Main*.)

CARTAGENA, SACK OF *(naval-buccaneer assault; Caribbean; 1697)* The French navy was joined by 650 BUCCANEERS during the third-largest pirate raid in the Americas. (Sir Henry MORGAN led about 2,000 to Panama in 1671. Edward DAVIS commanded about 1,000 in 1685.) Although the city yielded a rich booty, the buccaneers saw little reward. The naval commanders cheated them, and an enemy fleet captured much of their own plunder.

During the Nine Years' War (1688–1697), France fought England, the Netherlands, and Spain. Their Ca-

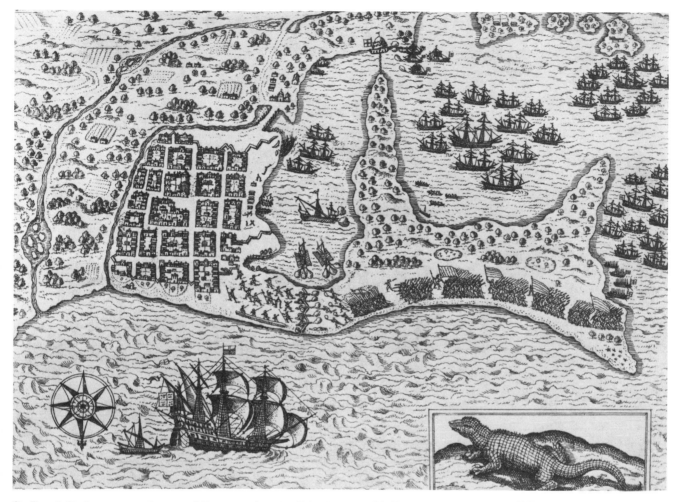

Sir Francis Drake captures the city of Cartagena (now in Colombia) in 1586. From Theodorus de Bry, *Collectiones . . . Americae pars VIII* (1599).

ribbean colonists carried out plunder raids against enemy islands. England and France also issued PRIVATEERING commissions on a grand scale, allowing private captains to devastate enemy merchantmen. Jean Du Casse, the governor of Saint Domingue, urged the conquest of Spanish Santo Domingo. However, the French government preferred one final plunder raid. With the war drawing to a close, French officials saw a golden opportunity to grab booty without fear of reprisals.

Cartagena was an inviting target, rich in hoarded wealth. The city's fortifications had scared off invaders, and it had last been attacked by Sir Francis DRAKE in 1586. Cartagena was a main port for the Spanish TREASURE FLEETS, and a timely assault might catch them in the harbor. The raid was organized as a business venture, with private individuals investing against a share of the booty.

In March 1689, Admiral Jean de Pointis (1645–1709) arrived at Saint Domingue with 10 warships and nine smaller craft holding 4,000 seamen and soldiers. The colonists supplied a separate 11-ship squadron. Four vessels carried about 300 local soldiers and colonists and 180 black slaves. Seven pirate warships held 650 buccaneers

under Captains Pierre, Blout, Galer, Pays, Macary, Cottuy, and Sales.

The arrogant Baron de Pointis infuriated the buccaneers, but Du Casse convinced them to stay with the fleet. To appease the pirates, Du Casse insisted upon a written agreement regarding booty. De Pointis quickly promised that the Saint Domingue forces would receive the same share as the king's troops.

The raiders arrived at Cartagena on April 13. The city was built on a landlocked bay with one narrow entrance. Massive forts guarded the city and harbor, but the Spanish garrisons were far under strength. In addition, none of the bastions could communicate with the others or with troops inside the city. Working together, the buccaneers and French soldiers took each of the forts in turn.

The causeways and bridges connecting the town to the mainland passed through the fortified island suburb of Imanie. De Pointis bombarded Imanie with 27 cannon and six immense mortars. On April 30, Du Casse and the buccaneers led the charge through a breach in the walls. During a fierce house-to-house battle, hundreds of defenders and at least 60 Frenchmen died.

French buccaneers loot Cartagena in 1697. Illustration by Howard Pyle in *Harper's Monthly Magazine,* December 1905.

Cartagena's governor and 2,800 Spanish troops surrendered on May 6, after de Pointis granted generous terms. The French were interested only in the richest treasures, and they wanted them in a hurry. The Spanish might send reinforcements to the town, and a British-Dutch squadron had pursued de Pointis from Europe.

The initial sack was carried out in an orderly and relatively decent way. Cartagena's inhabitants could keep half of their personal wealth, if they turned over an accurate inventory. To encourage the Spaniards to inform on each other, anyone reporting hidden treasure would receive 10 percent of its value.

The scheme worked well, and the Cartagenans brought their riches to the French in wagon loads. De Pointis said the take came to some 8 million *livres,* but Du Casse believed the real total exceeded 20 million. De Pointis stored the loot on his own warships, and he carefully stationed the buccaneers outside the city.

De Pointis had wanted to leave a garrison behind, but tropical diseases made this impossible. More than 800 of the soldiers from France fell ill, and most died. The Saint Domingue contingent now made up one-fourth of the total. When the fleet was ready to sail on May 29, Du Casse demanded one-fourth of the loot.

Du Casse expected to receive 2 million *livres,* and he was astonished when de Pointis handed over only 40,000. By offering the buccaneers the same share as the French

troops, de Pointis deliberately misled Du Casse. Almost all the booty was reserved for the investors and the crown. The regular soldiers had been promised only 10 percent of the first million and 5 percent of the rest, and de Pointis turned over a fourth of that amount. Even though Du Casse's followers had supplied their own vessels, de Pointis refused to increase their share before leaving on May 31.

Du Casse sailed the same day with two ships, promising the buccaneers that he would argue their case with the government. Most of the men from Saint Domingue decided to help themselves on the spot rather than waiting on French justice. Some captains wanted to follow and capture de Pointis' flagship, but the majority voted to plunder Cartagena for a second time.

The buccaneers occupied the city without resistance on June 1. They immediately locked the inhabitants in the main church, threatening unspeakable tortures unless they turned over 5 million *livres.* When the Cartagenans returned with a fraction of the ransom, the pirates invaded the town. They ruthlessly searched homes, looted churches, and robbed graves. However, there were relatively few cases of outright murder. About 1 million crowns were collected in four days. The buccaneers divided the gold and silver—giving the other raiders from Saint Domingue a smaller cut than themselves. They then sailed for Ile-à-Vache to divide up the slaves and other goods.

Meanwhile, some 30 English and Dutch ships under Admiral John Novalia caught up with de Pointis. The two fleets met south of Jamaica on June 6. Novalia pursued for several days, but the sturdier French ships outdistanced the enemy in a strong gale.

Not far from Cartagena, Novalia's fleet ran into the buccaneer squadron. Four warships attacked, and the freebooters fled in all directions. The English caught the ships of Captains Cottuy and Pierre loaded with most of the treasure. Another vessel was driven back to Cartagena and ran aground, and a fourth was wrecked on the coast of Santo Domingo. Captains Blanc (replacing Galer), Pays, Sales, Macary, and Blout made it back to Saint Domingue.

De Pointis brought home 7.7 million *livres* in gold and silver, more than a thousand pounds of emeralds, and many other jewels. Pleased with the entire operation, King Louis XIV awarded the buccaneers 400,000 *livres* instead of the paltry 40,000 de Pointis had offered. However, French officials embezzled most of the money before it reached Saint Domingue.

(See SELECTED BIBLIOGRAPHY: Crouse, *French Struggle;* Rogoziński, *Caribbean.*)

CASTLE OF COMFORT *(pirate ship; Atlantic, English Channel; active 1560s and 1570s)* A powerful 200-ton vessel highly prized as a private warship. The *Castle* was George FENNER's flagship during his 1566 gold and slaving expedition to West Africa. She was purchased in 1569 by Sir Henry Compton, who raided in the English Channel under a doubtful French PRIVATEERING license. In September 1571, the *Castle* was sailing with Jacques SORES' fleet, which captured a Portuguese prize in the Canaries. John GARRET used her as his flagship for West Indian raids in 1572 and possibly also in 1571.

Sir Richard GRENVILLE and William HAWKINS purchased the *Castle* in 1574 for their proposed South Seas adventure. When this scheme fell through, they used the *Castle* in the waters around England. Under various captains, she took many French and Spanish prizes in the 1570s, even though England was at peace with both nations.

CATALAN COMPANY (Spanish corsairs; Aegean Sea; 14th and 15th centuries)
A large band—some 7,000 men, many with families—of professional mercenaries from Catalonia in northeastern Spain. In 1303, the BYZANTINE emperor hired them to fight the Turks in Asia Minor. Following their leader's murder in 1305, they turned against the empire, plundering its inhabitants as they moved west and south. In 1311, they took Athens from its French lords.

Some Catalans became avid pirates, employing local sailors in their crews. Sometimes combining with Muslim corsairs from AYDIN in Asia minor, they attacked French and Italian merchant ships and the Venetian-controlled island of Euboea. Despite truces with Venice in 1319 and 1321, their sea raids continued even after a Florentine adventurer conquered their Athenian principality in 1388. Until about 1500, individual Catalan corsairs sailed from Greek ports and from islands, such as Lesbos, ruled by Italian families. They sometimes formed large squadrons, which carried out major raids against Chios in 1411 and Egypt in 1422 and 1438.

(See also FORMICAN, JAMES; MALOPOLUS, BARTHOLOMEW; TOCCO, ANTONIO DI.)

CAT-O'-NINE-TAILS (punishment; all oceans; 16th–19th centuries)
The special whip with which seamen were FLOGGED on naval and merchant vessels. Nine lengths of rope were tied to a rope or wooden handle. Each was perhaps a quarter-inch in diameter and from 18 inches to two feet long. Three knots were tied in each tail, but additional knots were added when a thief was flogged. Taken together, the tails weighed up to a pound.

CATRO, RICHARD (English pirate; Thames River; active 1613–1619)
A sailor from Kent known as "Dick of Dover." The English ADMIRALTY questioned him in 1613 about several piracies but could not prove its case. In 1619, he was overheard in a London tavern recruiting men to go down river. At Tilbury, his gang plundered a French ship carrying cloth and returned with the booty in two small boats. Catro was arrested, arraigned as "Dick of Dover," and sentenced to hang. A year later, a "Dick of Dover" led an attack on three more

Thames vessels. Either Catro had escaped from prison, or two persons had the same nickname.

CAUR ALI (Barbary corsair; Mediterranean; 1570s)
A Spaniard, he converted to Islam, became a corsair, and then supervised the governor's slave compound (BAGNIO) at ALGIERS. Describing Caur Ali's cruelty, Father HAËDO said he cut off a Christian's head at the mere rumor of a planned escape. Captured at the battle of LEPANTO in 1571, he was freed in a prisoner exchange.

CAVENDISH, THOMAS (English buccaneer; Caribbean, Pacific; 1560–1592)
Born into a land-owning family in Suffolk, Cavendish sought gold and glory during England's privateering war with Spain (1585–1603). He was the second English captain to circumnavigate the globe, following Sir Francis DRAKE.

In 1585, Cavendish financed and personally commanded a ship that joined Sir Richard GRENVILLE's expedition to Roanoke, Virginia. The fleet split up during storms, but the two vessels under Grenville and Cavendish reunited at Puerto Rico. On the way to Virginia, they captured two Spanish prizes and ransomed their passengers for large sums.

Cavendish probably broke even on this adventure. He immediately began to sell or mortgage his lands to prepare a plunder voyage, modeled on Drake's recent (1577–1580) Pacific raid. In July 1586, three small but heavily armed ships sailed with 123 men, some of whom had been with Drake. The little fleet reached the Pacific in March 1587 and headed north along the South American coast.

Cavendish found the Spaniards better organized than in Drake's day, and he failed to seize any of their silver ships. In all, his fleet captured 15 or so vessels and picked up a little bullion. Prisoners were brutally tortured with thumbscrews and other devices, and captured towns were burned to the ground. Whereas Drake usually had released captured ships, Cavendish burned his prizes and MAROONED their crews.

Cavendish's voyage was made by the lucky capture of a MANILA GALLEON carrying treasure from the Philippines to Acapulco. The English seized a ship at Acajutla, El Salvador, in July. Under torture, its French pilot revealed the expected arrival date of two galleons. In October, after sacking settlements along the Mexican coast, Cavendish reached Cape San Lucas, at the tip of the California peninsula. For the next month, his two remaining ships beat up and down the coast. (The smallest had been sunk for want of crew.)

On November 15, 1587, the English finally sighted the unarmed, 700-ton *Santa Ana*. The Spaniards put up an obstinate resistance and twice drove off boarding parties from the *Desire*, Cavendish's flagship. The *Desire's* cannon finally reduced the *Santa Ana* to ruins, and the prize was towed into a nearby bay. A Spanish priest was hanged from the mainmast yard, and other captives were

Thomas Cavendish's men slaughtering a large herd of sea lions during their 1587 raid on South America's Pacific coast. Their clothing and weapons are accurately depicted. From Theodorus de Bry, *Collectiones . . . Americae pars VIII* (1599).

stripped to the skin and marooned. The survivors managed to salvage the *Santa Ana*'s burned-out hulk and reached Acapulco the following January.

In addition to silks, perfumes, spices, and fine chinaware, the *Santa Ana* carried pearls and gold valued at 122,000 pesos. Her cargo had cost more than a million pesos in Manila, but the pirates could fit only part of the booty into their much smaller ship. A near mutiny among the suspicious seamen forced Cavendish to share the spoils on the spot. According to Spanish records, he took two-thirds and divided one-third among his men.

On November 19, Cavendish sailed east with the *Desire*, parting from his second ship, which was never seen again. After exploring many islands in the Philippines and other groups, he sailed to the south of Java and around the Cape of Good Hope, returning in September 1588. Cavendish's achievement brought him instant fame. He apparently squandered most of his captured wealth and borrowed money to outfit a second and larger expedition.

The *Leicester Galleon* and four other vessels sailed for South America in August 1591. Cavendish's luck had left him, and his weakness as a leader soon emerged. Purely by chance, the earlier venture had arrived at the Strait of Magellan during a mild season. This time, storms made the passage impossible. Cavendish developed fanciful grievances against the crew and his own following of gentlemen. His flagship abandoned the rest of the fleet, sailed back to Brazil, and made half-hearted and ineffective attacks on several ports. As he floundered about in the Atlantic, Cavendish died cursing his men as deserters.

(See also SELECTED BIBLIOGRAPHY: Gerhard, *Pirates*; Schurz, *Manila Galleon*; Spate, *Spanish Lake*.)

CAVO, GIOVANNI DE LO *(Italian corsair; Aegean Sea; active 1270s)*

Probably born on the island of Anáfi, he sailed from ANAIA on the Turkish coast. With the covert approval of Emperor MICHAEL VIII PALAEOLOGUS, he plundered Italian vessels as far north as Valona and Spinaritz in Albania.

Attracted by Lo Cavo's skills and daring, the emperor made him a naval captain and then commander of a squadron of 18 warships. In April 1277, the residents of

MENEMVASIA helped his warships plunder a Venetian merchant, who had sailed into the harbor with imperial permission. He became lord of Anáfi and RHODES by 1278 and—according to SANUDO—ended his career as commander of the entire imperial fleet.

(See also BYZANTINE EMPIRE; VENETIAN CLAIMS.)

CENTURIONE, NICCOLÒ (Italian pirate; Mediterranean; active 1513–1514) Sailing from RHODES with four ships carrying cannon and 400 men, Centurione caused serious losses to Genoese traders in the eastern Mediterranean.

(See also KNIGHTS HOSPITALERS.)

CERISOLA, BETTINO (Italian pirate; Mediterranean, 1496) A Genoese pirate operating with a 28-oar GALIOT and two smaller ships, Cerisola captured a Venetian trader near Alexandria, Egypt.

CERVANTES SAAVEDRA, MIGUEL DE (Spanish author; 1547–1616) The author of *Don Quixote de la Mancha* (published 1605–1615) and the most famous slave of the BARBARY corsairs. Little is know of Cervantes' youth. He went to Italy (largely under Spanish rule) in 1569, joined the regular army in 1570, and fought at LEPANTO in 1571.

A squadron under MEMMI "ARNAUT" REIS captured Cervantes as he returned to Spain in September 1575. He became the slave of MEMMI "DELLI" REIS, who sold him to HASAN VENEZIANO PASHA in 1577. Cervantes carried letters of recommendation that exaggerated his importance. This raised his RANSOM price but also protected him from physical mistreatment after four daring attempts to escape. He finally was freed in September 1580, after the REDEMPTIONISTS helped his family raise 500 gold escudos.

Cervantes' five years of captivity strongly influenced his literary works. While still a captive, he wrote to the Spanish secretary of state, lamenting the miseries of Christian slaves and calling for an invasion of ALGIERS. He returned to these themes in THE MANNERS OF ALGIERS, a play written between 1582 and 1587.

Cervantes earned little either from his plays or from the novel *La Galatea* (1585). He also was unsuccessful as a government purchasing agent in Seville (1588–1597). He finally achieved fame in 1605 with the first part of *Don Quixote*. It includes THE CAPTIVE'S TALE about a slave who escapes from Algiers.

In 1615, Cervantes published eight *comedias* (plays in verse) and eight one-act farces. Never staged in the author's lifetime, the comedias are seldom performed today. Three of the eight draw upon the author's remarkably persistent memories of his captivity 30 years earlier—THE SLAVE PRISONS OF ALGIERS, THE GALLANT SPANIARD, and *The Great Queen (La Gran Sultana)*.

CHAEREAS AND CALLIRHOE, THE ADVENTURES OF (Greek novel; second century) A ROMANCE by CHARITON written in the second century

A.D. and the oldest complete novel in any European language. Chariton writes in a relatively restrained style and quickly advances his plot. The major characters, including the pirate chief Theron, are well developed with distinct personalities.

An incredibly beautiful young boy (Chaereas) and girl (Callirhoe) live in Syracuse on Sicily during the fifth century B.C. They meet at a religious festival, immediately fall deeply in love, and marry. Callirhoe's disappointed admirers tell Chaereas she is unfaithful, stirring up his latent jealousy. In a rage, Chaereas kicks at Callirhoe, who is pregnant. She appears to be dead and is buried in the family tomb while Chaereas laments.

These opening scenes set the stage for the pirate kidnapping found in every Greek romance. Callirhoe had only fainted and is not really dead. Theron, a daring ARCHPIRATE, finds the girl alive when he robs her tomb and carries her off to Miletus in Asia Minor (present-day Turkey). Chariton portrays Theron as a cold and calculating villain. During Callirhoe's funeral procession, Theron is amazed by the wealth buried with the dead girl. He and his cut-throat band stake everything on one night's work of tomb-robbing, a horrible crime to the ancient Greeks.

While they are digging, Callirhoe awakens from a state of suspended animation. The other villains try to convince Theron to kill the girl. She is the only witness to their crime, and DEAD MEN TELL NO TALES. But Theron does not listen to his men and the pirates sail east with the beautiful captive and all of the gold. On the way, Theron ponders the risks involved in selling a girl who obviously belongs to a noble family. The archpirate convinces the other brigands to change course for Miletus, where he knows many people.

Theron cannot sell Callirhoe openly, since he has no legal proof he owns her. He sneaks into Miletus and runs into Leonas, chief steward to Dionysus, the city's widowed governor. Leonas agrees to consider buying Callirhoe. When Theron brings Callirhoe to Dionysus' palace, Leonas is struck by her beauty and pays a high price. The governor returns, also falls for Callirhoe, and forces her to marry him.

Theron and his men sail away for Crete before Leonas and Dionysus can find out that they've been tricked. A storm drives them into the Ionian Sea, the winds die down, and the pirates die of thirst on the motionless boat. Theron alone survives by stealing water from his dying comrades.

Somewhat later, Chaereas, who has discovered that Callirhoe's tomb is empty, sails in search of her. He comes upon the corsairs' derelict ship and finds the treasure previously buried with Callirhoe. Chaereas rescues Theron and takes him back to Syracuse, whose rulers investigate the strange incident. The crafty buccaneer almost convinces the court that he had been an innocent passenger on the corsairs' ship. However, a fisherman remembers seeing Theron in Syracuse before

Callirhoe's burial. Under torture, the archpirate confesses his crimes and is impaled on a spear in front of Callirhoe's tomb. However, Chareas and Callirhoe suffer through many other adventures before they are happily reunited.

CHAMBRAY, JEAN FRANÇOIS (Knight of Malta; Mediterranean; 1687–1756) The Knights' last outstanding captain, he saw combat soon after arriving at MALTA in 1700. Commanding a sailing ship, he defeated an Egyptian vessel near the island of Lampedusa in 1704, battled Tunisian warships in 1706, was wounded during the Algerian conquest of Oran in 1708, and captured a much larger Tripolitan warship in 1723. In 1732, during one of the order's last raids in the Levant, his squadron took a rich merchant ship near Egypt. He became governor of Gozo and wrote an autobiography, which remains unpublished.

CHANG PAO (Chinese pirate; South China Sea; 1786?–1822) A fisherman's son captured by pirates, he joined their ranks about 1801. The homosexual lover and adopted son of CHENG I, Chang became an influential and popular captain in Cheng's large Red Flag Fleet. When Cheng died in 1807, his widow Cheng I SAO took power and became Chang's lover.

Cheng I Sao controlled both the Red Flag Fleet and the larger pirate confederation Cheng had founded in 1805. Totally loyal to Sao, Chang managed day-to-day operations. He commanded in battle from a large seagoing JUNK carrying more than 40 cannon, two firing 24-pound shot.

Chang's pirates defeated every force sent against them. In July 1808 and July 1809, they destroyed Chinese naval squadrons protecting the Pearl River passage between Macao and Canton. In September 1809, they drove off two Portuguese warships sent in pursuit after European vessels were attacked near Macao.

Chang took more than 100 warships up the Pearl's main channel in August 1809, while KUO P'O-TAI's Black Flag Fleet attacked in the inner passage. Towns and villages resisting ransom demands were burned to the ground. More than 10,000 were killed, and thousands of women and children were taken captive. Chang was finally driven away by a British man-of-war. In November, he rejoined Cheng I Sao near Lantao Island, where the pirates beat off a fleet that included five Portuguese vessels.

The Chinese pirate empire suddenly collapsed at the end of 1809. Jealous of Chang's involvement with Cheng I Sao, Kuo P'o-tai refused to join in the battle near Lantao. To punish Kuo, Chang attacked his Black Flag Fleet in December and was badly defeated. Soon after, Kuo surrendered to the Chinese government.

Chang continued to attack Chinese and European shipping while he negotiated his own pardon. After some months, Cheng I Sao convinced the authorities to grant exceptionally generous terms. In April 1810, Chang and Sao surrendered the entire Red Fleet—260 junks carrying 14,000 crewmen and 1,000 cannon. Chang became an officer in the Chinese army, received a large sum of money, and was allowed to keep more than 20 junks. Soon after, he formally married Cheng I Sao.

Chang had a successful military career. In May 1810, he took part in an expedition that captured or killed the leaders of the other pirate fleets. When the Cantonese complained about his presence in their city, Chang was transferred to another province and later was promoted to colonel. At his death in 1822, he commanded the military forces on the Pescadores Islands near Taiwan.

An expert seaman and a bold tactician, Chang was an impartial leader who earned his followers' respect. With a tendency to fat, he dressed flamboyantly in a purple silk robe and black turban. He had dignified manners and used alcohol and other pleasures sparingly. He was devoutly religious, set up a temple on his flagship, and protected temples and priests on shore. The pirates believed the gods protected him and gave him superhuman powers.

(See also SELECTED BIBLIOGRAPHY: Murray, *Pirates*.)

CHARIDEMUS OF OREUS (Greek freebooter; Aegean Sea; died 333 B.C.) The adventurous Charidemus tried piracy before making his fortune as a mercenary soldier. He was born in Oreus (Histiaea), a city (on Euboea Island) allied with Sparta against Athens. From 378 to 376, Charidemus was an infantryman and then became the captain of a pirate boat preying upon Athenian shipping.

By 367, Charidemus reappeared as the leader of a body of mercenaries on land. For the next 10 years, he fought alternatively for the Athenians and for their enemies. While unemployed in 362, Charidemus tried to join up with pirates operating from Thrace in northern Greece, but his ship was captured by the Athenian fleet.

From 357, Charidemus fought as an Athenian general against Macedonia. When ALEXANDER THE GREAT sought his death in 335, he fled to Persia and worked for King Darius. According to legend, Darius executed Charidemus in 333 because of his plainspoken criticism of the Persian military.

CHARITON (Greek novelist; second century) Author of CHAEREAS AND CALLIRHOE, in which he describes himself as a secretary or assistant to Athenagoras, a lawyer resident in Aphrodisias (modern Kehre), a city in CARIA.

CHARLEVOIX, PIERRE FRANÇOIS-XAVIER DE (French historian; 1682–1761) A Jesuit priest who lived on Saint Domingue (modern-day Haiti) from 1717 to 1722. His *Histoire de l'isle espagnole ou de S. Domingue* (*History of Hispaniola also called Saint Dominque*) was published at Paris in two volumes (1730–1731). It describes BUCCANEER raids during the prior century and contains details not preserved by other authors. Generally

his statements are accurate. There is a Spanish translation by Roberto Guzmán and Gustavo Amigo (Santo Domingo, Dominican Republic: Editora de Santo Domingo, 1977).

CHENG CH'I *(Chinese pirate; South China Sea; 1760–1802)* Operating near the border with Vietnam, Cheng Ch'i (Cheng Yao-Huang) created a large gang bound to him by personal loyalty. At the urging of CH'EN T'IEN-PAO, he joined rebel forces in Vietnam with the rank of general in 1788. The pirates prospered by raiding Chinese shipping, but they also supported rebel assaults during yearly campaigns.

Cheng Ch'i and many other pirates went back to China after another faction defeated the Vietnamese rebels in 1801. Ch'en T'ien-pao persuaded him to return with 200 junks. After failing to recapture Hue, Cheng Ch'i shared the rebel defeat at Hanoi in July. The winning faction captured and beheaded him at Chiang-p'ing six weeks later. After some months of confusion, his cousin CHENG I emerged as the main pirate leader.

CHENG CHIH-LUNG *(Chinese pirate; South China Sea; active about 1625–1646)* From Fukien Province, Cheng Chih-Lung ran off to sea. He learned Portuguese and Dutch, was baptized as a Christian in Macao (as Nicholas Iquan), and then worked for a prominent Fukien merchant. About 1623, he married a Japanese woman near Nagasaki, who gave birth to KOXINGA.

Cheng left Japan soon after and operated from Taiwan and Amoy Island before returning to Fukien. By about 1630, he controlled the Fukien coast and was virtual overlord of the province. His fleet engaged in foreign trade and piracy and sold protection to other merchants. Unable to suppress him, the Ming emperor ruling southern China appointed Cheng "Admiral in Charge of Pirate Suppression."

The invading Manchus drove the Ming rulers out of their capital at Nanking in 1644. For a time, Cheng set up a Ming emperor in his own province of Fukien. However, he later came to terms with the advancing Manchu armies, and the puppet emperor was killed or committed suicide in 1646. Cheng's plot backfired, for the Manchus imprisoned him at Beijing.

CHENG I *(Chinese pirate; South China Sea; 1765–1807)* One of the master pirates of all time, Cheng I (Ching Yih, Cheng Yao-I, Cheng Wen-Hsien) created a powerful confederation controlling the sea lanes from Hong Kong to the Vietnamese border. Born into a family practicing piracy for several generations, Cheng fought with rebel forces in Vietnam. Returning to China in 1801, he made himself leader of the pirates in Kwangtung Province.

In 1805, Cheng brought other pirate leaders into an alliance. Six fleets flew banners with different shapes and colors—red, black, white, green, blue, and yellow. Although independent, the different gangs cooperated to prevent quarrels over booty. Each fleet cruised in specific sea lanes, usually located close to the leader's native place. Cheng's own group, the Red Flag Fleet, had 200 JUNKS and 20,000 to 40,000 men and continued to grow. By 1807, he commanded more than 600 junks near Hong Kong alone.

Cheng's confederation set up permanent bases at coastal villages and on uninhabited islands. Operating in organized squadrons, the pirates devastated trading boats and fishing craft and easily captured large ocean-going junks. They plundered villages, markets, and government forts, seizing cannon and gunpowder. By 1806, virtually every Chinese vessel passing the coast paid protection money. Merchants and government officials fenced their booty and furnished supplies, and the pirates also worked with criminals and secret societies.

Although Cheng's corsairs avoided large European vessels, they captured foreign sailors and held them for ransom. European vessels could not get supplies, and the Portuguese city of Macao was besieged for several weeks in 1804. Four Portuguese warships unsuccessfully chased after the pirates, and the British navy offered to protect local trade.

To prevent foreign interference, a Chinese general was sent to attack the pirates. In September 1805, 80 gunboats assaulted pirate bases in Kuang-chou Bay, near Vietnam. Only 26 vessels—a tiny fraction of the pirate's strength—were captured or destroyed. Since force had failed, the general gave a free pardon to those that surrendered. Perhaps 3,000 came in, before the government stopped offering pardons in December 1805.

Cheng died at the height of his success in 1807. One story relates that he was blown overboard and drowned in a gale. In another version, he was killed while fighting to recapture Vietnam for his former allies. His wife, Cheng I SAO, succeeded him as commander of the Red Flag Fleet and leader of the pirate confederation. Little is known about his personal appearance. Some European documents say, probably incorrectly, that he was a hunchback.

(See also CH'EN T'IEN-PAO.)

CH'EN T'IEN-PAO *(Chinese pirate; South China Sea; active 1788–1801)* A fisherman from Kwangtung Province who moved to Vietnam and enlisted with rebels in 1783. As the civil war dragged on, Ch'en took command of thousands of Chinese pirates working for the rebellion. Under his leadership, the pirates became a quasi-military organization with a structured chain of command.

From their Vietnamese bases, Ch'en's followers raided Chinese shipping and coastal villages. They were more effective as pirates than as a military force, and their Vietnamese allies were defeated by rival factions. Ch'en surrendered and was pardoned by Chinese authorities in November 1801.

(See also CHENG CH'I.)

CHETWOOD, WILLIAM RUFUS (British novelist; died 1766) Chetwood was a bookseller and the prompter at the Drury Lane Theatre. In addition to plays and a history of the contemporary stage, he wrote several popular novels of adventure and piracy. These include: *The Voyages . . . of Captain Richard Falconer* (1720), THE VOYAGES AND ADVENTURES OF CAPTAIN ROBERT BOYLE (1726), and *The Voyages . . . of William Owen Gwin Vaughan* (1736).

CHIDLEY, JOHN (English adventurer; Atlantic; 1565–1589) The leader of an unfortunate plunder venture, Chidley was born into an influential Devonshire family and was related to Sir Walter RALEIGH. (His aunt had married one of Raleigh's half-brothers.) He fought with distinction against the Spanish Armada in 1588.

In 1589, Chidley sold his lands and gambled on a voyage to South America's Pacific coast, hoping to imitate Thomas CAVENDISH's capture of a Spanish treasure ship. Although there were other investors—including Queen Elizabeth and Sir John WATTS—Chidley put up most of the money and was ruthlessly cheated by his suppliers.

Three large ships and two PINNACES sailed in August with Chidley commanding the flagship, the *Wildman*. His captains included experienced seamen, such as Benjamin WOOD and Abraham Kendall. Early in the voyage, the *Robin* became lost and went on alone toward Magellan's Strait. Failing to make it to South America, the ship ran out of food and turned back. Only six of 91 crewmen remained alive when the *Robin* was wrecked on the French coast.

The remaining ships and pinnaces sailed south along the African coast. Disease killed many of the men, and Chidley died in November. Benjamin Wood deserted and brought the *White Lion* safely back to England. The *Wildman* and her pinnace managed to reach Trinidad, where the survivors recuperated from the voyage. Kendall and others deserted in the pinnace and made it to Ireland, and the *Wildman* also returned in June.

(See also SELECTED BIBLIOGRAPHY: Andrews, *Elizabethan Privateering*.)

CH'ING YA-LING (Chinese pirate; South China Sea; 1857) See BROWN, EDWARD.

CHIVERS (SHIVERS), DIRK (Dutch pirate; Indian Ocean, Red Sea; active 1694–1699) In about January 1694, Dirk (sometimes Richard) Chivers sailed from Rhode Island on the *Portsmouth Adventure*. Under Joseph FARRELL, the *Adventure* helped Henry EVERY capture two rich prizes in the Red Sea in June 1695. On the way home, the *Adventure* was wrecked on Mayotte in the Comoro Islands. Every rescued Farrell and others, but Chivers remained at Mayotte. Late in 1695, he enlisted on the 28-gun *Resolution*. After some months without success, the crew elected Chivers captain and changed the ship's name to *Soldado*.

Chivers commanded the *Soldado* for three years and took rich prizes. In consort with John HOAR, Chivers seized two East India Company ships. One captive, Captain Sawbridge, suggested that the pirates ransom the prizes instead of destroying them. When the governor of Aden would not pay, the ships were burned. Chivers' men silenced Captain Sawbridge's constant whining by sewing up his lips with a sail needle.

In November 1696, Chivers boldly sailed into the harbor at Calcutta, seized four ships, and demanded £10,000. "We acknowledge no country," he wrote, "having sold our own, and as we are sure to be hanged if taken, we shall have no scruple in murdering and destroying if our demands are not granted in full." Despite this threat, the governor delayed payment. When 10 Indian vessels sailed into port, the pirates retreated after burning two of their prizes.

Chivers repaired the *Soldado* at SAINT MARY'S ISLAND during the summer of 1697. In April 1698, the British ship *Sedgwick* was captured. The pirates wanted to take over the *Sedgwick*, but her captain kept his ship "by merry management of a bowl of punch." In September, Chivers and Robert CULLIFORD jointly captured the *Great Mohammed* and some £130,000 in cash. Chivers and his crew of about 200 transferred to their prize, renamed the *New Soldado*, and went back to Saint Mary's.

The pirates sank the *New Soldado* to block the harbor when four English battleships arrived in September 1699. Chivers and some others accepted a royal pardon and arranged passage home on the merchant ship *Vine*.

(See also GLOVER, ROBERT; NORTH, NATHANIEL; SELECTED BIBLIOGRAPHY: Grey, *Pirates*; Jameson, *Privateering*; Ritchie, *Kidd*.)

CHRISTIAN PIRATES See KNIGHTS HOSPITALERS; SAINT STEPHEN, KNIGHTS OF.

CHUI-APOO (Chinese pirate; South China Sea; died 1850) After raiding with SHAP-NG-TSAI, Chui-apoo commanded 40 JUNKS and several thousand pirates based in Bias Bay (Ta-ya Wan), near Hong Kong. His fleet mainly raided east to Amoy Island, while Shap-ng-tsai controlled the sea lanes to the west. Shipping and coastal villages paid protection money to avoid attack.

While visiting Hong Kong in February 1849, Chui-apoo murdered two British officers who insulted him. In September and October, British warships destroyed his fleet in two encounters near Bias Bay. Although he fled to Chinese territory, Chui-apoo was kidnapped by the British and taken to Hong Kong. He committed suicide while in prison.

CIGALA (Italian corsair; Mediterranean; active 1551–1561) Probably from Genoa, Cigala sailed from Sicilian ports in a nimble GALLEON, which resembled a merchant ship but carried 300 men and 22 guns. He took several rich Venetian and French prizes near Cyprus and

CRETE from 1557 to 1559. In 1560, he contributed two galleys to the Spanish force defeated at DJERBA. He escaped the general defeat but was captured the following year by one of TURGUT's squadrons. (His beautiful galleon, commanded by a relative, ran aground on the Greek coast in 1561.)

Sent by Turgut to Constantinople, Cigala's 16-year-old son converted to Islam in the vain hope of securing his father's liberty. He eventually rose, as Sinan Pasha, to admiral of the Ottoman fleet. In 1598, he visited Messina under a flag of truce and received his mother and other relatives on board his flagship.

CILICIA *(pirate haven; Mediterranean; 150–67 B.C.)* Home to the largest and most aggressive pirate fleets of ancient times—possibly the largest pirate bands ever known. Through their skills in organization, seamanship, and warfare, the Cilician corsairs controlled the entire Mediterranean for more than two decades and humbled the mighty Roman empire.

The name Cilicia designated the southern coast of Asia Minor (present-day Turkey). Rich plains border the sea to the west in Cilicia Pamphylia. But the east—from Coracesium (Alanya) to Seleucia (Silife)—is dominated by the Taurus mountain range, which falls steeply into the sea. Throughout history, gangs of land brigands preyed on this wild and unfertile region, justly called "Craggy Cilicia" (Cilicia Tracheia). During the first century B.C., it also became the main HAVEN for Mediterranean sea robbers.

Cilicia seems as if designed to be a pirate fortress. Merchant ships traveling from the west to Syria, Palestine, or Egypt had to pass through the channel between Cilicia and Cyprus. The bold, precipitous foreland of the rocky coastline hindered approach by large warships while providing the pirates with hidden refuges and safe anchorages.

On these rugged crags or on the small islands just off the coast, the ancient corsairs built invulnerable fortifications. Coracesium, their most important stronghold, was perched on a steep ridge connected to the mainland only by a narrow isthmus. From their high lookouts, the corsairs could easily detect the approach of any vessel.

The Cilicians practiced wrecking and piracy from early on. However, to protect their commerce the kings of Egypt and the Seleucid kings of Syria patrolled the Cilician coast and held down the corsairs until about 150 B.C. For the next 70 years, piracy flourished unchecked. Its extraordinary growth was due to the misguided policies of the expanding Roman Empire. The Romans destroyed the navies of the existing empires but did not send Roman fleets to replace them.

By the Treaty of Apamea (188), the Romans expelled the Seleucid Empire from the western part of Asia Minor. More important, Rome no longer permitted the Seleucid navy to cruise along the coast of Craggy Cilicia, which

became practically independent. For a few decades, warships from RHODES continued to patrol the coastline, but Roman policies also weakened Rhodian sea power from the 150s.

While the pirates never ceased robbing merchant ships at sea, slave raids became their most lucrative business. Led by ISIDORUS, they extended their reach by 100 B.C. to the entire eastern Mediterranean. Their preferred prey was the coastal villages of the decaying Seleucid Empire, from eastern Asia Minor south to Egypt. The raiders let wealthy captives buy their freedom. But they carried away many thousands of peasants to slave markets at CRETE, DELOS and the Cilician town of Side (Selimiye).

Hoping to profit from the slave trade, many cities openly allied with the Cilicians and bribed them not to carry off their citizens. The pirates became the chief suppliers of skilled slaves to wealthy Roman senators. As long as they mainly raided Syrian territory, Rome took no steps to stop the pirates and allowed them to sell their captives—even those known to be free men—at slave auctions.

As in other great ages of piracy, men from many nations joined the corsair bands, attracted by their success and immunity from prosecution. Looking for fresh territories to raid, the growing pirate fleets began to attack shipping in the Aegean Sea and the western Mediterranean. Becoming bolder, they now attacked Italian and Roman tax collectors, merchants, and bankers.

After 50 years of indifference, the Roman government decided to take serious measures against the pirates. But they were now so strong that a bitter war raged for 35 years (102–67 B.C.) before Roman armies finally conquered the corsairs' Cilician bases. In 102 the Roman Senate sent a fleet under Marcus ANTONIUS (1). For the next two years, the Roman forces carried out naval operations along the Cilician coast. This expedition mainly sought to harass the pirates, and Rome did not set up a permanent base.

During the same years, the Senate passed the Pirate Law (101–100), which ordered kings and city-states in the eastern Mediterranean to close their harbors to pirates. The Senate earlier (in 104) had decreed that governors of Roman provinces should liberate all Roman allies of free birth now in slavery. The Pirate Law seriously threatened the corsairs, since it prevented them from selling their captives at city slave auctions. From then on, the pirates were Rome's bitter enemies.

In 89, MITHRIDATES, king of Pontus in northeastern Asia Minor, went to war to expel the Romans from the east. The Pontic armies soon took Asia Minor, and Mithridates made plans to march west into Greece. During the summer of 88, he personally led an unsuccessful siege of Rhodes, which had the only navy available to the Romans. Late in the same year, Mithridates became an ally of the anti-Roman faction at Athens. He sent a small force to defend the city and central Greece until his main armies attacked Thrace and Macedonia in 87.

The Cilician corsairs fought with Mithridates against Rome, and they made up a major part of his naval forces. The key to Mithridates' strategies was supremacy at sea, which would prevent Roman attacks on his bases in Asia Minor. Since Rome did not maintain a fleet in the region, Mithridates had the only naval forces. But he could not use his own navy to attack the Romans. His armies needed every ship for other purposes—to blockade Rhodes and to carry soldiers and supplies across the Aegean to Greece. Mithridates made a firm alliance with the Cilician corsairs, who served as his auxiliaries in battle and raided Roman shipping throughout the Aegean and the Adriatic.

A fleet of corsairs led by MENOPHANES sacked the wealthy island of Delos. Pirates manned the cruisers that sank a Roman fleet in 86 outside Brindisi in southeastern Italy. The corsairs also controlled the Mediterranean east of Greece. Their forces harassed the Roman general LUCULLUS, who wasted two years (87–85) trying to hire warships in Syria and Egypt.

The Roman leader Sulla destroyed the Pontic armies in Greece during the summer of 86. By the Treaty of Dardana (85), Mithridates gave up all his European and Asian conquests. Sulla could defeat Mithridates' armies on land, but the Cilician corsairs remained in control of the seas. The number of corsair ships had vastly increased to the point that they resembled regular war fleets rather than robber bands.

Despite the treaty, Cilician corsairs continued to raid throughout the Aegean. On Turkey's western coast, they captured the cities of Iasus and Clazomenae and the island of SAMOS. They audaciously attacked the island of Samothrace—taking booty worth 1,000 TALENTS—while Sulla himself was encamped on the island.

During the next two decades, until Pompey destroyed them in 67, the pirates were at the height of their power. They again served as Mithridates' allies during his third war with Rome (74–66). After the Romans evicted Mithridates' forces from the Aegean in 72, the Cilician corsairs withdrew to the Black Sea port of Sinope (modern Sinop). SELEUCUS, put in command of Sinope's defenses, managed to hold off a Roman seige for almost a year (71–70).

Although the pirates again fought on Mithridates' side, they were now a wholly independent force that operated throughout the Mediterranean. The pirates controlled the entire coast of Cilicia, and they turned Coracesium into a powerful fortress. The merchants of Side and Attalea were deeply implicated in their crimes, and the pirate chieftain ZENOCTES ruled the western shores of the Pamphylian Gulf. Like their successors on the BARBARY COAST, the corsairs maintained their arsenals with captured slaves, chained to their tasks.

Cilicia remained their headquarters, but the pirates built fortified bases, watchtowers, and beacons along all the Mediterranean coasts. (Pompey claimed he captured 120 forts during his anti-pirate campaign in 67.) Thousands of men from every nation, including those of noble birth, joined the corsairs.

Some pirate bands were based away from Cilicia, but the Cilicians provided organization and leadership. As piracy became their permanent occupation, the corsairs formed themselves into a regular navy. They kept their vessels clean and sailed in squadrons under admirals (strategoi), who were obeyed like military generals. As a token of their own grandeur, some captains ornamented their ships with masts gilded at the bottom, sails woven of purple cloth (a color reserved for royalty), and oars plated with silver.

The cooperation among various pirate bands was remarkable. The different groups coordinated their attacks, sending each other money and reinforcements as required. In fact, noted historian Dio Cassius (writing about A.D. 220),

> this was one of the chief sources of their strengths, that those who paid court to any of them were honored by all, and those who came into collision with any of them were despoiled by all.

The pirates manned a thousand ships, including large warships with two and three tiers of oars. Because of their exceptional seamanship, they easily escaped pursuers. Unlike ordinary sailors, they could sail even during the stormy winter season. Having swept commerce from the seas, they raided far inland, taking walled towns by storm or siege. During the 20 years following the First Mithridatic War (86–67), the pirates, it is said, ravished 400 cities and captured most of the islands in the Aegean Sea. Carved inscriptions excavated by modern archeologists provide proof of their raids on many islands, including attacks on Aegina and Tenos and the sack of Delos by ATHENODORUS.

During these years, the Cilicians also marauded throughout the western Mediterranean. In 72 a Cilician fleet agreed to carry SPARTACUS and 2,000 of his men to Sicily. Cilician squadrons aided the Roman general Sertorius when he set up an independent kingdom in Spain in 81.

By 70, the corsairs had driven Roman warships and merchants from the seas. HERACLEO entered the harbor of Syracuse, the capital of Sicily. The corsairs terrorized both coasts of Italy. Ships could not put out from Brindisi in the south, and the pirates controlled the coasts around Naples and Rome itself. A pirate squadron captured and destroyed a naval fleet in the harbor at Ostia, the city's port.

High government officials and Roman nobles were kidnapped along the Appian Way, the main road to Rome. Noble Roman ladies were held to ransom, including the daughter of the Marcus Antonius who had led the Roman expedition against Cilicia in 102. (However, the pirates seized Julius CAESAR and CLODIUS PULCHER while they were traveling away from Rome.)

The Roman government did not totally ignore the Cilician threat during the 80s and 70s. However, the Romans always were more interested in power on land, and they left the sea to the ineffective efforts of their subjects and allies. A Roman army attacked the pirates in 83 but accomplished little. The Romans turned western Cilicia (Pamphylia) into a province in 80. SERVILIUS, its first governor (79–74), fought the pirates, Roman style—campaigning inland rather than attacking the corsairs along the coast. After Servilius left for Rome in 74, the senate gave Marcus ANTONIUS (2) supreme command of all Roman naval forces. Antonius ignored Cilicia and sent his armies to Crete, where they were decisively defeated.

In earlier centuries, Rome had succeeded in crushing smaller bands of pirates—in CRETE, ILLYRIA, and the TYRRHENIAN SEA—by attacking their land bases. But Rome's traditional strategies, followed by Servilius and Antonius, was useless against the powerful Cilicians. Only combined land and sea operations of unprecedented size stood any chance of defeating the corsairs.

The Cilician threat finally was broken in 67 by GNAEUS POMPEIUS, one of Rome's greatest generals. Rich and poor now united to demand drastic action; the corsairs had cut off all imports into the city, including the wheat that fed its hungry mobs. Rome had ignored (or even welcomed) the pirates when they supplied slaves for Roman estates. Now the capital of the world itself was under siege. Pompey's masterful campaign broke the corsairs' reign over the Mediterranean. Individual pirates or small bands occasionally sailed from Cilicia during the following centuries, but the region never again became a major haven.

CIRIFFO MORO *(Barbary corsair; Mediterranean; 1675)*   Ciriffo sailed from TUNIS. The KNIGHTS OF SAINT STEPHEN caught up with his squadron near Elba, captured his galley, enslaved its crew of 117, and freed 250 Christian oarsmen.

CLARK, WILLIAM *(English pirate; Atlantic, Mediterranean; active 1614–1615)*   A bosun's mate in the English Channel naval squadron, he turned pirate, operating out of MARMORA and raiding ICELAND with James GENTLEMAN. After Spanish forces captured Marmora in 1614, he moved to ALGIERS and possibly suggested Jan JANSSEN's raid on Iceland in 1627.

CLARKE, THOMAS *(English buccaneer; Caribbean; 1689)*   Clarke was among the captains raiding Maracaibo and Gibraltar, Venezuela, with Sir Henry MORGAN.

CLIFFORD, GEORGE   See CUMBERLAND, GEORGE CLIFFORD, THIRD EARL OF.

CLIPPERTON, JOHN *(Irish pirate; Pacific; died 1722)*   Blunt, rough, and hard-drinking, Clipperton was loyal to his employers and an excellent seaman

who crossed the Pacific in 1704 with a small 40-ton ship and few or no maps. Clipperton first invaded South America's Pacific coast in 1703 as third-in-command of William DAMPIER's *Saint George*. The raiders took little booty, the *Saint George* rotted away, and many men accused Dampier of cowardice.

In August 1704, Dampier gave Clipperton command of a small prize with a crew of 21. All the ammunition and many other supplies were transferred to Clipperton's vessel while the *Saint George* was careened for repairs, Clipperton went hunting, captured a stout 40-ton ship, and decided to go off on his own. After putting some of the ammunition ashore for Dampier's use, he sailed from Costa Rica on September 12.

Clipperton took two prizes near Nicaragua and ransomed one for 4,000 pesos. After crossing to the Philippine Islands in 54 days, Clipperton captured more merchant vessels off the Chinese coast. The crew divided the booty and split up at Macao, and Clipperton returned home in a Dutch ship.

In 1714 or 1715, while England and Spain were at peace, Clipperton commanded one of two pirate ships that passed Cape Horn and cruised up the Pacific coast. Off Paita, they seized two Spanish merchantmen with merchandise worth 400,000 pesos. A Peruvian warship captured one vessel in the Gulf of Panama, recovering the loot and carrying off the crew to be hanged at Lima. The other pirate ship, probably Clipperton's, fled northward and was captured off Mexico early in 1716. Clipperton somehow made it back to England.

In February 1719, Clipperton was sent to the Pacific with the 36-gun *Success* and a crew of 180. The expedition initially had been entrusted to George SHELVOCKE. When he proved unsatisfactory, the investors put Clipperton in charge but left Shelvocke as captain of his second ship. Infuriated by the demotion, Shelvocke soon gave Clipperton the slip, and the two captains did not meet again until January 1721. This caused great hardship for Clipperton and his crew, since Shelvocke's ship carried the liquor supply for both vessels.

Clipperton reached the rendezvous at the JUAN FERNÁNDEZ ISLANDS in September with many sick men. "With their dying breaths," one officer wrote, the men "continually [cursed] Captain Shelvocke for running away with their liquors." Clipperton waited for a month and left behind several messages for Shelvocke before heading for Peru.

In only a few weeks, Clipperton captured four rich prizes carrying luxury goods, silver, and slaves. The passengers on one prize escaped, having overpowered the English seamen as they rummaged through the cargo. Clipperton loaded the captured goods on another small prize and ordered her crew of 23 to sail for Brazil. They were captured and killed by Indians before they could undertake the dangerous journey around Cape Horn. In January 1720, Clipperton took a ship carrying the Marquis de Villa Roche, the former governor of Panama.

Although his family was freed, Villa Roche was kept on board and agreed to pay a large ransom.

Clipperton had little success during the rest of 1720, although he cruised from Nicaragua to Chile and back. He sacked Trujillo with little profit, took no prizes of any value, and was almost captured by three warships off Chile. Villa Roche, his Spanish captive, stirred up at least one mutiny and encouraged 11 men to desert at Cocos Island. Clipperton became as despondent as the surviving crewmen and began to drink heavily.

Clipperton finally ran into Shelvocke in January 1712 off the Mexican coast. He tried to convince Shelvocke to join in hunting for the MANILA GALLEON that sailed from Acapulco. Shelvocke, who had no intention of sharing his booty, refused to return to partnership. Clipperton and the *Success* sailed for China on September 17, with the Marquis de Villa Roche still on board. Hard hit by SCURVY (1), the few remaining crewmen could barely work the ship. When they reached Guam, Clipperton was too drunk to bring the *Success* into the harbor.

Perhaps because of his drinking, Clipperton trusted Villa Roche and allowed him to go ashore to pick up the ransom money. The Spanish governor instead arrested two English officers and began to fire on the *Success.* Clipperton lay drunk in his cabin, singing at the top of his voice and unable to move. A Lieutenant Cook took command, but the *Success* drifted onto the rocks and was severely damaged.

The *Success* managed to reach the Chinese port of Amoy, where Cook led a mutiny and demanded that the booty be divided. Clipperton's 15 shares were worth about £1,500. Ever faithful to the ship's owners, Clipperton sent them more than £6,000 on a Portuguese vessel. He sailed home in a Dutch ship and died a week after arriving in Ireland.

(See also SELECTED BIBLIOGRAPHY: Burney, *History;* Gerhard, *Pirates;* Kemp and Lloyd, *Brethren.*)

CLODIUS PULCHER *(Roman noble; Mediterranean; 92–52 B.C.).* An ambitious member of the high nobility, Clodius Pulcher sometimes allied with Julius CAESAR during the Roman civil wars. The lover of Caesar's wife, he caused a famous scandal in 61. Dressed as a woman, he entered Caesar's house during religious festivities open only to women.

Clodius was notorious for his arrogance as well as his physical beauty. When pirates from CILICIA captured Clodius, the king of Cyprus offered two TALENTS for his ransom. Clodius nursed an undying hatred against the king because he considered this enormous sum an insultingly low evaluation of his own worth. (Julius Caesar set his own ransom at 50 talents after he was captured by Cilician corsairs.)

CLOISE, PETER *(African-American buccaneer; Caribbean, Atlantic, Pacific; active 1679–1688)* Edward DAVIS took Cloise, an African slave, from his Spanish owner in about 1679. Cloise became a close comrade and accompanied Davis on his expeditions in the Caribbean and along South America's Pacific coast. He was still with Davis when he was arrested at Philadelphia in May 1688.

CLOTHING *(all oceans, all eras)* Common seamen all wore the same type of clothing, whether they served on pirate ships or on merchant and naval vessels. Before the 19th century, clothes were extremely expensive, and most sailors had only one outfit, which they wore day and night until it rotted off.

While fashions fluctuated rapidly among the wealthy, the dress of sailors changed more slowly. Seamen usually went barefoot. From the 1500s, they wore loose, baggy trousers cut off between the knees and ankle. Both practices served functional purposes. Bare feet can grip a slippery deck or ladder more surely than shoes. Short, loose-fitting pants allowed the body to move freely, and their extra material provided protection against rain and spray.

During good weather, sailors in the ancient Mediterranean generally went naked when aboard ship. Officers and sailors on shore wore a knee-length tunic—a one-piece garment something like a gown or long shirt—belted around the waist. Medieval working men, including sailors, wore similar tunics over hose—long stockings, which might be joined like modern "tights." During the 16th century, English sailors adopted extremely baggy trousers call *sloppes,* closed just below the knee. On shore, they added stockings and a hip-length tunic, which

Wearing "petticoat trousers," Blackbeard battles Captain Maynard. An illustration to *The Lives and Actions of the Most-Noted Highwaymen, Street-Robbers, [and] Pirates* (London, 1839), a compilation of Daniel Defoe's writings on crime.

evolved into a shirt when tucked into the trousers. Captains dressed much the same as crewmen while aboard ship but might adopt more elegant garb ashore.

Sir Water RALEIGH, Sir Francis DRAKE, Thomas CAVENDISH, Jacques SORES, François LE CLERC, and other gentlemen dressed in costumes appropriate to their rank. They wore either hose or a combination of hose and breeches (close-fitting or baggy trousers tied with ribbons or garters near the knee). Over these came padded doublets (like a stiff, form-fitting shirt), jackets, and cloaks. Colors were bright, and clothes were ornamented with embroidery and jewels. A wide ruff surrounded the neck, and almost everyone wore a beard and mustache.

Like other 17th-century seamen, Caribbean pirates wore loose pants cut off just below the knee, woolen stockings, and a thigh-length blouse or coat. Many wore "petticoat trousers." Very full and open at the bottom, these resembled a divided knee-length skirt or the garment called culottes. During the 18th century, sailors in the colder Atlantic favored wide, ankle-length pants, checked linen shirts, and hip-length blue or gray jackets. (Dutch seamen wore longer trousers and coats in cold climates.)

Most clothing was of heavy wool, but sailors also sewed their own out of worn sail canvas. The cattle-hunting BUCCANEERS of Hispaniola sometimes turned the hides into crude shirts, petticoat trousers, and miniskirts. Dark colors were normal, and clothes often were covered with tar as protection against cold and damp. Jack RACKHAM was unusual, Daniel DEFOE wrote, because he wore only pants and shirts of white cotton.

Since they had no change of clothing, pirates were dirty and ragged while aboard ship. On shore, some captains scandalized observers by wearing expensive clothes reserved for the gentry. CILICIAN leaders wore long tunics and togas like Roman nobles. In 1603, Christopher OLOARD insisted on being hanged in velvet and silk. Bartholomew ROBERTS dressed for battle in a crimson damask waistcoat and trousers, a hat with a red plume, and a gold chain and diamond cross.

Few pirate movies accurately reproduce the clothing of the era portrayed. In films set in Elizabethan England, the heroes are clean-shaven and dressed far too somberly at court. Movies about the Caribbean do not show pirates in "petticoat trousers." This is understandable, since historically accurate clothing would work against a film's message. THE SEA HAWK (3), for example, portrays Errol FLYNN as hypermasculine, and Elizabethan costumes look very effeminate to modern eyes. In the same way, villains like BLACKBEARD would seem ludicrous rather than evil if they appeared in voluminous petticoat trousers.

COATES, EDWARD (British pirate; Indian Ocean, Red Sea; active 1692–1693)
Commanding the *Nassau*, Coates visited SAINT MARY'S ISLAND, near MADAGASCAR, in October 1692. There he divided booty of £500 per man taken in the Red Sea. Either the *Nassau*

was lost soon after or Coates changed ships. In April 1693, he was captain of the *Jacob* when it landed at Long Island, New York. Coates bargained with Governor Benjamin Fletcher and received permission to dock at New York. Governor Fletcher demanded a £700 bribe but settled for ownership of the *Jacob*.

(See also BURGESS, SAMUEL; MAY, WILLIAM; SELECTED BIBLIOGRAPHY: Jameson, *Privateering*.)

COBB, WILLIAM (English pirate; Red Sea; active 1635–1637)
Late in 1634, London merchants bribed King Charles I to grant a secret PRIVATEERING commission. This allowed them to capture any ship sailing below the equator from any country that did not have a formal peace treaty with England. (The commission was needed, since East India Company vessels had orders to sink any pirates they met.) Captain Cobb received command of two vessels. William Ayres was captain of his flagship, the *Roebuck*; but David Jones, the sailing master, was the real authority on board.

The two vessels became separated, and one was wrecked in the Comoro Islands, northwest of MADAGASCAR. The *Roebuck* captured an Indian vessel in the Red Sea in April 1635, even though it had a pass from the East India Company. With Jones leading the way, the passengers and crew were horribly tortured.

The pirates careened the *Roebuck* at the Comoros. They were caught by a Company ship, which seized £10,000 in booty but let them escape. Two more Indian vessels were taken in 1636, and the pirates returned to England in May 1637 with £40,000 in booty. King Charles and the promoters took most of the loot, leaving about £10,000 to be shared by the officers and perhaps 50 crewmen. Cobb and Ayres were arrested, released on bail, and briefly imprisoned in 1643.

(See also SELECTED BIBLIOGRAPHY: Grey, *Pirates*.)

COBHAM, ERIC (fictional English pirate; Atlantic; early 1700s)
A cold-hearted monster, Cobham sailed from Canada with his vicious lover, Maria LINDSEY. Eighteenth-century documents do not mention Cobham's crimes. His improbable biography appeared in print in the 1920s, in books for tourists visiting Canada.

As a teenager at Poole, Cobham enlisted with a gang smuggling brandy from France to England. After two years in jail, he stole a bag of gold coins while working at an inn, purchased a small ship at Plymouth, and recruited a crew of desperados. On his first voyage, Cobham captured an East Indiaman carrying £40,000 in cargo. His gang scuttled the ship, drowned the crew, and sold their loot in France. Cobham returned to Plymouth and joined up with Maria Lindsey.

Cobham and Lindsey sailed to Canada and set up a fort as a secluded anchorage in Saint George's Bay, Newfoundland. For many years, their gang preyed on vessels carrying furs from Canada to Europe. To remove witnesses to their crimes, they sank their victims and killed all hands.

The two lovers eventually settled in France and bought a large estate near Le Havre from the duke of Chartres. Sailing for pleasure on their small yacht, they ran into a BRIG becalmed in the channel. Taking it by surprise, the Cobhams murdered the crew and sold the ship and cargo at Bordeaux.

Cobham, now a wealthy and respectable landowner, served as a judge in French country courts. Although Maria Lindsey committed suicide, he died of old age. When the end was near, he confessed his crimes to a priest and asked him to publish the story. His family suppressed the book, but one copy supposedly survives in the French archives.

COBHAM, THOMAS *(English pirate; Atlantic; 1563)*
Cobham was a younger brother of William Brooke, seventh Lord Cobham, who held many royal offices. From 1562, England opposed the Catholic faction in France, and Queen Elizabeth issued PRIVATEERING licenses against French vessels. Early in 1563, Cobham was cruising in consort with Martin FROBISHER near the French border with Spain. There they captured a Spanish merchantman after a desperate battle.

England was at peace with Spain, and the ship contained royal tapestries as well as valuable wines. To conceal the crime, Cobham took the ship to Ireland, imprisoning the captive crew so cruelly that the chaplain and some others died. The cargo was sent to Cornwall and fenced by Peter KILLIGREW, who in turn sold the wines to WILLIAM (2) and JOHN HAWKINS at Plymouth.

The Spanish ambassador insisted that the goods be returned and the pirates punished. Neither demand was satisfied. The government allowed an agent of Martin Frobisher to take the wines. Frobisher and Cobham were imprisoned in Wales, but Frobisher soon was released. Cobham was brought to trial for piracy but refused to plea, thereby raising a nice legal point. Under the English common law, a mute defendant was pressed under heavy weights until he died or responded. Cobham's attorneys argued that this penalty did not apply because piracy was a statutory and not a common law crime. The judges ruled against Cobham, and he pleaded innocent.

Despite convincing testimony, a jury refused to convict Cobham. Although a second jury sentenced him to death, he later was pardoned. The wife of Lord Cobham interceded with the queen, as did Sir Robert Cecil, earl of Salisbury, who had married Cobham's sister.

COCKE, ABRAHAM *(English captain; Caribbean; active 1589–1593)*
As a crewman in 1580, Cocke deserted in Brazil after quarreling with the captain over a lack of food. In 1587, he was on a Portuguese merchantman captured off Argentina by the earl of CUMBERLAND's ships. Taken back to London, he went to work for John WATTS and took two ships back to Argentina in 1589.

In 1590, Watts sent Cocke to plunder the West Indies and to visit the ROANOKE colony in Virginia. His flagship was accompanied by the *Little John* under Christopher NEWPORT and Michael GEARE and a pinnace under William LANE. In the West Indies, Cocke's squadron was augmented by three prizes and a ship belonging to Sir Walter RALEIGH.

This large fleet hoped to intercept the homeward-bound TREASURE FLEET and did capture one valuable prize, the *Buen Jesus.* The raiders split up and Cocke took two ships to Roanoke, but the colony was deserted. The various sponsors sued each other, and the admiralty decided (probably as a result of bribery) that the *Buen Jesus'* cargo belonged solely to Cocke's ship.

In 1592, Cocke commanded the *Sampson* for the earl of Cumberland and was among the sailors pillaging the MADRE DE DIOS. He died after returning to the Argentine coast in 1593.

COCKLYN, THOMAS *(British pirate; Caribbean, Atlantic; active 1717–1719)*
Cocklyn sailed from NEW PROVIDENCE ISLAND in the Bahamas in about 1717. In early 1719, he briefly cruised off West Africa with Howell DAVIS and Olivier LA BOUCHE.

COLLIER, EDWARD *(English buccaneer; Caribbean; active 1668–1672)*
Although nothing is known about his earlier career, Collier was an experienced captain when he took part in Sir Henry MORGAN's expeditions. Many witnesses, both English and Spanish, claimed he tortured prisoners even more cruelly than Morgan and the other buccaneer captains.

Collier commanded a pirate vessel during Morgan's 1668 raid on PORTOBELO. At the end of 1668, the 34-gun *Oxford* was sent to defend Jamaica and to put down piracy. The island's governor gave Collier command, when her previous captain killed the ship's master during a quarrel. Collier captured Captain LA VEVEN, a French pirate, whose ship was seized and renamed the *Satisfaction.*

Soon after, Collier joined Morgan, who was gathering the buccaneers for his raid on Maracaibo and Gibraltar, Venezuela. The drunken pirates blew up the *Oxford* in January 1669, but Morgan and Collier were among the lucky survivors. Following this disaster, Collier went off on his own, taking the *Satisfaction* on an 18-month independent cruise to Mexico and possibly to Cuba.

In September 1670, Collier enlisted in Morgan's Panama expedition and was named "vice-admiral." While the pirates were gathering off southwestern Haiti, Collier took six ships to Venezuela to gather food and information. At RIO DE LA HACHA, he captured the fort and garrison and ferociously tortured his prisoners. He enjoyed his victims' agonies too much for efficient interrogation, for he missed 200,000 pesos hidden by the fort's commander. After extorting a ransom in salt, corn, and meat, he rejoined Morgan's main fleet early in December. When Morgan routed Panama's defenders in January 1671, Collier commanded the buccaneers' left wing. He and his men chased after and slaughtered the fleeing enemy. After the Spaniards surrendered, Collier killed one of their chaplains, a Franciscan friar.

Collier took ample plunder during his voyages. In 1668, Jamaica's governor gave him a 1,000-acre plantation next to one of Morgan's estates. Plantations of this size were granted only to men with substantial funds to purchase slaves and tools. Collier did not share Morgan's disgrace after the assault on Panama. Although a new governor arrested Morgan, Collier remained in Jamaica and led preparations to defend the island against a possible foreign invasion.

COMMISSIONS, PRIVATEERING *(licenses to commit piracy; about 1200–1865)* Rulers granted licenses, allowing raids on foreign shipping by private vessels. Until the 1680s, governments rarely enforced PRIVATEERING laws, and these licenses were simply an excuse for piracy.

(See also REPRISAL, LETTERS OF.)

CONDENT (CONGDON, CONDEN), EDMUND *(British pirate; Caribbean, Pacific; active 1718–1720)* From Plymouth, Condent was second-in-command of a pirate SLOOP that fled NEW PROVIDENCE when Woodes ROGERS became governor in 1718. When an Indian, beaten up by the other crewmen, threatened to blow up the ship, Condent leaped into the hold and shot him. "When he was dead," Daniel DEFOE writes, "the Crew hack'd him to Pieces, and the Gunner ripping up his Belly, tore out his Heart, broiled and eat it."

Soon after, the pirates captured a merchant ship. They quarreled, and the captain and half the crew left in the prize, while the rest chose Condent captain. At the Cape Verde Islands, he took a Portuguese wine ship, an entire squadron of small boats, and a Dutch warship, which he kept and renamed the *Flying Dragon*.

Condent marauded along the Brazilian coast, seizing many merchantmen. Hearing that the Portuguese had imprisoned a pirate crew, Defoe states, he cruelly tortured Portuguese prisoners, "cutting off their Ears and Noses." After taking more prizes along the West African coast, he reached MADAGASCAR in June or July 1719. At SAINT MARY'S ISLAND, he picked up some of John HALSEY's old crew.

Condent cruised in the Red Sea and along the Indian coast for more than a year. Near Bombay in October 1720, he captured a large Arab ship carrying treasure and precious cargo valued at £150,000. To avoid the East India Company's wrath, he ordered his men not to abuse the passengers and crew. The rich haul was shared out at Saint Mary's, each man receiving about £2,000. Condent and about 40 others went to Réunion Island and negotiated with the governor for a French pardon. About 20 settled on the island. According to Defoe, Condent married the governor's sister-in-law, migrated to France, and became a wealthy merchant in Brittany.

CONSERVA *(pirate partnership; Mediterranean; 16th through 18th centuries)* A written agreement between two or more captains, popular among corsairs sailing from MALTA. All the captains and crews shared—using various systems of disbursement—in prizes captured by any of the ships.

(See also BOOTY, DIVISION OF.)

CONSORT *(pirate partnership; all seas; 16th through 18th centuries)* When two or more ships agreed to cruise "in consort," the vessels divided all BOOTY taken, even if they became separated. The share assigned to each ship varied. Consortship rules were complex in 16th-century England, and disputes were common. Faithful to their rules giving each man an equal share, the BUCCANEERS and 18th-century pirates usually gave each ship a cut in proportion to the size of its crew.

(See also ADMIRALTY COURT; EATON, JOHN.)

CONSTANTINO, BROTHER *(Knight of Malta; Mediterranean; 1662)* Constantino was named captain of the TARTAN previously commanded by Aloisio GAMARRA.

CONTRERAS, ALONSO DE *(Maltese corsair; Mediterranean; 1580s)* A Spanish soldier-of-fortune, Contreras sailed for the KNIGHTS OF MALTA for two decades and had further adventures in Spain, Italy, Flanders, and the West Indies. His colorful autobiography provides a dramatic and not entirely believable account of the corsair's life.

Contreras ran away as a young boy and served with Spanish and Sicilian troops in Italy, Burgundy, Flanders, and Greece. He also went on several Sicilian naval expeditions, becoming an expert seaman and navigator. When one of his friends murdered an innkeeper, a Maltese knight rescued him and gave him a berth on his personal pirate ship.

On his first cruise, the corsairs took two Turkish sailing ships. Not content with his share of the BOOTY, Contreras sued before the TRIBUNALE DEGLI ARMAMENTI over a Turk he had captured. His Maltese mistress quickly relieved him of his riches. After sailing with the knight's GALLEYS, Contreras commanded FRIGATES sent by the grand master to spy on Muslim shipping. His voyages throughout the Near East and along the BARBARY COAST combined piracy with espionage.

Like other Maltese corsairs, Contreras ignored papal orders protecting Greek Christians. He seized Greek ships and tortured their crews to make them reveal treasures hidden by Muslim passengers. But he also paid friendly visits to Greek villages. After rescuing a Greek priest held for ransom by an Italian captain, he MAROONED the latter naked on an isolated island. His corsair days ended when he kidnapped the beautiful wife of the Muslim governor of Chios. The enraged husband posted Contreras' portrait and offered a large reward for his capture.

CONTROVERSIES *(Latin speeches; 50 B.C.–A.D. 400)* The ancient Romans highly esteemed rhetoric—the art of using words effectively in speaking or writing. As part of their training, students wrote speeches to the jury by the accuser or the defendant in imaginary court cases. Some adults continued to create similar exercises for entertainment, and professors of rhetoric composed examples to win customers. Two collections of these speeches survive: the CONTROVERSIES OF SENECA and the DECLAMATIONS OF PSEUDO-QUINTILIAN.

The speakers amused their audiences by presenting extreme cases. The surviving controversies deal with such sensational topics as piracy, sorcery, murder, insanity, cannibalism, incest, and homosexual rape. With their bizarre plots and flowery language, they present miniature versions of the ROMANCES written between 125 and 300.

CONTROVERSIES OF SENECA (Latin speeches; first century) CONTROVERSIES (fictional speeches) compiled by Lucius Annaeus Seneca the Elder (about 55 B.C. to A.D. 37). The collection preserves examples by more than 100 orators. Most are very short excerpts, containing fewer of the interesting details found in the DECLAMATIONS OF PSEUDO-QUINTILIAN.

Seneca's excerpts are taken from fictitious court cases involving bizarre situations. Four cases describe pirate captives whose families refuse to pay their ransom. In one case, a boy has been MAROONED and becomes a pirate. While the cases are imaginary, these situations are real enough, since kidnapping was the most profitable part of ancient piracy.

Seneca's pirates are less fiendish than in the *Declamations*. Compared to the captives' families, the pirates seem relatively humane. One group of pirates refuses when a father asks them to cut off his son's hands. Another captive is set free by the daughter of a pirate chief. In only one case do the pirates act cruelly. Here, as in APOLLONIUS OF TYRE, the corsairs sell a captured virgin to a pimp who turns her into a prostitute.

In another case, a man has two brothers—one a tyrant, the other an adulterer. Despite his father's pleas, he kills both. Later, the man is captured by pirates. The father informs the pirates that he will pay twice the ransom demanded if they cut off his son's hands. The pirates let the son go with his hands. The father sues to force the son to support him.

Another father believes that one of his sons wants to murder him. The father hands him over to his second son, who maroons the man on a boat without sails. The youth drifts into the hands of pirates and becomes their chief. Later he captures his father and sends him back to his country. The father disinherits the second son for not killing his brother.

A third father refuses to ransom his son, who is saved when the pirate's daughter falls in love with him and lets him go. They return to his home, and he marries the girl. The father disinherits the son when he refuses to divorce the pirate's daughter and marry another woman.

Another case invokes a villainous mother. A man is captured by pirates and writes asking for a ransom. His wife's weeping blinds her. The son wishes to go to his father but without the ransom. The mother demands that he be imprisoned because he will not stay and support her.

COOK (COOKE), EDMUND (English buccaneer; Caribbean, Pacific; died 1681?) Cook was among the few BUCCANEERS with a semi-legitimate excuse for his piracies. In December 1673, as he headed toward England with valuable goods (possibly smuggled out of Cuba), a Spanish vessel captured his ship near Havana and turned her crew adrift. Claiming that Madrid refused to reimburse his losses, Cook acquired a letter of REPRISAL. Early in 1679, he landed in Cuba, ambushed a Spanish ship, and sold her cargo in Jamaica.

William DAMPIER was hired as a surgeon by Cook and a Captain Lynch, who planned to sail together. However, Cook's small ship was alone when he reached the Panamanian coast in February 1680. There he ran into Bartholomew SHARP's company, which had just sacked PORTOBELO. Excited by their success, Cook and his men enlisted in a new adventure. Under John COXON's command, the pirates marched across the Isthmus and won a fierce battle near Panama City on May 3.

Soon after the battle, Cook received command of the 100-ton *Mayflower*, captured at Pueblo Nuevo. But her crew refused to accept Cook as captain, and he moved to Sharp's flagship, the *Trinity*. Cook joined in raids along the Peruvian coast and was still on board when they reached the JUAN FERNÁNDEZ ISLANDS in January 1681.

After another mutiny, John WATLING took Sharp's place as captain and immediately imprisoned Cook in irons for homosexual acts. Since HOMOSEXUALITY was commonplace among the buccaneers, Watling's act is difficult to understand. Cook is not mentioned again, and he probably died soon after.

(See also SELECTED BIBLIOGRAPHY: Kemp and Lloyd, *Brethren*.)

COOK, JOHN (English buccaneer; Caribbean, Atlantic, Pacific; died 1694) Born on Saint Kitts and "a sensible man who had been for some years a privateer" (according to William DAMPIER), Cook invaded the Pacific in 1680 with Bartholomew SHARP and John COXON. Off Ecuador in April 1681, 47 pirates (including Dampier and Lionel WAFER) deserted the main body. With Cook as leader, they survived a difficult 23-day journey across the Isthmus of Panama.

On the Caribbean coast, Cook and the others found at least nine pirate ships. Their party broke up, and Cook became QUARTERMASTER and second-in-command under a Dutch Captain YANKY. When Yanky's ship took a fine Spanish prize, Cook and the other Englishmen demanded it under pirate rules. Captain Yanky, however, "grutching the English such a vessel," took her back by force and MAROONED them on the Isle-à-Vache, off Haiti. A Captain TRISTIAN rescued Cook, Edward DAVIS, and a few others and took them to PETIT GOÂVE. After Tristian and his men went ashore, the English seized his ship and picked up their companions. Cook captured two French prizes, including the 18-gun *Revenge,* and fled to Virginia in April 1683.

Cook sailed for South America in August 1683 with 70 crewmen, including Davis, Dampier, Wafer, and William COWLEY. Since he needed a larger vessel in the Pacific, Cook sailed to Sierra Leone, stole a 26-gun Danish ship by trickery, and renamed it the *Batchelor's Delight.* According to an unlikely story, Cook exchanged the *Revenge* for 60 African girls, who died one by one in the icy wastes of the Antarctic.

Leaving Africa in mid-November, Cook was driven further south than any earlier captain and reached the Pacific in March 1684. On March 29, he ran into John EATON's *Nicholas.* Joining forces, the two pirate ships visited the JUAN FERNÁNDEZ ISLANDS, where they rescued WILLIAM, marooned by Bartholomew Sharp three years earlier.

Thanks to Charles SWAN's recent descent on the same coast, the Spaniards were on the alert. Giving up hope of surprising a Peruvian treasure ship, the pirates decided to raid Central America. On the way, they took four prizes and stored food on the Galapagos Islands. Off Costa Rica in mid-July, Cook died of illness, and the *Delight's* crew elected Edward Davis captain.

(See also SELECTED BIBLIOGRAPHY: Bradley, *Peru;* Burney, *History;* Kemp and Loyd, *Brethren.*)

COOKE, EDWARD *(English privateer; Pacific; active 1708–1711)* Second captain of the *Dutchess* during Woodes ROGERS' plunder voyage along South America's Pacific Coast. On their return with the loot from a MANILA GALLEON, he wrote *A Voyage to the South Seas* (London, 1712). Although his version is more detailed, it is poorly written and enjoyed less success than Rogers' *A Cruising Voyage.*

COOKE, WILLIAM *(English pirate; Atlantic; active 1540s)* Sailing from Exmouth early in 1545, he seized a merchantman off the Spanish coast and sold its cargo at Topsham. On the way home, he encountered James ALDAY, a fellow pirate who later testified to this crime in the ADMIRALTY COURT. Shortly afterward, Cooke ordered an officer on another Spanish prize to describe the cargo as French and therefore legal booty. When the officer said he could not see to write because he had lost his glasses, Cooke coolly sailed to Falmouth and borrowed a local parson's spectacles.

COOPER, JAMES FENIMORE *(American novelist; 1789–1851)* Cooper, the first successful American novelist, was born in Burlington, New Jersey. Best known for *The Last of the Mohicans* (1826), he also wrote THE WATER WITCH (1830) and THE SEA LIONS (1849). In *The Water Witch,* a New York merchant fences illegal cargoes brought in by a supernatural pirate ship. The hero of *The Sea Lions* goes treasure hunting with a dead pirate's map. Similar mysterious treasure maps reappear in TREASURE ISLAND and other pirate fiction.

"COPY OF VERSES, COMPOSED BY CAPTAIN HENRY EVERY, A" *(ballad; 1696?)* Thirteen four-line stanzas describing Every's career, probably published on the day six of his crew were hanged. The song (incorrectly) says Every slaughtered his prisoners. Pirates did not fly the JOLLY ROGER for another decade or two. When they refused to give quarter, they put up a solid red ("bloody") flag.

(See also "VILLANY REWARDED"; SELECTED BIBLIOGRAPHY: Firth, *Naval.*)

CORAL ISLAND, THE *(novel, 1858)* A popular adventure story by Robert M. Ballantyne (1825–1894), which influenced TREASURE ISLAND and PETER PAN. Ralph Rover, a boy of about 12, is wrecked on a desert island with two friends. After various escapades, they find a rotted stump bearing the letters J. S., a rude stone bridge, and a dilapidated hut. In the hut, a man's skeleton lies on a low bedstead, a dog's skeleton on his chest. (The meaning of all this is never explained.)

Seeing a schooner flying the JOLLY ROGER, the three comrades hide in a cave that can be reached only by swimming under water. Ralph, thinking the pirates have left, goes out to explore and is captured. Ralph stands up to the pirate captain, who admires his bravery and spares his life. The unnamed captain carries two PISTOLS and a CUTLASS in a shawl around his waist. "Of immense stature and fierce aspect," he is "a lion-like villain totally devoid of personal fear, and utterly reckless of consequences. . ."

Ralph makes friends with Bloody Bill, one of the crew. At Ralph's insistence, Bill warns the savages, the pirates' enemies, of a plan to massacre them. The savages kill all the pirates except Bill, who escapes badly wounded. Ralph has been left in charge of the boat, and he and Bill manage to board the schooner. Despite Bill's injuries, they head for Coral Island. Bill is killed during a storm, but Ralph gets to the island on his own. He is reunited with his friends and they reach home at last.

CORBELLI, VITTORIO *(Maltese corsair; Mediterranean; 1704)* Corbelli was captain of the *Holy Cross,* armed with 14 cannon and 20 breech-loading swivel-guns.

CORDES, BALTASAR DE *(Dutch captain; Pacific; active 1598–1600)* Cordes commanded one of five warships during the first Dutch raid on South America's Pacific coast, led by his brother Simon de CORDES.

CORDES, SIMON DE *(Dutch captain; Pacific; died 1599)* Cordes was second-in-command, under Jacob de MAHU, during the first Dutch raid on South America's Pacific coast. Outfitted by a private company and possibly licensed by the government, 500 men departed in June 1598 on five strong warships—*Faith, Hope, Love, Fidelity,* and *Good News* (*Hoop, Gellof, Liefe, Trouvw,* and *Blijde Boodschap*). Only *Fidelity* and 36 crewmen made it back to the Netherlands.

Despite their virtuous names, the ships carried a hundred cannon as well as weapons for Indians fighting the Spanish colonists. They also carried six English pilots, at least one of whom had sailed with Thomas CAVENDISH. Mahu and Cordes hoped to repeat Cavendish's capture of a richly laden MANILA GALLEON before going on to the East Indies. At war with Spain, the Dutch justified plunder raids as a way of weakening their enemy's finances.

The Dutch fleet moved down the African coast, where Mahu died and was replaced by Cordes. The journey was difficult, the Portuguese and Africans refused to trade for fresh food, and many men sickened and died. Worse was to come after the fleet reached the Strait of Magellan in April 1599. Cordes decided not to attempt the Strait in winter and waited nearby until August. More than 120 crewmen perished of cold and hunger.

As they emerged into the Pacific in September 1599, the five ships were scattered by high winds. By now, fewer than half the original crews were still alive, and the rest were seriously unwell. *Faith* and *Fidelity* remained at the Strait to help repair the *Good News,* and all three were pounded by savage storms. The *Faith's* commander, Sebald de Weert, gave up and went back to the Netherlands. *Good News* was driven far to the south before making it to Valparaiso, where the survivors surrendered to Spanish authorities.

Commanded by Baltasar de CORDES, Simon's brother, the *Fidelity* continued on alone. In April 1600, Baltasar reached Chiloé Island, where the Spaniards warred with the local Indians. Baltasar de Cordes apparently tricked the Spanish commander by offering to help him against the Indians in return for food. Once inside the fort, the Dutch killed or drove out the Spanish settlers. However, the Spaniards returned in June and ejected the Dutch after a hard battle. The *Fidelity* sailed west and reached the Moluccas in January 1601. There Portuguese forces captured the *Fidelity* and killed most of the remaining crewmen.

Meanwhile, unaware of the plight of his other ships, Simon de Cordes in the *Hope* had left the Strait of Magellan in September 1599. In November, he and 23 men were massacred by Indians as they visited the mainland. Those still on board the *Hope* went on to Santa Maria and rendezvoused with *Love.*

By this time, Spanish officials were well aware of the Dutch incursion and sent a ship to Santa Maria. Unwilling to challenge the alerted Spanish defenses, the *Hope* and *Love* made for the East Indies in November. The *Hope* was lost in a storm, perhaps north of Hawaii. The *Love* reached Japan in April 1600 with only five men still able to stand. The English pilot, William Adams, was kept in Japan for about 20 years until his death. Thanks to his tact and skills, subsequent Dutch ventures to Japan were favorably received.

(See also SELECTED BIBLIOGRAPHY: Bradley, *Peru.*)

CORNELIUS, JOHN *(fictional pirate; Atlantic; about 1700)* His imaginary life is inserted among the biographies of real pirates in Daniel DEFOE'S GENERAL HISTORY. Cornelius takes command when Captain LEWIS is killed. Soon after, he fights a fierce battle with a slaver. Joseph Williams, one of the crew, inspires the slaves to fight by telling them all pirates are cannibals. The pirates sink the slaver and fish Williams out of the water when he promises to join their company.

After looting many victims, Cornelius reaches MADAGASCAR. He is cordially welcomed by King Chimenatto, who had taken power with English help. However, 70 of the pirates die from their own excesses. "Having been long with fresh Provision, the eating immoderately, drinking Toke (a Liquor made of Honey) to Excess, and being too free with the Women, they fell into violent Fevers." Cornelius strengthens his crew with native warriors and unsuccessfully cruises in the Red Sea. On the way back, Joseph Williams leads a revolt that deposes Cornelius. He returns to Madagascar and dies five months later.

CORSAIR (1) *(licensed sea raider; Mediterranean; about 1300–1830)* A synonym for PRIVATEER, a person or a ship marauding with governmental approval. Privateering was called *corsa* in Italian, Spanish, and Portuguese and *la course* in French—all derived from the Latin word *cursus* meaning a race, march, or voyage. A person engaged in privateering was known as a *corsaro* (Italian), *corsario* (Spanish), *corsari* (Portuguese), or *corsaire* (French). The word was used in English from the 16th century in references to BARBARY raiders.

In theory, a corsair was not a PIRATE because his activities were approved and regulated by law. He supposedly attacked only ships from countries at war with his government. Booty was turned over to a prize court, such as the Maltese TRIBUNALE DEGLI ARMAMENTI. However, only the Barbary corsairs obeyed their government's rules, and Christian corsairs often looted ships from friendly and neutral nations. The worst offenders were the corsairs of MALTA, who regularly sacked Christian vessels and towns, despite complaints by Venice, France, and the papacy.

CORSAIR (2) *(novel; 1987)* Sailing with their beautiful mistresses, Dudley POPE'S Ned Yorke and Sir Thomas WHETSTONE scour the Caribbean. It is the early 1660s, and Yorke's royal pirates continue to battle Jamaica's governor, introduced in GALLEON (2). The Spanish government wants to reconquer Jamaica, whose BUCCANEERS endanger its TREASURE FLEETS. Although he has no troops or ships of his own, Governor Luce tries to drive away the buccaneers. He takes away their privateering licenses and even closes the brothels and taverns.

Yorke's pirates rescue smugglers imprisoned at RIO DE LA HACHA, where they capture the governor and bishop of Colombia. From their captives, they learn that ships are gathering along the SPANISH MAIN to invade Jamaica. Meanwhile, London orders Governor Luce to persuade the Spanish colonies to trade with England. Yorke and Whetstone take the governor's lieutenant to Santo Domingo. The Spaniards perfidiously attack at night but are driven off by the vigilant buccaneers.

The two captains visit Grand Cayman to seize four Cuban pirate ships. Avenging attacks on Jamaican villages, the buccaneers loot a Cuban town. In their final triumph, the pirates destroy or capture the Spanish ships assembling in Venezuela to invade Jamaica.

Yorke is cruel and bloodthirsty. He shows no remorse, for example, after butchering a sleeping garrison. To excuse Yorke's increasing brutality, Pope turns his Spanish opponents into devious murderers. But Spanish governors did not attack English envoys, and Spain never assembled a fleet to reconquer Jamaica.

(See also ADMIRAL (2); BUCCANEER.)

"CORSAIR, THE" *(Poem; 1814)* A historical
tale in verse couplets by George Gordon, Lord Byron (1788–1824). "The Corsair" enjoyed extraordinary success and inspired plays, operas, and ballets. Readers were entranced by the pirate chief, a romantic hero "of loneliness and mystery." The poem's message is ambiguous, which perhaps added to its appeal. Although it is set in the Aegean, "The Corsair" was inspired by a newspaper account of Jean LAFFITE's heroism at the battle for New Orleans.

Learning that Seyd, the Turkish pasha, plans to raid his island, Conrad, a corsair chief, decides to attack first and bids farewell to his beloved mistress, Medora. Disguised as a dervish fleeing the pirates, Conrad enters Seyd's camp. When his men set fire to the pasha's galleys before he gives the signal, the pirates are defeated. Conrad is captured and sentenced to death by impalement.

During the battle, Conrad saves Seyd's harem from the fire. Gulnare, the pasha's favorite slave, falls in love with Conrad and wants him to kill Seyd while he sleeps. Conrad refuses to take a step he considers cowardly.

Gulnare kills Seyd herself and escapes with Conrad. Disgusted by her act, he longs for the safe haven of Medora's tower. When they reach his island, Conrad finds Medora dead. She had faded away from grief at the news of his capture. Heartbroken, Conrad disappears and is never heard of again.

CORSAIRE, LE (1) *(symphonic overture; 1844)*
Lord Byron's poem partly inspired this piece by Hector Berlioz (1803–1869). The music, invoking the moods of the Mediterranean, is characterized by swiftness and brilliance. A beautifully expressive slow section is recalled, at a faster tempo, in the Allegro movement.

CORSAIRE, LE (2) *(three-act ballet; 1856)* The
most influential among the ballets inspired by Lord Byron's poem, *Le Corsaire* was presented at Paris with music

by Adolph Adam (1803–1856). Joseph Mazilier, one of the leading choreographers of the period, created inventive solo parts and *pas de deux* infused with dramatic expressiveness. These were combined with spectacular technical effects, especially in the final shipwreck scene.

Le Corsaire enjoyed great success at Paris and was revived from time to time up to about 1900. It also became a favorite of the star ballerinas in Saint Petersburg. Marius Petipa (1822–1910) staged it in 1868 with added music by Cesare Pugni and Léo Delibes. He again revived it in 1899, adapting it to his own style of choreography and adding a separate *pas de deux* often performed on its own.

The slave dealer Isaac sells Medora, a young Greek girl, to Säid Pasha. Conrad, a pirate chief, seizes Medora, takes her to his underground palace, and declares his love. Birbanto, Conrad's second-in-command, is jealous of his chief. He sends Medora back to Isaac, who once again takes her to the pasha.

Conrad and his men arrive in disguise. He is recognized, captured, and condemned to death. To save his life, Medora supposedly agrees to marry Säid. She secretly plots with the slave Gulnare, who impersonates Medora during the wedding ceremony.

That evening, Medora dances before Säid after having persuaded him to lay down his weapons. Conrad enters and takes Medora away, while Gulnare declares that she is the pasha's lawful wife. The ship carrying Conrad and Medora sinks in a terrible storm, but the two lovers miraculously reach safety on a rocky island.

CORSAIRE, LE (3) *(ballet pas de deux; 1899)*
When he revived Adolph Adam's 1856 ballet at Saint Petersburg, Marius Petipa added a *pas de deux* with his own choreography and music by Ricardo Drigo. A superb example of academic technique and a difficult test of virtuoso skill, Petipa's *pas de deux* is subdivided into the traditional adagio, solo variations, and coda. Detached from the parent work, it has been performed by many celebrated dancers including Margo Fonteyn and Rudolf Nureyev, Ekaterina Maximova and Vladimir Vassiliev, and Gelsey Kirkland and Mikhail Baryshnikov.

CORSARO, IL *(three-act opera in Italian verse; 1848)* An opera by Giuseppe Verdi (1813–1901), based on Byron's poem with the hero's name changed to Corrado for ease of singing. At the pirates' Aegean island, Corrado alternately rebukes the world and regrets his lost innocence. Learning of Pasha Seid's threats, Corrado rallies the pirates to attack Seid's city of Corone. Medora tries to dissuade him, but he assures her he will return safely.

At Corone, slave girls attend Gulnara, who sings of her hatred of Seid and her longing for freedom and love. Seid holds a banquet celebrating his expected victory. A dervish is brought in and questioned. Suddenly, flames light up the night sky, as Seid's fleet burns. The dervish reveals that he is Corrado, his men swarm into the banquet hall, and a fierce battle rages. By rescuing Gulnara and the other women from the burning harem, Corrado gives the Muslims time to recover. The pirates are routed. Corrado is imprisoned and condemned to death by torture.

When Gulnara pleads for Corrado's life, Seid threatens her in a jealous rage. Seeking revenge, Gulnara bribes her way into Corrado's prison. He refuses to murder Seid, and Gulnara kills him herself. She frees Corrado, and they flee together.

The opera's ending is significantly different from Byron's poem. In the opera, Corrado and Gulnara return to the pirate island. Before she dies in Corrado's arms, Medora confesses that she has poisoned herself because she thought he was dead. In despair, Corrado throws himself into the sea, as Gulnara and the chorus exclaim in horror.

Verdi wrote *Il Corsaro* to fulfill a contract and did not attend rehearsals. The critics were scathing, and only the set designer won a curtain call. Although much of the music is competent and enjoyable, *Il Corsaro* is considered one of Verdi's lesser works. It was not performed from 1854 until its revival in 1963.

COSTA, ALAMANNO DA *(Italian nobleman; Mediterranean; active 1200–1228)* A native of Genoa, Alamanno raided near Crete. In 1204, he led a flotilla that expelled Pisan merchants from Sicily. Declaring himself count of Syracuse, Alamanno pillaged shipping in the straits between Sicily and Africa. He again attacked Crete after Enrico PESCATORE was expelled in 1211. The Venetians captured him and 300 of his men, but released him in 1218 at the request of Pope Honorius III. The pope similarly protected Alamanno when Frederick II ejected him from Syracuse in 1221. He later prepared an expedition to help the Italian kings of Thessalonica in Greece, and he attacked Venetian ships near Tunis in 1228.

COTTON, RANDOLPH *(English captain; Atlantic; died 1595)* Captain of the BARK *Daintie* in Thomas CAVENDISH's unlucky 1591 expedition to South America, Cotton invested in and was second-in-command of Sir James LANCASTER's 1595 raid on Pernambuco, Brazil. The pirates, who spent a month loading their great booty, discovered that the Portuguese had built a redoubt blocking the mouth of the harbor. Lancaster sent Cotton and Jean LENOIR to destroy the fort, with strict orders not to venture beyond the range of the ship's guns. Disregarding this caution, Cotton and Lenoir chased the retreating enemy, fell into a trap, and were killed along with 35 of their men.

COTTUY, CAPTAIN *(French buccaneer; Caribbean; 1697)* Captain Cottuy took part in the Sack of CARTAGENA.

COURTENAY, SIR HUGH *(English pirate; Atlantic; active 1420–1471)* From Boconnoc and a cousin of the earl of Devon, Sir Hugh was among the Cornish gentlemen sponsoring piracy from Fowey. He had a share in a ship (principally owned by John TREVELYAN) that captured a Spanish galley in 1449. He personally owned and sometimes commanded a CARAVEL, whose well-armed crew captured several French and Dutch prizes.

In 1460, Sir Hugh seized a Dutch merchantman with John FENNELL's help. From Fowey, the pirates distributed its rich cargo throughout Devon and Cornwall. No local official dared to arrest Sir Hugh, and he ignored repeated orders to appear before the king's council. During the English civil wars, every government needed the support of landowners like Sir Hugh. He became a judge in 1465 and was later asked to recruit ships and seamen. While fighting for the Lancastrian side at the battle of Tewkesbury, he was captured and beheaded.

COWLEY, WILLIAM AMBROSE *(English buccaneer; Atlantic, Pacific; active 1683–1686)* A graduate of Cambridge University, Cowley in 1683 served as navigator of the *Batchelor's Delight*, which plundered along South America's Pacific coast under John COOK and Edward DAVIS. In September 1683, he switched to John EATON's *Nicholas* as master.

Cowley took the *Nicholas* across the Pacific from South America to Timor Island. "Finding the ship's company factious and not under command of our captain," he deserted, became navigator of a Dutch ship, and returned to England in October 1686. His journal of the voyage, published in 1699, primarily records details of navigation. Cowley tells less about the buccaneers' adventures than Basil RINGROSE and Raveneau de LUSSAN, and his book lacks the rich information about natural phenomena found in William DAMPIER and Lionel WAFER.

COXE, WILLIAM *(English pirate; Caribbean; active 1576–1578)* Coxe commanded one of Andrew BARKER's two ships during a raid on the SPANISH MAIN. In August 1577, Coxe led a mutiny and MAROONED Barker and a dozen others on a Honduran island, where Spanish soldiers killed them. Coxe's mutineers shared the contents of Barker's strongbox, plundered Roatán Island, and steered for home. But their largest ship, a captured Spanish FRIGATE, sank near Cuba with most of their booty and about 15 men.

The survivors returned to the Honduran coast, built a new frigate, and attacked Spanish shipping early in 1578. They had some success until a warship captured one of their boats and hanged its crew. Only Coxe and some 18 followers remained. They made it to the Scilly Islands (near Cornwall) in June 1578, divided the remaining booty, and sneaked into Plymouth. Coxe and other ringleaders were imprisoned for mutiny and as accessories to Andrew Barker's murder.

COXERE, EDWARD *(English seaman; Mediterranean, Atlantic; 1633–1694)* Coxere's diary was published in 1946. He was a seaman and gunner during the English civil wars, sailed with the Spanish against the French, and served on both sides in conflicts between the Dutch and English. In 1657, while aboard an English merchantman, he was captured off the IONIAN ISLANDS by the vice-admiral of TUNIS. He was held for five months, working as a boatswain, and was released in January 1658 by British warships visiting Tunis. On the return voyage, a Spanish warship captured his vessel, but he managed to escape in Cadiz.

COXON, JOHN *(English buccaneer; Caribbean; active 1676–1684)* Coxon sailed from Jamaica under a questionable French COMMISSION and was declared a pirate in 1676. To escape punishment, he promised to give up his crimes after assaulting Venezuela with Captain LAGARDE in early 1677. Despite the governor's efforts, most Jamaicans continued to tolerate piracy. In 1679, Coxon, Richard SAWKINS, and two other captains plundered along the Honduran coast and openly sold their booty at Port Royal.

Coxon and six other captains sailed for the Isthmus of Panama late in 1679. With Coxon as elected leader, the pirates captured PORTOBELO in February 1680 and took about £18,000 in booty. In April, Coxon was again elected to lead a march through the jungle against SANTA MARIA and PANAMA. Traveling in canoes and a small ship, the buccaneers reached Panama on May 3 and fought a savage battle with three Spanish warships. Although Coxon apparently helped to capture the 400-ton *Santisima Trinidad*, some of the men accused him of cowardice after the battle. While most of the company sailed into the Pacific, Coxon and about 50 men returned across the Isthmus and rejoined his ships.

Coxon continued to vacillate between crime and submission. In 1682, he obtained a Bahamian commission allowing him to capture Spanish ships. The Bahamian governor was replaced due to Jamaican complaints, and Coxon went straight for a time. In October, Jamaican Governor Thomas Lynch sent him with three vessels to bring the English LOGWOOD cutters back from Honduras. Lynch informed London that "His men plotted to take the ship and go privateering, but he valiantly resisted, killed one or two with his own hand, forced eleven overboard, and brought three here who were condemned last Friday."

Coxon reverted to piracy in November 1683. Following another promise to reform, the governor of the Leewards gave him a commission to catch pirates and Indians early in 1684. The Jamaicans arrested Coxon in January 1686, but he escaped and was cutting logwood in the Gulf of Campeche in 1687. In September 1688, he surrendered to the Jamaica authorities and was once again pardoned.

(See also SELECTED BIBLIOGRAPHY: Cruikshank, *Morgan*; Haring, *Buccaneers*; Kemp and Lloyd, *Brethren*.)

CRANE, THOMAS *(English pirate; Atlantic; 1286)* From Norfolk, Crane attacked a merchantman and killed its captain. Imprisoned at King's Lynn until trial, he escaped, took sanctuary in a church for 15 days, and then escaped to sea.

CRASTON, WILLIAM *(English privateer; Atlantic, Caribbean; born 1561?, active 1590–1601)* Craston began as an apprentice to John WATTS, the largest sponsor of West Indian plunder voyages. He became even more unscrupulous than other privateering captains. While a crewman in 1590, Craston helped embezzle gold from a captured prize. As captain of the *Hopewell* in William LANE's 1591 expedition, he was accused of the large-scale theft of prize goods. He again commanded the *Hopewell* during a 1597 expedition to Newfoundland. In 1601, he was tried for plundering vessels from friendly nations.

CRÉMEAULX, BROTHER FRANÇOIS *(Knight of Malta; Mediterranean; active 1628–1629)* CAPTAIN GENERAL OF GALLEYS. During the summer of 1628, Crémeaulx's squadron seized two large merchant ships near Crete, took a TARTAN off Sardinia, and captured USSEIN REIS' galleon off southern Sicily.

CRETE *(pirate haven; Mediterranean; 300–67 B.C. and 827–962)* A large island, some 60 miles south of mainland Greece at the southern limit of the Aegean Sea, Crete proved an excellent haven for pirates. The Aegean islands and Greece's eastern coast offered a nearby source of slaves. Ships plying between Italy and the east had to pass through the narrow channel between Crete and Greece's southern tip.

The deeply indented northern coast of Crete provides abundant harbors. Mountains cover 95 percent of the interior, and transportation remained difficult until after World War II. Their hard life as mountain herdsmen and warriors made the Cretans a proverbially tough race. Brigands probably always raided from harbors along the island's coasts. During several periods, piracy developed into a major industry.

Ancient Crete

Ancient Greek legends recall slaving raids by the legendary King MINOS. Until their power collapsed about 1350 B.C., the Minoans controlled trade with the Near East and imposed their rule on several Aegean islands and parts of Greece. During the 1100s, Dorian Greek warriors conquered the island and enslaved the Minoan population. The Dorians established a large number of sharply separated city-states, which fought endless wars. Initially the Dorians also took to the sea as buccaneers. HOMER, describing this early period, speaks of the Cretans as notorious pirates. In one of his adventures, ODYSSEUS pretends to be a Cretan pirate to hide his identity.

Later, as the economy declined from about 950, the Cretans retreated from the sea to mountain communities. Henceforth, trade routes with the Near East bypassed the island, as new ports developed in Greece and on islands such as RHODES. The Cretan city-states remained economically backward. They formed a loose confederation from about 500. But it received no powers, and it was up to the individual cities to enforce federal laws. The cities continued their wars, with Gortyn and Knossos tending to dominate the others.

Cretan pirates are mentioned in 331 under ALEXANDER THE GREAT. They became the principal marauders in the Aegean throughout the next century. Though evidence rarely gives the names of individual captains, Cretan pirates often raided for slaves, plundering the Aegean islands, ships at sea, the coast of Asia Minor, and the Greek mainland around Athens.

The corsairs held wealthy captives for ransom. Those without money were sold at DELOS and other markets. Cities like ALLARIA needed many slaves, and Crete itself developed into a major international market. The ancient sources describe a veritable "city of slaves," where thousands were kept for sale.

The Cretan cities encouraged piracy and openly taxed corsair booty. Since the island lay off the main sea routes, port cities found piracy more profitable than honest trade. Unlike the AETOLIAN LEAGUE, Crete did not use the corsairs to build up an empire. Several Greek cities and islands made treaties with the Cretan confederation and with individual cities. But these simply made it easier to ransom prisoners. They did not impose Cretan rule, nor did they require the Cretans to punish piracy.

The Cretan cities welcomed foreign as well as local corsairs. The AETOLIANS recruited Cretans for joint raids, assembled in Cretan harbors, and sold their captives in the island's markets. After raiding the Athenian coast in 229, BUCRIS carried his prisoners to Crete. To recover the captives, Athenian ambassadors paid the very large sum of 20 TALENTS.

Just as they hired Cretan mercenaries, rulers employed pirate bands during wartime—looking the other way when corsairs attacked neutral cities. King Philip V of Macedonia in 204 ordered DICAEARCHUS to help the Cretan pirates at war with Rhodes. From 204 to 195, King NABIS of Sparta systematically used Cretan pirate attacks to enlarge his empire.

The island state of Rhodes made itself the protector of the Aegean islands at the end of the third century. At first, the Rhodians tried to control piracy by allying with individual cities during Crete's interminable civil wars. In 205, Rhodes declared war following Cretan attacks on shipping and the island of Cos. The Rhodian-Cretan war involved a series of raids and counter-raids in the Aegean, with Philip of Macedonia supporting his pirate allies. When the Rhodians and Romans defeated the Macedo-

nian navy in 201, several Cretan cities thus came to terms with Rhodes.

As long as Rhodes maintained a strong naval presence, Cretan piracy declined, and slave dealers had to find other sources. Pirates again were active while Rhodes and Rome were preoccupied with their war (192–188) against the Aetolians and King Antiochus' Syrian Empire. NIKANDROS and other archpirates allied with Antiochus sold their captives in Crete, and the Cretans increased their raids in the Aegean. There they captured and enslaved thousands of Romans. In 189, a Roman general brought his fleet to Crete and demanded the release of Romans and other Italians. Several cities complied and freed 4,000 Roman captives. (The Romans did not ask the Cretans to free their thousands of Greek prisoners.)

Rhodian patrols kept down Cretan piracy until the 160s. Rhodes organized islands in the southern Aegean into a league, which created its own federal navy. The corsairs returned in great number after 168 when Rome unwisely weakened Rhodes' power by seizing Rhodian colonies and by making Delos a free port. Rhodes' new weakness became clear in 155–154, when it lost a full-scale war against the resurgent Cretan corsairs. The Cretans attacked Carpathos, and they savagely pillaged Siphnos and enslaved its inhabitants. The Cretans even defeated the Rhodians in a naval battle. The corsairs' host of nimble light ships smothered the large Rhodian warships, and Rhodes had to ask Rome to negotiate an end to the war.

In 74, MARCUS ANTONIUS (2) received a fleet and the authority to deal with piracy throughout the Mediterranean. General Anthony invaded Crete in 71, charging that the Cretans favored MITHRIDATES OF PONTUS and supplied him with mercenaries. He also accused them of openly assisting the Cilician pirates when the Romans pursued them. The war ended in total defeat for the Romans. As in 155, the pirate flotillas easily outmaneuvered Rome's heavy warships. The victorious Cretans used the chains from Roman ships to bind their captives, including officers of high rank. But this victory really marked the end of Cretan piracy and independence. In 68, the stubborn Romans sent three legions, which brutally conquered the island and united it to their empire.

Medieval Crete

Muslim adventurers, led by ABU HAFS, easily captured Crete in 827 from the BYZANTINE EMPIRE. The conquerors turned to piracy, joined by converts from the island's population. At a deep harbor on the island's northern coast, they built the fortress of Candia (present-day Iráklion) surrounded by a deep moat.

Two Byzantine expeditions against Crete in 828 failed disastrously. The corsairs pursued the second fleet and crucified its leader on the island of Cos. In 829, the Cretans briefly occupied several of the CYCLADES ISLANDS and then annihilated another Byzantine squadron off

Thasos. For more than a century, the corsairs carried out audacious raids against Byzantine territories. Like Cretan pirates during antiquity, they attacked Greece, the Aegean islands, and Asia Minor, where a band was massacred near Ephesus in 841. Until 875, they also roamed the Adriatic Sea.

In 838, a mixed fleet of Cretan and African pirates took Brindisi in southern Italy and destroyed 60 Venetian warships. They later gave up Brindisi but took TARANTO in 839, using it and BARI as bases for raids into the Adriatic Sea. In 841, marauders burnt Ancona, sacked the island of Cherso (east of ISTRIA), and seized Venetian merchantmen. The following year, they defeated another Venetian squadron in the Gulf of Quarnero.

In response, a powerful Byzantine fleet briefly occupied Crete in 843, until its general rushed home at rumors of a palace revolt. In 853 and 859, Byzantine fleets raided the Egyptian Delta, destroying arms intended for the Cretan corsairs. A fierce battle with the Sicilians in 858 or 859 also weakened the Cretans. Like other pirates, Muslim raiders often conducted joint raids. In this case, the Cretans apparently objected to Sicilian ambitions in parts of Greece they reserved for themselves.

Cretan corsairs returned to the attack from 860. In the Aegean, their bands raided from the Cyclades to Macedonia. Thirty ships ravished the Asiatic coast and the island of Lesbos. Raiders attacked Mont Athos, the Byzantine spiritual center. Semipermanent bases were set up on a nearby island and perhaps also at Athens. The corsairs also reappeared in the northern Adriatic. Raiders from Taranto and Crete besieged Dubrovnik for 15 months (866–867). A Byzantine fleet rescued Dubrovnik early in 868, and Bari was recaptured in 871. But Taranto served as a base in 875 for buccaneers that attacked Venice and destroyed the port of Comacchio.

A Byzantine expedition against Crete in 866 never sailed, because its commander was murdered for political reasons. In 873, Cretan and Syrian contingents jointly attacked Euboea. The Byzantines sent yet another fleet against the corsairs. It destroyed a large Cretan squadron in the gulf of Corinth, bringing the Aegean two decades of peace and helping to end the Adriatic raids.

The Cretans renewed their raids on the Cyclades in 901, even penetrating into the Sea of Marmora. In 904, they joined Syrian corsairs under LEO OF TRIPOLI in a great raid on Thessalonica, the Empire's second city. Byzantine counterattacks on Crete in 910 and 949 again met with disaster. Corsair raids continued until a vast Byzantine fleet reconquered the island in 961 and reimposed Christianity.

Burt Lancaster appears to be flying across the platform as Spanish soldiers climb up, trying to capture him. From *The Crimson Pirate* (1952).

CRIMSON PIRATE, THE *(motion picture; color; 1952)* In director Robert Siodmak's good-natured spoof of earlier SWASHBUCKLERS, particularly THE BLACK PIRATE, Burt Lancaster (playing Captain Vallo) tips off the audience as the movie begins. Soaring on the end of a line between the masts of two ships, he warns viewers, "Believe only half of what you see."

Captain Vallo plies the waves, joined throughout by his deaf-mute sidekick Ojo (Nick Cravat). Using a trick, he captures the ship carrying Baron Gruda, sent to suppress rebels on a Caribbean island. Vallo plans a double-cross. He will sell the captured guns and ammunition to the rebel leader, El Libre (Frederick Leicester). Then he will collect a reward for telling Baron Gruda where to find El Libre.

Disguising himself as Gruda (perhaps a reference to CAPTAIN BLOOD's mastery of disguises), Vallo rescues El Libre from jail. With him, he picks up Prudence, a scientist who concocts primitive machine guns, tanks, a balloon, and a submarine. Vallo's plot goes awry when he falls for El Libre's daughter Consuelo (Eva Bartok). Swayed by her charms, he decides to free his captives instead of selling them to Gruda.

Humble Bellows (Torin Thatcher), Vallo's villainous first mate, leads a mutiny at this violation of the "pirate code." After setting Vallo, El Libre, and Prudence adrift, Baron Gruda captures the drunken pirates. Vallo frees himself, leads the rebels to victory with Prudence's weapon, and rescues his unfaithful followers. Swimming underwater (as in the *Black Pirate,*) the pirates take over Gruda's ship. Vallo and Consuelo embrace in happy victory.

Filmed in an Italian fishing village, *The Crimson Pirate* includes many leaps from yardarms and SWORD DUELS. The fast-paced choreography incorporates countless sight gags, from Lancaster in drag to a pirate with a PEG LEG stuck in a grating. Lancaster, a former circus performer, tumbles and jumps with skill and grace.

CROMWELL, THOMAS *(English pirate; Caribbean; active 1643–1645)* A resident of Boston, Massachusetts, Cromwell joined William JACKSON's 1643 expedition as pilot. Although England and Spain were at peace, he obtained a PRIVATEERING license in 1645 from the earl of Warwick (who also had sponsored Jackson). After capturing several rich prizes in the West Indies, Cromwell returned to Massachusetts and was driven into Plymouth Harbor by adverse winds. Plymouth's government complained that Cromwell's 80-man crew "did so distemper themselves with drink as they became like madd-men;. . . they spente and scattered a great deale of money among the people, and yet more sine than money."

(See also SELECTED BIBLIOGRAPHY: Dow, *Pirates.*)

CROSSE, JOHN *(English captain; Atlantic, Caribbean; active 1591–1595)* In 1591, Crosse captured a Brazilian sugar prize with a Plymouth warship partly owned by Robert CROSSE, probably his brother. In January 1595, while Sir Francis DRAKE was raiding the West Indies, John Crosse sailed after Drake in the *Little Exchange,* owned by Robert Crosse and Sir Walter RALEIGH. Crosse carried messages warning Drake that he was being hunted by a Spanish fleet. However, Drake already had died, and it is not known whether Crosse actually made contact with the English ships. The pursuing Spanish fleet captured the *Little Exchange* near Havana on March 22.

CROSSE, SIR ROBERT *(English naval captain; Atlantic, Caribbean; active 1587–1595)* Crosse was captain of the 150-ton *Bark Bond* during Sir Francis DRAKE's 1585 West Indies expedition, and he commanded a private ship that joined Drake's Cadiz raid (1587). He was rear-admiral of Drake's squadron fighting the Spanish Armada (1588) and accompanied his failed assault on Lisbon (1589). In 1591, with Drake in disgrace, Crosse took part in a disastrous Azores cruise under Lord Thomas Howard and Sir Richard GRENVILLE. During these same years, he also financed privateering raids, including one by his kinsman John CROSSE.

In 1592, Crosse took the lead in capturing the MADRE DE DIOS, a great Portuguese treasure ship. Sir Walter RALEIGH had planned a West Indian raid, with Crosse as vice-admiral and Sir John BURGH commanding the land forces. However, the ships stayed nearer to home to intercept Portuguese CARRACKS returning from India, and Sir Martin FROBISHER replaced Raleigh as commander.

Crosse and Burgh refused to serve under Frobisher, sailed down to the Azores, and consorted with John NORTON (2) and Christopher NEWPORT. The *Madre de Dios* might well have escaped capture. But Crosse boldly—perhaps rashly—lashed the *Foresight* across the carrack's side and front until the other English raiders arrived. As soon as resistance ended, the seamen and officers wildly looted the cargo and passengers, rather than waiting to divide the BOOTY.

Crosse and his men could not dispose of more than £10,000 in illegal plunder, and they ultimately received nothing from this rich haul. Royal officials were searching ships at Dartmouth, and Crosse went on to Portsmouth. When dishonest buyers got his crew drunk and purchased jewels and gold for pennies, Crosse fled to Chatham, where the authorities confiscated the *Foresight.* He probably received little from Raleigh, the ship's owner, whose share of the booty had been grabbed by Queen Elizabeth. Crosse again hunted for East Indian carracks in 1595, but this time took no prizes of consequence.

CULLIFORD, ROBERT *(British pirate; Caribbean, Indian Ocean, Red Sea, South China Sea; active 1690–1698)* Culliford and other crewmen stole the *Blessed William* from William KIDD in February 1690. Electing William MAY captain, they sailed to MADAGASCAR in December and cruised near India with little reward. May and Culliford got off at the Nicobar Islands and somehow made it back to New York.

Culliford was QUARTERMASTER of the *Pearl* when May sailed in July 1693. The *Pearl* put in at Mangalore, India, in October 1694 and later departed without Culliford. While serving as a British gunner at Madras, he led a mutiny in June 1696 that seized the merchantman *Josiah.* Culliford was marooned at the Nicobar Islands when some of the crew retook the *Josiah.* Rescued by a passing ship, he joined Ralph STOUT on the *Mocha* (sometimes called the *Resolution*).

Culliford was chosen captain when Stout was killed about May 1697. The *Mocha* returned to the Strait of Malacca and pursued the richly loaded British ship *Dorrill.* When they came alongside, the *Dorrill* surprised the pirates with a cannonball into the *Mocha's* mainmast. The *Mocha* did capture several other prizes—Chinese, Indonesian, and European—before retreating to SAINT MARY'S ISLAND, near Madagascar, in May 1698. At Saint Mary's, Culliford plundered a French ship, taking £2,000 in cash. He also ran into and fraternized with his former captain, William Kidd. Almost 100 of Kidd's men enlisted with Culliford, who left late in June.

Soon after, the *Mocha* fell in with the *Pelican* and Dirk CHIVERS' *Soldado.* In September 1698, Culliford and Chivers captured the *Great Mohammed* in the Red Sea. The prize carried some £130,000 in cash, and each crewman received more than £700.

After taking a less valuable prize, Culliford and Chivers returned to Saint Mary's in February 1699. The pirates sank the *Mocha* in September, when four British warships arrived. Their commander offered the pirates a royal pardon. Although it had expired the previous June, he promised to have the date extended. About two dozen, including Culliford, accepted the offer and eventually arrived at London.

Culliford and several others were tried in May 1701 for robbing the *Great Mohammed.* When the court ruled that the pardon was not valid, all were hanged except Culliford, saved to testify against Samuel BURGESS in a separate trial. He vanished from the records and probably served on a naval ship.

(See also SELECTED BIBLIOGRAPHY: Grey, *Pirates;* Ritchie, *Kidd.*)

CUMBERLAND, GEORGE CLIFFORD, THIRD EARL OF (English pirate; Atlantic, Caribbean; 1558–1605)

Cumberland financed vast plunder ventures that appreciably influenced the course of England's sea war with Spain (1585–1603). In 1598, he captured San Juan, Puerto Rico, succeeding where Sir Francis DRAKE had failed three years earlier.

After studying at Oxford and possibly also at Cambridge, Cumberland in 1579 inherited one of the largest fortunes in the country. Through lavish expenditure and profligate gambling, he fell deeply into debt and, from 1586, turned to PRIVATEERING as a source of revenue. Seeking fame as well as booty, he led many expeditions in person—with experienced captains providing the naval skills he lacked. Ironically, Cumberland's 12 raids dramatically increased rather than reduced his debts. Professional corsairs grew rich on smaller ventures. Cumberland lavishly overequipped his ventures, borrowed expensive royal warships, and was ruthlessly cheated both by suppliers and by the buyers of captured cargoes.

In June 1586, Cumberland sent out three ships and a PINNACE under Captains Robert Withrington and Christopher Lister. They were ordered to imitate Drake by sailing through the Strait of Magellan and pillaging South America's western coast. However, the captains turned back before reaching the Strait and took only a few worthless prizes off Brazil. Cumberland was present at—but had no part in—the battle against the Spanish Armada in 1588. In October, he took a borrowed royal warship on a plunder cruise but captured only one small prize.

Cumberland's 1589 expedition made a small profit despite bad management. Assisted by Lister and William MONSON, Cumberland visited the Azores with a royal warship and three other vessels, hoping to intercept Spanish and Portuguese treasure ships. But the earl's badly supplied fleet had to keep landing for food and water. His ships captured several French and Portuguese vessels but only one rich prize—a GALLEON from the Spanish West Indian fleet worth some £100,000. Unfortunately, this was wrecked at Mount's Bay (in Cornwall) and sank with all hands.

Cumberland's warships seemed to do better when he was not present. Two of his vessels operating off Portugal in 1590 captured neutral Venetian and Dutch ships as well as several Portuguese prizes. In 1591, Cumberland personally led five ships to the Spanish coast. There they pillaged four German merchantmen of military supplies considered contraband of war. They also seized two Portuguese prizes carrying sugar and took spices from Dutch ships. But this more valuable booty was recaptured at sea together with Captain Monson.

In 1592, Cumberland stayed at home and entrusted his five ships to John NORTON (2). In the Azores, Norton joined Sir John BURGH and Christopher NEWPORT in capturing the MADRE DE DIOS, a Portuguese CARRACK loaded with precious goods. As they boarded their prey, the crews ransacked the cargo, pocketing most of the jewels and other valuables. Queen Elizabeth, a minor shareholder in Burgh's ships, took half of what was left. From a cargo worth half a million, Cumberland received only £36,000, barely enough to pay his expenses.

For his 1593 venture, the earl briefly cruised in the Azores with five ships, but caught only two French prizes and a Portuguese sugar ship. Before returning, however, he sent two of his vessels to the West Indies under James LANGTON, who brought back rich booty from Venezuela, Hispaniola, and Honduras.

Altogether, Cumberland had outfitted seven squadrons from 1586 to 1593. Only three (in 1589, 1592 and 1593) had made even moderate profits, and these gains were cancelled out by a great loss in 1591. From 1594, the earl no longer borrowed warcraft from the queen but instead depended on syndicates of London promoters for ships and financing. But his ventures remained unlucky, and he continued to fall into debt.

In 1594, Cumberland sent three powerful ships to the Azores. There they encountered the 2,000-ton carrack, the *Cinco Chagas* returning from the Far East with an even richer cargo than the *Madre de Dios* in 1591. During a desperate battle, the great ship caught fire and exploded. The raiders sighted another carrack, but were now too weak to attack one of these formidable opponents. Despite substantial losses on this voyage, Cumberland persisted and constructed the *Malice Scourge*, a very powerful 600-ton galleon. However, a cruise in 1595 (under Langton) and two more in 1597 all proved fruitless.

In March 1598, the earl personally led his final and largest expedition. Eighteen ships were assembled, four owned by Cumberland, the rest by London merchants. The original target was Recife in Brazil, but Cumberland later decided to occupy San Juan as a base for further attacks in the West Indies. On the way over, the fleet had poor luck in the Azores. It arrived too late to intercept the West Indian TREASURE FLEET but too early to capture the East Indian carracks, which stayed safely at Lisbon.

Cumberland struck swiftly and hard at Puerto Rico. San Juan and the El Morro fortress lie at the western end of an island, which blocks the mouth of a shallow bay and is separated by a lagoon from the mainland. In 1595 Sir Francis Drake had failed to force his way into the bay. Cumberland instead landed away from San Juan and attacked the two small forts protecting its eastern defenses.

An initial attack across the lagoon failed to take Fort San Antonio. (Cumberland led his men and almost drowned when he fell over wearing heavy armor.) At the earl's orders, a small boat ran itself onto the rocks near Fort Matadiablo, its cannon fire covering the English as they overcame the enemy. The Spanish forces gave up the town and retreated to El Morro, which surrendered on June 19 after a 10-day siege.

Cumberland's assault was superbly conceived and boldly carried out. But he succeeded partly because an epidemic had weakened San Juan's garrison. The conquerors soon succumbed to disease. Within three weeks, half of the 1,200 soldiers were dead or gravely ill, and the survivors fled in August.

San Juan held no treasures, and the Spanish—aware of the English plight—refused to pay a ransom. The expedition had taken only nine prizes and whatever hides, ginger, and sugar could be found in San Juan. The investors almost certainly lost money on the venture. Heavily in debt, Cumberland sold the *Malice Scourge* to the East India Company in 1600, lamenting that he had thrown his lands and other wealth into the sea.

(See also SELECTED BIBLIOGRAPHY: Andrews, *Elizabethan*; Corbett, *Successors*; Rogoziński, *Caribbean*; Williamson, *Cumberland*.)

CUNNINGHAM, WILLIAM *(British pirate; Caribbean; died 1718)* Raiding from NEW PROVIDENCE ISLAND in the Bahamas, Cunningham served as gunner for Edward TEACH (Blackbeard) in 1716 and 1717. After accepting a pardon from Woodes ROGERS in July 1718, he returned to piracy with John AUGER and was hanged in December.

CUP OF GOLD *(novel; 1929)* *Cup of Gold*, John Steinbeck's first published work, is very different from the realistic novels that won him the Pulitzer and Nobel prizes. In this complex study, Steinbeck (1902–1968) makes an ambitious attempt to understand a famous villain. Unfortunately, few copies were sold, and the book fails both as historical fiction and as allegory.

Cup of Gold is subtitled *A Life of Henry Morgan, Buccaneer, with Occasional Reference to History*. It presents several episodes during Morgan's life, but it is not a standard fictional biography. Steinbeck omits many events, and he gives only a few pages to Morgan's piracies before the Panama raid. The novel's many symbols often refer to legends about King Arthur. Morgan's obsession with Panama (the "Cup of Gold" of the title) becomes a version of the search for the Holy Grail.

Steinbeck's Morgan is a mediocre man driven by a strong will to power. He is completely absorbed in two goals: realizing his vision of himself and gaining "Elizabeth," his ideal image of female sexuality. Choosing piracy, he masters other men through the businesslike use of terror and intelligence. This Morgan resembles Satan, the cold deceiver, much more than the swashbuckling hero of writers like SABATINI.

Steinbeck tells the story entirely from Morgan's point of view, and he describes the background in interpolated essays. The young Morgan lives in rural Wales with his weak father and strong-willed mother, Elizabeth. A former farmhand returns with tales of pirate riches. Morgan decides to leave his first love, the farm girl Elizabeth. He consults Merlin, an aged seer who predicts he will gain greatness by remaining a little child.

Morgan sails for the West Indies. Tricked by the ship's captain, he is sold at Barbados as an indentured servant. His master, a kindly old planter, educates him and treats him like a son. Morgan runs the plantation with fearful efficiency but prefers to turn pirate. Snubbed by his titled relatives in Jamaica, he buys a pirate ship with funds filched from his trusting master. Despite many glorious victories, Morgan is lonely and despises the lesser men who fawn on him. Hearing rumors of Ysobel (the Spanish form of Elizabeth) the Red Saint, a fabled beauty all men desire, he plans to capture her love by seizing Panama.

Morgan successfully sacks Panama. (Steinbeck provides a detailed, compelling description of the battle.) But Ysobel is monstrously evil. She rejects Morgan as a childish beginner and humiliates him by preferring his lieutenant. Morgan concludes that money provides the only security. He gets his men drunk and single-handedly sails away with all the Panama plunder.

At Jamaica, Morgan sinks into respectability as lieutenant governor. He is deceived into marrying his cousin, another Elizabeth and a vicious badgering scold. As he dies, a fever-born image of the first (Welsh) Elizabeth appears, and he realizes that his lifelong search has failed.

CURTOGOLI   See KOURD OGLU REIS.

CUTIAR, PAOLO *(Maltese corsair; eastern Mediterranean; 1708)* Cutiar was captain of a TARTAN.

CUTLASS *(pirate weapon; all oceans; 16th–18th centuries)*   A heavy sword with a slightly curved, sharpened blade and a solid basket-shaped guard to protect the hand and wrist. The name is derived from a medieval French word (*coutelas, coutelace*) for a knife. The Caribbean BUCCANEERS used a cutlass up to three feet long. A shorter version was issued to seamen on British warships up to about 1920.

The cutlass' sharp edge made it ideal for cutting and slashing, which takes less skill than using a sword sharpened on the point only. Since the curve was slight and the point also was sharpened, an expert (and strong) swordsman could thrust at his foe as with a rapier.

(See also SWORD DUELS; WEAPONS.)

CYCLADES *(Greek islands; Aegean Sea; all eras)*   Some three dozen islands of various sizes north of CRETE. Their location made them an easy target for pirates sailing from ancient AETOLIA and CILICIA as well as from ancient and medieval Crete.

(See also BUTES; DELOS; SOCLEIDAS.)

CYGNET *(pirate ship; Atlantic, Pacific, South China Sea, Bay of Bengal, Indian Ocean; 1683–1689)*   Leaving England in 1683, Charles SWAN and Basil RINGROSE took the 16-gun *Cygnet* (Baby Swan) to South America's Pacific coast. Captain Swan took several small prizes but failed to catch the MANILA GALLEON. He sailed east in April 1686 and was marooned on Guam the following January.

John READ commanded the *Cygnet* during an 18-month cruise from China to Australia and west to the Bay of Bengal. After seizing a rich prize near Ceylon in April 1688, Read deserted and went back to America. Many of the crew left near Madras and became gunners for Indian princes. The 60 or so still aboard renamed the *Cygnet* the *Little England.* They took £25,000 from a vessel off India's western coast and arrived at MADAGASCAR by May 1689. Her hull eaten away by worms, the ship suddenly sank while anchored at Saint Augustine's Bay. Her crew presumably joined other pirate ships as they reached Madagascar.

(See also DAMPIER, WILLIAM.)

D

DAIMONOIOANNES FAMILY *(Greek corsairs; Mediterranean; 13th and 14th centuries)*
This family sponsored piracy from estates on CRETE and the MENEMVASIA, and several members were themselves renowned corsairs.

(See also VENETIAN CLAIMS.)

DALMATIA *(pirate haven; Adriatic Sea; 600 B.C. to A.D. 9; 800–1699)* A region along the eastern coast, from Fiume (Rijeka) to Kotor. Dalmatia formed part of ancient ILLYRIA until 180 B.C., when its inhabitants declared their independence from King GENTHIUS. Tiberius Caesar subdued Dalmatia in A.D. 9, and it became a province of the Roman and, later, BYZANTINE, empires.

During the seventh century, Slavic Serbs and Croats settled the coast, although some cities remained under Byzantine rule. As trade increased from the 800s, the NARENTANS preyed on merchants from Venice and other Italian cities. In 998, they were crushed by Venice, which annexed the entire coastline. The inland regions were divided between Croatia (in the north) and Serbia (in the south).

From the 1090s to 1382, Hungary (which ruled Croatia) disputed control of the region with Venice. The inland regions favored Hungary, while the maritime cities usually sided with Venice. Dubrovnik, the most important port, became an independent republic in 1358.

After a brief period of Bosnian rule, Venice in 1444 regained control of the entire coast, except for Dubrovnik.

Although never again as powerful as the ninth century Narentans, various pirate bands continued to prey on shipping. From the 1230s, Dubrovnik's government repeatedly promised Venice to stop receiving pirate goods. The inhabitants of Almissa (Omisa), between Split and the Naretva River, were reputed to live solely by piracy. Other pirate communities flourished at Ston and Kotor and further north in the region later home to the USKOKS.

The Venetians subdued the Almissans and other gangs in the early 1400s, but pirates returned in force during the 16th century. From the 1520s, the OTTOMAN EMPIRE occupied all of Dalmatia (and Croatia) as far north as Segno (Senj) and almost to Fiume. The Ottomans ruled the interior, and Venice retained a few maritime cities. Neither government effectively controlled the Dalmatian coast and islands, and piracy and slave-trading flourished from the 1540s. Many smaller gangs cooperated with the fierce Uskoks based at Segno in Austrian Croatia. Small-scale attacks on coastal shipping continued even after the Uskoks were expelled in 1618.

Piracy was suppressed after 1699, when Hungary regained control of Croatia (inland), while Venice reoccupied Dalmatia (the coast). The Austro-Hungarian Empire ruled both regions after 1815. After 1918, Dalmatia was absorbed into Croatia, which became a province of Yugoslavia. When Yugoslavia broke up in 1992, Croatia continued to rule the north, and Serbia seized most of southern Dalmatia.

DAMPIER, WILLIAM (British buccaneer and scientist; Caribbean, Pacific, South China Sea, Bay of Bengal; 1652–1715)

After two years (1676–1678) as a LOGWOOD-cutter and pirate in Mexico, Dampier joined plunder voyages to South America's Pacific coast and Asia (1680–1688). He commanded an expedition to Australia (1699–1701) and again raided South America as a privateer (1703–1711), completing his third voyage around the world.

Dampier published three books that describe his South American and Australian adventures. His accounts are a major source of information about the buccaneer expeditions. They also present richly detailed reports on natural phenomena, such as geographical features, winds, currents, plants, animal life and native peoples. With his striking yet conservative observations, Dampier helped to found the modern sciences of meteorology, botany, and zoology.

Dampier is famous as a scientist rather than as a pirate. He came home penniless, served as an ordinary seaman or subordinate officer, and never commanded a ship or an assault. Most other buccaneer-authors (such as Basil RINGROSE) do not mention him, and his own books provide all that is known about his piracies. But there is no question that he joined in the looting and murders he described. The buccaneers did not tolerate idle bystanders, and they ejected anyone who was "backward" in battle.

The son of a prosperous Somerset farmer, Dampier was educated at local schools. Seeking adventure, he went to sea in 1668, made a voyage to Indonesia, and briefly served on a royal warship. He went to Jamaica in 1674 and became a sailor on local trading voyages. He also began to keep the daily journal and detailed notes on which his books were based.

Dampier in 1675 was a crewman on a small ship that visited Campeche Bay in Mexico to purchase logwood, a profitable trade adopted by many pirates. Dampier joined their disreputable band from March 1676 to April 1678 and made a considerable amount of money. In the *New Voyage*, Dampier says that his fellow loggers frequently raided local haciendas and native villages and "brought away the Indian women to serve them at their huts." He admits taking part in one serious raid. After a severe storm halted operations in June 1676, the loggers raided Alvarado, Mexico, and battled Spanish warships.

Dampier decided the greatest profit lay in selling RUM to the cutters. He briefly visited England to set up his business (where he married a woman named Judith) and went back to Jamaica. While on a trading voyage in January 1680, his ship ran into Bartholomew SHARP,

John COXON, Richard SAWKINS and other buccaneer captains. The entire crew deserted to the pirates, and Dampier went with them.

The raiders sacked PORTOBELO, crossed the Isthmus of Panama to the Pacific coast, and defeated a Spanish squadron on May 3. Most sailed south in a captured ship, looting several towns with small profit. The pirates constantly quarreled, as Sawkins, Sharp, and John WATLING took turns as commander. In February 1681, after Sharp was reelected captain, about 50 pirates deserted under John COOK. Dampier and his friend Lionel WAFER joined this party and reached the Caribbean on June 3 without booty. Soon after, most of the English pirates took over a Spanish prize that sailed in consort with a Captain WRIGHT. Early in 1682, Dampier and 19 others left Wright, taking a captured ship as their share of the loot. Reaching Virginia in July, they received little for their prize and lived in poverty.

In August 1683, Dampier sailed with John Cook, who stole the *Batchelor's Delight* and reached the Pacific in March 1684. Dampier shared the *Delight*'s adventures under Cook and Edward DAVIS until January 1685. He transferred to Charles SWAN's *Cygnet*, not, he writes, "from any dislike to my old Captain, but to get some knowledge of the Northern Parts of this Continent of *Mexico.*"

Swan left in April for Guam and the Philippines, with Dampier aiding him in navigation. When Swan wanted to stay at Mindanao, the crew mutinied on January 24, 1686. With John READ as captain, the *Cygnet* aimlessly cruised to Cambodia, China, Formosa, and as far south as Australia. Only two small prizes were taken, and Dampier became "weary of this mad Crew." On May 16, 1688, Read put Dampier and seven others ashore at the Nicobar Islands without supplies. Using a pocket compass, Dampier steered a native canoe 150 miles to Sumatra through a savage storm.

After almost nine years as a pirate, Dampier was destitute. He visited Indochina, Malacca, and India as an ordinary seaman and also worked as a gunner at an English fort in Sumatra. Sneaking away from the fort in January 1691, he arrived at England the following September. Dampier brought home his diary (carried in a hollow bamboo tube) and a half-share in an elaborately tattooed South Sea islander. He apparently lived in the country for the next five years, revising his journal to give it an authoritative tone and inserting additional scientific details.

A New Voyage round the world, published in 1697, was an immediate best-seller. EXQUEMELIN had created a market for pirate books, and Dampier's book added descriptions of exotic places and scientific revelations. *A New Voyage* focused on the voyages from January 1681 to July 1688. *Voyages and Descriptions*, appearing in 1699, added a "Discourse on the Trade Winds" as well as accounts of Dampier's journeys to Campeche, Indonesia, and India.

In 1699, the government accepted Dampier's proposal to explore the unknown continent of Australia. His first command, at the age of 47, was the 292-ton *Roebuck,* a new but badly built ship.

Dampier arrived at Australia on August 11. He carefully surveyed the western coast before turning back to get fresh water at Timor. Dampier went on to New Guinea, but the *Roebuck* leaked badly, and his crew was hostile. He headed for home, and the ship sank at Ascension Island in March 1701. The crew managed to signal a passing convoy, and Dampier returned to England in August. The expedition is described in *A Voyage to New Holland,* published in 1703 and 1709.

Dampier had become a morose and cynical man, contemptuous of his crews and officers. On the way to Australia, he lost his temper, beat his second-in-command with his cane, confined him in irons, and deserted him in a public jail at Bahia, Brazil. Back in England, he was courtmartialed, fined three years' pay, and declared unfit to command any navy ship.

Dampier used his pirate experiences to win command of two small vessels sent to South America during a war with Spain and France. Sailing in September 1703, Dampier retraced his earlier voyages with Bartholomew Sharp and Edward Davis. The expedition was neither happy nor profitable. Dampier tyrannized over his officers and was overcautious, perhaps cowardly, in attacking enemy ships and ports.

Dampier took a few prizes on the way north from Cape Horn, but an attack on SANTA MARIA in Panama fell through. Captain Thomas STRADLING deserted with Dampier's second ship in May 1704, and John CLIPPER-TON and 21 crewmen took off in a Spanish prize in September. Dampier managed to locate the MANILA GALLEON but could not capture the much larger ship. Thirty-seven more men, including William FUNNELL, deserted in another prize. With fewer than 30 men, Dampier mercilessly sacked Puná, Ecuador. Exchanging his dilapidated ship for another prize, he sailed to Java and reached England in 1707. The ships' owners did not receive any booty and prepared a suit for fraud.

On his third voyage around the world from 1708 to 1711, Dampier accompanied Captain Woodes ROGERS as pilot and advisor. Rogers captured the smaller of two Manila Galleons and returned with booty worth £150,000. Dampier borrowed against his share (about £1,500) and spent his last years in relative comfort.

(See also SELECTED BIBLIOGRAPHY: Lloyd, *Dampier.*)

DANCING   (*pirate pleasure; 17th century and earlier*)   English and Anglo-American sailors enjoyed dancing something like modern "square dances." Some continued to dance with each other after they turned pirate. In his GENERAL HISTORY, Daniel DEFOE reports that—while holed up on a Caribbean island in about 1721—Thomas ANSTIS' crew "pass'd their time in Dancing and other Diversions."

DANIEL, CAPTAIN   (*French buccaneer; Caribbean; active 1700–1705*)   Father LABAT, a French missionary, describes Daniel's adventures. He raided enemy shipping during wars with the English and turned pirate during a truce from 1697 to 1702.

About 1700, Daniel took a ship and slaves owned by the Danish governor of Saint Thomas. Some time later, he stopped for food at the Saints Islands, between Dominica and Guadeloupe. The pirates asked the local priest to say Mass on board their ship and treated the ceremony with lavish festivity.

In fact, "only one incident slightly marred this ceremony." When the priest raised the consecrated bread, one pirate was disrespectful, and Daniel shot him on the spot. "Quite an effective method," Labat remarks, "to prevent the poor fellow repeating his offense." After the service, the pirates gave the priest valuable presents and one of the Danish governor's slaves.

In 1705, Labat journeyed from Martinique to Guadeloupe with Daniel, who was raiding as a licensed PRIVATEER. During the voyage, Daniel's ship captured four merchantmen and took them to Saint Thomas, where the English captains borrowed money to ransom their vessels' belongings. Daniel went on to Barbuda. Failing to capture the English governor, who already had left, Daniel's crew thoroughly sacked the island.

(See also SELECTED BIBLIOGRAPHY: Labat, *Memoirs.*)

DANN, JOHN   (*British pirate; Atlantic, Red Sea; active 1694–1695*)   Dann was among the crewmen on the warship *Charles* (renamed the *Fancy*), which mutinied and elected Henry EVERY captain. In June 1695, the *Fancy* captured two Indian treasure ships carrying gold and jewels. Dann returned to Ireland with Every in June 1696 and went to Dublin. Soon after, a maid at a hotel found his jacket, in which more than £1,000 in gold was "quilted up." Dann was captured, turned informer, and provided evidence about Every's crimes.

(See also SELECTED BIBLIOGRAPHY: Jameson, *Privateering.*)

DANSER, SIMON   Simon SIMONSON's nickname ("the dancer")—sometimes Danziker in English and usually Dansa in French and Italian sources.

DAPHNIS AND CHLOE (*Greek narrative poem; second century*)   A ROMANCE by LONGUS set amid the natural beauties of the island of Lesbos. Shepherds find and bring up a baby boy (Daphnis) and girl (Chloe). They gradually fall deeply in love and finally marry after being separated by various adventures and difficulties, including kidnapping by pirates.

The two youths—he is 15, she 13—spend their first summer together herding sheep and goats. Their innocent passion grows as they play childish games. In the early fall, PHOENICIAN pirates land on the shore (using a CARIAN ship to conceal their identity) and fill their boat with oxen, wheat, wine, and honey. As soon as they capture beautiful Daphnis (who would fetch a high price as a slave), the pirates immediately stop their plundering and set sail. The despairing Daphnis calls out loudly and often to Chloe as the brigands move out to sea.

Giving Chloe his pan-pipes, the dying oxherd Dorkon tells her to play a certain tune he always used to call his oxen. The animals recognize the familiar music. With a great bellowing, they rush to one side of the pirate boat and jump into the water, swamping the ship. The pirates drown, carried down by their heavy armor. But Daphnis, who is barefoot and half-naked, rides safely to shore by holding on to the horns of two oxen.

The story of Daphnis' rescue is similar to AELIANUS' tale of the pigs that rescued their master. Both versions must be copied from older literary sources, since piracy was uncommon during the second century. Two centuries earlier, during the CILICIAN heyday, a beautiful boy walking by the sea really did risk kidnapping by pirates.

DAVIS, EDWARD *(English buccaneer; Caribbean, Pacific; active 1680–1688)* Possibly of Flemish origin, he commanded the *Batchelor's Delight* and plundered South America's Pacific coast from 1684 to 1688. He was an excellent navigator (although illiterate) and successfully led the fractious pirates, who evicted many other captains.

Davis invaded the Pacific in 1680 with Bartholomew SHARP and John COXON. In 1681, he went back to the Caribbean with John COOK, who sold several captured prizes in Virginia in 1683. In August, Davis joined a new expedition as Cook's second-in-command. (William DAMPIER was among the crew and describes the voyage.) The pirates stole the 36-gun *Delight* in Africa, sailed around Cape Horn to the Pacific, and joined in consort with John EATON. Cook died in July 1684, and the *Delight*'s crew elected Davis captain. After the pirates failed to capture Realejo, Nicaragua, Eaton left because Davis insisted on a larger share of any booty.

Davis took the *Delight* back to Ecuador. On October 22, he encountered Charles SWAN's *Cygnet* and a smaller vessel under Peter HARRIS (2). The pirates took nothing of value at Paita, Peru, and called off an attack on Guayaquil, Ecuador. Some slave ships were captured, and about 15 slaves joined the pirates.

Davis went back to Panama to attack ships bringing Peruvian silver from Peru. While they waited, his company was joined by pirate bands under François GROGNIET, Captain TOWNLEY, and Captain LE PICARD. As they prepared for battle, the buccaneers had almost 1,000 men in the *Delight*, and *Cygnet*, and a variety of captured coastal craft. Davis, Swan, and Grogniet commanded the combined forces.

Aware the buccaneers were lurking in wait, Peruvian officials transported the kings' silver—worth over 500,000 pesos—in two galleons attended by three smaller warships. By taking a more westerly course than was usual, they evaded the raiders and secretly landed the treasure.

On June 8, 1685, the Peruvian fleet routed Davis' squadron. Afraid to face the pirates at close quarters, the Peruvians never boarded their ships but did chase them away to Coiba Island.

The buccaneers squabbled, with the English captains blaming Grogniet for the defeat. On July 30, Davis, Swan, Townley, Harris, and William KNIGHT took 640 men north in eight ships. Realejo and León in Nicaragua were sacked with little reward, and the pirates continued to separate into smaller groups. Swan and Townley went on to Mexico. After a visit to Honduras, where fever killed many crewmen, Harris also split off, while Davis and Knight went south to Peru in September 1685.

With fewer than 250 men, Davis and Knight terrorized the Peruvian coast throughout 1686. At least £25,000 pesos in jewels and silver were grabbed at Saña in March. Smaller booty was taken at Paita, but 39 black slaves joined the *Delight*'s crew. During May and June, the pirates sacked five more coastal towns, killing priests and officials who had hidden their treasures. After failing to drive off the raiders, Pisco's defenders paid them £5,000 in July.

At the JUAN FERNÁNDEZ Islands in November, each pirate received at least £1,250 (according to Raveneau de LUSSAN), and Knight left for the Caribbean. Davis and some 80 men took £10,000 in loot at Arica, Chile, in February 1687. From captured reports, he learned that the Peruvians were sending warships to rescue Guayaquil from Captain Le Picard's forces. Davis arrived at Guayaquil in May, helped fend off the Peruvian squadron, and shared £50,000 in booty.

Anxious to return home, Davis left Guayaquil on June 12. Stopping at the Galapagos and Juan Fernández islands (and possibly discovering Easter Island), the *Delight* reached the West Indies early in 1688 and anchored at Philadelphia in May. Accompanied by Lionel WAFER, Davis was imprisoned for a time in Virginia. He went to England in 1690 and much of his property was returned in 1692. One legal document lists his take after four years of piracy as three bags of Spanish money, 142 pounds of broken silver, and some dirty linen. (An Edward Davis, possibly the same man, met William KIDD at SAINT MARY'S ISLAND in 1697 and returned with him to America.)

(See also SELECTED BIBLIOGRAPHY: Bradley, *Peru*; Gerhard, *Pirates*; Kemp and Lloyd, *Brethren*.)

DAVIS, HOWELL *(Welsh pirate; Atlantic, Caribbean; died 1719)* A life-long seaman, Davis was a sociable man and a good actor, who often deceived his victims through clever tricks. About 1718, he was chief mate of a slave ship, captured near Africa by Edward ENGLAND. England killed the captain but took a liking to Davis. According to Daniel DEFOE in the GENERAL HISTORY, England gave the captured slave ship to Davis, who proposed to sell it in Brazil. The crew rejected the scheme and took the ship to Barbados, where Davis was jailed for three months.

Planning to turn pirate, Davis went to the Bahamas, only to find that Woodes ROGERS had subdued the rovers. Rogers put him on a SLOOP, manned by ex-pirates and loaded with cargo. At Martinique, Davis helped to raise a mutiny and was chosen captain "over a large bowl of punch." He drew up ARTICLES and made a short speech, "the sum of which was a Declaration of War against the whole World," Defoe writes. North of Hispaniola, Davis and his 35 men took two larger French ships. The second ship was bluffed into surrender. Davis made the first prize look like a pirate ship by forcing his prisoners to wave swords and by hoisting "a dirty Tarpawlin, by Way of black Flag."

Sailing to the Cape Verde Islands, Davis was royally welcomed by the Portuguese governor at Saint Nicholas, who was persuaded that the *Buck* was an English PRIVA-TEER. He went on to Maio Island, plundered the ships in the harbor, and recruited many followers. The pirates kept a 26-gun vessel, renamed the *Saint James,* and sailed to the Royal Africa Company's fort in the Gambia River. Dressing up like gentlemen, Davis and two other officers deceived the governor, took him prisoner during dinner, and made off with £2,000 in gold.

The *Saint James* now fell in with two other pirate ships under Captain LA BOUCHE and Thomas COCKLYN. Davis was elected admiral for a joint cruise. Defoe says that he gave up the post when they quarreled, "the strong Liquor stirring up a Spirit of Discord among them." *"Since we met in Love,"* Davis said, *"let us part in Love, for I find, that three of a Trade can never agree."*

During the next few months, Davis seized four large English and Dutch prizes loaded with slaves, gold dust, and ivory. The *Buck* was abandoned for the 32-gun *Rover.* Off Anomabu, Ghana, in June 1719, Davis seized three British slave ships. Bartholomew ROGERS, an officer on one of the slavers, joined Davis' band.

Davis went on to Principe Island. Along the way he took a Dutch prize and £15,000 but was forced to abandon the *Saint James.* Davis told the Portuguese governor and the islanders that the *Rover* was an English man-of-war chasing pirates. He even seized a French ship that came into the harbor, pretending that it had been trading with pirates.

A day before he planned to sail, Davis and several others were ambushed at the governor's palace. Defoe says an islander swam ashore and told the governor that the pirates planned to kidnap him. Others report that the governor feared the Portuguese government would learn he was friendly with pirates. Davis took five bullets before he dropped, and his assailants cut his throat to make sure he was dead. After electing Bartholomew Roberts captain, the *Rover's* crew avenged Davis by burning the fort and shelling the town.

DAVIS, JOHN *(English buccaneer; Caribbean; 1665)* Davis commanded a ship during Edward MANS-FIELD's expedition to Costa Rica and PROVIDENCE ISLAND.

DAVY JONES' LOCKER *(British sailors' slang; all oceans; 18th century to the present)* Davy Jones was an evil spirit living in the sea. His locker was the ocean, which received dead sailors. The usage first appears in print in Thomas Smollet's 1751 novel *Peregrine Pickle.* Smollet says that "This same Davy Jones, according to the mythology of sailors, is the fiend that presides over all the evil spirits of the deep." Some writers suggest that the phrase refers to the 17th-century pirate David JONES. This seems unlikely, especially since Jones did not throw his captives overboard.

DEAD MEN TELL NO TALES *(fictional pirate saying; 19th century to the present)* Phrase referring to the practice of killing captives to get rid of witnesses. Several variants exist, such as "Dead men don't pinch." There is no way of knowing whether a real-life pirate ever used this phrase.

Mediterranean pirates sold their captives as SLAVES until the 19th century. Ancient pirates, such as the CILICIANS, openly dealt with Greek and Roman slave merchants. From the 16th century, the BARBARY corsairs enslaved Christians. The KNIGHTS OF MALTA, the KNIGHTS OF SAINT STEPHEN, and other Christian pirates

Dead Men Tell No Tales. Howard Pyle's portrait of the imaginary "Captain Keitt" for *The Ruby of Kishmoor.*

enslaved Muslims. Wealthy prisoners were RANSOMED, poorer ones sold as workers or GALLEY SLAVES.

Most Caribbean BUCCANEERS also operated from havens, such as TORTUGA and PORT ROYAL, where colonial officials tolerated piracy against rival nations. They did not conceal their assaults until Britain and France outlawed piracy in about 1700. Since slavery for whites had died out, raiders simply released captives after plundering their vessel—sometimes cutting down the ship's masts to prevent pursuit. They did not have to kill their captives, and doing so would have been bad business. Since they knew they would not be harmed, sailors did not resist capture. Many even enlisted with the raiders, who usually needed skilled craftsmen.

Some (but not all) pirates killed victims after most havens were closed during the 18th century. Murders were most common during the early 1800s. Authors of pirate fiction exaggerated the crimes of these renegades and also transferred their practices to earlier eras.

For his GENERAL HISTORY (published in 1724–1728), Daniel DEFOE invented evil characters such as BLACKBEARD and Edward LOW. Charles Ellms' very successful PIRATES OWN BOOK (1837) popularized both the phrase and the myth that every captain killed captives. For centuries, Ellms wrote, pirates in the Atlantic and Indian Oceans murdered passengers and crew "thus obliterating all traces of their unhappy fate, and, . . . by practically adopting the maxim that 'dead men tell no tales,' enable themselves to pursue their diabolical career with impunity." Later authors of pirate melodramas repeated Ellms' unhistorical saying, and it also appears in movie SWASHBUCKLERS.

(See also DAVY JONES' LOCKER; TORTURE; "VILLANY REWARDED.")

DEANE, JOHN (English pirate; Caribbean; 1670s) Deane used Dutch, Spanish, and French flags to fool his victims. In 1675, he seized an English ship, stole some of her cargo, and carried his prize to Jamaica. Sir Henry MORGAN, Jamaica's lieutenant governor and a former pirate, refused to arrest Deane and encouraged him to escape. Jamaica's governor personally captured Deane and sentenced him to death as a pirate in April 1676. The English government pardoned Deane after reversing his sentence on a legal technicality.

DEBAUCHERY, PIRATE See DRINKING; FICTION; HOMOSEXUALITY; PROSTITUTES; RELIGION; WOMEN, TREATMENT OF.

DECLAMATIONS OF PSEUDO-QUINTILIAN (Latin speeches written before 400) Two collections of CONTROVERSIES (fictitious speeches), falsely attributed to Quintilian (about 40–96), a famous professor of rhetoric. The *Major Declamations* contains 19 complete speeches. The *Minor Declamations* presents briefer excerpts similar to the CONTROVERSIES OF SENECA.

Three of the surviving *Major Declamations* involve persons held for ransom by pirates. The speeches portray the pirates as heartless brigands who torture their victims. The captives write to their families, begging them to buy their freedom. These episodes are borrowed from earlier literary works, such as the Greek ROMANCES and the Greek plays copied by PLAUTUS and TERENCE. Rome had suppressed piracy when the *Declamations* were written. The speeches describe the practices of CILICIAN corsairs during an earlier era.

In one case, a man's two sons are captured, and one becomes deathly ill. The father goes to the pirates. He has only enough money for one ransom and chooses to free the sick son, who soon dies. The other son manages to escape and returns home. The father sues to force the surviving brother to support him, since he has spent everything rescuing his other son.

In a second case, a captive writes home for a ransom. His wife, who had lost her eyesight and sanity through constant weeping, tries to stop her son from helping his father. The son leaves the ransom money behind to support his mother, and he frees his father by taking his place in captivity. After the son dies, the pirates throw his body into the sea, and it washes up near his home. The mother seizes her son's corpse and allows it to rot on the shore. The father asks the court to force her to permit a burial. In this example, the pirates chained their captives in the hold of a ship moored to the Cilician shore. After the father was ransomed, he looked back and "picked out the curving shores, the sky traversed by the starry constellations, and the towering headlands with their craggy cliffs."

In a third case, a poor man and a rich man are enemies, but their sons are friends. Pirates seize the rich man's son. When his father is slow to pay his ransom, the pirates sell the son as a gladiator. After long searches, the poor man's son finds his friend at the arena, takes his place, and is killed in combat. On returning home, the rich man's son supports his dead friend's father. But his own father—wealthy and cruel—disinherits him to punish this charitable act.

(See also SELECTED BIBLIOGRAPHY: Quintilian, *Major Declamations*.)

DEFOE, DANIEL (British journalist and author; 1660–1731) Educated for the Presbyterian clergy, Defoe became a merchant and importer during the 1680s. He bought and sold ships that went to Europe, and he also traded with Boston and New York merchants. After going bankrupt in 1692, he owned a brickyard near London.

At some time in the 1690s, Defoe began writing political pamphlets for the leaders of King William II's government. The accession of Queen Anne in 1702 revived religious disputes. Defoe was imprisoned for publishing an ironic pamphlet on religious dissent. His brickyard failed, and he became a secret government agent and political journalist. In 1715, Defoe began to publish in a variety of fictional forms. In all, he is credited with more than 500 works. However, fewer than a dozen were published under his own name. His GENERAL HISTORY, for example, was credited to a "Captain Charles Johnson."

Defoe was fascinated by piracy. Several works have pirate heroes, and piracy plays an important role in other books. In ROBINSON CRUSOE, published in 1719, the hero is captured by a SALÉ rover, and a mutiny aids his escape from the island. THE KING OF PIRATES, also published in 1719, is a fictitious autobiography of Henry EVERY. It was intended as a tall tale even more outrageous than earlier stories about the fabulously successful raider.

CAPTAIN SINGLETON (1720) is a fictional pirate without a home, family, or scruples. The plot includes incidents from the lives of various unnamed marauders. In *Colonel Jacques* (1722), the hero is briefly captured by pirates. A NEW VOYAGE (1724) describes a plunder raid similar to William DAMPIER's expedition.

The first volume of the *General History*, in 1724, presented biographies of recent pirate captains. A second volume, in 1728, added the MADAGASCAR pirates active during the 1690s. For the *General History*, Defoe drew on his own knowledge of maritime trade as well as newspaper stories, official reports, and trial records. He also consulted sea captains such as Thomas Bowrey, who had explored the Indian Ocean and owned the *Prosperous*, later taken by John BOWEN. However, the *General History* includes several fictional biographies, and it adds imaginary speeches and conversations.

In The FOUR YEARS VOYAGES (1726), three famous pirates plunder Captain George Roberts. Roberts escapes with his life but lives for a time on a tropical island. MADAGASCAR; OR ROBERT DRURY'S JOURNAL (1729) describes the hero's 16 years of slavery on that island. Like the *General History*, it cunningly mixes fact and fiction.

DELANDER, ROBERT *(English pirate; Caribbean; active 1670–1671)* Delander commanded a ship during Sir Henry MORGAN's sack of PANAMA. Morgan left him in charge of the boats, when the buccaneers left the Chagres River to march cross country toward Panama.

DE L'ISLE, CAPTAIN *(French buccaneer; Caribbean; 1659 or 1661)* Nickname (meaning "captain of the island") of the man commanding a large raid by TORTUGA buccaneers. Claiming that a Spanish warship had killed some innocent Frenchmen, about 400 men elected De L'Isle and three other captains. A fraudulent letter of REPRISAL was purchased from an English adventurer, who functioned as governor of the island.

The pirates forced a French captain to lend them his FRIGATE. With this prize and two or three other boats, they landed at Puerta Plata in northeastern Hispaniola. Marching through the jungle for three days, they sneaked into Santiago at night on the Wednesday before Easter. Surprised in his bed, the governor turned over part of a promised ransom of 60,000 pesos. The raiders pillaged the town for a day, taking special care to strip the church bare.

After enjoying their victims' food and wine, the buccaneers made off, taking their plunder, the governor, and the other chief inhabitants. As they returned to the coast, they were ambushed by more than a thousand Spaniards, who had rallied from throughout the district. But the attack was given up when the raiders threatened to stab the governor and other prisoners.

Although the rest of the promised ransom never arrived, the invaders set their prisoners free. Delighted with their rich spoils, many gave presents to their lucky commander. Captain De L'Isle decided to retire to France and took passage in an English boat. Its captain picked a quarrel with him and threw him overboard in order to inherit his booty.

The Jesuit missionary Du TERTRE, who learned about the raid from the buccaneers, places it in 1659. A Spanish document dates it in 1661. The English and French governments both denied responsibility. The French said the raiders had an English commission, the English claimed they were mainly Frenchmen.

DELLI REIS *(Barbary corsair; Mediterranean, 1567)* A Greek convert to Islam, nicknamed Topal because he was lame, Delli Reis captured Juan GASCON's ship and vainly interceded with the BEYLERBEY of ALGIERS to save Gascon's life.

DEL MAR, NAPOLEONE *(Italian captain; Adriatic Sea; 1319)* Sailing his own warship, Napoleone led a convoy carrying the BYZANTINE emperor's son to Venice. After delivering him, he attacked and robbed ships almost in sight of Venice. The emperor disclaimed responsibility, saying he had simply hired Napoleone, a Genoese citizen.

DELOS *(pirate haven and target; Aegean Sea; 300–50 B.C.)* A small Aegean island (modern Dhilos) at the center of the CYCLADES group. The birthplace of the god Apollo, it contained a sanctuary and temple in his honor. In prehistoric times, the island was occupied by CARIAN sea-rovers, who were conquered by King MINOS of Crete. It was controlled by POLYCRATES OF SAMOS and (from about 454 to 314) by Athens, gained independence, but again fell under Athens in 168.

To punish the island-state of RHODES, the Romans made Delos a free port in 168. It became a major center of the slave trade, and Delian traders freely purchased human merchandise from the pirates of CRETE, AETOLIA, and CILICIA. Ironically, Delos became the victim of pirate raids during wars between Rome and King MITHRIDATES of Pontus. It was sacked by MENOPHANES in 87 and by ATHENODORUS in 69. Shortly afterward, the main trade routes altered, and Delos was abandoned.

DEMETRIUS OF PHAROS *(Greek buccaneer; Adriatic and Ionian Seas; died 214 B.C.)* Demetrius was a mercenary who gained power in ILLYRIA and sponsored piracy to further his ambitions. In 229, Queen TEUTA made him commander of her garrison on Corfu. Some months later, a Roman army invaded Illyria. Demetrius immediately handed over Corfu and joined the Romans. To reward his treason, Rome made Demetrius ruler of southern Illyria, with his capital on the island of Pharos (modern Havar). Prince SCERDILAIDAS ruled other parts of the Illyrian kingdom.

Demetrius was a man of action who recklessly gambled with fate. The still-powerful kingdom of Macedonia was next door, while Rome was far away and preoccupied with the Celtic War (225–222). Changing sides once again, Demetrius turned against his Roman patrons. He bid for the Illyrian kingship by making himself guardian of the previous king's son and marrying his mother. His own forces advanced on land, and his troops fought beside those of King Philip V of Macedonia.

Just as King Philip unleashed DICAEARCHUS in 224, Demetrius used piracy to finance his adventures. He encouraged Illyrian and ISTRIAN corsairs, who plundered Roman ships in the Adriatic. In 220, he and Scerdilaidas led an expedition to Greece and joined the AETOLIANS in attacking the city of Pylos. When this raid failed, Scerdilaidas split off and continued to raid with the Aetolians. Demetrius sailed around the tip of Greece with 50 ships, looting or holding to ransom islands in the southern Aegean. After taking substantial booty, he turned toward home when he learned that a fleet from RHODES was sailing to intercept him.

Demetrius' pirate raid had violated Queen Teuta's treaty of 228, which prohibited armed expeditions by the Illyrians. In 219, a large Roman army attacked Pharos. Demetrius, who had hidden several small ships, escaped and was welcomed by Philip V of Macedonia. He led new pirate raids in the Adriatic in 218 and was killed in 214 while commanding Macedonian land forces in Greece.

DEMOCHARES *(corsair captain; Mediterranean; died 36 B.C.)* A freedman (former slave) and captain of warships under Sextus POMPEIUS, whose corsair bands ravaged the coasts of Italy from bases in Sicily, Corsica, and Sardinia. Demochares was the lieutenant of MENECRATES, one of Sextus Pompey's chief commanders. He took command in the spring of 38, when Menecrates died during a naval battle off Cumae (near Naples) with the forces of Octavian (later emperor as Augustus Caesar). Although Demochares defeated Octavian's fleet, he allowed it to escape because of his grief over Menecrates' death.

Shortly afterward, Sextus appointed Demochares and APOLLOPHANES admirals of his warships, and they again routed Octavian's navy during a battle in the Strait of Messina. Although Demochares escaped by leaping onto another ship, the fight was broken off when the enemy commander rammed and captured Demochares' flagship.

The next day, a great storm destroyed most of Octavian's remaining warships.

Demochares and Apollophanes shared command of Sextus' warships until the pirates were driven from Sicily in 36. During the summer of 36, Demochares commanded a squadron of 40 warships when Sextus' fleet met Octavian's forces in an inconclusive battle off the Sicilian coast near Millazo. Octavian succeeded in landing part of his army in Sicily, and Apollophanes and Demochares almost captured the future emperor as he returned to Italy on a single ship.

Octavian's forces finally defeated Sextus' fleets at the battle of Naulochus in September 36. During the battle, Demochares killed himself rather than be captured. He thus proved to be unusually loyal, since Apollophanes surrendered to Octavian after this and MENAS already had betrayed Sextus Pompey twice.

DEMPSTER, EDWARD *(English pirate; Caribbean; active 1668–1669)* Dempster was among Sir Henry MORGAN's captains during expeditions against PORTOBELO (1668) and Maracaibo, Venezuela (1669).

DENBALL, SAMPSON *(Barbary corsair; Mediterranean; about 1606–1624)* A Dartmouth mariner, Denball accompanied John WARD to TUNIS in about 1606 but soon gained an independent command. Converting to Islam (as Ali Reis), he led many successful raids in the eastern Mediterranean and rose to CAPTAIN OF THE SEA. In 1624, with only three ships, he was captured by 14 Maltese and Sicilian galleys after a fierce six-hour battle and was condemned as a GALLEY SLAVE.

DERRICK, CAPTAIN *(English pirate; Atlantic; 1581)* Captain Derrick brought a captured French vessel into Studland Bay and imprisoned the crew in a royal blockhouse for 17 days while selling their cargo. After the vessel was empty, Derrick delivered it to the deputy VICE-ADMIRAL, Sir Christopher Hatton. He was arrested in Poole but bribed the mayor to release him and send carpenters to repair his ship.

DESMARAIS, CAPTAIN *(French buccaneer; Caribbean, Pacific; 1685)* With Captain LE PICARD and Jean ROSE, he brought 260 buccaneers overland across Panama to join a large raiding party gathering on the Pacific Coast.

D'ESTAMPES, BROTHER TEODOSIO *(Knight of Malta; Mediterranean; 1667)* Captain of a private sailing ship, D'Estampes was wounded capturing a large Turkish vessel and died soon after.

"DEVIL AND TOM WALKER, THE" *(short story; 1824)* A tale set in 1727 in Washington IRVING's *Tales of a Traveler*. CAPTAIN KIDD had hidden enormous booty at a swampy inlet near Boston. Like all BURIED TREASURE, it is guarded by the devil.

Walking through the swamp, the greedy miser Tom Walker meets the devil, about to cut down a tree holding a retired buccaneer's soul. Tom can have Kidd's treasure, if he will do the devil's work. After refusing to deal in slaves, Tom becomes a rich moneylender and (in his old age) a Bible-carrying religious zealot. The devil enforces his bargain and takes Tom to hell.

DEVIL-SHIP PIRATES, THE (British motion picture; color; 1964)

The ruthless Captain Robles (Christopher Lee) and his cut-throat crew briefly enlist with the Spanish Armada in 1588. After the Spanish defeat, Robles stops along the English coast to repair his vessel. Aided by some of the residents, the pirates terrorize a small village. Manuel (Barry Warren) finally deserts his shipmates and helps the villagers rebel against their evil rule. Directed by Don Sharp.

DEVIL'S OWN, THE (novel, 1975)

The second of five novels by Christopher Nicole (1930–), tracing the history of the Warner and Hilton families in the West Indies. The series mixes historical and invented characters, although Nicole takes many liberties with the actual chronology of events.

Devil's Own focuses on Christopher "Kit" Hilton, an illegitimate descendant of the Warners. In the late 1660s, Kit lives on TORTUGA with his grandmother, widow of Anthony Hilton, the island's first English governor. His best friend is Jean Du Casse (who commanded the French pirates sacking CARTAGENA).

Spanish troops invade and murder Kit's grandmother and Jean's mother. The boys escape by swimming to Hispaniola and joining the cow-hunting BUCCANEERS. Meeting up with Bartholomew PORTUGUES, they help seize a Spanish merchantman with an unarmed boat (a fictitious incident that EXQUEMELIN credits to Pierre LE GRAND).

The buccaneers sail to PORT ROYAL and join Sir Henry MORGAN's raid on PANAMA. When Morgan steals the booty, Kit ends up in Antigua and marries a beautiful, wealthy, and evil cousin. Other pirates, including Edward ENGLAND, show up during his sexually passionate but troubled marriage.

Devil's Own is packed with violence and lust, both heterosexual and homosexual. Murder, suicide, torture, starvation, cannibalism, gang rape, and leprosy—all are carefully described as is the Caribbean climate. Nicole pitilessly describes the horrors of Morgan's Panama raid. His pirates are not storybook fiends but normal men reduced to the lowest levels of brutality.

(See also AMYOT'S CAY.)

DEY (Barbary rulers; 17th and 18th centuries)

A Turkish word (meaning "maternal uncle") used of junior officers commanding OTTOMAN troops. After political revolutions, the same title was used by the head of the government in TUNIS (from 1591 to 1673) and in ALGIERS (from 1671 to 1830).

In Tunis, the JANISSARY garrison had 40 sections of 100 men, each under a dey. In 1591, the Janissaries rebelled, massacred several senior officers, and instituted the rule of a chief dey, elected for life by the other deys. Uthman Dey (1598–1610) and Yusuf Dey (1610–1637), both strong rulers, encouraged piracy and welcomed English captains to Tunis. However, they allowed the BEY, a hereditary officer governing the rural tribes, to build up an independent power base. After a military rebellion failed in 1673, the bey took control, and the office of chief dey was abolished in 1705.

In Algiers, Janissary officers remained in control until 1671, when the corsair's guild (TAIFE REISI) rebelled and elected a ruler with the Tunisian-style title of dey. In 1689, the Janissaries regained power and elected the dey from their own ranks. This elective monarchy survived in Algiers until the French conquest in 1830. Although deys became more autocratic during the 18th century, they remained members of the Janissary corps, liable to removal by assassination. Fourteen of the 30 deys ruling Algiers between 1683 and 1818 were murdered.

(See also SELECTED BIBLIOGRAPHY: Wolf, *Barbary*.)

DHOW (type of ship; Red Sea, Persian Gulf, Indian Ocean; ancient times to the present)

A trading vessel of 150 to 200 tons, with a single mast carrying one large lateen sail. Arab pirates raided in dhows armed with cannon.

(See also QAWASIM; RAHMAH IBN JABIR.)

DIABOLITO (Cuban pirate; Caribbean; 1823–1824)

In July 1823, an American squadron ran into Diabolito's new and heavily armed schooner near Matanzas, Cuba. About 30 pirates were killed, but Diabolito ("Little Devil") and 40 others escaped on shore. Acquiring another ship, he cruised off Cuba and the Yucatan Peninsula early in 1824.

DICAEARCHUS (Greek pirate; Aegean Sea, Mediterranean; died 196 B.C.)

A native of AETOLIA, Dicaearchus sold his services to several empires in the eastern Mediterranean. King Philip V of Macedonia had fought several wars against the Aetolians. Nevertheless, when Philip needed money in 204 B.C., he secretly hired Dicaearchus. Giving him 20 ships, the king ordered him to loot the Aegean islands and to help the pirates of CRETE, at war with RHODES.

For the next two years, pirate squadrons roamed the Aegean Sea in the largest raids since POLYCRATES. Dicaearchus' corsairs plundered independent islands and cities as well as those allied with Egypt (Philip's foe from 203). During the same years, Cretan pirates and those hired by King NABIS of Sparta also harried the Aegean. But Dicaearchus' corsairs were especially feared, and the pirate chief deliberately spread terror among his intended victims. Wherever he anchored his ships, he constructed two altars to Impiety and Lawlessness, worshiping these powers as gods.

Philip of Macedonia used his share of Dicaearchus' booty to purchase and construct a navy, which acted as lawlessly as the pirates. Alarmed by attacks on its allies and trading partners, Rhodes declared war on Macedonia in 202 and solicited the help of Rome and Pergamum. The Rhodian and Pergamene fleets defeated the Macedonian navy off Chios in 201. During the Second Macedonian War, the Roman army vanquished Philip's troops on land (200–196).

Escaping his patron's downfall, Dicaearchus switched sides and joined the forces of Ptolemy, ruler of Egypt. In 196, Dicaearchus and other Greek mercenaries unsuccessfully tried to overthrow Ptolemy's government. The Egyptians granted the other Greek leaders a merciful death by poison. But they savagely tortured Dicaearchus to punish his long history of treason.

DICK OF DOVER   See CATRO, RICHARD.

DIEGO THE MULATTO   See GRILLO, DIEGO.

DIODORUS OF SICILY   *(Greek historian; mid first century B.C.)*   A native of Sicily, Diodorus wrote a *World History*, relating historical events from the earliest times until his own. His narrative presents excerpts from the works of earlier Greek historians, many otherwise lost. Although Diodorus quotes various traditions without close analysis, he does suggest that certain stories are more fiction than fact. He is a major source for information about ancient pirates (including BUTES, POSTUMIUS, and TIMOCLES) and corsair havens such as CRETE and the LIPARI ISLANDS.

DIONYSUS OF PHOCAEA   *(Greek buccaneer; Mediterranean; fifth century B.C.)*   Dionysus commanded the fleets of PHOCAEA, a Greek city on the coast of Asia Minor, during the battle of Lade (495 B.C.) against the Persians. When the battle was lost, Dionysus knew that the enemy would soon capture his native city and decided to turn pirate. Seizing three Persian warships, he raided along the PHOENICIAN coast, sinking many merchant ships and collecting much booty.

Dionysus headed west to Sicily. A few years earlier, about 535, the Carthaginian and ETRUSCAN navies had destroyed a colony of Phocaean pirates on Corsica. After defeating the Phocaeans, they had killed captured seamen by stoning them. Dionysus hated these enemies of his people. From his Sicilian base, HERODOTUS relates, he ruthlessly plundered Carthaginian and Etruscan ships, but never attacked those belonging to Greeks.

DJERBA   *(Barbary corsair haven; Mediterranean; about 1504–1514, 1547–1551)*   An island off the coast of Tunisia. Djerba was ARUJ BARBAROSSA's first headquarters (about 1504), from which he occupied ALGIERS and other North African ports. It provided TURGUT REIS' main base from 1547 until the conquest of TUNIS in 1551.

DJERBA, BATTLE OF   *(corsair victory; Mediterranean; May 1560)*   The destruction of Spain's fleet at Djerba profoundly weakened its naval strength, thus ensuring the survival of the BARBARY STATES. By 1559, corsair attacks on merchant shipping had reduced Italy and western Spain to starvation. King Philip II dispatched 12,000 infantry on 50 galleys and 29 sailing ships to reconquer TRIPOLI. Gian Andrea Doria, Admiral Andrea Doria's great-nephew and only 20 years old, received command of the fleet, hired from Italian ports.

Rather than attacking Tripoli, the Spaniards occupied Djerba in March 1560. Alerted by ULUJ ALI, an OTTOMAN battle fleet suddenly arrived on May 11. Doria's panic-stricken captains fled in complete and utter disorder. Although this daring move exposed them to artillery fire, the Ottoman galleys gained speed by pursuing with their sails up. The Spaniards lost at least half their ships and 10,000 men, including many of their most experienced officers. TURGUT REIS arrived about a week later from Tripoli with 16 warships. After two months of bitter fighting, the Spanish garrison left behind at Djerba surrendered on July 29.

(See also SELECTED BIBLIOGRAPHY: Guilmartin, *Gunpowder.*)

DOBSON, RICHARD   *(English pirate; Caribbean; active 1668–1671)*   Dobson was captain of a ship during Sir Henry MORGAN's assaults on PORTOBELO (1668), Maracaibo (1669), and PANAMA (1671). During the Panama raid, he commanded the 15-ton *Fortune*, carrying six guns and 35 crewmen.

DOGLAR, JEAN   *(French pirate; Caribbean; 1668)*   Doglar was among the captains looting PORTOBELO with Henry MORGAN.

DOLOPIANS   *(Greek pirates; Aegean Sea; fifth century B.C.)*   Perhaps originally from north-central Greece, they occupied the island of SKIROS and lived by piracy. Shortly before 476, some merchants from northern Greece accused the Dolopians of enslaving them after stealing their ship and goods. The merchants subsequently escaped and won a suit against the Skirians in a law court at Delphi. When the Skirians refused to return their property, the merchants requested assistance from Cimon, commander of the Athenian fleets. In 476, Cimon's forces captured Skiros, expelled or enslaved the Dolopians, and set up an Athenian colony.

DORTOLO, GIOVAN PIETRO   *(Barbary corsair; Mediterranean; 1616)*   Dortolo purchased from the government of TUNIS permission to own a fellow Christian as his slave.

DOUBLE CROSSBONES   *(motion picture; color; 1950)*   Good-natured comedy directed by Charles Barton and containing lots of sight gags. Davy Crandall (Donald O'Connor) works for a Carolina shopkeeper, who fences pirate loot. Through various accidents and mistakes of identity, Crandall finds himself commanding a ship staffed with men headed for debtor's prison.

Crandall sails to TORTUGA and becomes friendly with the leading pirates, including Anne BONNY (2) (Hope Emerson) Captain Ben Wickett (Charles McGraw), CAPTAIN KIDD (Alan Napier), Henry MORGAN (Robert Barrat), BLACKBEARD (Louis Bacigalupi), and Ben Avery [Henry EVERY] (Glenn Strange). However, rather than marauding, Crandall devotes his time to rescuing Lady Sylvia Copeland (Helena Carter) from an arranged marriage. There are two song-and-dance numbers, one taken by O'Connor, the other by a chorus. The pirate captains are played as broad caricatures. They never met in real life, since some died a century before others were born.

DOWNES, JOHN *(English pirate; Atlantic, active 1606–1631)* Downs marauded from harbors in southern Cornwall, usually by bribing local officials. About 1611, he persuaded the captain of a Scotch ship to reveal hidden gold by whipping him and two young boys and by tying knotted cords around their heads.

"DOWNFALL OF PIRACY, THE" *(ballad; 1720s?)* A song about the battle between Lieutenant Maynard's vessel and that of Edward TEACH (BLACKBEARD), during which Teach was killed. Existing copies were printed in Britain, and the ballad draws on reports from British and American newspapers.

The song is evidence that Daniel DEFOE made up the stories about Teach's cruelty and invented a fictional character named Blackbeard. The lyrics refer to Teach as a lover of gold and "ill-got gain," but they do not mention any atrocities. Furthermore, Defoe wrote that Teach ravished countless females. But the ballad describes him as afraid of women and perhaps impotent. The second stanza relates how he took a pardon at Carolina.

> There he marry'd a lady, and gave her five hundred
> pound,
> But to her he prov'd unsteady, for he soon march'd
> off the ground.

In a military battle, it is the losing side that "marches off" or "gives up" the ground. In this context, "unsteady" refers to a defective performance.

(See also SELECTED BIBLIOGRAPHY: Firth, *Naval.*)

DRAGUT A version of TURGUT REIS' name often used by his Christian foes.

DRAKE OF ENGLAND *(British motion picture; black and white; 1935)* Sir Francis DRAKE (Matheson Lang) loots TREASURE FLEETS and defeats the Spanish Armada. The historical pageantry is enlivened by the story of Drake's secret marriage to Elizabeth Sydenham (Jane Baxter), a lady-in-waiting to Queen Elizabeth (Athene Seyler). Directed by Arthur Woods.

DRAKE, SIR BERNARD *(English captain; Atlantic; died 1586)* Born near Ashe in eastern Devonshire, Bernard possibly was related to Sir Francis DRAKE, who came from Tavistock. When the queen knighted Francis Drake in 1581, he tried to borrow Bernard's family crest, a red-winged dragon. Although Bernard complained, it is not true that he and Francis came to blows over the matter.

In 1585, Bernard Drake and Sir Amyas PRESTON jointly financed the 110-ton *Golden Royal* and planned to follow after and reinforce Sir Richard GRENVILLE's expedition, sent to ROANOKE, Virginia, by Sir Walter RALEIGH. The two men made a CONSORT agreement to split all prizes according to the amount of their investment. In July, along with one or more smaller ships, they instead were sent to plunder Spanish and Portuguese fishermen in Newfoundland.

On the way over, Drake and Preston captured a Brazilian sugar ship. Preston brought it back to England, while Drake went on and rounded up 17 fishing boats. Off Newfoundland, he encountered and entered into consort with George RAYMOND, who had slipped away from Grenville's main fleet. Drake and Raymond returned to England through the Azores, where they captured three or four Brazilian sugar ships and a French ship bringing gold and ivory from Africa. Taken together, Drake's prizes were extremely valuable, and Queen Elizabeth—thrilled by so much booty—knighted him the following January.

Drake brought back many of the captured ships, and their crews were jailed at Exeter until the spring of 1586. When they were brought to court, they spread "jail fever" (probably typhus) among those present. Drake caught it and died, along with the judges and 11 of the jury. Drake's son and Sir Walter Raleigh—the head of the entire Roanoke venture—apparently held on to the booty owed to Sir Amyas Preston under the consort agreements. Preston had to sue to get his fair share, and he held a grudge against Raleigh for years afterward.

DRAKE, SIR FRANCIS *(English admiral; Caribbean, Atlantic, Pacific; 1543?–1596)* The best-known Englishman of his day, Drake captured immensely rich prizes. A superb navigator and seaman, he was the second captain to circumnavigate the earth. (Juan Sebastián del Cano, Ferdinand Magellan's second-in-command, preceded Drake in 1522.)

The eldest son of a Devonshire farmer, Drake was related to John HAWKINS, who sent him on John LOVELL's 1566 slaving voyage to the Caribbean. In 1567, he served as an officer with a larger squadron, which Hawkins himself led. Hawkins' ships collected slaves by raiding African villages and plundering Portuguese vessels, and Drake received command of a captured CARAVEL. After forcing colonists in Venezuela to buy their cargo, the slavers were trapped at SAN JUAN DE ULÚA, Mexico, as they returned. Although the Spaniards destroyed most of their squadron, Hawkins and Drake made it back to England.

Raids on the Spanish Main

The failure of the 1567 adventure ended Hawkins' slaving voyages. Drake returned to the Caribbean each year from 1570 to 1572, openly bent on plunder. Although French corsairs previously had invaded the Caribbean, Drake's assaults were the first by an English captain. As a passionate Protestant, Drake hated the Roman Catholic Spanish, and he wanted to revenge the massacre at San Juan de Ulúa. However, the ADMIRALTY COURT refused to issue letters of REPRISAL. Legally, Drake's unauthorized raids in peacetime were nothing more than piracy.

Little is known about Drake's first expedition in 1570. His 1571 cruise was extremely profitable. With only the 25-ton *Swan*, he captured two FRIGATES and some 20 smaller vessels. Sailing up the Chagres River, he raided Venta de Cruces, only 20 miles from PANAMA.

These raids convinced Drake that the Panama Isthmus was the weakest point in Spain's defenses. Every year, American gold and silver were shipped to Panama and carried by pack-mule or by barge to the Caribbean port of Nombre de Dios. Although the Spanish Empire lived off this treasure, both Nombre de Dios and the trail across the Isthmus were undefended.

Sailing for Panama in May 1572, Drake suffered severe setbacks before finally plundering this "treasure of the world." He personally commanded Hawkins' 70-ton *Pascha*, and his brother John was captain of the *Swan*. Seventy-three crewman joined up for a chance at rich booty.

Landing on the Panamanian coast on June 29, Drake temporarily joined forces with John RAUNSE. A night raid captured Nombre de Dios on July 19. But the surprise was incomplete, some of the Spaniards put up a fight, and the raiders withdrew in disarray, with Drake wounded in the leg. Although they found heavy silver bars, the fleet already had left with the gold and jewels.

Raunse left the Americas, and Drake camped on a nearby island. For the next six months, his ships cruised along the coast. Although they seized some prizes, many men died of disease, and Drake had to sink the *Swan*. The expedition was saved by an alliance with the *Cimarrónes*, escaped African slaves familiar with the Spanish treasure trail. Late in January 1573, *Cimarrón* scouts learned that another treasure fleet had arrived at Panama. Drake set out with 30 Africans and 17 Englishmen. An arduous march brought Drake and John OXENHAM within sight of the Pacific, and they vowed to sail on its waters. Drake's gang ambushed the mule train in mid-February. But the Spaniards learned of the trap and escaped with most of the treasure.

Drake again cruised for prizes while waiting for another opportunity to attack. Early in April, he encountered a French ship under Guillaume LE TESTU. The two captains pooled their forces and agreed to split the take. (The *Cimarrónes* did not request a share.)

About a week later, Drake's force of English, French, and African raiders surprised the Spanish mule train only a mile from Nombre de Dios. They drove off the guards, buried the silver, and made off with as much gold as they could carry. Le Testu was killed during the assault, and Spanish troops recovered the bulk of the buried silver.

But most of the French and English pirates got back to their ships and divided their booty equally. Drake and his crew returned in August 1573 with a share worth perhaps £20,000.

Voyage around the Earth

In December 1577, Drake began what became his most famous voyage. Two years earlier, he had commanded ships in Ireland for the earl of Essex, Queen Elizabeth's favorite. Introduced to the court through Essex, Drake gained the support of the queen and high officials. Private investors financed the voyage, with the queen putting in, Drake later said, a thousand crowns.

Drake's 1577 expedition to South America's eastern coast had both a declared and a secret purpose. Officially, Drake was ordered to sail though the Strait of Magellan, look for likely sites for colonies, and return home the way he came. At the same time, the queen also expected him to raid the Peruvian ports where the Spanish treasure fleets originated. Since England and Spain were at peace, Drake's piratical plans were not mentioned in writing, and he did not receive a PRIVATEER's license. If he were captured, Elizabeth could pretend he had exceeded his instructions.

Drake sailed from Plymouth on December 13, 1577 commanding the *Pelican* (later renamed the GOLDEN HIND), four smaller ships, about 160 seamen and boys, and a dozen "gentleman adventurers" who had invested in the voyage. The fleet sailed down the African coast, taking half a dozen Spanish and Portuguese prizes. Off the Cape Verde Islands, Drake kidnapped a Portuguese pilot familiar with the route to South America.

After a difficult passage, the expedition reached Port Saint Julian, near the Strait of Magellan, on June 20, 1578. There Drake destroyed two of his ships and hanged Captain Thomas Doughty, whom he accused of treason, mutiny, and witchcraft. After they passed through the Strait, a ferocious storm drove the ships southward for 50 days. One sank and another turned back to England, leaving only the *Golden Hind*.

Drake turned north and reached Valparaiso, Chile, on December 5, capturing a valuable Spanish prize and sacking the town. A month was spent careening the *Golden Hind* and preparing for action. Drake had devoted a year to his official task of exploration. Now he was ready to plunder along the undefended coast. Since the Spanish did not expect to meet English pirates in the Pacific, Drake was able to take many vessels by surprise.

On February 5, 1579, Drake reached Arica, from which Peruvian silver was shipped to Panama. He seized only two relatively poor prizes and headed for Callao, the port of Lima. On the way, he captured other ships and learned that the CACAFUEGO had just left Callao, richly laden with treasure. Since none of the vessels in Callao harbor held a cargo, Drake feverishly pursued the *Cacafuego*. Along the way, he seized several more vessels. On one ship, he tortured the captain's clerk to make him reveal any hidden treasures.

On March 1, 1579, Drake caught up with the *Caca-fuego* near Cape San Francisco just north of the equator. Despite its riches, the ship was unarmed and surrendered after one volley. The cargo of gold, silver bars, and silver coins was immensely valuable, and the voyage was truly "made."

Drake still had to get home with his loot. It would be too dangerous to return past the angry Spanish and through the Strait of Magellan, and he continued north seeking an alternate route. In April, the *Hind*'s crew sacked Guatulco, Mexico, destroyed and desecrated its church, and took on food and water. The ship sailed far to the north, probably looking for the fabled Northwest Passage to Europe, until it was halted by extreme cold.

Drake returned south and repaired the *Hind* at a bay in northern California. Off Nicaragua, he had captured a prize with charts for the trans-Pacific voyage to the Philippines. The *Hind* sailed east in July 1589. With stops only at Mindanao, the Moluccas, Java, and Sierra Leone in West Africa, Drake returned to Plymouth on September 26, 1580.

Drake's voyage brought him instant fame as well as great wealth. But he also had bitter critics, including several shipmates and London merchants, who feared Spanish retaliation for his piracies. With his share of the booty (at least £10,000), Drake gave lavish presents to the queen's courtiers, and purchased an estate near Plymouth for £3,400. The queen gave him other estates and knighted him in 1581. He married a beautiful young heiress in 1585, was twice mayor of Plymouth, and served in Parliament in 1581, 1584, and 1593.

First West Indies Raid

On September 14, 1585, 25 or more ships left Plymouth carrying 2,300 seamen and soldiers. By sending this powerful amphibious expedition to the Caribbean, Queen Elizabeth began decades of open conflict with Spain. As she had in 1572 and 1577, Elizabeth played a double game. Drake's commission (the first he received) authorized him to release English prisoners in Spanish ports. But it was understood that he also would visit the West Indies.

The expedition was a plunder raid financed as a joint stock venture. Investors expected a large return if Drake captured a Spanish treasure fleet or sacked cities along its route. In the process, the assault would weaken Spain's finances and prestige in Europe. No permanent colony was planned, although Drake considered setting up a temporary base at Havana.

Drake fulfilled his official assignment by threatening Bayonna and Vigo in Spain. Without knowing it, he just missed intercepting a treasure fleet with one of the richest cargoes ever brought from the Americas. The English pressed on to the Cape Verde Islands and captured Santiago. Here, as later in the West Indies, Drake held the town for ransom. When none was paid, Drake burned Santiago to the ground and sailed for the Caribbean.

Within a few days, a virulent fever struck the fleet, killing hundreds and leaving the survivors weak and disoriented.

On December 31, 1585, the city of Santo Domingo was captured almost without a struggle and ruthlessly sacked. The former capital of the Indies was decayed and poor. Drake demanded a million ducats in ransom but finally accepted 25,000 after burning about a third of the city. CARTAGENA was richer and more strongly fortified. But its demoralized defenders were easily overcome and surrendered on February 11, 1586. Again the booty proved disappointing. By burning many buildings and threatening the rest, Drake extracted 107,000 ducats in ransoms early in March.

As his men continued to sicken and die, Drake abandoned any plan of using Cartagena as a base for a raid on Nombre de Dios and Panama. Before returning to England (on July 28), the fleet sailed north, devastated Saint Augustine, Florida, and visited the English colony on Roanoke Island, founded the previous summer by Sir Richard GRENVILLE.

Although Drake had proved himself a master at combining land and naval forces, the raid was not a financial success. Some 750 men had died, mainly of disease. The booty was estimated at about £69,000, with the crew dividing a third share. The backers, including the queen, got back only 75 percent of their investment, and Drake also lost money on the voyage.

In March 1587, Drake was ordered to attack the ships assembling for the Spanish Armada. Plunder remained a major goal. A joint-stock company financed the expedition, and Drake's fleet was accompanied by pirate ships belonging to John WATTS and other London merchants. Seizing a few prizes on the way, Drake took Cádiz completely by surprise and destroyed or captured some 30 ships. Soon after, off the Azores, Drake took his richest prize. A great Portuguese CARRACK, the *San Felipe*, carried East Indies treasure and goods worth £114,000, and Drake personally netted more than £17,000.

When the Spanish Armada sailed in 1588, Drake was appointed vice-admiral of the English fleet, and he had a major part in the battles that disrupted the invading force. In 1589, he received naval command of about 150 royal and private vessels, which landed troops at Lisbon and La Coruña, Spain. They accomplished little and were devastated by disease.

Second West Indies Raid

Drake's reputed good fortune deserted him on his disastrous last expedition. Partly because of his assault in 1585 and 1586, Spain had strengthened its Caribbean defenses. Moreover, the English military plans were over-ambitious and poorly executed. Drake and Sir John Hawkins shared command, with Thomas Baskerville leading the land forces. Drake's spirited opportunism was totally incompatible with Hawkins methodical caution, and the two commanders quarrelled bitterly from the beginning.

The fleet, even more powerful than in 1585, sailed on September 7, 1595. Six royal warships and 21 well-armed merchantmen carried about 1,500 sailors and 1,000 soldiers. Stockholders again financed the voyage and its sole purpose was plunder. The original plan was to capture Panama and to hold it for some time. However, news reached England that a damaged GALLEON with a large treasure had taken refuge at San Juan, Puerto Rico. The commanders resolved to capture it before heading for Panama. But the Spanish also knew of the wreck, and five Spanish FRIGATES left for Puerto Rico on September 25.

Drake insisted on attacking Las Palmas in the Canary Islands, partly because he had stocked insufficient provisions. The attack failed, and the Spanish learned of Drake's plans from English prisoners. The fleet arrived at Guadaloupe on November 9 but (at Hawkins' insistence) spent two weeks preparing for battle. In the meantime, the five Spanish frigates reached San Juan and warned of the attack.

Hawkins died as the fleet anchored off Puerto Rico on November 22. The Spanish had strengthened their defenses with cannon from the wreck, and the five frigates guarded the harbor behind a barrier of sunken ships. After several assaults were repulsed on November 22 and 23, Drake broke off the attack.

Instead of sailing straight for Panama, Drake leisurely toured the towns along the coasts of Venezuela and Colombia. RIO DE LA HACHA and Santa Marta were sacked but yielded little booty. Drake bypassed Cartagena, more strongly defended than in 1586. The English captured Nombre de Dios on January 6, 1596, but found no treasure in the abandoned town.

On January 8, Drake sent Baskerville with 600 or more soldiers along the overland mule track from Nombre de Dios to Panama. After they captured Panama, Drake planned to bring his ships up the Chagres River to Venta de Cruces. However, as Drake must have known, the overland route was almost impassible during the winter rainy season. The soldiers were repulsed with heavy losses and returned to Nombre de Dios on January 12.

The fleet stood westward for Nicaragua and Honduras, still seeking plunder. While it was delayed by bad weather, a deadly fever broke out. Drake himself died of dysentery on February 7 and was buried at sea near PORTOBELO. With Baskerville in command, the ships reached England in April and May, fending off a fleet sent out from Spain to destroy them.

(See also SELECTED BIBLIOGRAPHY: Gerhard, *Pirates*; Rogoziński, *Caribbean*; Sugden, *Drake*; SIR FRANCIS DRAKE REVIVED.)

DRINKING/DRUNKENNESS (pirate pleasures; all eras)

When alcohol was condemned during the 19th century, fiction writers invented the myth of pirate drunkenness. European and American pirates did drink freely, but so did most others in their societies. In real life, only Christian RENEGADES at the BARBARY STATES drank more than their nonpirate neighbors. Pious Muslims do not use alcohol. However, some Europeans converted to Islam simply to become corsairs and continued to imbibe.

As did other Europeans (including infants and children), pirates consumed alcoholic beverages during meals. Alcohol was shared at social gatherings (which often served a business purpose). In a few cases, it became an addictive drug.

Until the 19th century, water often was unhealthy and might carry lethal diseases. Everyone drank fermented beer, cider, and wine, with the rich enjoying better quality than the poor. Drinking was thought of as beneficial and desirable even by moralists and religious leaders. Roman Catholic monks and nuns received a generous liquor ration, with lesser amounts during Lent. English and New England Puritans, including the clergy, drank copiously at and between meals.

Since water stored in wooden kegs turned putrid, sailors preferred almost anything else. Mediterranean seamen drank wine, while the Elizabethan English consumed mainly wine and beer. From the 17th century, Caribbean RUM became more common than beer, which quickly becomes sour. But pirates happily consumed wine and brandy whenever they captured any.

Especially in the cold Atlantic waters, as Woodes ROGERS remarked, "good Liquor to Sailors is preferable to clothing." On longer voyages, men were reduced to eating rotten bread and salt meat or fish. Alcohol supplied easily digested calories and briefly warmed men who wore the same damp CLOTHING day and night. Nautical custom and written contracts guaranteed a daily liquor ration on both merchant ships and naval vessels.

Sailors drank for social reasons as well as for comfort. On shore, they gathered at taverns to cement old friendships and make new ones. With a population under 3,000, PORT ROYAL had 100 licensed taverns in 1680. Major ports such as London supported thousands of sailors' retreats. Wherever they were, seaman constantly drank toasts to "wives and mistresses," friends, comrades, voyages, and good luck. MADAGASCAR pirates, it is said, mixed gunpowder with rum when making especially solemn toasts.

Pirate crews were relatively undisciplined, and their business included tedious waits between victims. Some probably drank more than other seamen. George SHELVOCKE's vessel carried the normal liquor ration for two vessels for several years. When he was separated from John CLIPPERTON in 1719, Shelvocke's crew guzzled the entire supply in a few months. Despite this, the crew stayed sober enough to run the ship. (John Clipperton was himself one of the rare cases of incapacitating alcoholism.) All pirates caroused after capturing a rich prize.

Parties at sea or in captured towns sometimes turned unlucky. While Sir Henry MORGAN entertained his captains in 1668, a befuddled sailor set Morgan's vessel afire, blowing up 200 men. After Morgan occupied Panama in

1671, drunken pirates let a Spanish treasure ship sail away. A British warship defeated Bartholomew ROBERTS in 1722 partly because his crew had spent the previous night celebrating a prize. Debauchery was safer when pirates relaxed at a protected HAVEN, where townsmen eagerly sold them alcohol, rich food, and prostitutes.

Pirates often invited or forced others to join the party. When John HAWLEY seized French wine ships in 1399, all of Dartmouth, England, was drunk for a week. Caribbean towns were wide-open when the BUCCANEERS were in town.

Since drinking was condoned until the 19th century, fictional accounts either ignore it or mention it without pejorative comments. Exquemelin criticizes the buccaneers solely because they allowed tavernkeepers and whores to rob them. Daniel DEFOE also takes drinking for granted. Some 40 biographies in his GENERAL HISTORY rarely mention drunkenness. After taking a prize, Francis SPRIGGS' crew "spent the day in boysterous Mirth, roaring and drinking of Healths." When their ship was wrecked, John SMITH's men "resolved not to leave the Liquor behind them, rememb'ring the Proverb . . . and then came away in as drunken a Pickle as can be imagined." Both crews enjoyed innocent fun. Among Defoe's villains, BLACKBEARD alone turns unpleasant when drunk.

Drinking became a symbol of pirate wickedness only during the 19th century, long after piracy ended. English and American "temperance" movements taught that alcohol was evil in itself. Under their influence, writers invented the myth that pirates drank more than others. Drinking is bad, these authors reasoned, and pirates also are bad. Thus, they concluded, all pirates must have been drunks.

In "WOLFERT WEBBER" (1824), Washington IRVING created a retired buccaneer whose nightly drunks terrorize an inn. Irving's character became Billy Bones in TREASURE ISLAND (1883). Moreover, Long John Silver owns a tavern, and his pirates spend their nights carousing by a great fire after they reach the island.

Treasure Island established the myth of pirate alcoholism, and crewmen carouse in most later fiction. Rafael SABATINI's pirate novels added a curious twist to the pirate use of alcohol. Sabatini's Peter Blood is an honest man driven to piracy by oppression. Blood thus keeps his ship clean and disciplined, while all other pirate crews are slovenly drunks.

Although drinking occurs in some pirate MOVIES, drunkenness is not important to their plots. The first SWASHBUCKLERS, such as CAPTAIN BLOOD (1935), were based on Sabatini's novels. Their male leads have no vices. Later films either remade or spoofed these early classics. In the straight remakes, the pirate hero remains too manly to get drunk. For the many parodies, pirate captains are demented buffoons, who do not need alcohol to act foolishly.

(See also BAGNIOS; GROG; SELECTED BIBLIOGRAPHY: Bridenbaugh, *No Peace*; Defoe, *General History*; Exquemelin, *Buccaneers*; Lender, *Drinking*.)

DRINKING SONGS   See SONGS, PIRATE.

DRURY, ROBERT   See MADAGASCAR OR ROBERT DRURY'S JOURNAL.

DUCHESNE, CAPTAIN *(French buccaneer; Gulf of Mexico; 1683)*   Said to be from Saint Domingue (Haiti), Captain Duchesne sacked Tampico, Mexico.

DUDLEY, SIR ROBERT *(English adventurer; Caribbean, Atlantic; 1574–1649)*   Illegitimate son of Robert Dudley, earl of Leicester (1532?–1588), a favorite of Queen Elizabeth I. Although not recognized as Leicester's son, he received lavish financial support and attended Oxford University. In 1595, Dudley decided to invade the Pacific in imitation of Sir Francis DRAKE and Thomas CAVENDISH. When Queen Elizabeth vetoed his plans, he instead went to the West Indies in September, perhaps intending to thwart Sir Water RALEIGH's planned expedition to the same region.

On the way, Dudley's ships chased every vessel they encountered but took few prizes. His main force stayed in Trinidad from February through March (avoiding the Spanish colonists) while a small party explored the mouth of the Orinoco River in Guyana. As he returned to England, Dudley again hunted for Spanish ships but captured only one small merchant vessel.

In 1603, Dudley sued to prove that he was legitimate and thus the rightful earl of Leicester and Warwick. He fled to Europe when his case was dismissed in 1605, spending the remainder of his life in Florence, Italy.

(See also WOOD, BENJAMIN.)

DUPPA, MICHAEL *(English pirate; Mediterranean; 1613–1614)*   Duppa sailed from MAMORA in Morocco.

DUTCH IN THE AMERICAS *(pirate invasions; Caribbean, Atlantic, Pacific; 1594–1648)*   Influenced in part by their adoption of Calvinist Protestantism, various factions in the Netherlands rebelled against their Spanish king during the 1560s. The seven northern provinces declared their independence in 1581, and the war continued until a 12-year truce was signed in 1609.

French and English pirates were the first to invade the Americas. Following Jean FLEURY's capture of Montezuma's treasure in 1523, French captains carried their attack to both Brazil and the Caribbean. English raids steadily increased from the 1560s. Although pirate crews often included Dutchmen, Dutch captains were surprisingly slow to follow the French and English. Spanish sources report several Dutch pirates off Nombre de Dios in 1569 and 1572, and they mention a few ships during the 1580s. But Dutch smugglers and pirates invaded in force only after Dutch traders were expelled from the Iberian Peninsula in 1598.

From 1599, large fleets invaded the Caribbean to obtain salt and tobacco. A favored destination was the

A battle between a Spanish galleon and a Dutch warship. From Jurien de la Gravière, *Les corsaires barbaresques* (1887).

Araya Peninsula in Venezuela, which was visited by some 800 Dutch vessels during the next six years. While the large salt hulks were anchored at Araya, their crews marauded throughout the Caribbean in large armed boats brought over on the mother ships. So fierce were their assaults that Spanish coastal shipping was literally swept from the seas. At the end of 1605, a Spanish fleet visited the region, seizing salt ships at Araya and other ports and killing their crews.

The Spanish government also tried to prevent colonists trading with the Dutch enemy. Most drastically, armed troops depopulated northern and western Hispaniola and destroyed existing towns. The entire western half of Hispaniola lay open to occupation by bands of cattle hunters and pirates, soon to be known as BUCCANEERS.

Dutch captains visiting the Caribbean often were smugglers as well as pirates. In 1599, plunder was the sole objective of expeditions to the Pacific coast by Simon de CORDES and Olivier van NOORT. Both failed to repeat Thomas CAVENDISH's capture of the MANILA GALLEON in 1587, and their backers lost their entire investment.

A 12-year truce ended open warfare between Spain and the Netherlands in 1609. Although it was ignored in Africa and the Far East, the truce generally held in the Americas. Leading the only major Dutch expedition, Joris van SPILBERGEN took six vessels to South America's Pacific coast in 1614. The raiders destroyed a Spanish fleet and occupied several towns, but they took almost no booty.

As the truce expired in 1621, the DUTCH WEST INDIA COMPANY was created to coordinate naval warfare. The company licensed individual captains and also sent large fleets of warships to Brazil and the Caribbean. By destroying Spanish sea power, Dutch assaults protected buccaneer havens at TORTUGA and Hispaniola. Although peace with Spain ended this second Dutch invasion in 1648, freelance marauders thus continued to infest the West Indies into the 1700s. The Company usually ignored South America's Pacific coast. The Dutch government financed a failed expedition by Hugo SCHAMPENDAM in 1624. Hendrik BROUWER led an abortive Company assault on southern Chile in 1643.

DUTCH WEST INDIA COMPANY *(pirate patron; Atlantic, Caribbean; 1621–1648)* From the 1580s, the Dutch Republic was at war with the Spanish and Portuguese empires (united under the Habsburg crown between 1580 and 1640). Fleets of Dutch smugglers and pirates overran the West Indies from the 1590s until a 12-year truce began in 1609. From 1623, Dutch assaults were renewed on an even larger scale. The marauders took rich booty, although never enough to pay for their armadas of warships. By weakening Spanish strength in the Caribbean, Dutch raiders encouraged the invasion by freelance BUCCANEERS.

To coordinate naval attacks, the West Indies Company—created in 1621—was granted a monopoly in the Americas and along Africa's western coast. The Company, a blend of governmental agency and private corporation, was dedicated to piracy and conquest. In Asia, the older East India Company sought profits through trade but was willing to use force to gain market share. In the Americas, the West India Company invested in plunder raids. Although a scaled-down version survived until 1791, the Company became unimportant when peace was concluded with Spain in 1648.

Like other governments at that time, the West India Company licensed individual raiders. Operating with one ship or a small squadron, several (especially Cornelis JOL) took rich booty. In addition, the Company also mounted and directed expeditions by large armadas carrying hundreds of soldiers. Sailors on these Company warships served for wages only, although they expected a bonus when booty was taken.

These Company fleets enjoyed some striking successes. Piet HEYN captured an entire Mexican TREASURE FLEET in 1628, and Pernambuco (Recife) Brazil was occupied in 1629. Altogether, by 1636, Dutch warships had captured 547 ships and destroyed 62 more. The Spaniards lost cargo and supplies valued at 83 million guilders. Trade and communications in the West Indies came to a standstill. Despite this vast booty, the Company's overall financial record was abysmal. Its fleets were simply too large to pay for themselves. By the 1640s, the Company had sunk into hopeless bankruptcy, and its stock became virtually worthless on the Amsterdam exchange.

The West India Company struck first at the rich and seemingly weak empire of Portugal. In 1623, its directors drew up a "grand design" that called for assaults by several fleets. The Company's admirals were ordered to invade Brazil, to occupy the West African slave stations, and to capture the treasure fleets that sailed each year from Havana. Despite some initial triumphs, this bold plan ultimately failed. Given the communications technology of the 1600s, trans-Atlantic voyages by separate groups of sailing ships could not be coordinated.

In May 1624, a fleet under Jacob Willekens and Piet Heyn easily captured Bahia, Brazil's chief port. Meanwhile, Pieter SCHOUTEN explored the entire Caribbean and succeeded in taking one of the two Honduras treasure ships.

In 1625, the Company planned to use Bahia as a base for the capture of the even richer Peruvian and Mexican treasure fleets. When Boudewijn HENDRICKSZ arrived in Brazil, however, a Spanish armada already had retaken Bahia. Hendricksz went on to San Juan, Puerto Rico, but failed to capture the El Morro fortress. The Spaniards repelled an attack on Venezuela, and Hendricksz' fleet returned almost empty-handed.

Following the dismal failure of these expensive adventures, the West India Company temporarily set aside its "grand design" and concentrated on plunder. In 1626 and 1627, raiders took 46 prizes in the Caribbean, including a Honduras treasure galleon captured by Hendrick LUCIFER. Piet Heyn simultaneously captured 39 ships off Brazil.

Using the booty taken by Lucifer and Heyn, the company in 1628 outfitted two larger fleets to hunt Spanish treasure galleons. They enjoyed extraordinary luck. Piet Heyn captured the Mexican silver fleet, while Pieter ITA collared both Honduras treasure ships. Meanwhile, Dierck van UYTGEEST took notable booty in Brazil. Instead of reinvesting this enormous plunder, the Company paid out a 75 percent cash dividend in 1629. Wise investors sold their shares on the news, since the company again began to pursue overambitious dreams. Piet Heyn's triumph was made possible by a combination of skill and exceptionally good luck that never reoccurred.

In 1629 and 1630, Adriaen PATER attempted to repeat Heyn's success with 25 ships. Spanish authorities outwitted him by simply holding their treasure fleets in port until Pater's supplies were exhausted. An armada commanded by Hendrick LONCQ occupied Pernambuco in 1629. However, Portuguese colonists at Bahia and other southern ports continued to resist the invaders.

Loncq went on to the Caribbean in 1630, which also was invaded during 1630 by squadrons under Pieter Ita and Dierick RUYTERS. However, all three returned with few prizes, and 1631 was even more unprofitable. Pater took a large fleet to Pernambuco but went down with his flagship. Taking command of Pater's ships, Martin THIJSZ invaded the Caribbean in 1632, but took little booty.

From 1633, the West India Company ceased to send large fleets to the Caribbean. The Company instead tried to make its beleaguered Brazilian foothold profitable by importing African slaves. Expeditions in 1637 and 1642 (the later commanded by Cornelis Jol) occupied Portuguese slave factories in West Africa. Forts were set up in the Caribbean—at Curacao, Saint Martin, and Tobago—to facilitate voyages between Brazil and Europe. From Brazil, Hendrick BROUWER in 1642 vainly invaded Chile, swhitherto ignored by the Company.

Although the Company's grandiose ventures had ended, individual captains continued to plunder Caribbean shipping. Cornelis Jol scoured the seas from 1630 through 1638 and led the last Dutch attack on the treasure fleets in 1640. Jan van HOORN pillaged Honduras and the Bay of Campeche in 1633. Dozens of other captains, whose names have not survived, also took prizes.

The Company's schemes were overthrown in 1645 when the Portuguese in Brazil rose up in a devastating revolt. The Company soon lost most of its Brazilian territories, although it defended the Pernambuco fortress until 1654. Hopelessly in debt, the Company turned into a comparatively peaceful organization, which smuggled or sold slaves and goods into the colonies of other nations.

(See also SELECTED BIBLIOGRAPHY: Andrews, *Spanish*; Goslinga, *Dutch*; Rogoziński, *Caribbean*.)

DU TERTRE, JEAN BAPTISTE *(French missionary; 1610–1687)* Son of a Norman physician, Du

Dyak warship. From Francis Marryat, *Borneo and the Indian Archipelago* (London, 1848).

Tertre left school, sailed as a seaman on several long voyages, and fought with the Dutch army. Joining the Dominican order in 1635, he was a successful missionary priest in France's Caribbean colonies from 1640 to 1658.

Du Tertre published (Paris, 1667–1671) a four-volume *Histoire général des Antilles habitées par les Francais (General History of the French Antilles)*. Having personally witnessed many of the events he reports, Du Tertre provides accurate and fascinating descriptions of the BUCCANEERS raiding from TORTUGA and the French Hispaniola (Haiti). Historians and authors of fiction have borrowed from his *History*, which was reprinted in 1978 (Fort-de-France, Martinique: E. Kolodziej).

DYAKS *(Borneo pirates; South China Sea; 18th and 19th centuries)* The Dutch and British term for the indigenous peoples of northern Borneo, in contrast to the MALAYS. The largest group, known as "Sea Dyaks," lived on the rivers and traveled by canoe. The tribes continuously warred with one another and collected the heads of enemy males for ritual purposes.

During the 18th century, Malay bands such as the ILANUNS built forts along the Borneo Coast. These raiders taught the Sea Dyaks piracy and converted many to Islam. The Dyaks began as rowers in Malay PRAHUS. When a trading vessel was captured, they were rewarded with the heads of the dead and some captives. By the 19th century, the Dyaks cruised in independent bands. When they sailed together, Dyak chiefs had equal authority with Malay leaders. Plunder was evenly divided, but the Dyaks never willingly spared male captives.

While Malay bands lived in coastal forts, Dyak strongholds were located further up the rivers, usually too shallow for European vessels. Large gangs operated from forts on the Saribas and Batang Lupar rivers in Sarawak, about 60 miles east of the capital at Kuching. SARIBAS raiding parties elected commanders from their own people. Two half-Arab brothers, Sherip SAHAP and Sherip Mullar, led the raiders based on the Batang Lupar, who were known as the SEKRANG pirates.

During the early 1840s, the Sea Dyaks cruised in large parties that sometimes included 4,000 warriors. They were expert seamen and constructed oared warboats, called BANGKONGS, especially suited to surprise attacks. Sir James BROOKE, who became rajah of Sarawak in 1841, assaulted their forts with help from the British navy. His raids ended large-scale piracy, although small bands operated until late in the 19th century.

Brooke described the Sea Dyaks as "handsome, intelligent, powerful, well-made, beautifully-limbed, and clear-skinned." Their ears were decorated with several brass rings, and they wore oddly shaped caps of many colors, with red preferred.

(See also SELECTED BIBLIOGRAPHY: Keppel, *Expedition*; Runciman, *White*; Rutter, *Pirate*.)

E

EARRINGS *(fictional pirate ornament; 20th century)* Caribbean pirates sometimes are shown wearing one or two brass or gold "Gypsy" hoops. In real life, European men wore earrings—but not hoops—only during the 16th century. Even women's earrings disappeared during later eras, when long hair, wigs, or headdresses obscured the ears.

As hair styles became shorter during the 1500s, Spanish and English aristocrats sometimes sported earrings. The fad affected only court nobles, who displayed pearls and other jewels and not metal hoops. Sir Walter RALEIGH, Sir Francis DRAKE, the earl of CUMBERLAND, and Sir Anthony SHERLEY may have worn earrings at court, but they left them at home during voyages. In France, earrings briefly became fashionable under the homosexual King Henry III (1551–1589).

Earrings vanished during the 1600s, as aristocrats again adopted shoulder-length hair styles. In England, male earrings, unthinkable under the Puritans, were not restored with the monarchy in 1660.

The origins of the hoop earring myth are obscure. There are no earrings in EXQUEMELIN (1678) and Daniel DEFOE's GENERAL HISTORY (1724–1728). Earrings also are absent from 19th-century fiction, such as THE PIRATES OWN BOOK (1837), TREASURE ISLAND (1883), and PETER PAN (1904). During the 1890s, Howard PYLE was the first major author to put earrings in texts and illustrations.

His pirates sometimes flaunt silver and jeweled pendants rather than gypsy hoops.

Douglas FAIRBANKS wears hoop earrings in THE BLACK PIRATE, a 1922 comedy; but they are rare in the romantic SWASHBUCKLERS. Errol FLYNN is earringless, even in *The* SEA HAWK (1940) set in Elizabethan England. Tyrone POWER sports hoop earrings in *The* BLACK SWAN (1942), as does Anthony Quinn in the AGAINST TWO FLAGS (1952). Disney put earrings into TREASURE ISLAND (1950) but left them out of PETER PAN (1953).

(See also CAPTAIN BRAND; CLOTHING.)

EASTON (ESTON), PETER *(English pirate; Atlantic; born early 1570s, active 1608–1613)* Despite his argumentative nature and cruelty, Easton led large squadrons, captured rich prizes, and retired wealthy. From Dartmouth, he served on English and Dutch PRIVATEERING vessels, becoming skilled in gunnery. In 1608, he quarreled with Richard ROBINSON and made off with one of his ships. During the next five years, Easton robbed the English as freely as any other nation, telling a captured captain he considered Englishmen no better than "Turckes and Jews."

By the summer of 1609, Easton was "vice-admiral" of the pirate confederation led by Richard BISHOP and based in Ireland. Alone or with other captains, he plundered Dutch and English shipping in the Bristol Channel.

"The Pirate was A Picturesque Fellow." Illustration by Howard Pyle in *Harper's Monthly Magazine*, December 1905.

When Bishop retired in 1611, Easton became the pirates' "admiral," commanding as many as 17 ships during the summer of 1611. Powerless before their onslaught, King James I offered the pirates a general pardon, while he simultaneously allowed Dutch warships to patrol English waters. Instead of avoiding battle, Easton sought out the Dutch ships, taking two rich prizes during his search.

The pirate fleet alliance broke up in August 1611. Accompanied by William HUGHES and a Captain Harvey, Easton spent the winter of 1611–1612 off the coast of West Africa and captured several Dutch and English merchantmen. His squadron then crossed the Atlantic to Newfoundland looking for ships, crews, and supplies.

Commanding nine ships, Easton plundered the fishing fleets and conscripted some 500 British seamen. Despite these successes, he inspired little affection among his followers. Several hundred of his own crews deserted during the Newfoundland raid, and his officers quarreled and threatened one another.

Back from Newfoundland late in 1612, Easton stopped at SALÉ while he negotiated a pardon from CARLO EMMANUELE I, duke of Savoy. He entered Villefranche (today

in France) in February 1613 with four ships, 900 men, and booty valued at more than 100,000 crowns. Easton became a favorite with Savoy's ruler. Four Savoyard ships under his command sank in a storm. Nevertheless, the duke made him a marquis and gave an annual pension of £4,000 for his skillful use of artillery during a war with Mantua.

Like John WARD at Tunis, Easton retired to wealthy leisure. He treacherously rid himself of his old shipmates, leaving most of them penniless and forced to beg passage home. Publicly converting to Roman Catholicism, he built a fine palace, and married an heiress. Although the English agent in Savoy described Easton as "rude and savadge," the Savoyards were amused by the former pirate turned Italian courtier.

(See also SELECTED BIBLIOGRAPHY: Senior, *Nation.*)

EATON, JOHN *(English pirate; Atlantic, Pacific; active 1683–1686)* Late in 1683, Eaton and 70 crewmen left London in the 26-gun *Nicholas*. He attacked settlements in Brazil and Argentina and captured a Portuguese prize before passing through the Strait of Magellan. On March 19, 1684, he ran into John COOK's BACHELOR'S DELIGHT near Valdivia, Chile.

Joining in consort, Eaton and Cook continued north to the JUAN FERNÁNDEZ and Galapagos islands, taking four prizes but no gold or silver. Suspecting that Spanish officials knew of their presence, the pirates headed for Central America. Near Costa Rica, Cook died, and the *Delight*'s crew elected Edward DAVIS captain.

The pirates landed near Realejo, Nicaragua, but found the town too strongly defended to attack. While they were careening their ships at Fonseca Bay, Eaton and Davis broke off their consortship. Eaton had decided South America promised little booty. Moreover, the *Delight*'s crew would not agree to split prizes equally, since their ship was larger than the *Nicholas*.

Eaton sailed back to Ecuador, returned to Panama, and finally ventured into the Pacific on January 1, 1685. Although the *Nicholas* carried four surgeons, many men died of SCURVY before Guam was reached on March 25. Eaton traded gunpowder for food with the Spanish colonists and fought with the natives. Four captured Indians were thrown into the water and shot for sport.

After visiting Canton from May to June, Eaton unsuccessfully chased a Manchu ship carrying silver. Leaving Borneo in December, the *Nicholas* sailed south and east, picking up a few poor prizes. William COWLEY, the ship's master and pilot, deserted at Timor and took the log with him. The *Nicholas* was last sighted near Djakarta, Indonesia, in March 1686. Eaton somehow returned to England, but the fate of the *Nicholas* is not known.

(See also SELECTED BIBLIOGRAPHY: Kemp and Lloyd, *Brethren.*)

EBANKS, GIDEON *(Cayman Islands pirate; Caribbean; 1931)* Ebanks' gang attacked a Cuban ship, killed five of her crew, and fled back to Grand Cayman. The police subsequently found the pirate's dead body in a mangrove swamp.

ELFRITH, DANIEL *(English pirate; Caribbean; active 1614–1637)* Elfrith spent several years smuggling goods into Spain's American colonies. While on an expedition to Guyana in 1614, he received command of a captured Spanish CARAVEL, which he took to Bermuda early the next year. Although her cargo of grain saved the Bermudians from starvation, they arrested Elfrith as a pirate and sent him to England for trial.

By 1618 Elfrith became an employee of the earl of Warwick, a leader of the Puritan faction and one of the founders of Virginia. Warwick made Elfrith commander of the warship *Treasurer* and bought a commission from CARLO EMMANUELE I, the piratical duke of Savoy, even though King James I had outlawed foreign privateering licenses in 1605.

Returning to England in the summer of 1619, Elfrith visited Virginia in consort with a Dutch pirate ship and 100 African slaves robbed from a Spanish vessel. He sold part of the cargo in Virginia (the first slaves ever imported into British North America) and carried the rest to Bermuda. Although the Bermudians purchased Elfrith's slaves, the governor confiscated the *Treasurer*, claiming it was unseaworthy.

Elfrith managed Warwick's plantations and looked after his political interest in Bermuda from 1623. During a period of hostility toward Spain in 1627, Warwick obtained a royal commission (copied from that earlier given to the earl of CUMBERLAND) allowing him to attack any part of the Spanish Empire. Warwick called Elfrith back to England and gave him command of one of three ships during an unsuccessful plunder raid in 1628 and early 1629.

Elfrith and the governor of Bermuda convinced Warwick that his raiders would take more booty if they set up a base at PROVIDENCE ISLAND, near Panama. Elfrith took a small number of settlers to Providence in 1629 and brought a larger group in May 1631. The island was placed under the Providence Company, which also acquired the pirate base at TORTUGA in 1631.

Elfrith became the colony's admiral, and his daughter married Captain Philip Bell, Providence's first governor. England and Spain made peace in November 1630, but the Providence (and Tortuga) Puritans continued to tolerate piracy. Elfrith attacked and plundered any small vessel he came across. In 1631, he captured a Spanish FRIGATE at Jamaica, leaving his unseaworthy PINNACE in exchange.

After Spanish attacks on Providence and Tortuga in 1635, the Providence Company turned the island into an acknowledged pirate haven and reorganized its government. Philip Bell was fired as governor in 1636, and Elfrith (always Bell's strong supporter) was removed as admiral in 1637.

(See also SELECTED BIBLIOGRAPHY: Newton, *Puritans;* Rogoziński, *Caribbean.*)

EMO, PIETRO *(Italian pirate; Adriatic Sea; 1584)* Emo's Venetian squadron encountered three Turkish GALLEYS that were fleeing harsh weather and carrying immense treasure and the widow of the DEY of TRIPOLI. Pretending that the galleys were pirates, Emo captured them in a fierce battle and then ordered his men to kill their crews and passengers, including the Dey's son. The Venetians murdered more than 250, after raping the female slaves.

One of the Turks escaped the massacre and told his story at Istanbul. To avoid a war with the OTTOMAN EMPIRE, the Venetians beheaded Emo, profusely apologized, and bribed high Turkish officials. The captured galleys were repaired and sent to Istanbul, manned by Turks freed from slavery and carrying 400 Christian slaves to replace those Emo had slain.

ENGLAND, EDWARD *(British pirate; Caribbean, Atlantic, Indian Ocean; active 1717–1720)* Originally named Seegar, England was a good-natured but weak man, who disliked abusing prisoners but could not control the crew. While an officer on a Jamaican SLOOP, he was captured by Christopher WINTER and joined his band at New Providence. When Woodes ROGERS subdued the Bahamian pirates, England made off and took several prizes along the African coast as well as in the Azores and Cape Verde islands.

Exchanging his sloop for a larger ship renamed the *Pearl,* England returned to Africa in the spring of 1719. The pirates scoured the coast from Gambia to Ghana and took two dozen prizes, looting some, burning others. They kept one prize, renamed the *Victory* and commanded by John TAYLOR. Having stopped to careen their ships at an isolated bay, according to Daniel DEFOE, "they liv'd there very wantonly for several Weeks, making free with the Negroe Women, and committing such outragious Acts, that they came to an open Rupture with the Natives."

The *Pearl* and *Victory* took on provisions at MADAGASCAR early in 1720. The pirates looted several vessels along the Malabar coast of India, where England exchanged the *Pearl* for the 34-gun *Fancy.* They returned to Madagascar and then made for Johanna Island. In the harbor on August 27, they found three large English and Dutch ships trading with the East Indies.

Two of the ships ran off, but Captain James Macrae and the *Cassandra* fought off the pirates for several hours. Both the *Cassandra* and England's *Fancy* were grounded on the shore and pounded each other without mercy. Macrae and many others escaped ashore, leaving behind cargo worth £75,000, according to some reports. The *Cassandra* suffered 37 casualties, and more than 90 pirates were killed.

Macrae hid out for 10 days and then took a daring chance. Hoping that the pirate's anger had cooled, he went aboard the *Victory* and asked for mercy. Some wanted to kill him, but he was respected by several others, who had served under him. England and Taylor argued bitterly over Macrae's fate until Taylor was softened up with rum PUNCH. Allowed to sail in the half-ruined *Fancy*, Macrae and 43 others suffered terribly from hunger and thirst during a seven-week voyage to Bombay. The East India Company rewarded Macrae's bravery with a rapid promotion, and he became governor of Madras from 1725 to 1730. With a salary of £500 a year, he collected £800,000 in graft.

The pirate crew turned against England because of his clemency to Macrae. He was removed as captain and (early in 1721) put ashore on Mauritius with three others. The four men sailed to Madagascar in a little boat. England lived on the charity of other pirates at Saint Augustine's Bay and died a pauper not long after.

(See also SELECTED BIBLIOGRAPHY: Defoe, *General History*.)

EPHESIAN TALE, THE *(Greek novel; second century)*

In this ROMANCE by XENOPHON OF EPHESUS, many misfortunes separate two lovers, who finally are blissfully reunited. The story begins in Ephesus, on the western coast of Asia Minor. Habrocomes ("one with luxurious hair") and Anthia ("the one in bloom") probably are the most beautiful man and woman in the entire world. Still teenagers, they see each other at a religious procession and fall instantly into an all-consuming love that makes them physically ill. The two lovers marry and sail to Egypt for their honeymoon.

On the way, Habrocomes and Anthia stop at RHODES. Their ship is spotted by PHOENICIAN pirates, who have disguised their GALLEY as a merchant vessel. The corsairs plot to attack the Ephesian vessel, laden with gold, silver, and valuable slaves. Corymbos, the pirate leader, is "a young man of large frame and fierce aspect, and his hair was rough and unkempt."

The pirates quietly follow the lovers' ship and suddenly attack about noon. They easily massacre the crew, which had been "lying about sluggish with drink and idleness." Corymbos steals Habrocomes and Anthia and other valuable cargo. He then sets fire to the merchant vessel, burning its crew and passengers alive. (The first surviving example of DEAD MEN TELL NO TALES.)

The pirates land at Tyre and take their booty to the estate of the archpirate Apsytros for division into shares. Before Apsytros returns home, two pirates express their passion for their beautiful captives. Captain Corymbos has fallen violently in love with Habrocomes, and his friend Euxinos desires Anthia.

The pirates try to persuade their captives to submit. Speaking to Habrocomes as Corymbos' go-between, Euxinos both pleads and threatens. He tells Habrocomes that Corymbos loves him and will give him all his wealth. But he also reminds Habrocomes that Corymbos is a pirate, who has killed before and will kill again. In the meantime, Corymbos acts as Euxinos's go-between with Anthia. Praising his friend, Corymbos tells Anthia that Euxinos is even willing to marry her.

The return of Apsytros frustrates the desires of the two pirates. Realizing that he can sell the beautiful Habrocomes and Anthia for a high price, Apsytros takes them (and their two slaves) as his chief's share of the booty. The disappointed Corymbos and his crew are allowed to divide up the rest of the goods and girls they had seized.

Their meeting with the lusty pirates is only the first of many challenges Habrocomes and Anthia must face before they settle down in loving union. As the novel continues, they are separated and carried around the entire Mediterranean. Everywhere they go, they are maligned, tortured, captured by robber bands, falsely arrested, and condemned to death.

(See SELECTED BIBLIOGRAPHY: Hadas, *Three Greek Novels*.)

ESCRAINVILLE, BROTHER JACQUES DE JOINVILLE *(Knight of Malta; Mediterranean; 1664)*

Commanding a large sailing ship, Escrainville joined Gabriel TÉMÉRICOURT and Maximilien de TÉMÉRICOURT in pillaging an OTTOMAN convoy from Alexandria to Istanbul. A relative with the same name was CAPTAIN GENERAL OF GALLEYS from 1697 to 1699.

ESTON, PETER   See EASTON, PETER.

ESSEX, CORNELIUS *(English buccaneer; Caribbean; active 1679–1680)*

With other PORT ROYAL captains in 1679, he plundered Spanish vessels loading Indigo in the Bay of Honduras. On his return, Jamaica's governor informed London of Essex's arrest "with 20 of his men for riotously comporting themselves and for plundering Major Jenckes of Saint James parish . . . and two of them sentenced to death." Soon after, Essex invaded Panama with Bartholomew SHARP and was killed during the capture of PORTOBELO. (See also SELECTED BIBLIOGRAPHY: Cruikshank, *Morgan*.)

ETHIOPIAN ADVENTURES, THE *(Greek novel; third century)*

The *Aethiopica* is the longest of the surviving Greek ROMANCES. Although his characters remain undeveloped, HELIODORUS OF EMESA skillfully advances the complex plot. The mandatory piracy scenes are more probable than in other romances and show familiarity with seamanship.

Theagenes and Chariclea must triumph over many difficulties before they can marry. The novel begins as Egyptian bandits capture the two lovers, and a series of flashbacks present the preceding episodes. Chariclea was born with white skin because her mother, the queen of Ethiopia, stared at an icon of a white goddess during her conception. Fearing that her husband will accuse her of adultery, the queen exposes the newborn in the wilderness. Chariclea is rescued and ultimately becomes a priestess at Delphi in central Greece.

During the yearly athletic contests, Chariclea sees the noble Theagenes, and the two fall desperately in love. When the Delphic Oracle pronounces that the lovers will find happiness in Ethiopia, Theagenes kidnaps Chariclea from the temple. They flee on a PHOENICIAN ship, accompanied by Calasiris, an Egyptian sage pretending to be their father.

The Phoenician ship docks for the winter on the IONIAN island of Zacynthos. Calasiris and the two lovers lodge with an old man who, it turns out, supplies fish to pirates hiding in a concealed bay. Trachinus, the corsair captain, sees Chariclea and instantly loves her. In order to get both the girl and the booty, he decides to wait and seize her after the Phoenician ship has put to sea.

The pirates pursue the larger merchant vessel from Zacynthos to Libya. When the wind slackens, the pirates' lighter ship finally catches its prey. Kinder than the corsairs in the EPHESIAN TALES, Trachinus allows the Phoenician seamen to escape in a small boat—although he leaves them with only the shirts on their backs. Taking only Calasiris and the two lovers with them, the pirates sail the captured merchant ship to the Egyptian Delta.

Trachinus plans to marry Chariclea at a great feast celebrating the corsairs' safe arrival. The pirates strip the captured ship of its wines and fine furniture, and they lavishly overpay the neighboring farmers for cattle. While the crew happily gets drunk, Calasiris persuades Pelorus, Captain Trachinus' lieutenant, to want Chariclea for himself. Pelorus demands her as his share of the booty. For pirate law "gives first and unrestricted choice to the man who is first to board an enemy vessel."

When the love-stricken Trachinus refuses to give Chariclea to Pelorus, the pirate feast breaks up into a drunken brawl, "as clubs, stones, cups, torches, tables were hurled." Chariclea adds to the slaughter by shooting arrows from the ship. All the pirates are killed except Pelorus, who duels to the death with Theagenes. Although severely wounded, Theagenes is bolstered by his love for Chariclea and cuts Pelorus's arm off above the elbow. Theagenes and Chariclea are reunited for a time, but they face many other perils before reaching Ethiopia.

(See also SELECTED BIBLIOGRAPHY: Heliodorus, Ethiopian Romance.)

ETRUSCAN PIRATES (Italian pirates; Mediterranean; ancient legends) The Roman name for those living between the Tiber and the Arno rivers (approximately modern Tuscany). Ancient Greek writers called the same people TYRRHENIANS (Tyrrhenoi). The later name is still used for the Tyrrhenian Sea, which separates Italy from Corsica, Sardinia, and Sicily.

By about 600 B.C., the Etruscans had formed seven city-states, all on or near the coast. During the next century, they extended their empire northward and also to the south, where they ruled over Rome, Salerno, and other cities. During the 500s, Etruscan ships controlled the Tyrrhenian Sea (thus its name), keeping out Greek merchants and raiders and defeating the PHOCAEANS about 535. Etruscan hegemony ended about 500. The Romans and other Latin peoples threw out the Etruscan governors, and the Sicilian Greeks destroyed their sea power. From 396, the Etruscan cities themselves fell under Roman control, and their language and culture gradually disappeared.

In describing encounters with the Etruscans between 625 and 400, the Greeks routinely refer to them as "pirates." And they also use TYRRHENIAN—the Greek word for Etruscan—to refer to all pirates sailing from Italy from 325 to 200. However, most pirates—POSTUMIUS, for example—were not Etruscans and did not sail from Etruscan ports.

From the 700s, Greek cities founded colonies in the western Mediterranean. Greek merchants and corsairs (often the same individuals at different times) pushed aggressively into the region. Allied with the Carthaginians, the Etruscans tried to close the Tyrrhenian Sea to marauders from the LIPARI ISLANDS or Phocaeans from Corsica. The Etruscans wanted to control trade with the Near East, and their warships sunk Greek ships not authorized to enter their waters. The Greeks bitterly resented this Etruscan policy of exclusion and inaccurately described it as piracy. In the same way, they constantly brought charges of piracy against the PHOENICIANS, their main commercial rivals in the east.

EUMAEUS (fictional pirate victim; before 750 B.C.) A noble shepherd in HOMER's Odyssey, who remains faithful to ODYSSEUS during his 20-year absence. When he finally returns, Odysseus seeks refuge with Eumaeus, and the two men tell each other their histories.

Eumaeus was born on the island of Syros, ruled by his father. When he was very young, a PHOENICIAN merchant visiting the island became his nurse's lover. The nurse was herself a Phoenician, kidnapped by TAPHIAN pirates and sold to Eumaeus's father.

The treacherous nurse convinces the Phoenicians that Eumaeus is a "cunning child," who will fetch a high price as a slave. She entices Eumaeus on board, and the traders' ship carries him to Ithaca. There he is bought by Laertes, Odysseus's father.

(See also SELECTED BIBLIOGRAPHY: Homer, Odyssey, translated by Lattimore.)

EUPEITHES (fictional Greek pirate; about 750 B.C.) A nobleman from the IONIAN ISLANDS in HOMER's Odyssey. His son Antinous wishes to marry Penelope, ODYSSEUS's wife. She refuses, reminding Antinous that Odysseus had saved Eupeithes's life. The Ithacans wanted to lynch Eupeithes after he and TAPHIAN pirates raided Thesprotia, Ithaca's ally. Penelope's comments provide the oldest reference to a treaty between two cities limiting raids on each other's citizens.

EUSTACE THE MONK   *(French pirate and admiral; Atlantic, English Channel; died 1217).* Eustace's maritime skills became legendary and were honored by a long verse romance written in 1223. Some even said he could make his ship invisible through black magic learned from the Muslims of Toledo.

The younger son of a middling nobleman at Boulogne, Eustace spent some time in a Benedictine monastery and then served the count of Boulogne. He gained a reputation as a troublemaker, was outlawed, and became a freebooter. The "Black Monk" attracted followers from several nations, and his squadrons commanded the Straits of Dover.

Like the ancient ARCHPIRATES, Eustace sold his services to the highest bidder. King John of England and Philip II of France were at war after Philip seized John's French possessions. For seven years (1205–1212), Eustace worked for King John. His squadron repeatedly raided the French coast, several times penetrating far up the Seine. With his brothers and uncle, he seized the Channel Islands and used them as an independent base.

The Black Monk was temporarily outlawed for indiscriminately plundering King John's subjects as well as his enemies. But Eustace's services were indispensable, and John forgave his offenses and gave him generous gifts. With his booty, the former monk built a palace in London and placed his daughter in a school for highborn ladies.

In 1212, Eustace and other French corsairs left King John and went over to Philip of France. During the summer of 1215, he pillaged Folkestone to revenge the English capture of his Channel Islands haven. When civil war broke out in England in 1215, the rebels offered the throne to Prince Louis of France (later King Louis IX). While Louis's armies occupied southern England, Eustace kept the sea lanes safe for the invading forces. He tightly controlled the Channel, as Philip of France told the papal legate (who favored King John's cause). With obvious irony, the legate was warned not to be captured by the merciless Eustace the Monk.

After King John died (October 1216), many English rebels deserted Prince Louis' invaders and went over to John's son, Henry III. In August 1217, Eustace provided ships to carry French reinforcements across the Channel. Off Sandwich, the French flotilla met opposing English vessels. The English sailed close to and windward of Eustace's heavily laden flagship. Suddenly, they threw out powdered lime that was carried by the wind to blind the French sailors and knights. After boarding and overpowering the enemy ship, the English held several French nobles for ransom but immediately killed Eustace the Monk and his crew.

EVANS, JOHN   *(Welsh pirate; Caribbean; 1722)* While unemployed on Jamaica, this former captain turned pirate and stole a small SLOOP with several friends. The pirates pillaged at least five ships, recruited more

hands, and took £9,000 in booty. While they were careening at Grand Cayman Island, the boatswain shot and killed Evans during an argument.

(See also SELECTED BIBLIOGRAPHY: Defoe, *General History*.)

EVERSON, JACOB   *(Dutch pirate; Caribbean; 1680s)* In February 1681, Sir Henry MORGAN, Jamaica's lieutenant governor and a former pirate, sent out an armed vessel that captured Everson's ship. Twenty-six crewmen were hanged, but Everson escaped and continued to raid shipping throughout the Caribbean.

EVERY, HENRY   *(British pirate; Atlantic, Red Sea; active 1692–1695)* Sometimes called Benjamin Bridgeman (and nicknamed "Long Ben"), Every captured an Indian treasure ship and managed to escape with the loot. Although other pirates took more booty, his robbery endangered the British East India Company and aroused great public interest. Every was the hero of works by several authors, including Daniel DEFOE (who erroneously called him John Avery).

Every's admirers invented improbable stories about his early life. He is first mentioned in the early 1690s as an unlicensed slave dealer and pirate sailing from the Bahamas with the governor's protection. In June 1694, Every was second-in-command of a 46-gun private warship, licensed by the Spanish government to attack French smugglers. At Cadiz, the crew took the ship while the captain was dead drunk one night. Renaming her the *Fancy*, they elected Every captain.

Heading south along the African coast, the pirates plundered three British vessels at the Cape Verde Islands and destroyed two Danish ships near São Thomé. Early in 1695, they reached Johanna Island (Anjouan) in the Comoros, where Every seized a French pirate ship loaded with booty. Most of its crew joined his gang, bringing to it more than 170 men.

Reaching the Red Sea in May or June, Every ran into smaller pirate ships commanded by William WANT, Joseph FARRELL, William MAY, Thomas WAKE, and Thomas TEW. Cruising with Every as their admiral, the pirates waited for the treasure ships returning to India. Each year, Indian ships took rich luxury goods (and Muslim pilgrims) to Mecca and Jiddah and returned with gold and silver.

Most of the Indian fleet got past the pirates during the night, but Every took the last two vessels. Every easily captured the smaller *Fateh Mohammed* and then pursued the *Gang-i-sawai* (*Gunsway*), the largest ship in the Indian's fleet. The heavily armed *Gunsway* carried 400 to 500 soldiers. During a two-hour battle, both sides suffered heavy casualties.

Every's crew looted their prizes at the island of Socotra. In addition to gold coins, the pirates seized many jewels and a saddle and bridle encrusted with diamonds. They tortured prisoners and raped many women, including the aged wife of an important Indian official. Some jumped

Safely back in London, Henry Every sells jewels looted from an Indian ship in the Red Sea. Illustration by Howard Pyle in *Harper's Monthly Magazine,* September 1887.

into the sea to escape, while others died after being brutally handled.

The booty was split at Réunion Island, where most of the French pirates stayed. The East India Company estimated the plunder at £325,000. After giving small sums to the other pirate ships, each man received about £1,000 in cash plus some of the jewels. Every took two shares as captain, and he may also have grabbed some loose gems.

Before sailing to America, Every took on provisions at Sâo Thomé. One English captain reported that he paid the Portuguese governor with a check "drawn on The Bank of Aldgate Pump, attested by John-a-Noakes and signed by Timothy Tugmutton and Simon Wifflepin." In the Caribbean, the pirates sold some of their plunder at Saint Thomas and sailed to the Bahamas in April.

In return for some £2,000 in bribes, Governor Thomas Trott welcomed the pirates and entertained the officers in his own home. The pirates even gave Trott the *Fancy,* but she was wrecked during a storm. The British government fired Trott the following October but allowed him to take his loot to South Carolina.

Meanwhile, the Indian emperor took out his anger on the British East India Company. Indian officials seized the company's trading posts and imprisoned its officials, treating some so severely that they died in jail. The British government offered £500 for every man in Every's crew, and the East India Company doubled the reward.

Since the Bahamas were a privately owned colony, Trott could not grant a royal pardon, and the governor of Jamaica refused a bribe of £20,000. The *Fancy's* crew fled in all directions, while Every and several others bought a sloop and escaped to Ireland. Over the years, 14 were arrested, and six were hanged. But Henry Every vanished with his plunder. (See also DANN, JOHN; MIDDLETON, PHILIP; SELECTED BIBLIOGRAPHY: Botting, *Pirates;* Grey, *Pirates;* Jameson, *Privateering;* Pringle, *Jolly Roger.*)

EXPRESSIONS, SEAFARING See Account, Going on the; Ahoy!; A Soft Farewell; Avast!; Belay; Blow Me Down!; Brethren of the Coast; Davy Jones' Locker; Dead Men Tell No Tales; from the Seas; Grog; Keelhaul; Land Ho!; Lubber; Marooner; Mate; "No Purchase, No Pay"; Scurvy (2); "Shiver My Timbers"; Swab; Swearing; Wench; Yo-Ho-Ho.

Exquemelin glorified the exploits of Sir Henry Morgan. In April 1669, Spanish warships trapped Morgan's raiders as they entered the Caribbean from Lake Maracaibo, Venezuela. As pictured here, Morgan turned his vessel into a fire-ship and sailed it into the Spaniards' galleon. From Exquemelin, *Buccaneers of America*, first English edition (1684).

EXQUEMELIN, ALEXANDER OLIVER
(French surgeon and historian; CARIBBEAN; ABOUT 1645–1700) Exquemelin took part in major raids by the BUCCANEERS of Hispaniola and PORT ROYAL, serving under both François L'OLONNAIS and Sir Henry MORGAN. He drew upon his experiences to write the *Buccaneers of America*, which was published in 1678. His detailed account remains the most important source about both pirate customs and Morgan's 1671 conquest of PANAMA.

Exquemelin's book was a bestseller in many languages. (English editions sometimes spell his name as Esquemeling.) The book's success inspired Daniel DEFOE and other authors to write the first modern novels about pirates. "I assure the reader that I shall give no stories taken on hearsay, but only those to which I was eyewitness," he wrote. Some have questioned whether he remained faithful to this vow in recounting buccaneer adventures.

Exquemelin shared the buccaneer's risks and hardships, and his entire life was adventurous. He was born in Honfleur on France's western coast. In 1666, he sailed to TORTUGA, as an indentured servant. Exquemelin wrote that his first master—"the most perfidious man that ever was born of woman"—nearly starved him to death. Later, a barber-surgeon bought him and trained him in contemporary medical skills. After gaining his freedom in about 1669, he joined the buccaneers. "Naked and destitute of all human necessities," he wrote, "I determined to enter into the wicked order of the pirates, or robbers at sea."

Exquemelin spent the next five years under several French and English captains. At some point he moved from Tortuga to Port Royal and took part in Morgan's most famous raids. He was handsomely paid for his services as a surgeon, receiving 200 to 250 PIECES OF EIGHT plus his split of the booty.

Exquemelin broke with the pirates after Morgan's 1671 sack of Panama. The raid was harrowing, the men were reduced to eating buzzard eggs, and Morgan cheated them out of their fair share of the loot. Exquemelin returned to Europe in 1674, practicing his trade as a surgeon in Amsterdam while writing the *Buccaneers of America*. He reappeared in the Caribbean during the 1697 French sack of CARTAGENA, serving as a surgeon with the buccaneer forces.

Exquemelin's history appeared in Dutch in 1678 as *De Amerikaensche Zee-Roovers*. It met with instant success. Several printings quickly sold out, and translations into German, Spanish, English, and French soon followed. Each translation catered to the prejudices of its country's readers. While the Dutch original emphasized Spanish crimes in the New World, the Spanish translation naturally made the English the villains. It portrayed Henry Morgan as a monster of depravity and cruelty, and it pictured the Spaniards as innocent victims.

These nationalistic biases caused legal problems for the first English publishers, who had translated the Spanish rather than the Dutch version. Henry Morgan sued for libel, arguing that he was not a pirate since Sir Thomas MODYFORD had authorized his raids. The courts ruled for Morgan and ordered the English publisher to remove several sections. For centuries, publishers continued to reprint this revised English version of a Spanish translation. Only in 1969 was the Dutch edition directly translated into English.

EYE PATCH *(fictional pirate decoration)* Historically, there is no evidence whether or not pirates wore eyepatches. However, eyepatches became part of the pirate mystique during the 20th century. The villain wears an eye patch in *The* BLACK SWAN (1942) and in THE PIRATES OF BLOOD RIVER (1962). In illustrations to, and movie versions of, TREASURE ISLAND, both of Blind Pew's eyes usually are covered by black bandages.

F

FAENZO, AGOSTINO *(Maltese corsair; Mediterranean; 1607)* Commanding a BERTONE for the KNIGHTS OF SAINT STEPHEN, Faenzo and Jacques GERMAIN captured two Venetian merchantmen.

FAFFAELE, ANGELO DI *(Italian pirate; Black Sea; 1402)* Faffaele preyed with great success on Muslim shipping, passing on 10 percent of his take to Genoese officials at Constantinople.

FAIRBANKS, DOUGLAS *(American actor; 1883–1939)* With his 1920s action spectaculars, Douglas Fairbanks invented the SWASHBUCKLING romantic hero. Fairbanks' lithe grace, high-spirited athleticism, and broad-gestured acting were immensely popular. Functioning as his own producer, he chose (and sometimes wrote) the stories and lavished time and money on production and sets. No one has surpassed Fairbanks in making and selling adventure movies.

Fairbanks' swashbucklers drew on skills honed during his earlier career. Born in Colorado, he moved to New York and succeeded as a Broadway comedian with the era's florid style. Always a physical showman, he continued gymnastic training throughout his life.

Joining D. W. Griffith in 1915, Fairbanks soon became one of the first movie stars. In 30 comedies, he created the character of the all-American boy, who wins out through his innate optimism and moral courage. Wrenched from idleness or poverty in the big city, the hero overcomes the challenges of the American wilderness. By the end, he has proved his superiority over those sneering at him in early scenes.

In 1919, Fairbanks, Griffith, Charles Chaplin, and Mary Pickford formed United Artists to distribute their movies. Fairbanks married Pickford, "America's sweetheart," in 1920 and the two superstars reigned from Pickfair, their palatial Hollywood estate.

Douglas Fairbanks' dazzling swordplay holds off nine attackers in *The Black Pirate* (1926). In real life, Caribbean buccaneers used cutlasses and not fencing foils.

Fairbanks produced *The Mark of Zorro* in 1920. Encouraged by its success—and his own delight in costume drama—Fairbanks let rip with *The Three Musketeers* (1921), *Robin Hood* (1922), *The Thief of Baghdad* (1924), *Don Q Son of Zorro* (1925), THE BLACK PIRATE (1926), and *The Gaucho* (1927).

Fairbanks remained a comedian—a satirical swashbuckler who laughed in the face of danger. His films were escapist thrillers, set in the remote past to avoid mentioning current problems. In effect, the all-American boy of earlier comedies simply reappeared in costume.

Robin Hood had the grandest sets, and *Thief of Baghdad* had the most compelling visual tricks. *The Black Pirate* is distinguished by its energy and sense of fun. Shorter than several earlier films, *The Black Pirate* cut out all pageantry and emphasized fast-paced action sequences. It was meant solely as a joyous romp, as Fairbanks warned the audience in an opening title about the "playful habits" of pirates. A double took over when the hero slides down the sail on a knife. But Fairbanks was remarkably agile at 43, and there was no doubling in the vigorous SWORD DUELS.

Fairbanks' fame lessened with sound movies. In 1929, he and Pickford costarred in Shakespeare's *The Taming of the Shrew*. Its failure weakened their shaky marriage, and the two stars separated in 1933. Fairbanks retired after *The Private Life of Don Juan* in 1934.

FARRELL (FARO, FERRO), JOSEPH *(British pirate; Red Sea; 1694–1695)* Farrell left Rhode Island in about January 1694 in the *Portsmouth Adventure* and cruised in the Red Sea in consort with William WANT. In June 1695, he joined Henry EVERY in taking two rich Indian prizes. On the way home, the *Adventure* was wrecked on Mayotte in the Comoro Islands. Farrell reached Réunion Island, was picked up by Every, and went with him to the Bahamas. He was captain of the SLOOP that took Every back to Ireland.

FELUCCA *(type of ship; Mediterranean, Red Sea, Indian Ocean; Middle Ages to present)* A narrow, swift vessel, of Arab origin, propelled by lateen sails or oars, or both. Sea-going feluccas were decked and carried lateen sails on one or two masts. They are almost completely extinct. A smaller type, propelled by sails and six or eight oars, is still used on eastern Mediterranean rivers, particularly the Nile.

FENN, JOHN *(English pirate; Atlantic, Caribbean; active 1721–1723)* Fenn sailed with Bartholomew ROBERTS and then with Thomas ANSTIS. In 1721, Anstis captured the *Morningstar*, mounted her with 21 guns, and made Fenn captain. Sailing in consort with Anstis, Fenn wrecked the *Morningstar*, but was given command of another prize. A British warship caught Fenn, as he was careening his ship at Tobago. Fleeing into the woods, he was captured a day later and hanged at Antigua.

FENNER, EDWARD *(English pirate; Atlantic, English Channel; active 1567–1595)* From Sussex, Edward accompanied his brother George FENNER on an armed expedition to West Africa in 1567. In 1584, with his uncle William FENNER (1) and John CALLICE, Fenner pillaged French and Portuguese merchantmen. The two Fenners were indicted for piracy, and Edward was not formally pardoned until 1598.

Fenner commanded the 400-ton warship *Swiftsure* against the Spanish Armada in 1588. The following year, he and George Fenner took several prizes in the English Channel. In 1591, he commanded one of four warships outfitted by his kinsman Thomas FENNER and a London merchant. In 1595, while cruising in the Cape Verde Islands with his own *Peregrine* and another warship, he encountered a squadron under John LANCASTER. Fenner and his men joined Lancaster's raiders and split one-fourth of the rich booty taken from Pernambuco, Brazil.

FENNER, GEORGE *(English captain; Atlantic; active 1567–1590)* Fenner belonged to a family of Sussex merchants, shipowners, and captains. In 1567, he and Edward FENNER set out to acquire West African gold with the CASTLE OF COMFORT. (Queen Elizabeth ordered Fenner and John LOVELL not to sail, but both ignored her command.) They returned prematurely after battling a Portuguese squadron in the Cape Verde Islands. During several raids in the 1570s, Fenner plundered Dutch and Spanish shipping (possibly under cover of a foreign PRIVATEERING commission).

Fenner was captain of the *Galleon Leicester* under Admiral Lord Thomas Howard during the Armada battles in 1588. In 1589, with his brother Edward, he fitted out the Lord Admiral's 70-ton *Disdain* and brought in several legitimate prizes, including a rich Brazilian sugar ship. Later in 1590, commanding the queen's ship *Lion*, Fenner joined Howard in an Azores cruise. Although they failed to plunder the West Indian TREASURE FLEET, other prizes nearly paid for their expenses.

(See also GRENVILLE, RICHARD; FENNER, THOMAS; FENNER (1,2), WILLIAM.)

FENNER, THOMAS *(English admiral; Atlantic; active 1564–1591)* Member of a family of merchants and captains living around Chichester in Sussex. In 1564, he and Edward Cook, a Southampton pirate, voyaged to Guinea in West Africa. On their return, the ADMIRALTY COURT indicted Fenner for pillaging a Portuguese ship with sugar and brazilwood. During the early 1570s, he looted shipping under a dubious PRIVATEERING commission from Dutch rebels against Spain. His ships may have reached the West Indies in 1572.

Following the outbreak of the Spanish war, Fenner frequently commanded royal warships. Considered a daring and effective officer, he was a close friend of Sir Francis DRAKE. Fenner was captain of the 600-ton *Bonaventure*, which served as Drake's flagship during his 1585

West Indian venture. With the rank of rear admiral, he accompanied Drake's Cadiz raid in 1587 and commanded the 600-ton *Non Pareil* against the Spanish Armada in 1588. In 1590, as vice-admiral, he led one of five squadrons during Drake's disastrous attack on Lisbon. The following year, in partnership with a London merchant, he outfitted four powerful warships for plunder voyages, one commanded by his kinsman Edward FENNER.

FENNER, WILLIAM (1) (English admiral; Atlantic; died 1590)

From Chichester, he commanded a heavily armed PINNACE in 1576 and took a Danish ship off Elsinore in consort with John CALLICE. Obtaining a royal commission to take pirates in 1582, he instead gave command to Callice, who seized several innocent merchantmen.

By 1584, Fenner's family owned the *Galleon Fenner*, a large ship with 70 crewmen. He sailed in September with Callice and Edward FENNER (his nephew), captured a French warship in December, and made Callice its captain. After separating from Callice, the two Fenners were arrested in March 1585. While he admitted to plundering various French ships and a rich Portuguese sugarman, Fenner claimed that he held a PRIVATEERING commission from the claimant to the Portuguese throne.

After war broke out, Fenner plundered several Spanish ships (now legal prizes) in 1586. In 1588, he commanded the 250-ton *Aid* against the Spanish Armada. As rear admiral of the fleet, he accompanied Sir Francis DRAKE's disastrous Lisbon raid in 1590 and died of wounds received while attacking that city.

(See also FENNER, EDWARD; FENNER, GEORGE; FENNER, THOMAS.)

FENNER, WILLIAM (2) (English captain; Atlantic; 1590)

Son of William FENNER (1) and thus a cousin of George and Edward FENNER, members of a prominent Sussex family of merchants and captains. During Sir Francis DRAKE's disastrous Lisbon raid in 1590, he commanded a warship and plundered Puerto Santo in the Madeira Islands.

FENNICH REIS (Moroccan corsair; Mediterranean, Atlantic; active 1691–1695)

A member of a prosperous SALÉ family, Fennich Reis commanded his own ship but often joined BEN AÏSSA's squadron. His vessel sank with all hands in 1695.

FERLETICH, ANDREAS (corsair captain; Adriatic Sea; active 1618–1621)

In 1618, Austrian troops expelled the USKOKS from Senj in northern DALMATIA. Ferletich escaped to Naples, received a corsair's license from the Spanish viceroy (an Austrian ally), and captured several prizes. He planned to loot Venice itself in 1619, but was surprised off the Lido and had to flee. The viceroy provided Ferletich's Uskok corsairs with new vessels, which a Venetian squadron trapped at the Italian port of Manfredonia in 1620. Ferletich again escaped, and Venice in 1621 offered the large reward of 20,000 ducats for his assassination.

FERNANDES (FERNANDEZ, FERNANDO), SIMÃO (Portuguese pirate and pilot; Atlantic; born 1538, active to 1590)

Trained in Portugal, Simâo (sometimes Simon) Fernandes also worked for the Spanish, serving on one or more voyages to North America between 1561 and 1573. He moved to England and piloted at least five of the English expeditions to North America between 1578 and 1587. He was at least partly responsible for the destruction of the colony at ROANOKE ISLAND. Although powerful English officials prized his navigational skills, Fernandes' shipmates distrusted him because of his obsession with piracy and his unscrupulous and quarrelsome nature.

Fernandes came to England about 1573. In September 1574, at the request of Sir Henry KNOLLYS, he became pilot on the *Elephant*, commanded by Ferdinando FIELDING with John CALLICE as master. Off the Azores, they seized a rich Portuguese prize and sold it in Wales. The Portuguese ambassador alleged that Fernandes had personally killed seven sailors, but nothing was done to arrest him.

Fernandes subsequently bought a small BARK from William Herbert, VICE-ADMIRAL of Wales, which was outfitted by Cardiff merchants and officials. He took a Dutch FLYBOAT and brought it into Cork, Ireland, and thence to South Wales. In April 1576, his ship joined up with Callice's *Elephant* to seize a Portuguese caravel near the Canary Islands.

Fernandes claimed that he made no profit on this Portuguese prize. Perhaps for this reason, his former backers, the local ADMIRALTY officials, jailed him in May 1576. After some months, Vice-Admiral Herbert posted his bail, and the charges later were dropped. Fernandes lived quietly in Cardiff after his release, but the Portuguese sued to recover their goods. He was again arrested in February 1577, but was freed by Thomas Lewes, a Cardiff magistrate who fenced pirate loot.

Fernandes was sent up to London in April 1577. Although his guilt was obvious, the judges released him on a technical point thanks to Sir Francis Walsingham, the queen's secretary of state. Walsingham, who employed Fernandes soon afterward, ignored his crimes to obtain his skills and knowledge of American waters.

In November 1578, Fernandes piloted the *Falcon* (under Sir Walter RALEIGH) during Sir Humphrey GILBERT's abortive expedition to the New World. The other ships dispersed after turning pirate in English waters. The *Falcon* plundered as far south as the Cape Verde Islands, returning in the summer of 1579. Nevertheless, Gilbert sent Fernandes on a solo mission to explore Virginia in 1580. On his return, he operated as a pirate and captured at least one Spanish prize. Following the Spanish conquest of Portugal in 1580, he claimed to be working for the pretender to the Portuguese throne.

In May 1582, a GALLEON and a smaller ship sailed under Sir Edward Fenton, with Fernandes as copilot. The government ordered Fenton to sail east toward China. He instead went westward, sank a Spanish warship in Brazil, but returned home prizeless. Several officers blamed the mission's failure on Fernandes, alleging that his stories of Spanish gold had persuaded Fenton to turn pirate.

Despite the Fenton episode, Fernandes retained the confidence of Francis Walsingham and Walter Raleigh. He was the main pilot of Raleigh's three expeditions to Roanoke Island in 1584, 1585, and 1587. Roanoke was expected to serve both as a base for settlement and also as a port of call for English privateers preying on Spanish TREASURE FLEETS.

In 1584 Fernandes piloted two vessels that explored the Virginia coast and then cruised for Spanish prizes. The following year, Sir Richard GRENVILLE led seven vessels to Virginia with Fernandes serving as chief pilot. Grenville's ships attacked Spanish merchantmen both before and after landing colonists at Roanoke Island. After they returned, Queen Elizabeth granted coats-of-arms to Fernandes and the expedition's other officers.

John White took additional settlers to Virginia in 1587, with Fernandes as master of his flagship. The two men quarreled because Fernandes wasted time chasing every vessel they encountered. The expedition had planned to pick up earlier settlers at Roanoke and take everyone to Chesapeake Bay. But Fernandes refused to sail beyond Roanoke because he wanted to raid Spanish shipping before the summer season ended. His refusal to go on to the Chesapeake helped destroy the entire colony. Although Raleigh repudiated Fernandes after this incident, he retained some English friends. He fought under Sir Martin FROBISHER against Spain in July 1588, and he accompanied Frobisher during a raid on the Azores in 1590.

(See also SELECTED BIBLIOGRAPHY: Quinn, *England*; Taylor, *Troublesome*.)

FIAMENGO, GIORGIO *(Maltese corsair; Mediterranean; 1797)* Since Fiamengo was licensed to operate only off the BARBARY COAST, the TRIBUNALE DEGLI ARMAMENTI made him return a French ship taken in the eastern Mediterranean.

FICTION, PIRATE *(eighth century B.C. to the present)* Pirate literature has given birth to two major myths. One version makes heroes out of individual captains, such as Sir Francis DRAKE and Jean LAFFITE. Other stories, mainly about the Caribbean BUCCANEERS, portray pirates as depraved monsters. Rejecting all morality, they torture, rape, and murder everyone they meet. Between atrocities, they bury their booty and wallow in drunken debauchery. Both legends were created since the 18th century, after pirates virtually disappeared from the Carib-

bean and Atlantic. Earlier authors, when pirates still flourished, treated them as ordinary folk. Their pirates are secondary characters, important not in themselves but because of their effect on the hero and heroine.

For the Greeks and Romans, the marauders infesting the Mediterranean were not especially immoral. When he can get away with it, these ancient peoples believed, anyone will rob foreigners. Thus, every mariner potentially is a pirate. In ancient myths, NAUPLIUS, the first seaman, is also the first pirate and wrecker. In HOMER'S *Odyssey* (before 750 B.C.), ODYSSEUS and other rulers buy slaves captured from pirates such as the TAPHIANS. Odysseus and MENELAUS boast about their own piracies. The HOMERIC HYMNS (600–250 B.C.) assume that sailors will kidnap a pretty boy, if they get the chance.

Many ancient legends are preserved only by historians. HERODOTUS and THUCYDIDES, for example, collected stories about the CARIANS, who sailed for King MINOS of CRETE. DIODORUS OF SICILY wrote about BUTES and other legendary pirates. These authors coolly describe plunder raids as if they were military campaigns. Their attitude is logical, since ancient armies routinely pillaged and murdered civilians.

Most Greek plays have been lost, but some plots reappear in Latin comedies by PLAUTUS and TERENCE (second century B.C.). Less adventurous than those of earlier legends, these pirates are rather scruffy characters. Their main business is slave trading, and they prey only on the weak. In the Greek and Latin ROMANCES (written during the first three centuries A.D.), two young lovers undergo many trials, including kidnapping by pirates. As in ancient plays, most pirates are second-rate criminals interested in easy money. They treat their captives less cruelly than the merchants and officials that later buy them as slaves.

Pirates also appear in the Latin CONTROVERSIES, fictional speeches about lurid subjects. The brigands hold captives for ransom and torture them to gain information. However, they are only trying to make money, and they are kinder than the captive's own family.

Piracy at sea fell off when the Roman Empire collapsed but again flourished from about A.D. 1000. Medieval tales treat pirates as fantastic and magical figures. ALVILDA terrorizes the coasts with a band of WOMEN PIRATES. EUSTACE THE MONK could make his ship invisible through black magic learned from Spanish Muslims. The mast of STORTEBECHER's ship contains bars of solid gold.

RELIGION inspired both the BARBARY corsairs and Christian raiders, such as the USKOKS and the KNIGHTS OF MALTA and SAINT STEPHEN. Christian writers often accuse Barbary corsairs of atrocities. However, they describe the corsairs as evil not because they are pirates (after all, so were the accusers) but because they are Muslims. After escaping slavery at ALGIERS in 1580, CERVANTES unceasingly called for a war against the Muslims. Writing during the 17th century, Alonso de CONTRERAS and Fernao Mendes PINTO proudly boast of pillaging the subjects (including Christians) of Muslim rulers.

Sixteenth-century English raiders also believed that religion sanctified their piracies. A REPORT OF THE TRUTH (1591) and SIR FRANCIS DRAKE REVIVED (1621) both justify plunder raids because they harm the Roman Catholic Spaniards.

In popular belief, the Caribbean BUCCANEERS were the only important and interesting pirates. In fact, other raiders took greater loot and ventured on much longer voyages. Caribbean raiders owe their fame to EXQUEMELIN's *Buccaneers of America* (1678), immensely popular because of its gory tales of sadistic torture. Earlier pirate biographies described foul deeds, but they attributed them to the enemy. Exquemelin gloats over savage and even insane acts by his own heroes, François L'OLONNAIS and Sir Henry MORGAN.

Daniel DEFOE (1660–1731) enlarged on Exquemelin's themes to create enduring pirate myths. Defoe published three fictional autobiographies of pirate captains, and encounters with marauders are important in FOUR YEARS VOYAGES, MADAGASCAR, and ROBINSON CRUSOE. Defoe's GENERAL HISTORY convincingly mixes fiction and fact in some 40 pirate biographies. In these works, Defoe perfected the myth of pirate atrocities. Exquemelin's heroes mainly tried to make prisoners reveal their treasures. Defoe's fictional captains torture and rape merely to enjoy their victim's agonies. Several make a pact with the Devil—still considered a real person in Defoe's day.

These tales of demonic cruelty reach their peak in BLACKBEARD, Defoe's most enduring literary creation after *Robinson Crusoe*. At the same time, however, Defoe also created CAPTAIN MISSON and other heroes who turn pirate to escape a corrupt society. Although they steal, they treat their victims more fairly than do merchants, officials, and clergymen.

Into the 20th century, Defoe provided both plots and the characterization of pirates as uniquely evil. Sir Walter Scott's THE PIRATE (1822) and Sir Arthur Conan Doyle's "CAPTAIN SHARKEY" (1897) borrowed their villains from the *General History*. Defoe also influenced popular beliefs through anthologies, such as Charles Ellms' THE PIRATES OWN BOOK (1837). These reprinted only the goriest bits, without crediting their author. When Defoe's captains seemed insufficiently evil, the anthologies interpolated fictional incidents blackening their character.

Nineteenth-century authors added to the myth of pirate evil. Victorian society condemned DRINKING and unmarried sex as inherently evil. Since pirates were evil men, Ellms and others reasoned, they did evil things. These authors concluded that pirates must have indulged in alcohol and sex—even when Defoe and their other sources fail to mention any such thing.

Victorian authors also added the myth of buried TREASURE. Borrowing from popular legends about CAPTAIN KIDD's TREASURE, authors attached stories about booty and mysterious MAPS to other raiders. Tales by Washington IRVING, James Fenimore COOPER, and Edgar Allan Poe ("THE GOLD BUG") all feature ghosts haunting pirate spoil, curiously marked treasure caches, and sinister strangers bragging in seaside inns.

Pirates became stock characters in stage melodramas and adventure stories for young men. They provided the perfect contrast to the pure and manly heroes of PETER THE WHALER (1851) and THE CORAL ISLAND (1858). The pirates' bad example teaches the reader that swearing and arguing with parents inevitably lead to blacker crimes.

Robert Louis STEVENSON's TREASURE ISLAND (1883) is saturated with references to the *General History*, which provided Stevenson with LONG JOHN SILVER. Stevenson also borrowed freely from existing legends of strange maps and drunken captains. However, Stevenson excelled in analyzing psychological states, and his characters' motivations are unusually ambiguous. Howard PYLE similarly toned down existing legends. In THE STORY OF JACK BALLISTER'S FORTUNES (1907), for example, Blackbeard is dangerous precisely because he is not Defoe's grotesque satyr.

THE PIRATES OF PENZANCE (1) (1879) and PETER PAN (1) (1904) parody these myths about Caribbean pirates. Thus they deliberately present characters totally unlike any real-life raiders. *Penzance* mocks vaudeville pirates to soften its biting attacks on social foibles. *Peter Pan* is about the progression from childhood fantasies of "Pirates" and "Indians" to an adult's prosaic life of reality.

Film versions of *Treasure Island* and *Peter Pan* have made Caribbean buccaneers the best-known pirates. During the 19th century, however, Mediterranean corsairs were equally famous, thanks to Lord Byron's THE CORSAIR (1814), portraying the hero's relations with two women. Curiously, Byron's poem was based on newspaper reports of Jean Laffite's role in the War of 1812. Later works then projected Byron's invented love triangle back on Laffite. Pirates also became heroes in Charles Kingsley's WESTWARD HO! (1855), as brave Englishmen battle rapacious Spaniards during the 16th century.

Twentieth-century authors inherited two contradictory pirate traditions, both mainly centered about the Caribbean. For the *Westward Ho!* school, pirates are good men, their Spanish victims are the villains. In the myths invented by Daniel Defoe, a few pirates are daring heroes, but most are monstrously evil.

In his six pirate novels, Rafael SABATINI (1875–1950) successfully reconciled these conflicting legends. Sabatini's pure-hearted heroes are forced into piracy but never sink to the level of the brutish brigands around them. They also remain superior to the greedy Spaniards, who make piracy inevitable by refusing to trade with the English colonies.

Frank Yerby's THE GOLDEN HAWK (1948) and Dudley POPE's four novels during the 1980s also depict the Spaniards as cruel, dishonorable, and even physically repulsive. In FOR MY GREAT FOLLY (1942), Thomas Costain even uses the alleged Spanish threat to justify John

WARD's Mediterranean piracies. However, James Michener in CARIBBEAN (1989) breaks with this tradition and finds heroes and villains on both sides of the English/Spanish battle for the Caribbean.

Some authors have ignored mythology and tried to portray piracy as it really existed. In CAPTAIN MARGARET (1908), John Masefield creates Captain Cammock, a shrewd seaman who falls into piracy to make money. John Steinbeck's CUP OF GOLD (1929) accepts Exquemelin's stories but probes Henry Morgan's motivations. In Kenneth Roberts' LYDIA BAILEY (1947), the Christian RENEGADES in Tripoli during the First BARBARY WAR are cold-hearted businessmen. The heroine's lusts override her intelligence in Chloe Gartner's ANNE BONNY (1977).

Richard Hughes and Peter Benchley reject the myths of pirates as frightening fiends. Hughes' brigands (A HIGH WIND IN JAMAICA (1), 1929) are second-rate seamen, much less evil than the children they kidnap. Benchley (THE ISLAND, 1979) describes a band of degenerate buccaneers, who just barely survive into the 20th century.

FIELDING (FELDING), FERDINANDO (English captain; Atlantic; 1574–1578)

In December 1574, the *Elephant (Oliphant)*, owned by Sir Henry KNOLLYS, captured a Portuguese ship carrying valuable sugar and exotic woods. Fernando Fielding was the *Elephant*'s captain, John CALLICE served as master, and Simâo FERNANDES was among the crew.

Soon afterward, Callice later testified in court, Fielding sold him the *Elephant* for £110—even though Knollys was its rightful owner. Callice did use the *Elephant* in February 1576, but he had other ships after November. Perhaps the sale was fictitious to protect Knollys. In any case, the three men were on good terms during Sir Humphrey GILBERT's 1578 expedition to North America. The *Elephant* was Knollys' flagship, with Callice as pilot. Ferdinando Fielding, gentleman, is listed as an honorary member of the party.

"FIFTEEN MEN ON A DEAD MAN'S CHEST" (fictional pirate song; 1883)

While carousing at the Admiral Benbow Inn in TREASURE ISLAND, Bill Bones sings a song with the recurring ditty

Fifteen men on the dead man's chest
Yo-ho-ho, and a bottle of rum!
Drink and the devil had done for the rest.

These words were invented by Stevenson and not borrowed from seamen's SONGS. "Dead man's chest" does not refer to the trunk or box in which Bones hides his treasure map. Dead Man's Chest is a cay (now called Dead Chest Island) in the British Virgin Islands. Stevenson found the name in *At Last: A Christmas in the West Indies* (London, 1871), a travel book by Charles Kingsley, author of WESTWARD HO!

(See also SELECTED BIBLIOGRAPHY: Watson, *Coasts*.)

FILIBUSTER (sea raider; Caribbean; 17th and 18th centuries)

French writers used the term BUCCANEER only when referring to the cow hunters of Hispaniola. They called those turning pirate *filibustiers*, derived from either (or both) Dutch *vrijbuiter* (meaning PRIVATEER) or Dutch *vliebot* (FLYBOAT).

(See also FREEBOOTER.)

FILMS, PIRATE   See MOVIES, PIRATE.

FLAGS, PIRATE (pirate symbols; all eras)

In popular fiction, all pirates flew the JOLLY ROGER—a skull above crossed bones on a black background. However, this special flag was used only by British and British-American pirates from about 1700 to 1725. Other pirates attacked either under their own ruler's flag or under the flag of the prince issuing their PRIVATEERING commission. By flying a national flag, pirates made a symbolic statement (often false) that the attack was legal under that country's laws.

Some nations sponsored piracy and lived off pirate booty, including the BARBARY STATES, the KNIGHTS OF MALTA, and 17th-century England. In law, corsairs operating from one of these HAVENS had to fly its flag. This showed that the raiders recognized and paid taxes to the ruler's law courts.

While they were hunting, many pirates either flew no flag or used one that would fool their intended victim. Their battle flag was raised only when they were close enough to attack. Naval warships also used this trick. In 1815, American ships thus trapped HAMIDOU REIS by flying the British flag.

From 1805 to 1810, a large pirate confederation dominated the Chinese coast from Canton south to Vietnam. The raiders divided the coast into six territories, each belonging to a pirate fleet with its own banner—red, black, white, green, blue, and yellow. These flags allowed the pirates to recognize each other, but they had no symbolic meaning. Since China had no national flag, every shipowner devised a banner for the vessels he owned.

FLEGON, JOHN (English pirate; Atlantic; 1591)

Working for a Bristol syndicate that included Sir Walter RALEIGH, Flegon captured a French fishing vessel—a significant prize, since his sponsors sold both the fish and the captured ship.

FLEURY, JEAN (French corsair; Atlantic; died 1527)

From Normandy, Fleury commanded Jean ANGO's pirate fleets and waylaid Spanish vessels returning from the Americas through the Azores and Canary Islands. In May 1523, Fleury assaulted three ships, which Hernando de Cortés had dispatched with the finest spoils of Montezuma's palace in Mexico. In addition to jaguars and parrots, the booty contained treasures of unrivaled beauty and value—exquisite jewelry, religious objects in gold and silver, rare gems including an emerald as large as a fist, finely worked feather cloaks and headdresses, and thousands of large disks of gold.

In the Azores, the Spaniards ran into Fleury, who commanded eight ships with some 200 soldiers. Three Spanish warships came out to escort the treasure fleet, but Fleury pursued them in a long running fight. The two richest GALLEONS were finally taken after a brutal battle off Cape Saint Vincent in southwestern Portugal. In addition to all of the Mexican booty, Fleury's men seized Cortés' emissaries to the king, one mortally wounded.

Although prizes taken earlier had contained some gold, the yield from this haul astonished the corsairs and Jean Ango, their patron. For the first time, French raiders became aware of the extraordinary treasures being carried to Spain from the Americas. The hope of another such haul excited their greed. In some years, as many as 70 ships prowled the Atlantic approaches to Seville and its satellite ports. From the 1530s, French raiders extended their attacks to the Indies themselves.

Portuguese corsairs captured one of Fleury's ships and its Spanish prize in 1522. Although Portugal was neutral in the Spanish-French wars, the French pirates were imprisoned at Lisbon. To punish the Portuguese, Fleury in 1525 plundered their shipping along the North African and Spanish coasts.

In 1527, six Basque ships trapped Fleury while he was cruising with a single vessel. He surrendered after resisting so ferociously that 87 of the enemy were killed or seriously wounded. Fleury offered to pay 30,000 ducats for his freedom, but the Basques sold him to Charles V of Spain. The king, who still mourned the loss of Montezuma's treasure, hanged Fleury. His crew was released in 1531.

FLOGGING *(naval discipline; all seas; 16th to 19th centuries)* In this formal punishment, a seaman was WHIPPED with the cruel CAT-O'-NINE TAILS. It was the most frequent penalty in the English and American navies, imposed at the captain's discretion for minor and major offenses. Officers could be flogged after a court-martial reduced them to the ranks. Punishment took place the day after sentence was passed, and all hands had to be present.

The victim was spreadeagled against a grating or ladder and tied by the angles and wrists. He received up to six dozen lashes on his naked back, and the man inflicting the blows was changed after each dozen. Even a single dozen bruised and broke the skin and created severe pain in the lungs. Only a court-martial could order the worst punishment, "flogging round the fleet." The victim, given up to 500 lashes, was taken around in a boat and flogged before each ship present.

Originally, each captain set his own rules. In England, the Articles of War (1653) limited a flogging to 48 lashes. Under the 1731 regulations, a court-martial was needed to impose more than 12. However, few captains observed

these limits. Much more severe sentences were frequent up to the abolition of flogging in 1879. Flogging also was the main punishment in the United States navy until 1850.

FLOTA *(Spanish convoys; Atlantic, Caribbean; 16th–18th centuries)* A Spanish word meaning "naval fleet," the popular name for the TREASURE FLEETS that picked up Mexican silver at SAN JUAN DE ULÚA.

FLY, WILLIAM *(British pirate; Caribbean, Atlantic; died 1726)* Ignorant of most seamen's skills, Fly was noted for his cruelty and profanity. Joining a slaver bound for Africa, he led a mutiny. The brigands killed the captain and mate with an axe, chopping off the captain's hand as he clung to the rail.

Cruising off North Carolina, Fly took several prisoners, including Mister Atkinson, mate of a captured SLOOP. When Atkinson deliberately missed Martha's Vineyard, Fly threatened to shoot him. To save his life, Atkinson pretended to turn pirate. One day, most of the crew were off in the sloop chasing a prize. Atkinson and the other captives rebelled and captured Fly, who was hanged at Boston.

(See also SELECTED BIBLIOGRAPHY: Defoe, *General History*; Dow, *Pirates*.)

FLYBOAT *(type of ship; North Sea; 16th–19th centuries)* A flat-bottomed Dutch vessel (*vlieboot*) carrying 400 to 600 tons and mainly used for coastal traffic. It had a high stern and one or two masts, often square-rigged or the mainmast might carry a spritsail.

FLYNN, ERROL *(American actor; 1909–1959)* Born in Australia, Flynn became an American citizen in 1942. Exceptionally handsome and seemingly a superb athlete, he became the best-known SWASHBUCKLER since Douglas FAIRBANKS. Although plagued by illness, Flynn did many of his own stunts and became an adequate archer and swordsman. His favorite sports—sailing, swimming, and diving—involved his love for the ocean. He often lived aboard a 120-foot SCHOONER purchased in 1945.

The son of an eminent marine biologist, Flynn attended excellent schools and was expelled from most. Always contemptuous of authority, he was fired by his first employer for embezzlement. From 1927 to 1932, Flynn had various jobs in New Guinea. After a director saw him on the beach, he was cast in an Australian documentary in 1932. Moving to England in 1933, he performed with a provincial company and made a low-budget mystery for Warner Brothers, which shipped him to Hollywood in January 1935.

When a British star broke his contract, Warner gambled on Flynn as the lead in CAPTAIN BLOOD. His overnight stardom is part of Hollywood legend. Flynn's sensuality and animal vitality virtually leaped off the screen, while the movie's plot appealed to a world trapped

Errol Flynn in *The Sea Hawk* (1940).

to Flynn's reputation, *The Adventures of Don Juan* (1949) failed at the box office.

After leaving Warner Brothers in 1949, Flynn shuttled between Hollywood and Europe, making occasional movies. He had visibly aged by 1952, and AGAINST ALL FLAGS lacks the intensity of his earlier swashbucklers. He died of a heart attack in 1959, eulogized by Jack Warner as "all the heroes in one magnificent, sexy, animal package."

(See also MASTER OF BALLANTRAE, THE; SON OF CAPTAIN BLOOD, THE.)

FOOD, PIRATE   Like other seamen, pirates had to carry on board enough food and drink to reach the next port. In the days before refrigeration, almost all foods quickly became rotten. Even flour and dried beans soon spoiled in a ship's damp hull. Only heavily salted fish and meat lasted more than a few weeks. Since water stored in wooden casks also went bad, all sailors preferred to drink alcoholic beverages. Both fermented beverages (such as wine and cider) and distilled alcohols (such as RUM) remain safe to drink long after water has turned poisonous.

Food storage presented few difficulties in the Mediterranean, where friendly ports usually were close at hand. The problem became severe during the 16th century, when raiders chasing TREASURE SHIPS undertook long voyages from Europe to Asia or South America. Lacking sufficient protein from meat or fish, many men became feeble or died. Without fresh vegetables to provide Vitamin C, others succumbed to SCURVY (1).

Even when they remained in the Caribbean, 17th-century BUCCANEERS often had to limit or curtail raids because of a lack of food. All major Spanish ports were closed to the pirates, and uninhabited regions and small towns could provide only limited supplies. In the absence of other forms of meat, sea turtles were much prized. These were carried live on deck and killed when they were needed. Strongly spiced stews such as SALMAGUNDI concealed the taste of salted meats and pickled vegetables.

"FOR I AM A PIRATE KING"   The refrain of the Pirate King's song in PIRATES OF PENZANCE, THE.

(See also "OH, BETTER FAR TO LIVE AND DIE.")

FORMICAN, JAMES *(Spanish pirate; Ionian Sea; 1306)*   From Catalonia, Formican looted a Venetian merchant ship leaving the Gulf of Pátrai.

FOR MY GREAT FOLLY *(novel; 1942)*   The only pirate fiction by Thomas Costain (1885–1965), best-selling author of historical romances. The physical details of life in earlier times fascinated Costain. This novel captures the grim horrors of the sea, including amputation, SCURVY (1), and savage tortures. Weapons, food, and clothing are lavishly described. Unfortunately, Costain ties his plot to an inaccurate portrayal of John WARD, an English RENEGADE with the BARBARY pirates.

in economic depression. Flynn became a symbol of courage, freedom, laughter, adventure, glamor—everything audiences wanted for themselves but rarely could have. He was cast as a fearless leader of men in films such as *The Charge of the Light Brigade* (1936), *The Prince and the Pauper* (1937), *The Adventures of Robin Hood* (1938), *Dodge City* (1939), and THE SEA HAWK (1940). All were expensive spectacles that often ignored historical accuracy.

Colorful stories about his romantic escapades and barroom brawls enhanced Flynn's popularity. He became a living phallic symbol, associated with the slang phrase "in like Flynn." It is unclear how much truth lies behind these legends. Flynn exaggerated his exploits in two books, *Beam Ends* (1939) and *My Wicked, Wicked Ways* (1959). Later biographers portray him as an insecure, inhibited man who purchased male and female prostitutes.

Flynn's career had peaked by 1941. He divorced his first wife, was rejected by the army, and broke with Michael Curtiz, who had directed his most successful films. He was acquitted in February 1943 of raping two teenage girls. Although briefly revived by the trial, his wide popularity dwindled. Always a heavy drinker and smoker, Flynn became addicted to morphine, cocaine, and heroin. The derring-do of *Objective Burma* (1945) aroused more ridicule than enthusiasm. Although tailored

French settlers catching turtles, a favorite food of the Caribbean buccaneers. Also portrayed are various species of parrots and other tropical birds. From Jean-Baptiste Du Tertre, *Histoire générale* (1667–1671).

The story is told by Roger Blease, an educated lad of 18 when Ward visits England in 1608. Blease enlists and helps capture a Spanish GALLEON. Ward hangs the Spanish captain and falls in love with a captured Spanish noblewoman. But he cannot be faithful and continues to pick up women in every port.

Making Blease his secretary, Ward returns to TUNIS. Uniting the English captains as the "Free Rovers," he defeats the Spanish and Venetian fleets. However, King James I sells out to Spain and hangs any Rover caught in England.

Blease returns to England. Pursued by royal officials, he shows Ward's financial backers proof of King James' treachery. He also kills Sir Neville Macherie, a pirate who had betrayed Ward. Blease's bravery wins the love of his beautiful childhood sweetheart. They leave for Damascus to represent an English company. On the way, Blease warns off Ward, lured home by false promises of pardon. When he returns about 1613, he learns that the Tunisians killed Ward.

Neither fiends nor heroes, Costain's pirates maraud for booty. Although he appreciates gold, Ward is the exception. He risks his life to thwart Spain's arrogant plans to keep English shipping out of the Mediterranean. However, in real life, Spain did not try to monopolize Mediterranean commerce. Costain's chronology is faulty throughout. Ward never battled Spanish warships (or the Spanish Armada), and Spain was not allied with Venice. The real Ward converted to Islam and lived peacefully in Tunis. He was hated (and not idolized) by the English public. These glaring gaps between the real and fictional John Ward are disconcerting precisely because Costain plausibly depicts English pirate life.

(See also SEAMAN'S SONG OF CAPTAIN WARD, THE.)

FORTUNES OF CAPTAIN BLOOD (1)   *(motion picture; black and white; 1950)*   In this film directed by Gordon Douglas, the Marquis de Riconete (George Macready) is ordered to rid the seas of CAPTAIN BLOOD. A suave Spanish grandee, Riconete wears an elegant silk dressing gown while supervising acts of torture by his brutal prison overseer (Alfonso Bedoya).

When several of his crewmen are captured and enslaved at La Hacha, Blood penetrates the city disguised as a fruit peddler. Aided by Pepita Rosados (Dona Drake), an outrageously flirtatious tavern WENCH, Blood is admitted to the Spanish prison. There he gains the love of Riconete's niece, the haughty Isabelita Sotomayor (Patricia Medina), and teaches her to hate slavery. Blood and his men fight their way to freedom. Riconete pursues, and his vessel blows up as it attacks Blood's ship.

This version of Rafael SABATINI's novel emphasizes SWORD DUELS more than Blood's mastery of disguises. As Blood, Louis Hayward combats Spanish guards on the tavern's staircase, with several plunging through the banisters. He fights off two guards in the prison, and he kills George Fairfax (Lowell Gilmore), an unscrupulous English slave dealer, during a shipboard duel. Hayward and Medina recreated their roles in the 1957 film, CAPTAIN PIRATE.

FORTUNES OF CAPTAIN BLOOD, THE (2) (novel; 1936)

This sequel to Rafael SABATINI's CAPTAIN BLOOD ignores Blood's romance with Arabella Bishop. It is devoted to Blood the superhero, who outwits and annihilates his foes. Sabatini modeled Blood's initial adventures on those of Sir Henry MORGAN and other historical characters. Here Blood succeeds in impossible exploits, never attempted by a real-life BUCCANEER.

The six episodes celebrate Blood's genius for disguises. Fluent in Spanish and French, he passes for anything from a mulatto slave to a Spanish nobleman. Once again, Blood mainly fights the Spaniards, cowardly villains who ravish British cities and vessels. In one episode, he destroys an English pirate pretending to be Blood and soiling his reputation.

In the first adventure, Blood takes a marooned Spanish official to Santo Domingo, where the ungrateful Spaniards fail to trap his vessel. Next Blood travels to San Juan, Puerto Rico, disguised as a Spanish official. He takes command of the garrison, repels an invasion by his false namesake, and seizes two TREASURE SHIPS.

After returning to TORTUGA, Blood stages a mock battle between Spanish and buccaneer warships. Pretending to be a British naval captain, he rescues a friend from slavery at Nevis. He goes on to Havana, Cuba, where one of his men pretends to be an archbishop. Masquerading as a merchant, he spies out RIO DE LA HACHA, and saves a Spanish girl from a loutish lover.

(See also CAPTAIN BLOOD RETURNS.)

FOSCOLO, BARTOLOMMEO (Italian corsair; Aegean Sea; active 1270s)

Raiding with the approval of Emperor MICHAEL VIII PALAEOLOGUS, Foscolo plundered his fellow Venetians as well as merchants from Dubrovnik, Greece, and Crete.

(See also VENETIAN CLAIMS.)

FOUR YEARS VOYAGES OF CAPT. GEORGE ROBERTS (adventure story; 1726)

Published as a true story but attributed to Daniel DEFOE by literary critics. Captain Roberts undertakes a trading voyage from Virginia to West Africa. In October 1722, his vessel is captured by three pirate ships. Edward LOW leads the squadron, accompanied by Francis SPRIGGS and a Portuguese pirate nicknamed John Russell.

In the GENERAL HISTORY, also said to be by Defoe, Low is described as an unspeakable and bloodthirsty maniac, the very worst of the brigands. The *Four Years Voyage*, by contrast, portrays Low as a kindly and well-mannered pirate. He and Captain Roberts stay up late drinking wine and conversing about "*Church* and *State*, as also about *Trade*."

Although Captain Russell insists that the pirates kill Roberts, Low prevents the murder. Roberts gets back his plundered SLOOP without food or water. Since his men enlisted with the pirates, his only crew is two young boys.

Roberts manages to reach Saint Nicholas in the Cape Verde Islands. The older boy goes ashore, and Roberts is joined by several Africans. A sudden squall drives his boat south, and it is wrecked on Saint Johns. Thanks to help from his faithful black companions, he survives for two years, builds a ship, and reaches an inhabited island.

FOXCRAFT, SAMUEL (English pirate; Atlantic; active 1590–1591)

Foxcraft traded in Spain and Portugal until those nations declared war on England in 1585. In 1590, he commanded the 300-ton *Merchant Royal*, which cruised in the Azores with James LANCASTER. The two raiders captured a rich Dutch prize, and Foxcraft horribly tortured the Dutch seamen with Lancaster's approval. They were charged with but never tried for piracy. In 1591, Foxcraft and the *Merchant Royal* joined George RAYMOND's three-ship expedition to the East Indies. Foxcraft and many others died of disease as the fleet sailed south along the African coast.

FRANCE, SOUTHERN (pirate victim, Mediterranean; 800–1200, 1600s)

After Charlemagne died in 814, his empire separated into several dominions, none with a navy. The coast was unprotected against Muslim adventurers, sailing from the BALEARIC ISLANDS and the Spanish emirate of Saragossa (Zaragoza). In a "dark age" with little sea-going trade, the brigands concentrated on kidnapping prisoners for ransom or sale.

Spanish and Balearic raiders assaulted Marseilles in 838 and again in 846. From 842, their armed bands sailed up the Rhône River, plundering along both banks and capturing the bishop of Arles in 860. Slavers need HAVENS where they could assemble their captives. The Spaniards initially camped both at the Camargue Island (near the mouth of the Rhône) and at Maguelonne, a ruined city near Montpellier.

From about 890, the marauders moved east to LA FREINET. Their forays had depopulated the countryside, and it was difficult to assault the walled towns along the Rhône. From La Freinet, they could raid new territories in the fertile Alpine valleys of the Upper Rhône and Switzerland.

The destruction of La Freinet in 971 ended large-scale brigandage on land. But the Provencal coast remained exposed until the Christian reconquest of northern Spain in 1212. During the 11th century, the monks of Lérins bought back Christians carried to Spain. As late as 1178, Muslim pirates took many prisoners during a raid near Marseilles.

During the first half of the 17th century, BARBARY corsairs frequently took slaves and loot along the coast from Marseilles to Nice. A line of towers communicating by fires was built to warn of their raids. Majorcan, Italian, Sicilian, and British pirates preyed on coastal shipping, following their victims almost into the harbor of Marseilles.

FRANCKE, THOMAS (English pirate; Atlantic, Mediterranean; active 1608–1615)
One of Richard BISHOP's confederation sailing from Leamcon in Ireland and MAMORA in Morocco. Francke quickly became prominent after Robert STEPHENSON put him in command of a captured ship. (He later repaid Stephenson with one of his own prizes.) He took many merchant vessels off the French and Moroccan coasts, and Leamcon pirates elected him their "vice-admiral" in 1609.

In 1611, Francke was captured by some Flemish rovers, who released him but "spoyled him of all his welth, and also burned his fingers' endes of, and tormented him otherwise by the privy members." Seeking a larger corsair fleet, FERDINANDO I, duke of Tuscany, welcomed Francke to LIVORNO, Italy, in about 1613.

(See also SELECTED BIBLIOGRAPHY: Senior, *Nation*.)

FRANCO, CAPTAIN (French or Dutch buccaneer; Pacific; active 1685–1693)
Entering the Pacific through the Strait of Magellan, Franco cruised along the South American coast from Chile to Mexico. His mixed crew included 34 Frenchmen, five other Europeans, and about 50 blacks and Indians. Franco probably planned to join French buccaneers already in the Pacific. When he failed to find them, he operated from the Galapagos and JUAN FERNÁNDEZ ISLANDS. Although his crew was too small to attack coastal towns, he did capture several merchantmen—selling some to their owners for substantial ransoms.

(See also SELECTED BIBLIOGRAPHY: Bradley, *Peru*.)

FRANÇOIS, PIERRE (French pirate; Caribbean; about 1660)
EXQUEMELIN tells François' story. A native of Normandy, François sailed from Jamaica with a small ship and 26 men. Failing to take any prizes, he resolved to raid the pearl fishing beds off RIO DE LA HACHA, Venezuela. Every year, a fleet of small ships visited the beds guarded by a man-of-war.

François and his comrades rowed up without sails—like a Spanish coaster coming from Maracaibo—and overcame a pearling ship in a sudden rush. To their joy, it contained all the pearls taken by the entire fleet, worth some 100,000 pesos. To fool the other vessels, François left the Spanish flag flying and sank his own ship. However, when the raiders put to sea, the warship discovered the trick and pursued them.

Trying to escape, the pirates piled on too much sail and down crashed the mainmast. The Spanish warship caught up and attacked so fiercely that François bargained for his life. Rather than risk losing the pearls if the pirates' boat sank, the enemy captain agreed to try the captives in Spain instead of immediately enslaving them at hard labor.

FREEBOOTER (sea raider; all oceans; 16th century to the present)
Someone who goes about in search of plunder (from Dutch *vrijbuiter*). The word was popular among 19th-century writers of pirate fiction.

(See also FILIBUSTER.)

FREEMAN, CAPTAIN (English buccaneer; Caribbean; 1663–1665)
Captain Freeman assaulted cities in Mexico and Nicaragua with John MORRIS and Sir Henry MORGAN.

FREINET (LA) (Muslim corsair haven; France; 890–972)
A mountainous and forested site on the southern coast near Saint Tropez, fortified in about 890 by Spanish pirates. Armed bands devastated the countryside along the coast, kidnapping prisoners for Spanish slave markets. They also raided north into the Alpine passes between France and Italy. In 906, they sacked and burned a monastery above Susa on the road to Turin. Their assaults on pilgrims became frequent from 920, when they battered to death some Anglo-Saxons bound for Rome.

Muslim bands ventured far into the upper Rhône Valley and Switzerland. In 940, they burned the monastery of Saint Maurice d'Agaune in Valais. Another band killed several monks of Saint Gall—virtually in Austria—as they marched in procession round their church. (Swiss place-names derived from Arabic, such as Gaby and Algaby, commemorate their visits.) Little could be done as long as La Freinet received reinforcements from the sea. None of the local rulers had a navy, and nothing was achieved by BYZANTINE squadrons in 931 and 942.

In 972, however, the marauders kidnapped too illustrious a prize. On the road from the Great Saint Bernard Pass, they ambushed the abbot of Cluny, collecting a heavy ransom from his monastery. The abbot was the most famous churchman of his day, the spiritual advisor of kings. The count of Provence overtook and massacred the sacrilegious Muslims, gathered an army of nobles, and overpowered the fortress at La Freinet.

(See also FRANCE, SOUTHERN.)

FRENCHMAN'S CREEK (1) (novel; 1942)
Daphne Du Maurier (1907–1989) sets this "Gothic" romance during the reign of King Charles I. Lady Dona Saint Columb, beautiful and spirited, is bored by her flabby and stupid husband. In London, she flirts with his evil friend, Lord Rockingham, and plays at wicked games, sometimes disguised in male garb.

Disgusted with her dissolute life, Lady Dona takes her two young children to Navron, an isolated estate in Cornwall. Following after an enigmatic manservant, Dona runs across a French ship hidden in a nearby river. Dona and the pirate captain enjoy an idyllic month fishing and birdwatching. Again dressed as a man, she helps the captain seize a vessel owned by one of her loathsome neighbors. They consummate their love after the battle, but the Frenchman persuades her to accept her responsibilities as a mother.

Back at Navron, Dona finds her husband and Rockingham have arrived and are plotting to attack the pirates. Instead the Frenchmen temporarily capture the house and tie up the men. Rockingham loosens his bonds and attacks Dona, outraged to learn that she loves the captain and not himself. Dona kills him in self-defense.

Meanwhile, the pirate ship gets away, but the captain is captured. Again donning male clothing, Dona helps him escape, but then returns to her husband and children. She renounces the Frenchman (and her own zest for adventure) because their love has taught her to be a fully mature woman.

Du Maurier's many readers considered her a consummate master of love stories. A love story certainly is at the heart of *Frenchman's Creek*. As in other Du Maurier novels (notably *Rebecca* and *My Cousin Rachel*), however, the main characters are complicated and paradoxical, and varying interpretations are possible.

The well-made plot is aided by accurate descriptions of natural beauty and everyday life. Du Maurier's Frenchmen are not the debauched fiends of some pirate FICTION. Indeed, the novel ridicules pirate mythology when Dona first encounters the Frenchmen. Their ship is clean and freshly painted; the men are happy, hard-working seamen. This surprises Dona, who had been taught that pirates were "desperate creatures, with rings in their ears and knives between their teeth."

The French captain is appealing but normal—and not superhuman like the heroes of Rafael SABATINI. A landowner in a small way, he turned pirate both to escape boredom and to gain wealth. He robs any merchant ship he encounters, but then gives alms to the poor. He kills when he must but prefers to let his captives go. Like pirates in real life, he avoids battles, winning prizes by careful planning and seamanship and not by violence.

FRENCHMAN'S CREEK (2) *(movie; color; 1944)*

A lavish romance epic (Paramount's most expensive film up to that time), based on Daphne Du Maurier's 1942 novel. To get away from her stupid husband (Ralph Forbes) and lecherous Lord Rockingham (Basil RATHBONE), Lady Dona Saint Columb (Joan Fontaine) flees to a Cornish castle. She finds a French pirate (Arturo de Cordova) anchored in a nearby creek, falls in love with the brigand, and joins him in raiding the estate of pompous Lord Godolphin (Nigel Bruce).

The script and broadly sketched characterizations lack the complexity and ambiguity of the Du Maurier novel. Here the French pirate takes on the usual trappings of a movie SWASHBUCKLER, even fighting the inevitable SWORD DUEL against several attackers. In the film, the love-sick pirate begs the heroine to run away with him, but she nobly pledges her life to her children. This reverses their roles in the novel, where Lady Saint Col-

umb is eager to go to sea, but the pirate convinces her to remain with her family.

Mitchell Leisin directed the film, and Sam Corner won an Oscar for the sets. Victor Young provides a lush score, based on Claude Debussy's "Clair de Lune."

FRESSHOWE (FRYCHOWE), NICHOLAS *(English pirate; Atlantic; 1441)*

From Falmouth, Fresshowe owned and commanded several small ships. He captured a Breton ship on his own and raided off the Isle of Wight with Hankyn SEELANDER.

FRIGATE *(type of ship; all oceans; 1500 to the present)*

A name (Italian *fregata*, possibly derived from Latin *fabricata*, something built) for several types of ships. The Venetians gave this name to a small oared boat, about 35 feet long and seven feet wide. During the 17th century, the English used the same name for a larger ship with sails and sometimes also oars. Meanwhile, for 17th-century BARBARY corsairs, *fregata* was a generic term for any sailing ship (often also carrying oars) that had cannon for military purposes.

From the late 1600s, the English word was limited to a class of warships next in size to the battleship ("ship-of-the-line"). Frigates had three fully rigged masts and a raised quarterdeck and forecastle. They carried from 24 to 38 guns on a single deck.

Naval frigates were faster than battleships and accompanied them as lookouts and signal ships. They also escorted convoys and hunted for PRIVATEERS and merchantmen. Caribbean BUCCANEERS cruised in smaller ships and generally fled when they ran into a naval frigate. However, some successful pirates during the early 1700s took over and used frigates. Bartholomew ROBERTS' fourth *Royal Fortune* was a captured frigate.

The word was revived during World War II for a class of medium-speed vessels used to escort convoys. It now means any smaller, general-purpose warship.

FROBISHER, SIR MARTIN *(English explorer; Atlantic, Mediterranean; 1539–1594)*

After great success as a pirate, Frobisher explored Canada's northern coast. Born in Yorkshire, he lived in London with his maternal uncle, Sir John Yorke, an investor in many foreign ventures.

Frobisher went to sea at an early age. In 1553 and 1554, Yorke sent him with expeditions to West Africa. Most of his shipmates died, and the natives held Frobisher hostage for nine months during the 1554 voyage. Frobisher also made at least one excursion to MOROCCO, returning in 1559. From 1559 to 1662, he and a pirate named Strangways plotted to seize a Portuguese stronghold in Guinea.

Frobisher was back in Yorkshire by 1563. England opposed the Catholic faction in France, and a merchant fitted out three ships as PRIVATEERS. Frobisher commanded one ship, and the others sailed under Peter

KILLIGREW and Frobisher's brother, John. In about May 1563, Martin and John Frobisher brought five French prizes into Plymouth. Martin also captured an illegal Spanish prize in consort with Thomas COBHAM. He was arrested but quickly released, although the courts did seize some of his brother's property.

In 1565, Frobisher cruised in his own ship, captured two Flemish merchantmen, and was briefly arrested for other acts of piracy. He was freed in October 1566 and acquired a privateer's license from a French faction. He "haunted the seas" throughout 1568, taking several prizes in consort with five other pirate ships.

By 1569, Frobisher commanded two warships, which had a Dutch license to capture Spanish vessels. He also took at least two French prizes, and English merchants asked for protection against his raids. Arrested for piracy in August 1569, Frobisher was imprisoned in London for almost a year. He was freed through the influence of Lady Elizabeth Clinton, wife of England's ADMIRAL and a favorite of Queen Elizabeth.

Frobisher entered the royal service by 1571, but continued to take prizes for his own account. In 1572, he captured a German and several French vessels while traveling to Ireland for the queen. In January 1573, he took another French ship while cruising as a pirate. Warrants for his arrest apparently never were enforced.

Frobisher now withdrew from piracy, perhaps influenced by royal orders that prohibited the use of foreign privateering licenses. He long had been interested in the search for a northwest passage to the Pacific Ocean. In 1574 the crown licensed a venture by Frobisher and Michael Lok, a fellow enthusiast. Money came in slowly, partly because Frobisher's piracies were notorious. Frobisher finally sailed in June 1576 with two small ships, reaching Labrador and Baffin Island.

Frobisher claimed that he had discovered the northwest passage and also found gold. A Cathay Company was created, and Frobisher led a second expedition in 1577. It brought back ore supposedly containing gold and silver. (In fact, investors were shown fake samples.) In May 1578, Frobisher took 15 ships as far as Hudson's Strait. When he failed to establish a colony and returned with worthless ore, the Cathay Company collapsed leaving enormous debts.

Frobisher was again in favor at court by 1580. In 1581, he and Simâo FERNANDES prepared for a voyage to Asia by the eastern route. However, Sir Edward Fenton and not Frobisher commanded the ships that sailed in Mar 1582.

Frobisher was vice-admiral of Sir Francis DRAKE's 1585 West Indies expedition, and he led the assault on CARTAGENA. He was knighted in 1588 while fighting with Drake and Sir John HAWKINS against the Spanish Armada. He held other naval commands and was mortally wounded in 1594 battling Spanish troops in France.

(See also SELECTED BIBLIOGRAPHY: Andrews, *Trade*.)

FROM THE SEAS *(pirate slang; 17th and 18th centuries)* When they wished to conceal their identity, pirates declared they were "from the seas" and not from any particular country.

FRY, CAPTAIN *(British pirate; Mediterranean; 1615)* Captain Fry fled TUNIS in a stolen vessel with 80 British followers, many master gunners.

FUNNELL, WILLIAM *(English pirate; Pacific; active 1703–1706)* In September 1703, Funnell sailed for South America's Pacific coast as an officer on William DAMPIER's *Saint George*. While Dampier is famous as a BUCCANEER and scientist, he enjoyed little success as a naval commander. The *Saint George* took only a few poor prizes, and Dampier was accused of cowardice. Thomas STRADLING deserted with Dampier's second ship in May 1704, and John CLIPPERTON took off in a Spanish prize in September. Dampier located the MANILA GALLEON in December but was driven off by the larger ship.

By now the *Saint George* was rotting and in danger of sinking. Off the Mexican coast in mid January, Dampier told the crew he intended to raid as a pirate, keeping all the booty and ignoring the owners' rights. On February 11, Funnell and 36 others instead sailed for the East Indies in the *Dragon*, a 70-ton BRIGANTINE.

Funnell and his companions survived on a little flour and salt pork until the *Dragon* reached the Marinas Islands in April. Heading southwest, they arrived at Ambon (in the Moluccas) in June. The Dutch, jealous of their trading monopoly, confiscated the *Dragon* and jailed her crew for almost four months.

Funnell made it home on a Dutch ship in August 1706, a year before Dampier. Since Dampier's books about earlier voyages had been quite successful, Funnell rushed into print with *A Voyage Round the World, Containing an Account of Captain Dampier's Expedition . . .* (London, 1707). While closely imitating his style and descriptions of exotic places, Funnell blamed Dampier for the expedition's failure. Dampier ruined his own reputation by responding in the incoherent and ill-tempered *Dampier's Vindication of his Voyage . . .* (London 1707).

(See also SELECTED BIBLIOGRAPHY: Burney, *Chronological History*; Lloyd, *Dampier*; Kemp and Lloyd, *Brethren*.)

FUSTE (FUSTA) *(pirate ship; Mediterranean; 1500–1800)* A small ship driven by both sails and about 15 oars on each side. Long, low, and fast, it was a favorite of BARBARY and SALÉ pirates, who probably developed it from the TARTAN.

G

GADDALI *(Barbary corsair; Mediterranean; active 1510s)* Sailing from TUNIS, Gaddali raided Sicily, Sardinia, and the Italian coast. In 1516, he captured the flagship of a papal general, who was ransomed in 1519 for 6,000 gold ducats. The Italian records do not indicate whether Gaddali operated independently or under ARUJ and KHEIREDDIN BARBAROSSA.

GAFFORIO, ANDREA *(Italian corsair; Aegean Sea; active 1270s)* From Genoa, Gafforio pillaged Latin (non-Greek) shipping under a license from Emperor MICHAEL VIII PALAEOLOGUS. Keeping much of his booty, he lived in peaceful retirement at Athens (then under Latin rule) during the early 14th century.

(See also GAFFORIO, CAPTAIN; VENETIAN CLAIMS.)

GAFFORIO, CAPTAIN *(Italian corsair; Mediterranean; 1197)* A merchant and captain, he commanded a Genoese fleet in Syrian waters in the early 1190s. While in Constantinople in 1196 or 1197, Gafforio was unfairly fined by the BYZANTINE government. To take vengeance, he assembled a large flotilla and plundered Aegean ports and islands, taking away great booty from Atramyttium on the coast of Asia Minor. The imperial officials sent out 30 ships under Giovanni STIRIONE, a former corsair. But Gafforio surprised and seized Stirione's ships while their crews were ashore on the island of Sestos.

While assembling a new squadron of warships and Pisan corsairs for Stirione, the emperor pretended to want peace and offered Gafforio 80 pounds of gold and command of a province. Gafforio was still negotiating when Stirione suddenly attacked and killed him.

(See also GAFFORIO, ANDREA.)

GALER, CAPTAIN *(French buccaneer; Caribbean; 1697)* Galer took part in the siege of CARTAGENA.

GALERATI, FABIO *(Knight of Saint Stephen; Mediterranean; active 1578–1583)* Galerati came from Cremona, Italy. Although not sufficiently noble to join the knights, he was a skilled and highly aggressive seaman. Seeking to increase the knights' piratical cruises, Florentine Duke Francesco I dei MEDICI ignored the rules and made Galerati ADMIRAL in 1578. He led many raids on the Aegean islands and along the Tunisian coast.

GALILEE *(pirate haven; Mediterranean; 65)* Although the ancient Jews produced many famous warriors, history knows of only one band of Jewish pirates. In 66, various groups rose up against the Romans occupying Palestine. An army under Vespasian (emperor from 69 to 79) reconquered Galilee the following year.

When the war ruined the region and prevented farming, refugees seized the city of Joppa and turned pirate.

They built small ships and successfully plundered traders passing Syria, Phoenicia, and Egypt. But the Palestinian coast is treacherous, and these inexperienced sailors soon came to a bad end.

When he learned of their exploits, Vespasian sent an army against Joppa. The pirates fled to their boats and floated just off shore. In the morning a sudden squall rose, which local sailors call "the black north wind." It dashed the corsairs' ships against each other and against the rocks. Many drowned, and the Romans killed those carried to shore. According to the ancient historian Josephus, 4,200 died in all.

GALIOT/GALLIOT *(pirate ship; Mediterranean; 16th through 18th centuries)* The BARBARY and SALÉ corsairs favored this smaller and faster version of the GALLEY. The galiot was long and sleek with a flush deck, one large lateen sail, and two to 10 small cannon. Depending on size, it had a crew of 50 to 130 men. Twelve to 23 oars were manned by one to three rowers, usually free warriors and not slaves.

GALLANT SPANIARD, THE *(play in Spanish verse; published 1615)* CERVANTES' rarely performed *El Gallardo Español* presents the adventures of a Spanish soldier during the 1556 OTTOMAN seige of Oran, Algeria. Challenged to a duel by a Muslim, he leaves his camp and goes over to the other side under a false name, looking for his challenger. After all sorts of romantic encounters, the soldier joins the Muslims for the final attack on the Spanish camp. At the last minute, he reveals his true identity and singlehandedly saves the Spanish army.

GALLEASS *(type of ship; Mediterranean; 16th and 17th centuries)* Large vessels, 150 feet long and 25 wide, propelled by a single bank of oars and lateen sails on two or three masts. They were used for long voyages by Genoese and Venetian traders, who took them into the Atlantic during the calmer summer months. BARBARY corsairs sometimes armed them as warships, and the Spanish included six galleasses in the Armada that invaded England in 1588.

GALLEON (1) *(type of ship; all oceans; 16th through 18th centuries)* The Spanish used armed galleons to transport freight over long distances. Each year, one or two MANILA GALLEONS carried valuable Oriental products from the Philippines to Acapulco, Mexico. Annual TREASURE FLEETS took Peruvian and Mexican treasure from the Caribbean to Spain.

Spanish galleons were powerful and carried large amounts of cargo, but they were slow, difficult to handle and unable to sail into or near the wind. Pirate ships were faster and better sailers, but the galleon's size and heavy cannon made direct attack difficult. Few raiders

Fifteenth-century galleon. From Jurien de la Gravière, *Les corsaires barbaresques* (1887).

succeeded in capturing one of these immensely rich prizes.

The English word *galleon* usually refers only to these Spanish ships. This usage is somewhat capricious. England and other northern nations built similar vessels but did not call them galleons. Moreover, the Spanish themselves rarely used *galeón* and usually referred to this type of ship as *nao* or *navío*.

Whatever name was used, a galleon was a large, heavily built merchant or naval vessel with two or three decks. Most had three masts, with square sails on the forward masts, a lateen sail on the mizzenmast, and a small square sail on the high-rising bowsprit. The largest galleons sometimes had four masts.

The galleon evolved from the CARRACK during the 16th century. Architects kept the stern (or poop) castle but eliminated the high forecastle to make the ship more maneuverable. Some historians credit Sir John HAWKINS with the new design, but it may have developed independently in Spain. Sir Francis DRAKE'S GOLDEN HIND was a small galleon. Both sides fought with large galleons when the Spanish Armada invaded England in 1588. The English, French, Dutch, and Swedish navies built galleons up to about 1640.

Spanish galleons were about 100 to 150 feet long and 40 to 50 feet wide. Those in the Atlantic usually carried about 600 tons. Manila Galleons were larger and wider, and a few reached 2,000 tons. Over time, designers reintroduced the forecastle, and they increased the height of the elaborately decorated stern castle. Because of these towering castles and their shallow draft, later galleons were extremely top-heavy and cumbersome.

GALLEON (2) *(novel; 1986)* The further adventures of Dudley POPE's Ned Yorke and Sir Thomas WHETSTONE. Two years after ADMIRAL (2) in 1662, Yorke still leads the PORT ROYAL pirates, who have taken great booty in Cuba and at PORTOBELO. Jamaica's first royal governor is a physically and morally repugnant politician. Ignorant of Caribbean realities, he does not see that Jamaica needs the buccaneers to fend off a Spanish reconquest. When he takes away their licenses, most pirates sail to TORTUGA, while Yorke and Whetstone halfheartedly begin plantations.

Yorke learns that a TREASURE SHIP from CARTAGENA has gone aground between Saint Martin and Anguilla. With the beautiful Diana at his side, Whetstone sails for Saint Martin to loot the wreck. Yorke and his French mistress, Aurelia, follow after.

Whetstone stops for water at Boquerón, Puerto Rico, where the Spaniards suddenly turn on the BUCCANEERS and imprison them at San German. (Yorke admits there is a certain justice "when the Spanish play tricks on us; we play tricks on them.") The Puerto Ricans plan to garrote and shoot their captives at San German's main plaza. Yorke and Diana rescue their friends by disguising themselves and their crew as monks.

The two captains and their warrior women go on to Saint Martin, where the treasure ship is stuck. With the help of Saint Martin's French governor, they concoct a complicated plot that drives the Spaniards off the ship. The governor joins the buccaneers, and the raiders return to Port Royal with £400,000 in booty.

Pope is less faithful to the historical facts than in BUCCANEER. Jamaica's first governor was a handsome nobleman and a great friend to the buccaneers. Treasure ships did not sail northeast (against the prevailing winds) through the Lesser Antilles.

GALLEY *(type of ship; 3000 B.C.–18th century A.D.)* A commercial and combat vessel with one deck, primarily propelled by oars. They were common in the Mediterranean, where frequent summer calms halt ships dependent solely on sails. Galleys were seldom used in the Atlantic. They performed badly in the open sea, where large waves and poor weather are the rule rather than the exception.

Merchant galleys, used throughout ancient history to carry valuable cargoes, had deep, rounded hulls. The lighter war galleys were flat-bottomed with long, narrow hulls. They depended on short bursts of high speed (up to seven knots an hour) to ram or to close with an enemy vessel. The primary ships of battle in the Mediterranean from about 850 B.C. through the 16th century, galleys were last used during the Russo-Sweddish war of 1809.

A Phoenician war galley with two tiers of oars, carrying warriors and women. From a carving found at Kouyunjik, Iraq, and made about 700 B.C., when the Phoenicians were allied with the Assyrian Empire. From Austen Layard, *Nineveh and Its Remains* (New York, 1849).

Ancient Galley (2,000 B.C.–A.D. 500)

The MINOANS and the SEA PEOPLES had an undecked galley with rounded hulls. The Greek and Roman galley—with straight lines, angled ends, and a lofty prow—originated further north among the seafarers of the Aegean.

Homer's warrior pirates—men such as ODYSSEUS and MENELAUS—sailed in lightweight undecked galleys that were relatively low and narrow. The smallest, about 50 feet long, had 20 oars (10 on each side). The most common troop transport, the PENTECONTER, used 50 oars and reached a length of 125 feet. All carried a single square sail bent to a yard and set amidships on a mast that could be lowered or raised.

By about 700, two distinctive types of galleys had developed. Merchant galleys—some 150 feet long—had deep, rounded hulls and were relatively broad. In contrast, war galleys were low and narrow—about 10 times longer than wide—with a shallow draft and flat bottoms. The introduction of the ram had changed the war galley from a troop carrier into a man-driven torpedo that punctured the enemy's hull.

Unlike naval forces, pirates wanted to capture and not sink their quarry. Thus they continued to fight in the old-fashioned way, making fast to their prey and then leaping on board. To suit their special needs, they developed a variety of PIRATE SHIPS that were narrower and faster than merchant galleys but roomier and more seaworthy than war galleys.

To withstand the shock of ramming, naval men-of-war were built of heavy materials and provided with a deck about two feet above the rowers along the gunwale. This raised deck led the Greeks and PHOENICIANS to introduce *biremes*, ships with two levels or banks of rowers. Both soon placed the upper oarsmen along the gunwale, while the lower bank rowed through ports in the hull. The oars of the two banks were staggered, with each of the upper oars centered over the space between two of the lower. This left the raised deck as a true fighting platform.

During the 600s, naval architects took the next logical step and designed TRIREMES with a third bank of rowers. Built for maneuverability and the short bursts of speed needed to ram the enemy, the extremely slender, almost arrowlike trireme provided almost no storage room. POLYCRATES OF SAMOS, who confined his piracies to the Aegean, created the first large fleet of triremes in 525. But merchants and raiders continued to prefer the roomier penteconter for longer journeys.

The competing empires of the Hellenistic Age (323–31 B.C.) built very large galleys, known as POLYREMES. These added men to each oar in various combinations. More rowers gave the super galleys a wider deck to carry marines and catapults. And only the rower at the tip of the oar had to be skilled; the others merely supplied muscle.

Designed to fight each other in fixed naval battles, the triremes and supergalleys were not suitable for cruising on the high seas. They were expensive to operate and had almost no space for water or food. Because of their shallow draft, flat bottoms, and heavy load of oarsmen and soldiers, they were inherently unstable and capsized easily. Ancient warships seldom ventured far from land, and they avoided action during the stormy winter months.

The war galley's fragility made the open sea an unpoliced no-man's-land. Most strikingly, a pirate crew that accidentally ran into a war galley almost always escaped. (TIMOCLES apparently was the only ancient pirate captured on the high seas.) Corsairs such as NIKANDROS easily outsailed Greek and Roman warships. And, if they chose to stand and fight, groups of smaller pirate ships literally ran circles around the slower and heavier war galleys.

Only RHODES maintained a special anti-pirate fleet, which substituted the faster TRIEMIOLIA for the heavy galley. The Romans continued to use warships that could not defeat pirates at sea, and they had to send armies to attack the corsair HAVENS at LIGURIA, ILLYRIA, CRETE, and CILICIA. Ancient piracy ended only when Gnaeus POMPEIUS assembled an enormous force that simultaneously attacked along the entire Mediterranean coastline.

The Roman imperial navy founded in 31 B.C. was intended to provide communications and transport. It gave up heavy warships and relied on the trireme and the LIBURNIAN, based on a pirate design. But these fleets could hold down piracy only as long as Roman armies controlled the shores and destroyed budding pirate havens. When Roman land forces became weaker after A.D. 250, BLACK SEA pirates easily overran the Roman navy in the Aegean.

Medieval Galley (500–1500)

Until the 13th century, trade goods were carried in "roundships" moved by sails. Galleys continued to be used as warships by empires wealthy enough to support large numbers of rowers. During its flourishing days in the 10th century, the BYZANTINE navy favored the swift *dromon*, with two banks of 25 oars, each rowed by a single man. The largest were perhaps 130 feet long and 18 feet wide. The war fleets of Arab raiders—such as LEO OF TRIPOLI—also included galleys, but their design is unknown.

From about 1250, Venice and other Italian city-states developed "great galleys" for commercial and military purposes. These had one level of benches, with three men to each bench. Depending on design, each man pulled his own oar or all three shared one oar. The French, Spanish, and OTTOMAN navies imitated this design, which developed into the war galley of the 16th century.

Byzantine fleets used a lighter and faster ship to carry messages and spy on the enemy. Known as the *galea*, it was propelled by one bank of oars. This was also the favorite ship of Christian and Muslim pirates, who added a lateen sail to create something like the GALIOT of the BARBARY corsairs. The KNIGHTS OF RHODES also raided in fast oared vessels, although they maintained one or more "great galleys" for military purposes.

Modern Galley (1500–1800)

During the 16th century, the Ottoman and Spanish empires built large fleets of galleys, and smaller squadrons were operated by Venice and the Italian cities allied to Spain. After a lapse of 2,000 years, the Mediterranean empires re-created the navies of the ancient world. Battle tactics were different, however, thanks to the invention of artillery. Modern galleys carried heavy cannon and swivel guns on platforms at the bow. Rather than ramming their opponents, they tried to blow them out of the water and then closed for boarding.

Naval galleys were designed to destroy enemy galleys, transport troops, and bombard fortified places. They had a single deck and one bank of oars, with 21 to 27 benches and at least three oarsmen to a bench. Venetian war galleys were built for speed and were typically about 140 feet long, 17 feet wide, and five feet high. Spanish and Ottoman galleys tended to be somewhat larger and stronger with more rowers. In addition to oarsmen, galleys carried 30 to 40 sailors, soldiers, and artillerymen.

Although the galley was too costly and limited for everyday use, the Barbary corsairs and Christian pirates kept a few in their fleets. The KNIGHTS OF MALTA maintained three to five galleys, the KNIGHTS OF SAINT STEPHEN three or fewer. ALGIERS, the largest Barbary state, rarely supported more than six. These were used only for naval defense and the rare large-scale raid. Both Christian and Muslim pirates usually marauded in lighter, faster vessels propelled by both oars and sails.

Sixteenth-century galley, flagship of the admiral of a Christian state such as Malta. From J. Furttenbach, *Architectura Navalis* (Ulm, 1629).

Galleys provided the backbone of Spanish expeditions against Algiers and TUNIS. But they were notoriously ineffective at chasing pirates. Any North African galiot, BRIGANTINE, or TARTAN could outrun a Spanish galley hands down. Venetian galleys sometimes caught up with but rarely defeated pirates in the Adriatic. Ottoman galleys were equally powerless to stop Christian raiders.

The Spanish and Ottoman war fleets were enormously expensive, and both sides withdrew from battle during the 1580s. The war galleys and their ports decayed. Navies used galleys only to guard harbors and raid enemy commerce.

By the early 17th century, goods increasingly were carried in English and Dutch sailing ships, which held off Barbary galiots with cannon broadsides. Northern sailors also entered the Mediterranean as pirates. Some helped the North Africans master large sailing ships. Henceforth, Barbary fleets added a few warships with sails. However, they continued to rely on the galiot and other hybrids, which were sufficiently powerful to capture coastal trading vessels.

GALLEY, ATLANTIC *(type of ship; Atlantic, Indian Ocean; 17th and 18th centuries)* An English vessel with a level deck, primarily propelled by sails but fitted with oar ports for extra mobility. The name may be a contraction of "galley-built frigate." Galleys apparently were rigged like FRIGATES, but their deck was flush the entire length of the ship. The traditional frigate had a quarterdeck and forecastle four or five steps higher than the main deck.

Merchant galleys traded with North America and West Africa, and several were captured by pirates. The ship's oars proved useful when William KIDD took the *Adventure Galley* to MADAGASCAR in 1696. Kidd fell in with British warships and escaped by rowing away during a windless evening.

(See also SELECTED BIBLIOGRAPHY: Defoe, *General History*.)

GALLEY SLAVES *(captive oarsmen; Mediterranean; 1000 B.C.–A.D.1798)*

Ancient and Medieval

There is a common impression—fostered by movies such as *Ben Hur*—that ancient warships were moved by slaves flogged to their task. In fact, slaves did not serve as oarsmen on war galleys, which were rowed by free, paid workers. Slaves did work on warships—but not as rowers.

The poems of HOMER mention only oarsman-warriors, who rowed the ship and fought when it arrived. In later eras, merchant ships sometimes used slaves, but they were too expensive and untrustworthy for naval service. War galleys needed skilled oarsmen, rigorously trained to work together. Since their task was arduous and dangerous, expert rowers received high wages. But it was still cheaper to hire them for a single campaign then to support a slave for life.

The ancient Greek city-states depended on their poorer citizens, and hired additional manpower from neighboring islands and coastal towns. The Ptolemies of Egypt (304–44) hired skilled foreign rowers and conscripted peasants to fill out their crews. Republican Rome also relied on paid oarsmen, usually citizens, although foreigners were hired or drafted during emergencies. The pirate fleets of Sextus POMPEIUS did welcome runaway slaves. But they served him as free volunteers.

Under the Roman emperors, the navy relied on foreign seamen, who volunteered for long terms (at least 26 years). The BYZANTINE fleet, successor to that of imperial Rome, also used only free rowers, usually hired. The Arab governments drafted their Christian subjects, but paid them a money wage.

Modern

Although pirates preferred free rowers, naval squadrons began to use forced labor from the 15th century. Unable to fill their oars with convicts, official navies vied to purchase corsair captives. In many cases, captured crews brought in more than a ship's cargo. Partly because they needed slaves, European governments encouraged Christian piracy against Muslims.

Oared ships had several sources of manpower. Navies recruited professional seamen and conscripted rowers from seaside communities. Coerced oarsmen included both convicts and true galley slaves—prisoners of war condemned for life. Enslavement at the oars was justified by the religious war between Christianity and Islam. Christians usually enslaved only Muslim prisoners. In Muslim countries, Christian slaves served at the oars.

Economic considerations determined the choice between free and slave oarsmen. Slaves cost less per day. But paid rowers were more expert, did not tie up guards, and did double duty as fighters. Moreover, slaves must be fed year around, and galleys generally sailed only during the six warmest months.

Pirate captains fought for profit. Most preferred volunteer oarsmen both because they were cheaper and because their greater skills helped to bring in prizes. Free men rowed Italian, Spanish, Turkish, and Greek pirate ships. Many BARBARY corsairs (including the great KHEIREDDIN) insisted on paid rowers, especially on smaller ships. With less weight to pull and good prospects of booty, volunteers were easy to recruit. Corsairs sailing from MALTA also depended on volunteer crews, especially on cruises to the Levant.

Slaves were common on the large tax-supported galleys owned by governments, which cared less about profits. The Barbary States, the KNIGHTS OF MALTA, and the Florentine KNIGHTS OF SAINT STEPHEN all manned their galleys through slave raids. The tiny populations of these piratical states could not provide sufficient volunteers. The Maltese and Florentine knights (and the papal navy) used Muslim slaves as a religious duty. Malta had some 1,200 galley slaves in 1632, more than 1,000 in 1712.

Errol Flynn leads English galley slaves escaping from a Spanish vessel. From *The Sea Hawk* (1940).

(Earlier, sailing from more populous RHODES, the knights never used galley slaves and slaughtered captured Muslims.)

Other naval fleets also became dependent on unfree rowers during the 16th century. During the Middle Ages, navies maintained a small force of experienced rowers, supplemented by hired or conscripted short-term labor. For various reasons, many no longer could find enough volunteer rowers.

French galleys were allowed to impress vagabonds and criminals in 1443 and also purchased foreign slaves. By the 16th century, Spain and Spanish Naples relied almost exclusively upon convicts and slaves. The Ottoman navy preferred paid and conscript oarsmen, but Christian slaves rowed perhaps one-third of its galleys. The Venetians also favored volunteer rowers. Venice did use convicts from the 1550s, but never employed Muslim galley slaves.

Navies thus became a lucrative market for corsair captives. Demand swelled after 1660, as the French navy created a large galley fleet. By 1690, France had nearly 50 galleys, and its navy required 6,000 oarsmen in 1712. Although French captains also used criminals and religious minorities, they valued Muslim slaves and refused to release them even for high ransoms. Indeed, France's stubborn refusal to free galley slaves led to several wars with ALGIERS.

Since the Spanish also enlarged their fleets during the 1660s, slaves were scarce. The French government scoured the major corsair ports at Malta and LIVORNO.

Its agents bought up every likely male captured off North Africa or in the Levant, including crews and passengers from merchant ships. In addition to Muslims, they willingly took Jewish, Greek, and Russian captives.

During the 18th century, both Christian and Muslim piracy fell off partly because navies switched to sail and stopped buying captives. (The French suppressed their Galley Corps in 1748.) Algiers and Malta, the main pirate states, still supported a few oared warships. When Napoleon took Malta in 1798, he released 2,000 Muslim slaves, including the oarsmen for four galleys. The French freed a few hundred Christians at Algiers in 1830.

See also SELECTED BIBLIOGRAPHY: Bamford, *Fighting*; Casson, *Ships*; Guilmartin, *Gunpowder*.)

GALLIVAT, GALLEYWAT (type of ship; Indian Ocean; 18th century)

A 40- to 70-ton vessel, propelled by one or two sails and 20 to 40 oarsmen on each side. The ANGRIAN pirates armed the gallivat with two to eight swivel guns or small cannon.

GAMARRA, ALOISIO (Maltese corsair; Mediterranean; active 1659–1661)

A native Maltese, Gamarra rose through the ranks, serving on merchantmen, as pilot on warships, and as lieutenant and pilot on a corsair vessel. During the summer of 1659, he commanded an 11-oar BRIGANTINE that successfully cruised in North African waters. From August 1660, he raided in Barbary and the Near East as captain of a TARTAN. He returned to Malta in the summer of 1661, having taken only a few prizes of small value.

The seven Maltese merchants that had financed Gamarra's cruise sued him before the TRIBUNALE DEGLI ARMAMENTI. Charging him with incompetence, cowardice, and laziness, the merchants demanded that he repay the expedition's entire cost. Gamarra apparently won the case. But another captain received command of the tartan, and no one else ever employed Gamarra as a corsair.

(See also BOOTY; SELECTED BIBLIOGRAPHY: Earle, *Corsairs*.)

GANGA ROSSA REIS (Barbary corsair; Mediterranean; 1536)

Ganga Reis was a Maltese convert to Islam captured and hanged by the KNIGHTS OF MALTA.

GARRETT, JOHN (English pirate; Caribbean; active 1567–1572)

Garrett was a Plymouth mariner and captain of the 300-ton royal warship *Minion* during Sir John HAWKINS' 1567–1568 slaving expedition. Commanding the CASTLE OF COMFORT, Garrett in 1571 visited Morocco and possibly also the Caribbean. It is certain that he raided Central America in 1572. When Sir Francis DRAKE's raiders arrived in July 1572, they found a lead plate that Garrett had nailed to a tree a few days earlier. Garrett's message warned Drake that Spanish officials had discovered his haven.

(See also SIR FRANCIS DRAKE REVIVED.)

GASCON, JUAN (Spanish corsair; Mediterranean; active 1560s)

Captain of a BRIGANTINE, Gascon supplied the Spanish colony of Oran and plundered the BARBARY COAST. In 1567, he sneaked into the harbor at Algiers to burn the corsair fleet, laid up for the winter. More successful than Juan CANETE, he set fire to a few ships but was pursued and captured by DELLI REIS.

GASPARILLA (Spanish pirate; Caribbean, Gulf of Mexico; 1821)

Gasparilla's 14-gun pirate ship captured an American vessel off Cuba's western tip. He sailed, it was said, from the island of Boca Grande, near Fort Myers, Florida.

When Boca Grande became a winter resort in the early 20th century, someone prepared a pamphlet about Gasparilla for distribution to visitors. Gasparilla, the story goes, was a Spanish admiral who stole the crown jewels in 1782 and made for western Florida. He killed thousands and raped hundreds of women, including a Spanish princess. Jean LAFFITE joined him in attacking an American warship in 1822. Gasparilla was killed but left millions in buried treasure.

These incredible stories presumably were intended as a joke. Nevertheless, the city of Tampa holds an annual festival celebrating Gasparilla, and its football team is called the Buccaneers in his honor.

GATTINARO, BROTHER SIGNORINO (1) (Knight of Malta; Mediterranean; active 1543–1545)

As CAPTAIN OF GALLEYS, Gattinaro raided off North Africa in 1544, capturing a rich merchant ship as well as KARA MUFSA REIS. In 1545, his galleys attacked the coast near TRIPOLI (ruled by the knights at this time), taking a rich booty and 425 slaves.

Knights on active duty gave all their booty to the order. In this case, Gattinaro and the other captains turned over only one-third and divided the rest among themselves.

Determined to maintain the existing rule, the grand master removed Gattinaro from office and sentenced the other captains to two months of severe imprisonment.

GATTINARO, BROTHER SIGNORINO (2) (Knight of Malta; Mediterranean; active 1602–1620)

Gattinaro commanded a GALLEY and fought valiantly during a raid on Greece in 1603. Elected CAPTAIN GENERAL OF GALLEYS (1618–20) and ADMIRAL (1618–19). In 1618, his five galleys took two small ships off North Africa and joined a failed attack on Sousse, Tunisia. While raiding Greece in 1620, they captured a large Turkish GALLEON and then sacked the prosperous market city of Gastoúni (facing the island of Zante). The knights took rich booty and captured wealthy merchants who paid a high ransom.

(See also CAMBIANO ASCANIO.)

GEARE, SIR MICHAEL (English pirate; Caribbean; born about 1566, active 1585–1603)

Born poor in Limehouse, London, Geare raided the West

Indies during England's PRIVATEERING war (1585–1603) against Spain. On nearly every voyage, Geare was accused of taking more than his share of prize goods. He retired in about 1603 to an elegant home in the London suburb of Stepney, wealthy and honored by a knighthood.

After serving on two West Indian cruises for Sir George CAREY, Geare sailed annually from 1588 to 1591 for the London promoter John WATTS. During the 1590 voyage, he was sailing master of the *Little John* captained by Christopher NEWPORT. In 1591, Geare took command of the *Little John* in a five-ship fleet under William LANE. Geare was in the fore of most of the fighting. According to Lane, he grabbed a large part of the booty, both by pillaging prizes during capture and by smuggling goods into England.

With his loot, Geare bought a share in the *Little John* (renamed the *Michael and John*) and took her on four successful plunder adventures from 1592 to 1595. In 1595, Geare was bested by a Spanish warship near Havana. At least 50 of his men were lost together with his PINNACE and a Spanish prize. Geare escaped in the *Michael and John,* took another rich prize, and smuggled his booty into England.

In 1596, Geare shared command of the *Neptune* and its pinnace with Christopher Newport and John RILESDEN. In December, Geare made off with the pinnace and 15 men. He took numerous prizes, joined Sir Anthony Sherley at Jamaica, and accompanied Sherley and William PARKER to Honduras. Meanwhile, Newport fruitlessly searched for Geare's pinnace, since he needed a small ship to operate in shallow coastal waters.

Geare commanded the warship *Archangel*, accompanied by David MYDDLETON's pinnace, during a 1601 raid that captured three valuable prizes. He brought two back to England but lost contact with the third, sold in Morocco by its crew. In 1602, Geare's *Archangel* formed part of Christopher Newport's three-ship squadron, which captured two Spanish warships and several other vessels.

GENERAL HISTORY OF THE ROBBERIES AND MURDERS OF THE MOST NOTORIOUS PYRATES *(history/fiction; 1724–1728)*

Written in a compelling, colloquial style, this popular and influential book collected the biographies of contemporary English pirates. The title page names a "Captain Charles Johnson" as author, but many literary critics now credit Daniel DEFOE.

For three centuries, the *General History* has been a main source for both historians and authors of pirate fiction. Together with EXQUEMELIN, Defoe literally invented the conception of piracy found in the English-speaking world. Later authors picked up and elaborated Defoe's pirate myths, both negative and positive.

On the negative side, Defoe created the legend of pirate violence and cruelty. In his pages, Edward LOW, John MARTEL, and Francis SPRIGGS commit bloodcurdling atrocities. This myth reaches its peak with Edward Teach

Daniel Defoe created the fictional Blackbeard in his *General History of the Pyrates.* Illustration from the second edition (1725).

(BLACKBEARD), who is portrayed as an evil fiend, vile beyond belief. Defoe also invented the negative myth of pirates as sexual supermen. Some captains and crewmen are portrayed as insatiable brutes who rape every woman they capture. In addition to Blackbeard, rapist captains include Henry EVERY and Thomas ANSTIS.

In biographies of other captains, Defoe created the positive myth of pirates as virtuous outlaws. Captain MISSON, Samuel BELLAMY, Bartholomew ROBERTS, and others are acclaimed as free men escaping a corrupt and repressive society. Pirate crews from independent communities devise and enforce democratic rules that are superior to those in the world at large.

The *General History* is presented as history. In reality, it is a composite work that weaves factual accounts and fictional stories into one seamless web. When Defoe's facts can be checked, they usually prove to be accurate. But these true statements are mixed with others Defoe concocted. Several pirates in the *General History* never existed at all. Throughout, Defoe gives his captains invented childhoods and records imaginary speeches and conversations. Much information literally is unknowable, such as the final thoughts of dying men.

Defoe does not say which of his episodes are true, which invented. Successful as both a journalist and a novelist, he may have forgotten the difference. "By 1724," James Sutherland suggested, "he had become so accustomed to living in a twilight world between fact and fiction that the two mingle imperceptibly in his mind."

The first volume of the *General History*, published in 1724, discusses 17 captains, most of them active during the previous 10 years. The introduction tells how Woodes ROGERS subdued the NEW PROVIDENCE pirates in 1718. Chapter One describes Henry Every's Red Sea raid in 1693.

Defoe then narrates the lives of New Providence pirates, including Martel, Teach, Stede BONNET, Edward ENGLAND, Charles VANE, and John RACKHAM. He continues with captains who marauded near the African coast, such as Howell DAVIS, Bartholomew ROBERTS, Walter KENNEDY, and Thomas Anstis. The final chapters mainly discuss raiders off North America—Richard WORLEY, George LOWTHER, Edward Low, John EVANS, John PHILLIPS, Francis Spriggs, and John SMITH.

This first volume probably contains more fact than fiction. Every's chapter merely adds lurid fictional details to common gossip, now 25 years old. But other biographies draw on newspaper stories, trial records, and official reports. Defoe probably knew Woodes Rogers, and he used Rogers' official papers. He also consulted the officer who recorded the trial of Bartholomew Roberts' men.

Defoe does insert some fictional stories. The lives of Mary READ and Anne BONNY are entirely invented. All stories contain imaginary dialogue, and Defoe exaggerated pirate violence and cruelty.

The second volume, published in 1728, presents a complicated and dateless reconstruction of English raids in MADAGASCAR and Indian waters. Beginning with Captain Misson and William KIDD, it continues with interlinked accounts of John Bowen, John HALSEY, Thomas WHITE, Thomas HOWARD, Samuel BURGESS, Nathaniel NORTH, and others. Next Defoe recounts the story of a mulatto seaman kept for 16 years at Magadoxa, an African kingdom north of Madagascar. He concludes with four Caribbean captains: Samuel Bellamy, Captain LEWIS, John CORNELIUS, and William FLY.

Invented stories prevail in this second volume. Misson, Lewis, and Cornelius are wholly imaginary, as are the tales about Thomas TEW. The Madagascar episodes are historical but highly embellished. Having little evidence about events 30 years earlier, Defoe made up pirate communities and conversations with fictitious native chiefs. Oddly, Defoe copied the Magadoxa story—often considered fiction—from the captured sailor's own manuscript.

The second volume attacks the hypocrisy, injustice, and cowardice of English society. Captain Bellamy's speeches (invented by Defoe) sound the theme. The motives of pirates are the same as those of businessmen, bureaucrats, and clergymen. All want to get rich; pirates are simply more honest about their aims.

(See also KING OF PIRATES; SELECTED BIBLIOGRAPHY: Sutherland, *Daniel Defoe*.)

GENTHIUS OF ILLYRIA (buccaneer king; Adriatic Sea; reigned about 181–168 B.C.) In 181, Italian coastal cities complained of pirate raids from ISTRIA, across the Adriatic. The Roman governor for southern Italy was ordered to deal with the Istrians and sailed to ILLYRIA. On his return in 180, he brought serious charges against King Genthius. Genthius had organized the marauders. All the raiding parties had embarked from his realm, and he held Roman and Italian prisoners on the island of Corcyra—a reference either to Corfu or to Korcula. No independent sources mention raids by pirates allied with Genthius. But the Roman accusations may be true, since earlier Illyrian rulers—especially TEUTA and DEMETRIUS OF PHAROS—had tolerated and even personally commanded corsair raids.

GENTLEMAN, JAMES (English pirate; Atlantic; 1614) To revenge the islanders' mistreatment of Gentlemen's crew the previous year, Gentleman and William CLARK let their men devastate the Westmann Isles in Iceland for two weeks, pillaging homes and Danish storehouses, desecrating churches, and raping the local women.

GERMAIN, JACQUES (French corsair; Mediterranean; 1606) Germain commanded a BERTONE for the KNIGHTS OF SAINT STEPHEN. After a bitter fight lasting several days, his ship and that of Agostino FAENZO captured two Venetian merchantmen between Greece and Crete.

GHAZI (Turkish corsair; Black Sea; died about 1330) Lord of Sinope on the Black Sea's southern shore. In 1313 and 1314, Ghazi personally led attacks on Genoese ships near Caffa (Fedodosiya) in the Crimea. In 1319, his pirate band landed on the coast near Trebizond and plundered and burned the suburbs of that wealthy Christian port. A superb diver and swimmer, he once sank some Greek ships by piercing their hulls below the water line.

GIAFER (Barbary corsair; Mediterranean; 1536) Giafer raided southern Italy from ALGIERS with KHEIREDDIN BARBAROSSA. After the raid, he purchased a 16-year-old fisherman as a galley slave. His captive converted to Islam as ULUJ ALI and became one of the most famous BARBARY corsairs.

GIANNETTINES, BROTHER ECTOR (Knight of Malta; Mediterranean; active 1650s) Aloisio GAMARRA acted as Giannettines' lieutenant and pilot during successful raids.

GIBBS, CHARLES (American pirate; Caribbean; died 1831) A native of Rhode Island, Gibbs served in the U. S. Navy during the War of 1812. Some years later, he enlisted on a PRIVATEER commissioned by the newly independent government of Argentina.

Following a mutiny, he took command and plundered from Cuban bases.

Gibbs became famous, and newspapers told many tales about his atrocities. It was said he put to death any captive who refused to join his company. He burned at least one vessel with its crew, and he once hacked off a captain's arms and legs. His pirates captured a beautiful young woman, took advantage of her for two months at their Cuban stronghold, and then poisoned her.

The American government sent a squadron to patrol the Caribbean in 1821. In October, the BRIGANTINE *Enterprise* came upon four pirate craft looting American vessels near Cape Antonia, Cuba. After a sharp fight, the Americans captured 40 pirates, but Gibbs and 60 others fled to shore. Some accounts say he took his plundered gold along. He was caught and hanged in New York 10 years later.

(See also SELECTED BIBLIOGRAPHY: Botting, *Pirates;* Bradlee, *Suppression;* Marx, *Pirates.*)

GIBERT, PEDRO   *(South American pirate; Atlantic; died 1835)*   In September 1832, Gibert captured the American brig *Mexican,* sailing toward Argentina with $20,000 in silver. After they stripped the *Mexican* bare, Gibert told his men to kill her crew, remarking that "Dead cats don't mew." The pirates locked the sailors below, slashed the rigging and sails, filled the galley with combustibles, and set the ship afire. The sailors managed to break out and gradually doused the fire, letting enough smoke billow to fool the pirates until they were gone.

Some months later, a British warship captured Gibert as he loaded slaves in West Africa. He was extradited to Boston and hanged with four of his crew.

(See also SELECTED BIBLIOGRAPHY: Bradlee, *Suppression.*)

GILBERT, SIR HUMPHREY   *(English explorer; Atlantic; 1537?–1583)*   Born into a land-owning family in western England. His mother remarried after his father died, and Sir Humphrey thus became Sir Walter RALEIGH's half-brother. Gilbert strongly advocated foreign expansion. He tried to plant an English colony in southwestern Ireland from 1566 to 1572, using brutal genocide to suppress a rebellion in 1569.

After his Irish adventures failed, Gilbert became interested in attacking Spain's American colonies. In November 1577, he presented Queen Elizabeth I with various schemes for large-scale piracy. In one proposal, he offered to lead a fleet that would capture all foreign ships at the Newfoundland banks. Another proposal suggested one expedition to seize Cuba and Hispaniola and a second to waylay Spain's TREASURE FLEETS, using Bermuda as a base.

In the summer of 1578, the queen authorized Gilbert to explore and found colonies in the Americas. He brought together a 10-ship expedition and planned to plunder Spain's Caribbean possessions. Many of those sailing with Gilbert were pirates from England's West Country. Sir Walter Raleigh was captain of the *Falcon,* with Simão FERNANDEZ as his lieutenant. Henry KNOLLYS commanded three ships. John CALLICE was pilot of Knollys' flagship, on which Ferdinando FIELDING also sailed.

Gilbert never made it to the Caribbean. Knollys' three ships turned to piracy while the expedition was assembling. They continued to plunder after leaving for Ireland in November 1578 and never sailed for America. Gilbert's own seven ships tried to sail west but were forced back by bad weather. The government later investigated the expedition's piracies but took no action against either Gilbert or Knollys.

In 1583, Gilbert personally set out for Newfoundland with four ships. In this case, he apparently wanted to found a colony rather than to rob foreigners. However, the expedition returned without planting a settlement, and Gilbert was killed during the return voyage.

The ships on this Newfoundland voyage included the *Swallow,* previously (as the *Golden Chalice*) one of John Callice's prizes. Gilbert had seized the *Swallow* from Callice and kept the ship instead of returning it to its legal owners. He apparently inherited Callice's pirates along with his ship. The *Swallow* turned back before reaching Newfoundland. On their way home, its crew pillaged a fishing bark and tortured the men to make them give up their money.

(See also SELECTED BIBLIOGRAPHY: Andrews, *Trade;* Quinn, *Gilbert.*)

GILLIAM, JAMES (JOHN)   See KELLEY, JAMES.

GIOVANNI, CRISTOFORO DI   *(Maltese corsair; Mediterranean; active 1740–1741)*   Giovanni seized numerous small prizes (Muslim and Greek), cruising in a CONSERVA partnership with Geronimo PREZIOSI. On returning in February 1741, he was convicted of illegally taking a Venetian-owned ship and imprisoned for over a year by the TRIBUNALE DEGLI ARMAMENTI.

GLANVILLE, TOBY   *(Barbary corsair; Mediterranean; active 1606–1613)*   Glanville went to TUNIS with John WARD and served under Ambrose SAYER. He was captured with Sayer at SALÉ in 1613 and committed suicide.

GLAUKETAS   *(corsair chief; Aegean Sea; 300 B.C.)*   According to an ancient inscription, the Athenian navy drove Glauketas from Kithnos Island, capturing him and his pirate ships, "and making the sea safe for those that sailed thereon."

GLENHAM (GLEMHAM), EDWARD   *(English pirate; Atlantic, Mediterranean; active 1590–91)*   A prosperous gentleman from Suffolk, he sold his family home in 1590, outfitted two ships, and tried to conquer Saint George's Island in the Azores. His party of 86 men seized but could not hold the island, and he entered the Mediterranean. In separate engagements, he repulsed attacks both by six Spanish ships and by four French galleys.

After reprovisioning at ALGIERS (where he may have sold English captives into slavery), Glenham captured a large Venetian vessel, carrying sugar and other valuable goods. However, this booty did not repay Glenham's expenses, and he died heavily in debt.

GLOVER, ROBERT   (Irish pirate; Indian Ocean, Red Sea; active 1694–1695)   Glover was John HOAR's brother-in-law. He left New England in 1693 or 1694 and took the *Resolution* to Western Africa and MADAGASCAR. Arriving at the Comoro Islands late in 1695, he picked up Dirk CHIVERS and other crewmen from the shipwrecked *Portsmouth Adventure*.

After a profitless cruise in the Red Sea, the *Resolution* went to India and seized a small, decrepit Arab vessel at Rajapura. Some of the crew mutinied, elected Chivers captain, and changed the ship's name to *Soldado*. Chivers and the mutineers put Glover and 24 others on board the Arab prize. After a harrowing voyage, Glover reached SAINT MARY'S ISLAND in January 1696 and left for home the following June.

(See also SELECTED BIBLIOGRAPHY: Jameson, *Privateering.*)

GOLD   (pirate goal; all eras)   Every pirate craved BOOTY that was intrinsically valuable and easy to carry. Gold was best, since its value was known and relatively stable. Jewels, spices, medicine, and other rare Oriental goods also were desirable.

Mediterranean pirates rarely got a chance at gold, which seldom left government storehouses. From the 16th century, raiders cruised throughout the Atlantic and Caribbean and along South America's Pacific coast— all looking for Portuguese CARRACKS, Spanish TREASURE FLEETS, and MANILA GALLEONS. Hoping for gold, some sailed many thousands of miles in small, undersupplied ships.

John Ayre's 1684 history describes one raid across Panama, down the Pacific coast, and back around Cape Horn. Ayre bragged that "Gold was the bait that tempted a pack of merry boys of us, near three hundred number, being all soldiers of fortune, under command (by our own election) of Captain John COXON. . . ." During the expedition, Coxon and many others became frustrated and returned to the Caribbean. Those that stuck it out under Bartholomew SHARP made it back with perhaps £100, as pay for two years' work.

As the Coxon/Sharp raid shows, few raiders ever got their wish and seized great heaps of treasure. Most pirates had to be content with more mundane booty—agricultural products, fish, cloth, and ordinary manufactured goods. Still, if they stuck to their trade, they undoubtedly did better than seamen on merchant or naval vessels.

(See also MAPS; TREASURE, BURIED.)

"GOLD BUG, THE"   (short story, published in 1843)   Edgar Allan Poe (1809–1849) used legends about CAPTAIN KIDD while creating one of the first fictional detectives. Poe borrowed the main characters from Washington Irving's "WOLFERT WEBBER." Stevenson's TREASURE ISLAND copied Poe's device of a skeleton pointing to buried treasure.

"The Gold Bug" is set on Sullivan's Island, off South Carolina. BLACKBEARD would have been a more logical visitor than Kidd, who was never very near. Poe merely used Kidd as a generic pirate name and went on with his own story. The island is home to William Legrand and Jupiter, his old black servant. Legrand picks up a gold-colored beetle (which has nothing to do with the treasure). He also finds an old parchment, bearing a message in cipher written in invisible ink. Through various mental gymnastics, he solves the puzzle.

Legrand, Jupiter, and the story's unnamed narrator locate an old tree. Jupiter climbs the tree, finds a skeleton nailed to a branch, and lets the beetle drop through the skeleton's vacant eye socket. The three men dig and find nothing.

Legrand realizes that Jupiter has mistaken the skeleton's left and right eyes. Jupiter tries again and drops the beetle through the correct eye. The men dig up two more skeletons and a chest with more than $1.5 million in gold and jewels. Legrand explains that the treasure is Kidd's. The ruse of dropping an object through a dead man's eye was suggested by the skeleton on the pirate flag, the JOLLY ROGER.

GOLDEN HAWK, THE (1)   (novel; 1948)   The only pirate fiction among the 30-plus "costume novels" by Frank Yerby (1915–1991), a best-selling African-American author. *The Golden Hawk* was among Yerby's most popular works, with total sales of almost 3 million. Cristóbal "Kit" Gerardo has fled from Cadiz to the West Indies following the murder of his French mother. The bastard son of a Spanish nobleman, Kit is extraordinarily beautiful. His eyes are "as blue as a Norwegian fjord," his long blond hair "like Iberian sunlight, heavy with gold."

Kit learns the BUCCANEER's trade from an English captain deformed by leprosy. Taking command in 1692, he sails from French TORTUGA and PETIT GOÂVE, preying on Spanish and British shipping during the Nine Years' War. A skilled and lucky pirate, Kit takes seven Spanish prizes in only four months.

Kit's life (and the plot) are complicated by Kit's emotions. Kit intensely hates Don Luis de Toro, the governor of CARTAGENA and, it turns out, Kit's own father. He passionately loves two women, both unobtainable. Lady Jane Golphin, called Rouge for her bright red hair, thinks "all men are beasts." Resisting her love for Kit, she twice tries to kill him and ends up commanding her own pirate ship. Bianca, Don Luis' wife, loves Kit but refuses to break her marriage vows.

While raiding Jamaica in 1694, Kit is captured but breaks out of jail. He sneaks into Cartagena to kidnap Bianca and again is captured. After suffering fiendish tortures, he escapes and helps the French sack Cartagena in 1697. Bianca enters a convent, and Rouge accepts her love for Kit.

The Golden Hawk is characterized by fervent prose, fast-paced action, and graphic scenes of death and torture. Although Yerby does not describe sexual encounters in detail, the book is saturated with eroticism, both heterosexual and homosexual. Given all this, Yerby is remarkably accurate in describing the historical setting. He errs only in exaggerating Spanish power. By the 1690s, Spain's Caribbean colonies were poor and decayed. TREASURE FLEETS were rare, and they usually sailed in convoys and not singly.

(See also CARTAGENA, SACK OF.)

GOLDEN HAWK, THE (2) *(motion picture; color; 1952)*

Playing down the affair between Kit Gerardo (Sterling Hayden) and Bianca del Toro (Helena Carter), this adaptation of Frank Yerby's novel emphasizes Kit's love for "Rouge" Golphin (Rhonda Fleming). Kit rescues Rouge from archenemy Luis del Toro (John Sutton), whom Kit blames for his mother's death. Following several sea battles, Kit learns that del Toro is his own father. Rouge really is a noblewoman turned pirate to recover a stolen fortune. Sidney Salkow's directing is slow and stilted, but the battle scenes are spirited. (They were reused in PIRATES OF TRIPOLI.)

GOLDEN HIND *(English pirate ship; Atlantic; Pacific; 1577–1580)*

The ship, originally the *Pelican*, in which Sir Francis Drake circumnavigated the globe. As he entered the Strait of Magellan in August 1578, Drake changed the ship's name to honor Sir Christopher Hatton, whose family crest pictured a gold-colored hind (young female deer). Hatton was a sponsor of the expedition, and the new name also tied him to Drake's piracies. Moreover, Drake recently had beheaded Thomas Doughty, Hatton's secretary, after an unjust mock trial. By renaming his flagship, Drake pledged continuing loyalty to Sir Christopher, despite the execution.

The *Golden Hind* was about 70 feet long and 18 to 24 feet wide. Although not a large vessel for the time, the *Hind* was exceptionally well equipped and armed. Of the five original vessels, only the *Hind* completed the voyage and returned to Plymouth in September 1580. After her immensely rich cargo was landed, the *Hind* was taken to Deptford, where Drake was knighted on board in April 1581. Treasured as a symbol of England's maritime greatness, the *Hind* was laid up on land in a specially built shed, opened to the public for a small fee. The timbers eventually rotted away and were broken up in the 1660s.

(See also SELECTED BIBLIOGRAPHY: Andrews, *Drake's Voyages*; Sugden, *Drake*.)

GOPSON, RICHARD *(English buccaneer; Pacific; active 1680s)*

Among the seamen that crossed the Isthmus of Panama and invaded the Pacific with Bartholomew SHARP and John COXON in April 1680. A year later, he was with a group that deserted Sharp's

company and returned to the Caribbean. Exhausted by the journey, he dropped out and spent four months with Lionel WAFER as a guest of the Cuna Indians. He made it back to the Caribbean coast but died three days later of fatigue and a near-drowning.

Wafer, in his *New Voyage*, wrote that Gopson had studied pharmacy. "He was an ingenious Man, and a good Scholar; and had with him a *Greek* Testament which he frequently read, and would translate *extempore* into English to such of the Company as were dispos'd to hear him." His Christian beliefs apparently did not stop Gopson from murdering and stealing with the other buccaneers.

GOW, JOHN   See SMITH, JOHN.

GRAB *(pirate ship; Indian ocean; 18th century)*

This name (from Arabic *ghorab*, a raven) originally referred to a galley, rowed with oars. Under the ANGRIA pirate kings, a grab was a 150- to 300-ton ship with two masts and a shallow draft. The main deck was continued into a long overhanging prow. Two or three grabs would run along their victim at the same time, allowing the pirates to board along the prow.

GRAFF, LAURENS DE *(Dutch buccaneer; Caribbean; active 1682–1695)*

According to an unlikely legend, Graff was a renegade Spanish mulatto, originally named Lorenzo Jácome and nicknamed Lorencillo. Writing 50 years later, the French author CHARLEVOIX reports another version of his history. Graff had served the Spanish navy as a gunner and was advanced to captain. He was sent to America, captured by buccaneers, and joined their ranks. Charlevoix also says that Graff became engaged to his second wife in an unusual way. Enraged because she believed Graff had insulted her, the lady searched for and threatened to shoot him. Graff decided she was the perfect wife for a pirate.

Late in 1682, Graff captured a Spanish ship bound for Santo Domingo with about 120,000 pesos. The pirates took their prize to PETIT GOÂVE and bribed the French governor with part of their booty.

In 1683, Graff, Michel de GRAMMONT, Nicholas van HORN, and five other captains assaulted Veracruz, Mexico. Crowding most of the men into two vessels, they sneaked in before dawn on May 18. Veracruz and the fortress at SAN JUAN DE ULÚA were taken by surprise. About 150 of the leading citizens were held for ransom. The other townspeople were herded into the parish church while the pirates looted the town. The captives remained without food or water for almost four days, jammed together so tightly they could not sleep, wallowing in their own excrement. Some 300 died. At one point, Graff placed a barrel of powder in the church, threatening to blow up all the captives, unless they delivered their hidden valuables.

While the town was plundered, a TREASURE FLEET arrived from Cádiz, but the Spaniards did not dare to land or to attack the empty buccaneer vessels. On the fourth day, the pirates sailed across the path of the Spanish ships to a deserted cay. The booty was divided into a thousand or more shares of 800 pesos each.

These atrocities took place in peacetime, and the French government gave orders to suppress the Petit Goâve buccaneers. However, Jean de Cussy, governor from April 1684, instead treated Graff as a military hero and enrolled him in the colonial militia. (He received the title of major in 1685.)

Although de Cussy tried to persuade them not to sail, Graff and de Grammont again joined forces for a raid on Campeche, Mexico. In July 1684, they overran the town with 750 pirates, while another 550 stood by on 23 ships. Angered that the inhabitants had carried their treasures inland, the raiders vented their wrath in a 57-day orgy. They blew up the fort, burned the town, and took 200 prisoners, nine of whom they hanged.

A Spanish squadron caught the raiders as they were leaving on September 3. Two pirate vessels were captured or burned, but Graff was saved, when a Spanish cannon exploded. In the confusion, Graff escaped.

Graff sailed from Petit Goâve in November and took a Flemish (Belgian) vessel near Curaçao. Raveneau de LUSSAN, who was among the crew, states that Graff and de Grammont previously had captured off Havana two Dutch vessels taking 200,000 pesos to Spain. (De Lussan left Graff's ship in 1685 and invaded Panama with François GROGNIET.)

From May 1689, the Caribbean colonies were engulfed by a war between England and France. Sailing with a formal commission late in 1689, Graff raided Jamaica, seized eight or 10 English trading sloops, and plundered a plantation on the north shore. As the war progressed, Graff received command of the French forces at Cap Français (Cap-Haïtien). He was in charge when a joint English-Spanish fleet sacked Cap Français and Port-de-Paix in July 1695. In 1699, he piloted an expedition by Pierre d'Iberville, who founded New Orleans, Louisiana.

(See also SELECTED BIBLIOGRAPHY: Haring, *Buccaneers*; Rogoziński, *Caribbean*; Weddle, *Spanish Sea*.)

GRAMMONT, MICHEL DE (French buccaneer; Caribbean; active 1678–1686)

Fifty years after Grammont's death, CHARLEVOIX wrote that he was a Parisian who joined the French navy and excelled in several battles. He appeared in the Caribbean commanding a privateer, captured a Dutch vessel, but spent the entire value of his prize on gambling and debauchery. Not daring to return to France, he joined the BUCCANEERS and became one of their chiefs.

During a war with the Netherlands in May 1678, 1,200 buccaneers from Saint Domingue (present-day Haiti) joined a naval attack on Curaçao. The fleet was wrecked on a reef near the Aves Islands. Seven warships, several pirate vessels, and many lives were lost. The

French admiral left Grammont to recover what he could from the wrecks. The pirates later told William DAMPIER that "if they had gone to Jamaica with £30 in their Pockets, they could not have enjoyed themselves more." As the ships broke up, "they were never without two or three Hogsheads of Wine and Brandy in their tents, and Barrels of Beef and Pork."

After thoroughly plundering the wrecks, Grammont invaded Lake Maracaibo in Venezuela with about 700 men. They seized ships and sacked many towns but they took little booty from a region that François L'OLONNAIS and Sir Henry MORGAN already had plundered.

During a brilliant night assault in May or June 1680, Grammont occupied La Guayra, the seaport of Caracas, Venezuela. Only 47 men seized the town, despite its strong walls and two forts. The next day, the Spanish troops rallied, and the pirates learned that 2,000 reinforcements were approaching. Grammont was seriously wounded in the throat while he and a few friends covered the withdrawal under continuing Spanish assaults. Although the raiders kidnapped La Guayra's governor and many others, the prisoners paid only small ransoms.

De Grammont was among eight captains combining in Laurens de GRAFF's highly profitable raid on Veracruz, Mexico, in May 1683. Although this assault took part in peacetime, the governor of Saint Domingue ignored orders to suppress the pirates and gave Grammont a commission against Spanish shipping. During the summer of 1685, Grammont and de Graff again joined forces in a relatively profitless raid on Campeche, Mexico.

To retaliate for these pirate assaults, Spanish colonists raided their French neighbors from Santo Domingo (now the Dominican Republic). Needing Grammont's daring leadership, the French governor appointed him "royal lieutenant" for the coast of Saint Domingue in September 1686. Grammont planned one last pirate raid before becoming respectable. He armed a ship, sailed away with 180 men, and was never heard of again.

GRASSO, GUGLIELMO (Italian corsair and count of Malta; Mediterranean; active 1192–1201)

From Genoa, Grasso invaded the southern Aegean in 1192, with a squadron that included Pisan ships. Disguised as honest traders, the marauders sacked the town of Rhodes and then pillaged shipping in nearby waters.

Their prizes included a Venetian ship, carrying the BYZANTINE and Egyptian ambassadors and rich presents (including rare animals) being sent by the sultan to Constantinople. Pretending to need food, the corsairs suddenly attacked and killed everyone on board, sparing only a few Genoese and Pisans. Grasso's corsairs also captured an Italian ship carrying Byzantine ambassadors to Cyprus. They again massacred the crew and held a Greek bishop for ransom.

The Egyptian sultan's gifts contained a fragment of the True Cross, on which Jesus was crucified. One of the

Pisans fled with it to Bonifacio in Corsica. In 1195, a Genoese force captured Bonifacio and regained the relic, henceforth one of Genoa's most prized treasures.

Enraged by Grasso's crimes, a mob rioted in Constantinople, and the emperor seized Genoese and Pisan property until he was compensated. The Genoese government pretended that it had revoked Grasso's citizenship and was trying to arrest him. In fact, although the king of Sicily made Grasso his ADMIRAL and count of Malta in 1294, he was still living in Genoa in 1201. His daughter married Enrico PESCATORE, also count of Malta.

GRAVES, WILLIAM (Barbary corsair; Mediterranean; 1609) Joint master of a warship from TUNIS captured by a French squadron, Graves was executed at Marseilles.

GRAVIÉ, BROTHER (Knight of Malta; Mediterranean; 1660) Gravié was a sergeant-at-arms (nonnoble member) who captured a ship owned by the pasha of TRIPOLI.

GREAT MOOR, THE (Barbary corsair; Mediterranean; 1635) The nickname ("Il Grande Moro") for an Algerian pirate who captured a Neapolitan galley carrying silk, gold, and cannon.

GRECH, GIACINTO (Maltese corsair; Mediterranean; 1704) Grech applied for a corsair's license after serving for several years as a gunner for the KNIGHTS OF MALTA.

(See also TRIBUNALE DEGLI ARMAMENTI.)

GRENADES (pirate weapons; 16th through 19th century) Daniel DEFOE credits BLACKBEARD with inventing a "new fashion'd Sort of Grenadoes, viz. Case bottles fill'd with Power, and small Shot, Slugs, and Pieces of Lead or Iron, with a quick Match in the Mouth of it." However, hand grenades were used long before the 1720s.

Sixteenth-century sailing ships tossed grenades into the lower-lying galleys and GALIOTS of the BARBARY corsairs. EXQUEMELIN says Joseph BRADLEY's men threw grenades at the Chagres fortresses in 1671. The defenders of the MANILA GALLEON Disengaño dropped a "fireball" onto the deck of Woodes ROGERS' smaller vessel in 1710.

GRENVILLE, SIR RICHARD (English naval commander; 1541–1591) Born into the landed gentry, Grenville was sheriff of Cornwall and represented it in Parliament. Like several other Cornish landowners (Such as the KILLIGREWS), the Grenvilles financed local pirates and fenced their booty.

From the earlier 1570s, Sir Richard was an important member of the faction—mainly from the southwest—seeking to extend their piracies to the Americas. A partner of William HAWKINS and a close friend and kinsman of Sir Walter RALEIGH, Grenville also had ties

to Sir Francis DRAKE, Sir Humphrey GILBERT, and Sir Martin FROBISHER. He promoted and took part in ambitious adventures, although he was not himself a seaman, as his disastrous defeat in 1591 proves.

In 1574, Grenville and William Hawkins formed a syndicate with other West Country gentlemen and London merchants. They purchased the CASTLE OF COMFORT and other warships and recruited John OXENHAM, just back from raiding Panama with Drake. The adventurers planned to explore the Argentinean coast and then pass through the Strait of Magellan to the Pacific. Grenville hoped to capture Spanish treasure ships, and he may also have intended to set up bases for future raids. Queen Elizabeth ultimately stopped the expedition. But Grenville discussed his plans with Sir Francis Drake, who modeled his voyage around the world (1577–1580) on Grenville's 1574 scheme.

During the remainder of the 1570s, Grenville and Hawkins used the Castle of Comfort for piracy in European waters. He apparently was not involved in Sir Humphrey Gilbert's American adventures (1582–1583).

In 1585 and 1586, Grenville invested in and led expeditions to Raleigh's colony in ROANOKE, Virginia, planned as a HAVEN for raids on the Spanish West Indies. The Roanoke settlement failed and vanished. But Grenville made money by plundering any merchant ships that fell in his way during the voyages.

During the 1585 expedition, Grenville commanded seven vessels carrying some 600 men. Simâo FERNANDES was master of Grenville's flagship, and his captains included Thomas CAVENDISH and George RAYMOND. Bernard DRAKE and Sir Amyas PRESTON were expected to follow with reinforcements. Even though Spain and England were at peace, Grenville raided Spanish shipping on the way to Virginia, and he caught a straggler from the annual TREASURE FLEET on the way back. Though he told his partners that they were worth much less, Grenville's prizes brought in some £50,000—several times the expedition's cost.

Grenville returned to Virginia in 1586, but the disgruntled settlers already had left. (Drake had picked them up after his 1585 West Indies raid.) He diligently looked for but failed to find any treasure ships on this voyage. However, his squadron captured Spanish, French, and Dutch prizes and also pillaged an English merchantman. Although the ADMIRALTY COURT made him give back part of his loot, these prizes brought in large sums. Grenville enslaved many Spanish captives and forced them to rebuild his manor house at Stowe.

Grenville possibly sent ships to raid the Caribbean in 1587, but he never returned in person. He was fully occupied with military duties in southwestern England and with an English colony he had founded in Munster, Ireland.

In April 1591, Lord Thomas Howard took six of the queen's best fighting ships to the Azores. Grenville, as vice-admiral (second-in-command), commanded the 500-ton *Revenge*, Drake's flagship against the Armada in 1588. Perhaps half-a-dozen private warships trailed the squadron, hoping to share in the booty.

Howard's target was the annual West Indian treasure fleet. Phillip II of Spain had kept his ships in the Americas in 1590, and he desperately needed their golden cargoes. In August, King Phillip sent out a strong fleet—including more than 20 warships—to guard the returning treasure ships. The earl of CUMBERLAND, who also was hunting in the Azores, desperately tried to warn Howard that the Spanish warships were coming.

Trapped between the islands of Flores and Corvo, Howard just managed to escape with his five warships. As vice-admiral, Grenville left last and was caught by the enemy. Refusing to admit defeat, he was trapped trying to sail through the entire Spanish fleet. The *Revenge* surrendered only after a desperate 12-hour battle killed most of her crew. Grenville died of his wounds a few days later.

Sir Walter Raleigh's REPORT OF THE TRUTH enshrined Grenville as a national hero, and he was subsequently eulogized by the poet Alfred, Lord Tennyson. However, his entire career was marked by a stubborn impulsiveness. In 1585, he needed a small boat to board and capture a Spanish treasure ship. A raft was created out of the ship's chests. The substitute was so frail that it fell to pieces when Grenville and his men jumped to the Spanish vessel.

Because of his fierce temper, Grenville often was heartily hated by the gentleman serving him as well as by his crews. Like some later pirates, he apparently took pride in—and even helped to create—the legends about his savage rages. In one case, to terrify Spanish captives dining at his table, he chewed and swallowed glass as blood ran from his mouth.

(See also SELECTED BIBLIOGRAPHY: Quinn, *Set Fair*; Rowse, *Grenville*.)

GRILLO ("EL MULATO"), DIEGO *(African-Spanish buccaneer; Caribbean; active 1671–1673)*
Of mixed African-Spanish ancestry, Grillo escaped from Havana, Cuba. He commanded a small 10-gun ship in January 1671, when Sir Henry MORGAN sacked Panama. In August, Jamaica's new governor offered a pardon to all pirates abandoning their crimes. Diego refused the pardon, continued to prey on Spanish shipping, and sold his booty at the French colony of TORTUGA. After defeating three ships sent to capture him and massacring everyone of European ancestry, he was captured and hanged in 1673.

GRIMALDI, FRANCESCHINO *(Italian pirate; Mediterranean; active 1298–1302)* A native of Genoa, Grimaldi sailed from Cyprus and plundered ships from many countries. In 1298, he looted a Venetian

ship, which had put into Pistachi to escape him. He was captured, but the ADMIRAL of Cyprus set him free and allowed him to keep his loot.

GROG *(rum and water; 1740 to 1970)* Members of the British navy received a daily liquor ration, with RUM tending to replace beer after Jamaica was conquered in 1655. The 1731 Regulations called for either a gallon of beer, a pint of wine, or a half-pint of rum; a quarter-pint was issued from 1850 to 1970. In 1740, Admiral Edward Vernon ordered the rum diluted with a quart of water. Vernon's nickname was Old Grogram, and the sailors named the watered-down rum "grog" in his honor.

All navies (and merchant ships) gave out liquor, but only the English opted for rum. Dutch sailors received beer until the 18th century. Thereafter, a daily gin ration (about a quarter-pint) was provided until 1905. French sailors still receive wine, a beverage that protects against SCURVY (1).

(See also SELECTED BIBLIOGRAPHY: Pack, *Nelson's Blood*.)

GROGNIET, FRANÇOIS *(French buccaneer; Caribbean, Pacific; died 1687)* The least successful among the many captains invading South America's Pacific coast in the 1680s. His raids were described by Raveneau de LUSSAN, one of his company.

Leading about 280 French and English pirates, Grogniet and a Captain Lescuyer marched across Panama early in 1685. At the Pearl Islands, he joined a larger company under Edward DAVIS, who was expecting Peruvian treasure ships. Grogniet became the third-ranking officer of the combined force and received command of a captured Spanish vessel.

On June 8, the buccaneers were routed, while Grogniet's ship hung back from the battle. The pirates regrouped at deserted Coiba Island, in western Panama, where the French and English parties split up. William DAMPIER accused Grogniet of cowardice. For de Lussan, the quarrel was due to English arrogance and their sacrilegious pillaging of churches, which supposedly shocked the French pirates.

Davis and most of the English sailed off in July, leaving Grogniet and about 340 men at Coiba Island with three small ships. For the next 18 months, Grogniet's company pillaged ranches and small towns in western Panama, Costa Rica, and Nicaragua. They took no booty and hardly any food. Whenever they sighted the pirates, the Spanish colonists fled inland, carrying their valuables with them and destroying what was left behind.

The raiders attacked Realejo, Nicaragua, in November 1685 but found it deserted after a recent raid by Davis' band. On November 24, Spanish officials told them that a brief war had ended and suggested that they return to the Caribbean under a safe conduct. The pirates—who had never heard of the war—feared a trap and turned down the offer. In January 1686, in one of his few successful raids, Grogniet sacked Chiriquita (Alanje) in Panama. After several inhabitants were killed, the rest provided a ransom of food supplies. In retaliation, the Panamanians attacked Grogniet's camp and burned the pirates' only large ship while they hid nearby.

In March 1686, Grogniet's men paddled north in various small craft and met Captain TOWNLEY, returning from raiding Mexico with Charles SWAN. The two groups combined, marched inland, and occupied Granada, Nicaragua—previously plundered by John MORRIS (1665) and Lawrence PRINCE (1670). The Frenchmen chanted a hymn of victory in the cathedral. But the townsmen had taken their treasures to an island in Lake Nicaragua. They refused to pay ransom, and Granada was burned.

Back on their ships at Realejo's harbor, the buccaneers distributed 7,600 pesos to 10 crippled comrades—almost all they had after more than a year's buccaneering. The two parties again split up in May 1686. Half the Frenchmen (including Raveneau de Lussan) elected to go on to Panama with Townley's ship. About 145 pirates stayed with Grogniet, who camped on an island in the Gulf of Fonseca, Guatemala.

Grogniet's group carried out minor raids and made one big haul—450 pounds of gold captured at a mining camp halfway to Tegucigalpa. Soon after (possibly in July) more than half of Grogniet's men deserted and sailed north to Mexico, where they remained until 1690.

In January 1687, Grogniet's group—about 50 men in three canoes—met a party under Captain LE PICARD and George HOUT. About 90 of Le Picard's men chose Grogniet as captain, and he took command of one of the ships. Since no more loot and little food were available in Central America, the pirates went south to Guayaquil, Ecuador. More booty than usual was taken, but Grogniet died of wounds received during the assault.

GROMMET *(buccaneer slang; 16th and 17th centuries)* Name given by British seamen to an apprentice sailor or ship's boy. It is derived from the Spanish word *grumete*, which has the same meaning.

GUADAGNI DI BEAUREGUARD, GUGLIELMO *(Knight of Saint Stephen; Mediterranean; active 1608–1610)* His prizes were among the richest taken by any pirate. In 1608, his squadron—three galleys and five sailing ships—overcame a 42-ship OTTOMAN caravan carrying pilgrims to Mecca. Altogether, the corsairs captured 16 vessels, more than 600 prisoners, and 1 million ducats in merchandise.

Two years later, his three galleys followed the fleet carrying tax revenues from Egypt to Constantinople. They cut off stragglers and returned with an even richer haul—two GALLEONS, seven galleys, 2 million ducats in cash and goods, and 700 prisoners, many of whom fetched rich ransoms.

GUARCO, ANTONIO DI *(Genoese pirate; Mediterranean; 1401)* After Guarco seized a Muslim ship, the sultan of Egypt arrested all Christian merchants at Alexandria and Cairo and confiscated their goods.

"GUESTS FROM GIBBET ISLAND" *(short story; 1855)* Appearing in Washington IRVING'S *Wolfert's Roost*, this tale adds a ghost story to the legends about CAPTAIN KIDD. Yan Yost Vanderscamp is the SCALAWAG nephew of a Dutch tavernkeeper on the New Jersey shore. Accompanied by an aged black man named Pluto, Vanderscamp disappears and returns years later with great wealth. He and Pluto rebuild the inn and indulge in shocking festivities with their rough seafaring friends. Several of the wicked crew are arrested and hanged in plain sight on Gibbet Island.

Vanderscamp and Pluto vanish for several years, return for a second time, and take up smuggling. One night, as they return from visiting a ship, Pluto rows the former pirate close to the swinging skeletons of his companions. Making a drunken joke, Vanderscamp toasts the bodies and invites them to his inn. Finding them there when he arrives, he falls backward down the stairs and breaks his neck.

GUNS/GUNPOWDER See ARQUEBUS; BLUNDERBUSS; CANNON; MUSKET; PISTOL; WEAPONS.

HADJ AMIN REIS *(Barbary corsair; Mediterranean; 1664)* Hadj Amin Reis was nicknamed "Bruciacristiani" ("Roaster of Christians"). The KNIGHTS OF SAINT STEPHEN captured his large galley off northern Italy.

HADJ HUSSEIN REIS (MEZZOMORTO) *(Barbary corsair and ruler; Mediterranean; active 1670 to 1695)* Hadj Hussein Reis, a Turk, was nicknamed Mezzomorto ("in the middle of the dead") because he miraculously survived an explosion that killed many others. He was CAPTAIN OF THE SEA of the corsairs' guild (TAIFE REISI) in 1681, when France provoked ALGIERS into war. French warships under Admiral Abraham Duquesne bombarded Algiers in July 1682 and June 1683. Armed with a new and powerful mortar, they had orders to destroy the city.

Baba Hasan ruled Algiers for his aged father-in-law, the DEY Hadj Mohammed. Defenseless before the second bombardment, Baba Hasan offered to capitulate on French terms and surrendered Mezzomorto and other officials as hostages. Abject defeat was avoided when Duquesne demanded more money than the Algerians could pay. Mezzomorto promised that he would "settle everything" if allowed to return ashore.

Mezzomorto kept his duplicitous promise. He rallied the corsairs and part of the JANISSARY militia, murdered Baba Hasan, and had himself elected dey. (Hadj Mohammed escaped to TUNIS.) He then announced that he

would blow up every Frenchman in Algiers if Duquesne continued the shelling. For the next two months, the energetic admiral rallied the city as French bombs destroyed over 500 homes, several mosques, and a bathhouse. Twenty-one Frenchmen were tied to the mouth of a great cannon and blown apart.

Despite a new treaty in 1684, the French still refused to return Algerian galley slaves and even seized the crews from three more ships. Algiers declared war in August 1687, and a large French fleet attacked the city the following June. When Mezzomorto again blew up 10 French officials, Admiral Jean d'Estrées executed several Algerians and floated their bodies ashore on rafts.

Although shells destroyed more than 90 percent of the city, the Algerians would not surrender, and the French fleet left to fight a war in Europe. Since Mezzomorto faced a hostile alliance between Tunis and MOROCCO, he agreed to peace with France in September 1689. This treaty, which favored Algiers, remained in effect until 1830.

As soon as the treaty was signed, Mezzomorto led his soldiers to a disastrous defeat in Tunisia. When the Janissaries demanded his head, Mezzomorto fled to Istanbul and joined the OTTOMAN navy in its long war (1684–1699) with Venice. By 1695, he was admiral-in-chief (Kapudan-Pasha)—the office previously held by KHEIREDDIN, TURGUT, and ULUJ ALI. Under his command, the Ottoman fleet—including substantial Algerian contingents—defeated or stalemated the Venetians in several battles.

(See also ALGIERS; SELECTED BIBLIOGRAPHY: Anderson, *Naval*; Wolf, *Barbary*.)

HAËDO, DIEGO (*Spanish slave in Algiers; 1570s*)
A Benedictine monk, Haëdo described Algerian politics and society in a monumental work published in 1612. It begins with the *Topographia* (general description) and the *Epitome de los Reyes de Argel* (*History of the Kings of Algiers*). These are followed by several sections of religious propaganda, including the *Diálogo de la Captividad* (*Dialogue of Captivity*) and the *Diálogo de los Mártires* (*Dialogue of the Martyrs*).

Since Father Haëdo was an inquisitive and accurate observer, it is unfortunate that his works have not been translated into English. Containing a wealth of detailed information about the Algerian corsairs, they have been a major source for later historians. There are modern Spanish versions of the entire work (three volumes, Madrid, 1927–29) and the *Diálogo de los Mártires* (Madrid, 1990). Several parts have been translated into French, including the *Topographia* (*Revue Africaine*, 1860–1870), *Los Reyes de Argel* (Algiers, 1881), and *Diálogos de la Captividad* (Algiers, 1897).

HALSEY, JOHN (*British pirate; Red Sea, Indian Ocean; 1662?–1708*)
A Boston man, Halsey raided French and Spanish shipping as a PRIVATEER in 1704. Receiving a new commission in 1705, he turned pirate and went to MADAGASCAR with the 10-gun *Charles*. Late in 1706, Halsey trailed but refused to attack a larger Dutch ship in the Indian Ocean. Convinced that she was a harmless merchantman, the crew deposed Halsey for cowardice. They reinstated him when the Dutch vessel suddenly turned and fired.

Halsey seized two coastal traders at the Nicobar Islands in February 1707. Some crewmen left for Madagascar, while Halsey went on to the Straits of Malacca with little success. Because of their earlier encounter with the Dutch vessel, the pirates were afraid to assault any ship larger than their own *Charles*.

Halsey picked up reinforcements at Madagascar, and Nathaniel NORTH became QUARTERMASTER. Visiting Mocha (in the Red Sea) in August 1707, the pirates ran into five British ships with a total of 62 guns. Halsey showed greater daring this time and attacked the entire squadron. The largest British ship ran away, and the others scattered in all directions. Halsey captured two of his prey, taking £50,000 in cash and cargo.

In January 1708, the *Greyhound* came from India to Madagascar to barter liquor and other supplies for the goods captured at Mocha. While the British merchants were trading with the pirates, the *Neptune* arrived in port with Samuel BURGESS as first mate. Without warning, a hurricane destroyed the pirates' ships. With Burgess' help, the pirates took over the *Neptune* and plundered the *Greyhound*.

Halsey died of a fever soon after and was buried with great ceremony. "He was," Daniel DEFOE reports, "brave in his Person, courteous to all his Prisoners, lived beloved, and died regretted by his own People. His Grave was made in a Garden of Water Melons, and fenced in with Pallisades to prevent his being rooted up by wild Hogs."

(See also SELECTED BIBLIOGRAPHY: Grey, *Pirates*.)

HAMIDA BEN NEGRO (*Barbary corsair; Mediterranean; 1656*)
Sailing from ALGIERS, Hamida Ben Negro captured a Spanish galley carrying 800,000 *reales* in cash, valuable cargo, and many noblemen who paid heavy ransoms.

HAMIDAN REIS (*Barbary corsair; Mediterranean; active 1802–1808*)
Commanding a SHEBEC, Hamidan Reis often raided from ALGIERS with his brother HAMIDOU REIS.

HAMIDOU REIS (*Barbary corsair; Mediterranean; active 1790–1815*)
Of medium build and fair complexion with an enormous mustache, Hamidou was the last great BARBARY captain and commanded the ALGIERS fleet during the Napoleonic wars. Most corsairs came from the Near East or were Christian RENEGADES. However, Hamidou was a native Algerian, a tailor's son who amassed immense wealth through his piratical skills. The Europeans he met (including several captives) described him as highly civilized, with a commanding and even arrogant personality.

Hamidou shipped as cabin boy and rapidly rose to sailor, mate, and officer. Beginning in 1790, the BEY of Oran entrusted him with a SHEBEC, then with his entire fleet of small ships. Although he never learned to read, Hamidou was a natural navigator of great audacity. On one occasion, his little squadron literally sailed circles around two larger Genoese warships.

Hearing of Hamidou's exploits, HASAN DEY called him to Algiers and, in 1797, entrusted him with Algiers' largest ship, a 36-gun corvette. Sailing during all seasons and usually on his own, Hamidou reaped a rich harvest. Official Algerian records—which probably understate his booty—credit him with 19 prizes (18 Italian) during the next three years. In 1801, he took command of a superb FRIGATE that served as his flagship until his death. Built to his specifications, it was very fast and seaworthy, carrying 44 guns and 400 crew.

In 1802, Hamidou captured a 44-gun Portuguese frigate with almost no casualties. Using a traditional corsair ruse, Hamidou flew the English flag until he could grapple the enemy. His JANISSARY troops poured over the bulwarks, seizing the frigate and enslaving its 282 crewmen. Captured ships (but not their cargo) belonged to the dey. Renamed *El Portekiza* (*The Portuguese*), the frigate served the corsairs until she was destroyed during an 1816 British raid on Algiers.

Often sailing with his brother HAMIDAN, Hamidou took many more prizes from 1802 to 1808. The Algerian corsairs benefited from the anarchy brought by war between Britain and France. As Hamidou remarked, "God save Napoleon! As long as countries have to deal with him, they'll lose and won't dream of bothering us."

Hamidou mainly seized Portuguese and Neapolitan ships and sometimes sailed east to capture his own sultan's Greek subjects. In 1805—apparently unimpressed by U.S. efforts during the First BARBARY WAR—he also grabbed an American SCHOONER carrying beans and 58 men.

After he conquered Italy in 1800 and 1801, Napoleon pressed the Algerian government to stop molesting his new subjects, and he stopped the tribute money previously paid by the Italian states. The unpaid troops rioted, Hasan Dey was assassinated in 1805, and his successor fell in 1808. Hamidou Reis seemed too powerful, and the new dey exiled him to Beirut in 1808. The state treasury suffered without Hamidou's constant prizes. Another rebellion gave power to Hadj Ali, the minister of finances, who recalled Hamidou and named him admiral of Algiers. From then on, he rarely operated on his own but commanded a powerful squadron.

In 1809, Hamidou ventured into the Atlantic with a 20-gun BRIG and three 44-gun frigates. Returning through the Strait of Gibraltar, he found his way blocked by a strong Portuguese squadron. Hamidou ordered his ships to bear straight down on the enemy. Just as he was about to run down their flagship, the Portuguese lost their nerve and moved out of his way.

From 1810 to 1812, Algiers was at war with TUNIS. One of the few naval encounters ended in a bloody six-hour battle between Hamidou's frigate and the Tunisian flagship. Hamidou won and returned to Algiers in triumph, towing the second frigate he had captured in single combat. After the war, Hamidou's squadron continued to scour the seas, bringing in Danish, Swedish, Dutch, Spanish, American, and Greek ships loaded with booty.

In June 1815, the U.S. dispatched a fleet under Stephen Decatur. Near Cape de Gatt in Spain, the American warships ran into Hamidou's frigate, at sea without its normal supporting squadron. The Americans flew the British flag. Falling for the same trick he used against the Portuguese in 1802, Hamidou Reis let them approach and was cut in two by a cannon ball.

(See also SELECTED BIBLIOGRAPHY: Earle, *Corsairs.*)

HAMLIN, JEAN (French pirate; Caribbean; active 1682–1684)

Hamlin may have helped massacre 80 Carib Indians in 1674, including Thomas "Indian" Warner, illegitimate son of Antigua's governor. In the summer of 1682, with a sloop and 120 men, he pursued and captured *La Trompeuse* (*The Deceiver*), a large French merchant ship. He turned the *Trompeuse* into a powerful warship, took perhaps two dozen English vessels, and

cruelly abused their crews. While several ships searched for Hamlin, he escaped to Danish Saint Thomas. There he purchased a warm welcome from Governor Adolph Esmit, a former pirate who had seized power from his brother.

There is some uncertainty about Hamlin's movements in 1683. Hamlin was near Saint Domingue on January 25, and he was anchored at Saint Thomas on August 9. But English captains later testified that the *Trompeuse* was in Africa about mid-May disguised as naval vessel. According to this account, Hamlin cruised along the west coast for several weeks, capturing or destroying 17 English and Dutch ships carrying gold dust and slaves. If this testimony is accurate, then Hamlin made an extraordinarily fast passage returning from Africa. However, the English captains may have confused the *Trompeuse* with another pirate ship bearing the same name.

The English warship *Francis*, under Captain Charles Carlile, found the *Trompeuse* in the harbor at Saint Thomas on July 9. Either the *Trompeuse* or the Danish fort fired at the *Francis*, and Carlile's men burned the *Trompeuse* and another pirate ship. Governor Esmit helped Hamlin and his men escape and later sold them a SLOOP. A new governor arrested Esmit in October 1684, and the Danish government confiscated his property. Hamlin somehow acquired another ship, *La Nouvelle Trompeuse* (*The New Deceiver*), and was based at Île-à-Vache near Saint Domingue in June 1684.

(See also LE PAIN, PIERRE; SELECTED BIBLIOGRAPHY: Haring, *Buccaneers*; Paiewonsky, *Trompeuse.*)

HAMZA REIS (Barbary corsair; Mediterranean; active 1580s)

CAPTAIN OF THE SEA at Bizerte near TUNIS, Hamza Reis was captured off Rome in 1590, imprisoned at Naples, and escaped in 1591.

HANDS, ISRAEL (British pirate; Caribbean, Atlantic; 1718)

Second-in-command under Edward TEACH (BLACKBEARD), who made him captain of the SLOOP *Adventure* in March 1718. Hands settled in North Carolina with Teach after the siege of Charleston. When Teach was killed in December, Hands was away from the ship and was taken to Virginia for trial. He apparently was convicted but pardoned to reward his testimony against corrupt North Carolina officials. Daniel DEFOE wrote that he ended as a beggar in London.

According to another of Defoe's stories, Hands suffered from Teach's cruelty. One night in North Carolina, Teach was drinking in his cabin with Hands and another man. Teach quietly drew out a pair of small pistols, cocked them under the table, and fired. One pistol missed, but Hands was shot through the knee and lamed for life. "Being asked the meaning of this, [Teach] only answered, by damning them, that if he did not now and then kill one of them, they would forget who he was."

(See also SELECTED BIBLIOGRAPHY: Defoe, *General History.*)

HANGING   See PUNISHMENTS FOR PIRACY.

HANKYN, THOMAS   (English pirate; Atlantic; 1580)   Master of the *Prosperity*, a merchantman of Rye or London. Clinton ATKINSON, who served as Hankyn's purser, convinced him to turn pirate, and their ship seized a rich Italian prize.

HARRIS, CHARLES   (British pirate; Atlantic, Caribbean; died 1723)   Harris was second mate of a Boston ship, which George LOWTHER captured in the Bay of Honduras in January 1722. Joining the pirates, Harris received command of a captured SLOOP but lost her in Belize.

Harris went with Edward LOW when he left Lowther in June 1722. With Low, he cruised north to Nova Scotia and then across the Atlantic to the Azores. There Low moved to a larger ship and gave Harris command of an 80-ton SCHOONER. The two cruised in CONSORT for some months until Low's ship was wrecked on the South American coast in about December 1723.

Low gave command of his next prize to Francis SPRIGGS rather than to Harris. Perhaps Harris was wounded or sick. He is not mentioned again until May 1723, when he replaced Spriggs as captain of Low's consort. On June 21, the pirates chased the British warship *Greyhound*, thinking it was a merchantman. When the *Greyhound* turned and attacked, Low deserted under fire and left Harris to his fate. Thirty-seven men were tried at Newport, Rhode Island, where Harris and 26 others were hanged in July.

(See also SELECTED BIBLIOGRAPHY: Dow, *Pirates*.)

HARRIS, JAMES   (English pirate; Atlantic; active 1608–1611)   A ship's master redeemed from slavery in TUNIS by Richard BISHOP, Harris went to Ireland with Bishop in 1608 and commanded a ship marauding as part of his squadron.

HARRIS, PETER (1)   (English buccaneer; Caribbean, Pacific; 1671–1681)   Harris was among the pirate crewmen taking part in Sir Henry MORGAN's 1671 sack of Panama. In 1679, Jamaica's governor sent the FRIGATE *Success* in pursuit, when Harris seized and took for his own a powerful 28-gun Dutch ship. Harris lured the *Success* into the cays south of Cuba, where it was wrecked on a reef.

Cruising off Boca del Toro, Costa Rica, in his Dutch prize, Harris ran across Bartholomew SHARP's company soon after they pillaged PORTOBELO. He and his crew joined in the march across the Isthmus to Santa Maria and Panama City. The brigands reached the coast near Panama on May 3, 1681, and Harris was killed during a savage battle with a Spanish squadron.

HARRIS, PETER (2)   (English buccaneer; Pacific; active 1684–1686)   A nephew of Peter HARRIS (1) who invaded Panama with Bartholomew SHARP in 1681.

Leaving Jamaica in January 1684, Harris and about 100 men copied Sharp's crossing of the Isthmus and raid on SANTA MARIA. The pirates seized 150 pounds of gold dust at Santa Maria and a small BARK carrying an additional £1,000 in gold. They escaped five Spanish vessels sent out to catch them in July and met up with Charles SWAN on August 3.

Harris and Swan sailed south and joined up with Edward DAVIS in October 1684. The three captains returned to Panama to wait for Peruvian treasure ships, and Harris received command of a larger prize. After Spanish warships routed the pirates in June 1685, Harris raided Chilean and Peruvian ports in consort with Davis. Lionel WAFER wrote that Harris separated from Davis about September 1685. However, Richard ARNOLD later testified that Harris and Davis sailed in consort until April or even August 1686. What happened to Harris afterward is not known.

HASAN AGHA   (Barbary corsair; Algiers; active 1588–1624)   In 1588, Hasan commanded seven FUSTES that carried off 150 slaves from Pratica, 19 miles south of Rome. In 1624, his five ships ran into larger galleys from Naples, the papacy, and Florence. Hasan's vessel got away, but the Christians captured the rest of his squadron.

HASAN CALEFAT REIS   (Barbary corsair; Algiers; 1624)   The KNIGHTS OF SAINT STEPHEN captured six ships under Hasan Reis' command during a battle off Sardinia.

HASAN DEY   (Barbary ruler; Mediterranean; ruled 1791–1798)   A Turkish JANISSARY, Hasan Dey sailed on corsair cruises in his youth and was the official in charge of the navy before being elected DEY of ALGIERS. Recognizing the daring and skills of HAMIDOU REIS, Hasan gave him command of an Algerian warship in about 1797.

HASAN IBN RAHMAH   (Arab pirate chief; ruled 1814–1819)   See QAWASIM.

HASANICO REIS   (Barbary corsair; Mediterranean, Atlantic; active 1570s)   Hasanico Reis was a Greek RENEGADE at ALGIERS. Spanish sources accuse him of torturing his Christian slaves, disfiguring many for life. In 1574, he led six GALIOTS to western Spain—probably the first Algerian raid into the Atlantic. Near Cadiz, Hasanico's squadron surprised several hundred Spanish fishermen. When soldiers from Cadiz rode to the rescue, Hasanico discovered that the receding tide had grounded his flagship. He was captured and beheaded at Cadiz—renouncing Islam to avoid being burned alive by the Inquisition.

HASAN "IL MARABUTTO" REIS   (Barbary corsair; Mediterranean; active 1570s)   An Italian RENEGADE sailing from ALGIERS and nicknamed "Il Marabutto" ("The Holy Man"). Diego HAËDO, a Spanish prisoner, told a lurid story about Hasan's cruelty to Christian GALLEY SLAVES. Hasan was furiously driving his rowers to overtake a Sicilian GALLEY, when one of them collapsed from exhaustion. With one blow of his sword, Hasan cut off the man's arm, threatening and beating the other rowers with the bloody piece of flesh. (The KNIGHTS OF MALTA told the same story about the MURAT REIS they captured in 1556.)

HASAN REIS *(Barbary corsair; Mediterranean; 1677)* A Frenchman sailing from TRIPOLI, Hasan Reis commanded the 22-gun *Mary Magdalene*, captured from the Genoese.

HASAN VENEZIANO PASHA *(Barbary viceroy; Mediterranean; active 1565–1589)* Hasan Pasha was captured as a youth by TURGUT REIS (Veneziano means "The Venetian") and later became a follower of ULUJ ALI. CERVANTES was Hasan's slave at ALGIERS and describes him as proud, greedy, and cruel but also energetic and brave.

Hasan took charge of Uluj Ali's treasury, and he commanded a galley during the conquest of TUNIS in 1574. At Uluj Ali's suggestion, the OTTOMAN sultan made him BEYLERBEY of ALGIERS in 1574. He used terror to subdue the corsairs and the Turkish garrison, and he improved the city's fortifications. His attack on Majorca and Ibiza with 26 warships in 1578 was repulsed with little gain. In 1580, the sultan removed Hasan when the native tribes rebelled, embittered by his extortions during a period of famine and plague. However, the sultan spared his life thanks to Turgut Reis' generous bribes.

Turgut again intervened to restore Hasan Veneziano as beylerbey in 1582. His return marks the triumph of the corsair faction in its political struggles with Algiers' JANISSARY garrison. Hasan Pasha strongly encouraged independent expeditions. Soon after his return, he personally commanded a large fleet that took many slaves in Sardinia and Corsica and that also rescued 2,000 Moriscos (Spanish Muslims).

The sultan subsequently made Hasan beylerbey of TRIPOLI (1583–1585) and of Tunis (1585–1587). He became commander of the Ottoman navy after Uluj Ali died in 1587. During the summer of 1589, he returned to Tripoli to suppress a native revolt.

HASKOURI REIS *(Moroccan corsair; Atlantic; 1654)* Haskouri Reis was captain of a sailing ship captured by Dutch vessels attacking SALÉ.

HATLEY, SIMON *(British pirate; Atlantic, Pacific; active 1703–1722)* Hatley invaded South America's Pacific coast in 1708 as third mate of Woodes ROGERS' *Duchess*. In May 1709, while in charge of a tiny ship with nine men, Hatley lost contact with Rogers off the Galapagos Islands. After a harrowing ordeal, the ship reached Ecuador. The survivors were captured by Indians, flogged, and forced to march hundreds of miles to Lima.

They were imprisoned until at least 1711, sharing the dungeon with Captain STRADLING and a dozen others captured in 1704.

Hatley again sailed for the Pacific in April 1719 as second-in-command of George SHELVOCKE's *Spedwel*. Storms and mists plagued the passage around Cape Horn in December, and the *Spedwel* ran out of water. During the crossing, Hatley shot a large black albatross. Shelvocke recorded the incident in his *Voyage Round the World*, thus inspiring Samuel Coleridge's poem "THE RIME OF THE ANCIENT MARINER."

HATSELL, CAPTAIN *(English buccaneer; Caribbean; 1665)* Captain Hatsell commanded the garrison left at PROVIDENCE ISLAND after Edward MANSFIELD's conquest. He was captured when the Spaniards retook the island and presumably died in prison.

HAVENS, PIRATE *(3000 B.C.–A.D. 1850)* Pirates naturally prefer hideouts near major shipping channels, where merchant vessels are frequent. Ports not too far from narrow straits—which funnel ships through a limited channel—always have been pirate favorites. These include CRETE and TORTUGA. Even more than land bandits, sea robbers also seek safety. Their wooden ships needed constant repairs and periodic cleaning. In many regions, no ship can be at sea during long periods, especially when ferocious storms are frequent. Ancient pirates usually did not sail during the winter, and Caribbean BUCCANEERS sought secure ports during the summer hurricane season.

Pirate captains normally can choose from several harbors that are both safe and conveniently located. Political relationships usually decide which of these ports serve as pirate havens at any specific time. No outlaw group can exist unless it enjoys friendly, or at least neutral, contacts with the larger society. Every criminal band needs the help of merchants who fence its loot and provide it with food, weapons, and provisions.

Since pirates must have contacts outside their band, they seek havens where the government is either weak or corrupt. Whenever rulers actively suppress their activities, pirates flee the region. Many find refuge along rocky and barren coastal shores or on isolated islands. Ancient pirates preferred the coasts of CILICIA, LIGURIA, and ILLYRIA, while medieval pirates frequented Wales and the west coast of England. The mountain barriers along these coasts make attack from land difficult. Because they had few products to trade and little to lose when piracy disrupted commerce, the native inhabitants welcomed corsairs to their shores.

During the 16th century, the buccaneers initially assembled on Tortuga Island. Like the desolate coasts chosen by their European predecessors, this mountainous rock is both difficult to attack and near shipping lanes. When the French and British began to police the region, the buccaneers sought new refuges on islands not yet controlled by any government, such as NEW PROVIDENCE ISLAND and MADAGASCAR.

However, pirates operating from these barren coasts and isolated islands face several disadvantages. Only a small number of traders were available to take the pirates' booty back to a major port. Since there was little competition between the merchants fencing pirate loot, they could buy it at very large discounts. Operating out of a remote haven also hinders kidnapping and slave trading. Pirates could not make arrangements to ransom their captives, and slaves died off before they could be sold.

Pirates preferred to sail from major ports, whenever they could find dishonest governments that tolerated their presence. They found these havens along the edges of empires, far from the center of authority. Pirates never have operated out of the capital city of a state or empire. They always have sought refuge in ports on the periphery, where local governors were both autonomous and willing to cooperate in return for a share of the loot.

In the ancient Mediterranean, pirate gangs operated out of Crete, not out of Alexandria or Antioch. Medieval corsairs flourished in Wales, not in London. The OTTOMAN EMPIRE welcomed them to ALGIERS but not to Istanbul. In the Caribbean, PORT ROYAL thrived as a pirate haven for three decades (1650–1680) simply because it was very far from the British government in London.

Once pirates heard that a major port was open to them, they flocked to its protection, abandoning less convenient havens. Thus the location of a haven in itself tells us little about the nationality of the corsairs sailing from its harbor. Pirates rarely had a strong sense of patriotism, and pirate crews welcomed desperados of many nationalities and races. Most of the pirates sailing from Cilicia were not Cilicians. The most famous BARBARY corsairs were European renegades. And outlaws from every European nation (and African blacks) joined the buccaneers in the Caribbean.

HAWKINS, SIR JOHN (English pirate and naval official; Atlantic, Caribbean; 1532–1595) During four voyages (1562–1568), Hawkins was both the first English slaver and the first to invade the Spanish Caribbean. In later years, he played a major role in creating the Elizabethan navy.

Hawkins' father, a Plymouth merchant, had traveled to West Africa and Brazil and traded with the Canary Islands. Spain and England were at peace in the early 1560s. English pirates mainly preyed on French shipping in the Atlantic. English merchants could trade with Spain and the Americas, but were required to operate through the Casa de Contratación (Board of Trade) in Seville.

While visiting the Canaries, young John Hawkins smuggled slave captives from West Africa to the Caribbean, and took three small vessels of his own to Sierra Leone in October 1562. On this and later voyages,

Hawkins collected slaves by raiding native villages and looting Portuguese vessels. With the connivance of local officials, he sold his cargo on the northern coast of Hispaniola. One ship returned to England in August 1563. Two others sneaked into Seville, but Spanish authorities seized their cargoes. Despite this loss, Hawkins enjoyed a large profit.

Relations between Spain and England rapidly deteriorated from 1563. Pirate attacks in European waters led Spanish officials to suspend trade and to arrest English ships. Plans for an Anglo-French expedition to Florida had fallen through, and Queen Elizabeth switched her support to Hawkins, encouraging a second slaving expedition in October 1564. Courtiers and merchants financed the voyage. The queen contributed the 700-ton *Jesus of Lubeck*, and Hawkins also commanded three smaller vessels.

Hawkins assembled about 400 slaves by kidnapping and piracy and carried them to Borburata and RIO DE LA HACHA in Venezuela. Spanish officials tried to prevent and then to tax the illegal sales. But they backed down when Hawkins threatened to destroy the towns. Hawkins' squadron visited a French colony in Florida and returned to England in September 1655. His backers made at least a 60 percent profit on the voyage.

The Spanish ambassador persuaded the English to forbid Hawkins' next expedition. Despite the government's order, John LOVELL left for Africa in October 1566, commanding three small ships provided by Hawkins. (Sir Francis DRAKE was among the crew.) After stealing slaves from Portuguese slavers, Lovell arrived at Borburato, Venezuela, with Jean BONTEMPS, a French pirate. However Lovell's small squadron could not force the Spanish to trade, and the trip was a financial disaster.

Hawkins personally led a powerful squadron that sailed in October 1567. Backed by a joint stock company, it included the *Jesus*, another royal warship, and four smaller vessels. A larger fleet would facilitate illegal slave-trading, and Queen Elizabeth also may have wanted to demonstrate English power. Hawkins again raided the African coast and despoiled Portuguese vessels, with Drake receiving command of one prize. At Rio de la Hacha, Hawkins forced the Spanish to permit trade by taking hostages and burning part of the town.

The ships ran into heavy storms on the return voyage. On September 15, 1568, Hawkins stopped at SAN JUAN DE ULÚA in Mexico, occupied an island in the harbor, and took several hostages. A Spanish TREASURE FLEET arrived the next day, commanded by the viceroy of Mexico.

The viceroy could not allow a foreign squadron to occupy a Spanish port in his presence. Although he at first accepted a truce, he ordered the Spanish forts and ships to attack on September 23. Of the six English ships at San Juan, only the two captained by Hawkins and Drake limped into England months later. Three-fourths of Hawkins' crews were killed or missing, and the expedition lost large sums of money.

The queen forbade a voyage of retaliation, and Hawkins' slaving days were over. He succeeded his father-in-law as treasurer of the navy in 1577 and also became naval comptroller in 1588. Although not entirely honest in handling governmental funds, Hawkins was an excellent administrator. He rebuilt the older GALLEONS, helped design faster, more heavily armed ships, and improved pay and conditions for sailors.

Hawkins was knighted for his skill and bravery while commanding a squadron against the Spanish Armada in 1588. Early in 1590, Hawkins and Martin FROBISHER unsuccessfully tried to intercept the Spanish treasure fleet off Portugal. In 1595, he and Francis Drake jointly commanded an expedition to the West Indies. The two quarreled bitterly, and Hawkins died of illness as the fleet reached San Juan, Puerto Rico.

(See also SELECTED BIBLIOGRAPHY: Andrews, *Spanish* and *Trade, Plunder;* Unwin, *Defeat;* Wright, *Spanish Documents.*)

HAWKINS, SIR RICHARD (*English captain; Atlantic, Caribbean, Pacific; 1562–1622*)

The only son of Sir John HAWKINS, Richard soon went to sea in his family's ships. He accompanied his uncle, William HAWKINS, on a West Indian trading and plunder venture in 1582 and 1583. During Sir Francis DRAKE's West Indian expedition (1585–1586), he was captain of a small GALIOT financed by his family. He commanded the royal ship *Swallow* during the Spanish Armada battles in 1588, and he sailed with his father's expedition to Portugal in 1590.

During these years, Richard Hawkins planned a voyage around the world in imitation of those by Drake (1577–1580) and Thomas CAVENDISH (1586–88). His father had built the 350-ton GALLEON *Dainty,* a fine private warship that helped capture the MADRE DE DIOS in 1592. Hawkins purchased her and sailed in June 1593 with a PINNACE and a supply ship. After preying on Spanish shipping along the Peruvian coast, he planned to head east, perhaps stopping at China or Japan on the way home.

After a slow passage across the Atlantic, Hawkins refreshed his crews and burned his supply ship in southern Brazil. During a storm off Argentina, his shallow-draught pinnace deserted. The *Dainty* went on, sighted the Falkland Islands, fought its way through the Strait of Magellan in 46 days, and reached the Pacific on March 29, 1594.

In 1578 Drake had taken the Spaniards by surprise. Nine years later Cavendish found the Peruvian coast on alert but still managed to capture a rich MANILA GALLEON. By 1594, as Hawkins discovered, the Spaniards had built up an effective naval force to resist further raids. Aware that the ports were better defended, Hawkins planned to keep well out to sea until he was north of Callao, Peru's

chief seaport. But his crew was avid for loot and forced him to raid Valparaiso, Chile. Here they took four prizes, one carrying gold. Afraid that he would defraud them of their share (which many captains did), the men insisted that all captured treasure be locked up, with one of them carrying a necessary key.

Surprise now was lost. Thanks to bad weather, Hawkins managed to escape a Spanish squadron off Pisco, and fled to the Bay of Atacames in northern Ecuador. His insubordinate seamen ruined his chances of escaping to Mexico by chasing after a prize. Three Spanish warships trapped the *Dainty,* which surrendered on June 22 after three days of hard fighting.

The Spanish naval commander had promised to repatriate the survivors. But higher authorities kept Hawkins at Lima and Madrid until 1602, when the English paid a £3,000 ransom. The *Dainty* was exhibited as a trophy at PANAMA, the first prize the Spaniards had taken in the South Seas.

Despite this disastrous venture, Hawkins apparently was still wealthy. He was knighted in 1603 and was appointed VICE-ADMIRAL of Devon, performing his duties as dishonestly as many others holding that office. In 1614 and 1617, Hawkins was nominated to command voyages for the East India Company, and he was vice-admiral of a mismanaged expedition against the BARBARY states in 1620 and 1621. He is said to have died of a fit while vainly trying to persuade the Privy Council to pay his crewmen.

Hawkins' account of his Peruvian raid was rewritten and published (London, 1622) as *The Observations of Sir Richard Hawkins Knight.* James Williamson edited the book in 1933 (London: Argonaut Press). Although informative about nautical life, the work also contains many fictional anecdotes and factual blunders.

(See also SELECTED BIBLIOGRAPHY: Spate, *Spanish Lake;* Williamson, *Hawkins.*)

HAWKINS, WILLIAM (1) (*English captain and shipowner; Atlantic; died about 1554*)

The father of John and William HAWKINS (2), he was a prosperous Plymouth merchant and an occasional naval officer. In September 1544, one of his ships received letters of MARQUE against the French during wartime. The following spring, his men seized a vessel belonging to Juan Quintanadueñas, a wealthy Spaniard living at Rouen. Hawkins could not prove that the captured goods were of French ownership. (In fact, although Hawkins did not know it, Quintanadueñas earlier had taken French citizenship.)

While the ADMIRALTY COURT was hearing the case, Hawkins and the mayor of Plymouth sold the captured merchandise. By doing so, both men became guilty of contempt, when the court ruled against Hawkins. Although captains often sold disputed prizes before the courts ruled on their legality, the Privy Council decided to make an example in this case and imprisoned the defendants. Hawkins apparently also was a part owner of the *Mary Figge*, another PRIVATEERING vessel that seized illegal booty.

(See also WYNDHAM, THOMAS.)

HAWKINS, WILLIAM (2) *(English merchant and captain; Atlantic, Caribbean; 1519?–1589)* Son of William HAWKINS (1), elder brother of Sir John HAWKINS, and three times mayor of Plymouth. While Sir John was adventuring in the Caribbean during the 1560s, William promoted piracy in the English Channel. France was torn by civil wars between Calvinist and Roman Catholic factions. Hawkins' ships operated under PRIVATEERING commissions solicited from the Protestant party. Jacques SORES commanded one of his vessels in 1568 and 1569.

In addition to promoting the voyages of Sir Francis DRAKE, William and John Hawkins continued to sponsor Channel piracy throughout the 1570s. The French and Spanish ambassadors frequently complained of their piracies. In fact, the ADMIRALTY court indicted the CASTLE OF COMFORT—jointly owned by William Hawkins and Sir Richard GRENVILLE—more frequently than any other warship. Hawkins' lawyers usually got him off on technicalities, even though England was at peace with both France and Spain.

In 1582, Hawkins left Plymouth with seven ships, two belonging to Drake, with Richard HAWKINS as second-in-command. The fleet stopped at the Cape Verde Islands, where it was accused of helping to sack the city of Santiago. It then visited the pearl fisheries at Margarita Island (off Venezuela) and Puerto Rico, returning to England with pearls, gold, hides, and sugar. Hawkins may have obtained some of this treasure through illegal trade with Spanish colonists. But much of it was plundered from Spanish ships.

HAWLEY, FRANCIS *(English customs official; active 1581–1583)* Hawley was the deputy or lieutenant at Corfe Castle for Sir Christopher Hatton, the absentee VICE-ADMIRAL of Dorset. Hawley received stolen goods from many pirates, including Stephen HEYNES and William VALENTINE. He was accused of sending his servant to captains anchored in Studland Bay to see what they would give him for protection. On one occasion, Hawley became angry at Clinton ATKINSON when he failed to deliver a promised present of rich tapestry. He wrote to Thomas WALTON and asked him to abduct Atkinson. Walton told Hawley to catch Atkinson himself—if he could.

(See also ADMIRALTY COURT; SELECTED BIBLIOGRAPHY: Ewen, "Organized Piracy.")

HAWLEY, JOHN (1) *(English merchant and pirate; Atlantic; active 1399–1404)* Whether by lawful or by illegal trade, Hawley prospered as a merchant and landowner in Dartmouth and perhaps began piracy in reprisal for personal losses. In 1399, during peacetime, he led a massive raid on Normandy and Brittany that captured 34 merchant ships. Their cargoes included 1,500 tuns (378,000 gallons) of wine, which were largely consumed in a marathon public revel at Dartmouth.

Hawley continued to plunder the European shores of the Channel. In 1403, the Flemings complained of his activities. In the same year, he and Thomas NORTON commanded a squadron that seized seven vessels laden with goods from Genoa and Spain. He ignored royal orders to make restitution even though he had been the ADMIRAL's deputy and was commissioned in 1403 to investigate piracy. Hawley's attacks, and those by other pirates, enraged the Bretons, who sent a force against Dartmouth in 1404. Hawley took a leading role in driving off the invaders, and he received a royal commission in 1406 to survey and fortify Dartmouth's port.

HAWLEY, JOHN (2) *(English pirate; Atlantic; active 1406–1436)* Son of John HAWLEY (1), he inherited his father's wealth and political influence and was an able sea captain. He served in the king's fleet in 1406, held various royal offices under King Henry V (ruled 1413–1422), and received several commissions to arrest pirates.

During the same years, Hawley indulged in piracy on his own account. In 1413, he produced a letter of MARQUE to explain away the capture of a Spanish ship. It was harder to excuse the seizure of a Breton ship carrying English goods under a safe-conduct, and Hawley was briefly arrested in August 1413.

In 1427, Hawley thwarted justice through an ingenious trick. A Scottish merchant complained to the Royal Council that Hawley had seized his ship in time of truce. Hawley promised to restore the Scot's losses, if Hawley received a royal commission to arrest 40 other notorious criminals. Hawley got his commission, arrested several persons, and took large sums from them. But he gave the Scot nothing. He never was brought to account and held other royal commissions in 1430 and 1436.

(See also SELECTED BIBLIOGRAPHY: Kingsford, *Prejudice*.)

HAYS, WILLIAM *(American captain; South China Sea, Pacific Ocean; 1829–1877)* Nicknamed "Bully," Hays was born in Cleveland, Ohio, and went to sea from San Francisco. From 1854, he commanded various sailing craft along the Chinese coast, all bought on credit and never paid for. He carried illegal cargoes, sold guns to rebels and warlords, and transported kidnapped Chinese peasants to New Zealand and the South Sea islands. After helping a British warship catch the American pirate Eli BOGGS in 1856, Hays made off with much of the booty captured with Boggs.

From about 1860, Hayes prospered as a "blackbirder," kidnapping the inhabitants of small South Sea islands and selling them as plantation slaves at Fiji. He also sold guns and alcohol to native tribesmen and to the Maori on New Zealand. The United States and several European powers began to annex the Pacific islands during the 1870s and tried to suppress the illegal slave trade. The captain of an American warship arrested Hayes at Samoa in 1872 but let him go. Arrested by Spanish officials at Guam in 1875, he was freed after pretending to convert to Roman Catholicism. He was killed during a quarrel with one of his crew.

(See also SELECTED BIBLIOGRAPHY: Lubbock, *Bully Hayes.*)

HEGENBERT, CONRAD VAN See HIGGEN-BERTE, COURTE.

HELIODORUS *(Greek novelist; third century)*
A citizen of Emesa (Homs) in Syria, Heliodorus wrote the ETHIOPIAN ADVENTURES, the longest of the extant Greek ROMANCES.

HEMIOLA *(pirate ship; Mediterranean; fourth through first centuries B.C.)* A light, fast two-banked GALLEY, constructed so that the oars in the top bank behind the mast could be swiftly removed. Its name—Greek for "one-and-a-half"—derives from this peculiar arrangement of oars, designed to meet a pirate's special requirements.

A pirate SHIP needed sails as well as oars to catch merchant vessels. (If it relied solely on oars, then the rowers were too tired to fight.) When the corsairs caught up with their prey and were ready to grapple it, the top bank of oars was detached and stored. The men manning those oars also stowed the sail, yard, and mast. This provided the necessary room for the boarding party stationed along the gunwale. The navy of RHODES copied this innovative design for a warship, known as the TRIEMIOLIA.

(See also SELECTED BIBLIOGRAPHY: Casson, *Ships.*)

HENDRICKSZ, BOUDEWIJN *(Dutch admiral; Caribbean; died 1626)* Hendricksz commanded the third assault on San Juan, Puerto Rico, following earlier attacks by Sir Francis DRAKE (in 1595) and the earl of CUMBERLAND (in 1598). The El Morro fortress proved impregnable, and Hendricksz's expedition was an expensive failure.

Elated by their conquest of Bahia, Brazil, in May 1625, the directors of the DUTCH WEST INDIA COMPANY outfitted 42 vessels for Hendricksz, mayor of Edam and a director of the company. The fleet sailed in March 1625 with orders to reinforce Bahia, conquer Puerto Rico, and harass the Spanish TREASURE FLEETS. Delayed by storms, the Dutch flotilla reached Brazil at the end of May. Spanish forces had just reoccupied Bahia, and their ships refused to leave the safety of the bay and join battle at sea. Hendricksz sailed north into the Caribbean with 18 warships, while the rest of his ships returned with prizes or went on to raid Portuguese forts in West Africa.

The Dutch fleet sailed into San Juan harbor on September 25, firing incessantly at El Morro fortress. The Spaniards had greatly strengthened the fort after Cumberland captured it in 1598. Hendricksz' broadsides did little

damage and killed only four men. But they frightened the defenders, and many soldiers and almost all civilians fled into the woods with their best possessions. About 800 Dutch raiders landed, pillaged the abandoned town, and defiled the cathedral. Their officers tried to preserve some discipline by destroying San Juan's wine supplies.

Governor Juan de Haro—an experienced officer who had fought in Europe—withdrew into El Morro with 330 soldiers, many old and sick. Hendricksz tried to starve out the defenders, but small boats easily sneaked through with supplies. Haro turned down two Dutch demands for surrender, defying Hendricksz' threats to burn San Juan. Go ahead, Haro replied,

> the settlers have enough courage to rebuild their houses, for there is timber in the mountains and building materials in the land. And here I am today with people enough in this fortress to wipe out yours. Do not write any more such letters for I will not reply.

After destroying the town, Hendricksz prepared to leave but found that Haro had rearranged his cannon to cover the exits. The fleet finally escaped on November 2. Two ships ran aground and many had to be towed.

After his men had recuperated, Hendricksz turned on Margarita Island in February 1527. A small fort was burned, but the main city was too strong to attack. Hendricksz sailed east along the Venezuelan coast, looting and burning various small towns, and then headed back toward Cuba.

Hendricksz had been given a powerful and costly force, and the West India Company expected a return on its investment. His last hope was to capture the Spanish treasure fleets sailing from Honduras and Mexico. Stopping to pillage any vessels they encountered, the Dutch made for Havana, the fleet's last port of call in the Caribbean.

Havana was reached in June, but Hendricksz suddenly died. By now, the crews were thoroughly disgusted by their long cruise with little booty. Threatened with mutiny, the new commander returned to Europe. All together, Hendricksz had taken 24 prizes. But none contained valuable cargo, and the cruise was a financial disaster. Ironically, only one month after Hendricksz' fleet went home, Piet HEYN arrived with reinforcements and ran into the Mexican treasure fleet off the Dry Tortugas. Without Hendricksz's ships, he was outnumbered by the Spaniards and had to watch them reach safety at Havana.

(See also SELECTED BIBLIOGRAPHY: Goslinga, *Dutch*; Morales-Carrión, *Puerto Rico.*)

HENREID, PAUL *(American actor; 1908–)*
Born in Trieste, Henreid performed in Austrian plays and movies before receiving supporting roles in the British films *Goodbye, Mr Chips* (1939) and *Night Train to Munich* (1940). He moved to the United States in 1940 and became an American citizen. Hollywood initially

Paul Henreid (far right) in *The Spanish Main* (1945).

cast Henreid as a suave, aristocratic European lover. He starred with Bette Davis in *Now Voyager* (1942). In *Casablanca* (1942), he was the idealistic hero, Victor Lazlow, in a love triangle with Humphrey Bogart and Ingrid Bergman.

After *Casablanca*, Henreid played romantic parts in about 20 more movies. He saved Maureen O'HARA from the villainous Walter SLEZAK in THE SPANISH MAIN and starred as Jean LAFFITE, in LAST OF THE BUCCANEERS. As the BARBARY corsair Edri-Al-Gadrian, he rescued Patricia Medina in PIRATES OF TRIPOLI. During the 1950s and 1960s, Henreid frequently appeared as a television actor and also directed more than 300 TV plays or segments.

HERACLEO *(Cilician corsair; Mediterranean; first century B.C.)* Heracleo commanded four galleys that defeated a larger Roman fleet near Syracuse, the capital of Sicily. The pirates sailed into Syracuse's inner harbor, which was surrounded by the fortified city—a feat never previously achieved by an enemy of Rome.

Heracleo's raid occurred between 73 and 70, while Verres was governor of Sicily. The Roman orator Cicero (106–43) narrated the story of Heracleo's invasion as an example of Verres' dishonesty and incompetence. The governor pocketed the taxes raised to hire and feed sailors, so that the ships were undermanned and their crews half-starved. Verres also gave control of the Roman fleet to his mistress' husband, the incompetent Cleomenes.

Heracleo's pirate squadron was seen near Syracuse while the Roman admiral was drinking on shore. Learning of its arrival, Cleomenes hastily fled on his flagship, ordering the rest of the fleet to follow. The pirates cut off the two ships in the rear, and Cleomenes and the other captains ran their vessels aground. By nightfall, Heracleo's men had destroyed the entire Roman squadron.

The next day, the corsairs entered the city's fortified harbor. Sailing past its quays, they expressed their contempt by waving the palm roots that Cleomenes' starving sailors had gathered for food. Heracleo's men apparently filled their ships with booty, since—Cicero concluded—they left "not frightened away but simply satiated."

Cicero spoke as prosecutor when Verres was tried for extortion in 70. But the basic outline of Heracleo's invasion must be accurate, since Sicilian witnesses testified before the court. Verres was not the only Roman governor who stole taxes raised to support the navy. The pirates of CILICIA totally dominated the seas partly because widespread corruption left many provinces defenseless.

(See also SELECTED BIBLIOGRAPHY: Cicero, *Verrine Orations*.)

HERCKMANS, ELIAS (Dutch captain; Pacific; active 1642–1643)

Herckmans took command of a failed raid on southern Chile following the death of Hendrick BROUWER. Brouwer had brought 600 men around the tip of South America to Chiloé Island. After Brouwer died in August 1643, Herckmans took the Dutch forces and some 479 Araucanian Indians to Valdivia, Chile. There the tribes initially welcomed the Dutch invaders as allies against Spanish colonists. But relations soured. While addressing the local chiefs, Herckmans imprudently let slip the Dutch desire for gold. The native peoples remembered Spanish exactions with such bitterness that they were alarmed by any mention of gold.

The Indians refused to work for the Dutch. Their chiefs also claimed they could not provide meat and other food—which the Dutch desperately needed, since they had lost the ship carrying most of their supplies. There were other irritations, including the Araucanian custom of purloining everything movable.

Facing starvation, Herckmans left on October 28, reaching Brazil in December 1643 after the first west-to-east passage around Cape Horn. Following this expedition's failure and their expulsion from Brazil in 1654, the Dutch did not again try to invade the South Sea. Later raids were the work of individual buccaneers, including Bartholomew SHARP, William DAMPIER, and Lionel WAFER.

(See also DUTCH IN THE AMERICAS; SELECTED BIBLIOGRAPHY: Bradley, *Peru*; Spate, *Monopolists*.)

HERODOTUS (Greek historian; about 484–420 B.C.)

Herodotus wrote a *History* of the wars between the Greeks and the Persians from 560 to 478. The first major author of prose history, he largely based his work on oral traditions. Herodotus provided most of the information about Greek tyrants such as DIONYSUS OF PHOCAEA, HISTIAEUS, and POLYCRATES OF SAMOS. He also reported, sometimes skeptically, legends about piracy by the CARIANS, PHOENICIANS, and ETRUSCANS.

(See also LIPARI ISLANDS; MINOS; PHOCEANS.)

HERRIOT, DAVID (British pirate; Caribbean, Atlantic; died 1718)

Edward Teach (BLACKBEARD) captured Herriot's SLOOP *Adventure* early in 1718. While Israel HANDS took over the *Adventure*, Herriot and his crew joined Teach in raiding Charleston, South Carolina. Soon after, Teach wrecked the *Adventure* as part of a scheme to avoid sharing his booty.

Joining Stede BONNET as sailing master, Herriot was captured with Bonnet in October 1718. He agreed to testify against his shipmates and was imprisoned in a private house with Bonnet. The two men escaped, and Herriot was killed by their pursuers.

(See also SELECTED BIBLIOGRAPHY: Hughson, *Carolina*.)

HEYN (HEIJN, HEIN), PIETER (PIET) PIETERSZOON (Dutch admiral; Atlantic, Caribbean; 1577–1629)

Heyn gained enduring fame by capturing an entire Spanish TREASURE FLEET off Cuba, and he also took substantial loot in earlier raids on Bahia (São Salvador) Brazil. A popular, skilled, and sometimes brilliant commander, Heyn was Spain's most dangerous adversary at sea after the death of Sir Francis DRAKE. As an ardent Calvinist, he sought both wealth and the downfall of the Roman Catholic Spaniards. Constant study of the Bible nourished his zeal, and he FLOGGED crewmen that missed morning or evening prayer. Despite his hatred of the Spanish Empire, however, he did not torture or murder prisoners as did Drake, Jacques SORES and many other captains.

Born near Rotterdam, Heyn went to sea with his father, a fisherman, trader, and pirate. The Spaniards arrested him at least twice and he labored as a GALLEY SLAVE. Released about 1598 during a prisoner exchange, he was again captured and enslaved in the West Indies until about 1602. Between 1607 and 1622, he took part in at least two voyages for the Dutch East India Company. He rose to captain, amassed a considerable fortune, and fought in numerous assaults on Portuguese and Spanish ships and trading posts.

In 1623, Heyn was hired by the DUTCH WEST INDIA COMPANY, founded in 1621 to plunder the Spanish colonies. The Company directed its first expedition against Bahia, Brazil's chief port. Heyn was second-in-command of 16 ships and 3,300 men, which appeared before Bahia in May 1624. He led the attackers, who rapidly captured and thoroughly plundered the city and the ships in the harbor.

From Bahia, Heyn took a small squadron to join an assault on the Portuguese slave depot at Luanda in West Africa. However, the other Dutch fleet left before Heyn arrived. He went back to Bahia, found that it had been reoccupied by the Spanish, and returned to the Netherlands in July 1625. Although they took no rich prizes, Heyn's raiders looted Iberian shipping at each stop during this long cruise.

Promoted to admiral, Heyn sailed with 14 ships and 1,700 troops in May 1626. This time, he was sent to assist Boudewijn HENDRICKSZ, who had besieged Puerto Rico and terrorized the Caribbean. However, Hendricksz's fleet missed the rendezvous.

Heyn went on to the Dry Tortugas, west of Florida. While he was there, the Mexican treasure fleet—about 40 vessels, including 14 galleons—sailed past. Heyn lamented his inability to attack the much larger Spanish force. If only Hendricksz had been present, he wrote, "I would, with the help of God, have taken the whole fleet. It grieves me that I had to let so beautiful an opportunity slip through my hands only because of a lack of assistance."

Heyn decided to return to Bahia. Since the winds in the Caribbean prevail from the east, his fleet went back to the Azores, passed down the African coast, and recrossed the Atlantic to reach Bahia in March 1627. Heyn immediately attacked, sinking or capturing two dozen Spanish merchant ships. In July, four vessels richly laden with booty were dispatched to the Netherlands. After a profitable raid along the Brazilian coast, Heyn seized more Iberian ships at Bahia before returning in October 1627.

Although 1627 had been highly profitable, the Dutch West India Company was determined to make 1628 an even better year by capturing a Spanish treasure fleet. Three separate squadrons left for Spain each summer, carrying Peruvian and Mexican treasure and other valuable cargo. The largest, the Tierra Firme fleet, departed from PORTOBELO and CARTAGENA, while two smaller convoys left from Honduras and SAN JUAN DE ULÚA, Mexico. All three normally rendezvoused at Havana in July and sailed north through the Bahamas Channel and up the Florida coast.

After Piet Heyn's triumphant Bahia raid, the Company spared no expense in outfitting his second attempt on the silver fleets. Heyn commanded more than 31 vessels—several of unusually large size—carrying 2,300 sailors and a thousand soldiers. By August 1628, his ships awaited the Spaniards in the open seas between Havana and Cape San Antonio in western Cuba.

The Spanish ships were most vulnerable when passing through the straits between Cuba and Florida. When Spanish officials learned that Dutch raiders were in the area, they sent a warning to the Tierra Firme fleet, which stayed safely at Cartagena. Meanwhile, a separate Dutch squadron under Pieter ITA had attacked the Honduras galleons on August 1. The Spaniards were unaware that there were two Dutch fleets. When Ita left, the officers of the Mexican galleons made the disastrous assumption that all Dutch ships had left the area.

For more than a month, Heyn's ships maneuvered in the narrow Florida Straits. Belatedly learning of their presence, the governor of Havana sent out numerous dispatch boats, but they failed to find the Mexican ships. On September 8, Heyn's squadrons surrounded the Spanish vessels off the Cuban coast.

The Mexican fleet included four GALLEONS carrying silver and about 18 smaller ships. But only two galleons were men-of-war, and they were heavily laden with merchandise and passengers. Unable to run for Havana or to fight, the Spanish commander made for the Bay of Matanzas, 50 miles east of Havana, to disembark the treasure and burn his ships. Acting quickly and decisively, Heyn and his captains followed the enemy into the bay and opened fire. The Spanish crews panicked, many ran for

cover on shore, and the rest surrendered without a fight. The four galleons and 12 smaller ships were captured. The booty included 46 tons of silver, other valuable cargo, and the personal hoards of the passengers.

Heyn succeeded in maintaining discipline and limiting looting by his crews. It took eight days to transfer the cargoes from the smaller ships to the four galleons, which were taken back to Europe. Some crewmen embezzled gold and deserted in England on the way back. But there was none of the wild looting that accompanied the capture of other treasure ships (such as the MADRE DE DIOS). The Spanish prisoners were put ashore with food and water.

The raiders reached Amsterdam in January 1629. Heyn and his vice-admiral addressed the Dutch parliament and were feted at celebrations throughout the Netherlands. The booty was valued at 11 to 14 million guilders—enough to pay the cost of the entire Dutch army for eight months. After deducting expenses, the West India Company earned about 7 million. As ADMIRAL of the Netherlands, the prince of Orange took 10 percent.

Most of the West India Company's profit was paid out to shareholders, who received a 70 percent cash dividend. Only a small share was given to the seamen that had captured the silver, and they rioted at Amsterdam in protest. Heyn's own share was a miserly 7,000 guilders, less than 1 percent of the total take.

Heyn resigned from the Company in March 1629 and received command of the official Dutch navy, the first admiral who did not belong to the Dutch nobility. He was mortally wounded while attacking pirates operating from Dunkirk and Ostend under Spanish commissions.

(See also SELECTED BIBLIOGRAPHY: Goslinga, *Dutch*; Rogoziński, *Caribbean*.)

HEYNES, STEPHEN *(English pirate; Atlantic; active 1581–1582)* Sometimes calling himself Stephen Carless, Heynes operated from Studland Bay in southern England but also used Welsh and Irish ports. In 1581, he captured a French ship carrying rich goods from Brazil. Her cargo included 54 monkeys and apes, which Heynes sold at Studland and Torbay.

In July 1582, Heynes and William VALENTINE brought the German ship *Salvator* into Studland harbor. To discover their hidden money, Heynes tortured his captives so cruelly that some of his own crew fell on their knees and begged him to stop. He easily sold the *Salvator*'s cargo to local merchants and gentleman, who exchanged whole cattle at the pier for sugar and spices.

Royal officials shared in the spoils and protected Heynes, who boasted that he "had better friends in Englande then eanye alderman or merchants of London." He forced the *Salvator*'s master to borrow his ransom money from Francis HAWLEY, a deputy of the VICE-ADMIRAL of Dorset. Hawley demanded a bribe from the *Salva-*

tor's owners before he would release their plundered ship. On another occasion in 1582, Heynes looted an English vessel within gunshot of the royal castle at Sandown, whose captain kept part of the plunder.

HICKS (HICKES), ROBERT *(English pirate; Atlantic; died 1578)*

Hicks came from Cornwall. In February 1577, since both captains were short-handed, Hicks joined forces with John CALLICE. With Callice commanding Hicks' ship, they seized three Scottish and German vessels off southern England. Heading north, they joined up with William FENNER. Off Elsinore, the pirates captured the Danish-owned *Golden Lion*, an eight-gun 300-ton vessel. They took their prize to Weymouth, hiding 15 severely wounded Danes on board while they sold her cargo.

The pirates separated, and Callice was captured in May 1577. Commanding the *Golden Lion* (renamed the *Neptune*), Hicks seized various prizes including a German ship, and sold their cargo in Ireland. Hearing of Callice's incarceration, he wrote a sympathetic letter offering to surrender his ship (but not himself) to gain his friend's freedom.

Hicks was captured in Ireland in October 1577, tried by the ADMIRALTY COURT in London, and hanged. Despite the apparent friendship between Hicks and Callice, trial records suggest that Hicks had swindled Callice in dividing up their booty.

HIGGENBERTE, COURTE *(Dutch pirate; Atlantic; active 1572–1576)*

The English name of Conrad van Hegenbert, a merchant of Antwerp. He sailed in the *Flying Hart* from Wales and western England, selling his prizes to local landowners and officials. In August 1576, he joined forces with John CALLICE, and the two captains seized five or more French prizes during the next four months.

Many royal officials assisted Higgenberte. He was jailed at Cardiff in December 1576 but was released on bail by a friendly magistrate. He was arrested while making a Christmas visit to Wales in 1577, but was rescued by his crew. In April 1578, he was jailed in London for pillaging the French ships in 1576. He disappeared after being released on bail. Lord Charles Howard (later ADMIRAL of England) guaranteed Higgenberte's appearance, and he posted his own bond of £4,000. Although still a wanted man, he was comfortably retired on the Isle of Wight in 1584.

HIGH WIND IN JAMAICA, A (1) *(novel; 1929)*

High Wind (sometimes titled *The Innocent Voyage*) is a farce that ends in terror. Fictional pirates often capture young victims. In this novel, Richard Hughes (1900–1976) makes the children capture the pirates. Hughes outraged readers by portraying the youngsters as only half-human, without feelings or conscience.

Shortly after Britain freed the Caribbean slaves, probably in the 1840s, a hurricane devastates Jamaica. The Bas-Thorntons, a proper English couple, send their five children back to England on the *Clorinda*. John is about 12; Emily is 10; and Rachel, Edward, and Laura are even younger. Also aboard are two youngsters from the well-off but slovenly Fernandez family—Margaret, a sullen and sensual 13 and her younger brother Harry.

Caribbean piracy no longer prospered after DIABOLITO was killed in 1823. But a few poverty-stricken brigands languidly marauded out of backward rural havens in western Cuba. One such band, sailing without cannon, captures the *Clorinda* while her crew are preoccupied torturing a monkey. To fool their victims, the pirates carry transvestites disguised as female passengers.

While they loot their prey, the pirates remove the seven children to their own ship. They are caught aboard, vastly embarrassing their captors, when the *Clorinda* makes its escape. The pirates return to their refuge at a decayed Cuban city. No one will buy their booty or take the children off their hands. John, the oldest Bas-Thornton, accidentally falls and dies.

The pirates go back to sea with the remaining children. Captain Jonsen, tall and fat, is Danish. Otto, the smaller, thinner first mate, is Viennese by birth. Both took to the sea as boys, became inseparable companions while sailing on English ships, and drifted into piracy at Cuba. Most of their crew are drunken, unwashed simpletons.

As the pirates drift aimlessly about, the Bas-Thornton children quickly forget brother John. They enjoy life on board and like the pirates more than their own parents. ("They can't be pirates," one child remarks. "Pirates are wicked.") Margaret, the oldest Fernandez, voluntarily moves in with the captain and mate.

The pirates finally capture a little Dutch steamer carrying a mangy collection of circus animals. Emily, wounded by accident, is left alone with the Dutch captain, while the other children visit the animals. Ten-year-old Emily becomes terrified when the captured captain tries to cut the ropes binding him. She grabs the knife and slashes the tied man in a dozen places. Convinced that Margaret is the murderer, the crew throws her overboard, but she is rescued by the ship's boat.

Captain Jonsen stops a steamer and puts the children aboard, claiming he has rescued them. Emily tells the authorities about their capture. An English naval ship chases down the pirates. They are tried in London and executed solely because of Emily's testimony in court. Breaking down in tears, Emily lets the jury believe that the pirates (and not herself) murdered the Dutch captain.

HIGH WIND IN JAMAICA, A (2) *(motion picture; color; released 1965)*

Director Alexander Mackendrick's SWASHBUCKLER leaves out the dark brooding about the inherent immorality of children in Richard Hughes' novel. The movie makes the pirates more evil, the children more sentimentally innocent.

A High Wind In Jamaica (1965).

Captain Julian Chavez, played by Anthony QUINN, is a Spanish pirate who winds up baby-sitting the two Fernandez and five Thornton children. While his crew loots and burns their ship, the children crawl on board the pirate vessel. The brigands discover them and want to toss them overboard as bad luck. Chavez refuses and steers his ship to Tampico, Mexico. There he tries to leave the children with Rosa (Lila Kedrova), a whorehouse madame. She refuses, and John Thornton (Martin Amis) accidentally is killed.

Emily Thornton (Deborah Baxter) is injured, and the soft-hearted Chavez becomes more protective toward his unwanted charges. When the pirates spot a Dutch steamer, Chavez pulls alongside to drop off the children. First mate Zac (James Coburn) wants to pillage the ship. Chavez refuses, causing the crew to mutiny. Zac locks up Chavez, Emily, and the Dutch captain (Gert Frobe) while the pirates loot.

Desperate to escape, the Dutch captain excitedly approaches Emily with a knife, begging her to cut him free. Fearing that he means to kill her, she stabs him to death.

The authorities capture the pirates, who are tried for murdering the Dutch captain and young John Thornton. Under rough questioning, Emily lies and says Captain Chavez killed the Dutchman. Resigned to his fate, Chavez never refutes her testimony and is hanged.

HINGSON (HINSET), JOHN *(English buccaneer; Atlantic, Pacific; active 1680s)* Hingson was among the seamen that crossed the Isthmus of Panama with Bartholomew SHARP and John COXON in April 1680. A year later he was among a group that voted to leave Sharp's company and return to the Caribbean. Exhausted by the journey, he dropped out and spent four months with Lionel WAFER as a guest of the Cuna Indians. He again marauded in the Pacific from 1684 to 1688 under John COOK and Edward DAVIS. Hingson made it back to Virginia, where he was jailed with Davis and Wafer until July 1689.

HIPPON, ANTHONY *(English captain; Caribbean; active 1596–1602)* A resident of London, Hippon captured a Portuguese prize in 1596, while raiding with only a small PINNACE. The following year, as captain of the 150-ton *Golden-Dragon* (earlier commanded by Christopher NEWPORT), he sacked the pearling station near RIO DE LA HACHA (Venezuela) in consort with John WATTS' son. In 1602, he joined Newport and Michael GEARE in defeating two Spanish warships at PUERTO CABALLOS, Honduras. After privateering was outlawed in 1603, he sailed for the East India Company.

HISTIAEUS (Greek ruler; Aegean Sea; died 493 B.C.)

After they conquered western Asia Minor in 546, the Persians governed the Greek coastal cities through native rulers. Histiaeus, the tyrant of Miletus, was equally ready to make use of the Persians or to betray them. Like DIONYSUS OF PHOCAEA and POLYCRATES OF SAMOS, Histiaeus sent out pirate fleets, using his booty to subsidize land armies.

Histiaeus ruled Miletus by 513. Thanks to the collapse of its rival SAMOS, Miletus was prosperous, and Histiaeus also controlled silver mines to the north in Thrace. But the Persian king, Darius I, became suspicious of Histiaeus and summoned him to Persia, leaving his son-in-law Aristagoras to rule Miletus. When Histiaeus suspected that Darius never would let him return to Miletus, he advised Aristagoras to rebel against the Persians.

The rebellion began in 499, and Darius released Histiaeus, after he promised to bring the rebels to order. By the time he reached the Ionian coast, the rebellion was failing. The citizens of Miletus had expelled Aristagoras, and they refused to take Histiaeus back. During the general confusion, Histiaeus got eight warships from Lesbos and controlled the passage from the Black Sea to the Mediterranean at Byzantium. There he reigned as a pirate king, seizing passing merchant ships and forcing warships to acknowledge his authority.

In 493, Histiaeus' forces occupied Chios and sought to sack Thasos. However, when he heard that the Persian fleet was advancing north, he fled to the mainland, where Persian troops took him alive. Fearing that King Darius might yet forgive him, the Persian governor had Histiaeus impaled, cut off and embalmed his head, and sent it to Darius in Susa.

(See also SELECTED BIBLIOGRAPHY: Herodotus, *History.*)

HOAR (HORE), JOHN (British pirate; Indian Ocean, Red Sea; active 1695–1697)

Hoar captured a French ship in wartime, purchased it from the prize court, and renamed it the *John and Rebecca*. In December 1695, he sailed from Boston with a PRIVATEERING commission from Governor Benjamin Fletcher of New York. After visiting MADAGASCAR in April 1696, he cruised in the Red Sea. In consort with Dirk CHIVERS, Hoar took Indian and European prizes—including the *Rouparelle*, which William KIDD later destroyed. He went on to the Persian Gulf and captured a large Indian ship loaded with cloth.

Hoar arrived at Saint Mary's Island in February 1697. He was killed in July when local tribesmen attacked the pirates.

(See also BALDRIDGE, ADAM; SAMUEL, ABRAHAM.)

HOCQUINCOURT, CHEVALIER D' (Knight of Malta; Mediterranean; about 1640–1666)

Hocquincourt raided Muslim shipping in a 36-gun sailing ship, with the count of TOURVILLE as his lieutenant. After taking a large sailing vessel in 1665, they were surprised at Chios by 36 OTTOMAN galleys. The enemy fleet bombarded Hocquincourt's ship and landed soldiers to fire from the shore. His ship's masts and sails were badly damaged, and more than 150 cannon shots punctured its hull. Yet Hocquincourt beat off the Turks with tremendous slaughter. Early the next year, his ship struck a rock during a gale off Crete, and Hocquincourt drowned with 170 of his crew.

HOLLAND, WILLIAM (English pirate; English channel; 1579)

Holland captured a rich Spanish vessel and brought it into Purbeck in southwestern England.

HOMER (Greek poet; died before 700 B.C.)

The presumed author of the *Iliad* and the *Odyssey*, written in a form of early Greek. Although the ancient Greeks considered Homer their nation's greatest author, they knew nothing definite about his life or personality.

The *Iliad* narrates various events during the siege of Troy (in northwestern Turkey) by Greek warriors. The *Odyssey* tells how ODYSSEUS returned home after the war. The Greeks believed that the Trojan War was fought in about 1200 B.C. Modern archaeology confirms that a city at Troy was destroyed in about 1250.

The *Iliad* and the *Odyssey* preserve the earliest surviving account of Greek history. An earlier form of writing (Linear B) disappeared by about 1050. No written records were kept until the introduction, about 750, of a new alphabet, based on a PHOENICIAN model. Homer thus composed his epic poems about 500 years after the events they narrate. During those centuries, memories of the Trojan War presumably were handed down by oral tradition. Historians do not agree whether Homer's epic poems accurately describe the society of 1250 B.C. The major legends—such as the story of MINOS—apparently are based on real events. Details of everyday life may reflect the circumstances of the eight century, when the poems were completed.

Odysseus twice boasts of his piracies, and he expects his audience to praise his crimes. Obviously the Greeks did not condemn piracy when the *Odyssey* was composed. However, this does not necessarily imply that piracy was acceptable five centuries earlier, during the epoch in which Homer places Odysseus' journey.

HOMERIC HYMNS (poems in Ancient Greek; written from 600 to 250 B.C.)

Thirty-three hymns by unknown authors traditionally attributed to HOMER. The seventh-century *Hymn to Phytian Apollo* confirms that pirates infested the seas even at that early date. After various wanderings and adventures, Apollo builds a temple at Delphi. As he ponders who to bring in as his priests, the god becomes aware that a merchant ship is leaving Knossos, MINOS's city.

Disguised as a dolphin, Apollo guides the ship to Delphi's port. There, appearing as a beautiful young man, he asks the Cretans whether they are honest merchants or pirates. Cretans were considered a pirate race. But Apollo's question also implies that any men encountered at sea might be pirates in disguise.

The *Hymn to Dionysus,* written before 300, also describes kidnapping. But the god in the title turns the tables on the TYRRHENIAN corsairs. Appearing as a beautiful young man, Dionysus is walking along a promontory when the pirate ship suddenly appears. The corsairs leap out and grab him, hoping for a large ransom or a profitable sale. But their joy turns into horror, as Dionysus works many frightening miracles and then changes his unlucky captors into dolphins.

(See also SELECTED BIBLIOGRAPHY: Boer, *Homeric Hymns.*)

HOMOSEXUALITY *(all oceans; all eras)*
Since few pirates left diaries, rumors that they were homosexual are hard to evaluate. Two men enlisting together on several vessels were friends but not necessarily lovers. Since they considered homosexuality a defect, some observers brought false charges against their enemies. Although precise estimates are impossible, homosexuality clearly was found among seamen and pirates.

Ancient writers assumed that Greek pirates were attracted to all beautiful captives. The HOMERIC HYMNS relate how raiders grabbed the god Dionysus as he walked by the shore. When pirates capture a young couple in THE EPHESIAN TALE, the captain wants the man, while his friend desires the woman.

Christian slaves said that sodomy was widespread among the BARBARY corsairs. In the late 1500s, Diego HAËDO reported, "The man who keeps more male concubines is held in greater honor, and guards them more closely than his own wives and daughters, except on Fridays and feast days when they . . . parade through the streets richly attired." The REDEMPTIONIST FATHERS complained that young captives converted to Islam because it tolerated homosexuality.

Father Haëdo's statement is believable because he was relatively unprejudiced. During his stay in Algiers, four Greek RENEGADES failed to kidnap HASAN VENEZIANO PASHA because they quarreled over a boy. Despite their foolishness, Haëdo describes the four men as Christian martyrs.

Seventeenth-century BUCCANEERS formed permanent relationships as MATELOTS ("mates") and shared both hardships and possessions. During the 1680s, large gangs crossed the Panama Isthmus and cruised along South America's Pacific coast. Several pirate vessels included

educated men who kept diaries. They report lasting relationships similar to those between *matelots.*

Captain Edmund COOK sailed for many years with an unnamed servant. During a power struggle for command of a ship, John WATLING forced the servant to confess that "his Master had oft times Buggered him in England . . . in Jamaica . . .; and once in these seas before Panama." The confession did not offend the crew, but Watling imprisoned Cook. Peter CLOISE accompanied Edward DAVIS for nine years. When the ship's company dispersed in 1688, Davis and Cloise went on together to Virginia.

Some pirate captains carried off boys and young men. William DAMPIER reports that Charles SWAN kidnapped a boy of seven or eight, educated him for several years, and gave him a share of the loot. Bartholomew SHARP returned to England in 1682 with a 16-year-old Spaniard captured in South America. George SHELVOCKE infuriated his crew by promoting his cabin boy to first mate over older and more able mariners.

Captains during the early 1700s also had permanent consorts. John SWANN accompanied Robert CULLIFORD. George ROUNSIVIL died rather than abandon his captain on a sinking ship. During his trial, witnesses testified to John WALDEN's love for Bartholomew ROBERTS. Roberts' ARTICLES prohibited the introduction of a "boy or woman." Perhaps he feared that haphazard promiscuity would lead to quarrels among the men.

Large pirate fleets terrorized the South China Sea during the early 1800s. The leaders of at least three fleets were kidnapped as children, took to the pirates' trade, and were rapidly promoted. The sexual relations during their youth strengthened pirate alliances after they grew up. CHANG PAO was the lover both of CHENG I and of his widow, Cheng I SAO. KUO P'O-TAI and WU-SHIH ERH followed a similar path to advancement as fleet commanders.

HOOK (1) *(fictional metal hand; 1904 to the present)*
In J. M. Barrie's PETER PAN (1904), Captain Hook is named after the sharp, curved metal device replacing his hand. The same character reappears in the 1991 sequel HOOK. Because *Peter Pan* is well known, pirates with hooks are parodied in movie comedies, including THE PRINCESS AND THE PIRATE (1944) and THE CRIMSON PIRATE (1952).

The Neverland characters in *Peter Pan* are intended to represent figures from a child's dream, and Barrie took pains to ensure that the pirates do not resemble real people. Thus, it is not surprising that no real pirate is known to have worn a hook. However, a few pirates (Christopher NEWPORT, for example) did function with only one arm.

HOOK (2) *(motion picture; color; 1991)*
This sequel to James Barrie's PETER PAN (1904) offers a dual vision of Captain Hook (Dustin Hoffman) and his pirates. The movie treats Hook and First Mate Smee (Bob Hos-

In *Hook* (1991), Peter Banning (Robin Williams) pleads with his son to join him and leave Captain Hook (Dustin Hoffman).

kins) as figures of fun, but they also are evil villains, who actually murder a Lost Boy. The final battle between the boys and pirates alludes to earlier adventure movies, such as THE SEA HAWK (1935) and CAPTAIN BLOOD (1940).

Peter Banning (Robin Williams) is a middle-aged corporate lawyer with little time for his wife Moira (Caroline Goodall) and his children, Jack (Charlie Korsmo) and Maggie (Amber Scott). The family visits Granny Wendy (Maggie Smith) in London. The aged woman is Moira's grandmother and also raised Banning as an orphaned teenager.

When Captain Hook kidnaps Banning's children, Granny Wendy reveals that she is the "real" Wendy in Barrie's tale and that Peter Banning once was Peter Pan. Tinkerbell (Julia Roberts) leads Peter to Hook's pirate ship, where he agrees to battle Hook for the children.

Banning joins the Lost Boys, while Hook and Smee try to steal the affections of Banning's children. Led by Rufio (Dante Basco), the boys prepare him for the upcoming war by bringing out his former self. He regains his power to fly, momentarily forgets his adult life, and even kisses Tinkerbell. He soon remembers his wife and children, however, and leads the Lost Boys into battle against the pirates.

Hook murders Rufio and threatens to kill Banning/Pan. The battle is won when the gigantic crocodile that Hook had defeated and stuffed comes back to life and eats the villain. Banning returns to London. Having rediscovered the child within himself, he vows to spend more time with his family.

Steven Spielberg (who also directed *Star Wars, E. T.,* and *Schindler's List,* among others) spent lavishly to create Neverland and a replica of a pirate ship, 170 feet in length. Hundreds of stuntpersons took part in the final battle scene. *Hook* was nominated for Academy Awards for art direction and visual effects.

HOOK, CAPTAIN   See HOOK (1); HOOK (2); PETER PAN (1); PETER PAN (2).

HOORN, JAN JANSZOON VAN *(Dutch captain; Caribbean; active 1629–1633)* In 1629, Hoorn commanded a squadron in Adriaen PATER's war fleet, which unsuccessfully tried to copy Piet HEYN's capture of a Spanish TREASURE FLEET the previous year. In 1633, he assailed the American coast with four warships and six smaller vessels. Trujillo, Honduras, was quickly occupied on July 15, but the decayed town could afford only a beggarly 20 pounds of silver in ransom. Hoorn turned north to Mexico and assaulted San Francisco in the Bay of Campeche. The town put up a strong resistance and refused to pay ransom. Although Hoorn decided not to press the attack, he did seize nine ships and burned 13 more.

HORNIGOLD, BENJAMIN *(British pirate; Atlantic, Caribbean; active 1716–1717)* Hornigold sailed from NEW PROVIDENCE ISLAND in the Bahamas, with Edward TEACH (BLACKBEARD) among his crew. On one cruise, Hornigold gave Teach a captured SLOOP, and the two men sailed in CONSORT. In 1717, they pillaged six prizes off the American coast and then raided in the Caribbean. Late in the year, they captured a large French ship returning from Africa with gold, jewels, and other rich cargo. Teach left for America in the prize, while Hornigold returned to New Providence.

Hornigold submitted and was pardoned when Woodes ROGERS became governor in July 1718. He won Rogers' confidence and pursued John AUGER and other unrepentant pirates. About 1719, Rogers sent Hornigold to Mexico on a trading voyage. He and most of the crew died when their ship hit a hidden reef far from land.

HORSELEY, GILBERT *(English pirate; Caribbean; active 1574–1575)* Horseley sailed from Plymouth in November 1574 with a lightly armed, 18-ton vessel carrying 25 men. His ship took a Spanish fishing boat off Morocco, went on to Nombre de Dios in Panama, and attacked coastal shipping.

Between January and March 1575, Horseley's small force apparently joined a larger French band under Captain SYLVESTER. The combined crews ascended the San Juan River in Nicaragua and looted several boats. Their raid was unusually daring, since—unlike the open sea—the San Juan provided no safe escape route. Returning to western Panama, the pirates captured and cruelly plundered Veragua.

Horseley made it back to Plymouth in June, bribed an ADMIRALTY official, and landed his booty at Arundel. Only 15 of the original crew survived, but they divided substantial booty.

(See also BARKER, ANDREW; NOBLE, JOHN; OXENHAM, JOHN.)

HOUT, GEORGE *(English buccaneer; Pacific; active 1685–1686)* Among those crossing the Isthmus of Panama early in 1685 to join Edward Davis' larger company of raiders. A defeat by Peruvian ships on June

8 caused angry quarrels, and the pirates split up into small groups.

From May 1686 Hout was part of a band under Captain LE PICARD and Captain TOWNLEY. When Townley was killed on August 22, Le Picard assumed overall command of the gang. However, the Englishmen insisted on having their own ship and elected Hout captain. He led them in raids on Panama City, Nicoya (in Nicaragua), and Guayaquil, Ecuador.

HOWARD PYLE'S BOOK OF PIRATES (short stories; 1921)

Howard PYLE adds two additional stories and illustrations to the four stories in STOLEN TREASURE (1907). "Blueskin the Pirate" (first published in 1890) is set in 1750. Levi West returns to Delaware from nautical adventures and deals harshly with his half-wit stepbrother, Hiram White. When West is caught burying treasure, his scars prove that he is Captain Blueskin.

"Captain Scarfield" (1900) tells about a man with a split personality. Eleazer Cooper is a devoutly pacifist Quaker in Philadelphia, a "model of business integrity and of domestic responsibility." He is also Captain Scarfield, a murderous sea robber, who keeps a mulatto wife in the Bahama Islands. The young and dashing Lieutenant Mainwaring discovers Cooper's secret, kills him in battle, and marries his wealthy young niece.

HOWARD, THOMAS (British pirate; Caribbean, Atlantic, Indian Ocean, Red Sea; active 1698–1703)

Having squandered his inheritance, Daniel DEFOE tells us, Howard fled to Jamaica and stole a canoe with other drifters. Taking one vessel after another, the villains ended up with a 24-gun ship and elected Howard QUARTERMASTER. They marauded off North America in 1698, crossed the Atlantic, and plundered more victims along the West African coast.

Having arrived at MADAGASCAR about 1700, the pirates ran their ship onto a reef. While most of the crew were taking off cargo to lighten the ship, Howard and some others absconded with all the treasure. Howard in turn was abandoned one day, when his companion made off while he was hunting. He was picked up by George BOOTH and (after Booth's death) cruised with John BOWEN. When Bowen wrecked the *Speaker* late in 1701, Howard went back to Madagascar, left Bowen, and stayed for a time at Saint Augustine's Bay.

With some other brigands, Howard seized the 36-gun *Prosperous*, was chosen captain, and joined forces with Bowen in 1702. The pirates looted the British merchantman *Pembroke* in March 1703 at Johanna Island (Anjouan) in the Comoros. In August, Howard and Bowen again joined in consort in the Red Sea, where they captured two Indian vessels and more than £70,000 in booty.

The pirates divided their plunder at Rajapura, India, where both crews transferred to the largest Indian ship. Howard retired, a rich man, somewhere on the Indian coast. There, Defoe related, "Howard married a Woman of the Country, and being a morose ill natur'd Fellow, and using her ill, he was murder'd by her Relations."

(See also SELECTED BIBLIOGRAPHY: Defoe, *General History*; Grey, *Pirates*.)

HUDGA MOHAMMED SALAMIA REIS (Barbary corsair; Atlantic, Mediterranean; 1793)

Hudga Reis captured an American ship (flying the British flag) near Gibraltar and enslaved its crew at ALGIERS. John Foss, one of Hudga's captives, published an account of his adventures.

HUGHS, WILLIAM (English pirate; Atlantic; 1611)

Trusted lieutenant of Thomas HUSSEY, Hughs was one of Richard BISHOP's Irish confederation. Early in 1611, as he lay dying surrounded by the fleet's captains, Hussey willed Hughs his property and ship—probably the *Black Raven*, a 250-ton, 20-gun FLYBOAT. At the end of the summer, Hughs accompanied Peter EASTON's squadron to West Africa and across the Atlantic to Newfoundland.

HUSSAYN KALYGHI REIS (Barbary corsair; Mediterranean; active 1670s and 1680s)

A convert to Islam from southern Italy, Hussayn Reis became wealthy as a corsair, was named CAPTAIN OF THE SEA in 1682, and built an imposing mosque in an oasis outside TRIPOLI. He was executed in 1690, after an opposing political faction arranged a mutiny among the corsairs.

HUSSEY, THOMAS (English pirate; Atlantic; active 1610–1611)

One of Richard BISHOP's pirate confederation based in Ireland. In 1610, he bought a three-quarter share in Captain PARKER's warship and became its captain, capturing prizes off the French coast. At his death in 1611, he left his ship and other property to William HUGHS.

HYBRISTAS (Greek corsair; Ionian Sea; 190 B.C.)

An ARCHPIRATE from AETOLIA, Hybristas recruited men on Cephallania (Kefallinía) Island. His band controlled the Gulf of Corinth, preventing supplies from reaching Rome's eastern armies. Their raids took place during a war (192–188) that pitted Rome, Pergamum, and Rhodes against Aetolia and Syria. Hybristas may have worked for the Syrian king, Antiochus III, who hired NIKANDROS to harry the Romans in the Aegean.

I

IBRAHIM AL-HADJ REIS *(Moroccan corsair; Mediterranean; 1696)* Ibrahim Reis ran his ship aground on a sandbar while entering SALÉ harbor.

IBRAHIM "BECCAZZA" REIS *(Barbary corsair; Mediterranean; active 1630s)* A Frenchman from Marseilles and a pilot for the KNIGHTS OF MALTA, Ibrahim "Beccazza" Reis was captured, converted to Islam, and became a notable corsair at TRIPOLI. In 1638, the knights captured Ibrahim's three galleys after a fierce battle (more than 200 Muslims died) in the southern Adriatic.

IBRAHIM IBN RAHMAN *(Arab pirate; active 1816–1819)* See QAWASIM.

IBRAHIM LUBAREZ REIS *(Moroccan corsair; Mediterranean; early 1800s)* The emperor of MOROCCO respected Ibrahim and sent him as ambassador to Spain. In August 1803, commanding the 22-gun FRIGATE *Mirboka*, he took an American BRIG off Málaga, Spain. Soon after, the warship *Philadelphia* came upon the *Mirboka* and her prize. Threatened with hanging as a pirate, Ibrahim produced a letter from the governor of Tangier, directing him to capture vessels of the U. S. and other nations.

This incident during the First BARBARY WAR suggests that Morocco was supporting TRIPOLI. However, the em-peror came to terms when American frigates arrived at Tangier. Ibrahim's piratical cruise was blamed on the governor of Tangier, who supposedly had acted without the emperor's knowledge.

(See also PASSES.)

ICELAND *(pirate victim; Atlantic Ocean; 17th century)* Iceland was raided in 1614 by James GENTLE-MAN and William CLARK. Sailing from SALÉ, Jan JANSSEN carried off at least 400 prisoners in 1627.

ILANUNS *(Malayan pirates; South China Sea, Bay of Bengal, and adjacent waters; 18th and 19th centuries)* Sailing from Mindinao Island in the Philippines, the Ilanuns built forts throughout the Sulu Archipelago and along the coasts of Borneo. The fiercest and most powerful non-European corsairs, they plundered between the Philippines and India, often undertaking two- or three-year voyages. They attacked both native and European vessels and also raided coastal villages for slaves. Although they might show mercy to Asian crewmen, they slaughtered Europeans because of their hatred of Spanish authorities in the Philippines.

Precisely when the Ilanuns turned pirate is not known. William DAMPIER, who stayed with them during the 17th century, described them as a peaceful people. Although British forces invaded Malaya and Borneo from the 1840s, Ilanun pirates remained active into the 1870s.

Ilanun warship. From Francis Marryat, *Borneo and the Indian Archipelago* (London, 1848).

Their warships were large PRAHUS, built sharp in the brow and wide in the beam. Some exceeded 90 feet in length and carried a hundred rowers. Many had brass cannon and swivel guns, although Ilanun warriors preferred to overcome the enemy with spears and swords. Going into battle, they arrayed themselves in scarlet, with coats of mail and feathered headdresses (dyed, some said, in human blood).

The Ilanuns cruised in squadrons of 30 or 40 warships, although some fleets included 200 vessels of various sizes. One chief of high rank commanded the entire fleet. The captain and warriors on each ship usually were related. If needed, the rowers and other slaves fought alongside the free warriors. The chiefs and freemen plundered first, and the slaves took what was left.

In May 1838, six Ilanun warships assaulted Malayan, Chinese, and European vessels along the eastern Malay Peninsula. They were driven off by a British warship, which destroyed one Ilanun vessel and severely damaged the others. Seventeen pirates were captured and imprisoned in India for acts of piracy near western Borneo.

ILLYRIANS *(ancient pirates; Adriatic Sea, Mediterranean; 600 B.C.–A.D. 9)* The Greek and Roman name (*Illyrii*) for a group of related Indo-European tribes, living along the entire eastern shore of the ADRIATIC Sea, from Trieste to Durazzo. From this pirate coast, raiders attacked ships in the Adriatic and Mediterranean and pillaged along the coasts of Italy and Greece.

Piratical groups settled the islands of Corfu and Levkás during the second millennium B.C. As Greek commerce grew from the 600s, Illyrian raiders carried their attacks far into the Mediterranean. Since the Illyrian tribes never united into one state, their raids fell off during the fourth century, when strong rulers dominated neighboring Mac-

edonia. As the Macedonian Empire weakened, Illyrian pirates again attacked in force. They were especially aggressive under TEUTA, queen of the Ardiaei.

A Roman army defeated Queen Teuta during the First Illyrian War (229–228), and the Ardiaei agreed to a treaty forbidding pirate attacks. In 220, DEMETRIUS OF PHAROS, who had succeeded Teuta as ruler, joined the Illyrian chief SCERDILAIDAS in a piratical expedition. The Romans sent a second army to Illyria in 219 (the Second Illyrian War), which conquered Pharos and put Demetrius to flight.

Raids against cities on the east coast of Italy revived some 40 years later, in 181. The Romans blamed pirates from both ISTRIA and Illyria, and they accused King GENTHIUS of Illyria of encouraging the marauders. Roman armies again invaded southern Illyria in 168, when Genthius allied with King Persius of Macedonia during the Third Macedonian War.

The Romans divided Genthius' realm into three smaller regions, whose rulers apparently did not sponsor piracy. Sporadic minor raids continued from DALMATIA, the northern region of Illyria, until the Romans finally annexed the entire coastline along the Adriatic in A.D. 9.

"INCHCAPE ROCK, THE" *(poem, 19th century)* A short poem by Robert Southey (1774–1843), highly regarded during the 19th century. The Inchcape Rock is a dangerous sandstone reef off the Firth of Tay in southeastern Scotland. After 70 vessels (one a 74-gun battleship) were wrecked during a storm in 1799, a 100-foot lighthouse was erected.

Local legends say the abbot of Arborath monastery had set up a bell to mark the reef. As Southey's poem tells the tale, Sir Ralph the Rover cut the bell from its buoy to play an evil joke. As he returns with rich plunder years later, Sir Ralph is wrecked on the reef and drowns with his piratical crew.

INDJA MOHAMMED REIS *(Barbary corsair; Mediterranean; 1775)* Indja Reis captured a ship carrying hides, timber, and sugar. Its sale at ALGIERS yielded 341 shares, each worth more than 126 gold *reales*.

(See also BOOTY.)

INGHIRAMI, JACOPO *(Knight of Saint Stephen; Mediterranean; 1565–1624)* Under Inghirami's command as admiral (from 1599 to 1618), the Florentine corsairs scored their most striking successes. Inghirami's contemporaries praised him for spreading terror throughout the Mediterranean. He excelled as a military and naval commander, understood the value of espionage, and compiled extensive information about enemy territories.

Inghirami personally commanded many raids against the BARBARY COAST, Greece, and Turkey. Taking five galleys to Greece in 1605, he captured large merchant ships and looted PREVESA and Nisiros Island. (The squadron ransomed its prisoners in the IONIAN ISLANDS.) He cruised off southern Turkey and Syria in 1606, seized ships from the Alexandria-to-Istanbul convoy, and pillaged Anamur and Samandag. In September 1607, an assault on Bône in Algeria took 1,500 prisoners and extraordinarily rich booty.

Admiral Inghirami returned to the attack from 1610 to 1617, taking further rich prizes and plundering towns in Algeria, Greece, and Turkey. In 1615, the Florentines sailed in partnership with a Spanish squadron and kept 12 vessels as their share of the loot. Off eastern Greece in 1616, Inghirami's five galleys severely damaged MURAT THE YOUNGER's squadron carrying a new BEYLERBEY to Algiers. After retiring in February 1618, Inghirami returned to active service (as "General of the Sea") in 1621 and led several more cruises in the Near East.

IONIAN ISLANDS *(corsair havens; Ionian Sea; 13th through 15th centuries)* These islands are situated off Greece's western coast and include Corfu (Kérkira), Cephalonia (Kefallinia), Zante (Zákinthos), Leucadia/Santa Maura (Levkás), Ithaca (Itháki), Cythera (Kálamos), and Paxo (Paxoi). As the BYZANTINE EMPIRE weakened, they became bases for Greek and Italian pirates. Beginning with Corfu in 1386, Venice took over the islands, ruling them until 1797. The Greek republic imposed the current names as it took control during the 19th century.

(See also ILLYRIANS; MARGARITONE; SYBURTES OF PETRA; TOCCO, ANTONIO DI; VETRANO, LEONE.)

IRISH, WILLIAM *(English captain; Caribbean; born 1561?, active 1587–1591)* A gentleman from the Isle of Wight, Irish conducted at least three West Indian plunder raids for Sir George CAREY. He took several prizes in 1587 and probably returned in 1588. In 1587, he also may have visited the ROANOKE colony in Virginia. In 1590, commanding the *Bark Young*, he looted several vessels, possibly in consort with Abraham COCKE. As he returned to England via Newfoundland, several French ships snatched away his Spanish prize.

Commanding three ships in 1591, Irish sometimes consorted with squadrons under William LANE and Christopher NEWPORT. On June 13, a Spanish patrol attacked Irish's ships and one of Lane's (commanded by William CRASTON). The *Bark Burr*'s ammunition blew up, killing most of the crew. Without trying to rescue survivors, Irish escaped to the smaller *Swallow* and continued to accompany the Lane squadron. However, since their consortship agreement had expired, the ADMIRALTY court later denied Irish's claims to share in Lane's prizes.

(See also SELECTED BIBLIOGRAPHY: Andrews, *Elizabethan*; Quinn, *Roanoke*.)

IRVING, WASHINGTON *(American author; 1783–1859)* By preserving legends about William KIDD in three short stories, Irving helped create the myth of CAPTAIN KIDD'S TREASURE. "THE DEVIL AND TOM WALKER" and "WOLFERT WEBBER" appeared in 1824, "GUESTS FROM GIBBET ISLAND" in 1855. Among the first American writers, Irving used themes that later became standard in pirate stories, including ghosts haunting buried treasure, curiously marked treasure spots, and sinister strangers bragging in seaside inns. Although they were unsuccessful at the time, the 1824 stories inspired later books such as TREASURE ISLAND.

ISIDORUS *(Cilician corsair; Mediterranean; first century B.C.)* Isidorus reportedly was the first to lead large-scale raids throughout the eastern Mediterranean from bases in CILICIA. The Cilicians were allies of MITHRIDATES during his wars with Rome from 89 to 66. In 72, the Roman general LUCULLUS captured 13 enemy warships making for the Aegean island of Lemnos. During the battle, the Romans killed the enemy admiral—who was named Isidorus and who presumably was the Cilician corsair.

ISLAND, THE (1) *(novel; 1979)* Peter Benchley, author of *Jaws*, imagines a BUCCANEER colony surviving to the present with its way of life intact. Blair Maynard, a New York journalist, visits the Caribbean to investigate why hundreds of ships have vanished. Planning only a short stay, Maynard takes along Justin, his 12-year-old son. Their chartered plane crashes in the Turks and Caicos group, and they are captured by pirates living on an isolated island.

The pirates suspend Maynard's execution so he can console a dead pirate's wife. Maynard works at transcribing the pirates' records. He learns that François L'OLONNAIS—EXQUEMELIN's most bloodthirsty villain—founded

A colony of buccaneers—miraculously surviving to the present day—threatens to hang Blair Maynard (Michael Caine) in *The Island* (1980).

the colony in 1671. Exquemelin wrote that Indians ate L'Olonnais. *Island* assumes that he escaped to the Caicos with 20 men and six kidnapped whores. The little band settled the island, isolated in the dangerous Caicos banks. Ruled by hereditary chiefs, their descendants have pillaged passing ships for three centuries. Their crimes have increased in recent years because an unscrupulous American professor tells them when valuable prizes are coming.

Young Justin joins the pirate band, while Maynard suffers though various bloody adventures. Maynard is condemned to die but escapes to the hills. Just then, the pirates seize a coast guard cutter and massacre its crew. Maynard swims out to the vessel and kills everyone but son Justin with a 50-caliber machine gun.

The Island provides a historically accurate description of the buccaneer band. In more romantic novels, Caribbean pirates sailed on immaculate boats wearing elegant clothes captured from Spanish noblemen. Benchley depicts the buccaneer reality—mosquitoes, syphilis, alcoholism, bad food, rotten clothing, and primitive sanitation.

ISLAND, THE (2) *(motion picture; color; released 1980)*
Michael Ritchie directed and Peter Benchley wrote the script, which faithfully adapts his own novel. Blair Maynard (Michael Caine) and his son Justin (Jeffrey Frank) are captured by BUCCANEERS, whose chief (David Warner) is descended from François L'OLONNAIS. The pirates teach Justin their trade, and they allow Maynard to live until he can impregnate Beth (Angela McGregor). Though *The Island* lost money at the box office, it presents an accurate picture of buccaneer life.

ISOLA, FERRANDO DELL' *(Italian pirate; Mediterranean; 1497)*
Isola was captain of a large galley that attacked Christian and Muslim shipping along the North African coast.

ISTRIA *(pirate haven; Adriatic Sea; third and second centuries B.C.)*
Istria is a peninsula (modern Istra) at the Adriatic's northern end, inhabited toward the east by the Istri, an ILLYRIAN tribe practicing piracy by 300. Allied with DEMETRIUS OF PHAROS, the Istri in 221 seized grain ships supplying Roman armies in northern Italy. Two Roman armies devastated the pirate bases in 221 and 220 but did not occupy the region.

In 181, pirate raids again endangered Italian coastal areas. A Roman official accused King GENTHIUS of Illyria of sponsoring the marauders. The Istri also were blamed for attacks on the new Roman colony at Aquileia. Roman armies defeated the Istri in 178 and 177 and captured their chief settlement. In 168 the Romans also routed King Genthius and divided southern Illyria into three smaller regions, ending Istrian piracy.

ITA, PIETER *(Dutch admiral; Caribbean; 1628)*
Ita may have been an older brother of the Dutch admiral, Michiel Adriaenszoon de Ruyter. After visiting Guyana in 1616 and 1623, Ita took 12 ships to the Caribbean in 1628 for the DUTCH WEST INDIA COMPANY. They captured numerous Spanish prizes, but an unfortunate cannon shot sank another ship carrying African slaves. After reuniting off Cuba, the Dutch made for the Dry Tortugas to watch for Spanish TREASURE SHIPS. Since his own force was too small to attack the fleets leaving from CARTAGENA and SAN JUAN DE ULÚA, Ita hoped to capture the two GALLEONS from Honduras.

Warned of Ita's presence, the Cartagena and Mexican fleets stayed in port. After getting additional weapons from Havana, Commander Alvaro de la Cerda decided to sail with the Honduras fleet. His galleons carried several hundred crewmen and were armed with 20 cannon.

Ita attacked two miles from Havana. Cerda tried to escape along the coast into the port, but the faster Dutch ships prevented this maneuver. Throughout the morning of August 1, a terrible battle was fought in full view of Havana. Cerda finally beached his ships and began to disembark their crews. The Dutch continued to fire, killing more than half the Spanish crewmen.

Although the captured ships had to be destroyed, they contained rich cargoes of silver, indigo, ginger, and hides. After services thanking God for the victory, Ita sailed for home. His departure indirectly helped Piet HEYN capture the even richer Mexican galleons. Spanish authorities were unaware that the Dutch had two independent war fleets in the region. When Ita left, the commanders of the Mexican ships thought the coast was clear and sailed into Heyn's trap near Havana.

Ita returned to the West Indies in 1630 and assumed command of 25 Dutch warships in the region. His squadrons took only six or seven unspectacular prizes, and they failed to repeat Piet Heyn's capture of a treasure fleet in 1628. To escape detection, the Cartagena fleet avoided the sea lanes between Florida and the Bahamas and instead took an unusual route through the Windward Passage and the Caicos Islands.

(See also SELECTED BIBLIOGRAPHY: Goslinga, *Dutch.*)

IVAS REIS (1)   *(Barbary corsair; Mediterranean; 1679–1680)*   Of Greek origin, Ivas commanded the 38-gun *Flying Horse* at TRIPOLI.

IVAS REIS (2)   *(Barbary corsair; Mediterranean; 1679)*   A Greek nicknamed "Little Ivas," he was captain of the 22-gun *Tamberlain* at TRIPOLI.

J

JACKMAN, CAPTAIN *(English buccaneer; Caribbean; active 1663–1665)* Jackman assailed Mexico with Sir Christopher MYNGS in 1663 and raided Mexico and Nicaragua with John MORRIS and Sir Henry MORGAN in 1664 and 1665.

JACKSON, WILLIAM *(English pirate; Caribbean; active 1637–1645)* Jackson led the most ambitious assault on the Spanish Caribbean since Sir Francis DRAKE's 1595 expedition. While he took only moderate plunder, Jackson's raid exposed the military weakness of the Spanish colonies. His reports helped to persuade the English government to launch the invasion that conquered Jamaica in 1655.

In 1638, London and Cornish merchants (including the KILLIGREWS) financed a plunder voyage under letters of REPRISAL from the PROVIDENCE COMPANY. After stopping at PROVIDENCE ISLAND in April 1639, Jackson raided up the Nicaragua River, looted several Spanish ships, and sold their cargoes in Boston in September. At the end of 1640, he returned to England with a captured ship carrying indigo worth £15,000. His actual booty was much richer, since he had sold much of his cargo in Ireland to cheat his backers.

Pleased with Jackson's success, the Providence Company and London merchants supplied three large warships that sailed in July 1642, with Samuel AXE second-in-command. Jackson recruited four more ships and 800 men at Barbados and Saint Kitts and gave William ROUS command of the land forces.

Jackson headed for Venezuela in November. His squadron plundered the pearl fishers near Margarita Island but took little plunder. Maracaibo was captured and held to ransom in December, and several smaller towns were pillaged. After taking on provisions at Hispaniola, Jackson captured the Jamaican capital of Santiago de la Vega (modern Spanish Town) in April. The inhabitants had time to hide their valuables and paid only 7,000 pesos in ransom. But Jamaica's fertility impressed Jackson, and his men liked the island so much that 23 deserted to the Spaniards.

Guided by Thomas CROMWELL, Jackson's men captured Trujillo, Honduras, and pillaged coastal towns in Costa Rica and Panama. The winter of 1643 was spent in raids near CARTAGENA, the summer of 1644 in attacks against small towns in Guatemala and the Gulf of Mexico. After splitting the booty at Bermuda in November, Jackson returned to Plymouth in March 1645. Busy fighting a civil war, the government took no action against Jackson despite Spanish complaints.

JAFER REIS *(Barbary corsair; Mediterranean; active 1580s)* Jafer Reis was a French convert commanding a GALIOT at ALGIERS. Captured near Ibiza in 1586, he escaped from a Naples prison in 1591.

JAMES, MICHAEL *(English pirate; Atlantic; 1545)* Commanding the *Mary Figge* of Plymouth, James pillaged Flemish ships and seized a Spanish vessel sailing toward Chester. For more than two days, while he plundered its cargo of woad and iron, James imprisoned the captured crew "faste shytte uppe in the breadehowse . . . wher they had noo space to stande nor sytte but dyd lye one apon an other lyke hogges faste bounde in ropes and cordes." After threatening to sink the ship and men, James finally freed his captives. The cargo was sold to merchants in Cardiff and Bristol.

(See also SELECTED BIBLIOGRAPHY: SUMPTER, LEONARD; Connell-Smith, *Forerunners*.)

JANISSARIES *(Barbary soldiers; Mediterranean; 16th through 18th centuries)* An elite infantry corps in the OTTOMAN EMPIRE. Specifically, Janissaries comprised the military garrisons—recruited elsewhere in the Ottoman possessions—that ruled the three BARBARY states.

ARUJ and KHEIREDDIN BARBAROSSA instituted the Janissary system in ALGIERS, and it was extended to TUNIS and TRIPOLI as they were conquered. Authority was vested in the entire garrison, legally and socially set aside from the rest of the population. Aruj modeled the Janissaries after the KNIGHTS HOSPITALERS of RHODES, where he had been enslaved. Like the Knights, Jannissaries paid no local taxes and were subject only to their own laws and officers.

Corsair vessels collected new recruits each year at the principal ports in the eastern Mediterranean. Janissaries enlisted for about 20 years, rose through the ranks solely on seniority, and lived in elegant barracks. They served with city garrisons, on field expeditions that collected taxes from inland tribes, and on government galleys and ships.

When off duty, Janissaries could practice any legal occupation, including (after 1586 in Algiers) piracy. By the 16th century, all corsair ships carried Janissaries, who did most of the fighting. The soldiers took orders from their general (*agha*), while the seamen obeyed their captain (REIS). However, this dual system of command seldom caused problems during battles.

The Janissaries never enrolled native soldiers, and they restricted entry by the sons of Janissaries and native women. They did accept western Europeans as did the corsairs' corporation (TAIFE REISI). European RENEGADES had to convert to Islam. But this was a relatively easy step, since strict Muslim orthodoxy was not demanded of corsairs.

JANSSEN (JANSZ), JAN *(Dutch corsair; Mediterranean; active 1600–1631)* Born at Haarlem, Jansssen raided the Spanish under Dutch license and then turned pirate, attacking ships of any nation including his own. (From a strange patriotic sentiment, he still raised the Dutch flag when assaulting Spanish vessels.) Captured off the Canary Islands in 1618 by corsairs from ALGIERS, Janssen converted to Islam (as Murat Reis) and

sailed as mate for SOLIMAN REIS. After Soliman died in 1619, he moved to SALÉ and married a Moroccan, although he already had a Dutch wife.

During a cruise in 1622, Janssen put in at Veere in Holland for supplies. Despite the pitiful appeals of his wife and children, he refused to return. His crew also rejected pleas to desert, "as they were too much bitten of the Spaniards and too much hankering after booty." In fact, many seamen at the port flocked to join Janssen's pirates.

Over the next two years, Janssen captured several rich prizes—including at least three Dutch merchantmen—and Salé's corsairs elected him their admiral in 1624. In 1627, he raided ICELAND, a daring feat of navigation. Guided by an escaped Danish slave, his three ships (with English helmsmen) looted Reykjavik and enslaved at least 400 Icelanders. Four years later, an assault on Baltimore, Ireland, netted another 127 slaves.

Soon after he sold his Irish slaves at Algiers, Janssen was captured by the KNIGHTS OF MALTA. Free again in 1640, he returned to Morocco. As a kind of pension, the sultan named him governor of Oualidia, where Lysbeth Janssen, one of his Dutch children, briefly joined him.

(See also TAIFE REISI.)

JENNINGS, HENRY *(English pirate; Caribbean, Atlantic; 1715–1717)* Sailing from Jamaica, Jennings raided French and Spanish commerce during the War of the Spanish Succession (1702–1713). In July 1715, the Spanish TREASURE FLEET from PORTOBELO was destroyed by a hurricane off southeastern Florida. The governor of Havana sent a salvage crew, which had fished up considerable amounts of silver by 1716.

Aided by Jamaican merchants, Jennings got together three small ships and about 300 men. They swooped down on the salvagers, drove away about 60 soldiers, and made off with about 350,000 pesos awaiting shipment to Havana. As they returned to Jamaica, the pirates seized a Spanish ship carrying rich cargo and another 60,000 pesos.

The governor of Jamaica warned Jennings that he could not ignore Cuban complaints. After selling their booty at auction, Jennings and his followers found a haven on NEW PROVIDENCE ISLAND in the Bahamas. (Some sources indicate Jennings already had raided from New Providence in 1714.)

Though the Providence pirates soon broke up into various gangs, Jennings remained one of the leading captains. When the English government offered a general pardon in 1717, he and his crew surrendered at Bermuda. It is not known whether he returned to Jamaica or remained at Providence after Woodes ROGERS became governor.

JENNINGS, JOHN *(English pirate; Atlantic; active 1600–1612)* Jennings cruised under Dutch letters of MARQUE after England outlawed piracy in 1603. Hannibal Vivian, VICE-ADMIRAL of South Cornwall, arrested

Jennings and other pirates in 1607, but let them buy their freedom. (Jennings paid £140.) From 1608 to 1611, he joined Richard BISHOP's pirate confederation based at MAMORA and in Ireland. In 1612, Jennings surrendered his ship in Ireland, under a general pardon allowing him to keep his booty. It included clusters of pearls, rubies, and diamonds, as well as coins and goods worth thousands of pounds.

JEWISH PIRATES   See GALILEE.

JOL, CORNELIS CORNELISZOON (Dutch pirate; Atlantic, Caribbean; died 1641) Born at Scheveningen, Jol spent most of life at sea. While very young, he lost a leg in some battle or accident. He used his wooden substitute skillfully, moving as nimbly as most of his crewmen.

During at least 10 raids outfitted by the DUTCH WEST INDIA COMPANY, Jol's fiery attacks terrified Spanish colonists. Although Piet HEYN took more booty, Jol's assaults were so numerous and deadly that his Spanish enemies nicknamed him *el pirata*. He was "the pirate" above all others, and mere rumors of his arrival created panic.

With little education and fewer words—most of them unprintable—Jol's quick temper, roughness, and lack of tact were as legendary as his courage. Perhaps because of his own independent ways, he was among the few pirates embarrassed by slavery. At least twice, he set Spanish slave ships free to avoid dealing with their cargo.

Jol operated from 1626 to 1635 as captain and owner of the *Otter*—a swift Dutch YACHT as dreaded as its master. In consort with other Dutch marauders, he took several prizes off the Brazilian coast in 1626. He again assailed Brazil in 1627 with Dierck van UYTGEEST's squadron. There he led the capture of three CARAVELS with valuable tropical cargoes.

In 1630, Jol's *Otter* formed part of the fleets that raided Brazil and the West Indies under Hendrick LONCQ, Dierick RUYTERS, and Pieter ITA. He returned from mid-1631 until mid-1632, scouring the entire Caribbean and taking nine prizes alone or in consort with other raiders. During another cruise from the fall of 1632 to May 1634, he personally caught three prizes and was in the vanguard of squadrons that seized or destroyed at least 30 more.

Jol's daring exploits in 1635 increased his fame. He was ordered to wait at Curaçao for a Dutch fleet but soon tired of guard duty. Joined only by another small yacht, he determined to invade Santiago de Cuba. Jol's two ships flew the Spanish flag, and his crew wore the monks' robes. Thus disguised, the Dutch entered the harbor under the guns of the Spanish fort. Six or seven ships were pillaged, although most turned out to be empty.

From Santiago, the two Dutch yachts made for Havana and the Venezuelan coast. Near CARTAGENA, Jol had to run from four FRIGATES sent to arrest him. After accidentally meeting two other Dutch pirates, he convinced them to join him and returned to capture one of the frigates. He released his 150 prisoners and demanded that

the Spanish reciprocate. Disgusted to find that Cartagena contained only two Dutch prisoners, he burned the captured frigate in the harbor.

Altogether Jol looted at least 11 vessels in 1635, taking substantial amounts of silver, tobacco, copper, and indigo. As he neared his home port in Holland, he ran into a band of privateers from Dunkirk. Although he put up a stiff fight, his beloved *Otter* was captured, and he was imprisoned until a prisoner exchange in May 1636.

In the fall of 1636, Jol headed for Curaçao—which the Dutch had captured in 1634—commanding a 260-ton warship and two yachts. For the next six months, he cruised back and forth from the Gulf of Mexico to Île-à-Vache, off southwestern Haiti. One trip from east to west against the wind was made in only 17 days—to this day an extraordinary feat.

In August 1637, Jol hovered off Havana, hunting the TREASURE FLEET leaving PORTOBELO. When one of the Spanish vessels fell behind, Jol and seven other pirate ships—both Dutch and British—swooped down for the kill. In the confusion, with each of the greedy pirates trying to keep the others from the booty, their prey escaped.

Despite this setback, Jol stayed off Havana, hoping for better luck with the smaller Mexican treasure fleet. On September 6, he was suddenly trapped between the Portobelo and Mexican fleets, which left on the same day. Jol maintained his nerve and boldly attacked one of the smaller merchantmen in the windward Portobelo fleet. Although two Spanish galleons rallied to its support, Jol seized his prey and its cargo of lucrative tropical products.

After these successes, the Dutch West India Company believed that Jol could duplicate Piet Heyn's capture of a Spanish treasure fleet. With 17 or 18 ships, he reached the Dry Tortugas in the summer of 1638, where many other Dutch pirates joined up with his fleet. On August 30, the Dutch encountered the Portobelo treasure fleet of eight galleons and seven smaller vessels. Jol plowed his own ship into the side of Spanish galleon and tried to board her. But most of the Dutch captains were frightened by the huge Spanish vessels and refused to join the battle. Jol replaced five of the captains under his command, but the Spaniards managed to find refuge in SAN JUAN DE ULÚA.

Jol battled the Spaniards in the North Atlantic in 1639 (the "Battle of the Downs") and then returned to raids along the Brazilian coast. In July 1640, he commanded the final Dutch attempt—with 24 ships and almost 4,000 men—to capture a Spanish treasure fleet. However, the Spaniards learned of his mission and kept their fleets in port. Jol blockaded Havana and plundered Matanzas, but took little booty.

In 1641, Jol's fleet captured slave depots at Luanda and São Thomé. West African diseases proved more deadly than the Portuguese defenders, and Jol perished with hundreds of his men. He was buried with pomp at the main church, but the Portuguese dug up and dispersed his bones when they retook the town a year later.

(See also SELECTED BIBLIOGRAPHY: Goslinga, *Dutch.*)

JOLIFFE, EDWARD *(English pirate; Atlantic; active 1600s)* Joliffe sailed from Ireland with the help of Irish ADMIRALTY officers. Once, when the crew of a Dutch warship boarded his ship, he forced them to flee by threatening to set fire to his powder magazine.

JOLLY ROGER *(pirate flag; Atlantic, Indian Ocean; about 1700–1725)* A FLAG with a black background, portraying (usually in white) an item symbolizing death. In popular legend, every pirate flag displayed a skull above crossed bones. In fact, there was ample variation, since every crew wanted a unique flag. Some did portray a human skull or "death's head." But other symbols also were used, including skeletons, hourglasses, and weapons such as CUTLASSES, swords, and spears.

Only Edward ENGLAND showed the "skull and crossbones" in its pure form. Christopher CONDENT's banner repeated the same symbol three times. Henry EVERY's showed the skull looking to the right. John QUELCH was among the first to fly a black banner. In 1703, his flag showed a human body. One hand held an hourglass, the other a bleeding heart pierced by a spear. Edward TEACH (BLACKBEARD) used a similar design, replacing the body with a skeleton.

British and British-American pirates invented the black flag in about 1700. Before this time, pirates attacked under their national banner. During the 1600s, Caribbean BUCCANEERS flew the British or the French flag. Some also showed a red flag (symbolizing blood) when they refused to give quarter.

The Jolly Roger's origin is not known. A British warship saw a pirate with a black flag in 1700, and Henry JENNINGS probably flew the Jolly Roger in 1716. Thomas COCKLYN, Olivier LA BOUCHE, and Howell DAVIS all showed black flags off West Africa in 1719. Perhaps the usage was popularized at NEW PROVIDENCE ISLAND in the Bahamas, where all except Davis had lived. Black flags became common in the 1720s among pirates raiding in the Atlantic or from MADAGASCAR.

The Jolly Roger was meant to terrify the pirates' prey. In 1719, Captain SNELGRAVE noted that "said flag is intended to frighten honest merchantmen into surrender on penalty of being murdered if they do not." Some reports say the Jolly Roger was run up first, to signify an offer of quarter. If the victim refused to surrender, the red flag was flown to show that the offer had been withdrawn.

The symbols portrayed on the Roger have obvious meanings—death, violence, and limited time. The name Jolly Roger probably came from the English word *roger*, referring both to a begging vagabond and to the Devil ("Old Roger"). Several more fanciful origins have been suggested. According to one version, French buccaneers called the red flag the *joli rouge* ("beautiful red"), pro-

Captain Red (Walter Matthau) unfurls the Jolly Roger in *Pirates* (1986).

nouncing the final e. Another legend derives Jolly Roger from an Indian pirate named Ali Rajah, which British sailors pronounced "Olly Roger." (See also SELECTED BIBLIOGRAPHY: Botting, *Pirates*; Pringle, *Jolly Roger*; Rediker, *Devil*; Snelgrave, *New Account.*)

JONES, DAVID *(English pirate; Red Sea; active 1634–1636)* Jones was sailing master of William COBB's *Roebuck*, which captured three Indian ships with substantial booty. Jones led the crew in torturing captives.

(See also DAVY JONES' LOCKER.)

JUAN FERNÁNDEZ ISLANDS *(pirate haven; Pacific; 1624–1722)* Several islands about 400 miles east of Valparaiso, first discovered in 1574 and now owned by Chile. The largest (about 75 square miles) is Mas-a-Tierra ("Closer In"), renamed Alexander Selkirk Island in 1966. Although rugged and mountainous, Mas-a-Tierra provides ample wood, clear water, and meat from goats, seals, and sea-lions. The climate is mild year round, and a sheltered bay offers protection from strong winds.

Mas-a-Tierra was an invaluable base for raiders entering the Pacific around Cape Horn or through the Strait of Magellan. Many ships were damaged by the fierce southern storms, and crews were ravaged by SCURVY and other diseases. For pirates, the uninhabited Juan Fernández group was a safer stop than any Spanish port.

Dutch explorers rediscovered the islands in 1616, and Hugo SCHAMPENDAM visited them in 1624. Mas-a-Tierra was a major base for Bartholomew SHARP (1681–1682) and Edward DAVIS (1684–1687), whose crews included the pirate-authors William DAMPIER and Lionel WAFER. Dampier returned with his own squadron in 1704 and as pilot for Woodes ROGERS in 1709. John CLIPPERTON and George SHELVOCKE planned to rendezvous at the islands in 1719. A British naval squadron under George Anson launched devastating raids from Mas-a-Tierra in 1741. Not until 1751 did Spanish authorities build a fort that ended pirate visits.

Sailors deserted or were marooned on Mas-a-Tierra more than once. WILLIAM, a Mosquito Indian accidentally left behind in 1681, was the model for Friday in ROBINSON CRUSOE. He survived and eluded Spanish ships until March 1684, with only a knife, a rifle, and a few bullets. During Edward Davis' last visit to Mas-a-Tierra in 1687, nine white and four black pirates asked to be left behind. They had gambled away their booty and bet on rescue by another pirate ship. After beating off Spanish troops, they were picked up in September 1690 by John Strong, an English smuggler.

Alexander SELKIRK, who was marooned from 1704 to 1710 to escape a hated captain, was the model for *Robinson Crusoe*. In 1720, George Shelvocke's ship was wrecked on the island. Twenty-four men—including 13 blacks and Indians—deserted rather than leave in a small boat. They were caught and removed by a Spanish force by 1722.

(See also SELECTED BIBLIOGRAPHY: Woodward, *Crusoe's Island.*)

JUNK *(type of ship; western Pacific, South China Sea)* The junk (from Portuguese *junco*, adapted from Javanese *djong*, ship) has been used for many centuries by the Chinese and Malayans. The width is about one-third of the length, and the vessel has a flat bottom with no keel, a flat bow, and a high stern. A large rudder can be raised or lowered according to water depth, providing excellent steering qualities. Two or three masts carry four-sided sails, often made of bamboo, rattan, or grass matting, stiffened with poles.

The junk's sea-going capabilities are equal to those of any sailing ship. Commercial junks, carrying up to 800 tons of cargo, traded from China to the Philippine Islands. Junks of various sizes were armed with CANNON on deck as warships.

JUVARA, CARLO *(Maltese corsair; Mediterranean; 1661)* Juvara took several prizes, capturing many Algerians and their black slaves.

K

KARA ALI REIS *(Barbary corsair; Mediterranean; active 1546–1565)* The patron of MURAT "THE GREAT" REIS and MEMMI PASHA, Kara Ali fought with TURGUT REIS's Algerian squadron during the 1565 siege of MALTA.

KARA COGIA REIS *(Barbary corsair; Mediterranean; active 1630s)* CAPTAIN OF THE SEA at TUNIS, he owned and was immensely proud of a 500-ton sailing ship carrying 46 cannon. In 1640, three galleys of the KNIGHTS OF MALTA raided Tunis and captured his great ship, but Kara Cogia and his crew escaped on its small boat.

KARA DROMIS REIS *(Turkish corsair; Mediterranean; Aegean Sea; active 1503–1506)* In 1503, Kara Dromis Reis led 22 oared warships—mainly small BRIGANTINES and FUSTES—that sacked Mílos, looted Venetian possessions on the Greek mainland, and raided RHODES for slaves. A squadron of the KNIGHTS HOSPITALERS pursued his vessels. During the ensuing battle, the knights lost a galley but captured two Turkish ships and sank eight. Kara Dromis escaped and raided Crete in 1506.

KARA HASAN REIS *(Barbary corsair; Mediterranean; died 1577)* Kara Hasan Reis was a Turk sailing from ALGIERS. In 1577, he and MEMMI REIS (1) brought two GALIOTS to Tetouan, Morocco, close to Spain. As they were leaving port, his Christian slaves rebelled, and a carpenter buried his ax in Kara Hasan's chest. The corsairs on board fiercely defended themselves until Memmi Reis' crew could retake the ship. Memmi Reis cruelly tortured the rebellion's leaders until they died.

KARA KASSAM REIS *(Turkish pirate; Aegean Sea; active 1496–1506)* Kara Kassam Reis operated with a squadron of FUSTES. Captured but released by the OTTOMAN governor of Anatolia in 1496, he took numerous Venetian merchant ships and raided Chios between 1497 and 1499. During a war (1499–1502) between Venice and the Ottoman Empire, Kara Kassam led large squadrons against Venetian-owned Naxos and Cyprus.

After the Venetian war ended, Kara Kassam again sailed on his own account. He attacked Christian possessions in Greece and the Aegean in 1506. During a raid on southern Greece in 1514, two Venetian galleys surprised and captured his ships, and their crews fled into the mountains.

KARA MUFSA REIS *(Barbary corsair; Mediterranean; 1554)* One of TURGUT REIS' captains, Kara Mufsa Reis was captured by the KNIGHTS OF MALTA near the LIPARI ISLANDS. The knights killed him because he was a Christian convert to Islam.

KARA MUSTAFA REIS *(Barbary corsair; Mediterranean; 1529)* A native of Smyrna in Asia Minor,

Kara Mustafa Reis was captured by the KNIGHTS OF MALTA near the LIPARI ISLANDS.

KARA OGES REIS *(Barbary corsair; Mediterranean; 1660)*
Disgusted with his hard life as a dock worker at ALGIERS, Kara Oges Reis convinced some friends to sail with him in an old, abandoned ship. They captured a French merchantman with a rich cargo after only a few days.

KARA SAYM REIS *(Barbary corsair; Mediterranean; 1529)*
Taken by the KNIGHTS OF MALTA near the LIPARI ISLANDS, Kara Saym Reis guided his captors to and helped capture KARA MUSTAFA REIS.

KARA TORNUS REIS *(Turkish corsair; Aegean Sea; active 1497–1498)*
Kara Tornus Reis commanded several ships in the squadron of his brother, KARA KASSAM REIS.

KARA VILLI REIS *(Barbary corsair; Mediterranean; active 1676–1680)*
Kara Villi Reis was a Turk who commanded the 38-gun *Flying Horse* and was assistant CAPTAIN OF THE SEA at TRIPOLI in 1679. He died on a cruise the next year, reportedly from constantly drinking great amounts of wine.

KEELHAUL/KEELHAULING *(naval discipline; all seas; 17th century)*
A punishment in which the victim was hauled over or along the keel, the lowest lengthwise timber of a wooden ship. A rope was passed under the bottom of the ship from side to side or, in a small vessel, from the front to the back. The man was secured to it, suddenly dropped into the water, and dragged along to the other side, where the process might be repeated. Keelhauling was particularly painful and probably lethal when the ship's hull was fouled with barnacles and other sharp growths that lacerated the skin.

Some ancient Greek pictures may show pirates being killed in this way. Seventeenth-century Dutch and English naval captains sometimes imposed keelhauling, which was replaced after 1700 by FLOGGING with the CAT-O'-NINE-TAILS. There is no record of its use on board merchant ships or by pirates. However, the word is used as a threat and a curse in pirate FICTION and MOVIES.

(See also SWEARING.)

Men being keelhauled, painting on an ancient Greek vase.

KELES *(pirate ship; Mediterranean; fourth through first century B.C.)*
A small, fast GALLEY with a straight prow, one bank of rowers, and at least one sail. Despite its limited storage space, the keles' speed made it a favorite of Greek pirates as well as merchants with valuable or perishable cargoes.

(See also SHIPS, PIRATE.)

KELLEY, JAMES *(British pirate; Atlantic, Caribbean, Pacific, Indian Ocean, Red Sea; active 1680–1696)*
Kelley used the aliases James (or John) Gilliam and Sampson Marshall. While on a slave ship, he was captured off West Africa in 1680 by John WILLIAMS. Kelley enlisted with Williams, who returned to the Caribbean and rescued John COOK and other English pirates early in 1681. Kelley left with Cook, who quarreled with Williams over a Spanish prize.

Kelley joined Cook (and later Edward DAVIS) on the BATCHELOR'S DELIGHT, as it plundered South America's Pacific coast from 1684 to 1688. At his trial, Kelley said he left the *Delight* at Jamaica, accepted a pardon, and became a PRIVATEER. Some months later, he helped seize a SLOOP, was elected captain, and set out for the Indian Ocean.

Meanwhile, a gang of pirates had taken the *Delight* to the East Indies. Now known as James Gilliam, Kelley somehow was reunited with his old ship and served as QUARTERMASTER. In January 1692, the *Delight* seized the *Unity* near Bombay. The *Unity's* crew joined the pirates, set their officers adrift, and elected Kelley captain.

Kelley and 20 others were arrested as they stopped for water in northwest India. The Indians were angry because the *Batchelor's Delight* previously had visited without paying for supplies. They lavishly entertained the pirates, who were captured while in a drunken stupor. The local ruler forcibly converted the captives to the Muslim faith, several dying while being circumcised.

In about 1696, Kelley and some others stole a boat and reached Bombay. There they joined the East Indiaman *Mocha* and mutinied eight days out of port. Under Ralph STOUT and Robert CULLIFORD, the *Mocha* (also called the *Resolution*) took very rich prizes. When the pirates reached SAINT MARY'S ISLAND in May 1698, Kelley was loaded with booty and decided to return home with William KIDD.

This was an unfortunate decision, since the authorities were hunting for Kidd. Kelley was arrested, taken to England, and hanged (alongside Joseph BRADISH) in 1701. While in prison, he wrote an account of his adventures, taken to the printer by his wife and published as *A Full and True Discovery of all the Robberies, Pyracies and Other Notorious Actions of . . . James Kelley . . .* (London, 1701).

(See also SELECTED BIBLIOGRAPHY: Grey, *Pirates*; Ritchie, *Kidd*.)

KELLEY, THOMAS *(British pirate; Atlantic, Mediterranean; active 1610–1615)*
Kelley sailed

from MAMORA in Morocco until 1614, then operated from ALGIERS, capturing a British ship off Cadiz in June 1615.

KEMAL REIS *(Turkish corsair; Mediterranean; active 1487 to 1506)* Kemal Reis was the first major corsair to relocate from the Aegean to North Africa. His successful raids perhaps encouraged ARUJ and KHEIREDDIN BARBAROSSA to move west a decade later. In 1487, Spanish Muslims sent the OTTOMAN sultan, Bayezit II (ruled 1481–1512), a poetical plea for aid. The sultan provided Kemal with ships and sent him to look into their needs. After completing his mission, Kemal raided Christian Spain from bases at Bône ('Annaba), Bougie (Bejaïa), and DJERBA.

In 1495, the sultan recalled Kemal to Istanbul and appointed him a captain in the Ottoman fleet. Commanding a large sailing ship, he led squadrons that ravaged CRETE, RHODES, and Sardinia during a naval war with Venice (1499–1502). The war won, Kemal returned to freelance piracy. He marauded in the Aegean and as far west as Sicily in 1505. The following year, he took 20 ships west to Djerba, devastating Italian shipping during the crossing. In 1508, he crossed the Tyrrhenian Sea to sack Diano Marina, about 35 miles east of Monaco.

KENNEDY, WALTER *(English pirate; Atlantic, Caribbean; died 1721)* A pickpocket and housebreaker, Kennedy in 1718 sailed from NEW PROVIDENCE ISLAND in the Bahamas with Howell DAVIS. To revenge Davis' murder in June 1719, he led a group that attacked and burned the fort at Principe Island off West Africa. The crew of the *Rover* rewarded Kennedy's bravery by electing him second-in-command after Bartholomew ROBERTS.

The *Rover* made for Brazil and overpowered a Portuguese vessel carrying rich booty. Kennedy made off with both the ship and the prize while Roberts was away in a captured sloop. Since the pirates wanted to get home with their loot, Kennedy gave the Portuguese prize to a captive English captain. Off Barbados, the *Rover* seized a ship that took 10 of the crew to Virginia, where they were arrested and hanged.

Kennedy was illiterate and a poor navigator. Trying to reach Ireland, he wrecked the *Rover* on the Scottish coast. Most of the crew were captured and executed, but Kennedy got away to Dublin and spent his booty. He returned to England and set up a house of prostitution in Deptford, adding to his income by robbing houses. One of the prostitutes turned him in for robbery. He was recognized in prison, convicted, and hanged.

(See also SELECTED BIBLIOGRAPHY: Defoe, *General History*.)

KERCKHOVE, MELCHIOR VAN DEN *(Dutch pirate; Caribbean; 1597)* Kerckhove commanded four ships taking booty in the West Indies.

Kheireddin Barbarossa suppressing a rebellion by the inhabitants of Algiers, about 1520. Illustration by Léopold Flameng in Charles Farine, *Deux Pirates* (1869).

KHEIREDDIN BARBAROSSA *(Barbary corsair, viceroy, and admiral; Mediterranean; died 1546)* Properly Hizir (or Khizir) Reis; Kheireddin (Khayr-al-Din, "the gift of God") is an honorary title. The nickname Barbarossa ("Red-Beard") refers to his red facial hair. His forceful character, political skills, and military genius brought this son of an obscure soldier to the highest rank. A man of many abilities, he was skilled in engineering and fluent in at least six languages.

After ARUJ BARBAROSSA's death in 1518, Kheireddin fought hard to keep the North African territories his older brother had conquered. He was on good terms with Selim I (1512–1520). But the OTTOMAN sultan—occupied in conquering Syria and Egypt—probably did not send him an army. A savage storm destroyed a large Spanish expedition sent against ALGIERS in 1518. However, local opposition forced Kheireddin's flight to Djidjelli from 1520 to 1525. There he increased his funds through raids off Sicily and Spain.

By 1525, Kheireddin had reoccupied Algiers and constructed a formidable corsair fleet, acting in the name of Suleiman I (ruled 1520–1566). It is perhaps at this point, after Suleiman conquered RHODES in 1522, that Kheireddin received Turkish soldiers and more powerful cannon. In 1529, he finally captured and razed the Spanish fortress in the harbor of Algiers. A Spanish armada counterattacked but fled rather than fight Kheireddin's main corsair fleet.

Kheireddin imposed on Algiers a governmental system similar to one the Ottomans recently had introduced into Egypt. He acquired the title of BEYLERBEY (viceroy) of North Africa, received 2,000 elite Janissary soldiers, and could recruit additional troops from Turkey. This standing army ruled the city of Algiers, but it left the interior to tribal leaders, occasionally sending out military raids to collect tribute.

In 1533, Sultan Suleiman called Kheireddin to Constantinople and made him admiral-in-chief (Kapudan Pasha) of the Ottoman navy. His success in North Africa made Kheireddin a logical choice in wars against Spain. Suleiman may even have dreamed of reconquering Spain and liberating its Muslim population.

Kheireddin and his corsair captains rebuilt and reorganized the Ottoman navy. They then moved on TUNIS, which lay between Constantinople and their base in Algiers. In 1534, the corsairs and Ottoman troops easily overthrew Mulay Hasan, Tunis' unpopular sultan. The following July, the Spanish king, Charles V, personally led 400 ships with 30,000 men to Tunis. Despite fierce resistance, the Spaniards reconquered the city, murdered thousands, and reimposed Mulay Hasan as puppet ruler. Kheireddin took his revenge by sacking Majorca, taking 6,000 captives and an enormous loot.

From 1535, Kheireddin directed the Ottoman naval forces from Constantinople. In the summer of 1537, he and Lufti Pasha, the sultan's prime minister, commanded a vast fleet—perhaps 250 galleys plus many corsair ships—sent to conquer southern Italy. The Ottoman fleet devastated the region around Otranto. However, Sultan Suleiman decided not to bring the main Ottoman army across the straits from Albania.

The next year, Kheireddin led the Ottoman navy into the Aegean with TURGUT and SALIH REIS as his lieutenants. They subdued the islands controlled by Venice and Genoa, looted the southern coast of Crete, and then turned north into the Ionian Sea. At the Gulf of PREVESA they met the combined navies of Venice, the papacy, Genoa, and Spain. Kheireddin's tactical mastery of galley warfare resulted in a victory that confirmed Ottoman control of the sea.

For his last campaign, Kheireddin returned to the western Mediterranean. In 1542, both Sultan Suleiman I and Francis II of France were at war with Charles V. Since the French king had a negligible navy, he promised to subsidize the Ottoman fleet and invited it to spend the winter of 1543–1544 at Toulon in southern France.

On his way west with 150 warships, Kheireddin attacked Spanish territories in southern Italy and captured Reggio. There, legend says, he fell in love with the governor's daughter and made her his second wife. Passing north of Naples, the Ottoman fleet sacked Geta and other cities before meeting the French at Marseilles.

Assisted by the Ottoman warships, French troops captured Nice and burned the city after it had surrendered. Some French writers later blamed Kheireddin for this atrocity, but his fleet had already withdrawn.

After Nice fell, Kheireddin's main fleet withdrew to Toulon, where French observers unanimously praised the good behavior of his corsairs and soldiers. The French (but not the Ottomans) made peace with Charles V in 1544. Kheireddin's fleet sailed home—on the way raiding the islands of Procida, Ischia, and Lipari—to a triumphant victory parade in Constantinople.

(See also SELECTED BIBLIOGRAPHY: Fisher, *Barbary Legend.*)

KIDD, WILLIAM *(Scottish pirate; Caribbean, Indian Ocean, Red Sea; 1645?–1701)*

Kidd is among the best-known pirates. His trial incriminated royal officials and caused a political scandal. Generations of fiction writers have created a mythical CAPTAIN KIDD—bold and dashing, ruthlessly tyrannizing over his crew while terrorizing the seven seas. In fact, the real William Kidd was a mediocre and unlucky villain. As Philip Gosse commented, ". . . if Kidd's reputation was in just proportion to his actual deeds, he would have been forgotten so soon as he had been 'turned off' at Wapping Old Stairs." He made only one voyage and took only one significant prize. Other pirates roamed longer, took richer booty, and were far crueler.

There is no credible information about Kidd's early life. In 1689, he served on the pirate ship *Blessed William*, which surrendered at the Caribbean island of Nevis. During the Nine Years' War (1688–1697), the British and French used BUCCANEERS to loot the other side's colonies. The British governor of Nevis licensed the *Blessed William* as a PRIVATEER, and Kidd became captain.

Kidd joined a squadron that sacked Marie Galante in December 1689 and then battled French ships. Deciding that piracy was less risky than war, the *Blessed William*'s crew stole the ship in February 1690 while Kidd was ashore. (The deserters included Samuel BURGESS, Robert Culliford, and William MAY.)

Kidd was given the *Antigua* and chased the *William* to New York. He arrived during a civil war, helped the winning side, and married a wealthy widow in May 1691. For the next few years, he cultivated local political leaders and possibly raided French shipping on a small scale. Among his contacts was Robert Livingston, an ambitious entrepreneur.

In 1695, Kidd took the *Antigua* to England, hoping to get a privateering license from the ADMIRALTY COURT. In London, he and Livingston met with Richard Coote, earl of Bellomont, recently nominated as governor of New York and Massachusetts. The three men conceived a scheme to capture pirates and keep their booty, instead of returning it to its original owners.

In October 1695, Kidd, Bellomont, and Livingston signed a contract. Kidd was made captain, and Bellomont put up £6,000, four-fifths of the cost. Through separate secret agreements, Bellomont split his shares with four high-ranking partners—including the secretary of state and the heads of the admiralty and the judiciary. These sponsors would keep most of the loot, although King William III was promised 10 percent.

The king granted three commissions. A standard privateering letter allowed Kidd to capture French shipping. Under a special royal decree, Kidd could arrest pirates anywhere in the world. (William May, Thomas TEW, and Thomas WAKE were named as possible targets.) A third letter permitted Kidd to keep captured booty without going through the courts. To prevent him from cheating his partners, Kidd was ordered to surrender his loot to Governor Bellomont in Boston. He also had to post a £20,000 performance bond.

The partners bought the *Adventure Galley*, a 300-ton, 34-gun vessel that carried 46 oars. Leaving England in May 1696, Kidd recruited a crew in New York in July and August. The ship's ARTICLES promised the crew about 60 percent of any booty—even though Kidd already had pledged 60 percent to Bellomont. Kidd crossed the Atlantic in September and followed the African coast to the Indian Ocean. He aroused suspicions when he met a British naval squadron, but rowed away during a calm. Avoiding the Cape of Good Hope, he stopped at MADAGASCAR and careened his ship in the Comoro Islands. At Johanna (Anjouan) Island, he recruited more seamen.

Kidd turned pirate when the *Adventure Galley* left Johanna in April 1697. Had he wanted to honor his license, Kidd could have attacked John HOAR, Dirk CHIVERS, and other pirates at nearby SAINT MARY'S ISLAND. He instead sailed for the Red Sea to plunder the pilgrim fleets returning from Mecca to India.

On August 15, the *Adventure Galley* caught an Indian squadron accompanied by an East India Company ship. When the British vessel fired at the *Galley*, Kidd retreated to northwestern India. On August 19, he captured a small vessel near Janjira, tortured the Indian sailors, and took food and some money. The British captain was kidnapped and forced to act as pilot for several months.

Kidd continued south along the coast, stopping at Carwar and Calcutta. In September, the *Galley* fought off two Portuguese warships and visited the Laccadive Islands for repairs. Kidd's men forced the islanders to work for free, used their boats for firewood, and raped several women.

In early November, Kidd ran into another East India Company ship. Although most of the crew voted to attack, Kidd bullied and cajoled them into letting the British ship go. About two weeks later, the *Galley* was passing a Dutch vessel. William Moore, the *Galley*'s gunner, may have wanted to attack the other ship. During an argument, Kidd killed Moore by smashing a bucket down on his head.

Kidd took two more prizes off the Indian coast. At the end of November, he seized the *Rouparelle*. Although Dutch-owned, the *Rouparelle* flew the French flag, and her papers included a French "pass" (passport). Kidd took over the ship as the *November*, sold her cargo on the coast, and gave the crew their share. About a month later, the *Galley* or the *November* looted a small Indian vessel.

Off Cochin about January 12, 1698, Kidd took his only rich prize. The *Quedah Merchant* was leased to officials of the Indian government but carried a French pass. Kidd kept the *Merchant* and her crew and sold some of her cargo of cloth. Continuing south, he seized a small Portuguese vessel and unsuccessfully pursued the *Dorrill* and the *Sedgwick*, two East India Company ships. (Robert Culliford also chased the *Dorrill*, and Dirk Chivers later captured the *Sedgwick*.)

In April 1698, the *Adventure Galley* landed at Saint Mary's Island, where Robert Culliford's *Mocha* already was moored. Since Culliford had helped steal Kidd's ship in 1690, both men initially were cautious. But Kidd quickly reassured the pirates that "he was as bad as they."

The booty was divided when the *Quedah Merchant* arrived about a month later. Under the ship's articles, Kidd kept 40 shares, somewhat less then 40 percent of the take. Most of Kidd's crew enlisted with Culliford, who sailed in June 1698. In November, Kidd burned the rotted-out *Galley* and departed in the *Quedah Merchant*, renamed the *Adventure Prize*.

Kidd's capture of the *Quedah Merchant* threatened the East India Company. Already enraged by Henry EVERY's sack of the *Gunsway* in 1695, the emperor threatened to expel all European traders. Under pressure, the company compensated the owners of goods on the *Merchant*, paid large bribes, and agreed to patrol the South Indian Sea. But Indian officials continued to blame the company for new pirate attacks.

To answer Indian complaints, British officials had to punish Kidd's crimes. He was branded a pirate and omitted by name from a general pardon issued in 1698. In November 1698, the government ordered all colonial governors to conduct an all-out manhunt. Kidd learned the bad news when the *Adventure Prize* reached the Caribbean island of Anguilla in April 1699. After the Danish governor of Saint Thomas refused his protection, Kidd went to Mona Island and Savona Bay in Hispaniola. British traders bought cloth from the pirates, and one sold Kidd a SLOOP. The *Prize* was looted and burned after he left.

With stops at New Jersey and Long Island, Kidd headed for Boston. Governor Bellomont arrested him in July 1699, and he reached London in April 1700. His case became embroiled in British politics. The opposition party tried to impeach the sponsors of his voyage, and Kidd testified before the House of Commons in March 1701. Although the impeachment motion narrowly failed, only Kidd's execution would remove him as a dangerous witness.

In May 1701, Kidd was convicted of murdering William Moore and robbing the *Quedah Merchant* and other ships. He argued that the *Rouparelle* and *Merchant* were legal prizes because they carried French passes. (The war had ended, but the peace treaty applied south of the equator only after March 1698.) Kidd had given the passes to Governor Bellomont, and Admiralty officials hid them during the trial.

Because Kidd's trial was unfair, some have concluded that he was innocent of piracy. The two issues are not connected, and he unquestionably did assault innocent merchant vessels. He was hanged at Wapping on May 23, and his body was hung in chains farther down the Thames. His legend lived on, as did the rumors that he had buried fabulous booty somewhere between India and Boston.

(See also CAPTAIN KIDD(1); CAPTAIN KIDD'S TREASURE; SELECTED BIBLIOGRAPHY: Jameson, *Privateering*; Pringle, *Jolly Roger*; Ritchie, *Kidd.*)

KIDNAPPING See RANSOM OF CAPTIVES; ROMANCES, ANCIENT.

KILLIGREW FAMILY *(English pirate patrons; Atlantic; active 1500s)* A gentry family owning property in Cornwall from the late 1300s. By the 16th century, the Killigrews had extensive lands and were hereditary captains of Pendennis Castle, guarding the entrance to Falmouth harbor. They fenced stolen property by the 1550s or earlier, and several members personally indulged in wrecking and piracy.

The family's criminal activities flourished under Sir John KILLIGREW. Local officials belonged to or tolerated his closely knit syndicate of relatives, retainers, and agents, which operated freely in Ireland and throughout southwestern England.

(See also KILLIGREW, ELIZABETH; KILLIGREW, LADY; KILLIGREW, PETER; KILLIGREW, THOMAS.

KILLIGREW, ELIZABETH *(English pirate patron; Atlantic; active about 1560–1582)* Elizabeth Killigrew was the wife of Sir John KILLIGREW (1). In 1582, she led an assault on a Spanish merchantman driven into Falmouth harbor by a storm. Royal commissioners sentenced her to death for this crime, but the king pardoned her.

KILLIGREW, SIR JOHN (1) *(English pirate patron; Atlantic; active about 1560–1580)* Belonging to an ancient family in Cornwall, Sir John enlarged his parents' criminal syndicate and made Falmouth a notorious pirate HAVEN. In 1571, he built Arwennack, a fortified great house, connected to the harbor by a secret passage.

The Killigrews had connections throughout western England and Ireland as well as at Queen Elizabeth's court. Sir John was VICE-ADMIRAL of Cornwall, president of the Commissioners for Piracy, and hereditary governor of Pendennis Castle. Sir John Wogan, vice-admiral of South Wales, was his partner. His son, Sir Henry Killigrew, was an ambassador and an associate of Sir William Cecil, the queen's chief minister.

Sir John's political influence protected him, although the government knew that he sponsored piracy against English and foreign vessels. The entire family dealt in booty, and both Sir John's mother and his wife personally pillaged ships in Falmouth harbor. As a fence, Sir John took 80 percent of a cargo's value. But he also had large expenses, including Arwennack House, bribes, and a troop of armed guards. He died owing the enormous sum of £10,000.

(See also KILLIGREW, ELIZABETH; KILLIGREW, LADY.)

KILLIGREW, SIR JOHN (2) *(English pirate patron; Atlantic; active about 1580–1603)* From his parents (Sir John KILLIGREW (1) and Elizabeth KILLIGREW), Killigrew inherited a syndicate sponsoring piracy from Falmouth in Cornwall. He nevertheless became deeply indebted and personally led robberies on land and at sea. Accused of taking Spanish bribes, he sold to pirate captains ammunition the government had issued to defend against the Spanish Armada.

When some governmental officials tried to suppress piracy, Sir John diverted stolen cargoes to Irish ports. But he remained above the law. In 1588, Cornish juries obeyed Sir John's orders and released a pirate who had attacked two Danish vessels. The Royal Council expressed its disapproval but took no action. In 1597, a pirate brought a prize into Falmouth while royal vessels were anchored in the harbor. With the help of a £100 bribe, Sir John convinced the naval officers to ignore the pirate ship.

KILLIGREW, LADY *(English pirate patron; Atlantic; active about 1530–1570)* Lady Killigrew was mother and teacher of Sir John KILLIGREW (1). The daughter of Philip Wolverston, a Suffolk pirate, she helped fence pirate loot until her death. She was tried for leading boarders who plundered a German ship in Falmouth harbor, searching for two barrels of PIECES OF EIGHT supposedly on board. Although one crew member died during the raid, a bribed jury acquitted Lady Killigrew.

KILLIGREW, PETER *(English pirate; Atlantic; active about 1550–1563)* Peter Killigrew was from Falmouth in Wales and was the uncle of Sir John KILLIGREW (1). He commanded a pirate ship that captured prizes in the Irish Sea and near France. Escaping a royal fleet sent to suppress Welsh pirates in 1556, he disposed of wine from a Spanish prize taken by Thomas COBHAM in 1563.

KILLIGREW, THOMAS *(English pirate; Atlantic; 1464)* From southwestern England and possibly related to the KILLIGREW FAMILY of Cornwall, Killigrew attacked a Breton merchant ship with two other captains.

KING OF PIRATES, THE (novel; 1719)

A fictional autobiography of Henry EVERY by Daniel DEFOE. This version is very different from the equally fictitious account in Defoe's GENERAL HISTORY.

Every tells his story in two letters. As it begins, he is cutting LOGWOOD at Campeche but decides to give up hard work. He raids along South America's Pacific coast with Bartholomew SHARP and Richard SAWKINS, returns to Campeche, and hides out for two years.

Every buries his gold and enlists with a "Captain Redpath," noted for his bloodthirsty treatment of prisoners. Previously Every had robbed only Spaniards. Now he joins those who "listed in the service of the devil indeed, and, like him, were at war with all mankind." Redpath's raiders plunder the SPANISH MAIN and then (in 1691) sail around Cape Horn to the Pacific. In consort with Captain Guilotte (François GROGNIET), they capture several Spanish treasure ships. A cannon ball tears off Redpath's head, and Every is elected captain. Throughout, he succeeds as a leader because he focuses on the task of making money.

The pirates discover that they cannot trust each other. If they return to civilization, one of the men may betray the others. They decide to live at MADAGASCAR, because the climate is good and the people there are easily terrified.

Every reaches Madagascar in April 1693. His ship is wrecked, but the pirates land safely. After about a year, Every returns to England to fetch another warship. The men leave their booty at Madagascar, but Every stops at Campeche and digs up his buried treasure.

Since he cannot buy a ship in London, Every enlists on another vessel. Off the Spanish coast, he and his men mutiny and reach Madagascar after a three-year absence. Other pirates have swelled the colony, but no one has touched Every's treasure.

Every easily captures a ship carrying the daughter of the Indian ruler. Although he burst into the princess' cabin with his saber, Every denies raping her. "She was, in a manner, covered with diamonds, and I, like a true pirate, soon let her see that I had more mind to the jewels than to the lady." Every admits that four or five pirates ravished each of the princess' women, but he asserts that the young ladies were quite willing. The Indian ship is loaded with liquor, and his men stay drunk

"Captain Avery captures the Great Mogul's Grand-daughter." An illustration for a modern edition (New York, 1903–1904) of Daniel Defoe's novel, *The King of Pirates*.

for two weeks. Some fall over and drown, while others die of tropical fevers.

Every's pirates have more money that any "society of men ever possessed in this world before us." His main concern is to get his riches back to civilization. His gang offers the English queen a million pounds for a pardon. To encourage her to take his offer, Every spreads the rumor that he is setting up a pirate kingdom like that of the ancient CILICIANS.

As the pirates drift away, some are robbed by greedy captains. Others waste their money on luxury and alcohol, but not Every. He escapes to the Persian Gulf and turns merchant with one companion. Disguised as Armenians, the two men travel to the Persian capital and reach Constantinople. As his letters end, Every plans to enjoy his loot at some inland town in France.

KING'S PIRATE (motion picture; color; 1967)
The action scenes move quickly in director Don Weis' tongue-in-cheek remake of AGAINST ALL FLAGS (1952). Douglas McClure plays Lieutenant Brian Fleming, and Jill St. John is his fiery love, Jessica Stephens. Guy Stockwell is out to get the hero as John AVERY; Mary Ann Mobley is Princess Patma.

KNIGHT, WILLIAM (English buccaneer; Caribbean, Pacific; active 1680s)
About September 1684, Knight and some 50 men crossed the Panama Isthmus and built canoes. His band captured a Spanish ship off El Salvador, cruised south to Ecuador, and took other prizes before returning to Panama. In July 1685, Knight enlisted with Edward DAVIS' larger buccaneer force.

For more than a year, Knight joined Davis in assaults on Peruvian and Chilean ports. Leaving in November 1686, he sailed around Cape Horn to the Caribbean. In June 1688, he gave evidence in Jamaica against French marauders who had served under Captain TOWNLEY. He perhaps was the William Knight who—as William DAMPIER wrote—cruised in the Indian Ocean in 1689 with a West Indian BRIGANTINE.

KNIGHTS HOSPITALERS (Roman Catholic warrior-monks; 1070 to the present)
Founded to maintain a hospice in Jerusalem, the order received papal approval as an independent corporation in 1113. The knights, who wore an eight-pointed cross, were governed by a grand master elected for life. Brothers of any rank took vows of poverty, chastity, and obedience. After the crusaders lost Jerusalem, the headquarters was transferred to Syria (in 1187), Cyprus (in 1291), and RHODES (in 1308).

Following the OTTOMAN conquest of Rhodes, the knights occupied MALTA from 1530 to 1798. Although technically vassals of the kings of Sicily, their grand masters were recognized as sovereign rulers. The original order now makes its headquarters in Rome. Protestant offshoots exist in Britain and Germany.

Although the knights continued to maintain hospitals, they developed into a military force from the 12th century. While on Rhodes and Malta, the order operated squadrons of galleys. In principle, knights could be promoted only after serving four six-month cruises known as "caravans." When sailing ships were adopted about 1700, the caravan was extended to one year.

Perpetually at war with Islam, the knights attacked both Muslim shipping and Christian and Jewish vessels trading with Muslims. They maintained slave markets at Rhodes and Malta and pillaged the coasts of Greece, Turkey, and (after 1530) of North Africa. The order retained booty brought in by its own naval squadrons. In addition, the grand masters licensed private vessels—captained both by knights and by freelance pirates—and took a percentage of their loot.

As it evolved into a military body, the order became more exclusive. During the 13th century, its members were divided into brother knights and brother sergeants, with higher offices reserved for knights. By the 16th century, knights had to prove that all members of their families had been noble for several generations—although exceptions were made by papal dispensation.

The order's extensive possessions throughout Europe were administered by monasteries headed by commanders. Groups of several monasteries formed a larger unit governed by a prior. To join, an applicant needed merely noble birth and Roman Catholic baptism. After serving their caravans, most knights became commanders and priors and lived as country gentleman. A few, such as ROMEGAS and Jean de la VALETTE remained at Malta and became renowned corsairs.

(See also KNIGHTS OF MALTA; KNIGHTS OF RHODES; SELECTED BIBLIOGRAPHY: Bradford, *Shield*.)

KNIGHTS OF MALTA (monks and corsairs; Mediterranean; 1530–1798)
The OTTOMAN EMPIRE expelled the KNIGHTS HOSPITALERS from RHODES in 1522. In 1530, the order received Malta, Gozo, and Comino from Charles V, ruler of Spain and much of Italy. Until it was taken by TURGUT REIS in 1551, the knights also garrisoned TRIPOLI.

The knights owed their overlord only the token payment of one Maltese falcon annually. Most European and Muslim states recognized the grand master as sovereign ruler of Malta. There were, however, three limits on his freedom of action. Malta relied on Sicily for food. European rulers could seize the order's possessions in their countries. The order was responsible to the pope, who could overrule decisions by its courts or the grand master.

When the knights received Malta, Charles V was at war with the Ottoman Empire and the BARBARY corsairs. Except for France, many other Christian states also warred against the Muslims. In addition to defending Malta and Tripoli, the order was expected to join all Christian maritime expeditions against the Ottomans.

To meet its obligations, the order maintained a varying number of galleys. The knights provided four at PREVESA in 1537, five at DJERBA in 1559, but only three at LEPANTO in 1571. During the 17th century, the order usually had seven galleys. Sailing ships were introduced in 1704. The fleet still contained four ships-of-the-line, four galleys, and four FRIGATES in the 1750s, but thereafter fell in strength.

Between battles, the order's fleet went out on two or three cruises each year, sailing east to the Aegean or turning south to attack the Barbary coast and Egypt. In addition to soldiers and sailors working for wages, each galley carried some 30 knights. Every knight was expected to serve on four six-month cruises. Many then left Malta for the order's convents in Europe, but a few remained and became professional captains.

Although the knights denied that they were pirates, their victims considered them—as the Venetian ambassador charged in 1588—merely "corsairs parading crosses." Unlike most freebooters, the knights did not divide up their take. Booty and ransoms taken on active service theoretically went to the order, and the grand master in 1545 sternly punished Signorino GATTINARO's attempt to keep his spoils. But ways were found to reward knights (like ROMEGAS) who took rich prizes.

The order's galleys looted any Muslim merchant ships they encountered, and they also pillaged Christian and Jewish vessels trading with Muslim ports. They were especially eager to attack Venetian vessels with rich cargoes from the Orient. (Venice was at peace with the Ottomans from 1538 to 1571.)

A turning point came in the 1550s. The order's power reached its lowest point in 1551, when the Ottomans attacked Malta, plundered Gozo, and occupied Tripoli. The knights desperately needed money to build up Malta's defenses. Grand master Jean de La VALETTE (ruled 1557 to 1568) expected captains to bring back booty, and he ignored a 1555 papal order forbidding attacks on Venetian merchants. From then on, the order's squadrons attacked commercial vessels as freely as Ottoman or Barbary warships.

Valette and his successors also encouraged individual knights to cruise in their own ships, some of which were commanded by corsair captains. From the 1570s, grand masters licensed corsairs under both their own flag and that of the order. Both knights and corsairs disregarded a 1587 papal decree protecting Jews and Christians trading with Muslims, as long as they did not carry military stores.

To control the freelance corsairs sailing from Malta, the order set up the TRIBUNALE DEGLI ARMAMENTI in 1605. Henceforth, the island supported both the order's own galleys and a varying number of licensed corsairs. Both fleets were especially aggressive up to about 1650. From then on, France and the papacy increasingly sought to limit attacks on Christian shipping.

The Florentine KNIGHTS OF SAINT STEPHEN took the richest prizes during the early 1600s. The Maltese knights evened the score under BOISBAUDRANT, who in 1644 captured the sultan's favorite wife. Boisbaudrant's outrage precipitated the Ottoman invasion of Crete, which the knights helped Venice defend until 1669.

The knights cruised for prizes until 1697. By then, the Ottoman Empire posed no threat to European navies and was increasingly under French protection. With its fleet now a financial drain, the order suspended raids in the Levant after a final expedition in 1717. Cruises in North African waters continued on a limited scale until Napoleon occupied Malta in 1798.

(See also SELECTED BIBLIOGRAPHY: Anderson, *Naval;* Blouet, *Story;* Cavaliero, *Last;* Tenenti, *Piracy.*)

KNIGHTS OF RHODES *(Christian corsairs; Mediterranean; 1308–1522)*

After Muslim armies occupied Syria in 1291, the KNIGHTS HOSPITALERS fled to Cyprus and then (probably in 1308) seized RHODES and several smaller islands from the BYZANTINE EMPIRE. At Rhodes, the order was recognized as an independent state by many Christian and Muslim nations. (Western Europeans still controlled parts of Greece and the islands.)

The knights portrayed Rhodes as a forward base for the reconquest of the Holy Land, and they created a naval organization headed by an ADMIRAL. In fact, they rarely could afford to man more than a few galleys. Many among the few hundred knights residing at Rhodes had no interest in naval affairs. Few Europeans supported new crusades, and the order's available cash went into fortifying Rhodes itself.

During the 14th century, the knights did help to combat piracy from Turkish AYDIN and MENTESHE, occasionally fought in Greece, and joined raids on Syria and Egypt—including a major attack on Alexandria in 1365. From the 1420s, they were increasingly at odds with the expanding OTTOMAN EMPIRE.

During their Rhodian centuries, the knights followed two conflicting policies. As Europeans lost their other possessions in the Levant, Rhodes became a major base for merchants trading with Egypt and Syria. From the beginning, however, its ports also served as corsair havens. The order licensed cruises by individual knights and kept three-fourths of their profits. It also allowed Greek, Italian, French, and Catalan captains to operate from Rhodian harbors. Even during times of truce, pirates pillaged Muslim and Christian merchants from Cyprus and Italy.

A siege in 1480 by Mahomet II was repulsed with severe losses. Although they made peace two years later, both the sultan and the knights tolerated corsair raids. Hostilities escalated after a war between Venice and the Ottomans ended in 1502. The order's ships pillaged Turkish shipping as well as Venetian and Genoese vessels trading with Muslims. In addition, many knights armed private ships and joined the freelance corsairs in raiding on their own account.

Ottoman rulers could no longer tolerate piracy from Rhodes after the conquest of Syria and Egypt in 1516 and 1517. Constant Rhodian raids threatened communications between these new possessions and the capital at Constantinople. In 1522, Sultan Suleiman I personally led an army of about 200,000 men against the island's 7,500 defenders. During six months of siege, the Ottoman army lost half its force. The sultan offered the defenders honorable terms, and the grand master surrendered on December 18. The remaining knights sailed for Italy and took possession of MALTA in 1530.

(See also ASSANTI, LIGORIO; KARA DROMIS REIS; KOURD OGLU REIS; LA VALETTE, JEAN DE; VALDIVIESSA E MALDONATO, GUY; VIGNOLI, VIGNOLO DE; SELECTED BIBLIOGRAPHY: Setton, *Crusades.*)

KNIGHTS OF SAINT STEPHEN   (Italian corsairs; Mediterranean; 1562–1749)   A religious and military order founded in Florence by Duke Cosimo I dei MEDICI. Its rules imitated those of the KNIGHTS OF MALTA (except that its members could marry). Knights, who wore a white costume with a red cross, owed three years of service, including tours on the order's galleys. The Florentine dukes usually enrolled only sons of wealthy families and used the order to control the nobility. Although many knights treated the order as a social club, some pursued profitable careers in its squadrons.

Cosimo I supposedly founded the order to defend the Italian coast against BARBARY raiders. But he also expected his knights to imitate Maltese corsairs by bringing in rich booty. Since the order had its own flag and legally was separate from the Tuscan navy, the dukes hoped to escape responsibility for raids.

Like the Maltese, the Knights of Saint Stephen considered themselves at war with the entire OTTOMAN EMPIRE. They freely attacked any ships in Ottoman waters, including those owned by Jews, Greeks, and Venetians. The pope forbade attacks on Christians or Jews in 1587, but the Maltese and Florentine corsairs paid no attention.

There was one vital difference between the Florentine and Maltese orders. The Maltese knights were an independent and international order of adventurers. As their hereditary grand masters, the dukes kept the Florentine knights under firm control. Thus the policies of individual rulers determined the size and aggressiveness of the order's fleet.

Francesco I dei MEDICI encouraged raids against the eastern Mediterranean from the 1580s. The greatest successes came in the early 1600s under Admiral Jacopo INGHIRAMI, a captain of relatively modest birth. (The first admirals often represented minor branches of the Medici family.) Ferdinando I dei MEDICI and Cosimo II dei MEDICI appointed foreign adventurers (such as Jacques

PIERRE) as captains of the order's galleys, and they gave PRIVATEERING licenses to foreign pirates with their own vessels.

Ferdinando II (ruled 1627 to 1670) ended the order's buccaneering cruises. Ferdinando obeyed papal decrees protecting Christian traders, partly because Florentine merchants wanted to trade with the Ottoman Empire. The order played a small role in various naval wars until 1737, when Florence was attached to the Austrian Empire. It was suppressed in 1859.

(See also SELECTED BIBLIOGRAPHY: Braudel, *Mediterranean;* Tenenti, *Piracy.*)

KNOLLYS, HENRY   (English courtier; Atlantic; died 1583)   Eldest son of Sir Francis Knollys (1514?–1596), who held many offices and carried out delicate missions for Queen Elizabeth I. Henry Knollys attended Oxford and was elected to Parliament in 1562 and 1572. A sister married the earl of Essex (Robert Devereux), the queen's favorite.

By 1574, Knollys owned the heavily gunned *Elephant,* whose officers were notorious pirates. With Ferdinando FIELDING as captain, John CALLICE as master, and Simâo FERNANDES as pilot, the *Elephant* took a rich Portuguese prize in December. Soon after, Callice later testified, Fielding sold him the *Elephant* for £110. Since Knollys and not Fielding owned the ship, this was probably a fictitious sale to protect Knollys. The *Elephant* took several more prizes during 1575 and early 1576, but Callice commanded a different ship in November 1576.

In 1578, Knollys was Sir Humphrey GILBERT's principal associate in a planned expedition to North America. Knollys contributed three ships and personally commanded the *Elephant.* Callice—who had just escaped his parole officers—served as Knollys' pilot, Ferdinando Fielding as a gentleman-soldier.

During the summer of 1578, while Gilbert assembled his other ships at Plymouth, Knollys cruised for prizes in neighboring waters. He defeated the pirate Robert Holbourne, capturing his French prize and his warship, loaded with other plunder. Returning to Plymouth, Knollys released Holbourne and kept his booty. His two other ships cruised separately and apparently also took prizes.

Gilbert quarreled with Knollys, partly over his piracies, and the expedition broke up. Knollys took his three ships to Ireland and the Isle of Wight, taking another French ship on the way. The government investigated these crimes in 1579 but took no action.

Before leaving to attend the queen in February 1579, Knollys sent out the *Francis* with Richard Derifall as master. The *Francis* captured a French prize near Spain and sailed to Guernsey to meet Knollys. He sold part of his booty and transferred the remainder to a royal residence near Southampton. In 1581, he commanded a naval fleet sent to the Azores to assist the pretender to the Portuguese throne.

KOENIGSMARK, KARL JOHANN *(Knight of Malta; Mediterranean; 1657–1684)* A Swedish nobleman of Protestant background attracted by the knights' "Holy War" against Islam. Arriving at Malta about 1675, he demonstrated an exceptional command of galley warfare during both corsair cruises and the Venetian invasion of southern Greece.

KOMAZOTI REIS *(Turkish pirate; Aegean Sea; 1496)* Commanding a FUSTE, Komazoti Reis cruised for prey with KARA KASSAM REIS and RICHE REIS.

KOURD OGLU (CURTOGOLI) REIS *(Turkish corsair; Aegean Sea, Mediterranean; active 1514–1522)* Kourd Oglu Reis operated from Turkish and Greek bases but also used the pirate havens along the BARBARY COAST. On a lesser scale, his career as corsair and admiral resembles that of KHEIREDDIN BARBAROSSA.

After raiding in the Aegean in 1509 and 1510, Kourd Oglu crossed to North Africa in 1514 and 1515. Turning north against Italy's western coast, his squadron took rich prizes and many hundreds of slaves. Kourd Oglu apparently undertook these cruises on his own account. In 1516, he came to terms with Sultan Selim I; and commanded a much larger fleet—four galleys and 23 FUSTES. Taking on provisions in North Africa, the corsairs raided from Sicily to Florence. On their way home in September, they pillaged the Adriatic coast and captured more ships near Crete.

During Kourd Oglu's 1516 raid, an assault on the Roman coast terrified Pope Leo X, who was enjoying a hunting and fishing vacation. Panicked by seeing Turkish corsairs landing so near the city, the pope and his attendants abandoned their belongings and galloped back to Rome to spread the alarm.

Sultan Selim halted corsair activity in 1517, and Kourd Oglu commanded a naval squadron during the Ottoman conquest of Egypt. In 1521, probably at the order of Sultan Suleiman I, he almost captured the grand master of the KNIGHTS OF RHODES as he came from France. Kourd Oglu commanded the Ottoman fleet that besieged Rhodes in 1522. The sultan, enraged when a European ship slipped in, ordered that he be beaten aboard his own flagship.

(See also KEMAL REIS.)

KOXINGA *(Chinese pirate; South China Sea; 1624–1662)* Koxinga (Coxinga, Kuo Hsing Yeh) was born to CHENG CHIH-LUNG and a Japanese mother. By about 1630, his father controlled Fukien Province (across from Taiwan) as well as a large fleet engaged in commerce and piracy. Invading Manchu armies drove the Ming rulers from Nanking in 1644. Cheng Chih-lung initially gave a Ming ruler sanctuary in Fukien. He later submitted to the Manchus, who arrested and imprisoned him in Peking about 1646. Gathering a small band of followers, Koxinga went into exile and led a rebellion loyal to the deposed Ming dynasty. He soon commanded a large military force, regained control of Fukien Province, and conquered Amoy Island in 1650.

Koxinga's power was based on overseas commerce, and his JUNKS carried cargoes as far as Japan and southeast Asia. His fleet was stronger than the Manchu navy, and he controlled the entire coast from Vietnam to Shanghai. He was less successful on land. Allied with other Ming loyalists, he sent a fleet and army up the Yangtze in 1659, which were destroyed at the gates of Nanking.

The last remnants of Ming power collapsed, and Koxinga sought refuge on Taiwan. In 1661 he personally led an army that drove out the Dutch and set up a government that ruled Taiwan until 1683. While planning to invade the Philippines, Koxinga died of illness in June 1662. He became a mythical folk-hero, honored for his loyalty to the Ming and resistance to foreign invaders.

KRYVITZIOTES OF RHODES *(Greek corsair; Aegean Sea; active 1270s)* His squadron—including a large galley—captured a Venetian ship, took the captured merchants to RHODES, and imprisoned them at hard labor for eight months. One Venetian later obtained letters from MICHAEL VIII PALAEOLOGUS ordering Kryvitziotes to return his goods. Kryvitziotes ignored the emperor's orders, even though he was imperial captain at Rhodes.

(See also BYZANTINE EMPIRE; VENETIAN CLAIMS.)

KUO P'O-TAI *(Chinese pirate; South China Sea; active about 1800–1810)* From Kwangtung Province, Kuo P'o-Tai (Kuo Hsüeh-hsien) was a leader in the pirate confederation created by CHENG I in 1805. At its peak, Kuo's Black Flag Fleet had more than 100 vessels and 10,000 men.

Kuo was kidnapped and joined the pirates at the age of 14. A protege of Cheng I, he was rapidly promoted to squadron commander. He joined Cheng in aiding a Vietnamese rebellion and returned with him to China in 1801. After Cheng's death in 1807, Kuo and the Black Flag fleet remained loyal to his widow Cheng I SAO.

The Black Flag Fleet normally operated off Lei-chou peninsula near the border with Vietnam. However, in August 1809, Kuo carried out a six-week assault along the eastern tributaries of the Pearl River between Macao and Canton. (CHANG PAO's Red Flag Fleet simultaneously invaded the Pearl River's main channel.) Overcoming all resistance, the pirates came within 16 miles of Canton. Towns that refused ransom were devastated, and 10,000 deaths are recorded.

The pirate confederation collapsed in late 1809 because of rivalry between Kuo Po-tai and Chang Pao, who led the two largest fleets. Precisely why Kuo Po-tai turned on Chang Pao is not known. Chinese legends say the quarrel began because both men loved Cheng I Sao, and she preferred Chang Pao.

For whatever reason, Kuo's fleet refused to help Chang and Sao, when government forces trapped their ships near Lantao Island in November 1809. A month later,

Chang's fleet attacked Kuo's forces and was decisively defeated. Meanwhile, Kuo negotiated a pardon with the help of a Portuguese official at Macao.

Kuo and about 6,000 of his followers surrendered to the government in January 1810. He was appointed a military officer and joined an expedition against the other pirate leaders, who submitted or were captured in April and May. Soon after, Kuo resigned from the military and lived quietly as a scholar until his death. Some stories indicate he had loved learning even before his surrender. His flagship's hold, it is said, was filled with books, which he read between raids.

KYD, WILLIAM *(English pirate; English Channel; active 1430–1453)* From Devonshire, he seized French and English vessels, selling his booty at Exmouth, Plymouth, and the Isle of Wight. In November 1453, Kyd brought into Exmouth a ship owned by the bishop of Saint Andrews in Scotland. William de Kanete (Kennedy), a Scottish knight, appeared in town, pretended to own the ship, and connived with a local customs official to gain possession. The bishop never regained his vessel, even though he was a powerful man and the king repeatedly ordered its restitution.

(See also SELECTED BIBLIOGRAPHY: Kingsford, *Prejudice.*)

KYGHLEY, JOHN *(English pirate; Atlantic, English Channel; active 1403–1404)* In a 1403 truce between England and France, Kyghley was specifically mentioned by name when the two parties promised not to shelter sea-robbers. The following year, Kyghley carried off a ship from Bordeaux anchored in Weymouth harbor.

L

LABAT, JEAN-BAPTISTE (French missionary and author; Caribbean; 1663–1738)
A priest in the Dominican order, Father Labat served at Martinique and Guadeloupe from 1694 to 1705. His six-volume *Nouveau Voyage aux Isles de l'Amérique (New Voyage to the American Islands)* was published at Paris in 1722.

Labat was a devoted naturalist and student of engineering, who traveled throughout the islands to advise his fellow Dominicans. As the governor's request, he supervised the building of new forts on Guadeloupe in 1702 and helped defend the island against an English attack. Labat's *New Voyage* describes the natural environment and the customs of the Indians and settlers. His style is lively, and the accounts of his own experiences are interesting and believable. Unfortunately, since he gullibly trusted dubious legends and gossip, his historical narratives have little value.

During his voyages, Labat met Captain DANIEL and sailed with him and his buccaneers during raids. He took a lenient view of piracy and wrote about pirate crimes without comment. While at Saint Thomas, Labat found the shops filled with fine cloth brought back from India by William KIDD. He borrowed money to buy as much as possible for his fellow Dominicans and for "our friends, who, I felt sure, would be pleased to have them."

(See also SELECTED BIBLIOGRAPHY: Labat, *Memoirs*.)

LA BOUCHE, OLIVIER (French pirate; Caribbean, Atlantic, Indian Ocean; active 1716–1721)
Said to be from Calais, La Bouche (La Bous, La Buze) sailed from NEW PROVIDENCE ISLAND in the Bahamas. In 1716, he cruised in consort with a vessel commanded by Benjamin HORNIGOLD and later by Samuel BELLAMY. Bellamy and La Bouche captured British and French vessels near the Virgin Islands but were separated by a storm early in 1717.

After Woodes ROGERS became governor of the Bahamas in July 1718, La Bouche fled to the West African coast. In the spring of 1719, he cruised off Whydah (Ouidah, now in Benin) and briefly joined forces near Gambia with Howell DAVIS and Thomas COCKLYN. Heading toward the Red Sea, La Bouche wrecked his ship on Mayotte in the Comoro Islands in 1720. Early in 1721, he was living at SAINT MARY'S ISLAND, near MADAGASCAR, where John TAYLOR gave him command of the *Victory*. Cruising in consort, he and Taylor visited Réunion Island in April, captured a Portuguese ship carrying enormous booty, and divided their take at Saint Mary's.

The pirates split up in December 1721. Taylor sailed for the West Indies, while La Bouche went back to Madagascar. In one story he settled on Réunion and was hanged some years later.

LA CABANNE, MENJOUYN (French corsair; Caribbean; 1550)
La Cabanne took booty during an impulsive raid in the West Indies. A Gascon, he turned pirate as a youth, was captured, and labored for 18 months as a Spanish GALLEY SLAVE. In 1549, he spent

his remaining fortune on a small warship and set out to raid English shipping. At Bordeaux, he learned that England and France had ended hostilities. Rather than lose his investment in the ship, he sailed for the Americas early in 1550—even though he had no money left for supplies.

La Cabanne provisioned his vessel by stopping every ship he encountered in the Canary Islands. He gave promissory notes to the captains of French vessels and simply looted ships of other nations. Arriving at the city of Santo Domingo, he bombarded nine merchant vessels in the harbor until they paid ransom in sugar, wine, and cowhides. Since France and Spain were at peace, royal officials at Bayonne confiscated his ship, but the king released it after imposing a fine.

LA CARTE, BROTHER (Knight of Malta; Mediterranean; 1651) A Frenchman, La Carte plundered Spanish merchantmen while France and Spain were at war. Although the knights freely plundered Muslims, Jews, and Greek Christians, they spared French and Spanish vessels for fear of retaliation. The grand master ordered Maltese coastal batteries to drive La Carte out to sea when he attempted to return.

LAFFITE (LAFITTE), JEAN (1) (American pirate; Gulf of Mexico, Caribbean; 1780?–1821?) More of a businessman than a seaman, Jean Laffite excelled as a leader and maintained order among a large gang of criminals. In dealings with officials and naval officers, he had elegant manners and entertained lavishly. Until late in life, he was a romantic figure—tall, slender, and handsome, with dark hair and eyes. He charmed numerous aristocratic women.

Nothing certain is known about Laffite's ancestry and early life. He probably was born in France and became a seaman in his youth. By 1809, he and his brother Pierre owned a blacksmith shop in New Orleans, which fenced goods and slaves smuggled into Louisiana. (The United States had outlawed the slave trade in 1807.)

From about 1810, Laffite led the pirates based at Barataria Bay, a shallow body of water south of New Orleans. Some held privateering licenses from French governors in the Caribbean. Others had commissions from Cartagena (modern Colombia), which had rebelled against Spain.

Under Laffite's shrewd direction, 10 or more pirate vessels plundered in the Gulf of Mexico, sometimes attacking American and British as well as Spanish shipping. Laffite and his brother Pierre were arrested in 1812 but never showed up for trial. When the governor offered $750 for his capture in 1813, Laffite offered twice as much for the governor. Many in New Orleans traded with the pirates, and the U. S. government was occupied by the War of 1812.

Early in September 1814, British officers offered Laffite a pardon, financial rewards, and military rank if he would aid their attack on New Orleans. Laffite informed Louisiana officials of the British offer, but they spurned his advances at this time. Two weeks later, a small naval squadron captured the Barataria settlement and the ships in port. Laffite and his comrades escaped into the interior and returned as soon as the navy left.

In December 1814, General Andrew Jackson arrived and took command of New Orleans' defenders. Jackson was persuaded to meet with Laffite and accepted his offer of help. The pirates formed their own artillery units, and many fought in the battles around New Orleans in late December and early January. In February 1815, President James Madison pardoned past crimes by Laffite and his gang. However, the property confiscated during the September 1814 raid on Barataria was not restored.

Since naval forces were watching Barataria, the Laffite brothers pushed westward to Spain's turbulent province of Texas. For a time, Galveston was in the hands of an adventurer working for Mexico. When he left, Laffite took over early in 1817. In a game of triplecross, he bargained with (and perhaps took money from) Spain, the Texas insurgents, and the United States.

Criminals flocked to Galveston, which harbored 20 vessels and a thousand men by the summer of 1818. The pirates looted American as well as Spanish vessels and also raided Louisiana for slaves. An American warship chased one band to Galveston in November 1819, but Laffite pacified its officers by hanging the leading offender.

One of Laffite's cruisers captured and sank an American merchantman near Matagorda, Texas, in 1820. Early in 1821, an American warship visited Galveston. Laffite agreed to leave and burned the Galveston settlement. He and Pierre continued to raid from isolated ports in Central America. Some say that he died in 1821 and was buried near Mérida, Mexico, on the Yucatan Peninsula.

(See also SELECTED BIBLIOGRAPHY: Saxon, *Laffite.*)

LAFFITE (LAFITTE), JEAN (2) (fictional American pirate; 1816 to the present) Novels and fictional biographies have heightened the romantic elements in the life of Jean LAFFITE (1). After reading a newspaper account of the battle of New Orleans, Lord Byron wrote THE CORSAIR. Delighted by the idea of a pirate turned patriot, he did not try to describe the real Laffite. Byron's version of Laffite inspired Joseph Ingraham to write LAFFITE, THE PIRATE OF THE GULF, an 1836 novel that invents many lurid adventures.

In what was possibly a literary hoax, one George A. Pierce published a biographical sketch of Laffite in 1856. Before coming to Louisiana, Pierce's Laffite was a privateer and slaver in the East Indies. He reaches Barataria and becomes "The Terror of the Gulf." After leaving Galveston, he is chased by a British warship and dies in a horrendous duel.

Although both Ingraham and Pierce were harshly criticized at the time, their incredible stories became the basis for subsequent novels and movies. Following Pierce,

Jean Laffite (played by Yul Brynner) hangs the pirate captain who had destroyed the *Corinthian*. From *The Buccaneer* (1958).

subsequent writers inflate the $1,500 reward Laffite offered for the governor's arrest—sometimes to as much as $50,000. Although many have searched, Laffite's buried treasure has never been found and probably never existed. Barataria was looted by the navy, Galveston was wrecked by a hurricane in 1818, and Laffite's last years were profitless.

(See also SELECTED BIBLIOGRAPHY: Saxon, *Lafitte*.)

LAFFITE (LAFITTE), PIERRE (American pirate; Gulf of Mexico, Caribbean; active 1809–1821)
The brother and trusted partner of Jean LAFFITE (1). Mexican documents suggest that Pierre died in 1821 and that he, not Jean, was buried near Mérida, Mexico. However, Pierre is named as the father of a child baptized at New Orleans early in 1825.

LAFFITE, THE PIRATE OF THE GULF (novel; 1836)
One of dozens of sentimental romances, some widely popular, by the Reverend Joseph Holt Ingraham (1809–1860). Ingraham based his tale on Lord Byron's notes to THE CORSAIR, which give Jean LAFFITE as the model for Byron's own villain-hero.

Ingraham's Laffite is the handsome son of a fine old family. He becomes a wanderer after murdering his brother in a moment of rage. After various bloody crimes (during which he converts to Islam), Laffite builds a fort upon an "impregnable rock" at Barataria. Redeemed by the love of a good woman, he helps win the battle of New Orleans. He is stabbed for a crime he did not commit and dies just as he learns that his brother is not really dead.

The novel deals only incidentally with life at sea, and Ingraham apparently never visited Louisiana. The hero wanders through ruined monasteries and crumbling castles. Marble stairs lead down to still lagoons, and strong men duel with rapiers while frail females swoon.

LAGARDE, CAPTAIN (French buccaneer; Caribbean; 1677)
Lagarde occupied Santa Marta, Venezuela, with five or six French and English captains, including Captain BARNES and John COXON. To save the town, the governor and the bishop agreed to pay a ransom. Instead of money, the governor of CARTAGENA dispatched 500 men and three ships. The pirates fought their way back to their vessels with their hostages and about £20 each in silver.

The captains decided to take their prisoners to Jamaica, where they arrived early in July. France (but not England) was at war with Spain, and the pirates carried French PRIVATEERING commissions, obtained at TORTUGA. However, Jamaica had passed a law the previous April forbidding the use of foreign commissions by English subjects. The English captains promised to obey the law in the future, and the bishop was freed. (Sir Henry MORGAN gave him some richly embroidered vestments he had seized during his 1671 raid on PANAMA.) Lagarde fled to Tortuga with the other hostages—"being obstinate and damnably enraged the English had left them."

(See also SELECTED BIBLIOGRAPHY: Cruikshank, *Morgan*; Haring, *Buccaneers*.)

LAHE, CAPTAIN *(Maltese corsair; Mediterranean; active 1660–1661)* Captain Lahe took several prizes in CONSERVA partnership with Aloisio GAMARRA.

LANCASTER, SIR JAMES *(English captain; Atlantic, Pacific, Indian Ocean; 1554?–1618)* Born in Hampshire, Lancaster spent his youth in Portugal, traded in Spain in the early 1580s, and was financially hurt when war broke out in 1585. His subsequent sea raids were driven by an enduring hatred of the Spanish and Portuguese (united with Spain from 1580 to 1640).

Lancaster commanded private warships for London merchants against the Spanish Armada (1588) and during Sir Francis DRAKE's raids on Cadiz (1587) and Lisbon (1589). In 1590, he took the 250-ton, 25-gun *Edward Bonaventure* to the Azores in consort with Samuel FOXCROFT. There they captured a rich Dutch prize and brutally tortured its crew.

Commanding the *Bonaventure*, Lancaster joined Foxcroft and George RAYMOND on the first English voyage around the Cape of Good Hope. Although sponsored by London merchants, the expedition was not a commercial venture. Given soldiers but no cargo, the captains were expected to explore while plundering foreign shipping.

Many men perished of SCURVY (1) and fever along the African coast and during the difficult Cape passage. After Foxcroft died, his ship returned to England with the sick, and Raymond's ship sank in a storm. Lancaster went on alone with the *Bonaventure*, with Edmund BARKER second-in-command.

Lancaster made for southern India, where he hoped to intercept Portuguese merchantmen. Buffeted by contrary winds, he finally found a base on the island of Penang, off western Malaysia. During the next three months (June to September 1592), the English pillaged three Portuguese ships carrying pepper and rice.

As the crew continued to sicken and die, Lancaster feared Portuguese retaliation and retreated to the Nicobar Islands and Ceylon. In December 1592, the surviving men insisted on returning. The Cape was passed for a second time, and Saint Helena was reached in April 1593. Lancaster's men demanded that he try a direct course to England, but the ship was becalmed in the Doldrums. In June, Lancaster finally reached Mona Island, between Puerto Rico and the Dominican Republic.

The *Bonaventure* now tried for Newfoundland, but a gale forced it back to Mona in November. When Lancaster took 18 men ashore for water, the six sailors on board made off and wrecked the *Bonaventure* off Hispaniola. Left MAROONED for a month, Lancaster and 13 other survivors were rescued and carried to Europe by French pirates, including Jean LENOIR. Lancaster's three-year odyssey had killed nine-tenths of his crew and destroyed the sponsors' entire investment.

Despite this disaster, Lancaster soon received command of three small ships sent to raid Pernambuco, Brazil. An immensely rich booty rewarded his exemplary conduct of the entire venture. Edmund Barker and Randolph COTTON accompanied Lancaster. From prisoners taken in the Canary Islands, they learned that the Pernambuco warehouses temporarily held the cargo from a wrecked East Indian CARRACK. At the Cape Verde Islands, Lancaster's ships encountered four vessels under Edward FENNER. Happy to strengthen his squadron, Lancaster offered Fenner a fourth of the booty in return for his aid.

At Recife, the port city of Pernambuco, Lancaster found three large Dutch ships, sent to pick up the carrack's cargo. With the Dutch remaining neutral, Lancaster occupied Recife in a swift attack in April 1595. During the next month, his prudent management frustrated repeated efforts to retake the town.

The carrack's treasures and other booty were more than the seven English ships could carry, and Lancaster convinced the Dutch captains to take part of the haul on freight terms. Meanwhile, five French pirate ships arrived, including two under Jean Lenoir, Lancaster's rescuer in 1593. Lancaster invited them to help themselves from Recife's warehouses. As the raid ended, Cotton, Baker, and Lenoir disobeyed orders and were killed while impetuously charging a Portuguese fortification.

Fifteen ships stocked tight with loot sailed in May, but one was lost on the way home. In all, the English harvested well over £50,000 worth of plunder.

By its charter of 1600, the East India Company was granted a monopoly of Asian commerce. The company gave Lancaster overall command of its first expedition and five strong ships, headed by the *Red Dragon* (once the earl of CUMBERLAND's *Malice Scourge*). In contrast to Lancaster's 1591 venture, this was primarily a merchant voyage. Lancaster reached Sumatra in June 1602, captured a valuable Portuguese prize in the Straits of Malacca, and pressed on to Bantam. The expedition traded successfully—making good use of the captured Portuguese calicoes—and returned to England with a cargo of pepper.

Lancaster—knighted in 1603—had been enriched by the 1595 Pernambuco raid and was now in poor health. He made no more voyages but remained an active director of the East India Company until his death.

(See also SELECTED BIBLIOGRAPHY: Andrews, *Trade*; Foster, *Voyages*.)

LAND HO! *(nautical slang; uncertain origin)* The traditional report when the lookout sights land. Then he usually is asked "where away?" and replies with the direction, for example "on the port bow."

LANDLUBBER See LUBBER/LANDLUBBER.

LANDY, JOHN *(French pirate; Atlantic; active 1540s)* Landy settled in England by 1540 and commanded ships for prominent merchant-adventurers, including William HAWKINS and Thomas Winter. In 1545, as master of the *Mary Figge,* he captured a valuable Spanish prize in consort with Thomas WYNDHAM.

LANE, WILLIAM (English pirate; Caribbean; born 1555?, active 1590–1595)

By the 1570s, Lane was associated with Thomas WATTS, a London merchant and prominent sponsor of privateering cruises. In 1590, after sailing on several earlier ventures, Lane commanded a PINNACE, the smallest of three ships sent under Abraham COCKE to the West Indies and Virginia.

In 1591, Watts promoted Lane to command of five large ships and a pinnace. While in the West Indies, Lane's squadron sometimes operated in consort with separate expeditions under Christopher NEWPORT and William IRISH. Although it showed little heroism when attacked by a Spanish patrol, Lane's squadron captured eight merchantmen, including two richly laden ships detached from the Mexican TREASURE FLEET.

As Lane's sponsors, Watts and his partners took in some £40,000 and made at least a 200 percent profit on the 1591 raid. Captain Irish's backer (Sir George CAREY) sued Watts for a share, but he could not prove that Irish and Lane were in consort when the prizes were taken. Despite this rich haul, Lane complained that his subordinate captains—Michael GEARE, William CRASTON, and Stephen MICHELL—were crude ruffians who stole prize goods.

A return voyage with three ships in 1592 proved less profitable. Along with several other English privateers, Lane waited off Cuba for the Mexican treasure fleet. However, the Spaniards knew of their presence and delayed sailing until the English left to avoid the hurricane season. Lane's 1594 expedition captured several vessels off the Havana coast, even though Spanish patrols captured John MYDDELTON, one of his consorts.

While off Hispaniola during his 1594 raid, Lane seized a French ship, carrying survivors of James LANCASTER's unfortunate Indian Ocean expedition. Considering that the French captain had just rescued the English mariners, Lane's capture of his ship was grossly ungrateful piracy. The French owners sued before the ADMIRALTY COURT, but there is no record of its decision.

(See also SELECTED BIBLIOGRAPHY: Andrews, *English.*)

LANFRANC OF THESSALONICA, SIR (corsair; Mediterranean, 1276)

Probably of French origin, Lanfranc lived in Thessalonica in northwestern Greece. Sailing from ANAIA, he raided a village and captured a merchant ship at the tip of Greece.

(See also VENETIAN CLAIMS.)

LANGTON, JAMES (English captain; Atlantic, Caribbean; born 1558?, active 1593–1598)

Langton accompanied Sir Francis DRAKE's 1585 West Indian raid, probably as a junior officer. Fluent in Spanish and a brave and efficient military leader, he was the earl of CUMBERLAND's most trusted captain from 1593 to 1598.

As he returned from a cruise off Spain in 1593, Cumberland sent Langton to the West Indies with the *Pilgrim* and the *Anthony.* He reached Venezuela in August, plundered the pearl fishery on Margarita Island, but was repulsed before Cumaná and RIO DE LA HACHA. Hispaniola proved easier prey. After circling the island, Langton found a base just east of Santo Domingo. For the next two-and-a-half months, he kept that city virtually blockaded, capturing nine vessels and plundering and taking ransoms from plantations along the coast.

Langton took a few prizes near Jamaica in February 1594. The *Pilgrim* returned to England and was captured by French pirates along the way. With the *Anthony* and a captured frigate, Langton made for Honduras. During three days of hard fighting, six ships were taken at PUERTO CABALLOS. None contained treasure, but the best of the cargo was piled into the enemy flagship and sold in England for a good profit.

In 1595, Cumberland entrusted Langton with five vessels including the newly built *Malice Scourge,* a powerful 600-ton warship. The squadron cruised off the Azores but returned with little to show for large expenses. Langton commanded the 400-ton *Prosperous* during Cumberland's 1598 invasion of Puerto Rico. He received command of the *Malice Scourge,* the earl's flagship, on the return voyage.

(See also SELECTED BIBLIOGRAPHY: Andrews, *Elizabethan.*)

LARBI MISTERI, ABU ABDULLA MOHAMMED (Moroccan corsair; Mediterranean; active 1760s and 1770s)

A native Moroccan chosen by Sultan Mawlay Mohammed (ruled 1757–1790) to restore SALÉ as a pirate haven. In 1764, the sultan sent Larbi Misteri as ambassador to England to purchase cannon and rigging. He was named Salé's first governor by 1771, a new title intended to raise the corsairs' prestige. The next year, he commanded the best ship in the small Salé squadron, a 20-gun FRIGATE.

LASCHMI MISTERI (Moroccan corsair; Mediterranean; active 1770s)

Laschmi Misteri was a SALÉ captain captured in September 1772 by the KNIGHTS OF SAINT STEPHEN and imprisoned at Livorno.

"LAST BUCCANEER, THE" (poem; 1857)

In this poem Charles Kingsley (1819–1875), best-selling Victorian author and clergyman, describes the romantic life of the BUCCANEERS. Having escaped poverty in England, the buccaneers enjoy a tropical paradise. There they live as free men who make and obey their own laws. Like modern-day Robin Hoods, they steal from those who previously robbed others.

Daniel DEFOE and other authors had glorified pirates as brave men rejecting a corrupt social order. But the theme seems oddly subversive in a poem by Queen Victoria's personal chaplain.

(See also WESTWARD HO!)

LAST OF THE BUCCANEERS (motion picture; color; 1950)

Directed by Lew Landers, this tale about Jean LAFFITE (Paul HENREID) begins after the Americans have driven the British invaders from New Orleans. When the governor of Louisiana fails to return his ships, Laffite captures a vessel and escapes to Galveston Island. There he is joined by Sergeants Dominick (Jack Oakie) and Beluche (John Dehner) and by Swallow (Mary Anderson), a female freebooter who loves him.

Laffite's gang plunders Spanish shipping, leading to many complaints from merchants purchasing Spanish goods. But the government tolerates Laffite until one of his captains attacks an American vessel. Belle Summers (Karin Booth), who comes to Galveston to marry Laffite, finds the American goods. Government forces are told and raid the island before Laffite can clear himself. Laffite and Belle escape, planning to start over somewhere else.

Last of the Buccaneers contains all the standard pirate fare plus Indians fighting cavalry. As Dominick, Oakie sings the comedy song "Pirate from Kentucky."

LAUGHTON, CHARLES (American actor; 1899–1962)

Born in Yorkshire, England, Laughton became an American citizen in 1950. He broke away from his family's hotel business in 1925 to join the stage. A leading London star by 1930, he made his first movie in 1932. He achieved fame in American and British films throughout the 1930s while maintaining an equally commanding position in the theater.

The rotund actor had an affinity for roles as misfits, outsiders, and physical or mental cripples. To avoid repetition of these parts, he found ways of adding unusual facets, so that even his darkest villains enjoyed the audience's understanding.

Charles Laughton catches Randolph Scott rifling his cabin in *Captain Kidd* (1945).

Laughton's appearance and approach lent themselves to tyrannical roles. He starred in the 1933 *The Private Life of Henry VIII* (winning the first Oscar by an actor in a British film) and played the overbearing Captain Bligh in *The Mutiny on the Bounty* (1935). The most extreme of his deformed outsiders was Quasimodo in *The Hunchback of Notre Dame* (1939). He excelled in more complex roles, including Inspector Javert in *Les Miserables* (1935), the dignified butler in *Ruggles of Red Gap* (1935), and the artist in *Rembrandt*.

Laughton prepared an English version of *Galileo* with playwright Bertolt Brecht from 1943 to 1946. In 1945, he starred in CAPTAIN KIDD, probably the most chilling screen portrait of a pirate villain. Although mainly occupied with reading tours and directing during the 1950s, Laughton continued to appear in films, including ABBOTT AND COSTELLO MEET CAPTAIN KIDD (1952). He played the elderly barrister in *Witness for the Prosecution* (1957), Senator Gracchus in SPARTACUS (1960), and a viciously bigoted southern senator in *Advise and Consent* (1962).

LA VALETTE, BROTHER JEAN PARISOT DE (grand master of the Knights of Malta, 1494–1568)

A nobleman descended from the counts of Toulouse, La Valette became a KNIGHT HOSPITALER in 1515. Totally dedicated to the order, he never returned to France. After helping defend RHODES during the OTTOMAN siege of 1522, he followed the grand master to MALTA. An expert and inspired military leader, he was tall and handsome, had a cold and serene manner, and spoke several languages including Arabic and Turkish.

La Valette commanded a galley from 1534 to 1536 during raids along the BARBARY COAST and during the Spanish invasion of TUNIS. In 1540, he purchased his own GALIOT. While attacking merchant shipping, he was captured and made a GALLEY SLAVE by ABDUL-RAHMAN CASTAGLI REIS. TURGUT REIS, the great Barbary corsair, recognized La Valette at the oars and ordered that he receive better treatment.

The knights exchanged a high-ranking Turkish official to secure La Valette's release in 1541. He served for a time as governor of TRIPOLI. After the Ottomans conquered Tripoli in 1551, he commanded a galley during a vindictive raid that captured 1,500 slaves near the city.

From 1554 to 1556, La Valette led the order's squadrons as CAPTAIN GENERAL OF GALLEYS. In September 1554, the knights captured Abdul-Rahman, who now took his turn as a galley slave. Needing money and slaves to fortify Malta, the order encouraged piratical cruises, and La Valette also carried out solo raids on North Africa.

Elected grand master in 1557, La Valette served until his death in 1568. He intensified piracy and encouraged individual knights to acquire their own corsair warships. La Valette set an example by owning two galleys and a sailing ship, which he placed under ROMEGAS' command.

During the 1565 seige, La Valette brilliantly defended Malta and was wounded in battle. Ordering resistance to the death, he had his men shoot the heads of prisoners from CANNON. After the seige, he rebuilt the island's fortification. The slopes of the Sceberra Peninsula were leveled and work began on the city later named Valletta in his honor.

LA VEVEN (LA VIVION), CAPTAIN *(French pirate; Mediterranean, Caribbean; active 1660s)*
La Veven was captain of *Le Cerf Volant* (*The Soaring Stag*), a 14-gun warship from La Rochelle. Accused of looting a merchant ship from Virginia, he was captured near Haiti by Edward COLLIER in late 1668. In his defense, La Veven presented a privateering commission acquired while he cruised in the Mediterranean. He was taken to Jamaica, his ship was seized, and he was condemned to death but later reprieved.

LAZARIST (LAZARITE) FATHERS *(French missionaries; Mediterranean; 1643–1789)* Whether or not he was enslaved himself, Saint VINCENT DE PAUL was concerned about the Barbary SLAVES. About 1624, he founded the quasi-monastic "Congregation of the Missions," known as the Lazarists. The order set up permanent posts in TUNIS (1643) and ALGIERS (1646). From 1650, the pope made their leader at Algiers an apostolic vicar and titular bishop responsible for Christian slaves throughout North Africa. The REDEMPTIONISTS did not welcome the French Lazarists. Redemptionists already staffed chapels throughout Barbary, and the Spanish Trinitarians maintained a hospital in Algiers. They refused to obey the orders of the Lazarist vicar.

Lazarist priests also served as chaplains to the French consulates, and they sometimes acted for long periods as consuls. Having gone into debt to ransom captives, Father Barreau twice was imprisoned at Algiers during the 1650s. Father Le Vacher, the apostolic vicar, was acting consul when the French navy bombarded Algiers in 1682 and 1683.

The French admiral insulted the aged and ill Le Vacher when he tried to mediate. After MEZZOMORTO seized power, Le Vacher and 20 other Frenchmen were tied to the mouth of a cannon and blown to pieces. In 1688 the French again bombarded Algiers. The enraged Algerians castrated and half-lynched Father Montmasson, the next apostolic vicar, while dragging him to the cannon for execution.

LE BASQUE, MICHEL *(French buccaneer; Caribbean; active 1667 and earlier)* EXQUEMELIN says Le Basque fought as a soldier in Europe, joined the BUCCANEERS on TORTUGA ISLAND, and retired with rich spoils. Lured by the possibility of splendid booty, he joined François L'OLONNAIS in a successful assault on Maracaibo and Gibraltar, Venezuela, serving as commander during land battles.

LE CLERC, FRANÇOIS *(French corsair; Atlantic, Caribbean; died 1563)* From Normandy, Le Clerc financed voyages by other captains as well as commanding

his own ships. Always among the first to board the enemy, Le Clerc lost his leg and severely damaged an arm fighting with the king's forces (perhaps against the English at Guernsey in 1549). He was ennobled for bravery in battle in 1551.

Despite his wounds, Le Clerc led major raids against the Spanish, who nicknamed him Pié de Palo (PEG LEG). In 1553, he assumed overall command of seven pirate craft as well as three royal warships, the latter commanded by himself, Jacques SORES, and Robert BLONDEL. This strong fleet raided San Germán in Puerto Rico and methodically looted the ports of Hispaniola from south to north, stealing hides and cannon. Richer booty was taken on the return voyage, as the corsairs savagely plundered Las Palmas on Grand Canary Island and captured a Genoese CARRACK.

Le Clerc returned to the West Indies in 1554 with eight large ships and 300 soldiers. It was most likely this force that took Santiago de Cuba by surprise, occupied it for a month, and left with 80,000 pesos in booty. They devastated Cuba's first capital so completely that it remained a stricken struggling place, soon completely eclipsed by Havana.

In April 1562, Protestants in several Norman cities rebelled against their Roman Catholic king. Queen Elizabeth I dispatched English troops, who occupied Le Havre until June 1563. If he had any religious beliefs, Le Clerc probably was a Catholic. (Unlike Sores or Sir Francis DRAKE, he did not desecrate churches when he raided Spanish cities.) Nevertheless, he joined the English invaders and ravished French shipping. In March 1563, he asked for a large pension as a reward for his treachery. Wounded in his pride when Queen Elizabeth turned down his request, he sailed for the Azores and was killed hunting Spanish treasure ships.

(See also SELECTED BIBLIOGRAPHY: Andrews, *Spanish*; Wright, *Early Cuba*.)

LE GOLIF, LOUIS ADHÉMAR TIMOTHÉE
See MEMOIRS OF A BUCCANEER.

LE GRAND, PIERRE *(French pirate; Caribbean; about 1620)* A Norman nicknamed "Peter the Great" (his true name is unknown), Le Grand was the first BUCCANEER to settle on TORTUGA ISLAND. With one small boat and 28 men, he captured a great GALLEON, the flagship of a Spanish TREASURE FLEET, as it passed Cape Tiburon in western Hispaniola.

Pierre had been at sea a long time without meeting any prey. Food was short, and his boat was in bad shape. Suddenly he caught sight of a ship, which had fallen behind the rest of the Spanish fleet. He decided to board her, judging that the Spaniards would not expect an attack. His men swore an oath to fight to the death. Nevertheless, Pierre bored a hole in the bottom of his boat, thus preventing escape should the assault fail.

It was nearly dark when the raiders came alongside the galleon. Noiselessly, they clambered on deck, each

Pierre Le Grand and his brigands board the Spanish galleon and confront the captain in his cabin. Illustration by Howard Pyle in *Harper's Monthly Magazine*, August 1887.

carrying a PISTOL and a CUTLASS. Meeting no resistance, they made for the cabin, where the captain and some others were playing cards. Instantly a pistol was at his breast, and he surrendered the ship. Meanwhile, other raiders seized the arms in the gun room, killing some Spaniards who defended themselves. "What devils are these?" they cried out, startled by the pirates' savage appearance.

Spanish sailors had noticed the strange vessel earlier that day. But the contemptuous captain swore that he did not fear a warship of his own size, let alone such a small and tattered boat. Pierre kept as many Spanish sailors as he needed to run the ship, put the rest ashore, and set sail for France.

EXQUEMELIN reported this story, asserting that he had borrowed it from the "diary of a reliable person." There is no way of knowing whether Exquemelin's account contains any truth. Small raiding parties sometimes did take large ships by surprise. However, Spanish records do not mention the loss of a flagship, and Pierre's feat seems to be invented to point up the captain's arrogance.

LEMBOS *(pirate ship; Mediterranean; about 250 B.C. to A.D. 250)* A small GALLEY, especially built for speed by ILLYRIAN pirates, such as TEUTA, DEMETRIUS OF PHAROS, SCERDILAIDAS, and GENTHIUS. Shortly before 200, Philip V of Macedonia adopted the design for a special naval unit employed for spying, surprise attacks,

and troop transport. The Roman imperial fleet similarly included a type of lembos, called the LIBURNIAN.

Nothing is known about the lembos' shape, except that its prow was sharply pointed. Lemboi carried 15 to 50 rowers and might have one or two banks of oars. Those used in battle had a ram. The combat lembos would dart in among the enemy's heavier warships to break up their formation, interrupt their tactics, and damage their oars.

(See also SHIPS, PIRATE.)

LEMNOS *(pirate haven; Aegean Sea; 800–500 B.C.)* The island of Lemnos was inhabited by "Pelagasians" and "Tyrsenoi," immigrants from Asia Minor possibly related to the ETRUSCANS. According to legend, they raided the Greek mainland in 50-oared PENTECONTERS. On one raid, Lemnian corsairs ambushed Athenian women marching in a religious procession. They carried away many, but later killed the women and their children in a quarrel. Lemnos was still a pirate haven when the Athenians occupied the island in about 500.

LENOIR, JEAN *(French pirate; Caribbean, Atlantic; active 1594–1595)* In April 1594, Lenoir commanded a Norman warship that rescued James LANCASTER and Edmund BARKER, marooned on Mona Island (off Puerto Rico) after a disastrous East Indian voyage. Lenoir was an interloper in those waters, which were closed to foreigners. He traded illegally with the Spanish colonists and probably turned pirate whenever a good opportunity presented itself.

Lenoir commanded one of three French warships cruising off the Brazilian coast in April 1595. By coincidence, the French again ran into Lancaster, whose men had just occupied Recife. Since Lancaster had more booty than he could take away, he invited Lenoir to help himself from the Recife warehouses. As the English and French raiders prepared to leave, they learned that the Portuguese were building a redoubt to block the harbor. Lenoir was killed during an attack that destroyed the enemy fort.

(See also COTTON, RANDOLPH; LANE, WILLIAM.)

LEO OF TRIPOLI *(Muslim corsair; Mediterranean; active 900–923)* Born in CILICIA of Christian parents, he converted to Islam and settled at Tripoli in Lebanon. (Arabic chronicles call him Rashiq Al-Wardami or Gjulam Zurafa.) The most daring and skillful Muslim admiral before the 15th century, he sacked Thessalonica, the BYZANTINE EMPIRE's second city.

During the 840s, the Abbassid caliphs had created a navy based in Syria and at Tarsus in Cilicia. From 900, the caliph enlarged these fleets to reconquer Egypt and attack the Christian enemy. The Muslims ravaged the Aegean islands and northern Greece in 902 and attempted a landing near Athens. In July 904, Leo appeared in the Dardanelles with 54 large galleys—each with more than 200 men—drawn from CRETE and several Syrian ports.

Leo planned to capture Constantinople with the help of Greek traitors. When he met unexpected resistance, he retreated into the Aegean and instead attacked Thessalonica. Using flaming missiles, the Muslims captured and plundered the city after a three-day siege. Crammed with 22,000 prisoners, their ships withdrew to Crete. There the captives were sold (some later were ransomed), and the men divided their booty into equal shares.

Leo's corsairs terrorized the Aegean for a generation. Joining forces with Damian, another Christian renegade, he routed the Greek fleet near Chios in 911. He was undefeated until 923, when the revived Byzantine navy crushed his squadrons near Lemnos.

LE PAIN, PETER *(French pirate; Caribbean; 1682)* While captain of the French merchantman *La Trompeuse (The Deceiver)*, he seized the ship and cargo, took them to Jamaica in June 1682, and sought asylum as a Protestant. Without inquiring into his story, Jamaican authorities allowed him to settle and sell his cargo. When the truth came out, Le Pain was arrested and shipped to Saint Domingue for punishment. Meanwhile, Jamaican merchants hired the *Trompeuse* and sent her to Honduras. The pirate Jean HAMLIN pursued and captured the *Trompeuse*, made her his flagship, and devastated English shipping.

LEPANTO, BATTLE OF *(naval battle; Mediterranean; October 7, 1571)* Frustrated by the disastrous 1565 siege of MALTA, the OTTOMAN EMPIRE invaded the Venetian possession of Cyprus in June 1570. In response to Venetian appeals for help, Spain, the papacy, and the KNIGHTS OF MALTA sent ships to Cyprus. ULUJ ALI, corsair viceroy of ALGIERS, destroyed the Maltese squadron in July 1570, and quarrels between the Spanish and Venetian commanders prevented their taking action.

The pope, hoping to avoid the previous year's failures, joined Spain and Venice in a Holy League, created in May 1571. The league was planned as a permanent alliance. The three powers agreed to contribute 200 galleys and 100 sailing ships each year to raid both the eastern Mediterranean and the BARBARY STATES.

Under the overall command of Don Juan of Austria, the Spanish king's illegitimate brother, the allies assembled more than 200 galleys in Sicily. Pierre SAINT AUBIN led three Maltese galleys, while ROMEGAS helped to command the papal squadron. The Ottomans brought about 230 galleys and 70 GALIOTS to the Gulf of Patras, near Lepanto (Návpaktos), Greece—including about 40 ships commanded by ULUJ ALI's Algerian corsairs.

The two fleets met in battle, with Uluj Ali commanding on the left wing. After about four hours of fighting, the allies were victorious in the center. Although he captured the Maltese flagship, Uluj Ali's advance on the seaward flank came too late. Altogether the Ottoman navy lost seven ships, 30,000 dead, and 3,500 captured.

Almost as soon as Europe hailed this great Christian triumph, victory slipped away. Uluj Ali rebuilt the Ottoman fleet, and Venice accepted the lose of Cyprus in a 1573 treaty. The Spanish seized TUNIS in 1573, but the Ottomans recaptured it the following year. In fact, however, the reconquest of Tunis was their last major naval expedition, and the Ottomans and Spain signed a truce in 1577.

With Spanish and Ottoman withdrawal, Mediterranean piracy reached a peak not seen since the CILICIANS 1,600 years earlier. Until at least 1650, the Barbary and SALÉ corsairs raided from England to Sicily. In the east, Muslim and Venetian ships were plundered by the Maltese, the KNIGHTS OF SAINT STEPHEN, and rovers from Sicily and Naples. English pirates plundered every nation, as did hundreds of small gangs sailing from virtually every port between Majorca and Istanbul. The pirates' golden age lasted until Britain and France built up navies that imposed order on both Christian and Muslim marauders.

LE PICARD, CAPTAIN *(French buccaneer; Caribbean, Pacific; active 1685–1688)* Possibly the Pierre LE PICARD with François L'OLONNAIS in 1668. With Captains Jean ROSE and Desmarais, he brought 260 BUCCANEERS, mostly French, across Panama in April 1685. At the Pearl Islands, his band joined English raiders led by Edward DAVIS. The pirates formed groups based on nationality, and Le Picard and other Frenchmen came under François GROGNIET's command.

A defeat by Peruvian ships on June 8 caused angry quarrels. Most of the English raiders sailed off with Edward Davis. Without seaworthy vessels and adequate provisions, Grogniet's company stayed in Central America, attacking isolated ranches and small villages.

A year later, in March 1686, Grogniet's men joined a group under Captain TOWNLEY, captured Granada in Nicaragua, but won little booty. Le Picard and many others deserted Grogniet in May and went on to Panama with Townley. When Townley was killed in battle in August, Le Picard assumed overall command of the gang, although the English had their own ship under George HOUT.

While they recovered from the battle, the buccaneers wrote to Panama's governor, demanding immediate return of five captured pirates. Infuriated by the governor's refusal, they decapitated 20 Spanish captives. Their heads were sent to Panama with a warning that 90 others would die unless the pirates were released. The horrified governor sent out the five pirates and agreed to pay 10,000 pesos for the remaining Spanish prisoners.

Returning north, Le Picard and Hout sacked and destroyed Nicoya (La Mansión), Nicaragua, and then recombined with the remnants of Grogniet's group in February 1687. Thanks to unusually careful planning, the pirates captured the prosperous Ecuadorian port of Guayaquil on April 30 and occupied it until May 27. Grogniet died on May 2, and Le Picard took command of the French forces.

At Guayaquil, torture and terror were used to unearth hidden treasures, and the pirates again decapitated prisoners to speed up payment of a ransom. Fearing diseases from the corpses littering the streets, the raiders moved to a nearby island on May 16. Raveneau de LUSSAN, one of the company, describes their few weeks of debauchery, with ample food, drink, and women as well as music by the Guayaquil town band.

While Le Picard's men were relishing these rare luxuries, Edward Davis reappeared on May 16 and warned that the Spaniards were planning a counterattack. After threatening to kill more prisoners, the raiders received a ransom of 42,000 pesos. Three days later, a Peruvian fleet arrived and drove away the buccaneers. Le Picard and Davis distributed about 200,000 pesos taken at Guayaquil, with each man receiving at least 400.

Davis returned to the Caribbean around Cape Horn. Including prizes, Le Picard now had five small ships. But all had been badly damaged in the recent battle, and his band was forced to take the land route. After attacking towns along the Mexican coast, about 280 pirates crossed Costa Rica early in 1688. During the difficult two-month journey, Le Picard lost control, and the buccaneers broke up into small groups. Some lost their booty when their rafts turned over, and others were murdered by greedy companions.

LE PICARD, PIERRE *(French buccaneer; Caribbean; 1668)* Le Picard probably is a nickname, referring to the province of Picardy. Commanding a small ship, he took part in François L'OLONNAIS's unlucky voyage to PUERTO CABALLOS and San Pedro, Honduras. Disappointed with their small plunder, Le Picard and the other captains deserted L'Olonnais.

According to EXQUEMELIN, Le Picard sailed south to raid Costa Rican gold mines. The buccaneers grabbed only a few pounds of gold in Veragua, the home of the black slaves working at the mines. The presence of large Spanish forces blocked an assault on the richer town of Nata, on the Pacific coast.

LE SAGE, CAPTAIN *(French buccaneer; Caribbean, Atlantic; active 1684–1687)* His 30-gun *Tiger* was based at Saint Domingue in 1684. Soon after, he sailed for the Strait of Magellan, intending to join Edward DAVIS and other pirate captains ravaging South America's Pacific coast. The *Tiger* was driven back by contrary winds, and Le Sage instead cruised along West Africa for two years, returning to the Caribbean with great booty taken from Dutch ships.

LESCUYER, CAPTAIN *(French buccaneer; Caribbean; 1685)* Leading about 280 French and English pirates, Lescuyer and François GROGNIET marched across Panama early in 1685. Raveneau de LUSSAN wrote that Lescuyer died shortly after the pirates arrived at the Pearl Islands. His crew merged with Grogniet's and joined a larger company under Edward DAVIS.

LESSONE, CAPTAIN *(French buccaneer; Caribbean; active 1675–1680)* Captain Lessone was among the first buccaneers to attempt the overland route across the Isthmus of Panama. He led a small body of men toward the Pacific in 1675 but was driven back before the town of Chepo. In 1680, he sacked PORTOBELO with Bartholomew SHARP, but refused to go on to PANAMA because of the difficulties of the jungle trail.

LE TESTU, GUILLAUME *(French captain and navigator; Atlantic, Caribbean; 1509?–1572)* Born into a sea-faring family at Le Havre in Normandy, Le Testu studied navigation at Dieppe, the center of Jean ANGO's activities. He piloted a French ship that explored Brazil in 1551 and sailed with a 1555 expedition that founded a colony near Rio de Janeiro.

In 1556, Le Testu was appointed royal pilot at Le Havre and presented the king with a world atlas (*Cosmographie universelle*). His 56 maps carefully portrayed recent discoveries. They also depicted a nonexistent southern continent, described as "not imaginary even though no one has found it."

From 1567 or 1568, Le Testu raided for the Protestant side during the French Wars of Religion. Taken at sea, he was imprisoned until January 1572, when several pleas by King Charles IX secured his release. Off Panama in April 1573, Sir Francis DRAKE's raiding party ran into Le Testu commanding an 80-ton warship and about 70 men. Some mystery surrounded his presence in the West Indies. Spanish reports stated that a large French expedition was planned for 1572, but Le Testu apparently was cruising on his own.

Drake and Le Testu agreed to a joint attack on the mule train carrying treasure to the port at Nombre de Dios. The pirates drove off the surprised guards, buried a large amount of silver near the road, and made for the coast with all the gold they could carry. The French and English crews each took half of a haul estimated at £40,000.

Wounded in the stomach during the assault, Le Testu could not keep up with the retreating raiders. He stayed behind to regain his strength, and two of his crew voluntarily remained with him. Soon after, Spanish soldiers found them in the woods. One Frenchmen fled, but Le Testu and his other comrade were slain. His head was cut off and displayed in the marketplace at Nombre de Dios.

(See also SELECTED BIBLIOGRAPHY: Wright, *Documents.*)

LEUCIPPE AND CLEITOPHON, THE ADVENTURES OF *(novel in Greek; written between 172 and 194)* A ROMANCE by ACHILLES TATIUS. The complicated plot, told in the first person by Cleitophon, involves two separated lovers who remain faithful until their happy reunion.

During their many adventures, Leucippe appears to die on three occasions. The second false murder involves a band of bloodthirsty pirates. The couple has reached Alexandria, where a man named Chaereas falls in love with Leucippe and decides to steal her. He hires the pirates, who seize her and escape by boat. Although he is wounded, Cleitophon pursues in another ship. As he catches up with the pirates, they cut off Leucippe's head and throw the body into the sea. Two sailors rescue the headless body, and Cleitophon kisses the severed neck as he laments his sweetheart's cruel fate.

Cleitophon spends the next six months mourning in Alexandria. A woman named Melite persuades him to marry her. They return to her home in Ephesus, where Melite befriends a mistreated slave bought from pirates during her absence. The young slave turns out to be Leucippe. To stop their pursuers, the pirates had dressed another woman in Leucippe's clothes, cut off her head, and thrown over her body.

LE VASSEUR, JEAN *(French pirate; Caribbean; active 1642–1652)* Thanks to Le Vasseur, TORTUGA ISLAND, northwest of Hispaniola, became the capital of Caribbean piracy. A Norman nobleman, he mastered military engineering in 1627 and 1628 while defending the Protestant fortress at La Rochelle. After Royalist forces took the city, Le Vasseur fled to Saint Kitts. He became wealthy and often advised Philippe de Poincy, governor-general of the French colonies.

Protestant influence at Saint Kitts troubled the Paris government, which complained about Le Vasseur's power. In 1640, French settlers on Tortuga asked for help against English aggression. De Poincy used their request to get rid of Le Vasseur and the quarrelsome

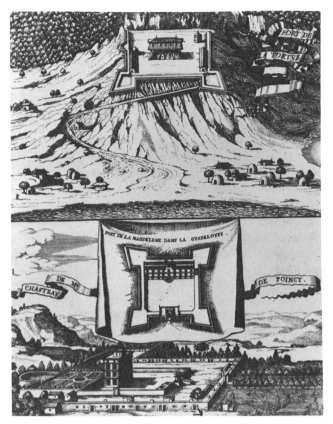

At the top is Jean La Vasseur's impregnable fortress on Tortuga. Below is the fortified estate on Guadeloupe belonging to Philippe de Poincy, governor-general of the French islands in the Caribbean. From Jean-Baptiste Du Tertre, *Histoire générale* (1667–1671).

Protestants. He sent Le Vasseur to conquer Tortuga, made him governor, and granted him a share in any future profits. Le Vasseur reached Tortuga in August 1642. (Some accounts erroneously place his arrival in 1640.) He commanded about 100 men, including BUCCANEERS picked up in Hispaniola. In a brief battle, the English easily were expelled.

Aware of earlier Spanish raids, Le Vasseur fortified a hill overlooking the harbor. The relatively flat summit of this hill was crowned by a steep rock, some 30 feet high. Le Vasseur shaped terraces on the flat hill that could hold several hundred men. On top of the rock, he placed his own palace, several cannon, and a storehouse for ammunition. A carved stairway reached halfway up the rock. Visitors had to climb the rest of the way on an iron ladder, raised or lowered from the top. Supplied with water by a natural spring, Le Vasseur had an impregnable fortress, which he jokingly called his "dove-cote."

In 1643, the Spaniards at Santo Domingo sent six ships with 500 men to destroy the new fort. Le Vasseur's artillery sank one of the enemy ships and scattered the rest. When the Spanish troops landed away from the harbor, they fell into an ambush, lost almost 200 men, and fled to their ships and back to Hispaniola.

This victory spread Le Vasseur's reputation throughout the Caribbean. Tortuga became a haven for anyone in trouble with the law. Dutch traders paid regular visits, paying for pirate plunder with guns, ammunition, brandy, and fancy clothing.

With total power over the less-educated men around him, Le Vasseur gradually lost any self-control. His character changed, he became suspicious and intolerant, and any opposition set off his cruel and overbearing temper. He prohibited services for Roman Catholics, burned their chapel, and turned out their priest. His mountaintop palace held an iron cage—nicknamed the "little hell"—in which his enemies could neither stand nor lie down.

These stories may be exaggerated, since they were reported by the Jesuits, Le Vasseur's religious foes. There is no question that Le Vasseur repudiated French authority and set himself up as an independent ruler. He took a percentage of all buccaneer loot, taxed the cowhides brought into Tortuga from Hispaniola, and amassed a fortune in jewels and treasure.

Le Vasseur refused to share his plunder with Governor de Poincy at Saint Kitts. When a Spanish prize yielded up a silver Madonna, de Poincy requested the statue for his chapel. Replying that Catholics were too spiritual to notice material differences, Le Vasseur sent him a wooden copy instead.

From his invincible eyrie, Le Vasseur could safely insult both the French and the Spaniards. He was killed, in 1653, by his heirs, two adventurers named Tibuat and Martin. Tibuat was enraged, probably because Le Vasseur had snatched away his young mistress. When Le Vasseur left his castle to inspect a warehouse, the two traitors wounded him with a musket, and finished him off with their daggers. A character named Le Vasseur appears in Rafael SABATINI's CAPTAIN BLOOD, HIS ODYSSEY (1922). Basil RATHBONE turns him into a sneeringly evil villain in CAPTAIN BLOOD (?), the 1935 film adaptation of Sabatini's novel.

(See also SELECTED BIBLIOGRAPHY: Cruise, *Pioneers*; Exquemelin, *Buccaneers*; Haring, *Buccaneers*.)

LEWIS, CAPTAIN (*fictional pirate; Caribbean, Atlantic; active early 1700s*)
This imaginary life is inserted among the biographies of real pirates in Daniel Defoe's GENERAL HISTORY. The story of Captain Lewis' pact with the devil frequently appears in 19th-century compilations such as THE PIRATES OWN BOOK.

Lewis served as a cabin boy for a pirate named Banister, captured off Jamaica in 1687. Still sailing from Jamaica, he was enslaved in Cuba but escaped and took command of a ship. By this time, he spoke French, Spanish, English, and Mosquito Indian.

At the bay of Campeche, Lewis captured several SLOOPS. When one captain gave up without fighting, Lewis whipped him about the deck for not taking better care of his employer's property. The pirates cruised off Florida and the Carolinas. Suspecting a mutiny, Lewis put the English crewmen in a boat "10 Leagues from Shore, with only 10 Pieces of Beef, and sent them away, keeping none but *French* and Negroes; these men, it is supposed, all perished in the Sea."

Lewis sailed boldly into Trinity Harbor in Newfoundland, plundered the fishing fleet, and took over the 24-gun *Herman*. The Canadians captured his quartermaster and fortified a point at the entrance to the harbor. Lewis sneaked past on a moonless night. Although the enemy could hear their shots striking the *Herman*, she vanished into the darkness. Lewis got his quartermaster back by threatening to kill all his prisoners.

Lewis went to the African coast and captured many ships. While chasing an English vessel, his topmasts were blown away. To catch his prize, Lewis made a pact with the devil. "Running up the Shrouds to the Main-Top, [Lewis] tore off a Handful of Hair, and throwing it into the Air, used this Expression, *Good Devil take this till I come.*"

Soon after, the English and French pirates quarreled. Lewis treacherously gave the Frenchmen their own ship and then sailed alongside and sank it, marooning them on the shore. The Devil warned Lewis that he would be murdered that night. The prediction came true when the Frenchmen sneaked aboard in canoes. John CORNELIUS managed to drive them off and took command.

LEWIS, WILLIAM (*British pirate; Caribbean; died 1718*)
A former prize-fighter, Lewis raided from NEW PROVIDENCE ISLAND in the Bahamas. He submitted and was pardoned when Woodes ROGERS became governor in July 1718. Sent out to trade for food, Lewis mutinied with John AUGER and was hanged in December. He showed no remorse at the gallows but instead asked for liquor to toast his fellow prisoners and the audience.

L'HERMITE, JACQUES (*Dutch admiral; Pacific; died 1623*)
L'Hermite commanded the largest and one of the least successful raids on Spain's South American colonies. He was sick in bed by the time the ships reached the Americas. Thus Hugo SCHAMPENDAM, his successor, must bear most of the responsibility for the expedition's failure. L'Hermite was buried on San Lorenzo Island near Lima, but the outraged Peruvians later dug up and burned his body.

LIA, JOSEPH (*Maltese corsair; Mediterranean; 1708*)
Lia repaid BOTTOMRY BONDS after selling his prizes.

LIANG PAO (*Chinese pirate; South China Sea; 1805*)
After working for Vietnamese rebels, Liang Pao commanded the White Flag Fleet in the pirate confederation CHENG I formed in 1805. Because his own fleet was very small, Liang often sailed in consort with Cheng I's Red Flag Fleet.

LIBYA See TRIPOLI.

LIBURNIAN *(warship; Mediterranean; about 250 B.C. to A.D. 250)* A fast, open-decked GALLEY with two banks of oars, similar to the LEMBOS and widely used by Roman provincial fleets. The Romans borrowed the design from the Liburnians, an ILLYRIAN tribe living on the DALMATIAN coast and islands.

LIGURIANS *(land and sea raiders; Mediterranean; about 300–181 B.C.)* The indigenous neighbors of the Greek city-state of Massilia (Marseilles). During the third century, they inhabited southeastern France and northeastern Italy, from Arles to Pisa. This region, today known as the Riviera, again became a pirate haven during the 16th and 17th centuries.

The country was rugged, poor, and difficult to penetrate. Many Ligurians became mercenary soldiers or brigands, and they often raided ETRUSCAN Pisa by land and by sea. The Romans destroyed the power of the eastern Ligurians (those in present-day Italy) between 238 and 230, but they left the western defenses to their allies at Marseilles.

In 181, Marseilles complained that growing numbers of Ligurian pirates were attacking ships as far west as the Strait of Gibraltar. For the first time, the Romans created a standing fleet, with 10 warships patrolling north of Sorrento. The Romans also sent a land army, which defeated the Ligurians in the region near Genoa. The Roman army imprisoned known pirates, while the reinforced fleet captured 32 pirate ships. There was little further piracy, although Rome sent armies between 155 and 122 to help Marseilles maintain control on land.

(See also CARLO EMMANUELE I, Cosimo I dei MEDICI.)

LINDSEY, MARIA *(fictional English pirate; Atlantic; early 1700s)* Lindsey was Eric COBHAM's lover and partner in crime. From a hidden fort on the Canadian coast, Eric and Maria ravished vessels carrying furs to Europe. After transferring the cargoes, they sank the ships with all hands. By killing the crews, the pirates removed witnesses to their crimes. But Maria also enjoyed murder and continually invented new forms of execution. She poisoned one ship's crew. Others were stuffed into sacks and thrown overboard or tied up and used for pistol practice.

Having made a great fortune, Eric and Maria bought a lavish estate near Le Havre in France. Eric lived for many years, but Maria committed suicide by taking poison and jumping off a cliff. She was ashamed of her crimes and depressed because Eric had abandoned her for younger women.

LINGGIR *(Malayan pirate; South China Sea; active 1845)* Linggir was the chief of an aboriginal tribe living along the Saribas River in Borneo. Angry at Sir James BROOKE's raids on the Saribas pirates, he invaded Brooke's home in 1846 with 80 armed men. When Brooke was rescued by armed followers, Linggir publicly announced that he would have the white rajah's head and displayed the basket made to contain it. He was killed in 1848 when his canoes attacked a British paddle steamer during a battle at Batang Maru.

LINT, PIETER ESAISZ DE *(Dutch pirate; Pacific; active 1598–1601)* Lint was captain of a 50-ton YACHT during Olivier van NOORT's South American plunder raid. Storms and disease buffeted van Noort's fleet during the Atlantic crossing and passage through the Strait of Magellan. When the captain of the warship *Hendrick Frederick* threatened mutiny, van Noort MAROONED him and gave command to Lint.

Lint and the *Hendrick Frederick* became separated from the other ships as they entered the Pacific in February 1600. He failed to keep a rendezvous with van Noort at Santa Maria and cruised up the coast as far north as Nicaragua. After taking only four small boats with little booty, Lint sailed for the East Indies. The *Hendrick Frederick* ran aground on Ternate Island and was sold to the sultan. Lint and the few surviving crewmen entered the service of the Dutch East India Company.

LION OF SAINT MARK *(Italian motion picture; color; 1967)* Manrico Masiero (Gordon Scott), son of the doge of Venice, dons a mask to fight plundering pirates. After a few battles, Manrico falls in love with female pirate Rosanna (Gianna Maria Canale) and frees her when she is captured. Learning that the "Lion of Saint Mark" really is Manrico, Rosanna renounces piracy. The corsairs are defeated, and Manrico and Rosanna marry. Directed by Luigi Capuano.

LIPARI ISLANDS *(pirate haven; Mediterranean; about 580–280 and 43–36 B.C.)* Seven volanic islands, directly north of eastern Sicily and thus well-located to harass merchant shipping. The islands attracted Greek buccaneers about 580. Fleeing RHODES and Cnidos in Asia Minor, one band tried to settle in western Sicily. When they were driven out, the survivors landed at Lipari, the main island, merging with or killing its inhabitants.

The Liparians became noted seamen and pirates and defeated TYRRHENIAN corsairs on several occasions. They drove off an Athenian fleet in 427 and repelled a Carthaginian invasion in 397. In 393, Liparian corsairs seized a Roman warship carrying ambassadors and gold to the temple at Delphi. TIMASITHEUS, the island's chief magistrate, convinced the people to free the Roman representatives.

Primarily living by piracy, the Liparians inhabited only the main island and crossed in boats to farm the others. Following pirate principles, they treated their possessions as common property. The proceeds of raids were divided up, and land also was held in common according to DIODORUS OF SICILY. From about 280 B.C., the Carthaginians and then the Romans annexed the islands. Two centuries later, they provided a base for pirates under Sextus POMPEIUS.

LI SHANG-CH'ING (Chinese pirate; South China Sea; 1805)
Also referred to as Li Hsiang-Ch'ing and nicknamed Hsia Mo-Yang (Son of a Frog), Li Shang-Ch'ing commanded the Green Flag Fleet in CHENG I's pirate confederation. He operated from the Lei-chou Peninsula, near Vietnam, and often raided in consort with WU-SHIH ERH.

LISLE, PETER (Barbary corsair; Mediterranean; active 1796–1815)
Lisle was admiral at TRIPOLI during the 1801–1805 war with the United States. A handsome blond Scot from Glasgow, Lisle became a skilled navigator. An unlikely legend tells how he learned Arabic while serving aboard a Mameluke (Egyptian) vessel. He had converted to Islam—taking the name Murat Reis to honor Jan JANSSEN—by September 1796, when he captured two American prizes.

Toward the end of 1796, Yusuf Qaramanli, pasha of Tripoli, gave Lisle command of the *Betsey*, a captured American SCHOONER. Renamed the *Meshuda*, she carried 28 guns and was gaily decorated. The following May, Lisle and his colorful ship defended Tripoli against a 40-gun Danish FRIGATE.

The first American consul arrived at Tripoli in 1799. By then, Lisle was admiral and had married the pasha's eldest daughter. He apparently loathed Americans and urged the pasha to repudiate the 1796 peace treaty. His galleys captured at least three American merchantmen during 1800, taking their cargoes but freeing the crews.

When Tripoli declared war in May 1801, Lisle cruised against American shipping with the *Meshuda* and a captured Swedish BRIG. His ships were caught at Gibraltar on June 29 and blockaded by the frigate *Philadelphia*. In August, Lisle abandoned both ships, sent the crews in small boats to Morocco, and sailed for Malta on a British ship. Crossing to Tripoli, he landed by night and walked 30 miles to the city to avoid the American blockade.

Lisle directed the Tripolitan fleet during the American blockade, and he commanded a galley during a gun battle with the *Constellation* in July 1802. He led the boarders that captured the *Philadelphia* in November 1803, supervised her refloating and repair, and helped defend the city against American bombardments in 1804.

Lisle remained admiral of the surviving Tripolitan ships after the war ended in 1805. But piracy had ceased to be a profitable trade. Without much to do, Lisle quarreled with the pasha, who banished him to Egypt. He returned in the 1820s but thereafter mainly served as a go-between and interpreter for foreign diplomats.

(See also BARBARY WAR, FIRST.)

L'ÎSLE DES PIRATES (four-act ballet; 1835)
Pirate Island was presented at the Paris Opera, with choreography by Louis Henry and music adapted from Rossini and Beethoven. Despite its unoriginal plot, the ballet's spectacular scenery drew large audiences for nearly three years.

The Marquise Isabelle agrees that Akbar—who is pretending to be a wealthy foreigner—can marry her daughter, Mathilde. At the wedding ceremony, Octavio, who loves Mathilde, reveals that Akbar is a pirate chief. Akbar and his men make their escape, taking Mathilde and her sister with them. Octavio follows them to their island and, unrecognized, joins their band.

When the pirates choose slaves from among their captives, Akbar and Octavio fight a duel for possession of Mathilde. The other pirates hear them fighting, and Mathilde tells them the reason for the duel. The pirate crew reproaches Akbar for breaking their rules about BOOTY. Akbar is enraged and threatens to fire his pistol into a barrel of gunpowder. Suddenly the sound of a cannon is heard. Sailors come ashore to rescue the captives, and Akbar stabs himself.

LIVORNO (pirate haven; Mediterranean; 1562–1796)
A port, called Leghorn by the British, on Italy's northwestern coast, about 12 miles south of Pisa. Livorno came under Florentine control in 1421. It developed into a major port from the 1560s under the Medici dukes, who spent freely to erect fortifications and harbor works.

The Medici dukes sponsored both legitimate trade and piracy. From Livorno, the KNIGHTS OF SAINT STEPHEN crusaded against the OTTOMAN EMPIRE by preying on commercial shipping. The dukes also welcomed freelance pirates and encouraged merchants to fence their goods. The city became a "free port" in 1590, open to traders of any European nation, including Protestants and Jews.

Ferdinando II (ruled 1627–1670) ended the knights' buccaneering cruises, and the dukes also regulated foreign pirates more closely. However, because of Livorno's free-port status, the city's merchants fenced corsair booty until the French conquest in 1796. Livorno was second only to Malta as a center for commerce in captives and property. At Livorno, Christian pirates sold Muslim captives for use as GALLEY SLAVES in European fleets. Livornese bankers transferred RANSOMS both for enslaved Muslims and for Christians held by the BARBARY corsairs.

(See also LASCHMI MISTERI; MURAT REIS.)

LOGAN, JAMES (English pirate; Atlantic; 1546)
In consort with James ALDAY, Logan looted Portuguese and Spanish ships in a Spanish port.

LOGWOOD (dyewood; Caribbean; 16th and 17th centuries)
A small thorny mahogany, with very hard, heavy, almost black wood. Logwood is native to tropical America, and it was abundant in the swamps of Honduras and Campeche, Mexico, both Spanish colonies. The wood produces a valuable purple dye that sold for a high price in Europe. It was one of the favorite prizes of 16th-century pirates, and English adventurers began harvesting the wood illegally soon after England conquered Jamaica in 1655.

A dangerous, lawless, and lucrative business, logwood cutting appealed to former or future pirates including Abraham BLAUVELT, John COXON, and Robert SEARLE. William DAMPIER, who cut logwood in Campeche from 1676 to 1678, described both the trade and the loggers' raids on Indian and Spanish settlements in his *Voyage to Campeache.*

(See also SHARP, BARTHOLOMEW.)

L'OLONNAIS, FRANÇOIS *(French buccaneer; Caribbean; 1630–1668)* Born Jean David Nau in western France at Les Sables d'Olonne (hence his nickname, "the man from Olonne"). Because of his inhuman cruelty, he also was called "Fléau des Espagnols" ("Flail of the Spaniards").

L'Olonnais went to the Caribbean in 1650. After three years as an indentured servant, he joined the cattle hunters at Hispaniola and then turned pirate. One legend attributes his hatred to a Spanish militia attack that slaughtered most of his fellow hunters.

In the early 1660s, L'Olonnais moved to TORTUGA ISLAND and received a ship from the governor, an adventurer who had finagled a French PRIVATEERING commission. L'Olonnais gained significant booty, although his psychopathic mistreatment of prisoners actually made it harder to take Spanish prizes. Instead of surrendering, EXQUEMELIN wrote, merchant ships "fought until they could fight no more, for he granted Spaniards little mercy."

During one voyage, L'Olonnais' ship was wrecked on the Campeche coast, where the Mexicans killed most of his men. According to Exquemelin, L'Olonnais escaped by smearing himself with blood and hiding under the corpses. He convinced some slaves to steal a canoe and made it back to Tortuga.

Returning to sea in a large boat, L'Olonnais attacked a minor port in northern Cuba. His band stormed a warship in the harbor, and L'Olonnais personally cut off the heads of the entire crew except one. He gave this man a letter for the governor of Havana, declaring that he would kill every Spaniard he captured. With his new prize, he seized a ship and large sums of money in the Gulf of Venezuela.

L'Olonnais committed these crimes during peacetime. A brief war between France and Spain (1667–1668) gave him an excuse to plan a larger expedition against the Venezuelan coast. Calling together the Tortuga and Hispaniola buccaneers, he set out in July 1667 with eight small ships and 660 men. Off eastern Hispaniola, the rovers took a prize carrying a rich cargo of cacao, silver, and jewels. At Saona Island, they seized a warship taking gunpowder and 12,000 pesos to San Domingo.

The buccaneers headed for Lake Maracaibo in Venezuela. They easily occupied the prosperous town of Maracaibo, but its inhabitants fled to the woods with their treasures. The raiders caught some 20 Spaniards with about 20,000 PESOS. They tortured their captives, and

François L'Olonnais portrayed as a French gentleman against a background of burning ships and cities. From Exquemelin, *Buccaneers of America,* first Spanish edition (1681).

L'Olonnais hacked one to pieces with his cutlass. But the other fugitives, knowing that the prisoners would be made to talk, already had moved their goods.

After two weeks, L'Olonnais moved on to Gibraltar, a small town across the lake. Despite fierce resistance, the buccaneers captured Gibraltar. They spent a month enjoying its food and women and extorted 10,000 pesos. L'Olonnais then returned to Maracaibo and exacted a 20,000-peso ransom. Altogether, the buccaneers divided up coins and jewels worth 260,000 pesos plus other merchandise.

Back in Tortuga, their spoils soon vanished. The governor bought the ship loaded with cacao for a twentieth of its real worth. As Exquemelin puts it, "The tavernkeepers got part of their money and the whores took the rest." Taking six ships and some 700 men, L'Olonnais headed for Lake Nicaragua, but his fleet was becalmed and drifted into the Gulf of Honduras. Pillaging the Indian villages along the way, the pirates reached the impoverished port at PUERTO CABALLOS.

The buccaneers plundered the warehouses and a Spanish ship. But most of the inhabitants had escaped, and they found little to steal. A few prisoners were tortured to obtain information. Exquemelin gloatingly describes the gory scene.

> When l'Olonnais had a victim on the rack, if the wretch did not instantly answer his questions he would

hack the man to pieces with his cutlass and lick the blood from the blade with this tongue, wishing it might have been the last Spaniard in the world he had thus killed.

Two prisoners finally agreed to lead the buccaneers to San Pedro, 30 miles away. Along the way, the pirates broke through a Spanish ambush. With his usual savagery, L'Olonnais asked his prisoners whether there was another road that would avoid further ambushes.

> Then l'Olonnais, being possessed of a devil's fury, ripped open one of the prisoners with his cutlass, tore the living heart out of his body, gnawed at it, and then hurled it in the face of one of the others, saying, Show me another way, or I will do the same to you.

Overrunning more ambushes and a valiant defense, the buccaneers took and burned San Pedro, but found little booty. After careening their boats, they captured a Spanish ship, which turned out to be empty.

Disappointed with their meager spoils, his captains deserted with the smaller boats. But L'Olonnais went on to Nicaragua in the captured Spanish vessel. As they sailed down the coast, the pirates ran the great vessel aground on a small cay. After five or six months, some of the men left in a small boat and were killed by Indians and Spanish troops. L'Olonnais pushed on to the Gulf of Darien, where he was captured by cannibals, hacked to pieces, and roasted limb by limb.

LOMELLINI, ANDREA DE *(Italian pirate; Mediterranean; 1395)* Himself from Genoa, Lomellini plundered a Genoese vessel near the island of Kithira (Cerigo).

LONCQ, HENDRICK CORNELISZOON *(Dutch admiral; Caribbean; active 1628–1630)* In 1628, Loncq was second-in-command to Piet HEYN, whose warships captured the Mexican TREASURE FLEET for the DUTCH WEST INDIA COMPANY. Commanding 65 vessels and 7,000 men in 1630, Loncq occupied Pernambuco (Recife), Brazil. From Brazil, he had orders to invade the Caribbean and chase Spanish treasure ships. However, he instead went back to the Netherlands, sending only a small and ineffective squadron under Dierick RUYTERS to the Caribbean. The West India Company never again entrusted him with a command.

(See also CORNELIS JOL.)

LONGBOAT *(nautical idiom; 16th–19th centuries)* A large ship's boat, without a deck and narrow in the beam, that might carry as many as 60 or 70 men. Normally propelled by oars, it often had a removable mast and sail.

LONG JOHN SILVER *(movie; color; 1954)* A sequel to the 1950 TREASURE ISLAND, made in Australia and directed by Byron Haskin.

Robert Newton in *Long John Silver* (1954).

Silver, played by Robert NEWTON, knocks around the Caribbean with a gang of shipless pirates. They rescue the governor's daughter from Captain Mendoza (Lloyd Berrell), Silver's bitter enemy. In a major double-cross, Silver's men collect the ransom for the daughter and also loot the governor's warehouse.

Silver gets his thugs aboard a ship taking Jim Hawkins (Kit Taylor) to England. Following a failed mutiny, Hawkins and the pirates are left on an island, which turns out to be Captain Mendoza's secret headquarters. They end up back on Treasure Island and once again take over Captain Flint's stockade. Silver almost is burned at the stake before they drive off Mendoza's attackers. He and Jim find Flint's hoard, and they return to England.

Robert NEWTON egregiously overacts in the role of Long John Silver. Some found his performance amusing, while others denounced it. For Bosley Crowther of the *New York Times*, Newton is "outrageously hammy, to the point of freakishness, with his squinting and popping of his eyeballs and growling in a bastard Irish brogue."

LONGUS *(Greek writer; second century)* Longus was author of DAPHNIS AND CHLOE, probably written between 150 and 225 and set on Lesbos. Longus' familiarity with Lesbos' landscape suggests that he lived on that island.

LOPEZ, CAPTAIN *(Spanish pirate; Mediterranean; 1506)* Sailing from Naples, Lopez plundered Venetian vessels between Malta and Cerigo. Venetian galleys pursued him to Sicily and burned his ship. He escaped and sold some of his booty at Barcelona, trying to disguise his raids as acts of REPRISAL.

LORD HIGH ADMIRAL *(English official; 14th century to 1964)* One of the king's chief officers, who administered naval affairs and judged all disputes about maritime matters. The title of ADMIRAL originally did not refer to command of ships at sea. The admiral instead received naval jurisdiction and authority to set up a law court.

By the reign of Henry VIII, the English navy was too large to be governed by one man. The king appointed an executive committee, which became the navy board. Its members were independent in their own spheres of influence, but the admiral continued to chair policy meetings. From the 15th century, the admiral delegated his judicial powers to the judge of Admiralty, who eventually became an independent official. In 1585, the crown declared that the Admiralty judge received his authority directly from the king rather than from the admiral.

When the incumbent lord high admiral was assassinated in 1628, his authority passed to a group of commissioners forming the Board of Admiralty. A lord high admiral was appointed from time to time until 1964, when the navy was merged into a single Ministry of Defence.

(See also ADMIRALTY COURT.)

LORENZI, GUGLIELMO *(Maltese corsair; Mediterranean; active 1780s)* A Corsican, he immigrated to MALTA as a youth and rose to captain. About 1787, he was licensed by Russia against the OTTOMAN EMPIRE, commanding his own ship and three vessels. After Russia and Turkey made peace in 1792, he returned to Malta. During the French occupation in 1799, he was captured and shot leading an unsuccessful revolt in Valetta.

LOVELL, JOHN *(English captain; Caribbean; active 1566–1567)* Commanding three ships for John HAWKINS, Lovell tried to smuggle slaves from West Africa to the Spanish Caribbean. (Sir Francis DRAKE was among his officers.) England and Portugal were at peace. Nevertheless, near the Cape Verde Islands, Lovell's squadron seized five Portuguese vessels carrying sugar and slaves.

Lovell may have acquired other slaves along the African coast. He went on to Borburata and RIO DE LA HACHA in Venezuela, arriving the day after Jean BONTEMPS. However, Lovell's small force could not make the Spanish colonist buy his illegal slaves.

LOW, EDWARD *(English pirate; Caribbean, Atlantic; active 1721–1724)* A quarrelsome and sadistic man, Low was born in London, went to sea, and then worked in Boston. While cutting LOGWOOD in Honduras, he received command of a boat and 12 men. During an argument, he shot the ship's captain. He and the others made off, captured a small ship, and arrived at the Cayman Islands in December 1721. There Low encountered George LOWTHER, and the two gangs joined forces until June 1722.

After he left Lowther, Low marauded from New Jersey to Newfoundland, plundering dozens of small ships and keeping an 80-ton SCHOONER for his own use. Riding out a hurricane on the way, Low went to the Caribbean, where he seized a damaged ship and £1,000 in money and goods.

About mid-August, Low went to the Azores Islands, where eight large merchant ships surrendered without resistance. Low moved to a large PINK and gave Charles HARRIS command of the schooner. Low disliked the food prepared by the cook of an earlier prize. He decided, Daniel DEFOE reported, to kill the cook, "a greazy Fellow, [who] would fry well in the Fire; so the poor Man was bound to the Main-Mast, and burnt with the ship."

With the pink and the schooner, Low took a dozen more vessels in the Azores and the Cape Verde Islands. The pirates then sailed for South America, where the pink was wrecked while being careened. Low went on to Grenada, seized another ship and gave his schooner to Francis SPRIGGS. (He had quarreled with Harris, who returned to the crew for some months.)

Low and Spriggs captured five or six prizes in the Caribbean in December 1722 and January 1723. Low became enraged when he learned that the captain of a Portuguese ship had dropped a money bag into the sea. Defoe told how he "ordered the Captain's Lips to be cut off, which he broil'd before his Face, and afterwards murdered him and all the Crew."

Entering the Bay of Honduras in March 1723, Low and Spriggs seized a Spanish ship, which had imprisoned six English captains cutting logwood. Although a few escaped into the woods, the pirates massacred more than 60 of the Spaniards. Low continued west through the Caribbean and up the U. S. coast, plundering at least a dozen more victims. The pirates whipped their captives, cut them with knives, and burned lighted matches between their fingers.

Early in June, Low appeared off South Carolina. Charles Harris once again was captain of the sloop recently commanded by Spriggs. On June 21, the pirates chased the *Greyhound*, a British warship somewhat weaker than the two pirate vessels combined. The *Greyhound* turned around and attacked. During a running gun battle, Low fled and Harris was captured.

This narrow escape enraged Low. Near Nantucket, Massachusetts, the pirates came upon a small whaling sloop. Before they shot the captain, the pirates stripped and savagely whipped him and cut off his ears. Two days later, the pirates caught two more whaling sloops near Rhode Island. A Boston newspaper reported that Low made one captain eat his own ears. He cut open the second captain, ripped out his heart, and made another captive eat it. (The USKOKS and François L'OLONNAIS also were accused of cutting out living hearts.)

Sailing north from Cape Cod, Low took 23 French fishing vessels near Cape Breton. He took over a 22-gun ship, and his two vessels pillaged 18 more victims. Early in August, he captured a larger 34-gun ship and made it his flagship. With this three-ship squadron, he reached the Azores in September, went on to Africa, and plundered at least four more vessels.

During his final days, Low apparently turned his insane sadism against his own crew. Francis Spriggs again was given a command but deserted and went off on his own. Low returned to the West Indies, quarreled with his fellow pirates, and was marooned early in 1724. In one account he was captured by a French warship and hanged.

(See also SELECTED BIBLIOGRAPHY: Dow, *Pirates*.)

LOWTHER, GEORGE *(English pirate; Caribbean, Atlantic; active 1721–1723)* Lowther's band seized or destroyed more than two dozen vessels but stole little booty. He arrived in Gambia in May 1721 as second mate of a ship carrying soldiers to a British fort. Lowther had quarrelled with the captain, and the soldiers received only small amounts of bad food. In June, Lowther and Colonel John Massey combined to seize the ship. The mutineers made for the Caribbean but took just four small prizes. Massey, being a soldier, wanted to land on some island to plunder the French settlements. But Lowther thought this too dangerous and sent away Massey and 10 others in a captured SLOOP.

After destroying three more ships, Lowther went to the Cayman Islands in December. There he ran into Edward LOW and 12 crewmen in a small boat. The two bands joined forces and captured seven more ships, sinking some and keeping others. At the Bay of Amatique in Belize, the inhabitants attacked and burned the largest ship. The pirates got away in a small sloop and seized another ship. Lowther and Low separated in May 1722, each taking about half the gang.

Lowther cruised off New York and Chesapeake Bay and took other small prizes. In August, his sloop was severely damaged in a battle with a larger ship near South Carolina. The pirates remained in North Carolina until the spring of 1723. They attacked shipping off Newfoundland in June and July and took prizes in the Caribbean in September. (Some sources indicate Lowther again consorted with Edward Low near the Cape Verde Islands and Africa in September. But this is impossible, given a sailing ship's speed.)

In October 1723, Lowther was careening his ship on Blanquilla Island, near Venezuela. An English merchant vessel took the pirates by surprise. Sixteen men were captured, and 11 were hanged at Saint Kitts. The Venezuelans caught and enslaved four others. Some time later, Lowther was found dead with his pistol beside him—either a suicide or killed by another pirate.

(See also SELECTED BIBLIOGRAPHY: Defoe, *Pirates*; Dow, *Pirates*.)

LUBBER/LANDLUBBER *(nautical slang; 14th century to the present)* An old name for a clumsy, stupid fellow, especially one who does not work. As used by sailors, the term described someone unfamiliar with sea life who acted in an awkward, "lubberly" way aboard ship.

LUCAS, JOHN *(Dutch buccaneer; Caribbean; 1663)* A Spanish squadron captured Lucas' BRIGANTINE off Campeche, Mexico.

LUCIFER, HENDRICK JACOBSZOON *(Dutch captain; Caribbean; died 1627)* In 1627, Lucifer's three ships transported colonists to Guyana for the DUTCH WEST INDIA COMPANY. Sometimes joined by two other pirates, Lucifer took several Spanish prizes. Off Cuba, his squadron almost collided with a two-ship Honduran TREASURE FLEET en route to Havana. One vessel was taken with cargo worth 1.2 million guilders, but Lucifer died of wounds received in the encounter.

LUCULLUS, LUCIUS LICINIUS *(Roman statesman and general; 110?–57? B.C.)* A Roman noble and supporter of the conservative faction led by Sulla, Lucullus served as Sulla's second-in-command during Rome's first war with King MITHRIDATES of Pontus (89–85). The corsairs of CILICIA, Mithridates' partners, quickly took control of the seas around Greece. In 87, Sulla sent Lucullus to borrow ships from Rome's eastern allies.

To avoid the Cilicians, Lucullus took an indirect route, traveling from Greece to Egypt by way of North Africa. Despite this precaution, the Cilicians seized most of Lucullus' vessels. He escaped capture only by frequently changing ship to conceal his movements from the corsairs. Lucullus finally did collect some ships in Egypt, but he brought them to Greece in the summer of 85, long after the war was over.

Lucullus' failure demonstrates the Cilician corsairs' extraordinary power rather than his own incompetence. He rapidly defeated King Mithridates' forces during the Third Mithridatic War (74–66), although political intrigues in Rome forced his return in 68. After retiring in 59, his life of exquisite ("Lucullan") luxury became legendary.

LUKKA, LUKKI *(sea raiders; eastern Mediterranean; 18th through 13th centuries B.C.)* It is unclear precisely where the Lukka lived in Asia Minor (present-day Turkey). Their exploits during the 13th century suggest a location in or near the region the Greeks later called CARIA and CILICIA. In both cases, the southwestern coast provided a natural base for pirates preying on merchant ships traveling from the Aegean to the Middle East.

Ancient Egyptian records say that the Lukka frequently raided Cyprus during the 14th century. They sometimes served as naval allies of the Hittite Empire, which ruled central Anatolia. (In the same way, the Cilicians latter provide a naval for King MITHRIDATES' inland empire. About 1286, the Lukka and Hittite forces battled against Egyptian forces at the Kadesh in Syria (near the modern city of Homs). They are last mentioned as allies of the Libyans, when the latter invaded Egypt in April 1220.

The entire eastern Mediterranean subsequently fell into a depression, which lasted for several centuries. The sparse surviving evidence suggests that piracy fell off simply because there were few merchant ships to attack.

However, it is possible that the Lukka survived and reemerged into history as the people called Carians, who often acted as mercenary soldiers and sometimes as pirates.

LUSSAN, RAVENEAU DE *(French buccaneer and author; Pacific; 1680s)* Lussan's adventures are described in his *Journal du Voyage fait a la Mer de sud avec les Filibustiers de l'Amerique . . . (Journal of a Pacific Voyage with the American Buccaneers).* Published in Paris in 1689, Lussan's *Journal* is the only source of information about his life. The book enjoyed some success in France, and it was translated into English in 1699.

Lussan says he was born into a wealthy family. He went to Saint Domingue (present-day Haiti) as an indentured servant, serving from 1679 to 1682. He sailed with Laurens de GRAFF in November 1684, hoping to steal enough Spanish gold to repay his debts. Since France and Spain were at peace, his activities were criminal.

After several months with only one prize, the buccaneers crossed the Isthmus of Panama to enlist with François GROGNIET's party. They arrived at the Pearl Islands on April 21. Grogniet and an English group under Edward DAVIS planned to seize a Peruvian treasure fleet and loot Panama.

Lussan's dreams of sudden riches soon vanished. Peruvian officials sent the silver on three warships, which routed the buccaneers on June 8, 1685. The defeated pirates squabbled, and Davis and most of the Englishmen sailed south. Grogniet (and Lussan) stayed in Central America, raiding north to Nicaragua with little gain.

In March 1686, Grogniet's men joined forces with Captain TOWNLEY. The pirates took almost no booty at Granada, Nicaragua, and the two groups split up in May. Lussan and many others deserted the unlucky Grogniet and went back to Panama with Townley. When Townley died, Captain LE PICARD took command and led a successful assault on Guayaquil, Ecuador, in April 1667.

Following further and profitless raids in Mexico, the pirates returned to the Caribbean in March 1688, after a harrowing two-month journey across Costa Rica. Lussan had shared in significant booty only at Guayaquil, where each man received 400 pesos ($100). Even if he multiplied this by gambling, he was miserably paid for three years of strenuous work, inadequate food, and physical suffering.

Lussan provides the sole buccaneer account describing the adventures of the groups under Grogniet and Le Picard. Judging by Spanish documents, his story is largely reliable. However, he sometimes is confused about the timing and geographical location of raids.

In sharp contrast to Lionel WAFER and William DAMPIER, Lussan says almost nothing about the natural environment or native inhabitants. However, his *Journal* is unique in describing an ordinary pirate's day-to-day life. (Wafer, Dampier, and Basil RINGROSE wrote from an officer's point of view.) Lussan's callous cruelty is striking. He coldly records, without any excuses or justification, the torture and murder of Spaniards, native Indians, and even his own companions.

(See also SELECTED BIBLIOGRAPHY: Lussan, *Raveneau de Lussan, Buccaneer.*)

LYDIA BAILEY *(novel; 1947)* In novels about the American Revolution, Kenneth Roberts (1885–1957) presented straightforward narratives unmixed with fantasy or romance. Roberts' heroes and heroines are ordinary persons caught up in exciting circumstances. During their adventures, they encounter historical characters, who are described with meticulous accuracy. Fact and fiction are effortlessly woven together, and Roberts enjoyed both critical praise and popular success. Sales of the hardback edition exceeded 1.4 million.

In *Lydia Bailey* Roberts quit North America and depicted the slave revolution in Haiti and the First BARBARY WAR. Albion Hamlin, a Massachusetts lawyer, believes that Lydia Bailey is her uncle's rightful heir and follows her to Haiti in 1801. The two fall deeply in love and are married. After suffering through Napoleon's failed invasion of Haiti, they escape and take Lydia's employer to France.

As they return home Murat Reis (Peter LISLE) captures their ship. For 15 months, Hamlin labors on Lisle's seashore farm while Lydia tutors the children of the pasha's estranged brother, Hamet Qaramanli. As Lisle's slave, Hamlin closely observes the Christian RENEGADES at TRIPOLI, and he is present when the U.S. warship *Philadelphia* is captured and burned. Escaping from Tripoli, Hamlin joins William Eaton and Hamet Qaramanli at the battle of Derna. When the Americans betray Hamet, Hamlin returns to Tripoli, rescues Lydia, and returns to a quiet life in the U.S.

Ⓜ

MACARY, CAPTAIN (French buccaneer; Caribbean; 1697)
Captain Macary took part in the Sack of CARTAGENA.

McCARTHY (MACARTY, MACARTHY), DENNIS (Irish pirate; Caribbean; 1690–1718)
McCarthy accepted a pardon when Woodes ROGERS landed at NEW PROVIDENCE ISLAND in July 1718. Told that McCarthy was a sober, responsible man, Rogers made him an officer in the militia. Despite this sign of favor, McCarthy helped lead a mutiny that seized three SLOOPS sent for provisions in October. With Phineas BUNCE, McCarthy cruelly abused and MAROONED the officers and men refusing to join the mutiny.

Spanish coast guards attacked the pirates near Long Island. McCarthy and several others escaped ashore but were recaptured and condemned to death. Determined to be hanged in style, McCarthy put on clean linen, tied his cap, neck, wrists, and knees with long blue ribbons, and lightly stepped up to the scaffold. Once there, he kicked off his shoes, having sworn, he said, not to die with them on.

(See also AUGER, JOHN; SELECTED BIBLIOGRAPHY: Defoe, *General History*.)

MACKETT (MAGGOTT), THOMAS (English buccaneer; Caribbean; 1680)
Mackett sacked PORTO-BELO in February 1680 with Bartholomew SHARP and five other captains. In April, the pirates marched overland across the isthmus to attack in the Pacific. Since they planned a swift raid, Mackett remained behind to guard their ships.

MADAGASCAR (pirate haven; Indian Ocean; about 1690–1722)
A large island, slightly smaller than California, some 250 miles southeast of Africa and inhabited by various African, Indonesian, Indian, and Arab peoples. From Madagascar, European pirates—mainly Anglo-American—devastated shipping in the Indian Ocean and the Red Sea for 30 years. (The island was occupied by France in 1885 and regained independence as the Malagasy Republic in 1958.)

The seas around Madagascar offered rich prizes. Each year, Indian ships carried Muslim pilgrims and rare luxury goods to Mecca and Jiddah. When the monsoon set in, they collected at Mocha and returned in a single fleet loaded with gold and silver. European shipping also offered tempting targets. Portuguese CARRACKS carried goods from Goa to Europe. Other large vessels were owned by the East India Companies of Britain, France, and the Netherlands. Ships for Europe were loaded with Oriental silks, cloth, jewels, spices, and drugs. Those heading east carried cash to finance trade.

Despite the wealth on board, no government protected vessels in the Indian Ocean. The navy of the declining Mogul Empire usually stuck close to shore, and Portuguese naval power in Africa also had collapsed. British warships did not venture east of the Cape of Good Hope. Although the East India Company's ships were well armed, their crews had little stomach for fighting. Only Dutch vessels put up much resistance and rarely were taken.

Madagascar provided a superb HAVEN. The native peoples had no central authority, and there were no European colonies. A British attempt failed in 1645, and the French abandoned Fort Dauphin at the island's southeastern tip in 1674. Power was divided among tribal states that fought continuous wars. The chiefs welcomed Europeans with firearms and rewarded them with prisoners-of-war that were sold to slavers.

Since it offered the first usable harbors east of the Cape, most European ships stopped at Madagascar where they fell prey to pirates. The island offered excellent harbors, ample fresh water and beef, and fruits that cured SCURVY. Even tropical diseases were less virulent than in Africa.

The first pirates, arriving at the end of the 1680s, were former BUCCANEERS. By the 1680s, there was little booty left in the West Indies, already pillaged for over a century. The CYGNET and John KELLEY'S BATCHELOR'S DELIGHT reached Madagascar in 1689 after raiding South America. Other buccaneers followed, including William MAY and Robert CULLIFORD in 1690.

Captains from British North America joined the move east. (Only a few, such as Henry EVERY, came from Europe.) The invasion gained force when Thomas TEW returned in April 1694 with extraordinary booty. In June 1695, Every took the *Gunsway* while cruising in consort with Tew, William WANT, Joseph FARRELL, William May, and Thomas WAKE.

At Bermuda and the Bahamas as well as at Massachusetts, Rhode Island, and South Carolina, colonial authorities shared in pirate booty. While Britain warred with France from 1688 to 1697, governors were allowed to license PRIVATEERS. The commissions usually authorized captains to attack the French in West Africa. But there were no complaints when they instead returned with booty from the East Indies.

Governor Benjamin Fletcher of New York openly befriended successful pirates. Thomas Tew's wife and daughters attended the governor's parties in rich silks and glittering diamonds looted in the east. Governor Thomas Trott allowed Henry Every to dock at the Bahamas. Governor William Markham of Pennsylvania welcomed Every's men for £100 per head, and married his daughter to one of the crew.

With official connivance, syndicates of merchants supplied ships for pirate voyages. Adam BALDRIDGE and others set up trading posts, where raiders could buy European goods at inflated prices. Seamen could remain at Madagascar or nearby SAINT MARY'S ISLAND while waiting for a ship, and some settled there permanently.

When he left for Madagascar in September 1696, William KIDD hoped to become as rich as Tew and Every. However, piracy was under attack when he returned in 1699. Lord Bellomont had replaced Fletcher in New York and Massachusetts, and the British government fired other governors fond of pirates.

The war with France ended in 1697, freeing the British navy for anti-pirate duties. Four men-of-war visited Saint Augustine's Bay in 1699 and reached Saint Mary's Island in September. The pirates did not resist the squadron. Some—including Robert Culliford and Dirk CHIVERS—accepted a royal pardon. Nathaniel NORTH and others fled into the interior. After visiting India, the warships cruised off Madagascar until December 1700. Two men-of-war also policed the island in 1703 and 1704 and captured David WILLIAMS.

With a new war in Europe in 1704, the naval patrols were recalled. Most captains settled down, enjoying their booty and trading slaves. John BOWEN moved to Mauritius Island, while Thomas HOWARD retired on the Indian Coast. John HALSEY of Boston was almost the only captain to cross the Atlantic (in 1704) to Madagascar. There were still plenty of pirates, but they preferred to operate closer to home in the Atlantic and Caribbean.

Woodes ROGERS' success in taming the Bahamas sent a new wave of raiders to Madagascar. Christopher CONDENT led the return to the eastern seas in 1719. Picking up the remnants of Halsey's crew, he took the richest prize in 20 years and then retired at Réunion Island. Edward ENGLAND, John TAYLOR, and Olivier LA BOUCHE followed in 1720. After they captured an East Indiaman, Taylor marooned England, who died penniless. Taylor then joined La Bouche in looting the richest prize taken from Madagascar—a Portuguese vessel carrying £500,000 in diamonds and cash.

Soon after, the two captains heard that a naval squadron under Commodore Thomas Matthews had rounded the Cape of Good Hope. Matthews' warships were not a serious threat. ANGRIA's pirate fleets defeated them in India, and they cruised harmlessly off Madagascar in 1723 without attacking. However, their mere presence in the Indian Ocean frightened away pirates. Taylor fled back to the Caribbean with his booty, while La Bouche retired at Réunion Island. Adventurers no longer came to Madagascar, although a few former pirates (such as John PLANTAIN) stayed there in retirement.

(See also BOOTY; SELECTED BIBLIOGRAPHY: Botting, *Pirates*; Pringle, *Jolly Roger*.)

MADAGASCAR; OR ROBERT DRURY'S JOURNAL (adventure story; 1729)

"I was not fourteen years of age when these miseries and misfortunes befell me." Thus begins Robert Drury's story of his ill-fated voyage to India and 13 years of captivity on MADAGASCAR. Drury was an apprentice seaman on the *Degrave* (wrecked in April 1703) and one of only four men escaping slaughter by native soldiers. For 10 years, he was enslaved at Adroy in the south. He learned the Malagasy language, herded cattle, and joined raids on neighboring tribes.

Drury finally fled across rivers teeming with crocodiles and found refuge near Youngoule (modern Morondava) under the kinder King Moume. He tried to escape by begging a visiting British slaver to buy his freedom. The captain instead sailed away with another castaway. Learning that Drury was alive, his father arranged for his rescue in 1716.

Drury's *Journal* long was accepted as true and important. The book mentions pirates such as Samuel BURGESS and Abraham SAMUEL. It also provides the only surviving description of the island's interior regions.

Since the 1940s, some critics have described the *Journal* as a fictional work by Daniel DEFOE. However, British records prove that a Robert Drury really was marooned on Madagascar. Most likely, Defoe edited Drury's rough manuscript and inserted additional information and fictional episodes. Whether fact or fantasy, the *Journal* provides a fascinating account of the great pirate HAVEN. A modern edition was published in 1897.

(See also SELECTED BIBLIOGRAPHY: Secord, *Robert Drury's Journal*.)

MADRE DE DIOS *(Portuguese treasure ship; captured August 3, 1592)* A CARRACK carrying spices and other precious cargo from India to Lisbon, she was one of the largest ships afloat, at 1,600 tons and 165 feet in length. Captured after a bitter fight by English raiders, the *Madre de Dios* probably was the richest prize ever brought into an English port. An exact estimate of her value is not known.

Three separate squadrons joined in CONSORT to seize the *Madre de Dios*. One squadron had been financed by Sir Walter RALEIGH, Queen Elizabeth I, Sir John HAWKINS, and various London merchants. The sponsors originally intended to raid the West Indies, but they changed their plans at the news that five Portuguese carracks were heading for Lisbon. While Sir Martin FROBISHER cruised off Portugal, Sir John BURGH made for the Azores with the *Roebuck*, the *Dainty*, and the *Foresight* (commanded by Robert CROSSE).

Meanwhile, the earl of CUMBERLAND had sent out John NORTON in the *Tiger* and Abraham COCKE in the *Samson*. At the Azores, Norton at once sighted one of the carracks. As he chased her, his squadron encountered and was joined by Burgh's ships. When the English attacked, the Portuguese captain deliberately wrecked and burned his ship on Flores Island. Under torture, the purser revealed the imminent arrival of the other carracks, including the *Madre de Dios*.

The English stayed to pick up water on Flores, where they were joined by a third squadron consisting of Christopher NEWPORT's *Golden Dragon* and *Prudence*. Burgh

assumed command of all nine ships and sent them out on patrol west of Flores. The *Dainty* sighted and chased the *Madre de Dios* but was driven off and severely damaged. Burgh and Crosse caught up but could not board the larger ship, and her captain pointed the *Madre de Dios* toward destruction on the shore.

Rather than lose his prize, Captain Crosse carried out a dangerous maneuver. He ran the *Foresight* up the side of the much larger carrack and tied her fast for two hours until the *Tiger*, *Samson*, and *Dragon* arrived. (This was doubly dangerous, since the *Foresight* was a royal ship, and her loss would have enraged Queen Elizabeth.)

Crazed by the prospect of so much booty, the English mariners swarmed aboard, and many died before their swords and pikes overcame the fierce Portuguese resistance. Pandemonium broke out as soon as the ship surrendered at about two in the morning. Throughout the night, both officers and men ran wild, stripping captives, breaking open chests, rifling the cargo, and briefly setting the ship afire with their candles. The seamen were at each other's throats, as each grabbed what he could before Burgh arrived and declared the ship royal property.

The *Madre de Dios* yielded a rich haul. To avoid Spanish customs duties, many passengers had converted their fortunes into pearls, diamonds, and rubies. The raiders made for ports in western England, where thousands of London merchants rushed to buy their loot for ridiculously low prizes. The government captured one jeweler, who had paid a sailor only £130 for 1,800 diamonds and over 500 rubies—some of great size.

According to English BOOTY rules, a ship's sponsors shared in two-thirds of a prize's cargo, while the crew got one-third and everything above deck. However, only £140,000 worth of plunder reached London, out of perhaps half a million. Queen Elizabeth grabbed about half. Cumberland received much less than he should have, and Raleigh actually lost money on the venture. Many seamen also lost out, especially wounded men unable to join in the mass looting after capture.

(See also SELECTED BIBLIOGRAPHY: Bovill, "*Madre de Dios*"; Williamson, *Cumberland*.)

MAHU, JACOB DE *(Dutch captain; Pacific; died 1598)* Mahu was the first Dutch commander to raid South America's Pacific coast. He died before the fleet crossed the Atlantic, and Simon de CORDES took command.

MAINWARING, SIR HENRY *(English pirate; Atlantic, Mediterranean; 1587–1653)* The most famous English sea rover of his day and among the most skilled in seamanship and naval warfare. Born into a well-known Shropshire family, he was graduated from Oxford in 1602, studied law, and joined the army for a time. In 1611, under an admiralty commission, he unsuccessfully tried to catch Peter EASTON in the Bristol

Channel. In July 1612, he purchased the *Resistance*, a fast ship of 160 tons, and solicited funds for a trading voyage to the West Indies. According to one tradition, he also was licensed to plunder Spanish shipping in the West Indies.

In the summer of 1613, Mainwaring instead sailed to MAMORA and "fell to takinge and spoylinge of shipps and goods." Fiercely anti-Spanish, he took dozens of prizes worth perhaps a million crowns. (Like Sabatini's CAPTAIN BLOOD, he swore never to seize his own country's ships.) His exploits brought Mainwaring recognition as the "admiral" of the Mamora captains. During the summer of 1614 (copying Peter Easton's 1612 raid), he led eight ships to Newfoundland. For three months, they pillaged the fishing fleet and forced or persuaded 400 English fishermen to join their crews.

During Mainwaring's absence, a Spanish fleet had captured Mamora. He found refuge at Villefranche with CARLO EMMANUELE I and continued to plunder Spanish commerce. In June 1615, with only two or three vessels, he outfought a larger Spanish squadron sent to catch him, forcing them to flee to Lisbon. The Spanish offered him a pardon and 20,000 ducats a year, and the DEY of TUNIS tried to recruit him for his corsair fleet.

Preferring to return home, Mainwaring sailed to Ireland to negotiate a pardon. King James I granted amnesty to Mainwaring and his band in June 1616 and allowed them to keep their booty. To show his gratitude, he helped to chase BARBARY corsairs in the English Channel. He also wrote *Of the Beginnings, Practices, and Suppression of Pirates*, which caught the king's attention. Knighted in 1618, Mainwaring became a courtier and personal friend of the king and Prince Charles.

Mainwaring was appointed lieutenant of Dover Castle and deputy warden of the Cinque Ports in 1620 and was elected to Parliament in 1621. In later years, he was a naval commissioner, held high command during several expeditions, and wrote several more books. These included the *Sea-mans Dictionary* (London, 1644), the first and, for over a century, the best treatment of naval terms.

(See also SELECTED BIBLIOGRAPHY: Senior, *Nation of Pirates*.)

MALOPOLUS, BARTHOLOMEW (pirate captain; Mediterranean; 1335) Possibly Genoese or Catalan, Malopolus raided shipping between RHODES and Cyprus.

MALAYS (sea raiders; South China Sea and adjacent waters; all eras) The seafaring peoples of the Malay Peninsula, who speak the Malay language and practice the Muslim religion. Living on the main trade routes between India and China, the Malays practiced both trade and piracy from ancient times. As early as 413, a Chinese traveler complained that the seas were "infested with pirates."

From the early 1500s, Malay rulers invaded regions to the east, including the Sula Archipelago and the coast of Borneo. As the power of the sultans weakened from the 17th century, effective power passed to local princes. Piracy increased after 1600, as political power became fragmented. Some historians also blame the Dutch East India Company, which conquered territories in Indonesia. The Dutch monopolized seaborne commerce and deliberately destroyed local trade. Piracy was the only career open to Malayan seamen, and rulers encouraged and taxed their raids.

Malay piracy peaked during the first half of the 19th century, after the Dutch navy was destroyed during the Napoleonic Wars. Several states in the Malay Peninsula sponsored seasonal raids in nearby waters and in the Straits of Malacca. The most ambitious cruises were carried out by the ILANUNS and BALANINI from bases in the southern Philippines and Borneo. These enterprising raiders sought booty and slaves from the Bay of Bengal to Canton.

(See also PENGERAN ANOM; TUANKU ABBAS.)

MALTA (corsair haven; Mediterranean; 870 to 1798) With Gozo and Comino, one of three small islands lying south of Sicily. Although lacking natural resources and even short of water, Malta is an exemplary pirate HAVEN. The island commands the passage between the eastern and western Mediterranean, and its superb deep-water ports can accommodate the largest fleet.

Malta's political fortunes were tied to those of SICILY. The island fell under Muslim rule from 870, was occupied by the Normans in 1091, passed to the Hohenstaufen emperors of Germany in 1194, and came under the kings of Aragon from 1282. In 1530, Emperor Charles V granted the island group to the KNIGHTS HOSPITALERS (often thus known as the KNIGHTS OF MALTA).

Under Muslim rule (870–1091), Maltese seamen joined Sicilian raids against southern Europe. After the Christian conquest, Sicilian nobles settled in the islands and raided Muslim North Africa. Sicilian rulers gave the lordship of Malta to corsairs who served them. Three pirates became counts of Malta between 1192 and 1203: MARGARITONE OF BRINDISI, Guglielmo GRASSO, and Enrico PESCATORE.

Despite complaints that the Maltese looted Christians as well as Muslims, the kings of Sicily favored their cruises. Until the early 1400s, corsair crews were exempted from import taxes on food. The vice-admiral of Sicily issued licenses, took 20 percent of the booty (from about 1409), and sometimes punished corsairs who sacked Christian vessels.

Alfonso V (1416–1458) especially encouraged attacks on Muslim commerce during wars with the North African states. Many foreign adventurers operated from the island with Maltese crews. So many men deserted farming that piracy was forbidden from 1449 to 1494. Despite this law, corsairs such as Michele de MALTA continued to raid near Cyprus, CRETE, and RHODES.

Malta's corsairs enjoyed their golden age under the Knights Hospitalers. Although the knights initially concentrated on military expeditions, their expenses soon outran revenues. The order's squadrons began to seek out and attack Christian as well as Muslim shipping in the Near East.

The decay of OTTOMAN naval power from the 1570s opened the seas to piracy. To increase their profits, the grand masters and other wealthy knights built their own warships. Both Ugo de Verdalle (ruled 1582–1595) and Alofio de Wignacourt (1601–1622) accumulated sizable fortunes from ships flying their personal flag as ruler of Malta. The grand masters also licensed private captains not connected to the order. At Rhodes, corsairs had received general licenses under the order's flag. Pietro del Monte (1568–1572) revived the practice, levying a set tax on captured booty.

By 1600, Malta supported so many corsairs that the order could not provision its naval squadron. To restrict their number, the grand master in 1605 created the TRIBUNALE DEGLI ARMAMENTI. Only corsairs it licensed under the order's flag could sail from Malta. Henceforth, the island supported two piratical fleets—the order's navy and a varying number of private ships.

The two fleets were financed in different ways. The official navy seldom took enough booty to pay for its operations. The order maintained it with revenues from its European estates or from trust funds that financed the building of galleys. Private cruises were a business that paid all expenses from captured loot. Sophisticated financial institutions provided the capital needed for each expedition. In addition to buying, outfitting, and arming a warship, the sponsors had to feed hundreds of men. They limited their risk by selling both BOTTOMRY BONDS and shares of stock.

Almost everyone in Malta invested in pirate cruises. Merchants, priests, nuns, and peasants took the safer bonds, which guaranteed them a fixed payment from booty. Stockholders got only whatever was left after paying off expenses. Owning stock thus was a gamble appealing to wealthy shipowners and knights.

While the naval and corsair fleets were legally distinct, they often shared the same personnel. Members of the order initially provided most captains. By the end of the 17th century, Maltese, French, and Corsican laymen predominated. The crews included Maltese, Italian, Spanish, and French seamen. During wartime, both captains and crews often served for pay in the order's navy, which also hired private warships for auxiliary service.

Both corsairs and the official navy usually stayed away from the Adriatic and the Spanish and French coasts. The Maltese primarily raided between Egypt and Constantinople, with the North African coast a second favored target. During the 17th century, the corsairs often

spent entire winters in the Greek islands and headed south in the spring.

Few Maltese took rich booty or collected large ransoms. Most prizes were merchantmen carrying bulk commodities. Enslaved crew members often brought in more than the cargo, and the corsairs also kidnapped Greeks from the mainland and islands. But really wealthy individuals and valuable cargoes traveled in "caravans" guarded by Ottoman warships. Most corsairs left these convoys to the order's navy, and they were attacked only by the most daring captains, such as Gabriel TÉMÉRICOURT and Maximilien TÉMÉRICOURT.

Malta, with a smaller population, supported about as many ships as Muslim ALGIERS. In some years, one-fifth of adult males sailed as corsairs, and many others were employed servicing pirate ships. As in the BARBARY STATES, fewer corsairs operated from the 1670s, as the larger European states actively protected their trade. Malta maintained about 20 to 30 ships to the 1670s, perhaps 10 to 20 until the 1740s, and fewer than 10 thereafter.

Both shipowners and captains promised not to attack Christian persons, ships, and merchandise. Enforcement of this oath (guaranteed by a money bond) would have ended Maltese piracy. To avoid capture, most Muslim merchants sent their goods on Greek or (from the 1660s) French ships.

In fact, however, the corsairs claimed the right to SEARCH any ships for Muslim passengers and property. They usually avoided the heavily armed British and Dutch ships, and they attacked fewer Venetian ships from the 1640s. But they plundered Muslims on French ships, and they seized the vessels of Jews and Greek Orthodox Christians. No European ruler protected these Ottoman subjects, who therefore sought help from the pope. The grand masters shielded the corsairs for more than a century. Ultimately the papacy and the French government won out, and Maltese piracy fell off from the 1740s.

Maltese attacks near the Holy Land led to Ottoman reprisals against Christian pilgrims. In 1647, the grand master prohibited cruises near Palestine and Syria. Many Maltese ignored this restriction. But the order needed French funds, and it usually enforced its 1673 decree forbidding the corsairs to search French ships.

The Maltese continued to pillage Greek vessels, and the grand masters used various tricks to thwart papal protection. Since the Armamenti was a religious court, Greeks could appeal its decisions to Rome. To avoid appeals, corsairs were licensed under non-Maltese flags or under the grand master's personal flag rather than the order's.

From the early 1740s, the order gave up and licensed corsairs only for Barbary. But even this did not totally end Maltese piracy in the Levant. Several large ships operated under the flag of Monaco. Captains licensed for

North Africa raided Greece, claiming that "strong winds" had blown them 500 miles off course. They attacked at least 45 merchant ships between 1764 and 1788 and eight in the Levant. Only the 1798 French occupation ended the order's Holy War against Muslims.

(See also SELECTED BIBLIOGRAPHY: Blouet, *Story;* Earle, *Corsairs.*

MALTA, MICHELE DE (*Maltese corsair; Mediterranean; active 1460s*)

The KNIGHTS HOSPITALERS of RHODES sought Michele's support in 1465, when Venice attacked to end the knights' piracies. He later switched his base of operations to Cyprus, whose king allowed Michele's large galley to prey on Christians sailing from Venice, Genoa, Cyprus, and Rhodes. In 1467, when he seized a Hospitaler GALIOT and a Venetian merchant ship, the enraged knights sent a war galley in pursuit. They found Michele's ship near Malta, loaded with spoils and towing the captured vessels. During a savage battle, the knights shot and killed Michele and imprisoned his men at Rhodes.

MALTA, SIEGE OF (*Christian versus Muslim corsairs; 1565*)

The KNIGHTS OF MALTA harassed the OTTOMAN EMPIRE by their own raids and by sponsoring freelance pirates. Following an attack on Greece in 1564, Sultan Suleiman II determined to take over the knights' haven. In Ottoman hands, Malta's superb harbor would provide an ideal base for raids on Europe. On May 18, 1565, an Ottoman fleet with more than 160 ships and 30,000 troops appeared before the island. TURGUT REIS arrived from TRIPOLI on June 2 with 45 additional warships and 2,500 soldiers. Some 2,500 fighting men defended Malta.

The Ottomans first attacked the small Fort of Saint Elmo, which guarded the Grand Harbor. Saint Elmo held out for 28 days against intensive bombardment and four major assaults. To capture it, Turgut Reis moved heavy cannon to a site—still called Dragut Point in his honor—only 500 yards from the fort. And he personally directed the construction of a wall down to the water's edge to cut off Saint Elmo. On June 18, while supervising the wall's erection, Turgut was wounded by cannon fire, dying on June 23 as Saint Elmo fell.

More than 6,000 Ottoman troops perished before Saint Elmo. From July 3 to September 7, the invaders turned their batteries on the main fortifications in the Grand Harbor. Despite the enemy's overwhelming artillery fire, the knights beat off massive land and sea assaults. On September 8, a relief expedition from Sicily reached Malta with 60 galleys carrying 11,000 fresh soldiers. With most of their best fighting men and rowers killed during the battle, the Ottoman commanders reembarked for Greece.

(See also SELECTED BIBLIOGRAPHY: Bradford, *Great Siege.*)

MAMET MEZZALUNA REIS (*Barbary corsair; Mediterranean; 1696*)

Sailing from TRIPOLI, Mamet Reis sold a Maltese ship to two Italians, promising not to recapture it before they reached their home port.

MAMORA (*Moroccan pirate haven; Atlantic; 1604–1614*)

A port on the Atlantic coast at the mouth of the Sibu River, not far from SALÉ. After Britain and Spain made peace in 1604, many British pirates used Mamora as a southern or winter base. In return for protection, the pirates shared their booty, taught the Moroccans sailing and gunnery, and sometimes transported Moroccan soldiers. The Spanish and Dutch navies unsuccessfully tried to blockade Mamora. In August 1614, a large Spanish expedition—99 ships and 7,000 troops—finally captured it, but most pirates escaped to sea.

MANILA GALLEONS (*Spanish treasure ships; Pacific; 1565–1811*)

Sea raiders hunted these extraordinarily rich merchant ships for more than 250 years. Only four were ever captured—two by English pirates, two by British naval ships.

Unlike the Portuguese and the Dutch, the Spanish Empire did not use the sea route around Africa. Goods and passengers traveled between the Philippines and Mexico in large ships, known to the English as the Manila Galleons. (The Spanish called them the *naos de China,* the "Chinese ships.")

Each year, one or two Galleons crossed the Pacific in both directions between Manila and Acapulco. The Spanish government owned the ships and heavily regulated their voyages. Cargoes from Manila could only be sold in Mexico, but many goods were illegally reexported. Direct trade between Europe and the Philippines was allowed after 1785, but the Galleons continued to sail until Mexican rebels raided Acapulco in 1811.

On the Manila to Acapulco voyage, the Galleons carried rare Oriental products. Until the 17th century, each ship was limited to 250,000 pesos in merchandise. But cheating was widespread, and the cargoes probably were sold for at least 10 times that amount. The Galleons always were packed with Chinese silks and porcelain, cotton cloth from India, and Persian and Chinese carpets. Most also carried gold bullion, jewelry, uncut gems, spices, and drugs. To pay for these Oriental imports, the vessels leaving Acapulco carried up to 3 million pesos in silver—worth several hundred times more in modern money.

The westward route was direct and easy. Leaving Mexico around March 1, the Galleons dropped south between the 10th and the 14th parallels. Carried along by the easterly trade winds, they reached Guam in three months or less, the Philippines a month later.

The voyage from Manila was among the most difficult and deadly in the world. The Galleons usually left between mid-June and mid-July. To catch the westerly

After capturing a Manila Galleon in 1587, Thomas Cavendish returned to England across the Pacific. Although Cavendish had only one vessel, this illustration shows several ships repelling a native attack in the Mariana Islands. From Theodorus de Bry, *Collectiones . . . Americae pars VIII* (1599).

trades, they ran far to the north of Tokyo and as high as the 40th parallel. No land was sighted during a voyage of four to eight months—perhaps six months on average. If all went well, the Galleons reached Oregon or California by about the end of December. They then traveled south to Acapulco along an inhospitable coast inhabited solely by impoverished Indians.

The Manila Galleons obviously were a pirate's dream come true. On both legs of the journey, much of the cargo was small, easily carried, and immensely valuable. Although warships sometimes came out to meet them, they largely traveled alone and without escort.

But the Galleons were hard to find in the vast wastes of the Pacific. Pirates waited for months along the California coast, and many ran out of food and water before the Galleon appeared. (Raiders did not dare to attack the ships at Acapulco, which was heavily fortified from 1617.) Once found, the Galleons strongly resisted attackers. Following English raids in 1578 and 1587, they were armed with large cannon. They also were defended by

their enormous size, much larger and higher than that of any pirate ship. Galleons of 700 tons were common, and some reached 2,000 tons. To survive the long voyage, they were strongly built of Oriental hardwoods. (Woodes ROGERS claimed that the *Begoña*'s tough sides absorbed over 500 cannon balls in 1709.) In addition to several hundred crewmen, they carried many passengers who could help to repel boarders.

The original Galleons did not expect to meet pirates and sailed without guns. Sir Francis DRAKE, the earliest raider in the Pacific, could have seized the Galleon at Acapulco in 1578. By that time, however, he was satisfied with looting the CACAFUEGO. Thomas CAVENDISH, who took the *Santa Ana* in 1587, became the first raider to capture a Galleon.

Once Cavendish had shown the way, many others tried to duplicate his feat. However, Spanish authorities strengthened coastal defenses and ordered that the Galleon carry cannon. None of Cavendish's imitators had much luck. John CHIDLEY died on the way to the

Pacific in 1589. Sir Richard HAWKINS was captured off Ecuador in 1594. Olivier van NOORT could not find the Galleon in 1600, and Joris van SPILBERGEN missed it by a few days in 1614. Hugo SCHAMPENDAM was repulsed at Acapulco in 1624. He was the last pirate to attack that city, although Captain TOWNLEY spied out the harbor in 1685.

During the buccaneer invasion of the 1680s, Charles SWAN and William DAMPIER missed the Galleon in 1685 because they were searching for food. After stealing Swan's ship in the Philippines, John READ (and Dampier) spent 18 months fruitlessly hunting for the Galleon throughout Asia. Dampier returned to California in 1704, but the *Rosario*'s heavy guns easily repulsed his attack.

Learning from the buccaneers' mistakes, Woodes Rogers captured the *Disengaño* in 1709, but the larger *Begoña* drove off his three ships. George SHELVOCKE and John CLIPPERTON in 1721 were the last pirates to threaten the Galleons. However, the two captains hated and distrusted each other, and Clipperton went off to the East Indies. A few days after Shelvocke left the sea lanes near Acapulco, a Galleon sailed for Manila.

Ships of the British navy captured two Galleons during wartime. Commanding a 60-gun frigate in 1743, Sir George Anson took an Acapulco Galleon east of the Philippines, seizing over 1.3 million pesos in silver. In 1762, a British squadron captured the 2,000-ton *Santísima Trinidad*, traveling from Manila with 2 million pesos in cargo.

(See also SELECTED BIBLIOGRAPHY: Gerhard, *Pirates;* Schurz, *Manila Galleon;* Spate, *Spanish Lake* and *Monopolists.*)

MANNERS OF ALGIERS, THE *(four-act play in Spanish; written between 1582 and 1587)* In *El Trato de Argel*, Miguel de CERVANTES (himself a former captive) depicts the misfortunes of Aurelio and Silvia, enslaved at ALGIERS. Izuf buys Aurelio as his servant and gives Silvia to his wife Zara. Inevitably Izuf falls for pretty Silvia, while Zara wants the handsome Aurelio. Since Aurelio and Silvia love each other, they cleverly sabotage their master's amorous plots. The play ends happily as the Christians are ransomed. A soldier named Saavedra (Cervantes' mother's name) befriends and sustains the other Christian captives.

Graphic and violent scenes portray the miserable fate of Christian slaves, who accuse the Spanish of giving up the struggle against the BARBARY states. *Manners of Algiers* is one of only two plays surviving out of more than 20 Cervantes wrote during the 1580s. While the work is a cry from the heart, it was not popular with Spanish audiences.

MANSFIELD (MANSVELT), EDWARD *(Dutch pirate; Caribbean; active 1663–1666)* Mansfield, like many other pirates, refused to discuss his past. Already elderly when he arrived in Jamaica after the English conquest in 1655, he successfully combined trade and piracy. Some rumors said he had come from Curaçao. In 1663, commanding his own four-gun BRIGANTINE and 60 men, he took part in Sir Christopher MYNGS' assault on San Francisco de Campeche in Mexico.

During the Second Dutch War (August 1665 through July 1667), Governor Modyford of Jamaica recruited buccaneers to attack the Dutch islands in the Caribbean. The first expedition, led by Edward MORGAN overcame the small islands of Saint Eustatius and Saba, but the pirates refused to go on to Curaçao. Despite this setback, Modyford invited captains to assemble in November 1664 at Bluefields Bay in southwestern Jamaica. Buccaneers of many nationalities came together and elected Mansfield their "admiral."

In December, the pirates raided Cuba, plundered and burned Santo Spirito, and routed 200 cavalrymen sent in pursuit. Spain and England were at peace, but several captains produced Portuguese PRIVATEERING commissions issued by the French governor at TORTUGA ISLAND. (Although some Spanish documents blame this Cuban raid on Pierre LE GRAND, it probably was the work of Mansfield's raiders.)

In mid-January 1665, Mansfield's fleet sailed for Curaçao—a hard voyage against the easterly trade winds. Along the way, ship after ship dropped off to attack Spanish settlements in Cuba and Hispaniola. Claiming that he was faced with a mutiny, Mansfield finally turned around and made for Boca del Toro on the border between Panama and Costa Rica. More captains split off, and Mansfield had only about seven or eight ships.

With about 600 men, Mansfield landed in Costa Rica and marched inland across the mountains to attack the city of Cartago. On the way, the pirates ran into vigorous resistance at Turrialba, 90 miles inland. With their food running out, they retreated to the coast and sailed back to Boca del Toro, where several more ships left him.

Rather than return to Jamaica without booty, Mansfield decided to attack PROVIDENCE ISLAND, off the Honduran coast. Providence had been settled by Puritan pirates in 1630 but reoccupied by Spanish troops in 1641. Mansfield still commanded four ships, which were joined by two French vessels. With more than 200 men, he easily subdued the small Spanish garrison on May 16. The raiders divided booty worth 55,000 pesos and also captured 150 blacks who could be sold at a high price. (Many actually had been free men, and one was an officer in the garrison.).

Leaving behind about 50 pirates, Mansfield returned to Jamaica in June 1665. He probably planned to use Providence during future raids, but Spanish forces from Panama recaptured the island in August. According to EXQUEMELIN, Mansfield quarreled with Governor Modyford soon afterward and died while at Tortuga. In another account he was captured and put to death at Havana.

(See also SELECTED BIBLIOGRAPHY: Cruikshank, *Morgan;* Earle, *Sack.*)

MAPS, TREASURE *(fictional pirate device; 19th century)* Since pirates did not bury their TREASURE, they did not need maps to find it. Maps with bizarre, misleading markings became part of stories about CAPTAIN KIDD. Drawing on these popular legends, Washington IRVING, James Fenimore COOPER, and Edgar Allan Poe (in "THE GOLD BUG") developed the mysterious map theme, which was perfected in TREASURE ISLAND.

MARCO, ANTONIO DI *(Italian pirate; Mediterranean; 1497)* Marco was captured by a Venetian warship while operating from Syracuse, Sicily, with a large galley and a GALLEON. He was fined and forced to post a large sum of money against future attacks on Christian ships.

MARGARITONE OF BRINDISI *(Italian corsair; Mediterranean, Ionian Sea; active 1187–1194)* Margaritone was born in Brindisi and also known as Margarito. By 1187, he commanded a fleet of warships for King William II of Sicily. (He presumably replaced SIPHANTOS, William II's corsair commander in 1185.) Margaritone was at hand when a BYZANTINE fleet arrived to recover Cyprus from a rebellious governor. He captured the Greek ships while their crews were fighting on shore and shipped their admirals to Sicily.

By 1192, Margaritone had seized and made himself lord of the IONIAN ISLANDS, and William II also named him count of MALTA. Henry VI took control of Sicily in 1194, imprisoned and blinded Margaritone, and gave the Ionian islands to his son-in-law. (Like William II, Henry VI hired corsairs rather than maintaining a navy, and he appointed Guglielmo GRASSO count of Malta and admiral of Sicily.)

MARINELLO, CAPTAIN *(Italian pirate; Aegean Sea; late 13th century)* Sailing from Crete, Captain Marinello raided for many years and boasted that his one ship had taken BYZANTINE loot worth more than 400,000 hyperpera, perhaps $10 million.

(See also SANUDO.)

MARINO, MANUEL DE *(Italian corsair; Aegean Sea; about 1276)* Outraged when the BYZANTINE emperor gave a valuable commercial monopoly to a rival Genoese family, Manuel brought two galleys to Constantinople. As they sailed past the imperial palace, his men gave a most improper salute. After seizing one of the rival family's ships, Manuel's crews again insulted Emperor MICHAEL VIII PALAEOLOGUS during the return voyage. Emperor Michael sent a flotilla in pursuit, cheered on his men from the shore, and blinded Manuel and his Genoese crew for insulting his imperial honor.

MAROON/MAROONING *(pirate punishment; all eras)* The act by which a person deliberately is abandoned as his ship sails away. The victim usually is left with few or no supplies, and he often is stripped naked. Marooning is an effective punishment only if the victim is abandoned at an unpleasant place from which he cannot escape or be rescued. (The word is inappropriate when unwanted crewmen were dismissed at a comfortable pirate HAVEN.)

When given a choice between marooning and execution, some victims preferred a quick death to abandonment. Marooning also had an obvious symbolic meaning. The crew cast out someone who had committed acts harming the pirate community. They left him behind because he had deserted their fellowship.

"Marooned." Illustration by Howard Pyle in *Harper's Monthly Magazine*, December 1905.

Maroon is derived from *cimarrón*, a Spanish word (meaning wild or untamed) for an escaped slave. William DAMPIER used it as a synonym for lost in 1699. Describing his Campeche adventures, Dampier wrote "I began to find out that I was (as we call it, I suppose from the Spaniards) Marooned, or Lost, and quite out of the Hearing of my Comrades Guns."

Although the word was first used during the 17th century, abandonment is an ancient punishment. In the CONTROVERSIES OF SENECA (first century A.D.) a man is marooned on a boat without sails. Alonso de CONTRERAS left a naked Italian captain on an isolated Greek island in the 1580s.

Abandonment was an established punishment among English pirates. During the early 1600s, William BAUGHE wanted to execute a crewman who had assaulted him. At the crew's insistence, he instead expelled the miscreant from the pirate crew and set him adrift in a boat with one oar and some water.

Andrew BARKER was marooned by mutineers in 1577. After Thomas CAVENDISH captured a MANILA GALLEON in 1587, he put the naked survivors ashore in the California wastelands. In 1688, William Dampier and seven others were left at the Nicobar Islands without supplies. Alexander SELKIRK, marooned at the JUAN FERNÁNDEZ ISLANDS in 1704, was the model for ROBINSON CRUSOE. Robert CULLIFORD was marooned at the Nicobar Islands in 1696, and Francis SPRIGGS was put ashore in Honduras in 1725.

Daniel DEFOE made marooning famous, and it became a staple ingredient in pirate melodramas. (The best-known fictional castaway is Ben Gunn in Stevenson's TREASURE ISLAND.) Defoe's GENERAL HISTORY (1724–1728) tells the story of John AUGER, who marooned eight men in the Bahamas without supplies or clothing. Defoe also printed the ARTICLES of John PHILLIPS and Bartholomew ROBERTS, which ordered marooning to punish desertion, cowardice, and theft. In Phillips' articles, the marooned man was given water and a pistol so he could kill himself when his loneliness and suffering became unendurable.

(See also MAROONER.)

MAROONER (synonym for pirate; Caribbean; 17th and 18th centuries)
Spanish colonists called escaped African slaves *cimarrónes*, meaning wild or untamed. The English and French shortened the word to *maroons*, referring to African bands that set up independent communities in isolated regions. As early as 1662, Jamaican pirates were called marooners—an appropriate name since they too lived in groups outside the law.

From the early 18th century, MAROON also referred to a punishment in which the victim is abandoned in the wilds. It is possible that the punishment received this name because it was common among the marooners (pirates).

(See also BUCCANEERS AND MAROONERS; SELECTED BIBLIOGRAPHY: Rogoziński, *Caribbean*.)

MARQUE, LETTERS OF (pirate commissions; 13th century–1856)
A variant name for Letters of REPRISAL, a government license to seize enemy property. Legal documents usually mention the license in the plural (as "letters"). They often combine the two names and refer to "letters of marque and reprisal." (*Marque* is an old French word referring to an object held as security for a loan.)

MARTEEN, DAVID (Dutch buccaneer; Caribbean; 1663–1665)
Sailing from PORT ROYAL, Jamaica, Marteen pillaged cities in Mexico and Nicaragua with John MORRIS and Sir Henry MORGAN. As the raiders returned, Marteen discovered that England was at war with the Dutch and went to French TORTUGA. He returned with his two FRIGATES when Governor Thomas MODYFORD assured him that pirates of any nation received a warm welcome in Jamaica.

MARTEL, JOHN (British pirate; Caribbean; 1716)
Martel probably sailed on a privateering ship during the War of the Spanish Succession (1702–1714). In September 1716, he pillaged vessels off Jamaica and Cuba, keeping the 20-gun galley *John and Martha* for his own use. He plundered several more ships near the Leeward Islands, including one carrying gold and slaves.

In November, the pirates careened the *John and Martha* at Saint Croix, then largely uninhabited. Trapped by a British warship, the pirates burned their vessel with 20 slaves still aboard, and escaped into the woods. Before the ship was lost at Saint Croix, according to one report, the crew deposed Martel because of his needless cruelty to captives. In this story, Martel took off in a captured sloop and went to NEW PROVIDENCE ISLAND in the Bahamas.

MARTELLI, BACCIO (Italian pirate; Mediterranean; 1562)
A Florentine cruising between TRIPOLI and Syria, Martelli captured a ship carrying African Muslims with rich gifts for the OTTOMAN sultan—precious stones, a gold cross, conquered Christian battle-flags, and a necklace made from amputated Christian noses.

MARTIN, CAPTAIN (Maltese corsair; Mediterranean; 1670s)
Martin enforced strict discipline during a cruise in the eastern Mediterranean. Many crew members mutinied, killed Martin and 14 supporters, surrendered their ship at the Lebanese port of Saïda (Sidon), and converted to Islam.

MASON, WILLIAM   See MAY, WILLIAM.

MASTER OF BALLANTRAE, THE (1) (novel; 1889)
Although it is less famous than TREASURE ISLAND, many consider this one of Robert Louis STEVENSON's best novels. When the supporters of Charles Stuart invade in 1745, a Scottish family supports both sides to protect its lands. James Durie, the rightful heir, fights for the Stuarts. Henry Durie, the younger son, stays home and

supports King George, whose troops defeat the Stuart forces.

After some years, Colonel Francis Burke arrives, announces that James is alive, and asks for money. When the battle was lost, Burke and James fled Scotland, and their ship was captured by pirates commanded by the Villainous William Teach (BLACKBEARD). Teach was "a horrible villain, with his face blacked and his whiskers curled in ringlets. . . . He stamped about the deck, raving and crying out that his name was Satan, and his ship was called Hell. There was something about him like a wicked child or a half-witted person. . . ."

Burke and James enlist with the pirates, who make the other captives WALK THE PLANK. These brigands are a scurvy lot indeed—"Drinking, roaring, singing, quarreling, dancing, they were never all sober at one time." In their drunkenness, they allow merchantmen to escape and even attack a warship.

To make more money, James convinces the men to make him QUARTERMASTER and takes control away from Blackbeard. Under his leadership, the pirates take many prizes, killing their captives after raping the women. However, they seize relatively little loot. When their ship stops in North America, James gets the pirates drunk, drugs their drinks, and ties Teach to the mast. He and Burke escape with the loot, taking along two seamen whom James murders. The two men argue and separate, and James buries the treasure.

James escapes to France, where his lack of morals guarantees political success. He returns to Scotland, quarrels with his brother Henry, who seemingly kills him in a duel. However, he survives, escapes to India, and returns with a servant named Secundra Dass.

Henry and James both move to New York. James goes after his buried treasure, and Henry sends a man to kill him. James pretends to die and is buried. To make sure he is really dead, Henry digs up James' grave. When Secundra Dass revives James, Henry dies of fright. However, the resurrection fails, and James also dies.

The Master of Ballantrae is a moral fable about two brothers. One is monstrously evil, the other begins as good and turns evil. The pirate sequence is intended as another example of James' wickedness, and the pirates are caricatures of foolish viciousness. Stevenson modeled his Captain Teach on the fictional Blackbeard in Daniel DEFOE's GENERAL HISTORY. The pirates' drunkenness and cruelty also are borrowed from fictional episodes in Defoe's work. However, the real Captain Teach never visited Scotland, and he died in 1718, long before the novel begins. Stevenson apparently realized his error; a footnote after the pirate episode explains that the novel's "Captain Teach" is a different man, who had borrowed the real Teach's name and bad manners.

MASTER OF BALLANTRAE, THE (2) (motion picture; color; 1953) James Durrisdeer (Errol FLYNN), heir to a Scottish title, joins a failed rebellion against the English in this film, directed by William Keighley. Accompanied by Colonel Francis Burke (Roger Livesey), James flees to the West Indies, convinced he was betrayed by his brother, Henry Durrisdeer (Anthony Steel). James and Colonel Burke outwit pirates, amass a fortune, and return to Scotland.

James plans to punish brother Henry and to marry Lady Allison (Beatrice Campbell). Instead, believing that James is dead, Allison has become engaged to Henry during his absence. James eventually learns that Henry really is not a traitor, escapes the British forces, and sails away with Lady Allison and Colonel Burke. The plot and characters are very loosely based on the novel by Robert Louis STEVENSON. At the age of 44, Flynn woos and duels with less verve than in CAPTAIN BLOOD or THE SEA HAWK.

MATE *(nautical word; 14th century to the present)* A habitual companion, fellow worker, partner, and comrade. The word (derived from *meat*) originally referred to persons who shared food. It was later used exclusively by laborers, including seamen. In TREASURE ISLAND, Long John Silver reminds Jim Hawkins that they had been mates.

Also, the title of an officer on merchant and naval vessels. The mate saw to it that orders by the captain or master were carried out, and he took command in their absence. In addition to navigational duties, he was responsible for stowing cargo and organizing the crew's work.

MATELOTS *(buccaneer friends; Caribbean, Pacific, Atlantic; 17th century)* Two men living together in a voluntary and permanent relationship. *Matelot* is an old French term for sailor, originally referring to men that ate together. The word can be translated as comrade, MATE, or buddy (as in, for example, a scuba diver's "buddy"). The relationship was known as *matelotage* ("comradeship," "buddyship").

Most BUCCANEER hunters and pirates at TORTUGA and Hispaniola lived with matelots. Similar relationships were found at PORT ROYAL, Jamaica, and other English islands. James Michener portrays matelotage in his novel *Caribbean*.

Matelots pooled their possessions, fought side by side in battle, and nursed each other when ill. Father DU TERTRE wrote that matelots formed a family, just like a man and wife. But matelots lived together without fussing or quarreling. Pierre CHARLEVOIX, a later missionary, also describes them as sharing their lives and all their goods.

According to EXQUEMELIN, young men became matelots when they finished their term as indentured servants. "They draw up a document, in some cases saying that the partner who lives longer shall have everything, in others that the survivor is bound to give part to the dead man's friends or to his wife, if he was married. Having made this arrangement, some go off marauding, others to hunt, and others to plant tobacco as they think best."

However, older men also became matelots, when, for instance, their previous matelot died. A written agreement was not always possible or needed. Without or without a contract, French settlers and their laws treated matelots as partners.

As matelots prospered, they jointly owned land, indentured servants, and slaves. Originally, Du Tertre wrote, they also shared women, but this became less common in later years. When a man married, the two matelots divided their property evenly. The one moving out received half the value of their house, and his buddy helped him build a new home and business.

MAULEON, SAVARY DE *(French corsair; Atlantic; active 1204–1230)* A noble from Poitou, Mauleon took advantage of French and English wars, switching with amazing ease to the most likely winner. Both sides relied on mercenaries and corsairs and overlooked his lack of loyalty.

After the French seized Poitou in 1204, Savary sold his services to King John of England. In July 1212, he apparently deserted to the French. A treaty with King Philip II gave him La Rochelle as a fief, if he could take it from the English. By 1224, he was back with the English as their governor of La Rochelle. In that year, he betrayed La Rochelle to the French, who let him continue as governor.

Savary now pillaged his former English friends and took several prizes. At the end of 1225, his oared galleys trapped a large merchant convoy near La Rochelle during a calm. As they attacked, a strong wind suddenly rose, allowing the sailing ships to escape. In 1230, he switched sides yet again (for at least the fourth time) when the English threatened to retake Poitou.

(See also EUSTACE THE MONK.)

MAURIZZI, CAPTAIN *(Maltese corsair; eastern Mediterranean; 1658)* Captain Maurizzi captured a large ship loaded with valuable foodstuffs and sent it back to MALTA under a prize crew.

MAY (MUES, MACE, MAZE, MASON), WILLIAM *(British pirate; Caribbean, Indian Ocean, Red Sea, Persian Gulf; active 1689–1699)* A former BUCCANEER, May became a PRIVATEER during the Nine Years' War (1688–1697). In 1689, he raided with William KIDD on the *Blessed William*. While Kidd was ashore early in 1690, the crew stole the ship (and £2,000 in booty) and elected May captain.

May fled to New York and attacked French shipping in the Gulf of Saint Lawrence. Moving to a prize renamed the *Jacob*, the pirates visited MADAGASCAR in December 1690 and then cruised off western India with scant success. Mason and Robert CULLIFORD got off at the Nicobar Islands (or possibly at Madagascar) and somehow made it back to New York.

May sailed in July 1693 with a privateering commission against the French slave stations in West Africa. Commanding the 16-gun, 200-ton *Pearl*, he instead went to Madagascar in about January 1694 and raided Muslim shipping in the Red Sea and Persian Gulf. In June 1695, May cruised in consort with Henry EVERY and shared in the rich plunder from the *Gunsway*. However, Every's men took back all except £2,000 because the *Pearl*'s crew cheated them. May looted at least three vessels off India's southwestern coast early in 1696. He returned to New York with some £200,000 in booty, his own share worth about £7,000.

In January 1699, May was back at SAINT MARY'S ISLAND, near Madagascar, waiting to attack Indian pilgrim fleets returning from Mecca. Hearing that a British squadron was pursuing the Madagascar pirates, May put out to sea and apparently had good luck. In some stories he arrived at New York in December with £300,000 in booty, shared out at £3,000 a man.

(See also BURGESS, SAMUEL; COATES, EDWARD; SELECTED BIBLIOGRAPHY: Grey, *Pirates;* Ritchie, *Kidd.*)

MAZZA, FILIPPO *(Knight of Malta; Mediterranean; active 1530–1534)* Commanding a GALIOT, Mazza was among the knights taking possession of MALTA in 1530. In 1534, the Venetians arrested him for attacking Christian ships in the Adriatic. He escaped and resumed his piratical cruises, but the Venetians recaptured and beheaded him.

MEDICI, COSIMO I DEI *(Italian ruler; Mediterranean; 1519–1574)* The duke of Florence and Siena and grand duke of Tuscany, Cosimo I dei Medici created the KNIGHTS OF SAINT STEPHEN in 1562 in imitation of the KNIGHTS OF MALTA.

MEDICI, COSIMO II DEI *(Italian ruler; Mediterranean; 1590–1621)* Cosimo II dei Medici was grand duke of Tuscany from 1609. Like his father (Ferdinando I dei MEDICI), he actively sponsored both the KNIGHTS OF SAINT STEPHEN and foreign adventurers. British pirates operating from MAMORA in Morocco sold their booty to Florentine merchants for shipment to LIVORNO. When a Spanish expedition wiped out Mamora in 1614, Grand Duke Cosimo II offered the British pirates asylum—despite the religious and diplomatic embarrassment this caused him.

(See also FRANCKE, THOMAS.)

MEDICI, FERDINANDO I DEI *(Italian ruler; 1549–1609)* Grand duke of Tuscany from 1587, Ferdinando I practiced an ambitious maritime policy and built up the port at LIVORNO. OTTOMAN naval forces withdrew from the western Mediterranean during the 1580s. With any real threat of invasion gone, the Florentine KNIGHTS OF SAINT STEPHEN devoted themselves to piracy. Before 1587, the knights mainly had raided along the BARBARY COAST. Led by Admiral Jacopo INGHIRAMI, they now turned east, raiding Greek and Turkish ports and attacking Christian as well as Muslim shipping.

In addition to sponsoring raids by the Florentine knights, Ferdinando also welcomed pirates from France, England, and other regions of Italy. Livorno carried on a thriving trade in captured goods and slaves, and Florentine merchants traveled to MAMORA in Morocco to fence pirate booty.

(See also FRANCKE, THOMAS; GUADAGNI DI BEAUREGUARD, GUGIELMO; SHERLEY, THOMAS; PIERCE, WILLIAM; SELECTED BIBLIOGRAPHY: Braudel, *Mediterranean*.)

MEDICI, FRANCESCO I DEI (Italian pirate patron; 1541–1587)
Grand duke of Tuscany from 1574, Francesco I pursued the maritime and piratical ambitions of his father Cosimo I dei MEDICI. To encourage trade, he completed the harbor and in 1577 founded a new city at LIVORNO. But he also sponsored raids in North Africa and the Levant by the KNIGHTS OF SAINT STEPHEN.

When forced to choose, Duke Francesco decided that piracy brought in greater profits than legitimate commerce. In 1577, he asked the OTTOMAN EMPIRE for a commercial treaty allowing Greek trading posts at Livorno. The negotiations failed because the duke refused to disarm the knights and halt their raids on Greece.

MEDICI, TOMMASO DEI (Knight of Saint Stephen; Mediterranean; 1586–1589)
Admiral of the knights' GALLEYS, Medici frequently raided RHODES, the Aegean islands, and the BARBARY COAST for booty and slaves.

MEHMED BEY (Turkish ruler; Aegean Sea; died 1334)
Emir of AYDIN and one of the first Turkish rulers to sponsor sea raids, although local Greek seamen manned his fleet. Mehmed captured the port of Altoluogo (near ancient Ephesus) in 1304 and the upper citadel of Smyrna in 1317. Despite opposition from the Genoese at Chios and the KNIGHTS OF RHODES, his ships preyed on merchantmen and plundered the Greek mainland and the Aegean islands. After taking the harbor at Smyrna in 1329, his son UMAR BEY built up a larger and more aggressive corsair fleet.

MEHMED ("TRICH") REIS (Barbary corsair; Mediterranean; active 1671–1675)
Son of the DEY of ALGIERS, Mehmed Reis commanded a 40-gun sailing ship captured by Francesco CARAFA in 1671. The KNIGHTS OF MALTA released him four years later. The dey paid an enormous ransom—more than 300 times the normal prize—in grain, always in short supply at Malta.

MEIZE REIS (Moroccan corsair; Mediterranean; active 1690s)
Meize Reis was a SALÉ captain called "the brave" and remembered for his cruelty to prisoners. In May 1691, a French PINK put up a savage fight against his much larger ship. Infuriated by their resistance, Meize ran among his wounded captives, stabbing them with a knife. The French captain received 200 lashes and was chained for 20 days, naked and fed only rotten bread and stagnant water.

The French consul at Salé reported these crimes. Two years later, a French warship captured Meize. Before exchanging him for their prisoners in Morocco, the French gave him 200 lashes in reprisal and as a warning against future atrocities.

MELATAS (Aetolian corsair; Aegean Sea; 276 B.C.)
Melatas sailed under AMEINIAS OF PHOCIS and led the pirates that stormed the walls of Cassandreia, a port city in Macedonia.

MEMADAM (Malayan pirate; South China Sea; 1852)
Memadam operated from the ILANUN settlement at Tunku, on Borneo's east coast. Off Marudu Bay, he and a dozen comrades boarded a British ship pretending to trade. They suddenly drew concealed swords and killed the captain and the owner, Robert Burns (a grandson of the poet). The rest of the crew agreed to sail the ship to Tunku. On the way, a Malayan chief captured and slaughtered the pirates, but Memadam escaped.

A British naval force attacked and burned the Tunku stronghold. However, most of the pirates were absent, and they continued their raids. A British warship again sacked Tunku in 1879, destroying the last of the Ilanun bases.

MEMMI "ARNAUT" REIS (Barbary corsair; Mediterranean; active 1573–1594)
Memmi Reis was an Albanian and CAPTAIN OF THE SEA at ALGIERS from 1573 or earlier. His squadron captured the Spanish author CERVANTES off the French coast in September 1575.

The equal of MURAT THE GREAT in seamanship, Memmi was as cautious as Murat was daring. He frequently fled rather than risk battle with Italian galleys, larger and better-armed than his GALIOTS. In 1592, he ran from Florentine galleys that had captured his much-loved nephew. He left Algiers by 1594, when he served as the OTTOMAN fleet's chief pilot during a raid on southern Italy.

In 1573, the BEYLERBEY of Algiers tried to retire Memmi as Captain of the Sea, naming Murat the Great as his replacement. He was reinstated after the corsairs' guild (TAIFE REISI) complained to the Ottoman sultan. It is not clear why the corsairs preferred to serve under Memmi. Perhaps they wanted a cautious commander, even if they admired the reckless daring with which Murat the Great risked his own life.

MEMMI "DELLI" REIS (Barbary corsair; Mediterranean; active 1570–1599)
A Greek sailing from ALGIERS, Memmi Reis' ship escorted HASAN VENEZIANO PASHA, sent from Istanbul as viceroy in 1574. Memmi purchased the Spanish author CERVANTES after his capture in 1575, and he plundered Sicily in 1591 with MEMMI "ARNAUT" REIS and MURAT THE GREAT. In 1599, while boldly raiding the KNIGHTS OF MALTA, his squadron captured seven Maltese grain ships in three days.

MEMMI PASHA *(Barbary governor; Mediterranean; active 1570s)* An Albanian, Memmi Pasha served at ALGIERS under KARA ALI and ULUJ ALI. The latter arranged for his appointment as BEYLERBEY of Algiers from 1583 to 1586.

MEMMI REIS (1) *(Barbary corsair; Mediterranean; 1570s)* Memmi Reis was a Venetian captured as a youth and trained at ALGIERS by KARA HASAN. In 1574, he was among the captains escorting HASAN VENEZIANO PASHA to Algiers. Resuming raids with Kara Hasan, he revenged his patron's murder by rebellious Christian slaves in 1577.

(See also ULUJ ALI.)

MEMMI REIS (2) *(Moroccan corsair; Mediterranean; 1630s)* A Dutch RENEGADE, Memmi Reis commanded a 13-gun sailing ship captured near SALÉ in 1636 by a French squadron.

MEMOIRS OF A BUCCANEER *(fictional autobiography in French; 1952)* The adventures of Louis Adhémar Timothée Le Golif, nicknamed Borgnefesse (One-Buttock) because of a wound suffered in battle. His writings were preserved, it is claimed, by a manuscript hidden in an old French house. They came to light when the house was destroyed during World War II. A. t'Serstevens, presumably the author, "edited" the miraculous find, which was published as the *Cahiers de Louis . . . Le Golif* and translated into English in 1954.

The *Memoirs* borrow from EXQUEMELIN, Raveneau de LUSSAN, and other 17th-century authors. In the story, Le Golif goes to TORTUGA as an indentured servant in about 1660. Disgusted with his master's cruelty, he turns pirate under the legendary Roche BRASILIANO. During the next 25 years, he takes many rich prizes and joins every major raid by Laurens de GRAFF and other French buccaneers.

Le Golif's *Memoirs* contain few details of sea or land battles. (T'Serstevens wrote that these were "edited out" of the manuscript discovered in the house.) Much of the book describes Le Golif's sexual encounters. The attractive hero made many conquests but never fell in love and died a bachelor. He also was in demand among the other buccaneers, when women were scarce.

Although Le Golif's exploits are fictional and sometimes incredible, the *Memoirs* accurately describe many aspects of buccaneer life. T'Serstevens' introduction notes that Le Golif's style and psychology are strikingly modern. Despite this warning, the hoax has fooled some writers on Caribbean piracy, who have accepted the *Memoirs* as a genuine product of the 17th century.

MENAS *(pirate admiral; Mediterranean; died 35 B.C.)* The leading seaman of his time, Menas commanded fleets for both Sextus POMPEIUS and Octavian (later Augustus) Caesar. Although he betrayed both men, Sextus and Octavian needed his services and thus overlooked his double-dealing.

Menas' name suggests that he was born in Asia Minor and practiced piracy from CILICIA. He was a freedman of Sextus' father, Gnaeus POMPEIUS, who may have enslaved and then liberated him in 67 while fighting the Cilicians. By 40, he was with Sextus' pirates in Sicily. In that year, he commanded a large fleet and 4,000 soldiers that conquered Sardinia.

Menas was a true corsair. He fought for profit and for fame, and he used unscrupulous methods to achieve his goals. From their Sicilian and Sardinian bases, Sextus' fleets controlled the seas. The price of food soared in Rome, and popular discontent led Octavian to seek peace in 39. Menas wrote to Sextus from Sardinia and advised him to continue the blockade. As the famine grew worse, Menas argued, Octavian would have to offer even better terms.

Sextus Pompey finally did agree to attend a peace conference with Octavian and Marc Anthony. While the three were feasting on Pompey's ship, Menas offered to trap and kill the enemy leaders. Pompey feared that such blatant treachery would soil his family's reputation. He replied that Menas should have killed Octavian and Anthony and then told him about their deaths.

By this and other treacheries, Menas earned a reputation as totally untrustworthy. In 38, he aroused Sextus Pompey's suspicions by returning a captured general to Octavian without demanding any ransom. When Sextus ordered Menas to come to Sicily, he instead murdered Sextus' messengers. After negotiating a deal with Octavian, Menas surrendered Sardinia and Corsica together with his army and 60 warships.

Octavian was delighted to receive Menas, who had his own ships and followers. He entertained the former slave at dinner, and enrolled him in the order of knights (the second-highest class below senators). Enraged by Menas's betrayal, Sextus Pompey renewed the war and sent MENECRATES, his other chief admiral, to ravage southern Italy.

Octavian placed Menas second in command of an invasion fleet that sailed for Sicily in the spring of 38. Off the city of Cumae, near Naples, Octavian's forces met Menecrates commanding Pompey's fleet. Menas and Menecrates had hated each other for a long time. Ignoring the fighting around them, the two corsairs became locked together in a battle to the death. The Greek historian Appian writing a century later, describes how the two men

> drove at once against each other with fury and shouting. . . . The ships came into violent collision and were badly damaged, Menodorus [Menas] losing his prow and Menecrates his oar-blades. Grappling-irons were thrown by both. . . . Showers of javelins, stones, and arrows were discharged, and bridges for boarding were thrown from one ship to the other. . . .
>
> Many men were already slain, and the remained wounded, when Menodorus [Menas] was pierced in the arm with a dart. . . . Menecrates was struck in

the thigh with a Spanish javelin, made wholly of iron with numerous barbs. . . . He remained there all the same, encouraging the others, until his ship was captured, when he plunged into the depths of the sea.

Despite the honors he received from Octavian, Menas stayed with him for less than two years. Early in 36, he returned to Sextus, this time taking only seven warships with him. Sextus had lost confidence in Menas. He took him back, but named Demochares commander of his fleets.

Menas remained with Sextus long enough to help burn Octavian's fleet, which had been damaged by a storm in July 36. Frustrated by Sextus' refusal to give him supreme command, he soon deserted to Octavian for a second time. To demonstrate his talents, he sailed his own warship to Italy, captured many merchant vessels, and raided Octavian's shipyards. Once he pretended to be stuck on a sandbank. When his enemies ran down to take him in, he rowed away, laughing with contempt.

Like Sextus, Octavian no longer trusted the turncoat. Menas thus did not play a major rule in the battle of Naulochus (September 36) that ended Sextus' occupation of Sicily. The following year, Octavian included Menas in an expedition against ILLYRIA (although again without major command). There he died in 35 B.C. during a naval battle on the Kulpa (Save) River near the city of Siscia (Siszeg) in Croatia.

MENDEZ DE VASCONCELLOS, BROTHER LUIZ *(Knight of Malta; Mediterranean; died 1628)* Of Portuguese origin, Vasconcellos was elected CAPTAIN GENERAL OF GALLEYS (1613–1614) and grand master (1622–1628). In 1613, while raiding PHOCAEA in Turkey, his squadron captured a large ship and held 20 merchants for high ransoms.

MENECRATES *(pirate admiral; Mediterranean; died 38 B.C.)* Menecrates commanded fleets for Sextus POMPEIUS, whose corsair bands raided from Sicilian bases between 43 and 36. Menecrates was a rival and personal enemy of MENAS, Sextus' chief admiral. Like Menas, he was born in Asia Minor and presumably learned piracy with the CILICIAN corsairs.

Early in 38, Menas betrayed Sextus and surrendered the ships under his command to Octavian (later the emperor Augustus Caesar). Enraged by his treason, Sextus sent Menecrates to ravish cities in the Bay of Naples. These raids gave Octavian an excuse to break the peace treaty with Sextus. Placing Menas second in command, Octavian launched an invasion of Sicily. The hostile fleets met near Cumae in the Bay of Naples. There the flagships of Menecrates and Menas met in fierce combat until Menecrates received a mortal wound.

MENELAUS *(king and sea raider; Mediterranean; ancient Greek legend)* Ruler of Sparta and warrior in HOMER's *Iliad* and *Odyssey*. The theft of Me-

nelaus' wife Helen led to the Greek siege of Troy. The Greeks could justify attacking Troy to defend the sanctity of marriage. However, Menelaus also raided foreign lands solely to gain booty.

In the *Odyssey*, ODYSSEUS' son Telemachus visits Menelaus' palace at Sparta. When the guests admire his rich possessions, Menelaus explains that he had acquired them during his voyage home after the Trojan War, but does not explain how.

(See also SELECTED BIBLIOGRAPHY: Homer, *The Odyssey*, trans. Latimore.)

MENEMVASIA *(pirate haven; Mediterranean; 13th–19th centuries)* A rocky peninsula at the tip of Greece frequented by Greek and Italian corsairs. Mentioned during the 1290s were George de Malvasia, John Curtese, John Scalo, and George Matricheri (Makrycheris), who operated in the Aegean and off the coast of Asia Minor.

(See also BYZANTINE EMPIRE; CRETE; CAVO, GIOVANNI DE LO.)

MENOPHANES *(Cilician corsair; Aegean Sea; first century B.C.)* Menophanes' squadron sacked DELOS Island in 87, during a war between Rome and MITHRIDATES of Pontus. The pirates allied with Mithridates sailed from CILICIA, but Menophanes' own nationality is unknown.

Writing about A.D. 150, the Greek author Pausanias describes Menophanes' raid.

> Knowing that the island was unfortified and the people unarmed, [Menophanes] sailed to it with a fleet, massacred the population . . . looted much of the merchandise and all the votive offerings, sold the women and children into slavery, and razed the town of Delos to the ground.

Delos was sacred to Apollo, who immediately chastised Menophanes' sacrilege. Some merchants, who had fled to sea while the pirates sacked Delos, lay in wait for Menophanes. As he sailed from the city with his loot, they attacked his ship and sank it.

Pausanias' account is not totally accurate. Menophanes obviously did not raze Delos, since ATHENODORUS plundered it again in 69. Nevertheless, Menophanes' men took rich booty in 87. Worshippers had made generous offerings to Apollo's priests for centuries, and Delos was a flourishing commercial port and slave market. Its warehouses were full of luxury goods, and its merchants kept substantial amounts of gold and silver in their homes.

MENTES *(pirate king; Ionian Sea; ancient Greek legend)* According to HOMER's *Odyssey*, Mentes was king of the piratical TAPHIANS at the time of the Trojan War. As the poem begins, the goddess Athena takes the form of Mentes when she appears to ODYSSEUS' son. Mentes is a "guest-friend" of Odysseus and his father Laertes, who ruled Ithaca in the IONIAN ISLANDS. Mentes

sold these kings slaves (including EUMAEUS) and other pirate plunder.

MENTESHE, EMIRS OF *(Muslim corsairs; 14th century)*

A warrior family that ruled CARIA in Asia Minor by 1300 and then attacked RHODES. The first Turks to take to the sea, they hired Christian sailors when the BYZANTINE EMPIRE disbanded its fleet. Because of opposition by the KNIGHTS HOSPITALERS, who occupied Rhodes in 1308, Menteshe raiders took less booty than those sailing from AYDIN further north. The OTTOMAN EMPIRE took over the principality during the 1390s.

MESMYN, GUILLAUME *(French pirate; Caribbean; 1556–1569)*

Mesmyn left La Rochelle in March 1556 with a warship and 150 crewmen. On the way to the West Indies, he captured a Spanish vessel and put his own men aboard. Near the Bermuda Islands, the Spanish prize was wrecked on a reef. Deciding that his own ship had too little food to feed the survivors, Mesmyn coldly abandoned them to their fate.

The shipwrecked French sailors reached the main island on crude rafts. Forty-two men built a larger boat and reached the Spanish colonies. There they seized a small ship, exchanged it for a larger, and finally captured a 160-ton warship near Léogane in Hispaniola. Two years later, they returned to La Rochelle, enriched by several prizes.

Meanwhile, Captain Mesmyn lost both his warship and another Spanish prize to Portuguese coast guards. Outfitting a small boat, he preyed on the Portuguese coast until he had more than recovered his losses. The French king rejected Portuguese complaints, since Mesmyn was an experienced captain who might be useful in wartime.

Unfortunately for the king, when a civil war broke out in 1567, Mesmyn joined the rebels. From 1569, he was captain of a warship in Jacques SORES's fleet, and joined Sores in taking several rich Venetian and Portuguese prizes.

MEZZOMORTO

The nickname of HADJ HUSSEIN, corsair and ruler of Algiers from 1683 to 1689.

MICHAEL OF ZACHLUMIA *(corsair ruler; Adriatic Sea; reigned about 913–926)*

Michael was prince of a Serbian tribe that occupied ILLYRIA from the Neretva River to Dubrovnik. In 913, he captured the son of the Venetian doge returning from Constantinople. In 926, his fleet crossed the Adriatic and sacked Siponto in Italy.

(See also DALMATIA; NARENTANS.)

MICHAEL VIII PALAEOLOGUS *(Byzantine emperor; reigned 1259–1282)*

Already ruler of northwestern Asia Minor, he conquered Constantinople in 1261 and southern Greece in 1262. However, Italian and French lords controlled most of Greece and the Aegean islands. These rulers tolerated or sponsored piracy and welcomed corsairs of many nationalities—Greek,

Italian, Spanish, and Slavic. According to SANUDO, Genoa furnished most captains, Venice the largest number among the crews.

Emperor Michael decided to use pirates to fight pirates. Taking advantage of rivalry between Venice and Genoa, he hired successful corsairs for the imperial fleet at Constantinople. The emperor allowed others to prey on foreign shipping in the Aegean, in some cases taking a share of their profits.

(See also BYZANTINE EMPIRE; VENETIAN CLAIMS.)

MICHELL, STEPHEN *(English captain; Caribbean; born 1570, active 1591)*

Michell commanded the 80-ton *Pegasus*, one of five ships raiding for Sir John WATTS. Michael GEARE and William CRASTON also joined the expedition, commanded by William LANE.

Michell was greedy and disloyal, although (according to Lane) he had lived with Watts for five years as an apprentice. On the way to the West Indies, Lane's ships captured a rich Spanish prize. Michell and Geare argued violently with Lane over the loot and even threatened to attack Lane's ship. After they reached the Caribbean, Lane's raiders captured seven more prizes. Michell, Geare, and Craston continued to grab valuable plunder rather than turning it over for later distribution.

(See also BOOTY.)

MIDDLETON (MYDDELTON), DAVID *(English pirate; Caribbean, Pacific; died 1615)*

The youngest of four brothers related to the wealthy London merchants Thomas and Hugh Myddelton. All four brothers took part in the initial voyages of the East India Company. David began his career with a plunder raid that provided excellent training for later battles in the East Indies.

In May 1601, David Middleton sailed to the West Indies with Michael GEARE, an experienced and unscrupulous captain. Geare commanded the *Neptune*, a warship originally built for Christopher NEWPORT. Middleton was captain of the PINNACE *James* needed for assaults in shallow waters. They unsuccessfully cruised along Venezuela and then took a prize near Cuba, which the *James* escorted back to England.

During the East India Company's second expedition (1604–1606), Middleton was second captain of the *Red Dragon* (formerly the *Malice Scourge*). After commanding a vessel during the third venture (1607–1608), he visited the East Indies with a single ship (1609–1611). Returning to England with a three-ship squadron in April 1615, his ship was wrecked and all hands perished off the MADAGASCAR coast.

(See also CUMBERLAND; SELECTED BIBLIOGRAPHY: Andrews, *Trade*.)

MIDDLETON, PHILLIP *(British pirate; Atlantic, Red Sea; active 1694–1695)*

Middleton was among the crewmen on the warship *Charles* (renamed the *Fancy*), who mutinied and elected Henry EVERY captain. In June 1695, the *Fancy* captured two Indian treasure ships carrying gold and jewels. Middleton escaped to Ireland with Every in June 1696, but he was caught as the pirates landed their booty. He turned informer and provided evidence about Every's crimes.

MINOS *(king of Crete; Mediterranean; ancient Greek legends)*

Ruler of CRETE before the siege of Troy, Minos was a son of Zeus, king of the gods. Centuries after Knossos was destroyed, Greek poets and historians described with wonder this Cretan king. Living in a time of rampant piracy, the Greeks remembered Minos as the lord of the seas, who lived in an unfortified palace and conquered the Aegean islands. However, their writings preserve two contradictory traditions about Minos' motives. One tradition portrays him as a grand monarch, whose navies suppressed piracy. In other legends, Minos himself was the pirate, whose fleets carried young Greeks to slavery and death in Crete.

HOMER's epic poems (before 700 B.C.) recount the siege of Troy by Greek heroes, including Idomeneus, Minos' grandson. Homer's Minos is a wise and majestic king, "who cared for his people." Unlike any other Homeric hero, Minos speaks directly with Zeus, and he rules as a king in Hades after his death.

Writing centuries later, the historians HERODOTUS and THUCYDIDES also held Minos in honor. Minos, says Thucydides, was the first person to organize a navy. He conquered the Aegean islands, installed his sons as governors, and drove out the merciless pirates. Minos, Thucydides comments, probably put down piracy to secure his own revenues. Nevertheless, his efforts brought peace to the Aegean. Before Minos, the Greeks had to build their cities far inland because of raids. Thanks to Minos' navy, those who lived on the coasts now could acquire wealth and live a civilized life.

Other ancient myths describe an evil Minos who was himself a pirate and slaver. The Athenians—who had lived on the Greek coast since Minos's day—preserved these darker stories, which told of the hero Theseus. After conquering the islands, Minos' fleets brought terror, not peace. They regularly raided the Greek coasts for tribute. As a punishment for killing his son, Minos forced the Athenians to hand over seven youths and seven maidens every nine years.

Minos' fleet carried these captives to his palace at Knossos. There they were eaten by the Minotaur, a monster with a bull's head and a human body kept in an underground labyrinth. The third time Minos' navy came to Athens, the 14 captives included Theseus, a son of the sea-god Poseidon. In Crete, Theseus won the love of Minos' daughter Ariadne, who showed him how to find his way out of the labyrinth. Theseus killed the Minotaur and sailed to Athens, taking with him Ariadne and the other young captives.

Beginning in 1873, Heinrich Schleimann dug up the ruins of Troy, while Sir Arthur Evans uncovered the remnants of elaborate palaces at Knossos and other sites in Crete. The Minos legends apparently were based on fact—up to a point. There really had been cities at Troy and Knossos. Since they have not yet translated the Cretan script, historians cannot give definite answers as to whether there was a King Minos and whether he was a pirate.

Believing that he had found Minos' palace at Knossos, Sir Arthur Evans gave the name Minoan to the entire Cretan civilization. Evans thought that Minos was not an individual's name but a general title used by many kings. Thus several Cretan kings contributed to the Greek legends—both good and bad—about Minos.

Evans's theory has one major weakness. Homer's Minos is dominant and forceful, and he traces his descent through the male line. But ancient Crete was a matriarchy controlled by women, and there is no picture of a male king or god in the Cretan ruins. If the powerful rulers called Minos were native Cretans, then they must have been priestess-queens (perhaps ruling through figurehead kings).

Judging by the material evidence, the Cretans were prosperous merchants who traded throughout the entire Mediterranean. Most Cretan cities were destroyed about 1500 B.C., when the volcanic island of Thera (Santorini) exploded. Although Knossos survived for a time, it was conquered by the Mycenaeans from southern Greece. About 1375 to 1350, a fire destroyed Knossos. The destroyers, also from mainland Greece, ravaged Crete and afterward subjected it to their rule.

If, as Homer says, Minos reigned three generations before the Trojan War, then he lived during the 1300s. The Minos of Homer and Thucydides thus was king after the Mycenaeans conquered Knossos. It is plausible that this Mycenaean Minos both fought pirates and also raided territories away from the areas he controlled. It is certain that foreign invaders destroyed Minos' great palace. The Theseus legends may describe (in poetical terms) either a massive pirate attack or a revolt by Minos' slaves.

MISSON, CAPTAIN *(fictional pirate; Caribbean, Atlantic, Red Sea; 1690s)*

Captain Misson was the hero of a long chapter inserted in Daniel DEFOE's GENERAL HISTORY among the biographies of real pirates. Defoe's clever trick has fooled many readers. However, Misson's biography is entirely fictitious, as are the stories about Misson's dealings with Thomas TEW. The meaning of Defoe's hoax is ambiguous. Defoe believed that many men became pirates to escape a corrupt society and live in a community of free men. But the chapter also may satirize Misson's communist beliefs.

Misson serves on board the French privateer *Victoire*. He travels to Rome and falls in with a Roman Catholic priest named Caraccioli. Disgusted with the papacy's hypocrisy and debauchery, Misson and Caraccioli turn PRIVATEER.

The two men fight various battles, one with a SALÉ pirate. Meanwhile, Caraccioli converts Misson and the crew to his ideology of rationality and human freedom. The dogmas of organized religion are absurd frauds,

Caraccioli teaches, and human government is a criminal conspiracy. The poor live in "the most pinching Necessity" solely because of the avarice and ambition of the rich. Rebellion is the only manly answer, since rulers destroy "the People's Rights and Liberties."

While battling an English ship, the officers are killed, and Misson takes command of the *Victoire*. The crew agree to make war on the whole world, which denies them their natural rights. Some want to fly the JOLLY ROGER, but Misson instead raises a white flag with the motto "For God and Liberty."

The raiders capture many ships in the West Indies and in Africa. Prisoners that surrender are courteously treated, but a ship that resists is sunk with a broadside. After taking a Dutch slaver, Misson frees the African slaves and gives a rousing speech about human liberty.

Misson visits the Comoro Islands. To keep the inhabitants under his thumb, he stirs up war between the various islands. Helped by a native queen, he sets up on MADAGASCAR the communist colony of Libertalia. His just laws ensure economic, political, and racial equality.

Near Zanzibar, Misson kills a Portuguese captain in a SWORD DUEL and captures £200,000 in gold. On the way home, he meets Thomas Tew, returning from the Red Sea with rich plunder. Tew joins Misson's colony and is elected admiral.

Some months later, the *Victoire* is wrecked. Tew is rescued by Misson, who describes Libertalia's sad fate. "Without the least Provocation given," the natives suddenly slaughtered most of the colony. Misson had escaped with two SLOOPS and ample gold and diamonds, which he shares with Tew. As the two captains head for Rhode Island, Misson's sloop sinks with all hands.

MITHRIDATES VI "THE GREAT" *(pirate patron; Mediterranean, Black Sea; reigned 121–63 B.C.)*
King of Pontus in northeastern Asia Minor, Mithridates was famous as a hunter, lover, and warrior. He fought three wars (89–66) with Rome, which had conquered Greece during the previous century. Against the Romans, Mithridates allied with pirates based in CILICIA. The pirates, now organized into large squadrons, raided throughout the Mediterranean until their defeat by POMPEY in 67.

The kingdom of Pontus, founded in about 302 B.C., occupied the BLACK SEA's southern coast. It was a wealthy state, and the governing nobility, primarily of Persian origin, provided excellent cavalry. Mithridates himself was of Persian descent, although he admired Greek culture and copied Alexander the Great in personal appearance and dress.

After seizing power from his mother, Mithridates conquered the northern coast of the Black Sea and regions east of Pontus, but failed to annex the neighboring kingdom of Bithynia, an ally of Rome. The Romans encouraged Bithynian raids into Pontus, leading to the First Mithridatic War (89–85). Helped by the Cilician corsairs, Mithridates quickly defeated the Romans in 88.

His forces occupied most of Asia Minor (welcomed as a savior from Roman tyranny), all the Aegean islands except RHODES, and (with Athenian aid) much of Greece.

The Roman general Sulla drove Mithridates' armies out of Greece in 86 and forced him to give up all conquered territory. Mithridates repelled Roman raids in 81 (Second Mithridatic War). However, he was defeated and died during the Third Mithridatic War (74–66), despite the continuing support of the Cilician corsairs.

The Cilician pirates furnished a ready-made navy that paid itself though booty. Corsairs swelled the naval forces that invaded the Aegean and Adriatic during the First Mithridatic War. The pirate captain SELEUCUS loyally defended the Black Sea ports during the third war. Mithridates' subjects were excellent horsemen but poor seamen. Greek cities could provide only a limited number of warships, while Egyptian and Syrian captains charged enormous sums for their services.

Mithridates completely trusted his corsair allies. For their part, the Cilician pirates gained a form of legitimacy, since the king's commission legally made them PRIVATEERS rather than criminals. At sea, the pirates formed the senior partners in their alliance with Mithridates, and the relationship closely resembles that between KHEIREDDIN BARBAROSSA and the OTTOMAN sultans.

MIXTOW, JOHN *(English pirate; Atlantic; active 1429–1433)*
Mixtow came from Cornwall and was perhaps related to Mark MIXTOW. In 1429, Mixtow helped seize a Breton ship in Penzance harbor under dubious legal claims. The government included him on a 1431 list of pirates, and he seized a Genoese CARRACK off Cape Saint Vincent in 1433. Though the Genoese crew offered no resistance, Mixtow marooned them in Portugal and brought the prize to Fowey. Several London merchants proved they owned the captured cargo. Royal officials, bribed by Mixtow, took no action against him.

MIXTOW, MARK *(English pirate; Atlantic; active 1402–1403)*
Mixtow came from Fowey in Cornwall. In 1402, while commanding three barges ordered to search for the king's enemies, he instead captured a German wine ship. The following year, the English government accused him of seizing Spanish ships during a truce, and the Flemish also complained of his piracies.

MODYFORD, SIR THOMAS *(English pirate sponsor; Caribbean; 1620?–1679)*
As governor of Jamaica from 1664 to 1670, Modyford encouraged pirates to sail from PORT ROYAL and freely granted dubious PRIVATEERING commissions. Modyford initially favored Edward MANSFIELD as the BUCCANEERS' leader. After Mansfield's death, he worked with Sir Henry MORGAN and authorized his raids on PORTOBELO, Venezuela, and PANAMA. Although the two nations were at peace, English officials privately condoned Modyford's actions to gain concessions from Spain.

Men sailed with Henry Morgan because they believed he would win booty, not because he held Modyford's commission. But Morgan needed Modyford's help to supply his raiders and to sell their booty. If Modyford had enforced the laws, Morgan and other pirates probably could have operated on a small scale, but their larger raids would have been impossible.

Born into a prosperous Exeter family, Modyford studied law and served with royalist forces in the English Civil War. He went to Barbados in 1647, bought a large plantation, and became a prominent leader of the royalist faction. In 1651, Oliver Cromwell—victorious in England—sent an expedition to subdue Barbados. Modyford at first resisted but then changed sides, allowing Cromwell's troops to take over the island.

Modyford was related to George Monck, duke of Albemarle, who restored Charles II as king in 1660. Modyford owed the Jamaican governorship to Albemarle, who protected him in London until he died in 1670. Morgan's Panama raid infuriated the Spanish government. With Albemarle dead, King Charles removed Modyford as governor and ordered his arrest. Sent to England in 1672, he was kept at the Tower for two years. No trial was held, and he returned to Jamaica as chief justice.

To justify his alliance with the pirates, Modyford claimed that they defended Jamaica. There was no threat of invasion, and the pirates were weak allies, since they refused to attack military forces. Modyford excused Morgan's Panama raid as retaliation for attacks by Manoel RIVERO PARDAL. However, Rivero acted in response to Morgan's unprovoked assault on Portobelo.

While governor, Modyford gave his own family more than 22,000 acres of land, and he set up his plantations with his share of pirate booty. Modyford admitted to receiving £1,000 a year in pirate bribes, and he probably got a great deal more. Modyford's brother headed Jamaica's admiralty court, which appraised prizes and took a fifteenth of their value for the king. According to his own accounts, Modyford collected only £860 for the king during six years as governor. This is a ludicrously small sum given the value of Morgan's plunder, and the king's share undoubtedly ended in Modyford's own pocket.

(See also SELECTED BIBLIOGRAPHY: Dunn, *Sugar*; Pawson, *Port Royal.*)

MOHAMMED AL-HADJ REIS *(Barbary corsair; Mediterranean; 1793)* Sailing from ALGIERS, Mohammed Reis' BRIG seized a Dutch ship loaded with cotton. After subtracting the government's and owner's portions, the crew split 490 shares, each worth more than 271 *reales*. Based on the Algerian records, these were the richest shares received by a corsair crew.

(See also BOOTY.)

MOHAMMED AL-SINCHOULY REIS *(Moroccan corsair; Mediterranean; 1760s)* Mohammed was a Christian RENEGADE who commanded a GALIOT at SALÉ.

MOHAMMED AL-TADJ REIS *(Moroccan corsair; Mediterranean; active 1680s)* Unlike most SALÉ corsairs, Mohammed often raided in the Mediterranean rather than the Atlantic. As he sailed to ALGIERS in 1683, a French warship captured his ship and made him a GALLEY SLAVE, even though he had a PASS from the French ambassador at Salé.

MOHAMMED ARRAEZ ROMELI *(Barbary corsair; Mediterranean; 1798)* Embarking from TUNIS with nine sailing ships and one GALIOT, Mohammed Arraez Romeli raided San Pietro Island, near Sardinia's western coast. The invaders plundered the island, ravished its women, and carried off some 900 prisoners—including five European consuls. The pirates spared only the consuls from the powerful French Republic, and they allowed the English consul to buy his freedom.

Some say a deceived lover inspired the raid. A sailor from another island had married a San Pietro girl, who proved unfaithful. To gain revenge, he joined the Tunisian corsairs and persuaded them to attack San Pietro.

MOHAMMED HADJ CANDIL REIS *(Moroccan corsair; Mediterranean; active 1686–1695)* A French RENEGADE at SALÉ, Mohammed mainly raided in the Mediterranean. He was twice captured by the French and made a GALLEY SLAVE. In 1686, Algerian corsairs seized a ship owned by Mohammed's French father and imprisoned its captain and crew. Soon after, the French captured Mohammed. They freed him in 1688 in exchange for his French father's captain. In 1695, he was taken near Minorca and again enslaved, while commanding a ship owned by Sultan Mawlay Ismail. This time he was exchanged for a young French girl with influential parents.

MOHAMMED REIS (1) *(Barbary corsair; Mediterranean; active 1557–1574)* A German drummer boy serving with Spanish invaders massacred in 1557 near Mostaganem, Algeria. Mohammed became one of ULUJ ALI's followers, and commanded a galley escorting HASAN VENEZIANO from Constantinople to ALGIERS in 1574.

MOHAMMED REIS (2) *(Barbary corsair; Mediterranean; 1679)* Mohammed was a Turk commanding the *Neptune*, a French vessel with six guns, based at TRIPOLI.

MOHAMMED REIS (3) *(Barbary corsair; Mediterranean; 1679)* A Turk and captain of a small sailing ship at TRIPOLI.

MOHAMMED REIS (4) *(Barbary corsair; Mediterranean; 1679)* A Turk commanding a 44-oar half-galley in the TRIPOLI fleet.

MOHAMMED REIS (5) *(Moroccan corsair; Atlantic; active 1695–1707)* This Mohammed Reis was the son of BEN AÏSSA REIS, a SALÉ corsair who gave him a captured ship in 1695. He continued piracy after his

father retired in 1698 and commanded a 16-gun sailing ship in 1707.

MOHAMMED ROUS REIS *(Barbary captain; Mediterranean; 1801)* Commanding the *Tripoli*, a 24-gun BRIG, Mohammed fought a three-hour gun battle at close range with the American ship *Enterprise*, a 12-gun SCHOONER. Two-thirds of the *Tripoli*'s crew were killed or wounded without a single American casualty. The Americans removed the ship's mast, and it returned to TRIPOLI. The pasha, enraged at Mohammed's incompetence, punished him with 500 blows after he was paraded through the streets mounted backward on a jackass.

(See also BARBARY WAR, FIRST.)

MOHAMMED SAKKAL DILISI *(Barbary corsair; Mediterranean; active 1684–1687)* Mohammed Dilisi was a Turk commanding the 38-gun *White Flying Horse*. During TRIPOLI's continuing political turmoil, one faction named him BEY of the land forces in 1587, and he took power by killing the previous bey in battle.

MOHAMMED "ZURNAGI" REIS *(Barbary corsair; Mediterranean; 1684)* Mohammed was captain of the *Santa Magharita*. Perhaps one of the three TRIPOLI captains named Mohammed active in 1679.

MOLETI, BROTHER FRANCESCO *(Knight of Malta; Mediterranean; died 1609)* An Italian, Moleti commanded one of five galleys in June 1595. Near Sicily's eastern coast, the Maltese ran into three smaller GALIOTS under MURAT THE GREAT. Murat drove off the stronger Maltese force during two days of battle that killed many on both sides. Moleti was criticized for firing his guns from a distance rather than closing with the enemy.

Moleti was elected CAPTAIN GENERAL OF GALLEYS in 1608. (He also held the ceremonial post of admiral from 1606.) In 1609, his squadron failed to catch a Tunisian galley carrying the captive son of the Sicilian viceroy. However, it did capture a large merchant ship, taking valuable foodstuffs from Alexandria to Istanbul.

MONSON, WILLIAM *(English captain; Atlantic; 1568–1643)* After taking part in four large raids for the earl of CUMBERLAND from 1589 to 1595, Monson served with the royal navy until 1616. As far as is known, he was the first English seaman to write a historical account (his *Naval Tracts*) analyzing the battles in which he had taken part.

Monson belonged to a family owning land near Lincoln, and he was enrolled at Oxford in 1581. In September 1585, he ran away to sea on a ship sent out by Sir George CAREY. After a bitter fight, Carey's raiders captured a French prize, which they tried to pass off as Spanish.

After sailing on another raid in 1586, Monson commanded two PINNACES in 1587. Presumably his family posted a bond with the ADMIRALTY, the only qualification needed to command an English raider. He disposed of a small Spanish prize in SALÉ, Morocco, and went on to the Canary Islands, where he tricked the Portuguese into selling him supplies.

Monson was a volunteer lieutenant on a royal ship during battles with the Spanish Armada in 1588. By 1589, he was working for Cumberland, who outfitted a series of ambitious plunder ventures. Monson was second-in-command of Cumberland's Azores raid in 1589. Captured in 1591 off the coast of Spain, he was released in 1592. He paid no ransom and apparently won his freedom by agreeing to work as a Spanish agent.

Monson accompanied Cumberland's fleet in 1593 and 1595. But he quarreled with the earl during the 1595 cruise and henceforth served in royal vessels. In 1602, he commanded one of nine ships sent to intercept the West Indies TREASURE FLEET. Although the Spanish fleet escaped, the English succeeded in capturing the *Saint Vincent*, a Portuguese CARRACK returning from the East Indies. According to his own version, Monson led the attacks on the great ship—which turned out to be less richly laden than usual.

Monson was admiral of the Channel fleet from 1604 to January 1616. He was removed from office when it was discovered that he and other officials had been taking Spanish pensions for some years. Aside from a brief command in 1635, he remained in retirement, devoting his time to the multivolume *Naval Tracts*.

MONTE GARIGLIANO *(Muslim pirate haven; Mediterranean; about 882–915)* A fortified camp on the Garigliano River, some 30 miles north of Naples, and the main forward base for Sicilian pirates raiding Italy. Troops from Naples, Capua, and Amalfi failed to capture it in 908. However, ties between Garigliano and SICILY were broken from 909, as the Fatamid dynasty fought to impose its rule on the island. Taking advantage of Muslim disunity, a joint Byzantine-Italian land and sea force assaulted Garigliano and wiped out its inhabitants in 915.

MOOR, THE GREAT *(Barbary corsair; Mediterranean; 1635)* The nickname ("Il Grande Moro") of an Algerian captain who captured a Neapolitan galley carrying silk, gold, guns, and ammunition.

MORETTI (MORETTO), JEAN *(Italian corsair; Adriatic; active 1557–1560)* Operating under a license from the duke of Savoy, his two galleys plundered Venetian shipping near the IONIAN ISLANDS. On at least one occasion, Moretti forced his victims to sign a statement that he had treated them well and had paid for the merchandise he stole.

(See also CARLO EMMANUELE I.)

MORGAN, EDWARD *(English military officer; Caribbean; died 1665)* Edward Morgan was a paternal uncle of Sir Henry MORGAN and a professional soldier.

He served for many years as a mercenary in the Netherlands and Germany and also fought on the royalist side during the English Civil War. In February 1664, he became lieutenant governor and commander of the English forces in Jamaica, when Sir Thomas MODYFORD was appointed governor.

England declared war on the Netherlands in February 1665, and Governor Modyford persuaded the government to make use of the PORT ROYAL pirates. With naive optimism, Modyford told Colonel Morgan to capture the Dutch colonies at Saint Eustatius, Saba, and Curaçao as well as the French settlements on TORTUGA and Hispaniola.

The BUCCANEERS were difficult allies, and they refused to sail until Morgan promised to divide all BOOTY equally, according to pirate rules. (The navy's regulations were much less generous.) Writing to London, Governor Modyford explained that this meant the pirates really were paying themselves.

> They are chiefly reformed privateers, scarce a planter among them, being resolute fellows, and well armed with fusees and pistols. . . . All this is prepared by the honest privateer, at the old rate of no purchase no pay, and it will cost the King nothing considerable, some powder and mortar pieces.

Morgan set a rendezous at the Isle of Pines off Cuba. After considerable delay, he sailed with nine small vessels crammed with 650 buccaneers. During the difficult eastward passage, two ships were separated in a storm, and a third deserted. Many of the crews slipped away when the fleet stopped at Montserrat.

Only 326 men remained when Colonel Morgan arrived at Saint Eustatius on July 23. The town and fort of Oranjestad were built on top of a low cliff behind a long, sandy beach. "The good old colonel," Modyford told London, "leaping out of the boat and being a corpulent man, got a strain, and his spirit being great he pursued over earnestly the enemy on a hot day, so that he surfeited and suddenly died. . . ."

Morgan's second-in-command took over and followed the pirates charging up the hill. The terrified Dutch garrison surrendered after firing only one volley. About three weeks later, the raiders seized the tiny island of Saba, 12 miles away. An easy victory had gained booty worth at least £25,000. After Curaçao, the island was the main Dutch trading post in the Caribbean, and its prisons held more than 900 African slaves, a valuable commodity at that time.

The buccaneers wanted to sell their human booty as soon as possible. They refused to make the 450-mile voyage to Curaçao, and only a few were willing to stay and guard Saint Eustatius. Although the Dutch garrison was deported, a French force from Saint Kitts reconquered the island early in 1667. The English government paid nothing for and gained nothing from the expedition.

Sir Henry Morgan, shown with the long hair (or wig) and elaborate costume of an English gentleman. There is no way of knowing whether this portrait accurately portrays the real Henry Morgan. From Exquemelin, *Buccaneers of America*, first Spanish edition, (1681).

MORGAN, SIR HENRY (1)   *(British buccaneer; Caribbean; 1635?–1688)*

Morgan is perhaps the best-known pirate, thanks to the Dutch author EXQUEMELIN, who vividly describes his raids. Exquemelin disliked his "admiral" although he respected his accomplishments. By exaggerating Morgan's villainy, he actually increased his fame.

Morgan assembled and kept together the largest expeditions ever undertaken by the West Indian buccaneers. He was an inspiring leader as well as a master politician. However, other pirate admirals took richer spoils. Morgan did occupy PANAMA, which Sir Francis DRAKE had failed to take in 1596. But no TREASURE SHIPS were captured, and the raiders brought home little booty from Panama.

Born into a family of Welsh landowners and farmers, Morgan never wrote or spoke about his early life. According to local tradition, he went to Barbados as an indentured servant and later moved to Jamaica, conquered by the English in 1655. Morgan presumably fought the Spaniards resisting the English invasion, and he also may have joined sea raids. His appointment as a militia officer in 1662 suggests some military experience. He received a PRIVATEERING commission in the same year and probably followed Sir Christopher MYNGS to Cuba and Mexico. In late 1663 or early 1664, he sailed for Central America with John MORRIS and other captains. During an epic 22-month voyage, they plundered three major cities.

Exquemelin incorrectly asserted that Morgan accompanied Edward MANSFIELD's 1666 expedition. He instead remained in Jamaica, invested in the first of several plantations, and married a daughter of Sir Edward MORGAN, his paternal uncle. He also formed close ties with Governor Thomas MODYFORD.

Spain and England agreed not to attack each other's possessions in 1667. However, Governor Modyford had heard rumors, he claimed, that the Spaniards planned to invade Jamaica. Defying the general peace, Modyford in early 1668 ordered Morgan "to draw together the English privateers and take prisoners of the Spanish nation, whereby you may gain information of that enemy."

Morgan's vaguely worded commission permitted the capture of Spanish ships at sea, but it did not allow land raids. In fact, this legal distinction partly explains why Morgan preferred to attack cities instead of ships. Under English rules, if he took booty at sea, about half went to the government and the ship's owners. Since Morgan's commission did not mention land actions, he and his men could split the entire take. Attacks on cities were illegal piracy—but extremely profitable.

Morgan assembled 10 small ships and 500 men in January 1668. As well as veteran pirates and former soldiers, the expedition attracted the expert marksmen and hunters of Hispaniola and Jamaica. With this fleet, he sailed to the "South Cays"—small islands east of the Isle of Pines. There he was joined by two larger ships and 200 men from Tortuga.

The pirates decided their force was too small to attack Havana. They instead hid their boats and marched against Puerto Principe, a prosperous town 30 miles inland. The Spaniards had learned of the raid and laid various ambushes, but the buccaneers' superb shooting overcame all resistance.

At Puerto Principe, according to Exquemelin, the raiders locked the inhabitants in the church. To make them reveal their treasures, the wretched prisoners "were pained and plagued by unspeakable tortures." Morgan agreed not to burn the town in return for a large ransom in cattle. Nothing bulky could be carried down the mountain trails, and Puerto Principe yielded only 50,000 pesos. Disappointed with this poor booty, the French contingent sailed off. However, another English ship joined Morgan, leaving his force close to 500.

Morgan proposed an assault on PORTOBELO, the port from which treasure ships left for Spain. Since its capture by William PARKER in 1601, three massive forts had been erected. However, Morgan had learned that their garrisons were undermanned and badly equipped. Some argued against this rash adventure. According to Charles Leslie, Morgan's reply paraphrased Shakespeare: "If our Numbers are small our Hearts are great; and the fewer we are, the better shares we shall win in the Spoils."

Morgan hid his fleet and transported his men in 23 canoes captured in Cuba. Sentries fired at the raiders and warned the city. But many Spanish cannon had no ammunition, and others were so poorly maintained that they blew up when fired.

In a series of savage assaults, the buccaneers took Portobelo and its three forts on July 11 and 12. To capture San Geronimo Castle, they forced prisoners—women, nuns, and old men—to carry ladders up to the walls through the Spanish cannon fire. After Portobelo was captured, Exquemelin describes how they made "merry, lording it with wine and women."

Spanish investigations confirm Exquemelin's stories of brutal torture. Women were burned on their genitals. One haughty lady was stripped and placed in an empty wine barrel filled with gunpowder. The grinning pirates held a lighted slow match to her face and asked her to remember where she had hidden her treasure.

The governor of Panama brought his militia across the Isthmus to within seven miles of Portobelo. Morgan demanded 350,000 pesos in ransom. After lengthy negotiations (and a small skirmish), Panama's citizens turned over 100,000. The pirates returned to Jamaica about August 17, after splitting some 250,000 pesos.

The Portobelo raid obviously exceeded the terms of Morgan's commission and violated the recent treaty with Spain. But English officials did not condemn Morgan or Governor Modyford. At that time, many agreed with Modyford that the pirates defended the island. They also hoped pirate raids would force Spain to open its empire to English merchants. In March 1669, the ADMIRALTY COURT decreed that the Portobelo booty was a legal prize.

Back at Port Royal, according to Exquemelin, the pirates ran through their money in drunken orgies. In October 1668, Morgan arranged a rendezvous at Île-à-Vache off southwestern Hispaniola. English and French pirate ships were joined by the Oxford, a 34-gun naval FRIGATE donated by Governor Modyford.

On January 12, 1669, the captains gathered on the Oxford and vowed to attack CARTAGENA. To celebrate their decision, writes Exquemelin, "they toasted their good success and fired off salvoes." A careless spark ignited the Oxford's gunpowder, and the ship blew up, killing some 200 crewmen.

No longer strong enough to attack Cartagena, Morgan's ships ran along the coast of Hispaniola. Several more ships deserted until he had just eight vessels and 500 men. A Frenchman suggested they repeat L'OLONNAIS' 1667 raid on Maracaibo and Gibraltar, located on Lake Maracaibo in Venezuela. At both cities, Morgan's pirates chased after the residents, who had fled into the jungle. Anyone they caught was tortured with psychopathic delight.

As Morgan sailed out of the lake on April 27, his fleet met three Spanish warships sent to intercept him. Twelve of Morgan's men ran his largest vessel into the Spanish flagship and blew up both ships. The pirates captured another warship, and the third was burned. Over 20,000 pesos in silver were salvaged from the enemy flagship.

The raiders reached Port Royal on May 27, 1669, with several captured ships and about 125,000 pesos.

Some crewmen again wasted their share in taverns. Morgan put his money into an 836-acre plantation, given him by Governor Modyford.

While Morgan was raiding Venezuela, England had adopted a friendlier policy toward Spain. On June 14, 1669, Governor Modyford unhappily proclaimed peace with Spain. However, small Spanish raids soon gave Modyford an excuse to renew Morgan's commission.

Outraged by the sack of Portobelo, the Spanish government copied the English practice of privateering by a decree of April 1669. For the first time, Spanish subjects were allowed to seize English ships and invade coastal towns. While few Spanish colonists took up piracy, Manoel RIVERO PARDAL seized several ships and attacked isolated villages.

In response, Governor Modyford gave Morgan ambiguous new orders on August 1, 1670. He was told to destroy enemy vessels and also "to doe and performe all matter of Exployts which may tend to the Preservation and Quiett of Jamayca." He was allowed to commission captains, and the raiders could split the spoils "according to their usual rules." To Modyford's credit, he also suggested that Morgan stop torturing prisoners.

Morgan again convened the raiders at Cow Island, and nearly every buccaneer in the Caribbean responded. About 33 ships and over 2,000 men sailed on December 18. Eight ships and about one-third of the crews were French. The fleet's ARTICLES contained elaborate rules about booty and gave Morgan 1 percent of the total take.

Panama was chosen as the richest and easiest target. Along the way, Morgan stopped to recapture PROVIDENCE ISLAND. Taking three ships and 500 raiders, Joseph BRADLEY captured the fortress of San Lorenzo at the mouth of the Chagres River. A ferocious battle killed some 300 Spaniards and 100 buccaneers.

On January 19, 1671, some 1,500 to 2,000 buccaneers set out, paddling up the Chagres River toward Panama in canoes and shallow-draught SLOOPS. After four days, they had to leave the boats and march on foot, cutting through the heavy jungle with machetes and fighting off ambushes. Their food and water soon ran out. On January 27, the pirates reached a broad savannah near the Pacific and captured a herd of cows, which they ate uncooked.

The following morning, the raiders routed Panama's defenders—1,200 untrained militia and 400 horsemen. When the pirate sharpshooters cut down impetuous cavalry and infantry charges, the defenders broke and ran for the city. The pirates chased after, slaughtering some 400 or 500 in their blood lust.

As Morgan's men rushed into the city, the fleeing militiamen started fires that destroyed almost all its buildings. The buccaneers spent four weeks picking through Panama's smoking ruins. But much of the city's wealth had been hurriedly carried away in three big ships that sailed to Ecuador.

Exquemelin tells us that Morgan let their richest prize escape—"a galleon, loaded with the King of Spain's silver together with all the jewels and treasure of the foremost merchants in Panama." When he was told that the galleon was close by, Morgan was "more inclined to sit drinking and sporting with a group of Spanish women he had taken prisoner, than to go at once in pursuit of the treasure ship."

Frustrated by their poor plunder, the buccaneers destroyed everything inside the few stone houses. They also tortured and raped their prisoners even more sadistically than usual. The Spaniards were accustomed to torture, which was used in judicial trials. But they were shocked at procedures that deliberately killed most of the victims.

Leaving Panama on February 24, 1671, the raiders gathered at Chagres and divided the booty. Morgan reported total plunder of only £30,000, and each man received a share variously estimated at from £10 to £16. The disappointed pirates accused Morgan of stealing their money.

Afraid they would attack him, Morgan sailed off alone. Most of the pirates continued to raid along the Central American coast, where many ships later were wrecked. The Spaniards abandoned the ruined city, rebuilding Panama (now Panama City) at a better and more defensible harbor six miles away.

By the Treaty of Madrid (July 1670), Spain officially recognized English holdings in the Caribbean, and both nations agreed to prohibit piracy against the other. Governor Modyford did not learn of the treaty until May 1671. But he certainly had exceeded his authority by declaring war on Spain and appointing Morgan as admiral. A new governor, Sir Thomas Lynch, arrested Modyford in August 1671, and he spent two years in the Tower of London.

To further appease Spanish outrage, Morgan was arrested and taken to England in April 1672. He never was imprisoned, however, and soon won influential friends. War was declared against the Netherlands, and Morgan was asked to write a memorandum on Jamaican defenses. In 1674, Lynch was ousted while Morgan was knighted and made lieutenant governor. (Modyford also returned to Jamaica as chief justice.)

Morgan was 39, immensely rich, and the owner of several plantations totaling 6,000 acres. He held several important posts and led the buccaneers and sugar planters who fought London's attempts to tax the island. In yet another political reversal, Lynch returned as governor in 1682 and removed Morgan from office. Always a heavy drinker, Morgan spent hours in taverns, cursing his enemies loudly and obscenely. His physicians' bizarre remedies also hastened his death.

(See also SEARLE, ROBERT; SELECTED BIBLIOGRAPHY: Cruikshank, *Morgan*; Earle, *Sack*; Pope, *Buccaneer*; Rogoziński, *Carribbean*.)

MORGAN, SIR HENRY (2) *(fictional villain; 20th century)* EXQUEMELIN's gory 17th-century history has remained popular. However, later fiction generally ignored Morgan, with his ambiguous mixture of charismatic leadership and selfish treachery. His raids are reen-

acted in CUP OF GOD (1929) and THE PRIVATEER (1952). The aged, pirate-fighting Morgan appears in Rafael SABATINI'S *The BLACK SWAN* (1932).

A character named Sir Henry Morgan appears in the 1942 film *The BLACK SWAN*, based on Sabatini's novel, and in other pirate movies. Morgan is a double-dealing villain in BLACKBEARD *The* PIRATE (1961), and he is hanged for his crimes in *The PIRATES OF TORTUGA* (1961). Only his name is used in MORGAN THE PIRATE (1961), a remake of CAPTAIN BLOOD. A Morgan character is part of the fun in DOUBLE CROSSBONES (1952) and BOY AND THE PIRATES (1960).

MORGAN THE PIRATE *(Italian motion picture; color; 1961)*

Although muscleman Steve Reeves stars as Sir Henry MORGAN, director Andre de Toth borrowed the plot from the 1935 movie, CAPTAIN BLOOD. Reeves's Morgan is a British royalist enslaved by the Spaniards at Panama. He is bought by the governor's daughter, Doña Inez (Valerie Lagrange), and falls in love with her. As punishment for this insolence, the governor condemns Morgan as a GALLEY SLAVE. He leads a mutiny and then plunders the Spaniards for the British. To revenge his mistreatment by the governor, he pushes on to Panama, conquering both the city and Dona Inez's heart.

MORISCO, ANDREA *(Italian corsair; Mediterranean; active 1304–1320)*

From Genoa and a noted

Steve Reeves in *Morgan the Pirate* (1961).

pirate, Morisco placed his two warships under the BYZANTINE flag in 1304 and was ennobled. The following year, he seized the island of Tenedos, at the entrance to the Hellespont, and evacuated its inhabitants. The emperor ignored this aggression because he needed Morisco's services.

In the summer of 1305, Morisco massacred some Turks fighting with the CATALAN COMPANY. The emperor made him an admiral and gave him and Ludovico MORISCO Rhodes, Kasos, and Karpathos—islands no longer under imperial control. Andrea supplied food to cities besieged by the Catalans in 1306 and molested Venetian shipping in 1307 and 1308.

MORISCO, LUDOVICO *(Italian captain; Mediterranean; active 1309–1319)*

In 1309, Ludovico tried to take possession of Karpathos, which the BYZANTINE emperor had given him and his brother Andrea MORISCO in 1305. The Venetians, who actually controlled the island, imprisoned him in Crete as a pirate. The emperor was still seeking his release in 1319.

MOROCCO *(pirate haven, 17th century)*

An Islamic nation in northwestern Africa facing the Atlantic and Mediterranean. Morocco's political system differed greatly from that of the BARBARY STATES to its east. While Turkish JANISSARY garrisons controlled the Barbary city-states, Morocco was ruled by native dynasties hostile to the OTTOMAN EMPIRE. Piracy began much later in Morocco and was less important than in Barbary.

The main HAVENS were on the Atlantic Ocean, and few native Moroccans joined the corsairs. European pirates, primarily from Britain, used MAMORA from 1604 to 1614. SALÉ was a base for Morisco refugees from Spain. The Dutch renegade Jan JANSSEN led the Salé fleet from 1619 to 1631, raiding as far north as Iceland. BEN AÏSSA, who retired in 1698, was the last of the independent captains at Salé. Piracy gradually disappeared as Sultan Malay Ismail (ruled 1672–1727) took over the remaining fleet and almost all the booty.

MORRIS, JOHN (1) *(English pirate; Caribbean; active 1663–1672)*

Sailing from PORT ROYAL in late 1663 or early 1664, he assaulted Mexico and Nicaragua with Sir Henry MORGAN, David MARTEEN, and Captains JACKMAN and FREEMAN. Although raids on Spanish possessions had been forbidden, the five captains pretended to act under PRIVATEERING commissions issued by Jamaica's previous governor.

The rovers anchored at the mouth of the Grijalva River. Aided by Indian guides, they marched 50 miles inland, using a round-about route to avoid swamps along the river. Taking the garrison by surprise, they sacked Villahermosa, capital of Tabasco Province.

When they returned to the coast, the pirates discovered that Spaniards had taken over their ships. They managed to capture two BARKS and four canoes, and paddled and sailed south against a strong current. Stopping to loot a small town on the way, they plundered Trujillo, Honduras, and captured a ship in the harbor.

Continuing south, they hid their vessels near the San Juan River and located Indian guides. Hiding by day and rowing by night, they went 100 miles up river to reach Granada on Lake Nicaragua. Jamaican Governor Thomas MODYFORD reported that they

> marched undiscried [undiscovered] into the center of the city, fired a volley, overturned 18 great guns in the Parada Place, took the serjeant-major's house, wherein were all their arms and ammunition, secured in the Great Church 300 of the best men prisoners, abundance of which were churchmen, plundered for 16 hours, discharged their prisoners, sunk all the boats, and so came away.

Returning in several captured ships, the pirates reached Port Royal by November 1665. During an epic voyage of several thousand miles, they had penetrated far inland and pillaged three important towns. However, Governor Modyford does not report the precise value of their substantial spoils.

Morris was at least an equal partner with Henry Morgan during this adventure. He took part in Morgan's raids on PORTOBELO (1668), Maracaibo (1669), and PANAMA (1671). While the pirates were gathering for the Panama raid, Morris attacked and killed the Portuguese corsair Manoel RIVERO PARDAL. With Lawrence PRINCE, he led the assault on Panama in January 1671.

Morgan had sacked Panama after a peace treaty had been signed. Thomas Lynch became governor, arrested Modyford and Morgan and sent them to England. However, Lynch gave Morris a frigate and ordered him to arrest captains refusing to give up piracy.

(See also SELECTED BIBLIOGRAPHY: Earle, Sack; Pope, Buccaneer.)

MORRIS, JOHN (2) *(English pirate; Caribbean; died 1670)* Son of John MORRIS (1), Morris commanded his own ship during Sir Henry MORGAN's PORTOBELO (1668) and Maracaibo (1669) expeditions. He was killed when Morgan's flagship blew up during a drunken party.

MOUGHAM, THOMAS *(English captain; Atlantic; 1546)* Licensed to prey on the French and Scots, Mougham instead joined James ALDAY in looting Portuguese and Spanish ships in a Spanish harbor. Although Mougham's men did not take part in the actual attack, they shared in the booty after their Spanish prize ran aground in Ireland.

MOVIES, PIRATE *(20th century)* Several types of pirate movies quickly developed, with each genre initially influenced by novels and plays. Spectaculars based on Rafael SABATINI's novels defined the SWASHBUCKLER between 1924 and 1942. Dozens of films in the same tradition appeared up to the late 1960s, when comedies and parodies became more common. Meanwhile, TREASURE ISLAND became the most frequently filmed novel in history, and movies also adapted PETER PAN and *The* PIRATES OF PENZANCE.

Swashbucklers emphasized action, including land and sea battles, SWORD DUELS, flogging and torture, mutiny and betrayal—and a few romantic kisses. Some also showed buried TREASURE. Almost all are set in the Caribbean between about 1680 and 1720. BLACKBEARD, CAPTAIN KIDD, and Sir Henry MORGAN appear most frequently, and they are the only pirates to receive film biographies.

In the classic swashbuckler, pirates provide villains of the darkest type. Against the background of their gross evil, the brave, unselfish male lead stands out starkly. Because of film production codes, pirates could not be depicted as heroes. Although he may temporarily join their band, the male lead is not a typical brigand. Some heroes only pretend to be pirates, while others were forced into piracy by cruel tyrants. Between battles, the hero romances a beautiful and spirited lady, whom he wishes to marry. Deceived by appearances, the lady initially believes the hero really is a criminal, but she melts into his arms at the end.

Rafael Sabatini fathered the swashbuckler. Sabatini's novels perfected the formula of the brave hero wooing the willful maiden. Immensely popular during the 1920s and 1930s, they were a natural source of scripts for adventure-romance features.

Silent film adaptations of Sabatini's CAPTAIN BLOOD and *The* SEA HAWK (2), both released in 1924, focused on sea battles and whipped GALLEY SLAVES. In *The* BLACK PIRATE (1926), Douglas FAIRBANKS retained the battles but emphasized athletic prowess. Every hero henceforth emulated Fairbanks by swinging down from the rigging and fighting long, acrobatic sword duels.

Romance was stressed when Warner Brothers remade *Captain Blood* in 1935. To Fairbanks' athleticism, Errol FLYNN added sexual charisma. The film was a box-office smash, making Flynn an instant star.

As Sir Francis DRAKE, Flynn again epitomized manly vigor and unselfish love in *The* SEA HAWK (3) in 1940. Seeking its share of box-office riches in 1942, the Fox studio starred Tyrone POWER and Maureen O'HARA in Sabatini's *The* BLACK SWAN (2), an exuberant romp through battles, duels, and lovers' quarrels. Once again the spirited maiden, O'Hara surrenders to Paul HENREID in *The* SPANISH MAIN (1945).

Few swashbucklers appeared during World War II, as movies stressed combat action. During this hiatus, Bob Hope starred in *The* PRINCESS AND THE PIRATE (1944). The first intentional parody of pirate movies, *Princess* introduced two fictional characters—the crooked Spanish governor and the demented captain—that became stock figures in later swashbucklers. As portrayed by Walter SLEZAK, the Spanish governor is a smooth, elegant villain—wealthy but greedy for more—who connives with

Bob Hope listens to the schemes of the crooked Spanish governor (Walter Slezak) and Hook, the demented captain (Victor McLaglen), in *The Princess and the Pirate* (1944), the first major pirate parody.

criminals. Slezak re-created the same role both for *The Spanish Main* and for *The* PIRATE (1948), a musical comedy in which Gene Kelly outswashes Fairbanks and Flynn.

The Princess and the Pirate also introduced Hook, the first pirate captain depicted not as a villain but as a vaudeville buffoon. Rolling his eyes and head, Hook stomps around bellowing out meaningless fake-nautical curses. He constantly threatens to murder everyone, but he is too dumb to pose a real threat. Demented captains like Hook often reappeared in later melodramas, and they were essential to later parodies.

Swashbucklers poured out during the 1950s and early 1960s. Flynn and O'Hara tried to re-create the magic in AGAINST ALL FLAGS (1952), but reviewers commented on their tongue-in-cheek attitude toward the plot. With one movie after another following the same stock formula, actors increasingly parodied their own performances, especially in low-budget Italian films.

As swashbucklers became less sincere, other movies caricatured the entire genre. In ABBOTT AND COSTELLO MEET CAPTAIN KIDD (1952), the two comedians adlib through vaudeville routines, befuddling Charles LAUGHTON. DOUBLE CROSSBONES (1950) also relies on

sight gags, while *The* CRIMSON PIRATE (1952) parodies all aspects of traditional swashbucklers. No one gets hurt in these early comedies. Their broad burlesque is mixed with graphic bloodletting in later parodies—SCALAWAG (1973), SWASHBUCKLER (1976), YELLOWBEARD (1983), and PIRATES (1986).

Pirates based on historical characters normally are villains or buffoons. Thanks to patriotic legends, however, Sir Francis Drake and Jean LAFFITE could be presented as heroes. Drake becomes the perfect Sabatini male in *The Sea Hawk* (1940) and SEVEN SEAS TO CALAIS (1963). DRAKE OF ENGLAND (1935) is more accurate, the hero less flamboyant.

Since Jean Laffite never fought a major sea-battle, Cecil B. De Mille wisely chose not to treat him as a swashbuckler in *The* BUCCANEER (1938; 1950). Both films emphasize Laffite's love affairs and the land battle for New Orleans. LAST OF THE BUCCANEERS (1950) continues the story after Laffite fled to Galveston.

While recreating Sabatini's adult novels, Hollywood also adapted fiction for younger audiences. With no love affairs and no sea battles, *Treasure Island* cannot be made into a swashbuckler. A 1934 British version stuck close to Stevenson's script. Borrowing from *The Princess and the Pirate*, Robert NEWTON portrayed Long John SILVER as a buffoon in 1952. In 1990, Charlton Heston returned to a more sober characterization of Silver.

J. M. Barrie's play *Peter Pan* was directed to much younger children than *Treasure Island,* and Barrie's pirates are characters from a child's game. They remain benign figures of fun in Disney's 1953 animated version, and they are comical but cruel in HOOK, a 1991 sequel to Barrie's play.

Gilbert and Sullivan's *The Pirates of Penzance* (1879) satirized both pirate melodramas and Victorian social customs. Some of Sullivan's music is incorporated in *The* PIRATE MOVIE (1982) and *The* PIRATES OF PENZANCE (1983). Downplaying piratical elements, both introduce popular music and topical jokes.

(See SELECTED BIBLIOGRAPHY: Fraser, *Hollywood;* Richards, *Swordsmen.*)

MOYSI, BROTHER FRANCESCO DE (*Knight of Malta; Mediterranean; 1546*) Moysi commanded a private warship, raiding from Malta.

MUCKILL, JOHN (*English pirate; Atlantic; 1605*) Muckill was said to be a "gentleman of London" sailing under Dutch letters of MARQUE. Nevertheless, he conspired with a Dutch captain to seize a Dutch merchant vessel in Portsmouth harbor. With the connivance of royal authorities, Muckill sold his share of the captured cargo in various Cornish ports and disposed of his prize in MOROCCO.

MULLINS, DARBY (*Irish pirate; Red Sea, Indian Ocean; 1661–1701*) Born in Londonderry, Mullins was an indentured servant, dockhand, and tavernkeeper in Jamaica before moving to New York. He enlisted on William KIDD's 1696 expedition, returned with Kidd in 1699, and was hanged on the same day as Kidd. His name possibly suggested Ben Gunn's weird chant ("Darby M'Graw! Darby M'Graw") in TREASURE ISLAND.

MURAT AL-FUSHALI REIS (*Barbary corsair; Mediterranean; 1683*) Murat Reis was a Turk active in the struggles between political factions at TRIPOLI.

MURAT "EL CHICO" REIS (*Barbary corsair; Mediterranean; 1577*) A Spanish convert to Islam at ALGIERS, Murat Reis was called "the little Murat" to distinguish him from MURAT THE GREAT and also known as Maltrapillo ("a small rag"). Commanding a GALIOT, he captured a galley from the KNIGHTS OF MALTA and held a Spanish priest for ransom. A mob killed his captive to revenge the murder of a Spanish Muslim by the Inquisition.

MURAT REIS (1) (*Barbary corsair; Mediterranean; died 1556*) Murast Reis was a Greek sailing from TRIPOLI. Murat's GALIOT was caught by the KNIGHTS OF MALTA near Stromboli Island, and he was hanged at

Malta. As his ship ran from their attack, Murat cut off the arm of a GALLEY SLAVE and beat the other rowers with it to encourage their efforts. (Father HAËDO tells the same gory story about HASAN "IL MARABUTTO" REIS.)

(See also SABCULI REIS.)

MURAT REIS (2) (*Barbary corsair; Mediterranean; 1570s*) This Murat Reis was a Corsican originally named Sebastian Paulo. According to Father HAËDO, he was a most engaging rogue. He became a corsair at ALGIERS, escaped to the Spanish at Oran, and reverted to Christianity. He was again captured by the Algerians, convinced them that he had remained a Muslim at heart, and resumed a corsair's life. When his GALLEY SLAVES mutinied, he persuaded them to take him along to Spain. There his ingratiating ways and skill with the Turkish bow won him a pardon and aristocratic favor. But life at court proved dull, and Paulo/Murat and some other ex-renegades tried to return to Algiers. This time, the Spanish caught and beheaded him as a warning to other turncoats.

MURAT REIS (3) (*Barbary corsair; Mediterranean; 1608*) He and REGEB REIS, both natives of Corsica, operated from TUNIS. They freed a captive who agreed to pay his RANSOM to Murat's mother and Regeb's sister, both still living on Corsica.

MURAT REIS (4) (*Barbary corsair; Tunis; 1612*) An Italian RENEGADE, Murat was born Agostino Bianco near Genoa. In 1612, he withdrew money from his Livorno bank account (through an Italian attorney) to purchase goods shipped to TUNIS.

MURAT REIS (5) The name assumed by Peter LISLE, who led the corsairs of TRIPOLI from about 1796 to 1815.

MURAT "THE GREAT" REIS (*Barbary corsair; Mediterranean; 1534–1638*) Murat the Great was the most renowned corsair after ULUJ ALI, as well as a successful diplomat. Probably an Albanian, he was captured in 1546 by KARA ALI and joined his band. On his first independent cruise in 1565, he sank his ship on a reef. But he soon redeemed himself by taking three Spanish merchant ships with a small BRIGANTINE.

Murat frequently raided the coasts of Italy and Spain, gaining great wealth and winning renown as an audacious warrior. Small in stature but always ready for a fight, he never turned down or lost a battle with Christian corsairs. While battling the KNIGHTS OF MALTA in 1570, he angered Uluj Ali by trying to be first to board the enemy's vessel. In 1578, he seized two Sicilian galleys carrying the retiring Spanish viceroy. In 1581, he captured two Breton merchant ships carrying more than a million ducats in gold and silver.

With only four smaller GALIOTS, Murat overwhelmed the papal flagship and another galley off northern Italy in 1580, and he similarly overcame two war galleys belonging to the KNIGHTS OF SAINT STEPHEN in 1594. On these occasions, he succeeded through a common corsair trick. Lowering the masts of two galiots, he towed them behind the other two to deceive the enemy about his strength.

The first BARBARY captain to venture into the Atlantic Ocean, Murat sacked Lanzarote in the Canary Islands in 1586, holding his captives until their families paid a large ransom. In 1589, with one galiot, he overpowered a much larger galley belonging to the Maltese knights.

The viceroy of Algiers nominated him as CAPTAIN OF THE SEA in 1574. But the sultan approved him as successor to MEMMI "ARNAUT" REIS only in 1594 or 1595. In 1594, Murat's Algerian squadron joined an OTTOMAN fleet in raiding southern Italy. The following year, he took many prizes, captured three Sicilian warships, and defeated five Maltese galleys. (These attacks were legally not piracy, since they aided England and France during wars with Spain.) He proved as successful a diplomat as a warrior, winning the respect of the Christian ambassadors with whom he dealt as captain of the sea.

Murat helped Ottoman generals put down rebellions in the Near East in 1603. He returned to Tunis in 1605 but went to southern Greece as BEYLERBEY before 1607. There, ironically, he savagely repressed Greek and Turkish pirates. He was killed in 1638 during a Venetian siege of Vlorë (Valona) in Albania.

MUSICAL COMEDIES   See FICTION, PIRATE; MOVIES, PIRATE; PETER PAN (2); SONGS, PIRATE; PIRATES OF PENZANCE; THE (1).

MUSKET *(firearm; 1550–1850)*   The word *musket* derives from Spanish *mosquette* (a sparrow hawk). A ball, usually of lead, was rammed in through the muzzle (the gun barrel's open end) on top of gunpowder. Applying a flame or spark caused the powder to explode, sending the ball forward.

Until the 19th century, military muskets were muzzle loaded and thus single-shot, with a smooth-bore barrel. Riffling (cutting spiral grooves inside the barrel) improves accuracy, and breach-loading (at the barrel's rear) is faster. However, although some sporting weapons incorporated these improvements, they were too fragile for battle conditions.

The first muskets weighed up to 20 pounds. With a bore (opening) up to an inch wide, they fired round balls weighing up to two ounces. The gun barrel—four to five feet long—was placed on a forked rest until the 1620s, when a somewhat lighter musket was introduced.

Armies relied on matchlock muskets during the 16th and 17th centuries. The "match" actually was a rope chemically treated to burn slowly, which was fastened to an S-shaped lever, or "serpentine" near the breech. When the firer pressed on one end of this serpentine, the other carried the match to priming power, which exploded and set off the main charge.

From the early 1500s, some muskets used a wheel-lock system, like a modern cigarette lighter. When the trigger was released, a spring-driven serrated wheel revolved against a piece of iron pyrite or flint to produce sparks. Complicated, expensive, and delicate, the wheel-lock mechanism was reserved for hunting rifles and some cavalry pistols.

The cheaper flintlock became standard from the 1690s. A flint was held in a small vise, called a cock. On pressing the trigger, the cock scraped the flint down a piece of steel, showering the priming power with sparks.

Smooth-bore military muskets were never very accurate. Most did not have gun-sights; the firer simply looked along the barrel. An 18th-century sharpshooter could expect to hit some part of a man 100 yards away. Accuracy was less during the previous century, when bullets were made on the spot, and powder varied in strength.

Especially with matchlock muskets, reloading and firing were time-consuming and required many separate movements. Matchlocks had other faults. The match's glow and smell warned off enemies, and a wet match could not be kept alight. Flintlocks could be loaded somewhat more rapidly, but sometimes misfired.

The musket was most effective against a massed enemy or in defending a fort. Military tactics called for volleys by rows of soldiers. If enough heavy balls were put into the air, some would hit the foe, producing ghastly wounds. However, muskets were not an effective weapon for naval warfare. Pirates (and other sailors) usually used swords, PIKES, and clubs to board and take over their victims.

(See also ARQUEBUS; WEAPONS, PIRATE.)

MUSLIM PIRATES *(sea raiders; Mediterranean; 651–1498)*   From 632 to 647, Muslim armies captured what today are Syria, Palestine, Egypt, and Libya from the BYZANTINE EMPIRE. After some setbacks, they pressed west, occupying TUNIS and MOROCCO (693–700) as well as Spain and southern France (711–720). While Christian armies gradually reconquered France (736–759) and Spain (1096–1212), North Africa remains under Muslim rule to the present time.

Although the name *Arab* sometimes is given to all Muslim states, their inhabitants belong to many ethnic groups. Non-Arab Syrians gave the Muslims their first navies, which temporarily occupied Cyprus in 651. And non-Arabs supplied the corsairs that assaulted Christian territories during the next 400 years.

Muslim governments in Syria, Egypt, and North Africa maintained organized navies, manned by volunteer or conscript sailors, which raided the Byzantine Empire each year. Autonomous pirate squadrons also harassed the Christian borders. Their crews of Muslim adventurers and Christian RENEGADES fought for booty after the host government took its cut.

During the ninth and 10th centuries, piracy was openly sponsored by the emirs ruling Saragossa in Spain, Tarsus in CILICIA, Candia in CRETE, and Palermo in SICILY. The corsairs set up more advanced bases deep inside Christian territories—at LA FREINET in Ssouthern FRANCE and at BARI, MONTE GARIGLIANO, and TARANTO in southern Italy.

Muslim raiders sometimes combined in large squadrons, like those LEO OF TRIPOLI led against Thessalonica. More often, they operated as individuals. Arab travelers painted an unflattering picture of the pirate quarter at Palermo. While professing scorn for the corsairs, Muslim merchants happily profited from their booty—just like merchants in Christian HAVENS.

Although they were independent, these forward corsair nests depended on the Muslim states for supplies and recruits. The Christians thus reconquered them as Byzantine naval power revived from the end of the ninth century. By 1050, the Italian cities of Venice, Genoa, and Pisa created navies, chased the Muslims from Corsica and Sardinia, and helped the Normans occupy Sicily from 1061.

The Italian city-states then turned east, taking advantage of the crusades to occupy the ports of Syria and Greece. Western Europeans dominated the Mediterranean and the Black Sea from about 1200. Muslim piracy never entirely ceased. But it again became a serious threat only from 1450, with the rise of the BARBARY states and the OTTOMAN conquest of Greece and the Balkans.

MUSTAFA MEMMI REIS *(Barbary corsair; Mediterranean; died 1616)* Mustafa Reis was a Portuguese convert and secretary to MURAT THE GREAT. He was killed off Greece by Jacopo INGHIRAMI while commanding the warship bringing a new governor to ALGIERS.

MUSTAFA "QUDAI" REIS *(Barbary corsair; Mediterranean; early 1680s)* Captain of the *Saint Louis*, a French prize, Mustafa sailed from TRIPOLI on 13 separate cruises without taking booty.

MUSTAFA REIS (1) *(Barbary corsair; Mediterranean; active 1560s)* Mustafa was an Albanian at ALGIERS, related by marriage to MEMMI "ARNAUT" REIS. Captured and imprisoned in Naples in 1565, he escaped in 1591.

MUSTAFA REIS (2) *(Barbary corsair; Mediterranean; 1574)* An Italian convert to Islam, expert seaman, and follower of ULUJ ALI, he commanded six GALLEYS that escorted HASAN VENEZIANO, the incoming BEYLERBEY, from Istanbul to ALGIERS.

MUSTAFA REIS (3) *(Barbary corsair; Mediterranean; active 1675–1681)* A Greek convert, he was captain of the 40-gun *Sun*, vice-admiral (1675–1679), and admiral (from September 1679) at TRIPOLI. In December 1681, the ruler banished him and confiscated all his property—valued at $10,000—because he had unnecessarily risked his ship the previous summer.

MUSTAFA REIS (4) *(Barbary corsair; Mediterranean; 1681)* Mustafa visited TRIPOLI while CAPTAIN OF THE SEA in TUNIS.

MUSTAFA REIS (5) *(Barbary corsair; Mediterranean; 1684–1685)* Mustafa Reis was the brother of TRIPOLI's vice-admiral and captain of the *Infant Jesus*, a French-built BARK.

MYDDLETON, JOHN *(English captain; born 1563; active 1589–1594)* Myddleton was a nephew of Sir Thomas Myddleton, a wealthy London merchant who financed many plunder raids. However, John Myddleton worked for syndicates formed by other merchants rather than for his uncle. He was twice captured by the Spanish.

With the 50-ton *Moonshine*, Myddleton raided in European waters in 1586, 1590, and 1591. In 1592, he visited the West Indies with the *Moonshine* and a prize taken near Spain. Off Havana, he and Benjamin WOOD tried to seize a Spanish FRIGATE that had run aground. The assault failed miserably. Myddleton's second ship capsized and sank, and the Spaniards captured him and other members of the raiding party.

In 1594, Myddleton raided in the Caribbean for Sir John WATTS. He briefly sailed in CONSORT with Christopher NEWPORT and then rendezvoused with other Watts ships under William LANE and Richard BEST. Near Havana, the three raiders took four prizes, two fairly valuable. The Spanish governor built two PINNACES and captured Myddleton and seven others. Myddleton was taken to Spain in 1595 and presumably kept prisoner until his death.

(See also SELECTED BIBLIOGRAPHY: Andrews, *English*.)

MYNGS, SIR CHRISTOPHER *(English naval captain; Caribbean; 1625–1666)* While a royal officer, Myngs recruited BUCCANEERS for profitable plunder raids. Henry MORGAN copied his tactics, especially the use of former soldiers to attack fortified cities.

Born in Norfolk, Myngs joined the royal navy as a cabin-boy and rose through the ranks. In January 1656, he brought the 44-gun FRIGATE *Marston Moor* to Jamaica, occupied by English forces the previous May. He took part in a profitless raid on Santa Marta, Venezuela, in May 1656 and assumed command of the Jamaican naval squadron in January 1657.

In October 1658, Myngs' squadron hid along the Central American coast and narrowly missed taking ships from a TREASURE FLEET. When the Spaniards arrived, most English ships had left to obtain fresh water. The *Marston Moor* and another vessel passed through the 29 Spanish ships, hung on their rear, and tried without success to scatter them. The English fleet later burned Tolú (today in Colombia), captured two large ships in the harbor, and devastated Santa Marta.

At rumors that pirates were in the neighborhood, Spanish colonists hid their valuables in the jungle. To take them by surprise, Myngs in 1659 sailed much further east, a difficult voyage against the prevailing winds. His efforts were rewarded with the largest haul ever brought into Jamaica. Taking only the *Marston Moor* and two other warships, he sacked Cumana, Puerto Caballos, and

Coro in Venezuela. At Coro, the raiders followed the inhabitants into the jungle and caught them with 5,000 pounds of royal silver. The entire plunder was estimated at £200,000 to £300,000.

Myngs split this booty with his men and refused to pass over the government's share. Captured goods were openly sold from the *Marston Moor* before the governor of Jamaica could make an accounting. Contrary to English regulations, the men broke into and divided up the chests of silver. The governor arrested Myngs and sent him back to England to be tried by the ADMIRALTY COURT. But the wealth Myngs had brought to the island made him immensely popular, and his success attracted dozens of pirate captains to PORT ROYAL.

In the confusion surrounding King Charles II's return to power, the charges against Myngs were ignored or dropped. In 1662, he was back in Jamaica commanding the *Centurion*. England and France had ceased hostilities in Europe. However, the Jamaicans persuaded themselves that the truce did not apply in the West Indies. In October, Myngs occupied Santiago, Cuba's second largest city. The raiders captured six ships, took substantial booty, and blew up the Spanish fortress. Myngs' pirate fleet was filled with former soldiers, who joined the buccaneers when there was a chance of good plunder.

Seeing that the Spaniards did not respond to the Santiago raid, the Jamaican government approved a second expedition. Myngs sailed with 12 pirate ships and 1,500 buccaneers, English, French, and Dutch. His reputation as a lucky leader attracted both veteran captains—such as Edward MANSFIELD and Abraham BLAUVELT—and younger pirates, including Henry MORGAN, John MORRIS, and Captain JACKMAN.

In February 1663, the raiders occupied San Francisco in the Bay of Campeche, a large town never previously attacked. They took the forts in one savage rush but spent a day capturing the stone houses, each a miniature fortress. Fourteen Spanish ships were seized as well as 150,000 pesos in booty.

The Spanish government strongly protested these illegal assaults on Santiago and San Francisco, and the Mexican treasure fleet remained in port until warships arrived. Without condemning the raiders, Charles II forbade future assaults in April 1663.

Back in Europe by 1665, Myngs was knighted while vice-admiral of a squadron fighting Dutch forces in the Channel. He was mortally wounded in battle in 1666. His will disposed of property in London and Norfolk, but it mentioned only small sums of money despite his share in very rich spoils.

(See also SELECTED BIBLIOGRAPHY: Cruikshank, *Morgan*; Haring, *Buccaneers*; Pope, *Buccaneer*.)

MYOPARO *(pirate ship; Mediterranean; 400 B.C. to A.D. 400)* An exceptionally swift open GALLEY, with one bank of oars and a detachable mast and sails. Cheap to build and maintain and easy to man, the Myoparo was favored by beginning brigands, who might graduate to a larger pirate ship if successful.

(See also SHIPS, PIRATE.)

(N)

NABIS *(Greek king; Mediterranean; 250?–192 B.C.)* King of Sparta from about 207, Nabis strengthened the city's forces and built new fortifications. Knossos and other cities in CRETE supplied him with mercenary soldiers. Over time, these alliances became so close that Nabis controlled some coastal cities in Crete.

From about 204 to 195, Nabis' Cretan allies attacked all along Greece's southeastern coast. King Nabis took a cut of their booty, and he sold captured soldiers and civilians in Cretan slave markets. Copying the AETOLIANS, he used the threat of pirate attacks to force Sparta's rule upon other Greek cities. By working with Nabis, the Cretan pirates gained access to the mainland ports he controlled. They especially needed safe havens during these years, as fleets from RHODES repeatedly raided their bases on Crete itself.

In 195, the Romans attacked Nabis. His conquests on land provided an excuse for war, and his pirate allies had seized Roman supply ships. The Romans forced Nabis to give up his navy and his Cretan alliances. But Cretan pirates found other patrons and roamed the seas for the next 150 years.

NARENTANS *(Slavic corsairs; Adriatic Sea; about 800–1000)* A tribe related to the Serbs and Croats. During the seventh century, they occupied the Dalmatian coast and islands from Split (Spalato) south to the Naretva River. Learning seamanship from the ILLYRIANS, they became expert navigators and buccaneers.

During the 800s, Narentan galleys preyed on merchants from Venice and ravaged coastal towns. The BYZANTINE EMPIRE had lost control, and the region was divided among several small principalities. Venice, the most powerful, also had to contend with Muslim pirates, who destroyed the Venetian fleet in 875. Dubrovnik, the other main port, often sided with the pirates, partly to maintain its independence from Venice.

Taking advantage of this anarchy, the Narentans fortified their islands, built up large fleets of galleys, and defeated at least three Venetian expeditions between 850 and 948. Although Venice paid them an annual tribute, Narentan captains attacked merchantmen and even raided Venice itself in 875.

Venetian Doge Pietro Orseolo finally decided to end their raids and refused to pay the annual tribute. A fleet in 991 forced several coastal towns to recognize Venetian sovereignty. In 1000, an even larger fleet brought all of Dalmatia under control. The Venetians surprised and seized 40 pirate galleys returning from a raid on southern Italy. With their Dalmatian allies, they then took the pirate island of Lastovo after a fierce fight and massacred its inhabitants. Although this attack broke the Narentan corsairs, other bands of Dalmatian pirates continued to prey on shipping throughout the Middle Ages.

NASSAU   The main city of NEW PROVIDENCE ISLAND in the Bahamas.

NASUF REIS   *(Barbary corsair; Mediterranean; 1556)*   The KNIGHTS OF MALTA captured Nasuf Reis, a TRIPOLI corsair, near the LIPARI ISLANDS.

(See also SABCULI REIS.)

NATALE, FRANCESCO DI   *(Maltese corsair; Mediterranean; active 1738–1760).*   A Corsican, Natale in 1739 received a five-year license from the KNIGHTS OF MALTA. He commanded *The Blessed Virgin of the Rosary,* a heavily armed sailing ship accompanied by two FELUCCAS and a small boat. By 1745, the knights had stopped licensing raids in the Levant. Natale looked for other patrons, and commanded a ship under the Sardinian flag in 1749. In the 1750s, he operated from Malta under a license from the prince of Monaco.

Natale's pilot sued him in 1742 regarding a wager. Two log books presented as evidence describe the routine followed by most Maltese corsairs. Natale wintered at one of the CYCLADES Islands. During the summer, he cruised—often in a CONSERVA partnership—in the waters between Turkey and Egypt.

The feluccas left the mother ship to attack Christian as well as Muslim victims. In the spring of 1740, they raided the island of Santorini and seized a ship belonging to Greek monks at Patmos. Natale sold his prizes and ransomed captives at ports in Cyprus, Syria, and Lebanon. He seldom encountered OTTOMAN warships.

(See also SELECTED BIBLIOGRAPHY: Earle, *Corsairs.*)

NATALE, GIACOMO DI   *(Maltese corsair; Mediterranean; 1738)*   A Corsican based in Malta, Natale commanded and owned a majority share in a heavily armed sailing ship. While flying the Spanish flag in 1738, he captured a Greek ship. Her captain sued him and demanded return of his vessel and cargo, both owned by Greek Christians.

The Spanish ambassador in Malta heard the case and ruled that Natale had taken a legal prize. The ship flew the Ottoman flag, the cargo belonged to subjects of the sultan, and it was bound from Alexandria to Smyrna. The following year, Giacomo turned command over to his nephew, Francesco di NATALE.

NAU, JEAN DAVID   See L'OLONNAIS, FRANÇOIS.

NAUPLIUS   *(pirate and wrecker; ancient Greek legends)*   Nauplius' story combines two different traditions: that of Nauplius the first seaman and that of a Nauplius associated with the Trojan War. Nauplius the first mariner was born in Argos in southern Greece and founded the city of Nauplia (Návplion). In this legend he was the son of Amymone—daughter of the king of Argos—and Poseidon, god of the sea. Amymone was herself descended from earlier encounters between humans and gods. In one of these, her grandmother also had given herself to Poseidon.

A son and a great-grandson of the sea god, Nauplius was an excellent seaman. His name means "sailor," and he discovered the constellation known as the Big Dipper or Great Bear. Unfortunately, he used his skills to gain wealth any way he could. According to Apollodorus, a historian of myths (second century B.C.), Nauplius was a notorious wrecker. He also was a slaver, who disposed of unwanted children for irate fathers. When Hercules raped Auge, her father (the king of Arcadia) gave her to Nauplius to drown or to sell abroad. Catreus, king of Crete, similarly asked Naplius to sell his two daughters, Aerope and Clymene. Nauplius took Aerope to Greece, where she fathered Agamemnon and Menelaus, the heroes of the Trojan War. But Nauplius kept Clymene for himself, and she bore two sons, Oeax and Palamedes.

Although he is not found in HOMER's *Iliad,* later Greek and Latin authors associated Nauplius with the Trojan War. To avoid joining the Greek army, ODYSSEUS pretended to be crazy. Nauplius' son Palamedes proved that Odysseus' insanity was a fraud. Odysseus subsequently framed Palamedes, who was executed as a traitor.

Nauplius wanted revenge for his son's murder. While the Greek warriors were in Troy, he sailed around persuading their wives to be unfaithful. (When she remained chaste, Nauplius tried to drown Odysseus' wife, Penelope.) As the Greek fleet returned after the war, Nauplius lit a signal fire on Mount Caphereus (Akra Kafirévs) at the southwestern tip of Euboea (Evvoia). Expecting a safe harbor, the Greeks sailed onto the rocks and drowned in great number. Nauplius killed any survivors reaching the shore. According to some legends, he later joined Jason and the other Argonauts who sailed to Asia to steal the Golden Fleece.

Nauplius stars in two plays—surviving only in fragments—by Sophocles (*circa* 496–406 B.C.). Both describe Nauplius' vengeance on the Greeks for their murder of Palamedes. *Nauplius the Fire-Kindler* deals with the beacon that lured the Greek ships onto the breakers. The second, *Nauplius Sailing Home,* tells how he also fell victim to false signals. *The* INCHCAPE ROCK by Robert Southey describes a Scottish pirate's similar fate.

Other ancient plays also mention Nauplius' destruction of the Greek fleet, including *Helen* and *Orestes* by Euripides (about 485–406 B.C.) and *Agamemnon* by Seneca (died A.D. 65). Perhaps Greek ships returning from the Trojan War did perish off Euboea. The entire eastern coast is rocky and without harbors, and the Caphereus Promontory attracts fierce storms.

NAUTICAL TERMS   See EXPRESSIONS, SEAFARING.

NAVARRO, PEDRO   *(French corsair; Mediterranean; active 1497–1511)*   Navarro was originally from southwestern France. Operating from Roccella (in southeastern Italy), with the local lord's connivance, he captured at least 10 merchant ships and hanged their crews. In 1497, Venetian squadrons attacked the pirate base at Roccella and bombarded nearby Crotone.

Navarro moved to Naples, came to terms with its king, and took command of a large galley with 400 men. In 1499, he plundered Venetian merchant ships off Sicily and in the Ionian Sea. A Spanish squadron captured his galley in Sicilian waters in July 1500, and he apparently worked with the Spanish navy for a time.

Navarro returned to piracy on a grand scale in 1507. Commanding four galleys, he attacked Venetian shipping near Sicily and then captured at least three vessels between Egypt and Crete. Returning to Spain early in 1508, he commanded fleets that captured the North African ports of Oran, Bougie (Bejaïa), and Tripoli between 1508 and 1511.

(See also ARUJ BARBAROSSA; BARBARY STATES.)

NECKERE, JONATHAN DE (Dutch pirate; Caribbean; 1631)

The DUTCH WEST INDIA COMPANY sent Neckere from Brazil to the Caribbean with a warship and two YACHTS, one commanded by Cornelis JOL. Despite his orders, Neckere failed to join Dutch fleets under Martin THIJSZ and Jan BOONETER. However, he did capture six prizes and made a profit—unlike Thijsz and Booneter, whose larger squadrons did not pay their expenses.

NEW ACCOUNT OF SOME PARTS OF GUINEA AND THE SLAVE-TRADE, A (sea captain's report; 1734)

In April 1719, Captain William Snelgrave was captured by Thomas COCKLYN near the Sierra Leone River in West Africa. Olivier LA BOUCHE and Howell DAVIS were anchored at the same harbor. In this report Snelgrave describes life on board the pirate ships during several weeks of captivity.

NEWPORT, CHRISTOPHER (English privateer; Atlantic, Caribbean; 1560–1617)

Newport rose from humble beginnings (in Limehouse, London) during the PRIVATEERING war against Spain from 1588 to 1603. As admiral of the Virginia Company's fleet (1606–1611), he helped secure England's foothold in North America.

As a crewman in 1580, Newport quarreled with his captain and deserted in Brazil. After serving on one of John WATTS' warships during Sir Francis DRAKE's 1587 raid on Cadiz, he conducted privateering voyages for London sponsors. In 1590, while traveling to ROANOKE for Watts, Newport lost contact with the main fleet. Off northwestern Cuba in July, Newport's crew tried to board a ship from the Mexican TREASURE FLEET. One of its defenders slashed off his right arm.

The loss of an arm did not slow down Newport. He led at least nine more raids on the West Indies, more than any other English captain. In 1591, he commanded three ships that traded with the BARBARY STATES before capturing a Spanish prize off La Yaguana in Hispaniola.

In 1592, Newport headed back to La Yaguana with the brand new Golden Dragon and three other ships.

Because the raiders lingered to loot a ship in the harbor, Newport failed to capture La Yaguana. In Honduras, PUERTO CABALLOS provided little booty, and Trujillo's defenders repulsed the raiders. But their luck changed during the return voyage. Off the Azores, Newport's ships joined in pillaging the MADRE DE DIOS, carrying the richest treasure the English had taken to date.

Newport was captain of the Golden Dragon during Sir John BURGH's 1593 expedition, partly sponsored by Sir Walter RALEIGH. The raiders were driven away from Margarita Island (off Venezuela) and then visited Trinidad and Guiana. Newport went back to Puerto Caballos in 1594, but took little booty from that much-plundered town.

After marrying the daughter of a wealthy London goldsmith in 1595, Newport constructed the formidable warship Neptune. Joined by Michael GEARE and John RILESDEN, Newport plundered shipping off Honduras in 1596. He took at least two prizes in the West Indies in 1598, captured Tabasco in Mexico in 1599, and took more prizes at Guava and near Havana early in 1602.

Newport immediately returned to the Caribbean with Michael Geare and Anthony HIPPON. In November 1602, joined by five French pirate ships, they attacked two warships guarding the Mexican treasure fleet at Puerto Caballos. After eight hours of heavy fighting, the raiders captured the two warships, a feat equalled by few other pirates. Rumors reached England that the warships held millions in gold. Newport apparently found no treasure, but he made a handsome profit from the ships and cargo.

Unlike many other captains, Newport returned to honest trade when King James I ended privateering. He visited the West Indies in 1604 and 1605, commanded the Virginia Company's fleet until 1611, and undertook three voyages for the East India Company between 1612 and 1617. He died at Bantam in the Cocos Islands, leaving his family considerable wealth.

(See also SELECTED BIBLIOGRAPHY: Andrews, Elizabethan.)

NEW PROVIDENCE ISLAND (pirate haven; Atlantic; about 1670–1718)

An island of some 60 square miles, 200 miles east of Florida. The chief city (called Nassau from 1695) is the capital of the Bahamas. British and American pirates careened their ships and obtained supplies at the Bahamas from the 1670s. From 1716 to 1718, Nassau briefly became the most important pirate HAVEN in the Americas.

Located near major trade routes, New Providence offered fresh water, wood, fruit, and meat from wild hogs and cattle. Nassau's harbor could take 500 small vessels but was too shallow for naval battleships. Hog Island divided it into two inlets, so at least two warships were needed for an effective blockade.

Although settlers arrived from the 1640s, plantations never prospered on the small and arid islands. Until 1717, the Bahamas were privately owned. The absentee landlords ignored their island possessions and sent ineffective governors who accepted pirate kickbacks.

Buccaneers, including John COXON, moved to Nassau during the 1680s as Jamaican authorities cracked down on piracy. After Thomas PAIN raided Florida, two Spanish expeditions sacked Nassau in 1684, but British pirates returned in 1686. Others moved in from French TORTUGA when France and Britain went to war in 1689.

These Nassau pirates operated on a small scale. Despite the island's natural riches and tolerant government, most raiders preferred ports in British North America. From 1680, pirates left the over-plundered Caribbean to raid in the Pacific or the Indian Ocean. To get a better prize, they fenced their exotic booty at major American ports, many of which condoned piracy. John COOK went to Virginia in 1683, while Edward DAVIS took his booty to Philadelphia in 1688. The governors of New York and Boston sold fake PRIVATEERING commissions, and prominent merchants openly bought pirate booty. Only Henry EVERY sold his loot at the Bahamas (in 1696), since he did not trust mainland officials.

Spanish expeditions raided New Providence in 1703, 1704, and 1706 during wartime. There was no governor after 1704, and the few remaining inhabitants appreciated the money pirates brought in. When the war ended in 1713, hundreds of former privateers turned marauder. Because mainland colonies had turned honest, they operated from Nassau.

Henry JENNINGS settled at New Providence in about 1716. By 1717, 500 or 600 pirates sailed from Nassau. Dozens of captains ravaged shipping in the West Indies and along the American coast from Florida to Maine. The roster includes Stede BONNET, Benjamin HORNIGOLD, John MARTEL, and Charles VANE.

In July 1718, Woodes ROGERS arrived as royal governor accompanied by three warships. Though the navy soon departed, Rogers managed to bluff the raiders into retiring or leaving New Providence. In December, he hanged John AUGER and seven others who had reverted to their wicked ways.

Convinced that Rogers meant business, the Nassau pirates looked for new havens. Christopher WINTER found safety at Cuba, but many others were captured or killed. Edward TEACH (BLACKBEARD) died in battle at North Carolina. Thomas ANSTIS, Jack RACKHAM, Mary READ, and Anne BONNY (1) were arrested and hanged in the West Indies. Samuel BELLAMY and Paul WILLIAMS were wrecked off New England. Thomas COCKLYN, Thomas CONDENT, Howell DAVIS, and Olivier LA BOUCHE sailed to West Africa, where Davis (and probably Cocklyn) was killed. Condent and La Bouche went on to Madagascar and later bought sanctuary from the French governor of Réunion Island.

(See also SELECTED BIBLIOGRAPHY: Marx, *Pirates*; Rogoziński, *Caribbean*.)

NEWTON, ROBERT *(British actor; 1905–1956)*
With his swarthy face, slow menacing voice, and mali-cious intensity, Newton was the cunning villain in major British films during the 1930s and 1940s. (He had more sympathetic roles in *Gaslight* [1940] and *This Happy Breed* [1944]). He adopted a broader, exaggerated style for his caricatures of pirate roguery in TREASURE ISLAND (1950), BLACKBEARD THE PIRATE (1952), and LONG JOHN SILVER (1955).

NEW VOYAGE ROUND THE WORLD, A *(novel; 1724)* Daniel DEFOE shows that pirates are morally superior to businessmen. Geographical details were taken from William DAMPIER's *New Voyage* and the journals of Dutch explorers.

An unnamed captain sets out for South America's Pacific coast, looking to make money through trade, piracy, and exploration. The captain secures a PRIVATEERING commission, even though the war against France and Spain is over when he leaves in December 1713. Although his ship loots many vessels, piracy is the least of the captain's crimes.

Driven back from the Strait of Magellan by harsh weather, the ship crosses the Atlantic and passes around the Cape of Good Hope. The captain finds out about a planned mutiny and tortures the ringleaders. At MADAGASCAR, he runs into a large pirate colony, buys a ship, and recruits crewmen. All of the pirates claim that they were forced to serve and want to return to England. The captain can take only 21 men and drives the rest off at gunpoint.

With two captured ships plus his own, the captain pushes on to Ceylon, Indonesia, and the Philippines, plundering along the way. Reaching South America, he takes several Spanish prizes and visits a large estate in Chile. From Chile, some of the crew march across the Andes to Argentina. True pirates, the men sign ARTICLES to share equally in any gold they find. Since they are acting for their personal profit, the men become ungovernable and pillage the countryside.

The ships pass around Cape Horn and pick up the party crossing overland. The captain sails to France, where both the explorers and the Madagascar pirates leave with their booty. The ships reach Dunkirk in April 1716, and the owners take the largest share of the voyage's fantastic profits.

NIKANDROS *(Greek archpirate; Mediterranean, Aegean Sea; active 190s B.C.)* During a war (192–188) between Rome and Antiochus III of Seleucia (Syria), Nikandros fought under Polyxenidas, Antiochus's admiral. Rome was allied with RHODES and Pergamum.

In 190, Polyxenidas attacked the Rhodian fleet based at SAMOS. His warships encircled the harbor at the Gulf of Vathí (ancient Panormos). Meanwhile, Nikandros took five ships east to Cape Prason (Palinourous) and landed soldiers. Nikandros led the troops across the fields to the harbor and took the enemy in the rear. The Rhodian seamen were trapped between the land and sea forces, which quickly sunk most of the enemy's ships.

Although not explicitly named as their chief, Nikandros probably led 15 pirate ships the Romans encountered off the island of Teos in 191. The pirates were heading toward CRETE, laden with plunder after raiding Chios. They easily outsailed the slower and heavier Roman warships.

NIKETAS OF RHODES *(Greek corsair; Mediterranean and Aegean Sea; 1270s)* Niketas cruised with the approval of Emperor MICHAEL VIII PALAEOLOGUS according to the VENETIAN CLAIMS.

NIÑO, PERO, CONDE DE BUELNA *(Spanish corsair; Mediterranean, Atlantic; 1379–1449)* A native of Castile, Pero Niño devoted himself to naval warfare and earned fame by raiding Muslim North Africa. In 1405, he commanded three galleys fighting for France against England during a time of truce. Joined by two galleys under Charles de SAVOISY, Niño attacked the English coast and devastated Poole in reprisal for raids by Harry PAY. The following year, Niño's ships twice defeated larger English naval squadrons.

Gutierre Diaz de Gamez, his lieutenant, wrote Niño's biography, virtually the only sea journal remaining from the Middle Ages. It contains both stories of amazing adventures and scrupulous accounts of seamanship.

NOBLE, JOHN *(English pirate; Caribbean; 1574)* After hiding his ship near the city of Veragua, Noble scoured the Panamanian coast with two small boats, capturing and burning many Spanish vessels. In June, a Spanish warship caught up with one of Noble's boats. Panicking, the English pirates deserted their vessel and were captured. After they revealed the mother ship's hiding place, Noble and his men were hanged. Two young boys were spared and condemned as GALLEY SLAVES.

(See also DRAKE, SIR FRANCIS.)

NOORT, OLIVIER VAN *(Dutch pirate; Atlantic, Pacific; active 1598–1601)* A Rotterdam tavernkeeper and pirate, Noort in 1598 set out to plunder South America's Pacific coast, perhaps with the approval of the Dutch government. Although he took little booty, he became the first Dutch captain to sail around the world.

A trading company provided van Noort with two warships and two YACHTS. Noort commanded the 250-ton *Mauritius*, while Jacob van Ilpendam was captain of the 300-ton *Hendrick Frederick*. The small fleet left in July and stopped in England to pick up a pilot who had sailed with Thomas CAVENDISH. After a rough crossing, the Strait of Magellan was reached in June 1599. To avoid the winter storms, the raiders did not enter the Strait until November, surviving meanwhile on a diet of penguins, their eggs, and fish.

Lashed by storms and fierce winds, the Dutch ships spent the next four months passing through the Strait of Magellan. To end a threatened mutiny, Noort MAROONED Ilpendam—a death sentence in that region—and re-

placed him with Peter de LINT. As the ships left the Strait, Noort lost contact with Lint and the *Hendrick Frederick*.

As he sailed north along Chile, Noort took a Spanish ship, but the crew already had thrown overboard her cargo of gold. He took three more ships in the harbor of Valparaiso, but they carried little of value. The MANILA GALLEON kept well away from the coast, and the Spaniards safely convoyed Peruvian silver ships to PANAMA.

Van Noort gave up and sailed west in May. By October he was in the Philippines, burning native villages and taking a few trivial prizes. Off Corregidor on December 13, Noort fought a savage battle with a Spanish ship sent out to catch him. The Spaniards boarded and almost captured the *Mauritius*. When she caught fire, Noort rallied his crew by threatening to blow her up. The enemy vessel began to sink as she sheered off to avoid the flames. The Dutch pirates brutally slaughtered Spanish soldiers trying to swim to safety.

Noort briefly traded at Brunei but was driven off by a MALAYAN squadron. He reached Rotterdam in August 1601 with little booty and only 45 of his 248 crewmen.

(See also SELECTED BIBLIOGRAPHY: Bradley, *Peru*; Gerhard, *Pirates*; Spate, *Monopolists*.)

"NO PEACE BEYOND THE LINE" *(diplomatic saying; Caribbean; 1559–1684)* A rule that European treaties did not apply beyond an imaginary line 100 leagues west of the Azores and Cape Verde Islands. West of this line (for example, in the Caribbean), mariners traveled at their own risk. Their own government would not protect them if they suffered violence. (In some eras, a similar rule also applied south of the Tropic of Cancer in Africa and the East Indies.)

To resolve conflicting Spanish and Portuguese claims, Pope Alexander VI in 1493 granted Spain all territories west of this line. No foreigner could cross the line without Spanish permission. Other European nations naturally opposed the Spanish claim to a monopoly in the Indies.

In negotiations for a 1559 peace treaty, France and Spain finally agreed not to mention the Indies. The two nations were at peace in Europe, but there was "no peace [treaty] beyond the line." Violence beyond the line would not break the treaty. Spanish authorities could hang French seamen as pirates, and the French king would not restore Spanish ships seized by his subjects.

Later treaties also ignored the Indies, and the "no peace" principle survived for more than a century. England and Spain were the first to extend their laws beyond the line. By the 1670 Treaty of Madrid, the Spanish government recognized England's American colonies, and both sides agreed to refrain from hostile acts everywhere in the world. Sir Henry MORGAN's raid on PANAMA infuriated Spain because it occurred after the Treaty of Madrid was signed. English officials arrested (but did not punish) Morgan and Jamaican governor Sir Thomas MODYFORD. Modyford's successor was ordered to suppress the PORT ROYAL pirates.

No purchase, No pay. Sir Henry Morgan's buccaneers are portrayed during the 1671 sack of Panama in this illustration by Howard Pyle for *Harper's Monthly Magazine*, September 1887.

A 1678 peace treaty between France and Spain continued to ignore the Americas, and French governors allowed pirates to operate from TORTUGA and PETIT GOÂVE. By the 1684 Truce of Ratisbon, France finally agreed to end hostilities "within Europe and without, both on this side of and beyond the Line." Piracy became illegal in all of the Caribbean colonies. Raiders sought new HAVENS, such as MADAGASCAR and NEW PROVIDENCE ISLAND in the Bahamas.

(See also SELECTED BIBLIOGRAPHY: Newton, *European Nations*.)

"NO PURCHASE, NO PAY" *(nautical slang; all oceans; 16th through 18th centuries)*
In this meaning (now extinct), the English word *purchase* referred to any plunder, loot, or BOOTY taken by force. "No purchase, no pay" in pirate ARTICLES meant that the crew would receive nothing until they seized booty. A similar phrase still survives in marine insurance. "No cure no pay," referring to salvage attempts, means there is no reward or pay unless the operation succeeds.

(See also ACCOUNT, GOING ON THE.)

NORMAN, RICHARD *(English pirate; Caribbean; active 1670–1671)*
Norman was captain of a ship during Sir Henry MORGAN's forays against PORTOBELO (1668), Maracaibo (1669), and PANAMA (1671). During the Panama raid, he took part in the bloody battle for Chagres.

NORTH, NATHANIEL *(British pirate; Red Sea, Indian Ocean; active 1696–1707)*
As a carpenter at Bermuda, North helped prepare Thomas TEW's *Amity* for its 1692 cruise. Aged 17 or 18, he shipped on a PRIVATEER attacking French shipping during the Nine Years' War. He was pressed into the royal navy but returned to privateering from Jamaica. He again was grabbed by navy press gangs but escaped by swimming ashore.

About 1696, North served on a privateer that captured the 18-gun *Pelican* off Newfoundland. The raiders bought a commission to raid the French in West Africa but instead headed for MADAGASCAR. They planned, Daniel DEFOE relates, "to cruise on the *Moors*, not intending to pyrate among the *Europeans*, but honestly and quietly to rob what *Moors* fell in their Way, and return home with clean Consciences, and clean, but full Hands."

Not finding any prizes, the pirates raided villages in the Comoro Islands. They returned to Madagascar (where North was elected QUARTERMASTER) and then cruised in the Red Sea in consort with Robert CULLIFORD and Dirk CHIVERS. In September 1698, Culliford and Chivers captured the *Great Mohammed* and large hoards of gold coins. However, they refused to share the booty with the *Pelican*, alleging that she had not joined in the battle.

Leaving her faithless consorts, the *Pelican* chased but could not catch another Indian ship. Going to India's Malabar coast, the pirates seized three small vessels, taking over one of their prizes as the *Dolphin*. They lost their masts in a hurricane, but made it back to Madagascar, where each man received about £700.

Sailing under a Captain Samuel Inless, the *Dolphin* plundered a large Danish ship in 1699. At Saint Mary's Island near Madagascar, her crew divided about £400 each in May. Four British warships arrived in September, and Captain Inless burned the *Dolphin* rather than surrender.

Some men accepted a pardon, but North did not trust the English commodore and fled to Madagascar. His small boat overturned during a storm, and he swam 12 miles to shore, losing everything he owned. From 1701 to late 1703, he sailed with George BOOTH and (after Booth's death) as quartermaster with John BOWEN.

When Bowen retired at Mauritius, North became captain of the pirates remaining at Madagascar, who intervened in native wars to gain slaves and women. Early in 1707, he became quartermaster of John HALSEY's *Charles*, which captured two valuable British ships. When Halsey went back to Madagascar in one of the prizes, North took command of the *Charles*, which was wrecked on a reef. He eventually made it home, was sailing in Madagascar waters in 1709, and was killed by local tribesmen some years later.

(See also SELECTED BIBLIOGRAPHY: Grey, *Pirates.*)

NORTON, JOHN (1) *(English pirate; Atlantic; 1449)* Norton was an officer on John TREVELYAN's ship, which seized a rich Spanish prize off Plymouth.

NORTON, JOHN (2) *(English captain; Atlantic; active 1591–1592)* Norton took part in several plunder raids financed by the earl of CUMBERLAND. He was captain of the 300-ton *Sampson* in a five-ship fleet personally led by Cumberland in 1591. The earl stayed at home the following year, and Norton had overall command of his ships during the plunder of the MADRE DE DIOS, a great Portuguese treasure ship.

NORTON, THOMAS *(English pirate; English Channel; 1404)* Norton, a Bristol merchant, and Thomas HAWLEY led ships from Bristol, Dartmouth, and Plymouth that seized seven richly laden merchant vessels.

NOVAGLIA, ARFANI *(Italian pirate; Mediterranean; 1498)* Sailing with his brother Franceschetto, Novaglia plundered shipping along the coast of Cyprus.

NOVELS See FICTION, PIRATE.

NUESTRA SEÑORA DE LA CONCEPCIÓN
The original name of the CACAFUEGO, a Spanish treasure ship captured in 1579 by Sir Francis DRAKE.

NUTT, JOHN *(English pirate; Atlantic, English Channel; active 1620s)* A Dartmouth man, Nutt sailed as a gunner with the Newfoundland fishing fleets in 1623 to escape the royal navy. With other refugees from the press gangs, he captured several ships and returned to terrorize the Devonshire coast, reappearing in Dartmouth in his victims' fine clothes. At the entrance to Dungarvan harbor, Nutt captured a bark carrying a dozen or more women, all of whom "were ravished by the pyrates' company." Nutt especially fancied the wife of a Cork saddler, carried her to his cabin, "and there had her a weke."

Sir John Elliot, VICE-ADMIRAL for Devonshire, tricked Nutt into surrendering and paying £500 for a pardon under a lapsed law. Taken to London, he was pardoned thanks to influential friends, including Sir George Calvert (afterward Lord Baltimore) who had estates in Newfoundland. Perhaps Nutt joined the BARBARY pirates. Some years later, a naval captain claimed he had encountered Nutt off the Irish coast commanding 28 Barbary ships. He definitely had retired (and been pardoned) by 1633, when he solicited a pardon for his brother, Captain Robert NUTT.

(See also SELECTED BIBLIOGRAPHY: Chew, *Crescent.*)

NUTT, ROBERT *(English pirate; Atlantic; active 1631–1633)* Nutt operated from Cornwall and northern Wales until 1633, when his brother John NUTT arranged for a pardon.

OCHIALI His Christian enemies gave this nickname to the BARBARY corsair ULUJ ALI PASHA—the latter a form of Ali-al-Uluj ("Ali the Renegade").

ODYSSEUS *(warrior and sea raider; ancient Greek legends)* HOMER's epic poem *The Odyssey* narrates the story of his return home after the Trojan War. Odysseus wanders the seas for 10 years and survives many strange and perilous encounters. The *Odyssey* relates the final six weeks of these adventures, and the poet brings in earlier events through stories related by Odysseus and others.

In two of his tales, Odysseus tells persons who have befriended him about his acts of piracy. Homer consistently portrays Odysseus as a consummate and crafty liar. However, at these points in the poem, Homer does provide some believable evidence about piracy in ancient Greece.

Both pirate stories relate similar events. Odysseus leads a corsair band that descends on a foreign coast. The pirates pillage the neighborhood, killing the men and seizing women and children as slaves. In both cases, warriors from inland regions arrive and kill many pirates.

The first pirate episode occurs after Odysseus escapes from the island paradise of the goddess Calypso. His raft sinks, and he finds refuge on Drepane Island with Alcinous, king of the Phaeacians. Alcinous gives a feast to honor Odysseus, who tells his hosts about his wanderings.

Shortly after leaving Troy, at the beginning of his journey, a wind drove Odysseus ashore. He landed near a small city in the land of the Kikones (near the modern Greek city of Lasomos). Odysseus' band took full advantage of this chance for plunder and sacked the city. Odysseus wanted to flee immediately afterward, but his men decided to stay and celebrate with a feast; several of Odysseus' men were killed by reinforcements summoned by the Kikonians.

This story is remarkably cold-blooded. Odysseus had no reason to attack the Kikonians, and his ship already was laden with loot from Troy. His hosts, the noble Phaeacians, do not criticize his brigandage, and they apparently accept it as perfectly natural behavior. They give Odysseus many presents and provide a ship that carries him home to Ithaca.

Odysseus tells a similar story after his return to Ithaca. During his absence, young princes tried to take Odysseus' throne by marrying his wife Penelope. Until he can kill these suitors, Odysseus (disguised as an old tramp) seeks refuge with his faithful shepherd EUMAEUS. He tells Eumaeus that he is a pirate from CRETE, the son of a rich man's concubine. Preferring war to work, he led nine profitable sea raids on various coasts.

Since Odysseus took much booty and spent it lavishly, his fellow Cretans feared and respected him. When King Idomeneus (grandson of King MINOS) joined the Greek siege of Troy, Odysseus commanded the Cretan ships.

Following the war, he returned to Crete but grew bored after only one month at home. Outfitting nine warships, he landed in Egypt.

There he was betrayed by the rashness of his men, who attacked too soon and were killed by the Egyptian army. Odysseus alone survived by throwing himself on the Egyptian king's mercy.

Odysseus' second pirate story is even more bloodthirsty than the first. Yet the shepherd Eumaeus, like the noble Phaeacians, finds nothing wrong in Odysseus' behavior. It is clear that Homer's audiences did not condemn piratical raids. Instead, like the Cretans Odysseus describes, they honored pirates who brought home rich booty.

Ancient pirates primarily looted coastal areas rather than merchant shipping. Until Rome defeated the CILICIAN corsairs, pirate attacks remained a constant threat. As the Greek ROMANCES show, pirates happily scooped up any good-looking youth walking by the shore.

Judging by Odysseus' stories, ancient pirates resembled more recent sea raiders. After looting the Kikones, the corsairs divided their booty equally. Once a raid succeeded, the corsairs immediately set about feasting and drinking, ignoring the risk of pursuit by local police forces.

"OH, BETTER FAR TO LIVE AND DIE" (fictional pirate song; 1879)

In The PIRATES OF PENZANCE, Act One, Frederic tries to persuade the pirates to give up their calling. Defending his profession, the Pirate King declares that he is simply more open about his villainies than so-called honest men.

> Oh better far to live and die
> Under the brave black flag I fly,
> Than play a sanctimonious part,
> With a pirate head and a pirate heart.
> Away to the cheating world go you,
> Where pirates all are well-to-do.

The music parodies operas by Giuseppe Verdi. The king's argument is an old one, strongly stated by Daniel DEFOE during the early 1700s. The song is important for its choral catch phrase "For I am a Pirate King." Later on, this is developed as "the very model of a Modern Major General" and as "an orphan boy." The melody of this statement became the signature tune of the cartoon character Popeye.

O'HARA, MAUREEN (American actress; 1920–)

A fiery green-eyed redhead born in Ireland, O'Hara was especially gorgeous in Technicolor. She acted in British plays and films before moving to Hollywood, where she played Esmeralda to Charles LAUGHTON's Hunchback of Notre Dame (1939). Appearing in more than 50 movies, she was particularly identified with those directed by John Ford, including Rio Grande (1950) and The Quiet Man (1952).

O'Hara frequently appeared as an explosive Irish lass, who rebels against a male-dominated society but is finally tamed by a John Wayne character. Although perhaps best known for her westerns, she played a similar role in three SWASHBUCKLERS: appearing with Tyrone POWER in The BLACK SWAN (1942); Paul HENREID in The SPANISH MAIN (1945); and Errol FLYNN in AGAINST ALL FLAGS.

OLOARD, CHRISTOPHER (English pirate; Mediterranean; 1603)

A Dartmouth man, Oloard brought a Venetian prize to Modone in southern Greece. The OTTOMAN governor normally tolerated Christian piracy against other Christians. Under pressure from higher officials in this case, he handed Oloard over to the Venetian governor at Zante, who hanged him from his castle's tower. Oloard was a colorful character, "rather small, dressed in black velvet trousers and jacket, crimson silk socks, black felt hat, brown beard, and shirt collar embroidered in black silk."

The Venetian governor retired soon after. As he left Zante, English pirates captured his ship and destroyed or stole his possessions. Four or five captains, one called Bully, led Oloard's avengers, "all young and beardless."

(See also IONIAN ISLANDS; SELECTED BIBLIOGRAPHY: Senior, Nation.)

O'MALLEY, GRACE (fictional Irish pirate; Atlantic; 16th century)

Grace's adventures are described by William O'Brien, a 19th-century writer who said he was retelling old Irish legends. Called Queen of the West, Grace buried more than nine tons of stolen treasure, still protected by her curse.

In the story, the O'Malleys hid their ships at coastal forts and on Clare Island, where Grace grew up. As a youth, she climbed a high cliff and killed eagles that had carried off her family's sheep. The talons of the great birds deeply gashed her forehead, leaving her scarred for life.

Grace went to sea with her father, who trained her as a warrior. Although she had a younger brother, Grace took command of the O'Malley forts and fleets after her father died. The pirates flourished under her leadership, and Queen Elizabeth I offered a reward of £500 for her capture.

Grace married twice and had many children. At the urging of her second husband, she became an ally of the English and was invited to visit the queen. While traveling to England, she gave birth to a son named Tibbot, who was knighted by the queen as Sir Theobold.

Grace possessed superhuman strength and magical powers. Just after Tibbot was born, a Turkish vessel attacked Grace's ship. The new mother climbed to the deck with a BLUNDERBUSS in each hand to repel the enemy. When more than 60 years old, Grace attacked a Spanish ship near Ireland. She came on deck in her nightgown, her gray hair flying in the wind, the scars on her face livid, waving a sword and a pistol. Convinced she was a fiend, the Spaniards instantly surrendered.

Grace was a harsh parent. One of her young sons fell out of a roll boat traveling to Clare Island. Grabbing the side of the boat, the boy began to pull himself back aboard. Grace chopped off his hand with a knife and left him to die in the waves. "If you had been a true O'Malley," she told her son, "you'd not have fallen overboard in the first place."

OMAR REIS *(Moroccan corsair; Mediterranean; 1760s)* Sailing from SALÉ in a 16-gun SHEBEC, Omar Reis took three French prizes in the Strait of Gibraltar in 1767. The sultan removed him from command, since these captures took place during negotiations for a peace treaty.

OMODEI VENTIMIGLIA, ANTONIO, BARON DE VALLONGA *(Italian pirate; Mediterranean, Ionian Sea; 1555)* Ventimiglia commanded a GALIOT outfitted by the son of the Spanish viceroy of Sicily and reinforced with a hundred soldiers. After looting two Venetian ships near the IONIAN ISLANDS, he was taken by a Venetian squadron while towing a captured Turkish vessel toward Messina.

(See also VARGAS, JUAN DE.)

ORANGE, PIERRE D' *(Belgian pirate; Mediterranean; active 1600–1601)* A native of Brussels, d'Orange plundered Venetian shipping with Michel VAIS.

ORDER OF THE HOSPITAL OF SAINT JOHN OF JERUSALEM See KNIGHTS HOSPITALERS.

ORDUÑA, DIEGO DE *(Spanish pirate; Mediterranean; 1492)* Warships of the KNIGHTS OF RHODES captured Orduña's CARAVEL, executed him, and made his men GALLEY SLAVES.

ORSINI DELL'ANGUILLARA, FLAMINIO *(Italian pirate; Mediterranean; 1558)* Orsini looted a Venetian ship near Alexandria, Egypt, seizing Jewish passengers and booty worth 12,000 ducats. Learning that Orsini was backed by a Roman nobleman, Venice unsuccessfully protested to the pope.

ORTIGUES, GABRIEL *(Spanish pirate; Mediterranean; 1445)* A Catalan merchant, Ortigues traded with Alexandria, Egypt, from 1428. In 1445, his galley captured a valuable Muslim merchant ship near the port. The sultan jailed other Catalan merchants in reprisal.

OSMAN, SHERIP *(Malay pirate; South China Sea; died 1845)* Half Arab by birth, Osman built a fort some distance up the Marudu (Langkon) River in northern Borneo. His prestige was enhanced by his marriage to a daughter of the rajah of Sula and his supposed descent from Mohammed.

Osman sold slaves to the sultan of Brunei and cooperated with ILANUN settlements in northwestern Borneo.

His 2,000 followers raided coastal villages and assaulted Asian and European vessels. In 1841 and again in 1845, they plundered British ships wrecked along the coast and enslaved members of their crews.

After bombarding Brunei, a British squadron attacked Osman's fortress in 1845. Although the pirates resisted fiercely, they were slaughtered by naval gunfire, and their fort and city were burned. During the battle, Osman stood atop a wall of the fort, directing his forces in full view of the enemy. He was shot through the neck, and his followers fled with his body.

(See also BROOKE, SIR JAMES.)

OSTA MURAT See USTA MURAT.

OTTOMAN EMPIRE *(pirate patron and victim; about 1288 to 1922)* The sultans of the Ottoman dynasty ruled vast territories in Asia, Africa, and Europe. Their empire sometimes is called "Turkey" and its inhabitants are described as "Turks." In fact, "the domain of the divinely-protected house of Osman" was a multiracial state unified by religion. The sultans had unlimited power, which they delegated to officials of many nationalities.

By the mid-15th century, the Ottomans conquered what are today Turkey, Bulgaria, Serbia, and Bosnia. They occupied Constantinople in 1453 and took most of Greece and the Aegean islands by 1500. Syria, Egypt, and Arabia were conquered by 1517. Croatia, Hungary, Romania, and much of DALMATIA were added after the Ottoman victory at Mohacs (August 1526). Although the seige of MALTA failed in 1565, Cyprus was taken from Venice in 1570, CRETE in 1669.

Ottoman territories were most numerous at the end of the 17th century, and the empire slowly contracted during the following centuries. In 1699, the Austrian Habsburgs took Hungary, and Venice reoccupied Dalmatia. Egypt, Serbia, Greece, Romania, and Bulgaria became independent during the 19th century. Syria and Arabia were lost in 1918.

The Ottoman sultans ruled all the lands surrounding the Black Sea and the eastern Mediterranean. During the 16th century, they aggressively sought maritime power, and they built up their navy by offering commands to successful pirate captains. KEMAL REIS, BURAK REIS, and PIRI REIS sought control of the Red Sea in the 1520s. Although they gave up the Red Sea, the sultans continued to staff their fleet with former corsairs, such as KHEIREDDIN BARBAROSSA, TURGUT REIS, and ULUJ ALI. After about 1580, however, the empire also turned away from the Mediterranean and let its navy decay.

The decline of Ottoman naval power helped to make the Mediterranean a pirate dominion. For centuries, both Muslims and Christians justified pillage for profit as a "Holy War." During their drive westward, Ottoman naval forces had supported corsair kingdoms at ALGIERS, TUNIS, and TRIPOLI. As the Ottoman navy weakened, the three BARBARY STATES conducted independent foreign policies.

With the help of Christian RENEGADES, piracy flourished until the 1670s.

While the Barbary corsairs were raiding Italy, Spain, and southern France, Christian pirates plundered the Ottoman east. The USKOKS dominated the Adriatic, and corsairs scoured the eastern Mediterranean. The dukes of Florence sponsored the KNIGHTS OF SAINT STEPHEN, while the Spanish viceroys of Sicily and Naples also opened their ports to corsairs, such as Jacques PIERRE, PAPACODA, and Michel VAIS. Ironically, many of their victims were Christians. Pirates considered any Ottoman subject or ally fair game, and they ruthlessly plundered Greek and Venetian vessels.

As other corsair bases became less important from the 1620s, Malta became the undisputed capital of Christian piracy. The KNIGHTS OF MALTA scoured the seas, and they also licensed hundreds of private captains. Although their attacks on Venetian shipping fell off from the 1640s, the Maltese plundered Christian Greeks until 1798.

(See also BYZANTINE EMPIRE.)

OXENHAM, JOHN *(English pirate; Caribbean, Pacific; died 1580)*

From Plymouth, Oxenham was the first English captain to sail the Pacific, having crossed the Isthmus of Panama. He took part in Sir Francis DRAKE's 1572–1573 raid and was second-in-command during the 1573 march to PANAMA. Climbing a tree, Drake saw the Pacific. SIR FRANCIS DRAKE REVIVED reports that he "besought Almightie God of his goodnesse to give him life and leave to sayle once in an English ship on that sea." Seconding Drake's vow, Oxenham "protested that unless our Captaine did beate him from his company he would follow him by Gods grace."

In the event, Oxenham returned before Drake, sailing in April 1576 with two vessels and 57 men, including John BUTLER. Some of Drake's men went along, but Drake himself was not involved. England and Spain had patched up their differences in 1573, and Oxenham's raid had no official license or sanction.

After preying on traffic along the Atlantic coast, the pirates spent the winter of 1576–1577 inland. Oxenham reunited with the *Cimarrónes*, escaped African slaves who had aided Drake. Building a light-draft PINNACE, his company descended a river into the Gulf of Panama in February 1577.

Oxenham's men looted the Pearl Islands, not far from Panama, and ridiculed and tortured a Franciscan friar. They then looted two unarmed ships traveling toward Panama with gold and silver. Oxenham actually took even more booty than Drake in 1573, but he never brought it home.

As the pirates withdrew toward the Atlantic, Spanish forces caught up with them, killed several, and recaptured the treasure. Oxenham, John Butler, and others escaped but were hunted down. In April 1578, 18 Englishmen and about 40 black Africans were taken to Panama. The blacks were returned to slavery, and 14 crewmen were hanged. The officers—Oxenham, Butler, and Thomas SHERWELL—were sent to Lima and executed in late 1580.

(See also SELECTED BIBLIOGRAPHY: Williamson, *Age*; Wright, *Documents*.)

P

PAIN, THOMAS *(English buccaneer; Caribbean; active 1680–1683)*   Pain accepted a pardon from Jamaica's governor in 1682 and promised to give up piracy. In March 1683, while they were pillaging a Spanish wreck in the Bahamas, Pain and four other captains decided to loot the Spanish colony at Saint Augustine, Florida. The Floridians drove them off, and they attacked small neighboring settlements. To end raids from the Bahamas, expeditions from Havana thoroughly plundered NEW PROVIDENCE ISLAND in 1684.

(See also SELECTED BIBLIOGRAPHY: Rogoziński, *Caribbean.*)

PALOMBO, CAPTAIN   *(Maltese corsair; Mediterranean; 1709)*   Captain Palombo attacked French and Muslim merchantmen along the Syrian coast.

PANAMA *(Spanish treasure port; 1545–1737)* The Isthmus of Panama provides the shortest route between the Atlantic and Pacific oceans. Founded in 1519, Panama became important when Peruvian silver mines were discovered during the 1540s. From 1564, it was one of three ports visited by the TREASURE FLEETS linking Spain to its American colonies.

Each year, Peruvian silver was brought to Panama and carried on mule trains across the Isthmus to Nombre de Dios or (after 1595) PORTOBELO. When the winter rainy season filled the Chagres River, goods also could be transported by water. From warehouses at Venta de Cruces, about 20 miles inland, small boats went downstream to the fort at Chagres at the river's mouth.

Merchants at Panama profited both from traffic across the Isthmus and also from the fair held when the fleet arrived at Portobelo. The city was richest when the fleet system flourished, and its prosperity faded after 1620. However, Panama was never as wealthy as covetous pirates imagined. The small houses, entirely built of wood, were closely packed together. In 1607 Panama's 6,000 inhabitants included about 1,000 whites and 4,000 black slaves. There were fewer whites by the 1670s, and most Panamanians were freedmen of mixed race.

English and French pirates invaded the Isthmus from the 1570s, including Andrew BARKER, Jean CAPDEVILLE, Gilbert HORSELEY, and John OXENHAM. Only Sir Francis DRAKE had much luck. Drake robbed Venta de Cruces in 1571 and captured a mule-train carrying silver to Nombre de Dios in 1573. But he had less success in later raids. He turned back before reaching the Isthmus in 1586 and was defeated at Vente de Cruces in 1596.

Following Drake's 1596 raid, the Spanish government strongly fortified Portobelo and Chagres. William PARKER sacked Portobelo in 1602, but the Isthmus was avoided both by the BUCCANEERS and by the DUTCH fleets invading from 1624 to 1640. The Dutch preferred direct assaults on the treasure ships, and the buccaneers considered the Isthmus too strong to attack.

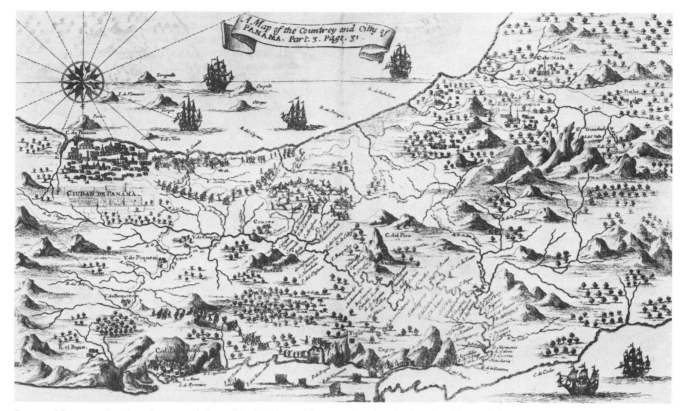

A map of Panama, showing the route followed by Sir Henry Morgan when he plundered and burned the city in 1671. From Exquemelin, *Buccaneers of America,* first Spanish edition (1681).

Pirates returned under Sir Henry MORGAN, who sacked Portobelo in 1688 and captured Panama in 1671. Morgan took significant booty at Portobelo, but his Panama raid yielded little profit. Morgan's pirates burned Panama to the ground, and the Spanish rebuilt the city (now Panama City) at a better harbor six miles away. The jungle had reclaimed the old city when William DAMPIER visited a decade later.

Bartholomew SHARP and other captains looted Portobelo in 1680 and then crossed the Isthmus to attack the new Panama. They defeated a naval squadron but were too few to assault the city. In 1685, Edward DAVIS gathered a large force near Panama. However, a Peruvian fleet sneaked the treasure into Panama City and then drove off the pirates. The buccaneers split up into several bands. Captain TOWNLEY and others raided near the city but did not attack it directly.

(See also LE TESTU, GUILLAUME; SELECTED BIBLIOGRAPHY: Earle, *Sack;* Haring, *Trade.*)

PAPACODA, CAPTAIN *(Italian corsair; Adriatic Sea; before 1560)* Operating from Bari, Captain Papacoda commanded three small ships sponsored by Duchess Bona of Savoy, former queen of Poland. The riches gained pillaging Venetian and other shipping brought Papacoda remarkable social advancement. He was ennobled with the title of marquis, married a niece of the Spanish viceroy of Naples, and lived in a splendid palace in Bari.

PARENT, JAMES *(English pirate; Mediterranean; 1595)* After visiting Venice as an honest merchant, Parent plundered every ship that came within range, including a Venetian vessel taken off Crete.

PARISIO, BROTHER FRANCESCO *(Knight of Malta; Mediterranean; active 1750–1752)* CAPTAIN GENERAL OF GALLEYS, Parisio raided the BARBARY COAST in 1752, capturing two Algerian SHEBECS.

PARKER, CAPTAIN *(English pirate; Atlantic; 1610–1611)* Captain Parker was one of the confederation under Richard BISHOP. In 1610, he sold Thomas HUSSEY a three-quarter share in the *Black Raven,* a 160-ton Flemish man-of-war with 23 guns.

PARKER, WILLIAM *(English privateer; Caribbean; died 1617)* A member of the lesser gentry near Plymouth, Parker took part in Sir Francis DRAKE's 1587 raid on Cadiz, Spain. He cruised in the West Indies each year from 1590, taking several prizes. In 1594 and 1595, he also looted PUERTO CABALLOS in Honduras.

Parker owned his own ship by 1596. After commanding a royal vessel during another raid on Cadiz, he left for the Caribbean in November and fruitlessly cruised in consort with Sir Anthony SHERLEY. Separating from Sherley, Parker attacked Campeche, Mexico. The Spanish forces rallied, drove out the pirates, and wounded Parker. But he did seize a frigate carrying silver to SAN JUAN DE ULÚA.

In February 1601, Parker captured PORTOBELO, the port from which Peruvian treasure left for Spain. En route to Panama, his two ships plundered Saint Vincent in the Cape Verde Islands, held the Cubagua pearl-boats to ransom, and captured a Portuguese slave ship. The Spanish recently had built two strong forts to defend Portobelo, but Parker took the town by trickery and held it for 24 hours. The English ships rendezvoused where Drake's coffin had been thrown overboard in 1596.

Although he missed by a week a large bullion shipment, Parker carried off substantial booty and two frigates from Portobelo. His spoils purchased two more warships, which took prizes under other captains in 1602. He made another voyage to Campeche and Honduras after the war ended in 1603. Spanish charges of piracy were dismissed in 1605.

His booty made Parker a prominent citizen of Plymouth. A follower of Sir Walter RALEIGH by 1595, he became a founding member of the Virginia Company in 1606. He died at Java as vice-admiral of an East Indies expedition.

(See also SELECTED BIBLIOGRAPHY: Andrews, *Elizabethan.*)

PARROTS Parrots flourished in the Caribbean islands and Central America. Although they are not mentioned in contemporary documents, it is possible that some BUCCANEERS kept them for pets. Illustrations to works of popular fiction often show a pirate carrying a parrot on his shoulder. In TREASURE ISLAND (1883), Long John SILVER's parrot constantly shrieks "PIECES OF EIGHT." Robert Louis STEVENSON said he borrowed Silver's parrot from ROBINSON CRUSOE. An alcoholic parrot appears in the movie parody SCALAWAG (1973).

PASSES (PASSPORTS), BARBARY *(safe-conducts; Mediterranean; 17th through 19th centuries)* An official document—sometimes called a "sea letter"—usually issued by a captain's native country or ruler and requesting friendly states to allow a vessel free passage with its crew, cargo, and passengers.

A Mediterranean pass system developed because the BARBARY corsairs were at war with some Christian states but not others. Rulers traditionally issued letters protecting their ambassadors. The practice was expanded to avoid conflicts whenever one ship sought to SEARCH another for enemy nationals or cargo.

Relatively minor officials began to give out passes that were easily counterfeited. Treaties between Britain and ALGIERS (in 1662 and 1682) recognized only passes issued by England's LORD HIGH ADMIRAL or by the governor of Algiers. The treaties guaranteed the safety of each nation's seamen, including those engaged in piracy. Only two men were allowed aboard a ship to inspect its cargo and passenger list.

British consuls received passes printed on a perforated form that could be matched against the detached counterpart. These were issued (for a fee) to a specific British captain and ship for a particular voyage. Although some consuls illegally sold passes to foreigners, the system was used until the 1840s, and it soon was copied in British treaties with TUNIS, TRIPOLI, and MOROCCO.

French treaties with Tunis (1665) and Algiers (1666) required all ships—including naval and corsair warships—to carry passes and produce them on demand. The admiral of France issued French passes, North Africans received them from their rulers or the CAPTAINS OF THE SEA. Other countries also included pass rules in treaties with the Barbary states, and they were almost universal by the 18th century.

Barbary rulers gave corsairs detailed passes, which listed both the countries they could attack and those protected by treaties or truces. Most corsair captains obeyed these pass laws, and the Barbary states promptly punished the rare offenders. Until the early 18th century, British, French, and Dutch captains were less scrupulous. Many seized Barbary ships even though they carried passes.

(See also ALI LUNEL REIS; IBRAHIM LUBAREZ REIS.)

PATER, ADRIAEN JANSZOON *(Dutch admiral; Caribbean; active 1628–1630)* From Edam, Pater commanded 12 vessels for the DUTCH WEST INDIA COMPANY. Arriving in the Caribbean in April 1629, he divided his fleet into two parts, which sacked and burned the poorly defended Spanish towns along the coasts of Puerto Rico, Hispaniola, Jamaica, and Venezuela. Freelance pirates and smugglers followed his warships and took whatever they left behind. In late summer, the raiders rendezvoused north of Cuba, where Piet HEYN had captured the Mexican TREASURE FLEET the previous year. Warned of his coming, the treasure ships remained in port.

The company's directors ordered Pater to stay in the region until God sent him richer prizes. For, they wrote, "the Lord has decided the times and places where and when it shall please Him to bless us." Pater sailed east, destroyed native villages in Guyana and Trinidad, and took Santa Marta, Venezuela, in a sudden slashing assault. The Dutch raiders totally devastated the town and fort, but the booty was meager. After promised reinforcements failed to arrive, Pater returned to the Netherlands in April 1630. During the entire voyage, God had granted him only five prizes.

In April 1631, Pater took his 900-ton flagship and 16 smaller warships to Pernambuco (Recife), Brazil, which the West India Company had occupied in 1630. There he encountered a Spanish armada. The battle became a single combat between the two flagships, during which the Dutch vessel caught fire. Pater, who could not swim, hung from a rope on the prow until he fell exhausted into the sea and was drowned.

(See also LONCQ, HENDRICK; THIJSZ, MARTIN; SELECTED BIBLIOGRAPHY: Goslinga, *Dutch.*)

PAY, HARRY *(English pirate; Atlantic; active 1395–1406)* From Poole on the southern coast, he scoured the Channel near Flanders and plundered northern and western Spain. (Spanish chronicles call him "Arripay.") During one audacious raid in 1395, Poole sacked the town of Gijon and carried off from the altar a crucifix famed for its holiness.

In 1402, Pay seized the *Marie* of Bilbao, laden with iron and rich clothing. The captured crew were beaten and tortured, and many died. Pay brought his prize to the Isle of Wight, put the survivors to sea in a little boat, and refused to make restitution when ordered. In reprisal for his outrages, Pero NIÑO, a Castilian corsair, brought a Spanish squadron to Poole in 1405 and devastated the town so thoroughly that it lost all commercial importance.

Although the English government denounced his Spanish raids, Pay served in an expedition under LORD HIGH ADMIRAL Thomas Berkeley in 1405. The following year, he sailed with a squadron of 15 ships that captured 120 French vessels (some merely fishing smacks). On one occasion, his ship was taken off the Norman coast. Minutes before they were to be executed, Pay and his men overpowered and massacred their captors. Flying the French flag, they took the enemy ship up the Seine, destroying the craft moored in the river. Pay later retired at Calais with a royal pension.

(See also SELECTED BIBLIOGRAPHY: Kingsford, *Prejudice.*)

PAYS, CAPTAIN *(French buccaneer; Caribbean; 1697)* Pays took part in the sack of CARTAGENA.

PECHELINGUE *(Spanish-American slang; 16th and 17th centuries)* The Spanish name (also spelled Pichilingue, Pechelinga) for Dutch pirates and privateers; it sometimes was broadened to include pirates of other nationalities. The word may be derived from the Dutch port of Vlissingen (Flushing).

PEG LEG *(pirate nickname and prosthetic; 15th century and after)* The name (*Pié de Palo* in Spanish, *Houtebeen* in Dutch) given to those replacing a lost leg with a wooden substitute. Among the best known are François LE CLERC and Cornelis JOL.

In fiction, Robert Louis STEVENSON created the peg-legged rascal, Long John SILVER, in TREASURE ISLAND (1883), and there is also a one-legged pirate in PETER PAN (1904). Although real pirates with one leg were rare, movie versions of *Treasure Island* have made peg-legged and pirate almost synonymous. These films were in turn spoofed by other movies, including *The* CRIMSON PIRATE (1952), RAIDERS OF THE SEVEN SEAS (1953), SCALAWAG (1973), and PIRATES (1986).

PELL, IGNATIUS *(British pirate; Caribbean, Atlantic; 1718)* Boatswain of Stede BONNET's ship, Pell testified against the other crewmen and was pardoned.

Kirk Douglas as a peg-legged pirate captain in *Scalawag* (1973).

PENGERAN ANOM *(Malayan pirate; South China Sea; active 1810s)* Illegitimate son of the sultan and actual ruler of Sambas, on Borneo's northwestern coast, Pengeran sponsored and probably led pirate raids. Sambas was a regular base for MALAY pirates, and it was frequently visited by the ILANUNS.

After Anom's raiders looted a British ship in 1811, gunboats attacked Sambas in October 1812. The invaders were repulsed by heavy fire from shore batteries and Ilanun vessels anchored in the river. The British sent a stronger force in June 1813, which captured and sacked the fort and city. However, Pengeran Anom escaped, became sultan in 1814, and continued to encourage piracy.

PENNANT, JEFFERY *(English buccaneer; Caribbean; active 1668–1669)* Pennant commanded a ship during Sir Henry MORGAN's assaults on PORTOBELO (1668) and Maracaibo, Venezuela (1669).

PENPONS, RICHARD *(English pirate patron; Atlantic; active 1450s)* An influential Cornish squire, Penpons managed property for a Cambridge college, was justice of the peace, and held royal commissions to suppress piracy. He used legal tricks to steal property from aged women, and he owned the pirate ship *Kateryn.* On Christmas Eve, 1451, the *Kateryn* captured an English vessel coming from France under a royal safe-conduct and carrying choice wines and other valuable goods. One of the owners, himself a powerful man, unsuccessfully tried for at least 10 years to recover his property. Although Penpons's guilt was obvious, his political influence protected him.

(See also SELECTED BIBLIOGRAPHY: Kingsford, *Prejudice.*)

PENTECONTER *(type of ship; Mediterranean; 1000–250 B.C.)* A GALLEY with one or two banks of oars rowed by 50 men (25 on each side) named from the Greek word for 50. With a relatively long hull, the penteconter was an efficient size for an armed cargo or troop ship. It was faster than the broader merchant galley with a rounded hull and roomier and more stable than the arrowlike TRIREME.

An undecked version is the main troop transport in HOMER's poems. From about 600, navies and sea raiders used a decked version, with or without a ram, as a warship and transport. In 535 the PHOCAEANS and the ETRUSCANS fought only with penteconters. The name disappears in about 250, but ILLYRIAN and CILICIAN pirates continued to use 50-oar ships, equivalent to penteconters.

(See also LEMBOS; SHIPS, PIRATE.)

PERGINANO *(Spanish corsair; Aegean Sea; 1270s)* With the approval of Emperor MICHAEL VIII PALAEOLOGUS, Perginano raided Venetian shipping off Euboea, taking prizes in the harbor of Negropont. In 1273, he offered to go over to Charles of Anjou (ruler of Sicily) with two galleys and 400 men. But he apparently stayed on the Greek side and captured another Venetian merchant vessel in 1274.

PERTUIZET, VINCENT *(Maltese corsair; Mediterranean; 1707)* The French ambassador at Istanbul protested Pertuizet's outrages on the island of Chios. He had broken into the French consul's home, insulted the French flag, and seized a slave already ransomed by French merchants.

PESCATORE, ENRICO *(count of Malta; ruled 1203–1231)* A member of the powerful Di Castello clan in Genoa, called Pescatore ("fisherman") because he "fished" for booty and crews on other people's ships. A follower of Guiglielmo GRASSO, Pescatore married Grasso's daughter, and made himself count of Malta after Grasso's death.

Pescatore often assisted his Genoese kinsmen. Assisted by Guiglielmo PORCO, he helped Alamanno da COSTA and other Genoese expel Pisan merchants from Sicily in 1204 and 1205. In the latter year, he sent three ships and 300 warriors to harass Venetian interests. Off Greece, his men seized two rich Venetian prizes bound for Constantinople. Continuing on to Syria, they helped the crusader lord of Tripoli defeat an insubordinate vassal.

From Malta, Pescatore sought to conquer CRETE, which Venice had purchased in 1204. In 1206, he arrived with a large fleet, occupied Candia and other forts, and declared himself king of Crete. Pescatore received substantial Genoese loans, but the Venetians reconquered the island by 1211.

Although Frederick II—ruler of Germany and Sicily—broke with Genoa in 1220, Pescatore retained his favor.

Frederick named him ADMIRAL of Sicily in 1221, responsible for maritime defense and corsair licenses. In that year, he led 40 galleys to defend crusaders at Damietta, Egypt. Blaming Pescatore for the expedition's failure, the emperor installed his own troops in Malta but left him his title of count. Pescatore gave up his piratical adventures and concentrated on his duties as admiral.

PESO *(silver coin; Caribbean; 17th and 18th centuries)* The main silver coin in Spain's American colonies, the peso was slightly larger than the 19th-century U.S. silver dollar and was also known as a PIECE OF EIGHT.

PETER PAN (1) *(play; first performed 1904; published 1928)* A children's play by the Scottish author J. M. Barrie (1860–1937). Many notable actors have appeared as Captain Hook, including Charles LAUGHTON, Alastair Sim, Sir Ralph Richardson, Sir Donald Wolfit, and Boris Karloff. In theatrical tradition, Peter Pan is played by a woman wearing male garb. The role has attracted such female stars as Fay Compton, Gladys Cooper, Margaret Lockwood, and Jean Arthur. Barrie edited the play in narrative format for a book published in 1911 (originally *Peter and Wendy* but now entitled *Peter Pan*). Other authors have adapted it for musical comedies and movies.

Peter Pan is a pastiche of fairy and adventure stories, such as CORAL ISLAND. The play is about the progression from childhood fantasies to adult reality. Barrie's pirates live only in Neverland and are not meant to resemble specific historical characters. The pirates are both evil and ludicrous. Captain Hook is introduced as "Blackbeard's bo'sun . . . the only man of whom Barbecue was afraid." His crewmen chant menacingly meaningless gibberish, as in the song AVAST BELAY. And Barrie deliberately made his Indians equally unreal. Members of the "Piccaninny tribe," they speak a vaguely Chinese form of gobbledygook.

One night, Wendy Darling and her two brothers are visited by Tinker Bell, a fairy, and Peter Pan, leader of the "lost boys." Having died in childhood, the lost boys live forever in an underground home (sepulchre) on the magical island of Neverland.

Joined by the Darling children, Peter and Tinker Bell fly to Neverland. There pirates endlessly pursue the lost boys; Indians chase the boys and pirates; and wild beasts hunt the Indians. The pirates, mainly from the SPANISH MAIN, are a "villainous-looking lot," crude and physically deformed. They are treated like dogs by Captain Hook, and obey his every command.

Hook himself is a higher class of villain. "Cadaverous and blackavized," his hair is "dressed in long curls which look like black candles about to melt." "Instead of a right hand, he has an iron hook, "and it is with this he claws." Peter Pan once threw Hook's arm to a crocodile, who hungrily pursues him to get the rest.

Dressed as a dandy from Charles II's reign, Hook is elegantly polite—especially while making victims WALK THE PLANK. His language is a melodramatic mimicry of

Victorian costume novels. "Brimstone and gall, what cozening is this?" "Back you pewling spawn."

Peter's battles with Captain Hook are typical of boys' adventure fiction. Peter is younger but cleverer, and children in the audience, however afraid, know that Peter will triumph in the end. As Act Four ends, Tinker Bell drinks medicine poisoned by Hook. She recovers when the audience claps to show it believes in fairies. The crocodile finally eats Hook, and the children go back to the nursery. But Peter stays at Neverland, the boy who will never grow up.

PETER PAN (2) *(motion picture; color; 1953)*
Walt Disney's animated cartoon presents a musical comedy adapted from Barrie's play. The opening scenes in London imply that Peter Pan already had visited the Darling children. Their adventures in Neverland (which Disney renamed "Never Never Land") also differ from those in the play. Thanks to the animated format, this was the first theatrical version in which Peter is not played by a woman and thus is unqualifiedly male. Tinker Bell and the Crocodile actually appear, and the audience does not clap to revive Tinker Bell.

Disney's *Peter Pan* drops any connection to piratical reality and earlier pirate legends. The pirates are harmless and even benign figures of fun. Although they are preposterous, Barrie's pirates are still evil and dangerous, and they thus refer back to historical pirates. Disney's brigands are figures from a child's game and do not resemble real pirates.

PETER PAN (3) *(musical comedy; 1954)*
Jerome Robbins directed and choreographed the comic ballets. Mark Charlap and Jule Styne provided the music, with lyrics by Carolyn Leigh, Betty Comden, and Adolph Green. This Broadway adaptation abbreviates Barrie's 1904 play about Peter and Wendy, the pirates, the Indians, and Neverland; and its mood is much gayer. Emphasizing constant comic movement, it leaves out Barrie's traces of sadness, as well as any vestiges of piratical reality. Mary Martin plays Peter Pan "sky-high with joy,"

Peter Pan balances on the sword of the evil Captain Hook in Disney's cartoon version (1953) of J. M. Barrie's play.

noted Walter Kerr in the *Herald Tribune*. As Captain Hook, Cyril Ritchard hatches his plots to tangoes and tarantellas, and his frolicsome and bouncy crew frightens no one on stage.

Following 82 performances on Broadway, this stage production was broadcast live over television in March 1955. An estimated 65 million viewers watched, the largest television audience up to that time. Additional live telecasts, with the same stars, took place in January 1956 and December 1960, and the latter performance was videotaped for home viewing.

PETER PAN (4) *(musical comedy; 1976)*
A lavish adaption of the Barrie play televised in December 1976, with music and songs by Anthony Newley and Leslie Bricusse. Mia Farrow played Peter, with Danny Kaye as Captain Hook. Julie Andrews sang the opening song.

The text took fewer liberties with Barrie's 1904 play than did Mary Martin's 1954 musical. Despite the sweetly sentimental songs, the voice-over narration (read by John Gielgud) presented Captain Hook as something more than a bumbling clown.

Critics inevitably compared this adaptation to the three television broadcasts with Mary Martin. Most found Mia Farrow less dynamic, while Kaye's comically menacing Hook received higher marks, as did most supporting actors.

PETER THE WHALER *(novel; 1851)*
A boy's adventure story by William Kingston (1840–1880). Peter's father is an Anglican clergyman in Ireland. Led astray by an Irish lout, Peter kills a pheasant and is sent to sea as punishment. He works on a merchantman, an Arctic whaler, and an American naval vessel. Among other adventures, he is abandoned in Greenland and on an iceberg.

While sailing from New Orleans to Havana, Peter is shanghaied by pirates. Until he agrees to enlist, he is guarded by an unpleasant runaway slave named Mark Anthony. The pirate captain, John Hawke, shows touches of noble dignity, like a watered-down version of Lord Byron's CORSAIR. At the same time, he operates like a businessman. The pirates run down small merchantmen, take their plunder to an uninhabited island in the Bahamas, and repackage it for later sale. (Hawke attacks under a solid red flag and not the JOLLY ROGER.)

Peter goes with Hawke's men, as they seize a large bark and tow it to their haven. The pirates plan to set their captives adrift but then set them to work unloading the cargo. It turns out that Peter knows the captured captain and loves his daughter. To help his friends, he agrees to the ship's ARTICLES—not to desert, not to betray a comrade, and not to leave before the band breaks up by mutual agreement.

Peter oversees the pirates guarding the prize, gets them drunk, and helps the captives retake the ship. Meanwhile, an American warship attacks the pirate vessel, which blows up. Tried for piracy with his vengeful pirate shipmates as hostile witnesses, Peter escapes hanging only by joining the navy.

Robert Louis Stevenson mentioned Kingston as one of his sources for TREASURE ISLAND. Peter's ambiguous relationship with John Hawke resembles Jim Hawkins' dealings with Long John SILVER. Before he meets the pirates, Peter is befriended by Silas Flint, a shrewd Yankee seaman who has some of Silver's cunning.

PETIT GOÂVE (pirate haven; Caribbean; 1659–1713)
A port in southwestern Saint Domingue (modern Haiti) frequented by BUCCANEERS. From the 1670s, Petit Goâve replaced TORTUGA as the most important haven for French pirates, including Laurens de GRAFF, Michel de GRAMMONT and Nicholas van HORN. Petit Goâve was farther from the centers of French government than Tortuga, and it was closer to the SPANISH MAIN.

PHILLIPS (PHELLYPPES), JOHN (1) (English pirate; Atlantic, Caribbean; 1540)
Phillips was the first English captain known to have committed piracy in the Americas. In March 1540, he took the *Barbara* from Portsmouth to Brazil. Her 100 crewmen included a dozen Frenchmen, several of whom already had raided the New World.

On the way to the Canary Islands, Phillips captured two prizes off Cape Saint Vincent, Portugal. One was a 40-ton French BARK carrying salt. The second was a small Spanish CARAVEL returning from the BARBARY coast with gold, amber, and other luxury goods. Phillips looted the Spaniard's cargo and took the French bark for his own use.

In May, the *Barbara* arrived north of Pernambuco (Recife), Brazil. No European ships were present, and the native peoples had nothing the pirates wished to steal. Phillips headed northwest and stopped in the "Land of the Cannibals." When eight men went on shore and vanished, Phillips moved on toward Hispaniola.

Near the city of Santo Domingo, the *Barbara* captured a 300-ton Spanish ship with valuable cowhides and sugar. Shortly afterward, the pirates encountered a Spanish GALLEON, which fired at and damaged the *Barbara*. Reaching western Hispaniola, they transferred their cargo to the Spanish ship and set her crewmen ashore. While still at sea, each man took a share of the gold.

After a rough crossing (possibly including a hurricane), the *Barbara* reached England in November with 32 survivors. In response to Spanish complaints, several crewmen were arrested and interrogated, but there is no record of an indictment or trial. Oddly enough, the insurers paid for the *Barbara*, even though she was lost while committing piracy.

PHILLIPS, JOHN (2) (British pirate; Atlantic; died 1724)
Thomas ANSTIS captured the ship in which Phillips, a carpenter, was migrating to Canada in 1721.

Phillips joined Anstis' pirate crew, briefly returned to England, and sailed to Newfoundland in 1723.

In September, Phillips and several others took over a SCHOONER anchored near Saint Pierre Island. During the next six months, Phillips cruised west into the Atlantic, south to Virginia, and perhaps into the Caribbean. He had a long string of good luck and plundered dozens of British, French, and Portuguese fishing boats and merchant ships.

In April 1724, Phillips captured two ships traveling together from Virginia to New York. Edward Cheeseman and John Fillmore (President Millard Fillmore's great-grandfather) were forced to join the pirates, who went back toward Newfoundland. Near Nova Scotia about two weeks later, Phillips took over Andrew Harradine's sloop and kept Harradine on board.

The next day, Harradine, Cheeseman, Fillmore, and others attacked the pirates with axes and hammers. Harradine killed Phillips with a carpenter's adz. His head was cut off, pickled, and hung from the masthead. Fillmore and Cheeseman were tried in Boston on May 12 and acquitted. The court awarded Fillmore some of Phillips's personal treasures, including two gold rings, a silver-hilted sword, and a tobacco box, shoe buckles, and knee buckles made of silver.

(See also SELECTED BIBLIOGRAPHY: Defoe, *General History*; Dow, *Pirates*; Jameson, *Privateering*.)

PHILLIPS, WILLIAM (British pirate; Atlantic; died 1724)
Captured by Captain John PHILLIPS (not a relative) about October 1723, Phillips joined the pirates on the *Revenge*. In February 1724, Captain John Phillips seized a merchantman. William Phillips and four others were put on board and ordered to sail in consort with the *Revenge*. Sometime later, they attempted to go off on their own but were caught by the *Revenge*. During the ensuing battle, William Phillips was badly wounded in the left leg, which had to be amputated.

Since the *Revenge* had no surgeon, the carpenter did the job. He brought up his largest saw, took the leg under his arm, and cut it in two like a board. The carpenter then heated his best axe red hot and cauterized the wound. Unfortunately, he also burned Phillips' body away from the amputated area, and that injury healed badly.

Phillips was among those captured in April when some prisoners took over the *Revenge*. He was hanged at Boston.

PHOCAEA (pirate haven; seventh and sixth centuries B.C.)
A Greek city (modern Foca) on Asia Minor's western coast, between the islands of Lesbos and Chios.

PHOCAEANS (Greek traders and corsairs; Mediterranean; seventh and sixth centuries B.C.)
Renowned for their enterprising seamanship, the Phocaeans traveled in fleets of 50-oared PENTECONTERS rather

than in sailing ships. Mainly dealing in luxury goods, they willingly sacrificed cargo space for speed and miliary strength, and their trading expeditions resembled naval invasions. As bases for their ships, Phocaean mariners founded colonies along the coasts of the Dardanelles and the BLACK SEA.

The Phocaeans made the first Greek voyages to the western Mediterranean, seeking bronze, tin, and silver. From about 640, Phocaean expeditions passed through the Strait of Gibraltar, traded with southwestern Spain, and possibly journeyed to Britain. Their colonies included Massalia (Marseilles) and Alalia (Aleria) on Corsica, close to ETRUSCAN cities.

The Persian Empire devastated PHOCAEA in 546, and many of its inhabitants fled west to Alalia. (But some, including DIONYSUS OF PHOCAEA, remained and again fought the Persians in 495.) The enlarged population of Alalia lived by piracy, "constantly harrying and plundering the neighboring peoples," according to HERODOTUS.

Alarmed by their raids, the Carthaginians and the Etruscans in 535 sent 120 warships against the buccaneers' 60 ships. Although the Phoceans drove off the enemy, 40 of their warships were lost, and the rest were crippled. While the survivors fled Corsica for Greek territories in southern Italy, the Carthaginians and Etruscans cast lots for the captured Phocaean crews. The Etruscan city of Ayglla-Caere won. Outraged by the Phocaeans' piracies, the Caerens stoned them to death, instead of enslaving them or killing them according to religious rituals.

(See also SELECTED BIBLIOGRAPHY: Herodotus, *History.*)

PHOENICIANS *(merchants and slavers; Mediterranean; 1000–600 B.C.)* The Greek and Roman name for the peoples of mixed origin inhabiting the Syrian and Lebanese coast. Never politically unified, the Phoenician city-states included Byblos (now Jubail), Sidon (Saïda), Berytus (Beirut), and Tyre.

From 1000, the Phoenicians replaced the Cretans and Myceneans as long-range sea traders. Highly skilled seamen, they willingly ventured into unexplored regions to trade Near Eastern manufactured goods for raw materials from Africa, Asia Minor, Greece, and the western Mediterranean. Several of their trading posts grew into major cities. Phoenician merchants remained active in the Near East under the Roman Empire. In the west, they were eclipsed after about 600 by merchants from Greece and their own colony of Carthage.

As the Greeks developed their own trading routes and colonies, they accused their Phoenician and ETRUSCAN rivals of piracy and kidnapping. In HOMER's *Odyssey* (before 750), EUMAEUS says that he was abducted by "Phoenicians, men famed for their ships, greedy knaves, bringing countless trinkets in their black ship." ODYSSEUS tells a similar story. He agreed to accompany a Phoenician to Libya, where the lying rogue intended to sell him.

HERODOTUS (about 450 B.C.) also describes the Phoenicians as notorious slave traders. Many years earlier, he relates, they had kidnapped the king's daughter and other women from Argos and sold them in Egypt. Other Phoenicians kidnapped Egyptian priestesses for sale in Libya and Greece. In DAPHNIS AND CHLOE (second century A.D.) Phoenician pirates again are the villains.

It is plausible that Phoenician traders did act as pirates, sinking the ships of rival traders and stealing women and children. Their semi-civilized customers probably overlooked an occasional kidnapping. The crew that stole Eumaeus presumably did not plan to return. And the islanders had to buy from other Phoenician merchants, who were their only source of many luxury goods.

(See also MINOS.)

PICAROON *(British slang; Caribbean; 17th century)* A synonym for BUCCANEER or PRIVATEER from a Spanish word (*picarón*) for pirate, used by novelists for its picturesque sound.

PIECES OF EIGHT *(Spanish coins; 17th through 19th centuries)* Another name for the PESO, with a value of eight *reales*. The Spanish government

"Pieces of Eight! Pieces of Eight!" As the *Hispaniola* prepares to leave the island, Jim Hawkins packs Captain Flint's treasure into bread bags. Illustration by Louis Rhead for a 1915 edition of *Treasure Island* by Robert Louis Stevenson.

minted such vast numbers that they were accepted almost as a world currency and are frequently mentioned in pirate FICTION, including TREASURE ISLAND.

PIERCE (PIERS), JOHN   (English pirate; Atlantic; 1581)
Operating out of Padstow, Cornwall—where his mother practiced witchcraft—Pierce plundered shipping and sold his prizes along England's southern coast. In 1581, royal officials captured him as he brought a prize into Studland Bay, usually a safe harbor for pirates. He bribed the jailer and escaped, but was recaptured and hanged.

PIERCE, WILLIAM   (English pirate; Mediterranean; active 1602–1603)
From a prosperous Plymouth family, Pierce sailed with letters of REPRISAL against Spain. He instead entered the Mediterranean, restocked at TUNIS and Modone, and captured the Venetian merchantman *Veniera* near Crete in May 1602. Its cargo of pepper and spices, worth some 100,000 ducats, was sold in OTTOMAN ports. Early in 1603, Pierce and Thomas SHERLEY seized a Venetian galley and two Dutch vessels. Sentenced to hang on returning to England, he was reprieved after he betrayed his accomplices and paid a fine to the Venetians.

PIERRE, CAPTAIN   (French buccaneer; Caribbean; 1697)
Took part in the Sack of CARTAGENA.

PIERRE, JACQUES   (French corsair; Mediterranean; about 1574–1618)
A Norman, nicknamed "Jacpier," who regarded himself as a Christian crusader against the OTTOMAN EMPIRE. He sailed for a time with the KNIGHTS OF SAINT STEPHEN and helped GUADAGNI DI BEAUREGUARD loot a rich Ottoman convoy in 1608. His fortune made, he retired to Nice in the duchy of Savoy.

In about 1612, Jacques Pierre moved his family and followers to Palermo, accepting lavish offers from the Spanish viceroy of Sicily. On the way back from the Levant in 1613, he captured an Ottoman convoy worth more than a million ducats. In July 1616, his six GALLEONS ran into and drove off 50 Ottoman galleys.

In the summer of 1617, Jacques Pierre suddenly fled to Venice and offered his services to the French duke of Nevers, who was planning the conquest of Greece. The following May, a close friend told the Venetians that Jacques Pierre really had not quarreled with the Sicilian viceroy. In fact, he and the viceroy were plotting to place Venice under Spanish control. Letters from the viceroy to Jacques Pierre seemed to confirm the accusation. The Venetians caught up with his squadron and stabbed him to death.

(See also CARLO EMMANUELE I; USKOKS.)

PIKE   (naval weapon; 3000 B.C. to 19th century)
A spear, up to 16 feet long, with a sharply pointed head of iron or steel, the pike was thrust at the enemy, not thrown. During the 17th century, bayonets attached to MUSKETS replaced pikes on land, but seamen continued to use them to repel boarders.

PILLAGE   (pirate custom; all eras)
Goods not belonging to the cargo proper were not part of the BOOTY, which was divided with the ship's owners and suppliers at the end of the voyage. Victorious crew members might share these small goods, or each man might keep his own loot. Under English customs, for example, the crew kept everything above the main deck as well as the possessions of the captive passengers and crew. Various pirate HAVENS followed different rules, and pillage also was regulated by contracts (ARTICLES) between the men and the ship's captain or owner.

PINK   (type of sailing ship; Mediterranean, Baltic, Atlantic, Pacific; 15th to 19th centuries)
A small vessel with a flat bottom, bulging sides, and a narrow stern. In Mediterranean usage, a pink (from the Italian word *pinco*), was a cargo ship something like a SHEBEC, only higher and flatter on the bottom. In the Baltic and Atlantic, the term (from the Dutch word *pincke*), was used for any small ship with a narrow stern. During the 17th and 18th centuries, large square-rigged pinks were built as merchantmen and warships.

(See also SELECTED BIBLIOGRAPHY: Defoe, *General History*.)

PINNACE   (type of ship; 16th through early 20th centuries)
During the 16th century, a light and narrow ship of about 20 to 60 tons. Propelled by both oars and a sail or sails, it often was used as a dispatch boat or tender for a larger vessel. In later centuries, a ship's boat with eight to 16 oars and a detachable mast.

(See also LONGBOAT.)

PINTO, FERNÃO MENDES   (Portuguese author; about 1510–1583)
Pinto's supposed autobiography was published (Lisbon, 1618) in Portuguese with the Latin title *Peregrinacam de Fernam Mendez Pinto* (*The Travels of Mendes Pinto*). His story of Asian adventures from 1537 to 1558 includes rollicking accounts of French, Malay, Portuguese, Chinese, and Japanese pirates.

Modern scholars agree that Pinto's book—intended as a satire of Portuguese imperialism—mixes fact and fiction. Although he recounts fictitious incidents, Pinto did travel to India, Malaysia, and Japan. In describing countries he did not visit, Pinto borrowed information from books by earlier travelers. Pinto's *Travels* was extremely popular during the 17th century. Like a modern historical romance, it presents a dramatic story set in a historical framework.

Pinto grew up, according to his *Travels*, beset by poverty and hardships that included capture by French pirates. He went to India in 1537, arriving as the Portuguese and the OTTOMAN EMPIRE struggled to control the spice trade through the Indian Ocean and Red Sea.

While traveling in the Red Sea and Ethiopia, Pinto is captured by the Ottomans and enslaved at Mocha and

Hormuz. He returns to India and then moves on to Malacca in Malaya. After an attack by a MALAY pirate, Pinto and other Portuguese turn buccaneer in the South China Sea and along China's northern coast. Arrested by the Chinese, the Portuguese are freed by Tartar invaders, and a Chinese pirate junk carries Pinto to Japan in 1542 or 1543.

Pinto returns to further adventures in Malaya, Sumatra, and Java. Sailing to China as a merchant, he is attacked by Japanese pirates, shipwrecked, and again enslaved for a time. After a stay in Siam, Pinto returns to Malacca. He makes three more voyages to Japan, where he assists Saint Francis Xavier and other Jesuit missionaries. He returns to Portugal in 1558, and the narrative ends four years later.

PIRATA, IL *(two-act opera in Italian; 1827)* A work by Vincenzo Bellini (1801–1835) about the final days of Count Gualtiero di Montalto, Sicilian nobleman turned pirate during the late 13th century. *Il Pirata* was immediately popular throughout Europe and North and South America. Revived in 1935, the opera has been staged as a vehicle for leading sopranos, including Montserrat Caballé and Maria Callas.

The libretto refers to events 10 years earlier, when Charles of Anjou and the king of Aragon disputed rule over Sicily. Gualtiero and the beautiful Imogene were deeply in love. Duke Ernesto di Caldora also loved Imogene. In his jealousy, Ernesto helped the Angevins win Sicily and drove Gualtiero from the island. By imprisoning Imogene's aged father, he forced her to marry him.

Gualtiero fled to Aragon, recruited a pirate squadron, and warred on the Angevins. To end his raids, Duke Ernesto attacked with the entire Sicilian navy. Defeated after a long battle, Gualtiero fled in a single vessel and was shipwrecked near Caldora, where Imogene languishes.

In the opera, Gualtiero meets Imogene and rebukes her for marrying his persecutor. He wants her to leave Ernesto and flee with him. Living together at sea, he sings, they will find relief for their misery. But Imogene replies that she sacrificed herself to save her father's life. As a wife and mother, she now belongs to her husband and infant son.

Informed secretly that his enemy is visiting his home, Ernesto bursts in upon Imogene and Gualtiero. The two men duel, and Gualtiero kills Ernesto. A council of knights condemns Gualtiero to death. Imogene becomes insane and raves about her love for Gualtiero. (See also PERGINANO.)

PIRATE, THE (1) *(novel; 1822)* Sir Walter Scott (1771–1832) describes the effect of outsiders on a closed community in about 1700. Scott borrowed the general plot and description of pirate life from Daniel DEFOE's GENERAL HISTORY, especially the biography of John GOW. Clement Cleveland, the pirate of the title, seems to be a demonic villain, who denies all civilized values. As the book ends, however, the reader learns that he is not as completely evil as he initially appeared. He stops his brutal crew from murdering and raping prisoners, and he dies bravely, fighting for his country.

The novel is set in the Zetland and Orkney Islands, near Scotland. The Zetlanders are fishermen who trade with passing ships and harvest the goods from wrecked ships. According to their superstitions, a stranger saved from drowning eventually will injure his rescuer. In defiance of Zetland prejudice, Mordaunt Mertoun saves the life of Clement Cleveland, a daring and glamourous raider. Cleveland has commanded corsairs, raided the SPANISH MAIN, and plundered TREASURE FLEETS. A worldly adventurer, he sees no difference between his own piracies and the Zetlanders' wrecking.

Welcomed into the home of Magnus Troil, Cleveland wins the love of Magnus' daughter Minna, who thinks of pirates as romantic heroes. More realistic than her sister, Brenda Troil distrusts Cleveland. Mordaunt also dislikes Cleveland and is jealous of his worldly glitter. (Without knowing it, the two men are half-brothers.)

Cleveland understands Minna far better than she does him. He knows that she loves an imaginary hero and not the bloody plunderer he has been. When he confesses his crimes, Minna is horrified and insists that he give up piracy. Cleveland learns that a vessel visiting Orkney is the consort of his own wrecked ship. He leaves to break with his former comrades.

The night before he sails, Cleveland serenades Minna. She hears and dimly sees a struggle. The next morning, both Cleveland and Mordaunt are gone. Believing that Cleveland has slain Mordaunt, Minna wastes away from melancholy guilt. Magnus Troil takes her and Brenda to Orkney to pray in the cathedral.

Meanwhile, Cleveland is forced to rejoin the pirates and then is taken hostage by the magistrates. As they voyage to Orkney, Magnus and his daughters are captured by the brigands. Minna's disgust swells when she see the drunken, blasphemous, and ferocious crew. Even if he repents, she can never marry a man involved in pirate deeds of cruelty and carnage.

Mordaunt, who was only wounded by Cleveland, saves Minna and Brenda from the pirates and restores them to their father. In a last stolen meeting with Cleveland, Minna renounces him forever. She is left an old maid when Mordaunt marries Brenda, her more sensible sister.

PIRATE, THE (2) *(motion picture; color; 1948)* In this spectacular musical comedy, directed by Vincente Minnelli, songs by Cole Porter (and others) make fun of theatrical life. Thanks to its extravagant choreography and stylish self-mockery, *The Pirate* has become a cult classic. Among its targets, *The Pirate* spoofs *The* BLACK PIRATE, *The* SEA HAWK, and other corsair epics. As Serafin, an actor/clown pretending to be a pirate, Gene Kelly walks tightropes, scales walls, and twirls a cutlass like a true SWASHBUCKLER. In the acrobatic "Pirate Ballet,"

Infuriated when she learns he is merely an actor and not a buccaneer, Manuela (Judy Garland) smashes a picture down on Serafin (Gene Kelly) during *The Pirate* (1948).

Kelly surpasses even the stunts of Douglas FAIRBANKS and Errol FLYNN.

Manuela (Judy Garland) lives on an island in the Spanish Caribbean, during the 1820s. Outwardly a demure young lady, Manuela secretly fantasizes about Macoco, a notorious pirate. Her Aunt Inez (Gladys Cooper) arranges Manuela's marriage to Don Pedro Vargas (Walter SLEZAK), their village's dull but wealthy mayor.

Manuela and Aunt Inez visit a coastal town to collect her trousseau. There Manuela meets Serafin, who leads a band of strolling actors. Intrigued by Serafin, she sneaks out that night to watch his performance. After Serafin hypnotizes her as part of his act, Manuela reveals her love for Macoco in a tempestuous song, "Mack the Black." Serafin breaks her trance with a kiss, and Manuela flees in humiliation.

Serafin and his troupe follow Manuela to her village, arriving on her wedding day. Serafin walks a tightrope across the town square and enters Manuela's bedroom. When Don Pedro comes to throw him out, Serafin realizes that the mayor is the former Macoco but agrees not to reveal his secret. Taking advantage of Manuela's infatuation with the pirate, Serafin pretends that he himself is Macoco. Overwhelmed, Manuela fantasizes the "Pirate Ballet," in which she sees Macoco (Serafin/Kelly) plundering ships and slaying all who oppose him.

Serafin takes over the mayor's house and threatens to sack the village if he does not get Manuela. Manuela is

thrilled to learn that "Macoco" loves her. She goes to the mayor's house, where one of Serafin's troupe accidentally reveals the ruse. Enraged, Manuela throws everything in sight at Serafin, who is knocked unconscious. She realizes that she loves him, even though he is only an actor and not a real pirate.

Meanwhile, Don Pedro has returned with the militia and the viceroy (George Zucco), who sentences Serafin to hang. Allowed to give a final performance, Serafin tries without success to hypnotize Don Pedro. Manuela pretends to fall into a trance and tells the crowd she loves "Macoco" (Serafin) and is disgusted by Don Pedro. As she sings "Love of My Life" to Serafin, Don Pedro is overcome with jealously, reveals his true identity, and is arrested. Manuela joins Serafin's troupe, and the film ends with the two lovers in costume, giving a rollicking performance of "Be a Clown."

PIRATE AND THE SLAVE GIRL, THE *(French/Italian motion picture; color; 1961)* During the 15th century, DRAGUT (Lex BARKER) has captured Bianca (Graziella Granata), daughter of the governor of RHODES. The governor releases Captain Diego (Massimo Serato) from prison, so he can rescue Bianca. Diego join's Dragut's band, but the pirates catch him staring at Bianca. Dragut is furious, since he plans to sell Bianca to Princess Miriam (Chelo Alonso), who will force her into prostitution. At Dragut's orders, the pirates beat Diego and leave him for dead. Helped by heroic fishermen, Diego recovers and rescues Bianca from Dragut and Miriam. Directed by Piero Pierotti.

PIRATE MOVIE, THE *(motion picture; color; 1982)* This film was rushed into production to beat Joseph Papp's The PIRATES OF PENZANCE (1983). Some original Gilbert and Sullivan songs are mixed with pop music, musical references to other movies, spoofs of SWASHBUCKLERS, and deliberately anachronistic wisecracks. Critics savaged the movie but liked Kristy McNichol as Mabel. Christopher Atkins plays Frederick, Ted Hamilton is the pirate king. Directed by Ken Annakin.

PIRATE OF THE BLACK HAWK, THE *(French/Italian motion picture; color; 1961)* Richard (Gerard Landry) leads the good pirates fighting Manfred (Andrea Aureli), whose evil pirates have seized the throne. Manfred forces marriage on Eleanor (Mijanou Bardot), the deposed duke's daughter. On their wedding day, Richard's band attacks, and a long battle ensues. When Eleanor and her attendants flee to the dungeons, Manfred orders the rooms flooded. Richard rescues the women, and Manfred is impaled on his own booby-trap. Directed by Sergio Grieco.

PIRATES *(motion picture; color; 1986)* A combination comedy and SWASHBUCKLER directed by Roman Polanski. Captain Thomas Red (Walter Matthau), a peg-legged old BUCCANEER, is adrift on a raft in the Caribbean. He is starving and tries to eat his companion, a

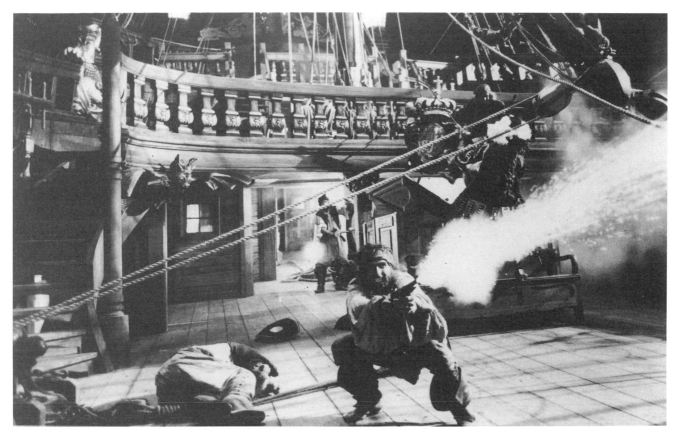

A mutiny breaks out aboard the Spanish galleon in *Pirates* (1986).

young and pretty French seaman known as Frog (Cris Campion).

The Spanish GALLEON *Neptune* appears, commanded by the dying Captain Linares (Ferdy Mayne). As Red and Frog clamber aboard, Red's wooden leg sticks in a crack, and he loses his treasure chest. Linares' lieutenant, the arrogant and elaborately overcostumed Don Alfonso (Damien Thomas), has Red and Frog imprisoned in the hold.

Red learns that the *Neptune* carries immensely rich Aztec treasure, the gold throne of Kapatek-Anhuach. Red and Frog are put to work, and they stir up a mutiny. They are forced to eat a rat, narrowly escape hanging, and finally take over the *Neptune*. Their prisoners include the lovely Dolores (Charlotte Lewis), niece of Maracaibo's governor, with whom Frog falls in love. When they reach the island where Red's crew are living, Red offers Dolores and the others to Dutch (Roy Kinnear), an unscrupulous trader.

Don Alfonso retakes the *Neptune*, and Red pursues him to Maracaibo. Using Dolores as a hostage, Red forces the governor to help recapture the Aztec throne. The scheme fails, and Red and Frog are imprisoned awaiting execution.

Red's crew rescues them, but Don Alfonso already has sailed away with Dolores and the throne. Catching up, Red scuttles his own ship, forcing his crew to board the *Neptune*. During the final battle, Frog and Don Alfonso

fight a wild duel. Alfonso and Dolores escape in a lifeboat, while flames engulf the galleon. Dawn finds Red and Frog once again adrift in a small boat. This time they at least have food as well as the captured throne.

Director Polanski spent substantial sums on *Pirates*, including $8 million to construct the *Neptune*. Critics considered the movie boring and unwatchable, and it was not widely distributed in the United States. However, some reviewers commended Walter Matthau who embodies icy and obsessive greed as the wily Captain Red. Polanski spoofs movie swashbucklers that had loosely adapted nonfactual romantic novels.

The pirates and Spaniards bear little resemblance to real life. Polanski said he wanted to lampoon pirate movies, especially the 1950 *Treasure Island*. Like Robert NEWTON as Long John Silver, Matthau constantly rolls his eyes and lips while roaring and cursing in a thick unclassifiable accent. There are many one-line jokes and sight gags, often scatological.

PIRATE SHIPS   See SHIPS, PIRATE.

PIRATES OF BLOOD RIVER, THE   *(British motion picture; color; 1962)*   In this film, directed by John Gilling, French Protestants have settled a West Indian island early in the 18th century. Their leader's son, Jonathan Standing (Kerwin Matthews), is falsely accused of adultery and banished to a penal colony. He escapes but falls into the hands of cut-throat corsairs led

Kerwin Matthews taken captive in *The Pirates of Blood River* (1960).

by LaRoche (Christopher Lee), an evil captain with an EYE PATCH and a useless left arm.

LaRoche persuades Jonathan to lead them to his island, where the settlers have buried hordes of treasure. After a lengthy battle, LaRoche takes over the island and kills many settlers to make them reveal the treasure's hiding place. Jonathan escapes with his stepsister Bess (Maria Landi) and her fiance Henry (Glenn Corbett).

LaRoche discovers that the statue of Jonathan's grandfather is made of pure gold. He orders his crew to drag it to the beach and load it on a raft. Jonathan's followers ambush the pirates on the raft. The statue falls overboard and sinks. Jonathan kills LaRoche, and the pirates leave.

This adventure movie stresses action and gory battle scenes. Kerwin Matthews is an adequately dashing SWASHBUCKLER, and Christopher Lee plays the cunning pirate chief with sinister aplomb.

PIRATES OF PENZANCE, THE (1) *(comic opera; 1879)*   A two-act opera, with libretto by W. S. Gilbert (1836–1911) and music by Sir Arthur Sullivan (1842–1900). *Pirates* opened in New York to thwart theatrical "pirates" who failed to pay royalties. An instant success, it has been translated into many languages. Sullivan's music wittily supports Gilbert's satire of British social foibles. The songs mimic Elizabethan and Italian tunes and operas by Beethoven, Bizet, Gounod, Purcell, Verdi, and various Italian composers.

Boisterous pirates, bumpkin policemen, unmarried daughters—all were stock characters in the Victorian melodramas and burlesques that *Pirates* parodies. Gilbert and Sullivan make it clear that their pirates are two-dimensional cardboard cutouts, not referring to any historical reality. The pirates wear something like 17th-century CLOTHING, but they plunder 19th-century Cunard liners. They genteelly sip sherry instead of guzzling RUM.

On a beach in Cornwall, pirates hold a sherry party celebrating Frederic's 21st birthday. Frederic intends to quit the group as soon as his term of duty expires. He became their apprentice through a mistake by Ruth, his nursemaid.

Frederic points out that the pirates are too tender-hearted. Being orphans themselves, they release anyone that says he shares the same predicament. In "OH, BETTER FAR TO LIVE AND DIE," the pirate king defends his profession as more honest than supposedly respectable careers.

After the pirates leave, Frederic hides as the daughters of Major-General Stanley appear. Frederic is starved for love, and Mabel, the youngest girl, falls for the "poor wandering one." Meanwhile, the pirates have crept up unseen. Each grabs a girl, demanding marriage. Stanley comes in and announces that he is "the very model of a modern Major-General." The pirates release their captives when Stanley pretends to be an orphan.

In Act Two, Frederic prepares to join a police assault on the pirates. Ruth and the pirate king appear. They explain that Frederic must rejoin them until he actually celebrates his 21st birthday. Since he was born on February 29, Frederic's birthdays are four years apart, and he will not be free until 1940! Bound by his sense of duty, Frederic agrees and tells the pirate king that Major-General Stanley is not really an orphan. Vowing to kill Stanley, the king rushes out. Frederic joins him, after he and Mabel promise to remain faithful.

The police hide as the pirates creep up, singing a loud chorus. Stanley and his daughters come in. The pirates seize them and overcome the police. All appears lost when the prostrate police sergeant tells the pirates to yield, "in Queen Victoria's name!" The pirates surrender since "they love their queen." However, Ruth explains that the brigands are all "noblemen who have gone wrong." Stanley instantly pardons them and gives them his daughters "because, with all our faults, we love our House of Peers!"

PIRATES OF PENZANCE, THE (2) *(motion picture, color; 1983)*   In 1980, producer Joseph Papp and director Wilfred Leach presented Gilbert and Sullivan's opera as a musical comedy with dance insertions. The very successful stage version won several Tony awards, and Papp and Leach created a movie adaptation. With one exception (Angela Lansbury as Ruth), the Broadway stars appear in the movie. Two soft-rock singers, Rex Smith and Linda Ronstadt, perform as Frederic and Mabel. Kevin Kline plays the Pirate King, George Rose appears as Major-General Stanley, and Tony Azito is the Police Sergeant.

The movie faithfully follows Gilbert's libretto. William Elliott, the arranger and conductor, significantly changes Sullivan's orchestration, speeding up the tempo and emphasizing brass over strings. Elliot retains Sullivan's allusions to 19th-century operas. He adds references to more recent music, from Elvis Presley songs to Jeanette Mcdonald-Nelson Eddy movie operettas.

This movie version presents a song-and-dance reinterpretation of Gilbert and Sullivan's mockery of 19th-century pirate melodramas. The original opera is a biting satire on Victorian social pretensions, softened in perfor-

The stars of the 1983 movie version of *The Pirates of Penzance* (1983).

Paul Henreid kills an enemy in *The Pirates of Tripoli* (1955).

mance by its daffy plot and the elegant acting of the D'Oyly Carte Opera Company. Papp's Broadway revival downplayed Gilbert's wit and focused on the plot's silliness. The movie adds visual references spoofing earlier pirate films. In a joking allusion to Douglas FAIRBANKS' gymnastic feats in *The* BLACK PIRATE, the Pirate King climbs the rigging but then falls down. The dancing policemen are photographed from above, as in a Busby Berkeley musical.

PIRATES OF THE SEVEN SEAS   *(British motion picture; black and white; 1941)*   Directed by Harold Schuster, this film was entitled *Queer Cargo* in England. Captain Harley (John Lodge) commands a freighter, whose crew mutinies. Just then, pirates led by Monty Cabini (Kenneth Kent) invade the ship looking for smuggled pearls. After some tense confrontations, Lodge's crew outslugs the pirates.

PIRATES OF TORTUGA   *(motion picture; color; 1961)*   Director Robert Webb's adventure-romance epic was intended for juvenile audiences. As does BLACKBEARD THE PIRATE (1952), it portrays Sir Henry MORGAN as an unredeemed villain.

The English government hires Bart Paxton (Ken Scott) and sends him to TORTUGA to destroy Morgan (Robert Stephens) and his gang of blackguards. On the way, he falls in love with a Cockney stowaway named Meg Graham (Leticia Roman). The wily Morgan is pre-

pared for Paxton's assault, and his pirates battle their attackers. Morgan and Paxton fight with swords and are knocked out. The governor of Tortuga is about to hang them both as pirates. Paxton is saved when Graham reveals his true identity, and Morgan goes to the gallows.

PIRATES OF TRIPOLI   *(motion picture; color; 1955)*   The wicked Malek (John Miljan) and his armies overrun the kingdom of Princess Karjan (Patricia Medina). In desperation, she turns to a lusty band of pirates led by Edri-Al-Gadrian (Paul HENREID). After several sea battles (some quite rousing) pasted against stock footage, they expel the ravaging hordes. Directed by Felix Feist.

PIRATES OWN BOOK, THE   *(horror stories; 1837)*   Charles Ellms' best-seller helped create the legend that all pirates were fiends. A former retailer in Boston, Ellms anonymously published almanacs and compilations with appealing titles. Ellms borrowed his materials from earlier authors without mentioning their names, and he inserted lurid fictional details to spice up the story. *The Pirates Own Book*, Ellms' most popular concoction, ran through at least nine editions.

Nineteenth-century readers liked violence in exotic foreign places, and they loved to be terrified by ghost stories and tales of buried TREASURE. Ellms cut and pasted his materials to appeal to these prurient interests. To placate the pious, he added moralizing statements suggesting that "crime does not pay."

The author's preface tells the reader what to expect. Throughout history, Ellms says, inhuman fiends have tortured and killed without mercy. Hence everyone fears the

> desperate exploits, foul doings, and diabolical career of these monsters in human form. A piratical crew is generally formed of the desperadoes and runagates of every clime and nation. . . . [who] pursue their diabolical career with impunity.

During their off hours, Ellms declares, pirates enjoy low pleasures in savage hideouts.

> The pirate is truly fond of women and wine, and when not engaged in robbing, keeps maddened with intoxicating liquors, and passes his time in debauchery. . . .

Stories about buried treasure are true, Ellms adds. Pirates always bury their booty, and many are captured before they can dig it up. Thus they leave behind

> rich plunder, caskets of buried jewels, chests of gold ingots, bags of outlandish coins, secreted in lonely, out of the way places . . . near rocks and trees bearing mysterious marks, indicating where the treasure was hid. . . . Immense sums remain buried in those places, and are irrecoverably lost.

Ellms took roughly half of his stories from Daniel DEFOE's GENERAL HISTORY. Defoe presents a mixed bag of biographies. He portrays some captains as brutes, others as virtuous refugees from a corrupt English society. Ellms copied only the goriest tales and left out heroic figures such as Captain MISSON.

In addition to Defoe's brigands, Ellms includes Charles GIBBS, Benito de SOTO and other 19th-century rogues. He also reprints materials about Jean LAFFITE and Arab, Malay, and Chinese pirates. Surprisingly, Ellms does not include any Caribbean buccaneers, despite EXQUEMELIN's grisly stories about François L'OLONNAIS and others.

When their villains were not sufficiently evil, Ellms attached fictional details to his borrowed biographies. For example, Ellms plagiarized Defoe's chapter on William KIDD (Ellms calls him "Robert"), with three additions. Always eager to play up buried treasure, Ellms fantasizes about Kidd's booty after Defoe's biography ends.

Earlier, Ellms asserts that Kidd was a monster from youth, "a nondescript animal of the ocean." (This contradicts Defoe, who says that Kidd was honest until his final voyage.) Before sailing, Ellms also claims, Kidd buried his Bible, which "condemned him in his lawless career." Readers liked Ellms' Bible story, which became part of the CAPTAIN KIDD legend.

PIRI REIS *(Turkish admiral; Mediterranean, Red Sea, Indian Ocean; active 1510–1552)* A nephew of KEMAL REIS, Piri may have served under ARUJ BARBAROSSA in North Africa. In 1517, he presented Sultan Selim I with a naval handbook (revised in 1525), which included accurate maps of recent Spanish and Portuguese discoveries in the Americas and Africa. In 1551–1552, Piri Reis brought 23 galleys through the Red Sea into the Persian Gulf. After sacking Muscat, Piri's squadron besieged for some weeks the Portuguese castle at Hormuz, although it was outnumbered by the defenders.

PISTOL *(firearm; about 1530–1850)* When gunpowder is ignited by a "slow match," the weapon cannot be fired with one hand. Smooth bore muzzle-loaders using the expensive "wheel-lock" system appeared from the early 1500s. The cheaper "flintlock" mechanism, perfected during the early 1600s, was widely adopted by 1650 and remained standard for two centuries.

Pistols had barrels up to a foot long and fired a relatively large ball. A few expensive guns were made with several barrels, but most were single-shot. Some cavalrymen carried pistols, but they generally were too inaccurate and expensive for combat. They were personal-defense weapons, which could be concealed.

Ship's records rarely mention handguns, since pirates owned their personal weapons. Portraits show aristocratic captains, such as Sir Martin FROBISHER, with wheel-lock pistols. As they became cheaper from the late 17th century, some corsairs of BARBARY and MALTA used flint-lock pistols.

Flintlocks also entered the Caribbean during the late 1600s—after the BUCCANEERS were suppressed. (EXQUEMELIN and other contemporary observers write of MUSKETS but not pistols.) About 1718, BLACKBEARD carried "three Brace [pairs] of Pistols, hanging in Holsters like Bandaliers," Daniel DEFOE wrote in his GENERAL HISTORY. More than one was needed, since pistols often misfired due to an incorrectly placed flint or damp powder.

PLAN, JUAN DE See SORES, JACQUES.

PLANTAIN, JOHN *(British pirate; Indian Ocean; active 1719–1721)* According to his own story (which cannot be verified), Plantain was born in Jamaica. He sailed on a pirate ship to West Africa and joined Edward ENGLAND's crew in 1719. When England was marooned, he stayed on the *Cassandra* under John TAYLOR and shared in his fabulously rich Portuguese prize.

After the loot was divided, Plantain retired at MADAGASCAR with a Scot named James Adair and a Dane named Hans Burgen. At Ranter (Antogil) Bay, the three pirates built a stockaded fort, visited by a British naval squadron in 1723. Calling himself the "King of Ranter Bay," Plantain had furnished the primitive rooms with rare Oriental treasures from his booty. His harem of local women were dressed in Indian silks and flaunted priceless diamond necklaces.

In some stories Plantain later conquered Fort Dauphin to the south and proclaimed himself king of Madagascar. Because of his cruelty, the native peoples rebelled and drove him out. These stories say he reached India and commanded a ship for ANGRIA.

(See also SELECTED BIBLIOGRAPHY: Downing, *Indian Wars.*)

PLAUTUS, TITUS MACCIUS *(Roman playwright; died about 184 B.C.)* Plautus wrote more than 130 plays (of which 21 survive), which are something like modern musical comedies. Spoken dialogue alternated with duets and arias in works with frequent verbal jests, slapstick farce, and exaggerated characters. Although he often borrowed his plots from earlier Greek authors, Plautus added new elements parodying his own time, and his works were extremely popular.

Judging by Plautus, pirate slave raids were a constant hazard. Many plots involve characters who had been carried off by corsairs and sold into slavery. In *The Braggart Warrior (Miles Gloriosus)*, pirates had captured Palaestrio's ship and sold him to the boastful soldier. Daemones's daughter suffered a similar fate in *The Rope (Rudens)*. In *The* TWO BACCHIDES, Chrysalus expects his master to believe his tale of an imaginary pirate attack.

Plautus' pirates are sinister figures. "Such are pirates: They never show mercy to anyone" is a fragment from the lost play *Caecus*. They are neither adventurous or figures of exceptional evil (as in modern legends of BLACK-BEARD), and they generally get their way by trickery. In *The Two Bacchides* and in *The Two Menaechmi*, pirates come on land to spy out the destinations of merchant ships. (CILICIAN corsairs used the same scheme.)

PLAYS See FICTION, PIRATE.

PLUMEN, CAPTAIN (British pirate; Mediterranean; active 1694–1697) Operating from LIVORNO, Captain Plumen captured French ships even though his COMMISSION forbade this. The French envoy demanded satisfaction from the grand duke of Tuscany. In court, Plumen argued that someone else owned his warship. Moreover, he was British, and Britain was at war with France. Unconvinced by these defenses, the grand duke jailed Plumen and fined him £6,000.

POLLACA/POLACRE (pirate ship; Mediterranean; 17th and 18th centuries) As used by the BARBARY corsairs, it had two or three masts, each formed from a single spar so it had neither a top nor crosstrees. The three-masted version usually was lateen-rigged on the fore and mizzen masts and square-rigged on the main mast. The two-masted version carried square sails.

POLYCRATES (Greek ruler; Aegean; about 570–522 B.C.) Polycrates became the sole ruler ("tyrant" in Greek) of the island of SAMOS about 535. Like many other Greek city-states, Samos' rulers had favored piracy, unless foreigners came from a city allied with them through a formal treaty. As ruler, Polycrates vastly expanded and sponsored Samian raids throughout the Aegean.

Polycrates took advantage of the political chaos following the Persian conquest (in 540) of Lydia on the western coast of Asia Minor. The Persian victory disturbed the traditional balance of power in the region and removed Samos' main rivals. The Persians had destroyed PHOCAEA, and Polycrates defeated Miletus, weakened by internal strife and civil war. Until the Persians conquered PHOENICIA in the 520s, Samos had the only large navy in the region.

Polycrates did not seek permanent conquests, and he simply expanded the Samians' traditional corsair adventures on an immensely larger scale. His warships raided cities on the Asian mainland controlled by Persia. They also looted the Greek islands in the Aegean, permanently occupying Lesbos and Rheneia (a small island near Delphi).

The Greek historian HERODOTUS describes Polycrates' cynical policy of indiscriminate piracy.

> For wherever he sent expeditions, everything went well for him. He possessed 100 fifty-oared ships and 1,000 archers. He raided and plundered all alike, drawing no distinctions between any. For, as he said, he would put a friend under a greater obligation by giving back things he had previously taken away from him than by not taking them in the first place.

Polycrates' captured wealth won him popularity at home. He built a magnificent temple to the goddess Hera, a new harbor and fortifications, and other public works. Many citizens also gained booty or were paid for serving with his fleet. Polycrates's power and wealth ultimately attracted the envy of the Persian viceroy of Asia Minor, who tricked him into a meeting on the mainland and then crucified him.

POLYREME (oared warships; Mediterranean; 399–31 B.C.) A large GALLEY derived from the TRIREME. No galley ever had more than three banks of oars. Naval architects instead added men to each oar in various combinations. For example, a Roman "five" might have one bank of rowers with five men on each oar. Or it could have two banks with three men on the upper oars and two on the lower. For practical reasons, eight men to each oar was the upper limit, and the "sixteen" was the largest galley used in combat.

With more oarsmen, polyremes had a wider deck with more space for carrying marines and catapults. But they were slow, heavy, expensive to operate, and unstable in bad weather. Most navies ultimately gave up the largest sizes, which were easily encircled by fleets of smaller, more nimble ships such as the pirate LEMBOS or LIBURNIAN.

POMPEY (Roman noble family; first century B.C.) The common English form of Pompeius. Two members played a large role in the history of piracy. In 67, Gnaeus POMPEIUS smashed the pirates based in CILICIA. From 43 to 36, his son Sextus POMPEIUS placed himself at the head of corsair bands that ravaged the Italian coasts.

POMPEIUS, GNAEUS (Roman general; Mediterranean; 106–48 B.C.) In 67, Gnaeus Pompey commanded a mammoth sea and land operation that crushed the pirates of CILICIA, perhaps the most powerful corsairs in European history. Unlike other leaders of anti-pirate campaigns, moreover, Pompey defeated the corsairs in large naval battles. (Naval forces almost never succeeded in forcing combat upon pirates, who usually escaped to fight another day.)

To deal with the Cilicians, the Roman Senate passed a law awarding Pompey unprecedented powers. He received unlimited military and judicial authority throughout the entire Mediterranean and up to 50 miles inland (thus giving him control of the wealthiest cities). The Senate also provided Pompey with 24 *legates* (assistants) with unlimited authority to carry out his orders anywhere in Rome's empire. The law granted Pompey the staggering sum of 6,000 TALENTS and empowered him to call up troops and requisition or construct ships as needed. He is said to have commissioned 270 ships and raised 120,000 soldiers and 5,000 calvary.

Many senators opposed so sweeping a grant of personal power, but popular pressure forced passage of the law. The Cilician pirates had harassed the eastern Mediterranean for many years. During the previous two decades, they had carried their attacks westward and assaulted Italy's coasts. On several occasions, the Romans had attacked pirate bases in Cilicia. But these partial efforts failed, since pirates driven from one port simply sail to another. By 67, the pirates controlled the seas, and prices soared as commerce came to a halt. Faced with actual hunger, the Roman mob demanded a massive naval campaign.

Seeking a chance to increase his military reputation, Pompey had made his plans long before his appointment as supreme admiral. His campaign was a masterpiece of strategy, carefully and rapidly carried out. Pompey divided the Mediterranean and Black seas into 13 districts and placed each under one group-commander. These legates simultaneously blockaded or attacked each of the major pirate havens. Through concerted action, they frustrated Cilician attempts to reinforce comrades threatened by superior forces. Pompey himself commanded a mobile force of 60 warships. This swept the western seas in only 40 days, driving the pirates toward the stationary fleets of the legates.

Many pirates surrendered themselves and their ships. Pompey treated them with moderation, pardoning their crimes in return for information. The most desperate retreated to the castles along Cilicia's bleak coast. Pompey gathered an enormous force prepared for mountain warfare and equipped with catapults and other siege-engines. In a major sea battle off the Cilician coast, the Romans defeated the corsair fleet. The survivors retreated to Coracesium, a fortress connected to the land only by a narrow isthmus.

But resistance was hopeless. After a short siege, Coracesium's defenders capitulated, and the pirates in other Cilician ports also threw themselves on Pompey's mercy. Pompey continued to treat them leniently. Instead of executing them—the normal punishment under Roman law—he settled his captives on inland farms in Cilicia itself or in Achaea, a region in Greece depopulated by war.

The entire campaign took only three months. The ancient historians say 10,000 pirates died in battle, and twice as many were captured. Pompey's forces captured more than 120 pirate fortress and bases, 98 warships, and hundreds of smaller craft. The main strongholds in Cilicia provided rich booty. They also contained many corsairs' victims, held for ransom or as slaves. Some returned home to read their own headstones, since their relatives had assumed they were dead.

His rapid and thorough victory greatly impressed Pompey's contemporaries. He received a second grant of extraordinary powers in 66 and spent the next four years establishing Roman power in the Near East. But Pompey proved a better general than a politician. On his return to Rome, he became at first an ally and then an opponent of Julius CAESAR, who defeated his troops in 48.

During this civil war, pirates again sailed from the ports of Cilicia, Syria, and ILLYRIA—with the largest fleet, ironically, being led by Pompey's son SEXTUS. Piracy finally ended only when the emperor Augustus established a permanent Roman fleet. But corsair bands never again were as large or as aggressive as those Pompey destroyed during the summer of 67.

POMPEIUS, SEXTUS *(Roman noble; Mediterranean; 76?–35 B.C.)* The younger son of Gnaeus POMPEIUS, Sextus from 43 to 36 commanded corsair bands based in Sicily. At its height, Sextus's fleet included more than 300 ships. The last major pirate navy during ancient times, it controlled the western Mediterranean and ravaged cities along both coasts of Italy.

Julius CAESAR's defeat of his father and older brother (in 45) left Sextus as the leader of the Pompeian faction. The civil war following Caesar's assassination in March 44 gave the young man an opportunity to vindicate his family's honor. After routing the Republican forces in 42, Octavian and Mark Anthony warily cooperated for several years and then fought for control of the empire. (Octavian defeated Anthony in 31 and assumed the title of Augustus Caesar in 27.)

During these years of strife, Sextus Pompey never aspired to rule the Roman Empire. From a base in Sicily, he instead fostered piracy on a grand scale. Caesar had seized Gnaeus Pompey's lands and possessions and sold them at a sham auction. Sextus relied on sea power to regain the wealth and respect due him as his father's son.

At first sight, Sextus' recourse to piracy seems bizarre, since his father had destroyed the CILICIAN corsairs in 67. He undoubtedly felt that piracy provided his best means of gaining power. Moreover, Gnaeus Pompey had sympathized with and shown leniency to the Cilicians surrendering to his forces. In the Roman tradition, the pirates pardoned by the elder Pompey became his family's hereditary clients and owed service to his son. Many were delighted to do their duty to Sextus by taking up their former trade.

Sextus survived the Pompeian defeat in 45 by raising troops in Spain and practicing robbery and piracy. The size of his fleet vastly increased in the spring of 43 when the Senate—not yet controlled by Octavian—made him commander of the Roman fleets and maritime coasts.

This command was similar to that held by Gnaeus Pompey during the Cilician war. It gave Sextus control of all shipping in the western Mediterranean, including at least 150 warships.

Octavian seized control of Rome in August 43, killed his political opponents, and seized their property. Shortly thereafter, Sextus occupied Sicily, and his lieutenants later seized Sardinia and Corsica. His forces became a refuge for Roman nobles and senators fleeing Octavian's persecution, and he also welcomed thousands of debtors and runaway slaves. Skillful sailors flocked to Sextus from Africa, Spain, and the East. All the ambitious pirates joined him, attracted by the large scale of his operations.

Sextus' senatorial appointment as supreme naval commander legitimized his activities, since Octavian's subsequent seizure of power was unconstitutional. However, his tactics differed little from those of the Cilician pirates 20 years earlier. Instead of aiding the senatorial forces fighting Octavian and Mark Anthony, Sextus' ships carried out massive raids on the Italian coasts. His admirals were former pirates. The most talented of them, MENAS and MENECRATES, were of Cilician origin and had been liberated from slavery by Gnaeus Pompey.

As in the days of the Cilicians, Rome suffered from famine, because Egyptian and African grain ships refused to sail. Octavian tried to invade Sicily in 42, but his admirals were no match for Sextus' more expert seamen. When the Roman mob rioted over the soaring price of food early in 39, Octavian was forced to make peace. The Treaty of Misenum strongly favored Sextus, who was promised southern Greece, high office in Rome, and an enormous sum of money in compensation for his father's property.

But neither Octavian nor Sextus kept his word, and pirate ships continued to prevent food from reaching Rome. According to Octavian, captured pirates confessed under torture that they acted under Sextus' orders. While these charges may be false, Sextus did not attempt to control the pirates. Most of his followers would have deserted, had he tried to stop their raids for booty.

Octavian renewed his attacks on Sicily in 38 after bribing Menas—Sextus' chief admiral—to surrender Corsica and Sardinia and 60 warships. The future emperor assembled two large fleets and several legions. But Sextus' forces defeated the invaders in battles off Cumae (near Naples) and in the Strait of Messina. In 36, Octavian assembled another fleet. Near the Bay of Naples, a great storm destroyed many ships. Octavian persevered. His troops managed to land in Sicily, and his admirals finally succeeded in defeating Sextus' corsairs off Naulochus (near Milazzo) late in 36.

Sextus fled Sicily as soon as he learned of this defeat and headed east. Stopping to loot a temple in southern Greece, he settled for a time on Lesbos and then moved to Asia Minor. There he was captured by Mark Anthony's soldiers and died, toward the end of 35.

Sextus' flight abandoned his followers to Octavian's cruel punishments. Octavian fined those of high social rank and condemned other free Roman citizens to service with the army. No mercy was shown to the many corsairs who were runaway slaves. A large number—one source says 30,000—were handed back to their owners for punishment. Those not claimed by any master, Octavian killed by the cruel death of impalement.

PONTALIER, BROTHER THALLEMEY DE *(Knight of Malta; Mediterranean; active 1624–1625)*
As CAPTAIN GENERAL OF GALLEYS, Pontalier raided Santa Maura in 1624 and captured 178 slaves. He was wounded in 1625 during a battle off Sicily between five Maltese GALLEYS and six from TUNIS.

(See also IONIAN ISLANDS).

POPE, DUDLEY *(British author; born 1925)*
Pope's novels feature two sea captains. Lord Nicholas Ramage is a naval officer during the Napoleonic period. Ned Yorke is the buccaneer hero of BUCCANEER, ADMIRAL, CORSAIR, and GALLEON. Pope also has written nonfiction books, including a biography of Sir Henry MORGAN.

Pope's writing is taut and fast-moving. Without interrupting the action, the Ned Yorke novels pass on information about the Caribbean, seamanship, weapons, and currencies. Pope brings naval and land battles to life while carefully describing 17th-century military technology.

While these technical details are fastidiously accurate, Pope is less careful about the general historical setting. To excuse Yorke's piracy, Pope describes his Spanish opponents as cruel, dishonorable, and physically repulsive. He presents Yorke's buccaneers as Jamaica's only defense against these Spanish invaders. In fact, Spanish officials never sent a fleet against Jamaica, and they did not license privateers until 1669. Spanish TREASURE FLEETS followed fixed routes, different from those in the novels. The PORT ROYAL pirates did not call themselves the BRETHREN OF THE COAST.

Pope's male characters are among the most realistic in pirate fiction. Yorke is not a romantic superhero. He doubts, questions his perceptions, and ponders his decisions. His friend Sir Thomas WHETSTONE is more flamboyant but still convincing. Their buccaneer followers are normal human beings who have fallen into crime.

Pope's female characters are less plausible. York and Whetstone cruise with their mistresses, Aurelia and Diana, and other female pirates. There is no evidence that large buccaneer fleets cruised with women on board during the 17th century. (Anne BONNY and Mary READ raided in Jack RACKHAM's small SLOOP in the 1720s, after Caribbean piracy had dwindled away.) Moreover, Aurelia and Diana expound feminist beliefs commonplace during the 1980s but not expressed during the 17th century.

(See also SELECTED BIBLIOGRAPHY: Rogoziński, *Caribbean.*)

PORCO, GUGLIELMO *(Italian corsair; active 1205–1221)* From a high-ranking Genoese merchant

family, Porco sailed as a pirate from Palermo, Sicily. As a reward for various services, the rulers of Sicily named him ADMIRAL by 1211. Ignoring a peace treaty, he captured two treasure ships from Marseilles. When Frederick II quarrelled with Genoa in 1221, Porco lost his post and fled Sicily.

(See also PESCATORE, ENRICO.)

PORTE, BROTHER PONZIO DE LA *(Knight of Malta; Mediterranean, active 1578–1610)* He commanded a galley and raided merchant shipping in the eastern Mediterranean. He was CAPTAIN GENERAL OF GALLEYS from 1609 to 1610.

PORTOBELO *(Spanish treasure port; Caribbean; 1595–1737)* A town in central PANAMA (its name sometimes spelled as Porto Bello or Puerto Bello) with an excellent harbor on the Caribbean Sea. Reacting to Sir Francis DRAKE's recent capture of Santo Domingo and CARTAGENA, the Spanish government in 1586 sent the Italian engineer Juan Batista Antonelli to strengthen the ports visited by the TREASURE FLEETS. Founded in 1595, Portobelo (which replaced Nombre de Dios) received the treasure carried across the Isthmus from the city of Panama on the Pacific coast. A stone highway connecting the two cities was built during the 18th century.

Drake's men destroyed Portobelo in 1596, but strong new forts were constructed. Despite its defenses, it was captured by William PARKER (1601), Sir Henry MORGAN (1668), and John COXON (1680) as well as by a British fleet under Edward Vernon (1739). The last treasure fleet arrived in 1737. The city became unimportant following the construction of the trans-Panama railroad (1848–1855) and the Panama Canal.

PORT ROYAL *(buccaneer haven; Caribbean; 1657–1680)* A series of cays and sandbars, forming a peninsula off Kingston in southern Jamaica. After they took Jamaica in 1655, English forces strongly fortified the peninsula, and the town sheltered some 3,000 persons by 1671. Port Royal offered a superb natural harbor, protected from storms and providing waters 30 feet deep a few yards from shore.

When the English fleet returned home, Governor Edward D'Oyley feared a Spanish reconquest. Beginning in 1657, D'Oyley lured buccaneer captains away from TORTUGA by setting up prize courts and offering PRIVATEERING commissions of doubtful legality. At least 12 captains—French, Dutch, and English—moved to Port Royal by 1660. Compared to Tortuga, the harbor was far superior and better defended, and the town offered a larger market for loot. Port Royal also lay at the very heart of the Spanish Caribbean, close to trade routes and near the treasure ports of PORTOBELO and CARTAGENA.

When the Spanish war ended in 1660, the pirates ignored D'Oyley's orders to halt hostilities. Lord Thomas Windsor, who became governor in 1662, received ambig-

The Port Royal buccaneers, led by Sir Henry Morgan, sack Puerto Principe, Cuba, in 1668. From Exquemelin, *Buccaneers of America,* first English edition (1684).

uous instructions. Privateers still had to obtain licenses from London. However, Windsor could erect admiralty courts and issue commissions to defend the island. Windsor and his successors took advantage of this legal confusion and publicly welcomed pirates. Declaring that the Spaniards were planning to invade Jamaica, Windsor unleashed the brigands. By 1663, Port Royal housed 22 ships carrying 1,200 men. Sir Christopher MYNGS led highly profitable raids on Cuba and Honduras.

Jamaican piracy reached its peak under Sir Thomas MODYFORD. As governor, Modyford ignored orders to suppress the raiders and allowed the sale of Spanish prizes. During a war with Holland (1665–1667), he commissioned raids against Spanish as well as Dutch colonists.

Even though the war ended in 1667 and England and Spain signed a commercial treaty, the pirates continued to devastate Spanish shipping and cities. With Modyford's commissions, Sir Henry MORGAN sacked Portobelo, Venezuelan cities, and PANAMA. Although the English government publicly scolded Modyford, officials privately condoned the raids to force concessions from Spain.

Morgan's Panama raid, occurring after a peace treaty in 1670, infuriated the Spanish government. Sir Thomas Lynch became governor, arrested Modyford and Morgan, and sent them to England. Lynch offered pardons to those quitting piracy and tried to suppress the others. However, pirates continued to operate surreptitiously until 1680.

Lynch and his successors lacked the naval force to pursue pirates. In 1675, Henry Morgan returned as lieutenant governor and admiralty commissioner. Morgan favored pirates and illegal slave traders and helped them escape justice. The earl of Carlisle, governor from 1678 to 1680, also tolerated pirates as protection against French attack. He thus allowed John COXON and Richard SAWKINS to sell goods plundered in Honduras.

After Carlisle left in 1680, Sir Henry Morgan (still lieutenant governor) turned against the pirates and sent out vessels to pursue them. Jacob EVERSON and others were caught and hanged. Thomas Lynch, who returned as governor from 1682 to 1684, continued Morgan's work. The Jamaican legislature finally passed an effective law against piracy in 1681. Lynch took strong action against Jean HAMLIN and tried to persuade Laurens de GRAFF to accept an English pardon.

When Jamaican authorities acted against them, the pirates sought other havens at the Bahamas or the Carolinas. The most ambitious followed Coxon, Bartholomew SHARP, and John COOK across Panama into the Pacific. After they returned to the Caribbean, Cook went to Virginia, Sharp to England, Coxon to the Bahamas.

The English conquest of Jamaica had proved a terrible blow indeed to the Spaniards. Between 1655 and 1680, Jamaican pirates sank hundreds of merchant ships, and they sacked countless villages and 22 major towns, several more than once.

Jamaica's governors told London that they needed their bloody allies to counter a Spanish invasion. Until Britain sent naval squadrons, they also claimed, the raiders would simply move to French Tortuga or Dutch Curaçao. It was better to keep the pirates at Port Royal, which was enriched by their booty. The first excuse obviously was false. There never was a real threat of Spanish invasion, and the pirates refused to fight military troops in any case. The second justification was more truthful, since pirate booty quickly passed to Port Royal's inhabitants.

Under English law, a tenth went to the LORD HIGH ADMIRAL, another fifteenth to the king. Cheating was widespread, and the government received only a tiny fraction of its share. Governor Modyford and other officials took large fees and bribes. The rest went for provisions and services to maintain the ships and crews. A few captains, notably Morgan and Lawrence PRINCE, used their loot to buy plantations. Most, as Exquemelin reported, squandered their shares.

Port Royal merchants profited at both ends. They bought stolen goods and treasure cheaply and resold them in London. With part of their profit, they brought in supplies and marketed them to the pirates at a very high markup. Pirate wealth made Port Royal a major city by 1680, larger than any other English or French settlement except Boston. Measured by its bustling commerce, per-capita wealth, and military strength, Port Royal equalled many ports in Europe. Taverns and PROSTITUTION flourished. But the town also included an elegant Merchants Exchange and stone dwellings built with pirate money.

In 1692, a powerful earthquake dissolved a huge slice of the peninsula, plunging much of the town to the ocean's bottom. Perhaps 2,000 persons perished, half or more of the inhabitants. Preachers throughout England and Europe rejoiced at God's punishment of this most wicked city. By then, however, the pirates had been gone for a dozen years, and Port Royal's citizens long since had laundered their booty.

(See also SELECTED BIBLIOGRAPHY: Dunn, *Sugar;* Haring, *Buccaneers;* Pawson, *Port Royal;* Rogoziński, *Caribbean.*)

PORTUGUES, BARTHOLOMEW *(Portuguese buccaneer; Caribbean; active 1650s)* Known only by his nickname ("the Portuguese"), he sailed from Jamaica soon after the English conquest in 1655. According to EXQUEMELIN, he was bold and ruthless but cursed by constant bad luck.

Prowling the coast of Cuba in a small boat with only 30 men and four guns, Bartholomew came upon a larger ship. The buccaneers boarded, were beaten back by the Spaniards, but took their prey on the second try. Half the pirates were killed or wounded, but they had won 70,000 PIECES OF EIGHT and 120,000 pounds of valuable cacao beans. Unable to return to Jamaica because of contrary winds, the pirates made for western Cuba. Near Cape San Antonio, three Spanish ships, sailing from Mexico to Havana, captured the pirates and stripped them of their plunder.

Bartholomew Portugues. From Exquemelin, *Buccaneers of America,* first English edition (1684).

Tyrone Power tries to trick two brigands, played by George Sanders and Anthony Quinn. Power sports gypsy-hoop earrings, while Quinn wears an eye patch. From *The Black Swan* (1942).

Soon after, a severe storm forced the ship holding the buccaneers to return to Campeche. The townsmen recognized Bartholomew as the leader of the marauders who had ravaged the Yucatan coast. Since he had previously given them the slip, the Spaniards kept Bartholomew on board the ship while they erected a gallows.

Bartholomew, who spoke good Spanish, overheard the sailors discussing the hanging. During the night, he killed the sentry with a stolen knife. Taking two earthenware wine jars, he leaped overboard and floated ashore. After a difficult journey through 120 miles of harsh wilderness, he reached Sad Gulf (*El Golfo Triste*), just west of Cape Catoche on the eastern tip of the Yucatan Peninsula. At this pirates' HAVEN, he found a ship with buccaneers from Jamaica.

With a canoe and 20 men, Bartholomew returned to Campeche and recaptured the ship on which he had been imprisoned. Since they thought his canoe was smuggling contraband from the town, the Spaniards did not resist. Although the gold had been taken out, plenty of merchandise remained on board.

Bartholomew's bad luck continued to haunt him. The ship ran aground on the Isle of Pines, south of Cuba. The survivors fled in their canoe to Jamaica and immediately set off in quest of new booty. According to Exquem-

elin, Bartholomew "made many violent attacks on the Spaniards without gaining much profit from marauding, for I saw him dying in the greatest wretchedness in the world."

POSTUMIUS *(pirate captain; Ionian Sea; died 339 B.C.)* Afer reconquering Syracuse, Sicily, the Greek general Timoleon seized and killed Postumius, who marauded with 12 galleys. Postumius put in at Syracuse because its merchants previously had welcomed him and his booty. DIODORUS OF SICILY calls Postumius a "TYRRHENIAN" (Etruscan), but his Latin name indicates that he was of Italian birth.

POWER, TYRONE *(American actor; 1913–1958)* Descended from a long line of actors, Tyrone Power appeared on stage in Chicago and New York before signing with Twentieth Century-Fox in 1936. Blessed with sweet-faced good looks and an insouciant manner, he was groomed as the studio's answer to matinee idols such as Errol FLYNN.

By 1943, Power was a top box-office attraction, having appeared in some 20 films. He was most often cast as the romantic lead in costume pictures, such as *Lloyds of London* (1937), *Marie Antoinette* (1938), *In Old Chicago* (1939), *The Mark of Zorro* (1940), and *Blood and Sand*

(1941). In 1942, he starred in *The* BLACK SWAN, a classic pirate spectacular with several stirring SWORD DUELS.

Power enlisted in the Marines during World War II and emerged from combat a tougher man, his baby-face gone forever. He received good notices for dramatic roles in *The Razor's Edge* (1946) and *Nightmare Alley* (1947), and he also appeared in lavish historical romances, including *Captain from Castile* (1947), *Prince of Foxes* (1949), and *The Black Rose* (1950). He died of a heart attack in Madrid, while filming a dueling scene in *Solomon and Sheba*.

PRAHU *(Malay warship; South China Sea; 16th century to present)* *Prahu* simply means "boat," but the word normally refers only to seagoing vessels of MALAY design. Pirate warships were built sharp in the prow and wide in the beam and could exceed 90 feet in length. They generally had two decks, and the space inbetween might be partly open. Most had one large sail, usually lateen, and up to a hundred rowers, who sat cross-legged, about a foot above the water line, on the lower deck or on strong outriggers. The warriors stood on the upper deck during battle, regardless of danger and ready to board their prey. By the 19th century, many prahus carried brass CANNON fore and aft as well as numerous swivel guns along the sides.

PRESTON, SIR AMYAS *(English admiral; Atlantic, Caribbean; died 1617?)* Preston was born into a gentry family in Somerset County. In 1585, he and Bernard DRAKE jointly commanded a squadron, partly financed by Preston's father. The two captains planned to follow and reinforce Sir Richard GRENVILLE's expedition, sent to ROANOKE, Virginia, by Sir Walter RALEIGH.

When the Spanish seized English ships in May, Preston and Drake instead were ordered to plunder Spanish and Portuguese vessels in Newfoundland. They captured a Brazilian sugar ship on the way over, and Preston immediately took it back to England. Bernard Drake continued on and took valuable booty. After Drake died, Raleigh and his partners refused to turn over Preston's share, under his consortship agreement with Drake. Preston sued, and the Privy Council eventually forced Raleigh to pay up.

After raiding in the Channel in 1587, Preston was seriously wounded while battling the Spanish Armada in 1588. In 1589, he marauded in the Azores with the earl of CUMBERLAND, and he also financed two warships that raided under George SOMERS, his friend and partner.

In 1595, Preston commanded an unusually powerful buccaneering venture. Assisted by Somers, William PROWSE, and a Captain Jones, Preston led four warships carrying 300 soldiers. Only Sir Francis DRAKE and Cumberland took larger forces to the West Indies. Preston's squadron was supposed to support Sir Walter Raleigh's Guyana expedition. After destroying Spain's Venezuelan bases, Preston was expected to keep a rendezvous with Raleigh at Trinidad. In fact, Preston left England five

weeks after Raleigh and made no attempt to catch up with him.

Thanks to Preston's bold and resolute leadership, the raiders sacked Puerto Sancto (in the Madeira Islands) as well as Caracas and Coro in Venezuela. But the loot and ransoms from these poor towns did not cover the venture's cost. Preston and Somers finally met up with Raleigh as he returned from Guyana and joined him in an unsuccessful hunt for Spanish ships. The entire incident makes sense only if Preston was still angry over Raleigh's unfair split of the booty in 1585.

As did George Somers, Preston became a high-ranking naval officer in later years. He commanded the flagship during a large raid on Cadiz in 1596, and he also took part in the 1597 Azores expedition. In 1601, he was vice-admiral of a fleet that battled the Spanish at Kinsale, Ireland. Preston challenged Raleigh to a duel after another quarrel in 1601, but the two men apparently never fought. He was knighted in 1596 and received a lucrative office at the Tower in 1603. He took an active part in founding the Virginia Company.

PREVESA *(battle site; Ionian Sea; 16th century)* A gulf (modern Préveza) in western Greece just north of the IONIAN ISLAND of Levkás and guarded by a powerful fort. It was the site of important land and naval battles between Christian and Ottoman forces.

PREVESA, BATTLE OF *(corsair naval victory; October 25–28, 1538)* Led by North African corsairs, the OTTOMAN battle fleet met and defeated Andrea Doria commanding the combined navies of Venice, the papacy, Genoa, and Spain. KHEIREDDIN BARBAROSSA was the Ottoman admiral, while TURGUT REIS commanded the right wing, and SALIH REIS led the left.

Doria commanded about 130 full-sized galleys as well as 30 sailing ships (including two GALLEONS). Kheireddin had only 90 galleys and 50 smaller GALIOTS. But he superbly managed his smaller fleet and forced Doria's retreat. Turgut and Salih's expert seamanship in holding to the line of battle (no easy task with oared galleys) advanced the Ottoman triumph.

The Venetians, losing confidence in their allies, made a separate peace and gave up their last Greek and Aegean strongholds. More important, by repulsing the fleets of the only Christian powers with significant navies, Kheireddin's victory gave the Ottomans control of the Mediterranean for more than 30 years. Thanks to the protection of the Ottoman battle fleet, the Spaniards could not reconquer the corsair bases at ALGIERS, TUNIS, and TRIPOLI.

(See also SELECTED BIBLIOGRAPHY: Guilmartin, *Gunpowder*.)

PREZIOSI, GERONIMO *(Maltese corsair; Aegean Sea; active 1739–1741)* When he returned from cruising in a SIAMBECCHINO, Preziosi's financial backers (including Francesco NATALE and Giacomo NATALE) sued

Forced to walk the plank, Bob Hope (dressed as a gypsy woman) is rescued by Featherhead (Walter Brennan). From *The Princess and the Pirate* (1944).

him, and his ship was auctioned off to clear his debts. The records from Preziosi's trial include his ledger of prizes sold while in Greek waters, the only surviving example of a document every Maltese captain was required to maintain.

(See also SELECTED BIBLIOGRAPHY: Earle, *Corsairs.*)

PRINCE, LAWRENCE (Dutch buccaneer; Caribbean; 1670)

A native of Amsterdam, Prince sailed from PORT ROYAL, Jamaica. In 1670, he took three ships up the Magdalena River in Colombia, hoping to sack the important town of Mompos, over 150 miles inland. The buccaneers were driven back by cannon fire from a Spanish fort, recently erected on an island in the river.

Determined to gain booty, Prince left in August for Nicaragua and succeeded in an almost identical adventure. The pirates went up the San Juan River, captured the fort, and paddled in canoes up to Lake Nicaragua. There they sacked the city of Granada, already raided by John MORRIS and Sir Henry MORGAN in 1664. According to the Spanish report, Prince "made havoc and a thousand destructions, sending the head of a priest in a basket and saying that he would deal with the rest of the prisoners in the same way unless they gave him 70,000 pesos [£17,500] in ransom." The previous assault had impoverished Granada, and the buccaneers secured only £12 per man.

Governor Thomas MODYFORD forgave this blatant act of piracy and sent Prince to join Henry Morgan's PANAMA expedition. Impressed by Prince's fighting spirit, Morgan made him third in command after himself and Edward COLLIER. Prince and John Morris led the buccaneer vanguard during the final battle with Panama's defenders.

Following the illegal Panama raid, Thomas Lynch became governor and arrested Modyford and Morgan. Without any military force of his own, Lynch tried to co-opt rather than to suppress Morgan's followers. Lynch made Captain Prince his own lieutenant, describing him as "a sober man, very brave, and an exact pilot." He settled in Jamaica and was given a substantial plantation.

(See also SELECTED BIBLIOGRAPHY: Cruikshank, *Morgan*; Earle, *Sack.*)

PRINCESS AND THE PIRATE, THE (motion picture; color; 1994)

Caribbean piracy, Hollywood-style, provides the setting for Bob Hope's one-liners in this film, directed by David Butler. Although the pirate background elicits sight gags, Hope's jokes mainly refer to celebrities and politics in 1944.

Hope plays a second-rate actor called "Sylvester the Great—Man of Seven Faces." Looking for work, Sylvester sails to Jamaica during the mid-1700s. In the next cabin is the British king's daughter, Princess Margaret (Virginia Mayo), who has run off to marry a commoner.

Loutish pirates attack their ship. Their dastardly leader is Captain Barrett (Victor McLaglen), called HOOK after the deadly weapon replacing his right hand. The pirates defeat the crew in a surprisingly straightforward battle scene. Hook kills his captives but spares the princess to collect a ransom. Sylvester, a self-described coward, survives by impersonating an aged gypsy woman.

A crazy, constantly cackling old pirate, aptly named Featherhead (Walter Brennan), steals Hook's treasure map and gives it to Sylvester. Escaping in a LONGBOAT, Sylvester and the princess arrive at the island of Casa Rouge, a tacky pirate town. To earn money, they take their vaudeville act to the Bucket of Blood, a louche bar filled with murderous cut-throats. The rowdy clients throw tomatoes at Sylvester. They toss gold coins at the beautiful princess, who sings the movie's one song, "Kiss Me in the Moonlight."

Governor La Roche (Walter SLEZAK) catches their act and recognizes Princess Margaret. The evil governor holds her for ransom, and he also keeps Sylvester, convinced that he is Margaret's lover. While La Roche lusts after the princess, crazy Featherhead shows up and tatoos the treasure map on Sylvester's chest.

Captain Hook arrives. He has been the governor's partner, but the two villains quarrel. Featherhead shoots Hook, and the pirates attack and overcome the palace guards. Masquerading as Hook, Sylvester takes the princess back to the ship, and the real Hook arrives soon after. The two captains drive the pirates crazy with conflicting orders until Sylvester and the princess are caught and imprisoned.

The two are saved when her royal father appears in a battleship and captures the pirates. The king (Robert Warwick) tells Princess Margaret he will let her marry whomever she wants. She walks past Sylvester and embraces her true love—Bing Crosby (playing himself).

The Hook character was borrowed from PETER PAN. He and his low-life crew also are reminiscent of the 1934 TREASURE ISLAND. Both Hook and Sylvester/Hope (when he impersonates Hook) strut about, SWEARING and bellowing out phrases such as "SHIVER MY TIMBERS." Walter Slezak recreated his character of the corrupt and greedy governor in *The* SPANISH MAIN.

PRIVATEER, THE (novel; 1952)

Using the pseudonym "Gordon Daviot," Elizabeth Mackintosh (1896–1952) narrates the story of Sir Henry MORGAN's raids. Mackintosh's historical novels, often ascribed to "Josephine Tey," enjoyed both popular success and critical esteem.

The novel's Morgan is unusually attractive. For EXQUEMELIN, Morgan was a greedy butcher who cheated his crewmen. As a secondary character in several movies, he is either corrupt or eccentric and overweight. Here, in contrast, Morgan is a resolute leader of men, as noble as Rafael SABATINI's heroes. (Exquemelin appears in the novel as a physically and morally unattractive man, whose lying stories are prompted by jealousy.)

Condensing the actual events, the novel leaves out Morgan's 1664 raid on Central America. Morgan is an indentured servant at Barbados. Set free when his owner's plantation fails, he runs into a small gang of cattle-thieves. With only a longboat, they overpower a Spanish vessel (a feat originally attributed to Pierre LE GRAND).

Morgan goes on to TORTUGA. Allied with John MORRIS, he captures other Spanish vessels and arrives at Jamaica as Sir Thomas MODYFORD becomes governor. Morgan attacks PROVIDENCE ISLAND with Edward MANSFIELD and then leads the assaults on Puerto Principe, PORTOBELO, Maracaibo, and PANAMA. The novel mixes fictional crewmen with real buccaneer captains, including Joseph BRADLEY, Bernard SPEIRDYKE, and Charles HATSELL.

Morgan's raids were inspired, in this version, by hatred of the Spaniards, who cruelly imprisoned his friends. Morgan easily overcomes Spanish soldiers and colonists, who are cowards as well as evil. He treats his prisoners honorably, forbids torture, and punishes rape. (Contemporary records suggest that Exquemelin came closer to the truth.)

Morgan did not cheat the men after looting Panama. Instead, Mackintosh says, the Spaniards stole back a chest with most of the treasure. Morgan's wife is a spirited woman who understands his ambitions. His followers are ordinary seamen—uneducated, footloose, and improvident—and not bloodthirsty fiends.

(See also CUP OF GOLD; MORGAN (2), SIR HENRY.)

PRIVATEERS, ANCIENT (Mediterranean; about 800–67 B.C.)

The Greeks and Romans used the same words for both PIRATES and privateers, and ancient states did not issue formal letters of MARQUE. Perhaps with less hypocrisy, ancient rulers simply used freebooters to hurt their enemies. Initially they invited captains to use their harbors as bases for plundering raids. From about 300, many rulers also hired pirates just as they retained mercenary captains on land.

Privateers are frequently mentioned from the fifth century. Often their activities grew out of the right of REPRISAL. Raids by one city's soldiers usually led to counter-raids and a declaration of war. In some cases, however, governments preferred to endorse private raids while theoretically remaining at peace.

A peace treaty in 421 temporarily halted a war between Sparta and Athens. In response to Athenian raids in 416, the Spartans, without renouncing the treaty, proclaimed that anyone on their side was free to plunder Athenians on land or at sea. During the fourth century, the Athenians, Spartans, and Macedonians continued to endorse pirate attacks on their enemies. And the AETOLIANS were notorious for using privateers without first declaring war and opening themselves to counterattacks.

Governments issuing these general invitations to piracy did not control the corsairs, who might attack neutral shipping or even their host's allies. It was somewhat safer to make a formal arrangement with an ARCHPI-

RATE. THEOPOMPUS worked for the Spartans as early as 405, and agreements with corsairs became common from the 330s.

The Macedonian kings frequently employed pirates, even though they had their own navies. GLAUKETAS acted for Antigonus I. TIMOCLES was the strongest of the pirates allied with Demetrius I, ANDRON the least loyal. AMEINIAS OF PHOCIS and MELATAS captured Cassandreia for Antigonus II. DICAEARCHUS looted the Aegean islands for Philip V.

The Seleucids of Syria and the Ptolemys of Egypt similarly retained pirate bands. In the first century, the pirates provided MITHRIDATES OF PONTUS with a ready-made navy. Although no evidence has survived, the Romans probably also used pirates since Roman generals had no scruples about employing land bandits.

Ancient authors refer to privateers as "allies" of Greek cities and kings. Most corsairs probably received some sort of up-front pay. The Macedonian king promised SCERDILAIDAS 20 TALENTS a year for the services of 30 LEMBOI. This was enough to give each crew member 5.5 drachmas a day—about five times more than mercenary soldiers received. Professional sea raiders were in an exceptionally strong bargaining position. They could sail away and offer their services to the enemy if he seemed more generous and more likely to win.

In addition to their wages, privateer crews always had the right—as did land soldiers—to split up captured booty. Some pirates probably remained independent during wartime and plundered both sides. But an alliance with one side guaranteed pirates turned privateers a friendly HAVEN where they could sell their loot and captives.

(See also ANDRON; CHARIDEMUS.)

PRIVATEERS, MODERN (Atlantic; Caribbean, Pacific; about 1200–1856)

Until the 19th century, most governments issued licenses allowing private vessels to plunder enemy merchantmen. The word *privateer* is first recorded in 1664 and became common a few years later. Sixteenth-century English raiders were known as "volunteers" or "voluntaries." (Mediterranean languages used the term CORSAIR.)

Privateering grew out of the ancient right of REPRISAL. From the 13th century, mariners seeking revenge needed a license, called a letter of MARQUE. English law continued to link reprisals and privateering, even after privateers no longer had to prove personal damages.

The French government rarely issued letters of reprisal after 1485. French law instead justified privateering under the king's absolute right to plunder and kill enemies, whether soldiers or civilians. After the ADMIRAL's office was abolished in 1627, the minister of the navy granted licenses. From 1681, privateers were treated as part of the navy and had to obey naval regulations.

Privateers and pirates are easily distinguished, according to legal theory. A pirate plundered ships of all nations and kept all his booty. A privateer attacked only enemy vessels during wartime. His actions were limited by the terms of his commission. Above all, he could not touch any plunder until a government court said the captured vessel was "good prize" (legally seized). The court also took 10 percent or more for the government and levied other fees.

The corsairs of MALTA and BARBARY legally were privateers. They carried commissions and registered their booty with prize courts. In fact, they were pirates. Their governments treated other nations as enemies until they signed a formal peace treaty. Plunder raids were the main source of income for these robber states.

Like the Barbary rulers; Queen Elizabeth I (1558–1603) of England promoted piracy disguised as privateering. Piratical privateers also flourished in 17th-century France during the religious wars. However, there were never as many French pirates, and fewer ventured into the western Atlantic and Caribbean.

Under English law, raiders had to get commissions from the ADMIRALTY COURT and post a bond. They were supposed to register prizes with the VICE-ADMIRALS, and the Admiralty Court settled disputes after 1589. King James I ended privateering in 1603, but it was revived during the 1620s.

Elizabethan raiders often attacked ships from neutral countries. In fact, most legally were pirates, since they seldom bothered to get a license before sailing. (Sir Francis DRAKE raided Panama and took the CACAFUEGO without commission.) Many did not bring prizes back to England, and they often looted the cargo before the courts appraised it. When they could not qualify for English licenses, raiders sailed under letters from foreign rulers.

During the 17th century, French and English governments were less generous with licenses in Europe. But their governors at PORT ROYAL and TORTUGA (and other Caribbean ports) freely issued commissions against Spain. Under the legal doctrine of NO PEACE BEYOND THE LINES, European treaties did not apply in the Caribbean. European rulers cynically let Caribbean governors grant licenses of dubious legality, even though the home countries were at peace. Governors gave commissions to pirates of any nationality, did not enforce any rules, and seldom collected the king's share of the booty.

BUCCANEERS liked to have commissions on board, although they sometimes treated them carelessly. When French or English licenses were unavailable, some bought Portuguese letters. (Spain and Portugal were at war from 1640 to 1668.) Others forged commissions, changed the dates, or bought letters from other pirates. Commissions often proved useful when pirates came before French or English courts. However, Spanish officials executed pirates, whether or not they pretended to be privateers.

Spain, the main victim of Caribbean privateering, was slow to retaliate. The Spanish government licensed raiders in Europe, especially during its war with the

Netherlands. But it was afraid of private warships in its distant American possessions. Privateers were difficult to control, and they often became smugglers, breaking the government monopoly of trade.

Colonial governors were allowed to grant commissions in 1669, following Sir Henry MORGAN's sack of PORTO-BELO. Few captains took up privateering, and their assaults did little damage. Spanish governors continued to license private *guarda-costas* (coast guards), which seized British ships accused of carrying Spanish goods. Their depredations were a major cause of the War of Jenkins Ear (1739–1748).

During their wars between 1688 and 1713, France and Britain freely licensed privateers. They also scoured European waters during the wars between 1740 and 1783, but both nations used regular naval units in the Caribbean. French privateers raided worldwide during the Revolutionary and Napoleonic Wars (1792–1815), and the United States issued thousands of letters of marque during the Revolution and the War of 1812.

In sharp contrast to earlier practices, governments brought privateers under much stricter regulation from the 1680s. Abuses still existed, especially when enemy cargoes were carried on neutral shipping. However, new rules were enforced that limited targets and made prize courts more effective. The distinction between pirates and privateers became clearer, since anyone without the required passes and certificates was a pirate. The seamen manning private warships usually were treated as prisoners of war when captured. In Europe, most raided only during wartime.

Some Caribbean raiders refused to return to peaceful pursuits when war ended in 1713. They turned pirate and operated from NEW PROVIDENCE ISLAND, other uninhabited islands, and MADAGASCAR. But they no longer were welcome in major ports. Colonial governors instead treated them as enemies of the human race and hanged any they caught. During the 1800s, privateering again turned into piracy, as the Latin American countries fought for independence from Spain. Rebel authorities sold commissions to mariners from any nation and made no effort to regulate their practices.

The development of specialized naval warships doomed privateering, and most European countries (but not the United States) gave up the practice under the 1856 Declaration of Paris. The Hague Convention of 1907 permits the arming of merchantmen for defense, but those used for aggressive purposes must be listed as warships. Efforts to revive privateering after 1856 failed in the face of modern navies. The Confederate States of America, for example, initially commissioned freelance raiders. By 1863, the privateers were brought under government control as the volunteer navy, complete with uniforms.

(See also GIBBS, CHARLES; LAFFITE, JEAN; SELECTED BIBLIOGRAPHY: McFee, *Law*; Ritchie, *Kidd*; Rogoziński, *Caribbean*; Stark, *Abolition*.)

PRIZE *(pirate prey; 16th through 19th centuries)* A ship captured by PRIVATEERS, PIRATES, or BUCCANEERS. The English word is derived from Latin *pretium* (prize, value, wages, reward).

(See also ADMIRALTY COURT; BOOTY.)

PROSTITUTES *(all eras)* Like other heterosexual mariners, successful pirates frequented women for pleasure when they reached a friendly port. Ancient Greece and Rome supported many kinds of prostitutes. A wealthy ARCHPIRATE had a wide choice—from educated courtesans to homeless street whores.

Prostitution was not openly practiced in the BARBARY STATES. Islamic law allows up to four wives. If Christian writers can be believed, the corsairs also enjoyed their male and female slaves. In contrast, Christian MALTA was renowned for prostitution as well as piracy. As in other cities at that time, the government regulated prostitutes to avoid disease. Before the great SIEGE OF MALTA began in 1565, the grand master transported the ladies to safety in Sicily.

Although they supposedly were monks, many Maltese KNIGHTS HOSPITALERS kept mistresses. When the grand master ordered their women expelled from the city in 1581, the knights rebelled, imprisoned the grand master, and elected ROMEGAS in his place. (However, political disputes also contributed to the rebellion.) Some secular captains also established long-term relationships. Every time he returned to Malta, Alonso de CONTRERAS wrote, he stayed with the same women until his money ran out. Although the records are silent, there probably also were low-class bars, where less-successful pirates bought women for an hour.

Prostitution was commonplace in England and its American colonies. Whores were ferried in from all over England, while the pirates made their home at Ireland between 1609 and 1611. Prostitution also flourished at PORT ROYAL, the BUCCANEER headquarters from 1660 to 1680. Jamaica was the main receiving point for criminals sent over as indentured servants, and some women already had worked the streets before they arrived.

As EXQUEMELIN reported, most women operated out of taverns, where the drunken buccaneers celebrated their victories. Visitors to the city complained that these "PUNCH-houses" were overrun by "vile strumpets and common prostratures." The most celebrated was Mary Carleton, nicknamed the German Princess, who was shipped to Jamaica in 1671 and taken back and hanged in England in 1673. Her alleged capacity for men gave rise to a great deal of fanciful literature. However, Jamaica also supported at least one full-time brothel, owned by John Starr. In 1680, 21 white and two black women lived and worked at his place. Several similar houses operated in New York, the HAVEN for many rovers during the 1690s.

Until the 19th century, fictional pirates are no more lascivious than any other suddenly rich and temporarily idle seamen. Daniel DEFOE's GENERAL HISTORY does not refer to prostitution. Defoe notes that some pirates operating from MADAGASCAR lived with native women, but they treated them as WIVES. In fictional comments on BLACKBEARD, Defoe accuses him of having 14 "wives," implying that he promised marriage to each woman. Defoe's imaginary biography of Captain CORNELIUS mentions sexual excess but probably not prostitution. Cornelius and his crewmen die of a fever "after being too free with the Women [of Madagascar]."

The myth of pirate debauchery was invented by Victorian writers, long after piracy disappeared. According to *The* PIRATES OWN BOOK (1837), the brigands were wholly devoted to drinking and dallying with "the unsophisticated daughters of Africa and India." "*The* LAST BUCCANEER" (1857) portrays the Caribbean as a paradise because the pirates shared their hammocks with "negro lasses."

In the late 19th century, sex became a taboo subject. Jim Hawkins' mother is the only woman in TREASURE ISLAND, and even romance novels avoid explicit details. A kiss is as far as anyone gets either in Rafael SABATINI's novels or in the MOVIES based on his works. Although unveiled eroticism was tolerated after World War II, novels like *The* GOLDEN HAWK focus on relations between the hero and heroine. Prostitution is discussed only in Dudley POPE's four pirate novels set at Port Royal. Pirate movies hint at but do not mention prostitution. In BLACKBEARD THE PIRATE, for example, crewmen go off with buxom native girls, but the script does not allude to their excursion's purpose.

(See also FICTION, PIRATE; HOMOSEXUALITY.)

PROVIDENCE COMPANY (English pirate sponsor; Caribbean; 1630–1650)
A corporation with governmental powers, which promoted and subsidized piracy from PROVIDENCE ISLAND and TORTUGA ISLAND.

PROVIDENCE ISLAND (pirate haven; Caribbean; 1631–1641)
Providence (Santa Catalina, Isla de Providencia) was a superb pirate base. About 250 miles northwest of PORTOBELO, Providence blocked the main route from Cuba to Venezuela. The large (about 24 square miles) and fertile island can supply a garrison and several warships. It is surrounded by reefs and easily fortified cliffs, making the one good port almost impregnable.

In 1630, the earl of Warwick and other Puritan politicians formed the PROVIDENCE COMPANY. Colonists were sent from Bermuda and England to Providence and the smaller island of San Andrés. TORTUGA ISLAND (northwest of Haiti) also came under the company's authority from 1631 to 1635.

The company advertised Providence as a refuge for godly Puritans, and some grew tobacco, cotton, and other crops. But Providence was always intended to be a pirate haven. Although not welcomed as openly as at Tortuga, Dutch pirates frequently purchased provisions and sold their booty. Some of the English colonists also plundered Spanish shipping.

In 1635, CARTAGENA's governor personally led 300 soldiers against Providence. The islanders had strongly fortified the only harbor, and the Spaniards were beaten off with heavy losses. During the same year, a force from Santo Domingo successfully sacked the pirate colony at Tortuga.

The Providence Company never made money from farming, since the settlers sold their crops to Dutch traders. Using the Spanish raids as an excuse, the company turned the island into an open pirate base. From January 1636, the king allowed the company to grant letters of REPRISAL, and Providence became a favorite stop for Dutch, English, and New England raiders. In 1639, Governor Nathaniel BUTLER raided Honduras and collected 16,000 pesos in ransom at Trujillo. The islanders also outraged Spanish colonists by keeping captured Franciscan missionaries in a harsh dungeon.

In May 1640, a GALLEON, six FRIGATES, and a thousand men were sent from Cartagena. Spanish soldiers managed to reach the island in small boats, but they were driven back during a savage battle. Although the English governor had promised them mercy, he brutally murdered dozens of unarmed Spanish prisoners. The remnants of the defeated Spanish army returned to Cartagena just as the annual TREASURE FLEET arrived in port. In May 1641, the fleet's commander led nine warships and 2,000 soldiers against Providence's 600 defenders. The dangerous reefs were navigated with guidance from Spanish renegades and a BARBARY corsair who had raided with the pirates.

The islanders put up a fierce resistance but had to surrender to overwhelming force. The booty was immense—600 black slaves and more than 500,000 ducats in treasure and goods previously robbed from the Spaniards. Showing more mercy than his English foes, the Spanish commander sent the male prisoners to Spain and allowed the women and children to return to England.

The Spanish victory left the Providence Company with enormous debts. Until 1650, the investors tried to recoup their losses by issuing privateering commissions in return for 20 percent of the loot. Armed with its letters of reprisal, William JACKSON scoured the Caribbean from 1642 to 1644, plundering several towns and occupying Jamaica for three weeks.

Spanish authorities maintained troops on Providence Island to keep English or French buccaneers from returning. As years passed without an attack, the garrison was undermanned, and the forts decayed. Edward MANSFIELD easily captured Providence in May 1666, but a Spanish squadron retook it in August. Sir Henry MORGAN occupied the island in 1670 and 1671 during his attack on Panama.

(See also SELECTED BIBLIOGRAPHY: Earle, *Sack*; Hamshere, *British*; Newton, *Puritans*; Rogoziński, *Caribbean*.)

PROWSE, LAWRENCE *(English captain; Atlantic; active 1589–1598)* Prowse was born in London but financed raids from Southampton, using small ships staffed at low cost. Although he never took a really rich prize, Prowse made a steady profit throughout the Spanish war (1585–1603) and was elected mayor of Southampton in 1617.

In 1586 and 1587, Prowse was captain of the *Eleanor*, owned by several Southampton merchants. He captured two valuable Portuguese ships and was condemned (but not punished) for also looting French vessels. Again commanding the *Eleanor* in 1591, he took Spanish and Portuguese prizes worth £4,000.

Prowse invested his profits with various syndicates sponsoring piracy. From 1589 to 1598, he also owned ships that were commanded by members of his family, including Thomas and William PROWSE. Raiding off the Spanish coast, his vessels plundered merchantmen with cargoes of moderate value.

(See also SELECTED BIBLIOGRAPHY: Andrews, *Elizabethan*.)

PROWSE, WILLIAM *(English captain; Atlantic, Caribbean; died 1595)* A kinsman and probably the brother of Lawrence PROWSE. With the 60-ton *Minion*, partly owned by his family, Prowse captured two Spanish wine ships in 1590. As captain of the *Desire* in 1592 and 1593, he took a prize in the Cape Verde Islands in 1592 worth almost £2,000.

Toward the end of 1593, Prowse was made captain of the 80-ton *Angel*, also partly financed by his family. After seizing various prizes in 1593 and 1594, Prowse and the *Angel* went with Sir Amyas PRESTON to the West Indies, where Prowse was killed assaulting Coro, Venezuela.

PUERTO CABALLOS, SAN JUAN DE *(Honduran port; about 1550–1668)* A town, now abandoned, near the Guatemala-Honduras border. From the mid-16th century, ships from the annual TREASURE FLEETS stopped to offload Spanish goods and pick up hides, dyes, cacao, and some silver. Compared to the treasures shipped from SAN JUAN DE ULÚA in Mexico and Nombre de Dios and PORTOBELO in Panama, these cargoes had little value, and Puerto Caballos was poorly defended. Pirates assaulted the city precisely because the risks were fewer even if the pickings were slimmer.

Christopher NEWPORT attacked in 1592, and Puerto Caballos suffered three raids in 1594. In April, James LANGTON captured six prizes in the harbor. Two weeks later, Christopher Newport found no ships present and sailed away. On May 17th, William PARKER and Jeremias Raymond seized the town and took substantial booty from its warehouses. Parker returned with Sir Anthony SHERLEY in 1597 but gained no loot at "the most poore and miserable place of all India." Joined by five French ships, Christopher Newport captured two heavily armed warships in the harbor in 1602. The Spaniards created a new regional port in 1604, but some vessels continued to call at Puerto Caballos, and François L'OLONNAIS sacked it in 1668.

PUNCH *(alcoholic beverage; 17th century to present)* A drink enjoyed on land and sea by all segments of British and American society, including BUCCANEERS and PIRATES. The number and variety of ingredients were almost unlimited. All punches began with some kind of distilled alcohol or wine. Water, tea, or milk was added as well as sugar, spices and (usually) lime juice. Since it takes some effort to make, punch was especially common at parties. The revelers mixed the components in a bowl, either hot or cold as desired, and drank from a ladle or dipper.

(See also DRINKING; RUM.)

PUNISHMENTS FOR PIRACY *(official deterrents; all eras)* Most legal systems punished pirates in the same ways as other thieves. Some ancient laws allowed robbers to pay penalties to their victims; others imposed physical punishments.

The Greeks and Romans initially accepted piracy as a normal way of treating foreigners. After they conquered the entire Mediterranean region, the Romans condemned pirates as enemies of the human race. Governors were ordered to catch pirates and publicly kill them by beheading, crucifixion, or exposure to savage animals—standard Roman punishments imposed for other crimes as well. Medieval and modern governments also treated pirates like other thieves and murderers. Under the BYZANTINE EMPIRE, pirates were blinded and had their noses cut off. The Chinese cut off their heads with a sword during a public ceremony at the city gate.

In England, public hanging became the penalty for all felonies. Particularly vicious criminals, such as murderers, were hung up in chains near the scene of their crime. Like other thieves, pirates initially were hanged immedi-

Punishments for piracy. Tyrone Power is stretched on the rack in *The Black Swan* (1942).

ately after trial. The first known hanging for piracy took place in 1228; the most recent occurred in 1840.

An act of 1536 made the ADMIRALTY COURT responsible for crimes at sea, with hanging the punishment for piracy and other felonies. Pirates had their own place of execution in London. While other criminals were taken to Tyburn or Tower Hill, pirates died at Execution Dock, located at Wapping on the left bank of the Thames.

After execution, the body was left hanging, chained so it would still look human as it rotted. The corpse was placed at the low-tide mark with the toes almost touching the water. This practice had several motives. The man's body was near the sea, the scene of his crimes. The body was placed over the low-tide mark as a symbol that the Admiralty had jurisdiction, because the offenses occurred outside England. The gruesome corpse was supposed to discourage passing seamen from turning pirate.

By the 18th century, this supreme penalty was reserved for officers and ringleaders. Although still sentenced to death, most crewmen were reprieved or pardoned. William KIDD and Darby MULLINS were hanged at Wapping in 1701, but several of Kidd's crew were pardoned after sentencing.

Kidd's hanging expressed the English government's new determination to suppress pirates. Anti-piracy laws were passed in the colonies, which also adopted the English ritual. In an unusual mass execution, 54 of Bartholomew ROBERT's crew were hanged in Africa in 1722 and left in chains for months. Public hangings at the waterfront also occurred in North America, and the practice continued when the United States became independent. A Confederate PRIVATEER was hanged for piracy in 1862, but his body was not displayed in chains.

(See also BRIGGEHO, WILLIAM DE.)

PURCHASE *(English slang; 13th through 18th centuries)* In this meaning (now extinct), the word *purchase* originally described the process of hunting (chasing) animals. It later referred both to the act of robbery or piracy and also to the booty taken by robbers or pirates.

(See also ACCOUNT, GOING ON THE; NO PURCHASE, NO PAY.)

PUXOL, JAYME *(Majorcan corsair; Mediterranean; 1509–1564)* After many raids along the BARBARY COAST, Puxol was captured by corsairs from ALGIERS. He was burned alive to revenge the death of an Algerian killed in the same way by the Majorcan inquisition.

PYLE, HOWARD *(American author and illustrator; 1853–1911)* Pyle is best remembered for his illustrations in several artistic styles. He initially worked in pen and ink and black-and-white oil colors. After 1900, as printing technologies improved, he used color to heighten the sensual appeal of his drawings.

Pyle's illustrations combine accurate physical details and emotional drama. Pyle believed that he could mentally project himself into the scenes he painted. He

"Attack on a Galleon." Illustration by Howard Pyle in *Harper's Monthly Magazine,* December 1905.

deliberately sought to portray raw emotions: the ruthlessness of pirate greed, grief in defeat, smug pride, a humble prayer for mercy. His illustrations bring to life and give a polished form to many old legends about the BRETHREN OF THE COAST, CAPTAIN KIDD (1), BURIED TREASURE, and WALKING THE PLANK.

In addition to creating thousands of drawings accompanying other authors' works, Pyle wrote and illustrated his own poetry and fiction. Despite his own life of quiet domesticity, Pyle identified with the adventurous heroes of earlier eras. He was especially attracted to pirates, medieval legends, and America's colonial era. Librarians often assign all Pyle's books to the children's section. However, the novels were fables for all ages, and the stories appeared in general-circulation magazines.

The Merry Adventures of Robin Hood, published in 1883, retold the old legends in simple prose accompanied by drawings modeled after 16th-century engravings. Like James Barrie in PETER PAN, Pyle tried to entice his readers into a fanciful "No Man's Land," divorced from reality. Between 1886 and 1895, Pyle wrote and illustrated five books of fairy tales and a children's novel (*Otto of the Silver Hand*) set in medieval Germany. From 1903 to 1910, he produced four volumes narrating various legends about King Arthur. *Rejected of Men* (1903) sets the life of Jesus Christ in Pyle's own day.

Piracy fascinated Pyle, and he collected a large library of pirate books. The introduction to BUCCANEERS AND MAROONERS (1891) defends his devotion to pirate adventures. Inside all of us, Pyle wrote, is an "old-time savage." This inner self lusts after wealth. It also hungers for "a life of constant alertness, constant danger, constant escape," for "blood and lust and flame and rapine."

In *The* STORY OF JACK BALLISTER'S FORTUNES (1895), ROSE OF PARADISE (1888), STOLEN TREASURE (1907), and other pirate fiction, Pyle revised earlier accounts, created his own plots, and reinterpreted the motives of pirate captains. Pyle's biographies often are less fantastic than those of EXQUEMELIN and Daniel DEFOE. Even when he could not prove that they invented details, Pyle felt that some of their stories are inherently implausible.

Q

QAWASIM *(Arab pirates; Persian Gulf, Indian Ocean, Red Sea; about 1750–1830)* A tribal confederation ruled by the Qasimi dynasty. Qawasim (Joasim, Jauasem) is plural; the singular form is Qasimi (Joasimi). From fortified bases at Ras al-Khaima and Sharjah, near the Gulf of Hormuz, Qawasim war fleets cruised the Persian Gulf. Due to their continuing assaults, the region from Hormuz to Bahrain became known as the "Pirate Coast." From 1808, the Qawasim also raided northern India and the Red Sea.

The Qawasim are known only from British documents, which may be biased against them. In part, their piracies grew out of a political struggle against the rulers of Muscat and Oman. Since the Qawasim usually did not attack merchants if they paid protection money, Gulf shipping prospered during these years.

Vessels flying the British flag were seized from 1778, but their crews were released unharmed. Pirate attacks increased from 1805, when the Qawasim occupied islands at the entrance to the Gulf of Hormuz. Raiders also became more ruthless when the Qawasim converted to the ultraorthodox Wahhabi branch of Islam.

The Wahhabi took the Koran literally and rejected later commentaries. They considered it legal to exterminate other Muslims, who were worse than infidels. Because the Koran forbids plundering the living, Qawasim pirates routinely killed captives before robbing them.

Their attacks on neighboring Oman and Muscat became a religious war, as those regions remained loyal to more traditional forms of Islam.

The Qawasim agreed not to attack East India Company vessels in 1806, but the truce lasted only two years. In 1808, the Wahhabi ruler replaced the Qawasim ruler, Sultan ibn Saqr, with his own vice-regent. The Qawasim were ordered to attack all non-Wahhabi, whether Muslim or unbeliever. As the Koran required, the Wahhabi ruler took 20 percent of all plunder.

The Qawasim cruised in squadrons of 15 to 20 vessels, each commanded by a *naib* (lieutenant), responsible to a Wahhabi vice-regent. A standing fleet of 70 to 80 warships was joined by hundreds of fishing boats and up to 25,000 fighting men. Booty was fenced at Bahrain, which also provided supplies.

In May 1808, the Qawasim captured a British merchant vessel. Most of the crew and many passengers were butchered, and a British officer's wife was sold at Bahrain. In the autumn, an East India Company cruiser was taken, and its crew was murdered. Qasimi war squadrons appeared off the Indian coast in November and captured 20 merchant vessels.

To punish the Qawasim, 10 British warships bombarded Ras al-Khaima in November 1809, and British troops sacked the town. Most of the pirate fleet had escaped before the attack. However, the Wahhabi ruler was busy with other wars and guaranteed the safety of British vessels.

Pirate squadrons returned to the Gulf in 1812 and raided the Indian coast from 1813. In October 1814, Hasan ibn Rahman, the new Qasimi ruler, again promised not to assault British shipping. From 1816, however, the pirates seized European as well as Indian and Arabian vessels. Their war fleet had increased to 100 large DHOWS, carrying 800 cannon and 8,000 fighting men.

Ibrahim ibn Rahman, the ruler's brother, led one squadron into the Red Sea late in 1816. His ships captured three Indian vessels flying the British flag and carrying £100,000 in booty. The pirates killed all on board two vessels and 60 crewmen on the third. When the British complained, Hasan explained that he could not admit that Indians were British subjects. If he did, the Qawasim would have no one left to plunder.

Qawasim piracy was at its height in 1818, even though Egyptian troops defeated the Wahhabi inland. In December 1819, the British attacked Ras al-Khaima with a battleship, 10 other warships, and 3,400 troops. Ibrahim ibn Rahman was killed during the battle. Sheikh Hasan surrendered with most of the surviving fighting men, and the British restored Sultan ibn Saqr to power.

The British squadron attacked other ports along the coast, razed their fortifications, and burned pirate vessels. In January 1820, the coastal rulers signed a general peace treaty, outlawing piracy and the slave trade. A British cruiser squadron henceforth patrolled the Gulf. Several cases of piracy occurred during the 1820s, but the British forced the Qasimi sheiks to reimburse the victims.

(See also RAHMAH IBN JABIR; SELECTED BIBLIOGRAPHY: Kelly, *Persian Gulf*.)

QUARTERMASTER (pirate officer; about 1680–1725)

British and Anglo-American pirates delegated unusual authority to the quartermaster, who became almost the captain's equal. Pirates disliked rigid rules, and there were exceptional situations. Generally, however, the captain had unlimited power during battles, but he was subject to the quartermaster in many routine matters. In this way, as Walter KENNEDY explained at his trial, pirate crews avoided putting too much power in one man's hands. As was the captain, the quartermaster was elected by the crew and received an extra share when the booty was divided. If the pirates decided to keep a captured ship, the quartermaster often took over as its captain.

The quartermaster represented, as Daniel DEFOE noted, the "Interest of the Crew." Above all, he protected the seamen against each other by maintaining order, settling quarrels, and distributing food and other essentials. Serious crimes were tried by jury, but the quartermaster could punish minor offenses. Only the quartermaster could flog a seaman and only after a vote by the crew.

The quartermaster took part in all battles and often led attacks by boarding parties. If the pirates won, he decided what loot to take. He was compelled to seize gold, silver, and jewels. But he took more bulky cargo at his discretion, depending on storage space and distance from markets. He guarded the plunder and supervised the final share-out of goods at the masthead.

Pirate quartermasters had gained their exalted status by the 1720s and perhaps somewhat earlier. The BUCCANEERS did not give the quartermaster special powers or extra shares of booty according to EXQUEMELIN, who wrote in the early 1670s. By 1681, however, John COOK was considered second-in-command as quartermaster and had first claim on any captured ship. Whenever it was invented, this system could spread rapidly because pirates often joined forces during cruises, and men freely moved from ship to ship.

(See also SELECTED BIBLIOGRAPHY: Defoe, *General History*; Pringle, *Jolly Roger*; Rediker, *Devil.*)

QUEEN OF THE PIRATES (Italian/German motion picture; color; 1961)

During the 16th century, Duke Zuliam (Paul Muller) rules as a tyrant over the Duchy of Druzzo, aided by his daughter Isabella (Scilla Gabel). The duke unjustly sentences Captain Mirko (Jose Jaspe) to be hanged. Sandra (Gianna Maria Canale), supposedly Mirko's daughter, is to be sold to a harem. Cesare, count of Santa Croce (Massimo Serato) secretly frees Mirko and Sandra and then is sent to recapture them.

Cesare instead falls in love with Sandra. Leading the pirates and oppressed peasants, they assault Duke Zuliam's palace. Mortally wounded, Zuliam reveals the truth. Sandra is his real daughter and the next rightful ruler. Many years earlier, Zuliam had ordered Mirko to kill the girl, but Mirko instead raised her as his own child. The wicked Isabella is sent to a convent, and Cesare and Sandra will marry and right all wrongs. Gianna Canale displays some adequate fencing ability while dressed in male attire. Directed by Richard McNamara.

QUELCH, JOHN (Anglo-American pirate; Atlantic; 1703)

A Massachusetts captain, among the first to fly the JOLLY ROGER, the pirates' black flag. In 1703, Quelch was second-in-command of the BRIGANTINE *Charles*, commissioned as a PRIVATEER during wartime. While the ship was anchored off Marblehead in August, the crew mutinied, elected Quelch commander, and threw the original captain overboard—whether alive or dead is not known.

Quelch took the *Charles* to Brazil and captured nine vessels carrying gold and silver as well as fine cloth, food, and rum. These attacks were outrageously illegal, since Great Britain and Portugal had just become close allies. When the *Charles* returned to Marblehead in May 1704, suspicious officials rounded up the crew. The pirates were tried in Boston with the governor presiding, and Quelch and five others were hanged.

(See also SELECTED BIBLIOGRAPHY: Jameson, *Privateering.*)

QUINN, ANTHONY *(American actor; 1915–1994)* Born in Mexico of Irish and Mexican parents, Quinn lived in the United States from childhood and entered films in 1936. The next year, he married Cecil B. De Mille's adopted daughter Katherine (divorced 1965).

Quinn is associated with more major pirate movies than any other male actor. He starred in HIGH WIND IN JAMAICA (1966) after supporting Frederic March in *The* BUCCANEER (1938), Tyrone POWER in *The* BLACK SWAN (1942), and Errol FLYNN in AGAINST ALL FLAGS (1952). When De Mille became ill in 1958, Quinn directed *The Buccaneer* with Yul Brunner. (In 1946, he appeared in the equally swashbuckling although nonpiratical *Sinbad the Sailor* with Douglas Fairbanks, Jr.)

Altogether, Quinn performed in well over 100 movies, usually in a co-starring or supporting role. Thanks to his dark, exotic looks and his broad, earthy acting style, he usually was cast as a foreign heavy or (in his early years) as a ferocious Indian chief. He received Oscars as best supporting actor for *Viva Zapata* (1952) and *Lust for Life* (1956). He also performed in *La Strada* (1958), *The Guns of Navarone* (1961), *Requiem for a Heavyweight* (1962), *Lawrence of Arabia* (1962), and *Zorba the Greek* (1964), his most memorable role.

Captain Chavez (Anthony Quinn) visits a decayed Mexican pirate haven in *A High Wind in Jamaica* (1965).

(R)

RACKHAM, JOHN *(English pirate; Caribbean, Atlantic; hanged 1720)* Nicknamed "Calico Jack" because he wore CLOTHING made of calico (a coarse white cloth imported from Calcutta, India). He sailed from NEW PROVIDENCE ISLAND with Charles VANE, who refused the royal pardon offered by Governor Woodes ROGERS in August 1718. By early 1719, Rackham was second-in-command as Vane's QUARTERMASTER. When the pirates seized a large ship, Rackham was chosen captain.

Soon after, Vane and Rackham quarreled, and Rackham went on alone with the booty. Two SLOOPS sent from Jamaica surprised the pirates on a deserted island and seized their vessel. Rackham made it back to Providence Island in May 1719 and convinced Governor Rogers to grant him a belated pardon.

At Providence, Rackham became infatuated with Anne BONNY, James Bonny's wife. With other former pirates, Rackham and Bonny stole a sloop late in 1719. Cruising between Haiti and Bermuda, Rackham plundered several small ships without taking significant booty.

A sloop armed by the governor of Jamaica captured Rackham's ship in November 1720. He was tried on November 27 and hanged the next day. Although some reports indicate Anne Bonny stayed in Cuba while Rackham cruised, both she and Mary READ were with him when the pirates were captured.

RAHMAH IBN JABIR *(Arab pirate chief; Persian Gulf; died 1826)* Rahmah was the ruling sheikh of the Al Jalahimah tribe and the outstanding pirate in the Gulf. In 1783, the Al Jalahimah helped the Al Khalifah conquer Bahrain from Persia, and the two clans argued over the spoils. The Al Jalahimah retired in disgust to Khaur Hasan (Al Khuwayr) at the tip of the Qatar Peninsula.

Rahmah ibn Jabir, the ablest of their chiefs, conducted a savage war of atrocities against the other Gulf rulers for almost 40 years. Khaur Hasan became a haven for all who wanted to live by the sword, and Rahmah's personal hatred of the Al Khalifah never diminished. His vendetta grew to include all their allies, including the Al Sabah of Kuwait and the QAWASIM pirates located to the east. To pursue his quarrels, Rahmah and his followers converted to the Wahhabi sect. An ultraorthodox branch of Islam, the Wahhabi condemned other Muslims as heretics and routinely massacred captives.

Thanks to his alliance with the Wahhabi, Rahmah's power was at its peak from 1809 to 1816. With 40 warships, he helped the Wahhabi impose their authority on Bahrain in February 1810. Late in 1809, he led a squadron that captured 20 Kuwaiti vessels. His warriors slaughtered their crews, including a son of the Al Sabah ruler of Kuwait. Meanwhile, a British fleet sacked Qawasim strongholds late in 1809 but left Rahmah and his followers alone. Rahmah never attacked a vessel flying the British flag, perhaps because he hoped for British help against his Arab enemies.

J. S. Buckingham, a British captain, traveler, and writer, met Rahmah at about this time. Though old and crippled by wounds, he was still formidable. His lean body was

> cut and hacked, and pierced with wounds of sabres, spears, and bullets, in every part. . . . He had, besides, a face naturally ferocious and ugly, and now rendered still more so by several scars there, and by the loss of one eye. This Butcher Chief, who is said to have 200 wives, affects great simplicity in garb and manners. . . . His usual dress is a shirt which is never taken off until it is worn out, no drawers or covering for the legs, a large black goat's skin wrapped over all, and a close-fitting handkerchief on his head.

A blast of grapeshot had so shattered his left arm that the elbow was connected to the shoulder by withered skin and tendons stiffened with silver wiring. Even this boneless arm, he proudly boasted, could still slit the throats of his enemies.

Rahmah refused to sign a general peace treaty sponsored by the British in 1820 and continued to attack Arab shipping. By 1826, he had alienated every ruler in the Gulf. He earlier had lost Khaur Hasan, and the Al Khalifah of Bahrain besieged his remaining base at Dammam.

Nearly 70 and totally blind, his fleet reduced to one vessel, Rahmah sailed out and battled the Bahraini ruler's nephew. Both ships suffered heavy casualties, and the enemy pulled back to pick up more men. Rather than be captured, Rahman ordered his warship to grapple with the enemy. Holding in his arms his youngest son, a boy of eight, he set fire to his gunpowder, instantly blowing up both ships.

(See also SELECTED BIBLIOGRAPHY: Kelly, _Persian Gulf._)

RAIDERS OF THE SEVEN SEAS _(motion picture; color; 1953)_

After being caught in the sultan's harem, Barbarossa (John Payne with an appropriately red beard) flees MOROCCO, seizes a Spanish prison ship, and liberates the convicts. Under his spirited leadership, the men capture several vessels. Their prisoners include an ambitious Spanish officer, Don Salcedo (Gerald Mohr), and his fiancée, Alida (Donna Reed), whom Barbarossa romances.

One of the pirate crew, Renzo (Anthony Caruso) turns traitor and kills Peg Leg (Lon Chaney Jr.), Barbarossa's second-in-command. Learning that Don Salcedo had bribed Renzo, Barbarossa threatens to destroy Havana. In the final minutes, however, Barbarossa smells a trap and decides against the invasion. Humiliated, Salcedo tries to justify his maneuvers to his superiors. Directed by Sidney Salkow.

RALEIGH, SIR WALTER _(English adventurer and author; Atlantic, Caribbean; 1554?–1618)_

Widely disliked during his glory days, Raleigh gained popular approval while imprisoned for treason from 1603 to 1618. He remains an enigmatic figure, portrayed by his many biographers both as a hero and as a villain. However, there is no question that he promoted piracy on a grand scale.

Raleigh, who easily became seasick, was not himself a seaman. In contrast to some other courtiers, including the earl of CUMBERLAND, he rarely commanded in person. When he did take command during the two Guyana adventures, they proved expensive failures.

Raleigh treated piracy as a form of financial speculation. By investing with several professional captains, he gained a large income not dependent on the queen. As Robert Lacey noted, "Even if Walter Ralegh had never won the favour of the queen of England he would have made himself wealthy, and probably famous, as a buccaneer in his own right, and a most businesslike buccaneer at that."

Raleigh was a younger son of a country squire and his third wife. Through blood and marriage, he was related to many Devonshire families long involved in seafaring and piracy. He fought on the Protestant side in the French civil wars from about 1568, briefly attended Oxford University, and moved to London in 1575.

In 1578, Raleigh commanded a warship during the failed West Indies raid led by his half-brother, Sir Humphrey GILBERT. Raleigh's ship was the only one that actually sailed for the Americas. Most of the other captains were professional pirates, who lingered in English waters to pillage merchantmen.

In 1580, Raleigh became an infantry captain with English troops invading Ireland. There he gained booty and a reputation for courage and cruelty. Some 400 Italian and Spanish mercenaries landed at Smerwick and were joined by 200 Irish men and women. The English forces besieged Smerwick, which surrendered in November. Commanded by Raleigh and another officer, English soldiers stripped the helpless prisoners and slaughtered them with swords and knives.

Raleigh returned to England early in 1582, a mature, handsome, and engaging man determined to rise. He rapidly won the affection of Queen Elizabeth I and remained her favorite for almost a decade. The queen knighted Raleigh in 1584, gave him a London palace and extensive lands, and granted him lucrative monopolies over wine sales and cloth exports. In addition to other offices, he served as VICE-ADMIRAL of Cornwall and Devon—thus controlling efforts to suppress smuggling and piracy in western England.

Though the English people attributed Raleigh's wealth to the hated monopolies, he actually gained substantial income from piracy. Ships were hunting on his behalf as early as 1582, sometimes under cover of licenses from

Sir Walter Raleigh makes a treaty with an Indian chief while unsuccessfully exploring for gold in Guyana in 1595. From Theodorus de Bry, *Collectiones . . . Americae pars VIII* (1599).

factions in the French civil wars. Probably using booty taken in France and Ireland, he constructed the *Bark Raleigh*, a sleek 200-ton private warship. In 1584, he added the 300-ton *Roebuck*, named after the symbol on his new coat of arms.

In 1585, Raleigh founded England's first North American colony at ROANOKE, Virginia. Roanoke was planned as a HAVEN for raids on the West Indies and Spanish TREASURE SHIPS. It was abandoned when Raleigh and the other sponsors discovered that a land base was not needed for successful piracy.

In May 1585, Queen Elizabeth began to license attacks on Spanish and Portuguese vessels. Raleigh's warships became more aggressive, and he built the 800-ton *Ark Raleigh*, the most advanced warship of its time. Renamed the *Ark Royal*, it served as the English flagship against the Spanish Armada in 1588.

Raleigh's captains attacked neutral as well as enemy shipping. The *Roebuck*'s captain took a French prize in 1585 in consort with John CALLICE. In 1590, his ships

joined others in carrying off £25,000 in spices, jewels, and ivory from two Italian vessels. The ADMIRALTY COURT and the queen's Privy Council ordered restitution, but the pirates had already disbursed the loot.

In 1586, two small PINNACES hired by Raleigh raided the Azores. Their prisoners included Don Pedro Sarmiento de Gamboa, governor of the region around the Strait of Magellan. (In 1579, Sarmiento had pursued Sir Francis DRAKE off the coast of Peru.) Instead of demanding a high ransom for Sarmiento, Raleigh offered to betray England for a Spanish pension, perhaps planning to act as a double agent.

Raleigh spent 1588 preparing western England for possible invasion, and he visited his Irish estates in 1589. The scale of his privateering adventures dramatically increased after he became associated with Sir John WATTS. In 1590, Watts dispatched ships that took rich prizes before visiting the deserted Roanoke colony. In 1591, Raleigh became a shareholder in Watts' syndicate, which financed William LANE's highly profitable West

Indies raid. But he also continued to invest in pirate cruises sponsored by other syndicates.

The year 1591 also saw Raleigh's first published book, which immortalized Sir Richard Grenville. The queen named Raleigh vice-admiral of a plunder venture in the Azores. Grenville took Raleigh's place and lost the *Revenge* during a foolish battle with a Spanish fleet. Written in superb prose, Raleigh's REPORT OF THE TRUTH turned the incident into an enduring legend of British heroism. The sponsors, including Raleigh, lost the money they had put into the failed raid.

In 1592, Raleigh invested heavily in and commanded a planned assault on PANAMA. At the last minute, the queen again refused to part with her favorite, and the ships went on under Sir Martin FROBISHER and Sir John BURGH. In the Azores, Burgh's squadron joined other English raiders in taking the MADRE DE DIOS, an immensely rich Portuguese CARRACK.

In the meantime, Queen Elizabeth discovered that Raleigh secretly had married her maid of honor. To punish him for loving another woman, she snatched away his booty from the *Madre de Dios*. Taking into account the interest charges on their loans, Raleigh and his partners actually lost money by capturing the richest prize of the century.

Banished from court, Raleigh tried to recover his fortunes by looking for gold in Guyana. Many Spanish colonists believed that a fabulously wealthy Indian city existed deep inland. Its legendary ruler was called *El Dorado* ("the gilded one") because he covered his body with gold dust before bathing.

Obsessed by the legend, Raleigh sent out several major expeditions to find El Dorado's treasures. In 1593, four ships under Sir John Burgh attacked Spanish settlements in Venezuela and Trinidad, which guarded the sea lanes to Guyana. In 1595, Raleigh set out with four ships and some 300 men. Another squadron under Sir Amyas PRESTON and Sir George SOMERS was supposed to join Raleigh in the Caribbean.

After burning the Spanish settlements on Trinidad, Raleigh's party sailed up the Orinoco River until it was blocked by waterfalls. Convinced that he had discovered gold ore, he turned back to England to recruit a larger force. On the way home, he sacked two towns in Venezuela and unsuccessfully hunted for treasure ships off Cuba.

The Guyana expedition paid only half its costs, and tests of Raleigh's ore samples were inconclusive. To encourage investment in future ventures, Raleigh published the *Discovery of the Large, Rich, and Beautiful Empire of Guiana* in 1596. Although it was a best-seller, the book did not persuade doubters. (In fact, Guyana did possess gold mines, but they were not worked until the 19th century.)

English adventures preferred targets nearer than Guyana. In 1596, 150 vessels joined a great plunder raid on Cadiz, Spain. Seconded by Robert CROSSE, Raleigh led one of four squadrons. Soldiers and sailors poured into Cadiz in an orgy of looting, while their officers bargained over the ransom due from ships in the harbor. As the English and shipowners haggled, the Spanish military commander set the vessels ablaze. The troops pocketed most of the booty, and the queen and Raleigh made only small profits.

In 1597, Raleigh, by now reconciled with Queen Elizabeth, was second-in-command of a futile raid on Portugal. Its commander, the earl of Essex, decided not to attack the Portuguese ports and just missed several treasure ships in the Azores. However, Raleigh continued to benefit from smaller-scale privateering cruises until the Spanish war ended in 1603.

Raleigh's enemies slandered him to King James I, who succeeded Elizabeth in March 1603. Sentenced to death for his part in a conspiracy to dethrone James, Raleigh was reprieved at the last minute and imprisoned in the Tower of London. In 1616, the king released him to lead a second Guyana expedition, which hoped to find gold mines and trap Spanish TREASURE FLEETS.

Private investors financed over a dozen ships carrying a thousand men. A severe fever prevented Raleigh from leading his forces up the Orinoco River. His lieutenant burned a Spanish settlement but found no gold. On the way home, most of his captains deserted and turned pirate. King James implemented the suspended sentence of 1603, and Raleigh was beheaded. (See also SELECTED BIBLIOGRAPHY: Lacey, *Raleigh*.)

RANSOM OF CAPTIVES *(Barbary states; Mediterranean; about 1520–1830)* Kidnapping was always the most profitable part of Mediterranean buccaneering. During three centuries of North African piracy, slave emancipation developed into a major international industry involving a complicated network of individual entrepreneurs and organizations.

A fortunate few were freed through prisoner exchanges or by charitable organizations. European governments sometimes swapped Barbary captives for Muslim slaves in Christian countries, usually on the basis of three or four Muslims for one Christian. But these deals often fell through because Christian captains hated to part with seasoned GALLEY SLAVES. The REDEMPTIONIST FATHERS were the most famous, but many smaller religious and secular organizations also ransomed captives. Cities and provinces set up charitable trusts, and the British government spent nearly £40,000 on ransoms during the 1640s.

The majority of captives had to buy their freedom. Some raised the money themselves by working as craftsmen, surgeons, or by running the taverns in the slave barracks (BAGNIOS). Their masters allowed them to keep a percentage until the ransom was accumulated. But most slaves, dependent on money from home, sent powers of attorney to Europe authorizing the sale of property or borrowing on future inheritances.

However it was raised, the ransom had to be transferred to North Africa. Cash money sometimes was entrusted to a merchant or sea captain. Most often, captives borrowed the ransom from Jewish traders with business connections on both sides of the Mediterranean. Dealing with bankers in Christian cities such as LIVORNO and Marseilles, these ransom dealers collected the amount of the loan plus heavy interest and a 14 to 15 percent fee. The Lomellini family scrupulously handled most Tunisian ransoms during the 17th century for a modest fee. But some dishonest merchants inflated a ransom (to get a higher fee) or were slow in paying it.

To avoid problems, owners often let slaves return to Europe to arrange ransoms for themselves and friends. Most actually did return with the money, since they often left hostages in Barbary. During the 1600s, the grand duke of Tuscany guarded slaves waiting to collect their ransoms at a kind of bonded warehouse at Livorno. If they did not pay within a set time, the grand duke returned them to their owners.

(See also SELECTED BIBLIOGRAPHY: Clissold, *Barbary*.)

RAPE See WOMEN, TREATMENT OF.

RAPIER See SWORD DUELS.

RATHBONE, BASIL *(American actor; 1892–1967)* Born in South Africa, Rathbone became an American citizen in 1930. During 45 years in Hollywood, he appeared in 150 movies, ranging from adaptations of classic novels to low-budget horror films. He is most strongly identified with two contrasting roles—as a SWASHBUCKLING villain and as Sherlock Holmes, the proponent of justice.

After appearing as a Shakespearean actor, Rathbone fought in World War I. Tall, dark, and handsome, he had an excellent profile and a distinguished voice. During his first years in Hollywood, he appeared as a romantic lead. Then in 1935, thanks to his cold portrayal of a villain in *David Copperfield*, producers began to cast him as the heavy in costume dramas.

Rathbone had taken fencing lessons as a young man; his sword play was highly skilled and theatrically brilliant. In the 1935 CAPTAIN BLOOD, he outfenced (in real life and in the film) Errol FLYNN during a long SWORD DUEL down the beach and into the water. (During one take, he cut Flynn's face. For added realism, the director had taken the guards off the foils.) Rathbone again fenced with Flynn as Sir Guy of Gisbourne in *The Adventures of Robin Hood* (1938). As Captain Esteban Pasquale, he fought a spirited duel with Tyrone POWER at the end of *The Mark of Zorro* (1940). He was viciously menacing as Lord Rockingham in FRENCHMAN'S CREEK (1944).

Rathbone probably is best remembered as Sherlock Holmes to Nigel Bruce's Doctor Watson. On radio and in 14 films between 1939 and 1946, Rathbone defined Holmes as a master of scientific logic—sardonic, playful, and proud.

RAUNSE (RANCE), JOHN *(English pirate; Atlantic, Caribbean; active 1566–1572)* Raunse was a captain during two of Sir John HAWKINS' expeditions, which plundered Portuguese vessels and smuggled slaves into the Spanish Caribbean. In 1566–1567, he commanded the 100-ton *Solomon* in John LOVELL's squadron, which captured at least five Portuguese prizes near Africa. He was master of the 150-ton *William and John* during Hawkins's disastrous 1567–1568 expedition. Separated during a storm, his ship escaped the massacre at SAN JUAN DE ULÚA.

Sailing from the Isle of Wight in a BARK, Raunse captured several prizes in the Caribbean in 1572. In July, he joined Sir Francis DRAKE in an unsuccessful raid on Nombre de Dios. Fearing arrest by Spanish troops, Raunse went his own way and thus did not share in Drake's subsequent capture of Spanish treasure.

(See also SIR FRANCIS DRAKE REVIVED.)

RAYMOND, GEORGE *(English adventurer; Atlantic, Pacific; active 1584–1591)* A native of Sussex, Raymond was captain and owner of the *Lion*, which sailed for Virginia with Sir Richard GRENVILLE in 1585. Raymond became separated from Grenville and went on from Virginia to Newfoundland. There he met and consorted with Bernard DRAKE, and the two captains took a rich haul of Portuguese sugar ships and French fishermen on the way home.

In 1586, George SOMERS and Raymond raided as co-captains of the *Swiftsure*. Raymond sailed with Sir Francis DRAKE's 1587 raid on Cadiz and battled against the Spanish Armada in 1588. By 1589, he owned the *Swiftsure* and cruised in the Azores in consort with Somers and another captain. The little squadron took two prizes worth £30,000, and Raymond and Somers fought over their shares in the ADMIRALTY COURT.

From 1590, Raymond used his own booty to finance voyages by other captains, most of which also were highly profitable. In 1591, commanding his own ship *Penelope*, he both promoted and led the first English expedition around the Cape of Good Hope. The *Penelope* disappeared during a fierce storm in September, and James LANCASTER took command of the expedition.

(See also PRESTON, SIR AMYAS.)

REDEMPTIONIST FATHERS *(liberators of Barbary slaves; 1520–1789)* Several Roman Catholic monastic orders ransomed Christians enslaved by Muslims, especially (after 1520) in the BARBARY STATES. The most important were the Order of the Most Holy Trinity (incorporated in 1198) and the Order of Our Lady of Mercy (founded in about 1218).

The Paris-based Trinitarians were most numerous in France. Their striking costume included a white tunic carrying a cross with a red upright and a blue cross-bar. The Fathers of Mercy (or Mercedarians) originally were Spanish and Italian but later had French convents. If necessary, members promised to surrender themselves as hostages until captives could pay their ransoms.

The two orders controlled large amounts of land, and the Mercedarians also received grants from the Spanish government. But administrative costs ate up most of their revenues, and they became famous for their fund-raising propaganda, preaching, and processions. The Redemptionists scoured the provinces for money—as did charlatans pretending to be monks. They carried banners flying from ships' masts and marched to trumpets, flutes, and cymbals. Plays and tableaux showed the Moors brutally torturing their Christian slaves. After they were ransomed, captives spent several months with these processions, loaded with chains much heavier than those worn by Barbary slaves.

Some of the money collected did help to ransom Christian slaves. Altogether, over several centuries, the Trinitarians ransomed perhaps 90,000 Christian captives, while the Fathers of Mercy freed another 50,000. In addition, Trinitarian brothers maintained hospitals in North African slave prisons (BAGNIOS).

Barbary rulers welcomed the Redemptionists, charged them high fees, and guaranteed the safety of ships carrying captives back to Europe. However, corsairs from another Barbary state sometimes recaptured ransomed prisoners and returned them to slavery.

(See also SELECTED BIBLIOGRAPHY: Clissold, *Barbary Slaves*.)

READ, JOHN *(English buccaneer; Pacific, South China Sea, Bay of Bengal; active 1680s)* A Bristol seaman, Read plundered South America's Pacific coast from 1684 to 1686 with Charles SWAN. Having taken little booty, Swan took the CYGNET west to the Philippines and arrived on July 2. Swan wanted to remain as a merchant, but Read and many other crewmen preferred to return to piracy.

The crew mutinied on January 23, 1687, when Read got hold of Swan's journal. As William DAMPIER described the incident, Swan sent a man aboard to fetch something from his cabin. Read "was a pretty Ingenious young Man, and of a very civil carriage and behaviour. He wass also accounted a good Artist, and kept a Journal, and was now prompted by his Curiosity, to peep in to Captain Swan's Journal, to see how it agreed with his own. . . ." Informed of Swan's contemptuous criticisms, the crew seized the ship, left Swan ashore, and sailed with Read as captain.

Henceforth, Dampier writes, "our business was to pillage," and Read cruised around, hoping to meet up with the MANILA GALLEON. But only two small prizes were taken during the next 18 months, as the *Cygnet* visited Manila, Cambodia, southern China, Formosa, and the Celebes Islands. In January 1688, Read and his crew became the first Englishmen to reach Australia, visiting the regions still known as Dampier Land and the Buccaneer Archipelago.

Sailing northwest, Read reached the Nicobar Islands in May, where he MAROONED Dampier and several others.

The *Cygnet* made for Ceylon but was driven ashore on the Cormandel coast of India. More than half the crew deserted. Some enlisted at an English fort, others "went up and down plundering the Villages, and fleeing when they were pursued."

Read went on to the Bay of Bengal. He finally took a rich prize in April 1688, deserted with his loot, and left on an American slave ship. Electing a James Smith captain, the *Cygnet*'s crew returned to India. Some joined the armies of native princes. The rest looted an Indian ship and went to MADAGASCAR, where the wormeaten *Cygnet* suddenly sank while at anchor.

(See also SELECTED BIBLIOGRAPHY: Dampier, *New Voyage*.)

READ, MARY (1) *(British pirate; Caribbean; 1720)* Read and Anne BONNY were arrested near Jamaica with Jack RACKHAM's pirate crew, and Rackham and the other men were hanged. Since the court knew they were women, Read and Bonny received a separate trial. When witnesses testified that they had been as bloodthirsty as their male comrades, the two women also were sentenced to hang. Because they were pregnant, their execution was put off, and their fate is unknown.

READ, MARY (2) *(fictional pirate; Caribbean; 1720)* In his GENERAL HISTORY, Daniel DEFOE invented fictional biographies for both Mary Read and Anne Bonny. According to Defoe, they successfully disguised themselves as men until after they were sentenced. Bonny wore male clothing for about a year, while Mary Read had been a transvestite since birth.

Mary's mother, who had a legitimate son, became pregnant after her husband died. She fled to the country, where the son died, and Mary was born. When the mother returned, she brought Mary up as the dead son to get money from her husband's parents.

Still pretending to be male, Mary joined first the navy and then the calvary during the Nine Years' War. (Defoe's story makes Mary quite middle-aged by 1720.) She loved and married a fellow soldier. When he died, she again became a transvestite, went to the West Indies, and ended up as a pirate with Jack Rackham and Anne Bonny.

Before long, Mary loved a man forced to join the pirates. She let him know her secret, Defoe wrote, "by carelessly shewing her Breasts, which were very white." The forced man, "being made of Flesh and Blood," wanted to go further, but Mary resisted. Soon after, he quarreled with another pirate and was challenged to a duel. Mary deliberately picked a fight with the same man and ran him through with her CUTLASS.

Having thus proved her love, Mary and the forced man "plighted their troth to each other, which Mary Read said she look'd upon to be as good as a Marriage, in Conscience, as if it had been done by a Minister in Church." But their happiness lasted only a little time before the pirates were captured.

REGEB GHIELIPOGLÙ REIS *(Barbary corsair; Mediterranean; June 1555)* Captain of a GALLEON taken by a Maltese galley under Jean de LA VALETTE.

REGEB HAMZAH REIS *(Turkish captain; Mediterranean; 1556)* While carrying a rich cargo from Egypt to Constantinople, Regeb was waylaid by five galleys of the KNIGHTS OF MALTA. He surrendered after a bitter fight.

REIS *(Barbary corsair title; Mediterranean; 1500–1830)* An Arabic word (the same in the singular and plural) referring to a ship's captain or commander.

RELIGION, PIRATE *(all eras)* Although fiction writers created the myth that pirates rejected God and served the devil, many real pirates were God-fearing men. Their religious habits included belief in statements about God, the application of moral principles, and attendance at ceremonies. Pirates usually shared the faith of their neighbors, who accepted them as fellow worshipers. As long as the pirates plundered members of other faiths, clergymen applauded their cruises. Raiders often were extremely pious, and some were priests or monks.

Piracy agreed with the religious beliefs of ancient Mediterranean societies. Some pirates (BUTES, for example) were themselves descended from a god. All raiders expected their gods to help them plunder foreigners. They thanked them with a share of their booty, used to build temples and statues.

During the holy wars between Christianity and Islam from the eighth century, both sides plundered in God's name. MUSLIM rulers encouraged attacks from pirate bases in CRETE, SICILY, and southern Italy. From about 1050, the BYZANTINE EMPIRE and the Italian city-states drove out the Muslim invaders, and Christian crusaders occupied Syria and Palestine.

When Muslims reoccupied the Holy Land, the KNIGHTS HOSPITALERS moved to RHODES in 1308 and turned pirate. Until 1798, the knights remained at war with Islam—and with Christians who traded with Muslims. After the OTTOMAN EMPIRE took Rhodes in 1522, the knights went on to MALTA, where they sold port facilities to hundreds of pirate captains. Copying the Knights Hospitalers, ARUJ and KHEIREDDIN BARBAROSSA set up a Muslim military government at ALGIERS by 1525. Similar regimes were erected at TUNIS and at TRIPOLI, and Muslim pirates also raided from SALÉ in Morocco. Meanwhile, until 1618, the USKOKS scoured the Adriatic from bases in Croatia.

For both the Maltese knights and BARBARY corsairs, piracy was a religious service. The knights reported directly to the pope, just as Barbary rulers acted in the name of the sultan-caliph at Istanbul. Perhaps some corsairs privately considered religion merely an excuse for plunder. But all publicly thanked God after looting and enslaving their victims.

The Maltese knights took monastic vows, and some were priests. Freelance pirates attended Mass, and the devout Uskoks walked on their knees praising God for their booty. Barbary Muslims obeyed Islamic rules and built mosques, and only Christian RENEGADES had a reputation for impiety. Christians and Muslims both financed nuns and holy men who prayed for their success. (Thus, it is not surprising that Persian Gulf piracy increased when the QAWASIM adopted the strict Wahhabi form of Islam.)

Religious hatreds also justified piracy in the Caribbean, where French, Dutch, and English Protestants attacked the Roman Catholic Spanish. Sir Francis DRAKE, Jacques SORES, and other captains desecrated Catholic churches and spurred hatred at daily religious services. From the 1620s, Protestant pirates founded Caribbean settlements to prey on the Spanish. English Puritans occupied PROVIDENCE ISLAND. French Protestants (Huguenots) under Jean LE VASSEUR settled TORTUGA, and the DUTCH WEST INDIA COMPANY occupied Curaçao. Adriaen PATER and William ROUS thanked God for every captured ship and murdered Spaniard.

Piety and piracy also were combined by the BUCCANEERS sailing from Tortuga and PORT ROYAL after 1655. French priests said Mass for Catholics like Captain DANIEL (who shot a disrespectful crewmen during the service). Jamaican buccaneers were as religious as other English settlers, and some preached to their comrades between battles. Caribbean pirates continued to be devout after they moved to the North American mainland. William KIDD owned a pew at and helped to build Trinity Church in lower Manhattan.

Eighteenth-century Europe witnessed widespread religious revivals, which stressed personal piety rather than formal ceremonies. As Christians began to condemn piracy, fiction redefined pirates as enemies of God. Daniel DEFOE's GENERAL HISTORY (1724–1728) helped invent the myth of pirate satanism. Defoe's BLACKBEARD calls himself the devil and turns his ship into a mock hell. The equally fictional Captain LEWIS gives the devil a lock of hair as a token of his allegiance.

Changes in CAPTAIN KID'S FAREWEL show how fiction increasingly portrayed pirates as irreligious. During the 18th century, Americans added a verse to the original 1701 ballad. The new verse tells how William KIDD buried his Bible to reject God. Charles Ellms' PIRATES OWN BOOK (1834) popularized this story, which would have surprised the rector of Kidd's Trinity Church.

Fictional pirates enlisted with the devil until the end of the 19th century. TREASURE ISLAND (1883) is more accurate, since Long John Silver observes the conventional pieties and chastises George Merry for mutilating a crewman's Bible. Curiously, religion is ignored in Rafael SABATINI's five pirate novels, written between 1915 and 1936.

Recent fiction depicts pirates who are as religious as anyone else. Several buccaneers are believers in James

Michener's CARIBBEAN and Dudley POPE's novels. Perhaps because they are based on Sabatini's novels, SWASHBUCK-LER movies do not refer either to belief or to satanism. Pirate religion also is not mentioned in children's fiction or in musical comedies, such as PETER PAN and *The pirates of penzance.*

(See also BOOTY, CAPTAIN KIDD (1); GOPSON, RICHARD; IRVING, WASHINGTON; PIRACY, ACCEPTANCE OF; POLYCRATES OF SAMOS.)

RENEGADES *(Christian converts; Barbary states; 1520–1830)*   Islam welcomed converts, who often rose to high office. (In contrast, Christian governments distrusted converts. No former Muslims are found among the corsairs of MALTA.) KHEIREDDIN chose renegades to serve as his personal bodyguards, and several became corsair captains. TURGUT also favored converts including ULUJ ALI and HASAN VENEZIANO. Two-thirds of the Algerian captains listed by Father HAËDO in the 1580s were converts.

Before about 1600, the majority of renegade corsairs were Italian, Spanish, and Greek. English pirates entered

Pirate religion. "And they knelt all together and received the Holy Communion. . . ." English raiders in the Caribbean pray for God's help before assaulting their Spanish prey. Illustration by Charles Brock for an 1896 edition of Charles Kingsley's *Westward Ho!*

the Mediterranean during the war with Spain (1588–1604). After King James I outlawed piracy in June 1603, many found new havens in the BARBARY STATES. Drawn by John WARD's success, perhaps 300 Englishmen sailed from TUNIS by 1607. They were less welcome at ALGIERS, where the Dutch captain Simon SIMONSON led the corsairs from 1606 to 1609. Jan JANSSEN, another Dutch renegade, became admiral of the SALÉ fleet in the 1620s.

English, Dutch, and French captains taught the Muslim corsairs how to build and navigate "round" sailing ships and how to handle artillery. However, their dominance of Barbary piracy was short-lived. More than 150 English sailors were killed when Ward's flagship, the *Soderina,* sank early in 1608. This loss, the riotous behavior of Christian sailors, and Simonson's treasonous flight from Algiers made foreigners unwelcome unless they converted.

The corsairs were quick learners and soon mastered the sailing ship. Later renegades were less influential than Ward, Simonson, or Janssen. But Barbary continued to attract some Christian adventurers, usually from Mediterranean countries. Five of the 13 captains at Tripoli in 1679 were renegades.

(See also ALI BITCHNIN; MAMORA; LISLE, PETER; SINAN REIS.)

RENEGER, ROBERT   *(English merchant; Atlantic, Caribbean; active 1543–1545)*   The first Englishman to plunder a Spanish TREASURE SHIP, a feat previously accomplished only by French raiders. The incident embittered Anglo-Spanish relations and encouraged other English captains to attack Spanish shipping.

Reneger traded with Spain from Southampton. He received letters of MARQUE against French vessels early in 1543, but these did not apply to Spanish vessels. On March 1, 1545, near Cape Saint Vincent at Portugal's northwestern tip, Reneger and his brother John looted the *San Salvador* with several armed vessels. Their prize carried gold, silver, and pearls worth at least 19,000 ducats. Some time earlier, Reneger had taken a French prize in a harbor near Cadiz as well as a Spanish ship carrying cloth. He returned to England by April, when his ships joined the royal fleet during the naval war (1545–1546) against the French.

Reneger's presence at Cape Saint Vincent suggests that he was hunting treasure ships. He claimed that he acted in REPRISAL for the Spanish seizure of one of his French prizes—even though Anglo-Spanish treaties forbade reprisals. In response, Spain imposed an embargo and seized English goods and ships. In 1548, Reneger agreed to pay 6,000 ducats (one-third of his take) to owners of the *San Salvador*'s cargo. King Henry VIII kept his share of Reneger's booty.

(See also SELECTED BIBLIOGRAPHY: Connell-Smith, *Forerunners.*)

REPORT OF THE TRUTH OF THE FIGHT ABOUT THE ISLES OF ACORES THIS LAST SOMMER, A *(English pamphlet; 1591)*   This

pamphlet was written by Sir Walter RALEIGH after the defeat of Sir Richard GRENVILLE, his friend and cousin. A much larger Spanish fleet had trapped English ships plundering the Azores. The commander, Lord Thomas Howard, ordered a retreat. All obeyed and got away except Grenville and the *Revenge.* Rather than surrender, Grenville fought the entire Spanish fleet for some 15 hours until he was mortally wounded, his munitions were exhausted, and most of his men were dead or wounded. The *Revenge* was the sole English warship captured during the entire Spanish War (1585–1603).

The incident had no military significance, yet it presented the English government with a difficult problem. Grenville had lost an expensive battleship and many experienced seamen. Furthermore, rumors quickly spread that Lord Howard refused to aid the *Revenge* out of cowardice or personal animosity.

Raleigh may have written as a governmental spokesman, and he also sought to defend his quarrelsome cousin. Drawing upon interviews, letters, and official reports, Raleigh created a masterpiece of war propaganda. The *Report* succeeded in simultaneously justifying both Howard's decision to avoid battle and Grenville's refusal to follow orders. Raleigh's superb prose made this comparatively obscure event the best-known story in British naval history. For three centuries, dozens of lesser works drew upon the *Report* to praise "Grenville of the *Revenge*" as the finest model of heroic courage.

REPRISAL, LETTERS OF *(pirate license; 12th century to 1856)* A governmental license allowing a private individual to seize persons and property from a specific foreign country. Letters supposedly were granted to someone harmed by citizens of that country. In England, they became a convenient legal fiction that encouraged piracy. The ADMIRALTY COURT and colonial governors gave licenses to anyone promising to attack the enemy—whether or not they personally had suffered losses. Private warships were not regulated and also attacked neutral and friendly vessels. (Documents usually refer to these licenses in the plural, as "letters." They also were called letters of MARQUE.)

Reprisals originally occurred on land and at sea, during both peacetime and wars. Reprisals were condoned during the Middle Ages as well as in ancient times. A medieval city or village was a small, self-contained community. It seemed natural to take REPRISAL against any citizen who could return home and sue the real culprit. From the 12th century, the self-helper first had to get a license. By about 1300, property taken at sea could be kept only with the approval of a nation's ADMIRAL or his deputies. In England, formal letters of reprisal are first mentioned in 1293.

To encourage trade, rulers signed treaties forbidding private reprisals. Letters of reprisal were rare in France after 1485, and other European governments also limited their use. In times of war, however, they granted other types of licenses to private warships.

England continued to issue letters of reprisal, which became a ruse to hurt enemy nations. During the Spanish war (1585–1603), the Admiralty Court granted letters to anyone claiming he had been injured by Spaniards, with no proof required. These licenses allowed any English corsair to attack any Spanish ship or city, and some also seized non-Spanish and even English vessels. King James II (1603–1625), who disapproved of piracy, refused to issue letters of reprisal and forbade the use of foreign licenses. Charles I (1625–1649) revived the sale of privateering commissions. He also let the PROVIDENCE COMPANY grant unlimited letters of reprisal.

From the 1650s, officials in the Caribbean and North America issued letters and often tolerated piracy. During the Second Dutch War (1665–1657), governors and vice admirals were permitted to grant commissions against enemy shipping. Even though not at war with Spain, Jamaica's governors also permitted attacks against the Spaniards. After Sir Henry MORGAN's 1668 PORTOBELO raid, Spanish colonial governors, for the first time, also issued letters of reprisal.

During the Nine Years' War (1688–1697), colonial governors licensed private warships, which often turned pirate at MADAGASCAR. From then on, however, the fiction of reprisals was given up, and commissions simply authorized the recipient to assault the king's enemies. Most European countries (but not the United States) abolished all forms of privateering commissions by the 1857 Declaration of Paris.

(See also PRIVATEERS; REPRISAL, RIGHT OF; RIVERO PARDAL, MANOEL.)

REPRISAL, RIGHT OF *(Mediterranean; 3000–67 B.C.)* Belief in an "international law" binding all nations is relatively recent. In the ancient world, each community's law applied only to its own citizens. Since they could not enforce their own laws outside their boundaries, the Greek city-states allowed their citizens to defend themselves against foreigners. Roman law also distinguished between its own citizens, treaty allies, and the rest of the world. But this distinction became meaningless after the Romans conquered the entire Mediterranean world.

In direct contrast to the modern letter of MARQUE, a right of reprisal existed unless two communities made a treaty (called *symbola*) specifically outlawing reprisals and setting up some means of legal relief. These treaties themselves became a form of blackmail. The AETOLIAN LEAGUE encouraged outright piracy by its citizens and benefited either way. When no one complained, the Aetolians received part of the pirates' booty. If a foreign state wanted to limit pirate attacks, it had to sign a treaty recognizing the Aetolian League's authority.

(See also PRIVATEERS, ANCIENT.)

RHODES *(pirate foe and haven; 300–150 B.C., A.D. 1308–1522)* A large island (some 420 square miles) and the most easterly in the Aegean Sea, Rhodes lies about 10 miles from the coast of Asia Minor. Merchant ships traveling from Greece to the Middle East tended to stay close to the coast. Rhodes' location made it a natural center for both commerce and piracy.

Rhodes prospered from the seventh century B.C. and established colonies in Sicily, Italy, and Spain as well as along the coast of Asia Minor. In 408, the island's inhabitants came together in a newly founded city-state, also called Rhodes. The new town, laid out on a fine site with an excellent harbor, was famed for its beauty.

Rhodes became one of the richest cities of the ancient world, attracting much of the trade previously controlled by Athens. The conquests of Alexander the Great gave Greek merchants unrestricted access to Egypt, Cyprus, and Syria. With the partition of Alexander's empire after 323 B.C., the Rhodians asserted their political autonomy. Living by commerce and on imported grain, they consistently sought to suppress piracy in the eastern Mediterranean.

For more than a century, Rhodes maintained a large navy, which escorted merchant ships and destroyed pirates and pirate havens. However, the expanding Roman Empire crippled the city's trade and revenues by proclaiming DELOS a free port in 167. The Rhodians ceased to police the seas after about 150, and pirate fleets based at CILICIA and CRETE freely plundered merchant ships and coastal cities.

Captured and pillaged by the Roman general Cassius in 43 B.C., Rhodes remained relatively prosperous under Roman and BYZANTINE rule. In 1308, the KNIGHTS HOSPITALERS captured the city and converted it to a great fortress. The knights both encouraged honest trade and also sponsored piracy against vessels owned by Muslims. In 1480, a small force of knights repulsed an OTTOMAN invasion fleet. After a second hard-fought siege in 1522–1523, the knights surrendered to Sultan Suleiman I and (in 1530) transferred their activities to MALTA.

Rhodes was taken by Italy in 1912 and ceded to Greece in 1947. Under OTTOMAN rule, the population had dwindled, reaching its lowest point during the 19th century. Because of this economic stagnation, the knights' picturesque fortifications survive virtually unchanged and attract thousands of tourists each year.

RHODES, KNIGHTS OF   See KNIGHTS OF RHODES.

RICHE REIS *(Turkish corsair; Mediterranean; died 1502)*   Joining with KARA KASSAM REIS, Riche attacked a Venetian ship off northern Greece in 1496. Soon after, the OTTOMAN governor of Anatolia sent out ships that captured Riche's FUSTE at Lesbos. Although he impaled 23 of his men, the governor spared Riche and gave him a command the following year.

Riche led a corsair squadron in the Ottoman war with Venice (1499–1502). Returning from North Africa late in 1501, he stopped at Milos Island during a storm. A pilot betrayed him to the Venetians, who roasted him alive on a bonfire of galley oars.

RILESDEN, JOHN *(English captain; Atlantic, Caribbean; born 1560?, active 1587–1596)*   From Barnstable, he owned and commanded the *Prudence*, which took valuable prizes near Spain in 1587 in consort with John WATTS' ships. Acting for a syndicate of London merchants in 1595, he captured three vessels in the Caribbean. In a 1596 raid, he shared command of the warship *Neptune* with Christopher NEWPORT and Michael GEARE.

"RIME OF THE ANCIENT MARINER, THE" *(poem; 1798)*   In the poem an aged seaman tells how a storm drew his ship toward the South Pole. The ship is cursed when the seaman shoots an albatross, and all the other crewmen die of thirst. The seaman is condemned to travel endlessly, teaching love and reverence for all God's creatures.

The poem by Samuel Taylor Coleridge (1772–1834) is based on a real incident in December 1719. During a miserable passage around Cape Horn, George SHELVOCKE recorded, his ship was buffeted by a "continued series of contrary tempestuous winds which oppressed us ever since we had got into this sea." Simon HATLEY, Shelvocke's second-in-command, felt so depressed that he shot the only other living creature in sight—"a disconsolate black Albatross who accompanied us for several days as if he had lost himself." (See also SELECTED BIBLIOGRAPHY: Shelvocke, *Voyage*.)

RINGROSE, BASIL *(English buccaneer; Caribbean, Pacific; died 1686)*   His journal or diary describes the first buccaneer invasion of the Pacific from 1680 to 1682. Ringrose apparently went to the West Indies in 1679 as an indentured servant. Early in 1680, he joined raiders who had just sacked PORTOBELO.

Ringrose and the other pirates hiked across the Panama Isthmus, plundered SANTA MARIA, and defeated a Spanish squadron near PANAMA. Following the battle at Panama, one group returned to the Caribbean under John COXON, and others deserted later, after Richard SAWKINS was killed. Ringrose says he also wanted to leave, but he feared the "wild Indians" and heavy rains of the Isthmus more than a voyage on the Pacific Ocean. Ringrose sailed with Sharp on the *Trinity*, raided along the Peruvian coast, and returned to the Caribbean around Cape Horn, reaching England in April 1682.

In London, Ringrose met Charles SWAN, who had sacked Panama in 1671 with Sir Henry MORGAN. Trading on their knowledge of the region, the two men persuaded some merchants to outfit the 16-gun CYGNET for a smuggling voyage to Spanish America. Ringrose put his booty into the venture and sailed as "super cargo" to protect his investment. Swan and the *Cygnet* left England in October 1683, reached the Pacific through the Strait of Magellan, and joined Edward DAVIS' pirate squadron. Ringrose remained with the ship until his death in February 1686, during a raid on Tepic, Mexico.

Ringrose prepared his journal for publication between his two Pacific adventures. It was added (as "Part IV") to EXQUEMELIN's *Buccaneers of America* in the 1685 edition and most later versions in English.

Away in the Pacific, Ringrose did not receive credit as author, and passages were added praising Sharp's leadership.

Ringrose never took a leading role among the pirates. He sometimes commanded a boat or a small party, but he was never a superior officer. He is important because of his diary, which presents a graphic account of the buccaneers' raids, hardships, jealousies, and quarrels. To all this, Ringrose adds descriptions of places and native peoples, charts of harbors, and drawings of features interesting to seamen. His observations are accurate and insightful, although not as detailed as those of his shipmates, William DAMPIER and Lionel WAFER.

RIO DE LA HACHA *(pirate victim; 16th and 17th centuries)*

A port in western Venezuela that exported grain, livestock, and pearls taken in nearby waters. It housed a hundred Spaniards and an unknown number of slaves and mixed-race freemen in 1628, but the population fell during the 17th century.

Although Rio de la Hacha never was wealthy, its location made it an easy target for pirates invading the SPANISH MAIN. Jacques SORES took prizes there in 1555, and the harbor also was visited by Sir John HAWKINS in 1564 and by Jean BONTEMPS and John LOVELL in 1567. The Spaniards repulsed James LANGTON in 1593, but Sir Francis DRAKE sacked the town (with little reward) in 1595. In 1670, Edward COLLIER made its inhabitants supply food for Sir Henry MORGAN's raid on PANAMA.

The pearl fishing station was plundered by Anthony HIPPON in 1597. According to EXQUEMELIN, Jean FRANÇOIS attacked the pearl fishers in 1660 and took rich booty. If this assault took place at all, Exquemelin exaggerates the spoils, since the pearl banks were much depleted by that era.

RIVERO PARDAL, MANOEL *(Portuguese pirate; Caribbean; died 1670)*

For three centuries, pirates attacked Spanish shipping and colonies. Rivero was among the small number of buccaneers on the Spanish side. Although they issued PRIVATEERING commissions in Europe, Spanish officials forbade private warships in the Americas. However, in April 1669, following Sir Henry MORGAN's PORTOBELO raid, colonial governors received permission to commission privateers. Rivero was almost the only Spanish colonist to respond. His feeble assaults gave the English pirates an excuse to renew their own raids, much larger and more effective than Rivero's.

Leaving CARTAGENA in January 1670 in the *San Pedro*, Rivero headed for Jamaica but was held back by adverse winds. Attacking the impoverished settlement on Grand Cayman Island, he carried away to Cuba two small boats and four children. In Cuba, Rivero learned that Bernard

SPEIRDYKE was visiting Manzanillo. On this visit, the Dutch pirate apparently confined himself to smuggling, but Rivero captured his ship after a savage battle.

Spanish victories were rare. When Rivero returned to Cartagena in March, he received a hero's welcome and was made "admiral" of the Spanish corsairs. Taking the *San Pedro* and a captured French vessel, he went to Jamaica, seized a SLOOP, and raided isolated settlements in the north. In July, he landed on the southern coast and left behind a pompous challenge to Henry Morgan.

> I come to seek Generall Morgan with two shippes of twenty gunns and, haveing seene this, I crave he would come out uppon ye coast to seeke mee, that hee might see ye valour of ye Spaniards.

In response, Governor Thomas MODYFORD commissioned Morgan to take whatever steps were needed to defend Jamaica. Morgan collected all available English and French pirates. Instead of looking for Rivero, Morgan used Modyford's commission as an excuse to sack PANAMA.

While the pirates gathered for the Panama raid, John MORRIS accidentally ran into Rivero off the Cuban coast. The English boarded the San Pedro and shot Rivero dead. Seeing their valiant captain fall, the Spanish and Indian crew panicked and jumped into the sea, where some drowned and the rest were shot. With Rivero's ship, the English captured an epic poem he had written in praise of his own exploits.

(See also SELECTED BIBLIOGRAPHY: Earle, *Sack.*)

RIZZO, ANTONIO *(Maltese corsair; Mediterranean; active 1715–1741)*

In 1720, Rizzo applied for a two-year extension of his five-year license, since he had captured only a few poor prizes. In 1741, he sailed under Francesco di NATALE and took a captured prize back to Malta.

ROANOKE ISLAND *(pirate haven; Atlantic; 1585 to 1590)*

The first English settlement in the Americas, originally part of Virginia but today in North Carolina. In April 1585, Sir Walter RALEIGH dispatched seven vessels under Sir Richard GRENVILLE's overall command. Financing was provided by Grenville, Thomas CAVENDISH, and other gentlemen from western England interested in piracy. All the 300 settlers were men, and most were professional soldiers.

The Roanoke expedition grew directly out of previous investments in piracy by Raleigh and the other sponsors. As Roanoke's all-male population suggests, Virginia was not planned as a commercial or agricultural colony. It was intended to be a base for assaults on the West Indies and Spanish TREASURE FLEETS.

Roanoke appeared to be ideally located for piracy—close enough for quick raids but far enough from Spanish Florida for safety. Although the two nations were still at peace, English captains had been attacking Spain's West Indian colonies since the 1560s. In 1584, ships exploring the Roanoke region hunted Spanish prizes as they returned to England.

The Roanoke settlement apparently was part of a larger scheme to pillage Spanish America, and Raleigh timed his Virginia venture to coincide with other English raids. Bernard DRAKE and Sir Amyas PRESTON were expected to follow with reinforcements. After sacking cities in the Caribbean in 1585, Sir Francis DRAKE turned north, attacked Spanish Florida, and brought supplies and settlers to Roanoke.

Founded as a pirate HAVEN, Roanoke failed because Raleigh and the other investors decided an American base was not needed for successful plunder raids. The land settlement became merely an expensive nuisance that wasted resources more profitably devoted to forays from England. Both Grenville and Bernard Drake had taken very rich booty during the 1585 expedition. Meanwhile, Roanoke did not possess a deep-water harbor, and conflicts with the Indians frustrated the search for a better site. When Francis Drake reached Virginia in June 1586, after his West Indies raid, he took the disgruntled colonists back to England.

Sir Richard Grenville found the colony deserted when he arrived with reinforcements a few weeks later. It is significant that Grenville was late because he had stopped to loot merchant shipping on the way over. He left behind 15 men, who were driven off by the Indians and never seen again by English eyes. Grenville could not leave a stronger force, since his crews preferred piracy and refused to stay.

Sir Walter Raleigh decided to set up a new colony in the Chesapeake Bay region. In 1587, he sent out a more civilian expedition that included farmers and 18 women. Unfortunately, Simâo FERNANDES, a notorious pirate, served as the fleet's pilot. Anxious to be off cruising for prizes, Fernandes dumped the settlers at Roanoke rather than taking them on to Chesapeake Bay. Somewhat later in 1587, Captain William IRISH stopped in Virginia returning from a Caribbean raid, but he apparently was unable to find the colonists.

Raleigh could not send a major expedition in 1588 because Queen Elizabeth kept shipping in port for use against a Spanish invasion. He did manage to dispatch two small PINNACES, but their captains stopped to chase every merchant vessel they sighted. One was badly mauled while attacking a French ship, and both abandoned the voyage. By 1589, Raleigh had given up on Virginia. Although he financed various plunder raids in the West Indies, he made no attempt to contact the colonists abandoned in 1587.

In 1590, Sir John WATTS wanted to send Abraham COCKE to the Caribbean, but the queen again kept all ships in port. Raleigh arranged for a license to sail, and Watts in turn promised that Cocke would visit the Roanoke colony. After taking several rich prizes, Cocke

finally did make it to Roanoke, but the settlers had vanished. Their fate remains a mystery to this day.

(See SELECTED BIBLIOGRAPHY: Quinn, *Set Fair*.)

ROBERTS, BARTHOLOMEW *(Welsh pirate; Atlantic, Caribbean; 1682?–1722)*

Born (as John Roberts) to a poor family in Pembroke County, Roberts rose to mate of a Barbados SLOOP by 1718. Turning pirate, he cruised from Brazil to Canada to Africa. Altogether, he captured some 400 vessels, including several substantial prizes. Almost alone among pirate captains, he rarely drank alcoholic beverages.

In June 1719, Roberts was the third mate of a ship captured off Ghana by Howell DAVIS as its crew bought slaves for the Royal Africa Company. Roberts joined Davis' crew and took the name "Bartholomew." Tall, dark, and handsome, he was called "Black Barty" by his shipmates.

The pirates proceeded south and careened their ship at Principe Island. Toward the end of July, they were ambushed by the Portuguese governor, and Davis was slain. Roberts was elected captain of the *Rover* and revenged Davis by bombarding the town and burning the fort.

Roberts plundered a Dutch vessel and burned an English slave ship before making for Brazil. In September, he fell in with a convoy of 42 Portuguese traders escorted by two 70-gun warships. In a bold attack, he captured a larger and better-armed vessel with £30,000 in gold coins and other rich cargo. However, both the *Rover* and his prize were snatched by Walter KENNEDY, left in command while Roberts was off in a captured sloop.

Roberts renamed the 10-gun sloop *Fortune*, looted four small vessels, and outsailed a British ship sent in pursuit. After selling his booty in New England, Roberts reached the Newfoundland fishing banks in June 1720. Roberts' raiders spread terror along the coast, captured 26 sloops and 150 fishing boats, and wantonly destroyed sheds and machinery along the shore.

With the *Fortune*, Roberts seized an 18-gun galley and then traded her for a 28-gun French ship, renaming each in turn the *Royal Fortune*. As he returned south with his two ships, Roberts pillaged at least a dozen English merchantmen. The raiders fell upon the London ship *Samuel* like a "parcel of furies," destroying her cargo and taking away £8,000 in booty. Many seamen from his prizes voluntarily enlisted, and the pirates recruited others by force. Roberts preferred English seamen, and some reports say he tortured and killed French captives.

After taking on food at Deseada and Saint Bartholomew in the Caribbean, Roberts made for Africa. Through inept navigation, the pirates sailed to the south of the Cape Verde Islands and could not go back against the trade winds. Forced to return to the Caribbean, they ran out of water and survived on one mouthful a day.

Reaching the West Indies in September 1720, Roberts attacked the harbor at Saint Kitts, seized and looted one

Bartholomew Roberts. In the background are his *Royal Fortune* and *Ranger* and the 11 merchantmen Roberts captured off the African coast in January 1722. Each of Roberts's vessels displays a different flag, contrary to the myth that all pirates flew the Jolly Roger. From the second edition (1725) of the *General History of the Pyrates* by Daniel Defoe.

ship, and set fire to two others. The *Fortune* returned the next day, but was driven off by cannon fire. With his usual bravado, Roberts sent an insulting letter to the English governor.

> Had you come off as you ought to a done, and drank a glass of wine with me and my company, I should not harmed the least vessell in your harbour. Further, it is not your gunns you fired that affrighted me or hindered our coming on shore, but the wind. . . .

After repairing his ships at Saint Bartholomew, Roberts returned to the attack in late October and plundered 15 French and English vessels. In January, he captured a 32-gun Dutch slaver and played a clever trick on the inhabitants of Martinique. The Dutch ship sailed past the harbors and signaled the Frenchmen to visit Saint Lucia, where Dutch smugglers sold slaves. The pirates seized and burned 14 French ships and tortured their crews. They severely whipped some victims and cut off their ears. Others they hung from the yard-arm and used for target practice.

Roberts looted another French vessel and then careened his ships at an island off eastern Hispaniola. The *Fortune* was replaced by an 18-gun BRIGANTINE, renamed the *Good Fortune*. Soon after, his two ships captured a French man-of-war carrying the governor of Martinique. Roberts hanged the governor and took over his 52-gun ship, the third to be named the *Royal Fortune*.

In April 1721, Roberts sailed to Africa to trade his plundered goods for gold. The *Royal Fortune* at this time had a crew of 228, including 48 blacks. The *Good Fortune* carried 100 white and 40 black seamen. To keep control of these large and often drunken crews, Roberts became increasingly autocratic. On the way to Africa, Thomas ANSTIS deserted with the *Good Fortune*, but Roberts had kept the best loot on board his own ship.

Roberts arrived at Africa in June, captured four prizes, and kept one, renamed the *Ranger* (later called the *Little Ranger*). After resting at the Sierra Leone River, the rovers headed for Liberia. There they captured the Royal Africa Company's *Onslow* (with £9,000 in cargo), which became the fourth and last *Royal Fortune*.

Roberts cruised southeast to Nigeria and Gabon and then went back to the Ivory Coast, taking at least six prizes along the way. On January 11, 1722, he reached Whydah (Ouidah, now in Benin) and captured 11 slave ships, each of which paid eight pounds of gold dust in ransom. When one Portuguese captain refused to pay, the pirates burned up both his ship and its cargo of 80 slaves. A 32-gun French warship was retained as the *Great Ranger*.

Rogers decided to return to Brazil to disband his crew. Meanwhile, two British men-of-war had been pursuing the pirates along the coast. On February 5, the *Swallow*, under Captain Challoner Ogle, caught up with Roberts' squadron near Cape Lopez in Gabon. Mistaking the warship for a Portuguese trader, the *Great Ranger* chased the *Swallow* and surrendered after a gun battle.

The *Swallow* returned to Cape Lopez on February 10 and found the *Royal Fortune* at anchor. The pirates had taken a prize the previous night, and most were either helplessly drunk or hung over. Roberts dressed for battle in a crimson damask waistcoat and trousers, a hat with a red plume, and a gold chain and diamond cross.

Giving his orders with his usual boldness, Roberts sent the *Royal Fortune* toward the *Swallow* to escape with the wind. Grapeshot from the *Swallow*'s broadside brought instant death. Loyal to his last wish, the pirates threw Roberts' body overboard, rather than let it be hanged in chains from the gallows.

The *Royal Fortune* surrendered about three hours later. Captain Ogle's men found about 300 pounds of gold dust (worth around £14,000) in Roberts' three ships. The captain of Roberts' last prize had escaped after stealing other booty from the *Little Ranger*. Captain Ogle took his prisoners to Cape Coast in Ghana, where a Vice-Admiralty court was set up. Seventy black pirates were returned to slavery. Fifty-four crewmen were hanged, 37 received lesser sentences, and 74 were acquitted.

(See also SKYRME, JAMES; SELECTED BIBLIOGRAPHY: Defoe, *General History*; Richards, *Black Bart*.)

ROBERTS, CAPTAIN *(British seaman; Mediterranean; 17th century)* Roberts' ship was wrecked near the Aegean island of Nio (Ios) in 1692. Captured by a "crusal" manned by Italian corsairs, Roberts was compelled to serve as their gunner. His account of his experiences (published in London in 1699) describes the yearly schedule and methods of Christian pirates in the eastern Mediterranean.

ROBINSON, RICHARD *(English pirate; Atlantic; 1607)* Robinson and his crew (which included Peter EASTON) brought a rich prize into Baltimore, Ireland, and spent their profits in riotous drunkenness. His wife and children lived in Plymouth, England.

ROBINSON CRUSOE *(novel; 1719)* Daniel DEFOE's *The Life and Strange Surprising Adventures of Robinson Crusoe of York, Mariner* was among the first novels in

Friday's footprint in the sand startles Robinson Crusoe. An illustration for a modern edition (New York, 1903–1904) of Daniel Defoe's novel.

English. Young Robinson runs off to sea to gain wealth. On his second voyage, a SALÉ pirate captures his ship. Crusoe becomes the captain's slave, catching fish alongside a Moor and Xury, a Morisco (Spanish Muslim) boy.

One day, Crusoe sails the boat out of sight of land, throws the Moor overboard, and persuades Xury to run away with him. They journey south along the African coast and are picked up by a Portuguese vessel. Crusoe sells faithful Xury along with the boat and supplies.

Crusoe lands in Brazil and raises tobacco. In September 1659, he sets out with 16 other men in a small ship. All the rest are killed, and Crusoe lives for 28 years on an island off the Brazilian coast. With great ingenuity and a few supplies from the wreck, Crusoe builds a house and canoe and tames goats, cats, and a PARROT.

During his 25th year of exile, Crusoe rescues one of the cannibals that visit the island. Crusoe names the savage Friday, converts him to Christianity, and teaches him to speak English, to shoot, and to wear clothes. An English ship arrives. Its crew has mutinied and tries to MAROON the captain and two other men. Crusoe helps the captain overpower the mutineers and returns to England in June 1686.

The book enjoyed immediate and permanent success and inspired many imitations. In late 1719, Defoe published a sequel, *The Further Adventures of Robinson Crusoe.* Crusoe revisits his island, where he finds a flourishing colony of shipwrecked Spaniards and the mutinous English sailors. Friday is killed when savages in canoes attack near the Brazilian coast. Crusoe visits MADAGASCAR and lives in India for six years. The unwise purchase of a ship from a former pirate leads to pursuit by irate English and Dutch sailors. Crusoe makes it to China and returns to England through Mongolia, Siberia, and Russia.

Defoe modeled Robinson Crusoe and Friday on Alexander SELKIRK and WILLIAM, whose adventures were described by William DAMPIER and Woodes ROGERS. Many aspects of Crusoe's tropical island also are taken from Dampier, Lionel WAFER, and other explorers. Defoe used these factual details in creating an extraordinarily convincing account of Crusoe's exile. By skillfully evoking Crusoe's states of mind, Defoe draws the reader into the fantastic situations coolly described by Dampier and Rogers.

(See also JUAN FERNÁNDEZ ISLANDS; SELECTED BIBLIOGRAPHY: Bonner, *Dampier.*)

ROCHE, PHILIP *(English pirate; Caribbean; active 1576–1577)* Roche commanded one of Andrew BARKER's two ships during a raid on the SPANISH MAIN. In August 1577, he went along when William COXE, the other captain, mutinied and marooned Barker. Roche was killed when his ship capsized as the mutineers made for England.

ROGERS, WOODES *(English privateer; Pacific, Caribbean; 1679–1732)* After a highly profitable raid on South America's Pacific coast, Rogers suppressed the pirate haven in the Bahama Islands. His father, a prosperous sea captain, moved from Poole to Bristol in about 1697. In 1705, Rogers married a daughter of the naval commander in the West Indies. He took over his father's business interests and sent out PRIVATEERS to raid French shipping during the War of the Spanish Succession.

To encourage private looting of enemy commerce, the English government in 1708 gave up its 20 percent share in their booty. Rogers proposed an expedition to plunder South America and to capture the MANILA GALLEON. Basil RINGROSE and William DAMPIER had recounted buc-caneer attacks along the same coast. Rogers avoided the failures they described by careful planning and tight discipline.

Wealthy merchants in Bristol generously provisioned two 300-ton FRIGATES, and the 333 English and Dutch crewmen received wages as well as shares in the BOOTY. Rogers commanded the *Duke,* with Thomas Dover as second captain. Stephen Courtney and Edward COOKE took charge of the slightly smaller *Dutchess.* William Dampier was pilot and navigator, and a council of officers decided major issues.

Despite his relative inexperience, Rogers proved a superb commander. Both brave and physically tough, he won the support of his officers through honesty and diplomacy. The crew got decent food, medical care, and daily prayers. They also received a generous alcohol ration, since Rogers knew that "good liquor to sailors is preferable to clothing." But discipline was strict and maintained with the CAT O' NINE TAILS. A mutiny early in the voyage—Rogers refused to loot a neutral vessel—was firmly suppressed, and gambling was forbidden.

The two ships left Ireland in September 1708, took a Spanish prize in the Canaries, and entered the Pacific around Cape Horn. In February 1709, they rendezvoused at the JUAN FERNÁNDEZ ISLANDS and rescued Alexander SELKIRK, the original ROBINSON CRUSOE. To maintain secrecy, Rogers avoided ports in Chile and Peru. He captured several Spanish and French prizes, keeping the largest as the *Marquis.* Guayaquil, Ecuador, was taken by surprise in May. Atrocities were avoided, as Rogers' men pillaged the town and collected about 27,000 pesos in ransom.

Rogers learned that PANAMA was prepared for invasion. With stops at the Galapagos and Gorgona Islands, he made for Lower California to await the Manila Galleon. His three ships and a captured bark rendezvoused in October and spent seven weeks cruising off Cape San Lucas. Rather than run out of food, he reluctantly decided to leave for Asia. The next day, the lookout sighted *Nuestra Señora de la Encarnación Disengaño,* the smaller of two ships sent from Manila that year.

On January 1, 1710, the *Duke* captured the *Disengaño* in a running gunfight. During the battle, a musket ball pierced Rogers' left cheek and smashed out much of his upper jaw and many teeth. The *Disengaño* carried valuable Chinese goods and news that the even richer *Nuestra Señora de Begoña* was not far behind.

The *Dutchess* and *Marquis* sighted the *Begoña* on January 4, and the battle continued for three days. Despite his wound, Rogers and the *Duke* joined the fight on January 6. But the 900-ton *Begoña* carried guns throwing 12-pound shot, twice the size of the largest English shells. Rogers estimates that at least 500 shots struck her strong hull without piercing it.

The *Begoña's* passengers and 450 crewmen resisted fiercely. Rogers writes that "150 of the Men on board this great Ship were *Europeans,* several of whom had been formerly Pirates, and having now got all their Wealth aboard, were resolved to defend it to the last." The *Begoña's* defenders dropped firebombs onto the lower English vessels. One exploded some ammunition on the *Duke.* A splinter entered Rogers' left foot, "part of my Heel bone being struck out and all under my ankle cut above half thro'."

Rogers broke off the attack on the *Begoña* before his ships were destroyed. The *Disengaño,* renamed the *Batchelor,* was added to his squadron. Sailing in January 1710, Rogers returned to England in October 1711 via Guam, Java, and the Cape of Good Hope. The ships and booty were sold in 1713 for nearly £150,000. Of the owners' two-thirds, half went on expenses (including bribes), but the net profit was nearly 100 percent. Ordinary seamen got their wages, whatever PLUNDER they had picked up, and about £200 each in booty. As a captain, Rogers received more than £1,600 but went bankrupt before the money was distributed.

Rogers published *A Cruising Voyage Round the World* in 1712. Although based on his journal, the book was edited by a professional author and perhaps by Daniel DEFOE. It was widely successful, and served as a guidebook for later expeditions.

From late 1713 to mid-1715, Rogers commanded a ship carrying slaves from Africa to Sumatra. On his return, he unsuccessfully recommended the creation of a law-abiding colony at MADAGASCAR. He had more success with a similar plan for the pirate base in the Bahamas.

Late in 1717, the lords-proprietors of the Bahamas leased their property rights to Rogers for 21 years. Rogers was named the first royal governor and empowered to pardon pirates surrendering before September 1718. However, he did not receive a salary, and he and other private investors paid for the troops and settlers sent to the islands.

Rogers arrived at NEW PROVIDENCE ISLAND in July 1718, accompanied by a royal frigate, and two sloops. Under the warships' guns, only Charles VANE put up any resistance. Some pirates left for other ports. Several hundred accepted the royal pardon and were given jobs building a fort and clearing roads. However, as Daniel Defoe put it, "it did not much suit the inclination of the Pirates to be set to work." Many sneaked away and resumed their former trade. When John AUGUR was sent for provisions, he instead pillaged two vessels and MAROONED their crews on an uninhabited cay.

Since the three royal warships had left, two other ex-pirates, Benjamin HORNIGOLD and a Captain Cockram, were sent in pursuit. Although he had no authority to do so, Rogers convicted Augur and eight others on December 16 and hanged them the next day. Early in 1719, Rogers FLOGGED three islanders, who were plotting to murder him.

After this rigorous and speedy justice, pirates avoided New Providence, but Rogers faced other threats. England went to war with Spain in December 1718, and a strong Spanish force attacked in February 1720. The presence of English ships prevented a frontal attack, and the musket volleys of the former pirates repelled a landing east of Nassau.

English officials ignored the Bahamas, and Rogers returned in February 1721 to ask for aid. Both his partners and the government refused to pay for the defense of New Providence. He was imprisoned for debt and forced into bankruptcy.

Rogers' successor as governor was less forceful, and his overbearing wife monopolized retail trade. Rogers was reinstated as governor in October 1728 and granted a salary. He died at Nassau in 1732.

(See also SELECTED BIBLIOGRAPHY: Defoe, *General History;* Kemp and Lloyd, *Brethren;* Little, *Crusoe's Captain;* Lloyd, *Dampier;* Rogers, *Cruising Voyage,* edited by Mainwaring; Schurz, *Manilla Galleon.*)

ROLANDO OF THESSALONICA, SIR *(Italian corsair; Aegean and Ionian Seas; 1270s)* A Pisan knight based in Thessalonica in northwestern Greece, Rolando plundered merchant vessels together with a Spanish son-in-law named Pardo. According to the VENETIAN CLAIMS, he also robbed Venetian merchants on land near Thessalonica.

ROMANCES, ANCIENT *(Greek and Latin epics; 50 to 300)* Pirates are crucial to the plot of the five Greek romances: CHAEREAS AND CALLIRHOE, LEUCIPPE AND CLEITOPHON, DAPHNIS AND CHLOE, THE EPHESIAN TALE, and THE ETHIOPIAN ADVENTURES. The pirate episode is less important in the Latin romance APOLLONIUS OF TYRE. These ancient novels remained immensely popular until about 1800 and were translated into many modern languages during the 16th century.

The romances present adventure stories with ingeniously constructed plots. Events follow each other in rapid order, and the scenes change frequently. Their authors devote less attention to individual personalities. In their concentration on action, movement, and setting, the romances often resemble modern motion pictures more than novels written since 1800.

The surviving romances share similar plots. Each focuses on extremely beautiful young lovers. Separated by fate, they remain faithful through many adventures, including shipwreck, enslavement, forced marriage, battles, false accusations, torture, and death sentences. Ultimately, the lovers overcome all their trials, are reunited, and live happily ever after.

In these novels, kidnapping forms the main business of pirates, who capture one or both of the beautiful lovers. Most plan to sell their prisoners. In the *Ephesian Tale* and *Ethiopian Adventure,* the captain and first mate attempt to keep their captives for themselves. Here the corsairs seize ships at sea after learning their destination on land—a trick also described by PLAUTUS and attributed to the CILICIANS. Pirates in the other novels grab victims walking along the shore.

The romances portray sea raiders as second-rate villains—greedy, cruel, and often rather stupid. Only Theron in *Chaereas* is as monstrously evil as the BLACKBEARD or CAPTAIN KIDD of more recent legends. CAPTAINS have little authority and must persuade their men to act. Corsairs divide booty equally, with the man first on board an enemy vessel getting first choice. In the *Ephesian Tale*, the pirates endorse the principle that DEAD MEN TELL NO TALES.

These novels were written during one of the few eras without piracy, thanks to imperial Rome. Their authors drew on descriptions of piracy in older works. The marvelous, erotic, and violent incidents in the romances already are found in works by HOMER, other epic poems, and fictional biographies of great men. Pirates and kidnapping are depicted in the Greek plays imitated by PLAUTUS and TERENCE. Kidnapping also provides the plots of speeches in the CONTROVERSIES OF SENECA and the DECLAMATIONS OF PSEUDO-QUINTILIAN. Drawing on these sources, ancient novelists accurately described piratical practices during the last three centuries B.C.

ROMEGAS, BROTHER MATHURIN D'AUX DE LESCOUT- *(Knight of Malta; Mediterranean; died 1581)*

Member of an ancient French family descended from the counts of Armagnac, Romegas was the greatest seaman among the KNIGHTS OF MALTA, and TURGUT's only equal in sea warfare. According to legend, he captured or sank every ship he attacked.

Romegas was lieutenant on a galley when a typhoon struck Malta in October 1555. Hearing sounds from the overturned ship, rescue workers opened a hole in its bottom. Out came the sailors' pet monkey, followed by Romegas. He had clung to the keel for many hours, his head in an air pocket, the water up to his shoulders. For the rest of his life, a nervous disease caused his hands constantly to tremble.

Romegas raided as a solo corsair in 1557. After commanding a galley at DJERBA in 1560, he took command of galleys owned by grand master Jean de LA VALETTE and turned them against Muslim and Jewish commerce. His raids devastated shipping between Alexandria and Constantinople and precipitated Sultan Suleiman's attack on Malta.

In the fall of 1561, Romegas took valuable prizes near Egypt and then turned north toward CILICIA. At the Gulf of Alexandretta (Iskenderun), he caught up with a large sailing ship separated from its convoy. Romegas slaughtered its crew with cannon fire and enslaved 33 prisoners of the highest rank. One of these, an aged woman returning from a pilgrimage to Mecca, was the former nurse and great favorite of Mihrmah, the sultan's daughter.

After scouring BARBARY waters during 1562, Romegas returned to the Levant in 1563. Cruising with two galleys, he captured eight ships (sinking six, keeping two) near Alexandria. Off Kárpathos, his galley outmaneu-

vered a much larger GALLEON, thanks to calm winds. The venerable Sanjak of Alexandria, one of Islam's most famous lawyers, was taken and held for an enormous ransom.

Romegas again enjoyed good hunting in 1564 before joining up with the order's naval fleet. Between the islands of Zante and Cephalonia, the knights captured a great galleon. Owned by the sultan's chief eunuch, it was returning from Venice with luxury goods worth 80,000 ducats. Repeated losses of this magnitude reminded Sultan Suleiman that Malta commanded the major trade routes, and he assembled the army that invaded Malta in May 1565.

Romegas fought valiantly during the siege of Malta. Trying to rescue Fort Saint Elmo's defenders, he led five open boats through intense gunfire. After the knights' victory, he returned to piracy along the Barbary coast and in the Levant—both as an individual corsair and as CAPTAIN GENERAL OF GALLEYS from 1575 to 1578. He played a major role at LEPANTO in 1571 and brought news of victory to Pope Pius V.

Romegas gained great wealth, purchased his own galleys, and built a splendid palace. Held in high honor, he was almost certain to be elected grand master. But he wrecked his career in 1581. Dissident knights arrested the existing grand master and put Romegas in his place. The pope reinstalled the ousted head and ordered Romegas to apologize publicly. He died in Rome, either of poison or of shame at his humiliation.

(See also MALTA, SIEGE OF; PROSTITUTION; SELECTED BIBLIOGRAPHY: Bradford, *Great Siege*; Schermerhorn, *Malta*.)

ROSE, JEAN *(French buccaneer; Caribbean; active 1680–1685)*

Rose sacked PORTOBELO in February 1680 with Bartholomew SHARP, but did not follow Sharp's party across Panama and into the Pacific. In January 1685, the buccaneer-author Raveneau de LUSSAN ran into a pirate squadron that included Jean Rose commanding a captured Spanish SLOOP. After running to Curaçao and Venezuela without taking prizes, Captains Rose, LE PICARD, and Desmarais decided to cross the Panama Isthmus.

About 264 buccaneers arrived at the Pearl Islands on April 21 and joined up with other groups. During their adventures in the Pacific, Edward DAVIS assumed overall command of the English pirates. Jean GROGNIET took charge of the Frenchmen, including Rose and his crew.

ROSE OF PARADISE, THE *(novel, 1888)*

The writer-illustrator Howard PYLE describes Captain John Mackra's bloody battle near MADAGASCAR with Edward ENGLAND's pirates. The novel (serialized in *Harper's Weekly* in 1887) includes eight halftone illustrations.

Using Daniel DEFOE's GENERAL HISTORY as a point of departure, Pyle invented his own plot. Mackra is entrusted with an enormous ruby, the Rose of Paradise. England steals the gem through treachery, and Macra successfully recovers it. *Rose* is as much a novel of self-revelation as it is a tale of adventure. Captain Mackra, who narrates the story, carefully records his reactions and emotional states as events occur. A sensitive and high-strung man, he is devoted to duty and honor. Although he has faults, he is fundamentally unselfish as well as honest, generous, loyal, and resourceful.

Edward England is a more ambiguous character. Like Long John Silver in TREASURE ISLAND, he is wicked yet attractive because of his courage, intelligence, and occasional moral sensitivity. Totally self-centered, England feels no loyalty to his men and knocks them about. The men copy England's cold-heartedness and abandon him on Mauritius Island when he falls ill.

One of Mackra's passengers steals the ruby and betrays the ship to the pirates. England doublecrosses the traitor and pockets the gem rather than sharing it as booty. When he discovers the theft, Mackra goes back to the pirate ship—to secure the safety of his passengers and crew as well as to recover the gem. England saves Mackra's life, but he is disgraced and exiled when he returns to Bombay.

Following England's trail, Mackra finds him on Mauritius Island and nurses him through a deadly fever. Apparently thankful for Mackra's help, England grudgingly gives him the ruby. The novel ends ambiguously. As Mackra leaves, England fires a shot—perhaps to murder Mackra, perhaps to hurry him on his way.

ROSE, THOMAS *(English pirate; Atlantic; 1545)*
Rose and another captain captured a Spanish wine ship anchored in Ireland. They tortured the crew by twisting bowstrings around their hands and genitals.

ROSSI, GIOVANNI *(Maltese corsair; Mediterranean; active 1715–1741)*
Lieutenant and pilot for Francesco di NATALE from 1739 to 1741, Rossi frequently commanded one of the FELUCCAS that left the mother ship to hunt for prey. It was his crew that pillaged the boat of a Greek monastery. Rossi sued Natale in 1742 to collect a wager. The trial records state that he became a corsair in 1715.

ROUNSIVIL (ROUNSEVELL), GEORGE *(British pirate; Caribbean; born about 1690)*
From Dorset, he was at NEW PROVIDENCE ISLAND in 1718, when Woodes ROGERS became governor. Rounsivil, aged 18, was among the crew when Rogers sent three SLOOPS to buy food in October. Phineas BUNCE and others mutinied and seized the ships but were recaptured. At their trial, witnesses said that Rounsivil joined the mutineers, changed his mind, but was afraid to desert. Rogers reprieved Rounsivil at the last minute, after he was brought to the scaffold.

Daniel DEFOE wrote that he later went PRIVATEERING with a Captain Burgess. Rounsivil got safely away when their ship was wrecked, but Burgess was stuck aboard.

"Upon which," Defoe reported, Rounsivil "jump'd into the Water, and swam to the Vessel, and there perished with his Friend since he could not save him."

(See also SELECTED BIBLIOGRAPHY: Defoe, *General History*.)

ROUS, WILLIAM *(English pirate; Caribbean; active 1631–1643)*
Born into a land-owning family in Cornwall, Rous was the half-brother of John Pym (1584–1643), a prominent Puritan politician. In 1631, Pym sent him to the pirate haven at PROVIDENCE ISLAND. Rous governed Providence's main fort and also raided in small ships. In October 1636, he was captured while attacking Santa Marta, Venezuela, with the 200-ton warship *Blessing*. Thanks to money sent by Pym, he escaped from a Spanish prison in 1639 with the surviving crewmen from the *Blessing*.

Rous commanded the land troops when William JACKSON's raiders sailed from England in 1642. After helping sack several Venezuelan cities and occupy Jamaica, Rous left the expedition in April 1643, having learned of his election to Parliament.

ROUSSAY REIS *(Moroccan corsair; Mediterranean; 1690s)*
Roussay was an unsuccessful SALÉ captain. In 1693, a Portuguese CARAVEL without cannon held off Roussay's 14-gun warship for more than two days. Roussay captured no prizes during two long cruises in 1694, and he took only a small Spanish vessel in 1695.

ROY, LEONARDO *(Maltese corsair; Mediterranean; 1707)*
Appointed captain by a warship's owners, Roy applied to the TRIBUNALE DEGLI ARMAMENTI for a five-year license to raid in BARBARY and the Near East.

RUBY OF KISHMOOR, THE *(novel; published 1908)*
Howard PYLE published this tale to spoof pirate novels. The earnest Quaker hero suffers through extravagantly romantic adventures, and the impressionistic color illustrations emphasize the story's nightmare quality.

A prologue explains that Captain Keitt stole a great ruby and later was murdered with all of his crew, except three men. Years later Jonathan Rugg visits Jamaica. Rugg is a Philadelphia Quaker, whose "sedate and sober demeanor" hides romantic desires for adventure and excitement.

A mysterious veiled woman asks Rugg to guard a small ivory ball. A small gentleman with one eye, a foreigner with silver EARRINGS, and a sea captain with a flattened nose try to kill Rugg when they learn he has the orb. Each of them dies in their struggles with the astonished Quaker.

Rugg returns the ivory ball to the woman, who turns out to be Keitt's daughter. She has been harassed by the three treacherous pirates, who had killed her father to get the fabulous ruby hidden in the ivory ball. To thank Rugg, she offers him her ruby, her wealth, and herself. He refuses in alarm, flees back to Philadelphia, and

Anne Bonny (Jean Peters) and Blackbeard (Thomas Gomez) enjoy a glass of rum in *Anne of the Indies* (1951).

marries plain Martha Dobbs. On his wedding day, a rope of pearls mysteriously arrives. The money from its sale makes Rugg one of the city's leading merchants.

RUM *(Caribbean beverage; 1600s to the present)* A distilled liquor made from sugar by-products. English and French colonists grew Caribbean sugar cane from the 1640s, and production steadily increased until the 19th century. Before shipping, many growers cured or semi-refined sugar in clay pots. As the sugar crystallized, large amounts of a brownish liquid called molasses drained out containing remnant sucrose. Planters recycled this liquid into a potent drink with a sweetly burnished taste.

Molasses and skimmings from the boiling kettles fermented naturally and then were distilled. The clear liquor turned darker if aged in wooden casks. All rums were full-flavored; rums with a "lighter" taste were a 19th-century innovation. French colonists called the liquor *tafia*. The English initially named it kill-devil or rumbullion, soon shortened to rum.

Along with everyone else, Caribbean and North American pirates drank vast quantities of rum, mostly because it was inexpensive. During the 1700s, large amounts went to British North America and England, which also made more from imported molasses. However, Spanish Cuba and Puerto Rico produced significant amounts of sugar cane and rum only from the late 1700s.

Early rums probably were stronger than modern versions, although no way of measuring "proof" existed until the 1820s. Rum was mixed with other liquids, both hot and cold, depending on personal taste and what was available. (Adding fruit juices prevented SCURVY.) To test rum, water and a few black gunpowder grains were added, and the mixture was heated with a magnifying glass. If too much water was added, the gunpowder did not explode.

(See also BUMBOO; DRINKING; GROG; PUNCH; RUMFUS-TIAN; SELECTED BIBLIOGRAPHY: Rogoziński, *Caribbean*.)

RUMFUSTIAN *(beverage; Caribbean, Atlantic, Indian Ocean; 17th and 18th centuries)* A hot drink generally made of beer, gin, and sherry mixed with raw eggs, sugar, cinnamon, and nutmeg.

(See also DRINKING.)

RUYTERS, DIERICK *(Dutch captain; Atlantic, Caribbean; active 1618–1630)* Ruyters was briefly imprisoned while raiding Brazil in 1618, and he visited the West Indies in 1619. A student of astronomy and mathematics, he drew upon both his own experiences and Portuguese accounts to write the *Torch of Navigation*, published in 1623. The DUTCH WEST INDIA COMPANY, which plundered the Spanish Empire from 1621, depended on Ruyters and his *Torch* for accurate information about the seas around Africa, Brazil, and the West Indies.

Ruyters served as navigator during Piet HEYN's first voyage (1624–1625) to Brazil and West Africa. In 1630, following the Dutch conquest of Pernambuco, Brazil, Ruyters took six ships to the Caribbean. There he linked up with Pieter ITA's squadrons but took few prizes.

(See also SELECTED BIBLIOGRAPHY: Goslinga, *Dutch*; Rogoziński, *Caribbean*.)

RYSWAN REIS *(Barbary corsair; Mediterranean; 1679)* A French RENEGADE at TRIPOLI, Ryswan commanded the 16-gun *Souls in Purgatory*, captured from Venetians.

S

SABATINI, RAFAEL *(British author; 1875–1950)* Sabatini wrote plays, movie scripts, and more than 40 novels and biographies. His works were immensely popular even though critics complained of his melodramatic plots, and historians attacked his frequent errors of fact. In several novels, he invented a type of pirate romance, imitated by later writers. THE SEA HAWK (1915) is set in 16th-century England and the Mediterranean. The 17th-century Caribbean provides the background for CAPTAIN BLOOD (1922), CAPTAIN BLOOD RETURNS (1931), THE FORTUNES OF CAPTAIN BLOOD (1936), and THE BLACK SWAN (1932).

Sabatini's pirate novels combine romantic entanglements and daring deeds. For Sabatini, piracy provided a perfect setting for love affairs between admirable women and misunderstood men. Forced to turn pirate, his heroes excel at the trade but retain their sense of honor. Sabatini's plots turn on the hero's efforts to win the affections of a beautiful and virtuous woman. She initially rejects him because of the gap between his chivalrous manner and his dealings with criminals. Before they can come together, the hero must both prove he is honorable and also end the evils that involved him in piracy. Moments of courtship thus alternate with periods of vigorous action.

Sabatini's romances reconcile two conflicting myths, which began with Daniel DEFOE's GENERAL HISTORY. One myth portrays pirates as heartless fiends. In the other, they are brave rebels against a corrupt society. Sabatini has it both ways. He describes most pirate captains as brutes and murderers. Although they associate with these brigands, his heroes remain pure at heart and combine all manly virtues.

Piracy allowed Sabatini to place his hero's adventures in exotic locales. He treated history as mere background and freely revised the lives of historical characters to suit his plots. Sabatini revealed his attitude in an author's comment after Blood's lieutenant tells an outrageous lie. Sabatini remarked that "there was a great historian lost in Wolverstone. He had the right imagination that knows just how far it is safe to stray from the truth and just how far to colour it so as to change its shape for his own purposes."

Sabatini's novels inspired movie scripts partly because he excelled in painting word pictures. After one battle in *Captain Blood, His Odyssey*, Blood's "head-piece was gone, his breastplate dinted, his right sleeve a rag hanging from his shoulder about a naked arm. He was splashed from head to foot with blood. . . , mixing with the grime of powder on this face." From that horrible mask, two vivid blue eyes looked out, "and from those eyes two tears had ploughed each a furrow through the filth of his cheeks."

SABCULI REIS *(Barbary corsair; Mediterranean; died 1556)* A Turk sailing from TRIPOLI for

TURGUT REIS, Sabculi was enslaved for a time by the KNIGHTS OF MALTA. In 1556, he commanded one of three GALIOTS that ran into Maltese GALLEYS near Stromboli Island. The knights vanquished MURAT REIS and NASUF REIS. But Sabculi escaped by pretending to surrender and lowering his sails. Suddenly ordering his slaves to began rowing at full speed, Sabculi made a 360-degree turn and rowed off directly into the wind. The Maltese galleys, still under full sail, could not follow.

Sabculi tried the same trick against some Venetian galleys a few days later, but an enemy ship headed him off. This time, the Christians cut off Sabculi's head rather than enslaving him.

SACCOGLI REIS *(Barbary corsair; Mediterranean; about 1496 to 1556)* Saccogli was a Turk who became a corsair, rose to captain, and roamed the Mediterranean and Adriatic for more than 30 years. By the 1540s, Saccogli was based in DJERBA. He quarreled with TURGUT REIS, who sequestered his ship from 1546 to 1551, probably because he refused to serve with the OTTOMAN fleet during wartime. He was killed when a Venetian squadron took his large GALLEY by surprise.

SACHETTI, IGNAZIO *(Maltese corsair; Mediterranean; early 19th century)* When Britain occupied Malta in 1800, Sachetti renamed his ship *La Gran Bretagna* and marauded under a British PRIVATEERING license.

SAHAP, SHERIP *(Malay pirate; South China Sea; 1840s)* Partly Arab in origin, Sahap claimed descent from Mohammed. He led about 5,000 MALAY and DYAK pirates from a fort about 50 miles up the Batang Lupar River in western Sarawak. His brother Sherip Mullar commanded a smaller fort 15 miles further upstream. The English called their followers the Sekrang pirates, referring to their original home on a tributary of the Batang Lupar.

Cruising in small squadrons, the Sekrang raiders looted trading and fishing boats and scoured the coast for heads and plunder. In August 1844, Sir James BROOKE led an assault that destroyed the Batang Lupar forts as well as other Dyak settlements. Sherip Sahap fled to Dutch Borneo (now part of Indonesia). His brother Mullar joined other pirates on the SARIBAS River and probably was killed during another of Brooke's anti-pirate raids in 1848.

(See also SELECTED BIBLIOGRAPHY: Keppel, *Expedition*; Runciman, *White*; Rutter, *Pirate*.)

SAINT AUBIN, BROTHER BERNARDO ROCQUELAURE DE *(Knight of Malta; Mediterranean; active 1569–1583)* Saint Aubin commanded naval squadrons but also owned ships that raided for his individual profit. In 1575, his GALIOT raided in the Near East under Captain Nicolo COSTA. In 1578, commanding his own galley, he captured a richly laden merchant vessel. In 1582 and 1583, Saint Aubin com-manded the grand master's personal galley during successful piratical cruises. His own galiot (under another captain) formed part of the squadron in 1583.

SAINT AUBIN, BROTHER PIERRE ROC-QUELAURE DE *(Knight of Malta; Mediterranean; active 1560–1598)* In 1565, Saint Aubin commanded a galley owned by Grand Master Jean de LA VALETTE. (ROMEGAS, Malta's greatest corsair, commanded La Valette's other galley). In late May, back from raiding the BARBARY COAST, he found an OTTOMAN fleet besieging MALTA and ran for safety.

Six enemy galleys gave chase, but only one could match Saint Aubin's speed. Seeing that the other five had dropped away, he suddenly turned his galley around—a difficult maneuver for an oared ship. His pursuer fled back to Malta. Saint Aubin went on to Sicily to persuade the Spanish viceroy to reinforce Malta. On June 30, he returned with four galleys and several hundred soldiers.

After the siege ended, Saint Aubin went back to piracy, usually operating alone except during wartime. (He commanded a Maltese galley at LEPANTO in 1571.) After a 1597 cruise, Saint Aubin returned to Malta with five prizes, much gold, and more than 270 captives—including Ottoman officials and Jewish merchants who could pay high ransoms. His piratical skills brought Saint Aubin both riches and honor. He built a fine palace and was elected CAPTAIN GENERAL OF GALLEYS from 1595 to 1598.

SAINT MARY'S ISLAND *(pirate haven; Indian Ocean; about 1690–1722)* A narrow island about 35 miles long (modern Île Sainte-Marie, also called Ambodifototra) off MADAGASCAR's northeastern coast, Saint Mary's was favored by pirates cruising in the Indian Ocean and Red Sea. Europeans could control the island's relatively small population, and its landlocked and bottlenecked harbor was easily defensible. Between 1691 and 1697, Adam BALDRIDGE built a fort and warehouses where booty and slaves were traded for European products. Although Baldridge was driven off, other traders took over his fort. Saint Mary's remained a major base and a refuge for shipwrecked and retired pirates.

SAINT STEPHEN, KNIGHTS OF See KNIGHTS OF SAINT STEPHEN.

SALÉ *(pirate haven; Atlantic; 17th century)* Located at the mouth of the Bou Regreg in MOROCCO, Salé (today known as Rabat and *not* the modern city of Salé) was the main Atlantic base for Muslim pirates. About 1609, it became a haven for Moriscos, Muslims expelled from southern Spain. The Moriscos, who elected their own government, expelled the Moroccan authorities in 1627 and erected an independent pirate republic. (Other Morisco refugees set up a smaller piratical principality in Tetouan, east of the Strait of Gibraltar.)

As in TUNIS, Europeans often served as captains and officers, particularly after 1614, when the pirate base at

MAMORA was destroyed. The Moriscos provided the fighting men; the sailors and rowers were unarmed Christian slaves. By the 1620s, Salé supported more than 40 warships, most small, light CARAVELS.

Salé corsairs usually stayed in the Atlantic, where they rivaled raiders from ALGIERS as the main threat to Christian shipping. (It often is difficult to know which city corsairs came from, since Salé welcomed Algerian rovers.) The Salé rovers initially attacked Spanish vessels near the Strait of Gibraltar, the Azores, Madeira, and the Canaries. From the early 1620s, they also raided in the English Channel, near western England, and as far north as Ireland. They carried out slave raids on the English coast, held Lundy Island for two weeks, and sometimes crossed the Atlantic to capture men from the Newfoundland fishing fleet.

The French (in 1629, 1630, and 1635), the English (in 1637), and the Dutch (in 1649 and 1650) all sent naval expeditions against Salé. None of these ventures hampered the pirates for long, and Muslim fleets again raided England's west coast in 1639 and 1640. Because they could not defeat the corsairs, the European powers sent consuls to Salé, and the Dutch signed a treaty with its rulers in 1651.

The glory days of Salé piracy ended in 1668. The corsairs' republic disappeared as Sultan Mawlay Ishmail (ruled 1672–1727) imposed his authority over Morocco. Despite peace treaties with France and England in 1682, piracy continued on a smaller scale until BEN AÏSSA retired in 1698. Stronger English and French navies ended raids to the north, Spanish commerce and shipping declined, and the sultan heavily taxed the remaining corsairs. Sultan Mawlay Mohammed (ruled 1757–1790) unsuccessfully tried to revive the Salé fleet under state control. Piracy was outlawed in 1818 and disappeared after 1829, when Austrian gunboats destroyed the Moroccan fleet.

(See also BARBARY WARS.)

SALES, CAPTAIN *(French buccaneer; Caribbean; 1697)* Captain Sales took part in the Sack of CARTAGENA.

SALIH REIS (1) *(Barbary corsair; Mediterranean; died 1556)* Born in Egypt, of middling height, corpulent, and dark-skinned, Salih became BEYLERBEY of ALGIERS thanks to his naval successes. Brought to North Africa—probably in 1517 as the OTTOMANS conquered Egypt—he became a great favorite of KHEIREDDIN BARBAROSSA. In 1529, second-in-command to AYDIN REIS, Salih raided the BALEARIC ISLANDS and Spain, defeating a larger Spanish squadron.

When Kheireddin became Ottoman admiral-in-chief in 1533, Salih accompanied him to Constantinople and remained one of his main advisors. He commanded the left wing during Kheireddin's victory at PREVESA in 1538, and he was with the fleet visiting France in 1542. After the Franco-Ottoman forces took Nice, Kheireddin sent Salih's squadron to sack cities on the Catalonian coast.

Hasan Pasha, Kheireddin's son, who ruled Algiers from 1544, did not inherit his father's passion for sea warfare. In 1551, war again broke out between the Ottoman Empire and the Habsburg rulers of Spain and Austria. Sultan Suleiman's French allies highly esteemed Salih Reis as a warrior and a man of "noble courtesy." They had hoped that Salih would succeed Kheireddin as Ottoman admiral, and they now persuaded Sultan Suleiman to make him beylerbey of Algiers, replacing Hasan Pasha.

Salih imposed Ottoman control on the territory inland from Algiers to the Sahara. Just as he arrived in April 1552, the Tuggurt and Ouaregla tribesmen refused to pay tribute. Aided by the Beni-Abbas, fierce mountain warriors, Salih crushed the rebellion and seized large amounts of gold and 5,000 black slaves.

The following June, Salih personally commanded 40 warships. Although they had little luck along the Spanish coast, the corsairs captured a Portuguese squadron carrying the pretender to the throne of Fez in Morocco. Salih's captives proved useful during battles with the Moroccans a few months later.

Salih could not suppress the Beni-Abbas, who turned against him thanks to Moroccan and Spanish bribes. But he won the support of the Koukou tribe, their traditional enemies. During the winter of 1553, the Koukou provided cavalry for a lightning-swift raid on Fez that ended Moroccan incursions.

Salih was now ready to attack the Spanish territories in North Africa. His corsairs occupied the island of Valez in 1554. In June 1555, he personally led a land and sea attack on Bougie (Bejaia). The Spanish governor saved himself and his officers by surrendering. As soon as he arrived home, the Spanish government beheaded him for cowardice.

Once in control of Bougie, Salih planned to conquer the remaining Spanish forts at Oran and Mers-el-Kebir. Sultan Suleiman sent 40 galleys from Constantinople, while Salih brought 30 corsair vessels from Algiers. Oran was saved when Salih died of the plague while at sea, forcing the sultan to call off the attack.

SALIH REIS (2) *(Barbary corsair; Mediterranean; 1571)* Sailing from ALGIERS, Salih's BRIGANTINE was seized by a Venetian galley near the LIPARI ISLANDS.

SALIH REIS (3) *(Moroccan corsair; Mediterranean, Atlantic; 1760s)* This Salih Reis was famed for his bravery. In 1767, commanding a 14-gun SHEBEC, he captured a French ship after a fierce battle. Most of the French crew died, and 40 of Salih's corsairs were killed or wounded. In 1769, the sultan, trying to rebuild SALÉ's corsair fleet, named Salih ADMIRAL of Morocco and gave him command of a newly constructed 30-gun warship.

SALMAGUNDI/SALMAGUNDY *(pirate food; Caribbean, Atlantic, Indian Ocean; 17th–18th centuries)* The colloquial French name for a highly seasoned cold salad. Salmagundi was a favorite food of the Caribbean BUCCANEERS, who carried it north to the Atlantic and east to West Africa and MADAGASCAR. Bartholomew ROBERTS was eating salmagundi for breakfast when he was surprised by British warships off West Africa in 1722.

The strong seasonings and chopped vegetables both prevented SCURVY (1) and added variety to a diet of dried and smoked foods. Meat of any kind—including turtle, duck, or pigeon—was roasted, chopped into chunks, and marinated in spiced wine. Imported salted meat, herring, and anchovies also were added. When ready to serve, the smoked and salted meats were combined with hard-boiled eggs and whatever fresh or pickled vegetables were available, including palm hearts, cabbage, mangoes, onions, and olives. The result was stirred together with oil, vinegar, garlic, salt, pepper, mustard seed, and other seasonings.

SALMAN REIS *(Turkish corsair; Mediterranean; active 1490–1525)* Born on Lesbos, Salman won fame warring on Christian shipping. Shortly after 1500, he became an officer in the Egyptian navy and helped protect Egypt's Red Sea territories against Portuguese attack. He directed the construction of an Egyptian fleet at Suez in 1513 and led it against Yemen in 1516. Joining the OTTOMAN navy when Selim I (ruled 1512–1520) conquered Egypt in 1517, he commanded the fleet that defeated the Portuguese at Jedda (Jiddah) in that year.

(See also SELECTED BIBLIOGRAPHY: Guilmartin, *Gunpowder.*)

SALTER, THOMAS *(English buccaneer; Caribbean; 1669)* Salter commanded a ship during Sir Henry MORGAN's raid on Maracaibo and Gibraltar, Venezuela.

SAMOS *(pirate haven; Aegean Sea; 700–400 B.C., A.D. 1600–1800)* A large island opposite the ancient city of Miletus in Asia Minor. Samos lies near the main sea lanes between Greece and the Near East. Its Greek inhabitants prospered through trade and piracy in antiquity and—on a lesser scale—during more recent times.

During the seventh century, Samian merchants were noted for the daring of their long-range voyages. Samians helped to reopen trade with Egypt and were the first to reach Spain's southwestern coast. Like other early traders, they also engaged in slave-trading and seized foreign ships. By the 600s, Samian pirates preyed on Cypriote and Aegean commerce from camps in CILICIA.

Samian corsairs even attacked vessels belonging to foreign rulers. When the Spartans attacked Samos in 525, they cited two such acts of piracy to justify the invasion. In about 505, the Samians had seized a richly embroidered breastplate given to Sparta by the king of Egypt. The next year, they had captured a Spartan ship

and taken a valuable drinking-cup being sent to King Croesus of Lydia.

As in many other Greek city-states, Samian rulers encouraged piracy, unless a foreign city had signed a treaty of alliance. At least during some eras, the government took 10 percent of the corsairs' booty. About 540, Aeakes (Aikes)—a public official and probably POLYCRATES' father—erected a statue of the goddess Hera. Aeakes, the inscription states, paid for the statue with the city's share of booty taken during wars or from foreign ships.

SAMSON, CAPTAIN   See DENBALL, SAMPSON.

SAMUEL, ABRAHAM *(African-French pirate; Indian Ocean, Persian Gulf; active 1693–1699)* Said to be from Martinique, Samuel was QUARTERMASTER of John HOAR's *John and Rebecca.* After a profitable voyage, the pirates retired in February 1697 to SAINT MARY'S ISLAND, near MADAGASCAR. About July, the natives rebelled against the pirates, killing Hoar and 30 others.

Samuel and the other survivors reached Fort Dauphin, an abandoned French settlement at Madagascar's southeastern tip. Some months later, the local queen decided that he was her long-lost son—taken away when the French fled 20 years earlier. She claimed him as her child and made him chief.

Samuel remained suspicious of his new relatives, for he ruled with 20 pirate bodyguards. He traded with visiting ships and once sold a captured vessel to some pirates, attaching a large wax seal as "King of Fort Dauphin." How long King Samuel's reign endured is unknown. In December 1706, a Dutch vessel found his fort deserted and a native chief in charge.

(See also BALDRIDGE, ADAM; SELECTED BIBLIOGRAPHY: Ritchie, *Kidd.*)

SAN JUAN DE ULÚA *(Spanish treasure port; Gulf of Mexico; 16th–18th centuries)* A wharf and fortifications were erected from 1535 on this island off the Mexican coast, which became the port for Veracruz. The coast is flat and sandy without a natural harbor. Ships are exposed to the full force of storms, and Spanish captains always tried to make it to Havana, Cuba, before the hurricane season.

Despite its disadvantages, San Juan de Ulúa was one of only three ports visited by the annual TREASURE FLEETS taking American wealth to Spain. At San Juan, the galleons collected the king's share of the silver from Mexican mines. They also picked up valuable Oriental goods brought to Acapulco by the MANILA GALLEONS and shipped across Mexico. (Although technically illegal, Spanish authorities tolerated this traffic.)

Like PANAMA, San Juan lived for the fleet's annual visits. During most of the year, it was a relatively small town without great wealth. Pirates seldom raided San Juan. The treasure fleets were too strong to attack, and the pickings were slim when they were absent. In 1568,

Sir John HAWKINS and Sir Francis DRAKE visited San Juan to make repairs after a storm. The Spaniards assaulted their squadron and destroyed four of the six ships. Other raiders from England and the Netherlands hunted treasure ships in the waters between San Juan and Havana until 1640, but they did not attack the port itself.

The buccaneers based in the Caribbean also left San Juan alone. Since it was far to the northwest of their Jamaican and Haitian bases, they faced a long return voyage against the prevailing easterly trade winds. In 1683, Laurens de GRAFF and seven other captains finally raided San Juan and Veracruz and took substantial booty.

SANTA MARIA *(pirate victim; Caribbean; 17th century)* A small fortified town (near present-day El Real) in eastern Panama, where Spanish colonists collected gold dust and stored it for shipment to Panama City. BUCCANEERS raided Santa Maria with varying success. In 1680, Bartholomew SHARP arrived just after the gold had been shipped. Peter HARRIS was luckier in 1684, and his crew took a rich haul. Captain TOWNLEY in 1685 found the town deserted after Harris' raid. The Spaniards subsequently strengthened the garrison, which drove off an assault by William DAMPIER in 1704.

SANTO HIZO, GIUSEPPE DE *(Italian pirate; Adriatic Sea; 1558)* Sailing from Messina in a GALIOT owned jointly with the head of the Sicilian treasury, Santo Hizo sacked a Muslim vessel near the Albanian port of Alessio (Lezhë), taking 15,000 ducats in booty.

SANUDO, (TORSELLO) MARINO *(Italian historian; 1260–1338)* Related to the Venetian dukes of Naxos, Sanudo wrote a history of Greece (*Istoria del Regno di Romania*), which draws on official documents and eyewitness reports in describing Mediterranean piracy.

SAO, CHENG I *(Chinese pirate; South China Sea; early 19th century)* An outstanding woman pirate, Sao controlled fleets that plundered shipping and looted villages near Canton between 1807 and 1810. In her management of subordinates and in her deliberate use of terror, Sao equaled any western captain.

Pirates infested the South China seas whenever the central government in Peking was weak. The Manchus, the last imperial dynasty, had lost control of the southern provinces by 1800. Pirates (called *landrones* by Europeans) took a heavy toll on both Chinese and European shipping. The most powerful band was led by CHENG I, one of the master pirates of all time. Unlike Europeans, some Chinese sailors brought their wives on board. By all accounts, these women pirates were as cruel as their menfolk.

When Cheng was drowned during a typhoon in 1807, his captains elected his widow, Cheng I Sao, as their new chief. Sao expanded the force until it included 800 large junks and nearly a thousand smaller ones, crewed by 70,000 men. Sao's own JUNK boasted 38 CANNON, two of them 24-pounders.

Sao's pirates frightened most of the villages in Canton Province into paying tribute money. Villages that fell behind in their payments suffered devastating raids. The brigands cut off the heads of men killed during these attacks, slinging them round their necks by a cord through the victim's pigtail.

This force of disciplined marauders also captured European ships. In September 1809, they seized and held for ransom seven men from an East Indiaman anchored at the mouth of the Canton River. The fourth officer, Richard Glasspoole, kept a detailed account of his three months in captivity. Sao's pirates, Glasspoole reports, held wealthy merchants for ransom. They gave captured crew members a choice between joining their band or dying painfully (FLOGGING).

Those joining the pirates submitted to a code of conduct, similar to the ship's ARTICLES signed by European marauders. However, Sao imposed more rigid rules and more severe penalties than European codes. Chinese *landrones* had to register all the booty they took. Sao's officers seized four-fifths of each haul for a general fund, kept in a well-guarded storehouse. A seaman going ashore without permission had his ears slit. A second offense brought death. The code also imposed the death penalty on sailors who raped captives without permission. ("No person shall debauch at his pleasure captive women. He must first ask the quartermaster for permission and then go aside in the hold.") Sao herself took several lovers from among her officers.

Sao routed three fleets sent by the Chinese imperial government, even though these had the aid of Portuguese warships. In 1808, she annihilated the imperial fleet by concealing the main body of her ships behind a headland. During a 16-hour battle, these squadrons came out of hiding and attacked the enemy fleet from behind. The imperial admiral, shamed because he had survived the disaster, committed suicide at Sao's feet.

A second Chinese fleet sent to avenge this rout fared no better. Its commander (a general), frightened by the sight of Sao's armada, ordered his captains to retreat. The pirates followed and overtook the imperial ships. When they caught up with them, the wind had dropped to a dead calm. Hundreds of *landrones* swam the distance to the imperial ships, swarmed aboard, and killed the general and most of his crews.

Sao could not keep so enormous a fleet together indefinitely. By 1810, bickering among the admirals of the pirate squadrons led to mutiny. After the imperial viceroy offered an unconditional pardon, several of Sao's captains surrendered. Finally, with a Portuguese doctor acting as negotiator, Sao herself bought an imperial pardon. Although some of her followers began honest life ashore, Sao spent several decades as the director of a large smuggling operation.

(See also CHANG PAO.)

SARIBAS *(Borneo pirates; South China Sea; 19th century)* A confederation of DYAK tribes living on the Saribas River, about a dozen miles north of the Batang Lupar River in Sarawak. By the 1840s, the Saribas raided in hundreds of boats carrying several thousand warriors. Sir James BROOKE led two expeditions that destroyed their villages and ended large-scale piracy.

SAUMUR, PAUL DE *(French corsair and Knight of Malta; Mediterranean; 1597–1668)* Known as Le Chevalier Paul ("Sir Paul"), Saumur was the illegitimate son of a washerwoman and the governor of the Chateau d'If, a fortress off Marseilles. Born on board a ship taking his mother to her lover, his seamanship and audacity earned him ennoblement (in 1649) and high rank in the French navy.

Paul ran away to sea as a boy, and killed his corporal during a duel in Malta. He fled on a corsair BRIGANTINE, distinguished himself in battle, and took command when his captain was killed in action. In one battle, his single ship defeated five OTTOMAN galleys. From a base in a ruined castle on Lesbos, he devastated Aegean shipping, and (prior to 1637) plundered the annual convoy from Alexandria to Constantinople.

Paul's exploits attracted the attention of the KNIGHTS OF MALTA who raided in the same waters. In 1637, the grand master received him as a sergeant-at-arms (non-noble member) and made him captain of a galley. The French government gave him command of a French warship the following year.

In 1647, during a war with Spain (which ruled southern Italy), Paul led five ships in a raid on Naples. Pursued by 13 sailing ships and 11 galleys, Paul outsailed and drove off the enemy during a bloody three-day battle. When French corsairs insisted on immediate payment in advance, he personally financed another attack on Naples in 1649. In 1652, he was named lieutenant-general for Near Eastern waters. Nearly always successful, he was still in command of the Toulon fleet when he died of gout.

SAVOISY, CHARLES DE *(French corsair; Mediterranean; early 15th century)* Banished for three years following bloody quarrels at the University of Paris, Savoisy spent his exile plundering Muslim North Africa. With the wealth and slaves captured during these forays, he built a magnificent château at Seignelay near Auxerre. In 1405, he joined PERO NIÑO in raiding the English coast.

SAWKINS, RICHARD *(English buccaneer; Caribbean; active 1679–1680)* Joining John COXON and other captains, Sawkins looted Spanish ships at the Bay of Honduras in 1679. Although Jamaica's governor tried to keep them away, the pirates managed to dispose of much of their loot.

Early the next year, Sawkins was cruising off Costa Rica with a small 16-ton ship with only one gun. There he joined Bartholomew SHARP's company, which had just looted PORTOBELO. Led by John Coxon, the pirates marched across the Isthmus to assail SANTA MARIA and PANAMA.

Sawkins displayed a crazy courage that impressed the pirates but ultimately took his life. At Santa Maria, he rushed the fort before most of the pirates had arrived, obviously hoping to secure the pick of the plunder. He was again first into the fight at Panama, where the pirates attacked three Spanish warships on May 3.

During an unusually savage battle, Sawkins ran his small boat against the larger Spanish ship commanded by Francisco de Peralta. (Peralta had escaped with a treasure ship when Sir Henry MORGAN assaulted Panama in 1671.) The combat between the two crews, Basil RINGROSE wrote, "was very hot, lying board on board together, and both giving and receiving death unto each other as fast as they could charge."

The buccaneers applauded Sawkins' savage fearlessness. Accused of cowardice, Coxon left for the Caribbean. Sawkins became the new commander and prepared to invade the Pacific. Needing fresh meat, he crossed to Pueblo Nuevo on June 2. He again rushed into battle before the other ships arrived and was killed by the town's defenders.

SAXBRIDGE, TIBALT *(English pirate; Atlantic and Mediterranean; active 1608–1609)* One of Richard BISHOP's confederation based in Ireland in 1608. Bishop and John JENNINGS rescued Saxbridge in August, when an English warship attacked off Baltimore, Ireland.

Saxbridge was a "little fellowe" with a ship of only 35 tons, but he took his crew on a far-flung adventure. In September 1608, he seized a French ship returning from Africa and sold her rich cargo in Ireland. Sailing to MOROCCO and on to the West Indies, he lost eight men trying to send a landing party ashore. Hungry and ill, the pirates went north to Newfoundland and attempted to take a French ship at night. But the Frenchmen drove them off, demolishing their ship and killing Captain Saxbridge. The survivors begged passage home on other vessels.

SAYER, AMBROSE *(English corsair; Mediterranean; active 1600–1613)* A gentlemen from Cornwall, Sayer was arrested for piracy in Italy, spent seven years in jails in Florence and Rome, and was then condemned as a GALLEY SLAVE with the Sicilian fleet. With other Protestant prisoners, he seized a ship and escaped to ALGIERS in 1610. There he became commander of a corsair squadron, taking several French and Spanish prizes. In 1613, his galley was captured at SALÉ by an English corsair resident in LIVORNO, Italy. Sent back to England for trial, he was convicted of piracy, but apparently once again escaped.

SAYINGS, PIRATE See EXPRESSIONS, SEAFARING.

SCALAWAG *(motion picture; color; 1973)*
Kirk Douglas both directed *Scalawag* and played the role of Peg, a one-legged pirate whose men died after burying treasure. An alcoholic PARROT knows where the gold is, but he won't tell. Peg and his cut-throats befriend young Jamie (Mark Lester) and his sister Lucy-Ann (Lesley Anne Down). Together they search for the treasure, while battling a mutiny, hostile Indians, and deadly rapids.

SCALAWAG/SCALLYWAG *(slang word; 19th century to the present)* A contemptuous and insulting term, which has nothing to do with sailors, the sea or piracy. Originally American and of unknown origin, it refers to a rascal or scamp, especially one who refuses to work and is good for nothing.

SCERDILAIDAS *(buccaneer king; Mediterranean; died about 207 B.C.)* A warrior chief in ILLYRIA and probably a brother of King Agron, Scerdilaidas fought for plunder and changed sides with amazing ease. When TEUTA, Agron's widow, took power in 230, Scerdilaidas led her forces south against Epirus. After the Romans defeated Teuta, he shared power in Illyria with DEMETRIUS OF PHAROS.

In a peace treaty in 228, the Illyrians had agreed not to sail south into the Ionian and Mediterranean. In the summer of 220, Scerdilaidas and Demetrius of Pharos broke the treaty and embarked with 90 warships. They first joined the AETOLIANS in raiding Pylos, on Greece's southwestern tip. When this attack failed, Demetrius took 50 ships and looted the Aegean islands, while Scerdilaidas returned toward Illyria.

On the way home, Scerdilaidas put in at Naupactus, an Aetolian port, to visit his wife's kinfolk. There he joined forces with some Aetolian chieftains. The brigands successfully sacked a city just south of Aetolia, carrying off many slaves and cattle. But the Aetolians refused to give Scerdilaidas his promised share of the loot. Enraged, Scerdilaidas made a treaty with Philip V of Macedonia. For an annual payment of 20 TALENTS, Scerdilaidas promised to attack the Aetolians with 30 ships.

The next year (219), when the Romans defeated Demetrius of Pharos, Scerdilaidas returned to Illyria and made himself king. However, owing to disturbances throughout Illyria, he sent Philip of Macedonia only 15 ships in 218. Since he had provided half the ships promised, Philip refused to pay the full subsidy.

Feeling that he again had been cheated, Scerdilaidas in 217 dispatched a pirate fleet to punish Philip. By pretending they were still allies, his corsairs captured four Macedonian warships in the harbor of Levkás. They then turned east into the Aegean, plundering and capturing any merchant vessels they could find. This was Scerdilaidas' final pirate raid. Impressed by Roman power, he stood firmly by his new allies until his death.

SCHAMPENDAM, HUGO *(Dutch admiral; Pacific; died 1625)* Schampendam commanded during the largest Dutch plunder raid on South America's Pacific coast. After a truce with Spain expired in 1621, the government created the DUTCH WEST INDIA COMPANY to coordinate plunder raids on Africa and the Americas. However, the company's directors concentrated on Brazil and the Caribbean and refused to attack in the Pacific. Thus the Dutch government directly outfitted a fleet to sack South American ports and, if possible, to establish a military colony.

The government assembled 11 great ships—five of 600 tons or more—carrying 1,600 men. This was the strongest force of sailing ships ever seen in the Pacific. Since it took almost no booty, the expedition also holds the record as the most expensive failure in the history of sea raids.

The fleet left in April 1623, cruised leisurely down the African coast, and sailed around the recently discovered Cape Horn. (Earlier raiders had entered the Pacific through the Strait of Magellan.) The Chilean coast was reached at the end of March 1624.

Jacques L'HERMITE initially commanded the expedition. Schampendam took over in April 1624, when l'Hermite became mortally ill. The admiral apparently died of natural causes, even though a physician—in league with the devil—later was convicted of poisoning seven sailors. Schampendam proved an unpopular and irresolute leader.

The Dutch ships headed for Arica, where Peruvian silver was collected for shipment to Panama. They just missed capturing the annual treasure fleet thanks to the cunning of a Spanish captain. The viceroy had dispatched the king's silver on May 3. Learning of the Dutch incursion, he sent out two ships to discover whether the second part of the fleet could safely depart with private hoards. One ship was captured on May 7. Under interrogation, the Spanish captain convinced his captors that the treasure fleet had sailed weeks instead of days earlier.

Fooled by his prisoner, Schampendam changed plans and attacked Lima and its port of Callao. Although Callao was weakly fortified, the Spaniards beat off several landing parties. Schampendam blockaded the port for three months, but his ships captured only small coastal traders carrying foodstuffs. Another detachment captured and burned Guayaquil, Ecuador, but took little booty.

During the blockade, the invaders acted with great brutality. When the viceroy refused to negotiate, Schampendam hanged 20 prisoners. Another time, while returning from Puná Island, the squadron, threw 17 captives into the sea tied back-to-back. According to Spanish accounts, one of the prisoners, a Franciscan friar, was tortured before he was drowned. "The privateers took him by surprise, split his head with a cutlass and opened up his stomach, removing his entrails whilst he was still alive."

Schampendam left Callao at the end of August and made for Mexico to intercept the MANILA GALLEON. Following an assault by Joris van SPILBERGEN in 1616, the Spaniards had strongly fortified Acapulco, which repulsed the Dutch assault on October 28. At the end of November, Schampendam gave up efforts to find the Manila Galleon and sailed for the Moluccas. There the various ships split up and entered the service of the East India Company. Schampendam's attack frightened the Spanish government, which erected strong forts at Callao and Lima. Although some of these still exist as impressive ruins, they were never tested in battle, as future raiders bypassed Callao.

(See also SELECTED BIBLIOGRAPHY: Bradley, *Peru*.)

SCHOONER *(pirate ship; Caribbean, Atlantic; 18th century)* A vessel of less than 100 tons with a narrow hull and two masts. The characteristic rig had two large sails suspended from gaffs (spars) reaching from the top of the mast toward the stern. Other sails might be added, including a large headsail attached to the bowsprit. The schooner was extremely fast but large enough to carry a substantial crew. Its shallow draft allowed pirates and smugglers to navigate shoal waters and hide in remote coves.

SCHOUTEN, PIETER *(Dutch captain; Caribbean; 1624–1625)* After earlier excursions to the West Indies, Schouten in 1624 led the first Caribbean raid by the DUTCH WEST INDIA COMPANY, founded in 1621 to loot the Spanish Empire. With three ships, Schouten made a thorough reconnaissance of the Lesser Antilles, the Venezuelan coast, Haiti, Jamaica, and Cuba. His squadron plundered the Yucatan, destroying at least two towns and capturing at least six prizes.

As the squadron returned to Cuba, one of Schouten's ships became separated from the other two. After a fierce battle, it captured a GALLEON from the Honduras TREASURE FLEET. While towing this glorious prize home, the Dutch warship was wrecked at the Dry Tortugas, and its crew returned aboard the Spanish vessel. Schouten himself arrived home in April 1625, rich in information and booty.

SCURVY (I) *(naval disease; all oceans; 1500–1800)* An illness caused by a lack of vitamin C. After 12 to 16 weeks, dark blotches and sores cover the skin, pimples appear on the gums, and teeth fall out. Severe symptoms include internal bleeding, brittle bones, and deep lethargy.

Mediterranean and Caribbean sailors did not suffer from scurvy, since they returned to port frequently. The disease became deadly during long voyages to Asia or from Europe to South America's Pacific coast. Since men became feeble before they died, many shipwrecks resulted. Altogether scurvy may have killed some 2 million sailors between 1500 and 1900.

Scurvy defeated or hampered some pirate cruises. During the 1500s, scurvy ended raids on South America by Sir Thomas CAVENDISH and Sir Richard HAWKINS, and it crippled Sir James LANCASTER's East Indies expedition. Many also died during voyages from South America to Asia during the 1680s.

However, pirates probably suffered less than men on naval and merchant vessels. Experienced captains understood the disease's causes. As early as 1593, Richard Hawkins wrote, ". . . that which I have seen most fruitful for this sickness is sour oranges and lemons." The JUAN FERNÁNDEZ ISLANDS and MADAGASCAR became pirate bases because they provided fresh food. SALMAGUNDI enabled pirates to eat even unappetizing vegetables.

In contrast, accepting the advice of physicians and scientists, the British navy was especially slow to provide anti-scurvy foods. When Admiral George Anson took 1,955 men around the world (1740–1744), 1,051 died, most of scurvy. British naval vessels provided lemon juice only in 1795, merchant vessels from 1854. (When lime juice later was substituted, British sailors were called Limeys.) The American navy was even less careful, and seamen died during the BARBARY WARS. The disease became less important beginning in the 1930s, when vitamin C's benefits were discovered.

SCURVY (2) *(derogatory word; 15th century onward)* An extremely insulting adjective. *Scurvy* originally referred to someone whose skin was covered with scurfs (scales) or scabs, and it later meant any sorry, worthless, and contemptible person or thing. Although it appears 19 times in William Shakespeare's plays, the word was obsolete by about 1650. Pirate comedies use *scurvy* and other somewhat archaic but nasty-sounding words because books and movies cannot repeat the insults sailors really used.

(See also SWEARING.)

SEA DYAKS See DYAKS.

SEA HAWK, THE (I) *(novel; 1915)* A pirate romance by Rafael SABATINI, author of CAPTAIN BLOOD. Sales were limited in 1915, because paper was rationed during World War I. When a new edition appeared in 1923, *The Sea Hawk* was among the 10 best-selling books in the United States. Two movie adaptations were equally popular. Despite some factual errors, Sabatini's description of the BARBARY corsairs is plausible. However, Sabatini is too kind to Sir John KILLIGREW and fails to mention his crimes as a pirate and receiver of stolen goods.

Sir Oliver Tressilian, a "tall, powerful fellow of good shape," lives in Cornwall near the Killigrews. Tressilian is a pirate, who fought with Sir John HAWKINS at SAN JUAN DE ULÚA and later battled the Spanish Armada. Throughout, Tressilian is obsessed by his love for Rosamund Godolphin. Rosamund stubbornly rejects Tressilian because she believes (erroneously) that he killed her brother.

Tressilian is kidnapped by Lionel, his half-brother, and ends up as a Spanish GALLEY SLAVE. When his vessel is taken by the pasha of ALGIERS, Tressilian converts to Islam and joins the corsairs. His valor and fury in battle earn him the name Sakr-el-Bahr ("Sea Hawk"). He commands the Algerian fleet and seems destined to rule the city, as did ULUJ ALI and other worthy RENEGADES.

But the Sea Hawk still loves Rosamund. Like Captain Blood, the Hawk refuses to war on his countrymen, and he buys and frees captured Englishmen. Through one of these captives, he sends a letter to Rosamund proving his innocence. She burns it unread and even plans to marry Lionel, his weak and cowardly brother. At news of this, the Sea Hawk's embittered love swells up. His corsairs sail a captured CARRACK to Cornwall, the first Algerians to enter the Atlantic (an honor actually held by MURAT THE GREAT). They abduct Rosamund and Lionel and carry them to Algiers.

The pasha's Sicilian wife is insanely jealous of the Sea Hawk's power. The time comes to auction the Sea Hawk's captives and divide the receipts among the corsairs. The Sea Hawk buys his brother Lionel to use as a galley slave. He also wins Rosamund in a frenzied bidding war against agents acting for the pasha and for his wife.

At the Sea Hawk's palace, he and Rosamund express their love-hate until Lionel finally confesses his crimes. The pasha arrives, lusting after Rosamund. To save her, the Sea Hawk marries Rosamund in a Muslim ceremony. The next day, he smuggles her aboard his vessel, concealed in a palmetto bale. He is about to lead a raid and plans to free her on the French coast.

The pasha takes command of the Sea Hawk's vessel and is infuriated when Rosamund is discovered. At the BALEARIC ISLANDS, their ship is trapped in a narrow cove by Sir John Killigrew. Killigrew's men attack, Lionel is wounded, and the Sea Hawk threatens to blow up his vessel. Killigrew agrees to take the Sea Hawk and Rosamund and spare the Muslims.

Killigrew and a royal official judge the Sea Hawk, once again Sir Oliver Tressilian. He cannot be convicted of piracy outside of English waters—the actual English law at the time. Rosamund, finally recognizing Tressilian's innocence, defends him, and the dying Lionel confirms her words. Tressilian is saved and falls into Rosamund's passionate embrace.

SEA HAWK, THE (2) *(motion picture; black and white; 1924)*

This action-filled silent film follows the plot of Rafael SABATINI's novel. Milton Sills plays Sir Oliver Tressilian, renamed the "Sea Hawk." Lloyd Hughes is his wicked brother Lionel Tressilian, and Enid Bennett plays his fiancée, Rosamund Godolphin. Wallace Beery is Jasper Leigh, the sea captain who kidnaps Sir Oliver.

Errol Flynn romances Brenda Marshall in *The Sea Hawk* (1940).

The Sea Hawk cost about $800,000 to make, an extraordinary sum of money in 1924. Four large wooden ships were converted into replicas of 17th-century vessels. In four separate seafights, the ships duel with CANNON, the men swing across the deck, and individuals fight long SWORD DUELS. Some of these battle scenes were reused in the 1935 CAPTAIN BLOOD.

Director Frank Lloyd took pains to make the GALLEY SLAVE sequences seem realistic. The sweaty, unshaven slaves look tired and weatherbeaten, and they appear to feel real pain as the whip strikes.

SEA HAWK, THE (3) *(motion picture; black and white; 1940)*

Again under the direction of Michael Curtiz, Errol FLYNN recreates the swashbuckling character he played in CAPTAIN BLOOD. Warner Brothers had planned a sequel based on Rafael SABATINI's SEA HAWK (1). When World War II broke out, only Sabatini's title was kept. The studio substituted a patriotic story (loosely based on Sir Francis DRAKE's exploits) that links the Spanish Armada to Hitler's planned invasion.

As the story begins in 1585, King Philip's shadow looms over an enormous map of the world. The evil ruler explains that Spain, having conquered the rest of the world, now must suppress England. To fool Queen Elizabeth, Don José Alvarez de Cordoba (Claude Rains) goes to England as ambassador, accompanied by his gorgeous niece, Doña Maria (Brenda Marshall).

During the movie's one major sea battle, Captain Geoffrey Thorpe (Errol Flynn) captures a Spanish GALLEASS. Thorpe frees the English GALLEY SLAVES in a moving sequence possibly inspired by Charles Kingsley's WESTWARD HO! He then takes the indignant Don José and Doña Maria to Queen Elizabeth (Flora Robson).

The queen pretends to be outraged at Thorpe's attack. Secretly, she agrees to a raid on the mule trains bringing treasure from PANAMA to Nombre de Dios. Thorpe and Doña Maria reveal their mutual love in a rose garden.

Lord Wolfingham (Henry Daniell) is a royal advisor and a secret Spanish agent (an allusion to Nazi collaborators). Wolfingham and Don José spy out Thorpe's destination and set a trap. In Panama, Spanish troops ambush Thorpe's band, and the few survivors retreat through the deadly tropical jungle. They reach their ship but are captured by the Spaniards.

When Thorpe proudly admits to plundering nine cities and 54 vessels (including CARTAGENA), a Spanish judge sentences him as a galley slave. Thorpe and his men toil at the oars, exhausted and beaten (with real whips, the story goes). On the way to Cadiz, they break loose, scoop up the plans for the Armada invasion, and swarm over the side of a Spanish galley. Singing a lusty patriotic song, they row back to England.

Aided by Doña Maria, Thorpe fights his way to the queen. Wolfingham bars his path, and the two men fight a wild SWORD DUEL. Casting gigantic shadows, they battle down flights of stairs and through cavernous halls, smashing furniture and lopping off the tops of chairs and candles. After Thorpe runs the traitor through, six guards attack him until Queen Elizabeth bursts into the room.

Thorpe hands the queen the Spanish invasion plans. Elizabeth declares war and orders the building of a new war fleet. As the crowd cheers, she knights Thorpe, who will lead the British to glorious triumph. A smiling Doña Maria stands at Thorpe's side as the seamen sing "For England—and the Queen!"

The Sea Hawk drastically revised Sir Francis Drake's biography. Before release, the studio dropped Drake's name to avoid offending the British public. Characters named Sir Martin FROBISHER and Sir John HAWKINS briefly appear. Galley slave sequences were popular, and they may refer back to Sabatini's *Sea Hawk*. However, Drake never was enslaved. In Panama, the Spaniards repeatedly fire MUSKETS without reloading. They often call themselves British, a name not used in the 1500s.

The Sea Hawk is now considered a classic SWASHBUCKLER. Flynn did his own rope swinging and fencing, although doubles fought the final duel. The stars are seconded by superb character actors, and Erich Wolfgang Korngold provided one of his lushest scores.

SEA LIONS, THE; OR, THE LAST SEALERS, (novel; 1849)
James Fenimore COOPER's novel, which mixes whaling and buried treasure, was influenced by folk legends about CAPTAIN KIDD. Young Roswell Gardiner (descended from the man who welcomed Kidd back to New York) sails to the Antarctic for whales. On the way home, he visits a Caribbean cay and finds treasure buried near a tree and a small sand hill. Cooper's theme of treasure hunting with a dead seaman's map was borrowed in TREASURE ISLAND.

The story begins in 1819 at Oyster Pond (Oyster Point) in northeastern Long Island, where Thomas Dagget is dying. A former pirate or friend of pirates, the penniless sailor had been left behind by a passing ship and owns only a sea chest. Deacon Ichabod Pratt visits Dagget to learn his secrets. The seaman tells Pratt that his sea chest hides two maps, one describing a rich whaling ground, the other locating pirate treasure.

When Dagget dies, Pratt grabs the chest, copies the maps, and erases important directions from the originals. Roswell Gardiner leaves in the *Sea Lion* to find the seals and the treasure. The dead sailor's relatives discover the maps and send a second ship, also named *Sea Lion*, to pursue Gardiner. Dropping the pirate story, Cooper devotes the rest of the novel to the perils of whaling and the rivalry between the two vessels. At the end, Gardiner tells the dying deacon that he had found $2,300 in gold coins after searching the island for a month.

"SEAMAN'S SONG OF CAPTAIN WARD, THE" (ballad; 1609)
Fifteen six-line stanzas condemning John WARD, an English pirate who marauded from TUNIS with great success. Ward is depicted as a totally evil man who denies God and spends his wealth in drunkenness and debauchery. He will find, the song predicts (incorrectly, it turned out), that his riches will waste away.

> This wicked-gotten treasure
> Doth him but little pleasure;
> The land consumes what they have got by sea,
> In drunkenness and letchery,
> Filthy sins of sodomy,
> Their evil-gotten goods do wast[e] away.

(See also SELECTED BIBLIOGRAPHY: Firth, *Naval*.)

SEA PEOPLES, THE (sea raiders; Mediterranean; 12th century B.C.)
The name given to several unrelated tribes that invaded from the northeast and were defeated by Egyptian forces about 1186. Their destruction is recorded in carved inscriptions and pictures on the walls of a large temple at Medinet Habu, near Thebes. The detailed carving of this sea battle is unique. It is the only pictorial representation of an actual naval combat to have survived from any part of the ancient world.

Ramses III (about 1195–1164) built the Medinet Habu temple, and its carvings praise the pharaoh's military genius. According to the inscription describing the 1186 attack, the Sea Peoples were great warriors and sea raiders. They had destroyed the armies of every other nation before they fell to Ramses' invincible might.

Some modern authors—accepting the pharaoh's pompous boasts—describe the Sea Peoples as pirates who had come together in a massive raid. However, the great land and sea attack described by the Medinet Habu inscriptions seems to be a hoax. There is no evidence that any of the "Sea Peoples" practiced piracy before they invaded Egypt in 1186. And, of the six peoples mentioned, only the TJEKER (or some of them) became seamen and pirates after their defeat in 1186.

Modern scholars are not certain about the meaning of the names given to the individual Sea Peoples in the ancient Egyptian writing. However, it is likely that the Peleset, Shekelesh, Denyen, and Weshesh fled back north and became farmers in Palestine. There the Pelesets' descendants may have become the Philistines mentioned in the Old Testament. Like their Hebrew enemies, the Philistines were never a sea-going people, and their cities did not have harbors.

The Tjeker also settled in Palestine, in the region around Dor. From this base, they carried out piracy on a large scale around 1100. Some of the Shardana went to Palestine, but others escaped to Cyprus, and their descendants later colonized and gave their name to Sardinia. In the Medinet Habu inscriptions, Pharaoh Ramses brags that he alone could defeat these mighty buccaneers. What really seems to have happened is that various northern groups—fleeing some unknown disaster—sought refuge in Egypt. Some marched south along the coast, while others traveled in small boats. Most were farmers, and they brought with them their wives, children, and cattle.

The Medinet Habu carvings portray the Egyptians' cruel tactics in graphic detail. The so-called Sea People actually had smaller boats than the Egyptians, and their warriors had no armor. Most important, unlike Ramses' forces, the invaders lacked bows and arrows. The Egyptians encircled the enemy vessels. Coming to a halt just within bow range, they poured arrows into the ranks of the defenseless enemy oarsmen. Those who managed to swim toward shore were met with further volleys. The encounter ended in an ugly slaughter and not a battle between warriors.

The Egyptians easily defeated the Sea Peoples because they were migrating farmers rather than true sea raiders. Real corsairs do not travel with their families and cattle, and professional warriors would have known that the Egyptians fought with bows and arrows. The story told by the Medinet Habu carvings is as much fantasy as historical fact.

(See also SELECTED BIBLIOGRAPHY: Breasted, *Ancient Records*.)

SEARCH, RIGHT OF *(pirate procedures; Mediterranean; about 1650–1830)* Unlike most pirates, the BARBARY corsairs practiced a trade regulated by their own government. To protect their commerce, some Christian nations signed peace treaties with Barbary rulers. Thus Barbary pirates legally could attack the nations of some ships but not of others.

Sea captains from treaty nations often carried goods and persons belonging to Barbary's enemies. To prevent such chicanery, the treaty nations allowed Barbary corsairs to stop and search their ships. The corsairs could seize enemy passengers and property found on friendly

ships. But they had to pay the captain the full freight charge to their destination.

A different problem was posed by friendly passengers and property found on a captured enemy ship. The corsairs could confiscate the cargo and enslave the crew, but they were supposed to free passengers from nations protected by treaties. A system of PASSES was created to identify the latter.

SEARLE, ROBERT *(English buccaneer; Caribbean; active 1662–1671)* Searle's career suffered during frequent quarrels with Governor Thomas MODYFORD of Jamaica, who normally befriended buccaneers. Searle may have invaded Santiago, Cuba, with Sir Christopher MYNGS in 1662. The political situation changed, and Modyford outlawed attacks on Spanish colonists in June 1664. Searle brought in two Spanish ships in August and began to unload sacks of gold and silver. Governor Modyford seized his prizes and ordered his rudder and sails brought ashore.

Searle got his ship back with the outbreak of the Anglo-Dutch War (1665–1667). In 1665, Searle joined Edward MORGAN's expedition against Saint Eustatius and Saba. The next year, Searle and Captain STEDMAN took two small ships and 80 men to Tobago and destroyed everything they could not carry away.

Governor Modyford forbade further raids in June 1669. Ignoring his order, Searle attacked Saint Augustine, Florida, early in 1670. Although he acted, he said, to revenge a Spanish raid on the Bahamas, Searle was arrested and imprisoned. He was freed after some months and took part in Sir Henry MORGAN's sack of PANAMA.

While he was at Panama, according to some reports, Searle missed an extremely rich prize because his crew was drunk. Searle was pursuing Spaniards who had fled to islands near Panama. On one island, his crew found and emptied a store of Peruvian wine. Soon after, the raiders captured a boat from a Spanish GALLEON fleeing with Panama's treasures. Searle ordered his men to pursue the galleon, but they were in no shape to obey.

EXQUEMELIN faulted Morgan for the galleon's escape. However, according to William DAMPIER, its Spanish captain told him Searle was to blame. In later years, Dampier wrote, Searle moved to Honduras, where an English LOGWOOD cutter killed him during a quarrel.

(See also SAWKINS, RICHARD.)

SEELANDER, JOHN (HANKYN) *(English pirate; English Channel; active 1436–1456)* Sailing from Falmouth and Fowey, Seelander raided with other West Country pirates and captured Breton, Flemish, English, and Portuguese ships. He apparently had friends throughout the region, since nothing came of frequent royal orders to arrest the pirates and restore stolen goods. In 1441, for example, Seelander captured several Breton ships off the Isle of Wight and openly sold their cargoes of wine and salt in Newport.

(See also SELECTED BIBLIOGRAPHY: Kingsford, *Prejudice.*)

SEKRANG *(Borneo pirates; South China Sea; 19th century)* DYAK raiders living on the Sekrang River, a tributary of the Batang Lupar River, about 60 miles east of Kuching, Sarawak's capital. Sekrang raiders were especially aggressive in the 1840s, under Sherip SAHAP (whose main fort actually was located on the Batang Lupar and not the Sekrang).

SELEUCUS *(Cilician pirate; Mediterranean, Black Sea; first century B.C.)* Seleucus led a corsair force that fought for King MITHRIDATES during his third war with Rome (74–66). During the first part of the war, Seleucus' fleet maneuvered in the Aegean alongside Mithridates' regular navy. When a storm destroyed his fleet and flagship in 72, Mithridates leaped aboard Seleucus's own vessel, which carried him safely to the BLACK SEA port of Sinope (modern Sinop).

After the Romans defeated Mithridates's armies the following year (71), the CILICIAN corsairs continued to defend Sinope. Led by Seleucus and a eunuch named Clechares, they routed the Roman navy and held off LUCULLUS' besieging army for almost a year. Rather than surrender to the hated Romans, the corsairs burnt Sinope and their heavier warships after cramming their small boats with loot. Although Seleucus and many others escaped during the night, Lucullus is said to have killed 8,000 Cilicians left behind in the burning city.

SELIM TRABLESI (TRIPOLISSY) REIS *(Barbary corsair; Mediterranean; active 1760s)* Captain of a 45-gun FRIGATE at TRIPOLI in 1766, Selim also sailed from SALÉ.

SELKIRK (SELCRAIG), ALEXANDER *(Scottish seaman; Atlantic, Pacific; 1676–1721)* The real-life model for the marooned sailor in ROBINSON CRUSOE. The seventh son of a country shoemaker, he fled arrest for "indecent behavior" in church. Thanks to a keen mind and aptitude for mathematics, he rose from common seaman to respected navigator.

In April 1703, the buccaneer-author William DAMPIER sailed for South America's Pacific Coast. Dampier's own vessel was accompanied by the 90-ton *Cinque Ports,* a heavily armed and overcrowded warship. When the *Cinque Ports'* captain died off Brazil, Thomas STRADLING advanced to captain, with Selkirk second-in-command.

Stradling was a tyrannical and mediocre captain. When the two ships reached the JUAN FERNÁNDEZ ISLANDS in February 1704, the *Cinque Ports'* crew mutinied. Dampier persuaded the men to go on, but they took few prizes and were defeated at SANTA MARIA, Panama. Stradling and Dampier argued, and the two ships separated. By the time the *Cinque Ports* returned to Juan Fernández in October, Selkirk hated and distrusted Captain Stradling. The two men almost came to blows, and Selkirk insisted on going ashore.

Although he acted impulsively in the midst of an argument, Selkirk's decision was not irrational. He took his sea chest, weapon, tobacco, and navigational instruments. English and French ships entering the Pacific usually stopped at Juan Fernández for food and water. A few months alone seemed far better than close quarters with Captain Stradling. As it turned out, the *Cinque Ports* soon sank off the Peruvian coast. Stradling and a few survivors were imprisoned in a Lima dungeon.

Unfortunately, friendly ships reached Juan Fernández only in February 1709, more than four years later. When Woodes ROGERS' expedition visited the island, his boats returned with Selkirk "cloth'd in Goat-Skins, who look'd wilder than the first Owners of them." Selkirk had been tormented by loneliness for months, Rogers reported; but he eventually learned to live alone. He tamed baby goats and hundreds of cats, "and to divert himself would now and then sing and dance with them." Unable to tolerate fish without salt, the hermit existed on spring water, lobsters, goats, and fruit. He had forgotten how to speak, but was so healthy that he could outrun goats as well as men and dogs.

Rogers wrote down Selkirk's stories in his journal, published in 1712 as *A Cruising Voyage.* Additional details were provided by Sir Richard Steele (1672–1729), a pioneer journalist who interviewed Selkirk in 1713. These accounts inspired Defoe's novel, although he located Crusoe's island off Brazil.

Selkirk joined Dampier's raiders, who captured a MANILA GALLEON and returned to England in October 1711. After living for a time on his £800 share of the booty, Selkirk became a naval officer in 1717 and died at sea. He reportedly was sorry he had ever left his beloved island.

(See also SELECTED BIBLIOGRAPHY: Little, *Crusoe's Captain;* Kemp and Lloyd, *Brethren;* Rogers, *Cruising;* Woodward, *Crusoe's Island.*)

SENZARAXON, GIOVANNI *(corsair captain; Aegean Sea; 1270s)* Senzaraxon was member of a Latin (non-Greek) family (whose name means "the Crazy") based in Thessalonica in northern Greece. Joined by his brother Julian and several nephews, he preyed on Latin shipping. In 1273, he killed a Thessalonica merchant's young son to persuade the man to give up hidden gold coins. Senzaraxon and his companions were arrested and detained in Constantinople for a brief time. But he was freed by August 1274, when he plundered a Venetian ship.

(See also MICHAEL VIII PALAEOLOGUS; VENETIAN CLAIMS.)

SERVILIUS VATIA (ISAURICUS), PUBLIUS *(Roman general; Mediterranean; 134–44 B.C.)* Servilius was a member of an important noble family and first governor (79–74) of the newly created province of CILICIA Pamphylia in southwestern Anatolia. The nature of Servilius' military campaigns suggests that the Romans under-rated the threat posed by the Cilician corsairs.

During the summers of 80 and 79, Servilius' ships defeated some pirate squadrons in the Gulf of Pamphylia. But he made no attempt to attack the corsair bases further east along the Cilician coast. Instead, he turned to land warfare, using his legions to take ZENOCTES' western strongholds. He then spent the next two or three summers conducting a laborious campaign inland, far to the north of Cilicia.

Servilius' inland campaigns presumably sought to open a northern land route for Roman attacks on MITHRIDATES. No Roman army could have turned south against the Cilician coast through the high mountains. Thus, Servilius' campaign did not weaken the pirates, who dominated the sea until GNAEUS POMPEIUS attacked in 67.

SEVEN SEAS TO CALAIS *(Italian motion picture; color; 1963)* Rudolph Mate directed this fictionalized biography of Sir Francis DRAKE, which portrays his 1573 raid on PANAMA, his voyage around the world, and the battles against the Spanish Armada. "As Drake," *Variety* commented, "Rod Taylor emotes with the swashbuckling ardor and assurance of an embryo Errol Flynn."

SEXUALITY, PIRATE See HOMOSEXUALITY; WOMEN, TREATMENT OF.

SHABAN REIS (1) *(Barbary corsair; Mediterranean; 1646)* Shaban was a Portuguese RENEGADE at ALGIERS. Although he commanded a 16-gun sailing ship, he seized only two small boats during three months in the Atlantic. After restocking at SALÉ, he was captured off the coast of Holland by a Dutch corsair.

SHABAN REIS (2) *(Barbary corsair; Mediterranean; active 1682–1684)* A nephew of the ADMIRAL of Majorca and originally named Giuseppe Vich, Shaban reached TRIPOLI in 1682. He took prizes on every voyage, married a local official's daughter in 1684, but lost his ship during a quarrel with the CAPTAIN OF THE SEA three months later.

SHAP-NG-TSAI *(Chinese pirate; South China Sea; active 1845–1849)* From about 1845, Shap-ng-tsai commanded 70 JUNKS based at Tien-pai, 180 miles west of Hong Kong. From Macao to Vietnam, coastal villages and traders paid protection money to escape attack. Chinese naval vessels sent in pursuit were captured, and their officers were held for ransom. To end Shap-ng-tsai's raids, the government unsuccessfully offered him a pardon and an officer's rank in the military.

Pirate raids increased during the spring of 1849, and Shap-ng-tsai was blamed for the loss of one American and three British ships carrying opium. In September a British squadron visited Tien-pai and found more than 100 captured craft held there for ransom. However, it failed to locate the pirates' main fleet.

In October, three British ships pursued the pirates to the islands and channels north of Haiphong, Vietnam.

After two days of unequal combat, they reported the destruction of 58 junks carrying 1,200 cannon and 3,000 crewmen. Shap-ng-tsai escaped with six smaller junks and 400 men. He later surrendered to the Chinese government and accepted its offer of a military commission.

SHARES, EQUAL DIVISION OF See BOOTY.

SHARP, BARTHOLOMEW *(English buccaneer; Caribbean, Pacific; 1650?–1688)* During much of the voyage from 1680 to 1682, Sharp commanded a major raid along South America's Pacific coast. A superb navigator, efficient, and also lucky, he was the most capable but the least popular of the captains joining in the expedition. The company included Basil RINGROSE, William DAMPIER, and Lionel WAFER, who wrote books describing their adventures. (The diaries of Sharp and John COXON have not been published.)

After Sir Henry MORGAN in 1668, Sharp's group was the second to cross the Isthmus of Panama, and it was the first to invade the Pacific since Hendrick BROUWER in 1643. By successfully surviving on a hostile coast and returning with booty, Sharp attracted many imitators. Eastern Panama, never settled by the Spaniards, became virtually a highway for the buccaneers. This region offered a much easier route than the provinces northwest of Panama City. Its Indian inhabitants, generally hostile to the Spanish colonists, willingly guided the buccaneers through the low-lying jungle and swamps.

Sharp left PORT ROYAL in December 1679 accompanied by John Coxon, Robert ALLISON, Thomas MACKETT, Cornelius ESSEX, Jean ROSE, and Captain BOURNANO. The seven captains had Jamaican commissions permitting them to cut LOGWOOD in Honduras. Their true purpose was piracy, and they rendezvoused at the Isle of Pines, near eastern Panama.

Electing Coxon leader, the buccaneers decided to copy Morgan's 1668 assault on PORTOBELO. Leaving their ships at a deserted cay, where Captain LESSONE joined up, about 250 pirates traveled by canoe and on foot to the town's undefended rear and took its garrison by surprise. Captain Essex and 30 men were killed, but the buccaneers took about £18,000 in booty.

Heartened by this success, the pirates decided to attempt the Isthmus crossing. Captains Rose and Bournano dropped out, but Edmund COOK, Peter HARRIS, and Richard SAWKINS joined the company. On April 5, Coxon, Sharp, Harris, Sawkins, and Cook set out for the Pacific Ocean, with Coxon still leading. (Allison and Mackett stayed behind guarding the ships.)

Guided by a son of the Cunas' "emperor" and 50 other Indians, the buccaneers reached the Gulf of San Miguel in a record-setting nine days. Their first target was SANTA MARIA, where gold mines recently had been opened. Sawkins rushed the fort, but the gold dust had just been sent to Panama. The Indians massacred 50 prisoners, and the surviving Spaniards were tortured until they gave up 20 pounds of gold and some silver.

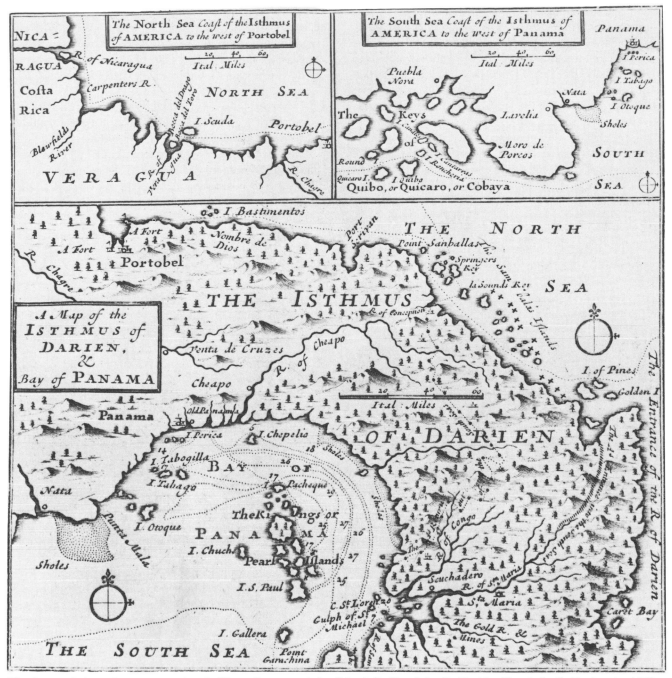

The Panama Isthmus lies between the Caribbean (here called the "North Sea") and the Pacific (the "South Sea"). During the 1680s, Bartholomew Sharp and other buccaneers crossed to the Pacific by the southern or Darien route passing near Santa Maria. Peruvian silver was carried from the city of Panama ("Old Panama") through Venta de Cruces to Nombre de Dios or (after 1595) to Portobelo. From Lionel Wafer, *New Voyage* (1699).

The disappointed buccaneers pressed on to Panama in canoes and two small craft commanded by Sharp and Harris. Sharp went on to the Pearl Islands for water. About 70 buccaneers in Harris' vessel and some canoes reached Perica Island, near Panama's harbor, on the morning of May 3. There they found five merchant ships and three warships commanded by Francisco de Peralta, who had evaded Morgan at Panama in 1671.

Some 250 defenders (mainly free blacks and mulattoes) resisted the pirates' attack, "giving and receiving death

unto each other as fast as they could charge," Basil Ringrose wrote. A hundred or more Spaniards died before two warships were taken and the third put to flight. Twenty buccaneers (including Captain Harris) were killed, and most of the rest were wounded. One of the merchant ships, the 400-ton *Santísima Trinidad* (renamed the *Trinity*) became their flagship.

Although the pirates now controlled all the ships at Panama, they were too few to attack the city. After Sharp returned on May 4, fierce arguments broke out.

John Coxon was accused of cowardice and left for the Caribbean with 50 men. The remaining buccaneers elected Sawkins commander and voted to plunder the Pacific. Several more prizes were taken, including an unarmed bark carrying 51,000 pesos and 1,400 jars of wine and brandy. Sawkins crossed to Pueblo Nuevo to obtain meat, where he was killed in an impetuous attack.

After renewed disputes, Sharp was elected overall commander, but 70 more men decided to follow Coxon's group back across the Isthmus. Sharp took command of the *Trinity*, while John cox became captain of another prize, the 100-ton *Mayflower*. After careening his two ships, Sharp led about 150 men south on August 4.

On September 4, a small Spanish vessel was taken with 3,276 pesos. (Ringrose wrote that the pirates shot one of the passengers, a Franciscan friar, out of boredom.) Learning that the Spaniards were prepared for their assaults, Sharp avoided large cities and attacked minor ports and coastal shipping. At Ilo, Peru (November 6), and La Serena, Chile (December 13), the churches were looted of silver and jewels.

On January 4, 1681, Sharp reached the JUAN FERNÁN-DEZ ISLANDS, intending to restock the *Trinity* (the *Mayflower* had been lost along the way) before returning home. Sharp and a few others had won most of the booty at cards and dice. The penniless losers, who wanted to remain in the Pacific, turned him out and elected John WATLING captain.

Driven northward by a Chilean squadron, 90 buccaneers invaded Arica, Chile, on February 10. The pirates were beaten off, even though they attacked, as a Spanish document reported: "with . . . the valor and ferocity of lions, fighting recklessly with an unnatural disdain for all risks and making light of death." Along with many others, Watling was killed, and his head was exhibited by the victors.

Although Sharp was reelected captain, the pirates continued to quarrel over their course. John COOK and some 50 others seceded off Ecuador on April 26 and made their way back across the Isthmus of Panama. Sharp and about 70 buccaneers returned south in the *Trinity*, looting a minor town and a few small ships.

On July 20, after more than a year in the Pacific, Sharp captured the *San Pedro*, carrying more than 37,000 pesos in silver. Three weeks later, he took the *Santa Rosario*, bound from Callao to Panama. The captain's young wife was, Ringrose wrote, "the most beautiful woman that I ever saw in all the South Sea."

Presumably beguiled by her beauty, the buccaneers ignored nearly 700 bars of crude silver, thinking they were merely tin. One sailor took a bar to make bullets; he later sold a small piece for £75. However, Sharp did stop the Spanish captain from throwing overboard an invaluable set of maps of every port along the Pacific coast.

After a failed raid on Parita, Peru, Sharp made for home about September 7. Driven far to the south by extreme gales, he missed the Strait of Magellan and sailed around Cape Horn. The *Trinity* arrived at Barbados on February 7, 1682, after traveling some 10,000 miles and three months without sight of land. Sharp was the first English captain to round Cape Horn, only the second (following Hendrick Brouwer in 1643) to pass it from west to east.

While Sharp's company had been away, the English government had become stricter about piracy. Forbidden to land at Barbados or Antigua, the pirates split up after sharing out the remains of their plunder. The various diaries give conflicting estimates of their haul. Spanish reports indicate the pirates destroyed 25 ships, killed more than 200 civilians, and caused 4 million pesos in damage.

Sharp and several others went to England, arriving on March 26. He had unwisely brought home one of his Chilean captives, a 16-year-old boy who told his story to the Spanish ambassador. The ADMIRALTY COURT tried Sharp and three of his officers in May but found them innocent. Sharp owed his life to the captured Spanish charts of the Pacific, the first ever seen in England. The admiralty knew about the maps before the trial, and Sharp presented King Charles II with an ornately decorated copy in September.

Sharp returned to piracy but never again undertook a long voyage. The navy made him a captain in November, but his ship later sailed without him. In one account he ran out of money and robbed a French vessel in the Thames.

Sharp was back in the Caribbean by February 1684, when the governor of the Leeward Islands commissioned him to catch pirates and Indians. He took a ship off Jamaica in October, used it to raid a Spanish settlement at Campeche, and sold his captives as slaves. At Nevis, the governor condoned his crimes and probably took a share. A zealous naval officer arrested Sharp, but he was acquitted at trials in December 1686 and February 1688. He is mentioned in 1688 as commander—not quite governor—at the tiny and waterless island of Anguilla, often used as a pirate base.

(See also SELECTED BIBLIOGRAPHY: Bradley, *Peru*; Gerhard, *Pirates*; Kemp and Lloyd, *Brethren*; Lloyd, *Dampier*.)

SHEBEC/XEBEC *(pirate ship; Mediterranean; 15th–19th centuries)*

Originally a fishing boat, the shebec was favored by the BARBARY corsairs, who transformed it into a formidable warship. During the 18th century, the French and Italians borrowed its design for shore patrols.

Shebecs could reach 200 tons and carried four to 24 cannon and 60 to 200 crewmen. They had a distinctive hull with a pronounced overhanging bow and stern, three masts (usually lateen-rigged), and up to 15 oars on each side. Both fast and stable, they featured a narrow floor for speed and a relatively wide beam to carry extensive sails.

SHELVOCKE, GEORGE *(British pirate; Atlantic, Pacific; active 1718–1722)*

Hoping to duplicate

Woodes ROGERS' profitable voyage, English merchants outfitted two ships in 1718 to plunder South America's Pacific coast. Overall command was given to Shelvocke, a naval lieutenant related to one of the investors. Shelvocke spent lavishly while visiting Europe to buy a PRIVATEERING commission from the Holy Roman Emperor. When England and Spain went to war, the investors transferred leadership to John CLIPPERTON, who already had raided South America with William DAMPIER.

Clipperton and Shelvocke sailed in CONSORT in February 1719, with Shelvocke in charge of the 24-gun *Spedwel* and a crew of 106. Partly because of the change in authority, Shelvocke hated Clipperton and the owners. He kept their share of the booty and also deserted or MAROONED most of his men to increase his cut.

The *Spedwel* was an unhappy ship throughout the voyage. Shelvocke was an arrogant captain. His permanent state of drunkenness also irritated the men, since he refused to share his enormous liquor supply. The crew constantly threatened mutiny, and the officers were not on speaking terms.

Shelvocke soon gave Clipperton the slip. Avoiding the planned rendezvous, he instead crossed to Brazil. There he looted a Portuguese ship after threatening its captain with BLOODING AND SWEATING. He also issued new ARTICLES reducing the owners' share of any plunder.

After a rugged passage round Cape Horn, the *Spedwel* was out of water when it reached the Pacific in December. Shelvocke looted Indian settlements on Chiloé Island and headed for Chile. Near Concepción, the *Spedwel* took two ships carrying silver plate and 6,000 pesos. Shelvocke burned the two ships when the governor offered only 12,000 pesos in ransom. He converted a smaller prize into an auxiliary renamed the *Mercury*.

Shelvocke reached the rendezvous at the JUAN FERNÁNDEZ ISLANDS on January 15, long after Clipperton had left. He returned to Peru, captured a few poor prizes, and burned the town of Paita. He also managed to lose the *Mercury* with two officers he disliked.

Shelvocke went back to Juan Fernández in May. During a sudden storm, the *Spedwel* was wrecked and sank with much of the booty. Despite low morale and possibly a mutiny, the crew built a tiny ship and sailed to Peru in October. Shelvocke left behind 24 men, who later were captured by the Spaniards. A new set of articles totally cut out the owners and gave all booty to Shelvocke and the crew.

Near Pisco, Shelvocke took over a 200-ton Spanish ship. On January 25, 1721, he accidentally ran into Clipperton in the Bay of Panama. The two captains remained enemies and parted after fierce arguments.

Shelvocke seized another and larger Spanish ship in Mexico—even though he knew the war had ended. Soon after, he took a prize carrying 108,636 pesos and made for China. The ship was sold at Canton, and Shelvocke soundly cheated the 36 surviving crewmen in dividing the booty. He reached England in July 1722 and hid more than £7,000 before his arrest.

Shelvocke was acquitted of piracy because the Spanish and Portuguese ambassadors failed to bring witnesses to England. He was rearrested for defrauding the *Spedwel*'s owners but managed to escape to France with his loot. His history of the expedition, published in 1726, blames its failure on Clipperton. However, several other officers kept journals, which document his crimes.

(See also DRINKING; "RIME OF THE ANCIENT MARINER"; SELECTED BIBLIOGRAPHY: Burney, *History*; Kemp and Lloyd, *Brethren*; Shelvocke, *Voyage*.)

SHERLEY, SIR ANTHONY **(English adventurer; Caribbean, Mediterranean; 1565–1636?)** A persuasive and haughty rogue, Sherley practiced piracy while pursuing chimerical schemes on four continents. The second son of a bankrupt Sussex landowner, Sherley took to soldiering after attending Oxford and perhaps the Inns of Court. In 1591, he went to Normandy under the earl of Essex, the queen's favorite. He accepted a French knighthood, and was imprisoned in 1593 until he renounced this foreign title—although he afterward still called himself Sir Anthony.

Hoping to regain Queen Elizabeth's favor, Sherley married a cousin of Essex. But he soon loathed his wife and left England to escape her as well as to recoup his family fortune. Using borrowed money and Essex's patronage, he assembled an expedition to capture the Portuguese island of São Thomé off the African coast. Eight ships carrying some 400 soldiers sailed in May 1596. The fleet was struck by disease, and Sherley never reached São Thomé. Turning north, he captured Santiago in the Cape Verde Islands but took little booty.

The much reduced force made for the West Indies and took Santa Marta, Colombia, with little reward. Early in 1597, Sherley's men stripped Jamaica's one poor settlement, Santiago de la Vega, of every scrap of food or goods they could find. Two professional pirates, William PARKER and Michael GEARE, joined in consort with Sherley at Jamaica. Even with their help, Trujillo (Honduras) proved too strong to capture. The raiders easily took PUERTO CABALLOS, but found it a destitute and miserable place.

Refusing to return without booty, Sherley and Parker tried to march across the Guatemala mountains to the Pacific. When this failed, he planned (copying Sir Francis DRAKE) to take the surviving men through the Strait of Magellan. However, the other ships now deserted him, and he reached England still alive but deeply in debt.

Sherley continued to dream up grand schemes that came to nothing. At the end of 1597, Essex sent him to Ferrara, Italy, with a company of English troops. By the time they arrived, Ferrara's political disputes were settled, and Sherley could find no other employment in Italy.

With money raised on Essex's credit, Sherley moved on to Persia in an attempt, entirely unofficial, to establish diplomatic relations with the new shah. The Persian ruler appointed Sherley his ambassador to win allies against the OTTOMAN EMPIRE. However, the English government repudiated his mission and would not allow him to return.

Sherley wandered from court to court, always leaving behind large debts. In 1607, as a Spanish agent, he wrote to John WARD and Simon SIMONSON, trying to turn them against the Ottoman Empire. In 1609, the Spanish decided to attack the BARBARY corsairs and allowed Sherley to assemble ships in Sicily. However, instead of joining a Spanish raid on TUNIS, Sherley's squadron looted European merchantmen and pillaged the Greek islands.

After this fiasco, the Spanish government had little further use for Sherley. An Englishman, visiting Spain about 1619, described him as still a "great plotter and projector in matters of State." He died in poverty some time after 1636.

(See also SELECTED BIBLIOGRAPHY: Andrews, *Elizabethan*; Chew, *Crescent*; Davies, *Elizabethans*; Rogoziński, *Carribean*.)

SHERLEY, SIR THOMAS (English pirate; Atlantic, Mediterranean; 1564–1630?)
The older brother of Sir Anthony SHERLEY, he attended Oxford and fought as an officer in the Netherlands and Ireland. Meanwhile, his father fell into hopeless debt, and Sherley turned pirate to gain funds.

In 1598, Sherley outfitted the 34-gun *Golden Dragon*. Four substantial German ships were taken, but the *Dragon* was badly mauled, and Sherley had to borrow money to get home. Later in the year, he tried again and took seven prizes—the best haul of his career. Although the ADMIRALTY COURT forced him to release the German vessels, his neighbors elected him to Parliament in 1601. In April 1602, he took out four ships and cruelly sacked two poor hamlets in Portugal.

Jealous of his younger brother's notoriety, Sherley resolved to gain publicity by attacking the OTTOMAN EMPIRE. The government tried to hold him in England, but his desperadoes managed to overpower the guards and sail for Italy in the *Dragon*. At LIVORNO, Sherley replenished his crew with Italian and Greek bandits. Using the flag of Ferdinando dei MEDICI, grand duke of Tuscany, he raided the Greek islands in consort with William PIERCE. In January 1603, the two pirate ships pillaged several vessels, including two Dutch grain ships and a Venetian galley.

Pierce sailed off, and Sherley's men descended upon the small island of Kéa. Sherley wrote the English government that he stopped at Kéa to repair a leak. But he told Grand Duke Ferdinand that his men mutinied and forced him to land. In any event, the Greek islanders captured Sherley and two others. His crew made no effort to rescue their captain before resuming assaults on Christian and Muslim commerce.

Sherley was imprisoned in Greece and later in Istanbul, and he claimed that his captors tortured him to find out how much ransom he could pay. King James I tried to arrange Sherley's release, but the foreign service procrastinated, happy to have him in jail. He was finally ransomed in December 1605, settled at Naples, and apparently returned to piracy.

Sherley was back in England before September 1607, when he was jailed for interfering with English shipping in the Levant. His later life was unadventurous and forlorn. Remarriage and a large family increased his financial woes, and he was twice jailed for debt. While in prison in 1617, he wrote a *Discours of the Turkes*, not published until 1936. He was forced to sell his English estates, and he retired to the Isle of Wight as keeper of the royal park.

(See also SELECTED BIBLIOGRAPHY: Chew, *Crescent*; Davies, *Elizabethans*; Tenenti, *Piracy*.)

SHIPS, PIRATE (all oceans; all eras)
Pirates preferred smaller, lighter ships. Fast enough to catch merchantmen and escape pursuers, these also were less expensive to build and maintain and needed smaller crews. When pursued by heavier warships, pirates escaped by entering shallow waters or by carrying their ships across reefs or peninsulas.

In antiquity, Greek pirates favored the MYOPARO, KELES, and HEMIOLA. The ILLYRIANS developed the LEMBOS and LIBURNIAN, while BLACK SEA pirates used the exceptionally light CAMARA. A successful ARCHPIRATE later might add larger ships to his corsair fleet. The CILICIAN corsairs began with *myoparones* and *hemioliai* and graduated to *biremes* and TRIREMES. By working together, pirate craft defeated larger war GALLEYS. In 201 B.C., Macedonian *lemboi* darted in among RHODES' warships, breaking up their formations and damaging their oars. Fleets of small corsair ships from CRETE routed the battleships sent by Rhodes in 154 and by Rome in 71.

With the fall of the Roman Empire, commerce and piracy vanished from the Mediterranean. From about 1000, pirates again developed swift raiders that outsailed naval galleys and warships. The GALIOT was a light fast galley that also carried one large sail. TARTANS, FUSTES, BRIGANTINES, POLLACAS, PINKS, and SHEBECS were adapted from fishing craft and coastal traders. In addition to sails, they carried oars for maneuverability and extra bursts of speed.

The BUCCANEERS raided in SLOOPS or small FRIGATES captured from Spanish traders. Pirate movies incorrectly show Caribbean pirates aboard large warships. When Sir Henry MORGAN sailed for PANAMA in 1670, his men were packed into 38 small vessels. The largest, Morgan's 120-ton flagship, carried only 140 men. During the early 18th century, Atlantic pirates cruised in sloops and in SCHOONERS, even on voyages to Africa and MADAGASCAR. A few captured and cruised in BRIGANTINES and three-masted square-riggers.

Shallow-draft Arab DHOWS, Indian GRABS, and Malayan PRAHUS eluded European warships by sailing up rivers or into remote coves. Into the 19th century, native raiders were more than a match for the largest British warships. In every case, the British defeated the pirates only by sending land troops to storm their HAVENS.

SHIPTON, CAPTAIN (British pirate; Atlantic, Caribbean; active 1724–1725) Captain Shipton sailed under Francis SPRIGGS, who gave him command of a captured SLOOP. Spriggs and Shipton cruised in consort until they were overthrown in a mutiny and MAROONED by their crews.

"SHIVER MY TIMBERS" (fictional seaman's saying; 19th and 20th centuries) An expression of surprise or disbelief, presumably referring to a vessel that strikes a hidden rock so hard that her hull "shivers" (shatters). There is no evidence that real-life seamen ever used this picturesque phrase. It was invented by Robert Louis STEVENSON for TREASURE ISLAND and copied in later pirate FICTION and MOVIES.

SHORT STORIES See FICTION, PIRATE.

SIAMBECCHINO (pirate ship; Mediterranean; 18th century) BARBARY raiders mounted several cannon on this vessel, lateen-rigged on two masts—the main mast formed from a single spar like a POLLACA, and the mizzen mast shortened.

SICILY (pirate haven; Mediterranean; 700–500, 43–36 B.C., A.D. 831–1060) The largest Mediterranean island, separated from the Italian mainland by the narrow Strait of Messina, whose peoples have been pirate victims throughout history. In contrast to many other islands (such as CRETE), Sicily was a pirate HAVEN only during several widely separated eras.

Ancient Sicily

In the *Odyssey*, HOMER described Sicily's peoples as both slavers and victims of slavers. DIODORUS OF SICILY noted that they lived high in the mountains for fear of pirates. From 735 B.C., various Greek cities established colonies throughout the island, whose inhabitants (like the PHOCAEANS in Corsica) raided to the north in the Tyrrhenian Sea.

In later periods, although they sometimes fenced corsair booty, Sicilian cities usually abstained from piracy. As a Roman province (from 211), Sicily suffered from CILICIAN raids. From 43 to 36, the northeastern coast provided the main base for the corsair fleets of Sextus POMPEIUS.

Muslim Sicily

In 827, the Aghlabid rulers of Tunisia began the conquest of Sicily, until then ruled by the BYZANTINE EMPIRE. Although some cities held out until 878, Palermo fell in 831 and became the center of an independent Muslim state.

Sicilian corsairs generally attacked along Italy's western coast, while bands from CRETE plundered in the Adriatic. In 846, Naples, Amalfi, Gaeta, and Sorrento combined to retake pirate bases on the island of Ponza

off Naples and at Licosia near Sorrento. Thwarted in that direction, the freebooters from 846 raided Rome and other papal territories until the pope bought them off. They also carried out major raids on Gaeta and Salerno in 868 and 872. Once the threat to their own coast was gone, Naples and neighboring ports openly traded with the Sicilians.

Naples returned to its Byzantine allegiance in 884, and the pirates raided from MONTE GARIGLIANO, north of the city. When that haven was crushed in 915, Italy's western coast was secure. However, Muslim corsairs continued to loot merchant ships until the Normans conquered Sicily during the 11th century.

(See also HERACLEO; POSTUMIUS; ZANKLE.)

SIDI ALI REIS (Ottoman captain; Mediterranean, Persian Gulf; 1538–1554) Sidi fought at PREVESA under KHEIREDDIN BARBAROSSA in 1538. In 1554, he commanded an OTTOMAN fleet that sailed into the Persian Gulf from Basra in Iraq. He lost some vessels in battles with the Portuguese, suffered severe damage in a storm off the coast of Makran, and disbanded the remnants of his fleet at Surat in western India.

SILVER (pirate objective; Caribbean, 16th–18th centuries) Spanish TREASURE FLEETS transported immensely rich cargoes of silver coins and bullion through the Caribbean and on to Europe. Silver is bulky and less valuable than an equal weight of GOLD. To score, a pirate crew had to take over the treasure ship and carry it to a friendly HAVEN. Several English raiders accomplished this feat during the war with Spain (1585–1603), and Dutch raiders captured entire treasure fleets during the 17th century. However, no BUCCANEER based in the Caribbean ever captured a silver ship.

(See also PESO; PIECE OF EIGHT).

SILVER, LONG JOHN (fictional pirate; 1883 to the present) The villain in Robert Louis STEVENSON's novel, Silver also is the most important character in the movie versions of TREASURE ISLAND and in LONG JOHN SILVER (1954).

SIMAIN REIS (Barbary corsair; Mediterranean; active 1580s) After many slave raids on southern Italy, Simain was captured in 1586 by Tommasso dei MEDICI, ADMIRAL of the KNIGHTS OF SAINT STEPHEN.

SIMONSON, SIMON (Barbary corsair; Mediterranean; active 1606–1609) A native of Dordrecht in Holland, nicknamed *der Tantzer*, "the Dancer." About 1606, he moved to ALGIERS from Marseilles, where he had married and was a shipbuilder. Within three years, he had become the city's leading and most audacious corsair, earning the name of Delli Reis ("Captain Devil").

Using captured prizes as models, Simonson taught Muslim captains how to manage and navigate "round" (sailing) ships. He personally captured 40 prizes, which were incorporated into the corsair fleet. Simonson also led the corsairs through the Strait of Gibraltar and into the Atlantic. There they preyed on Spanish TREASURE FLEETS and later raided as far north as ICELAND. (MURAT REIS already had attacked the Canary Islands with galleys in 1586, but Simonson's larger sailing ships were safer in Atlantic waters.)

Simonson again changed sides in 1609, using Jesuit priests captured off Valencia to negotiate with the French court. He fled back to Marseilles, rejoined his family, and was restored to full citizenship. He took with him four ships and booty worth 400,000 crowns as well as two large brass CANNON belonging to the Algerian government. He left behind 150 dead Algerians with whom he and his men had quarreled.

Simonson in 1610 presented the king and the Marseilles city council with a bold plan for an expedition against Algiers. Given his inside knowledge of the city, it might well have succeeded; but the French government had more pressing concerns at home. Marseilles paid him to maintain a squadron patrolling against the Barbary corsairs. He was captured and executed at TUNIS in 1616.

SINAN REIS *(Barbary corsair; Mediterranean; active 1524–1544)* A convert from Smyrna in Asia Minor (nicknamed Chesout, "the Jew"), Sinan was an expert pilot who could determine a ship's latitude using a crossbow rather than an astrolabe. Sinan joined KHEIREDDIN BARBAROSSA at ALGIERS by 1524. With TURGUT REIS, he soon became one of Kheireddin's most important lieutenants and commanded as many as 30 ships in raids on Italy and Sicily.

Sinan followed Kheireddin to Istanbul in 1533 and helped his patron occupy TUNIS in 1534. When Spanish troops reconquered Tunis in 1535, Sinan led three desperate sorties against the invaders before fleeing the city. During the Spanish siege, according to legend, he persuaded Kheireddin not to kill 6,000 Christian slaves imprisoned in the citadel.

Sinan fought with Kheireddin at PREVESA in 1538. He did not accompany Kheireddin to France in 1543–1544, but instead prepared a Suez squadron for an attack on Portuguese forts in the Red Sea. On his way back to Istanbul in 1544, Kheireddin took his fleet to Elba solely to free Sinan's son, enslaved on that island.

SINOP *(pirate haven; Black Sea; first century B.C., third and 14th centuries A.D.)* An excellent harbor on the BLACK SEA's southern coast. In ancient times, it was a base for CILICIAN and Gothic brigands. Turkish invaders took Sinop from the BYZANTINE EMPIRE in 1214, and its emirs frequently promoted or took part in piracy. In 1340, a Genoese counter-raid from Caffa (Fedodosiya) in the Crimea sank 10 pirate galleys and murdered their crews.

(See also GHAZI; SELEUCUS.)

SIPHANTOS *(Greek corsair; Adriatic and Aegean Seas; 1285)* Siphantos' band assisted William II

of Sicily in an unsuccessful invasion of the BYZANTINE EMPIRE. After ferrying the Sicilian army across the Adriatic to Durazzo, the corsairs sailed to Thessalonica and joined in besieging that city. On August 24, the invaders blew up the defending walls. One of the pirates was the first to mount the rubble heap, triumphantly waving his spear.

While the disorderly Sicilian soldiers massacred Thessalonica's citizens, Siphantos showed his skills as a professional looter. At the racetrack, he carefully assembled his valuable booty and captives—including a Byzantine general and bishop—and guarded them from horseback. Perhaps Siphantos died soon afterward, for MARGARITONE was William II's pirate admiral by 1287.

SI RAHMAN *(Malayan pirate; South China Sea; 1863)* An ILANUN commanding eight warships, Si Rahman attacked the *Lizzie Webber*, a six-gun BRIG, near Brunei. Directing his warriors from a high platform, he ignored bullets and cannon fire and (the British captain says) "pranced about like a scarlet demon."

After a three-hour battle, Si Rahman's ship was alongside, his warriors ready to board. In desperation, the British captain and crewmen lifted the end of a gun carriage with a spar. Firing down into the water, they blew up Si Rahman with his ship and crew. Although the remaining pirates regrouped and renewed the attack, a breeze sprang up, and the *Lizzie Webber* escaped.

(See also SELECTED BIBLIOGRAPHY: Rutter, *Pirate Wind*.)

SIR FRANCIS DRAKE REVIVED *(report of pirate raid; 1628)* The source for later descriptions of Sir Francis DRAKE's 1572–1573 assaults on PANAMA and Nombre de Dios, written by Drake's nephew. The author based his narrative on oral reports by crewmen, which Francis Drake had reviewed and amplified. *Drake Revived* presents a fluent and compelling account, and contemporary Spanish documents confirm its accuracy. It was republished in 1932.

(See also SELECTED BIBLIOGRAPHY: Andrews, *Drake's Voyages*; Wright, *Documents*.)

SITIA *(corsair ship; eastern Mediterranean; 15th–19th centuries)* A single-decked ship with a long, sharp bow and two masts, both lateen-rigged.

SKIROS *(pirate haven; Aegean Sea; fifth century B.C.)* A large island on the main sea routes between northern and southern Greece. Its inhabitants, the DOLOPIANS, were accused of living solely by piracy.

SKULL AND CROSS(ED) BONES See FLAGS; JOLLY ROGER.

SKYRME, JAMES *(Welsh pirate; Caribbean, Atlantic; 1678?–1722)* Skyrme was chief mate of a ship captured in November 1720 by Bartholomew ROBERTS. Skyrme joined the pirates, and Roberts later made him captain of the 32-gun *Great Ranger*, seized in West Africa

Christian slaves at Algiers during the 16th century. Illustration by Léopold Flameng in Charles Farine, *Deux Pirates* (1869).

in January 1722. On February 5, Skyrme attacked the warship *Swallow*, having mistaken it for a Portuguese merchantman. The pirates fiercely resisted for four hours, with Skyrme urging on his men even after his leg was shot off. Skyrme was hanged at Cape Coast, Ghana, on April 13, and his body was hung in chains near the harbor.

SLAVE PRISONS See BAGNIO.

SLAVE PRISONS OF ALGIERS, THE *(four-act play in Spanish; 1615)* CERVANTES' verse drama (*Los baños de Argel*) rarely is performed today. Its loosely knit plot resembles that of the same author's CAPTIVE'S TALE. A series of tableaux portray the life of Christian slaves, inspired by Cervantes' own captivity in ALGIERS. Many episodes are humorous in contrast to the caustic tone in the earlier The MANNERS OF ALGIERS.

(See also BARBARY STATES.)

SLAVES *(corsair captives; Mediterranean; 1500–1830)*

Christian Slaves

Like the ancient Greeks and CILICIANS, Barbary pirates gained substantial sums through slave trading. Islamic tradition recognized several forms of slavery, and the BARBARY STATES contained many slaves purchased from African and Near Eastern traders. The corsairs' captives were exceptional since they were considered prisoners of war and thus could be repatriated. (The corsairs could not enslave captives from nations with peace treaties.) In most cases, the corsairs wanted quick profits through a fast RANSOM rather than permanent slaves.

The corsairs took perhaps a million captives over all—at least 4,000 each year before 1680, perhaps 2,000 annually in later years. Ransomed captives and foreign visitors provide estimates for different eras. In about 1630, ALGIERS held 25,000 slaves. TUNIS had 7,000, TRIPOLI about 500, SALÉ some 1,500. The British consul counted 1,559 at Tunis in 1671. Corsair raids and the number of captives fell after the 1680s, and Algiers held only 500 slaves in 1787. But business picked up during the Napoleonic wars, and the British freed 3,000 captives in 1816.

Slaves came from all parts of Europe. The corsairs harvested a rich crop from Spain, Italy, and the larger islands such as SICILY, Majorca, Sardinia, and Corsica. Their constant raids totally depopulated large sections along the Italian and Spanish coasts. They took thousands of British and French captives during the 17th-century wars. From the east came Venetians, Russians, and Christian Greeks—even though the latter were subjects of the OTTOMAN sultan. More exotic prisoners showed up from time to time—Canary Islanders from MURAT THE GREAT's 1586 raid, 800 Icelanders captured by Jan JANSSEN in 1631.

The captives included nobles, officials, merchants, and seamen as well as peasants taken in coastal raids. The wealthy and important were quickly ransomed. Others (like CERVANTES) had to wait for years. An unfortunate few spent their lives in captivity.

A captive's skills largely determined his or her fate. Thousands of government-owned slaves—imprisoned in vast BAGNIOS—labored as GALLEY SLAVES or repaired the mole in Algiers' harbor. But most slaves did not sweat at the oars or in the quarries. The entire Barbary economy depended on slavery. Slaves worked as household servants, clerks, shopkeepers, artisans and government officials. The conditions of those living in private homes varied with their owners.

Captives often converted to Islam. Only Christians could be used as galley slaves, and RENEGADES could earn promotion and eventual freedom. During all eras, the corsairs encouraged skilled seamen and strong young men to join their ranks. Especially during the 16th century, many famous captains were renegades—including ULUJ ALI, SINAN REIS, and HASAN VENEZIANO.

Muslim Slaves

Freelance pirates and the crusading orders—the KNIGHTS OF MALTA and KNIGHTS OF SAINT STEPHEN—routinely enslaved the crews and passengers of merchant ships. Both also raided for slaves in Greece and North Africa, taking women and young children as well as males. In addition to Muslims, other OTTOMAN subjects were considered legitimate prey, including Greek and Slavic Christians, Armenians, and Jews. The corsairs' polyglot haul ranged from blue-eyed Berbers to African oarsmen captured with their galleys.

The number of Muslim captives cannot be precisely estimated. Some private captains ransomed their captives on the spot in Greece, Palestine, or North Africa. Many were taken back to the corsair ports of MALTA and LIVORNO. As with other BOOTY, the Maltese knights kept all the slaves captured by their fleets and 10 percent of those taken by freelance pirates. The remainder were sold at auction.

Many men ended as galley slaves. Spain, the popes, several Italian city-states, and the Knights of Malta used galleys into the 18th century. Maltese pirate captains also employed some slave oarsmen on the smaller boats that accompanied their sailing ships.

Britain, France, and the Netherlands stopped direct slave trading after 1650, as they signed peace treaties with ALGIERS, TUNIS, and TRIPOLI. But agents for these major powers continued to buy and sell slaves at Malta and Livorno. British and Dutch convoys sold large numbers of captives, and British officials purchased slaves for the galleys based at Tangier from 1662 to 1684. French galleys held about 2,000 slaves in 1719, and French agents bought up every likely male.

Slaves at Malta and Livorno who escaped the galleys could expect to be ransomed eventually. Some wealthy merchants or Barbary corsairs fetched huge sums. As in Barbary, Malta had professional ransom agents, often Jews or Greek Christians. Payment also was made through Christian ambassadors in Muslim nations or through the French representative at Malta. Some slaves were allowed home to arrange their own ransoms.

Slaves without wealthy family or friends might not be ransomed for many years. The Maltese owned slaves, marketed them to Italian cities, and presented them as gifts to European rulers. The Maltese knights employed captives to maintain their fortresses and as servants, and almost every household had slaves. Most worked as domestic servants, but some ran stores, taverns, and barber shops. Altogether, Malta (with a population of 60,000) held 6,000 slaves in 1723, and 2,000 were liberated in 1798. The number of slaves at Malta usually was larger than the Christian slave population in major Barbary cities.

The treatment of Maltese slaves was remarkably similar to that of Christian slaves in the Barbary states. The pirate kingdoms of Barbary and Malta enforced an unofficial international law of slavery. If the Maltese or the Algerians heard that the other side was mistreating slaves, the offended party meted out similar treatment to its own captives.

Slaves owned by the Maltese knights lodged at night in large prisons (BAGNIOS) similar to those in North Africa. They went to work chained in pairs, wore iron rings around their ankles, and had their heads shaved clean except for a long pigtail from the center. In times of emergency—for example, following a suspected slave revolt in 1749—the bagnios also imprisoned all private slaves, Greek Christians, and Jews.

The knights treated slaves in their hospital, but Muslim captives had their own mosque, and they settled internal disputes before their own judges. Only regarding religious conversions did the Maltese differ significantly from their Barbary rivals. The Barbary states prized converts to Islam, and RENEGADES became corsairs or held high government offices. By contrast, the Maltese did not encourage captives to turn Christian, and converts remained slaves.

(See also MEHMET REIS; NATALE, GIACOMO; SELECTED BIBLIOGRAPHY: Cavaliero, *Last Crusaders*; Earle, *Corsairs*.)

SLEZAK, WALTER (American actor; 1902–1981)

The son of Leo Slezak, a noted operatic tenor and character actor, Walter Slezak was born in Germany and became a movie actor in 1922. He played romantic leads in German plays and films, but his tendency to gain weight soon forced him into character parts. He moved to the U.S. in 1930, became a Broadway actor, and began making movies in 1942. Hollywood typecast him either as a menacing heavy or as a bumbling idiot. He continued to appear on stage and won a Tony and the New York Critics award for his role in the musical *Fanny* in 1956.

Slezak added to the pirate movie tradition in 1945 by creating the greedy, smooth-talking Spanish governor in the Bob Hope comedy, *The PRINCESS AND THE PIRATE*. He recreated this character the same year for an adventure-romance, *The* SPANISH MAIN. In the 1948 Gene Kelly and Judy Garland musical, *The* PIRATE, Slezak presented a toned-down version of the same role as the greedy but dull mayor of a Caribbean town. He played Squire Trelawney in the 1972 TREASURE ISLAND starring Orson Welles.

SLIMAN REIS *(Barbary corsair; Mediterranean; 1778)* Sailing from ALGIERS, Sliman captured a ship with a rich cargo of tobacco.

SLOOP *(pirate ship; Caribbean, Atlantic; 17th and 18th centuries)* A fast vessel favored by Caribbean BUCCANEERS and Atlantic pirates. In modern usage, a sloop is a sailing vessel with one mast, usually serving as a pleasure YACHT. Earlier the name implied a specific form of rigging. The large mainsail was attacked to a gaff (spar) above, to the mast on its foremost edge, and to a long boom below. To achieve additional speed, the sloop could add another sail from the main mast, triangular sails attached to a very long bowsprit, and a square topsail. These vessels could be as large as 100 tons and had a relatively shallow draft.

SMITH, JAMES *(British pirate; Pacific, South China Sea, Bay of Bengal, Indian Ocean; active 1683–1689)* Smith was among the crew of the CYGNET, as it raided along the coast of South America, crossed the Pacific, wandered through the South China Sea, and visited India in 1688. Smith was chosen captain, captured a rich Indian prize, and reached MADAGASCAR in May 1689. The *Cygnet*, her hull eaten away by worms, sank at anchor.

Pretending to be an honest merchant captain, John Smith (alias John Gow) welcomes the Portuguese governor of Madeira aboard his vessel. On several occasions, Howell Davis also captured victims by disguising his ship and men. An illustration to a modern edition (New York, 1903–1904) of Daniel Defoe's *Account of John Gow.*

SMITH, JOHN *(British pirate; Atlantic; died 1725)* Smith often used the alias John Gow. While sailing from Morocco to France in November 1724, Smith and several others mutinied and seized a merchant ship. The rebels murdered the captain and three other officers and elected Smith captain.

After looting British ships off Portugal, Smith visited Madeira, seized the governor, and forced him to provide supplies. In February 1725, he made for the Orkney Islands near Scotland—solely to visit his girl friend according to some reports. Some of his prisoners escaped and raised an alarm.

The pirates raided several villages, but wrecked their ship on one of the islands. A local landowner turned down a bribe, and Smith and his crew were captured. Following a trial that aroused intense public interest, Smith and eight others were hanged in London.

(See also ACCOUNT OF JOHN GOW; SELECTED BIBLIOGRAPHY: Defoe, *General History.*)

SMYRNA   See AYDIN.

SNELGRAVE, WILLIAM   See NEW ACCOUNT OF SOME PARTS OF GUINEA.

SOCLEIDAS *(corsair captain; Aegean; mid-third century B.C.)* "Pirates came into our land at night and carried off young girls and women and other persons, free and or slave, to the number of thirty or more." So begins the inscription on a monument erected by the city of Aigiale on Amorgós Island. "Having destroyed the ships in the port [presumably to prevent pursuit], they seized Dorieus' boat and escaped with their captives and the rest of their booty."

Fortunately, two of the captives—honored by the monument—made a deal with Socleidas, the pirate chief. The sons of a prominent islander, they persuaded Socleidas to send the other free citizens of Aigiale home. (Socleidas kept the slaves he had captured.) The two men remained his captives until a large ransom was paid.

SOLIMAN REIS *(Barbary corsair; Mediterranean; 1610)* Soliman was a Tunisian raider ransomed from the KNIGHTS OF MALTA, who had captured and enslaved him some months earlier.

SOMERS, SIR GEORGE *(English privateer; Atlantic; 1554–1610)* The discoverer of the Bermuda Islands, often called the Somers Islands in his honor. Born in Lyme Regis, Dorsetshire, which he represented in Parliament from 1604 to 1610, Somers became a professional raider. He was master of George RAYMOND's *Lion*, which visited Portugal and the Canary Islands in 1584. The following year, the head of royal customs at Chichester entrusted him with a warship.

From 1587, Somers promoted as well as conducted PRIVATEERING cruises. In 1589, he and Sir Amyas PRESTON financed two warships, which Somers took to the Azores. In consort with two other vessels, Somers amassed very rich prizes, worth some £30,000. Although Somers and Preston later sued the other captains to obtain a larger share of this booty, they made a huge profit on the voyage. Joining Preston in a pirate foray in 1595, Somers was among those sacking towns in the Canary Islands and along the Venezuelan coast.

Somers subsequently commanded royal warships during several large expeditions. He took part in raids on the Azores in 1597 and 1602, and he fought against a Spanish fleet in Ireland in 1601. He was knighted by King James I in 1603.

By then a wealthy man, Somers became an active member of the Virginia Company. In May 1609, he commanded nine ships bringing settlers to Jamestown. On the way, a hurricane scattered the fleet, Somers' flagship was wrecked in the Bermudas, and he reached Virginia a year later. Somers' companions in this adventure included Christopher NEWPORT and the colony's secretary, William Strachey, whose description of the shipwreck inspired Shakespeare's *The Tempest*. Somers revisited the Bermudas to procure fish and hogs for the starving Virginians. He died there in November 1610 after eating immense amounts of pork, and his heart was buried where the town of Saint George now stands.

"SONG OF DANSEKAR THE DUTCHMAN, THE" *(ballad; 1609)*
Fourteen six-line stanzas about Simon SIMONSON (nicknamed "the Dancer"), often sung as the second part of the "SEAMAN'S SONG OF CAPTAIN WARD." Simonson's piracies would be glorious if he robbed Muslims, "the foes of Christ." He is a fiend only because he plunders Christians for the BARBARY corsairs.

> But their cursed villanies,
> And their blood pyracies,
> Are chiefly bent against our Christian friends;
> Some Christians so delight in evils
> That they become the sons of divels,
> And for the same have many shameful ends.

(See also SELECTED BIBLIOGRAPHY: Firth, *Naval.*)

SONGS, PIRATE *(1600 to the present)*
Sailors sang chanties or work songs during their labors. Half-sung, half-chanted in a call-response pattern, chanties included ample profanity. The leader improvised, commenting on recent events and insulting the officers. After working hours, sailors entertained themselves with ballads. Many were sad songs of separation from home and family, known generically as "the sailor's lament." Also popular were ballads of danger and adventure, sea battles, storms, and shipwrecks.

At least some seamen continued to enjoy music after they turned pirate. In the early 1600s, Captain STEPHENSON kidnapped a man because he was expert on some kind of pipe. On Bartholomew ROBERTS' warship—much larger than most pirate vessels—"musicians" entertained or accompanied the men. Roberts' ARTICLES allow "The Musicians to have Rest on the Sabbath Day, but the other six Days and Nights, none without special favour." Whether they sang or played instruments is unknown.

Some sailors' songs were written down from the late 17th century. Some individual mariners probably remained faithful to their favorite ballads after turning pirate. But others may have preferred foreign ditties learned during their travels or from captives.

Pirates may have celebrated each other's exploits. However, the only surviving songs about pirates are ballads, composed by professional (although usually anonymous) authors. From the early 1600s, these ballads were sold to the London public, often in connection with hangings. Since their authors knew little about individual brigands, each ballad tells the same story. Pirates are bad men, who slaughter their victims and spend their money "in drunkenness and letchery," to quote "*The* SEAMAN'S SONG" (1609). "CAPTAIN KID'S FAREWEL TO THE SEAS" (1701), the most successful ballad, remained popular in America for two centuries.

Bill Bones sings "FIFTEEN MEN ON A DEAD MAN'S CHEST" at the Admiral Benbow Inn in TREASURE ISLAND. In *The* PIRATES OF PENZANCE (1879), the Pirate King soars in "OH, BETTER FAR TO LIVE AND DIE," while the pirates in PETER PAN (1904) chant "AVAST BELAY." The lyrics and music were invented for these works and are not based on sailor's ballads.

(See also YO-HO-HO; SELECTED BIBLIOGRAPHY: Defoe, *General History.*)

SON OF CAPTAIN BLOOD, THE *(motion picture; color; 1964)*
The 1935 CAPTAIN BLOOD made a star of Errol FLYNN. In a publicity ploy, this made-in-Spain sequel stars Flynn's son Sean as Robert, son of Peter Blood. The *Variety* reviewer noted that Sean had inherited his father's good looks and athletic prowess. "When he learns to act," he remarked, "Flynn fils could become a popular screen personality in romantic adventurer roles." This never became a reality, as Sean Flynn was killed in 1970, covering the Cambodian war as a photographer.

Robert Blood's mother Arabella (Ann Todd) wants him to be a physician, but he would rather turn pirate like his father. Robert becomes a seaman and romances a passenger named Abbigail (Alessandra Panara). The evil pirate De Malagon (Jose Nieto), an enemy of Robert's father, takes over their vessel. The young couple is rescued by Peter Blood's old crew, and young Robert leads them in action-packed sequences. They return home, save everyone from a tidal wave, and become heroes. Having had enough of the pirate life, Robert settles down with Abbigail, planning a career as a doctor. Directed by Tulio Demicheli.

SON OF THE RED CORSAIR, THE *(Italian motion picture; color; 1963)*
Enrico di Ventimiglia (Lex BARKER), the Red Corsair's exiled son, returns to avenge his father's death. Enrico's pirate crew captures a

galleon carrying the man who betrayed his father. The man tells Enrico that his sister, Neala (Vira Silenti), is not dead but working for Countess Carmen de Montelimar (Sylvia Lopez), the governor's sister. However, Neala actually is imprisoned by the evil governor, who will go to any lengths to force her to marry him. Enrico arrives just in time, kills the governor, and rescues Neala and the countess. Directed by Primo Zeglio.

SORES, JACQUES   *(French corsair; Caribbean; active 1553–1570)*   A fanatical Huguenot (Calvinist) from Normandy, Sores brutally sacked Havana, Cuba, in 1555. But he found no treasure in the town and apparently never returned to the West Indies.

Sores commanded one of three royal warships during a 1553 plunder raid by François LE CLERC but later quarreled with his commander. In 1555, he raided with his own three ships and some 200 men. Juan de Plan, a Spanish renegade, was second-in-command. Sores looted harbors along the Venezuelan coast at La Margarita, RIO DE LA HACHA, and Santa Marta. Guided by two former residents (one a traitorous Portuguese pilot), he descended on Havana on July 10. With a population of only a few thousand, Havana did not offer rich pickings. But Sores expected to find treasure stored in the fort from vessels recently wrecked in Florida.

Havana's governor and many residents fled at the sight of the corsairs. The little fort surrendered after two days, but it contained only one emerald ring and a little silver plate. After agreeing to ransom negotiations, the governor changed his mind and attacked at night with a force of 35 Spaniards, 220 slaves, and 80 Indians. Some of the corsairs were killed, but the Indians' war cries awakened those sleeping at Sores' headquarters in the largest house. Maddened by the governor's treachery, Sores slaughtered his prisoners (some two dozen in all) and drove the defenders from the town.

Sores scorned the paltry thousand pesos now offered as ransom. He burned the town to the ground, destroyed the boats in the harbor, and systematically ravaged the surrounding countryside. Black slaves were hanged since they formed part of their masters' property. Before he destroyed the church, Sores desecrated the altars and gave the priest's vestments to his soldiers as cloaks. Havana was so devastated that another band of French raiders found nothing left to steal the following October. But Sores had taken little booty, and he also had to give up plans to attack Santo Domingo on the way home.

His talents as a seaman earned Sores a leading role in the French religious wars. In 1562, he joined Protestant rebels in Normandy. Profiting from the English invasion and occupation of Le Havre, he plundered merchant ships belonging to French Catholics. By 1569, the Protestant factions throughout France had drawn together around Henry of Navarre (later King Henry IV), who made Sores head of his naval forces. William HAWKINS outfitted eight warships that joined Sores' fleet.

Led by Jacques Sores, French raiders capture, plunder, and burn Havana, Cuba, in 1555. From Theodorus de Bry, *Collectiones* (1590–1634).

Under Sores' leadership, the Protestant marauders became notorious for unrivaled brutality. In December 1569, his squadron surrounded a much larger Venetian CARRACK armed with 45 cannon. Sores murdered the ship's master and purser when they went to his cabin to discuss terms. Terrified by his ferocity, the Venetian seamen surrendered. Soon after, Sores captured an even larger Venetian carrack. With these two magnificent ships, he took cargoes worth some 300,000 *écus*.

While his lieutenants sacked Catholic towns in northern France, Sores returned to the hunt for Iberian treasure ships. Near the Canary Islands in July 1570, he caught up with a Portuguese ship taking 40 Jesuit missionaries to Brazil. Maddened by his religious hatred, Sores led the boarders in person. Living or dead, the Jesuits were thrown into the sea with their holy images, pious books, and relics of saints. All but six of the 500 passengers and crew were coldly massacred.

(See also SELECTED BIBLIOGRAPHY: Wright, *Early Cuba*.)

SOSTRATUS   *(Greek pirate; Aegean Sea; about 345 B.C.)*   Sostratus' corsairs seized Halonnesos, a tiny island off northeastern Greece previously ruled by Athens. King Philip of Macedonia sent soldiers to the island to expel the pirates. Philip's occupation of Halonnesos provided a pretext for war between Athens and Macedonia. In 343, an Athenian embassy demanded that Philip return the island. Philip's response offended the Athenians' pride, since he offered to "give" (rather than to "restore") Halonnesos to Athens. Soon afterward, men from the neighboring island of Peparethos drove away the Macedonian garrison. Philip's forces attacked Peparethos, the Athenians retaliated, and war broke out.

SOTO, BENITO DE   *(Portuguese pirate; Atlantic, Caribbean; died 1832)*   De Soto was a seaman on

an Argentinean slaver in 1827. Off the African coast, he and the mate took over the ship and renamed her the *Black Joke.* As the mutineers celebrated, de Soto shot the mate and was elected captain. Eighteen crewmen refused to join the pirates. They were set adrift in a small boat and drowned when it capsized.

De Soto made for the Caribbean, sold the slaves, and plundered a dozen vessels, sinking them with their crews locked below deck. He then cruised in the South Atlantic, on the route between Europe and the East Indies. To avoid capture, homeward-bound Indiamen formed convoys at Saint Helena before heading north.

In February 1832, de Soto captured the BARK *Morning Star,* returning from Ceylon with invalid soldiers. Having looted their prey and raped the female passengers, the pirates locked everyone below and bored holes in the ship's bottom. The survivors kept her afloat until they were rescued the next day.

De Soto sold his booty in Spain, and the *Black Joke* was wrecked off Cadiz. A soldier from the *Morning Star* recognized him as he passed through Gibraltar. At the gallows, he coolly arranged the noose around his own neck.

(See also SELECTED BIBLIOGRAPHY: Bradlee, *Suppression.*)

SPANISH MAIN, THE (1) *(pirate victim; Caribbean; about 1520–1730)* A geographical term referring to the Spanish possessions in the Americas. For 16th-century English raiders, "The Spanish Main" meant only the northern coast of South America (and the adjacent waters), from Panama to Trinidad. The term distinguished this region from the islands in the Caribbean—perhaps as a translation of the Spanish name *Tierra Firme* (The Mainland) for the same area.

The English word *main* can mean a broad sweep of sea as well as a stretch of land. For some BUCCANEERS of the late 17th and early 18th century, the "Spanish Main" meant the Caribbean Sea itself. (They thus exactly reversed the original definition.) Authors of pirate fiction employ the phrase to add local color to stories and movies. In this loose usage, "Spanish Main" can refer to any place in the Caribbean or along the coast from Florida to Brazil.

(See also TREASURE FLEETS.)

SPANISH MAIN, THE (2) *(motion picture; color; 1945)* Spirited battles and energetic performances enliven this SWASHBUCKLER directed by Frank Borzage. Laurent Van Horn (Paul HENREID) commands a Dutch ship shipwrecked near CARTAGENA. The villainous Spanish governor, Don Alvarado (Walter SLEZAK), orders his men to enslave the Dutch crew and hang Van Horn. He and several others escape and plunder Spanish shipping.

One of their prizes carries Francisca (Maureen O'HARA), daughter of the viceroy of Mexico and Governor Alvarado's fiancée. Seeking revenge, Van Horn

Paul Henreid leans against Maureen O'Hara in *The Spanish Main* (1945).

forces Francisca to marry him. His fellow pirates are afraid that the Spaniards will retaliate by destroying TORTUGA, the buccaneer haven. The crew steals Francisca and takes her back to Governor Alvarado. By now, she has fallen in love with Van Horn. With her help, he fights off the governor's guards and carries her away from Cartagena.

SPARTACUS (1) *(commanded slave revolt; died 71 B.C.)* Spartacus and 70 others broke out of a gladiatorial school near Capua in 73 and set up a camp on Mount Vesuvius. Like ancient pirates, Spartacus divided BOOTY equally, and thousands of discontented slaves and farm workers joined the rebels' ranks. Early in 72, Spartacus defeated two Roman armies, devastated southern Italy, and then marched north to escape across the Alps. But many among his followers preferred to plunder in Italy. Spartacus accordingly turned south again, conquered two more Roman armies, and was finally trapped near Reggio di Calabria at the bottom of the peninsula.

As Spartacus withdrew south through Lucania (modern Basilicata) in 72, the Greek historian Plutarch (first century A.D.) says he ran into some Cilician pirate ships. Spartacus

> had thoughts of attempting Sicily, where, by landing two thousand men, he hoped to newly kindle the war of the slaves, which was but lately extinguished, and seemed to need but little to set it burning again. But after the pirates had struck a bargain with him, and received his earnest [deposit], they deceived him and sailed away.

This incident, not mentioned by any other ancient historian, has tarnished the reputation of the corsairs, perhaps unfairly. The pirates of CILICIA usually kept their word, and they delivered prisoners when their ransom was paid. During his third war with Rome, SELEUCUS and other corsairs remained loyal to King MITHRIDATES after his own soldiers deserted that unlucky monarch.

This band of Cilicians simply may have been less trustworthy than other squadrons. But it also is possible that they fully intended to pick up Spartacus at Brindisi. Spartacus was marching toward Brindisi when another Roman army suddenly arrived, blocking his retreat. In this case, the Cilician corsairs did not break their word, since Spartacus never arrived at the agreed rendezvous.

(See also SELECTED BIBLIOGRAPHY: Plutarch, *Lives*; *Crassus*.)

SPARTACUS (2)   *(motion picture; color; 1960)*
Spartacus, directed by Stanley Kubrick and based on the novel by Howard Fast, recreates a slave rebellion that panicked the Roman Empire. Dalton Trumbo wrote the screenplay. Critics generally regard it as one of Hollywood's best epics about the ancient world. The all-star cast includes Kirk Douglas (also producer), Laurence Olivier, Jean Simmons, Charles LAUGHTON, Tony Curtis, and Peter Ustinov (Academy Award winner as best supporting actor). More than 8,000 Spanish soldiers filled out the ranks of the slave and Roman armies.

Before the final battle, SPARTACUS (Douglas) arranges for CILICIAN pirates to carry his army away from Italy. He pays the Cilicians with great chests jammed full of looted treasure. However, when he arrives at the coast to meet their ships, the pirates have accepted an even bigger Roman bribe to stay away.

The Cilician commanders who betray Spartacus are portrayed as fast-talking, vaguely Oriental racketeers dressed in flamboyant garb. This accurately reflects stories told by ancient historians. Cilician captains were immensely rich, and their ships and HAVENS were lavishly decorated. Accepting a story by Plutarch, the movie suggests that the pirates cheated Spartacus. However, Plutarch's version may be incorrect since Spartacus never reached the port where the Cilicians had promised to meet him.

SPEIRDYKE, BERNARD CLAESEN   *(Dutch pirate; Caribbean; died 1670)*   Nicknamed both Captain Bart and Captain Barnard by his English comrades, Speirdyke sailed from PORT ROYAL in June 1663. He cruised along Venezuela, plundered the town of San Tomas, and returned the following March. Early in 1670, he visited Manzanillo, Cuba, to release some Spanish prisoners and present a letter of peace from the governor of Jamaica. While there, he smuggled European luxury goods into the town. As he was leaving, his ship was attacked by the Spanish corsair Manoel RIVERO PARDAL. Even though he had only 18 men to Rivero's 70, Speirdyke put up a sharp fight and was killed during the battle.

SPILBERGEN (SPEILBERGEN), JORIS VAN   *(Dutch admiral; Atlantic, Caribbean, Pacific; 1568 to after 1616)*   Van Spilbergen took part in African

and Caribbean expeditions, visited the East Indies from 1601 to 1604, and helped defeat Spanish vessels near Gibraltar in 1607. In August 1614, he commanded a large fleet that invaded the Pacific coast of South America and the East Indies.

Peru and Mexico were the source of silver for Spanish TREASURE FLEETS and the destination of the rich MANILA GALLEON. The region already had been invaded by individual pirate captains, such as Sir Francis DRAKE, Thomas CAVENDISH, Sir Richard HAWKINS, Simon de CORDES, and Olivier van NOORT. But Spilbergen led the first expedition with official backing. Although a 12-year truce (1609–1621) had halted hostilities with Spain, the Dutch government licensed the raid. The East India Company sponsored Spilbergen and intended to keep all loot. The crew sailed for wages only, and every ship carried a merchant who recorded all spoils.

Hoping not to repeat the mistakes of earlier raids, the East India Company lavishly outfitted Spilbergen's force. Eight hundred sailors and professional soldiers manned four warships and two YACHTS. The ships carried a three-year supply of salted meat, fish, and biscuits.

The fleet reached Brazil in December 1614. When Portuguese settlers at São Vicente refused to provide supplies, Spilbergen burned a church and a sugar mill and seized a ship. To end talk of mutiny, two men were hung up at the yardarm and riddled with MUSKET balls.

After a rapid passage through the Strait of Magellan (April 2–May 4), the Dutch fleet sailed north, sacking and burning Santa Maria on May 31 and Valparaiso on June 12. They briefly visited Arica on July 2 but found no silver galleons in the harbor. The citizens made a great deal of noise, convincing Spilbergen that a large force guarded the unarmed town.

The Spanish viceroy had already collected Arica's silver and sent it to Panama guarded by three galleons. Although this left only two warships along the Peruvian coast, the Spaniards hastily armed five merchantmen. The two fleets fought a confused and bitter battle throughout the night of July 17 and the following morning. One Spanish warship and merchantmen sank with some 500 men. Only 40 of Spilbergen's crews were killed, while his ships were practically unharmed.

The whole coast of America lay open to attack. On July 20, Spilbergen invaded Callao, the port of Lima. As earlier at Arica, the Spaniards fooled Spilbergen with a fine show of banners, trumpets, and countermarching. Most of Callao's guns had been removed to reinforce the fleet. Only one Franciscan priest knew how to fire artillery, and he got off two or three shots with an ancient cannon before it disintegrated. When one lucky shot hit a Dutch ship, Spilbergen called off the attack.

The Dutch captured and burned Paita, Peru, in early August. Acapulco put up no defense and was peacefully occupied for a week in October. After cruising along the Mexican coast until December 2, Spilbergen left for Asia convinced that the MANILA GALLEON had been warned to keep off shore. In fact, a warning had been sent but never received, and the Dutch missed the galleon by only a few days. With unrewarding stops at Manila and Ternate, the fleet made it home in July 1617.

Unlike Cordes and Noort 16 years earlier, Spilbergen managed to keep his fleet together and lost few men. But his expedition was highly unprofitable. One prize carried 7,000 pesos in silver, the rest were small boats with fish or foodstuffs. Neither Arica or Callao was captured, and both the Peruvian silver galleons and the Manila Galleon escaped. Nevertheless, Spilbergen's raid revealed the weakness of Spanish defenses, and the wealth of Peru continued to tempt raiders.

(See also SELECTED BIBLIOGRAPHY: Bradley, *Peru;* Spate, *Monopolists.*)

SPITERI, PAOLO *(Maltese corsair; Aegean Sea; active 1739 to 1741)* A Turkish CARAVEL captured Spiteri's ship in 1741 while it was anchored at Santorini Island. He escaped with many of the crew in his FELUCCA. On his return to Malta, the ship's owners sued him for incompetence, and he was jailed until trial.

SPRIGGS, FRANCIS *(English pirate; Atlantic, Caribbean; active 1721–1725)* Spriggs left London in March 1721 with George LOWTHER and willingly followed him into piracy. When Lowther and Ned LOW parted company in May 1722, Spriggs went with Low and was made QUARTERMASTER. With Low, he devastated shipping off New England and Canada, visited the Azores, and went back to the West Indies. Low gave Spriggs command of a SCHOONER late in 1722. However, Charles HARRIS was captain of Low's consort in May 1723, and Spriggs again served as quartermaster.

A warship captured Harris in June, and Low returned to the Azores and West Africa. In January 1724, Low made Spriggs captain of the 12-gun *Batchelor's Delight,* taken off the African coast. Two days later, Spriggs slipped off during the night and was elected captain by the *Delight*'s crew.

Spriggs headed west and seized a dozen vessels in the Caribbean and as far north as Bermuda and Rhode Island. The captured crews were tortured; their ships were sunk or burned. Spriggs told one captured captain that he planned to revenge Charles Harris' death by ravaging the American coast and destroying every ship he captured.

One of Spriggs' followers named Shipton received command of a captured SLOOP. Late in 1724, Spriggs and Shipton were caught near Cuba by a British warship, and Shipton's vessel was wrecked on the Florida coast. Boston newspapers reported that 49 pirates were captured, and the Florida Indians killed another 16. About £2,000 in booty was found on Shipton's sloop. Spriggs outsailed the warship and later rescued Shipton and a few others.

In January 1725 Spriggs and Shipton looted 16 ships cutting LOGWOOD in the Bay of Honduras, and they took other prizes during the next few months. Philip LYNE, Spriggs' quartermaster, apparently led a mutiny, and

Spriggs and Shipton were marooned among the Mosquito Indians in Honduras.

(See also SELECTED BIBLIOGRAPHY: Dow, *Pirates.*)

STEDMAN, CAPTAIN *(English buccaneer; Caribbean; 1666)* Captain Stedman operated from PORT ROYAL, Jamaica. With two small ships and 80 men, he and Robert SEARLE devastated the Dutch colony on Tobago in about January 1666. Later that year, after war broke out with France, a French FRIGATE trapped Stedman near Guadeloupe. His much smaller vessel was becalmed and unable to escape, and Stedman's buccaneers boldly boarded the French ship and fought for two hours. Stedman and many others were killed.

(See also SELECTED BIBLIOGRAPHY: Haring, *Buccaneers.*)

STEPHEN, CLAYS *(English pirate; English Channel; active 1448–1456)* Stephen was one of William KYD's company during numerous piracies.

STEPHENSON, ROBERT *(English pirate; Atlantic; active 1608–1611)* Among the captains sailing from MAMORA and Leamcon, Ireland, Stephenson commanded a 28-gun FLYBOAT. Stephenson sometimes forced skilled men to join his crew. He once gave a carpenter the choice of enlisting or being "shot off in a piece of ordinance." While at Mamora, the sounds made (on some type of pipe) by a man from another ship so delighted him that he refused to let the musician leave.

(See also BISHOP, RICHARD.)

STEVENSON, ROBERT LOUIS *(British author; 1850–1894)* Robert Louis Stevenson was born and raised in Edinburgh, Scotland, the only child of a prosperous engineer. Although often in poor health, Stevenson attended Edinburgh University and studied law. In 1877, he fell in love with Fanny Osbourne, 10 years his senior and married to another man. She returned to California in 1878, Stevenson followed a year later, and they were married in 1880, after she divorced her first husband.

The couple spent the next years at health resorts in England and Europe. A winter (1887–1888) in the Adirondack Mountains seemingly arrested Stevenson's tuberculosis, but he still sought a healthful climate. In May 1888, he left San Francisco in a sailing yacht, with his wife, mother, and stepson. After visiting various South Sea islands, the family settled at Samoa.

Stevenson's sole ambition was to be a writer, and he began with essays and short stories. TREASURE ISLAND (1883) was slow to achieve success, but *The Strange Case of Doctor Jekyll and Mr. Hyde* (1886) instantly caught the public fancy. Stevenson followed *Treasure Island* with other adventure stories for young adults. *The Black Arrow* (published as a serial in 1883) is set in 15th-century England. In *Kidnapped* (1886), David Balfour, a Scottish boy of 16, is cheated, shipwrecked, and pursued through the harsh Highland mountains during the 1750s. Balfour's

"I can't have these colors, Mr. Hands; and, by your leave, I'll strike 'em." Jim Hawkins lowers the jolly roger after taking possession of the *Hispaniola*. Illustration by Louis Rhead for a 1915 edition of *Treasure Island* by Robert Louis Stevenson.

story is continued in *Catriona* (1893, called *David Balfour* in America).

Stevenson's later works are intricately plotted psychological studies of mixed motives. Many consider THE MASTER OF BALLANTRAE (1889) the fullest achievement of his narrative art. Two other Scottish novels—*Weir of Hermiston* (1894) and *St. Ives* (1897)—were incomplete at his death.

Stevenson's South Seas tales present adult versions of *Treasure Island*. In *The Wrecker* (1892), Loudon Dodd and Jim Pinkerton fail in business. Setting out to salvage a supposedly valuable wreck, they instead learn of a horrible and irrational slaughter. *The Ebb-Tide* portrays three failed men who steal a worthless hulk. They arrive at an unregistered island ruled by a cruel religious fanatic, plan to steal his pearls, but instead submit to his dictatorship.

Stevenson's literary reputation has fluctuated widely. Adulated as a saint and genius immediately after his death, he later was dismissed as merely an author of children's books. Since the 1950s, his reputation has soared and his writings have been praised as original and powerful. At their best, as in *Treasure Island*, his works illuminate the equivocal nature of human character during unforeseen and dangerous situations.

STIRIONE, GIOVANNI *(Italian corsair; Aegean Sea; active 1190–1206)* Originally from Calabria, Stirione raided so successfully that the BYZANTINE emperor, Isaac II Angelus (reigned 1185–1195), lavishly bribed him to join the imperial navy. In 1196 or 1197, Stirione raised taxes in Athens to outfit a fleet, which soon was captured by the Genoese corsair, Captain GAFFORIO (2). The Byzantines got together another squadron, and Stirione took Gafforio by trickery.

After Constantinople fell to a western European force in 1204, Stirione commanded the small navy created by the Greek emperor-in-exile at Nicaea. In 1306, he led 17 galleys in an abortive attack on the Latin Christians at Cyzicus (Erdek) in the Sea of Marmara.

STOLEN TREASURE *(short stories; 1907)* Four stories with colorful illustrations, which Howard PYLE originally published in magazines. Three stories feature a young hero, basically moral and brave. After sharing the adventures of a courageous but conscienceless adventurer, the hero rejoins civilized society. The fourth contrasts two brothers, one sedate and domesticated, the other a lawless adventurer.

"With the Buccaneers" borrows from EXQUEMELIN but portrays Sir Henry MORGAN more favorably. Harry Mostyn, aged 16 and the son of a prosperous Barbados sugar planter, enlists with Morgan and watches him kill a man in cold blood. Harry helps capture a warship, risks his life as the pirates battle other Spanish vessels, and dallies with a beautiful French girl. Back at PORT ROYAL, Harry is reclaimed by an older brother and settles down as a respectable sugar merchant.

The hero of "Tom Christ and the Treasure-Box" is an orphan. One night, Tom sees CAPTAIN KIDD burying treasure by moonlight. He returns and steals Kidd's fortune and his ship's log books. Later he consults a wealthy and influential New Yorker, who turns out to be his uncle. Tom settles down in marriage with his uncle's daughter, while the log books help to convict Kidd.

Barnaby True is the hero of "The Ghost of Captain Brand." Twenty years earlier, Barnaby's grandfather, the pirate William Brand, was killed by Captain Jack Malyoe. While in Jamaica on business, Barnaby joins one of his grandfather's partners to avenge the murder and secure the treasure. In the final battle, Malyoe dies of fright after seeing a ghostly vision of Captain Brand, who reappears later when Barnaby marries Malyoe's niece.

In "The Devil at New Hope," Obadiah Bedford is a former pirate and slaver, reputed to be in league with the devil. To torment William, his pompous brother, Obadiah engineers the marriage of William's only child to an imposter. However, Obadiah's scoundrel turns out to be a real aristocrat. Revolted by Obadiah's depravity, he returns to virtue and inherits the family title and wealth.

STORTEBECHER (STERTEBECKER), JOHAN *(German pirate; Baltic, Atlantic; executed 1402)* According to legend, Stortebecher was a ruined noble from Frisia, whose nickname ("gulper of glasses") refers to the unusual ordeal imposed upon his captives. A prisoner was killed unless he emptied at one swallow the pirate's drinking mug, which held as much as four wine bottles.

The city of Lubeck employed Stortebecher during a war with Denmark. When a 1395 peace treaty left his pirates without work, they formed the Brotherhood of Suppliers. Portraying himself as a sea-going Robin Hood, Stortebecher adopted the motto "Friends of God, Enemies of the World." Outwardly pious, he gave a cathedral a stained-glass window portraying the seven deadly sins. Gluttony was represented by his coat of arms—two crossed drinking glasses.

Operating from Frisia and Gotland Island, Stortebecher's band plundered throughout the Baltic, and many legends surround their exploits. The Swedish and English governments and the Hanseatic League all financed expeditions, which failed to arrest the pirates. In 1402, the admiral of Hamburg captured Stortebecher's flagship. Its mast was hollow, the story goes, and contained bars of gold. Using some of the gold, the citizens of Hamburg erected a crown of thanksgiving atop the spire of Saint Nicholas' church.

STORY OF JACK BALLISTER'S FORTUNES, THE *(novel; 1895)*

An adventure story with black and white illustrations by Howard PYLE. At the age of 16, Jack Ballister is adopted by his unscrupulous uncle, who sells him as an indentured servant. He is carried from England to Virginia, flees a brutal master, and joins BLACKBEARD's gang.

Jack is spiritually reborn when the kidnapped Eleanor Parker unsuccessfully tries to flee her captors. Jack and an older pirate, Christian Dred, rescue Eleanor. The marauders pursue them, Dred is killed, and Jack saves the girl on his own. Hailed as a hero when they return, Jack claims his fortune, returns to Virginia and marries Eleanor.

Mixing history and romance, *Jack Ballister's Fortunes* gives an intimate portrait of pirate life. Pyle relied on Daniel DEFOE's GENERAL HISTORY for the outline of Blackbeard's life. However, he ignored Defoe's fictional stories about a bizarre monster with a plaited beard. Pyle's Blackbeard is an unruly adventurer, who takes a pardon but cannot accept a quiet, domestic life. Although wicked, he is physically brave, resourceful, and articulate.

STOUT, RALPH *(British pirate; Indian Ocean, Bay of Bengal; died 1697)*

While serving with James KELLEY in 1692, Stout was arrested by an Indian ruler. In 1696, the prisoners stole a boat and found their way to Bombay. There they enlisted on the East Indiaman *Mocha*, many crewmen having deserted because of Captain Edgecumbe's cruelty.

Eight days out of Bombay, Stout and the other pirates seized the *Mocha*. Twenty-seven officers and men reached shore in the ship's boat. Captain Edgecumbe was pounded

"The combatants cut and slashed with savage fury." Blackbeard's final battle, portrayed by Howard Pyle in this illustration to *The Story of Jack Ballister's Fortunes.*

to death with broken bottles and thrown to the sharks. The pirates shared out £19,000 found aboard the *Mocha* and elected Stout captain.

Stout took the *Mocha* to the Mergui Archipelago, southeast of Burma. There he ran into a merchant ship that had arrested Robert CULLIFORD and other pirates. Stout freed the captives who joined his crew. For almost a year, Stout cruised between India and the Strait of Malacca in consort with the CHARMING MARY. The two ships plundered at least seven victims, some with considerable treasure.

While the pirates usually released their plundered prizes, they tortured and murdered prisoners in two cases. In February 1697, they brutally abused the crew and passengers on a Portuguese ship. After hoisting up a priest with his hands tied over his head, the pirates sliced off part of his head with a cutlass. Shortly afterward, they seized a Malayan or Indian vessel, locked up her crew and passengers, and burned them alive with their vessel.

The *Mary* went to Sumatra in April or May 1697, while Stout took the *Mocha* to the Laccadive Islands. In one story his men murdered him because he wanted to retire. In another version he was slain by Malay seaman visiting the islands. Robert Culliford, the *Mocha's* QUARTERMASTER, replaced him as captain.

(See also SELECTED BIBLIOGRAPHY: Grey, *Pirates*.)

STRABO *(Greek historian; 64/63 B.C. to about A.D. 21)* A native of Pontus in what now is Turkey, Strabo came from a distinguished local family that supported first MITHRIDATES and then LUCULLUS. He studied in Rome and traveled in Asia Minor, Egypt, Ethiopia, and Arabia. His *Geography* provides information about the history, legends, and peoples of various regions, including the TAPHIANS, TYRRHENIANS, and CILICIANS.

STRADLING, THOMAS *(English privateer; Pacific; active 1703–1709)* Stradling was QUARTERMASTER of the 90-ton *Cinque Ports*, a heavily armed warship propelled by both oars and sails. In September 1703, the *Cinque Ports* sailed for South America's Pacific coast in consort with William DAMPIER's *Saint George*. When the captain died near Brazil, Stradling took over, with Alexander SELKIRK as second-in-command.

After passing around Cape Horn, the two vessels rendezvoused at the JUAN FERNÁNDEZ ISLANDS in February 1704. Heading north along the coast, Dampier and Stradling took a few small prizes and reached Panama in May. After an abortive attack on the gold mines at SANTA MARIA, they seized a large Spanish vessel loaded with food and cloth.

From letters on the captured ship, the English raiders learned that two Spanish warships were pursuing them. Stradling broke off the consortship on May 19 and went back to Juan Fernández to pick up supplies. Alexander Selkirk quarreled with Stradling and marooned himself on the island in October. Selkirk was picked up by Woodes ROGERS four years later, and his story inspired ROBINSON CRUSOE.

Stradling went back to the Mapella Islands but failed to make contact with Dampier and sank the badly leaking *Cinque Ports*. Her crew survived but were discovered by Spanish sailors. Chained hand and foot, they were imprisoned at Lima as pirates.

In 1709, French officials (France was Spain's wartime ally) took Stradling to Brittany as a prisoner of war. He convinced his jailers that he had buried treasure on a Pacific island, and they improved his conditions to encourage further revelations. Stradling instead tied his bedclothes together, climbed over the castle wall, and made his way back to England.

(See also SELECTED BIBLIOGRAPHY: Lloyd, *Dampier*.)

STROZZI, BROTHER LEONE *(Knight of Malta; Mediterranean; 1515–1554)* Among the leading mercenary warriors of his time, Strozzi belonged to an ancient Florentine family. He was a nephew of Pope Clement VII, who made him an officer of the KNIGHTS OF MALTA at the age of 13. Still only 21, Strozzi was elected CAPTAIN GENERAL OF GALLEYS in 1536. The following year, he commanded four Maltese galleys that

joined a Spanish squadron. Near Corfu, the allies gave battle to an OTTOMAN fleet, and two enemy ships attacked Strozzi's Galley. Strozzi maneuvered superbly, sinking one and capturing the other.

Despite marriage ties, the Strozzi opposed Medici hegemony in Florence. In 1537, during an unsuccessful assault on the city, Filippo Strozzi was captured and tortured to death by Cosimo I dei MEDICI. To revenge his father's murder, Leone left Malta and served with the fleets of France, the Medicis' chief enemy. He thus changed sides, since France was allied with the Ottoman Empire against Charles V of Spain, Malta's protector.

Late in 1551, having quarreled with the French king, Leone returned to Malta with his own two galleys. When the grand master refused entry to the port, he went corsairing in the Levant and returned to Malta towing rich prizes. The knights (who had meanwhile placated Charles V) now welcomed Leone and hired his ships for their own fleet. He is reported to have kept a reckoning of the booty captured from Christians, promising to repay them when he had accumulated sufficient funds.

Commanding the order's four galleys and one of his own, Strozzi in 1552 led a slave raid on Zuara, west of TRIPOLI. Although the raid failed, he was reelected captain general in June 1553 and was almost elected grand master the following September. Early in 1554, he again left Malta to accept command of the French forces fighting the Medici in Italy. After escaping death in many sea battles, he was killed by a sentinel while spying out the Medici positions around Porto Ercole.

STROZZI, BROTHER SCIPIONE *(Knight of Malta; Mediterranean; active 1550–1553)* Strozzi arrived at MALTA with a superb galley, which was hired by the knights. Sometimes sailing with the squadrons of his uncle, Leone STROZZI, he captured numerous merchantmen and warships off the BARBARY COAST.

STUKELEY (STUCLEY), SIR THOMAS *(English adventurer; Atlantic, Mediterranean; 1525?–1578)* Stukeley belonged to a landowning family in northern Devonshire. An extraordinarily persuasive rogue, he claimed to be Henry VIII's bastard and victimized many experienced rulers and statesmen.

Stukeley fought in France from 1544 to 1550. In 1551, he was arrested during political intrigues but escaped to France. He spied for the French in England, became a double agent, was jailed (1552–1553), and served with the armies of Germany and Savoy (1553–1557). Turning pirate early in 1558, he seized several Spanish ships but was released without trial by the LORD HIGH ADMIRAL.

Stukeley's wife inherited substantial wealth in 1559. After squandering her fortune, he assembled six warships in 1563, supposedly to colonize Florida. Queen Elizabeth and some of the other investors probably knew that Stukeley's real game was piracy. Stukeley's squadron spent the next two years taking Spanish, French, and Portuguese prizes at sea and along the Spanish coast. Foreign complaints forced Elizabeth to disown Stukeley and send ships to capture him. He was seized in Ireland in March 1565 and brought to London, but was released without trial in September.

In 1566 and 1567, Stukeley tried to buy estates and royal offices in Ireland with his pirate booty, but Queen Elizabeth refused her sanction. It later turned out that Stukeley, possibly a sincere Roman Catholic, had been a Spanish agent since 1563. He was arrested in 1569 but released for lack of evidence.

In 1570, Stukeley fled to Madrid and was generously received by King Philip II. A proposed invasion of Ireland fell through, and Stukeley commanded three Spanish galleys at LEPANTO in 1571. He continued to plot an invasion of England, and the pope gave him a GALLEON and 600 soldiers in 1578. Stukeley abandoned the dilapidated vessel in Lisbon, joined a Portuguese invasion of Morocco, and was killed in battle.

STYLES, ANTHONY *(English pirate; Atlantic; active 1582)* While anchored in Wales, Styles lured Thomas WALTON and his crew ashore by burning some houses and then sailed away with Walton's prize.

SUCCESSFUL PIRATE, THE *(play; performed 1712, published 1713)* Charles Johnson (1679–1748) reworked and added comic episodes to a 17th-century tragedy to meet the craze for stories about Henry EVERY. *The Successful Pirate* had some success at the Drury Lane Theatre. The audience enjoyed (and officials protested) satirical comments on the government's efforts to catch pirates.

The pirate king Arviragus (Every) lives at MADAGASCAR and loves Princess Zaida, daughter of Aureng-Zebe. These persons reside in grand surroundings, and Arviragus makes bombastic speeches describing his crimes as "heroically great." Comedy is provided by a "Mobb" of pirates named Herring, Porpoise, Shark, and Codshead.

SUITTO, NICOLI *(Italian pirate; Mediterranean, Aegean Sea; 1820s)* From Genoa, Suitto moved to Kardhamili in southern Greece and looted coastal shipping with the approval of the local authorities. In January 1827, a British warship captured his four-gun schooner at anchor, but Suitto fled to shore. After the British commander threatened to bombard the town, Greek officials surrendered Suitto. He escaped, seized an Austrian vessel, and took it to Kardhamili in June. This time, the British shelled the city, but Suitto again got away.

SULTAN IBN SAQR *(Arab pirate chief; active 1805–1808)* See QAWASIM.

SUMPTER, LEONARD *(English pirate; Atlantic; 1546)* Near Waterford, Ireland, Sumpter's vessel ran into a Spanish merchantman carrying woad and iron. Since they had just been robbed and tortured by Michael JAMES, the Spaniards were terrified of Englishmen and abandoned ship. Sumpter's men took the deserted vessel to Wales and sold whatever cargo James had left behind.

SWAB *(nautical insult; 16th century to the present)* A swab is a rope-yarn mop with which common seamen cleaned a ship's deck. In nautical slang, a swab (or swabber) is a term of contempt, used to describe or address a crude, uneducated person, who acts like the lowest type of sailor.

SWAN, CHARLES *(English buccaneer; Caribbean, Pacific; died 1687?)* Already an experienced captain, Swan commanded a ship during Sir Henry MORGAN's 1671 sack of Panama. In 1682, he brought a merchant vessel from Jamaica to London. There he became friendly with Basil RINGROSE, and the two men arranged financing for a smuggling venture to Chile and Peru, which left in October 1683. The *Cygnet* carried 16 guns so Swan and Ringrose may have intended piracy from the beginning.

In October 1684, Edward DAVIS encountered Swan and Peter HARRIS off northern Peru. Swan had prepared a story, which he told to William DAMPIER, one of Davis' officers. After passing through the Strait of Magellan, Swan said, he stopped at Valdivia, Chile. The Chileans refused to trade and even killed two men carrying a flag of truce. Swan continued on to Costa Rica, where he ran into Harris. Seeing Harris' buccaneers with gold in their pockets, his crew forced Swan to turn pirate.

Swan and Harris joined up with Davis. Their three ships entered the Gulf of Panama in February 1685, hoping to intercept Peruvian treasure ships. While they waited, several hundred French pirates arrived as well as a group under Captain TOWNLEY. On June 8, Spanish warships defeated the buccaneer forces, and the French and English contingents split up.

The English captains raided cities in Nicaragua but took little loot. In September 1685, Swan and Townley left Davis and went on alone toward Acapulco, Mexico, looking for the MANILA GALLEON. In November, they failed to capture a Peruvian treasure ship guarded by Acapulco's guns, and they also missed the Galleon in January. Townley's ship left for Peru, while Swan contained north, trying to find gold or silver mines. On February 26, 1686, the pirates occupied Tepic, Mexico, about 15 miles inland. As they returned to their ships, the Mexicans ambushed the party and killed 50 men, including Basil Ringrose.

Swan sailed east on April 10, 1686, to invest his booty in Asian goods. With William Dampier's assistance, the *Cygnet* reached Guam in only 54 days. As the food ran out, the crew plotted to eat the officers. "This made Swan say to me after our arrival at Guam, 'Ah! Dampier, you would have made them but a poor meal'; for I was as lean as the captain was lusty and fleshy."

Swan headed for Mindanao in the Philippines, where his men spent their money on drink and women. When Swan refused to leave, the crew mutinied, abandoning him and 36 others in January 1687. Swan later quarreled with the sultan's general, who arranged his murder.

(See also READ, JOHN; SELECTED BIBLIOGRAPHY: Bradley, *Peru;* Dampier, *New Voyage;* Gerhard, *Pirates;* Kemp and Lloyd, *Brethren.*)

SWANN, JOHN *(British pirate; Indian Ocean, Red Sea, South China Sea; active 1697–1698)* Swann lived on the *Mocha* as Robert CULLIFORD's "great consort" (homosexual lover).

(See also HOMOSEXUALITY.)

SWASHBUCKLER (1) *(literary term; 19th century to present)* A boastful and noisy brigand, eager to use his sword. A *buckler* is a small round shield carried on the arm. *Swash* refers the sound made by a heavy blow, like that of the waves crashing on the shore. A swashbuckler came to mean someone who makes a loud noise by striking his own or his opponent's shield with his sword. Sixteenth-century writers invented this picturesque word to describe any loud, swaggering bully, or ruffian. Revived in the 1800s, it now refers mainly to pirates or to pirate movies, especially those presenting many dynamic SWORD DUELS.

SWASHBUCKLER (2) *(motion picture; color; 1976)* Ned Lynch (Robert Shaw) and Nick Debrett (James Earl Jones), come to Jamaica and get rid of the tyrannical governor, Lord Durant (Peter Boyle). Although the governor is a flamboyant homosexual, some of his henchmen have wronged Jane Barnet (Genevieve Bujold). Helped by Major Folly (Beau Bridges), a seemingly foppish British officer, the two genial pirates set things straight. In addition to the kinky goings-on at court, there are several action and mob sequences with lots of Technicolor blood. Directed by James Goldstone.

SWEARING *(pirate speech; all eras)* Sailors always had nimble tongues, and volleys of curses accompanied both work and play. Sometimes jokingly, often seriously, they hurled insults at each other, at their officers, and at landsmen crossing their path. Historians believe that blasphemy and swearing were considered more offensive after the Protestant Reformation. By using "rough talk," Caribbean BUCCANEERS and Atlantic pirates expressed their contempt for middle-class notions of gentility.

Some persons today take offense to "dirty words." Hence pirate FICTION and MOVIES cannot repeat the expressions sailors actually employed. Fictional pirates instead use obsolete but ugly-sounding words in ways that seem nautical to non-seamen. These fictional curse words include AVAST, BELAY, BLOW ME DOWN, KEELHAUL, LUBBER, SCURVY, SHIVER MY TIMBERS, SWAB, and WENCH.

SWORD DUELS *(fictional pirate habit)* In MOVIES about Elizabethan England and Caribbean pirates, combatants thrust at each other with thin swords, using the elegant gestures of modern fencing. However, pirates did not fight chivalrous two-man duels using fencing movements. Seamen used CUTLASSES and sabres; officers carried rapiers. These weapons had sharpened edges, and opponents mainly hacked at each other rather than lunging with the point.

Sword duels were reserved for gentlemen. Medieval knights duelled with heavy, thick swords. (Fencing matches in most Robin Hood films are totally anachronistic.) As armor disappeared during the 15th century, flat swords were replaced by the rapier, a long and slender two-edged weapon with a wide, cuplike hilt.

Intended for combat as well as for personal defense, the rapier was too heavy for modern fencing tactics. Opponents faced each other and slashed more often than they thrust. They ducked or sidestepped attacks and parried with a dagger in the left hand. Some sought to trip or grab their foe.

From the 1660s, noblemen abandoned the rapier for a shorter lighter sword, without a cutting edge and designed solely for thrusting. The new weapon, not meant for combat, developed into the fencing foil, requiring a nimble wrist rather than muscular strength.

Whether fought with rapiers or foils, the duel of honor was a private fight between two noblemen. Dueling rules first appeared in 16th-century Italy, and the fad spread to France. There duels became an essential part of noble life, killing 4,000 men between 1589 and 1610. In England, sword duels became popular during the 1600s and were most numerous at the century's end.

The two-man duel was part of a system of manners by which nobles sustained each other's dignity. Duels replaced law cases when a nobleman's honor was attacked. Since both opponents had to be honorable, a gentleman almost never dueled with a commoner. Courtesy and fairness were reserved for these ceremonial duels. In battle, even noble pirates (such as François LE CLERC) used ruthless tactics.

Fencing became a standard feature of pirate movies during the 1920s, thanks in part to Rafael SABATINI's novels. A sword fight by the hero's brother determines the plot of Sabatini's SEA HAWK (1915). Sabatini's sword duels, not described in the novel, become fencing matches in the 1924 film adaptation. Douglas FAIRBANKS excelled at sword play in movies about Zorro and the Three Musketeers, and he naturally included fencing in *The* BLACK PIRATE in 1926.

Each SWASHBUCKLER tried to outfence its predecessors. For extra realism, the foils carried no caps when Errol FLYNN defeated Basil RATHBONE in CAPTAIN BLOOD (1935). Since *Blood* is set in the 1680s, their characters could have known how to fence. As Sir Francis DRAKE, a century before foils were invented, Flynn fights an even wilder duel in *The* SEA HAWK (1940). Tyrone POWER, a former Zorro like Fairbanks, displays his skill in *The* BLACK SWAN (1942).

Henceforth, every pirate movie included at least one fencing match, although few equal the Fairbanks, Flynn,

A sword duel between Errol Flynn and Basil Rathbone being filmed for the 1935 movie version of *Captain Blood*.

or Power duels for bravura athleticism. WOMEN PIRATES fence in ANNE OF THE INDIES (1951) and QUEEN OF THE PIRATES (1961).

(See also WEAPONS; SELECTED BIBLIOGRAPHY: Richards, *Swordsmen.*)

SYBURTES OF PETRA *(Greek pirate; Mediterranean; 189 B.C.)* Syburtes came from Petra, part of the city of Elis (near modern Loutra) in southern Greece. Near Cephalonia Island (Kefallinia) in 189, he captured a ship carrying the AETOLIAN ambassadors to Rome. Syburtes disposed of his prisoners in Charanda, a town in the kingdom of Epirus.

Since they were at war with Aetolia, the Epirots demanded a large ransom. Although the prisoners were wealthy, they refused to pay five TALENTS and bargained with their captors. The Epirots accepted three talents, because they wanted their money before their Roman allies heard of the affair. But one of the prisoners balked at paying anything and stayed in jail until the Romans freed him. This captive, a man named Alexander, thus confirmed his reputation as both the richest and the stingiest man in Greece.

SYCONIAN, THE *(play in Greek; fourth century B.C.)* Only a few sections survive of this comedy by the Athenian playwright Menander (about 342–293/289). In the prologue, a young girl and her maid, captured by pirates, are offered for sale at a slave market in CARIA. (The same pirates also had seized an old woman, but they left her behind because she had little value as a slave.) There they have the good luck to be purchased by Sicyonius, a decent and wealthy officer.

Greek audiences considered piracy and the slave trade realities of everyday life. Sailing from the Aegean islands, AETOLIA, CRETE, and CILICIA, corsairs robbed ships and coastal communities throughout the third and second centuries.

SYLVESTER, CAPTAIN *(French pirate; Caribbean; active 1574–1575)* Sylvester left Le Havre in September 1574 with a hundred fighting men and unsuccessfully attacked Veragua in western Panama. Some slaves deserted to the raiders and told them that valuable shipping came down the San Juan River in Nicaragua. Between January and March 1575, Sylvester's band was joined by English raiders under Gilbert HORSELEY. Perhaps planning to attack the Nicaraguan settlements, the mixed force ascended the San Juan, and captured several vessels. The pirates returned to Panama and cruelly sacked Veragua.

TAIFE REISI *(pirates' professional association; Mediterranean; about 1525–1830)* In the BARBARY STATES, the corsairs formed a legally recognized guild, which combined the features of a corporation, labor union, and trade association. The Taife Reisi regulated corsair recruitment, organization, financing, and operations. It also played a significant role in politics and government. Originating in ALGIERS, the guild system was copied in TUNIS, TRIPOLI, and SALÉ. These Barbary corsair associations are unique. Pirate captains often formed temporary confederations. But nowhere else did pirate groups become legal (and even constitutional) institutions enduring for centuries.

Under the OTTOMAN EMPIRE, the government actively supported craft guilds, and it enforced guild rules controlling the price, quality, and sale of goods. At least in theory, Barbary corsairs only attacked Christians at war with their state. Barbary governments thus treated the pirates as legitimate professionals, organized into a guild just like any other skilled craftsmen.

The corsair's guild was governed by a council (*divan*) of ship captains chaired by the CAPTAIN OF THE SEA. Seamen advanced by merit through a series of established ranks. The captain (REIS) of a corsair ship was chosen by the ship's owner for each cruise. But he first had to pass an examination by the guild's *divan* before he could serve as captain.

The guild's governing council could certify any captain that met its established standards. Especially during the 17th century, many corsairs were Christian converts to Islam. Muslim captains came from all parts of the Ottoman Empire and many ethnic backgrounds. (Despite this, Christian enemies erroneously referred to them all as "Turks.") Very few native North Africans became captains in the corsair fleet.

The Taife's regulations also governed ship ownership and the division of booty. As business fell off during the 18th century, the Barbary governments owned most ships and underwrote their cruises. Private ownership again became common during the highly profitable war years from 1792 to 1815.

TALENT *(unit of measurement; ancient Greece and the Near East)* The talent was used both to weigh commodities and as a unit for counting money. Weights varied from place to place and time to time. In theory, the talent was equivalent to about 57 (Athens standard) or 83 (Aegean standard) pounds of gold or silver.

Obviously no government ever minted a coin of this weight, and the talent was a fictitious unit in accounting. Its equivalent value in modern money would be enormous. Assuming that gold has a market price of $350 an ounce, then the ancient gold talent was worth about

$300,000 to $500,000. But its buying power was immensely greater.

TALISMAN REIS *(Barbary corsair; Mediterranean; active 1540s)* Talisman owned a GALIOT trapped by the KNIGHTS OF MALTA in 1541 after frequent raids on southern Italy. He was captured by the Maltese the following year while commanding a BRIGANTINE.

TAPHIANS *(Greek pirates; Mediterranean; ancient legends)* A people given to piracy in HOMER's *Odyssey*. STRABO describes them as sharing the small Ekhinadhes Islands with another group of pirates called Teleboans.

At the time of the Trojan War, according to Homer, MENTES ruled the Taphians, who sold captives as slaves at the IONIAN ISLANDS. Taphian pirates cultivated good relations with the Ionian nobles, and EUPEITHES joined one of their raids. Their exploits took them as far as the Syrian coast, where they kidnapped PHOENICIAN men and women, such as EUMAEUS.

In a later legend, the Taphians and Teleboans raided Mycenae (near modern Argos) in the Peloponnesian Peninsula. There they killed King Electryon's eight sons and stole his cattle. Either Electryon or his nephew followed the Taphians and burned their villages. Differing versions of this story are told by Hesiod (sixth century B.C.) and by Apollodorus (first century A.D.).

Homer's stories and later legends about the Taphians probably have some factual basis. The Ekhinadhes Islands are an ideal HAVEN near the Gulf of Corinth. During the 18th and 19th centuries, they sheltered Christian and Muslim pirates, greatly feared by travelers and merchants.

TARANTO *(Muslim corsair haven; Mediterranean; about 839–875)* A city on Italy's southern tip, situated on a rocky peninsula made into an island in the late 1400s. Its citadel provided an advanced base for corsairs, mainly from CRETE, raiding along Italy's Adriatic coast. Retaken by the BYZANTINE EMPIRE, it was totally destroyed by Muslim raiders in 927, rebuilt in 967, and occupied by the Normans from 1063.

TARTAN *(pirate ship; Mediterranean; about 1500–1800)* The name (from Arabic *taridha*) of a fishing and trading vessel popular among the pirates of BARBARY and SALÉ. Fast, maneuverable, and relatively narrow, it usually had one mast with a lateen mainsail and a small foresail set on a bowsprit. The tartan often carried four to 15 oars on each side. To gain greater speed, some pirate captains added a small mizzen mast with a lateen sail.

(See also FUSTE.)

TATTOOS *(body markings; 18th century to the present)* Scarring the skin by punctures accentuated by pigment (from Tahitian *tattau*, to mark). Tattooing was an ancient practice in parts of Africa, Asia, and the Pacific islands. However, although they marked criminals and slaves for identification, European peoples loathed decorative tattooing. All forms of body scarring are prohibited in the Jewish, Christian, and Muslim religions. (See, for example, *Leviticus* 19:28).

Tattooing was introduced to Europe after 1700 by sailors who had been to Asia. William DAMPIER imported a tattooed Pacific islander in 1691 and planned to exhibit him to the public. A London author met sailors with tattooed biceps in 1698. Tattooing spread slowly, and it was still novel in 1764, when a sailor was tattooed while visiting Tahiti with Captain James Cook. Until the 1960s, it remained a rebellious practice among criminals, madmen, and other social outcasts.

Mediterranean pirates probably never were tattooed. A few tattooed seamen may have visited the Atlantic and Caribbean before piracy died out about 1830. Tattoos occasionally appear in pirate films and fiction. In PETER PAN (1) (1904), Hook's crew includes Bill Jukes, "every inch of him tattooed."

TAYLOR, JOHN *(British pirate; Atlantic, Indian Ocean; active 1719–1721)* Taylor was among Edward ENGLAND's crew, which seized a 30-gun ship off Africa in 1719. Taylor took command of the prize, renamed it the *Victory*, and raided the Indian coast in consort with England. In September 1720, England and Taylor captured the East Indiaman *Cassandra* after a fierce gun battle. England was deposed and later put ashore for showing mercy to the captured captain, and Taylor left for India with the *Victory* and the *Cassandra*.

On the Indian coast, Taylor took some small European and Arab prizes and chased away a British naval squadron (which he at first thought was Conajee ANGRIA's pirate fleet). After paying a heavy bribe to buy provisions at the Dutch port of Cochin, Taylor and his men spent the Christmas of 1720 at sea in "carousing and forgetfulness."

The pirates repaired their ships at Mauritius and SAINT MARY'S ISLAND, where Olivier LA BOUCHE assumed command of the *Victory*. Taylor and La Bouche arrived at Réunion Island in April 1721. There they captured the Portuguese CARRACK *Nostra Senhora de Cabo*, which had stopped for repairs. On board was the retiring viceroy of Goa carrying diamonds valued at £500,000, as well as another £375,000 in rare Oriental products.

Taylor took his two ships and the *Coba* to MADAGASCAR. Counting earlier plunder, about 240 pirates divided more than a million pounds. Daniel DEFOE wrote that each man received up to 42 diamonds, depending on their size. The *Victory* was burned and replaced with the *Cabo*, also renamed the *Victory*.

Learning that a British squadron was on the way to Madagascar, the pirates stayed in East Africa until December 1722 and then split up. Some returned to Madagascar and burned the *Victory*. Sailing in the *Cassandra*, Taylor and 140 others reached Panama in May 1723. In return for the *Cassandra*, the governor of PORTO-BELO pardoned Taylor and his crew. Each pirate reportedly still had £1,200 in gold and silver in addition to diamonds and other plunder. In one account, Taylor later became a captain in the Panamanian coast guard.

(See also SELECTED BIBLIOGRAPHY: Course, *Pirates*.)

TEACH, EDWARD *(English pirate; Caribbean, Atlantic; died 1718)* Famous as BLACKBEARD, but 18th-century records call him Teach, probably also an assumed name. Daniel DEFOE, who reported the only information about his early career, paints an exaggerated picture. Defoe's Teach is a superhuman and totally evil fiend. In fact, Teach had a brief career (some 15 months) and took few and comparatively poor prizes. There is no evidence that he ever harmed his captives.

Teach was tall, strong, and broad-shouldered. Literate and a skillful navigator, he was a strong leader with a charismatic air of authority. Other captains were impressed by the discipline among his crew and the deference shown by his officers. On shore, he associated easily with colonial landowners and governmental officials.

Born in Bristol, Teach served on Jamaican vessels raiding French and Spanish shipping during the War of the Spanish Succession (1702–1713). In 1716, he enlisted with Benjamin HORNIGOLD at NEW PROVIDENCE ISLAND in the Bahamas. On one cruise, Hornigold made Teach captain of a captured SLOOP.

On their last voyage together in 1717, the two captains pillaged several prizes off the American coast and in the Caribbean. Late in the year, they captured a large, well-built ship trading between Martinique and Africa. Hornigold and Teach parted amicably after dividing the cargo as well as gold dust, coins, and jewels. Teach took over the prize, renamed her *Queen Anne's Revenge,* and installed 40 cannon.

Cruising near Saint Vincent, Teach took a large British merchantman, put the crew ashore, and burned the ship. Defoe wrote that he also fought off the warship *Scarborough,* but the captain's letters and the ship's log do not mention a battle with pirates. During December and early January, the *Queen Anne*—now carrying a crew of 300—took several sloops off Crab Island and Saint Kitts.

In January 1718, Teach arrived at Bath, one of the few towns in North Carolina. (The entire colony had fewer than 8,000 white inhabitants.) Governor Charles Eden pardoned Teach and his crew after they took the oath to give up piracy. Eden allowed the pirates to keep their loot and prepare for a new cruise.

The Bath region provided an excellent HAVEN. Traffic between the Atlantic and Pimlico Sound had to pass through Ocracoke Inlet, south of Ocracoke Island. (The present Hatteras and Oregon inlets were opened by storms in 1846.) The struggling colonists willingly paid more for pirate booty than the professional fences Teach had used in the Bahamas.

About March 1718, Teach sailed for the Bay of Honduras. On the way, he met Stede BONNET with the 10-gun *Revenge.* Teach seized the *Revenge,* put a man named Richards in charge, and made Bonnet his involuntary guest. Soon after, Teach captured the sloop *Adventure.* Israel HANDS took over the *Adventure,* and Captain David HERRIOT and his crew joined the pirates. At some point, Teach added a fourth and unnamed sloop.

With this squadron, Teach plundered several vessels in Honduras Bay. He burned one Boston ship because some pirates recently had been hanged in that city. Several more prizes were taken as Teach headed north.

In May 1718, Teach blockaded Charleston, South Carolina, and plundered eight or nine vessels. One carried several prominent citizens and £1,500 in coins plus other cargo. Teach demanded that the governor send out a medicine chest and certain specified drugs (worth less than £400). The captives became frantic when the boat carrying Teach's envoys overturned, delaying them for five days. They finally returned, and Teach released the ships and prisoners unharmed. Charlestonians wondered why Teach demanded so small a ransom. It also is odd that he requested medical drugs obtainable at Bath. Prurient historians have guessed that the pirates needed mercury to treat syphilis.

From Charleston, Teach made for North Carolina. Sailing through Topsail Inlet (now Beaufort Inlet), both the *Queen Anne* and the *Adventure* ran aground on a sandbar. Teach apparently wrecked the ships to avoid splitting the booty. Several dozen crewmen protested and were marooned on a sandbar. Teach gave the *Revenge* back to Stede Bonnet. With about 40 men and all the loot, Teach made off in his unnamed tender sloop.

At Bath, Teach was welcomed as a respected member of the community. Governor Eden gave him a second pardon. A VICE-ADMIRALTY court certified his ownership of the sloop, stolen from English merchants. Teach bought a house across from the governor's home and anchored his sloop at the southern tip of Ocracoke Island. He married a plantation owner's 16-year-old daughter, was feasted by the local gentry, and lavishly entertained them in return.

After some months at Bath, Teach visited Philadelphia, where a warrant was issued for his arrest. He went on to Bermuda and captured two French ships, one loaded with sugar and coca and the other in ballast. After transferring both crews to the empty vessel, he took the sugar ship back to Bath in September.

Governor Eden convened a Vice-Admiralty court, presided over by Tobias Knight, the colony's chief justice. The court ruled that the French ship was a derelict found at sea and allowed Teach to burn it after he removed the cargo. For playing their parts in this charade, Governor Eden took 60 barrels of sugar, and Knight received 20. This was Teach's last act of piracy on the high seas, although he may have molested small trading vessels in inland waters. In October 1718, Charles VANE visited him at Ocracoke. There, some say, the pirates enjoyed a drunken festival.

Governor Alexander Spotswood of Virginia disliked this flourishing pirate colony immediately to the south. William Howard, Teach's former quartermaster, was arrested in Virginia and testified to his crimes. Governor Spotswood claimed that North Carolinians had complained about Teach's continuing robberies.

Since he expected to find rich treasure at Teach's hideout, Governor Spotswood hired two sloops with his own funds. The crews of two British warships were promised liberal rewards for defeating the pirates. One force traveled overland, while Lieutenant Robert Maynard commanded the two leased sloops.

Maynard arrived at Ocracoke Inlet on December 2, 1718, and attacked the next morning. Maynard had about 60 men, while Teach had fewer than two dozen, including servants. Maynard's two sloops, which had no cannon, tried to board Teach's vessel. According to Defoe, Teach raised a glass of liquor and toasted Maynard with the oath "Damnation seize my Soul if I give you Quarters, or take any from you." When the two royal sloops ran aground on a sandbar, Teach fired a broadside. One sloop was disabled, and about 20 attackers were killed or wounded.

Maynard ordered his men to hide below, their pistols and cutlasses ready for close fighting. Only the pilot and helmsman remained on deck. As Maynard's boat drifted closer, Teach's men threw GRENADES, but these did little damage.

When Teach and a dozen others boarded, the hidden men swarmed on deck and began a furious battle. Teach and Maynard met in personal combat. Both fired, and Maynard's shot plowed through the pirate's body without apparent effect. The two men charged with their swords, and a powerful blow from Teach's CUTLASS snapped off Maynard's blade near its hilt. As Teach moved in for the finishing blow, a British seaman attacked from behind and wounded him in the neck and throat. With blood spurting from his neck, Teach continued to swing his heavy cutlass as his foes attacked from all sides. Teach finally fell after receiving five pistol shots and 20 severe sword wounds. Maynard cut off Teach's head and displayed it from the front of his sloop.

Thirteen prisoners were hanged at Williamsburg the following March. One was acquitted, and Israel Hands was saved when a royal decree pardoning pirates arrived at the last minute. Lieutenant Maynard confiscated booty valued at £2,238. Many have tried to find Teach's buried treasure. But he never captured a prize with much gold or silver, and he spent everything he took.

(See also SELECTED BIBLIOGRAPHY: Lee, *Blackbeard*; Pringle, *Jolly Roger*.)

TÉMÉRICOURT, GABRIEL D'ABOS DE
(Knight of Malta; Mediterranean; 1646–1672)
Téméricourt was a Frenchman who cruised from 1663 with his elder brother Maximilien TÉMÉRICOURT each commanding a FRIGATE with more than 20 guns. An exceptionally handsome blue-eyed blond nicknamed "Flail of the Seas," Gabriel became a Protestant but was allowed to remain in the Roman Catholic KNIGHTS OF MALTA.

In addition to pillaging the Greek isles, the brothers combined with other corsairs to assault the OTTOMAN convoys traveling between Alexandria and Istanbul. In 1664, joined by ESCRAINVILLE's large sailing ship, the brothers captured four vessels from the convoy near Rhodes. Together with 11 other corsair ships, most smaller, they again met the Alexandria convoy in June 1669. Although it was protected by seven large warships carrying 60 or 70 guns, they attacked at once. Gabriel was severely wounded, but the corsairs captured a GALLEON and some smaller ships.

In 1668, the brothers and two other knights repulsed with considerable losses an Ottoman battle fleet that attacked them in the harbor at Nios. In 1671, after Maximilien's death, Gabriel and four other corsairs beat off an attack by 50 Ottoman galleys. The following year, after a fighting retreat from five Tripolitan ships, he was wrecked on the African coast and captured. He was taken to Adrianople and put to death after refusing all inducements to convert to Islam.

TÉMÉRICOURT, MAXIMILIEN D'ABOS DE
(Maltese corsair; Mediterranean; 1645–1669) A Frenchman who cruised with his younger brother Gabriel TÉMÉRICOURT. Joined by other corsairs, the two brothers pillaged the strongly guarded Alexandria to Istanbul convoy in 1664 and 1669 and drove off an OTTOMAN battle fleet in 1668. In 1669, Maximilien took a 40-gun Ottoman ship near the island of Kárpathos and transferred to his prize. Accompanied by another corsair, he engaged two large Turkish ships south of Crete. He burned one of the enemy but was killed during the battle.

TERENCE **(Roman playwright; about 190–159 B.C.)** Publius Terentius Afer wrote six Latin comedies derived from Greek originals. Unlike PLAUTUS, he does not mention contemporary conditions and makes fewer references to piracy. In *The Eunuch*, Thais' supposed sister had been carried off by pirates from Sunnium (near Athens) and sold to slave dealers.

TERRY AND THE PIRATES **(comic strip; 1935–1973)** Milton Caniff (1907–1980) created *Terry* in 1934 as a daily and Sunday comic strip for the *New York Daily News* and national syndication. *Terry's* popularity built up slowly and reached its peak during World War II. The strip was reissued as a monthly comic book from 1941 to 1957, adapted as a radio drama and movie serial in the early 1940s, and made into a television series during the 1950s. Caniff left at the end of 1946 to create the *Steve Canyon* comic strip. George Wunder took over and produced *Terry* until 1973.

Terry initially was a blond-haired American boy, perhaps 10 years old. Accompanied by Pat Ryan, a handsome adventurer, he headed to China to find an abandoned mine. Going up river, Pat and Terry ran into Chinese pirates led by the Eurasian Poppy Joe. While still at sea in the Sunday strip (which followed a different continuity), Pat and Terry were captured by pirates serving the sinister half-Oriental Dragon Lady. One of the strip's strongest and most long-lasting characters, the Dragon Lady simultaneously embodied voluptuous beauty and the essence of evil. Other pirates also appeared among *Terry*'s colorful rogues, including the suave, seagoing Captain Judas and the blustering smuggler Captain Blaze. Except for the Dragon Lady, most were comic vaudeville villains, created to amuse rather than to frighten readers.

Terry grew older over the years. When the United States entered World War II in 1941, he became an air force pilot, while Pat Ryan joined the navy. Terry, from then on the strip's main star, found a new father-figure in his commanding officer, Colonel Flip Corkin.

During the war years, *Terry* diligently promoted military causes and loyalties. Even the Dragon Lady enlisted on the American side, although her allegiance often seemed doubtful. In one Sunday page, Colonel Corkin lectured Terry on the values inspiring U.S. participation in the war; the sequence was inserted in the *Congressional Record*, the only comic strip ever so honored. Caniff also designed a special version of *Terry* for military camps, full of sexy women and inside jokes about military life.

Caniff introduced new artistic and literary techniques to the adventure strip genre. Movie makers as well as other cartoonists imitated his lighting, framing, and editing. His inspired use of solid black shadows helped create moods, reinforced the effect of colors, and suggested three-dimensional depth. The main characters had strong and multifaceted personalities, expressed through individual speech patterns, accents, and mannerisms. Caniff's continuities were unusually complicated, and he employed sexual motivations more frequently than almost any other American cartoonist.

Under George Wunder's pen from 1947, *Terry* continued to stress patriotic loyalty. Promoted to a major in the air force, Terry valiantly defended the United States from Communist aggression and espionage.

TEUTA (pirate queen; Adriatic Sea; third century B.C.)

As queen of the Ardiaei from 230, Teuta ruled ILLYRIA from Split to Epirus. She fostered pirate raids against Roman traders, leading Rome to invade Greece during the First Illyrian War (229–228).

Piracy formed the chief industry of the ancient Illyrians. During the 230s, King Agron built up a large state centered at Scodra (modern Scutari) and raided Greek cities in Epirus. His forces thus threatened commerce passing through the Strait of Otranto, the narrow body of water separating Epirus from Italy.

Agron died in 231 during a drunken orgy celebrating his military victories. Teuta, his second wife, seized the throne as regent for Agron's young son. Queen Teuta continued Agron's aggression on land. The Greek historian Polybius (about 200 to after 118 B.C.) wrote that Teuta also allowed pirates to pillage any ships they met. Illyrian raiders ravaged the Italian coast and killed Italian merchants.

In 230, the Roman Senate sent two of its members to meet with Teuta, who was besieging the Greek city of Issa. The queen, in Polybius' account,

> listened to them in a most arrogant and over-bearing manner, and when they had finished speaking, she said she would see to it that Rome suffered no public wrong from Illyria, but that, as for private wrongs, it was contrary to the custom of the Illyrian kings to hinder their subjects from winning booty from the sea.

The Roman ambassadors left, threatening to force Teuta to curtail piracy. On the way home, pirates attacked their ship—possibly at Teuta's command—and one Roman envoy died. Angered by this attack on its envoys, the Senate in 229 sent out 200 warships with 20,000 soldiers. When the Roman fleet reached Corfu, the island's Greek commander, DEMETRIUS OF PHAROS, quickly surrendered. The Roman force then turned toward Issa, and Teuta agreed to leave Illyria.

By a treaty signed in 228, the Ardiaei gave up their earlier conquests on land, and Rome gave many cities to the traitorous Demetrius. The Illyrians also promised not to send more than two unarmed ships into the Straits of Otranto at any one time. But this treaty hardly ended Illyrian piracy, which continued until the emperor Augustus in 31 B.C. established a permanent fleet.

(See also SELECTED BIBLIOGRAPHY: Polybius, *Histories*.)

TEW, THOMAS (English pirate; Atlantic, Red Sea; died 1695)

A sea captain from a respected Rhode Island family, Tew went to Bermuda and possibly committed piracy in the Caribbean. While England was at war with France in 1692, he bought a share in the *Amity*, an eight-gun SLOOP. The governor commissioned Tew and another captain to attack French slaving stations in Africa.

Tew lost his consort in a storm and turned pirate. Tew told his men, Daniel DEFOE reported, that it was better to risk their lives for plunder rather than for the English government. Easily convinced, they "cry'd out one and all, 'A Gold Chain, or a wooden Leg, we'll stand by you.'"

The *Amity* rounded the Cape of Good Hope, probably stopping at MADAGASCAR. At the entrance to the Red Sea, the pirates captured an Arab ship carrying gold. They returned to Madagascar in October 1693 and reached Rhode Island the following April. Each crewman received about £1,200, and Tew kept £8,000. He sent £5,000 to his partners in Bermuda, who purchased plantations on the island.

Thomas Tew (left) being entertained by New York Governor Benjamin Fletcher at the governor's home about 1694. Fletcher later described Captain Tew as "agreeable and companionable," perhaps because Tew gave him jewels captured in the Red Sea. Illustration by Howard Pyle in *Harper's Monthly Magazine*, November 1894.

Tew got a new license from the governor of New York and sailed in November 1694 in consort with William WANT and Thomas WAKE. Reaching the Red Sea by June 1695, Tew joined the pirate squadron cruising under Henry EVERY. He was killed while assaulting an Indian treasure fleet.

(See also SELECTED BIBLIOGRAPHY: Defoe, *General History*; Jameson, *Privateering*; Pringle, *Jolly Roger*.)

THEOPOMPUS OF MILESIA *(Greek archpirate; Aegean Sea; 405 B.C.)* A native of Milesia, a Greek city on Asia Minor's western coast. His corsairs cooperated with Spartan forces during a war against Athens (the Peloponnesian War). In 405, Lysander, the Spartan admiral, sent Theopompus to Sparta to report his destruction of an Athenian fleet in the Dardanelles.

THIJSZ, MARTIN *(Dutch admiral; Caribbean; active 1629–1631)* In 1629 and 1631, he raided for the DUTCH WEST INDIA COMPANY as Adriaen PATER's second-in-command. Following Pater's death, Thijsz took 22 ships to the Caribbean in May 1632. He seized only

a few, poor prizes and—partly due to his carelessness about security—failed to molest the Spanish TREASURE FLEETS.

THUCYDIDES *(Greek historian; 460/455– about 400 B.C.)* Thucydides wrote a *History of the War* between Athens and Sparta from 431 to 404. The second major Greek historian (after HERODOTUS), he sought to produce a factual account and reported with reservations the surviving legends about MINOS, the CARIANS, and other early pirates.

TIERI REIS *(Barbary corsair; Mediterranean, Adriatic Sea; active 1560s)* Tieri was an Italian from Gaeta, who ravaged both coasts of Italy. In June 1562, the ADMIRAL of Venice reported that his five FUSTES had been captured in the Adriatic.

TIMASITHEUS *(corsair commander; Mediterranean; fourth century B.C.)* While leading the pirate community on the LIPARI ISLANDS, Timasitheus convinced his fellow citizens to free captive Roman ambassadors and their treasure. After conquering Veii in 396, the Romans turned one-tenth of their loot into a great gold bowl, which three Roman nobles carried to Delphi as an offering to Apollo. Just west of the Lipari Islands, pirate galleys seized the Roman warship and towed it into the harbor. There the Liparians planned to auction off the captives and treasure, dividing the receipts according to pirate custom.

Timasitheus did not want to antagonize the powerful Roman state. He finally persuaded the corsairs to let their captives sail on, and he sent his own vessels to escort the Roman ship to Delphi. The Roman Senate granted Timasitheus public honors and exempted his descendants from taxation when they conquered the Lipari Islands in 255.

TIMOCLES *(Greek archpirate; Aegean Sea; about 305 B.C.)* Timocles was employed by Demetrius I Polorcetes, one of the successors to Alexander the Great and later king of Macedonia (294–288). In 305 and 304, during wars to divide up Alexander's empire, Demetrius besieged RHODES. Timocles was considered the strongest of the pirates fighting as Demetrius' allies. Nevertheless, in 304, the Rhodians captured Timocles and his three warships during a battle off the coast of Asia Minor.

(See also ANDRON.)

TJEKER *(Near Eastern pirates; Mediterranean; 12th century B.C.)* One of the SEA PEOPLES, they invaded Egypt about 1186 and became buccaneers along the Palestinian coast during the following century. Historians have transliterated their name into the English alphabet in many ways, including Thekel, Zalkkar, Zakkal, Djakaray, and Zakkaray.

The Tjeker possibly came to Egypt from CILICIA, which later became a major center of piracy. Ancient Greek legends refer to a hero called Teucer or Teucros. Teucer's father, the Greek warrior Telamon, named him after the people of his mother, a princess from Asia Minor. In HOMER's *Iliad*, Teucer fought beside Telamon and his half-brother Ajax during the Greek invasion of Troy.

Telamon banished Teucer after the Trojan War. He had many adventures and founded the city of Salamis on Cyprus, not far from the Cilician coast. Teucer's son (called Ajax after his uncle) later erected a temple in Cilicia. For many centuries, a long line of priest-kings, who claimed descent from Teucer and Ajax, continued to rule a region called Teukria.

There may be some truth to these legends that Cilicia was the home of a people named something like Tjeker or Teuker. Most of the tribe remained in Cilicia, and their descendants later became famous buccaneers. However, some Tjeker found themselves among the Sea Peoples that unsuccessfully invaded Egypt in 1186. After their defeat, they settled in Palestine, at Dor and Tel Zeror, near present-day Haifa. There the Tjeker (like their Cilician cousins) made their living both as merchants and as pirates.

A vivid picture of Tjeker piracy survives in a papyrus diary kept by the Egyptian priest WENAMON. Archaeological evidence indicates that the Tjeker maintained their separate ethnic identity and pirate ways until perhaps 1000. Since the Hebrew scriptures do not mention them, they presumably were absorbed by the more numerous Philistines, who lived south of the Tjeker territory in Palestine.

TOCCO, ANTONIO DI (Italian corsair; Ionian Sea; 1452–1484)

His family ruled the IONIAN ISLANDS of Leucadia, Cephalonia, and Zante from 1353 until 1452, when they were conquered by the OTTOMAN EMPIRE. Antonio— the last ruler's younger brother—assembled a force of Italian and CATALAN corsairs, recovered Cephalonia and Zante, and had great success as a pirate. Since his raids halted their trade with the east, Venetian naval forces evicted him. Venice returned Cephalonia to the Ottomans, but paid an annual tribute to retain Zante.

TOMASO, ZUAN (Italian corsair; Mediterranean, Aegean Sea; about 1500)

From Naples, Tomaso commanded a large galley. He was licensed to prey only on Muslim shipping and left his brother in Sicily as a guarantee of good behavior. Nevertheless, he seized at least four Christian vessels in the Aegean.

TOMPKINS, THOMAS (English pirate; Mediterranean; 1603)

A gentleman and former page to the earl of Essex, Tompkins sailed from La Rochelle with a crew of French, Dutch, and English adventurers. Near Cyprus, he captured the *Balbiana*, a Venetian ship with textiles worth 300,000 ducats. Although six pirates were caught and hanged, the booty was landed safely in England. Tompkins' share was £2,600 in silver.

Tompkins was captured seven years later only because King James I recognized him as he presented a petition at court. At his trial, he regretted not having killed the entire Venetian crew (several died during the attack) to get rid of witnesses. Sentenced to be hanged, he was pardoned thanks to his influential connections.

TORGHUD REIS See TURGUT REIS.

TORTUGA ISLAND (pirate haven; Caribbean; about 1620–1713)

A large (about 85 square miles) and rocky island, separated by a narrow channel from the northwestern coast of Hispaniola (modern Haiti). The island's name (Île de la Tortue, "Turtle Island") refers to its shape. Viewed from Haiti, it resembles a monster sea turtle floating upon the waves.

Tortuga initially served as a haven for cattle hunters (BUCCANEERS) on Hispaniola. The Spanish government, based at Santo Domingo, had abandoned western Hispaniola in 1605, but the colonial militia continued to attack the hunters. Mountainous and inaccessible to the north, and with only one harbor on the south, Tortuga offered safe refuge. By the 1620s, cattle hunters had a rough place of settlement near the harbor, where they sold hides to visiting traders.

Sea rovers passing through from Europe found Tortuga a convenient harbor. The island provides good access around northern Hispaniola to the coast of Central America. To the south, Cuba and Mexico are easily reached through the Windward Passage, although the return journey against the wind is difficult. The Tortuga huntsmen soon began to supplement their income by piracy. By the late 1620s, DUTCH fleets had weakened Spanish naval power, encouraging freelance marauders. According to EXQUEMELIN, a certain Pierre LE GRAND was the first to turn pirate. To end raids from Tortuga, troops from Santo Domingo invaded the island in late 1630 or early 1631. But the islanders simply fled to the hills, returning as soon as the Spanish ships had left.

From 1631 to 1635, Tortuga was protected by the PROVIDENCE COMPANY, which already had a base on PROVIDENCE ISLAND, off the Honduran coast. Anthony Hilton, a former ship captain, persuaded the Company to adopt Tortuga and was appointed governor. Hilton, a most persuasive rogue, had quarreled with the Barbados government and founded a colony on Nevis in 1628. He was chased away by the Spaniards the following year, leaving behind large debts in Nevis and Saint Kitts.

The agreement with the Company was a ruse to protect Hilton's buccaneer associates. Hilton (who died in 1634) never paid the Company for the cannon and ammunition it supplied. He recruited lawless men fleeing from the French and English colonies at Saint Kitts and Barbados. The Puritan minister sent by the Company fled after two years to escape his unruly flock.

Guided by an Irish sailor who had quarreled with Hilton, a force from Santo Domingo sacked the Tortuga settlement early in 1635. Spanish galleons again swooped down in 1638 and killed any of the residents they could find. Soon after, a Captain Roger Flood arrived with 300 settlers from Nevis. The Frenchmen still living on Tortuga claimed that Flood abused them, forcing them to flee to Hispaniola.

The French inhabitants requested aid from Philippe de Poincy, the French governor-general at Saint Kitts. To solve his own political problems, de Poincy appointed Jean LE VASSEUR governor in 1642. Le Vasseur, a skilled engineer, built an impregnable fortress near the harbor and cut all ties with France. During the next 12 years, the island became the capital of West Indies piracy.

Le Vasseur was killed by two of his henchmen in 1652, but the new governor sent by de Poincy also welcomed buccaneers. In January 1654, Spanish troops again drove out the pirates and this time tried to found a permanent colony. However, when an English fleet invaded in 1655, the Spanish government withdrew its troops to defend Santo Domingo.

In 1656, soon after the English occupied Jamaica, Elias Watts acquired a commission as governor and recruited English and French settlers. The islanders soon returned to piracy, and a Captain DE L'ISLE led a major raid against Santiago in Hispaniola. Watts was expelled in 1659 by a French adventurer, and Tortuga fell under French control in 1665 when Bertrand D'Ogeron became governor.

D'Ogeron encouraged French settlement along the northern and western coasts of Hispaniola, creating the French colony of Saint Domingue (modern Haiti). He also imposed some order on Tortuga but never tried to suppress the pirates, who formed the French colony's best defense in wartime. François L'OLONNAIS and Michel LE BASQUE attacked Venezuela in 1667 from Tortuga, and pirates continued to visit the island until France outlawed piracy after 1713. From the 1670s, however, PETIT GOÂVE replaced Tortuga as the main pirate haven in the French islands.

TORTURE (pirate persuasion; all oceans; all eras)
During many eras, courts tortured prisoners to get confessions. Like judges, pirates tortured prisoners to make them reveal concealed information, usually about the location of their valuables. Most pirates used whatever methods were usual at the time. Only the Caribbean BUCCANEERS went beyond normal practices.

No doubt some pirates (and some judicial officials) enjoyed their victims' pain. EXQUEMELIN describes deliberate sadism by François L'OLONNAIS and Sir Henry MORGAN. Daniel DEFOE'S GENERAL HISTORY tells equally gruesome tales about Edmund CONDENT, Bartholomew ROBERTS, Francis SPRIGGS, and others.

Mediterranean corsairs treated prisoners with relative restraint. Ancient authors accused Greek and CILICIAN pirates of torture, but their stories do not supply specific details. There are almost no documented accounts of torture by the BARBARY pirates. (Christian slaves report abuse, but only after the pirates sold them to new masters

Fictional pirates delight in fiendish tortures. Here François L'Olonnais forces a Spanish captive to eat the living heart he had just ripped out of another captive's chest. From Exquemelin, *Buccaneers of America,* first English edition (1684).

on shore.) The MALTESE and other Christian corsairs used violence to gain information from Greek and Muslim seamen. No sophisticated forms of torture are mentioned, and captives often gave in at the mere threat of a beating.

From the 15th century, there are many reports of torture by English pirates, such as Clinton ATKINSON, Thomas ROSE, and John CALLICE. These raiders lit matches between the fingers of prisoners. They also used sticks to tighten cords tied around a captive's head, hands, and genitals. Thomas CAVENDISH and Sir Francis DRAKE used thumbscrews during their raids on South America's Pacific coast.

Protestant pirates and buccaneers were unusually cruel to Spanish captives. Spanish observers were not surprised by torture. But they were horrified that the pirates went on until their victims died, long after they already had confessed. Hatred of the Roman Catholic religion inspired atrocities. Jacques SORES threw 40 Jesuit missionaries overboard in 1570. Under Hugo SCHAMPENDAM, Dutch raiders cut open a Franciscan friar and tore out his entrails.

Exquemelin wrote that François L'Olonnais stretched prisoners on the rack, cut off pieces of their flesh, and once ate a captive's living heart. Exquemelin says Morgan's men were equally sadistic at Puerto Principe, Portobelo, and Panama. While he probably exaggerated, the buccaneers did employ the rack, which they found in captured Spanish prisons.

Daniel Defoe described diabolical tortures by the pirates roaming the Atlantic in the early 18th century. Defoe is even less trustworthy than Exquemelin. Some pirates did beat their prisoners to make them talk. But there is no mention of unusual torments in the trial records regarding Edward TEACH and other raiders.

Indian and Arab prisoners were tortured by William COBB, Henry EVERY, William KIDD and other pirates raiding from MADAGASCAR. However, non-European pirates were unlikely to practice torture—or at least torture for pleasure. British observers do not mention cruelty toward prisoners in histories of Arab and Malayan piracy. Under Cheng I SAO, Chinese pirates beat Chinese seamen but did not torture Europeans.

(See also BLOODING AND SWEATING; CAT O' NINE TAILS; DEAD MEN TELL NO TALES; FLOGGING; KEELHAULING.)

TOURVILLE, ANNE-HILARION DE CONTENTIN, COMTE DE (Knight of Malta and French admiral; Mediterranean; 1642–1701)
Tourville was a French nobleman famed both for his beauty and elegant dress and also for his passion for the sea. Tourville came to MALTA in 1660 and raided in the Aegean under the Knight of HOCQUINCOURT. In 1666, their warship was wrecked near Crete. Tourville, a superb swimmer, survived the turbulent seas.

Reputedly a great lover, Tourville was released from his monastic vows in order to marry. He transferred to the French navy and fought against TUNIS in 1671 as well as in the Third Dutch War (1672–1674). Earning a reputation as a complete seaman, he became an admiral in 1683 and was named commander-in-chief during a war with Great Britain from 1689 to 1697.

TOWNLEY, CAPTAIN (English buccaneer; Pacific; died 1686)
Townley led 180 English pirates across the Panama Isthmus early in 1685. He attacked the mines at SANTA MARIA, but found them deserted following raids by Bartholomew SHARP in 1680 and Peter HARRIS in 1684. With two captured BARKS, he joined larger groups assembling near Panama City under Edward DAVIS and François GROGNIET. On June 8, Peruvian warships routed the buccaneers, and the French and English pirates soon separated. Their quarrel began—according to Raveneau de LUSSAN—when Townley tried to seize Grogniet's ship.

The English pirates went north and attacked León, Nicaragua, in August. William DAMPIER wrote that Townley led the advance party "with 80 of the briskest men." They fought so savagely that the town's 700 defenders ran away. However, León provided little loot, and the governor was slow in paying the demanded ransom, so the pirates burned it as well as nearby Realejo.

The pirate captains again separated, with Davis and several others returning to Peru. Townley and Charles SWAN went north with four small ships and 340 men, unsuccessfully searching for gold mines and the MANILA GALLEON. A captive told them about a Peruvian treasure ship, which visited Acapulco to purchase goods from the Manila Galleon. In December, Townley and 140 men in canoes silently paddled into the harbor but found the ship anchored under the fort's guns. The pirates also missed the Galleon, which sailed by in January while they were hunting cattle.

While Swan stayed along the Mexican coast, Townley returned south with one ship and 120 men. In March 1686, he ran into Grogniet's Frenchmen. Patching up a temporary alliance, the two groups occupied Granada, Nicaragua, but found little to steal. After their small booty was divided, Townley continued south toward Panama, taking along 150 men who had deserted Grogniet's unlucky company.

On June 23, Townley's band burned a town on the west side of the Gulf of Panama, seizing 15,000 pesos in gold and silver. But the Spaniards ambushed the party returning with the loot, taking back their gold and sticking the pirates' heads on sticks. Perhaps this massacre enraged Townley's men, for they began to treat their prisoners with great cruelty. The pirates decapitated four Spanish prisoners in revenge, and they cut off the heads of two more to force payment of an 11,000-peso ransom.

The buccaneers moved to the Pearl Islands, blockaded Panama for several months, and captured two Spanish ships sent against them on August 22. Townley died of wounds received during the battle, and the buccaneers elected Captain LE PICARD in his place.

(See also SELECTED BIBLIOGRAPHY: Gerhard, Pirates.)

TREASURE, BURIED (pirate booty; all eras)
Treasure chests frequently occur in pirate FICTION and MOVIES, and hunters have scoured the earth looking for pirate gold. No one has found hidden riches because pirates did not bury their BOOTY. (Divers have recovered treasure from sunken wrecks, but these were Spanish TREASURE SHIPS and not pirate vessels.) When they were captured, some pirates tried to buy their acquittal with stories of hidden wealth. There is no evidence to support taking these tales seriously.

When pirates operated from HAVENS with tolerant rulers, they returned home and divided their take with the government sponsoring them. Most spent their share on necessities or pleasures. A few invested in businesses and property. After 1700, some pirates operated outside the law from refuges such as NEW PROVIDENCE ISLAND and MADAGASCAR. These brigands also shared out their loot as they got it. Pirates distrusted each other too much to leave their plunder in a common horde. Each man expected his cut before the ship's company separated, and the crew would have killed anyone keeping booty aside.

Novels often describe pirate gold buried on Caribbean islands. However, EXQUEMELIN and other observers wrote that the BUCCANEERS spent their take as soon as they reached shore. They had nothing left to hide, as a pirate complains in Frank Yerby's The GOLDEN HAWK. "If there is any buried gold in the Antilles, it was by the hands of whores and rum-sellers that it was hidden. God knows they get it all."

Perhaps a buccaneer did avoid the taverns, hide his share, and was killed before he could dig it up. If found

To protect its treasure fleets, the Spanish government built large fortresses guarding the ports of Cartagena, Portobelo, San Juan de Ulúa, Havana, and (pictured here) San Juan, Puerto Rico. Begun in the 1580s, this massive structure repelled Sir Francis Drake in 1595 but fell to the earl of Cumberland three years later.

today, one of these individual caches would seem relatively meager. Pirate fiction refers to vast treasures buried by tyrannical captains. In real life, captains did not enjoy despotic powers, and their share usually was only twice that of ordinary seamen.

Nineteenth-century authors borrowed stories of buried gold from popular legends about CAPTAIN KIDD'S TREASURE. (Henry EVERY temporarily buries his loot in *The* KING OF PIRATES [1719], but Daniel DEFOE does not emphasize these incidents.) These tales of mysterious MAPS and weirdly marked sites were perfected in TREASURE ISLAND.

(See also ADMIRALTY COURT; BARBARY STATES; MALTA; PORT ROYAL.)

TREASURE SHIPS/FLEETS, SPANISH *(convoys; Atlantic, Caribbean; 16th–18th centuries)*
Goods and passengers traveled between the Caribbean and Spain in two yearly convoys. This system protected the immense amounts of Peruvian and Mexican silver collected by the Spanish government. It also enforced the Spanish monopoly on trade with the Americas.

Spain created the convoy system in direct response to pirate attacks. Many ships sailed together from the 1520s to defend against French corsairs. In 1564, the government compelled merchant ships to join two annual fleets bound for New Spain (Mexico) and Tierra Firme (Central America). Each convoy was guarded by the special naval squadron known as the ARMADA DE LA GUARDA DE LA CARRERA DE LAS INDIAS.

The treasure ships were at the richest between 1580 and 1620, and the convoys carried some 25,000 tons of silver to Spain by 1600. During the sea war with England (1585–1603), the fleets sometimes skipped a year when corsair attacks were especially fierce. However, the total amount of treasure remained high until the 1620s, when the convoy system entered a period of rapid decline.

By 1650, the treasure fleets were a shadow of their former greatness. Aging and unsafe ships left late in the season or failed to sail for years at a time. Although silver shipments revived somewhat after 1670, the system again fell apart during the War of the Spanish Succession (1701–1714). Convoys to Mexico and Tierra Firme ended in 1736 and 1737. The Mexican fleet was revived on a small scale from 1754 to 1789.

The treasure ships sailed between Spain and four Caribbean harbors. At CARTAGENA, the convoys stopped for gold, emeralds, and tropical products from Colombia and Venezuela. Mexican silver was picked up at SAN JUAN DE ULÚA, the harbor for Veracruz. Silver from Peru was taken to the city of Panama, transported across the Isthmus, and collected at Nombre de Dios or (after 1594) at PORTOBELO. On the way back to Europe, ships assembled and took on supplies at Havana, Cuba.

The two convoys had set schedules but often were delayed. At its height, the Central American fleet (popularly called "the Galleons") brought together from 30 to 90 merchant vessels, guarded by eight or more warships. Leaving Spain about August, the convoy usually entered the Caribbean between Trinidad and Tobago. It then sailed along the Venezuela coast, dropping off merchant ships at various ports. The fleet stopped at Cartagena for a month or more and arrived at Nombre de Dios or Portobelo in November or later. It left Panama in March, returned to Cartagena, and reached Havana during the summer.

The Mexican convoy (called the *flota*) contained 15 to 20 merchantmen. Protected by two GALLEONS, the ships left Spain in April or May. They passed between Guadeloupe and Dominica and sailed south below Hispaniola and Cuba, with merchant ships leaving along the way. The convoy reached San Juan de Ulúa in late summer, remained over the winter, and headed for Havana in March or April. Until 1633, two additional warships sailed with the Mexican convoy, went to Trujillo in Honduras, and rejoined the Mexican ships in Havana.

The Mexican and Central American convoys might return to Spain separately or join together in one great fleet when pirate attacks were particularly fierce. In either case, the heavily laden ships made their way through the narrow channel between Florida and the Bahamas. At the Carolinas, they caught the westerly trades across the Atlantic.

The convoy system accomplished its main goal, that of safeguarding the king's silver. Year after year, pirates prowled the broad channel between Cuba and Mexico as well as the narrower Florida strait. As long as the Spanish ships stayed together, they were protected by the galleons' size and armament. Although ships were destroyed by storms or wrecked on reefs, few were lost either to enemy navies or to pirates.

An entire fleet was captured on only three occasions, each time by a large squadron of warships. Piet HEYN overpowered the Mexican fleet in 1628. Three English warships took a small Central American fleet near Cadiz in 1656. Another naval squadron destroyed the Mexican fleet in the Canary Islands in 1657, but the Spaniards managed to get their treasure ashore.

Pirates followed the fleet, hoping to pounce on stragglers separated by a storm or accident. But even individual ships were difficult prey. Raiders sailing from England and the Netherlands enjoyed the most success. As far as is known, no buccaneer based in the Caribbean ever took a prize from the convoys. (There is no evidence support-ing EXQUEMELIN's story that Pierre LE GRAND seized a galleon.)

Several treasure ships were taken during England's 16th-century sea war with Spain. In 1585, Sir Richard GRENVILLE captured the *Santa Marita* off Bermuda with treasure worth at least £50,000. Abraham COCKE plundered a merchantman in 1590. Cocke's raiders also boarded but were driven off a Mexican treasure galleon. In 1591 William LANE looted two richly laden ships separated from the Mexican convoy. In 1597, William PARKER captured a FRIGATE carrying silver to San Juan de Ulúa.

The DUTCH WEST INDIA COMPANY outfitted large squadrons that preyed on the treasure ships with some profit. Hendrick LUCIFER seized one of the two Honduras galleons in 1627. In addition to Piet Heyn's success in 1628, Pieter ITA took both Honduras galleons. With only a small YACHT, Cornelis JOL in 1637 captured a merchant ship from the Tierra Firme fleet.

The Caribbean buccaneers avoided the treasure ships because other plunder—although not as rich—was easier to snatch. By concentrating all its efforts on the treasure fleets, Spain left its colonies open to attack. During some eras, raiders seized almost all the vessels carrying goods between Caribbean ports. With little booty left at sea, pirates turned to raids on coastal cities.

The four ports visited by the treasure fleets presented the richest and best-guarded targets. Like the convoys themselves, these normally were raided only by large bands under a daring leader. No buccaneer ever dared to attack the forts at Havana. Sir Francis DRAKE seized a mule train carrying silver to Nombre de Dios in 1573. Portobelo was sacked by William Parker (1601), Sir Henry MORGAN (1668), and John COXON (1680). Morgan captured the city of Panama in 1671. Laurens de GRAFF and seven other captains raided Veracruz and San Juan de Ulúa in 1683. Cartagena was plundered in 1697 by a fleet combining French warships and pirate vessels.

Some pirates entered the Pacific and attacked along South America's western coast. In addition to looking for the MANILA GALLEON, these raiders hoped to bypass the convoy system by capturing the ships carrying silver from Peru to Panama. Several captains sacked Spanish cities, but only Drake plundered a Peruvian treasure ship.

(See also COOK, JOHN; DAVIS, EDWARD; DUTCH IN THE AMERICAS; FLEURY, JEAN; SHARP, BARTHOLOMEW; SELECTED BIBLIOGRAPHY: Andrews, *Spanish Caribbean*; Earl, *Concepción*; Haring, *Buccaneers* and *Trade*; Rogoziński, *Caribbean.*)

TREASURE ISLAND (1) *(novel; 1883)* A tale of treasure buried on an imaginary Caribbean island. Robert Louis STEVENSON (1850–1894) began *Treasure Island* to amuse his 12-year-old stepson. Although unsuccessful as a magazine serial in 1881, an 1883 revision quickly became popular and strongly influenced later pirate fiction.

"I'm poor Ben Gunn, I am. . . . Marooned three years agone, and lived on goats since then, and berries, and oysters." Illustration by Louis Rhead for a 1915 edition of *Treasure Island* by Robert Louis Stevenson.

The story is narrated in the first person, mainly by Jim Hawkins. It begins in western England at the Admiral Benbow Inn, owned by Jim's parents. There the aged Bill Bones waits for a one-legged man. Drunk on RUM, he tells lurid stories and sings wild songs, including one recurring ditty, "FIFTEEN MEN ON THE DEAD MAN'S CHEST."

Although the one-legged man never arrives, Bones fights with a seaman named Black Dog. Soon after, Pew, a deformed blind man, gives Bones the "black spot" death notice, frightening him to death. Jim and his mother search Bones' sea chest for the money owed them. Inside they find a MAP locating the treasure horde of Captain Flint, "the bloodthirstiest buccaneer that sailed."

Squire Trelawney and Doctor Livesey decide to collect Flint's treasure, with Jim going along as cabin boy. At Bristol, Trelawney buys the *Hispaniola*, retains Captain Smollet, and hires a cook named Long John SILVER. A tavernkeeper with one leg and a PARROT, Silver assembles a crew of his own friends.

Just before the *Hispaniola* reaches Flint's island, Jim overhears Silver and others plotting a mutiny. When Silver and most crewmen go ashore, Jim sneaks along and escapes into the woods. While Jim watches, Silver kills two men that refuse to join the mutiny. Jim then runs into Ben Gunn, who helped Flint bury the treasure. Gunn was MAROONED three years earlier when his shipmates failed to find Flint's gold.

Discovering Silver's treachery, Livesey and Trelawney move to Flint's stockade with a few loyal crewmen. Israel HANDS, formerly Flint's gunner, shells the stockade with little effect. Leaving Ben Gunn, Jim sees the JOLLY ROGER atop the *Hispaniola* and joins his friends.

Visiting under a flag of truce, Silver offers the fort's defenders a safe passage home in return for the treasure map. When Captain Smollet contemptuously refuses, Silver leaves in a rage. The pirates attack and are driven back with heavy casualties. Only Jim, Smollet, Trelawney, Livesey, and one sailor remain alive in the stockade.

Jim steals off and boards the *Hispaniola*. The only guard is Israel Hands, wounded while fighting with another pirate. Jim takes command and beaches the ship. Pursued by Hands, he climbs to a crosstree, and Hands' first knife misses him. Another knife pins Jim to the mast, but he manages to shoot Hands.

Returning to the stockade, Jim finds his friends gone and Silver in control. Silver protects Jim and shows the other pirates the treasure map. Doctor Livesey secretly gave Silver the map, knowing that Ben Gunn already had taken the treasure.

When the pirates find the gold gone, they turn on Jim and Silver. Gunn and Jim's friends rescue them, and the group escapes in the *Hispaniola*. At the first port, Gunn helps Long John Silver get away with a bag of coins. The survivors return to Bristol and divide the treasure. "Drink and the Devil had done for the rest."

Stevenson drew his plot—the drunken Billy Bones, treasure map, and deserted island—from many earlier authors. Stevenson's prefatory poem placed *Treasure Island* within the tradition of "Kingston, or Ballantyne the brave, or COOPER of the wood and wave." The buried treasure scenes also borrowed, he later wrote, from Poe's "GOLD BUG" and stories by Washington IRVING. Silver's parrot and Ben Gunn came from Daniel DEFOE'S ROBINSON CRUSOE. The phrase "dead man's chest" in the song "Fifteen Men" came from an 1871 travel book.

Stevenson was most indebted to Defoe's GENERAL HISTORY, which provided Long John Silver. After Edward ENGLAND captured Captain Macrae's *Cassandra*, many pirates wanted to hang Macrae, who was saved by a former shipmate. Defoe wrote that "a Fellow with a terrible Pair of Whiskers, and a wooden Leg . . . comes swearing and vapouring upon the Quarter-Deck . . .; *shew me the Man,* says he, *that offers to hurt Captain Mackra, for I'll stand by him.*"

While inciting the mutiny, Silver describes his adventures with England. The surgeon who removed his leg later joined Bartholomew ROBERTS and was "hanged like a dog, and sun-dried like the rest, at Corso Castle."

Silver earlier told Jim that his parrot sailed with England and learned to say "PIECES OF EIGHT" from Charles VANE. There are many other references (not always accurate) to the *General History*. "Even minor bits of phraseology," Harold Watson pointed out, "and the . . . prose rhythm of Jim Hawkins' narrative go back to . . . Defoe."

Above all, Stevenson drew upon Defoe in creating Long John Silver's psychology. Silver dominates the book, raising it from a mere adventure story to a timeless myth. Silver is an ambiguous character, both bad and good, cruel and generous, despicable and admirable.

A Victorian author could not portray pirates as heroes, especially in a book for young adults. Stevenson thus made Silver into a good/bad figure set against truly evil villains like Israel Hands. However, Stevenson's study of Defoe also contributed to Silver's ambiguity. Although Defoe created memorable monsters, many of his pirates are normal persons with families and friends. Pirates, Defoe emphasized, steal for a living, but so do many respected citizens. Pirates are simply bolder in their crimes. With his conflicting good and bad qualities, Silver is both artistically compelling and true to Defoe's history.

Treasure Island is a "coming of age" story describing Jim Hawkins' transition to manhood. His own father having died, Jim works next to other adult males (Livesey, Silver, Trelawney)—all of whom also became wiser during their shared adventure. Although today children are its primary readers, *Treasure Island* is not a "children's book." In the 1880s, almost all youths had left school and worked at full-time jobs by the age of 12. Like Jim Hawkins, they were apprenticed to adults. In *Treasure Island*, Stevenson created a believable adventure story for anyone trying to be grown-up.

In reworking earlier stories, Stevenson perfected a powerful pirate mythology. Because of the novel's success, Stevenson's myths are accepted as true history. Pirates had wooden legs, carried parrots, ranted and raved, and buried their TREASURE. Intended for a younger audience than Stevenson's novel, some later novels and films emphasize these bizarre aspects. In place of Stevenson's ambiguous villain, they offer a Silver as demented as Ben Gunn.

(See also PEG LEG; SWEARING; SELECTED BIBLIOGRAPHY: Bonner, *Pirate*; Defoe, *General History*; Watson, *Coasts*.)

TREASURE ISLAND (2) *(motion picture; black and white; 1920)* Director Maurice Tourneur's silent movie is among the least faithful to the plot and spirit of the novel. Stevenson's Jim Hawkins narrates his own story, and he is an adventurous young man, who initiates actions with important consequences. The movie tells its story about Jim, who is played by a girl (Shirley Mason). He is a passive object to whom events happen.

In the novel, for example, Jim slips away from the stockade and cuts the *Hispaniola*'s cable because he feels

useless washing dishes while real men battle. Tourneur has Doctor Livesey (Charles Hill Mailes) send Jim on an errand to the ship, where his adventures are forced upon him. Miss Mason's performance emphasizes Jim's passivity. Her gestures and manner are feminine, where Stevenson's Jim is distinctly a sturdy young male.

As Long John Silver, Charles Ogle is strong and wicked and less florid than in some later movie versions. However, he leaves out the sunnier side of Silver's complicated character. The novel's climax depends on the mutual, if ambivalent, affection between Jim and Silver. But this version does not even hint at their feelings, partly because Tourneur leaves out the scenes at Silver's tavern.

While it is not faithful to Stevenson's novel, Tourneur's *Treasure Island* is a classic silent movie with excellent composition and photography as well as some fine acting. Tourneur created a fast-paced melodrama full of constant action. Silver's crew is immensely villainous, and Lon Chaney is fiendish both as blind Pew and then as the surly George Merry. In comparison, Squire Trelawney (Sidney Dean) and Doctor Livesey are duller and seem less interesting.

Treasure Island's success partly inspired the evil brigands in *The* BLACK PIRATE (1926). Together, the two movies helped establish the pirate action adventure or SWASHBUCKLER as a major movie genre.

TREASURE ISLAND (3) *(motion picture; black and white; 1934)* The first sound version is faithful to Stevenson's novel and treats it as serious fiction about

Long John Silver (Wallace Beery), Jim Hawkins (Jackie Cooper), and Silver's parrot in *Treasure Island* (1934).

events that might actually have occurred. The script faithfully abridges Stevenson's plot. Victor Fleming (who later directed *Gone With the Wind*) supplies striking visual effects at the Admiral Benbow, the besieged blockhouse, and the *Hispaniola*, as Israel Hands pins Jim to the mast.

As Long John Silver, Wallace Beery is bluff, plausible, and sly as he wheedles and conspires. Jackie Cooper, a former child star, plays Jim Hawkins emerging into manhood. Nigel Bruce is foolish and greedy as Squire Trelawney. Otto Kruger (Dr. Livesey) and Lewis Stone (Captain Smollett) also provide sober performances.

TREASURE ISLAND (4) *(motion picture; color; 1950)* Walt Disney filmed Stevenson's novel in England, with Bobby Driscoll (Jim Hawkins) the only American actor. The lavish settings are saturated with pastel colors, even in early sequences supposedly set on a stark and craggy coast.

The script abridges some episodes, adds explanatory comments in other scenes, and significantly changes the finale. Long John Silver and Jim are alone in a rowboat, which sticks in the sand. Silver cannot bring himself to shoot the boy, and Jim cannot bear to see Long John in prison. Jim suddenly pushes the boat (and a large treasure chest) out to sea and waves farewell to Silver. In the novel, Silver escapes without Jim's knowledge, taking only a small sack of coins.

Stevenson's novel describes the hero's transition to adult manhood. Stevenson began the book to amuse his 12-year-old stepson, and it was serialized in a magazine for boys about that age. Disney aimed this version at a less mature audience. Bobby Driscoll looks and acts younger than 12. More significantly, director Byron Haskin declared the novel a "children's story" and decided that "Kids don't go in much for subtleties."

Haskin kept Basil Sydney (Captain Smollett), Walter Fitzgerald (Squire Trelawney), and Denis O'Dea (Doctor Livesey) under control. But (according to both Haskin and the stars), he told Robert NEWTON (Long John Silver) to "let it rip," and he gave Ralph Truman (George Merry) "full scope to out-ham Newton whenever he could." Newton played Silver with a full barrage of broad grimaces, eye rolling, and expressions, such as YO-HO-HO and "SHIVER MY TIMBERS." His version resembles the fairy-tale Captain Hook in PETER PAN rather than Stevenson's Silver, a clever BUCCANEER who outwitted intelligent adults as well as young Hawkins. Like Hook, Newton's Silver calls his pirate crew "dogs" and treats them as such.

(See also SELECTED BIBLIOGRAPHY: Maltin, *Disney Films.*)

TREASURE ISLAND (5) *(motion picture; color; 1972)* Director Harry Alan Towers made this version solely for children under 12 years of age. Although the script usually follows Stevenson's novel, the actors posture with arch gestures. Orson Welles stars as Long John Silver, with Kim Burfield as Jim Hawkins and Walter SLEZAK as Squire Trelawney.

TREASURE ISLAND (6) *(motion picture; color; 1990)* Filmed in England and Jamaica, this big-budget cable-television movie stars Charlton Heston as Long John Silver. Director Fraser Heston, the actor's son, respects both the letter and the spirit of Stevenson's novel. The script generally follows the original and incorporates some of its text. At the end, Silver sails away in a small boat. In the novel, he drops over the side at night.

Charlton Heston plays Silver as a vigorous and charismatic rogue who can swindle anyone. Jim Hawkins (Christopher Bale) is appropriately serious as a young adult learning how to be a man. As Stevenson intended, Doctor Livesey (Julian Glover) and Squire Trelawney (Richard Johnson) also become somewhat wiser during the voyage.

By treating Stevenson's novel as historical fiction rather than as comedy, the movie presents believable characters. Silver's piratical crewmen resemble 18th-century mariners, who even are seen working the ship.

TREBELLIANUS *(Cilician archpirate; Mediterranean; mid-third century)* As the Roman navy disintegrated, the peoples of CILICIA returned to their buccaneering practices. Like ZENOCTES three centuries earlier, Trebellianus proclaimed himself emperor, built a palace high in the Cilician hills, and issued an independent coinage. He was overthrown by an officer of the emperor Gallienus (ruled 253–268).

TRETI, CAPTAIN *(Maltese corsair; Mediterranean; 1676)* Captain Treti received partial payment of his share of captured booty.

TREVELYAN, JOHN *(English pirate; Atlantic; active 1440s)* Trevelyan had considerable property in Devonshire and was highly regarded by King Henry VI. He was the main owner of a ship that made a rich haul in 1449. A large Spanish galley, sailing from Sluis and Southampton, carried cargo valued at the enormous sum of £12,000. The pirates captured the vessel without resistance after a storm trapped it near Plymouth. Trevelyan was briefly arrested, but the stolen property was never restored. The investigating royal commissioners were corrupt, and one was the pirate Thomas BODULGATE.

TRIBUNALE DEGLI ARMAMENTI *(Maltese prize court; Mediterranean; 1605–1798)* The administrative and judicial body—five magistrates and their staff—that regulated corsairs flying the FLAG of the KNIGHTS OF MALTA. (Since *armamento* refers to the total investment in a voyage, the court's name translates as "Tribunal of Corsair Cruises.") The Tribunal was a religious court that could enforce oaths and contracts sworn before its judges. Appeals went first to the grand master and then to the papal courts in Rome.

Maltese law forbade corsairs to sail under foreign flags. In principle, the Tribunal dealt with all private captains and every aspect of their cruises. (However, it had no jurisdiction over piracy by the knights themselves, who reported directly to the grand master.) The Tribunal investigated captains and their ships before the grand master licensed them to practice piracy (*ad exercendam pyraticam*). Both shipowners and captains swore before the court (and posted a money bond) not to attack Christians or infidels with a safe conduct.

While their ships were being outfitted, owners registered with the Tribunal the amounts due to their creditors. In addition, every ship carried a purser who kept a detailed register of expenses incurred and booty taken while at sea. The purser took an oath to the Tribunal and lost his right hand if he cheated.

When a corsair returned, the Tribunal's staff recorded his captured ships, cargoes, and prisoners. Prizes and booty were sold, usually by public auction, and the sales price was registered. The proceeds might be directly paid out or deposited in the Tribunal's own bank for later distribution.

As a court, the Tribunal judged all disputes related to pirate voyages. The magistrates also decided whether prizes had been lawfully taken under its rules. Many suits were brought by Greek Christians pillaged by the corsairs. From the 1680s, the Tribunal tended to rule against these victims, and papal courts often overturned its verdicts.

To avoid appeals to Rome, 18th-century grand masters sometimes ignored the law and allowed corsairs to operate with foreign licenses judged by foreign courts. They also issued licenses under their personal flag as secular rulers of Malta. These were regulated by the Consuls of the Sea (*Consolato di Mare*), created in 1697 to regulate normal maritime commerce. Since the Consolato was a secular court, litigants could not appeal to the pope. However, many corsairs continued to receive licenses under the order's flag, and they thus remained subject to the Tribunal.

(See also BOOTY, DIVISION OF; SELECTED BIBLIOGRAPHY: Blouet, *Story*; Earle, *Corsairs*.)

TRIEMIOLIA (anti-pirate warship; Mediterranean, Aegean Sea; about 304–42 B.C.)
The island-state of RHODES was the main enemy of piracy in the eastern Mediterranean. Traditional Greek warships were too slow to catch a pirate HEMIOLA, which carried both sails and two banks of oars. Just as corsairs created the hemiola to chase merchantmen, so Rhodes's naval architects designed the triemiolia to run down hemioliai. They took one of the faster open-decked models of their three-banked TRIREME. Copying the hemiola, they rearranged the oars in the after part of the upper row so that they were easily removed before a battle.

TRINITY, ORDER OF THE MOST HOLY (TRINITARIANS)
See REDEMPTIONIST FATHERS.

TRIPOLI (1) (Barbary corsair haven; Mediterranean; 1551–1835)
A port city and the capital of modern Libya. Occupied by the KNIGHTS OF MALTA in 1530, it was attached to the OTTOMAN EMPIRE by TURGUT REIS in 1551. Like the other BARBARY STATES, Tripoli lived by piracy, leaving inland tribes to rule themselves. The Ottoman BEYLERBEY lost power to the JANISSARY garrison, which elected the DEY governing Tripoli and the BEYS commanding troops in the interior.

Conflicts between the Janissary soldiers and the corsairs led to frequent rebellions during the 17th century. In 1711, Ahmad (or Hamid) Qaramanli, a cavalry commander of mixed Turkish-Tripolitan origins, seized power. The Ottoman sultan recognized him as pasha, and the Qaramanli family ruled until 1835.

Tripoli supported its largest fleet (perhaps 30 ships) under Turgut Reis during the 1550s and 1560s. After 1600, corsairs raiding in the western Mediterranean concentrated at ALGIERS. Tripolitan corsairs normally operated to the east of Sicily, chiefly against the KNIGHTS OF MALTA and the Venetians.

During the 17th century, Tripoli became involved in conflicts pitting France and Britain against the larger corsair havens at Algiers and TUNIS. The number of corsairs fell, as the city's rulers enforced the resulting peace treaties with England (1658), the Netherlands (1662), and France (1685). In 1679, Tripoli supported 13 captains, five of them Christian RENEGADES and almost all commanding sailing ships. Between 1679 and 1685, the entire fleet took only 75 prizes.

Tripolitan corsairs took a relatively limited part in the British-Tunisian war of 1655. When a peace treaty was signed in 1658, the city held only about 150 British captives. Four years later, a Dutch fleet toured the BARBARY COAST and concluded commercial treaties with Tripoli and Tunis. In 1672, the dey declared war on Britain, which had failed to present the customary gifts at his election. A new treaty was imposed in 1676 after a British squadron burned four warships in Tripoli's harbor.

From 1679, the French navy cruised the Mediterranean to punish Tripolitan piracy. In 1681, French ships shelled the island of Chios (part of the Ottoman Empire), forcing the Tripolitans to release two prizes. They bombarded Tripoli itself in 1685 and 1692, dictating a treaty that gave French merchants the same privileges as the British and the Dutch. Visits by naval squadrons during the following century compelled the Tripolitans to respect French shipping and consuls.

Tripoli's naval forces reached their lowest point during the 1760s. A small Venetian squadron forced the pasha to punish violations of a 1764 treaty. Nevertheless, some European nations continued to pay tribute to Tripoli's rulers, since this was cheaper than sending a fleet to the city.

Piracy increased under Ali (1754–1793) and Yusuf (1795–1832) Qaramanli, who treated corsair captains as national heroes. By weakening European surveillance, the British-French wars (1792–1815) allowed the corsairs to take more prizes, and many nations paid the annual tribute. Since they feared these two great powers, the corsairs mainly attacked ships from smaller states. Following an ineffective assault in 1797, Denmark agreed to a larger tribute.

Perhaps encouraged by this success, Yusuf Qaramanli declared war on the United States in 1801. When hostilities began, Peter LISLE, a Scottish renegade, commanded five sailing ships and two galleys, carrying 106 guns and 840 men. During this first BARBARY WAR, the U.S. fostered a rebellion by the pasha's brother, forcing Tripoli to sign a new peace treaty in 1805.

The war destroyed most of Tripoli's ships, and the second Barbary War in 1815 increased American prestige. As piracy became unprofitable, Yusuf Qaramanli became deeply indebted to British and French bankers. To prevent European intervention, the Ottoman sultan removed the Qaramanli dynasty and reimposed Turkish rule from 1835 to 1911. Tripoli remained the capital of the Italian colony of Libya (1911–1943), independent since 1951.

TRIPOLI (2) *(motion picture; color; 1950)* Directed by Will Price, this low-budget costume melodrama combines romance, touches of comedy, and one major battle scene. During the First BARBARY WAR, Countess D'Arneau (Maureen O'HARA) is a French diplomat's daughter and the ward of Hamet Qaramanli, brother of TRIPOLI's ruler. While trying to land a native prince, the countess falls for dashing Lieutenant O'Bannon (John Payne). Disguised as a dancing girl, she crosses the desert with Payne's marines, Hamet's native forces, and Greek cut-throats led by Captain Demtrios (Howard Da Silva). Surviving a howling sand storm, this disparate band finally reaches and conquers a coastal city blocking the invasion of Tripoli.

TRIREME *(warships; Mediterranean; seventh century B.C. to fourth century A.D.)* A decked GALLEY with three banks of rowers, derived from earlier two-banked galleys called *biremes*. The PHOENICIANS simply made their ships higher, while the Greeks (and later the Romans) added an outrigger projecting laterally above the gunwale. The long, narrow trireme was a man-powered torpedo that sought to ram its opponent. Fourth-century Athenian triremes were about 115 to 120 feet long and 16 feet wide (at the deck), with a depth of 4.5 feet and a height above water of 8.5 feet.

The trireme was a naval warship that rarely went far from land. Pirates almost never used them, and they were not effective against many types of pirate SHIPS. They were unstable in bad weather, had very little space for provisions or cargo, and required a large and highly skilled crew.

(See also POLYREMES.)

TRISTIAN, CAPTAIN *(French pirate; Caribbean; active 1681–1682)* After returning from the Pacific in May 1681, John COOK and several other English seamen sailed with Captain YANKY. In an argument over

a prize, Yanky marooned the Englishmen on the Île-à-Vache, off Haiti. Captain Tristian rescued Cook, Edward DAVIS, and a few others and took them to PETIT GOÂVE. Cook and Davis rewarded Tristian's kindness by stealing his ship.

TUCKER, THOMAS *(English pirate; Atlantic, Mediterranean; active 1611–1615)* A skilled mariner from Newcastle, Tucker rose to master's MATE aboard Peter EASTON's flagship. Easton retired with a fortune at Villefranche in 1613, but dismissed his crew with a pittance. Tucker briefly became a solider, escaped to the pirate haven at MAMORA about 1614, and gained his own command.

According to one account, he and Captain John Woodland planned a voyage of plunder in Russia. A storm wrecked Tucker's ship off the Faro Islands, and Woodland stole everything he owned. Tucker returned to England in 1615, was pardoned the following year, and took a job as a common seaman.

TUNG-HAI PA *(Chinese pirate; South China Sea; active 1805–1810)* Leader of the Yellow Flag Fleet in the pirate confederation created by CHENG I in 1805. Pa (also known as Wu Chih-ch'ing) operated from his home territory on the Lei-chou Peninsula, near Vietnam.

In early 1810, CHANG PAO and KUO P'O-TAI, who commanded larger fleets, surrendered to government forces. Joining an attack on his former colleagues, Chang Pao captured both Pa's right-hand man and WU-SHIH ERH, leader of the Blue Flag Fleet. Finding himself isolated, Pa surrendered with 12 officers and 3,400 crewmen,

The imperial governor was willing to pardon Pa. However, the region's inhabitants protested so loudly that his death was ordered. Just before the sentence was carried out, an imperial pardon arrived, and Pa returned home.

TUNIS *(Barbary corsair haven; Mediterranean; 1574–1830)* A city strategically situated on the narrow channel between Sicily and North Africa, second only to ALGIERS as a center of Muslim piracy. By the 1530s, the rulers of Tunis had lost the interior and fallen under Spanish control. To protect his base at Algiers, KHEIRED-DIN BARBAROSSA occupied Tunis in 1534. A Spanish expedition retook the city in 1535, but ULUJ ALI PASHA returned Tunis to Muslim rule in 1574.

Uluj Ali installed a political system similar to that in Algiers. A BEYLERBEY represented the OTTOMAN sultan, assisted by the BEY of Tunis, who collected taxes and policed the city. But control soon passed to the city's JANISSARY garrison. In 1591, the junior officers rebelled and forced the pasha to recognize rule by a DEY, whom they elected.

At this time, most corsairs preferred to sail from Algiers. Uthman Dey (ruled 1598–1610) and Yusuf Dey (ruled 1610–1637) consolidated their power by turning the Janissaries against insubordinate native tribes. They also built up a strong corsair fleet with the help of English and Dutch pirates led by John WARD. Since Ward and the other foreign captains had to sell their booty at low prices, Uthman Dey and other Tunisian leaders made enormous profits by backing their voyages.

The Christian RENEGADES taught their Muslim hosts how to build and navigate large sailing ships. The city sheltered only two or three oared GALIOTS when Ward arrived in 1606. By 1609, the fleet included 12 large sailing ships, six galleys, and many smaller vessels. The great influx of English sailors ended about 1609, although individual renegades continued to settle at Tunis. The Tunisian corsairs had mastered the art of sailing ships, and they built lighter and faster vessels than their opponents. Mediterranean piracy flourished, and the city's rulers embellished Tunis with mosques and other public buildings.

Corsair raids diminished from the 1660s. The Tunisian corsair fleet usually stayed east of Sicily and mainly attacked Italian vessels. When English, French, and Dutch merchants took over trade with the Near East, their governments imposed treaties protecting their shipping.

Great Britain and Tunis signed a formal peace treaty in 1622. A quarrel arose in 1651 because a British captain allowed the KNIGHTS OF MALTA to seize Tunisian merchants. Admiral Robert Blake surprised and destroyed nine Tunisian ships at anchor in 1655. The "firm and perpetual peace" called for in a 1662 treaty was achieved, and the two nations remained on good terms until the early 1800s. Meanwhile, French and Dutch traders also acquired trading rights at Tunis. In 1662, the Netherlands and Tunis concluded a treaty guaranteeing the safety of each country's shipping. The French government negotiated substantial commercial privileges in 1665.

The few corsairs remaining at Tunis attacked only ships from the smaller European states without treaties. Austria signed a commercial agreement in 1725, Denmark in 1751. The mistreatment of Tunisian passengers by Venice led to a short war (1784–1786) followed by a peace treaty in 1792. Spain finally made peace in 1791. European states helped keep the peace by offering "gifts" to the Tunisian rulers. Treaties with Austria, Sweden, and Denmark in 1784 specifically called for annual tribute.

European states could impose their will during the 17th century partly because of continuing political disorder in Tunis. Ultimately the dey—elected by the Janissary soldiers—lost power to hereditary civilian beys. Hussein ibn Ali, who organized the Tunisian resistance to an Algerian invasion in 1705, founded the Husainid dynasty of beys. These rulers emphasized agriculture and legitimate commerce. They turned away from piracy, since they gained more by taxing trade and accepting European tribute.

Although the most adventurous corsairs sailed from Algiers with HAMIDOU REIS, Tunis rebuilt its corsair fleet during the Napoleonic Wars (1792–1815). A British fleet bombarded the city in 1816. After a second show of force three years later, the bey outlawed piracy and reiterated its suppression in an 1830 treaty with France. The Ottoman Empire reasserted its authority over Tunis after 1836. In 1881, French troops occupied the city and imposed a protectorate on the Husainid beys. Tunisia regained its independence in 1956 and became a republic in 1957.

(See also OSTA MURAT; TAIFE REISI.)

TURCHA, PERCIVAL DE LA (Genoese pirate; Mediterranean; 1303) Turcha was captured near RHODES after seizing several Venetian ships and taken to Cyprus for trial.

TURGUT (TORGHUD, DRAGUT) REIS (Barbary corsair; Mediterranean; died 1565) Unsurpassed in seamanship and audacity, Turgut established TRIPOLI as a major corsair base. Probably born of Greek parents, in Asia Minor or on RHODES, he turned pirate at an early age and became a superb pilot and gunner. Moving to North Africa in the late 1520s, he enlisted under KHEIREDDIN BARBAROSSA, attacking shipping and ravaging the Italian and Sicilian coasts.

Turgut became—with SINAN REIS—one of Kheireddin's chief advisors and commanded the OTTOMAN right wing at PREVESA in 1538. In 1540, Giannettino Doria (nephew of the Spanish admiral, Andrea Doria) caught Turgut's ship at anchor and made him a GALLEY SLAVE. Four years later, while encamped at Toulon in France, Kheireddin paid Andrea Doria 3,000 gold ducats to secure Turgut's release and named him commander of the North African corsairs.

Andrea Doria later regretted his bargain. When Kheireddin died in 1548, his son, Hasan Pasha, ruled Algiers, while Turgut remained the corsairs' commander. The Ottomans and Spain had concluded a truce in 1547. Turgut's corsairs left Algiers and operated from DJERBA, ARUJ BARBAROSSA's old haunt.

Imprisonment had sharpened Turgut's appetite for Christians, and his squadrons harried the Italian coasts. In 1548, his corsairs entered the Bay of Naples and seized a galley and 70,000 gold ducats belonging to the Knights of Malta. In 1550, they occupied the fortress of Mahdiya, directly threatening the Spanish at TUNIS.

Charles V of Spain considered Turgut a major threat. In September 1550, Andrea Doria's fleet and Sicilian troops recaptured Mahdiya, destroyed the city, and killed or enslaved its inhabitants. The following year, Doria returned and trapped Turgut's ships in the shallow straits between Djerba and the mainland. But Turgut brought his squadron out by dredging canals through an unnavigable bog on the southern side of the island.

From Djerba, Turgut steered for the Aegean and joined an Ottoman battle fleet that unsuccessfully attacked Malta. Seeking a victory to compensate for his defeat, the Ottoman commander turned on Tripoli—occupied by the Spanish in 1510 and ruled by the Knights of Malta since 1530. The knights surrendered in August 1551.

Turgut spent the next five years with the regular Ottoman navy, which again cooperated with France against the Spanish and Austrian Habsburgs. In 1552, he was second-in-command of an Ottoman armada that defeated Andrea Doria's fleet off the western coast of Italy. In 1553, he returned to Italy as commander of a squadron that attacked Elba and sacked Corsica.

Dismissed as admiral-in-chief through palace intrigues, Turgut in 1556 returned to Tripoli as governor. Punitive expeditions forced the local tribes to end their attacks and recognize Turgut's suzerainty. At sea, his corsairs repeatedly raided Italy, in 1558 carrying away most of the inhabitants of Reggio as slaves. In Tripoli itself, Turgut used pirate booty to build housing, a fort, and a mosque. By 1559, corsair attacks on shipping had reduced Italy and western Spain to starvation. Philip II, Spain's new king, dispatched a large expedition. Its destruction during the battle of Djerba in May 1560 confirmed corsair control of Tripoli.

Turgut commanded warships until his death. With eight galleys in 1561, he captured seven warships from the Knights of Malta. He led the fleet that unsuccessfully besieged Oran in 1563. In 1565, Sultan Suleiman ordered his commanders to consult Turgut on all major decisions during the siege of Malta. He was killed by cannon fire during the heat of battle.

TWO BACCHIDES, THE *(comedy in Latin; about 189 B.C.)* A play by PLAUTUS set in Athens.

Two years before it begins, Nicobulus has sent his son Mnesilochus and his slave Chrysalus to Ephesus, to collect a debt from Archimides. Calling at SAMOS on the way, Mnesilochus falls in love with Bacchis, a professional courtesan. But a sea captain hires Bacchis' services for a year and takes her to Athens.

In the first act, Bacchis arrives in Athens and expresses her willingness to be purchased by Mnesilochus. As the second act begins, Mnesilochus and Chrysalus return from Ephesus with the money collected from Archimides. But Chrysalus pretends that he no longer has the money, so that Mnesilochus can use it to buy Bacchis.

To explain the disappearance of his master's funds, Chrysalus tells Nicobulus an elaborate story. Archimedes and a pirate gang jointly owned a warship. After paying the money to Chrysalus, Archimedes resolved to get it back. He told the corsairs the exact route Chrysalus and Mnesilochus would take back to Athens, and the pirate ship followed its prey out of the harbor.

Chrysalus' story would be believable only if pirates were a frequent hazard. Archimedes, a legitimate merchant, provides the pirates with a ship and takes a cut of their booty. Like Chrysalus' imaginary pirates, corsairs from CILICIA and other ports spied out on shore a ship's cargo and destination.

TYRRHENIAN *(Greek word for pirate; Mediterranean; from 300 B.C.)* Originally the Greek name for the ETRUSCANS, its meaning gradually expanded to include pirates of any nationality sailing east from Italy or Sicily to raid in the Aegean.

U

ULUJ ALI (EULJ ALI, OCHIALI) PASHA
(Barbary corsair; Mediterranean; 1520–1587) Uluj Ali was born Giovan Dionigi, the son of a fisherman in southern Italy. Captured by the Algerian corsair GIAFER, he became a GALLEY SLAVE (hence his Arabic nickname Farta, "scurvied"). According to legend, he converted to Islam so that he could retaliate against a soldier who had struck him. In another story, he converted in order to marry Giafer's daughter.

Rapidly rising to officer, Uluj Ali purchased a GALIOT and joined TURGUT REIS at TRIPOLI in the late 1550s. In 1560, his squadron ran into a Spanish expedition and rushed north to alert the OTTOMAN fleet, returning with it to destroy the invaders off DJERBA. Piali Pasha, the Ottoman admiral, applauded his boldness during this battle.

Uluj Ali again fought bravely at the siege of MALTA in 1565. At Piali Pasha's suggestion, he replaced Turgut as governor of Tripoli. Raids on Sicily and southern Italy brought in considerable booty, which Uluj shared with officials in Istanbul. In 1568, he was appointed BEYLERBEY of the more important port of ALGIERS.

Uluj Ali's first concern at Algiers was the Moriscos of Granada, who rebelled in 1569 and 1570 against Spanish rule. Although some Algerians sent weapons and supplies, Uluj Ali's government offered no official aid. (He did refuse to change sides, even though the Spanish offered him the rank of marquis.) In January 1570, Uluj Ali instead overthrew Spain's puppet king in TUNIS.

Once the Morisco War was won, Philip II of Spain joined Venice and the papacy in a Holy League against the Ottomans. As the Christians assembled, Uluj Ali seriously weakened the KNIGHTS OF MALTA. In July 1570, his squadron captured three Maltese galleys and killed or enslaved more than 80 knights off Sicily's southern coast.

On October 7, 1571, the allied and Ottoman navies met at LEPANTO, with Uluj Ali commanding 95 warships on the left wing. Although the Ottomans were defeated, Uluj Ali fought brilliantly. He outmaneuvered the opposing commander, shot through the gap, and fell on the enemy's center with devastating force. Had he arrived a half hour earlier, the Ottomans might have won. As it was, he managed to lead a dozen galleys away from the general destruction.

The sultan at once made Uluj Ali commander of the Ottoman navy. By the following spring, he had created a new armada of 220 lighter and sturdier warships. The Holy League's campaign in 1572 came to nothing. Again outmaneuvering his opponents, Uluj Ali barred their entry into the eastern Mediterranean at Modone in Greece. The next year, the Holy League fell apart and no longer threatened to invade the Ottoman Empire.

Spain again turned her attention toward North Africa and reoccupied Tunis in October 1573. Uluj Ali and the

Ottoman navy retook the city the following June. In 1577, Spain and the Ottomans signed a truce that effectively ended their wars in the Mediterranean. Uluj Ali, who remained naval commander until his death, led several small raids in the west and in the Black Sea. In 1581, he assembled a fleet in Algiers for a campaign against Morocco that was aborted by political disputes.

UMAR BEY *(Turkish corsair patron; Aegean Sea; 1309–1349)* Umar conquered and ruled Smyrna in western Asia Minor in 1329, and he succeeded MEHMED BEY as emir of AYDIN in 1334. Umar continued his father's piracy on a larger scale. He built up a fleet of 250 to 300 ships, most manned by Greek Christians or recent converts to Islam. From Smyrna, they attacked shipping and plundered the Greek mainland, the Aegean islands, and CRETE.

The Venetians, whose rich Oriental trades passed through the Aegean, sought allies to fight the pirates. After much discussion, the BYZANTINE EMPIRE, the KNIGHTS OF RHODES, France, and the papacy formed an alliance against Umar Bey. In 1334, a joint fleet of some 40 galleys defeated the emir's warships but failed to take Smyrna. In 1335, the Byzantine emperor cut his losses and made a treaty with Umar, who helped the emperor raid Bulgarian territory in 1341.

The Knights of Rhodes, Venice, Cyprus, and the papacy formed a new league against Umar in 1344. In October, the allied fleet took some of Umar's warships by surprise, captured Smyrna's port and its fortress, but failed to take the upper citadel. The Latin patriarch of Jerusalem insisted on holding mass in the former cathedral in January 1345. Umar attacked during the service and killed the crusade's leaders.

Umar died in 1349 while leading an attack on the lower city. His brother made peace, and the pirate threat became less serious. The Knights of Rhodes defended Smyrna until its conquest by the Mongols in 1402.

UMAR REIS *(Barbary corsair; Mediterranean; 1677)* Umar was captain of the six-gun *Palm*, a captured French ship at TRIPOLI.

USAIN REIS *(Barbary corsair; Mediterranean; 1574)* A Sicilian convert and follower of ULUJ ALI, Usain commanded one of six ships escorting HASAN VENEZIANO, the incoming BEYLERBEY, from Istanbul to ALGIERS.

USKOKS *(Slavic pirates; Adriatic Sea; 1537–1618)* Christian refugees who settled at Senj, about 85 miles south of Trieste, and carried on guerilla warfare against the expanding OTTOMAN EMPIRE. (Uskok means "escapee" without referring to a specific ethnic group.) Joined by adventurers from western Europe, they scoured the Adriatic from the 1560s, attacking Muslims and Christians alike.

By the 1530s, Ottoman forces had occupied the Balkan Peninsula and ruled much of the Adriatic coast. Venice retained several coastal garrisons, Dubrovnik remained independent, and the Austrian Habsburgs held the coast from Senj northward. In 1537, the Habsburgs settled refugees at Senj as auxiliary soldiers. The entire border region received a separate military government, with its capital at Graz.

None of these states effectively controlled the Dalmatian coast. Except for the Cyprus conflict (1570–1573), Venice avoided war with the Ottomans from 1540 to 1645. And the Habsburgs and Ottomans were at peace from 1562 to 1593. But the three empires remained bitter rivals and condoned land and sea raids by their nominal subjects.

The Uskoks turned to piracy during the late 1540s. Habsburg officials never delivered the promised subsidies, and the Ottomans fortified their frontiers against land raids. Senj's poor soil could not be farmed, but the town provided an excellent corsair haven. Shallows, jagged cliffs, and savage winds prevented the approach of heavily gunned warships. Ottoman armies could not bring their artillery down through the steep and barren cliffs on the land side.

Although mainly from inland regions, the Uskoks made themselves into a formidable naval power. Using the hard weather against their enemies, they devised small, shallow-draft oared boats that ran before the wind and were easily concealed on shore. At first they attacked only Muslim vessels. They grew so successful that the Ottomans cited Venice's failure to stop assaults by the Uskoks (and the KNIGHTS OF MALTA) to justify the 1570 conquest of Cyprus.

From the early 1560s, the Uskoks also pillaged Christian shipping. After the Habsburgs and Venice made peace with the Ottoman Empire, most Muslim and Jewish goods were carried on ships from Dubrovnik, Ancona, or Venice. (In the 1573 peace treaty, Venice guaranteed the safety of property owned by Ottoman subjects.) As long as they could find (or sometimes plant) the smallest scrap of infidel merchandise aboard a ship, the pirates regarded themselves as Christian crusaders.

With a total fighting force estimated at 1,000 to 2,000, the Uskoks controlled the entire coast of the Adriatic down to Dubrovnik. The pirates rarely operated far from land and continued to rely on small boats. But their squadrons now included a dozen or more vessels carrying hundreds of men, and they often captured large galleys and GALLEONS as well as smaller coastal traders. Between 1592 and 1600, Venetian companies alone lost more than 30 ships, most of considerable size.

The entire population of Senj financed raids and shared in the profits, with one-tenth reserved for the clergy. Unhappy with their Ottoman and Venetian overlords, other coastal communities cooperated with the Uskoks, who savagely punished anyone who betrayed them. Spies along the coast and in Venice itself notified the Uskoks when merchant vessels departed. If by chance they ran into a Venetian naval force, they fled inland to hiding places prepared by their supporters.

Since a conspiracy of silence protected them, we rarely know the names of individual Uskok captains. New refugees continued to arrive from the Ottoman zone, and Uskok successes attracted adventurers, criminals fleeing punishment, and deserters from the Venetian fleet. Only Muslims were unwelcome; and Greeks, Albanians, and Italians joined the pirates. One band, hanged in Venice in 1618, included nine Englishmen, six of high social rank.

Their enemies describe the Uskoks as both pious Christians and bloodthirsty killers in league with the devil. In 1601, a Venetian spy reported, the people of Senj crawled to the churches on their bare knees to give thanks for their uninterrupted robberies. Priests and monks, who sometimes sailed with the pirates, preached sermons whipping the people into a frenzy. Wives incited their husbands and children to violence, and the Uskoks were said to eat the living hearts of their victims. (EXQUEMELIN told the same story about François L'OLONNAIS.)

Only a full-scale military invasion could have crushed the base at Senj. The Uskoks were protected by both official corruption and Austrian rivalry with Venice. They regularly bribed Habsburg officials at Graz, where merchants saw great ladies wearing jewels that had been snatched by pirates. By tolerating the Uskoks, the Austrians upset Venetian-Ottoman relations, damaged Ottoman subjects, and inexpensively affirmed their sovereignty over part of the coast. Austria did send a small force to Senj in 1580, but the unpaid troopers soon deserted to the pirates.

Venetian naval commanders immediately cut off the heads of any Uskoks they could catch. But other officials marketed their prizes, and Venice hesitated to mount an invasion, which might lead to war with Austria and also invite Ottoman intervention. In 1600, as the Uskoks grew bolder, the Venetians took advantage of a Habsburg-Ottoman war (1593–1606) to burn several towns and massacre their inhabitants. However, Venice did not occupy Senj or sink the main Uskok flotilla.

After lying low for a few years, the pirates again raided throughout the Adriatic as far south as Brindisi. Venice took more aggressive action from 1611, blockading Trieste and Fiume and seizing several ports further south. In 1615, the Uskoks provided the pretext for a full-scale war between Venice and Austria. The Venetians imported Protestant mercenaries from Britain, Holland, and Germany. Austria received Spanish troops, and the Spanish viceroy of Naples sent a fleet into the Adriatic. (The viceroy may have conspired with Jacques PIERRE to seize Venice.)

Faced with more serious wars elsewhere, Austria made peace with Venice in 1618. The Uskoks at Senj were expelled or transferred inland into Croatia. Their removal eliminated piracy in the northern Adriatic, although smaller bands still operated from Ottoman territories to the south.

(See also BRAZZERE; FERLETICH, ANDREAS; SELECTED BIBLIOGRAPHY: Gracewell, *Uskoks;* Tenenti, *Piracy;* West, *Black Lamb.*)

USSEIN REIS *(Barbary corsair; Mediterranean; active 1620s)* The KNIGHTS OF MALTA captured Ussein's 24-gun sailing ship in 1621 and enslaved him at the oars. Ransomed by his wealthy family at TUNIS, he again was captured in 1624 (by Francis de CRÉMEAULX), while commanding the Tunisian flagship.

USTA (OSTA) MURAT *(Barbary corsair; Mediterranean; 1640)* Usta Murat was a Genoese RENEGADE captured as a youth in the Near East. By the 1590s, Murat was a protégé of the Tunisian ruler, Uthman Dey. He remained scrupulously loyal to Uthman's successor, Yusuf Dey. At TUNIS, political power was disputed between the corsair captains and the JANISSARY soldiers. Murat managed to win the esteem of both factions, and he was the only corsair to become ruler of Tunis. (Usta is an honorific title meaning "Master.")

A very successful pirate, Murat became rich by selling and ransoming captured Christians. As "General of the Galleys" at Bizerte (home port of the Tunisian state fleet) from 1615, Murat led audacious raids on Italy and Sicily. In 1625, his squadron captured two galleys from the KNIGHTS OF MALTA during a pitched battle off Syracuse. He commanded the Tunisian forces during a war with ALGIERS in 1628, and was elected DEY in 1637.

(See also BARBARY STATES.)

UTHMAN REIS *(Barbary corsair; Mediterranean; active 1680s)* Uthman was captain of the *Golden Sun,* a French prize taken off Crete. After several unsuccessful voyages, he traveled to Albania as a merchant's employee and then was named captain of the port at TRIPOLI.

UYTGEEST, DIRCK SIMONSZOON VAN *(Dutch captain; Atlantic; 1627)* Raiding along the Brazilian coast for the DUTCH WEST INDIA COMPANY, Uytgeest took at least a dozen Spanish and Portuguese prizes but lost two vessels from his 12-ship squadron.

(See also JOL, CORNELIS.)

UZUN IBRAHIM REIS *(Barbary corsair; Mediterranean; active 1676–1679)* Captain (in 1676) of the *Europa*—captured near Venice—and (in 1679) of the *Sun,* a 40-gun warship based at Tripoli.

UZUN REIS *(Barbary corsair; Mediterranean; 1679)* Born to a Turkish father and a Libyan mother, Uzun commanded the *Dolphin,* a six-gun Maltese prize in the TRIPOLI fleet.

V

VAIS, MICHEL (French pirate; Mediterranean; early 1600s)
With Pierre d'ORANGE, Vais chartered a French ship and captured two Venetian merchantmen about 1600 or 1601. The count of Lemos, the Sicilian viceroy, received 30,000 ducats, while his wife took an equal amount. The viceroy subsequently treated Vais as an intimate friend, and he commanded a squadron of GALLEONS. Vais also owned a merchantman, which the Venetians rescued from five "Muslim" corsair vessels in 1602. To punish Vais' piracies, the Venetian captain sold this ship and cargo and kept the receipts for his crew.

VALDIVIESSA E MALDONATO, GUY BOREL (Spanish corsair; Mediterranean; 1504)
Valdiviessa's ship captured a high-ranking officer of Kurkut Chelebi (son of the OTTOMAN sultan and governor of southern Turkey). Taken as a slave to RHODES, the captive escaped but fell into the sea and drowned.

VALENTINE (VAUGHAN), WILLIAM (English pirate; Atlantic; active 1582–1583)
Often using the alias Vaughan (Baugh), Valentine sailed from harbors in Dorsetshire and Wales. In 1582, he and Stephen HEYNES pillaged a rich German prize and tortured her crew. The next year, he captured a ship carrying Bibles. He gave them as gifts to Anglican priests and to Francis HAWLEY, a deputy VICE-ADMIRAL. Valentine was captured in 1583, tortured to discover his accomplices, and hanged in London.

VALI REIS (Barbary corsair; Mediterranean; 1684)
Vali was lieutenant to the commander of TRIPOLI's garrison and captain of the *Infant Jesus*, a French vessel taken near MALTA.

VANE, CHARLES (British pirate; Caribbean and Atlantic; died 1719)
Among the Jamaicans raiding Spanish wrecks with Henry JENNINGS in 1716, Vane later cruised from NEW PROVIDENCE ISLAND in the Bahamas. Most Providence pirates accepted a pardon when Woodes ROGERS arrived in August 1718. But Vane had just taken a French merchantman and wanted to keep his plunder. He set fire to his prize and sent it toward Rogers' ships, which escaped to sea. As they fled, Vane sailed away in a BRIGANTINE with much of his loot.

Soon after, Vane seized a SLOOP and gave command to Captain YEATS. The pirates looted four ships near South Carolina, but Yeats quarreled with Vane and deserted. While he was chasing Yeats, Vane captured two more ships.

Two sloops sent to arrest Stede BONNET looked for Vane in September. He escaped with his prizes to Green Turtle Cay near Abaco, arriving on about September 23. On the way, according to some accounts, Vane stopped to visit Edward TEACH at Ocracoke, North Carolina. During the largest pirate gathering in North America, his crew and Teach's enjoyed several days of feasting and DRINKING.

354

Vane pillaged two ships off Long Island, New York, in early November and then cruised south to the Windward Passage between Haiti and Cuba. In February or March 1719, he seized the London ship *Kingston*, and John RACKHAM became its captain. Vane and Rackham quarreled and parted because Rackham refused to share the liquor found on the *Kingston*. After taking several more prizes, Vane went to the Bay of Honduras. A storm caught his ship and wrecked it on a small island. A captain stopping for fresh water recognized Vane and took him to Jamaica, where he was hanged in November.

VAN HORN, NICHOLAS (Dutch buccaneer; Atlantic, Caribbean; active 1681–1683)
Late in 1681, Horn left England in command of a merchant ship. At Cadiz, he put his passengers ashore and stole four Spanish cannon. He then sailed to the Canaries and along the African coast, plundering ships and stealing slaves. After unsuccessfully trying to sell his slaves at Santo Domingo, he went to PETIT GOÂVE (now in Haiti) in November 1682, picked up 300 men, and joined a squadron under Laurens de GRAFF.

In May 1683, the pirates thoroughly sacked Veracruz, Mexico, taking 800,000 pesos in booty. Horn is said to have received 2,400 pesos. He and Graff, who were on bad terms, quarrelled over the division of the booty. They crossed swords, and Horn was wounded on the wrist. The wound seemed so slight that Horn proposed an attack on a nearby Spanish fleet, offering to board the flagship himself. He died of gangrene two weeks later, and willed his ship to Michel de GRAMMONT.

(See also SELECTED BIBLIOGRAPHY: Haring, *Buccaneers*.)

VARGAS, JUAN DE (Spanish pirate; Mediterranean; 1555)
Commanding a GALIOT sponsored by the son of the Spanish viceroy of Sicily, Vargas sacked several ships in Cretan ports.

VENETIAN CLAIMS (pirate raids; Aegean Sea; 1267–1277)
By a treaty in 1277, Venice and the Byzantine emperor, MICHAEL VIII PALAEOLOGUS, agreed to compensate each other's subjects for acts of piracy during the previous 10 years. In March 1278, Venice sent a list of 271 individual cases submitted to its courts. The Venetian merchants claimed enormous (and possibly exaggerated) damages for attacks by Italian and Greek corsairs, often licensed as PRIVATEERS by the emperor. Judging by this list, the most active were Giovanni de Lo CAVO, Andrea GAFFORIO, Giovanni SENZARAXON, and ROLANDO OF THESSALONICA.

VENEZIANO REIS (Moroccan corsair; Mediterranean; active 1680s)
An Italian sailing from SALÉ, Veneziano was noted for his audacity and mastered a much larger English ship during a fierce battle in 1683.

VENIER FAMILY (Venetian pirates; Aegean; 13th and 14th centuries)
A large Venetian clan with extensive properties in Greece and Crete. One branch ruled the island of Cerigo just south of Greece until 1364 and joined their subjects in piracy. Wars that pitted Venice against Pisa and the CATALAN COMPANY made their assaults legal during some years, but they remained zealous raiders during times of truce. In 1335 and 1340, they refused to appear before the Venetian Senate to answer the charges against them.

VERNEY, SIR FRANCIS (Barbary corsair; Mediterranean; 1584–1615)
Verney was an Oxford graduate and the eldest son of Sir Edmund Verney (died 1599). Tricked out of an inheritance by his stepmother, he sold his estates in 1606 and wandered about Europe. By 1608, he was in ALGIERS, a convert to Islam. His prizes included English merchant vessels—one carrying French wine for the king's table. Captured by a Sicilian corsair, he spent two years as a GALLEY SLAVE, was ransomed by an English Jesuit about 1611, and died in poverty at a hospital at Messina, Italy.

VETRANO, LEONE (Genoese corsair; Adriatic, Mediterranean; 1206)
Making himself lord of Corfu, Vetrano pillaged Venetian shipping as far south as Crete. In 1206, a Venetian naval force sent to expel Enrico PESCATORE from Crete stopped at Corfu, defeated Vetrano's troops, and hanged him.

(See also IONIAN ISLANDS; MARGARITONE.)

VICE-ADMIRALS (British officials; about 1525–1890)
The LORD HIGH ADMIRAL had jurisdiction over everything at sea, and cases were tried by his ADMIRALTY COURT sitting in London. From about 1525, vice-admirals represented the admiral in coastal counties. After 1673 (or when there was no admiral), the king directly appointed vice-admirals. They collected fees for the admiral and the king, and they also enforced the laws regarding PRIVATEERING and piracy. However, some vice-admirals took bribes from raiders or were themselves pirates.

Beginning with the Spanish War (1585–1603), vice-admiralty officials supervised private warships with royal commissions (letters of REPRISAL). They collected cash bonds from owners and captains as security for their good behavior. They inventoried and appraised prizes and booty, collected the government's share, and enforced decisions by the Admiralty Court when there were disputes over booty.

Vice-admirals also were expected to fight piracy. They supposedly checked all cargoes brought into port and arrested persons accused of piracy. When the Admiralty Court ruled that goods had been taken illegally, vice-admiralty officials were ordered to return them to their owners.

Piracy flourished in 16th-century England with the active support of many vice-admirals. While vice-admiral of Cornwall, Sir Peter CAREW personally raided merchant shipping, and Sir John KILLIGREW fenced pirate plunder. In Wales, Vice-Admiral George Herbert trafficked with

John CALLICE and sold a ship to Simâo FERNANDES. During the Spanish War, vice-admirals often ignored the rules governing privateering. Sir Walter RALEIGH was vice-admiral of Devonshire and sometimes of Cornwall, and Sir George CAREY served in Hampshire. Using their offices, they fenced the spoils when captains plundered a ship from a friendly nation.

Vice-admiralty officials continued to sponsor piracy after the war ended. As vice-admiral of Devonshire from 1603 to 1610, Sir Richard HAWKINS conspired with almost every pirate of note. When pirates fell into his hands, Hawkins simply took their loot and released them. He also sold them blank pardons for use at a later date.

Piracy from England decreased only when raiders moved their operations to the Caribbean and North America. Since colonial governors connived with pirates, vice-admiralty courts were erected in nearly all the colonies from about 1700. Some early vice-admirals were as corrupt as their English predecessors. The North Carolina court allowed Edward TEACH (BLACKBEARD) to keep captured English and French vessels. From the 1720s, however, most courts were at least honest, if not always efficient.

VIGNOLI, VIGNOLO DE (Italian pirate; Mediterranean; active 1300–1306)
A native of Genoa, Vignoli preyed on shipping and raided Cyprus from RHODES, where he owned a small castle. In 1306, he commanded the ships on which the KNIGHTS HOSPITALERS invaded Rhodes, then under BYZANTINE rule. Prior to embarking, Vignoli and the order's grand master drew up an ambitious plan to conquer the Aegean islands. Their scheme fell through, the Hospitalers took only Rhodes, and Vignoli got nothing.

"VILLANY REWARDED" (ballad; 1696)
Eight four-line stanzas that celebrate the hanging of six of Henry EVERY's men. The pirates confess (inaccurately) to slaughtering their victims.

> Thus for some time we liv'd and reigned as masters of
> the sea;
> Every merchant we detain'd and us'd most cruelly.
> Their treasures too, we sunk the ship, and those that
> in it were
> That would not unto us submit. Let pirates then
> take care.

(See also "COPY OF VERSES.")

VINCENT DE PAUL, SAINT (French priest; 1581–1660)
Saint Vincent de Paul was founder of the LAZARISTS, a Roman Catholic order active among Christian slaves in ALGIERS and TUNIS. There is no evidence about two years (1605–1606) in Saint Vincent's early life. Writing to a patron in 1606 and 1607, he claimed that BARBARY corsairs had captured and enslaved him at Tunis. He escaped with his last master—a French RENEGADE who wanted to return home—by sailing a small open boat more than 1,000 miles to France. The renegade and his wife had repented after hearing Vincent chant Christian prayers.

Most historians do not believe this story. Saint Vincent later tried to destroy these letters, and he never mentioned the alleged captivity in subsequent writings or recorded conversations.

(See also SELECTED BIBLIOGRAPHY: Clissold, *Barbary*.)

VINCIGUERRA, GIACOMO (Knight of Malta; Mediterranean; active 1599–1609)
Already considered an expert on the Levant, Vinciguerra helped raid Egypt and the BARBARY COAST in 1599. Early in 1601, he joined in a joint raid by Maltese and Neapolitan squadrons. Soon after, with two large BERTONES financed by the wife of Naples's Spanish viceroy, he and Ferdinando d'ARAGONA captured two richly laden Venetian ships. They plundered the first, enslaving Muslims and Jews and leaving the Christians naked. The second was taken back to Naples, where the pirates were greeted as great heroes.

In January 1603, Vinciguerra took part in a massive Maltese raid on Greece led by Ascanio CAMBIANO. He commanded a smaller squadron that raided Muslim shipping in the Aegean in 1604. In 1609, after Simon SIMONSON absconded with large sums, ALGIERS launched savage assaults on French shipping. The city of Marseilles made Vinciguerra one of two commanders of her war galleys. In 1617, he took five large sailing ships and 1,500 soldiers to TUNIS, forcing its rulers to sign a short-lived peace treaty with Marseilles.

VOYAGES AND ADVENTURES OF CAPTAIN ROBERT BOYLE, THE (novel; 1726)
Sometimes attributed to Daniel DEFOE but probably written by William CHETWOOD. The cynical hero turns pirate after escaping from BARBARY corsairs.

Orphaned at the age of 10, Robert Boyle is bullied by his master's adulterous wife. A wicked uncle steals his inheritance and sends him to sea. Captured by an Irish RENEGADE, he is enslaved at SALÉ in Morocco. There Boyle gains his master's affection by building a complicated fountain. By drugging his keepers, he escapes in a small boat with an Italian and a beautiful French woman. A ship carrying the French ambassador rescues the party and carries them to MAMORA. Boyle and the French woman declare themselves married and consummate their passion.

Separated from his mistress by a servant's treason, Boyle goes to Rome with his Italian companion. The Italian's father gives Boyle a ship, which he takes to South America's Pacific coast (meeting William DAMPIER along the way). Boyle captures many Spanish prizes, returns to England, and buys a country estate. One day, he rescues a woman from attackers and a child from gypsies. The woman is his long-lost mistress, the child is the result of their brief union.

W

WAFER, LIONEL (English buccaneer and scientist; Pacific, Caribbean; 1660?–1705?)

Wafer took part in two plunder voyages along South America's Pacific coast between 1680 and 1688. His *New Voyage*, published in 1699, focuses on four months spent with the Cuna Indians in 1681. Scientists still study Wafer's accurate description of Panama's natural environment and the Cuna way of life. But the *New Voyage* is more than a catalog. Like EXQUEMELIN, Wafer carefully selected telling details that make incidents come alive.

Wafer sailed to East Asia in 1677 as servant to a ship's doctor and returned to England early in 1679. He again shipped as a surgeon's assistant but deserted in Jamaica. Enjoying little success as a physician, he joined Edmund COOK's small pirate crew as ship's doctor. Off the Panamanian coast in February 1680, Cook ran into Bartholomew SHARP and other captains, who had just sacked Portobelo. Cook (and Wafer) joined their company, which crossed over to the Pacific and defeated a Spanish squadron on May 3. Soon after, a group under John COXON went back across the isthmus, while the rest sailed in the *Trinity*.

Quarrels continued as Richard SAWKINS, Sharp, and John WATLING took turns as commander. The *Trinity* voyaged far to the south, looting several towns but taking only moderate booty. When Sharp was reelected captain in February 1681, 47 buccaneers elected to return home with John COOK. Wafer and William DAMPIER accompanied this group. Leaving Ecuador on April 27, the men reached Panama on May 11 and began the land journey.

On the fifth day, a careless buccaneer, drying some gunpowder on a silver plate, caused an explosion that burned Wafer's knee to the bone. When gangrene set in, he threw himself on the mercy of the Cuna Indians. Exhausted by the march, John HINGSON, Richard GOPSON, and two others stayed with him.

The Cuna tribesmen cured Wafer in only 20 days by chewing herbs and applying the paste to his wound. But many were hostile because the main group of buccaneers had kidnapped several Indians as guides. The Cuna waited a month and then prepared to burn the Englishmen alive. Fortunately, Chief Lacenta passed by and suggested that Dampier's party go north for news. After an agonizing eight-day march with no food, they learned that Captain Cook had sent the Cuna guides back with generous pay.

Wafer went on to Lacenta's palace, where he cured one of the chief's wives by skillful bleeding. Lacenta became Wafer's warm friend, showered him with gifts, and insisted he stay with the Cuna. Wafer won his freedom only by promising to marry one of Lacenta's daughters after returning with English hunting dogs.

Wafer and his four companions reached the Caribbean a week later. After briefly rejoining Dampier, he moved to Captain YANKY's ship with John Cook. Cook and Edward DAVIS seized a French vessel, renamed it the

The wounded Lionel Wafer was rescued by Chief Lacenta of the Cuna Indians in southern Panama. Lacenta, his wife, and his warriors are shown dressed in their finest necklaces and nose-rings for a feast or ceremonial visit. From Wafer's *New Voyage* (1699).

Revenge, and rejoined Dampier in Virginia in April 1683. (Jamaica no longer tolerated pirates.)

In August 1683, Wafer and Dampier set out on a new raid with John Cook as captain. Cook stole the *Batchelor's Delight* in Africa, sailed around Cape Horn, and reached the Pacific in March 1684. Wafer remained with the *Delight* under Cook and later under Edward Davis during four years of raids from Chile to Nicaragua.

The *Delight* made it back to the West Indies early in 1688. Wafer, Edward Davis, and John Hingson went on to Virginia, where they were arrested and jailed. The governor freed them in July 1690 under a royal proclamation pardoning pirates. Their property was not returned until 1694, and part was kept to build the College of William and Mary. A legal document lists Wafer's booty after almost 11 years as a pirate: 1,158 silver pesos, 162 pounds of silver, 1½ ounces of gold, and cloth worth £40.

Wafer settled in London in 1690 and wrote an account of his adventures. Dampier's *Voyage Around the World* appeared in 1697 and became immensely popular. Efforts to set up a Scottish colony in eastern Panama also aroused public interest. Published in 1699 as a sequel to Dampier's book, Wafer's *New Voyage* was a success although not a best-seller.

(See also BASIL RINGROSE; RAVENEAU DE LUSSAN; SE-LECTED BIBLIOGRAPHY: Severin, *Golden;* Wafer, *New Voyage.*)

WAKE (WEAK), THOMAS   *(British pirate; Atlantic, Red Sea; died 1696)*   Wake's earlier piracies

were pardoned about 1688, and he became a captain at Boston. In November 1694, he sailed from Rhode Island in consort with Thomas TEW and joined Henry EVERY in the Red Sea. Wake had no luck, but Every gave him a small share from his rich prize. He returned to SAINT MARY'S ISLAND near MADAGASCAR in October 1695 and died of disease the following April.

WALDEN, JOHN   *(English pirate; Atlantic, Caribbean; 1699?–1723)*   Walden was among the crew of a fishing vessel plundered by Bartholomew ROBERTS during the summer of 1720. An expert seaman, a reckless fighter, and a good-looking man, he became Roberts' confidant and bedfellow. Behind his back the crew called him "Miss Nanny," which was 18th-century slang for a passive homosexual.

After they were arrested, many pirates blamed Walden for burning alive 80 black slaves. In January 1722, Roberts captured 11 ships loading slaves at Whydah (Ouidah) in western Africa. A Portuguese captain refused to ransom his vessel, and Roberts sent boats to carry the slaves to his own ships. Deciding that unshackling the slaves was taking too long, Walden and others burned the Portuguese ship while many were still in chains.

Walden's leg was struck off as the pirates battled the British warship *Swallow* in February. He was tried and hanged at Cape Coast, Ghana.

(See also SELECTED BIBLIOGRAPHY: Richards, *Black Bart.*)

Walking the plank. Illustration by Howard Pyle in *Harper's Monthly Magazine*, September 1887.

WALK THE PLANK *(fictional pirate practice; Caribbean; 17th and 18th centuries)*

One legend about Caribbean piracy describes a cruel punishment called "walking the plank." The pirates blindfolded the victim, tied his hands behind him, and stood him upon a plank cocked over the gunwale. Telling him to step out, they either let him fall off or shot him on route to his watery grave.

No contemporary description of a BUCCANEER raid mentions this bizarre practice. Pirates did not kill off people who could be useful to them. They often talked captured crew members into joining their band, and they might force reluctant prisoners to serve them. They were more severe in their treatment of captured officers, sometimes MAROONING or feeding them to the sharks. Pirates TORTURED captives to make them reveal the location of hidden riches. But they did not make them walk the plank.

This myth became popular during the 19th century. Several famous illustrators, including Howard PYLE, showed fiendish buccaneers goading a blindfolded captive to the end of a wooden plank.

During the first century B.C., the CILICIAN pirates terrorized the Mediterranean. According to the historian Plutarch (about A.D. 100), these pirates terrorized arrogant Romans by telling them to walk home across the ocean. However, Plutarch wrote that the ancient corsairs used a ladder and not a plank during their game. Plutarch's story was retold by Daniel DEFOE in his GENERAL HISTORY.

Nineteenth-century pirate buffs avidly read Defoe's works. One of them transferred this tale from ancient Rome to the 17th-century Caribbean. Adding the plank and the blindfold was a stroke of inspired fancy and vicarious sadism.

(See also BRAND, CAPTAIN.)

WALL, GEORGE *(American pirate; Atlantic; active 1780s)*

With his wife, Rachel WALL, and a few crewmen, George Wall sailed from Massachusetts in a SCHOONER and captured other small ships by trickery. The brigands anchored in a safe harbor during storms. After the weather cleared, they disarranged the sails and spars and hoisted a distress signal. Conspicuously dressed in female garb, Rachel stood on deck, looking like a pathetic survivor on a storm-battered hulk.

On several occasions, a small coastal vessel stopped to offer help. The pirates killed the crewmen, transferred the cargo, and sank the ship. Their cruel game ended when they misjudged the strength of a storm. George and one other crewman were killed, and their schooner was turned into a genuine wreck.

WALL, RACHEL *(American pirate; Atlantic; died 1789)*

Rachel was the wife of George WALL. After he died, she returned to Boston, worked as a servant, and was convicted of robbery. At the gallows, she confessed to piracy and various thefts on land but denied the specific crime for which she was hanged.

WALSINGHAM, ROBERT *(English pirate; Atlantic, Mediterranean; active 1613–1618)*

Walsingham was one of Henry MAINWARING's captains at MAMORA in Morocco. After the Spanish seized Mamora in 1614, he followed Mainwaring to Villefranche and took Spanish prizes worth a million crowns in only six weeks. When Mainwaring returned to England in 1615, Walsingham joined the corsairs at ALGIERS and captured a British ship. He fled from Algiers and surrendered in Ireland with his men in 1618.

WALTON, THOMAS *(English pirate; Atlantic; active 1581–1583)*

A native of Norwich, Walton (alias Purser) sailed from Dorsetshire and Wales. He was on bad terms with some of his fellow pirates. About 1581, William VAUGHN and another captain fired at Walton's ship and drove him from Studland Bay. In 1582, he lost a captured ship and loot to Anthony STYLES in a Welsh port, but rejoined his own warship at Lundy Island.

Soon afterward, sailing in consort with a Captain Ellis, Walton captured a much larger French vessel laden with Newfoundland fish. Walton traded fish for cattle and bread at Studland and then repaired his prize at Baltimore, Ireland. In 1583, he attacked English and French ships in Weymouth Road and captured a French

BARK. The outraged townsmen slew seven of his men and maimed others.

WANT, WILLIAM (British pirate; Atlantic, Red Sea; active 1693–1695)

Commanding the *Dolphin*, Want sailed from Philadelphia about January 1694 and joined Henry EVERY's squadron in the Red Sea in June 1695. The *Dolphin*, in poor shape, was burned. Her crew enlisted with Every and helped plunder two Indian treasure ships. Soon after, Want somehow acquired another vessel and went cruising in the Persian Gulf.

WARD, JOHN (English pirate; Caribbean, Mediterranean; 1553–1623)

Said to be "a poore Fisher's brat from Kent," Ward was jailed in 1602 for plundering a Danish ship in the Caribbean. In 1603, he was impressed into the navy, deserted with 30 others, and helped steal a small BARK at Plymouth. The gang captured a larger vessel and then took a six-gun French ship.

Ward made himself the band's leader and sailed into the eastern Mediterranean. During the next two years, his pirates captured a 32-gun warship, renamed the *Gift*, as well as Italian, Flemish, and Dutch merchantmen loaded with spices and silks. In 1605, while he was at SALÉ, Morocco, many English and Dutch sailors joined his crew, including Richard BISHOP and Anthony Johnson.

By August 1606, Ward had come to terms with Uthman Dey, ruler of TUNIS. From this new haven, his squadron took rich Venetian prizes, including the *Reniera e Soderina*, a 600-ton sailing vessel carrying £100,000 in cargo. Ward's pirates returned in June 1607 as rich men, even though Uthman Dey bought their booty for one-fifth of its true value. Ward was now at the height of his success and notoriety. In June 1608, an English seaman described him as

> Very short with little hair, and that quite white, bald in front; swarthy face and beard. Speaks little, and almost always swearing. Drunk from morn till night. Most prodigal and plucky. Sleeps a great deal, and often on board when in port. The habits of a thorough "Salt." A fool and an idiot out of his trade.

A series of disasters struck Ward's squadron during the winter of 1607. When the *Soderina* began to rot, Ward deserted his men and secretly transferred himself and some close friends to a new French prize. The *Soderina* sank off Greece, killing 250 Muslim and 150 English sailors. Soon after, his French prize was lost at sea, and the Venetians captured two warships commanded by Jan CARSTEN, one of his leading captains.

The *Soderina* disaster naturally outraged the Tunisians, although Uthman Dey protected Ward. He apparently thought of returning to England in 1608 and offered King James I £40,000 for a pardon. The scheme fell through because the Venetians insisted that Ward also reimburse their losses.

Ward made himself at home in Tunis, converting as Yusuf Reis and taking part in raids until 1622, when he was close to 70. He married an Italian (but also sent money to his English wife) and lived in great luxury until his death, probably of the plague. In 1615, he entertained William Lithgow, a Scotch traveler, in a "faire Palace beautified with rich Marble and Alabaster stones." They were served by 15 English servants, all circumcised converts to Islam.

The English idolized the PRIVATEERS who attacked Spanish shipping under Elizabeth I. But they loathed corsairs sailing from the Barbary states, who attacked English ships and rejected Christianity. Ward's well-known exploits made him especially hated, and he was viciously attacked in pamphlets and ballads that probably exaggerated his crimes. At least twice, Ward freed Englishmen enslaved at Tunis. Lithgow, who harshly criticized other RENEGADES, wrote of him as "Generous Waird."

(See also "SEAMAN'S SONG OF CAPTAIN WARD, THE"; SELECTED BIBLIOGRAPHY: Senior, *Nation*.)

WATER WITCH, THE; OR THE SKIMMER OF SEAS (novel; 1830)

James Fenimore COOPER's historical novel refers both to CAPTAIN KIDD'S TREASURE and to the trade between New York merchants and the MADAGASCAR pirates. The complicated plot includes a ghostly ship, perhaps modeled on legends of the *Flying Dutchman*.

During the early 1710s, Alderman Van Beverout receives smuggled goods at Lust in Rust, his summer house on the Jersey Shore. He deals mainly with Tom Tiller, the "Skimmer of the Seas," whose *Water Witch* magically eludes all pursuers. The vessel owes her name and safety to a green-clad female figurehead with a malign smile. The figurehead, which answers questions through a metal book, may embody a goddess or spirit. At moments of danger, the long, graceful, black ship vanishes. Nothing is seen but the illuminated face of the figurehead, which finally also disappears.

Van Beverout's contact with the freebooters is an effeminate youth named Seadrift, who turns out to be his illegitimate daughter in disguise. When her secret is revealed, the female smuggler marries Tom Tiller. Throughout, Tiller is an unusually mild-mannered and gentle outlaw. Both physically and mentally strong, he combines daring courage with moods of poetic melancholy. His crimes are forgivable, Cooper suggests. As a smuggler, he breaks immoral laws that enrich Britain but harm the American colonists.

WATLING, JOHN (English buccaneer; Caribbean, Pacific; died 1681)

Watling apparently gave his name to Watling's Island (San Salvador) in the Bahamas, where Columbus first landed in 1492. He was among those invading South America's Pacific coast in 1680. In January 1681, the raiders reached the JUAN FERNÁNDEZ ISLANDS, west of Chile. Captain Bartholomew SHARP planned to return home around Cape Horn. Since many crewmen wanted to keep on raiding in the Pacific, they threw out Sharp and elected Watling commander.

Watling was a religious zealot, and he began his rule by imposing Sunday prayer, throwing the dice overboard, and imprisoning Edmund COOK for sodomy. On February 9, he died during a disastrous assault on Arica, Chile. The town's inhabitants killed or wounded half of the 90 pirates.

WATTS, SIR JOHN *(English sponsor of piracy; Atlantic, Caribbean; 1550?–1616)* Since Watts did not personally command his vessels, the Venetian ambassador was perhaps unfair in calling him "the greatest pirate that has ever been in this kingdom." But he was certainly the greatest promoter of piracy by others.

Watts became a merchant and shipowner by marrying the daughter of the mayor of London. When the Spanish arrested English ships in their ports in 1585, the ADMIRALTY COURT granted him letters of REPRISAL. Until privateering was outlawed in 1603, his powerful warships, singly and in substantial fleets, continuously warred on Spanish shipping and coastal ports.

Many prominent captains worked for Watts, including Thomas LANE, Christopher NEWPORT, and Michael GEARE. In addition to sponsoring his own expeditions, Watts' ships joined Sir Francis DRAKE's raid against Cadiz (1587), James LANCASTER's Brazilian venture (1595), and the earl of CUMBERLAND's invasion of Puerto Rico (1598).

Although Watts made immense profits from these privateering cruises, he also diversified into more peaceful ventures. He joined the Levant Company in 1592 and was governor of the East India Company in 1601. He was an active member of the Virginia Company, and his ships brought tobacco from Guyana in 1610. He was knighted in 1603, was lord mayor of London in 1606, entertained King James I in 1607, and left his eldest son extensive landed estates.

(See also SELECTED BIBLIOGRAPHY: Andrews, *Elizabethan.*)

WEAPONS *(pirate tools; all oceans; all eras)* Although they tended to use the same weapons, pirates used them differently and sometimes better than naval forces. Pirates wanted to loot the enemy vessel, and they often kept it to sell or for their own use. Unlike a warship, pirates did not try to sink the enemy, but had to close in and board. Pirate ships carried heavy weapons, such as catapults, rock-throwers, and CANNON. But these were used only to frighten the enemy or for self-defense. Cannon duels were rare, since pirates simply sailed away when attacked by a warship.

Once they boarded their victims, pirates relied on swords and spears, even after the adoption of gunpowder. Until the 19th century, firearms usually fired only one shot, could not be rapidly reloaded, and were extremely inaccurate. During battle, anyone firing across a crowded deck was as likely to hit one of his comrades as the

Using the weapons of that era, 16th-century English raiders in the Caribbean repel boarders attacking from a Spanish warship. Illustration by Charles Brock for an 1896 edition of Charles Kingsley's novel *Westward Ho!*

enemy. Guns, gunpowder, and matches easily get wet at sea and become useless.

The BARBARY corsairs used bows and arrows well into the 18th century because these fired more rapidly and accurately than guns. After boarding, they fought with the scimitar, a curved sword sharpened on the outer edge. The KNIGHTS OF MALTA and other Christian raiders in the Mediterranean used MUSKETS rather than bows. After boarding, they relied on bludgeons, CUTLASSES, and occasionally rapiers.

Arab raiders in the Persian Gulf also favored the scimitar. Malayan and DYAK pirates used spears and the *kris*, a short sword with a wavy, double-edged blade. A distinctive weapon was the *kampilan*, a large sword whose blade curved sharply during the final third of its length. This was wielded with two hands and brought down with a sweeping motion on the foe's skull or shoulder, ensuring death at a single blow.

The matchlock musket was the main weapon of the Caribbean BUCCANEERS, many of whom also were hunters. To enhance accuracy, this had a smooth-bore barrel more than four feet long; it fired 60-caliber lead balls weighing an ounce. A few carried large-caliber flintlock pistols, accurate only at short distances. Once aboard the enemy, Caribbean pirates attacked with boarding axes, PIKES (long spears), knives, machetes, and cutlasses.

While none of their guns were rifled, the buccaneers reportedly were expert marksmen. EXQUEMELIN wrote that they devoted their time to "target-shooting and keeping their guns clean." They probably were better shots than untrained Spanish militiamen, who often still carried the ARQUEBUS, an earlier version of the musket. However, Spanish troops poured down accurate and deadly musket fire when Joseph BRADLEY assaulted the fortresses at Chagres in 1671.

Muskets were less important among the pirates sailing from MADAGASCAR or NEW PROVIDENCE ISLAND during the early 17th century. Pistols remained common, and the cutlass replaced the machete. Some raiders also used GRENADES, although these risked setting fire to the prey.

Early SWASHBUCKLER movies give a true picture of pirate tactics, given the inaccuracy of smooth-bore cannon and muskets. In *The* BLACK PIRATE (1926) and both versions of CAPTAIN BLOOD (1924, 1935), the pirates storm the enemy's deck and fight hand to hand. Since he cannot hit them at any distance, Blood bravely sails right between two French ships.

Some later films take more liberties. Before they are captured in Panama, the English raiders in *The* SEA HAWK (1942) are attacked by Spanish troops, who repeatedly fire their muskets without reloading. The cannon fire is too accurate in CAPTAIN KIDD (1945) and BLACKBEARD THE PIRATE (1952). However, no film makes the mistake of showing a ship sunk at long range.

Almost every pirate movie shows at least one SWORD DUEL. Often, the two opponents adopt a fencing stance and thrust at each other with thin foils pointed only at the tip. European nobles adopted this difficult weapon only from the 1660s, and its mastery required years of practice. Both navies and pirates continued to prefer the more versatile cutlass, a heavy slashing weapon sharpened on the edge as well as the point.

(See also BLUNDERBUSS; SHIPS, PIRATE; SELECTED BIBLIOGRAPHY: Exquemelin, *Buccaneers*.)

WEERT, SEBALD DE *(Dutch captain; Pacific; active 1598–1600)* Weert commanded one of five warships during the first Dutch raid on South America, led by Simon de CORDES. After a disastrous crossing, Weert was separated from the rest of the fleet. With most of his men dead, and the rest near mutiny, Weert returned to the Netherlands in July 1600. Thirty-six of 109 crewmen survived, the only members of the original fleet to make it home from this unlucky venture.

WENAMON *(Egyptian traveler; Mediterranean; 12th century B.C.)* A papyrus manuscript, written about 1100 B.C., contains the travel journal of Wenamon, a priest in Amon's temple at Karnak. Found during the 19th century, the diary describes the exploits of TJEKER buccaneers along the Palestinian coast. Wena-

mon's account is unique. Ancient historians wrote extensively about piracy; and fictional sea voyages occur in poems, novels, and plays. But the papyrus with Wenamon's adventures is the only first-hand description of ancient piracy surviving to the present day.

Temple officials at Karnak sent Wenamon to Byblos in Syria. They gave him a substantial amount of gold and silver to buy cedar. When his boat reached Dor, a Tjeker town, a sailor ran away with all of Wenamon's money, and the Tjeker prince ruling the city refused to take any action.

Wenamon continued on to Byblos. On the way, he ran into a different Tjeker and somehow robbed him of seven pounds of silver. "I have seized upon your silver," Wenamon told him, "and it will stay with me until you find my silver or the thief who stole it." His action provides the first recorded example of the right of REPRISAL in maritime law.

After many adventures, Wenamon reached Byblos and purchased the needed wood. Just as he was about to leave, 11 ships sailed into the port, filled with angry Tjeker eager to seize the Egyptian priest. The ruler of Byblos had taken the disputed silver from Wenamon to pay for the cedar, and he did not want to give it back to the Tjeker. He came up with a cunning solution. "I cannot arrest the messenger of Amon inside my land," he told the corsairs. "Let me send him away, and you go after him." Wenamon did escape the Tjeker. But he apparently lost his cargo and wrote this unique 3,000-year-old journal to explain why he returned with empty hands.

(See also SELECTED BIBLIOGRAPHY: *Ancient Near Eastern Texts*.)

WENCH *(fictional pirate word)* A very ancient word, recorded since the ninth century and probably related to a Germanic term meaning unsteady, insecure, changeable. Wench usually was used in an affectionate way to describe or address someone to whom the speaker was intimately related. Originally spelled *wenchel*, it denoted a child of either sex, a servant or slave, or a mistress or concubine.

From the 13th century, wench was applied only to females. It also was used when referring to a PROSTITUTE, usually qualified by an adjective, such as common, light, or wanton. However, every prostitute was not also a wench. The word implied that the woman was warmhearted and enjoyed her work.

Wench dropped out of formal, written English from the 16th century, but it survived in some rural districts both in England and in North America. In American dialects, from the 18th century, it referred only to black or colored women. There is no way of knowing whether Caribbean or North American pirates used wench to describe either white or African women. It is not found in written sources such as EXQUEMELIN, but some pirates may have employed the word in spoken slang.

Tavern wenches entertaining Captain Singleton, who wasted on "folly and wickedness" the vast fortune he had stolen in Africa. Illustration to a modern edition (New York, 1903–1904) of Daniel Defoe's 1720 novel *Captain Singleton*.

In its original meanings, wench is extinct in colloquial English. However, humorists occasionally revive the word as an arch and flippant euphemism for prostitute. In *The* PRINCESS AND THE PIRATE, BLACKBEARD THE PIRATE, and other pirate comedies, wench is a fictional curse word. Employed without specific meaning, it replaces the scabrous terms 18th-century sailors actually used when SWEARING about women.

WEST INDIA COMPANY   See DUTCH WEST INDIA COMPANY.

WESTWARD HO!   *(novel; 1855)*   A historical romance by Charles Kingsley (1819–1875), an Anglican priest and novelist. The bloodthirsty nationalistic sentiments expressed by *Westward Ho!* met with immediate success. By 1900, sales exceeded half a million in Britain alone (with a population of some 30 million). The book remained popular for decades, inspiring subsequent novels and movies about the Elizabethan corsairs.

Amyas Leigh attends school at Bideford in western England. After striking a teacher, he sails with Sir Francis DRAKE in 1577. (The voyage is not described.) Amyas is welcomed home by Frank Leigh, "as delicately beautiful as his brother was huge and strong." He also meets his cousin Eustace. Educated by the Jesuits, Eustace is a lustful coward who embodies Roman Catholic cunning and treachery.

While visiting Sir Richard GRENVILLE, Amyas encounters Salvation Yeo, who had invaded the SPANISH MAIN with John OXENHAM. Crossing the Isthmus of Panama, Oxenham captured a treasure ship carrying a Spanish noblewomen and her six-year-old daughter. The daughter was his own child, conceived during an earlier raid on the Spaniards.

The raiders were caught, the Spanish lady committed suicide, and Oxenham was hanged. Tortured by the Inquisition and condemned as a GALLEY SLAVE, Yeo escaped and made it back to England. He longs to return to South America to kill Spaniards and search for Oxenham's young daughter.

Amyas and Yeo instead join Sir Walter RALEIGH at the siege of Smerwick in Ireland. Led by Raleigh, the English soldiers slaughter their captives, sparing only the officers to pay ransom. During the battle, Amyas captures Don Guzman, a Spanish captain. While Amyas remains in Ireland, Guzman is imprisoned at Bideford and woos Rose Salterne, Amyas's childhood sweetheart. In 1583, Guzman's ransom is paid, and he becomes governor of La Guayra, Venezuela. Amyas returns to Bideford and learns that Rose has eloped with Guzman. Joined by his brother Frank and Salvation Yeo, Amyas chases Guzman to La Guayra.

After plundering a Spanish ship carrying pearls, Amyas and Frank slip ashore and spy on the governor's palace.

Attacking near the Margarita Island (Venezuela) pearling banks about 1584, Amyas Yeo and his English raiders capture a Spanish caravel. The cowardly Spaniards flee without fighting. Illustration by Charles Brock for an 1896 edition of Charles Kingsley's novel *Westward Ho!*

They overhear Rose and Amyas' cousin Eustace, who wishes to separate Rose and Guzman. When the Spaniards notice them, the brothers run for the beach. Amyas is knocked cold and rescued by his crew. Frank, wounded, is left behind.

Amyas' crew fight their way past three Spanish ships, but their own vessel is severely damaged. The sailors move inland in search of El Dorado, the city of gold. Meanwhile Frank and Rose, betrayed by Eustace, are killed by the Inquisition.

After three years, Amyas' crew has not found any treasure. They plan to steal a Spanish ship and return to England. On the way to the seacoast, they meet an Indian tribe, and Ayancanora falls in love with Amyas. However, the Englishmen attack without the Indians because the savages plan to eat captured Spaniards.

Soon after, Amyas' crew surprise Spanish troops cruelly driving slaves loaded with gold. When they have killed the Spaniards and taken their treasure, they discover that Ayancanora has followed them and joined the battle. Amyas seizes a Spanish galleon and hangs the bishop who had sentenced Frank and Rose to death.

As Amyas heads for home, Salvation Yeo realizes that Ayancanora is Oxenham's long-lost daughter. The girl tries to become worthy of her English blood, but the discovery hardens Amyas against her. While Ayancanora may be half-English, she is also half-Spanish.

Amyas fights the Spanish Armada in 1588, hoping to kill Guzman who commands an enemy vessel. As he closes on his foe, a storm sinks Guzman's ship. Enraged because his vengeance is thwarted, Amyas is blinded by lightning. Repenting of his crazed hatred, Amyas is reconciled with Guzman in a dream and accepts Ayancanora's love.

Westward Ho! presents historical characters inaccurately. There is no evidence, for example, that John Oxenham loved a Spanish lady. However, Kingsley shared the religious and ethnic beliefs of the Elizabethan raiders. He thus understood how they were able to justify their crimes against Roman Catholic Spaniards.

Westward Ho! consistently asserts England's divinely ordained duty of "replenishing the earth and subduing it for God and the Queen." Except for Eustace Leigh, all English characters are depicted as admirable, while all Spaniards are arrogant, heartless, and cunning. Both national characters are shaped by religion. Spain is ruled by "Popish priests and friars, who . . . get their bread shamefully and rascally." The Church of England makes "men good Christians by making them . . . good Englishmen." Anything advancing English power is forgivable—including piracy and the massacre of captives. Charles Kingsley believed this just as strongly as Elizabethan corsairs.

WHETSTONE, SIR THOMAS (English captain; Caribbean; died about 1667)

Although he was a nephew of Oliver Cromwell, who led the Republican forces, Whetstone followed King Charles II into exile. After Charles regained power in 1660, Whetstone lived lavishly and was imprisoned for debt. Because of his former services, the king paid off his creditors and sent him to Jamaica about 1661.

Whetstone ran into and joined Sir Christopher MYNGS' fleet, which assaulted Santiago, Cuba, in 1662. Many of his crewmen were said to be Indians. He commanded a seven-gun Spanish prize and was the leader of a small squadron of pirates that joined Myngs' 1663 Mexican raid. He was elected to the Jamaican parliament the following year and chosen as its first speaker.

After Edward MANSFIELD seized PROVIDENCE ISLAND in May 1665, Whetstone's ship took a Jamaican garrison to the island. He was captured when the Spaniards retook Providence in August. Whetstone and two other officers were paraded through the streets of Panama while the Spaniards threw stones and dirt. The three prisoners were chained in a Panama dungeon for 17 months, where Whetstone probably died. One of the other English officers was taken to Havana and later released.

WHIDDON, JACOB (English captain; Atlantic, Caribbean; died 1595)

Whiddon was a trusted follower of Sir Walter RALEIGH, who described him as "a man most valiant and honest." Raleigh's brother Carew was captain, and Whiddon was master of the *Hope*,

Jacob Whiddon commanded the flagship during Sir Walter Raleigh's 1595 raid on Trinidad. Raleigh's forces burned cities and captured the island's governor on the way to Guyana, where they unsuccessfully explored for gold. From Theodorus de Bry, *Collectiones . . . Americae pars VIII* (1599).

during Sir Humphrey GILBERT's 1578 West Indies expedition. He also may have sailed with Raleigh's ROANOKE expedition in 1585.

While battling the Spanish Armada in 1588, Whiddon commanded Raleigh's *Roebuck,* a fast private warship used to scout out the enemy. The *Roebuck* accompanied Sir Francis DRAKE's vessel when it captured the crippled flagship of a Spanish commander. The *Roebuck* towed the prize ashore and presumably shared in Drake's booty.

Commanding Raleigh's *Pilgrim* in 1590, Whiddon captured a valuable Brazilian prize in consort with George RAYMOND. In 1591, the *Pilgrim* was among the private warships raiding the Azores when Sir Richard GRENVILLE was killed. Whiddon also played a leading role in Raleigh's first Guyana expedition. In 1594, he took a scouting party to Trinidad, made contact with the Indians, and was ambushed by the Spanish governor. Whiddon commanded the flagship during Raleigh's 1595 expedition and accompanied him up the Orinoco River. He died on the return journey to Trinidad and was buried there by a grieving Raleigh.

(See also SELECTED BIBLIOGRAPHY: Rogoziński, *Caribbean.*)

WHIPPING *(nautical punishment; all oceans; all eras)* The act of striking another person with a whip, stick, or some other object. Whippings took place at sea for several reasons. GALLEY SLAVES were whipped to make them row harder. Pirate captives were beaten to make them reveal hidden treasure. Sailors frequently were FLOGGED on naval vessels and merchantmen, but less often on pirate ships.

Ancient and medieval GALLEYS were rowed by free men, who were not whipped. From the 15th century, European navies drove slave oarsmen with whips. Although free oarsmen remained common on smaller vessels, the KNIGHTS OF MALTA and the BARBARY corsairs also employed captives on some warships. According to their Christian enemies, the Barbary pirates horribly whipped and abused their rowers.

During all eras, pirates beat captives suspected of hiding valuables. These whippings generally ended when the prisoners gave up their loot. Mediterranean pirates tried not to harm captives, who could be sold as slaves. Most Caribbean pirates also avoided killing captives.

Whippings also were inflicted to punish crewmen. In ancient times, disciplinary floggings were imposed in the Roman navy but probably were rare on merchant ships. An officer's powers were limited during the Middle Ages, when all on board often held shares in the cargo. A maritime law of 1063 specified that "the master of a ship may not strike a mariner and . . . the mariner may defend himself if the master persists in striking him."

Physical punishments were revived from the 1500s. On English naval vessels, petty officers "started" slow-moving sailors by striking them with rope ends or rattan canes. Flogging with the cruel CAT O' NINE TAILS was imposed to punish almost any crime. On merchant ships, officers constantly beat sailors with canes, ropes, belts, sticks, and whatever else came to hand. Some captains copied the navy and held formal floggings with the cat.

A captain's authority supposedly had limits. In England, the ADMIRALTY COURT sometimes punished exceptionally brutal masters. But many captains literally got away with murder, while ships were away at sea for many months. Rebellion and mutiny proved the only effective check on a captain's powers. Pirates often claimed that they turned outlaw to escape brutal floggings, and some were telling the truth.

Whipping was a less frequent punishment on pirate vessels. The powers of pirate captains always were limited, and officers were elected from the 1680s or earlier. The entire crew tried serious crimes and usually MAROONED the guilty. Only the QUARTERMASTER could flog a man, and only with the crew's approval.

Although not stressed in written FICTION, whippings are a major feature of pirate MOVIES. Mentioned in passing by Rafael SABATINI, flogging become more important when his novels were adapted for the screen. These early films are accurate in showing beatings of GALLEY SLAVES (*The* SEA HAWK) and indentured servants (CAPTAIN BLOOD). To achieve believable grimaces, director Michael Curtiz used real whips on stars such as Errol FLYNN.

Hollywood believed that audiences enjoyed seeing muscular men lashed until blood flowed. Later films continued to show floggings on galleys (MORGAN THE PIRATE) and on warships (AGAINST ALL FLAGS; PIRATES). However, some (for example, BLACKBEARD THE PIRATE) instead show pirate captains whipping crewmen, which is less true to history.

(See also DEAD MEN TELL NO TALES; TORTURE; SELECTED BIBLIOGRAPHY: Sanborn, *Origins*.)

WHITE, THOMAS *(British pirate; Indian Ocean, Red Sea, Persian Gulf; died 1708)* From Plymouth, White migrated to Barbados after serving in the royal navy. In about 1698, he commanded a vessel taken by the French pirates who also captured John BOWEN. Refusing to join their gang, White worked as a "forced man" during cruises in the Red Sea under Bowen and George BOOTH.

Bowen's crew split up after their ship was wrecked in 1701. Enlisting on the *Prosperous* under Thomas HOWARD, White was QUARTERMASTER when Howard (in consort with Bowen) took several rich prizes in 1703. Many crewmen retired in India or at Mauritius Island, while the rest headed back to MADAGASCAR under Nathaniel NORTH. Their ship was blown off course toward Cape Dauphin in the south, where North abandoned White and 30 others who had gone ashore for provisions.

Sometime in 1704, after traveling from port to port, White became captain of a small ship abandoned at the island, and cruised in the Red Sea. Several Indian craft, a Portuguese merchantman, and (in August 1706) two British vessels were taken. In all, the pirates gained about £1,200 each. In 1707, White sailed as quartermaster with Thomas HALSEY and again shared in rich booty. He died at Madagascar early in 1708, reportedly of "excessive drinking and other irregularities."

(See also SELECTED BIBLIOGRAPHY: Grey, *Pirates*.)

WHITE, WILLIAM *(British pirate; Atlantic; died 1724)* With John PHILIPPS, White stole a ship off Newfoundland in September 1723 and marauded along the Atlantic coast until April 1724. He was hanged at Boston in June.

(See also ARCHER, JOHN ROSE.)

WIJN (KLIJN), MOISE VAN *(Dutch buccaneer; Caribbean; 1668)* Commanding a small ship, Wijn took part in François L'OLONNAIS' unlucky raid on PUERTO CABALLOS, Honduras. According to EXQUEMELIN, Moise was left in charge, when L'Olonnais took part of the force to San Pedro. Following the San Pedro foray, Moise deserted L'Olonnais and returned to TORTUGA ISLAND in a ship captured at Puerto Caballos.

WILCOX, JOHN *(English pirate; Atlantic; active 1469–1471)* Sailing from Fowey, Wilcox pillaged 16 ships near France in 1469 and seized the goods of Bristol merchants in 1471.

WILLERS, CHARLES DE *(Knight of Malta; Mediterranean; 1696)* The grand master extended Willers' license as captain of two oar-driven ships for five years.

WILLIAM *(American Indian buccaneer; Caribbean, Pacific; 1680s)* Said to be a Mosquito Indian (from Nicaragua or Honduras), William was accidentally MAROONED while marauding along South America's Pacific coast. In January 1681, the pirates stopped at the JUAN FERNÁNDEZ ISLANDS to repair and restock their vessels. Two weeks later, they left in a great hurry to avoid Spanish warships, abandoning William who was hunting goats.

In April 1684, John COOK and John EATON stopped at Juan Fernández and ran into William. After his ammunition ran out, William had cut up his gun barrel and used the pieces to make a crude saw, fishhooks, and a long knife. He had almost forgotten how to speak and had survived on fish, seals, goats, and wild vegetation.

William DAMPIER, who was present in both 1681 and 1684, told William's story in his *New Voyage*, published in 1697. It is likely that William was the model for Friday in Daniel DEFOE's ROBINSON CRUSOE.

WILLIAMS, DAVID (Welsh pirate; Indian Ocean, Red Sea, South China Sea; died 1709?)

A merchant ship accidentally left Williams on MADAGASCAR, where he fought for native chiefs. Sailing on the *Pelican* about 1698, he also served on the *Mocha* under Robert CULLIFORD and possibly helped loot the *Great Mohammed.*

The *Mocha*'s crew broke up at Madagascar late in 1699. Williams joined George BOOTH in seizing a French ship and then cruised with the *Speaker* under Booth and John BOWEN. When the *Speaker* was wrecked in 1701, Williams went back to Madagascar. He enlisted with Thomas HOWARD in 1702 but was left ashore when the pirates attacked a Dutch trader on the island. Arrested by a British warship in November 1703, he escaped at the Comoro Islands the following February. As QUARTERMASTER with Thomas WHITE in 1704 and with John HALSEY in 1707, he shared in substantial booty.

After Halsey died in 1708, Williams became the *Neptune*'s captain, but a hurricane wrecked the ship before he left Madagascar. Daniel DEFOE reported that an Arab governor killed Williams about 1709 "by throwing hot Ashes on his Head and in his Face, and putting little Boys to beat him with Sticks."

WILLIAMS, JOHN See YANKY, CAPTAIN.

WILLIAMS, MAURICE (English buccaneer; Caribbean; active 1664–1666)

Governor Thomas MODYFORD of Jamaica forbade attacks upon Spanish subjects in June 1664. Despite the ban on piracy, Williams in November asked permission to dock at PORT ROYAL with a rich prize. Although Modyford refused to promise him safety, Williams came in with his prize eight days later. The goods were seized and sold on behalf of the Spanish owner. In 1666, commanding the 16-gun *Speaker*, Williams sacked Saint Eustatius and Saba with Edward MORGAN.

WILLIAMS, PAUL (British pirate; Caribbean, Atlantic; active 1716–1717)

Williams raided with Benjamin HORNIGOLD and later with Samuel BELLAMY, who made him captain of a captured SLOOP. In March 1717, Bellamy and Williams captured the *Whydah*, a slave ship returning to England with rich cargo. In May, Bellamy wrecked the *Whydah* during rough weather, killing almost all aboard. Williams, still commanding the sloop, had lost contact with Bellamy. He visited the site of the wreck two days later and possibly salvaged some of the booty. He returned to the area a month later, pillaged two ships, and entered Cape Cod harbor on June 6.

WINTER, CHRISTOPHER (British pirate; Caribbean; active 1716–1717)

Winter surrendered to Cuban officials in 1717, when Woodes ROGERS suppressed the pirates at NEW PROVIDENCE ISLAND. In 1722, while a captain in the Cuban coast guard, he was accused of robbing English vessels and stealing slaves from Jamaican plantations.

(See also ENGLISH, EDWARD.)

WIVES OF PIRATES (spouses; all oceans; all eras)

Many pirates were wanderers, with little emotional attachment to home life. William DAMPIER, for example, wrote four large books without even mentioning his wife's family name. While they cruised for prey, married pirates left their wives behind for years at a time. John KELLEY was off marauding for 16 years, although his wife did manage to sell his gallows confession when he returned. Kelley and other real-life pirates were gone even longer than ODYSSEUS, who wandered for only 10 years, according to HOMER's poem. "One can only marvel," Robert Ritchie comments, "at the long-suffering wives who endured at home awaiting the return of their husbands while left with the burdens of providing for and rearing children."

Few wives joined their husbands on board ship. Sir John KILLIGREW's mother (Lady KILLIGREW) and his wife (Elizabeth KILLIGREW) joined him in piracy. However, both women plundered victims anchored in the nearby harbor. Rachel WALL and George WALL also raided very close to home. Anne BONNY (1) was the only European woman to accompany her lover on long cruises. (Her "marriage" to Jack RACKHAM was not really legal.) In China, Cheng I SAO helped her husband manage his pirate fleet and took over control when he died in 1807. But there is no evidence that she actually went into battle with him.

Like the sailor of the proverb, some pirates kept "a wife in every port." This was especially true of Christian RENEGADES who sailed from the BARBARY states and MOROCCO. After Jan JANSSEN married a Moroccan in 1619, he lost interest in the wife left behind in Europe. She showed up on the dock with his children when Janssen visited Holland in 1622, but he coldly rejected her tearful pleas. (Since Muslim law permits up to four wives, Janssen could have taken her with him.)

During the same years, John WARD lived in great luxury at Tunis with an Italian woman. Unlike Janssen, he at least sent small sums of money to his English wife. Simon SIMONSON's French wife was luckier, since he fled Algiers after only three years and returned with enormous booty.

Sarah Kidd, William KIDD's wife, did not make money from her husband's crimes. The governor, Lord Bellomont, threw her in jail when Kidd returned from his three-year voyage. Bellomont soon freed Mrs. Kidd and gave back her own property, but he continued to hound her while he searched for CAPTAIN KIDD'S TREASURE.

Pirate FICTION paints a harsh picture of relationships between husband and wife. In legend, Sir Anthony SHERLEY turned pirate solely to get away from his nagging wife. Daniel DEFOE tells the same story about Stede BONNET. Defoe wrote that Edward TEACH (BLACKBEARD) allowed his friends to rape his wife while he watched. Pirate MOVIES do not mention wives.

(See also HOWARD PYLE'S BOOK OF PIRATES; WOMEN, TREATMENT OF; SELECTED BIBLIOGRAPHY: Ritchie, *Kidd*.)

"WOLFERT WEBBER, OR GOLDEN DREAMS" *(short story; 1824)* Published in *Washington* IRVING's *Tales of a Traveller,* this story introduces topics developed in later pirate FICTION, including TREASURE ISLAND. Wolfert Webber, a fat, pipe-smoking Dutchman, lives in New York during the early 18th century. After ruining his farm by digging for CAPTAIN KIDD'S TREASURE, Webber visits an old Dutch inn on the waterfront. There he finds a bragging, foulmouthed BUCCANEER dominating the owner and guests.

This strange mariner suddenly appears one dark and stormy night seated on a large oaken sea chest. Scarfaced, square, and muscular, he is immensely strong. He disappears for days at a time on mysterious errands. On other days, he sits in his pistol-hung room with a short pipe, a RUM toddy, and his telescope, studying the small boats in the harbor. At night, he roars and drinks and tells hair-raising stories about the SPANISH MAIN.

During Webber's visit, the captain argues with the other drinkers about Kidd's treasure. When Peechy Prauw, one of the company, starts to tell a story, the buccaneer cuts him off. With "the grin of an angry bear," he warns his audience to "let buccaneers and their money alone. . . . They fought hard for their money; they gave body and soul for it, and wherever it lies buried, depend upon it he must have a tug with the devil who gets it."

After the stranger leaves, Peechy tells his yarn about Sam, a black fisherman who witnessed a weird burial on the Manhattan shore. Six men, five in red woolen caps, land a small boat at a place marked by an iron ring. Sam thought they were murderers, especially since they shot at him to drive him away.

Just as Peechy finishes his tale, MUSKET shots and wild shouts ring out from the shore. Carrying his heavy chest, the horrid seaman lunges out into a wild storm. By lightning flashes, Webber and the other customers see a boat bobbing about a rocky point. The buccaneer heaves one end of the chest onto the boat's gunwale. When the vessel suddenly surges away from the rocks, the heavy chest sinks, pulling the scarred pirate after it.

Webber seeks out Black Sam and finds the spot where the boatmen landed. Three crosses chiseled near the seaside rocks match three crosses at the burial spot. Webber returns with a learned "High German Doctor." With the help of many magical spells and a divining rod, they dig up a chest but are driven off by the drowned buccaneer's ghost. All agree the mysterious seaman was either a smuggler or "one of the ancient comrades of Kidd or [Joseph] BRADISH, returned to convey away treasures formerly hidden in the vicinity."

WOMEN OF PITCAIRN ISLAND, THE *(motion picture; black and white; 1957)* After the mutiny on the *Bounty,* only women and children have survived. They are terrorized by shipwrecked cut-throats, led by Page (James Craig). While searching for a bag of black pearls, the pirates abuse Maimitia (Lynn Bari) and the other women. Most die fighting over the pearls, the islanders kill the rest. *Variety* found the film tedious, "a dull programmer with little to recommend it." Directed by Jean Yarbrough.

WOMEN PIRATES *(female sea raiders; 3000 B.C. to the present)* Pirates are mariners who prey on other ships or on coastal cities. By this standard definition, piracy was a male activity. However, several women sponsored piracy as rulers of corsair HAVENS. Queen TEUTA governed the ILLYRIANS during the third century B.C., and Elizabeth I of England also profited from pirate raids.

There is no truth to the myth that sailors considered women at sea unlucky. Throughout history, women went to sea as passengers and wives of mariners. In some countries, women joined men on fishing vessels, merchantmen, and whalers. During the 18th century, British warships routinely carried female servants, who received government wages. But these female mariners rarely turned pirate.

A few women sailed with the pirates of the Atlantic and Caribbean. During the 16th century, the KILLIGREW FAMILY sponsored piracy from southwestern England. Lady KILLIGREW and her daughter-in-law, Elizabeth KILLIGREW, were both accused of leading attacks on ships in Falmouth harbor. Neither was found guilty, but the juries probably were bribed. In 1720, a Jamaican jury did convict Anne BONNY (1) and Mary READ (1) of joining their male comrades during battle. Rachel WALL confessed to minor acts of piracy before she was hanged in 1789. Although other women were arrested on pirate ships, they were acquitted because they did not take part in attacks.

Female pirates may have served in combat in 19th-century China. Cheng I SAO commanded large pirate fleets during the 1810s. Some witnesses said her own warship took part in sea battles. Europeans also reported rumors that female crew members joined in assaults.

However, there were no women among the pirates executed by the Chinese government.

In pirate fiction, female raiders were rare before the 18th century. All pirates in Greek and Latin ROMANCES are male, and women are presented as their victims. ALVILDA of Sweden is the sole female pirate in medieval literature.

Daniel DEFOE, who fathered many other pirate legends, invented the myth of female piracy with his stories about Anne BONNY (2) and Mary READ (2). Both actually existed and were convicted of piracy in 1720. However, Defoe gave them fictional biographies that went far beyond the facts. Defoe portrayed Anne as highly promiscuous, and he depicted both women as ferocious amazons, "very ready and willing to do anything." Defoe's story made Bonny and Read famous. The two women are mentioned in most histories of piracy, which often present Defoe's fiction as fact. Bonny also appears in novels and movies, such as ANNE BONNY and AGAINST ALL FLAGS.

Following Defoe's lead, fictional female pirates often are portrayed as even more depraved than BLACKBEARD or other male monsters. Grace O'MALLEY kills her own son, while Maria LINDSEY delights in finding new ways to murder captured crews. Dudley POPE's female pirates are an exception. In Pope's novels, two captains cruise from PORT ROYAL with their mistresses on board. The two women dominate but are no crueler than their male partners.

WOMEN, TREATMENT OF   (pirate etiquette; all oceans; all eras)   Daniel DEFOE, who invented many pirate myths, created the legend of lust-crazed brigands, especially in his stories about BLACKBEARD. Real pirates tortured male captives to make them give up their treasures, but they almost never harassed females. In fact, the reverse was true. European and North African raiders protected women and treated them with care. (There is too little information to generalize about Arab and Chinese pirates.)

In the Mediterranean, captives usually were worth more than captured cargo. Pirates ransomed those of high rank and sold the rest as slaves. Only a stupid pirate would have brutalized captives and reduced their resale value. The ancient historians do not mention rape among the crimes of the CILICIANS, CRETANS, and other pirate folk. Abused women also are absent from ancient fiction. In some ROMANCES, the pirates want to marry the heroine, in others they plan to sell her off.

The BARBARY corsairs also treated females gently. Captives were part of the BOOTY, distributed only after the ship returned to port. A corsair who raped a woman was punished for damaging property that did not belong to him. Peter Earle describes corsair kindness as good business.

Indeed, kind and flattering words were a good way of getting a captive to . . . reveal his station in life [and thus pay a higher ransom]. Women were almost invariably well treated. Anyone who touched a woman in a sensual manner ran a very great risk of being bastinadoed.

For similar economic reasons, corsairs from Malta and other HAVENS for Christian pirates also were considerate of captured women. They did not need to commit rape, since PROSTITUTION flourished in the Christian ports and Greek islands.

The Caribbean BUCCANEERS also respected woman captives. EXQUEMELIN frequently describes the torture of prisoners. He refers to rape only twice—after François L'OLONNAIS seized Gibraltar in 1667 and again when Sir Henry MORGAN sacked PANAMA in 1671. If Exquemelin is telling the truth about Panama, Morgan's behavior was unusual. During earlier assaults on PORTOBELO (1668) and PROVIDENCE ISLAND (1670), Morgan had female captives locked up and guarded.

There is no evidence of harassment by the pirates invading the Pacific during the 1680s. None is mentioned by the pirate journalists William DAMPIER, Basil RINGROSE, and Lionel WAFER. There are no accusations of sexual abuse in Spanish documents from the cities they sacked.

The first reported gang rape occurred after Henry EVERY took the Gunsway in 1695. An Indian historian (but not an eyewitness) says the pirates ravished both young and old so savagely that many women killed themselves. Daniel Defoe does not tell this story in his GENERAL HISTORY. However, he does describe gory rapes in his biographies of Edward ENGLAND, Thomas ANTIS, and other pirates. Defoe's Blackbeard had at least 14 wives and watched his friends rape them.

At least in Blackbeard's case, Defoe's stories are untrue, and the real Edward TEACH probably was frightened of women. The ARTICLES signed by John PHILLIPS's crew punish rapists with the death penalty. Other articles do not mention the crime, perhaps because it was rare.

Defoe created the myth, which later writers expanded. Charles Ellms inserted fictional rape stories when he reprinted Defoe's stories in 1834 in THE PIRATES OWN BOOK. Newspapers accused Benito de SOTO and other 19th-century raiders of raping every female captive. By the early 1900s, when tales about GASPARILLA were being embellished, pirates routinely were described as raping hundreds of women.

(See also SELECTED BIBLIOGRAPHY: Earle, Corsairs.)

WOOD, BENJAMIN   (English captain; Atlantic, Caribbean; active 1584–1597?)   An expert but unlucky seaman, Wood took few major prizes and sailed with several expeditions that failed utterly. He is first mentioned as one of Sir Walter RALEIGH's captains. He took part in a voyage that explored the Virginia coast in 1584 as well as in the 1586 Azores raid.

Wood was master of the 340-ton *White Lion* in 1589, when John CHIDLEY planned to cross through the Strait of Magellan and raid South America's Pacific coast. As the ships sailed past Africa, disease killed Chidley and most of the sailors. Wood deserted and managed to take his ship back to England.

In 1592, Wood raided the Caribbean with three ships owned by Lord Thomas Howard, a naval commander. No prizes were taken, and one of Woods' ships disappeared during a storm. Near CARTAGENA he joined forces with John MYDDLETON and unsuccessfully assaulted a FRIGATE that had run aground. The Spaniards captured 13 of the raiders, including Myddleton.

Wood accompanied Sir Robert DUDLEY's venture to Trinidad and Guyana in 1594. While Dudley explored the Orinoco River, Wood apparently cruised along the Venezuelan coast but took no prizes.

Two years later, Dudley placed Wood in command of a squadron that—like John Chidley's in 1589—intended to raid in the Pacific. This plan apparently was abandoned, and Woods made his way to the Indian Ocean around the Cape of Good Hope. His expedition suffered the same fate as that of Sir James LANCASTER. Woods plundered several vessels, but disease killed off his crews until his last ship was wrecked. Only one sailor made it back to Europe.

(See also GRENVILLE, SIR RICHARD.)

WOODEN LEG   See PEG LEG.

WORLEY, CAPTAIN *(British pirate; Atlantic; 1718)*   Worley left New York in about October 1718 in a small boat with a crew of eight. The daring band plundered shipping on the Delaware River, took over a SLOOP, and captured several more vessels.

Worley was off Charleston, South Carolina, in November. Because of recent raids by Edward TEACH and Stede BONNET, his presence alarmed the city. The governor personally commanded four ships that captured Worley's sloop and one of his prizes. Worley and most of his crew died during the battle, and 25 others were hanged at Charleston.

(See also SELECTED BIBLIOGRAPHY: Hughson, *Carolina.*)

WORRALL, CAPTAIN *(English pirate; Atlantic; about 1582)*   Sailing from Dorset in a small ship, Worrall lost half his crew while capturing a much larger French merchantmen. He was later captured and jailed. At his trial, Worrall claimed he had served under Sir Francis DRAKE.

WRIGHT, CAPTAIN *(English pirate; Caribbean; active 1675–1682)*   When John COOK's pirate band returned from the Pacific in May 1681, they found Wright and at least eight other pirate captains hovering off the Caribbean coast. While Cook joined Captain YANKY's crew, the pirate-author William DAMPIER sailed with Captain Wright, who operated under a dubious French PRIVATEERING commission.

Captains Wright and Yanky cruised in consort until April 1682, taking several valuable prizes along the Venezuelan coast. Soon after, Dampier resigned from Wright's ship and went to Virginia. Dampier wrote that Wright had sacked La Guaira, Venezuela, some years earlier. He had been a pirate since at least 1675.

WU-SHIH ERH *(Chinese pirate; South China Sea; died 1810)*   Wu-shih Erh (Mai Yu-chin) led the Blue Flag Fleet, the second largest in the pirate confederation formed by CHENG I in 1805. Wu was captured as a youth, joined the pirates, and helped extort protection money in the ports of Kwantung Province. He rose to squadron leader and then fought with rebel forces in Vietnam. After their defeat at Hue in June 1801, Wu accompanied the rebel emperor in his flight to Hanoi. There he joined forces with CHENG CHI in raids on Chinese salt fleets.

When Cheng Chi died, Wu affiliated with his nephew, Cheng I. His power was second only to Cheng's, and he commanded more than 160 JUNKS by 1805. Operating from the Lei-chou Peninsula, near Vietnam, he often raided in consort with TUNG-HAI PA's smaller Yellow Flag Fleet.

After Cheng I died in 1807, CHANG PAO took command of his fleet. Chang accepted a government pardon in 1810 and joined an assault on his former colleagues. Wu also wished to surrender but feared treachery. In June, Chang Pao defeated Wu in a battle off Hainan Island. Chang's forces seized 86 junks, 291 cannon, and 490 prisoners, including 128 women. Soon after, Wu-shih Erh and seven of his squadron leaders were beheaded at the town gate.

WYNDHAM, THOMAS *(English pirate; Atlantic; 1510?–1553)*   Related to a prominent Norfolk family, Wyndham settled in Somerset, took to the sea, and commanded royal ships against the Scots (in 1544 and 1547) and the French (1545–1546). Like other Tudor captains, he combined these naval commissions with piracy against friendly nations.

By 1545, Wyndham helped lead a syndicate in western England that outfitted raiders and fenced their loot. Early that year, he commanded a warship owned by Sir John Russell, lord privy seal. In consort with John LANDY, he captured a Spanish ship loaded with costly wines and dyes. The mayor of Plymouth pretended the stolen goods were French. However, the ADMIRALTY COURT ruled against Wyndham, and (in 1546) confiscated one of his legal prizes to reimburse the Spanish owner. In May 1546, Wyndham again was censured for looting a Portuguese ship.

Wyndham was captain and part-owner of the first ship to trade with Morocco in 1551. (James ALDAY later claimed credit for arranging the excursion.) In January

1552, the Privy Council rebuked him for plundering Danish vessels, probably during this voyage. Wyndham returned to Morocco late in 1552. On the way home, he put in at Lanzarote in the Canary Islands. His men clashed with the Spanish, and Wyndham captured but later released the governor.

In 1553, Wyndham and a renegade Portuguese captain took two ships to West Africa. The venture was sponsored by London merchants and supported by the government. But Wyndham conducted it like a pirate raid, plundering Portuguese shipping and raiding African villages. Ignoring the advice of his Portuguese pilot, Wyndham stayed too long in Africa and died of fever along with three-fourths of his crew.

(See also SELECTED BIBLIOGRAPHY: Andrews, *Trade*; Connell-Smith, *Forerunners*.)

XEBEC   See SHEBEC.

XENOPHON OF EPHESUS   *(Greek novelist; second century)*   Xenophon was the supposed author of *The* EPHESIAN TALE, a ROMANCE written between 125 and 200. Nothing is known about him, and the name could be a pseudonym. As it exists, the novel may be only an abbreviated summary and not the entire work as originally written.

Y

YACHT *(type of ship; 16th century to the present)* The word *yacht* (from Dutch *jaght*, short for *jaghtschip*, a vessel for chasing) originally referred to light, fast pirate ships of several designs. It was borrowed into English to describe royal pleasure craft and now refers to any pleasure boat more than 30 feet long.

YAHYA REIS *(Barbary corsair; Mediterranean; active 1558–1562)* Operating from ALGIERS and the former Spanish fortress at Bougie (Bejaïa)—recently captured by SALIH REIS—Yahya ravaged both coasts of Italy, bringing in more than 4,000 captives.

YALLAHS (YELLOWES), CAPTAIN *(Dutch pirate; Caribbean; 1672)* In August 1671, the governor of Jamaica offered to pardon pirates who promised to end their crimes. Yallahs refused to submit. He fled to Campeche, Mexico, sold his frigate for 7,000 pesos, and acquired a Spanish commission. During the next 12 months, he captured more than a dozen English ships carrying LOGWOOD.

YANKEE BUCCANEER *(motion picture; color; 1952)* Commander David Porter (Jeff Chandler) disguises his vessel as a pirate ship and searches for freebooters terrorizing Caribbean shipping. Porter is a rock-solid officer who lives by the manual. His second-in-command, Lieutenant David Farragut (Scott Brady),

is a happy-go-lucky man, always breaking the rules. The two inevitably clash and finally duel with swords.

Soon after, Countess Margarita (Susan Ball) comes on board. Her group of Portuguese patriots are plotting to overthrow the king. But the wicked Spanish governor, Count Domingo del Prado (Joseph Callela), and the Caribbean pirates are working together to steal the patriots' gold. The governor captures Farragut and Countess Margarita and stretches them on the rack in his torture chamber. Commander Porter and his hardy U. S. sailors rescue them, destroying the pirates' malicious plot. Directed by Frederick de Cordova.

YANKY, CAPTAIN *(Dutch buccaneer; Caribbean; active 1681–1687)* "Yanky" is a nickname; his original name probably was John Williams. When John COOK's pirate band returned from the Pacific in May 1681, they found Yanky and at least eight other pirate captains assembled on the Caribbean coast. Cook joined Yanky's ship as QUARTERMASTER and second-in-command. Several French captains had dubious PRIVATEERING commissions, but Yanky operated as a freelance.

Cruising in consort with Captain WRIGHT, Yanky captured several ships off Central America. The two captains argued over a prize but stayed together until about April 1682. William DAMPIER (who sailed with Wright) portrays Yanky as greedy or at least tight-fisted. Soon after he left Wright, Yanky seized a fine Spanish prize, which

Cook and the other Englishmen demanded under pirate rules. However, Captain Yanky lusted after the prize, took her back by force, and MAROONED the English on the Île-à-Vache, off Haiti. (They were rescued by Captain TRISTIAN.)

In February 1683, Jean HAMLIN was devastating English shipping in the *Trompeuse*. To ensure Hamlin's destruction and to "sow dissension among the pirates," Jamaica's governor wrote London, "I have sent Captain [John] COXON to offer to one Yankey (who commands an admirable sailer) men, victuals, pardon, naturalization and 200 pounds in money to him and Coxon if he will go after *La Trompeuse*." Yanky apparently rejected the governor's offer. He operated from Saint Domingue in 1684 and continued to raid Caribbean shipping until at least 1687.

(See also SELECTED BIBLIOGRAPHY: Paiewonsky, *Trompeuse.*)

YEATS, CAPTAIN (British pirate; Caribbean, Atlantic; 1718)
Captain Yeats sailed from the Bahamas in August 1718 with Charles VANE. Soon after, Vane seized a sloop and gave Yeats command. The pirates looted four ships near Charleston, South Carolina; but Yeats quarreled with Vane and deserted. In Daniel DEFOE'S GENERAL HISTORY Yeats surrendered at Charleston, but South Carolina records do not mention this.

YELLOWBEARD (motion picture; color; 1983)
Mel Damski directed this raunchy, frenetic spoof of TREASURE ISLAND (1) that emphasizes slapstick and one-line jokes. The large comedy ensemble includes many players from the Monty Python and Beyond the Fringe groups, Cheech and Chong, Marty Feldman, Madeleine Kahn, James Mason, and Susannah York.

Yellowbeard (Graham Chapman) seizes and buries the fabulous treasure of El Nebuloso (Tommy Chong). He is betrayed by his one-handed mate, Mr. Moon (Peter Boyle), and escapes from prison 20 years later. Using a map tattooed on the head of his son, Dan (Martin Hewitt), Yellowbeard sets out, pursued by other treasure-seekers. After overcoming various comic obstacles, father and son dig up the loot. Dan kills Yellowbeard, who comes back to life and takes over a man-of-war.

YO-HO-HO (fictional seaman's expression; 1883 to the present)
In TREASURE ISLAND, Bill Bones' drinking song FIFTEEN MEN ON A DEAD MAN'S CHEST includes the line "Yo-ho-ho and a bottle of rum." Stevenson used the nonsense syllables "Yo-ho-ho" because he liked their rhythm. They reappear in movie comedies. Stevenson may have been thinking of the seaman's work-chant, "Yeo heave ho," used to unify action. If the sailors shout in unison and exert their muscles on "heave," a strong effect results.

YUSUF KUCIUK REIS (Barbary corsair; Mediterranean; 1550s–1562)
From southern Italy, he converted to Islam and sailed from ALGIERS. He frequently raided Sicily and Italy for slaves, treating his captives with great cruelty. In 1562, the Maltese corsair ROMEGAS captured Yusuf's GALIOT, and he was torn apart by his Christian oarsmen.

YUSUF REIS (Barbary corsair; Mediterranean; active 1574–1579)
Yusuf was an Italian from Genoa nicknamed Borrasquillo ("stormy"). One of ULUJ ALI's followers, he commanded a ship escorting HASAN VENEZIANO to Algiers in 1574. In 1579, while he was ashore in Bône (modern Annaba) purchasing food for ALGIERS, his Christian GALLEY SLAVES seized his ship and took it to Majorca.

YUSUF TRABLESI (TRIPOLISSY) REIS (Barbary corsair; Mediterranean; 1760s)
Yusuf operated from TRIPOLI, then became a captain in the SALÉ fleet, in which he commanded a 12-gun SHEBEC in 1766, a 24-gun sailing vessel in 1769, and a GALIOT in 1772.

Z

ZANKLE *(pirate haven; Mediterranean; seventh century B.C.)* A city (present-day Messina) in Sicily supposedly founded about 700 by Greek pirates from Cuma near Naples. Ancient sources describe the Zankleans as even more piratical than the Greek settlers colonizing other sites. The town's advantageous position on the Strait of Messina aided their raids.

(See also DIONYSUS OF PHOCAEA; ETRUSCANS; LIPARI ISLANDS; PHOCAEANS.)

ZENOCTES *(Cilician archpirate; Mediterranean; died 77 B.C.)* Zenoctes was the most important chief in the Gulf of Pamphylia (modern Antayla Korfezi). From 80 B.C., he could scan the coastline for many miles from his fortress high in the Solyma Mountains (Tahtali Beg). He controlled all the major ports, including Phaselis, Corycus, and Olympus. After capturing these three coastal cities, the Roman general SERVILIUS stormed Zenoctes' mountain stronghold in 77. When the battle was lost, Zenoctes set fire to his fortress, killing himself, his soldiers and servants, and his entire family.

(See also CILICIA.)

SELECTED BIBLIOGRAPHY

This list gives the sources of quotations and also includes books recommended for further information on individuals and specific topics. It is far from a complete record of all the primary and secondary sources I have consulted. Only studies that will be of wide interest are cited. I have not included most works in languages other than English, books long out of print, or articles in specialized journals with limited circulation.

For individuals with many biographers, I normally list only recent works when these provide bibliographies of earlier books and magazine articles. Works of fiction are included only when I have quoted or referred to a specific edition.

Ancient Near Eastern Texts relating to the Old Testament. Edited by James Pritchard. Third edition. Princeton, N.J.: Princeton University Press, 1975.

Anderson, Roger C. *Naval Wars in the Levant 1559–1853.* Princeton, N.J.: Princeton University Press, 1952.

Andrews, Kenneth R. *Drake's Voyages: A Re-assessment of their Place in Elizabethan Maritime Expansion.* New York: Scribners, 1967.

———. *Elizabethan Privateering: English Privateering during the Spanish War 1585–1603.* Cambridge: Cambridge University Press, 1964.

———. *English Privateering Voyages to the West Indies, 1588–1595.* Cambridge: Hakluyt Society, 1959.

———. *The Last Voyage of Drake & Hawkins.* Cambridge: Hakluyt Society, 1972.

———. *Ships, Money, and Politics: Seafaring and Naval Enterprise in the Reign of Charles I.* New York: Cambridge University Press, 1991.

———. *The Spanish Caribbean: Trade and Plunder 1530–1630.* New Haven: Yale University Press, 1978.

———. *Trade, Plunder, and Settlement: Maritime Enterprise and the Genesis of the British Empire, 1480–1630.* Cambridge: Cambridge University Press, 1984.

Apollodorus. *The Library of Greek Mythology.* Translated by Keith Aldrich. Lawrence, Kans.: Coronado, 1975.

Appian. *Appian's Roman History.* Translated by Horace White. Four volumes. Cambridge, Mass.: Harvard University Press, 1912–1913.

Bamford, Paul. *Fighting Ships and Prisons: The Mediterranean Galleys of France in the Age of Louis XIV.* Minneapolis: University of Minnesota Press, 1973.

Biddulph, John. *The Pirates of Malabar. . . .* London: Smith, Elder, 1907.

Blouet, Brian. *The Story of Malta.* London: Faber and Faber, 1967.

Boer, Charles. *The Homeric Hymns.* Chicago: Swallow Press, 1970.

Bonner, Willard. *Captain William Dampier, Buccaneer-Author.* Stanford, Calif.: Stanford University Press, 1934.

———. *Pirate Laureate: The Life and Legends of Captain*

Kidd. New Brunswick, N.J.: Rutgers University Press, 1947.

Botting, Douglas. *The Pirates.* Alexandria, Va.: Time-Life Books, 1978.

Bovill, E. W. "The *Madre de Dios,*" *The Mariner's Mirror,* volume 54 (1968), pages 129–152.

Bradford, Ernle. *The Great Siege.* New York: Harcourt, Brace & World, 1961.

———. *The Shield and the Sword: The Knights of Saint John: Jerusalem, Rhodes, and Malta.* New York: Dutton, 1973.

Bradlee, Francis. *Piracy in the West Indies and its Suppression.* Salem, Mass.: Essex Institute, 1923. Reprinted, Glorieta, N.Mex.: Rio Grande, 1990.

Bradley, Peter. *The Lure of Peru: Maritime Intrusion into the South Sea, 1598–1701.* St. Martin's, 1989.

Braudel, Fernand. *The Mediterranean and the Mediterranean World in the Age of Philip II.* Translated by Siân Reynolds. New York: Harper & Row, 1973.

Breasted, James. *Ancient Records of Egypt.* . . . Five volumes. Chicago: University of Chicago Press, 1906–1907.

Bridenbaugh, Carl, and Roberta Bridenbaugh. *No Peace Beyond the Line: The English in the Caribbean, 1624–1690.* New York: Oxford University Press, 1972.

Bry, Theodorus de. *Collectiones Peregrinationum.* . . . *Americae Pars VIII: Continens Primo, Descriptionem trium itinerum Noblilissimi et fortissimi Equitis Francisci Draken, qui Peragrata Primum Universo Terrarum Orbe.* . . . Frankfurt-am-Main, 1599.

Burney, James. *Chronological History of the Discoveries in the South Seas.* Five volumes. London, 1803–1817. Reprinted, Amsterdam (N. Israel) and New York (Da Capo), 1967. Volume Four reprinted in part (as *History of the Buccaneers of America*), New York: Norton, 1950.

Casson, Lionel. *The Ancient Mariners.* New York: Macmillan, 1959.

———. *Ships and Seamanship in the Ancient World.* Princeton, N.J.: Princeton University Press, 1971.

Cavaliero, Roderick. *The Last of the Crusaders: The Knights of St John and Malta in the Eighteenth Century.* London: Hollis & Carter, 1960.

Chew, Samuel. *The Crescent and the Rose: Islam and England during the Renaissance.* Oxford: Oxford University Press, 1937. Reprinted, New York: Octagon, 1965.

Cicero, Marcus Tullius. *Verrine Orations.* Translated by L. H. G. Greenwood. Two volumes. Cambridge, Mass.: Harvard University Press, 1928–1935.

Clissold, Stephen. *The Barbary Slaves.* Totowa, N.J.: Rowman and Littlefield, 1977.

Connell-Smith, Gordon. *Forerunners of Drake: A Study of English Trade with Spain in the Early Tudor Period.* London: Longmans, Green, 1954.

Contreras, Alonso de. *The Life of Captain Alonso de Contreras, Knight of the Military Order of St John, Native of Madrid, Written by Himself (1582–1633).* Translated by Catherine Philipps. New York: Knopf, 1926.

Corbett, Julian. *The Successors of Drake.* London: Longmans, Green, 1900. Reprinted, New York: Burt Franklin, 1967.

Course, A. G. *Pirates of the Eastern Seas.* London: Muller, 1966.

Coxere, Edward. *Adventures by Sea of Edward Coxere: A Relation of the Several Adventures by Sea with the Dangers, Difficulties and Hardships I Met for Several Years.* . . . Edited by E. H. W. Meyerstein. New York: Oxford University Press, 1946.

Crouse, Nellis. *French Pioneers in the West Indies, 1624–1664.* New York: Columbia University Press, 1940. Reprinted, New York: Octagon, 1977.

———. *The French Struggle for the West Indies, 1665–1713.* New York: Columbia University Press, 1943. Reprinted, New York: Octagon, 1966.

Cruikshank, E. A. *The Life of Sir Henry Morgan.* Toronto: Macmillan, 1935.

Dampier, William. *A New Voyage Round the World.* London: Knapton, 1697. New edition by N. M. Penzer, London: Argonaut, 1927. Penzer edition reprinted, London (Black), 1937; New York (Dover), 1966.

———. *A Voyage to New Holland.* London: Knapton, 1703–1709. New edition by James Spencer, Gloucester, England: Alan Sutton, 1981.

———. *Voyage to Campeache.* London: Knapton, 1699. New edition by Clennell Wilkinson, London: Argonaut, 1931.

Davies, D. W. *Elizabethans Errant: The Strange Fortunes of Sir Thomas Sherley and his Three Sons.* Ithaca, N.Y.: Cornell University Press, 1967.

Defoe, Daniel. *A General History of the Robberies and Murders of the Most Notorious Pyrates.* Two volumes. London, 1724–1728. New edition by Manuel Schonhorn, Columbia: University of South Carolina Press, 1972.

———. *The Life, Adventures, and Pyracies, of the Famous Captain Singleton.* . . . London, 1720. New edition by Shiv Kumar, New York: Oxford University Press, 1990.

———. *The Four Years Voyages of Captain George Roberts.* London: Bettesworth, 1726. Reprinted, New York: Garland, 1972.

———. *Madagascar; or, Robert Drury's Journal, during Fifteen Years' Captivity on that Island.* London: Meadows, 1727. New edition by Pasfield Oliver, London: Unwin, 1897. Oliver edition reprinted, New York: Negro Universities Press, 1969.

Dictionary of National Biography. Edited by Leslie Stephen and Sidney Lee. Oxford: Oxford University Press, 1885–1901.

Dio Cassius. *Dio's Roman History.* Translated by Earnest Cary. Nine volumes. Cambridge, Mass: Harvard University Press, 1914–1927.

Diodorus Siculus. *The Library of History of Diodorus of Sicily.* Translated by C. H. Oldfather and others.

Twelve volumes. Cambridge, Mass.: Harvard University Press, 1933–1967.

Dow, George, and John Edmonds. *The Pirates of the New England Coast.* Salem, Mass.: Marine Research Society, 1923. Reprinted, New York: Argosy, 1968.

Downing, Clement. *A History of the Indian Wars. . . .* London: Cooper, 1737. New edition by William Foster, London: Oxford University Press, 1924.

Dunn Richard. *Sugar and Slaves: The Rise of the Planter Class in the English West Indies, 1624–1713.* Chapel Hill: University of North Carolina Press, 1972.

Earle, Peter. *Corsairs of Malta and Barbary.* London: Sidgwick & Jackson, 1970.

———. *The Sack of Panamá: Sir Henry Morgan's Adventures on the Spanish Main.* New York: Viking Press, 1982.

———. *The Treasure of the Concepción: The Wreck of the Almiranta.* New York: Viking, 1980.

Ellms, Charles. *The Pirates Own Book, or Authentic Narratives of the Lives, Exploits, and Executions of the Most Celebrated Sea Robbers.* Boston: Dickinson, 1837. New edition, Salem, Mass.: Marine Research Society, 1924.

Ewen, C. L'Estrange. "Organized Piracy Round England in the Sixteenth Century," *The Mariner's Mirror,* volume 35 (1949), pages 29–42.

Exquemelin, Alexander O. *The Buccaneers of America.* Translated by Alexis Brown. Harmondsworth, England: Penguin, 1969.

Farine, Charles. *Deux pirates au XVIe siècle: Histoire des Barberousse.* Paris: Ducrocq, 1869.

Firth, C. H. (editor). *Naval Songs and Ballads.* London: Naval Records Society, 1908. Reprinted 1987.

Fisher, Godfrey. *Barbary Legend: War, Trade, and Piracy in North Africa 1415–1830.* Oxford: Oxford University Press, 1957.

Foster, Sir William. *The Voyages of Sir James Lancaster to Brazil and the East Indies, 1591–1603.* London: Hakluyt Society 1940. Reprinted, Nendeln, Liechtenstein: Kraus, 1967.

Fox, Grace. *British Admirals and Chinese Pirates, 1832–1869.* London: Kegan Paul, 1940. Reprinted, Westport, Conn.: Hyperion, 1973.

Fraser, George MacDonald. *The Hollywood History of the World.* New York: William Morrow, 1988.

Friedman, Ellen. *Spanish Captives in North Africa in the Early Modern Age.* Madison: University of Wisconsin Press, 1983.

Gerhard, Peter. *Pirates on the West Coast of New Spain, 1575–1742.* Glendale, Calif.: Arthur H. Clark, 1960.

Goslinga, Cornelis. *The Dutch in the Caribbean and on the Wild Coast, 1580–1680.* Gainesville: University of Florida Press, 1971.

Gosse, Philip. *The History of Piracy.* New York: Tudor, 1932. Reprinted, Glorieta, N.Mex.: Rio Grande, 1988.

Gracewell, Catherine. *The Uskoks of Senj: Piracy, Banditry, and Holy War in the Sixteenth-Century Adriatic.* Ithaca, N.Y.: Cornell University Press, 1992.

Grey, Charles. *Pirates of the Eastern Seas (1618–1723): A Lurid Page of History.* London: Low, Marston, 1933. Reprinted, Port Washington, N.Y.: Kennikat, 1971.

Guilmartin, John. *Gunpowder and Galleys: Changing Technology and Mediterranean Warfare at Sea in the Sixteenth Century.* London: Cambridge University Press, 1974.

Hadas, Moses. *Three Greek Romances: Longus' Daphnis and Chloe; Xenophon of Ephesus's Ephesian Tale; Dio Chrysostom's Hunters of Eurboea.* New York: Doubleday, 1953.

Hamshere, Cyril. *The British in the Caribbean.* Cambridge, Mass.: Harvard University Press, 1972.

Hanson, Bruce. *The Peter Pan Chronicles: The Nearly 100 Year History of The Boy Who Wouldn't Grow Up.* New York: Birch Lane, 1993.

Haring, Charles H. *The Buccaneers in the West Indies in the XVII Century.* London: Methuen, 1910. Reprinted, Hamden, Conn.: Archon Books, 1966.

———. *Trade and Navigation between Spain and the Indies.* Cambridge, Mass.: Harvard University Press, 1918. Reprinted, Gloucester, Mass.: Peter Smith, 1964.

Heliodorus of Emesna. *An Ethiopian Romance.* Translated by Moses Hadas. Ann Arbor: University of Michigan Press, 1957.

Herodotus. *The History.* Translated by David Greene. Chicago: University of Chicago Press, 1987.

Hinrichs, Dunbar. *The Fateful Voyage of Captain Kidd.* New York: Bookman Associates, 1953.

Homer. *The Odyssey.* Translated by E. V. Rieu. London: Penguin, 1951.

———. *The Odyssey of Homer.* Translated by Richmond Lattimore. New York: Harper and Row, 1965.

Horwood, Harold, and Edward Butts. *Pirates & Outlaws of Canada, 1610–1932.* Toronto: Doubleday, 1984.

Hughson, Shirley. *The Carolina Pirates and Colonial Commerce 1670–1740.* Baltimore: Johns Hopkins University, 1894. Reprinted, New York: AMS Press, 1992.

Jameson, John. *Privateering and Piracy in the Colonial Period.* New York: Macmillan, 1923. Reprinted, New York: Kelley, 1970.

Jurien de la Gravière, Jean. *Les corsaires barbaresques et la marine de Soliman le Grand.* Paris: Plon, 1887.

Kelly, John. *Britain and the Persian Gulf, 1795–1880.* Oxford: Clarendon, 1968.

Kemp, Peter, and Christopher Lloyd. *Brethren of the Coast: Buccaneers of the South Seas.* New York: St. Martin's, 1961.

Keppel, Henry. *The Expedition to Borneo of H. M. S. Dido for the Suppression of Piracy.* Revised edition in two volumes. London: Chapman and Hall, 1847. Reprinted, London: Cass, 1968.

Kingsford, Charles. *Prejudice and Promise in Fifteenth Century England.* London: Oxford University Press, 1925.

Labat, Jean-Baptiste. *Nouveau Voyage aux Isles de l'Amérique.* Paris, 1722. Translated and abridged by John Eaden as *The Memoirs of Pere Labat.* London: Constable, 1931.

Lacey, Robert. *Sir Walter Ralegh.* New York: Atheneum, 1974.

Lee, Robert E. *Blackbeard the Pirate,* Winston-Salem, N.C.: Blair, 1974.

Lender, Mark, and James Martin. *Drinking in America: A History.* New York: Free Press, 1982.

Leslie, Charles. *A New History of Jamaica.* London, 1740.

Little, Bryan. *Crusoe's Captain, Being the Life of Woodes Rogers, Seaman, Trader, Colonial Governor.* London: Odhams, 1960.

Lives of the Most Remarkable Criminals, Who Have Been Condemned and Executed. . . . London: Osborn, 1735. New edition by Arthur Hayward, New York: Dodd, Mead, 1927.

Lloyd, Christopher. *William Dampier.* Hamden, Conn.: Archon, 1968.

Lubbock, Basil. *Bully Hayes, South Sea Pirate.* Boston: Lauriat, 1931.

Lussan, Raveneau de. *Raveneau de Lussan, Buccaneer of the Spanish Main and Early French Filibuster of the Pacific.* Edited by Marguerite Wilbur. Cleveland: Arthur H. Clark, 1930.

Lydon, James. *Pirates, Privateers, and Profits.* Upper Saddle River, N.J.: Gregg, 1970.

Maltin, Leonard. *The Disney Films.* New York: Crown, 1973.

Marx, Jenifer. *Pirates and Privateers of the Caribbean.* Malabar, Fla.: Krieger, 1992.

Marx, Robert F. *The Capture of the Treasure Fleet: The Story of Piet Heyn.* New York: McKay, 1977.

McFee, William. *The Law of the Sea.* London: Faber and Faber, 1951.

Means, Philip. *The Spanish Main, Focus of Envy 1492–1700.* New York: Scribner's, 1935.

Meijer, Fik. *A History of Seafaring in the Classical World.* New York: St. Martin's, 1986.

Mitchell, David. *Pirates.* London: Thames and Hudson, 1976.

Morales-Carrión, Arturo. *Puerto Rico and the Non Hispanic Caribbean: A Study in the Decline of Spanish Exclusivism.* Rio Piedras: University of Puerto Rico Press, 1952.

Murray, Dian. *Pirates of the South China Coast, 1790–1810.* Stanford, Calif.: Stanford University Press, 1987.

Newton, Arthur. *The Colonising Activities of the English Puritans.* New Haven: Yale University Press, 1914.

————. *The European Nations in the West Indies, 1493–1688.* London: Black, 1933. Reprinted, 1966.

Ormerod, Henry A. *Piracy in the Ancient World.* Liverpool, England: University Press of Liverpool, 1923. Reprinted, New York: Dorset Press, 1987.

Pack, James. *Nelson's Blood—the Story of Naval Rum.* Annapolis, Md.: Naval Institute, 1982.

Paiewonsky, Isidor. *Account of the burning of a pirate ship, La Trompeuse, in the harbour of St. Thomas, July 21, 1683.* Saint Thomas, Virgin Islands, 1961. Privately published.

Pausanias. *Pausanias's Description of Greece.* Translated by J. G. Frazer. Six volumes. New York: Biblo and Tannen, 1965.

Pawson, Michael, and David Buisseret. *Port Royal Jamaica.* Oxford: Clarendon, 1975.

Pinto, Fernão Mendes. *The Travels of Mendes Pinto.* Edited by Rebecca Catz. Chicago: University of Chicago Press, 1989.

Plutarch. *Plutarch's Lives.* John Dryden's edition revised by Arthur Hough Clough. Three volumes. London: Dent, 1910.

Polybius. *The Histories.* Translated by W. R. Paton. Six volumes. Cambridge, Mass.: Harvard University Press, 1922–1927.

Pope, Dudley. *The Buccaneer King: The Biography of Sir Henry Morgan, 1635–1688.* New York: Dodd, Mead, 1978. (Published in England as *Harry Morgan's Way.*)

Pringle, Patrick. *Jolly Roger: The Story of the Great Age of Piracy.* New York: Norton, 1953.

Pyle, Howard (editor). *The Buccaneers and Marooners of America.* London: T. Fisher Unwin, 1891. Reprinted, Glorieta, N.Mex.: Rio Grande Press, 1990.

Quinn, David B. *England and the Discovery of America, 1481–1620.* New York: Knopf, 1974.

———— and A. N. Ryan. *England's Sea Empire, 1550–1642.* London: Allen & Unwin, 1983.

————. *Set Fair for Roanoke: Voyages and Colonies, 1584–1606.* Chapel Hill: University of North Carolina Press, 1985.

————. *The Roanoke Voyages.* Two volumes. London: Hakluyt Society, 1955. Reprinted, Nendeln, Liechtenstein: Kraus, 1967.

————. *The Voyages and Colonising Enterprises of Sir Humphrey Gilbert.* Two volumes. London: Hakluyt Society, 1940.

Quintilian. *The Major Declamations Ascribed to Quintilian.* Translated by Lewis Sussman. Frankfurt-am-Main: Peter Lang, 1987.

Rediker, Marcus. *Between the Devil and the Deep Blue Sea: Merchant Seamen, Pirates, and the Anglo-American Maritime World, 1700–1750.* Cambridge: Cambridge University Press, 1987.

Richards, Jeffrey. *Swordsmen of the Screen, from Douglas Fairbanks to Michael York.* London and Boston: Routledge and Kegan Paul, 1977.

Richards, Stanley. *Black Bart.* Llandybie, Wales: Christopher Davies, 1966.

Ritchie, Robert C. *Captain Kidd and the War against the Pirates.* Cambridge, Mass.: Harvard University Press, 1986.

Rogers, Woodes. *A Cruising Voyage Round the World.* London, 1712. Reprinted, edited by George Manwaring, London: Cassell, 1928. Manwaring edition reprinted, New York: Dover, 1970.

Rogoziński, Jan. *A Brief History of the Caribbean: From the Arawak and the Carib to the Present.* New York: Facts On File, 1992.

Rowse, Arthur L. *Sir Richard Grenville of the 'Revenge': An Elizabethan Hero.* London: Cape, 1937.

Runciman, Steven. *The White Rajahs: A History of Sarawak from 1841 to 1946.* Cambridge: Cambridge University Press, 1960.

Rutter, Owen. *The Pirate Wind: Tales of the Sea-Robbers of Malaya.* London: Hutchinson, 1930.

Sanborn, Frederic. *Origins of the Early English Maritime and Commercial Law.* New York: Century, 1930.

Saxon, Lyle. *Lafitte the Pirate.* New York: Century, 1930. Reprinted, New Orleans (Crager), 1950; Gretna, Louisiana (Pelican), 1989.

Schermerhorn, Elizabeth W. *Malta of the Knights.* New York: Houghton Mifflin, 1929.

Schurz, William L. *The Manilla Galleon.* New York: Dutton, 1939.

Secord, Arthur. *"Robert Drury's Journal" and Other Studies.* Urbana: University of Illinois Press, 1961.

Senior, C. M. *A Nation of Pirates: English Piracy in its Heyday.* Newton Abbot, England: David & Charles, 1976.

Setton, Kenneth, general editor. *A History of the Crusades.* Six volumes. Madison: University of Wisconsin Press, 1969–1989.

Severin, Timothy. *The Golden Antilles.* New York: Knopf, 1970.

Shelvocke, George. *A Voyage Round the World by way of the Great South Sea.* London: J. Senex, 1726. New edition by W. G. Perrin, London: Cassell, 1928.

Sherry, Frank. *Raiders and Rebels: The Golden Age of Piracy.* New York: Hearst Marine Books, 1986.

Snelgrave, William. *A New Account of Some Parts of Guinea and the Slave Trade. . . .* London: Knapton, 1734. Reprinted, London: Cass, 1971.

So, Kwan-wai. *Japanese Piracy in Ming China During the 16th Century.* East Lansing: Michigan State University Press, 1975.

Spate, Oskar. *The Spanish Lake.* Minneapolis: University of Minnesota Press, 1979.

———. *Monopolists and Freebooters.* Minneapolis: University of Minnesota Press, 1983.

Stark, Francis. *The Abolition of Privateering and the Declaration of Paris.* New York: Columbia University Press, 1897. Reprinted, New York: AMS, 1967.

Sugden, John. *Sir Francis Drake.* New York: Henry Holt, 1990.

Sutherland, James. *Daniel Defoe: A Critical Study.* Boston: Houghton Mifflin, 1971.

The Tel El-Amarna Tablets. Edited by Samuel Mercer. Two volumes. Toronto: Macmillan, 1939.

Tarn, W. W. "The Greek Leagues and Macedonia," *The Cambridge Ancient History.* Volume Seven, edited by S. A. Cook and others. Cambridge: Cambridge University Press, 1928.

Taylor, Eva. *The Troublesome Voyage of Captain Edward Fenton 1582–1583.* Cambridge: Hakluyt Society, 1959.

Tenenti, Albert. *Piracy and the Decline of Venice.* London: Oxford University Press, 1967.

Unger, Richard. *The Ship in the Medieval Economy, 600–1600.* London: Croom Helm, 1980.

Unwin, Rayner. *The Defeat of John Hawkins.* New York: Macmillan, 1960.

Wafer, Lionel. *A New Voyage and Description of the Isthmus of America.* London: Knapton, 1699. New edition by L. E. Elliott Joyce, London: Hakluyt Society 1934. Elliott Joyce edition reprinted, Nendeln, Liechtenstein: Kraus, 1967.

Wagner, Henry R. *Sir Francis Drake's Voyage around the World.* San Francisco: Howell, 1926.

Watson, Harold. *Coasts of Treasure Island.* San Antonio, Tex.: Naylor, 1969.

Weddle, Robert. *Spanish Sea: The Gulf of Mexico in North American Discovery, 1500–1685.* College Station: Texas A & M University Press, 1985.

West, Rebecca. *Black Lamb and Grey Falcon.* New York: Viking Press, 1941.

Williams, Lloyd. *Pirates of Colonial Virginia.* Richmond: Dietz, 1937. Reprinted, Detroit: Grand Rapids, 1971.

Williams, Neville. *Captains Outrageous: Seven Centuries of Piracy.* New York: Macmillan, 1962.

———. *The Sea Dogs: Privateers, Plunder, and Piracy in the Elizabethan Age.* New York: Macmillan, 1975.

Williamson, George C. *George, Third Earl of Cumberland.* Cambridge: Cambridge University Press, 1920.

Williamson, James A. *The Age of Drake.* London: Black, 1938.

———. *Hawkins of Plymouth: A New History of Sir John Hawkins and of the Other Members of his Family. . . .* London: Black, 1949. Second edition, New York: Barnes and Noble, 1969.

Winston, Alexander. *No Purchase, No Pay: Sir Henry Morgan, Captain William Kidd, Captain Woodes Rogers in the Great Age of Privateers and Pirates, 1665–1715.* London: Eyre & Spottiswoode, 1970.

Wolf, John. *The Barbary Coast: Algiers under the Turks 1500 to 1830.* New York: Norton, 1979.

Wood, Peter. *The Spanish Main.* Alexandria, Va.: Time-Life Books, 1979.

Woodward, Ralph. *Robinson Crusoe's Island: A History of the Juan Fernández Islands.* Chapel Hill: University of North Carolina Press, 1969.

Wright, Irene Aloha. *Documents Concerning English Voyages to the Spanish Main 1569–1580.* London: Hakluyt Society, 1932.

———. *The Early History of Cuba 1492–1586.* New York: Macmillan, 1916. Reprinted, New York: Octagon, 1970.

———. *Further English Voyages to Spanish America 1583–1594.* London: Hakluyt Society, 1951.

———. *Spanish Documents concerning English voyages to the Caribbean 1527–1568.* London: Hakluyt Society, 1929.

PHOTO
CREDITS

INDEX

Vessels are listed alphabetically under the heading "Ships." In all references to historical time, "Ancient" indicates the years before 500 A.D. "Medieval" means after 500 and before 1500 A.D. "Modern" refers to the years since 1500.

Pirates, The; Buccaneer, The (1938); *Buccaneer, The* (1958); *Buccaneer's Girl; Captain Blood* (1924); *Captain Blood* (1935); *Captain Kidd; Captain Kidd and the Slave Girl; Captain Pirate; Caribbean; Crimson Pirate, The; Devil-Ship Pirates, The; Double Crossbones; Drake of England; Fortunes of Captain Blood; Frenchman's Creek; Golden Hawk, The; High Wind in Jamaica, A; Hook; King's Pirate; Last of the Buccaneers; Lion of Saint Mark; Long John Silver; Master of Ballantrae, The; Morgan the Pirate; Peter Pan; Pirate, The; Pirate and the Slave Girl, The; Pirate Movie, The; Pirate of the Black Hawk, The; Pirates; Pirates of Blood River, The; Pirates of Penzance, The; Pirates of the Seven Seas; Pirates of Tortuga; Pirates of Tripoli; Princess and the Pirate, The; Queen of the Pirates; Raiders of the Seven Seas; Scalawag; Sea Hawk, The* (1924); *Sea Hawk, The* (1940); *Seven Seas to Calais; Son of Captain Blood, The; Son of the Red Corsair, The; Spanish Main, The; Spartacus; Swashbuckler; Treasure Island* (1920); *Treasure Island* (1934); *Treasure Island* (1950); *Treasure Island* (1972); *Treasure Island* (1990); *Tripoli; Women of Pitcairn Island, The; Yankee Buccaneer; Yellowbeard*

Moysi, Francesco de 233
Muckill, John 233
Mullins, Darby 233
Murat al-Fushali Reis 233
Murat "el Chico" Reis 233
Murat Reis (died 1556) 233
Murat Reis (active 1570s) 233
Murat Reis (active 1608) 233
Murat Reis (active 1612) 233
Murat Reis (active 11796–1815). *See* Lisle, Peter
Murat "the Great" Reis 233
Musical comedies. *See Peter Pan; Pirates of Penzance, The*
Musical compositions. *See* Ballets, Musical Comedies, Operas, Symphonies
Musket 234 (illustration 45)
Muslim Pirates 234–235
Mustafa Memmi Reis 235
Mustafa "Qudai" Reis 235
Mustafa Reis (active 1560s) 235
Mustafa Reis (active 1574) 235

Mustafa Reis (active 1675–1681) 235
Mustafa Reis (active 1681) 235
Mustafa Reis (active 1684–1685) 235
Mutiny 41, 47
Myddleton, John 235
Myngs, Sir Christopher 235–236
Myoparo 236

N

Nabis 237
Narentans 237
Nasuf Reis 238
Natale, Francesco di 238, 298
Natale, Giacomo di 238
Nau, Jean David. *See* L'Olonnais, François
Nauplius 238
Navarro, Pedro 238
Neckere, Jonathan de 239
New Account of Some Parts of Guinea and the Slave-Trade, A 239
Newport, Christopher 239
New Providence Island 172, 188, 200, 207, 239-240, 296, 298, 354
Newton, Robert 240 (illustrations 28, 203)
New Voyage Round the World, A 93, 240
New York, New York 20, 48, 77, 162, 208, 338
Nicole, Christopher 9, 100
Nikandros 240
Niketas of Rhodes 241
Niño Pero, conde de Buelna 241
Noble, John 241
Nombre de Dios, Panama 103
Noort, Olivier van 241
No peace beyond the line 241
No purchase, no pay 227, 242
Norman, Richard 242
North, Nathaniel 242–243
Norton, John (active 1449) 243
Nortom, John (active 1590s) 243
Norton, Thomas 243
Novaglia, Arfani 243
Novels. *See Admiral; Amyot's Cay; Anne Bonny; Apollonius of Tyre; Black Swan, The; Buccaneer Surgeon; Buccaneer; Candide; Captain Blood, His Odyssey; Captain Blood Returns; Captain Brand of the "Centipede"; Captain Margaret: A Romance; Captain Singleton; Caribbean; Chaereas and Callirhoe; Coral Island, The; Corsair; Cup of*

Gold; Daphnis and Chloe; Devil's Own, The; Ephesian Tale, The; Ethiopian Adventures, The; For My Great Folly; Fortunes of Captain Blood, The; Four Years Voyages of Capt. George Roberts; Frenchman's Creek; Further Adventures of Robinson Crusoe, The; Galleon; Golden Hawk, The; High Wind in Jamaica, A; Island, The; King of Pirates, The; Lafitte, The Pirate of the Gulf; Leucippe and Cleitophon, The Adventures of; Lydia Bailey; Master of Ballantrae, The; New Voyage Round the World, A; Peter the Whaler; Pirate, The; Privateer, The; Robinson Crusoe; Rose of Paradise, The; Ruby of Kishmoor, The; Sea Hawk, The; Sea Lions; Or, The Last Sealers, The; Story of Jack Ballister's Fortunes, The; Treasure Island; Voyages and Adventures of Captain Robert Boyle, The; Water Witch; Or, The Skimmer of the Seas, The; Westward Ho!. See also Fiction; Romances

Nutt, John 243
Nutt, Robert 243

O

Ochiali. *See* Uluj Ali Pasha
Odysseus 114, 244
Odyssey, The 114, 162, 221, 244, 334
Of the Beginnings, Practices, and Suppression of Pirates 210
Officers, ship's. *See* Admiral; Archpirate; Captain; Mate; Quartermaster
Ogeron de la Rivière, Bertrand d' 340
Ogle, Challoner 294
O'Hara, Maureen 245, (illustrations 5, 324)
"Oh, better far to live and die" 245
Oloard, Christopher 245
O'Malley, Grace 245
Omar Reis 246
Omodei Ventimiglia, Antonio, Baron de Vallonga 246
Operas *See Pirates of Penzance, The; Pirata, Il*
Orange, Pierre de 246
Orduña, Diego de 246
Orsini dell'Anguillara, Flaminio 246
Ortigues, Gabriel 246
Osman, Sherip 246
Ottoman Empire 172, 178, 184, 196, 212, 246–247, 352